F E L I K S T O P O

F O U R T E E N L E … S

CW01670068

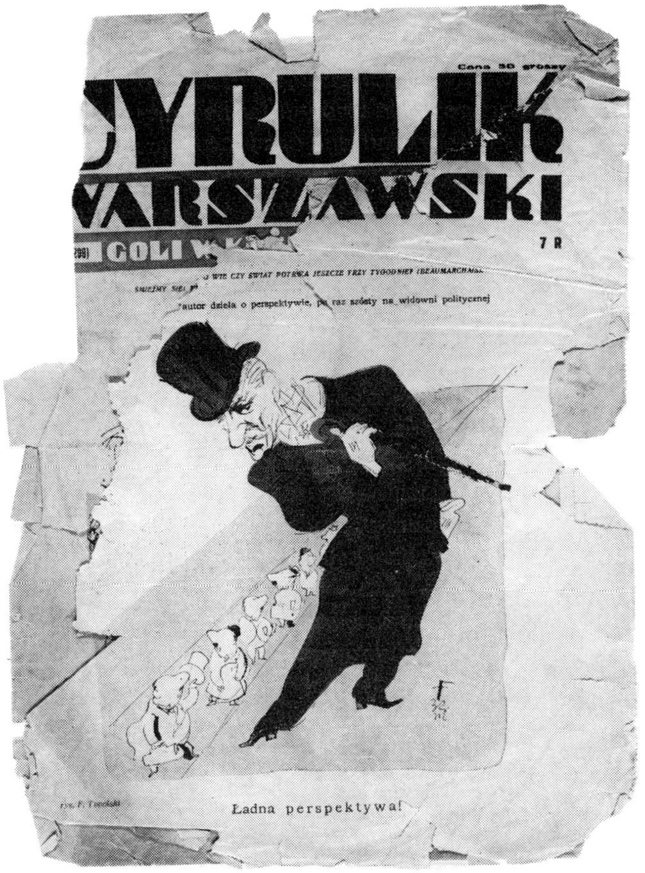

Cyrulik Warszawski

Anyway, why fourteen letters? Still an art student, summoned by the lofty pederast–dandy–poet–editor Jan Lechoń to join his prestigious satirico-literary weekly *Cyrulik Warszawski* (*The Barber of Warsaw*), I met this opening question: 'How many letters in your name?' The elongated long-nosed chic editor and compact-small, casually chic, shy-panachious I counted out fourteen. The satirico-lyricist: 'Marvellous, it means the life of **fulfilment** – always use/sign your full name to keep fuelling the magic!'

This playful 'motto' casually informed a lot of my life:

(a) Holding to ks in Feliks, thus (perhaps a childishly major point) to my Polishness.

(b) Meticulously signing in full my exhibited work – to the smallest drawing, thus causing a mean London critic to mock my swollen egocentricism.

But more significantly:

(c) The 'life of fulfilment' propped up a – possibly already budding – *je m'en foutisme* of confidence, disregarding the obligatory tactics for an artist in obtaining patronage and institutionalized prestige; a pseudo-aristocratic (that is, of assured security/dignity background) disdain towards the market, without any other justification, but the blind faith in my 'fulfilment'. Hence not only cold-shouldering the indeed endless offerings of 'career' connections, but also, distressingly, not straining the whole of my gifts (and beyond) towards that very 'fulfilment'.

(d) Circumstance (London planners demolishing my studio) arrested my work's growth towards 'fulfilment' – it didn't

First published in 1988 by **Faber and Faber Limited** 3 Queen Square London WC1N 3AU Photoset by **Parker Typesetting Service**, Leicester Printed in Great Britain by W S Cowells Ltd Designed by **Charlie Riddell** All rights reserved © **Feliks Topolski** 1988 This book is sold subject to the condition that it shall not, by way of trade or otherwise, be lent, resold, hired out or otherwise circulated without the publisher's prior consent in any form of binding or cover other than that in which it is published and without a similar condition including this condition being imposed on the subsequent purchaser. *British Library Cataloguing in Publication Data* **Topolski, Feliks** Fourteen letters. 1. Topolski, Feliks 2. Artists – England – Biography I. Title 760'.092'4 NC242.T/ISBN 0-571-13889-6

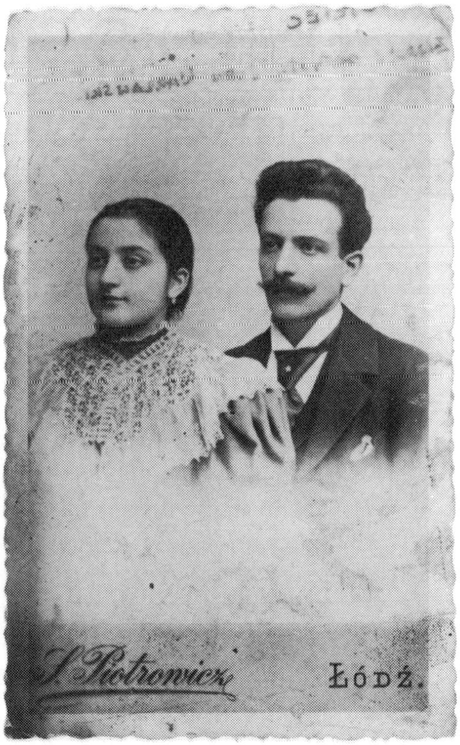

Stanisława and her brother

recover till well into post-middle-life – but in stepped the comforting delusion/proposition of **promise**. 'Promise' neatly embraced/justified my prolonged preoccupation as a chronicler: it bagged me for the globe and its history of clashes in an amassment of serviceable references, before, eventually, I plunged into my 'Memoir'.

The origin-lore: noble pure and optimistic socialism in step with patriotic liberation arose in **the 1905 revolution** – the Polish an upshot of the Russian. It threw up in **Warszawa** (Warsaw) a minor 'activist' – **Edward**, twenty years old, a sonorous platform speaker; and in Łódź, **Stanisława**, a girl of twenty-one, marching in a street demonstration – pulled to safety by a worker-comrade from under the hoofs of a Cossack horse.

She came to Warszawa and yielded her virginity enthusiastically to his seductive (noble) recitations and his free-love (purity) creed; thus the century conceived me at Edward's parents' '*salon*' in a humble armchair (as I was repeatedly told) – a mock-reverent inheritance, with me till I departed West. The century, I say, because it began the revolutionary ecstasy which faded in defeat, with, when I was born in 1907, Edward – defeat's aftermath – in a Russian prison. But, before then, Stanisława's brothers, Łódź ('the Polish Manchester') industrialists, descended on Edward in a two-horse-drawn carriage and chained him into marriage.

Thus 'normality' submerged the anguish of the fallen revolution; thus my father's declamatory voice settled for the unsettled career of an actor – a free-loving truant from the sluggish stability embodied in the son – mostly away in the country – or touring 'reps'. Thus my mother was set on the drudgery of jobs – but her unused reserves of enthusiasm, a desperate need for a metaphoric substitute for buried ideals, lodged in her faith in her son's high compensatory destiny: he must be uniquely worthy, a replacement for the thwarted hopes. Death of one hope – birth of another. Thus the son, born out of the collapse of a conglomeration of faiths (rational and holy) had to be an all-round disbeliever, at best – a Stoic; and so, more or less, his generation in that country.

But this rather negative and spoilt individual may be redeemed by his inheritance. It renders him tender towards promethean urges (albeit passively when it comes to extrovert demonstrations – son of an actor fearful of staging himself), decisive in his overpowering instinct for out-of-step–ism; this last, of course, one ingredient within an alloy of averseness to dogmatic and tribal groupings.

But first:
The child grows, demands, is given food, warmth, paper to draw, squatted, so many Napoleons on. The child becomes a boy and his head levels with the table; hundreds of suns having risen over the horizon, his eyes rise over the table's top; above the window's ledge. Now his eyes are given the stage with his father upon it: Bonaparte pointing/commanding victory.

Childhood is a meticulous events-crowded time of life, hence apt to absorb much autobiographical attention. It must not usurp it here – a batch of loose set-pieces sufficing:

– Well implanted in memory: circuiting the whole flat seated on the chamber pot, panties down, feet working speed and direction; this would encompass for long stretches of time the multitude of undertakings: games, drawing, books, surveys.

– Earliest demonstration of the gift of **eye-witness-recorder**: a series of drawings, a strip (I can see them clearly) showing stages in two dogs' courting, in coitus, finally held together back to back unable to separate – observed though not understood. I remember the joy of the grown-ups and my lack of curiosity at the dogs' odd games.

– Aunt, student in Zurich (anthropology?) on vacation. I look through the keyhole, impatient as she readies herself for ages, locked in her room; and I exclaim '*Tyle tyłka!*' ('So much bottom!'). Remembered, or passed on by family anecdote?

– Women servants: one, Jagusia, taking me to the red-bannered Steelworkers' Union meetings at their headquarters in my street opposite *Pogotowie Ratunkowe* (the Ambulance Service). Another, to the church services – Roman Catholic – in the same street. Later, obligatorily, the round Lutheran church.

– Visiting maternal grandparents in Częstochowa in the shadow of Orthodoxy: the grandfather at prayers – the white black-striped shawl on his head; leather strap pressed into bare arm, a mysterious box centred on the forehead; candlelit chants out of another millennium/world.

– Illness. Still, if the memory holds, in a bed with liftable netted sides. There was a new beautiful/large/costly book in the friendly bookshop which I craved without hope. My father (a rare presence) puts this book on my pillow. And the inexplicable: I burst into tears.

– Down below the back balcony – the courtyard unveils the thrills of alien manifestations in continuous progress: mighty peasant wenches-maids beat bedding/carpets. Jewish rag pedlars, long-black-coated, long-ringleted-bearded and black-peak-capped, cry out '*Handel! Handel!*' ('Business! Business!'); beggars disport distortions; acrobats and conjurors strip off the everybody-ordinariness to disclose tinsel magic of outlandishness; gypsies with their hurdy-gurdies on sticks, a parrot or a monkey on their shoulder, their women, colours and skirts swishing, strut ('Tell your fortune? Come upstairs?') and scare/tempt. Beckoning other world – a thrill to the humdrum-held bourgeois child.

– Shadowy-oaky dining room. A large sideboard to discard my part-eaten chunks of larded bread behind.

– **The 1914 'War Artist'**, seven years old, in earnest: a growing batch of coloured drawings; the first: a German plane over Warsaw with passers-by swept by Stójkowy into a porchway in Żelazna Brama; the second: Siberian furry cavalry on shaggy little horses; the third: strings of peasant horse-carts loaded with Russian wounded.

– A tiny memory-bracket: my mother, when dressing, would fold lengthwise a small hand towel and tuck it in the corset-top to simulate/compensate period-required breasts.

– My harassed mother, back from her German Occupation office, challenges my grandmother about money given to her for my food – I don't seem to be well. Some of the money goes stealthily to fatten up my student aunt in Switzerland.

– Saxon Park: children under statues; my shyness, my 'well-behavedness' – yet, one day I fall under boycott by mothers and nannies – girls must not play with me, the boy who kicked one of them. I remember only my segregation, not the cause of it.

– This must be my earliest, most intense **germination in visuality**: a compulsion towards art of enigma mostly buried neglected, quickened now, when this grand oblong Napoleonic album, glory of my childhood, found in London, is in my hands, perhaps – why not – even the same copy. A single picture matters here, better described as remembered than as seen anew, since the working of its magic on a child can be resurrected, while now the reality of the very page exposes its forgotten semi-circularity laid out ploddingly with two medallions and *Uniforme de Bonaparte, Consul* when looked at with an old man's jaundiced eye.

So to the eye of memory: the amassed soldiery moving fast and away all in chaos-crowding into the depth of some mountain gorge, the snow blowing over and exposing rocks. And against this military onrush the reproductional mishandling, or a naturalist-painter's stumble, bring out a miracle of enigmatic intervention: from an officer's three-cornered hat there draws out – elongates plasmatically – the vast and as if wind-twisted dark stretch of something earthy

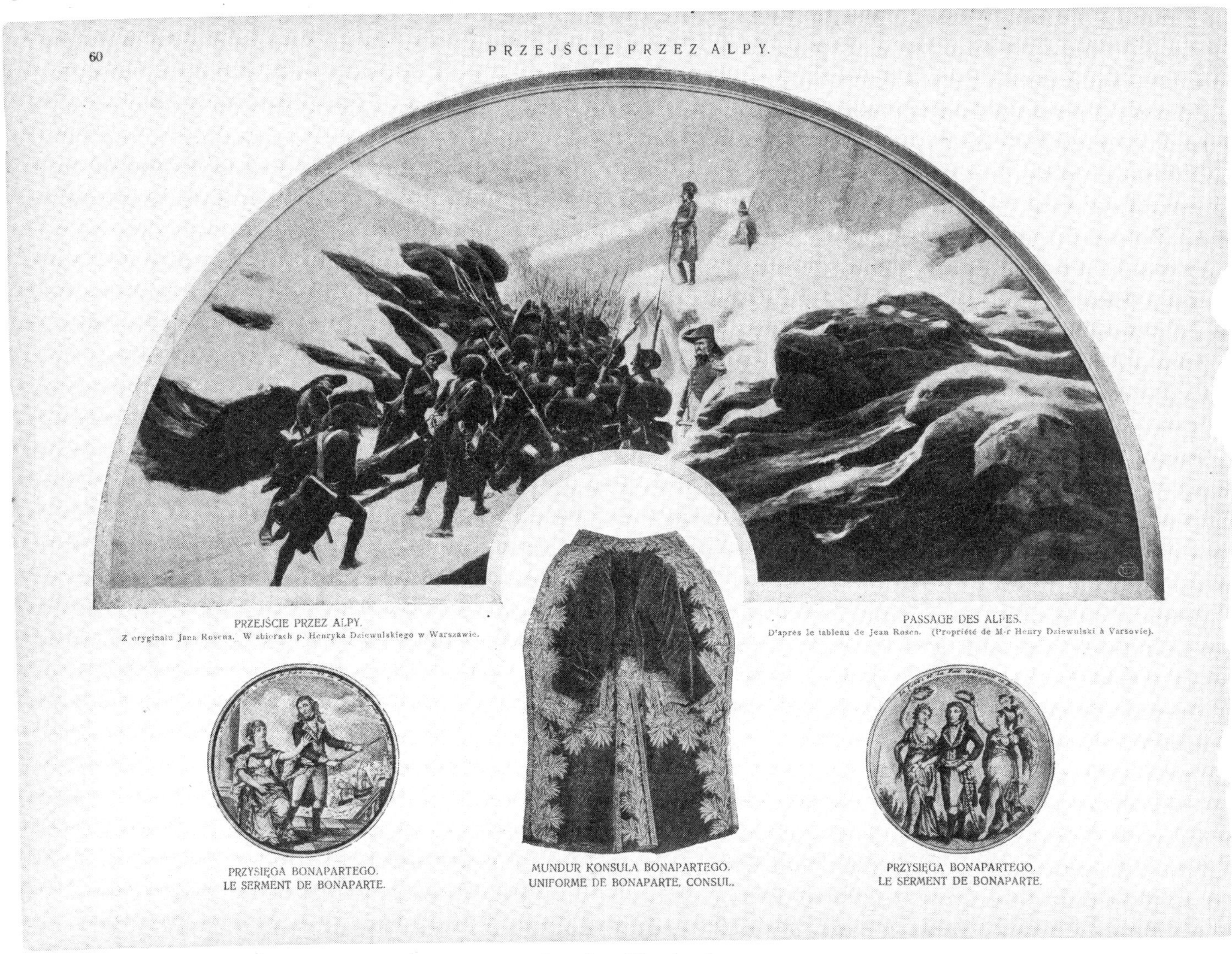

Page from 'Napoleon'

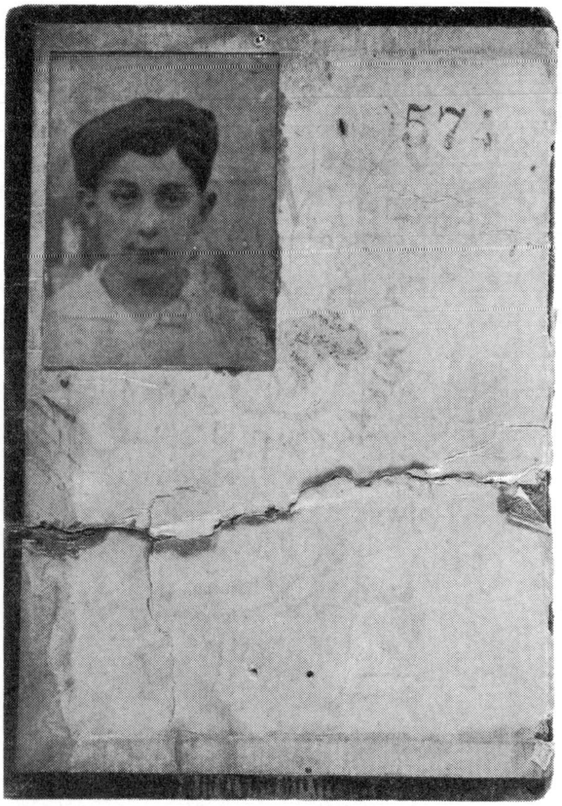

Schoolboy Feliks

that tugs at the man, bends his head, the whole of him, away from the order and the purpose of the comradely march, as if, having caught ensnared trapped him, it seemingly enmeshes, binds him to the cragginess of the rocky ground . . . and more: a sort of enlivened arm of the earth claims, tears him out of his ranks. The eye of this child saw this inexplicable weirdness, heart-breath held: and the call of the power of imagery, let loose and soaring when unchained, will stay with him.

Even looked at now those sur-real elements far from the painter's intention still emerge, although, examined closer, the black elongated patches of ground, issuing from under the snow, cling to two, not one, straining soldiers. And the title of the picture: *Passage des Alpes d'après lę tableau de Jean Rosen*.

– Dusty hamlet vacation: the village fool (torn hat? stick?) sways up the dust-road barking at the tailing dust-cloud of children customarily pestering him; but this boy is awestruck: brush against the threat of the unrationalizable.
– My father averts his eyes from me, ignores me – a young actor, on provincial circuits as far as the Baltic Kołobrzeg, towing one actress after another.
– I am detached – a child without religion; atheism – the remaining virtue of my parents' defeated world. This detachment stays, serves the watchful eye.
– Play with a neighbours' son in his parents' storage room piled to the ceiling with wooden boxes: gravitation-defying leaps/flights, super-human-winged, and, finale: I stand superior and Olek reverentially squats and, memorably but inexplicably, whines repeatedly, '*Pocałować w kolanko*' ('Kiss! Kiss! your dear knee'). Puzzling, yet solid in memory.
– Drawing solely on narrow cut-off strips of office paper brought by the mother, working then in the German-run *Kohlen-Centrale Ost*: a multitude of pencilled illustrations to the patriotic *Trylogja* ('Trilogy') by Sienkiewicz.
– The dark-brown Warsaw flat (the salon chairs under dust-covers round grandfather's body laid in state) left behind for two rooms, bathroom, kitchen and maid's alcove on the sixth, top, floor of a 'tall' new block – with a lift.

Changes, but blurred, since early certainties gave in to multi-pressures of grey times within alien war. A scene remembered: my godless parents on their knees flanking me kneeling on a chair, faced by the bearded Lutheran pastor sprinkling water over my head; conversion? return to faith? hardly; an act in the chain of confirmations of the *status quo ante*.

There are two versions of **our school cap** – the ambition is to secure the old, vanishing shape (the ear-flaps held on top with one button, not two) from Tuczyn in the old town; and then to whiten the blue edges with chalk for a faded look.

My school was considered the best in Warsaw, and in consequence, though attached to the Protestant community and Church, contained schoolboys of all religious denominations (mostly in name only, in those 'progressive' days). Strict attendance at the circular eighteenth-century church on Sundays and at *religja*, religious-instruction lessons in falsity: the chorally repeated declarations of 'I believe . . .' were never, from the outset, true. But, alongside this **training in hypocrisy**, there seeps in and sets a moral stance, unaccountably based, without religion and within the war, on loose humanism.*

Christianity as fair-choice. I moved in enough layers of Poland's life in the between-the-wars years to know that my schoolboy atheism (alongside institutionalized lip-service) matured into a way of life, not as an isolated case but as a universal phenomenon: the young of the then-Poland moved away from dogmatic religiosity, thus most massively from the dominant Roman Catholicism – birth (and such) certificates declaring, naturally, 'no change', as did school – and forced prayers, and church attendances, demanded by the establishment rules.

The school, the Art Academy, the School of Officers, gave the widest social cross-section, but (since the obstinate may claim that these were select groups) my closeness, when serving later in a regiment, to the largest variety of ordinary young soldiers (and thus to their backgrounds) confirmed this flight from religion; and so did endless random encounters.

And this argument bulges out with, to me, an astonishing conclusion: the good temper of the nation in those years must have had a link, paradoxically, with this loosening up of better-than-thou divisivenesses.

The obvious, but necessary to state here: the return to a hold over the Poles of the Roman Catholic religion came with the anti-Nazi and, later, the anti-Soviet needs for display of unifying national emotions – in the only available place: the church.

*Not unlike my son's progress within our atheistic life: his school, attached to Westminster Abbey, demanded the filling in of old rubric sections, old deadwood, following Marion's and my register-enforced classification: Protestant (the oft-applied justification, used without conviction: 'The child must be given the chance of choice'). And in consequence Daniel's long inattentive passage through ritualized days: one day, I sneaked at 9 a.m. into the Abbey and there, submerged in beauty and picked up by dust-rays, Daniel (by then *Princeps oppidanorum* – Monitor) in grey, high in the pulpit reading the lesson to the vast uniformally grey-suited congregation of boys.

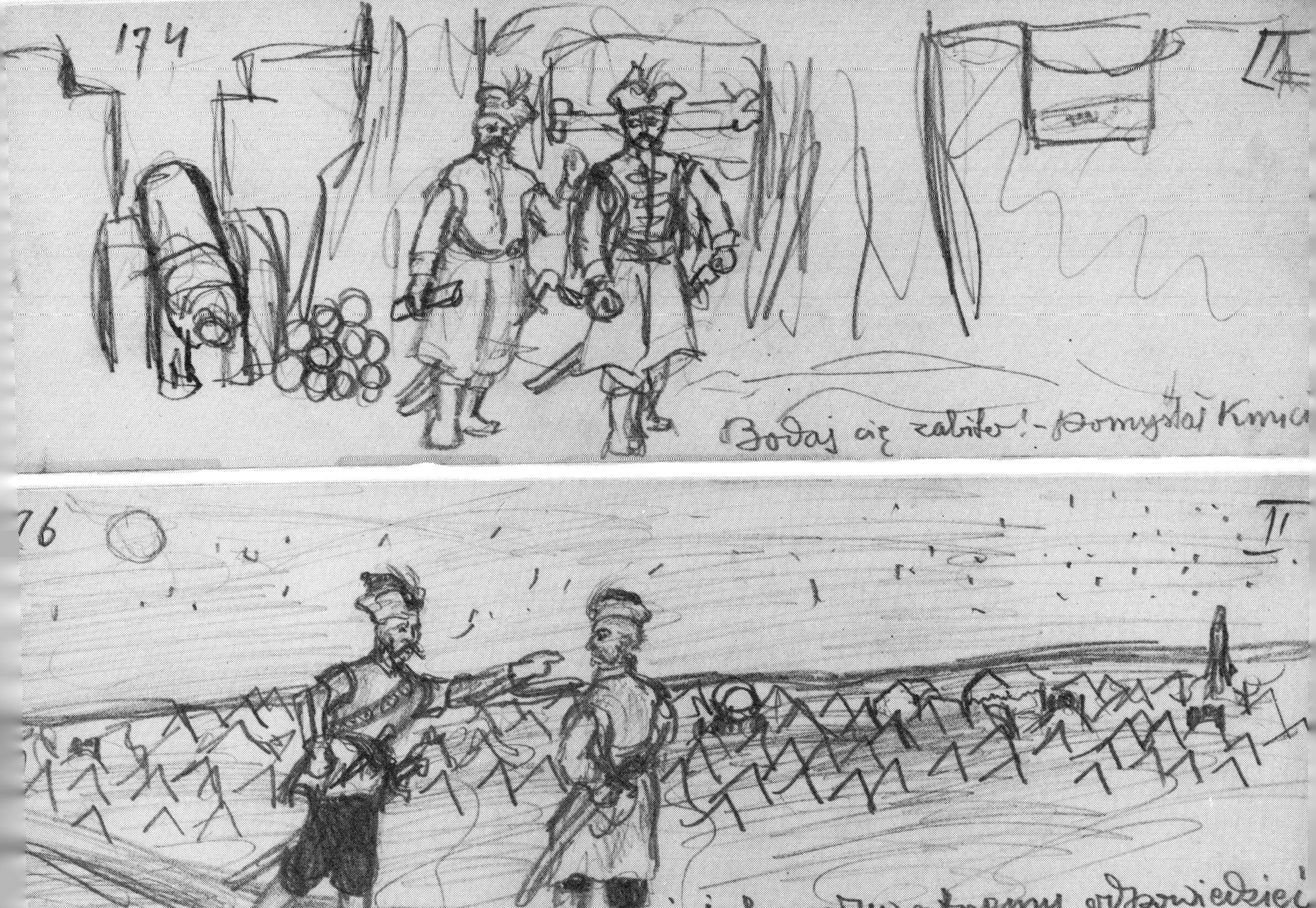

Childhood illustrations to *Trylogja* (and overleaf)

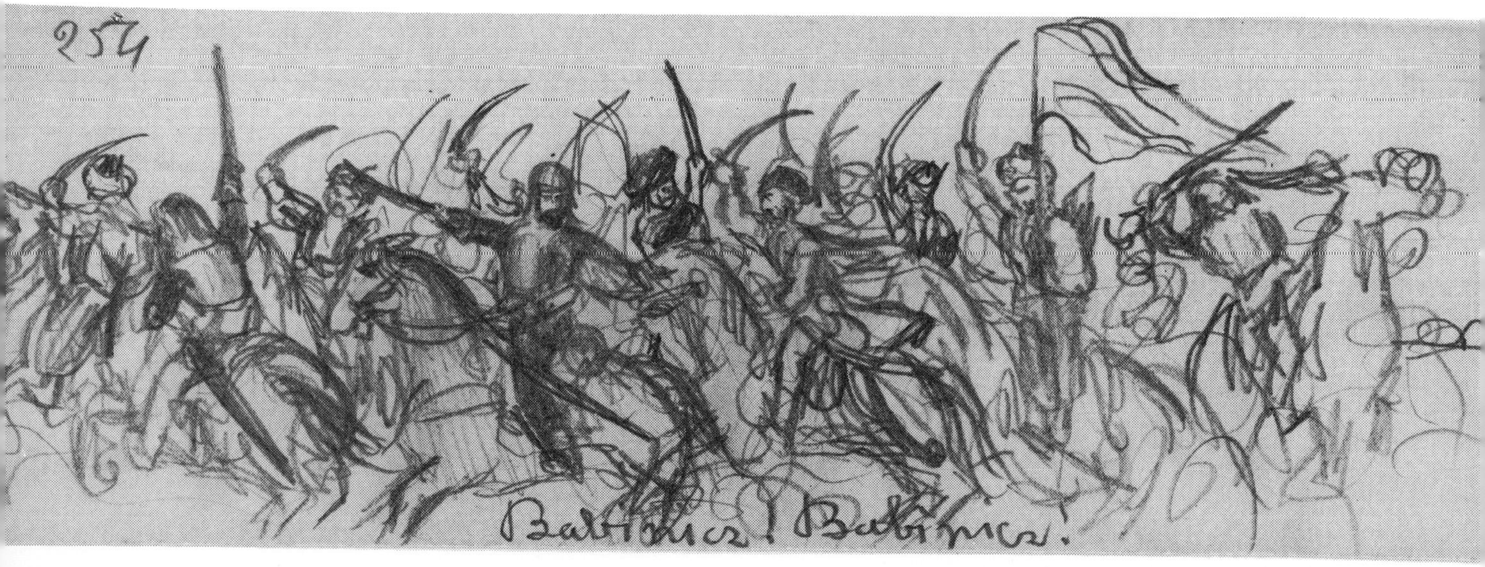
Babinicz! Babinicz!

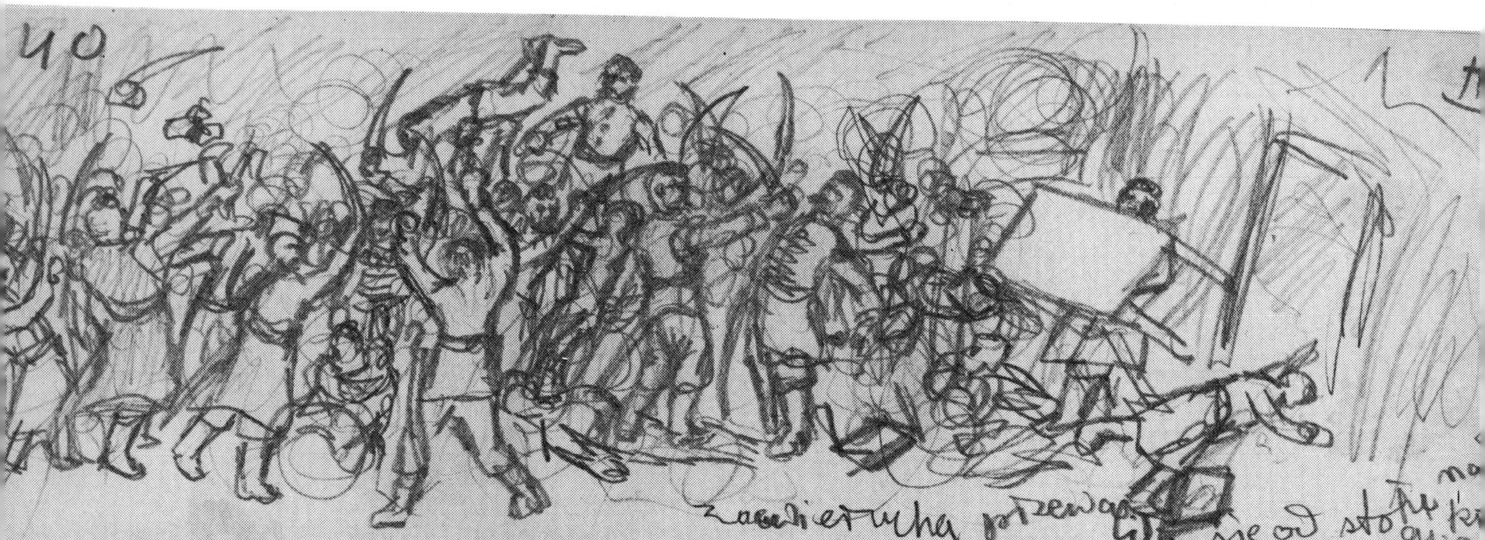

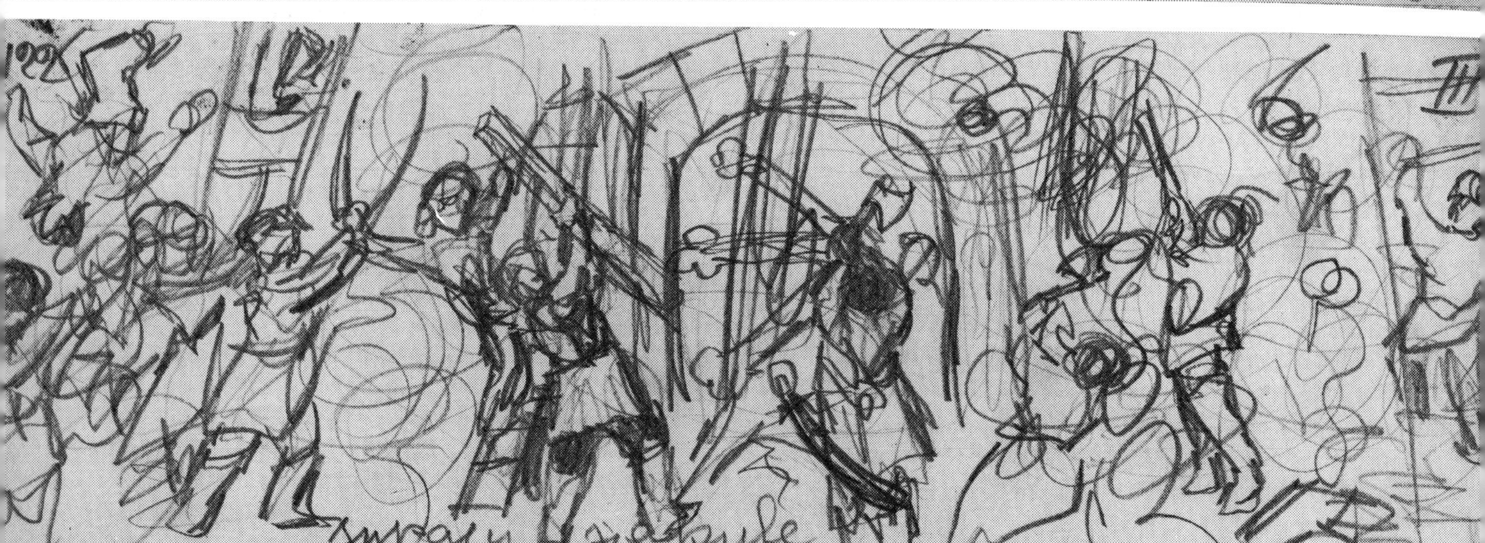
sypały się kule

German soldiers being disarmed in Warsaw streets. And then the boys, swept from Russia by the maelstrom of the October Revolution, educationally retarded, much older and blue-bearded, filled up the back benches among the boys of eleven. I and my permanent partner in our double seats, the timid innocents, therefore year after year hugging the rear of our schoolroom, found ourselves in an instant swamped amongst those unleashed brutes/survivors to cope at close quarters with unpredictable maturity, but also to learn about and from it.

They also accelerated my sexual progress* – innocence (I was not even aware of masturbation in those early years) harmoniously applied to reality. I, twelve years old, and that paragon German-colonist girl – not much older than I – who graduated from looking after me to a living-in seamstress-trainee, are on our own in the flat during my vacations. **Helenka**, weak in Polish language, strong of elongated bone structure; we reached the point of invented-by-me strip-a-garment for each linguistic mistake. Then, with me pulling her shift down below her hips, she slid off the bed to the floor (conscious of the window) and there was, cowering below me but also upright-ascending, this marvel of a long pale back, evoking my possibly first-ever aesthetic rapture in a prolonged suspense (the games buried now) – possibly setting for life, against one another, the competitive spheres of desire and contemplation.

The glassy-doored bookcase provided theory. The boy kept on sneaking, ever ready to escape, into forbidden books (packed below the shelves of an imported German encyclopaedia with passages thickly blacked out – censored): *The Hygiene of the Honeymoon* booklets, a great amassment of back copies of progressive weeklies, their socialist theorizing embracing short stories woven around sexual freedom. The boy learned all but, in naked embrace upon the German receptivity, he took considerate care in his goodness not to lay his unwakened penis on the pubic blondness, sure that mere touch would spark conception.

Later that day, or was it the next day, the games returned to single-mindedness. Both in our underwear, she, now aggressive, on top of me chasing my baby cock – dipping with her hand into my panties buttoned up to a childish bodice, roll/undulation intensifying – until, the startling unquenchable impulse made me push her off and rush to the loo – to pee, I thought. But that must have been my first-ever orgasm. Then, the knock at the door, and the reappearance of that subjugated playmate ('Kiss your little knee!') back from the Russian upheaval: education in lawlessness – the playmate-now-brute. He senses the aura, winks at the hero in pretended alliance (the hero to observe and learn, he to instruct), and, preliminaries bypassed, he leaps at the girl (now buttoning up), an immense (to my eye) phallus already dangling outward. She, a long strong Nordic, fights off, in fury, the little Bolshevik. Feliks – humiliated, but enlightened.

For this growing boy the most marked thrills on increase were the supremely emphatic stabs of **confrontation with alienness** – that is, the acutely upsetting instant *mélange* of seduction/repulsion in the face of any human bordering on exotica – that is, otherness; even the revelation of sex.

The earliest of these were, as aforesaid, the courtyard invaders. Then this circus with my father:

All outlandish, each group and each single performer displayed otherness (many othernesses) in the minutest detail of their physique, their movements/gestures, their voices, their clothes. But then the climax: the high rope was stretched and upon it stepped this magic female creature, beyond imaginings of desires; her pale almost-nakedness tenuously athletic, her unmatchable and awesome antipodality indeed of flesh, not of mythology. Rope-raised and contorted she began to shed her meagre glittering coverings . . . The boy felt at one with the father – both leaning forward, transported. The act ended, she danced out; she ran back again to the applause – and, in the centre of the ring, tore her blond wig off, revealing herself as a tall, not uniquely handsome boy.

The upsurge of **independence**. Prezydent Paderewski, top-hat subduing floating locks, side by side with Komendant Piłsudski saluting, glimpsed, in a landau, amongst the horseback guard of honour: blue-grey, post-Napoleon Polish *chevaux-légers* – amaranthine lapels and high square shakos.

Father absent most of the time, before the war with provincial or touring companies, now **an actor manager at a front-line theatre**. I look at a photograph of his troupe: he in the centre, and at its edge my father's girlfriend, also his leading actress – eyes locked in fascination with a smart officer.

The military also enter our life, courting my mother.

Piłsudski worship, but every morning's ten-to-eight trot to school: after the passage of Russian-German-Austrian-Polish high-booted metal-clanking 'regular' uniforms, the post-First-World-War days of US missions. A heavy wide man, luxuriously pistoning under more a safari than a military outfit, crosses a Warsaw street; his shape/cut (from the back) – no Germano-Slavonic goose-stepping land-locked power, but the outward-flung light-footed force/energy, globe-trotting/taking sweep – MODERN. The kerb is low enough to stroll flabbily over, but the American: his every step manhood's challenge, an obstacle to overcome, an opportunity for a trial of strength – his front foot springs upwards, his back foot in support lifted on the toes and off the asphalt, so that the act of landing from above, and lightly, is a literal *tour de force*.

This leap-toe conquest of the street's gutter, this conqueror of sidewalks the world over, gave me plenty of America – more than Hollywood's streamlined seductions. I imitated this step – perhaps it took me round the globe.

But also the pale blue French uniforms and the same cloth and cut on the Polish soldiers of General Haller, who volunteered in France; and the greenish post-German cut of men from the western provinces (under Germany's 'civilizing' rule since the end of the eighteenth century), who,

*Undoubtedly the commonplace stirrings: first, recurring sets of dreams around my mother's femaleness; second, after the traumatic crowded nude bathing in boys' holiday camp, dream serials, piling up entangling of male-adolescent bodies. Then came clinical reading on sex – clinical and erotic – and Helenka.

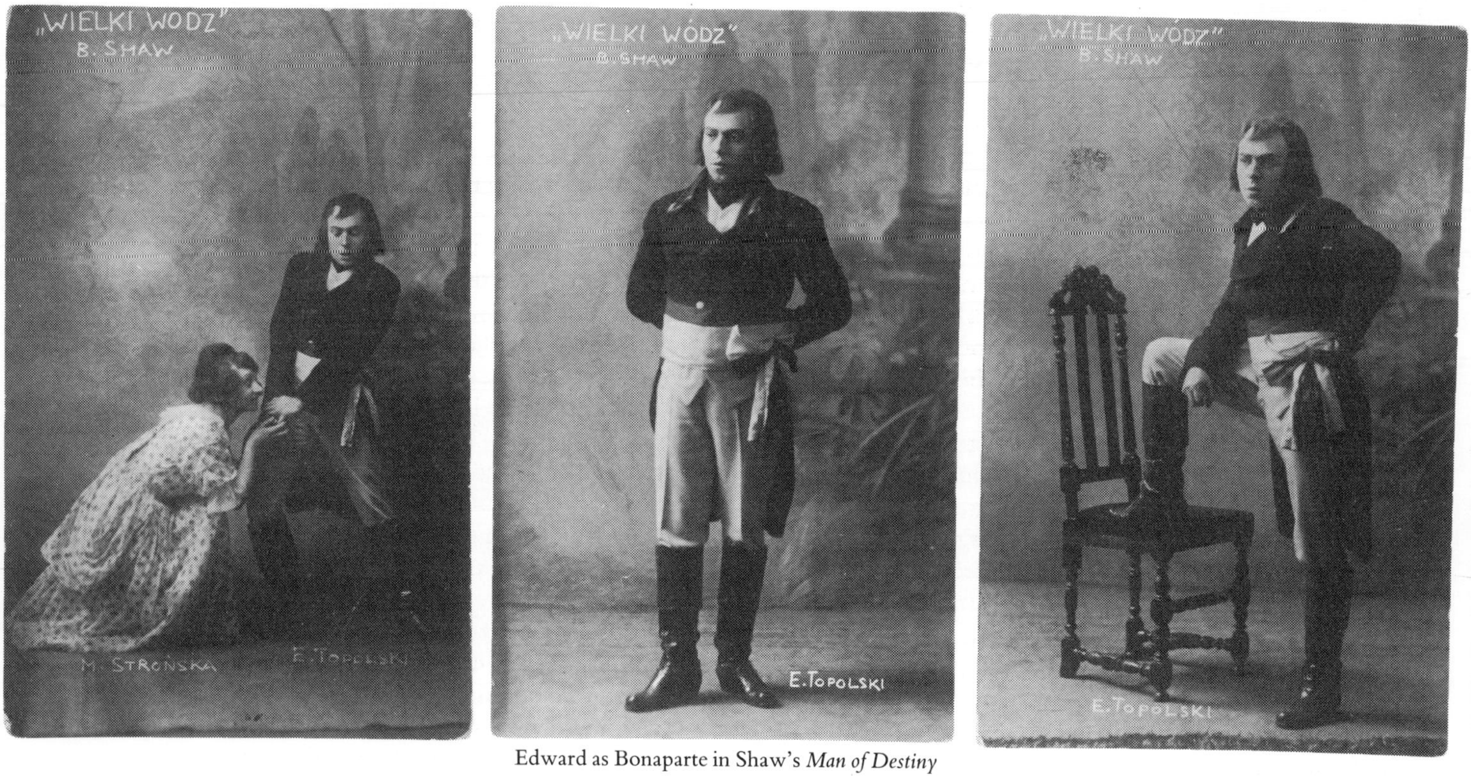

Edward as Bonaparte in Shaw's *Man of Destiny*

confronted by the unknown-to-them black-coated and -capped Orthodox Jews of central Poland, would have brutish flings at tearing/lopping off their beards and side-curls.

In 1920 the Russians pressed on to the Vistula, towards Warsaw. So near, that for nights of respite, the commander of the 3rd Division, Colonel Fabrycy, would stay with one of his officers at our tiny flat: glistening equipment and huge man, his feet overhanging the end of the bed.

The dream begins then and recurs: all within our two-room-kitchen flat (in faithful replica of reality), out of the passage-narrowness and the loo, grimy fully armed Polish soldiers press and crouch stealthily, break through in bayonet-charge, belying the impossibly minute kitchen space round stove/sink, at the backstairs door – it bursts open and a fierce tight landing/staircase battle, bizarrely compressed, swings back and forth, the Russians pressing from below, into the kitchen – all-in: heroic gestures, banners, trumpets and drums, firing, shouts, songs, the wounded, the tangled. But, is reality already intermingling? Under and beyond struggling feet the skimpily curtained alcove with the naked pair: our new peasant maid lodged there and the batman of the Lieutenant, the Colonel's ADC, also on one night's leave, camped in the kitchen for lack of space – his humble boots lined up with the officer's for polishing.

This day crowds the memory. A night sharing my room with the ADC – the Lieutenant, my future stepfather – his naked bare thin shape watched sliding out towards my mother's bedroom. The morning's unexpected arrival of my father from the front and his son's shaken and revengeful half-disclosures. In the evening the rooms were packed, as most often, but this time in the mood of extremity.

War and threatened defeat – tensions, despondency, courage, suspense erupted in tragedy: military belts with weapons attached left in the hall, the boy's juvenile bravado, and a schoolgirl cousin, Zosia, shot dead. They were both there round my mother: my father and the Lieutenant. The bemedalled officer broke down in tears – the actor, calm, comforted him.

This **sacrificial girl** (the minute red dot on her forehead) and the bloody victory, to be called 'Miracle of the Vistula'. And the boy pampered/comforted by parents, friends, the police, teachers, schoolmates, even later by her parents destroyed utterly – an accident, yet he sees himself undeserving of all this, unable though to grip at this shame, at this unease, since it is not plain and definable guilt, but the sympathetic verdict 'innocent' which could not rub out the fact of death at his hand.

Soon after Poland's liberation it must have been, my father acted in Warsaw: he played Starosta in the patriotic melodrama *Kościuszko pod Racławicami* at the Teatr Mały ('Small Theatre') and then, at the Teatr Nowoczesny ('Modern Theatre'), **Napoleon Bonaparte** in Bernard Shaw's *Man of Destiny*. Stiffly posed photographs, when I put them before Shaw himself years later in London, drew an uncommitted 'He must have made a **good Bonaparte**'. He must have, with his speech-making and declamatory voice and his actor's clean-shaven face – no whiskers (early photographs show him, when not yet on the stage, as a tribune-speaker, with a narrow moustache), as it behoved an actor open to transformations.

A man of books (his poetry recitals, his bookshop browsing, his rare reading to me, a mere child in bed about to fall asleep, long passages from *Pan Tadeusz*), he would, with studied grace (his proudly beautiful hands), spray his joint thumb and index with a dash of spit for turning a page – a gesture assumed to be refined and hygienic. Papers in his desk drawers (part of a Biedermeier set of furniture assembled piece by piece over years) he organized so meticulously that my secret incursions into their contents, however guarded and intent on exact repositionings, were always detected and punished: those elegantly shaped palms descended on the backs of mine with unexpected paining force.

Around my sixteenth, seventeenth year my father began to warm to me – a sort of **camaraderie** ensued, with the son tending to feel fatherly tolerance towards the other's weaknesses. The divorce and my mother's marriage to the Lieutenant-become-Captain caused a *contre-danse* shift: the Captain mostly absent (as previously my father) at his garrison town would, on collecting his monthly pay, rush secretly to Warsaw's race course, propelled by precise calculations, lose the money and sneak back; my father, having absented himself from Warsaw and home almost throughout his acting life with his theatrical and romantic engagements in distant towns, chose now to settle in Warsaw and to become an unfailing everyday caller on his one-time wife.

From *Wśród autorów i Książek* ('Amongst Authors and Books'), published by KSIĄŻKA I WIEDZA, 1975, by Władysław Grzelak, Poland. Władysław Grzelak, whose memoirs as a life-long assistant, then manager, at leading Warsaw bookshops, contain this and other passages about my father:

> Our bookshop could boast only one client of the true bohemian sort. But he was a truly **thoroughbred bohemian**. We owed his visits mainly to his old acquaintanceship with the head of the bookshop. He served Melpomene, therefore only when he had time to spare would he drop in to chat on the way from his nearby flat. He was treated not so much as a client, but rather as a guest, though it would happen that sometimes he bought a book. A guest happily received by the whole staff and always ready to offer a witticism or the latest joke. Such a bohemian was Edward Topolski, an enchanting man, always serene, word-spinner of resonant voice and clear delivery. He would bring into the bookshop a calm and carefree atmosphere. His shape could remind one somewhat of Napoleon and indeed he created the great leader in Bernard Shaw's play on the boards of Teatr Nowoczesny with considerable success. Later he played some dignitary, I believe Starosta, in *Kościuszko pod Racławicami* ('Kosciuszko at Raclavitze') on the stage of Teatr Mały. . .
>
> By the by, it may be worth adding that, at times, there would come with Mr Edward his juvenile son Feliks who, as it is known, grew into a draughtsman, caricaturist and painter famed in our country and abroad. . .

At not yet forty Edward was becoming a stylishly mellow bachelorish personage: dandyish clothes made by the best Warsaw tailor; a chained watch and a massive ring dressing his soft hand, and pride in the smallness of his feet, forcing them into too-tight shoes, thus to a half-gait/half-skid when proceeding along the Warsaw pavements, ever assisted by one or other of his female acolytes, the hyper-tailored tight-waisted flaring-out autumnal (*jesionka*) top-coat or, well above his station, the winter number sealskin-lined (*foki*) with an otter skin (*wydra*) collar. The wide-brimmed black hat and a silver-topped stick gave his son imperishably his backview silhouette, ever returning re-entering in a sorrowful troubled **chain of dreams** – thirty-five years after his death – in which the son, certain that his father is in London and easy to reach, yearns to make amends but stays benumbed – horrified at himself. And then – the dream continues – his father's back appears receding along a London street – hat/tight-waisted/stick – still painfully attainable as long as the dream holds. In reality he – his acting career squandered – by then touchingly performed in life, which became chequered into almost sealed-off compartments – '**plays**', almost, because somehow his son transgressed the borders, was admitted as the sole audience of most, watchful, with the tender bond of comprehension.

The schoolboy son's Sunday visits at his bachelor one-room flatlet would entail attendance at prolonged act of levee amidst his treasured suite of Biedermeiers: the ablutions, the nail trimming, the fastidiousness of his dressing, and vocalities (poetry included).

With my privileged circumstance, I would, with my father, partake of lunches or fluent evening gatherings at his sister's and her lawyer husband's home. I would join modest editorial meetings of the small theatrical magazine now run by him with Madame Marcinkowska, a do-all devotee (heavy *maquillage* and blackened hair) at a humble café glued to the side of Teatr Polski. In various settings I would accompany him and the young former leading actress of his front-line theatre – a very thin and determined girl; and my mother and I would see him every day at our home. Once (I was not expected) I entered his bachelor room, left unlocked, and, even then, the performance was well produced. A *tableau vivant*: in the depth of the pretty room, opposite the door, on a decoratively unmade bed, he held, in a static embrace, fully clothed, an ample painted and peroxided female.

One day in 1926, in good form, Edward lunched at his sister's, but next morning he was dead on his bed, dressed, with a basin at his side, as if in anticipation of sickness. The family persuaded me, whose decision it had to be, to refuse the sordid routine of autopsy. Thus his death remained **a mystery** – perhaps his carefully divided life had overlapped this once.

Immediately after his funeral his actress lover pressed with urgency to see me alone in her rooms and appeared to wish to pass her attachment on to me.

Saski Ogród (Saxon Park) – a child skipped in from the eastern end – a schoolboy left through the other gate (edging his *gymnasium*) after football games, aloofly bypassing **the regular skirmishes** of his colleagues, expressing themselves thus with the comparative ruffians of the enemy school, Kopernik's – their black headgear modelled on Austrian military 'pots'.

These nasty excesses (stones the ammunition) were beneath my classroom *milieu*, but the fashion for jousts between schools spread unpredictably: one afternoon, strolling home after school, I entered my street routinely – the first after Saski Ogród, turning from a leading avenue, and emerging at the other end into a large square: a stage for the urban confrontation between a handsome church and the pressing of a proletarian, mostly Jewish quarter.

Beyond the towering Telephone Centre, there stood across Próżna Street **two bellicose lines**, facing one another, of – now, as I closed in on them, recognizable – *Koperniki* with their backs to me and, opposing them at a few steps' distance, the local boys, sons of wretched Jewish menials and tradesmen, from the far end of the street and beyond.

However this battle order came into being – a challenge, surely not by chance – this was the classical moment of pre-engagement invective. And my home being beyond these lines, I walked on, did not slow down, rapidly assessing the situation (was I ten then?): the proletarian warriors must have known me by sight as a native of the street, while the blatantly different schoolcap on my head – a distinguishing emblem of the acclaimed, established adversaries of Kopernik's – should also be acknowledged by them; yet the same cap (and the leather-strapped books under my arm) marked me for the *Koperniki*, I hoped, as neutral in this conflict . . .

And, indeed, the *Koperniki* opened their line for me in recognition of the knightly code – mere seconds and two or three steps to reach the opposing 'front' – when a large dusky brute (the tinsmith's son) landed his fist in my eye – the first blow of this encounter, of a proletarian revolution even, against the 'class' personified by this schoolboy 'representative'.

But in Saski Ogród's topography this was the rarest of incidents (the school battles were of an entirely different kind – ritualized jousts); the other edge of the park – linked with my school, the eighteenth-century circular church of the Lutheran community, and the turn-of-the-century Art Gallery – opened through colonnaded entrance winged left and right by the Saxon Palace, led into the huge Plac Saski (Saxon Square), surmounted, filled up to the brim (during the first years of my schooling) by the Sobór – the Russian Orthodox cathedral – an alien white mammoth bulging on top with a multitude of gold-glowing, bulbous onions.

As the earliest deed, the Russian rule banished from Poland, the Sobór was swept away, leaving a never-resolved dreary flatness, planting early seeds of contrariness in me.

And so, in today's Warsaw, raised from the German-inflicted ruins at speed, with large sections obedient to the blank Stalinist pseudo-classicism reigning in Soviet Russia in disregard of the talented and mostly ambitiously 'modern' architects of Poland, the Russians offered – to top this – a scale-upsetting, sky-scraping 'Palace of Culture' – a 'generosity' at odds with the past fate of the Sobór.

All these became for the Poles habitual objects of truistic hate and mockery – and my counter-arguments would be received as *faux pas*. I claimed the need for gratification: cities grow over centuries, illustrating history by their changes and accumulations of shapes – Warsaw and its past was wiped out, but the short yet crowded sequence of moods, political suppressions, interpolated with surges of creative liberation and Western inroads, have all produced their architectural evidence; one moves through this new Warsaw as if through the history of those not-quite-forty years, with the upsurge of patriotism in re-creating a new/old city, with the everyday/symbolic reminder of the country's dependence, with continuously varying urban sections – not a commanded city, but grown in layers through its compressed revival.

My growing **classroom popularity** reached its zenith in the sixth form (at sixteen) when, at its yearly **self-government** elections I got the highest (in fact, everybody's) vote, but declined the Presidency and offered to serve instead as mere Secretary recording the progress of its functioning.

Why such esteem? Not the particular gift of my hand. Not my everyman's averageness – not too small, not too tall, not too bright a scholar (though good at reciting/reading poetry and prose in Polish literature lessons) – well supported by respect-causing physical strength, revealed in frequent sparring bouts (according to unwritten rules: always fair, never hitting below the waist, but also not the head – and the adversary's shoulders on the ground ending the contest; all this with one exception: Focht fought in anger and his hooligan out-to-kill style was to tuck the other's head under his arm and slam it against any hard edge – he was resented and ostracized). The sole possible reason for this build up of popularity must have been my public silence. To recite my homework was a necessity but taking upon myself to stand up and declare myself, in front of my forty or so colleagues, was beyond me. And so, during the self-government debates I could only whisper my views/protestations to my nearest neighbour, nudging him to voice them for me. My muteness then, coupled with a generally recognized soundness, put me into leadership – perhaps a unique case.

Why refuse? Not noble modesty for sure. It was the same triviality: shyness, shrinking from any exposure – to preside at a meeting, thus to have to utter conventional opening words, caused secret panic; and all other functions in self-government would have demanded pronouncements, except that of a recorder-secretary: reading out written matter was within my equipment.

With the school years accumulating, so was **my talent's reputation** – based on what? Because it seemed to be emerging solely in the senselessly, persistently and meticulously rendered (amongst the notes in my exercise books) feet of my schoolmates, as they stood/shuffled on the platform at the front of the class, by the blackboard (the routine for presenting homework) –

amounting to some half-a-dozen feet up to half-shin or so per lesson. Year after year these foot portraits were accumulating, but, in justice, the feet variations, thus descriptive challenges for the draughtsman, were enormous: the war and post-war shortages, the multi-national military-surplus sources, the greatly differing backgrounds of the wearers – not mitigated yet by stability's convenances. The footwear of a peasant, a plutocratic Jew, an aristocrat, a refugee from Russia, a football fan, a pastor's son, an academic's son, a tradesman's son, an officer's stepson. The portraits were recognizable – and, perhaps, with such an obsessionally limited subject, led the hand/eye to accuracy.

Anyway, the fame spread. The gym master, of immense chest and noble moustache, in the earlier years animose, began to give the artist the top mark of five. And, at the finale of my schooling, Director Ronthaler offered me the post of art master. Deliberations with my mother at this honour cum security chance for ever followed – and the proposal was declined.

Very early, **the collusion** of two discordant musings played, I suppose, the 'identity' game.

One – play-acting: that is, rubbing out the assumption of being oneself – as an ineradicable **individuus**, a solid opponent – a **myself** – to non-existence – except by taking on roles. This was and is strongly present in any sort of intercourse, but, puzzlingly, did not eradicate trust in one's gifts as an artist, having settled early for the comfort-irresponsibility of 'promise' – possibly as one of the roles. To clarify this, even for my own mind, it must mean simply a fundamental doubt as to the 'identity' concept as such and particularly when applied to me; the unimportance of myself, ever ready to accept others' right of way, not prepared to enter any competition, astonished at marks of appreciation and tending to suppose them to be a sort of mistake or befuddlement (all this again concerns only my physical, not artistic self – as said above, this was shelved out of the way as 'promise'), denying myself any validity for self-assertion, but seeing my progress through life as a gaseous plasmatoid's erratic and continuous reshaping to accommodate/flow over or round other more solid forms.

Alongside, a child's contrasting fantasy, faded out later (but entirely?): the only *real* living being, ME, within the world of still puppetry, so that only my advancing through it stirs the dormant perspectives to response; people, animals, machines act, plants sway and exhale scents, clouds bustle; I encounter and involve – or am commanded, wronged by parents, neighbours, teachers, but all this living activity, when out of my sight, instantly relapses into staticality – in waiting readiness for the return of my attention, maybe never to come its way.

Cornered very recently (June 1984!) as never before: **the old boys' reunion** lunch in London of my Mikołaj Rey School in Warsaw; Rey – the sixteenth-century's first writer in Polish, not Latin, and a convert to Protestantism, thus the right patron for a school founded by the Augsburgian-Evangelist congregation and attached to their circular church.

Astonishingly as many as eleven old boys (and some wives) of various ages assemble in London's Polish House – the oldest, a ramrod figure, having matriculated in 1915, the youngest in the thirties, myself in 1925; and quite a number of fraternal messages arrive from the far ends of the globe. The wives may be assumed guilty of disrupting the flow of remembrances, which soon run dry into mere litanies of teachers' names. Another diminishing factor: each of us belonged to a different vintage. But although the Sunday-groomed men round the table manage to sentimentalize, I find it hard to make out any communally worthy themes: my school was a bondage to me.

History – eruptive in the extreme during those years; pouring into our streets and lives – trickled meekly through the schoolboy's daily ordeals, the 'milestones' of his growing pains. The Russians in possession; the Germans triumphant, then disarmed in the streets of freed-Poland's Warsaw; the defeat of Trotsky's armies marching on Europe.

But: each morning's trotting over the short distance, almost always late (for luck skipping over the joints of paving stones), mumbling repetitious private prayers, 'Let me not be called . . .', against that day's expected threats (each day renewed, but all nauseating in their relentless indifference towards life outside) of calls to the blackboard; of written class tests; of, hour after hour, dodging the teacher's eye; of ill-prepared passages/problems/ exercises – crammed ahead and bit by bit – throughout the course of a day, in case of an unpredictable challenge; of cribbing or, when singled out by a pitiless master, straining an ear towards co-operative corner-of-the-mouth promptings. This from eight to two or three in the afternoon, only a few hours in the week (Polish literature, history, gym, geography) easy-going or even engrossing, but some (drawing, religion) used solely for stealthy catching up on following oppressive subjects. Then rush home with an overload of homework – never surmounted: either too much (Latin, Latin, Latin) or plainly above my head (geometry, trigonometry, physics) – struggled with helplessly till late hours, to be followed by the next day's almost uninterrupted panic.

Yet we acquired, truly, a general knowledge from A to Z, our curriculum embracing the wholeness of each subject, however thinly spread within each term's practice, to the last page of prescribed textbooks. None of the British specialization in minute sectors. But the essence of those eight, no, nine years, six to seven hours of each classroom day, was consumed mainly by self-training in tactics of evasion.

Thus my 'public' school years would not, as in boarders' England, stand out as the nostalgia-loaded climax of life, but the opposite: the unavoidable and precarious springboard to life, or rather a semi-open prison eventually unlocking its gates to earthly paradise.

A love-making device to counter youthful hasty ejaculations, worked by shut-eyed imaginings/ recollections of cross-lovely-country horseback racing over and towards a tree-banked edge of grassery: there, under the lids, would strain to living clarity, in transferred elation, the rhythms of the horse's head/ears/ mane, the streaking of the ground underneath, the rub of the saddle, the acceleration, spurs and reins pressed, gaining on adversaries and on further horizons and skies (also in competition) – all glowing in the day's height.

Precise, the details and the motion had to be, to divert the ravishment without loosing it. And the past reality of such a ride, stimulated by the sweep of a meadow into an impulse race: its crowded camaraderie, yet the startling manifestation of the fierceness of one's will to win – all this, implanted in memory, carried onward (above its side uses) the love of **horsemanship**.

There were those early, repressed, rides with the Colonel's wife. Fourteen, fifteen years old? An ugly, spotty, curly-low-over-the-forehead, small, shy specimen. An Eastern Poland vacation within the military complex of the 3rd Division on the move; the ADC and his new family are billeted in a village house on the ground floor, with Colonel Fabrycy, the new CO of the 3rd Division, and his wife, above. She, an imposing – and of spectacular dignity – raven-haired caryatid, rode every morning, assisted by another adjutant, a singularly red-faced gallant. And – a shock of disbelief – one evening our ceiling reverberates with bawling, banging, clanging, shrieks.

The next day the boy is commandeered by the Colonel to accompany his wife on that adjutant's horse, and from then on she and he, an incongruous pair, hack regularly, almost in silence, with her now and again exploding: 'Keep off me! Your stirrup! Don't bloody ride over me!' as the well-drilled horse nudges in.

There were later rides, jolly but of necessity soaked: the reconstituted Poland gave to her defenders modest plots of land in the Ruthenian East – a gratitude gesture and a 'colonial' gain at one swoop. General Berbecki, one of the élite of Piłsudski's *Legiony* and the first CO of the Division, was given a plot of the prescribed size, but in the centre of a parcelled estate containing a tenderly aged timber mansion: it was natural that his devoted adjutant – my stepfather – chose to have an adjacent plot to be part of the larger whole. Thus, during the school vacations we lived with the Berbeckis; thus, in this modest establishment, the few retired cavalry horses worked, and were free for our (the general's two sons' and my) equestrianism only under heavy rains.

Still a schoolboy, moderately diligent in the classroom, earnest at reading and pencilling, a jot adventurous in artless reachings towards sexuality, but essentially solitary; the penchant welded to a gift concocts/fortifies the most promising concentration and develops the furthest. But

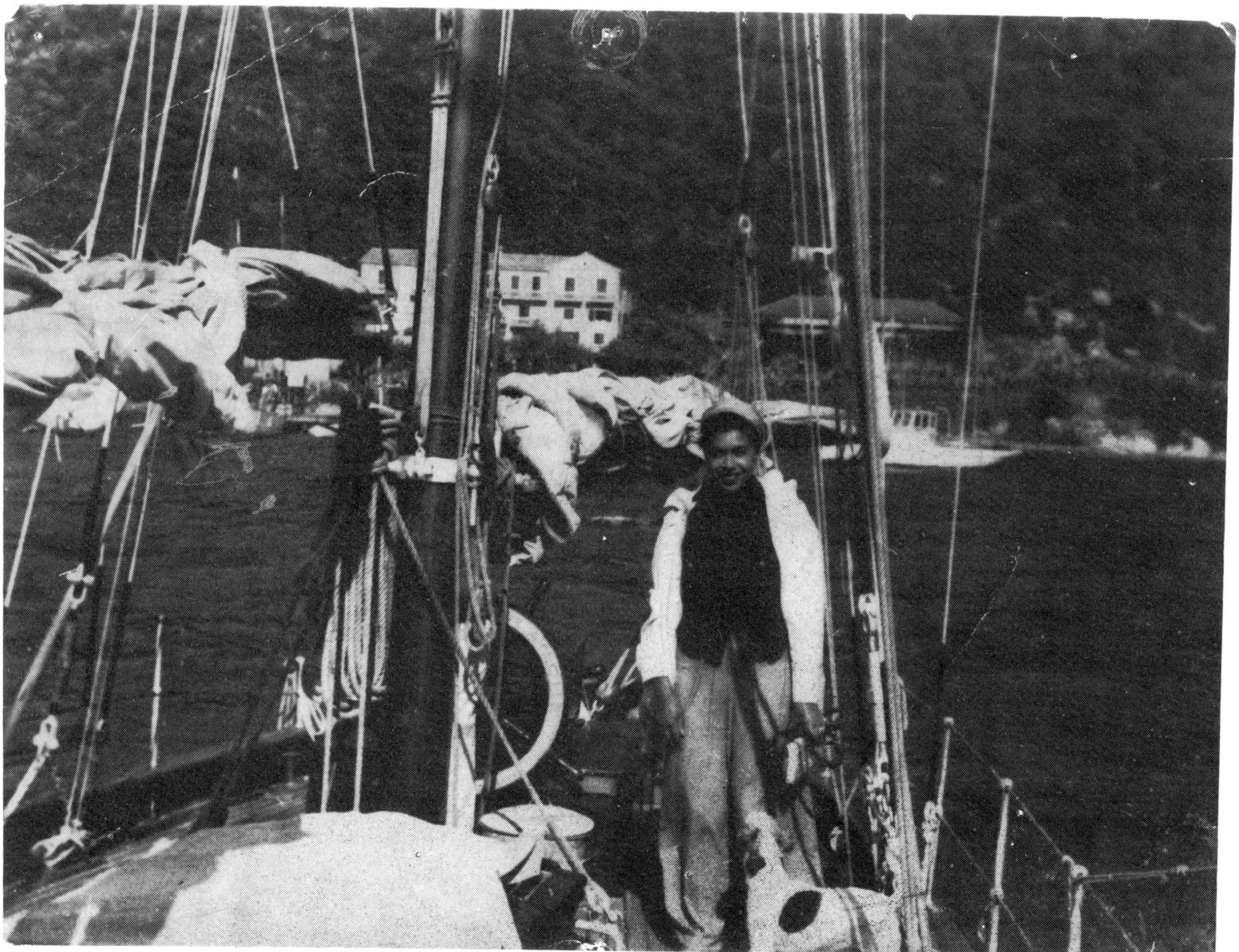

Dolly on the Riviera

my anxious mother heading a chorus of aunts fought to bring the boy to a supposedly desirable sociability. They won: pushed out of withdrawn shyness, at first clumsily ill-fitting, I developed a dependence on 'mixing'; perhaps gaining eventually in scope, but losing in attentiveness: a different artist emerging from the one intended by nature.

During the self conscious adaptation stage, staying with an aunt at a summer resort, although I carried out a covert and daring affair with her peasant maid (in the woods, on a kitchen table), when encompassed by a dashing group of my contemporaries my clumsy clothes stitched out of old uniforms consorted well with this awkward boy. And the most worldly and intimidating amongst them was **Dolly**. She and they all looked down at me from their well-off sophistication.

Each autumn Dolly, after her school hours, would turn herself into a mystery black-lace-veiled female and roam/intrigue the café life of Warsaw fashion. Her striking uniqueness intrigued even more: her physique was almost that of a svelte Creole – her features had a negroid touch (unaccountable in Warsaw). She could have been a mulatto; but how? Her parents were Russian – a Pushkin connection? They were rather grand – he a Russian banker who had stayed on in Poland, the mother a calm elegant woman who, in the Tsarist time, in close alliance with Madame Sempołowska (imposingly draped in long folds), laboured bravely aiding Polish political prisoners. And so Dolly Kamienka combined her panache with social privileges: equipped with languages and moving around Europe – her style, prematurely mature (outside school), a shadow-play.

So it should be clear that in those earlier encounters she stood out within her crowd and hardly condescended to notice me, while I did not consider any of them singly, including her, as my mates or desirables, but, as a group, giving me an unwelcome sense of inferiority.

How did the *volte-face* of the whole commerce perform itself? Myself, a self-assured and eccentrically dressy gallant cum art student; and Dolly following me devotedly to my *Kazimierz*, stricken by jealousy and tearsome and burdening me, unwilling, with deflowering her.

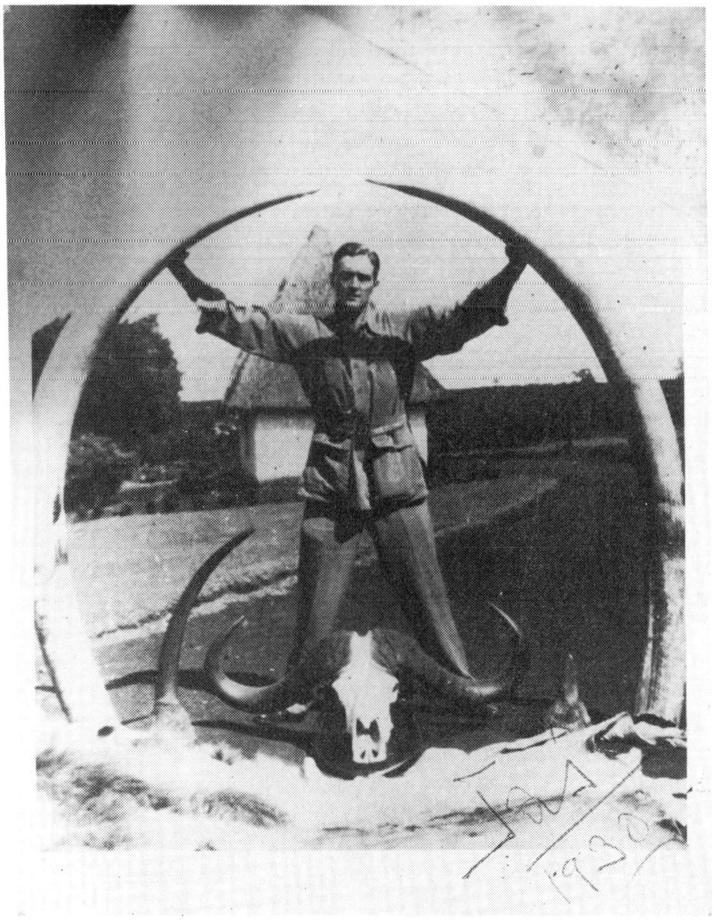

Jaś Tarnowski

Finding my grown-up feet: the widespread applause given to my emerging performance in art and society and manhood, to me (doubting myself) all verging on fraudulent – made verifying/testing my young years' dominant compulsion.

Well carved in memory, exhilaration over a corporeal engagement: Andzia, a massive peasant girl of great sexual ardour and catholicity arrived at a *rendezvous* with me, hours late and befuddled; the first encounter over, the long sleep – and, both half awakened, clasp again – she crying out, 'Kubuś! Kubuś!' or some other pet name with a plebeian/rustic connotation. And so my orgasmic explosion is enhanced by rapturous self-laudation: in bringing out Andzia's fervour for a 'Kubuś' I am proved to equal an *everyman*.

Thus many a competitiveness must be sparked. Unsure, I would tend to trust my nerve, rather than muscle, preferring to team with a horse's strength – and arriving first. But there was this long chaotic swim-become-race along a stretch of the Vistula, which I had to win – conscious of a rising heat, and still so on emerging from the cold river; did it permeate the depth of the body or burn the skin only?

But how does this assurance testing and all its contradictory deliberations fit with this sample (my final Warsaw year) on the theme of corrupted swankiness – ingrained to become my nature, or still put on?

The top night-club has engaged an impressive dancing pair of Hungarians: she, a grand blonde; he, a stringy dark smoothie. I am paired (it is not a regular operative team but friendly camaraderie) with an exquisitely and handsomely aristocratic homosexual 'Jaś' Tarnowski ('Count', but titles were officially abolished in the new Poland and honestly shrugged off in social practice) back in Poland after legendary culture-cum-hunting dandying between Peking and Nairobi – Europe thrown in. We two are perched at a bar (chain of *wódki* and salty nuts) in the shut-off emptiness above the floor show and crowded tables below, our conversation minimal, humour minimal – there is even some *wódka*-soaked grimness. Indeed, we lay in wait, as it were marksmen-hunters, for the completion of the pair's performance – to captivate them and – cleave them.

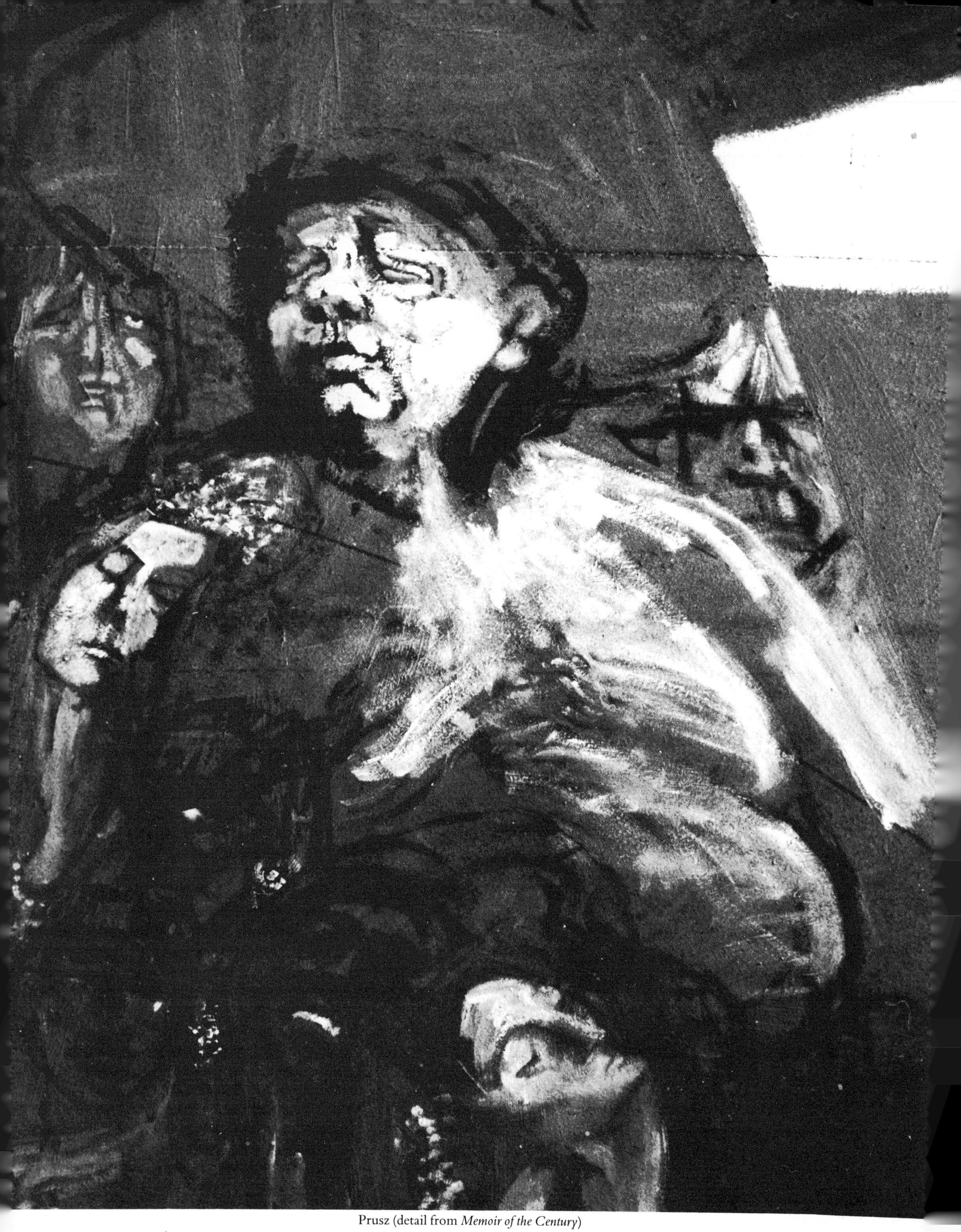

Prusz (detail from *Memoir of the Century*)

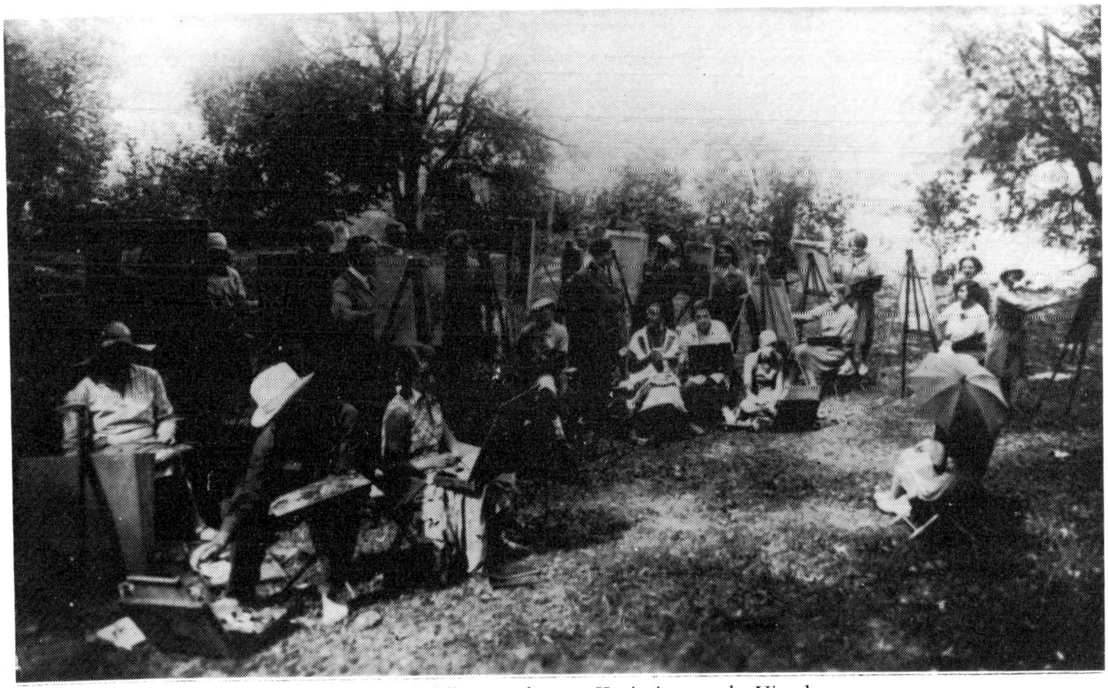

Summer with fellow students at Kazimierz on the Vistula

I have to write about PRUSZ*, to flatten GRUBAS ('Fatty'), that bulkiness, 100 kilos of supreme vitality, Janus in his curiosities, the unquestionably three-dimensionalist – into the flounder of a notepaper sheet. Also to write about the most serene being, whose buoyant life was cut short by a grim murder. The cruel discordance of his tragic death at the enemy's hands gauges the substance of peace and war of our days, but how hard to apply the epic scale to familiar matters; and to settle to dilettante scribbling about the human tragicomedy, enlarged by history to immensity. . .

Fanning out faded photographs. The first shows (in the smudge of a sunray that broke into the flimsy camera) the summer-flushed Vistula at Kazimierz with near-bare formation of bathers graded from waist deep to heads afloat in the river, a clowning 'group allegory': Grubas and we, his disciples crowned by body-perfect Halszka. Allegory of what? Perhaps of the young, hope-winged Polish Art, the New Warsaw Academy of Art, and, particularly, the Prusz education.

Next snap: Prusz strolls through the *galimatias* of the Market Square in Kazimierz, shortish, square and of huge dimpled chubbiness, hugely brimmed hat, hugely original here-and-there wrinkled belted jacket, boots laced up to the knees over huge calves. The flock of pupils follows, cuts into, contrasts with, the Jewish and peasant trading: our girls-nymphs draped in rustic capes, decorated fastidiously with strings of corals and flowers, lanky beggary barefooted boys topped by straw hats, 'new' pups hung over with painters' paraphernalia, spellbound by the master – Grubas strolls and teaches.

And this one: a plum orchard, sun-sprinkled, Vistula-girded. Again these girl-ornaments, the pseudo beggarboys and the show-off peacocks – all at easels (Prusz at hand), all diligently splashing their canvases with greeny flourishes: a ***plein-air* in Kazimierz-on-the-Vistula**, year 1927, and my second summer with Grubas. For my first summer with him I slid straight from school, ahead of my acceptance at the Academy. And to relate how it all happened will tell a lot about Prusz, although also weaving in my mother's merits.

My good mother respected her son's daubing/scribbling predilections and when, some time around my seventh year at school, I commenced artistic revolts against wasting two more years, she made the rounds, with a pile of my drawings, of the high priests of the painterly cult to learn the truth about my 'vocation'. Devotedly she pilgrimmed, received civilly with praises and good advice, until she arrived at Pruszkowski. Prusz's opinion was in accord with the others', but what is essential is that, faced with the work of a promising youngster, he reacted 100-per-cent – in that, while several others offered noncommittal encouragements, he gave spontaneously of himself, his time, his talent as a pedagogue. They all said: he must get his matriculation first – only then the Art Academy. Prusz said the same, but did not wish to lose sight of me in the meantime. He made me a present of a few evenings a week. He instructed me, setting pictorial tasks and revising the results regularly and minutely, generous with his time, which he, more than anyone else, could use in a thousand beguiling ways. Wondrous evenings. My schoolboy's cap pocketed, the loaded climb up to his attic (legend had it that the young Prusz-student similarly worked his way each morning up the backstairs to the studio of his master Krzyżanowski, 'visiting' kitchenmaids systematically one after another, floor by floor – and, diligent pupil, still reaching it before all the others). Grubas's door, not easy to grope for in the dark confusion of the two flats glued together into one, would be opened by him, or his **Pani Zuzia** (Madame Pruszkowska), lovely, decorative doll, or, better still, by **Jola**, their ward, flaxen hair round a wilful face.

The overworked schoolboy plunged into this domain of the sources of all heavenly delights – art, enchanting beautiful women, bohemian interiors opening up sesame-like: to the

*Fragments (in translation) of my text: 'Tadeusz Pruszkowski, executed by the Germans in 1942', from *Straty Kultury Polskiej 1939–1944* ('Losses in Polish Culture 1939–1944'), published in Polish by Książnica Polska (Glasgow, 1945).

left the master's workshop, oil aromas and holy disarray, canvases and books; to the right the fairyland of frills and flutters, Biedermeiers and Zuzi's chirrupings – the sphere of Taste not of Art. And, in the shade of passageways, halfway in between, Jola – sullen, overcast – a promise of the raptures of disharmony, fascination of blunders, temptation of digressions into murky but frolicsome corridors of *la vie de bohème*. The wholeness of the 'art world', as anticipated by me.

Thus, in Prusz's quarters, I was instructed not only in art, but in finding my way around the world of 'taste', and also in living. My father died at this time: Prusz stepped in during those vital years: I matured within his aura. I speak, apparently, in his idiom; I think now and again along his 'line of thought'. Prusz gave munificently his energy and heart to this stripling. And this is not all. My mother would tell him, with some naivety, of my cinematic urges – that not painting alone but interweaving film-making might strengthen the fabric of her treasure's future. And look, one more photograph: Prusz turns the handle of a *Debris* film camera against the background of Kazimierz quarries – Zygmunt Jurkowski and I round him, directors, scriptwriters, editors, text-mounters of a film, silent and comic, titled *The Happy Hanged Man or California in Poland*, acted by our colleagues. The film is shown in the 'Splendid', Warsaw's largest cinema; critics write 'new epoch in film', 'jejeune'; the distributors trip us up, resentful at the amateurs' intrusion; the public keeps away – one week's run, a flop. Prusz dismisses film-making as business corrupted. [. . .]

He carried about *Pickwick Papers*, discussed *Candide*, quoted *Colas Breugnon*, read aloud long passages from *Manuscrit trouvé à Saragosse*. Settled broadly within the charms of his countrified Kazimierz interior, he would perorate most wittily and most wisely. To be with him was a sublime ceremonial but of hellish verve! Ribald robustness interlaced with the finesse of an uncommon taste: cynicism with the visionary. Prusz taught us 'renaissancism', objectivism, irony – altogether a 'liberated' life.

One more snap – the last I possess: Prusz-airman stands sturdily on the Vistula beach in front of his overturned 'Moth'. In the lengthy collection of his passions (his always overflowing energy) flying was probably the last to arrive. [. . .]

Have I managed in this disjointed (how otherwise) piece, to show a living man? Alive enough, for the death meted out to him to testify to the boundless ignominy of the invaders, the enemies of light.

This is and reads as an obituary. So some living tissue of those days: Matriculation won – just just, I set out for the first time ever on my own, still in my schoolboy's approximation of plus-fours (I had nothing else) but provided with my mother's parting gift – a package of condoms.

Prusz thoughtfully alerted his students to me, his newest whimsy, with *Kazimierz* lodgings reserved, as was their way, in a villager's thatched roofed cottage – already partly occupied by two senior star pupils of the graphics department. Instructed to introduce myself, I knocked at their door: a ravishment, as if staged for my eye – a *tableau* of idealized rusticity; the interior's true modesty (timber walls and small-paned windows) lifted (the folk paintings on glass and the galaxy of flowers and dry grasses in support) to the most achieved work of art-of-the-interior.

The homespun riches expertly hunted out from villages (sashes, capes, skirts, kerchiefs, sequined waistcoats, shawls, rugs – wisely selected for patterns and stages of fadedness); the country-fair strings of beads, necklaces, rings – the gaudy glitter of glass-and-tin jewellery: all this draped over the room in tumultuous harmony – ascending enwrapping embellishing the beautiful being seated crosslegged on the bed: immobile, only her hands carving a woodblock in small deft movements; and, yes, she offered a smile.

There is a proverbial Tatra-mountain type of beauty most respected in Poland: it is evolved not so much from heredity as from folklore ballads about a breed of never-enslaved rock-leaping robbers, benefactors of the poor with the alertness – given by the heights – of a bird-of-prey's nature – and features. They do not all match this image; but the ideal is unmistakable – and **Bogna** Krasnodębska had this face: tightly boned, hawk-eyed, dark hair parted at the centre smoothly bunned back ; and there, suitably folk-embellished, she squatted – an icon.

An icon, holiness to worship. In came her room-mate also a distinguished graphic artist **Janka** Konarska, an incarnated blonde daintiness – my eyes felt free to wander over the whole of her admirable construction, texture, detailing; she also wore folklore attire (including the local peasantry's straw hat), but, unlike Bogna's 'authenticity', hers was a 'regulation' style, turned by her advantages into elegance.

Men's damaging duality: awed by Bogna, I became glued to Janka throughout the summer, stepping close behind her along the narrownesses of the path (a meagre stream ran in the middle of our street leading to the Grubas' house), my eyes on her amazing ankles. Her numerous admirers (artist-colleagues and the celebrated poets, Słonimski and Wierzyński, descending from Warsaw) – and, indeed, she herself – were victimized by this schoolboy's blockade.

During that first summer I was cosseted as **Prusz's protégé** – thus, rather than feeling impelled to work, I gave my best attention to mastering the huge oar-poles which propelled heavy fishing boats over the fast tides and depths of **the Vistula** (Thames punting was child's play after that): the boats were hired from local fishermen for the summer – indispensable as transportations to the mid-river sandbanks or for diving from, after the early-morning painting sessions, which I attended erratically.

The Grubas' village house was open to all – an every-evening 'service', as indeed it was a temple of liberal rites. A countrified blend of his and Zuzi's aesthetic habits within one interior, it was, to me (to all of us) an ideal of unaffected, graceful ease; the bulkily moulded master – a lay-papal presence (no religion institutionalized or otherwise was ever scrutinized or followed – his genealogy was that of the Age of Self-indulgence and Reason) – never ponderous yet profound, deliberately provoking contradictions and distortions from the young circle, easily involving his contemporaries (visiting artists, pedagogues, writers). Joy for everybody, but for me – straight from school-home narrowness examination-dulled – the admission to **earthly paradise**.

Spoiled, softened by all this, I underwent the Academy's admission examination accepted *a priori* – the lazy bliss of favouritism jetpropelling me out of the chrysalis of awkwardness into rather facile but intoxicating aerobatics.

And consequently, not that first winter term, which should have been given to hard work, but the **Kazimierz** that followed was my time of fullness. This first proper student's summer was given over almost entirely to **film-making** (conceived between Prusz and my mother) – into which I brought another partner – **Zygmunt** Jurkowski. At the examination easels I fell into a lasting complementary friendship with Zygmunt – complementary because I think now that his spare handsome manliness and minor-gentry-bred brutality countered my soft-centred neatness, possibly because he, being much older than me, echoed those hard/large educationally backward school colleagues squeezed out from Russia by the Revolution, seated round me and bridging my passage from child to adulthood; perhaps there was in Zygmunt's strength (touching on evil) a counterpoint to Prusz's education in sensitivity? And what attracted him to me must also have rested in that obvious complementary otherness. And perhaps another link: his impressively uncouth aloofness emanating from his impressive he-man physique, though strangely knuckled and knotted, suggested a cover for unease.

He held back from the female students, as if defensively. In later Kazimierz summers he worked out devilish intrigues round my attachments. He also carried on to Warsaw schemes of envy and self-punishment centred round a girl-colleague he was attracted to, and suspected of being one of Prusz's liaisons, not meant to draw out any gain, not even her attention. There was a chain of these but only one I remember: he had secreted out an observation nest on a staircase (or was it an attic) in a house across the road, angling with mirrors and binoculars into her window. Long hours given to tracing her and Prusz's daily habits; still longer to the vigils at his post. Then his report, forced on me, reluctant to listen, amounting to her pincushioning his buttocks; I don't recollect any embroidering details – probably, like Renia (later), I recoiled from listening further.

Only with me was he at ease with such disclosures, besides initiating me, hitherto a rather private boy, into the Warsaw circuits of whoring, drinking and brawling. At the Academy though he was largely respected, and much later proved to be a very talented, ruthlessly satirical writer.

We contrasted still further in our style of dress. Zygmunt, from his entry into Art School and throughout his Warsaw progress, never abandoned his provincial (that is, unfastidiously ready-made) tweeds, collar-tie, high boots – all this, including black gathered under his nails, shoddy and sweaty.

I, when eventually out of adaptations of my stepfather's discarded khaki uniforms, was still in breeches-and-stockings, but, on the way to later dandyism, via an ambitious wardrobe inherited from my father, followed the arty-folksy fantasies of the elder students with shirts made from patterned cottons bought in Kazimierz market place – the affordable contribution. By then my boyish physique had established itself to last many years unchanged; somehow in that shortish structure resided unexpected strength, perhaps fostered by attentiveness (given top marks by imposing Professor Olszewski) to school gymnastics and proven in frequent wrestling with towering boys. Boating on the Vistula helped it further, so that the torso was praised, though legs were declared lacking. Just the same, my fussiness in dress and self-esteem (cohabiting with shyness) grew, bolstered by popularity and the girls' banal verdict 'the poor man's Ramon Navarro'. In sum: a sort of sensitivity and a gift, coupled with ardent appetites and acceptability – on credit; thus I pulled Zygmunt along into the Prusz circle, while he helped me to develop an outward muscle to cope

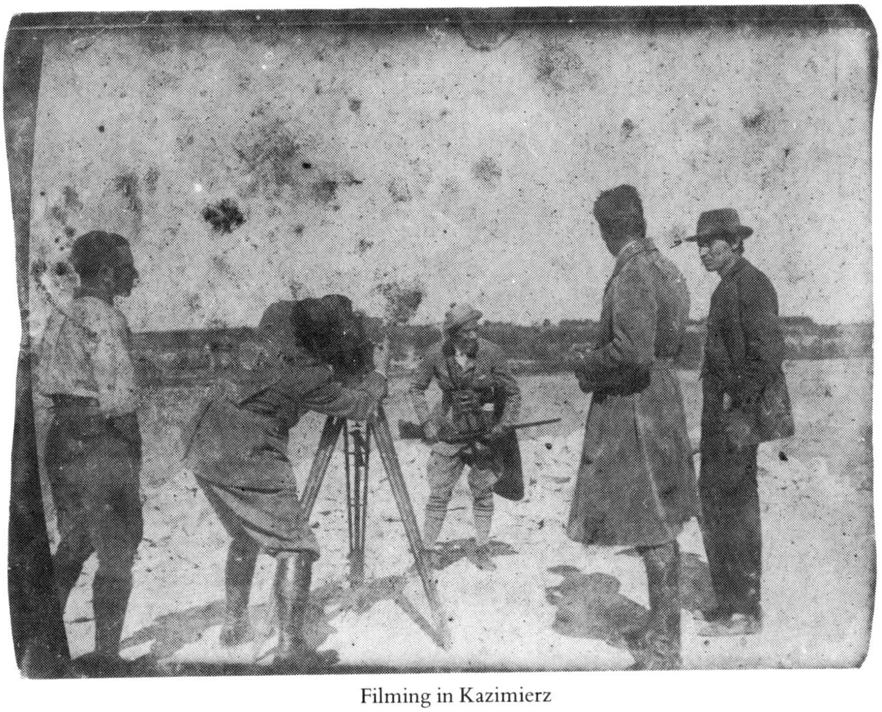

Filming in Kazimierz

with the rough-and-tumble of manly brotherhood.

On my leaving Poland we lost contact. After the war I heard that Zygmunt had been killed by the Nazis.

But it is still early days – my first proper student's summer, filming. And myself still romanticizing over and courting my female colleagues while lodging this year in a loose timber structure of cubicles built for farmhands, but inhabited now only by to my left **a model girl** brought from Warsaw for our open-air painting sessions, bedded with her girlfriend – and to my right – Zygmunt. What follows I record as the most pointed (in my early life that is) parable on the pestering theme of duality and its subdivisions. The model was a module of sinful attraction – her importuning muscled physique (appropriately her back's whiteness spot-sprinkled for emphasis) was endowed with a head (straight neck-held) and features of arresting coarseness: her bridgeless upturned and bulging nose, her brow shadowing set-back cross-eyedness, the whole effect that of dour single-mindedness. Her partner seemed an appendage: crippled by a slum case of rickets, her trunk contained what was needed. The partitioning of our cells was made of horizontal ill-fitting boards with wide crevices in between, over which we chalked on my side crude drawings, with circled and captioned climactic accents, marking the two of them in perpetual entanglement – this performed dutifully in reality within our outline: the little legs shaped for knotting round the other's head, their candle lit as if for us, the audience. Such nightly peep-shows would have made enough of a contrast to our daily purities, but a consummation had to come.

One evening I looked through the gap as the model (her candle on the table against the partition) moved forward (the partner's paleness passive on the shadowed bed) to light a cigarette (perhaps?), so that the limits of my vision held the slice of nakedness from waist to half-thighs, her uneven lips, as if signalling out of the hair-jungle which concluded in a thinned climb up to her navel. I called to her. She had to gain accord for my proposal from her reclining 'spouse'. And, after a while, she entered, proudly outfitted now for her idea of a temptress: high heels, black stockings and suspenders round the bushy middle, with alert spotted nipples above. Reduced by this, I sent her on to Zygmunt's cubicle, but soon she was back – he dismissed her; so I, having commanded her to strip, plunged.

And a tragicomic and prolonged aftermath: soon after, the itch – my hunting sessions for the crab lice (even applying a mirror) could not compete with their breeding urge; and the only chemist in Kazimierz was a friendly gossip – to approach him was out of the question. So this eventful summer went on, my platonic dalliances with our nymphs mitigated shamefully by my secret and progressing humiliation ('they' conquered my armpits, never the head-scalp. The eyebrows? I don't remember) – until the autumn return to Warsaw.

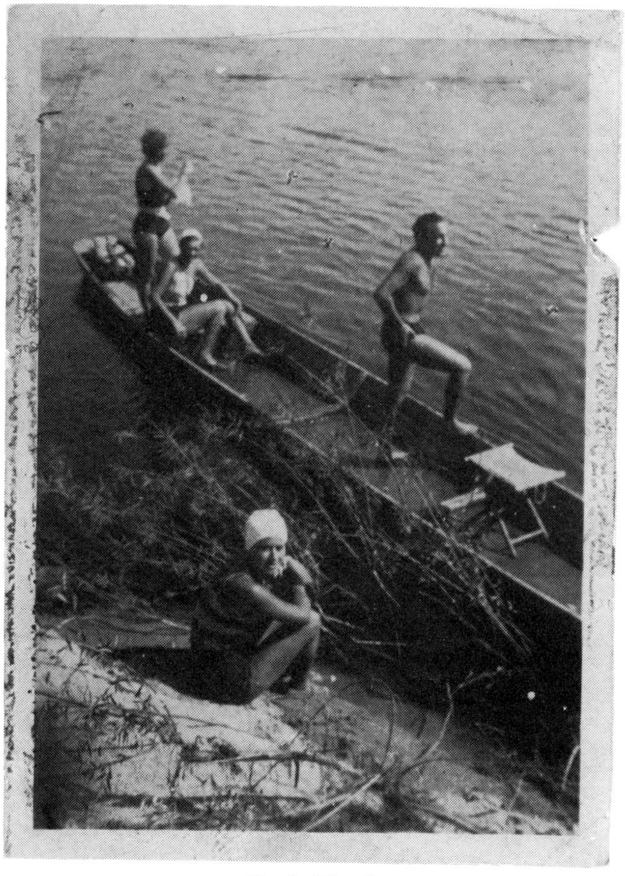

On the Vistula

Through the next academic year and its Kazimierz sequel I advanced:

– as a painter, into sharply overstressed images, 'legitimized' by strong brushwork and colour (my painting sprang out then in some completeness, but later, in the forties, forceful contents began to challenge and stretch it);

– into a sort of young parody of bon-viveurism acting ease within a wide Warsaw territory of café society cum *bohème*, which embraced all ages;

– towards discovering the wholeness of young women round me (more often encouraged than venturing).

The period began in a Parnassian sphere, the evocation of which is appropriate for a fellow art student, **Renia**, perhaps a year older: 'Greek profiled', of Athene's loftiness, dressed in trailing drapes (in *Empire* interpretation), unbending and inattentive in the mould of the great not lesser goddesses, thus not earthly-haughty but of a higher plane, and surely virginal.

This rarity asked me to a dinner at her home. I was prepared for a family function, but her mother was away; yet expected formalities were observed over the quite Epicurean meal for the two of us in impressive though ponderous rooms viewing the river. We moved to the salon, our art talk habitually plentiful, although the formality of the opulent-cultured décor of an earlier generation dominated – until Renia excused herself most politely to return after a long pause – and without any indication, any pre-sign of her intentions – in a negligée (again *Empire*), to embark on the most accomplished abandon.

Her courtly surface (gently mocked at the Academy) – and the secrecy of her untrammelled passions beneath; her preciosity, indeed, of *les précieuses* of an earlier time, which came together with *méchancetés* into a blend of exquisiteness, were appropriately enclosed in the Phidias – to Botticelli – to Fragonard – to Ingres – to the Pre-Raphaelites shape. Even her minor fraility – her classically tiny mouth amazingly engulfing at speed vast (in size and quantity) cakes – smacked of the eighteenth century.*

That summer, wisely holding to her marble hue, even on the beach she would promenade under a parasol and never sunbathe. We both lodged in a Renaissance burger's stone house, in low white-washed rooms, one above the other, I joining her nightly; memorably, her legs straining up, toes drumming at the ceiling (their length? its lowness?).

But **Dolly** also arrived in Kazimierz, by then a pleader – often crysome. Sometimes Renia would ask me simply and courteously not to come that night because Janusz, her dashing airman cousin was claiming her on a night's leave – which would make it Dolly's turn with me.

All this, far from insensibility, followed the honourable and rational code of libertinism, which I and my peers advocated and pursued fanatically – its roots set in abomination of sentimentalisms in deeds and language.

Mostly in language: above all the possessive word *love* banned; my lifelong man–woman preoccupations, loving to the fore, seemed not hampered by this persistent declaratory gap.

Sadly, committed Dolly was not responsive.

And here Zygmunt stepped in. He concentrated his energies on spying out my secret entanglements, lengthily tortured Dolly to tears with disclosures, and proceeded to 'inform' Renia; but she, unerringly ladylike, stopped him at the start, as not being interested in whatever it was he wished to say. I don't think he spread his tales any further: his purpose was not malicious gossip, but to disrupt my well-being.

Yet the summer continued without perturbations though punctuated by similar intrigues – such were the tolerancies of our particular society. Nor did Zygmunt's malevolence harm our friendship. I learned early that closeness is not sustained on virtues but attractions – thus the devilish urges in Zygmunt had to be lived with.

And so, our devotion to Kazimierz widened, with Prusz's house less at the centre of things.

Over the gullies edging one side of Kazimierz a gentle hill bore a new but 'traditional' house, built by **the Kuncewicz family** – she, one of the best novelists of the country. Her book *Two Moons* grew out of her pondering of life below – a fable of apartness: the constant-ancient village blend of peasants and Orthodox Jews permeated/upset/disregarded by the invading mavericks.

The Vistula, the orchards, the Mounts of Three Crosses and of fourteenth-century Castle Esterka (the legendary Jewish mistress of King Casimir the Great) moated the village appurtenances: the haughty Baroque parish church, the Monastery, the Synagogue, the marketplace's St Christopher's Town Hall, the two timber-roofed wells, the timber-arcaded house, the backs and the prominences.

Round, across, on to the cobbled compactness of the marketplace – the stage – peasants' carts brought plentifulness once a week, the few village burghers paraded their air of moustachious gentry – masters of the municipality, the Law, Medicine, the Hotel. But the black-clad Jews' toings and froings, hurried by market and solemnified by their religious calendar, prevailed.

Long coats, round peaked caps, beards and side curls – reverential around the rabbi's fox-fur hat at the entry to the inner Synagogue-world; there, secretive, with wailful chants and rockings and biblical white black-edged prayer shawls. In the market, they engaged an outsider in other voices.

In 1957 my *Chronicle* came out with several drawings, captioned thus:

> Poland (and all Europe) is gutted out of its **black Jewish folklore**. In my Polish youth I went, incurious, by that world – now irretrievable. Therefore the fleeting, make-believe resurrection of it, brought to London by the Polish State Jewish Theatre, is recorded here not as theatre but as remembered reality.

A few years later, at their Warsaw theatre's most accurate reconstructions, I drew again – as if facing reality; and, with fullest devotion, when in Israel, particularly in the streets of Jerusalem's Mea Shearim quarter and, breaking through the rules against strangers, in the Hassidim praying houses, catching up on early neglect.

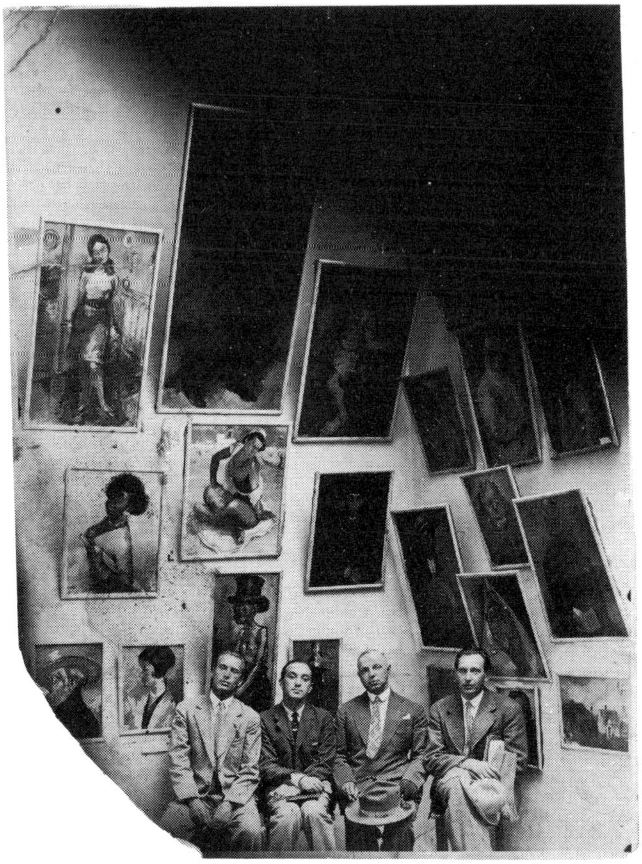

My end-of-year paintings at Warsaw Art Academy

*Twenty-two years later, an escapee living in New York, she was sadly fattened – yet ever 'classical'.

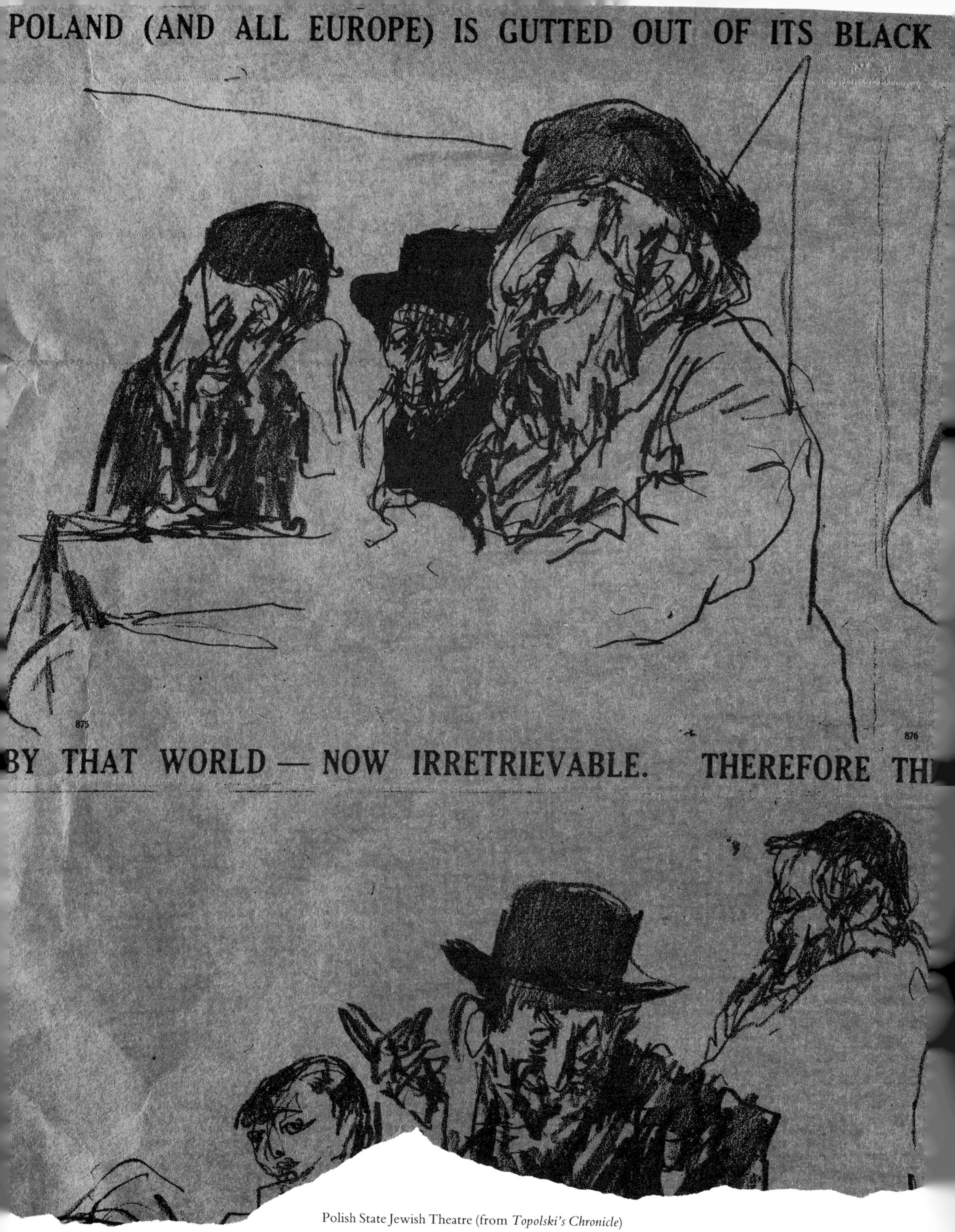

Polish State Jewish Theatre (from *Topolski's Chronicle*)

WISH FOLKLORE. IN MY POLISH YOUTH I WENT, INCURIOUS,

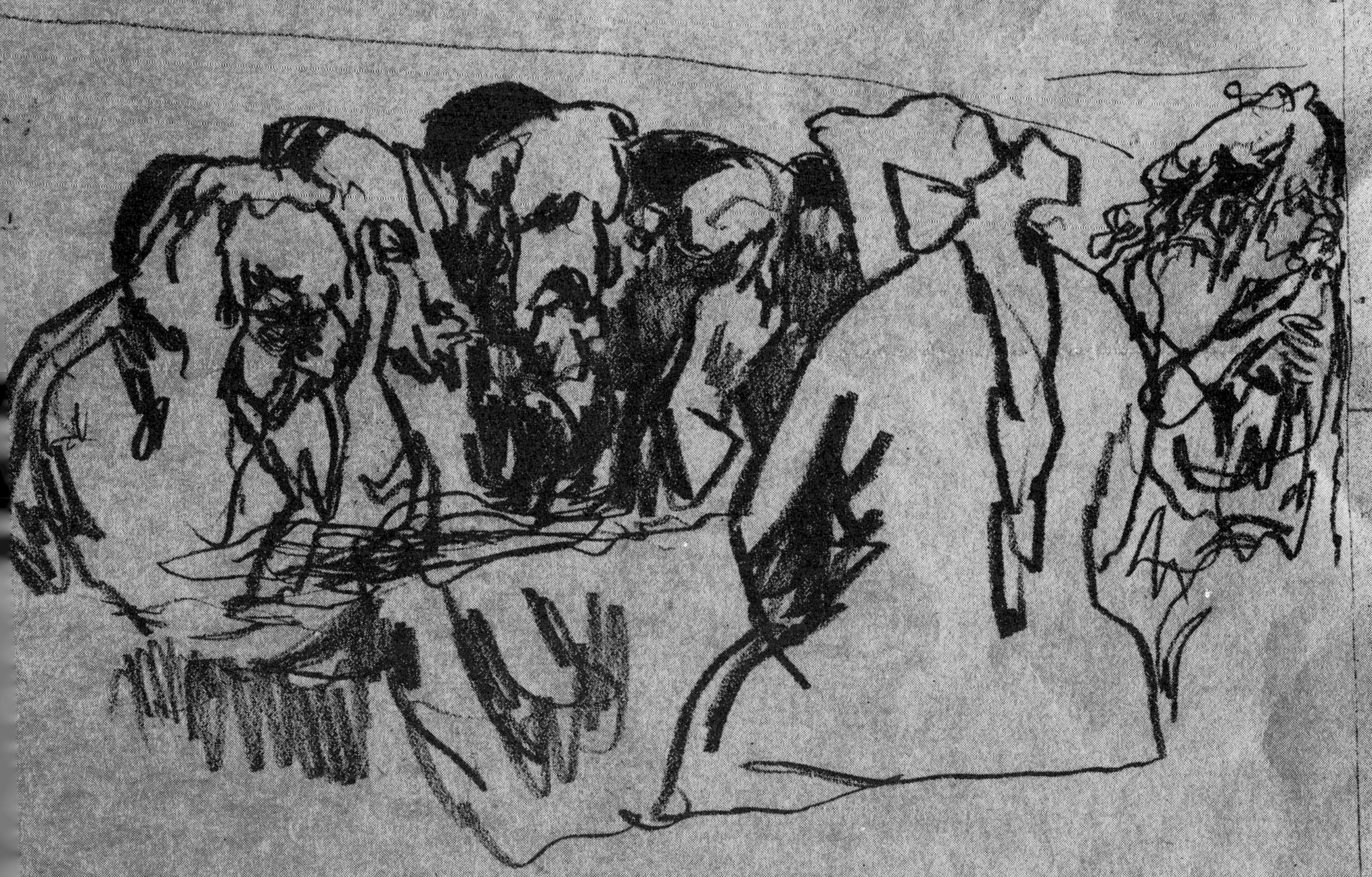

FLEETING MAKE-BELIEF RESURRECTION OF IT, BROUGHT TO

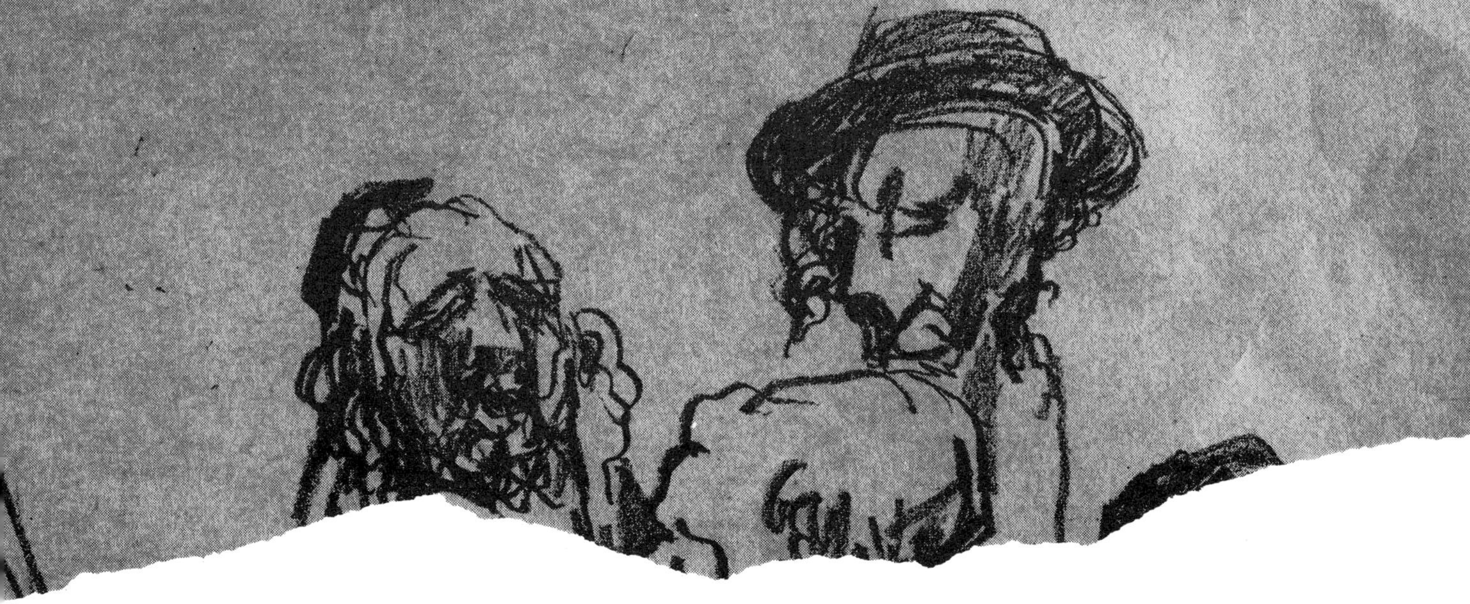

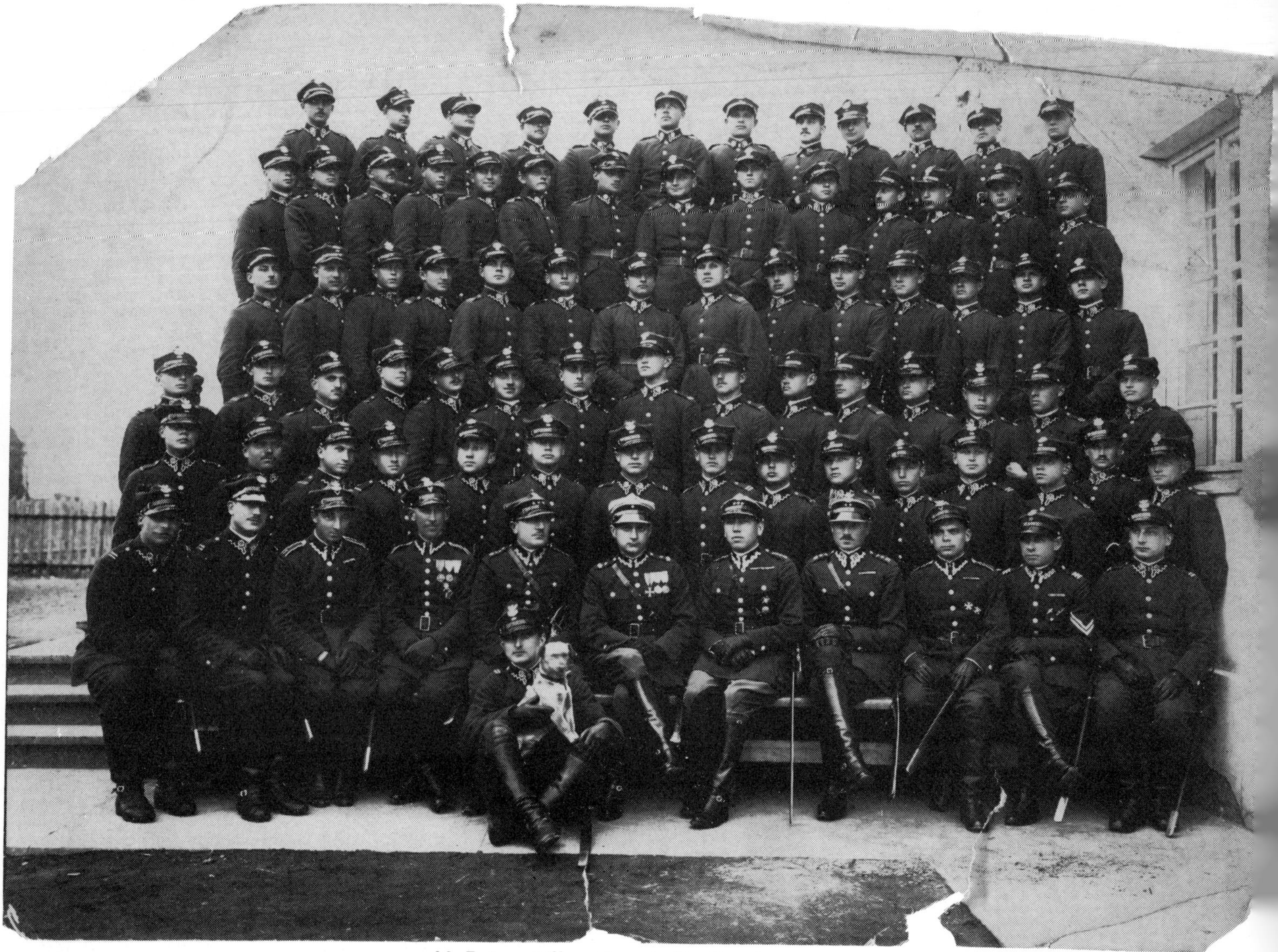

My Battery, Officers' School of Artillery Reserve

Sense of theatre, of pretending games. Having emerged from our parents' revolution, and from our childhoods' wars (always their echoes only, however close the fighting) we, the prancing young, must have mindlessly taken the newly emerged Poland as our *status quo* for good, as Utopia at the end of history – must have, because all our involvements (outside art-commitment, which was earnest) were conviction-lacking masquerades – even for those few performing publicly as Marxist plotters.

And so, my soldiering: it was not difficult for the 'educated' (destined for Schools of Reserve Officers) to dodge the Service, but, ever curious – assuming this, as most of us did, to be, not a preparation for the impossible but, **playing at soldiers** – I wished to try my hand at the fading-away remnants of style on horseback.

Hair clipped to the skin, much-laundered but unpressed generations-inherited denim uniforms and weary high boots – the double line ranked according to height down the great length of the 5th Battery's barrack room: the first morning of the three-month **'recruit' period**. The diversified arrivals of the night before reduced to a hundred artillerymen. An officer, a sergeant-major and a corporal sort them out: divide into three gun sections, select section leaders. When the third (the smallest men) is reached, I (the schoolboy's shyness no longer monolithic, but chipped by the eulogizings and prospects dished out at him by the Academy and Warsaw café society) am galvanized, Darwin-prompted, into stepping forward and surfacing – out of this drowning/submerging reductive equality – my uniqueness. Thus I became the third section leader – and gained one place up in the line above my taller subordinate.

And the same evening, at the line-up, my climb up continued to advance with the ceremony of the mail: the Command in front of the Battery would call out the names of letter recipients; each would march stiffly, come to a halt (the last three steps beating the floor hard), receive his mail, about-turn and stamp his return to his place in the ranks. This I repeated every evening of my Service, the only man in the history of the School to receive letters – one or several – daily.

The 900 standardized recruits began soon enough to particularize, the processes of self-assertion buzzing over the vast quadrangle of shabby redbrick post-Cossack barracks: talents, backgrounds, age/experience – but, hierarchy having restarted from scratch, physical shape/prowess properly (as of old) headed the virtues.

My increasing stature in the barrack square, it must be

made clear, was not that of a paragon, and resulted not from deliberate tactics but from being true to my criss-crossing appetites, purchasing my energies in one direction to pay out in the opposite. Erratically, even farcically, shaping myself into an applauded anarchistic protagonist – enticing to those locked in absolute military stringency.

Some evidentials: the recruits' three months' confinement in the broadness of the muddy square; crowded, but in step, harassed/blunted by the din of commands.

But for some reason I am given the unique privilege of a few hours' leave on an errand into town. The brushed and shined-up decorum of the long cavalry greatcoat, the sword, the spurs and, out of the guarded gates, a long walk to Włodzimierz in the Wołyń flatness. The hunched timber humilities, the after-the-rain cobbled guttered sidewalks, the ultra-grey drudgery of living – yet, for me, with the sky clearing and the puddles responding, with the voices of children, women and dogs, every step brings transport, every humble sight elation in sharpened receptivity of its orchestration, in the compound of the living and the still-life; in all the senses promising responses.

This puddle-dotted walk through the modesty of Wołyń, bounced into poetic impulse off the grimness of the barracks, gave me a mechanical device for the 'high': always counter your mainstream by a harsh routine-imposition to give it an edge. But predictably I neglected to do so – my seldom troubled 'freedom' mellowing my days.

The first harshest month of recruit drill and, indeed, those letters from the hedonistic world, made me plan an escape: I asked for a medical examination, and, throughout the previous week, drank endless coffees during the day and masturbated during the night, to turn, as I imagined, into a palpitating wreck. But medical differentiations, not general condition, apparently decisive, declared extra-fit, I leapt on a contrasting chance just opened: selections were made from all the Officers' Schools for the Air Force School. This, whatever the outcome, offered a – blissful, and undreamed of by the imprisoned recruits – summons to Warsaw for an interview.

But I was already marked as the **master dodger**, and the Major in command of the Battery kept me standing at attention while promising me, in a prolonged roaring harangue, a terrible time when back, rejected – which was more than probable since I was already twenty-three. The fierceness emanating from the wiry little Major, the irrepressible shaking in my calves, the whiff of regret in anticipating an ungainly Air Force uniform replacing horses, ankle-length greatcoat, sword, and spurs . . .

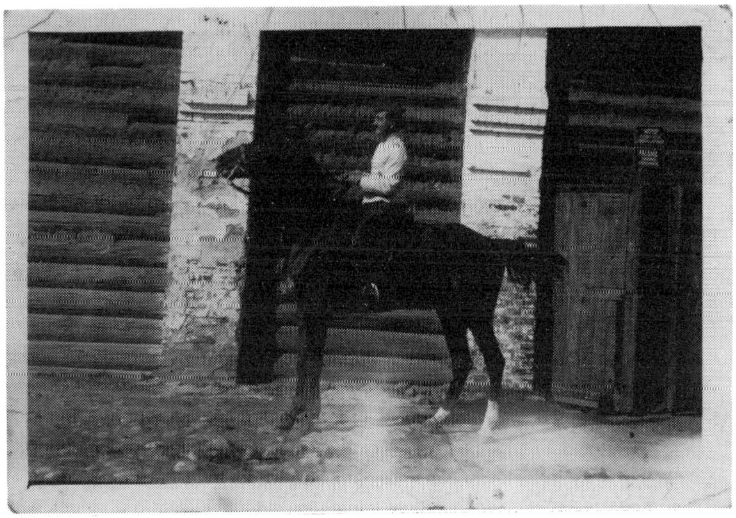

As Cadet Officer

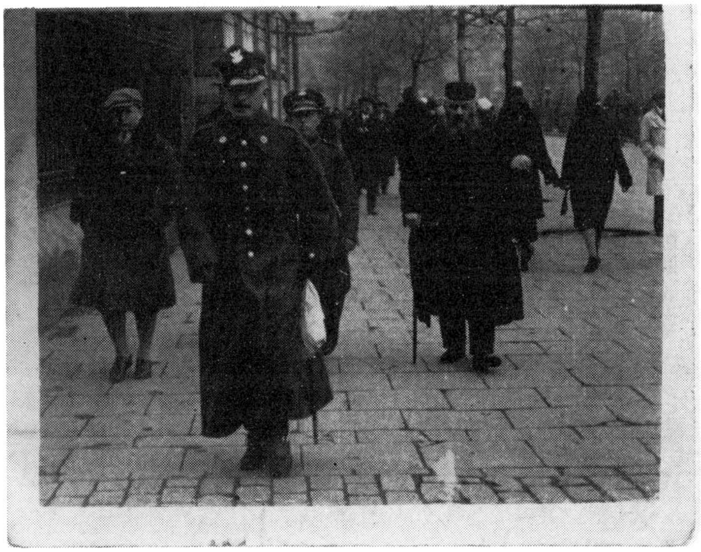

On leave

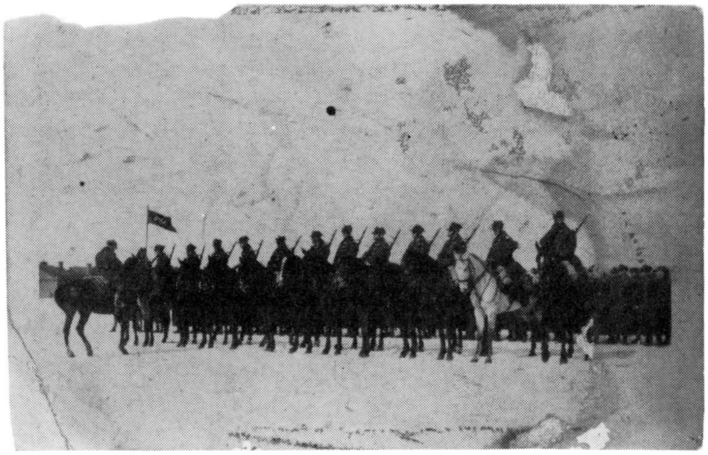

The ceremonial patrol to Warsaw

Rejected and back (now well into the next stage of Service), and almost instantly another twist. Captain Porębny, the Battery's riding master, put me forward as his best horseman for an honour (and a many-months-long almost-total evasion of the barrack-square routine and of the abomination, the classroom artillery-mathematics): inclusion in the horsemanship extra-training in preparation for a **ceremonial patrol of twelve**, selected from the 900 cadets,

Overleaf: Cadet Officer with regiment

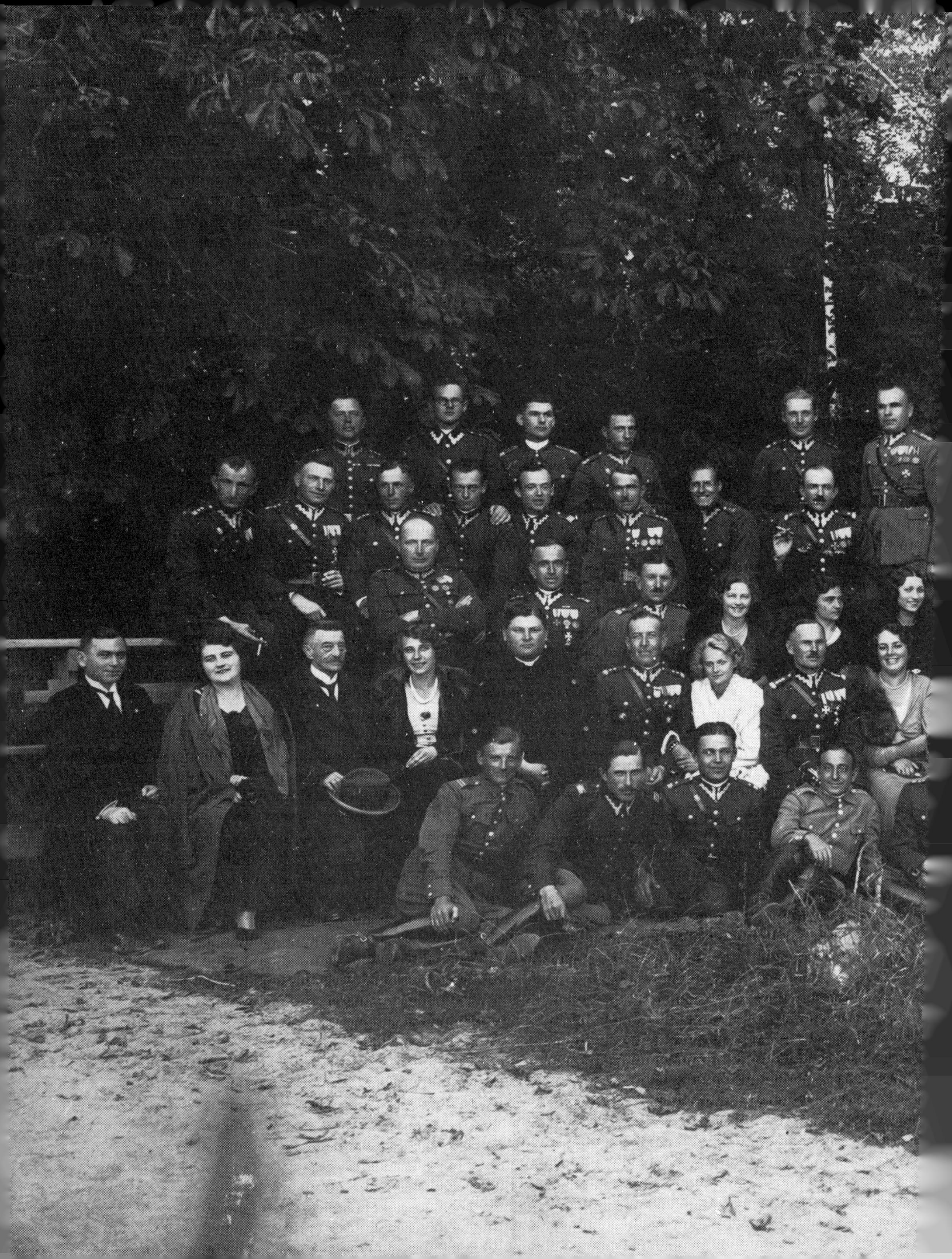

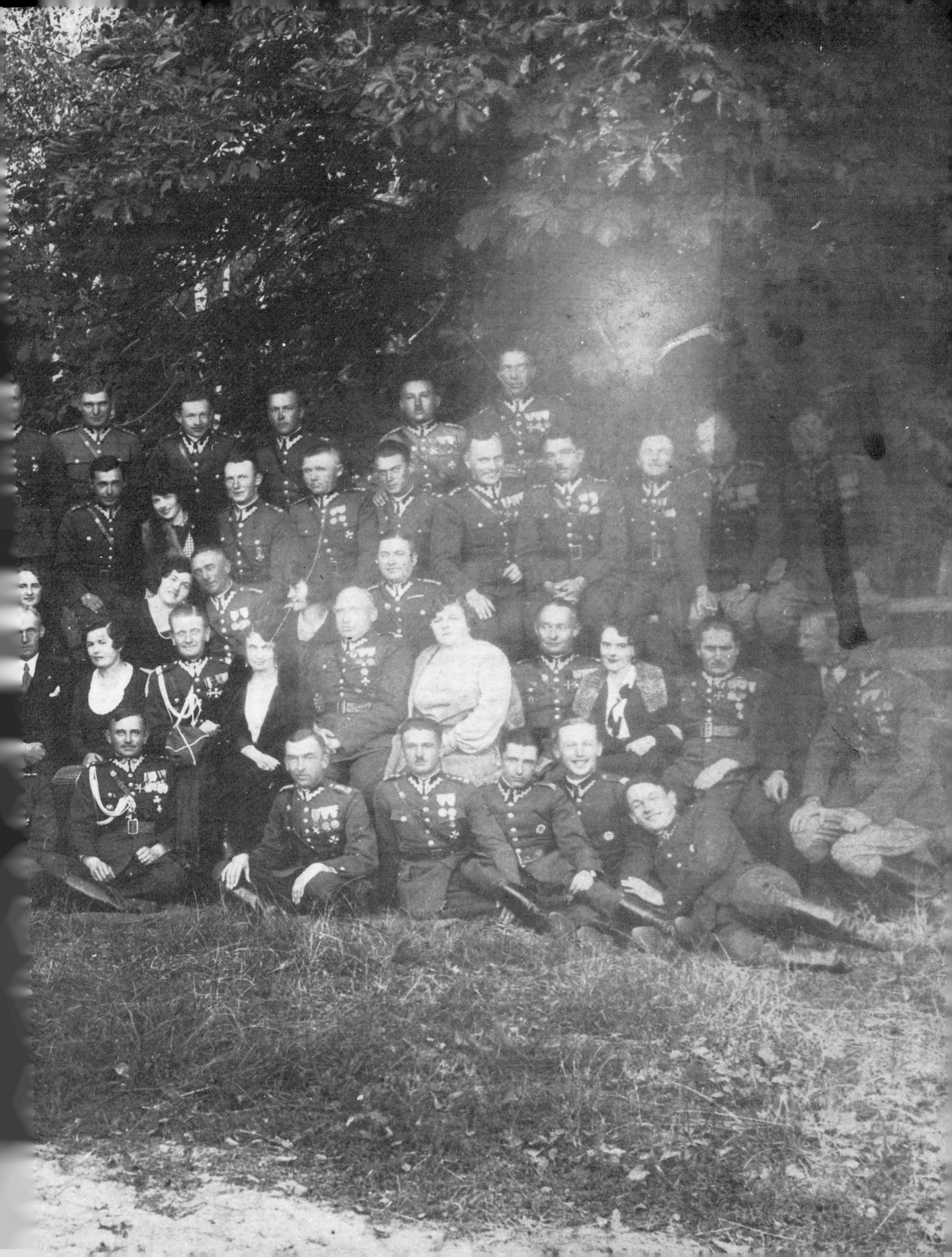

to ride the five days to Warsaw in the traditional contribution of the School **to Marshal Piłsudski's nameday celebrations** on 19 March. [. . .]

But for me the culmination came when (squared, eagled, and brass-edge-peaked hat, the gun across my back, the post-Cossack black-and-brass sword at my side, spurs) I squeezed through the revolving door **into the Café Ziemiańska** at noon with *le tout* Warsaw present and turning their heads at me. The mock-but-real soldier, incongruous in this bohemian setting, yet, underneath his moustachious martial make up, belonging. Was it a childish act of ostentation, or, more likely, an equally childlike dressing-up make-believe – which the whole army service was to me – incomplete without being staged in front of my own kind?

Dry heat over the sands. The feet-dragging, gun-and-rucksack-loaded progress to **the 'poligon'** – the live-shooting range – and manoeuvres. Sweat streaming, blouse/flies unbuttoned for air; knotted dampened handkerchiefs on the clipped recruit heads; the limit!

Taking turns at the observation post in command of firing, watched by staff officers; utterly vacant. My own Captain Poręby at my side whispers a series of prompting figures. I parrot them. The guns fire submissively and accurately.

I scurry from the crowded barn straw lairs towards the nightly mandolin sound. I know my way to that log cabin's little high window (one of a cluster in the hamlet), in the latticed frame of which a girl, with camp-follower inclinations, on vacation from the province's capital of Równo, moons and lilts Ruthenian songs, the mandolin twittering. Out of many hundreds, I am the only one who responds; and **the duetto** stabilizes thus: she leans downward out of the high narrowness, I below outside, my arms (can it be rightly remembered?) almost full-length in the depths of her loose *décolleté*, caressing in prolonged passes her naked breasts from below upward (the memory says so, and there is nothing in it about lips meeting – perhaps left free to express thwarted desires).

Next to the barn was lodged a young peasant woman mothering a baby, distinguished by one of her calves carrying a bandage; the Ruthenian leg-sturdiness, emphasized by the wrapping, brought me out on another dark night, in search of her doorway.

The village men seemed to have been absent for the duration and possibly this, as well as the lack of daytime privacy, made me omit preliminaries: I went in, no better than a rapist. And, justly, in the dark partitions' commotion, having found her by touch, not sight, with the baby in her arms, I got the only possible reaction – screams of panic, and my resulting **flight**.

These manoeuvres in the wilderness of Ruthenia lasted only some two weeks and were full of exhausting exercises. Yet, after the barracks, the open land and its **monumental maidens** . . .

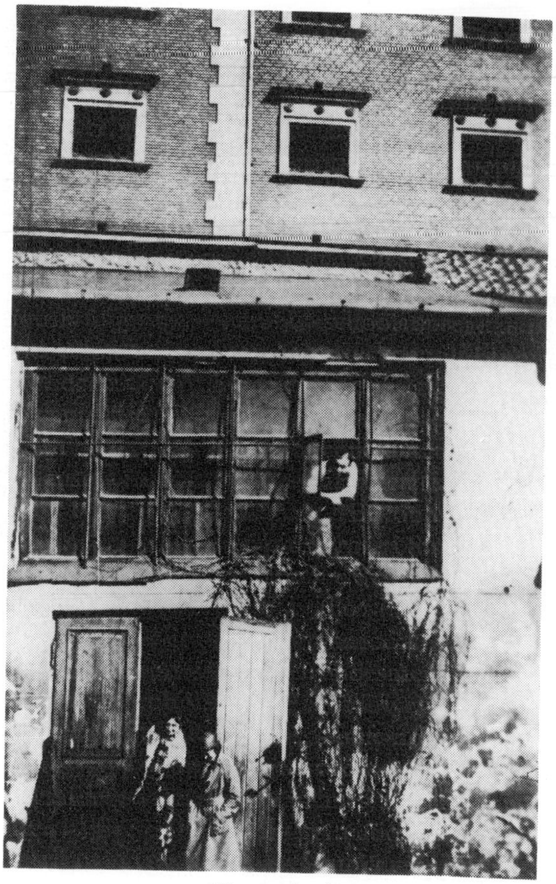

Warsaw Studio

This one stood out – physically of that world, but dressed with the touches of a city. Eloquent and aware, indeed, politically; she had even, I believe, crossed the Soviet border. We made an evening date – she did not come. Next day I found a pretext for staying behind, and, at noon, marched to her gate. Already from afar I saw her bare feet topped by mighty calves hastily climbing a ladder to a hayloft – she must have seen me, and either it was an escape, or the time-honoured invitation on to the hay and away from hinderers. Did I, or did I not, see my chance to get in after her? The memory is blurred, but what clearly remains is me stepping up a few rungs of the ladder to show my head and announce loudly that I had seen her and that I wanted to talk to her down on the ground!

She came down, a fine girl, dignified – devoid of false modesty – thus, probably at that point, making me show respect and not want to go for a doubtful tumble.

We sat harmoniously on the grass by the streamlet, yes, under the willow tree, and her statement impressed: she had met, last night, and would continue to meet, the batman of our Commanding Officer; she would not be my lover because I, the cadet and future officer, belong to a different world: she likes me, but there is a gulf.

My mother was never less than honourable and humdrum-heroic, darning/patching the ends to meet – her son her justification.

Amongst her early but long-lasting aspects, besides her office hours, in gathering small earnings: her handwriting's

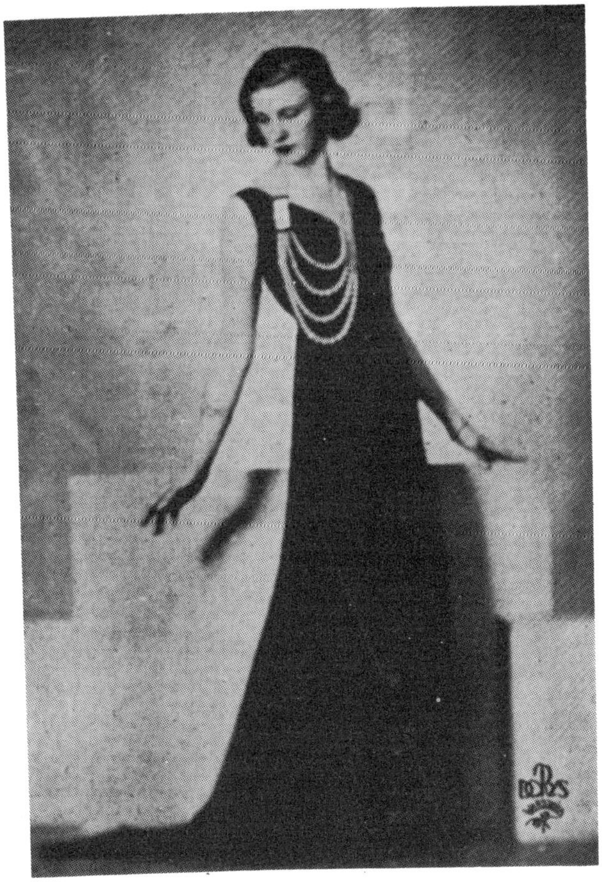

Vera Bobrowska

precision and slanting elegance held her to a desk into the early hours writing out/splitting into parts the plays to be produced by her husband's company; the 'cues' were neatly underlined in red.

Living under the domination of her unreliable mother-in-law had to be ended. On her own (her unsupporting and ever-absent husband) in a cramping flat, she queened in the evenings over a growing entourage of friends and relations – all drawn to her unobvious modesty-shielded qualities, which inspired devotion. And during the week, between the kitchen where the sewing girls worked and the son's room-become-a-waiting-room, she conducted in her bedroom, pluckily, evolved out of nothing and without any previous professional knowledge, a made-to-measure exclusivity in *négligés*. So the son, when back from school, had to sit out her clients, perched in the darkness on the edge of the bath.

Because of her vast expectations of me and her sacrifices, impatience would burst out of tiredness or exasperation at my childish insensitivities into pathetic eruptions. I, no longer a child, but conscious of my deficiencies, submitted to this and crouched on the floor in my superior strength under her innocuous blows.

But we were to become truly friends very early; and I her trusted adviser. I eventually accepted and was accepted by the Captain, although, when this second marriage degenerated and a deserving admirer declared himself, the son gave counsel, even help, throughout the affair, culminating in a dramatic conclave between him and her lover's son pleading for her not to break up their family.

Unaided by any influential connections or sufficient money, entirely on the strength of her own determination, she managed to place me in one of the best Warsaw schools, to place my drawings in the *Child's Art* travelling show organized by the Ministry of Art and Culture, and, when the time came, to peddle a large portfolio of my work round the leading professorial figures in art to resolve the dilemma of whether her son's future could be entrusted to the risky road of art, or should be set on the safer one of architecture. She raised the enthusiasm of Professor Tadeusz Pruszkowski of the Warsaw Academy of Art – but that is a separate story.

This mother piece, hesitant and material-poor, evokes the miserable truth that gradually her self-effacing virtues, meeting my advancing self-assertion, reduced her in my inattentiveness to a convenience. Even her last: to spare me trouble, she chose to undergo a long-postponed routine operation in my absence with my regiment.

Yet I could try to escape this cruel conclusion:

True, I have little to say about my good mother, more about my unimpressive father, because . . .

Because I am keyed up (to receive and to transform into my reactions – pictorial, verbal) to disharmonies, sophistries, clownery – all humanly contributions to life; because (I touch on this elsewhere) perfection, thus natural purity, disarm me – my faculties fall away, replaced by, to me, uselessness of worship. I fend all this off in instinctive self-defence – hence THE mother, as a subject, falls outside my 'creative' scope.

The most diversified Warsaw blend – **Plac Teatralny**: the colonnaded opera house and, still within the colonnade, Teatr Narodowy (National Theatre) and Reduta – the daring yet respected theatre of Osterwa, later of Jaracz, both actor-managers of the highest order, particularly the latter in astounding productions by Leon Schiller, the anti-Establishment director. To one side, *recherché* shops and Oaza, the elegant and arty restaurant/night-club which we, Kanarek and I, decorated. And, across the wide expanse of grass and flowerbeds and the circulating traffic, spreading pompously, the high-towered City Hall – its prison wing overhanging the deep cobble-stoned courtyards of the contrastingly pontificating eighteenth-century Dom Panien Kanoniczek (The Lay Convent of Canonesses).

This was a semi-convent for aristocratic spinsters who would not marry beneath their station: they wore no habits, but their chapel-and-daily routines were strict. Their furthest courtyard contained **the studio barn** occupied by the three young painters Eljasz Kanarek, Aleksander Żyw and myself – a gently disreputable cleavage deep into the blessed domain of canonesses reached daily (and nightly) by a traffic of women and men, high and low – ladies twisting their high heels on the cobblestones.

One of them, **Vera Bobrowska** – a chauffeur-driven car belonging to her Armenian boyfriend waiting round the corner★ – was a star singer in his revue theatre thanks to her beauty and 'glamour' (she unfailingly won the first prize at

★The secrecy of our intimacy was strangely not maintained when on one occasion – the car was not available – she and I, with my two dogs (defining our point of departure), rode through town in an open two-horse *dorožka*.

the yearly Ball of Elegance), not to her lesser gift. Half-Russian, spoilt and romance-craving, she settled her fantasies on me, announcing to my impecunious embarrassment her readiness to accompany me on my forthcoming travels abroad: my first 'grand tour' possible only on a shoe-string and alone – unrealizable on her grotesquely glittering level. I went alone.

But back after nearly a year, I phoned her to resume our loving. She met me, but at a café, not at my studio, and declared matter-of-factly and convincingly that her former assumption that uplifting loving was to be found only among artists was wrong; the same or higher communion of minds and bodies could be found without moving out of the sphere of rich males. Thus I was no longer required.

My 'grand tour' in 1933 tripped at the first stop. Giving Germany a wide berth, it was in a small Czech town called **Morawska Ostrawa** that, I remember vaguely, a neglected endorsement for my passport was to be stamped by a friend, the Polish Consul there.

To keep the lustre of that voyage untarnished, I did not relate to anybody how, when the train had wobbled to a stop by the town's nameboard, still amongst tangled rails, I mistakenly jumped down from the great height, watched the train move onward and had to drag my hefty case the long mucky distance to the platform proper – no longer a Warsaw sophisticate, but a small country's small boy abroad.

My next stop was **Vienna**, where I regained composure at my cousin's flat*, heavy with well-being and decorated by probably my best painting (oddly, I have just come upon a full-page colour reproduction of it in a brittle aged copy of a Polish magazine). The bumptious Austrian baroque has receded in my memory, but a narrowly elongated phonily Polish-style bar with an endless array of vodkas and spicy open sandwiches remained.

Now the phantasmagoria: all parochial conceits shed, the clever-clever skip-giggle voyager, afloat on the Grand Canal, turns pilgrim to flawless – paradisiac – nonpareil (those ornamental words-evoked, but inadequate) beauty: the first sight of **Venice**, first time out of Central Europe's sameness into uniqueness.

And consuming Italy alone, the intensity of its strangeness carves deep – including even such accumulations of clashes foreign to me: was it **Fiesole**? The Roman amphitheatre, nature invaded in Piranesi enchantment (the sun at the zenith and the Italian folklore siesta dotted over the lower plain) with me perched contemplatively on its stones – and the sudden entry from above – not just entry but balletically fanning-out descent – of, to me keyed up for non-familiar Arcadian raptures, arch-nymphs matrixed in identical leggy ginger **Anglo-Saxon ideal**, blazered straw-hatted emphatically English/Scottish schoolgirls, their shrill laughter and guttural nasal calls compelling still further my childhood-rooted thrill at confronting outlandishness.

Rome – only a backcloth for Black Shirts performing: stepping or at a trot-run in unified tempo, high-and-fast, in long formations, ejaculating *tutti con brio* 'Giovanezza, Giovanezza, Primavera di Bellezza! Della vita nell'ebrezza il tuo canto squilla e va! Per Benito Mussolini Alala! Alala!', arms shooting three-quarters forward-up – bulky men (these most emblazoned), small boys; in line-ups shouting *con bravura* 'DU-CE' *tempo rubato*, inducing a swelling crescendo to clamour – 'DU-CE, DU-CE, DU-CE, DU-CE' – leading into the giantesque depths of semi-darkness of which the memory retains nothing visual, but as its epicentre the hammering of 'DU-CE, DU-CE, DU-CE' in perpetuity, its mass *fortissimo* chorus amplified, rendered superhuman 'sonic boom' – the innermost chamber of the **Decennale del Fascismo**.

Dolly joins me from Paris, reduces the rest of my Italian epic to a private idyll – Italy its background; and, in repercussion, her departure makes me elegiacally lonely, the initial potent receptivity lost for a time.

The Riviera: the indelible memory – a bus ride along the coast, an impassive donkey in mid-road, the unfalteringly *au ralenti* driver: corpulent black-moustachious descent, stroll to the animal and gently efficient persuasion – not force – clears the road.

Marseilles' sinister waterside vice quarter – some years later flattened out of existence as there was no way to curb its dangers. Marked as an easy-prey foreigner by my rot-green Austrian hat, only a short stroll amongst mild molestations in tight streetlets culminates in the hat being snatched off my head (perhaps the usual procedure) and my chasing after it into a doorway and up a stairway – hats were *de rigueur*. A foul scramble follows: a gruesome screaming clutch of naked women, a pair of gyrating buttocks pinning me to the corner of the landing while I, the recovered hat to my chest, work my way to freedom – luckily none of their men about.

Paris, home-from-home: the cosiness of Dolly's flat, numbers of old friends, guiding over 'sights'.

Le Dôme's terrace in the thirties – the key to Paris of the arts. We, the interloping foreign youngsters, don't feel out of place and chat away in Polish – this particular time Dolly and I – with habitual pranksterish shots about our neighbours, the nearest being certainly not a Pole, not even French, but, with her bony carroty elegance, perhaps a Scandinavian-American. She walks indoors, returns and unfolds demonstratively (inside were hung a choice of European papers set in timber spines) a Warsaw daily. Instant friendship. Yes, she's Polish-Jewish living in Paris. Next winter she causes a sensation with her outlandish handsomeness when I host her, first skiing in Tatras, then round Warsaw café society. Back in France, engaged to a French naval officer, they are both, under German occupation, in the Underground; are caught and executed.

*That branch of the family recently hiccuped with a young granddaughter who traversed, at first with her parents, then alone, Poland and Australia, to settle as a doctor in Hamburg.

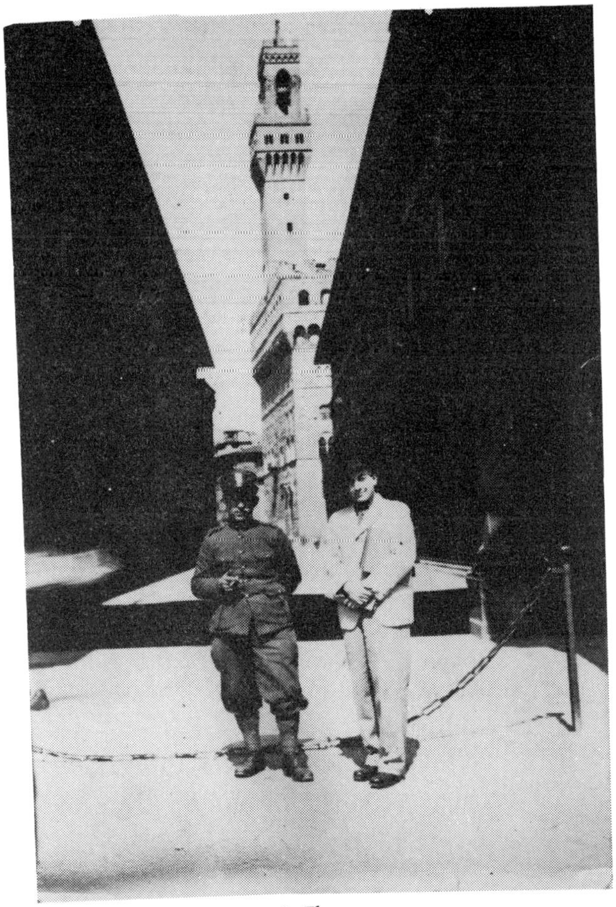

In Florence

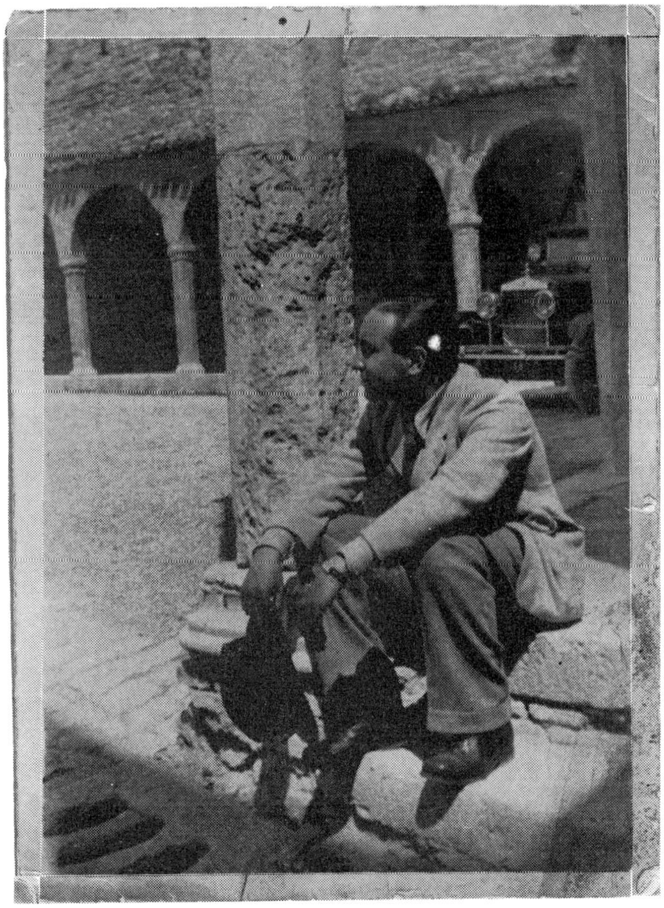

In Assisi

Bleak morning, bleak progress from the station up **Victoria Street**, naturally expecting it to be hotel-filled – entering Artillery (House?) as the only possibility to be dismissed by an aloof uniformed figure. Return to the station and its mean backs: rows of sleazy lodgings.

Polish Embassy girls living in Southampton Row instruct on the phone: *bus 38*. Not a word of English, it proves impossible until there to get the conductor (or friendly passengers) to resolve my need for 'Suzamton Rov'. But then the colour scheme (green – parks, red – buses/uniforms/letterboxes; above all – the stained blackness of architecture), utterly unlike the standardized Europe, the exotic otherness, clicked with my draughtsman's eye, in that period focused on the nineteenth-century's masters.

The stay ended with a minor providential promise: with a former colleague, a Londoner for a while, strolling on a Sunday round the City, I stepped (left-hand traffic and a dearth of people and cars) off the kerb and – bang – am wedged over the front bumper of a miraculously tiny low car; scramble off apologetically – unharmed, but, the car gone, there remains on the road one of its headlights.

The last of Paris. While deciding on the return route – obviously the shortest being across now **Nazi Germany** – I encounter a Warsaw pair, whom I know, Jewish and recognizably so, about to drive in an open car to Poland through Germany. I fill in the back, not looking very Aryan either. And, to cap our (strangely blind) provocation, a large PL (for Poland) is stuck at our rear.

We ride almost continuously through the gauntlet of abuse – those wide-gaping/roaring mouths; of arms outstretched or fist-bearing; of this isolated highest-pitched non-Europe (Fascist Italy tame beside it); of brownness, high-stiffened headgears, high boots, frenzied women – the land, the towns draped – masked, smothered, pullulating with black-hacken-crossed redness.

Stop for the night we must and it is **Berlin**, at the back of the Kurfürstendamm, amid scowling roughness – but, as if still controlled, short of rough-handling. This whole rapid panorama of German mass-puppetry posing as spontaneity amounts to **a demonic carnival** over-hammed by a sinister command with a taste for 'comics': not lived, but of deadly artifice.

A survival trick, practised later, in Nazi Germany then carried out only by good fortune: our cross-country fast moving was in our favour – any power-machine gathers momentum ponderously, leaving a gap of time before it strikes.

Close to the Polish border the roads narrow and show neglect. And out of this misty almost-no-man's-land file at us on both verges of the road, enclosing our wariness, on horseback, fully armed helmeted **Wehrmacht cavalrymen**; they trot/clatter by relaxed – men returning from a dawn border patrol? manoeuvres? an ominous exercise for things to come?

In six years . . .

Young men, given to bunching, evolve, in the absence of meaning, rituals and a nomenclature of unity. And so the **Group of Six**, a random collection, played – tongue in cheek – the 'game', centred mainly on nocturnal immersions, drinking challenges, presenting a pretence of complicity – a modicum of justification for the exclusion of women: timidity masked as manliness; that is, paradoxically, the exclusion of *les princesses lointaines* of their own sphere – not of women of the people or of the streets.

The Group was put to the test on that level once when an inconsequent seduction, as the mores of class division dictated, by one of them culminated in a spirited working-class girl hedged in her room, gun in hand, prepared to shoot her lover and herself. The loyal five climbed the stairs, knocked at the door and, sure targets, entered to resolve the love drama.

At a more extended, thus more absurd, touchline of the same fidgety social inconsistency I staged in my rooms, some years later, **the Kitchen Maids' Ball**, Warsaw maids being recruited mostly from the countryside, its folklore fragrance tending to cling to them. It all began unexceptionally: within the code of gay bachelorism of the time I had an eye on the lovely peasant maid of my dentist. My wicked serving pair Mr and Mrs Warszawski, the able messengers in my intrigues, having failed to overcome her pride and inveigle her, came up with the idea of a maids' ball, their widespread chumminess with the breed commending it; the idea caught on and, the young Leś (Count) Breza being my cohabitant, it reached bedrock purification by restricting the male invitees, except for the host, to aristocrats only. Oddly this childishly clumsy and close-to-unsavoury confection, kitchen-conceived, did not turn out bathetic but became a joy – because there unexpectedly appeared two distinguished gate-crashers: the country's exalted poet, **Julian Tuwim**, reassuringly courteous and grey-haired, and **Mira Zimińska**, the most attractive and popular cabaret comedienne in Warsaw. The youthful maids gathered expertly by my servants from neighbouring flats were decorous and at ease; the titled males both singularly handsome and forthcoming – whether hetero- or homosexual. And, with the feasting time, there formed an adorational tableau round the two royally gracious personages – though the girls were probably charmed by them, rather than by their art – clamour happily mounting.

The two celebrities having grandly departed, the occasion rapidly deteriorated due to a third, late, gate-crasher – an actor (and a commoner!) best known as a drunkard; his drunkenness mounting into chasing the girls rowdily – his main prey the dentist's maid – upsetting, destroying the perhaps overdone decorum – forging a middle-of-the-road vulgarity cum lust of no return.

The ball of the kitchen maids might seem unsavoury if it had not been an unconscious item in the politics of joy: **śmieszność**; and perhaps fuelled by the turn-of-the-century idealization of the peasantry by the Cracow creative élite. It could even be seen, within the local conditions, as a precursor of the present day's racial and social *rapprochements*.

Śmieszne: 'funny', limiting it to dictionary celibacy, would not translate it – rather 'laughter-worthy' or 'joy-worthy', since this modest word, elevated by the cliquy slang of those days, ennobled what it stamped. Those young people of Warsaw were not mere pranksters – their pursuit of things **śmieszne** amounted to a zest for life's gratifications: things dionysian/aphroditian/artemisian; also: fraternal/liberal/christian (as fair play without liturgy or miracles).

Yet the governing power was inherited/snatched by Piłsudski's Colonels, who intensified unavoidably the detainment of political opponents – even so, though these did not seem extreme actions, they upset our shortsighted tranquillity.

And worse: Nazi Germany's hate cult began to seep in. The proletarian Orthodox Jew had lived in harmony with the Slav peasant; the assimilated Jew of general education was an accepted Pole;* but pollution now enveloped a sphere of university students, both competitive and eager for foreign fashions. Yet until 1935, when I went abroad, this 'tendency' was still marginal. The seekers for **śmieszne** still kept their innocence.

And so these 'Arcadians', unarmed but for the weapon of mockery at the rising monsters, entered the heroic age unaltered: the first victims of conquering grimness were the writer who satirized 'Herr Hitler' by instalments in a popular paper and an actor who played Hitler in the world première of Shaw's *Geneva*. The others carried their **śmieszne** appraisals on to the battlefields, under the bombs, into the prisons, labour camps and escape routes – and in the camaraderie of perdition/frustration.

Decades later, a voice, rooted in the comforts of 'at home' English progressiveness: '. . . the terrible years between 1919 and 1939 . . .'; '. . . the years 1930 to 1939 were horrible both publicly and privately . . .' (*Leonard Woolf, 'An Autobiography'*.)

From a learned American book: '. . . the coming depression will . . . outstrip the great depression of 1926–1940 . . .' This for the Americans? Or for the Western world? Depression as an all-embracing overpowering climate – historically, thus socially, thus individually. Yet those are precisely **MY years**, that is the span of my crest, the reaching out towards untrammelled joys and tests within, yet not governed by, 'the depression', rising in some valour to the challenges however deadly.

Summarizing scholars, when stamping their bleak generalities on the progress of generational/organic vitalities, as well as those voices, which, declaring that period 'the end of civilization' (Woolf again), elevate their fugitive domestic comforts to the status of permanent universality, should be checked.

Surely history's high dramas ought to be paralleled with Nature's elements in motion; 'progress' is upset by generational restlessness – which sweeps away dug-in absurdities together with worthinesses. Messy matters, but

*A Polish poet friend, too young to have tasted the between-the-wars Warsaw 'intelligentsia', tells me that a London girl editor, who read my manuscript and talked to me over some months, informed him that 'Topolski said there was no anti-Semitism in Poland'. An amazing generalization; what hopelessness. I wrote and talked to her about differentiations in Polish, as anywhere, personal attitudes and social spheres – all apparently missed by even that person well introduced to my views. I just received a book tribute by several writers published in Warsaw this year (1985) and, in an essay by a Kazimierz Błeszyński, I read (my translation) '. . . they say that there was anti-Semitism in Poland. Likely; on the outskirts of culture . . .'. This view falls close to mine.

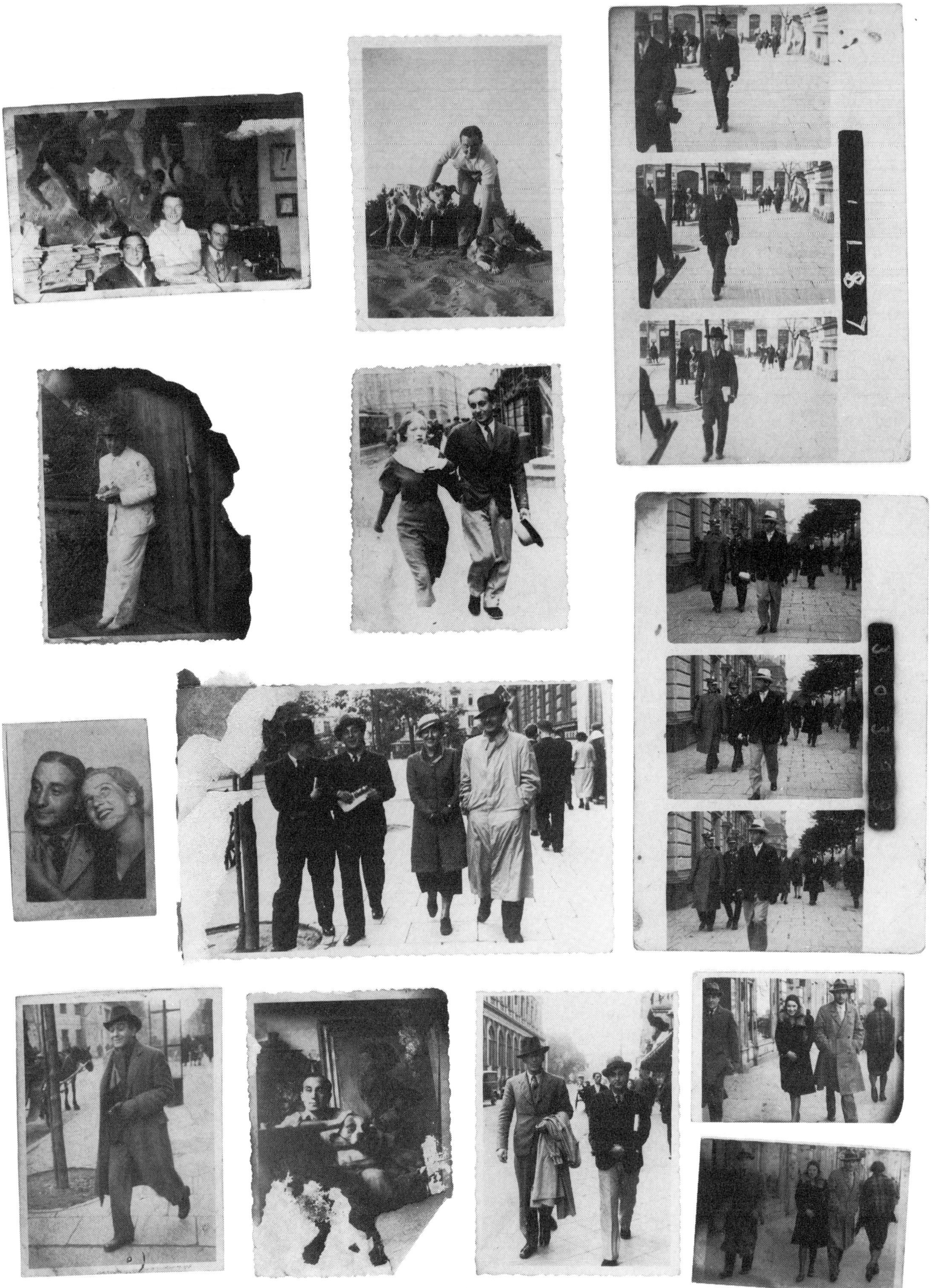

In Warsaw

their recurring rhythms are crossed by the opposite natural function (must this truism be put down?) – that of breeding/growing/flourishing life, given a chancy moment, on the paused slopes of lava.

Must then the surge of young energy within the murkiest uncongenial circumstances be apologized for?

Hindsight renders those carefree years of ours more unbelievable than condemnable. We must have been proceeding in blindfold momentum along the sidelines of tolerant 'European values' in our unguarded unpreparedness amongst the threats of bellicose fanaticisms erupting around us. Or was it the usual phenomenon of 'fiddling . . . etc.'?

The feeble fences/frontiers of Poland must also have served to becharm us enough for our disbelief, even when training in soldiering, in any future application for it. In France, with its three borders ablaze with fascisms, our 'kind' were devoted to art and playfulness – both there and in Britain (Channel-isolated) Communism and Spain were side motifs. One was even inclined to argue that in my country bellicose patriotic/leftist fervour had been spent with my parents' generation, with us, generationally reacting, made free for the aftermath's irresponsibilities, while in Britain political longings arose only with my contemporaries (again, a generational reaction) – and only in a few of them; the majority (of 'the cultivated') stayed *sans souci*.

But it would have been much more astonishing to stand aside and watch 'us' in London under the **imminent invasion threat**. The sure material for Nazi killers' ruthlessness, we did not fuss about the chances of escape from this island, or search for any precautionary/camouflage/suicide measures. We did not even talk about the prospects but, if not signed up with the Forces or in defence activities, went on playing.

After the Continent's spreading monotone, pre-war England seemed – **exotic**! And then the enchantment of finding there the nineteenth-century uniforms (be it of a later period) strutting singly, parading-prancing in formations; and framing, the joy of it, the fantasy yet unerring world of court sartorials arrested in Victorian pomp-and-circumstance. And all this followed by dressing down to all occasions of life and seasons – with caste divisions rooted in tradition of all spheres of life – and astonishing to a foreigner. My dominant, at that time, **receptivity for 'human comedy'** exaggerations fully gratified – somewhat prepared, hence the thrill of recognition at the source. The worldwide manhood's snobbery over 'Old England' paraphernalia made the visitor melt towards the sporty/tweedy/Burberry/Lock/Brigg realities. But there was more: their spindly posturings; their sartorial unerring subtleties – out of uniform and in (not excluding the field-cum-tropics uniforms, blend with safari eccentricities, flourishing in distant campaignings) – all perfectly in accord with their long-boned pear-shapes; with the land's greenness and Georgian bricks' blackness of London and the interwoven red.

Costumologist's enchantment with the unbroken line of evolutionary dressing . . . down to cavalier hats and striped jackets of street cleaners and buttoned-up policemen's tunics unchanged for a century because arrived at perfection. All this is gone; some inferiority-complex-ridden busybodies impose American-cum-white-collar pretences – the costume echoes of bastard vulgarities from mammoth Ruritanias.

But in recent decades new panache leaps from the distant past – young 'fashions', significantly, leave out the nineteenth century of stabilized style and again shape people correctly – to match the new wider society – and readjust, or maybe enrich my devotions.

In my old Poland, even when at a trot, naked sword up at the shoulder – eyes right, in tight formation of clanging/clutter-flutter/horsey tumult against brass-and-drums; even when within the cleaner-cut harder-edged drill of stamping spurred boots – I held out to **the pose of outsiderism**, attracted merely by the nostalgia fun of it all.

Years later I saw England, still in the imperial shape, customarily **arming its soldiers for real** – the recruit would have been bloodied in one or another of somewhere or other ever-erupting skirmishes, under the never-setting sun. Thus the parades, the marching past, trooping the colour, had solemnity and elation of martial liturgy of patriotism as faith.

But the Danish, the Monégasque, the Italian uniformed drills ceased long ago to emanate this tension – now curiosities (showpieces), animated toy soldiers.

Exotic England – the reverse of the British gaze at abroad. More compellingly so, when for the second time I entered London in 1935 aboard a Polish ship **up the Thames** morning-mists-trailing, into the narrowing mounting grim-mighty apotheosis-parade of a Sea-Trade Empire, its gorging-purpose patina-ed black by the nineteenth-century chimneys of its lofty destiny.

This sootiness persists, shapes escalate, culminate in the bizarre two-fold hoisting giant-of-a-bridge of welcome-yet-threat; and instantly to the left the landing stage – all of its nautical litter and its busy dockers in the, now accepted by the voyager, colour of London (water and sky only variations of it) – throws forth a strident counterpoint: a bright shape, as if a cut-out, incongruously tacked against the blackness.

Closer: it is **a stereotype English gentleman** posturing with studied grace; the great pear-shaped length, the eye-catching hat tipped over the nose, the brush moustache, the sloppy unpadded-shouldered flared/slit jacket, a handkerchief in the cuff, narrow trousers, umbrella-cum-gloves-and-newspaper, waistcoat not in accord with the suit, but echoing the shirt's stripes, red carnation . . . Closer: but this is **Tony**. Tony Sobański. Count Sobański, schooled in England like many young Polish aristocrats, emerged shaped and dressed *à l'anglais* – more, surpassing his models; but, still more, one of the finest subtlest intelligences and best-natured friends about. He and I are to write and draw a reportage on the Royal Jubilee celebrations for *Wiadomości Literackie* ('Literary News') and he will, beginning now, guide me dedicatedly over London.

This tableau an all-important object lesson in **Old England** of the mid-Thirties.

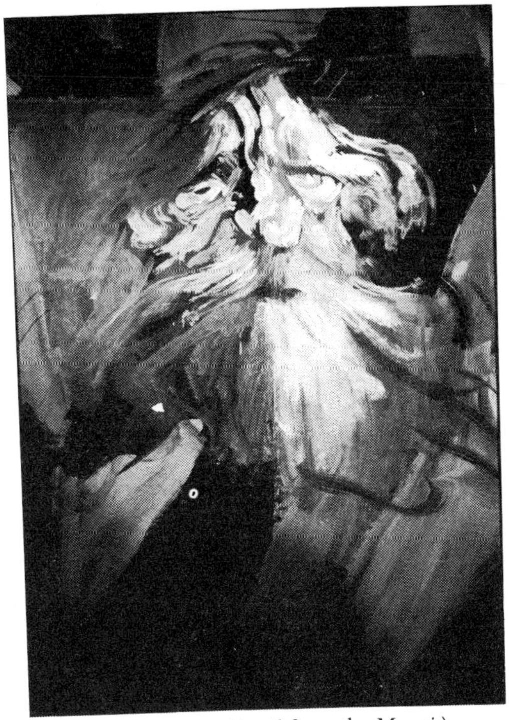

Augustus John (detail from the *Memoir*)

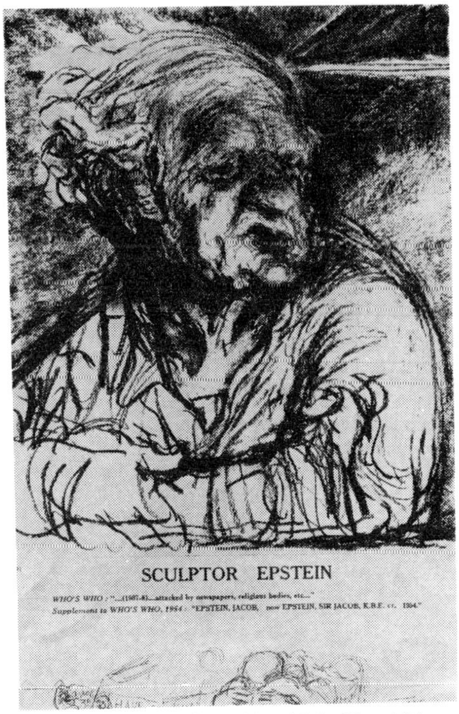

Jacob Epstein (from *Topolski's Chronicle*)

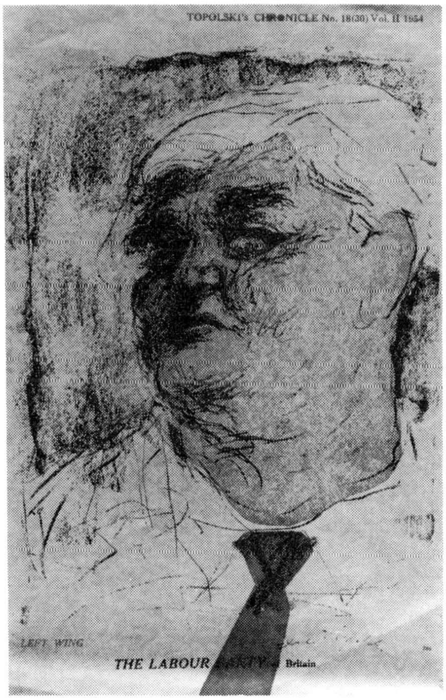

Nye Bevan (from *Topolski's Chronicle*)

Tony's Polish papal countship and an English public schooling, with his best years having been the London Gay Twenties, formed an unselfconscious over-perfection of homosexual gentlemanliness, sensitive and generous in friendship – practising snobbery seriously, hence etiquette paired with honourable ethics.

Funds minimal (Poland restricted allowances for travel abroad), he procured a room for me next to his in a humblest lodging house, run by an Italian, one of many such in Ebury Street, then a semi-slum, but for him satisfactory because of its good phone number: SLOane.

His initiating me to London attractions: first the depth of dockland's back streets lined narrowly with one-storey working-class terraces, their unique grace in the Georgian system minimalized to perfection. Those streets and their liveliness were (they are now despoiled by the bombing but even more by planners' 'clearances') to him close to the architectural backgrounds in Italian primitives' paintings. Second, to help me in bridging the two Englands (which I already did) to cavort down Bond Street, to the carillon bells clanging from the Atkinson's towerlet, along with the parade (very effective then) of vanities.

A Napoleonic 'N', the muddledly imperial emblem of the **Café Royal**, focused on entering in 1935. The traditional turn-of-the-century grand room bypassed, a twist to the left opens up on to the huge ungainly balconied room, painted ochre and red-plush-banquetted (a close relation to the Paris Coupole). It forgoes segregational airs, in its oneness half of it given to tablecloths and high feeding, and the other to bare marble tops and beer/coffee. But the overall clientèle: the treasure trove of London's *rarae aves*!

The young foreigner, even unpossessed of the language, is in no time acquainted on terms of equality with his neighbours at the marble tops: Augustus John and his ladies, Jacob Epstein and his, Nye Bevan, John Rothenstein, Claude Cockburn, Gerald Barry, the Duke of Sutherland, Michael Redgrave, Constant Lambert, Allen Lane, Matthew Smith; and an array of the amiable best in young arts and sheer bloom.

In some of my progress in those early years there may have been instrumental good friends like **'Jusuf'** Retinger with his advice, **Tony** making rounds with a valise of my drawings, a senior Polish press correspondent interpreting at my lunch (this in the table-cloth section of the Café Royal) with the director of John Lane The Bodley Head over my *The London Spectacle 1935*.

But the main flow of impromptu friendships, loves, patronage, commissions – and achievements – had their source at those marble tops.

They germinated plenty: the Forbes-Robertson-Hale twins, **Robin and Clement**, cropped-haired *garçonnes*, immense and of immense vitality – both (but independently) my best friends; Clement married to John Davenport and in turn to William Glock – she died young. The 'Night and Day' circle: John Marks, **Graham Greene**, Walter Goetz. **Nye Bevan**, my proposer, later, for British citizenship – Jennie sadly fell, when Minister for the Arts, for the charms of smooth art manipulators.

Another modest usage was that of meeting place before forays on the town for the bubbling-over young Warsaw intelligentsia of **śmieszność** persuasion, oddly transferred by chance (and fluctuating) to London.

Still another, later, when love-bound to **Marion** Everall, banquette-bound for hours waiting for her grand veil-hatted evening arrivals, always delayed by the supreme *maquillagerie*.

Those first London years: trusting acceptance of the very young gate-crasher, bountiful patronage given to his gifts. Such bizarre occurrences as the Editor of the ***News Chronicle***, **Gerald Barry**, and his wife accepting my invitation to dinner at my boarding-house room (a Polish

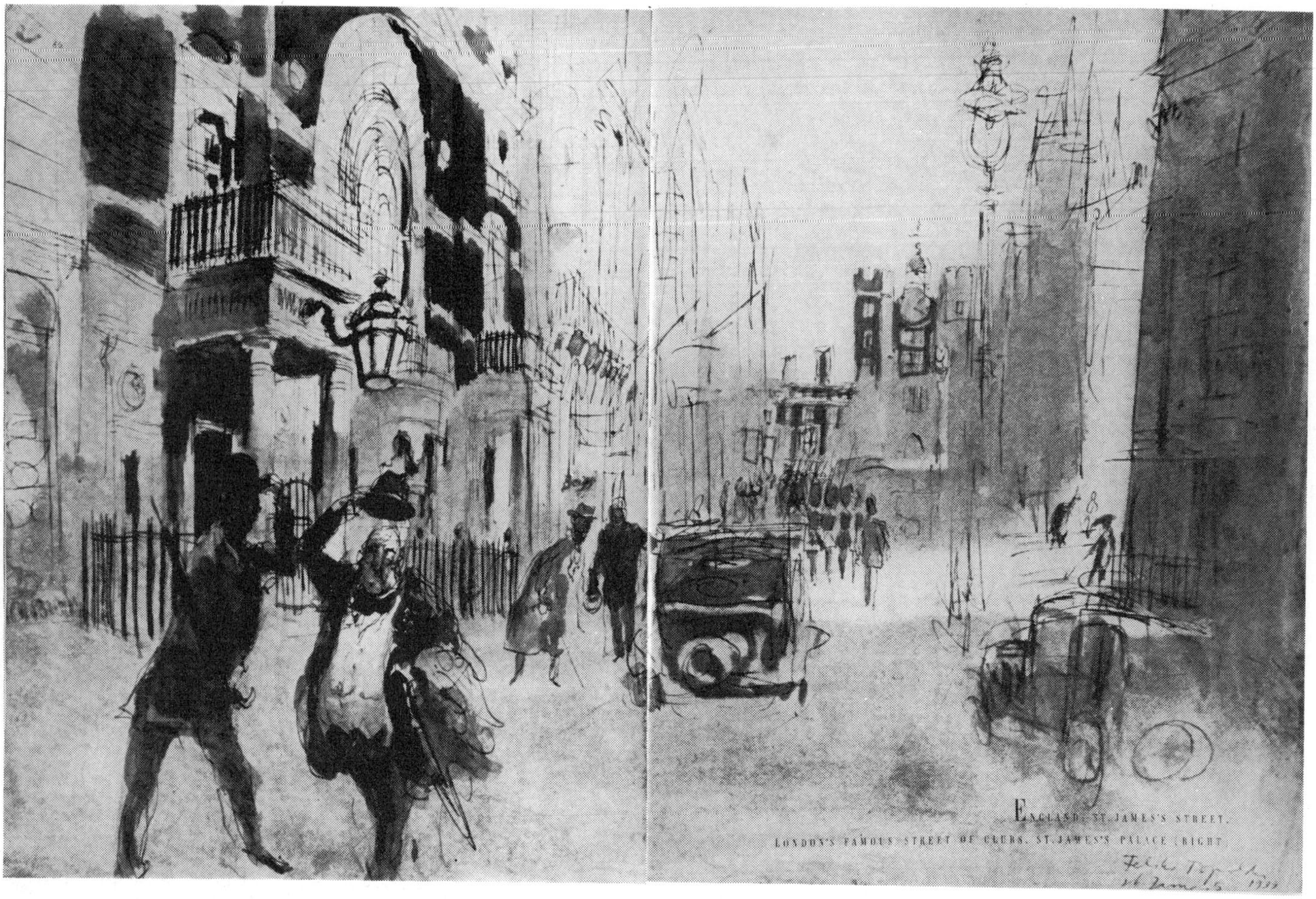

Pre-war London (from American *Vogue*)

journalist friend, Mr Bauer-Czarnomski as go-between – I still hardly spoke English); he forgot (my landlady fussing over the wasted roast), but a telephone call after an hour's wait brought them, touchingly apologizing, and the feast fulfilled itself, resulting in a chain of cartoons.

But being immersed in news and deadlines and particularly having to sort out the urgency of subjects and ideas (interpreted over the phone, often in the midst of love-play, by my skinny cockney young landlady) did not fit in with my lackadaisical rhythms; and I soon settled to **Shy (D. B. Wyndham-Lewis) and Topolski see the Sights** on the Saturday green pages of the paper.

London Transport's profuse patronage given to the arts incorporated my contributions and resulted, at the *Exposition Internationale des Arts et des Techniques, Paris 1937,* in a *Diplôme commémoratif, décerné à Felix Topolski, Sélection Nationale Britannique*★.

And I was embraced mainly by bohemian London: the whole pleiad of today's exalted worthies (now knights, lords, emeriti or departed) formed my young circle (Anthony Hippisley-Coxe, Lord Reilly, Sir Hugh Casson, Sir William Glock, Lord Elwyn-Jones, Clive Entwhistle, Anthony Greenwood, Walter Goetz, Anthony Lousada). And there was, always milling around, my Polish sphere – both the more formal and my fellow *flaneurs*. Also outflung diversions among the glittering – both of 'class' and dandy-homosexual.

In the summer of 1936, the Julian Trevelyans lent me their **Durham Wharf**. They entrusted me with all their minutest *preciosa* except for their padlocked little Morris. This was my dream home fulfilled, fleetingly, and never attained again: the lovely but nonchalantly accommodating shack-shabbiness, its workshoppy spread dwindling into a humble shop window on to the calm street; here lay the core of my joy – echoing my years of communion with the Vistula: the whole, overhung/clung to the Thames wall, his dinghy moored at the widest of windows. I would swim out and about, call on A. P. Herbert, a neighbour, for a chat (holding to the side of his sailing boat) – and, towards the evening, shyly woo **Jocelyn**, his daughter.

But a more rumbustious domesticity developed alongside. A Polish friend Eugeniusz ('Genio') Cękalski, a film director, moved in for a while with his wife Janka (now married to the Nobel-ennobled Czesław Miłosz) and, affected by just having won his driving licence, tantalized me with the – not very sinful, one thought – play of giving me a driving course; we broke into the garage, and soon I drove the open car, filled up with friends, to the Rochester Medway, to visit Anthony Hippisley-Coxe on his rusty-red-sailed barge. Jollities beer-propelled; the return drive in the dark, my right arm smartly overhanging the curved door; a nasty swish-rub, incoming car shooting by; after a while, cold draught at my elbow turns my head: no sleeve and black/red bare elbow. The aftermaths

★But the more momentous accent: the Spanish pavilion unfinished, unopened. I broke in and faced Picasso's commissioned contribution – the *Guernica* – propped against an empty wall.

were plentiful: a large slice of flesh scooped out (astonishingly the joint undamaged), **the arm in plaster** – and, amongst commiserating visitors, starlet **Marion** and I set on the path of a fruitful life. The car's body speedily repaired, but the smooth redder patch discloses all, Julian understandably even more enraged by the ruination of the nicely aged wholeness of his antique Morris than by my dishonourable misdemeanour.

And there was more at stake: under the wing of Ian Parsons of Messrs Chatto and Windus, there had been brewing for some time plans for a weekly satirical-literary paper, which was to supersede, in the scope of its recruited talents and in the originality of its form, all the sundry Anglo-American periodicals. The writers, already acclaimed – and to become the greatest of that generation – included Graham Greene, Evelyn Waugh, John Betjeman, Anthony Powell, V. S. Pritchett, T. F. Powys, Christopher Isherwood, Rose Macaulay, Elizabeth Bowen, William Empson. The artists – James Thurber, Brian Robb, Paul Crum, Eric Fraser – with myself distinguished by being given the cover of No. 1 (and of the paper's prospectus) and a regular individual feature under the heading **Fe Fo Fi Fum** (incomprehensible to me – and apparently jumbled up for some reason?) of one or two pages picturing my view of the British. Dates and contracts were about to be settled when my right arm was stricken and the alarming tales of my having ceased to be 'Topolski' went round.

The scene not to be forgotten: a habitual Soho pub, a group of ***Night and Day*** editors-in-making, and I, my arm just out of plaster. The subject of my accident is not raised, but there is a gentle move towards the dartboard – deliberate? And I am expected to play, naturally. But, when posed for my first throw, I sense a tension closing round me. Never an outstanding player (and not a devotee), I tended to play erratically – but luck had it that that night I did well at this, clearly a test of my 'Topolski' wrist.

Night and Day came out, but – its looks disappointed me greatly. The oft-confirmed determination was not to fall into the *New Yorker* format; but, page by page, it came out as its imitation, thus provoking adverse comparisons. This British self-relegation, accepting American models as unsurpassable, puzzled my newcomer's eye at the time – it used to be the other way round, I thought, even in that narrow domain: the *New Yorker* followed *Punch*. Texually unchallengeable, the paper did not do well, I am sure, because of its layout unadventurousness – and a face-saving mishap precipitated its end: Graham Greene, writing on cinema, gave Shirley Temple some epithet like 'sexy little bit', and her mighty Hollywood studios pounced.

A photograph on my kitchen wall in Whitehall Court: its unchanged entrance seen from the street – **GBS**, hat-and-gloves, steps out, a kneeling char pausing at washing the tiled steps, as if worshipful.

I suppose it was about then that Shaw summoned me there, having seen my drawings, to his presence.

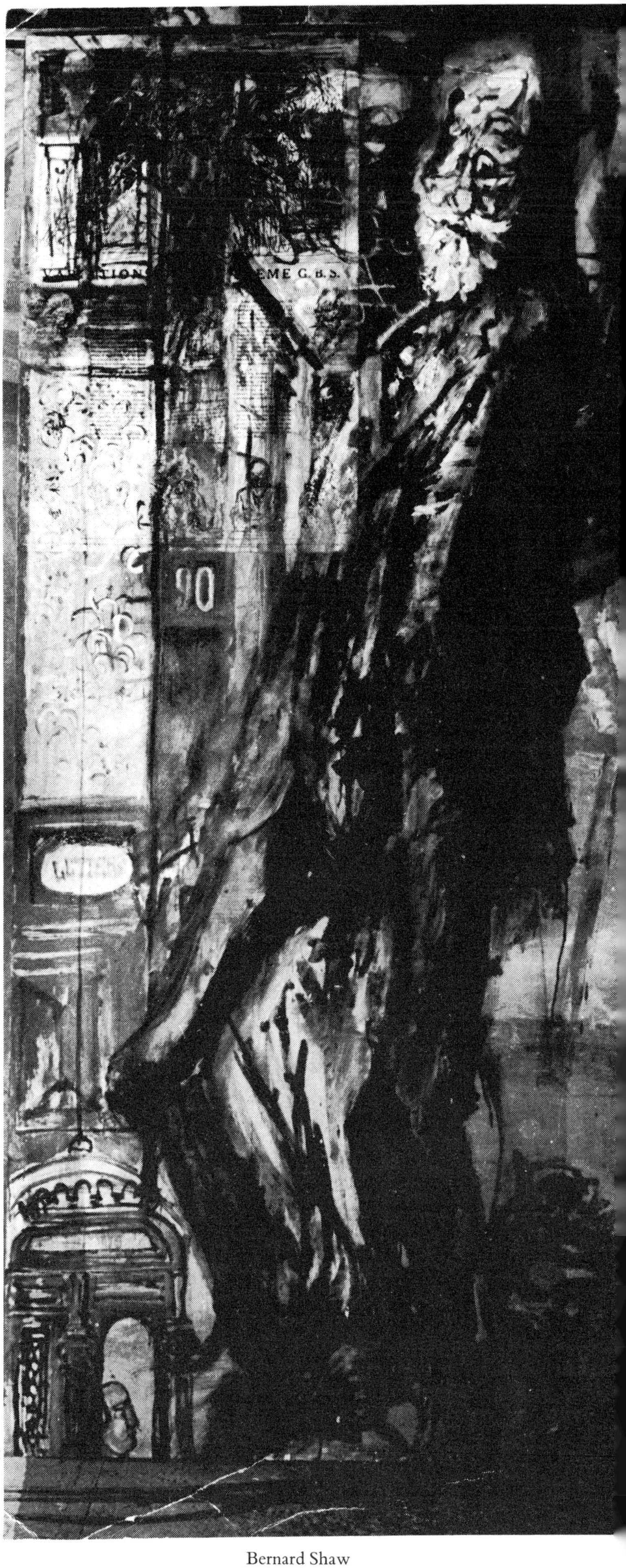

Bernard Shaw

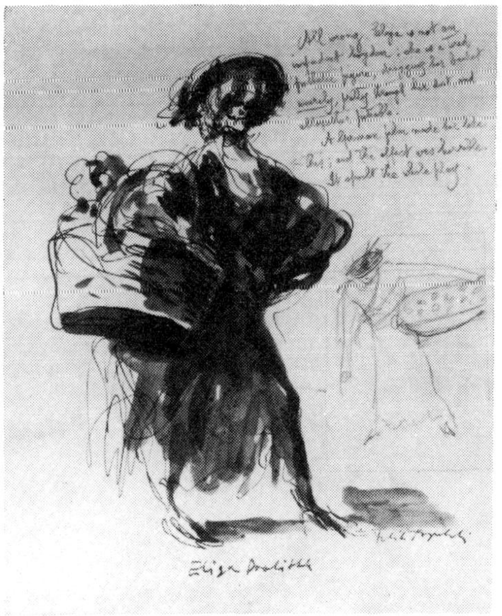

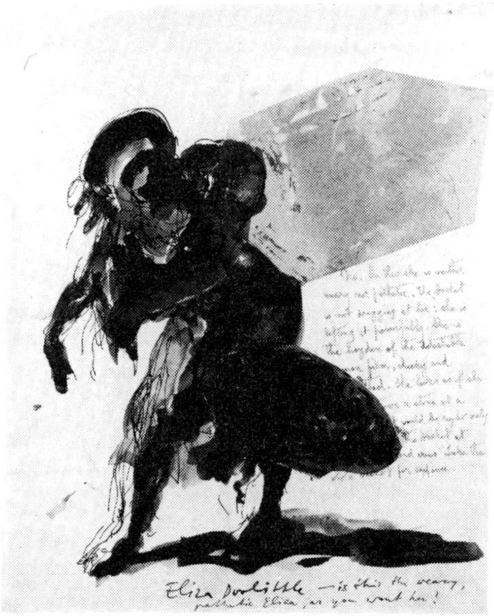

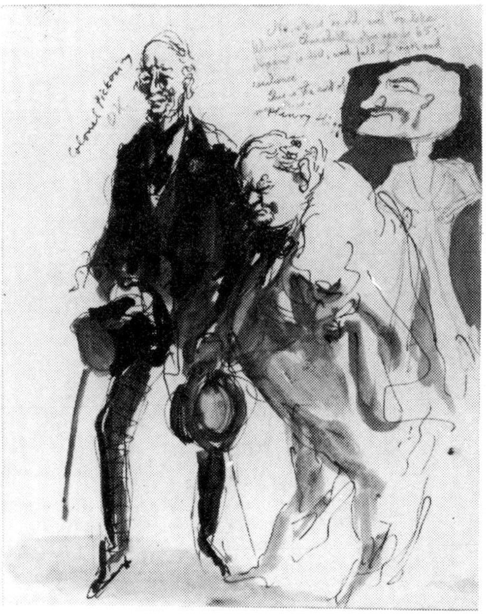

My sketches for *Pygmalion* illustrations, written and drawn over by George Bernard Shaw (Collection of University of Texas, Austin)

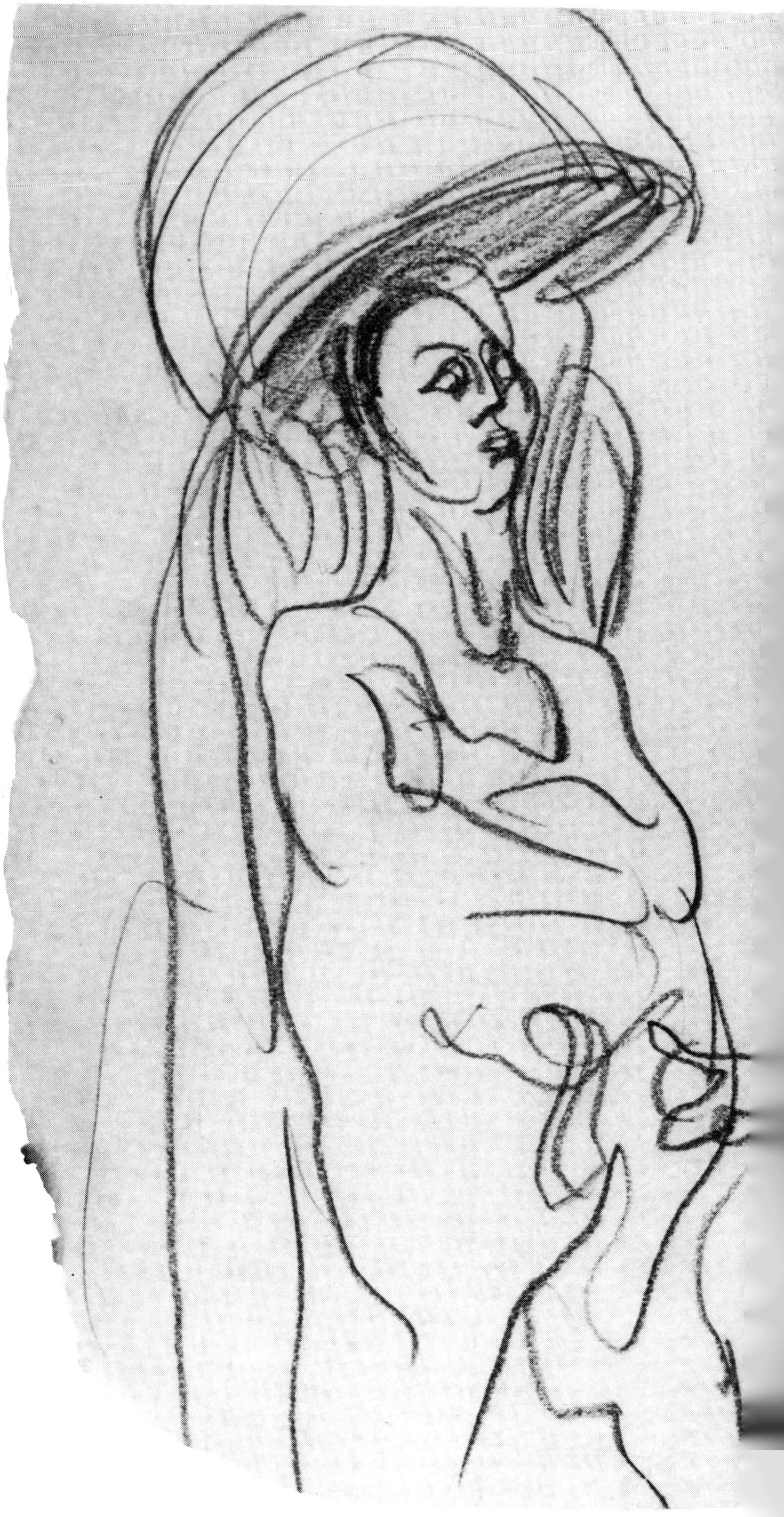

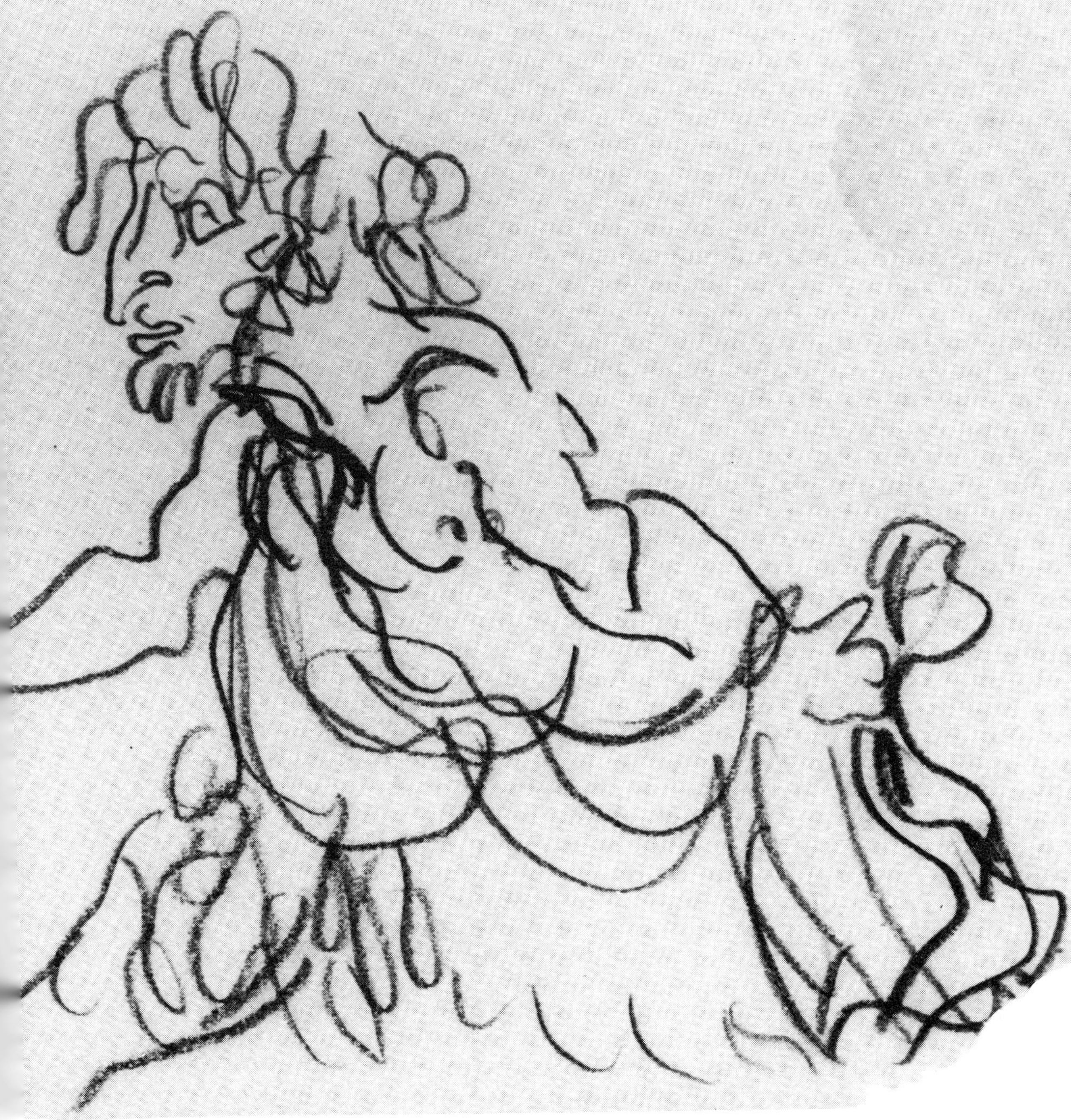

Farfetched Fables sketch during performance

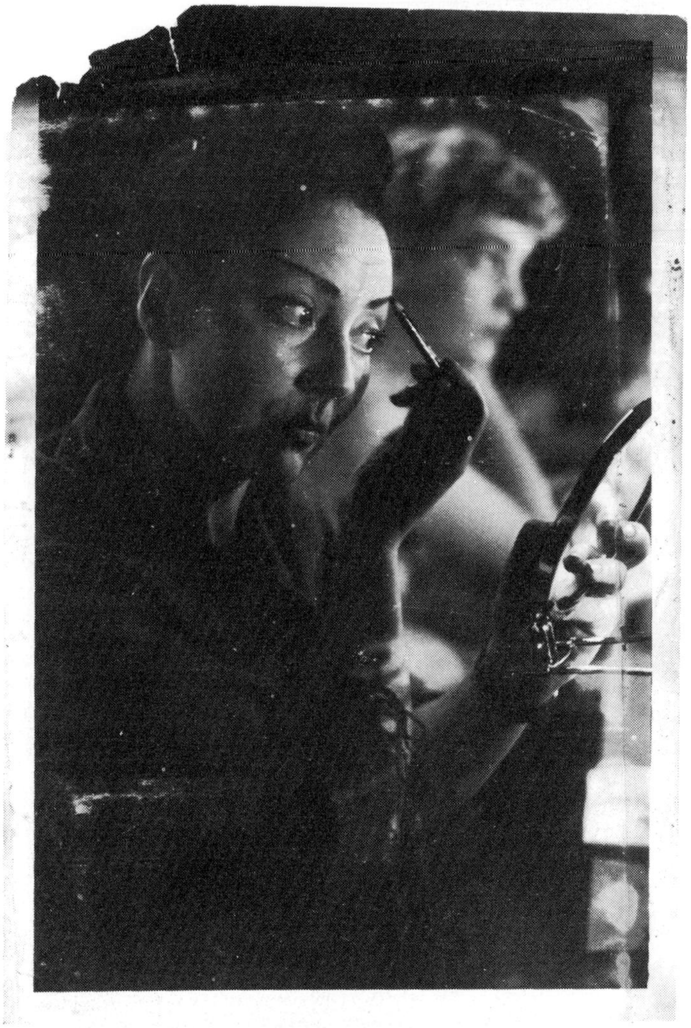

Farfetched Fables on stage dressing room (Marion)

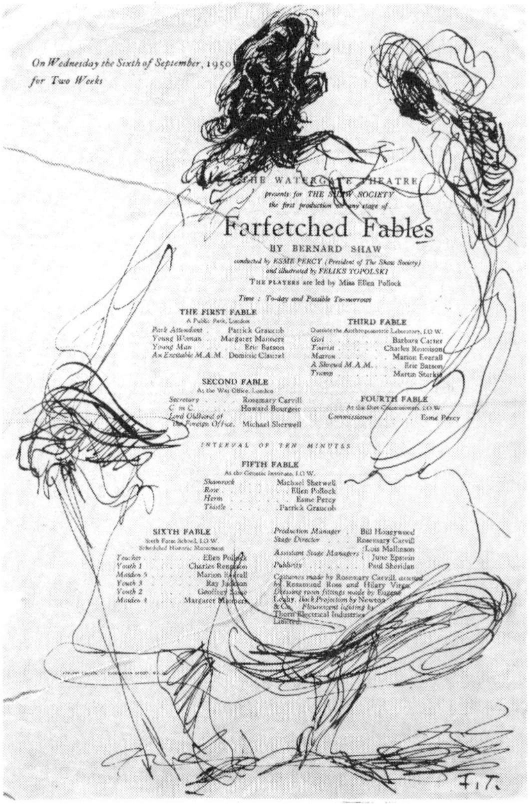

On Wednesday the Sixth of September, 1950
for Two Weeks

THE WATERGATE THEATRE
presents for THE SHAW SOCIETY
the first production on any stage of

Farfetched Fables

BY BERNARD SHAW

conducted by ESME PERCY *(President of The Shaw Society)*
and illustrated by FELIKS TOPOLSKI

THE PLAYERS are led by Miss Ellen Pollock

Time : To-day and Possible To-morrows

THE FIRST FABLE
A Public Park, London

Park Attendant	Patrick Graucob
Young Woman	Margaret Manners
Young Man	Eric Batson
An Excitable M.A.M.	Dominic Clancel

SECOND FABLE
At the War Office, London

Secretory	Rosemary Carvill
C in C.	Howard Bourgeois
Lord Oldhilead of the Foreign Office.	Michael Sherwell

THIRD FABLE
Outside the Anthropometric Laboratory, I.O.W.

Girl	Barbara Carter
Tourist	Charles Rennison
Matron	Marion Everall
A Shrewd M.A.M.	Eric Batson
Tramp	Martin Starkie

FOURTH FABLE
At the Diet Commissioners, I.O.W.

Commissioner	Esme Percy

INTERVAL OF TEN MINUTES

FIFTH FABLE
At the Genetic Institute, I.O.W.

Shamrock	Michael Sherwell
Rose	Ellen Pollock
Hern	Esme Percy
Thistle	Patrick Graucob

SIXTH FABLE
Sixth Form School, I.O.W.
Scheduled Historic Monument

Teacher	Ellen Pollock
Youth 1	Charles Rennison
Maiden 5	Marion Everall
Youth 3	Ray Jackson
Youth 2	Geoffrey [illegible]
Maiden 4	Margaret Manners

Production Manager	Bill Honeywood
Stage Director	Rosemary Carvill
Assistant Stage Managers	Lois Mallinson, June Epstein
Publicity	Paul Sheridan

Costumes made by Rosemary Carvill, assisted by Roseamund Rose and Hilary Virgo. Dressing room fittings made by Eugene Leahy. Back Projection by Newton [illegible] & Co. Fluorescent lighting by [illegible] Thorn Electrical Industries Limited.

F.T.

Programme

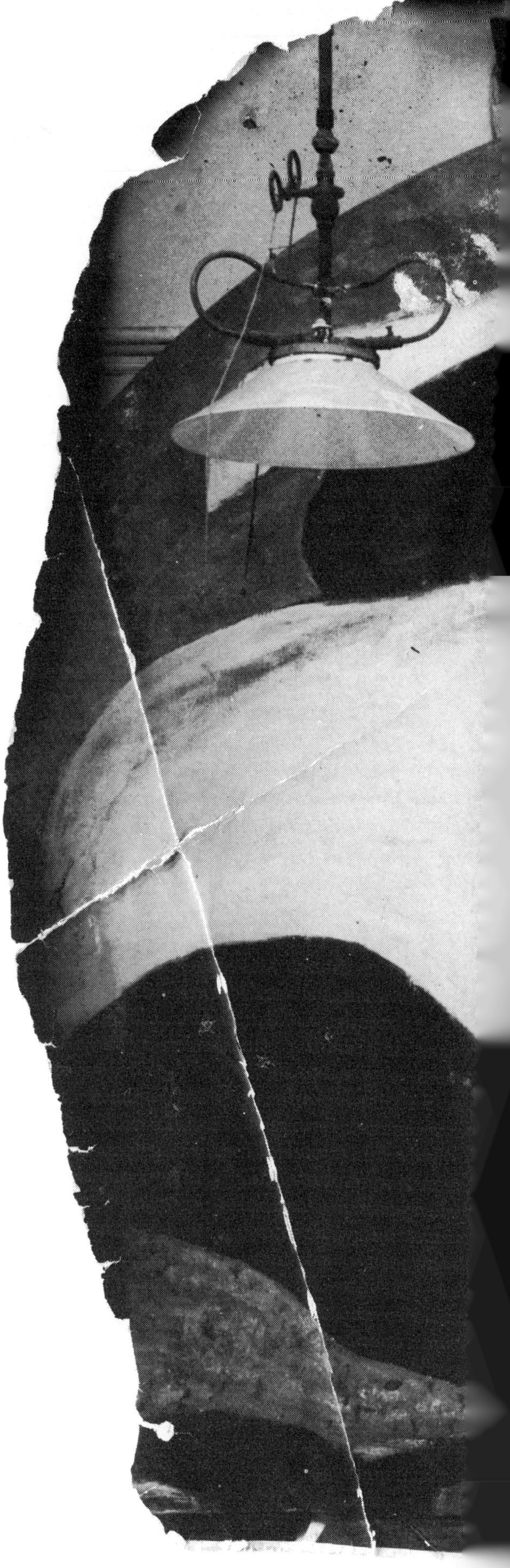

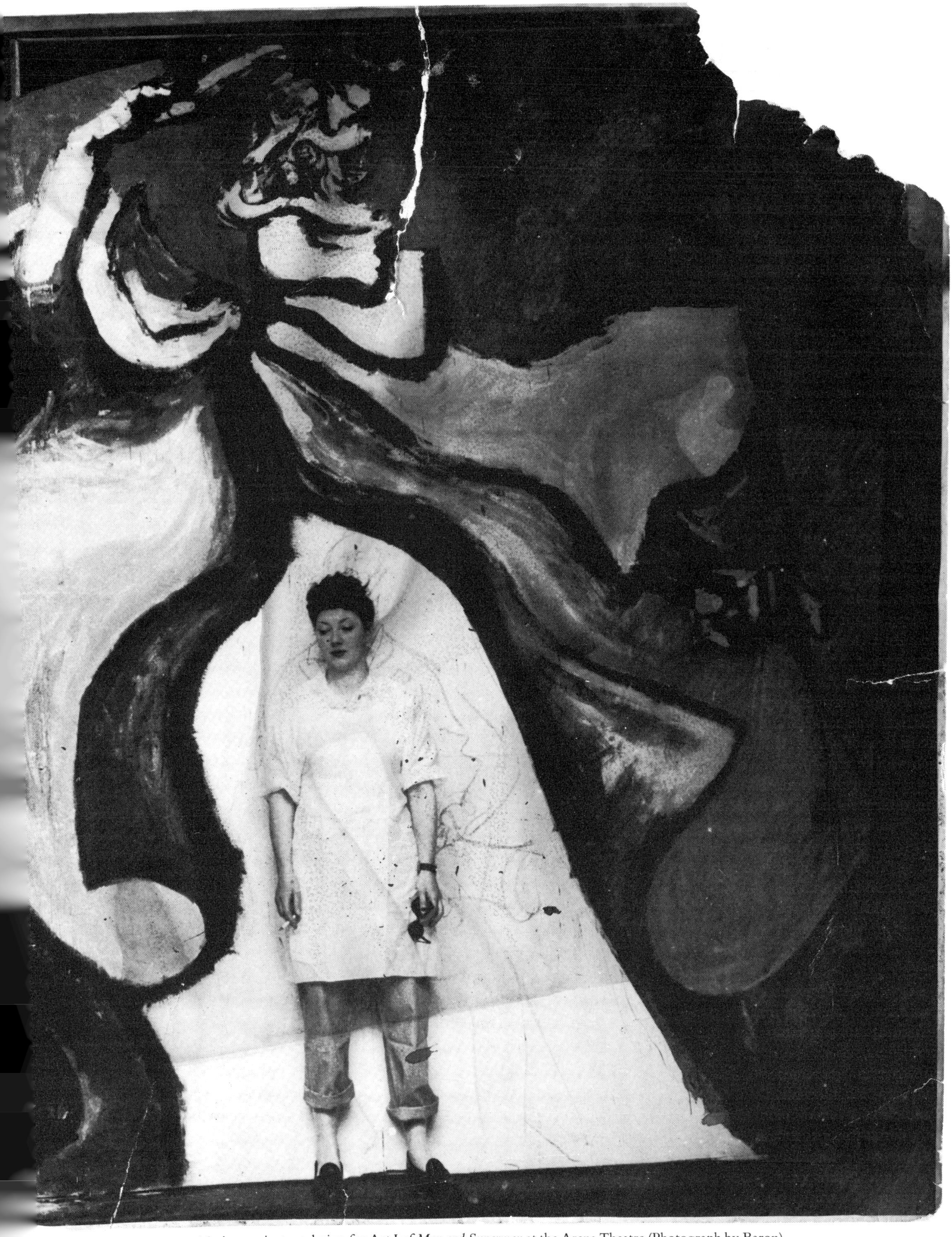

Marion against set design for Act I of *Man and Superman* at the Arena Theatre (Photograph by Baron)

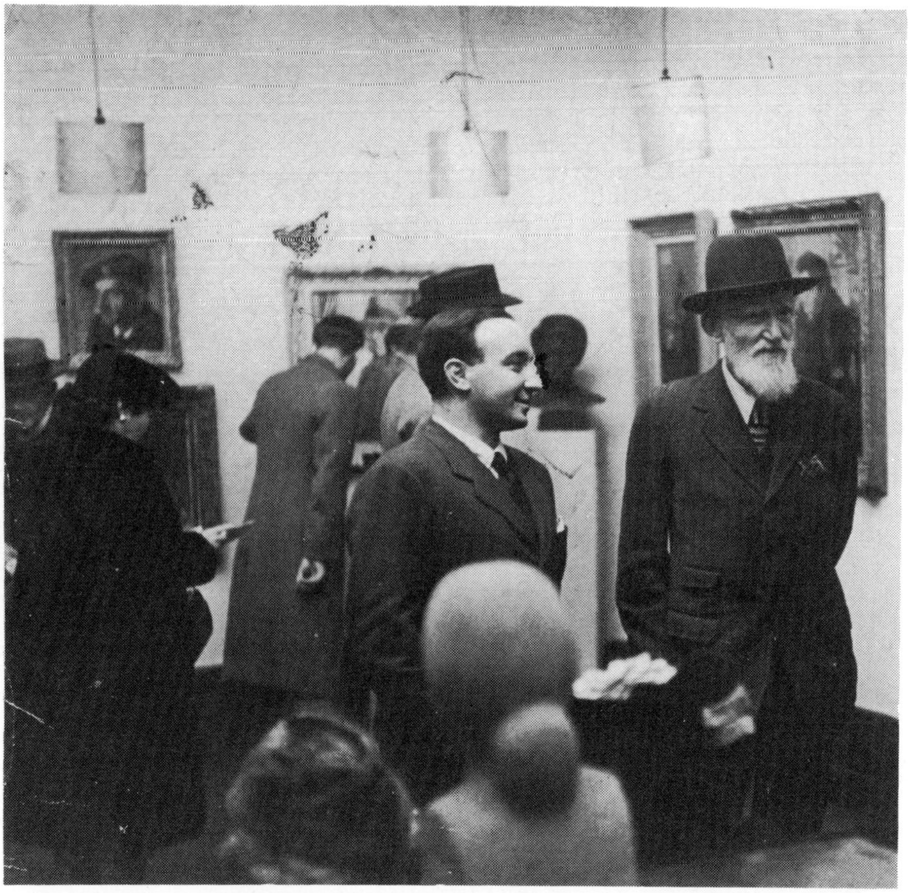
With GBS at Leicester Gallery examining his portrait

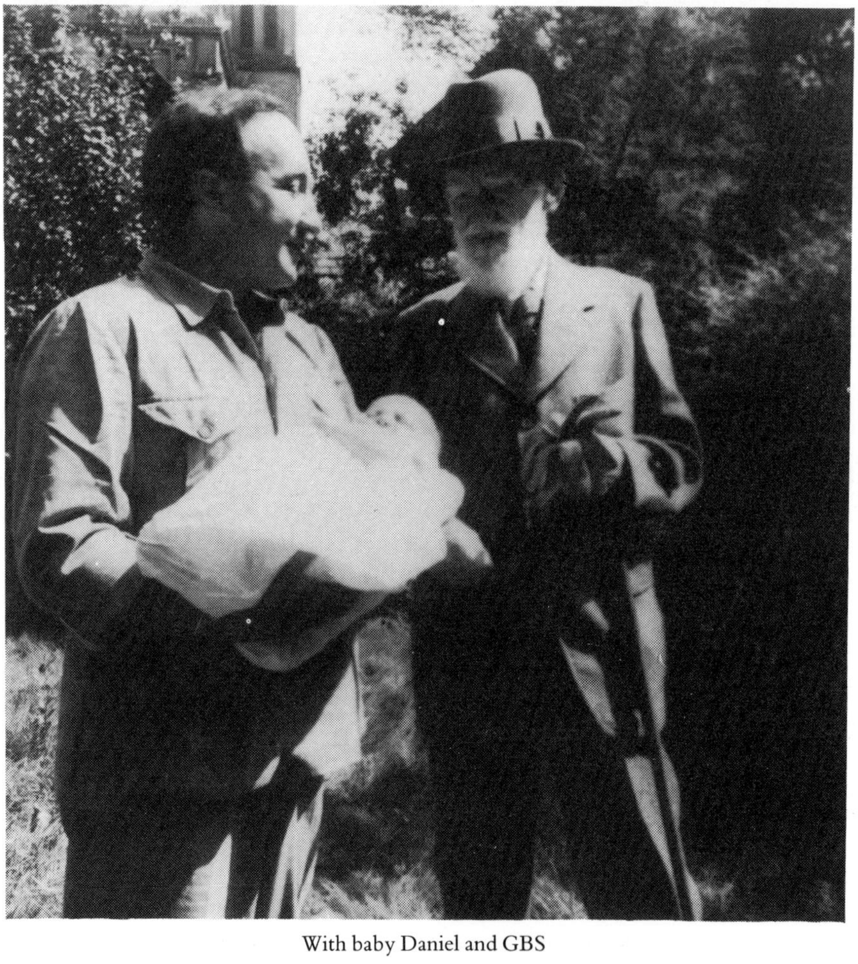
With baby Daniel and GBS

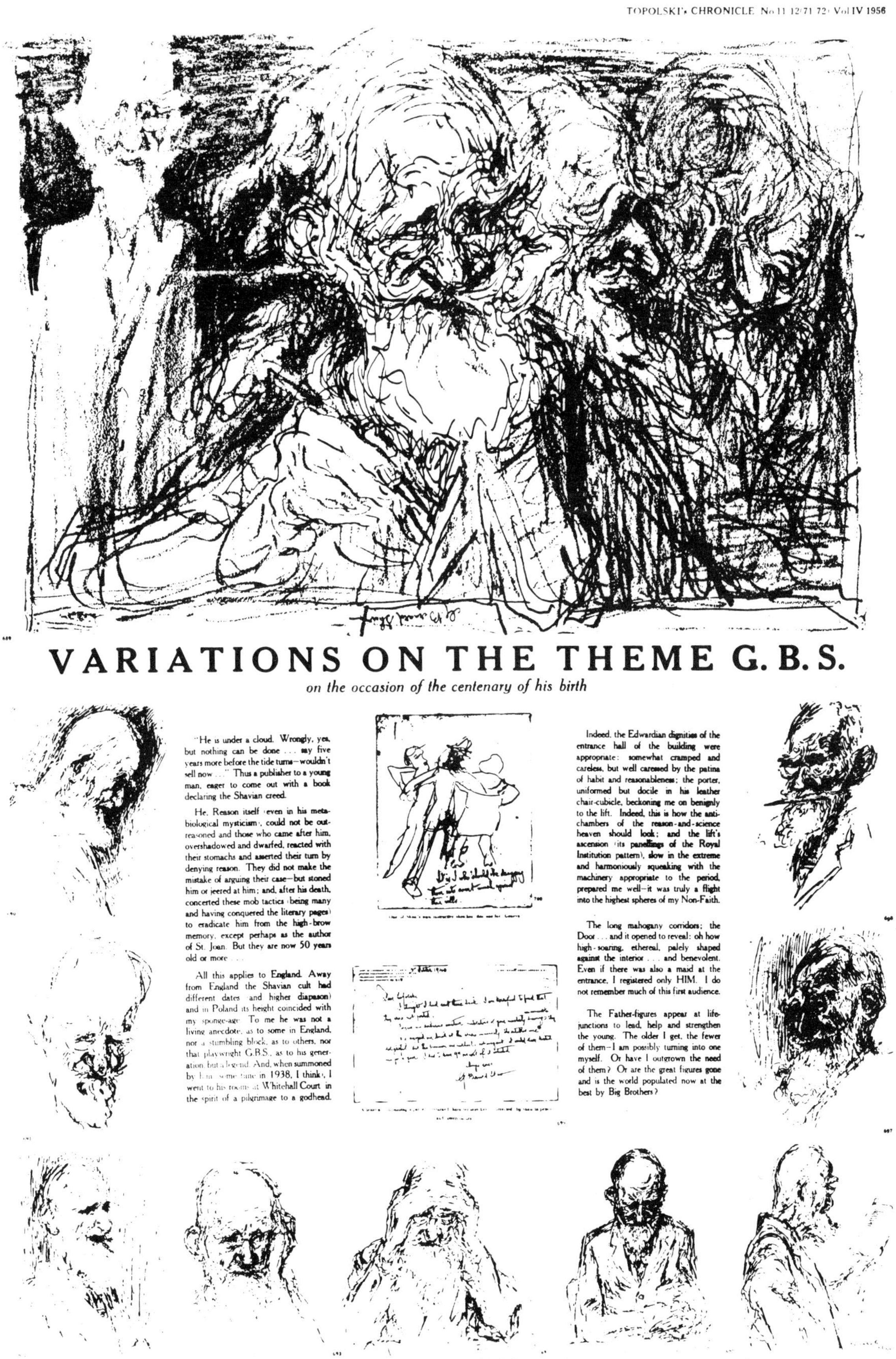

TOPOLSKI'S CHRONICLE No 11 12(71 72) Vol IV 1956

VARIATIONS ON THE THEME G.B.S.

on the occasion of the centenary of his birth

"He is under a cloud. Wrongly, yes, but nothing can be done . . . say five years more before the tide turns—wouldn't sell now . . ." Thus a publisher to a young man, eager to come out with a book declaring the Shavian creed.

He, Reason itself (even in his metabiological mysticism), could not be outreasoned and those who came after him, overshadowed and dwarfed, reacted with their stomachs and asserted their turn by denying reason. They did not make the mistake of arguing their case—but stoned him or jeered at him; and, after his death, concerted these mob tactics (being many and having conquered the literary pages) to eradicate him from the high-brow memory, except perhaps as the author of St. Joan. But they are now 50 years old or more . . .

All this applies to England. Away from England the Shavian cult had different dates (and higher diapason) and in Poland its height coincided with my sponge-age. To me he was not a living anecdote, as to some in England, nor a stumbling block, as to others, nor that playwright G.B.S., as to his generation, but a legend. And, when summoned by him (some time in 1938, I think), I went to his rooms at Whitehall Court in the spirit of a pilgrimage to a godhead.

Indeed, the Edwardian dignities of the entrance hall of the building were appropriate: somewhat cramped and careless, but well caressed by the patina of habit and reasonableness; the porter, uniformed but docile in his leather chair-cubicle, beckoning me on benignly to the lift. Indeed, this is how the antichambers of the reason-and-science heaven should look; and the lift's ascension (its panellings of the Royal Institution pattern), slow in the extreme and harmoniously squeaking with the machinery appropriate to the period, prepared me well—it was truly a flight into the highest spheres of my Non-Faith.

The long mahogany corridors; the Door . . . and it opened to reveal: oh how high-soaring, ethereal, palely shaped against the interior . . . and benevolent. Even if there was also a maid at the entrance, I registered only HIM. I do not remember much of this first audience.

The Father-figures appear at life-junctions to lead, help and strengthen the young. The older I get, the fewer of them—I am possibly turning into one myself. Or have I outgrown the need of them? Or are the great figures gone and is the world populated now at the best by Big Brothers?

Edition of *Topolski's Chronicle* devoted to GBS

31 1956

The Arts

POLAND'S LONG C[illegible] WITH SHAW'S PLAYS

FROM OUR SPECIAL CORRESPONDENT

WARSAW

The Teatr Polski (Polish Theatre) here is celebrating the centenary year of Shaw's birth in two ways—by a new production of *Saint Joan* (close on the heels of Polish *premières* of *The Dark Lady of the Sonnets* and *The Man of Destiny*) and by an absorbing exhibition which recapitulates, with justifiable pride, the theatre's long and intimate connexion with the dramatist.

The Teatr Polski was founded in 1913 by Dr. Arnold Szyfman, who, at the age of 75, is still directing it with a youthful vigour that Shaw would have been the first to admire. Dr. Szyfman early recognized Shaw as a force in the European theatre. He first produced Shaw (*Pygmalion*) in March, 1914. This was followed, especially between the wars, by a long succession of Shaw's plays, some old and some new. When the thirty-fifth anniversary of the opening of the theatre came to be celebrated in 1948 Shaw wrote him on a characteristic typewritten postcard, "I hope you will remind your audience that you were the first to perform some of my most famous plays. I think this places you as the most farseeing manager in Europe (including England) and the Teatr Polski above London as a centre of dramatic culture!"

No doubt Shaw had particularly in mind *The Apple Cart* which had its world *première* in the Teatr Polski in June, 1929, and *Too True to be Good* and *The Simpleton of the Unexpected Isles* which had their European *premières* there in 1932 and 1935. The commemorative brochure put out for the exhibition claims that "no other theatre not even Malvern . . . has produced a greater number of Shavian *premières*."

Altogether 20 of Shaw's plays have been produced under Dr. [illegible]zyfman's direction, [illegible] in the Teatr Pol[illegible] or in its associated [illegible] Theatre, with [illegible] total to date of about [illegible] performances—a record which might [illegible] even [illegible] but for the difficul[illegible] [illegible] in Poland had to face, [illegible] under the German occu[illegible] and under arbitrary Communist censorship in the post-war years. Shaw's re[illegible]earance in familiar surroundings last J[illegible] was a sign of the greater intellectual and cultural freedom which Poles like to believe has been consolidated in the "October days" when Mr. Gomulka took his stand against Stalinism.

The Shaw repertory of the Teatr Polski is an interesting study in national taste. *Pygmalion*—ripe for a new production, since it was last seen in 1937—was much to the liking of Warsaw audiences. In all it has been performed 179 times, and was outstepped in popularity only by *Arms and the Man* (last produced, in the Little Theatre, in 1935) with 214 performances. On the other hand, there are curious gaps. *Mrs. Warren's Profession*, *Candida*, and *The Devil's Disciple* have not been produced at all.

Except for the present version, which is by the producer, Mr. Bohdan Korzeniewski, all the translations of Shaw's plays for Dr. Szyfman have been done by Mr. Florian Sobieniowski. One of the Shaviana in the exhibition is an undated handwritten letter from author to translator accompanying an amended version of *Geneva* (produced in Warsaw in July, 1939). "I do not know," Shaw wrote, "how long a performance is expected to last in Warsaw, but this version, with the cut on pp. 21-43, makes it possible to finish in a little over three hours."

In this letter Shaw wrote of having seen Feliks Topolski, whose drawing of the dramatist is the centrepiece of the exhibition. He continued: "An astonishing draughtsman: perhaps the greatest of all the Impressionists in black and white." The letter concluded with a sharp Shavian transition to business—"An edition of the play in which your translation is used is subject to your copyright and to mine. Any alterations would introduce the artist's copyright."

There are two leading ladies in the present production of *Saint Joan*: Miss Nina Andryez, who in private life is the wife of Mr. Cyrankiewicz, the Prime Minister of Poland, and Miss Katarzyna [illegible]aniewska, an actress in her early twenties, who is playing her first important part. Miss Andryez may not have the intensity of a Sybil Thorndike, but she makes a very human saint in her earthly tribulations, a very blithe spirit in the rehabilita[illegible] scene, the irony of which has a special[illegible]ness for a Polish audience to [illegible]

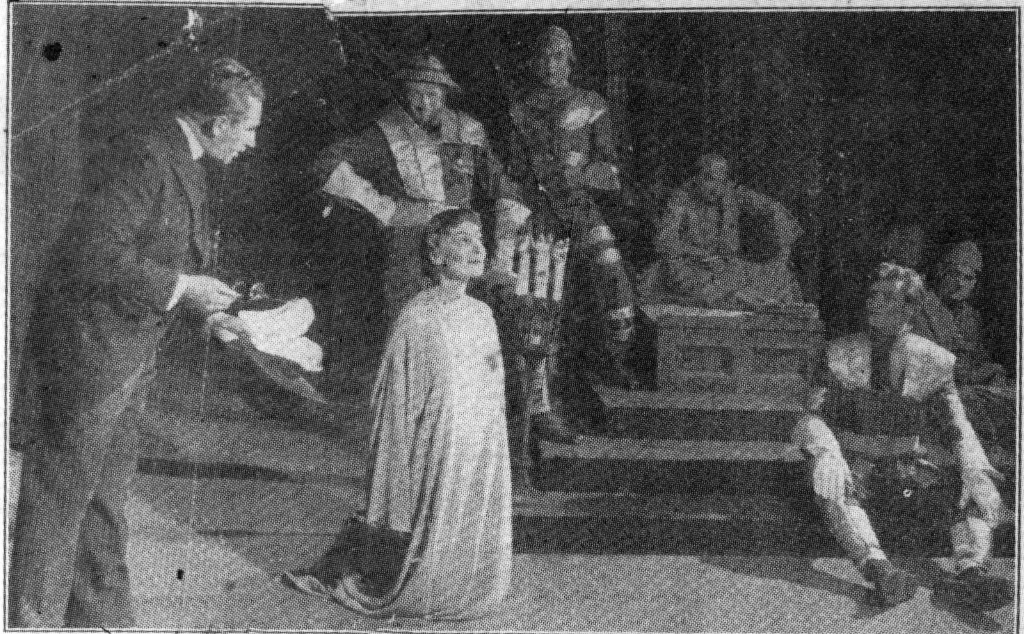

Miss Nina Andryez in the production of *Saint Joan* at the Teatr Polski.

Cutting from *The Times*

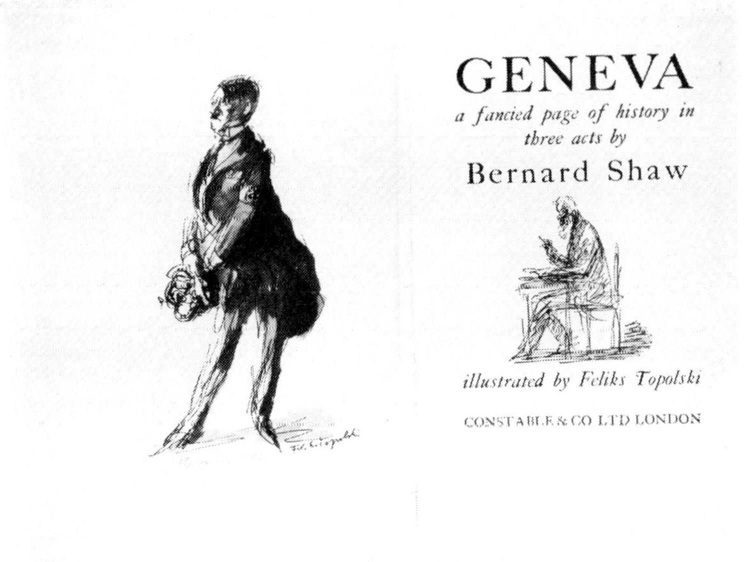

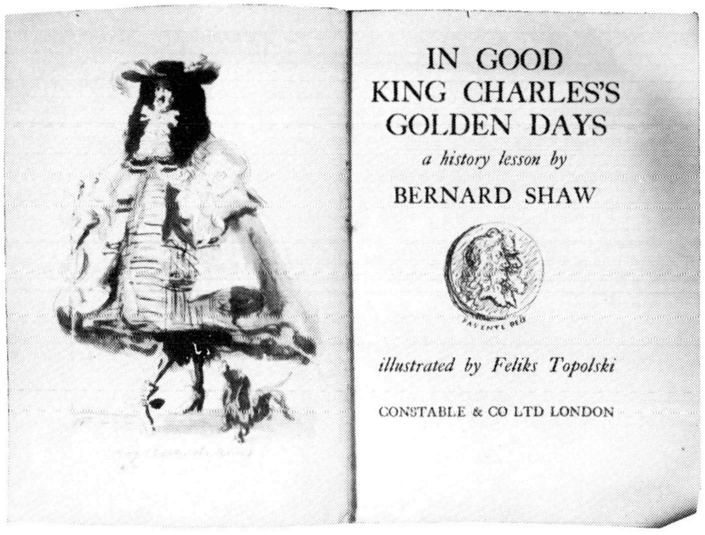

Frontispieces and title pages

'He is under a cloud. Wrongly, yes, but nothing can be done . . . say five years more before the tide turns – wouldn't sell now . . .' Thus a publisher to a young man, eager to come out with a book declaring the Shavian creed.

He, Reason itself (even in his metabiological mysticism), could not be outreasoned and those who came after him, overshadowed and dwarfed, reacted with their stomachs and asserted in their turn by denying reason. They did not make the mistake of arguing their case – but stoned him or jeered at him; and, after his death, concerted these mob tactics (being many and having conquered the literary pages) to eradicate him from the highbrow memory, except perhaps as the author of *St Joan*. But they are now fifty years old or more . . .

All this applies to England. Away from England the Shavian cult had different dates (and higher diapason) and in Poland its height coincided with my sponge-age. To me he was not a living anecdote, as to some in England, nor a stumbling block, as to others, nor that playwright GBS, as to his generation, but a legend. And, when summoned by him (some time in 1938, I think), I went to his rooms at Whitehall Court in the spirit of a pilgrimage to a godhead.

Indeed, the Edwardian dignities of the entrance hall of the building were appropriate: somewhat cramped and careless, but well caressed by the patina of habit and reasonableness; the porter, uniformed but docile in his leather chair-cubicle, beckoning me on benignly to the lift. Indeed, this is how the antechambers of the reason-and-science heaven should look; and the lift's ascension (its panellings of the Royal Institution pattern), slow in the extreme and harmoniously squeaking with the machinery appropriate to the period, prepared me well – it was truly a flight into the highest spheres of my Non-Faith.

The long mahogany corridors; the Door . . . and it opened to reveal: oh how high-soaring, ethereal, palely shaped against the interior . . . and benevolent. Even if there was also a maid at the entrance, I registered only HIM. I do not remember much of this first audience.

The father figures appear at life-junctions to lead, help and strengthen the young. The older I get, the fewer of them – I am possibly turning into one myself. Or have I outgrown the need of them? Or are the great figures gone and is the world populated now at the best by Big Brothers?

The settled Constable's conveyor belt of the standard edition of GBS's plays (preceded by a few rehearsal/proof copies) would be upset by his whimsy to publish the initial edition of ***Geneva*** in a different format with my illustrations. Otto Killman of Constable's fought against this, but Shaw, seduced by my draughtsmanship, persisted. And went still further into the fun of it. I sent him sketched-out suggestions for the play's characters for his comments. After a while, not having heard from him, I telephoned Miss Patch, his faultless secretary, and got this reassurance: 'It's all right. He has bought himself a box of coloured pencils and is working hard on your drawings.' And I soon received most thorough criticisms: my drawings were redone, added to, drawn anew, his versions emphatically more true to the characters, with textual argument pencilled along the margins. This enchantment–exchange went on and was repeated over my illustrations to his next play ***In Good King Charles's Golden Days*** (by then Constable's won over) and to the Penguin edition of ***Pygmalion***.

And a contributory tale: the Polish translator of Shaw, Mr Sobieniowski, well liked by Shaw, but also gently mocked for his scrounging inclination, pushed Poland's admiration for Shaw by translating his plays at speed from the rehearsal copies Shaw sent, thus achieving for a number of them world premières in Warsaw.

With ***Geneva*** on the way,* he wrote to me from Poland that GBS had scribbled in the margin of the copy of the play: 'Topolski . . . an astonishing draughtsman; perhaps the greatest of all the impressionists in black and white', and that this being in his view of value to me, he proposed to sell the copy to me for (if I remember) £100. Not moneyed and full of myself, I declined, but went on quoting this pronouncement – though without any proof in hand, war having separated us seemingly for good. But some years after the war I read in *The Times* its Warsaw correspondent's report about an

**Geneva* was staged in Warsaw not long before the Germans marched into Poland – one of their first acts on occupying Warsaw was to arrest the leading actor, Józef Węgrzyn, who had played Hitler in it.

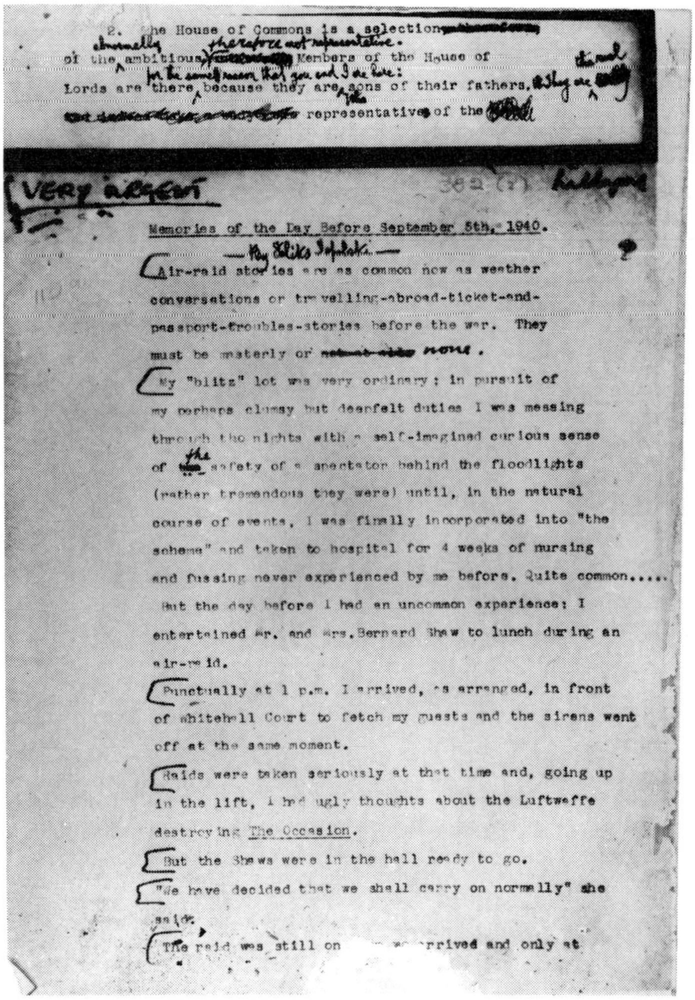

2. The House of Commons is a selection abnormally therefore not representative. of the ambitious Members of the House of Lords are there, because they are sons of their fathers. representative of the

VERY URGENT Lilliput

Memories of the Day Before September 5th, 1940.

— by Feliks Topolski —

Air-raid stories are as common now as weather conversations or travelling-abroad-ticket-and-passport-troubles-stories before the war. They must be masterly or none.

My "blitz" lot was very ordinary; in pursuit of my perhaps clumsy but heartfelt duties I was messing through the nights with a self-imagined curious sense of the safety of a spectator behind the floodlights (rather tremendous they were) until, in the natural course of events, I was finally incorporated into "the scheme" and taken to hospital for 4 weeks of nursing and fussing never experienced by me before. Quite common....

But the day before I had an uncommon experience: I entertained Mr. and Mrs. Bernard Shaw to lunch during an air-raid.

Punctually at 1 p.m. I arrived, as arranged, in front of Whitehall Court to fetch my guests and the sirens went off at the same moment.

Raids were taken seriously at that time and, going up in the lift, I had ugly thoughts about the Luftwaffe destroying The Occasion.

But the Shaws were in the hall ready to go.

"We have decided that we shall carry on normally" she said.

The raid was still on ... arrived and only at

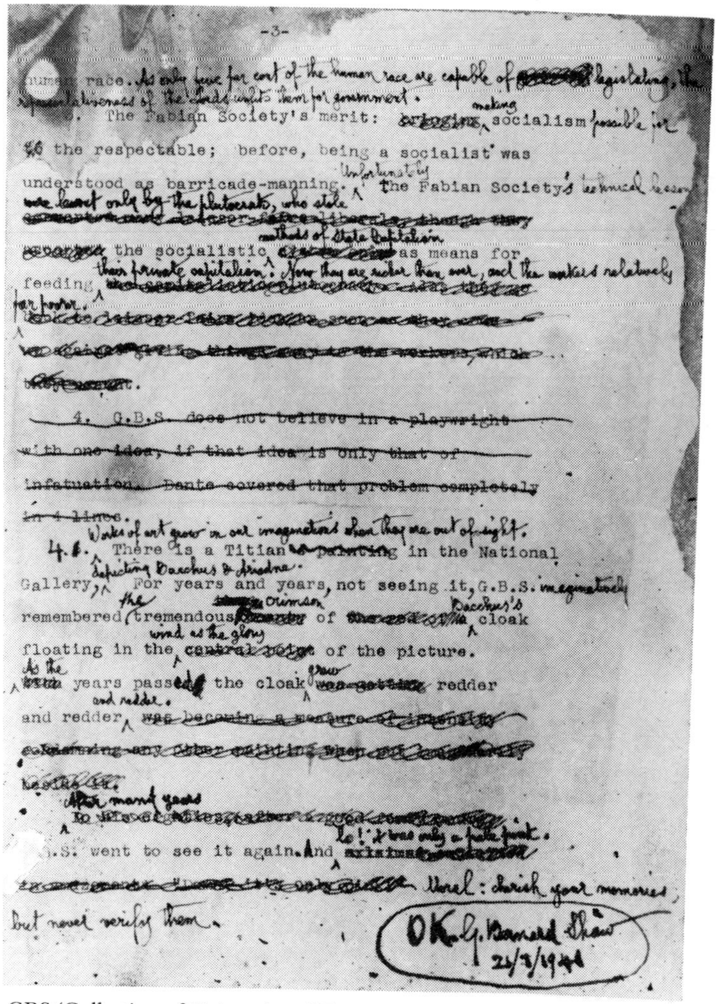

-3-

human race. As only four per cent of the human race are capable of legislating, the representativeness of the Lords unfits them for government.

3. The Fabian Society's merit: making socialism possible for the respectable; before, being a socialist was understood as barricade-manning. Unfortunately the Fabian Society's technical lessons were learnt only by the plutocrats, who stole the socialistic methods of State Capitalism as means for feeding their private capitalism. Now they are richer than ever, and the workers relatively far poorer.

4. G.B.S. does not believe in a playwright with one idea, if that idea is only that of infatuation. Dante covered that problem completely in 4 lines.

4. Works of art grow in our imaginations when they are out of sight. There is a Titian in the National Gallery, depicting Bacchus & Ariadne. For years and years, not seeing it, G.B.S. imaginatively remembered the tremendous crimson of Bacchus's cloak floating in the wind as the glory of the picture. As the years passed the cloak grew redder and redder. After many years G.B.S. went to see it again. And lo! it was only a pale pink. Moral: cherish your memories but never verify them.

OK G. Bernard Shaw 21/3/1941

Typescript for article in *Lilliput* with corrections by GBS (Collection of University of Texas, Austin)

exhibition at the Teatr Polski of 'teatralia' including a rehearsal copy of *Geneva* with, written in by GBS – and there came word by word the complete quote.

Touchingly **Augustus John** sat for me, having insisted that I do a drawing of him in the **Festschrift** for Sir John Squire. And he gently admonished me by saying only that I made him look a Volga boatman. A much fiercer reaction came unexpectedly from Bernard Shaw. With his full approval, and his lively draughtsmanship helping, I illustrated *Pygmalion* for Penguin. It was to be brought out long enough after having been written to justify the simplistic idea of *two heads of GBS*: one white-faced and red-bearded, and the other red-faced and white-whiskered (their cover then allowed only red colour added to black). He vehemently protested, sent me a set of photographs to emphasize the tidiness of his grooming with approximate dates scribbled on their backs, to prove that: 'I was perhaps not quite as good-looking as the Hermes of Praxiteles; but I was at least presentably clean and decent'; wrote angrily to Allen Lane – and eventually insisted that his wife would not have any of my offensive portraiture and that anyway a pretty girl on a cover sells a book best. The cover was duly replaced by a drawing of Eliza.

But endearingly, soon after this storm, I was placed in the corner of his Whitehall Court study, drawing and painting endless likenesses of him while he wrote, strolled round the room dictating, received. This resulted in the book ***Portrait of GBS'**** – and some larger paintings; a full-length one, which he came with me to examine at the Leicester Gallery, was bought by Alexander Korda and, after his death, went to join my other Shaviana at the University of Texas.

In 1941 a London periodical, ***Lilliput***, proposed to come out with an issue of *Blitz* stories. I wrote for it a piece on the Shaws' visit to my studio, but first sent the manuscript to GBS for approval. The returned manuscript had the thoughtful inclusion in his hand under the title 'by Feliks Topolski', and was unmarked up to the pages in which were recorded (in my interpretation) his views – these were entirely remoulded; and at the end in red ink the letters 'OK', his signature and the date, encircled with a flourish.

The receding pleasures at/blessings of the towering elders as they faded away. My **studio on the Canal** in the late Forties. A spring afternoon packed pleasantly with flagging-yet-racing **Polish talk** – because a singularly

*But his contrariness showed up again; I noted down on the edges of the drawings bits of what he said during the sessions; he insisted that all this should be erased: 'I made your publishers take your pencil notes of my conversation out of the plates because their publication would discredit you professionally. The most frightful breach of etiquette a painter can commit is to exploit a sitting as a journalist's interview. It is like a priest selling a confession. If you were thought capable of it nobody of any public standing would sit for you.'

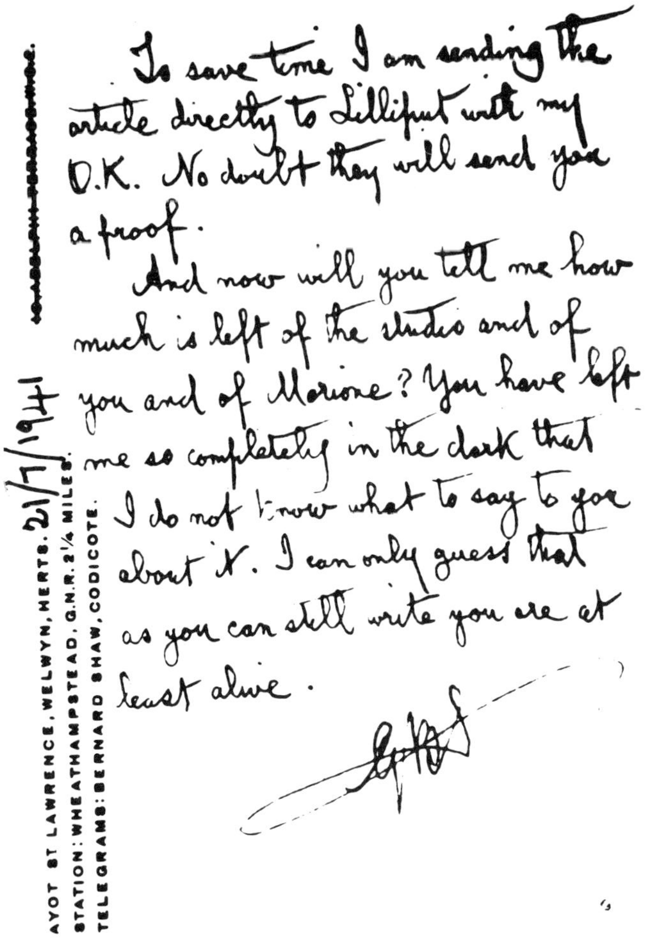
AYOT ST LAWRENCE, WELWYN, HERTS.
STATION: WHEATHAMPSTEAD, G.N.R. 2¼ MILES.
TELEGRAMS: BERNARD SHAW, CODICOTE.

21/7/1941

To save time I am sending the article directly to Lilliput with my O.K. No doubt they will send you a proof.

And now will you tell me how much is left of the studio and of you and of Marion? You have left me so completely in the dark that I do not know what to say to you about it. I can only guess that as you can still write you are at least alive.

Blitz-time postcard from GBS (Collection of University of Texas, Austin)

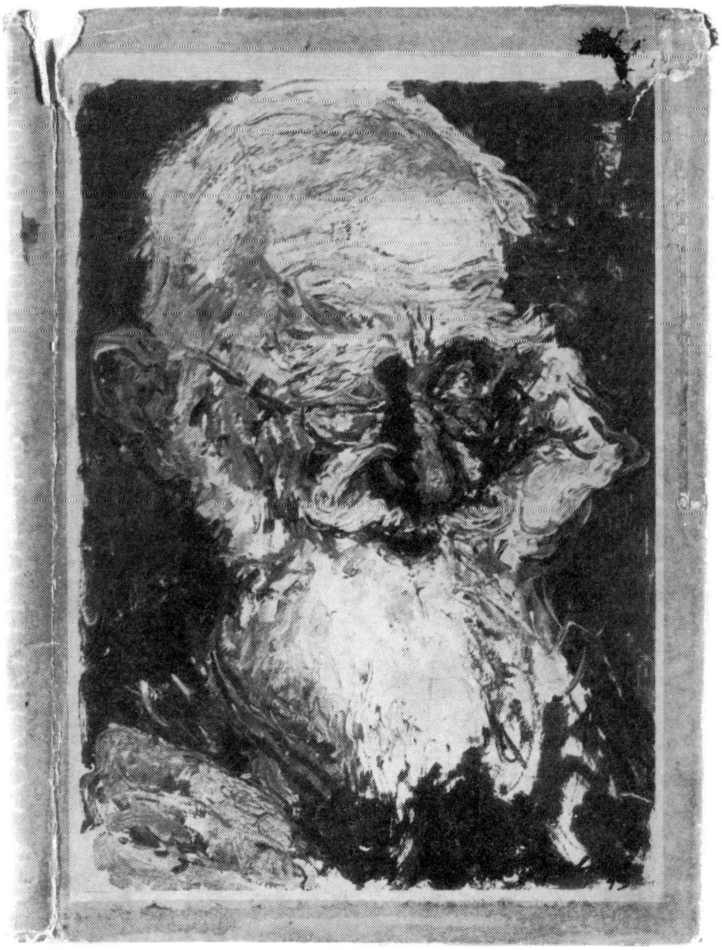

Frontispiece to *Portrait of GBS*

sympathetic choice of company suffices: the harmony rests on short-cut idiom; we all know one another and fill in the gaps.

The open entrance from the garden, hidden from us, lets somebody into the little lobby, our heads turn, and there, in the narrow/low doorway, bending lower still, the long narrow shape of GBS (not expected) comes at us, head first, unbends in clicks to his fuller-than-need-be straightness, and now, 'on the stage', with us a tightly grouped audience, opens his monologue and his gestural charms. A chair: he gives it a swing to ensure the old arm's success, hence a wider arc than needed, and sits himself in front of us, apart. Entranced, we listen: he, in flamboyant contrast to our hitherto murmurings, lilts rounded/rhythmical/ uninterruptable wisdom – our well-composed receptivity obviously pleases/prompts him – for an hour at least . . .

He is up and gracefully ready to go – masterly well timed: we far from satiated, ample for more.

I offer to get a taxi – the studio is buried in the depths of Maida Vale, the whole of London from Whitehall; but he (another of his overstated gestures to fob off the lurking inadequacies of old age) dismisses the idea. Unbelievably light-footed (though ever so creaking), he steps up from my garden into the undemanding/ungiving Warwick Avenue, turns determinedly right, and there, positively bounces – those bony shoulderblades, that shrivelled/straight neck, stiff Homburg over uneven ears – down and round the dreariest bend of the most dismal Harrow Road.

London critics were moving in a body at the old man overstaying his welcome. This piece, **Farfetched Fables**, intelligent above their aptitudes, gently nonchalant but overflowing with benevolent/humorous tolerance (unlike Wells's end-fury), they called a charade, meaning dismissiveness. This was London farewelling its majestic but never bombastic sage.

In the tiniest – pre-Fringe – basement in Villiers Street, called the Watergate Theatre, the little platform had to hold a lapidary set of fables playfully reaching into millennia ahead. And there was no money, which helped, because I was at ease designing this 'charade' to its deliberately mini-measure: and so, the actors (amongst them Ellen Pollock and Marion) boldly changed and made up – in view of the audience – facing the side walls of the acting area backed only by painted quadrangles – different for each millennium, as were also the performers' shapes, reaching maxi-oddities within the cardboard and speediest-change limitations. **Esmé Percy**, the angelic-stylish Shavian veteran – a lovable homosexual – his shape/upper lip/hands/movements those of my father – directed and led. It was all lovely, except for the sour critics and, in consequence, nightly not enough people to fill up some fifty seats. Shaw stayed then continuously in Ayot St Laurence; did not come; and (am I right?) his fabled life ended during this short run.

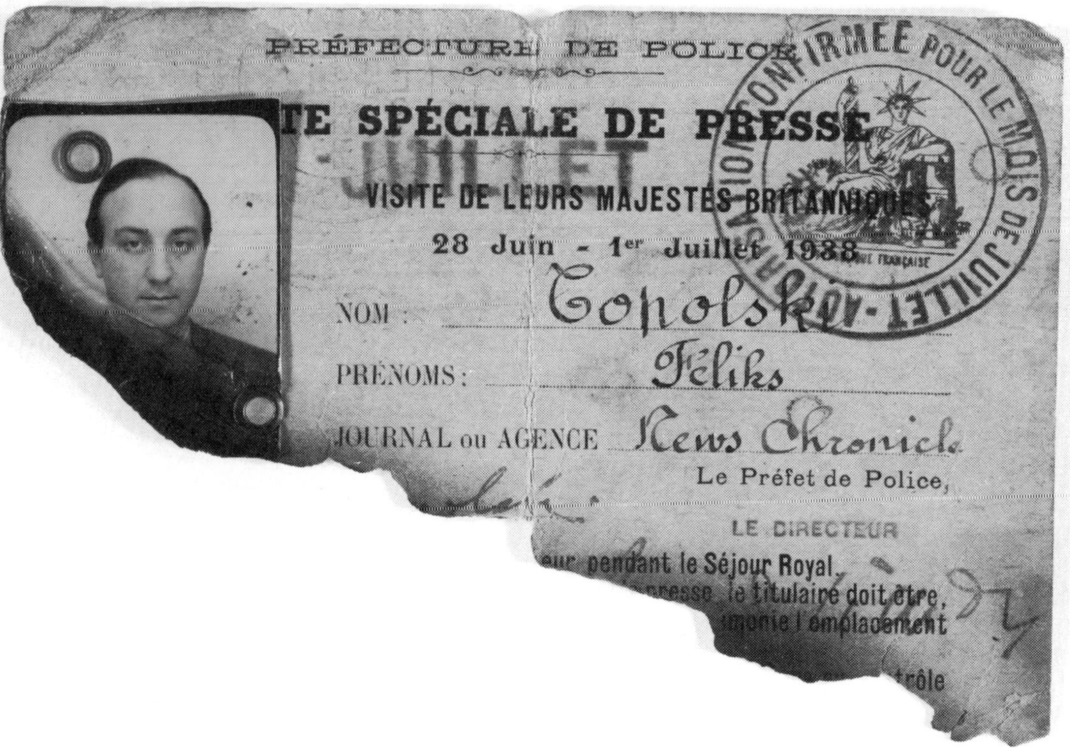
PRÉFECTURE DE POLICE
TE SPÉCIALE DE PRESSE
VISITE DE LEURS MAJESTÉS BRITANNIQUES
28 Juin - 1er Juillet 1938
NOM : Topolski
PRÉNOMS : Feliks
JOURNAL ou AGENCE News Chronicle
Le Préfet de Police,
LE DIRECTEUR
eur pendant le Séjour Royal.
presse, le titulaire doit être,
mente l'emplacement
trôle
CONFIRMÉE POUR LE MOIS DE JUILLET

Royal Paris visit, 1938 – Press Card

Paris Lost: Excerpts from Jonathan Stone's Introduction*

He met a Spanish Academician of great distinction, **Eugenio d'Ors** – professor, novelist, 'foremost among contemporary art critics', according to Léon Daudet, philosopher and diplomat – who was Permanent Secretary of the Spanish Institute. Señor d'Ors, a Catalan by birth, but a natural cosmopolitan who had aptly described himself as 'the Wandering Catholic', was living in Paris at the time. He enormously admired Topolski's work and proposed collaboration between them on a book – a medley of Parisian drawings and words. [. . .]

By the end of 1938, Topolski had completed a remarkable collection of just over two hundred drawings of Paris and d'Ors wrote four dialogues of imaginary discussions between himself and the artist to accompany them. Arrangements were made for the publication of what was originally entitled ***Paris Scenes and Secrets*** – *Recorded and Revealed by the pen of Eugenio d'Ors and by the pencil of Feliks Topolski* by the Minerva Publishing Company in collaboration with Przeworski's Publishing House, a leading firm in pre-war Warsaw. The drawings, of which satisfactory proof pulls had been provided by the printers in Cracow, were to be reproduced in two-colour offset. The text was translated from d'Ors's original French by John Marks of *Night and Day* fame. [. . .] It was set by Lund Humphries . . . and progress was such that a prospectus was prepared by the proposed publishers, promoting the trade edition of twenty-five copies, signed by Señor d'Ors and Mr Topolski, offered at five guineas. Publication in England was fixed for 15 September 1939, and further editions were planned for Paris and Warsaw. None of the editions ever appeared, and the outbreak of war saw all the drawings in Poland.

On the fall of France in 1940, Eugenio d'Ors returned to Madrid. From his office as the Secretario Perpetuo of the Instituto de España at the Palacio del Sacramento, he made contact with the German Embassy in Madrid in the hope that through wartime diplomatic channels he would be able to use his influence to have the original drawings prised out of Poland and sent to him in Madrid; and, indeed, his standing was such that he was initially successful in his efforts. Two members of the **Gestapo in Warsaw** presented themselves at the offices of Przeworski to the utter terror of the proprietors for whom a visit from the Gestapo spelled – as they thought – certain arrest, and probable death; the story of the visit was recounted to Topolski after the war by Dr Przeworski, the brother of Marek, the head of the publishing firm who had died in the ghetto uprising. Their requirements were, however, less demanding – quite simply the portfolio of Topolski drawings. [. . .]

In d'Ors's first surviving letter, of 19 May 1941, he tells Topolski that in letters which he had written to him in the previous autumn (and which never arrived at their destination) he had told him how the drawings had been finally retrieved. [. . .]

According to d'Ors, 'they' (presumably the Germans) were prepared to release the drawings to him on condition that he presented himself as proprietor and at the same time – according to his last information (10 May 1941) – that he deposited with 'them' a sum equivalent to the value of the drawings according to the publishing contract. [. . .]

Eventually after several months of discussions between d'Ors and the German Embassy, d'Ors was told that the drawings would no longer be available since their withdrawal to Berlin had been ordered by a higher authority: his ceaseless representations availed nothing. What is totally unclear is whether the order to **the German Embassy in Madrid** came from the *Reichskanzlei* in Berlin – in other words from Hitler – or from Goebbels, the Reich Minister of Propaganda, and what the purpose of the order was. There are two conjectures: first, that Hitler had heard that the

*1973; and as *Paris disparu*, 1974.

drawings were of architectural or artistic interest and sought them in his 'artistic' capacity – since he regarded the Paris Opéra as the height of architecture. Perhaps he had even seen the drawings on their journey from Warsaw to Madrid. The second possibility is that Goebbels required the drawings for wartime propaganda purposes. Certainly the suggestion that the drawings might have propaganda value makes eminently good sense. Topolski was an Official British War Artist and at least one of his *Blitz* drawings, namely that of a tired ARP warden, which was originally reproduced in *Illustrated London News*, and subsequently as one of the Penguin *Topolski Prints*, was used by the Nazis (without payment of royalties!) in some of their propaganda to demonstrate the plight of wartime Britain. Unfortunately, our best potential sources of information have run dry: none of the German ambassadors to Madrid during the war (Dr Eberhard von Stohrer, Hans Adolf von Moltke, and Dr Hans Heinrich Dieckhoff) is still alive; both José Janés and John Marks (press attaché at British Embassy in Madrid during the war) died about six years ago; and Eugenio d'Ors died in 1954.

When d'Ors and Topolski met again in 1951 for the first time since the war, d'Ors was unable to shed any light on the fate of the drawings and they both resigned themselves to the inevitability of their destruction and the non-appearance of their book. [. . .] What Topolski never knew when he was tramping the ruins of Berlin in 1945 as an Official War Artist was that the drawings were soon to be – or were already – safely in the hands of one **Dr Hans Cürlis**, the Director of the Kulturfilm-Institut GmbH in Berlin, who is now in his eighty-fifth year and who has, in the last fifty years, filmed over seventy painters and sculptors at work, starting with Louis Corinth. On 15 May 1963, Dr Cürlis wrote to Topolski for the first time to say that he had **bought a parcel of drawings** shortly after the end of the war **from a Russian soldier** near Kochstrasse, which is now in East Berlin, and that they were all in very good condition. It is for conjecture why four of the originals of which we possess proof pulls only have never been recovered; perhaps they were at the printers in Cracow, whereas the originals were with Przeworski in Warsaw. The soldier had been extremely selective and out of all the property available for looting, he had, with a connoisseur's eye, picked the Topolski drawings out of the ruins of Berlin. Dr Cürlis, 'found the pictures extraordinarily beautiful' and, for obvious reasons, had directed his inquiries about the drawings in a French direction. In view of the markings on the back of the drawings for the layout of the frustrated pre-war publication, Dr Cürlis asked M. Frechet, the Director of the French Institute in Berlin, whether a book of them had already been published. He also consulted the French Embassy but neither was able to assist on either the book or the artist. Finally Dr Cürlis approached the Keeper of the Department of Engravings – das *Kupferstichkabinett* – of the Berlin Museum where an assistant, Mr Anzelewsky, was able to decipher Topolski's signature and to tell him that the artist was British and living in England. Mr Turner of the Information Services Branch, British Military Government, Berlin, told Dr Cürlis about Topolski's work and gave him his address. It was, however, not until November 1963 that Topolski received Dr Cürlis's letter of 15 May following the artist's extensive uninterrupted world travels. In February 1965, thanks to the warm co-operation of Dr Cürlis, the drawings were returned to Topolski who had not seen them for a quarter of a century or more.

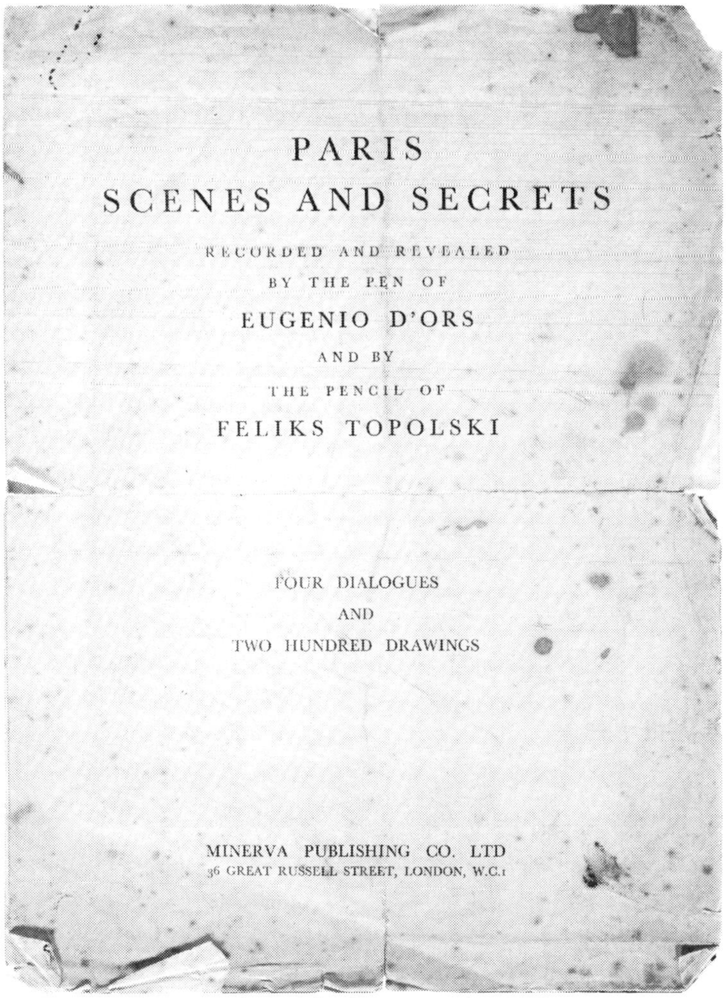

PARIS
SCENES AND SECRETS
RECORDED AND REVEALED
BY THE PEN OF
EUGENIO D'ORS
AND BY
THE PENCIL OF
FELIKS TOPOLSKI

FOUR DIALOGUES
AND
TWO HUNDRED DRAWINGS

MINERVA PUBLISHING CO. LTD
36 GREAT RUSSELL STREET, LONDON, W.C.1

Prospectus for Paris book in preparation, 1939

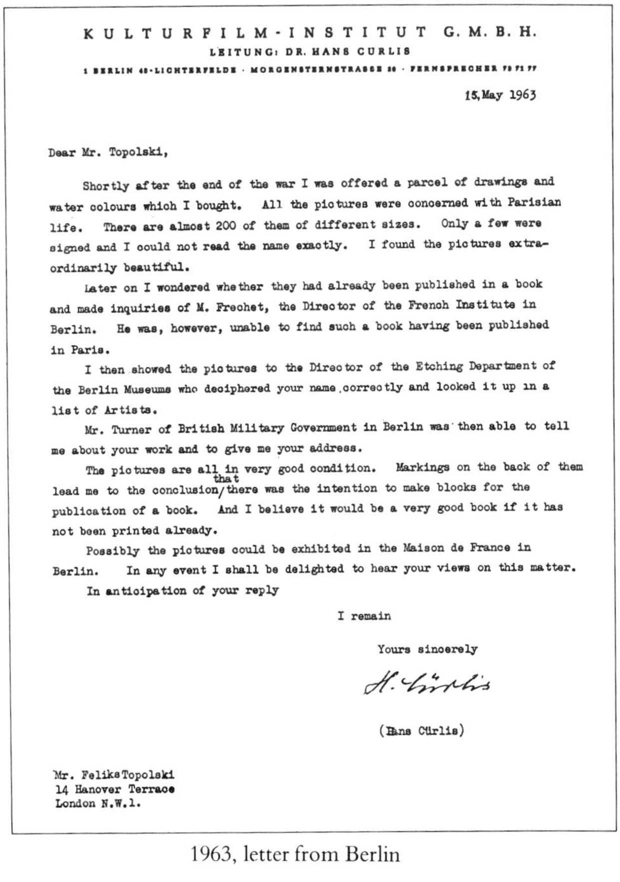

KULTURFILM-INSTITUT G.M.B.H.
LEITUNG: DR. HANS CURLIS
1 BERLIN 45-LICHTERFELDE · MORGENSTERNSTRASSE 30 · FERNSPRECHER 73 71 77

15, May 1963

Dear Mr. Topolski,

Shortly after the end of the war I was offered a parcel of drawings and water colours which I bought. All the pictures were concerned with Parisian life. There are almost 200 of them of different sizes. Only a few were signed and I could not read the name exactly. I found the pictures extraordinarily beautiful.

Later on I wondered whether they had already been published in a book and made inquiries of M. Frechet, the Director of the French Institute in Berlin. He was, however, unable to find such a book having been published in Paris.

I then showed the pictures to the Director of the Etching Department of the Berlin Museums who deciphered your name correctly and looked it up in a list of Artists.

Mr. Turner of British Military Government in Berlin was then able to tell me about your work and to give me your address.

The pictures are all in very good condition. Markings on the back of them lead me to the conclusion that there was the intention to make blocks for the publication of a book. And I believe it would be a very good book if it has not been printed already.

Possibly the pictures could be exhibited in the Maison de France in Berlin. In any event I shall be delighted to hear your views on this matter.

In anticipation of your reply

I remain

Yours sincerely

H. Cürlis

(Hans Cürlis)

Mr. Feliks Topolski
14 Hanover Terrace
London N.W.1.

1963, letter from Berlin

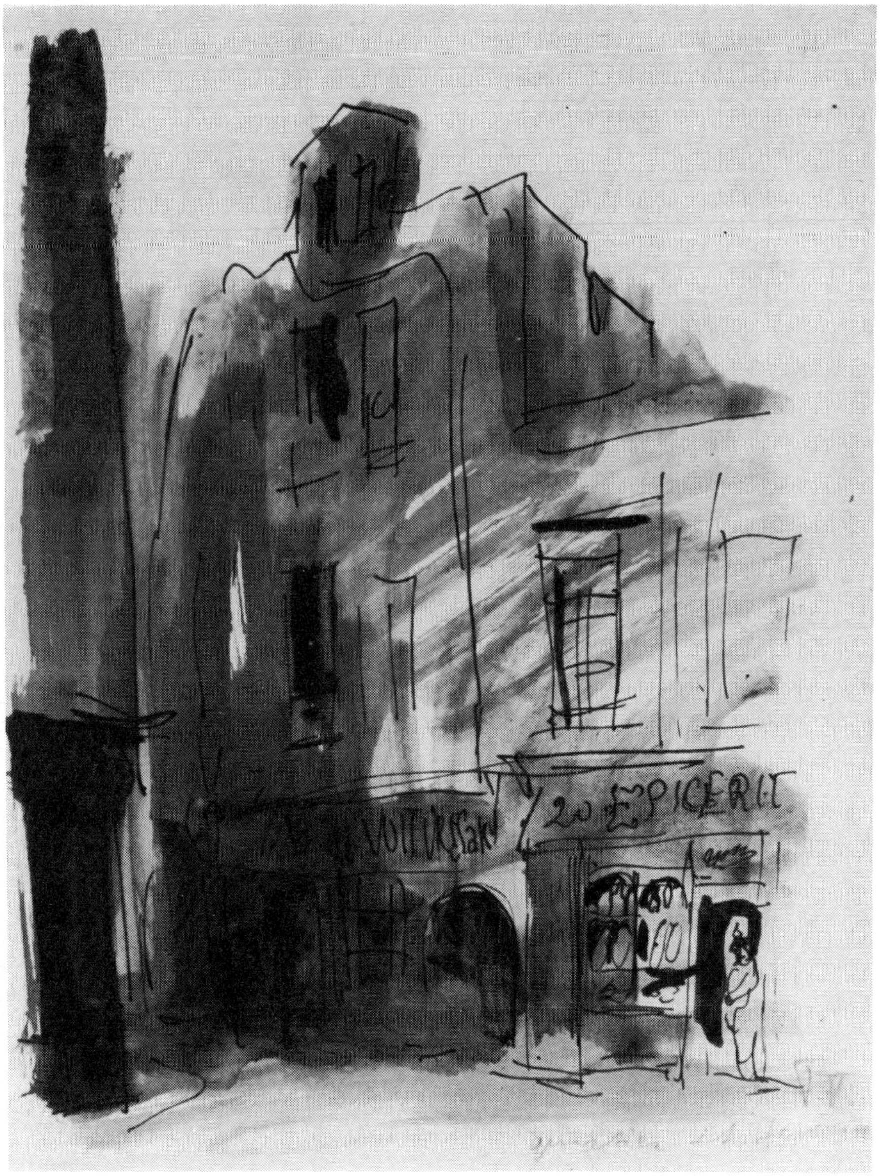

Quartier St Severin (from *Paris Scenes and Secrets*)

So there: **Paris of the thirties**.

– For Parisian emblem, correctly over-emphatic: over-middle-aged/over-dressed/over-panachious – deliberately not shaped/attired as if of English-bent society, but consummately French, *Le Grand Comédien, Le Prince de Théâtre* – Sasha Guitry.

– And the feminine professional heights: Suzy Solidor, Josephine Baker, Madame Schiaparelli.

– Confident connoisseurs at the heart of the world art market's confidence, their outrageous modern paintings reassuringly on canvases, gaudily/comfortingly framed, conveniently sized, reliably oily; and *les peintres surréalistes en vogue* assuringly backed by *Les Marchands, Les Éditeurs* and *La Société*. But also: La Salle du Jeu de Paume: carved age-patinaed frames round some precious brush strokes. Le Grand Palais: white statuary circled *au ralenti* by black-suited/hatted or cassocked dignities (also *pince-nez* and *barbiches* and heavy-hatted/bottomed *mesdames*).

– Le Quartier St-Sévérin – its calm and its *épicerie*, its *boucherie chevaline*.

– Le Quartier St-Paul: *une fille* leads upstairs, undoing her slip; soaps your cock diligently; obligingly climbs on top to avail you of the horizontal mirror above the bed.

– Rue Blondel, Rue de Lappe and Rue St-Denis cornucopias.

– Au Faubourg St-Antoine: *une poule* successfully fights off an unruly *client*.

– Le Concert Mayol files ladies *à poile* – their hair-dos ambitious; le Bal Tabarin sets them prancing; le Casino de Paris admixes black ones.

– Les Halles and la Place de la Bastille display *les forts* – la Sorbonne, bowler-hatted massives after *Soutenances de Thèses*; La Bibliothèque Nationale, those *à barbe; la banlieue*, the bereted moustachious siestas, la Seine *et les pêcheurs*, ditto; le Pont des Arts *le repos des clochards* on the benches. Women of *les marchés* are from one mould, but le Café du Dôme and La

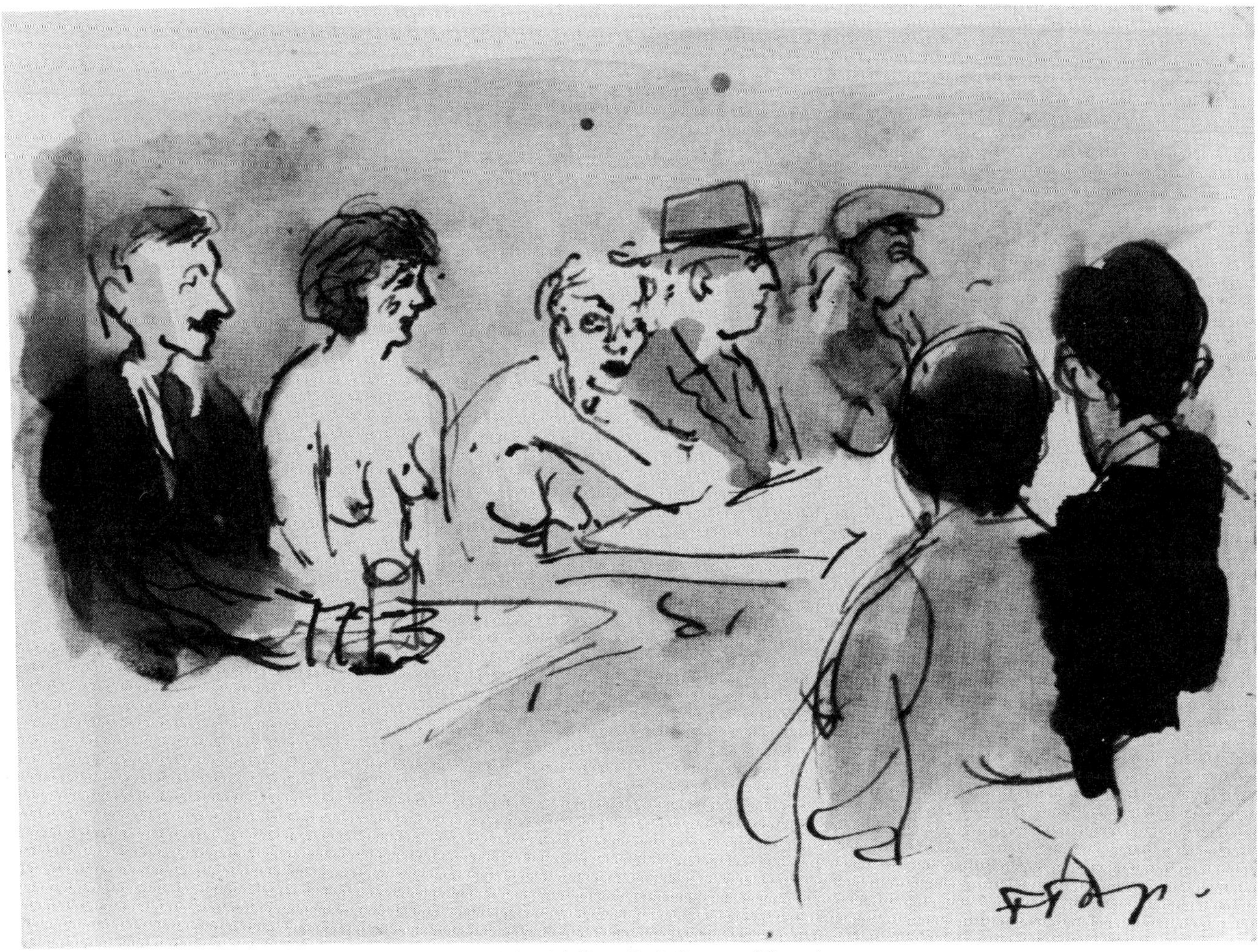

Rue Blondel (from *Paris Scenes and Secrets*)

Coupole – bohemian multiplicity. Le Palais Bourbon symbolically/peacefully guarded/defended; but *la banque's Salles des Coffres-Forts* grille-and-padlock their commerce; and *concierges* watch.

– Variegated hats – feathered, curved, pot-reversed; padded-shouldered knee-skirted black numbers, gloved braceleted ringed, long cigarette-holders – that's Place Vendôme – the same ladies attend *le 'fiv-o-clock'* à l'Hôtel George V; but le Café de la Paix serves befurred ostentation, and Chez Nina unrestrained *bijouterie* and *voilettes*.

– Antoine, *Le Grand Maître de la Coiffure*, peasant-handed Pole, prepares round and thin ladies for hand kisses *aux entr'actes* à la Salle Pleyel and à l'Opéra; his lesser concurrents make up young girls (they are nowhere seen *au naturel*) into middle-aged *élégantes* – feminine youth cannot be fashionable in the Paris of the thirties.

– *Les bistros et les boîtes et les patrons/patronnes.*

– And le Louvre.

– And le Boul' Mich.

– And *la foire* – Place de la République.

– And Chez Fouquets – mini-dogs and their *mesdames.*

– And à Métro *apache* (the widest: tie, trousers, lapels).

– And le Prunier.

– Le Lapin Agile ever rude.

– *Le Tombeau de l'Empereur* ever pensive-making.

– *Le gala à* l'Hôtel de Ville ever *Troisième-Empire.*

– Le Bal Musette ever *bal louche.*

– Herriot presides in La Chambre.

– *14 juillet* 1938 celebrates the past with Saint-Cyr's plumes, veterans' standards, Arabic cavalry, the Eiffel Tower. . .

– Longchamps ever Proustian.

– Le Bois de Boulogne also.

– Le Rond Point des Champs-Élysées the same.

– And la Rue Castiglione with a 1900 old gentleman.

– And so Rue du Faubourg St-Honoré and Avenue Foch.

– And mostly so the *acte de présence chez* Madame de La Rochefoucauld embellished by Messieurs Valéry et Mauriac, and Señor Eugenio d'Ors.

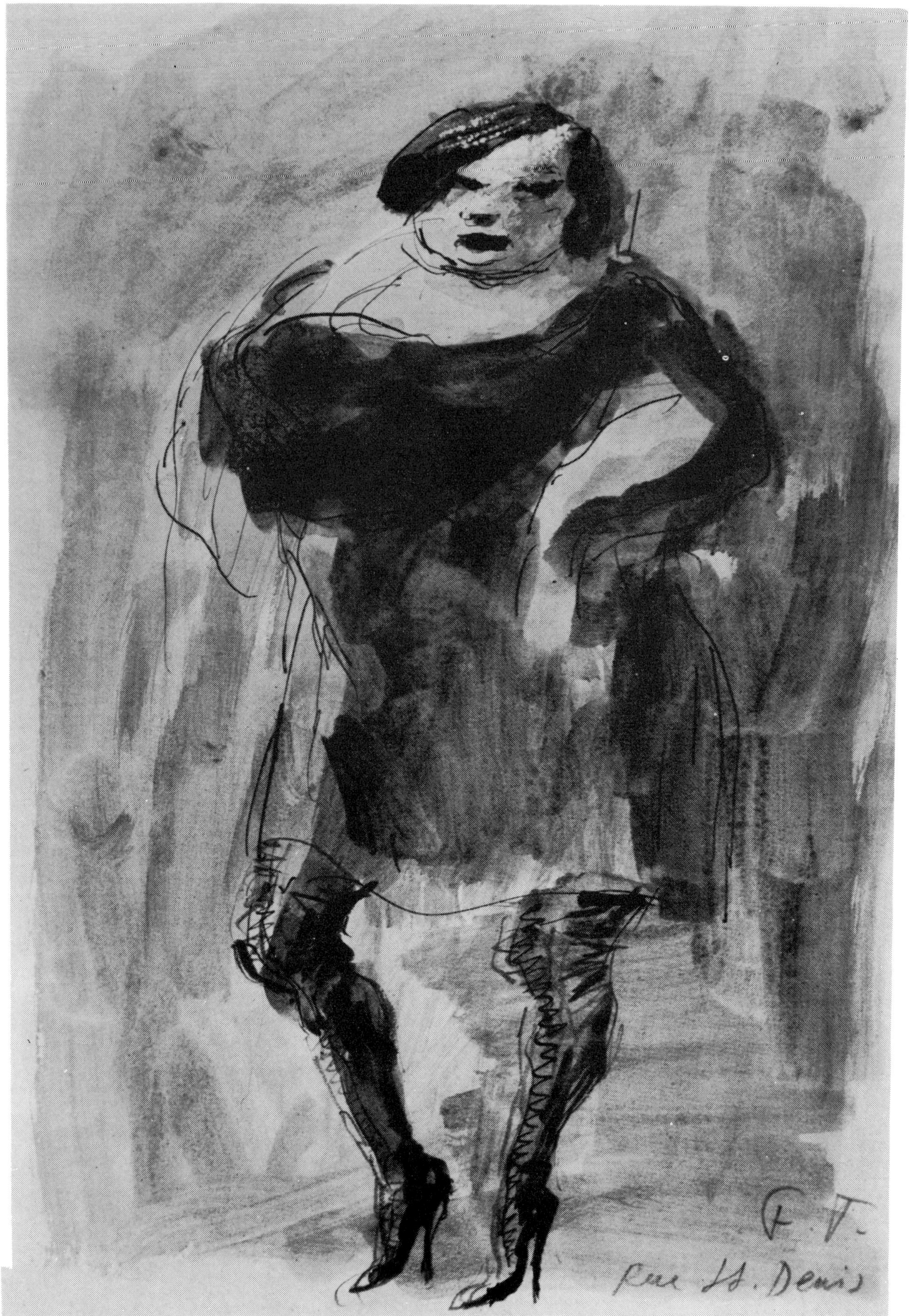

Rue St Denis (from *Paris Scenes and Secrets*)

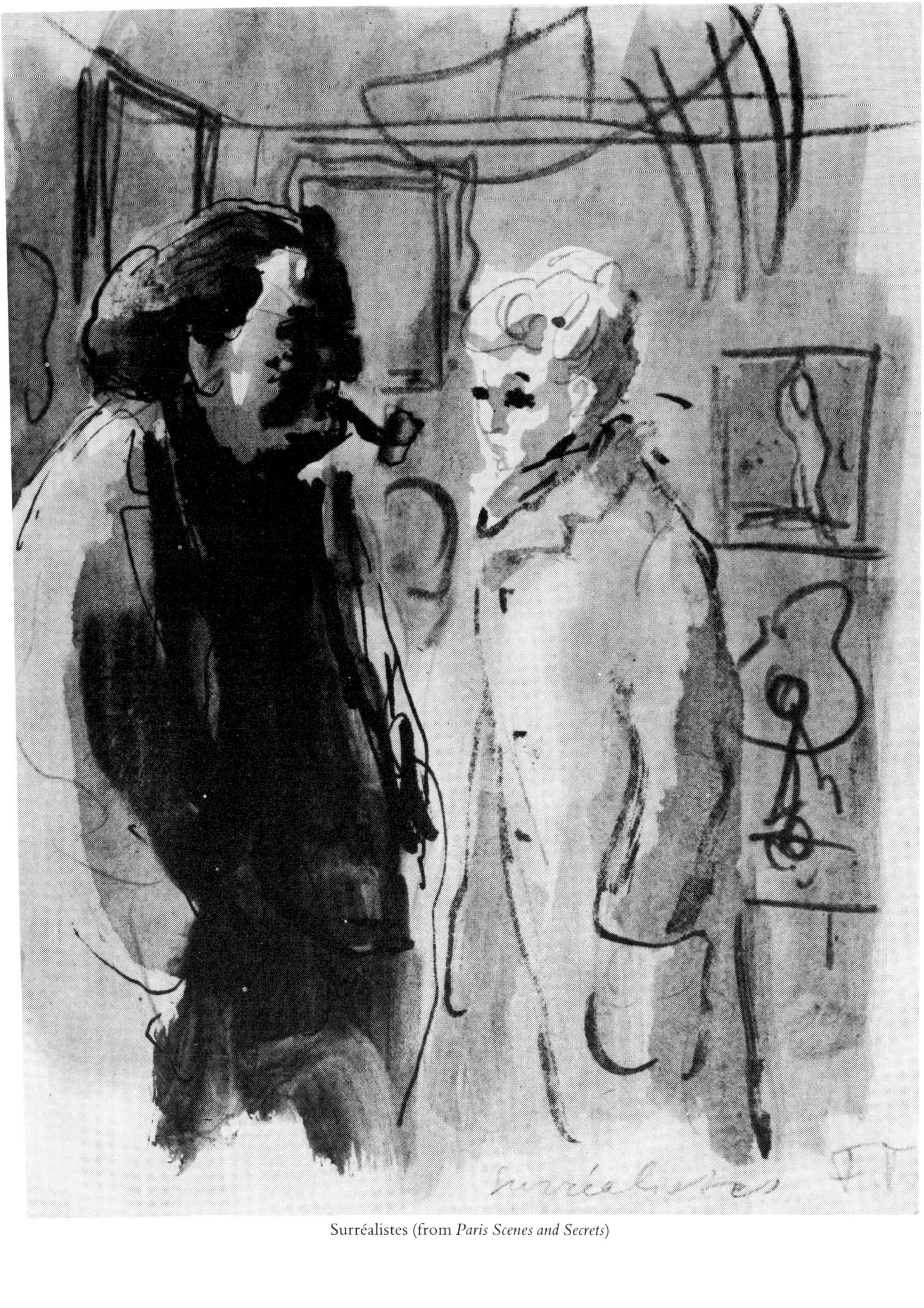

Surréalistes (from *Paris Scenes and Secrets*)

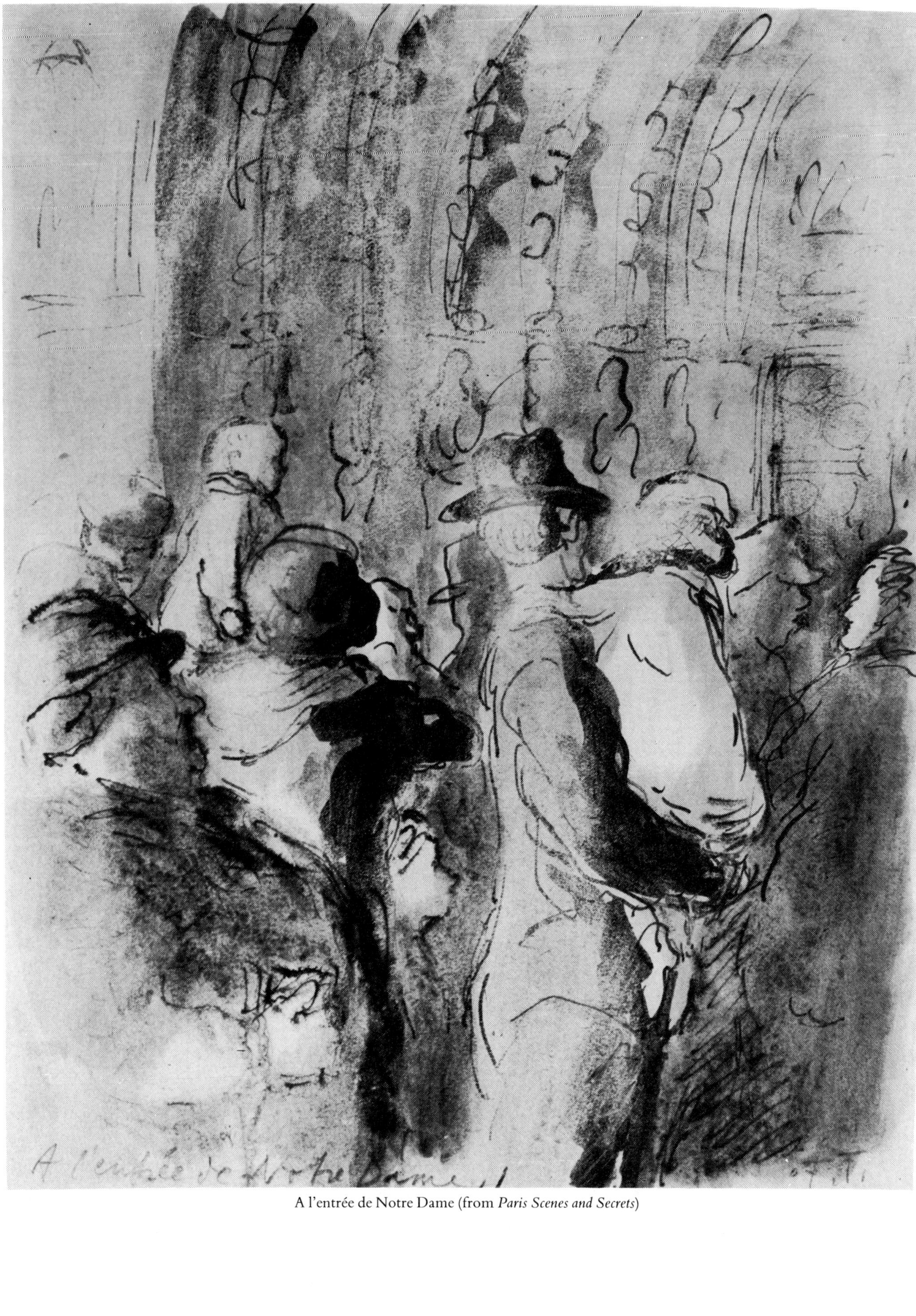

A l'entrée de Notre Dame (from *Paris Scenes and Secrets*)

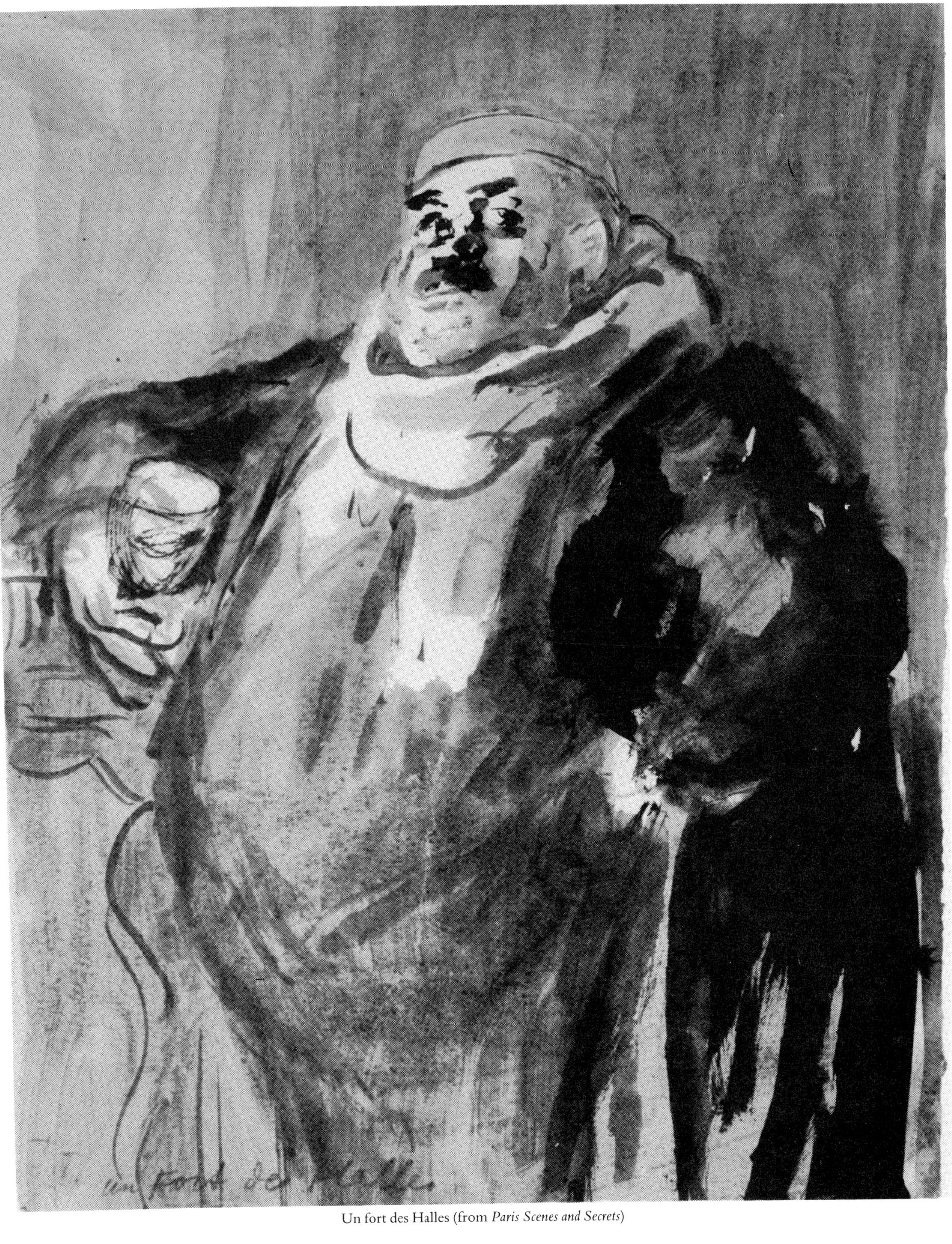

Un fort des Halles (from *Paris Scenes and Secrets*)

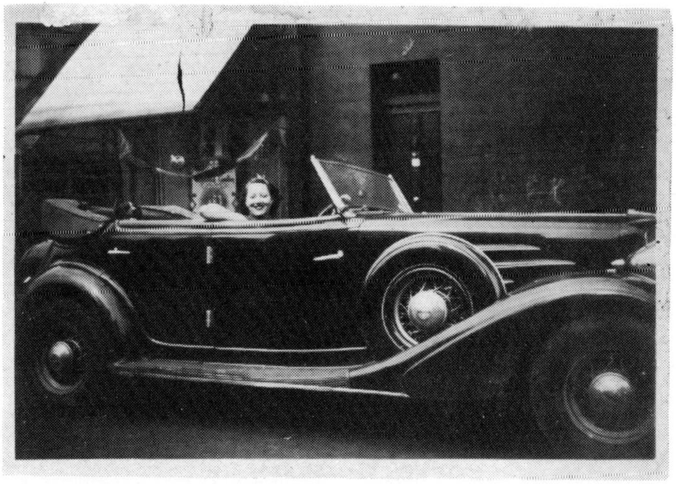

Marion in the Auburn

Marion, an exuberant Korda starlet, brought to the wharf studio borrowed from Julian Trevelyan, extended/overacted her natural flow of charitableness: threw all of her part-true act at my arm-in-plaster, and all of herself at me in a performance of nursing devotion, followed by several months or a year without follow-up from her.

I recovered, Marion forgotten; moved to another borrowed studio (this time Tristram Hillier's at the World's End in Chelsea) and – during the usual bachelorish lull's ever-repeated fidgeting through telephone numbers – having come upon hers, phoned. Her vitality at first surpassed my libertine code; later her emotional capacity took over, also irresistibly.

The first stage at Hillier's studio: upstairs, a rather formal reception introducing a Polish pianist friend, staying with me, to London; in the meagre ante-room below Marion's legs/arms/mouth, my trousers at ankles, withhold me from hosting; this capped by the blatant *faux pas*, thus enchantment, of stealing us both out to her distant flat – her sense of priorities. But then, the next afternoon, returning to the studio to meet her, I bump into her in the long passage leading from the King's Road: she banged the studio door shut, and rushed out passing me without a word, her lipstick smudged over her face, splotched with a genuine flush breaking in odd patterns through her white make-up and, inside, my pianist (a very pretty boy) Kazimierz Kranc: devoutly married and, his all-important recital at the Wigmore Hall starting shortly, in need of calm.

My sandwiching Marion sessions with non-emotional casual stands did not disturb my conscience, but did not shield me from new-to-me jealousy-tortured nights – when alone – of phoning with no reply. And my up-to-then-uncommitted sex-gamesmanship moved, led by her, into deeper thus deceitful entanglements. After one night and morning with me, she sent me ahead for our lunch with a trusting friend and rushed home, to arrive late having put on her riding clothes – as if straight from trot-and-gallop. Or I would have to hide in her attic on the expected arrival of . . . who? and why? Or the insomniac Alex Korda (her boss and god) would phone in the middle of the night demanding her presence – she being, as she had persuaded me, his platonic confidante of the early hours – I at peace in her bed to which she would return, having performed her good deed. How come? How pitiful was Alex? How did all this reflect on my free love *modus vivendi*? Well, I accepted, not ungladly, this role of a clandestine and therefore truest lover – my 'standards' not upset.

And this *quid pro quo*, in the swept-under-the-carpet mode of our time's pretences (its all-round frivolity worthy of eighteenth-century comedy plots) was, in the thirties as ever, practised but not preached: its stage is one of my frequent Paris visits, amassing friends and drawings for my book with Señor Eugenio d'Ors, *Paris Scenes and Secrets*, about which more has been said. Marion (busy at her film studios) was to join me on the day after my arrival for a weekend (was it to be her first in Paris?) and, as a treat for her, I picked a hotel on the strength of the view alone, on the Quais, with the best angle on Notre-Dame, the Seine, the bridges.

But that first afternoon was to be spent with an art dealer of genius, **Mr Salz**. A year earlier, exiled, for not-immaculate transactions over works by Ensor amongst others, from Belgium, he had come to London and, penniless but purposeful, took the cheapest room in Piccadilly (was it Hamilton House?) and filled it up with Ensors – having persuaded Ensor himself (or were they Ensor's inheritors?) that he would establish him in England, if he could borrow these marvellous paintings.

Salz had originally leapt into the West straight from a Polish-Jewish village marketplace – a *parvenu manqué*. He was expensively/ostentatiously dressed, *chutzpah*-mannered, his spoken Polish and French appalling, *ergo* persuasive, his confidence as a salesman *non plus ultra*. He began by extricating single pounds from such as me – impecunious young artists – on the strength of clumsily worded fantasies of future glories which would materialize by the magic of his supreme middleman's gifts; we did not take it all seriously but he amused us and we pitied him – and also liked the paeans of Ensor-adoration, delivered in his comic lingo, but lifted to inspired heights by his earnestness. And, with our incognito pocket money (there were enough of us to pull him through), thus shrewdly without blemish when confronting **COLLECTORS**, his uncouth shamanism worked. He began to sell, and *presto*, his little room (but a good address) had on the walls Pissarros, Vlamincks, Vuillards – Ensors no longer. When asked, his gesture more explicit than his words dismissed/buried Ensor as of no account; now the hymns of praise went to his new gods-goods – and the all-important revelation dawned on us that a great salesman is not a precise calculating rationalist, but a maniac preacher of the trade-gospel, on his knees at the altar of his full shelves.

Now he moved to Paris (later to New York) and a large suite at the George V – round him works of the highest names and prices. But, being rather isolated, he was insatiable of showing off his triumphal peak; and I was given The Treatment. And so: Salz guides round his gilded rooms and gilt-framed Impressionists; Salz orders champagne cocktails; Salz returns his debts in kind by swaggering into the top **maison de rendezvous** with a 'take your pick' flick of the wrist, impossible to resist. We sit in the salon: it is *five-o'clock* and these are not prostitutes but adventurous females (independent or on wages or wives) entering and exiting one by one – all in armours of *haute couture* and classy *maquillage*, the highly deserving and quite disdainful earners of extra pocket money. I choose a svelte *élégante*, rather surprise her by not wishing her to keep on any inventive négligés, and, after some initial sense of inadequacy, embark on the simplest copulation, which gratifyingly brings out a rhythmical long-lasting 'C'est ça, c'est ça, c'est ça . . .' I find Salz waiting in the salon, impatient.

Then a lone stroll along the Faubourg St-Honoré, arrested by a shop window bursting with a magnificently hairy/orangey short fur coat – as if meant for Marion.

Marion arrives; the room with the view roars/trembles with the night-long heaviest lorry traffic to Les Halles – weary, we augment it (now only a viewing room) with one at the back for sleeping, and emerge on to Paris. There are many sights for Marion to see, appointments with friends to show Marion off. And a Schiaparelli fashion show (on the way we drop in at that fur shop: she adores the coat, looks fine in it, but its price bars me from making it a present to her): Marion and I sit in the semicircle of *politesse* while little but tall-hatted (hat-on-one-eye) Madame Schiaparelli surveys the event – models entering singly and diagonally swishing/swinging over the floor, as it happens at us. And the inevitable (almost predictable) makes it memorable to me: my *maison de rendezvous* partner of yesterday reproduces her paddock performance – and strolls at me, a fraction closer than the others, so that her flawless spin/turn brushes my knees.

Marion returns to London; my duties having retained me in Paris a week longer, I meet her wearing the orange shaggy-furred coat.

The wide-cast nets of a glamour girl – the film studios' camaraderie of beauties outbidding one another in 'gilded admirers' games, in leaps from starletism to stardom – had with her a different mettle, superior to that of the other girls with her enthusiasms for good causes – humane and political (plain gold-digging, the sole *modus operandi* of most of them, being beneath her). Undoubtedly these were an extra bonus in her as a companion for her film and rich admirers, but just the same (is it clear yet that she, with her background pulling her down, was an exceptional girl?) they were in essence the authentic overflow of temperament and appetites, which encompassed and carried out a plentitude of variations. And those enthusiasms were roughly channelled in two, not always concordant (with each other or with her way of life) directions: **Communism and philosemitism**!

Marion Everall (her full name), Ever-All – ever and all of her on injustice scent; she and her schoolteacher sister – a party-card Communist – broke out miraculously from the tight Wolverhampton ring of parochial phobias. Marion, a 'starlet' (that is, one of the under-exercised stable of contracted girls), would speechify on prejudice/injustice, and on Jesus=Stalin in London Films canteens, at plushy night-clubs (befurred and bemaquilléed) with golden boys, in a Maida Vale back-of-delicatessen (the term not yet in use) mucky eatery, frequented by her 'to relax', choicily ragged or dressy, amongst the quarter's riff-roughs and tarts, where one afternoon an elderly untypical habitué declared from the next table 'You're not a Communist, little lady, but **a sentimentalist**.'*

She discovered the Jews, as appealing underdogs, and they her – this rarity: a young stunning long-boned short-nosed *shiksa* girl with a softness for the Jewish predicament, yet who, brown-eyed black-haired and made-up (lipsticked enormous mouth) into a pale southern mystery dame, could also seem related to that race. But happily for us (because truly her gypsy aura and flowing draperies did not appeal to me) my first morning awakening, after an energetic night with her, had disclosed a very youthful pink-cheeked/freckled/narrow-lipped face, little troubled by eyebrows and lashes, in accord with a generous white-skinned shape – a touching revelation of what she really was: peasanty Irishness crossed with the refining of Midlands suburbia.

Once, when drawn, by a persistent unfamiliar bell, to my door, there was joy and not much surprise at finding her facing me in the corridor – atop a bicycle: a kerchief round her head (it was always tied back off her pretty ears), a 'revealing' worn-out vest, shorts rolled up to the limits (as far as only she would dare in those days) above the imposing longitude of immaculate white thigh and calf, aged bedroom slippers open-seamed and toe-gaping: the costume meant that she was on her revolutionary path; and, indeed, later that day she got herself arrested for chalking ARMS FOR SPAIN on the walls. That was still peacetime. But, two years gone, with the war hotting up in the West and the refugees from France arriving in London, she, in the same outfit, stood in Piccadilly Circus encircled by a sympathetic crowd – this time an endearing bedraggled escapee.

I am aware that my relating palpable exuberances unfurled in private intrigues/strategies may label me by many a cad – discretion the supreme virtue – only, perhaps, acceptable under the guise of 'fiction', while vices of public personages are the lappable beverage.

I am aware of, yet I dare to attempt to give in full, without application of gilding, an admirably contradictory personality in her variable progress, with me fused (in all senses) alongside on her way. We are in London still untouched by the war. Her entries into the Café Royal: always unbearably late as her preparations' ritual meant transfiguration from one of her other selves and so the most serious application of

*One Blitz night, in a short mean street across from there, this scene: a shower of little flames (fire-bombs?) bouncing over its width/length, and – out of their lodgings, out of the shadows – a flock of pale-nightgown-floating tarts/angels in a fast ballet – the street a stage – of voluntary fire-fighters.

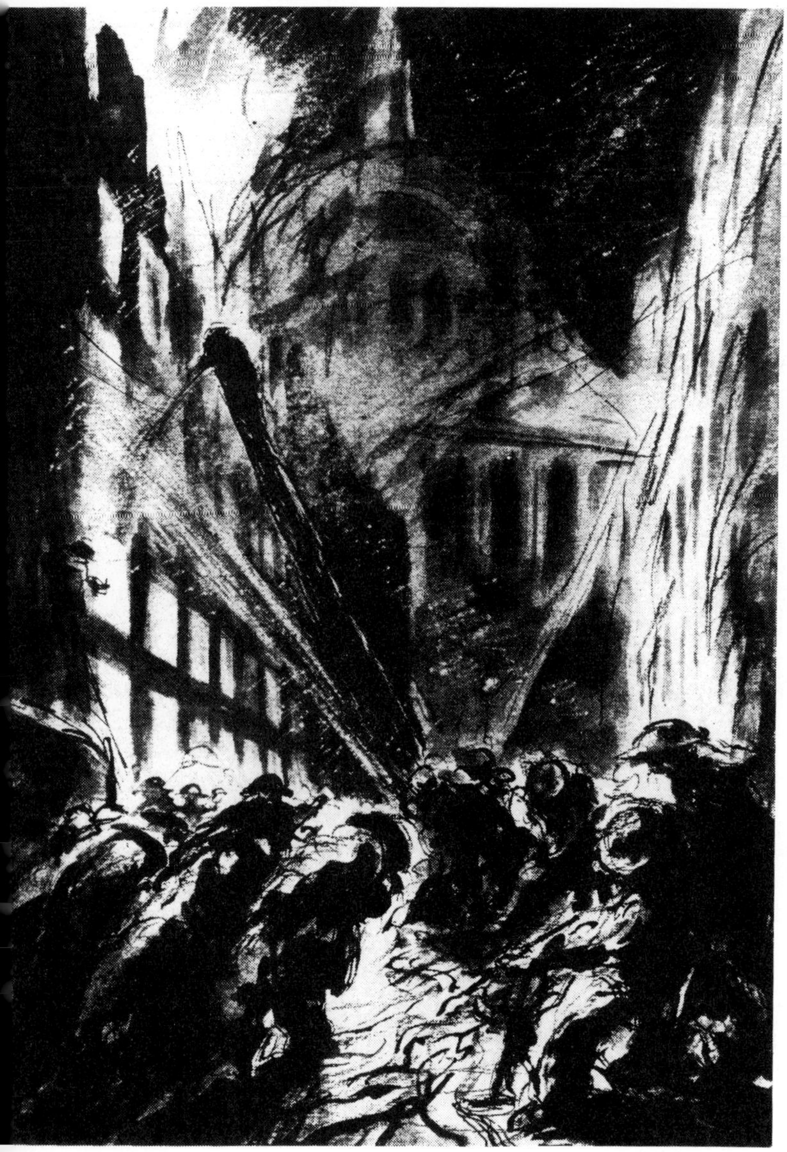

London, 29 December 1940 (from *Britain in Peace and War*)

costume and make-up for this particular role – **Reigning Belle** for the evening. I confess that the entries of this unequivocal glamour made me, their recipient, uneasy. But a further confession stems from the duality of my appetites contending with my standards: the sybaritic streak, that is the pleasure in the outward trappings of dress styles, appeared very early in my student time, perhaps sparked off pathetically by inheriting my father's fastidious wardrobe; and my first short visit to London had as musts, already ingrained by Warsaw snobberies, purchases of a Briggs' umbrella and a Lock's hat. But Marion, in our earliest months together, that is before she adjusted herself to my bohemian level of 'cost of living', tended to voice the assessments of men, applied by the coterie of starlets and their usual admirers, as 'mean' or 'generous'. Her let's-call-them 'aspirations' extended her towards me, but, in turn, she still pressed extravagant extensions on me – not unwelcome, since my backwater 'dandyism' offered receptive soil. I became the owner of an immense American convertible four-door Auburn, second-hand and (but in the class of American Rollses) unwieldy and costly to run, chosen for its handsomeness, but embarrassingly stare-catching, its uses amounting to racing Marion's Studebaker along the A4.

So much for my 'unease'. Marion's heavily painted, veiled, lace-draped, false-bejewelled, furred persona would be offset, without much tremor, by her contrapuntal stripped honesty; by her girlishly disarrayed rooms; by her array of 'undress'; by her mink coat having been stolen.

In the 'phony' war year came the progress towards maturing – she emerged from a stagnant starlet as a **stage actress** in Peter Ustinov's first play, directed by Michael Redgrave and designed by me, and, with the first wave of Poles (refugees and sailors), **Marion-the-noble** came to the fore – cooking and setting out that immense Christmas feast for ninety Poles at my studio* and disappearing before its start. The nobility prelude to knightly valour. Even her earlier 'irresponsible' darings compelled a *sui generis* respect; her potential was on the heroic scale and the Blitz gave it a fair field.

With the Polish forces, spread over Britain and at sea, demanding attention, my War Artist's duties varied, but the dominant assignment was a series on London under the bombs, for which Marion and I developed a routine. The mighty Auburn, its hood down, Marion at the wheel and I at her side with my sketchbook, would carry us over destruction (all this in the blackout, but bright with fires/searchlights/explosions – **the Blitz** proper went on every night for over three months from sunset to sunrise) hunting **incidents** – a neat 'filing' word for the moment of encounter between a spot on London's grid and a whining/striking/exploding bomb. We zigzagged continuously within the bomb-showered city, but instant nosing on to an 'incident' would give most for the recording pencil.

I was in the throes of my 'mission', but Marion was led by her devotion to me, to my purpose, and by the testing of her stamina. This was **her 'service'** – and proven in unpredictable clashes too: one night we (with my Honourable reporting partners Theodora Benson and Betty Asquith) began to explore Chislehurst Caves, natural shelters; but fear-enraged locals – publicized by us, they thought, the caves would become the enemy's targets – mobbed me, drawing, and moved in for a lynch. Marion dashed in front of me, arms legs outstretched, fiery and shouting condemnations – a demi-goddess, **a fury**, an Amazon, ready to fight them all (the other girls in meek support – Theodora: 'You call yourselves MEN?' – me behind). And she held these ordinary suburbanites-turned-killers until their priest arrived and, in a true Christian solution, pushed us out into the night under the bombs.

No longer a game, now in earnest – the cataclysm enforced gravity; her feelings hotted up – became more demanding and

*Her supreme gesture: buying for it, from Fortnum and Mason, the whole of the last pre-war supply of famed Baczewski liqueurs – the last ever: the city of Lwów is now in Russia, and I heard only recently that the make is taken on in Vienna.

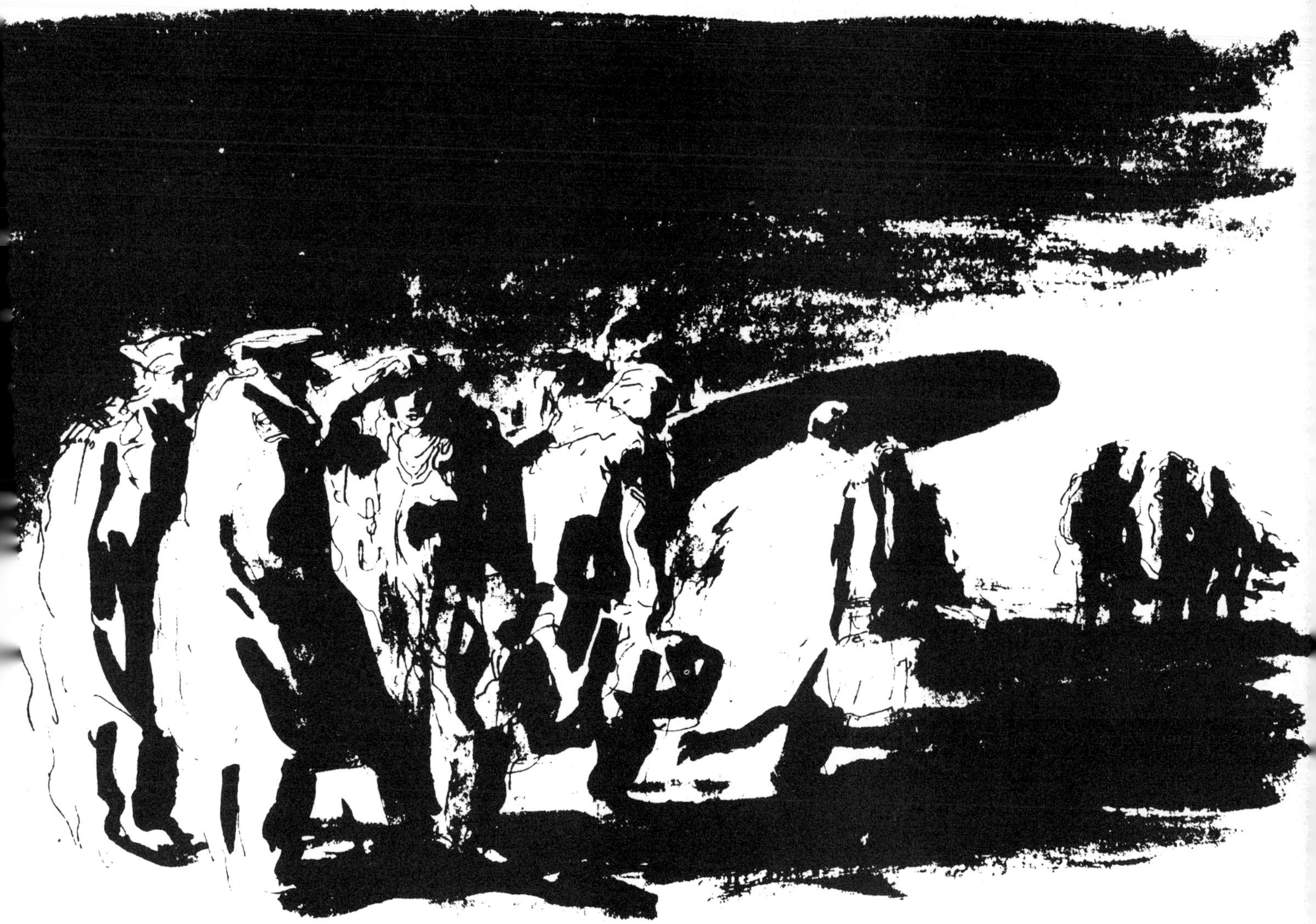

Night Mission. Polish Crews, Winter 1940 (from *Britain in Peace and War*)

thus, with my stay-put levity, brought forth clashes (other men, to my mind, merely stratagems) and frequent partings.

The London-at-war period is packed with speeding-up changes, challenges, transits, pleasures and pains – all maximalized, impossible to disentangle into consecutiveness: it must stay a bundle. **Marion's** grace, **hospitality** – and cooking for Bernard Shaw and his wife at my studio, under the sky window and the lunchtime air-raid threat. Late-morning **Marion concealed**, still in the bed set up in the crashed-open house edging my garden (where we slept in comparative safety, away from the glass overhead), while I parleyed inside the studio with her brothers on a surprise foray to London to catch us *in flagrante* and pin us down (the story repeats itself – as with my mother's brothers). With Marion, at the basement Players' Theatre, at night-clubs, shelter-crawling from the Dorchester to the dockland warehouses, and on our nightly motoring survey over the length and breadth of the London apocalypse (a mundanely 'English' occurrence: in the car precariously perched on the Chiswick/Thames bank, as I note down the sweep of conflagration under the closest roaring path of whistling-down and exploding bombs, a phlegmatic policeman drawls a routine questioning at us, to end with, 'Your licence's out of date').

At first scattered separations; then Marion perhaps with her 'fiancé', and I on the loose. And into those breaches, becoming entrenched, protracted, step other attachments for me too – Marion detaches herself from me prolongedly until: the last massive night air-raid, after a lull, hits London and me loitering on foot in Soho. Foreboding; my telephone not answering; she, **a brave woman in love**, runs, literally runs, through the smouldering ruined transportless town from one hospital to another, finds me in a ward of the Middlesex Hospital full of wounded, brushes aside my current girlfriend, **Barbara** (helped by our doctor who knows Marion's right of precedence), and resumes her dominance.

Overleaf: Blow your own trumpet – Finale with drop curtain

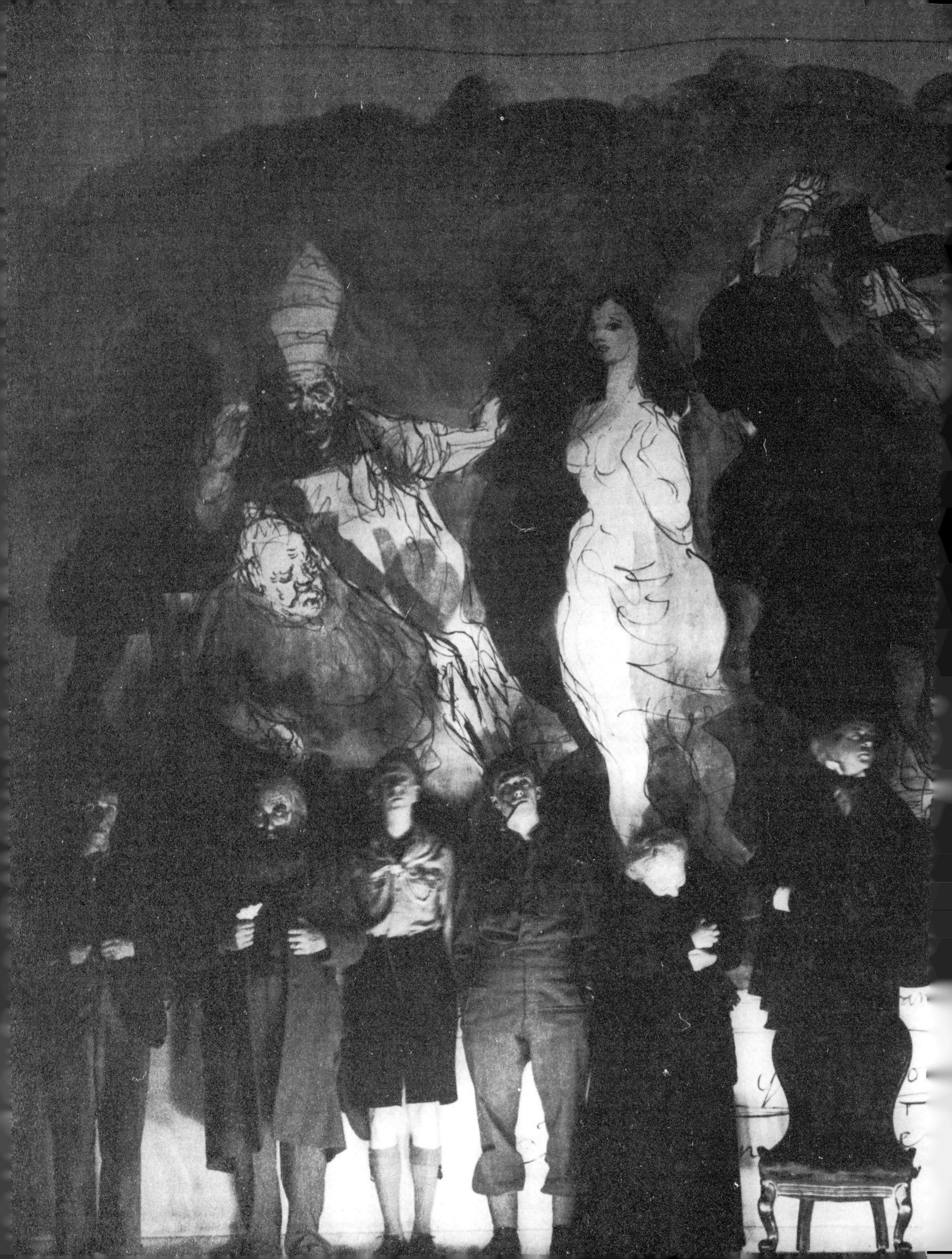

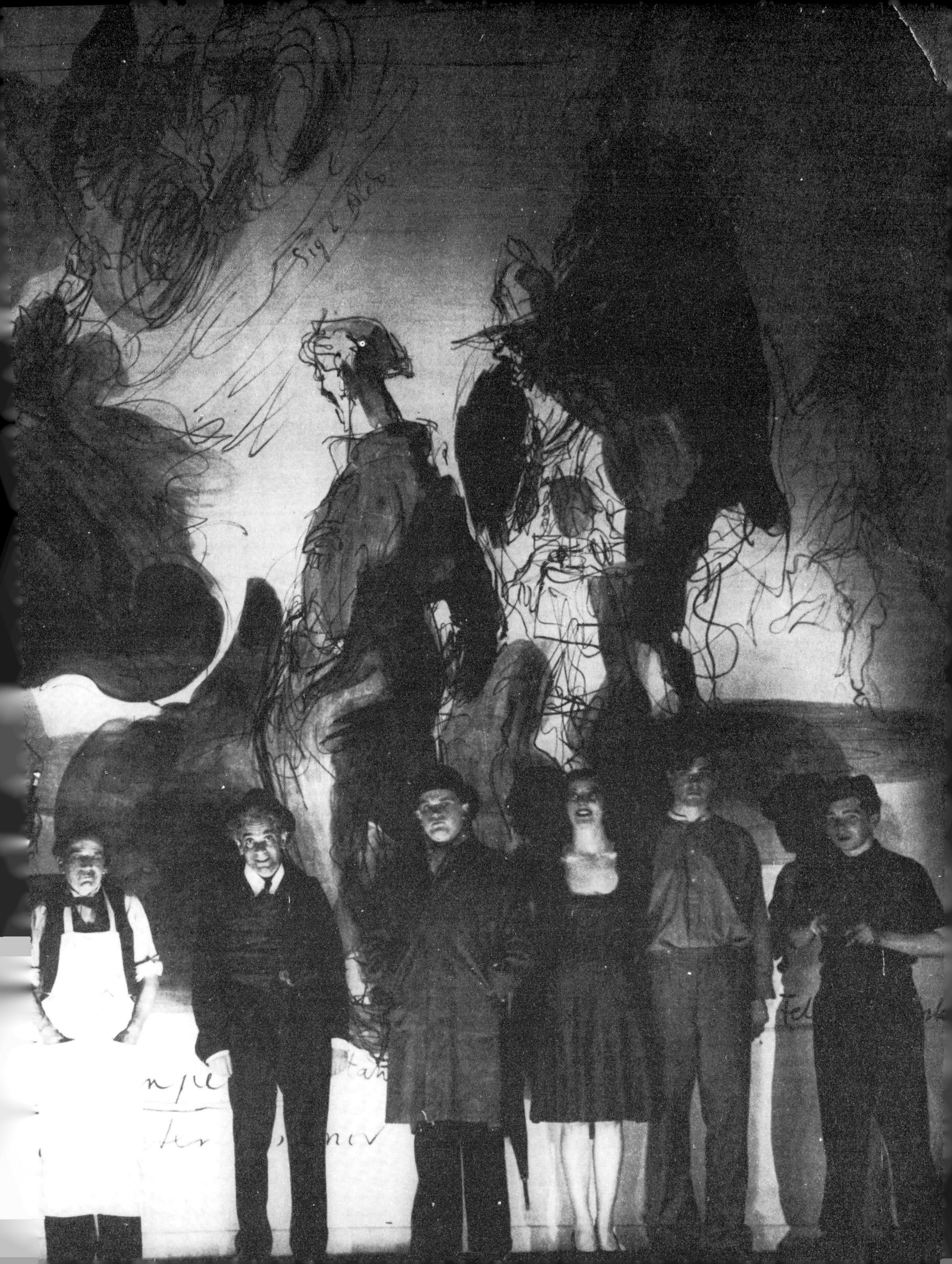

Yet on recovery and rediscovery of the taste of freedom, I ease out, aided by history: Germany invades Russia; and I am to embark on the first British convoy across the Arctic seas, with the Germans poised for attack, and, more, all the looming risks of Soviet Russia. At the train's departure for Liverpool and enshipment, **Marion's histrionic last words** – which might be last in more ways than she means – at me in the already-moving-away window: 'Goodbye for ever!'

Between my return from Russia in 1942 and the major and long-lasting assignment of 1944, Marion grew in dignity and, strangely, although most of the time distanced, became indispensable to me (her respect for and attachment to my work somewhat compensating for her my personal inadequacies) so that, when going back again 'to war', it was to her I entrusted my studio, London being still far from safe; and, indeed, soon the attacks by V-bombs meant, at the least, an unnerving trial. Marion met it as the guardian of my work with **foolhardy fortitude**: she procured for the studio a so-called Morrison shelter – a steel table-like structure steel-netted on all sides – filled it up with my paintings and drawings and settled herself to live and sleep at its side, unprotected under the glass roof, in constant imperilment.

I learned of this on my return after the Vs had ceased. The sweep and length of this '**overseas service**' had been considerable: convoys, Egypt, the Levant and East Africa, India, the Burma front, China and the Italian campaign – almost an entire year of, however erratic, 'soldiering'. Because a '**soldier's return**' it was: to face closed 'civilian' ranks with no room/need for one, almost denied recognition. Except from Marion. She waited, and was there for me, even a dash of identification with my mother in features and colouring percolating in (or had it been there from the start?). It was not my enfeeblement of the moment, though it brought this intuition, but her by then proven and unreserved commitment which wedded me to it, cavalier *laissez-faire* eschewed. I rushed to Oxford, where she was in another Ustinov play, we merged in loving without reservations and undoubtedly conceived Daniel. '**Jusuf**' Retinger, a supreme strategist in international politics but also my fond personal prompter, on my telling him (in a taxi in Park Lane) about me marrying Marion, exclaimed '**Katastrofa**!' I didn't ask from what point of view: of a social/riches climber (the potentialities for which, he may have imagined, we both possessed); or, for both of us, the clash of our characters; or, for me, the marriage *tout court* . . .

Her company moved to London; **we wedded** (a bleak Harrow Road registry, Marion in a specially made dress and matching head-adornment by Mme Przeworska, I in full uniform, a taxi driver one of the witnesses); and, her part in the play being that of newly married expectancy, the play a success (Ustinov's sights lowered from his earlier ambitions), she gradually shed the padding as her own belly swelled.

From now onward all goes **her way**. My sufficiency within one room/studio, that is, my non-marrying-sort habits, overcome. Her woman's essence commanded and I complied happily: my subjugation springing perhaps from a seed of guilt implanted by her rapidly sprouting-out righteousness – assured by now. Nothing unique – **a marriage classic**. The growth: children – nanny, house – servants, responsibility – lodgers; simultaneously the splitting begins with pressure – reaction; the studio becomes my retreat for some days and nights nearly every week; Marion – on top; the wife and mother handsomely nested – the loser. I cannot trace the ingredients of clashes in those early years: why, on my return from a *bona fide* stay in Ireland, perhaps delayed by a day before reaching – on the heights of Welsh mountains – the ideally secluded farmhouse well serving, for one summer, the substantial family (a new baby, Teresa), with Arthur Koestler 'round the corner' below in Ffestiniog, why the mountaintop Marion turned erupting volcano. Her genuine hot-headedness, previously kindling eccentricities, now bounced off the solid atavistic-genetic ground in burning accusations/condemnations. Succinctly, and a touch obviously: marriage prods/distils/culminates/brings to the boil **female–male polarities**.

But in between, to be sure, plenty of harmony. Her generosity without bounds and gift for cooking materialized in supreme feasts, her physical/dress decorativeness giving an enchantment-status to our **studio Thursdays**.

Perhaps Marion's wife-party-giving was accelerated by **Daniel's first** massive **birthday party** and its uncalculated mark on the media. By chance or as our 'dues' there appeared in *Picture Post*, in 1946, a page headed **One Year of Peace** displaying Daniel eyeing a one-candled cake and in other photographs his guests: young Redgraves – Vanessa, Lynn and Corin, Cassons' daughters . . .

Marion did not become a proverbial 'salon hostess' – the rough studio, the guests of variety never conforming, and above all the motivation not snobbish or purposeful, but of pleasure – receiving people who interested us was for her a valid outlet.

But children submerged her acting and inevitably took over almost the whole of her attention – except for her **fanaticism about my art** (my person more and more often in disgrace) – her commitment to my working on the Festival of Britain mural (and, later, on the emerging *Chronicle*) was total.

The studio's existence probably reached its crest with a 200-strong **reception for Picasso**, soon followed by its **destruction** by the local borough councillors (determined to assert their communal power) – a chain-gang brutality engendered by higher planners. We held, in those condemned interiors, surrounded by advancing demolishers, an enormous **retrospective exhibition** (cum symbolic protest-sale of chattels) – which may have been **her dedication's supreme moment**, yet, with the encircling ruins, also the prognosis of decline. Throughout long days friends swarmed, friendly celebrities marking their sympathy (Prince Philip; Harold Macmillan, the Minister who had signed the destruction verdict – funereally apologetic: 'I *have* to obey civil servants' submissions', but officially buying something; Nye Bevan; Ken Tynan emerging with a handful of theatrical drawings off the cut-price tray; Christopher Fry; John Rothenstein; Maurice Collis; Redgraves . . .), the curious, hunters for bargains (Joseph Herman never looked at the exhibition, but bee-lined predatorily to my easel to try to buy

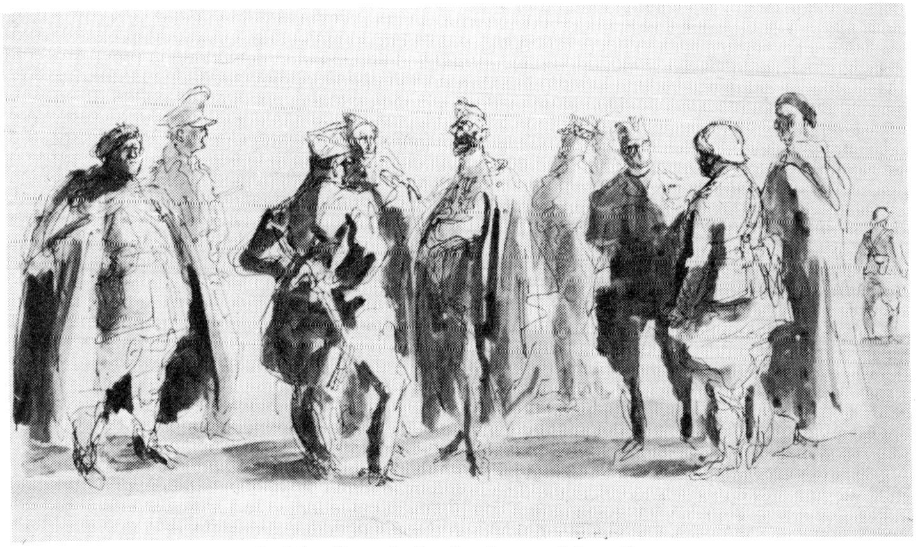

Polish officers in Scotland rescued from France

it – the essential tool of an obviously still-working painter – as if at a posthumous sale). She 'received' upright, undaunted and resplendent in her long, exotically flared Afghan carpet-coat, black-biretta-ed, made-up to the utmost precision of her starlet days.*

S**ummer Sunday 1939**, the Thames at and above Richmond gliding past to punting's unhasty rhythms, the motorized traffic still mitigated, the banks still unmunicipalized – it is crowded, yet private when fancy downs the canopies over the moored punts.

I, in charge of the pole, hold to the aloofness of a skipper, and **Robin**, cushioned at the other end, becomes stiffened/put out, as her elder sister **Sanchia** (a stunningly shaped actress and an overindulgent *poseuse*, affected by belated reading of D. H. Lawrence into erotic chases in their cottage-surrounding woods under the rain) tops herself with a shy Foreign Office young man in earnest coupling, heads and all under a rug, only four bare feet monitoring action – uncomfortably too definitive for the passive others. But Sanchia, in an inspired impulse, atoned for or rather crowned all: she sprang in pure-in-boldness nakedness on to the boat's edge, stretched arms gathering in the whole busy sun-glittering riverscape to witness her 'I'm so happy!' and leapt in. The finale of peace?

The end of August did not bring preparedness for war; nor grand banner-thoughts; nor even private escaping/burying plottings. Only minute trivialities like ordering new riding boots from a top bootmaker and reporting to the Polish Consulate my second-lieutenant readiness for the sea-transport to Poland, unbelievably now anticipating **the banalities of war**, none of its disasters. Only when (the sea passage cancelled), with **the calamitous fall of Poland** in a few days, the apocalyptic/manic purpose of Germany was revealed, the belated shock came.

With **London unmolested** the too-agonizing-to-absorb rash of reports on destruction, streaming refugees, the back-entry of the Soviets, and the arrests – all raised to a giant-vortex scale, but all made tangible by the real, close people within – reports buffeting without respite, until, soon, knocks at the studio door announced the first **friends-turned-refugees**: my Warsaw, left behind five years earlier, had followed me to London.

And, with the dust of disaster on them, they confirmed the abnormal ordinariness, already present in England from the first day of the war with the expectation of instant annihilation, of the co-existence of trifles alongside the drama, or even the patchwork of trifles being the fabric of the awesome draperies of history. They and their host had to set up their day-to-day existence, the distribution of functions – and had to talk.

Perhaps, for those first months of Polish diaspora, this will do: *Christmas Eve 1939*; Marion's single-handedly mounted feast for ninety Poles: having lighted the candles she left for her Midlands family, not to be in the way.

But the guests and their aura. Firstly, Warsaw's creative core in its full range of arts and ages, that is the largish slice of it which reached London, and all more-or-less acquainted with young Feliks in his Warsaw days; then my other friends, who in the normal past formed the outer yet overlapping layers of arts-receptive intelligentsia – some already in uniform; and then those close to me in professional military and official spheres; besides, finally, a fringe of submarine crewmen.

The Poles were and are thought by others to be fired solely by romantic passions. Perhaps this is close to true now in Poland itself, with highly emotional restlessness abounding.

There exist, no doubt, multiple justifications for a summary outsider's view of a nation/race; but, in the day-to-

*Marion reading this piece – approving: exiled from thirty years of Regent's Park, in this humbler sitting-kitchen room, back to a wall of books on a tired red sofa amongst the amassment of my collecting past – only leftovers, but seeming much because scraped from a tall house into a modest one; she operation-wasted, looks-façade and fight abandoned – though in pain, mellowed? resigned? at peace? I, as guest (and my chapter about her), well received in this semi-mausoleum of our past, now accepted after years of non-admittance.

day practice within a country, these characteristics hardly surface – until its average citizen finds himself abroad facing the foreign cliché view of his kind; this Pole then, if average, that is held up by leaning on his tribality (not on his personal propensities or aptitudes), will act, nay **overact the recipient-modulated persona**: Poles would then, ejected but received/labelled here *en masse*, perform the romantic, chivalresque handkissing-heelclicking relics for their hosts.

But not among themselves. And, anyway, most of those gathered in my studio were individualists.

War artist now, I rushed in **July 1940** (but still in civvies) to the Scottish moors patterned by the assemblage of the Polish formations rescued from France lined up – with great gaps: the retained mementoes, the only remnants of Poland's uniforms – the giant cloaks of the mountain-*chasseurs* a-blow. But only the military could be present at the next morning's **sombre review**, and so I was lent a two-starred (one above my rank) uniform. Afterwards at the evening gathering General Sikorski sought me out. 'Topolski, how is it that yesterday you were a middle-aged civilian and today you're a young lieutenant?'

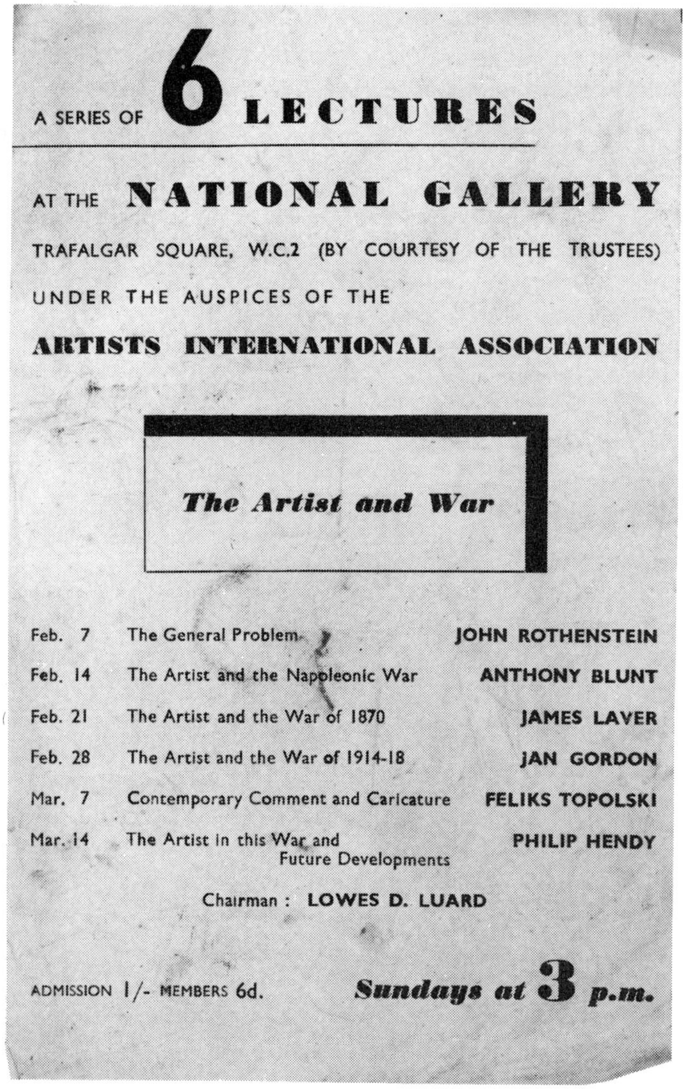
A SERIES OF 6 LECTURES

AT THE NATIONAL GALLERY

TRAFALGAR SQUARE, W.C.2 (BY COURTESY OF THE TRUSTEES)

UNDER THE AUSPICES OF THE

ARTISTS INTERNATIONAL ASSOCIATION

The Artist and War

Feb. 7	The General Problem	JOHN ROTHENSTEIN
Feb. 14	The Artist and the Napoleonic War	ANTHONY BLUNT
Feb. 21	The Artist and the War of 1870	JAMES LAVER
Feb. 28	The Artist and the War of 1914-18	JAN GORDON
Mar. 7	Contemporary Comment and Caricature	FELIKS TOPOLSKI
Mar. 14	The Artist in this War and Future Developments	PHILIP HENDY

Chairman : LOWES D. LUARD

ADMISSION 1/- MEMBERS 6d. *Sundays at 3 p.m.*

Split divisions: some fall in for faraway lands to fire and be fired at; some battledress to sit at home-bound desks or to command home guards or traffic; some stay-put civilians – like a friend of heroic features – serve the London wireless – his supreme war act 'servicing' in the blackout an unknown faceless girl at the foot of Piccadilly Eros; some, like me, nature's harlequins but also gluttons, play-act as many parts as costume changes and circumstances offer, that is dodging not climaxes and dangers but entanglements in duties, the flat grey inbetweens; thus, in the time-honoured **survivors' way**, shaping within disaster and conflict the tissue of free living, however irresponsibly and in trivially minute doses.

Survival, amongst death abounding and closest-striking, reinforces itself shamefully (or, why shamefully? – inevitably); zest goes along with sorrow, and fear is ridden by the show-off. At a distance of time the minutiae of senses acting upon seconds become incidents, the incidents merge into events, events congeal into the bulk of history's tides, opposing ideologies and consequent summary judgements and emotions; grandchildren see mass horrors, mass sufferings, mass resistance, massive mistakes, failures in the 'history' preceding them, but are repelled or puzzled when told of their grandfather's past **frivolities in the eye of a cyclone**.

Throughout those five and a half years or more I was given the privilege (or sometimes orders) to touch, as **witness or witness-participant** (never having fired a gun or held a weapon in war), upon a vast range of war fronts (perhaps more than anyone else: all – land sea and air – except for the American Pacific) and war-infected – the odd word is – theatres. This word fits with my many roles, which made the wide scope possible.

A so-called war artist, both British and Polish, thus wearing uniform with either war correspondent or Polish second lieutenant of artillery insignia (battledress; the formal version worn with a Sam Browne belt made by my Savile Row tailor; and a variety of tropical styles and hats) – this being my proper rank, earned at a School of Officers and with a regiment in the early thirties; then the civilian clothes when in diplomatic involvements or more prolonged engagements in the London Blitz, or in journalistic assignments requiring more neutral less demonstrative appearance. Some of these almost-disguises necessitated at times quick changes even within the same day. All this loaded me with bulky and growing luggage – drawings accumulating outrageously as I traversed continents at one swoop.

The last of **London dockland's backstreets**: held by the high wall (ocean-going nautical testimonials jutting atop from behind it) of a longshoremen's preserve. A medieval township of architectural modesty and clarity, as if modelled on Giotto's townscape backgrounds (Tony's view) – calm in the dockers' working day but for women's and children's voices.

This humble low-strung perfection was soon to be subjected to the first of many assaults to come from the sky. More so than the more elevated precincts, terraces and

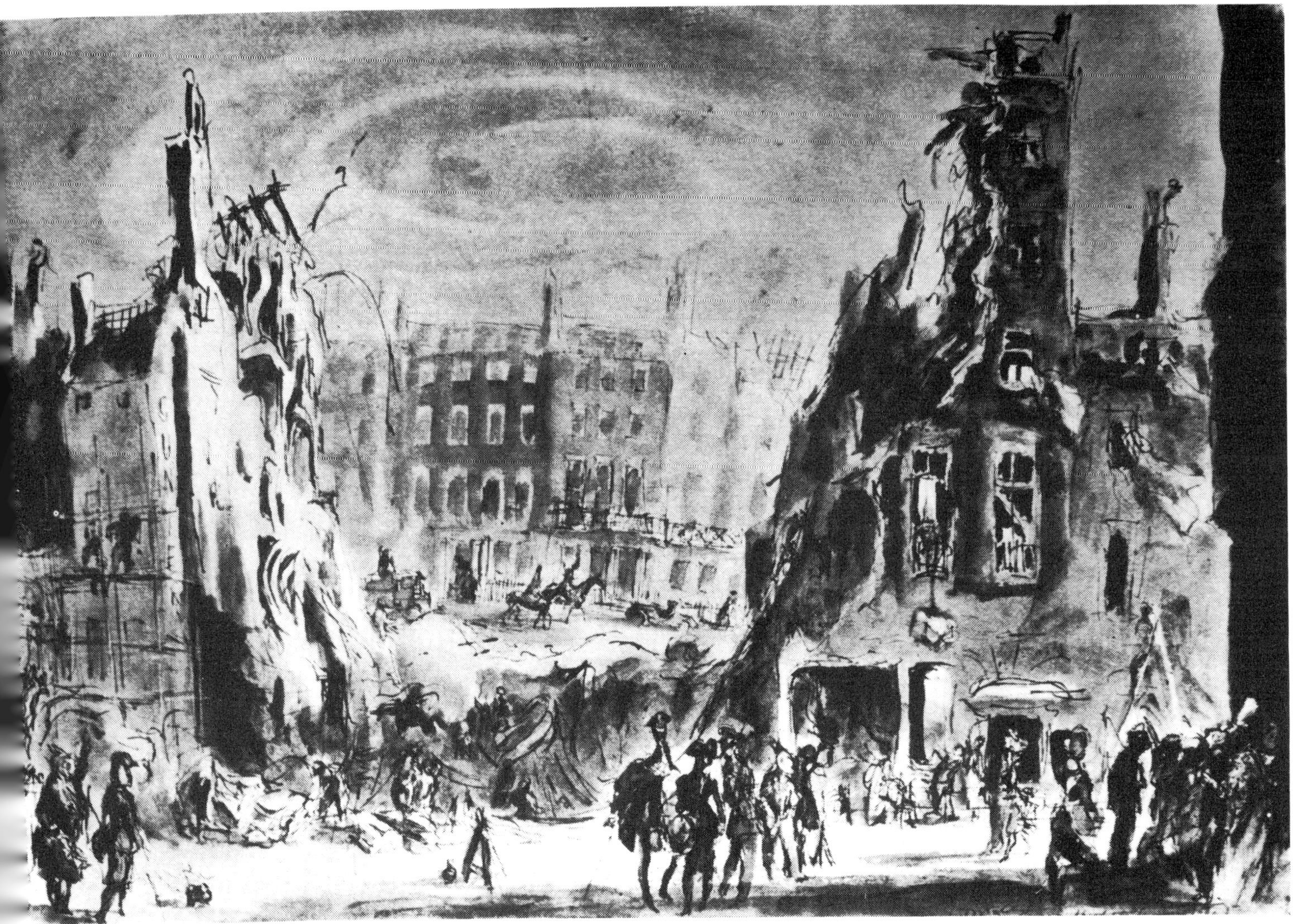

Air raid over London (from *88 Pictures*)

crescents shaped on the same model of blackened simplicity.

But before then, further West, in September 1939 there were only modest pointers: newsvendors' hand-scribbled placards (they had a freer way with their texts then): HITLER INVADES POLAND, backed by gold-braided doormen imposing above the new khaki soldiers shuffling along; and the compulsory gasmasks, the windows criss-crossed with paper strips, the sandbags, the coupons, the blackout. Because, when the expected annihilation had not come on the first day of war, old and new jobs settled to the rush-hour and opening/closing-time routines.

And **the night life**: The *Sketch* called up a *bon-viveurs*' team – two Honourable girl writers (Betty Asquith and Theodora Benson), a chic photographer (Baron Nahum), and a draughtsman (myself) – to make the rounds of and report on clubs shows cabarets, all very active, while awaiting more dramatic themes; a pathetic, imposed angle on the year of suspense.

But gravity was mounting, with frivolities in undiminished attendance: the chorus in a tragedy *à la grecque*, if written now, should grotesquely reflect the ever-sipping insouciance. This obviousness, astonishing at first, does not need excuses or reasoning – **young people serve war and are served by its stimulation.** It is significant that for Shakespeare the comic interludes had to be a class apart from the diapason of their betters – today's theatrical-social structure would be almost the opposite: the upper strata are playful in the face of tragedy, while the lower respond genuinely to its stimuli.

This is rushing ahead of events, but to clarify: in **1940 London**, under the regularized **bombing continuous and dense** from sunset to sunrise, **the masses** moved assiduously to shelters for the night; **the 'highlifers'** carried on on the surface in night-clubs, parties, coming closest to the others in their shelter-crawling-as-a-game, assessing the cave-dwellers' varieties from 'above'.

The argument I evolved at that time, perhaps stretched, went thus: for the poor the threats of hunger, homelessness, injury are always real – the disaster-signalling nerves are thinly under the surface, ready to respond; thus they reacted positively to Blitz-dangers and sought shelter. The well-to-do had existed in safety, hence the fatty layers of comfort/security stultified their responses – the resulting sense of immunity, of attending, as it were, a show, but not participating in it, produced a foolish bravado, easily boosted by the cowed background of fear, which was not bravery.

Overleaf: Blitz-time sketchbook

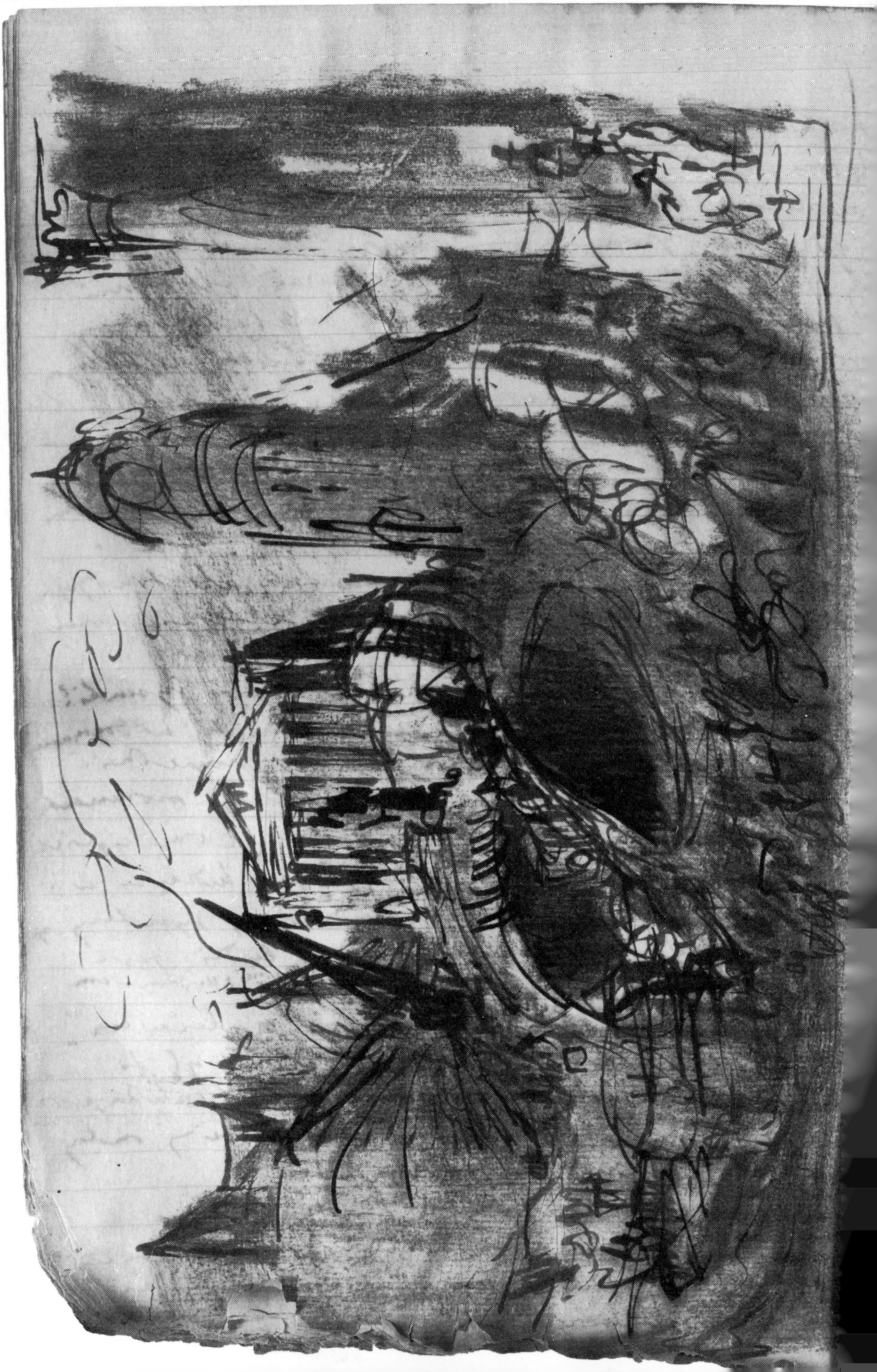

mość" nie ginęły w schronach, ale w bójkach
własnych, — oznaczało co? Albo pokłady
waty-komfortu co opatulały nasze nerwy
nie dopuszczały prostej zdrowej reakcji: instynktu
strachu, ale kazały wierzyć, że to wszystko
nas nie tyczy. Albo, co szlachetniej sprawdziło
się w przód "okazjach", up-bringing, ~~[illegible]~~ sportowego
braku kodeksu moralno-religijnego, i "stylu"
zawsze nie-wykazania — ta sama co prowadziła
przez zabiegi savoir-vivre — obawa
"faux-pas". Najważniejszy sztandar cywilizo-
wanego człowieka: gentlemaństwo — a więc
wobec innych nie zawiedzenie, nie "stracenie twarzy".
Musi ~~od~~ inteligenta, hrabiego, ~~urzędnika~~ księdza,
urzędnika, ~~[illegible]~~ dandysa że zachowa się
"tak należy" w obliczu katastrof, przy widoku
świadków swej "sfery" (ma przed kim grać) nie jest sam wobec strachu.
Ale jaka ~~długa~~ jest wytrzymałość owej
waty-poczucia bezpieczeństwa, czy owego standardu
"trzymania się". Napór "prób" powoli (przezwyciężył [illegible]
mimo fanfaronady) szeregi kokieterii z mas
, ~~[illegible]~~ 1939 wytrenowana żyła (tu ~~[illegible]~~ zabójstwo — w chudości
zbawionej owej Warszawy-Hańcza-wały) obnażając
wszystko prostym reakcjom głodu, strachu,
chłodu, spłynęły naturalnie w podziemiu.
Mówiło się tylko o złamaniu "morale",
bombardowaniu jako strategii wobec zmobilizo-
wanego narodu. Wiem mi, bzdura. Bombar-
dowanie wzmacnia morale i jedność —
(nawet dziś z tanto)
po złamaniu trzeba zmienić się przedtem
a wynik zdecydował ~~[illegible]~~ wahadło losu — [illegible]
niespotykanym w jakimś [illegible]
~~[illegible]~~ wszystko inne jest przypadkiem, i [illegible]
pamiętam mój, jeniec ~~w polsce~~ [illegible]
wszystko [illegible] i [illegible]

No one who was not in London in the autumn and winter of 1940 and up to May 1941 can absorb/comprehend that ambience, the multifariousness of heightened everydayness in company with: cataclysm havoc carnage immolation. The hecatomb expected, rather placidly, on the first day of war, did not come; a year passed, occasional air-raid warnings hardly upsetting, with London a capital traditionally far behind the lines; the Dunkirk drama in accord. But then **the air Battle of Britain** began.

Throughout those months every sunset brought **continuous** – this must penetrate – lull-less **bombing**, seemingly untroubled by the defence, to last each night until sunrise. The evening sirens rushed crowds into the shelters and underground stations/tunnels, burdened with bundled belongings, mattresses, blankets, camping utensils – the morning ones brought people out to make the return trek at sunrise, to resume '**business as usual**' or to find it and their homes smashed and burned out.

Days amazingly would seem to close the brick-and-mortar ranks over the gaping destructions; heartening in a way: after the total night-long ceaseless whizz-and-blast flak-and-shrapnel flaming hell, the sizzling damage seemed lesser.

But a lot of daily routines and **romping flippancy** continued into nightly perils. A bomb found its way to the Café de Paris, killing a large number of revellers, but not destroying that way of life: perhaps even the incomparable accumulation of hazards pushed many beyond the threshold of fear? And then the added thrill of decamping from blitzed houses to camp on friends, the sexual *quid-pro-quos* thrown in.

The cataclysmic 'blitz' crushed the very structure of social routines, which should have given rise – out of this fundamental waste – to new unpredictable growths as nature demands . . . had it not been for the ubiquitous continuity-mongers.

This generalization may be narrowed to the sphere of culture profiteers who continued *ad infinitum* their pre-war mastery of 'taste', reinforced by their assumption of ultra-Olympian postures to cover-and-justify their well-sheltered Service-dodging absenteeism. My token immersion in 'action' (that is, the war), past and continued, loosened me from the sphere of cultural armchair superiors – hence compensations. Amongst these, a clear conscience and none of their sense of 'civilian' (but cleverly hidden) shame, when, for instance, it was announced that the Polish submarine, on which Witold served, had been destroyed. **Witold** swam to safety in the punishing North Sea – and soon came to my London studio, a **perky sailor**.

Should I embark on the theme of Witold? – one in a multitude of accumulated (but also dispensable) devotions – in need, as with most of them, of a great length in telling because deserving, ordinary lives are 'fictional' in their subtleties and coarsenesses, their ebbings low and high in accord with history – which cannot be compressed into a few reductive, thus inevitably commonplace, words. Or should I omit him (them) altogether, to rely on the crammed name-dropping supposedly so satisfying to 'wide readership': the shop-soiled ready-made epithets surrounding 'fame' – little else could be added.

Just the same – Witold: in front of me a paled snapshot: a sandy islet in mid-Vistula, mid-Poland; I, in my youngest art-student days, seated on a tripod at a field easel, painting, bare but for swimming trunks and sunburn; and, posing for me, a tiny baby boy, bumptious stuck-out belly, little cock dangling, white-piqué-hat-topped.

I represent the summer *plein-air* of the Warsaw Academy of Art and little Witold is the son of the youngish (but to me, then, middle-aged) Mr and Mme Kuncewicz – he, a political theorist; she, Maria, one of the finest novelists in the country. They built themselves a flamboyant house on a steepness above the tender village of Kazimierz – to us (there every summer, art students and pedagogues) a mongrel house; but, after forty years of unimaginable upheaval, it seems now a miracle of charmed survival, strong, handsome, cosy – a period piece of the late twenties, not of the Bauhaus variety but of Slav folklore swollen into a villa. My inattentive galloping of those years took in and left behind Kazimierz, Warsaw dandyism, army service, and during years abroad I was puzzled on hearing that, when entering his teens, Witold, distant and almost forgotten, declared **me his exemplar** over his parents' heads, set himself to imitate me, and persisted at it, and that his mother accused me (countries away) of leading her child astray. He hardly ever encountered me, even in my

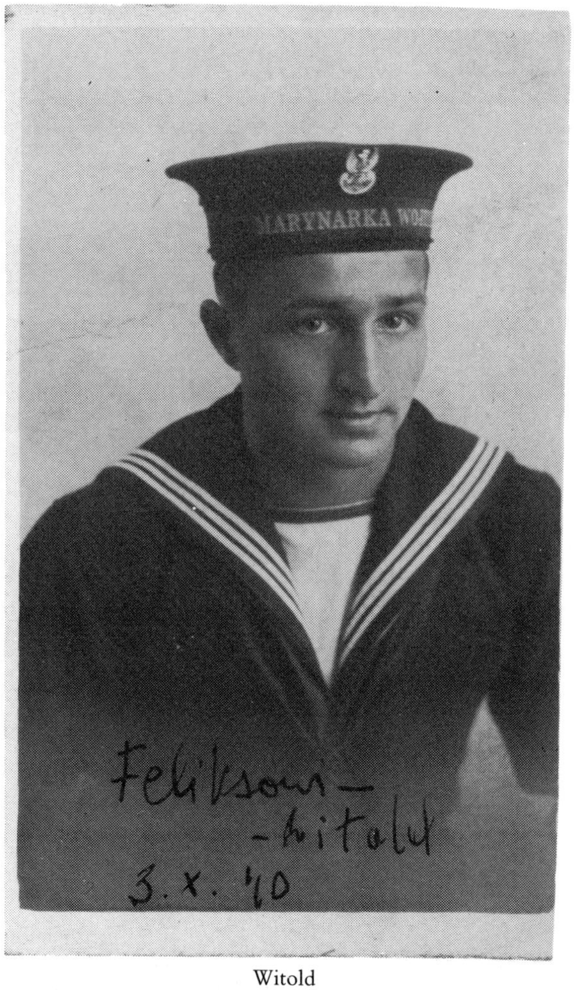

Witold

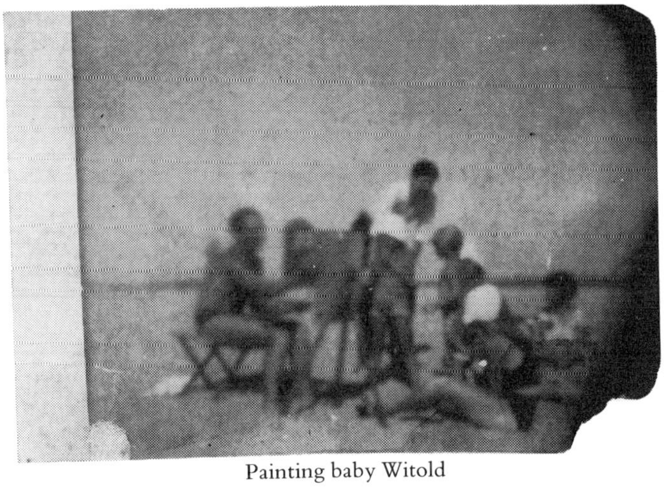

Painting baby Witold

Polish past – except in his imaginings of an ideal for his adolescent needs; which must have been shaped by the rejection of the culture-munching preciosities of his home, by his tossing about – a tough strong boy – for the way out to adventure – funnily, within their circle, I was apparently the only approximation to a necessary hero.

Between the autumn of 1939 and the Dunkirk débâcle, and again later, waves of escaped Poles – a great many old friends amongst them – descended on Britain. Witold, not seen for years, entered my studio one of the first, his idea of himself fulfilled: the Polish ordinary seaman's uniform true to the pugnacious young man inside it, his long crooked nose (inherited from his father) well structured into the forceful face; brutal head and neck; the whole toned in darkish hue (his mother's proud admixture of Tartar blood); his assured stance of strength – a going-places, ultra-sexy sailorman. And, as if of right, he grabbed, for the first time in reality, the position of my loving closest liegeman – that is, between his submarine 'action stations'.

His worshipful loving extended to Marion, my lady, but no mark of enslaved humility would ever germinate from him; his cheek and readiness to take advantage were modelled, I think, on his imagined me – but we were also the nearest available objects for his experiments in self-assertion. And so, when Marion was away acting in Liverpool and let him use her neat Hyde Park Corner cottage when on leave, on return she confronted pigsty leavings of easily detectable camping/feasting/fucking by a largish crew of naval ratings and their pick-ups. Even a few days ago, in the piles of old papers dumped on me by my children emptying the old house: a note left by Witold listing, without promises though of mending his ways, several utilitarian objects he took/borrowed while camping at my studio during my absence. All this was the preamble; Marion in her immense generosity prepared single-handed the first Christmas dinner of the war (described before) for my ninety Poles of all kinds, and, whilst most tactfully withdrawing beforehand as an English outsider, was set on and almost raped by the early-arrived cluster of submarine sailor pals of Witold.

And so his liberation from the parental milieu, speeded up by the naval regime, was completed – with myself, as his guiding figurehead, overtaken, left standing. And it must be added that the presence of this model (if not quite authentic) of young rough manhood enhanced my studio gatherings and drew admiration from the contingent of blue-blooded homo-*cognoscenti*.

With all this, Maria-Marysia, his mother (the parents also improbably rescued from the Continent and in London) went on feuding against my destructive influence on him. A great many odd disputes were held (while Witold plunged the seas), with me pleading alibi cum innocence but also jusifying his right to eschew culture-conventionality.

Under the surface of war, its multi-governmental bureaucracies 'in exile' and the bombing, the business of usual dealings and wheelings went on hardly interrupted, stimulated, even, in the case of the arts, by the rarity of international presences. Maria, her status as an outstanding writer recognized and her linguistic elegancies aiding, did well in the PEN Club friendships with such as Storm Jameson *et al.* The Blitz moved the Kuncewiczes to the West Country, writings poured out, the intellectual aura undiminished. With the end of the war, an unmatchable *salto mortale* was performed by the parental couple: Marysia became a professor of Slavonics at the University of Chicago and their home in Kazimierz, for a while in the hands of some cultural trade union, was returned to them unblemished. Thus they divided their time to the rhythm of academic terms, part in the States – part behind the Iron Curtain, rare specimens of private landowners; and they ignored animosities on both sides.

Another look at my 'documentation': only a few years ago, Polish Television made a film about me; I have a copy here and respond tenderly to a sequence embracing all three of them (Witold impressively preserved but mellowed into the role of devoted son) in their Kazimierz interior – a rare family reunion – eulogizing for the camera about 'their' Feliks.

This apotheosis of friendship and happy ending would be more correct as the finale if the divisions (with my muddled interpolations) had not persistently gone on.

Witold's progress at the end of the war and after sustained his buccaneering momentum (my undeclared, because hardly provable, suspicion: that he was activated greatly by the motive of proving himself to me, his by-default 'spiritual father') in alternating marketable inventions (of fishskin as leather, for instance) with shipping/smuggling arms to North Africa. But, simultaneously, he partly regained his ever-watchful mother's approval: he lodged in London with our common friend, a dancer and teacher in the Wigman School of Berlin tradition, Pola Nireńska, and merged with her circle to surface in a high-powered love affair (his emotional diapason was of the widest and highest, as it should have transpired from this tale) with another lodger at Pola's, Eileen Hurlie, an outstanding young actress and the finest being, moving then to the pinnacle in the London theatre. And so he-manism merged with grace and artistry – Mars and Venus – the foolproof fusion.

But no; they were equal in ambitious aims: Europe/England having failed for him, he had to move to the land of limitless opportunity for a natural explorer; for her, acclaimed and having just begun her assured ascent, London was essential. He left for the States, stayed at the bottom a mere labourer, pressed her, desolate, to join him; then began to blame her for his buoying up by a sympathetic American girl, met in a provincial pub over a common interest in horses. Eileen fought for her stay-put theatrical future, but the yearning for him and fear of loosing him to another made her brush aside contracts and prospects in England. But she came too late – to a by then bitter man. Dramatic stuff.

I am not sure of the sequence of events, but here is my memory of their truce, or initial almost-harmony: she had a good part, though not of the deserved highest order, on the New York stage; he emerged, as usual with him – never in placid permanency – out of still another eccentric ploy into sudden prosperity. They took a country cottage in an area studded by similar ones tenanted by theatrical 'celebrities' – the nearest: Rex Harrison and Kay Kendall – British colonizing exclusivity. In New York for a while, I insisted on bringing young Maggie Smith for the weekend, blinded by her *vis comica* outshining all the rest of the acclaimed *New Faces* revue. (I pleaded with her to stay in the great tradition of solo clowns, unique as such, being a female of grace and grotesquerie; but this is not done nowadays, and she moved to trot out her lines on cue in 'straight' theatre, no more a wonder.)

Saturday evening brought to the cottage a sparkling crowd – Eileen shone, but Witold, although outwardly harmonious and indeed respected for his manhood and conviviality, even though a somewhat out-of-line choice for an actress on a career track, poured out, when alone with me, discomfiture at his inferior marital status, merged with other paraphernalia of diminishing love, while enumerating the attractions (comparisons starting with the feet) of the simple girl who had stood beside him in his trying days. Though socializing was to go on till Monday, I left on Sunday evening weary of tensions, of the incessant theatrical shop-talk, of Maggie – ceasing to notice me – in pursuit of valuable connections.

My next New York visit found the drama, tragedy now, almost concluded. Eileen, less and less in demand as an actress, yet no longer possessing the strength to move back to England, abandoned and given to drinking. Witold settled with the other girl at her level. Madame Kuncewicz, the mother in despair over her son descending into triteness, perhaps for good, from the elevating companionship with talent and aspiration; Maria's and Eileen's devotion to each other prolonging this close entanglement. My inconsequential, bedside-mannered encounters with both the ladies useless, though, accepting the inevitabilities of it all, my sympathies moved into line with those of Maria. Witold seemed neither an adventurer nor a part-bohemian any more, but disappointingly flattened out of the horizon of heroics.

Some years later, in 1968, I stayed with him in Virginia – a complete family, including a domineering ginger-haired native, one year old, adopted. Complete merging, without escape, with the American 'majority': erstwhile Pole-sailor-intellectual, now horse-breeding industrialist, monologuing on his creativity-through-business, prospects, past-as-status, love, achievement – regrets erased: there goes a brand-new American . . . The races at Fair Hill. His mare does her utmost: loses rapidly a good start, falls on her nose at a fence and gives up before the last. 'Very good,' my owner friend instantly exclaims; he miraculously builds this débâcle up into a success – he must and so he does advance at his first racing entry.

Even (again, some years later) a gesture of independence through falling in with his childlike/plain stable-girl (he brought her to London – touchingly trying to lift her from her silences) seemed condemned to fit in with the usual. Has he lost all his battles, or simply settled into middle age? Either would be odd in this everlasting – to me – youngster.

The weekend at **the Dean of Windsor's.** Courtly personages come to tea. The conversation is keen and minutely detailing of **Princess Elizabeth**'s **first formal engagement** yesterday: she had reviewed some foot guards unit – a routine royalty function but, it appeared, **a test.** Its professionalism was revealed by the gravity with which this group of specialists assessed her preparedness and passed her approvingly for her job.

The Dean, at breakfast, declares that porridge should be eaten not with sugar but with salt – the Scottish manner; the guest does not believe: the old mountainous thing streaming to the ground with a great length of pink silkiness must be, he thinks, economizing on rationed sugar: true or false, the idea of grandiose Scots meanness within the tradition-weighty panelled world appeals; and, on Sunday morning, robed into an icon, the Dean performs in the Royal Chapel.

But there is an odd scheme under the surface: he desires to meet **Polish airmen**, young they must be – not the higher ranks. And so, a painfully arranged return visit. The Studio (still the only one – later it doubled along the Little Venice lagoon), vulnerable and crammed, was supplemented by the pretty house across the street owned by Lord Kinross (or then still the Hon. Patrick Balfour), who went to serve in Cairo and lent it to me, all in, including the aged-prim butler-and-cook pair (very different from the Warsaw pair that served me before 1935). There the Dean arrived to stay the night and undergo the most conventional evening, surrounded respectfully, as he desired, by young Poles in blue uniform with their figher-pilot eagle badges dangling on their left breasts.

The clearest memory stays of a bleak post-breakfast early morning over empty and humble Warwick Avenue (seen from a window) with this incongruously grand personage (in pink, not black) stepping ponderously up and down the pavement – his constitutional – fulfilled, or not?

But there stands out in those years this tale of more intensity, hence, by postponement, less rewarding. I was benumbed by **Janetta**'s sublimity; my not uncommon brashness, easily winning in commoner encounters, here evaporated in adoration; yet not conforming to the old, home-bred division between the loved pure and the desired bawdy: she was a *desideratum tout court*, but unavailable. Until on my first evening back after Russia and the battling month on a British cruiser in the Arctic, she

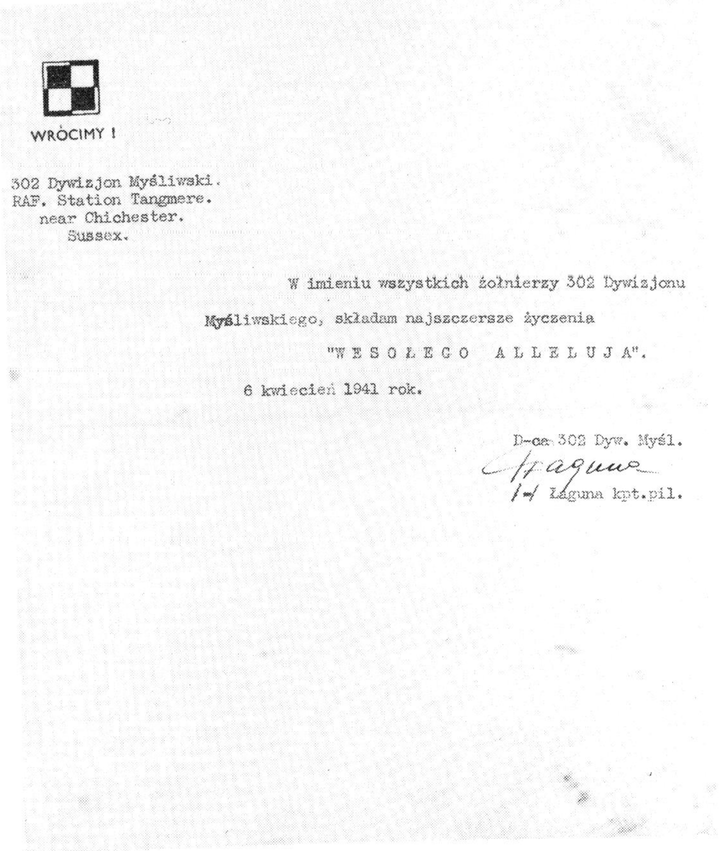

WRÓCIMY !

302 Dywizjon Myśliwski.
RAF. Station Tangmere.
near Chichester.
Sussex.

W imieniu wszystkich żołnierzy 302 Dywizjonu Myśliwskiego, składam najszczersze życzenia
"W E S O Ł E G O   A L L E L U J A".
6 kwiecień 1941 rok.

D-ca 302 Dyw. Myśl.
/-/ Łaguna kpt.pil.

Letter from Łaguna, Captain-Pilot, Commander of 302 Fighter Squadron

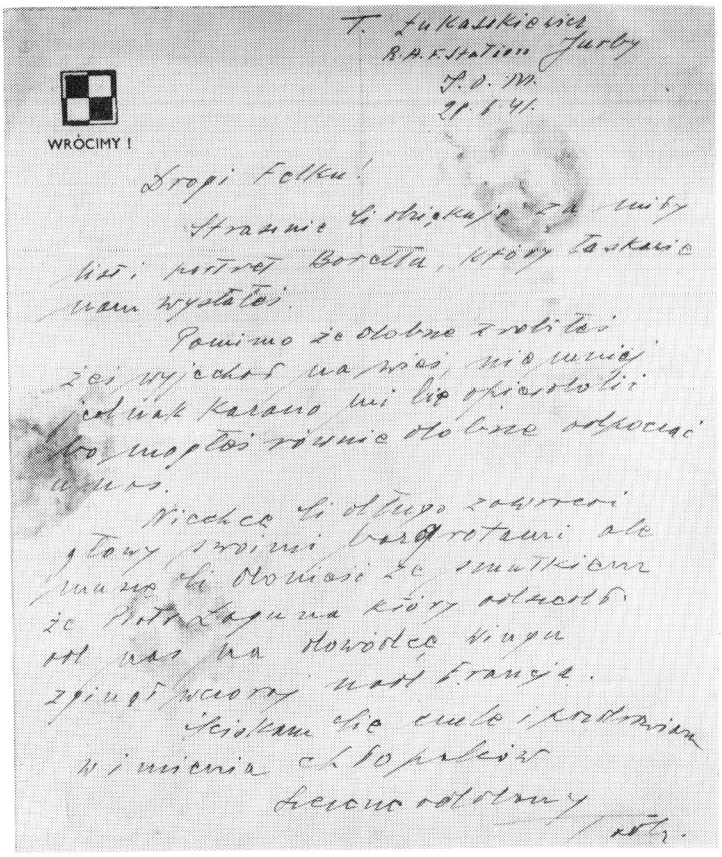

WRÓCIMY !

T. Łukasikiewicz
R.A.F. Station Jurby
I.O.M.
21.6.41.

Drogi Felku!
Strasznie Ci dziękuję za miły list i portret Borella, który łaskawie nam wysłałeś.
Pomimo że [illegible]
Nie chcę Ci długo zawracać głowy swoimi kłopotami ale muszę Ci donieść ze smutkiem że Kpt Łaguna który odszedł od nas na dowódcę Wingu zginął wczoraj nad Francją.
Ściskam Cię mile i pozdrowienia w imieniu chłopaków
Serdeczny [illegible]
Tolek

Letter reporting: '. . . commander lost over France yesterday . . .'

appeared at my studio drenched, hair dripping, overhanging her face and shoulders (one of the progenitors of this bohemian, later universal, style), enchanting – accessible as never before – and becoming more so, while my trophies from besieged Moscow (caviare and vodka) were consumed. But, the night progressing, my contrariness and timorousness besmirched my 'reputation'. With phony dignity I drove her to her one-night address.

Quite a few years later, flipping through my book of addresses in face of an empty evening (my attachments severed), I chanced to phone her (not my first call). She arrived, shortly, on a bicycle with a bulging rucksack, to stay, having meant anyway to leave her man on that day.

These turned out to be a charming and calm seven days of courteous bed-sharing – technically proficient. The single instance which breached the distancing almost-monotony with some glow happened momentarily at a distance: I, on a bus to the West End, spotted her, long-striding in the opposite direction – home to my studio through the mean Edgware Road crowding, uniquely unaffected, blonde, undeniably my mate, very beautiful, very desirable.

The farce of daily pointlessness (warnings plentiful, unheeded) went on; the catastrophe descended – but trivialities picked up in no time (perhaps even, sustained by the *esprit de corps* of cynics-about-town), the small-change pursuits – within the eye of history.

A textbook heading emphatically states 'London under Bombardment' and, selectively, Marion's and my exploits fit in with the timbre, but what about this: days, weeks later, she and I once more parted, each time irreversibly, and not seeing one another, I lunch with **Tony Sobański** (whose bachelor flat in Albermarle Street I am using since, in the safety game, it seems more of a shelter than my studio, while its bricky old fabric unnerved Tony, who is not well, and made him move to something more 'concrete' off Piccadilly) at **the French pub**, upstairs, in Soho.

The shabby room, somehow in vogue, filled up with *cosmopolitains*, allies and 'knowing' natives, focuses for me, extricated from the furthest end and seen through the transparent (for me) shape in the blue French uniform, on a singularly 'English rose'.

Soon the pair begin to make their way out: he, a bald-headed, bemedalled French staff officer; she, abundantly encompassing the quintessence of her breed: the uncannily conquering disharmony of supreme, almost tripping, anti-graceful, all-loose, un-ablebodied allure, only possible within precision of structure to the minutest fingernail detail; all this countered by, high-neck held, supremely inattentive *hauteur*.

This alluring essentiality of beauty not to be encountered anywhere but in this island – elsewhere beauty is of aggressive barbaric strength, as if steel-clad – lies in its duality: the physique cultivated by inbreeding to its pitch – a turning point at which the inevitable decline begins infolding – softening into vulnerability.

I, seated by the door, with her floating by me and out, assuredly to be never seen again, my senses bundled into exclaiming at Tony 'Why don't I know such masterpieces?'

Blitzy London's *bon-viveur*ism was locked in a very tight circuit. Not many evenings later a largish party was already crowded round the night-club table when I came in – and the seat waiting for me was next to **the quintessential English girl** from the French pub.

We even danced. And out in the blackout, holding hands, we ran away from the shepherding calls. The surprise 'imperfection': we were a few corners only from my Albemarle Street '*garçonnière*', but she pressed for a taxi – her feet troubled her! Black night, no taxis, and my manly command. Of that night the memorable item: lying on her side, her volant body almost floated – resting only on the rib cage and the hip – the space between did not sag, did not touch the bed.

She pressed mutely (her sole/toes signalling through my thigh) for spinning out the deed, to conclude with apologetic whisper 'I only need it twice – first thing, and in the morning.'

Then her room on top of a Mayfair house was blasted and she was left with a basketful of essentials hanging from her arm (perhaps the first to introduce the style), unconcerned. Suitably homeless now, her attachments being multifarious and multiple – and constant but in need of moratoriums, she should conclude a tiff by walking out of a morning to reappear after some days and re-establish herself, as if of right, to be off again at the arising of friction.

Perhaps also she was the first to introduce the Blitz-time erotic *contre-danse* fluctuations.

The double personae of civilized upper echelons of Oxbridge men: their untrammelled drunken-brawling abandon of the early hours and the precisely phrased (every 'Englishman' writes well), law-of-libel trammelled, best-of-manners autobiographies.

The rough and tumble of **Peter** Quennell's and my struggle over **Barbara**, literally 'tumble' when at **the Blitz-time Gargoyle**, drunken Peter cornered us by the lifts with his fist shooting out at my face but never landing, my untrained hands having somehow gripped at his chest and pushed him away; seeing him bundled in the corner and on the floor, imagining that (appropriate film sequences flashing by) I should make the finishing-off move, I trotted to him, bent over, indecisively roughed his hair and backed, amongst John Davenport's applauds, into the just-arrived lift with John and Barbara – a victor. I heard (but not confirmed) much later that one or two of Peter's ribs were cracked – and earned confirmation of his and his exclusive pals' solid animosity: personal and as an intruding foreigner. (Now, in old age, we are friends.)

Yet in his autobiography *The Wanton Chase* he says (though denying me the name identification):

> Hazlitt's main rival . . . had been a fellow lodger, Mr Tomkins.* My own Tomkins, an ambitious and adventurous young foreign artist, inhabited the opposite end of London; but Julia, although she quarrelled with him, still refused to give him up; and it was Tomkins' shadow, cast across our meetings, that often caused our bitterest disputes . . . at the cottage . . . I was free from the obtrusive Tomkins and the dangers that he represented. Or so I thought, and foolishly continued to think long after we had said goodbye . . . Yet, although jealousy may outlive passion, it loses something of its previous power to wound; and by the time I heard a diverting piece of gossip about a rival's sojourn at the cottage, so far was I from retrospective anguish that I enjoyed the story's comic details.

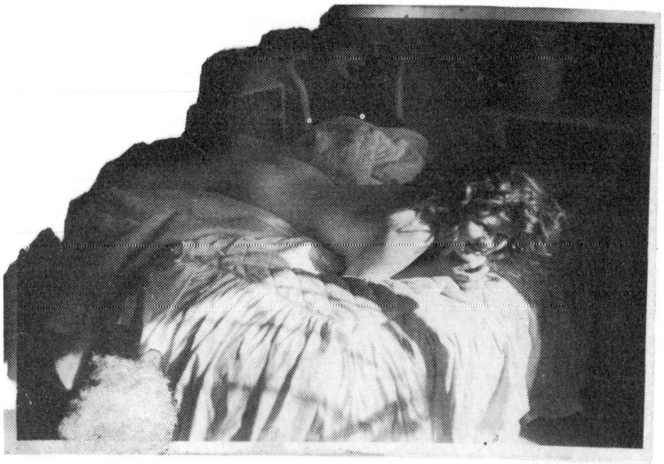

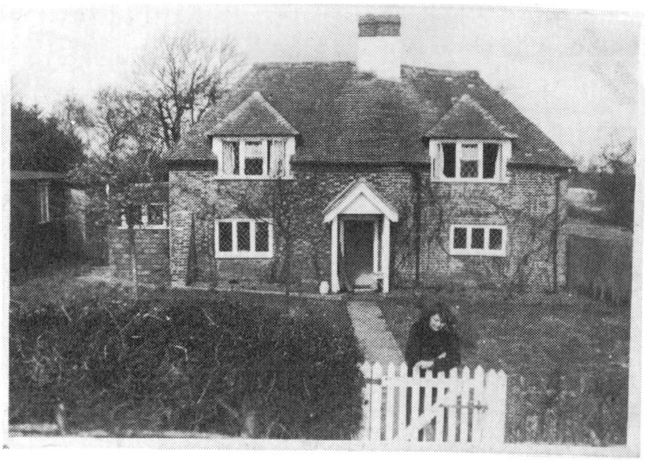

Barbara

Comic details in plenty. But he may not have known that the cottage had me many more times than once – though these weekends, started in harmony, tended to deteriorate into thunderous Mondays. One of these: loading into a country taxi about to depart for the London train, Barbara explodes with vehement abuse at the driver; corrects herself – 'I'm sorry, I confused you with my friend.'

There had been a prolonged lull in night bombing. But, with the darkening of **10 May**, the sirens preambled what was going to be the fiercest and the last attack of this series. Bug-bombs were to follow much later to unnerve terminably – but to no effect. Alone that evening and keen on catching up on rest I went to bed, in Tony's flimsy Mayfair '*garçonnière*'; the rumble of bombs not a deterrent – this was the routine: no shelters for 'us'. But the ring of screeches/

*William Hazlitt's *The Liber Amoris* (1823); his infatuation with Sarah compared with Peter's with 'Julia' (Barbara).

whistles/explosions was tightening, the blasting multiplying into near-continuity – as if, eventually, to con-centre overhead.

The little bricky house swayed, not just trembling as usual, and there was no pause. A stretch of some half-hour given to stubborn clinging to the bed (being alone did not help) was enough. This was to be THE night.

I was conscious of a tinge of shame at the retreat, when, out of bed, I dressed – plus an extra layer of tweedy overcoat and, usually a neglected item, the tin-hat – and went out into pandemonium.

A bundle of ridiculous brain-buzzes: displeasure at myself not resisting being pushed out, coupled with excuses that, **the attack-monstre** progressing, I am duty bound to be in the streets. Engulfed in the chaos, blunted beyond sight's, hearing's and, indeed, nervous system's receptivities, I moved mechanically towards Piccadilly Circus; no fear surfacing.

It may be of some worth to establish the minutiae of my behaviour within the unfathomable, rather than to line up mere dry facts, which would amount to yet another 'my bomb' story. And so, why unhesitatingly that direction? Obviously because my habitual peacetime walk would not take me to the parks, but rather to my spheres of interest: rough crowds and Soho – now, thus conditioned in spite of the sky-high roar giving out flashes of explosions, the town's outlines a-fire in all directions, the street level sprinkled with firemen and wardens, still I move doggedly and with outward composure into Soho.

And why no panic? It must be said again that there is no determination, or even daring, in me, but, on top of the 'civilization'-blunted self-preservation instinct, the vocational watcher's absurd sense of immunity. Those engaged in rescue and fire-quenching form purposefully active clusters; but also, bizarrely, next to my sluggish gaper's posturing, justified by my scribble-recording, there are unhurried others.

The narrow streets and my having stopped intensify, bring closer, 'the effects': the streaming flames, the crumbled and in-the-act-of-crumbling walls; above all, indeed apocalyptically above, the bursts showering/clanging down shrapnel, fast-wandering searching bars of whiteness; the unbearable frequency of swish-whistles-screams, followed by roaring blasts of illumination.

Yet, all this the vicious backcloth to the corner of Old Compton and Dean Streets, smudgy as always but more so, with mushy wetness streaming out muck/plaster thrown from a monstrous gap where St Anne's Church had stood earlier that evening – a crashed gate thinly outlining its instant memory this side, with the other, Wardour Street, and – just discernible – marked similarly. This being a novel deed, we stand loosely, almost cosily, on the opposite, undamaged, unaffected pavement (holding to this remnant of familiarity), staring, not differing from matter-of-fact passers-by halted, but hardly curious, at the sight of a trivial accident: two unremarkable pub-goers, **two tarts** *en pantouffles*, a dosser, and I, hazily making up my mind whether to pull out my small sketchbook – the scene is not very drawable. And a thought limps through my head that the ordinariness of us exposed here gives the lie to my neat concept of dividing the vulnerability of common shelterers from the bland swagger of 'us' others, when –

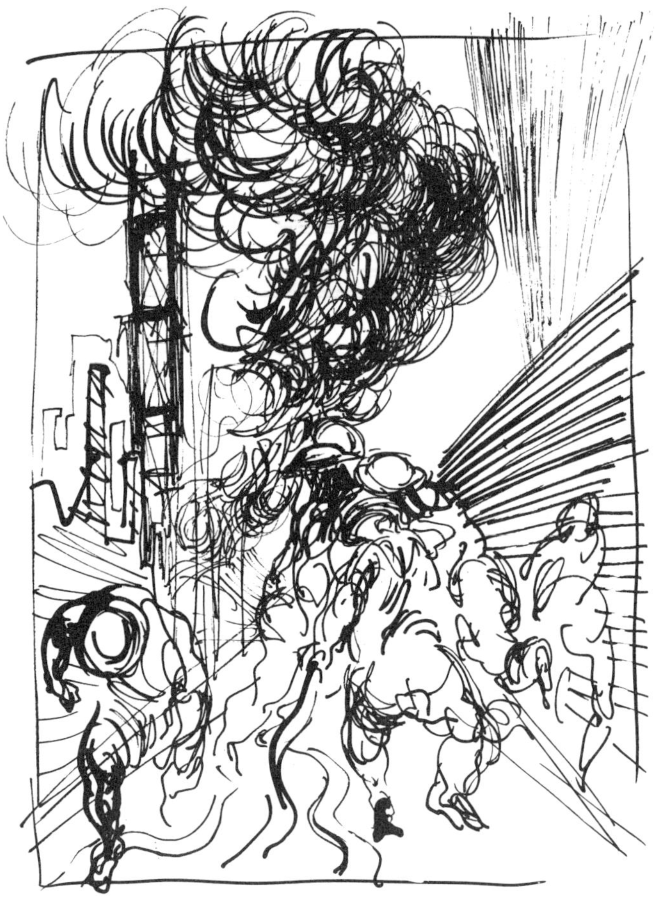

Blitz

I suppose that second should have alerted me momentarily to the descending blast and cosmic glare, but no . . . my next awareness is of myself on my hands and knees amongst the dust-raising débris: and of scattered irritations over the indignity of tripping and falling, over my coat soiled, over how-on-earth.

The vague, unfocused taking in of the dirt-clouded unrecognizable ruinscape* and figures (prone, crawling, advancing) round me, and getting to my feet, not aware of the débris falling off my back. An aimless wobble across the street, and, conscious of feeling a bit unsteady, taking a seat ('only for a moment') on the doorstep of the Gamba shoe shop. But agitated groups drag by: warden-supported, warden-carried 'victims' – hackneyed Blitz images; and somebody bends over me: 'Are you all right?', hastes on.

The porch has a mirror above me (still there till recently) and, why not? just as well to check, I lift myself to face – a monster: scarecrow mask, over all white-grey powdered, top oozing redness which clots on-end hair, streams down in plaster-lined rivulets over inflammation-ringed swelling-closed eyes; drips down the whole shredded ill-defined coat-

*This bomb landed next to the earlier one and smashed the whole street corner.

shape. I slide down to sit, to digest my *status quo*. And there is no pain whatsoever.

Again solicitous voices: 'The hospital' . . . 'Take you' . . . 'Soho Square'. But, 'No thanks, I'll manage.' My refusal contains an ulterior motive: the tin-hat! It's lost and, conscious of the ridiculousness of it, I cunningly steal back on to the smouldering ruin, in vain search for it, soon abandoned.

Now, on my own ('No thanks') I conquer the short distance to Soho Square, turn right, as I know the Women's Hospital and its entrance. And from then on my initiative ceases – I become one of the sacrificial lambs of the 'most recent incident'. I am instantly turned into a bandaged-head-to-foot Lazarus-mummy and laid on the floor of the entrance hall in line with other males, to be shifted from this strictly female hospital.

A long wait, until: Chelsea 'lady-like' voices round me, my stretcher shoved in an ambulance's bunks, we move off. And my turgid, thus inconsequentialities-bound brain alerts: Chelsea; yes, I have an appointment with Theodora, who belongs to Chelsea Ambulance Service: out of the tightly wrapped head of an obviously serious 'case' comes clearly and loudly (not to be ignored): 'You're from Chelsea. Do you know the Honourable Theodora Benson?' Sounds of stupefaction. Ever so calmly in social ordinariness: 'Would you please pass on to her my regrets – T–O–P–O–L–S–K–I is the name – that I can't come to lunch today–

Middlesex Hospital is round the corner but buildings fallen into the roads, unexploded bombs, fires, make it a longish trip – comfortable though, without pain – to a different school of thought: my bandages cut open, I am to mend by exposure to the air.

I am stuffed to capacity with glass, shrapnel, wood, concrete – head and back mostly, the right arm and the face black-blue; otherwise in one piece. And the pain will arrive with the healing.

The drama of Marion's entry into the ward, brushing Barbara out of her way and taking sole possession of my bedside! Then the flood of visitors and 'tokens' – from Tom Hopkinson a tall pile of Trollopes. And of letters, telegrams. The widest sweep of my 'popularity'.

After six weeks I began to treat the hospital as a convenient pad (a walking stick justifying my claim on it) promenading out for lunches in Charlotte Street and for afternoon assignments.

But reviewing the stream of my well-wishers, I was acutely alerted to the large proportion of those uninvolved in the war. And, perhaps encouraged by the simpleness/ease of dealing with wounds and death, I began to think of volunteering for the utmost active service – the Air Force. But my visitors included Polish fighter-pilot friends, who, brushing my idealized readiness aside, listed for me the prosaics: of piercing continuity of motor-noises, of the fuel-stinks, of the crippling confinements, of longitudes of waiting and sleep-denying, of sweat . . .

I stuck to my War Artist commission, but to be pursued energetically.

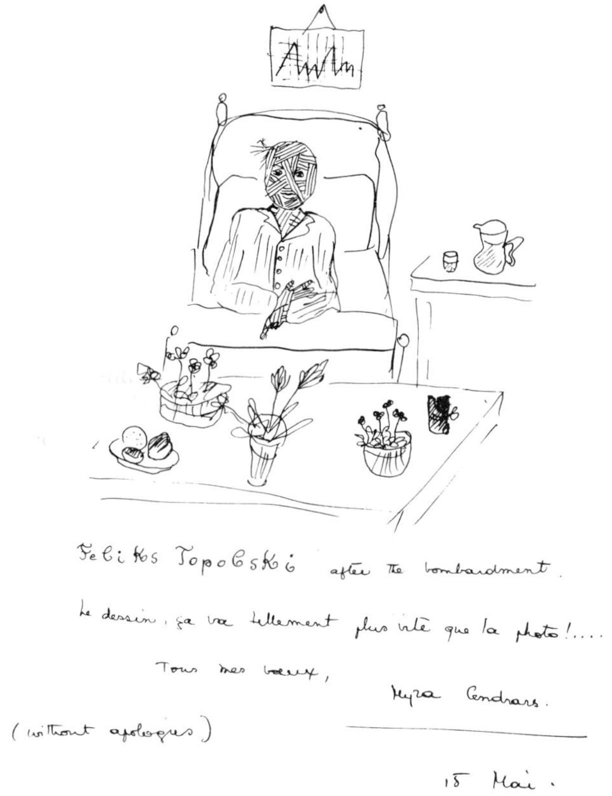

Friend's drawing of myself in hospital wounded in the Blitz

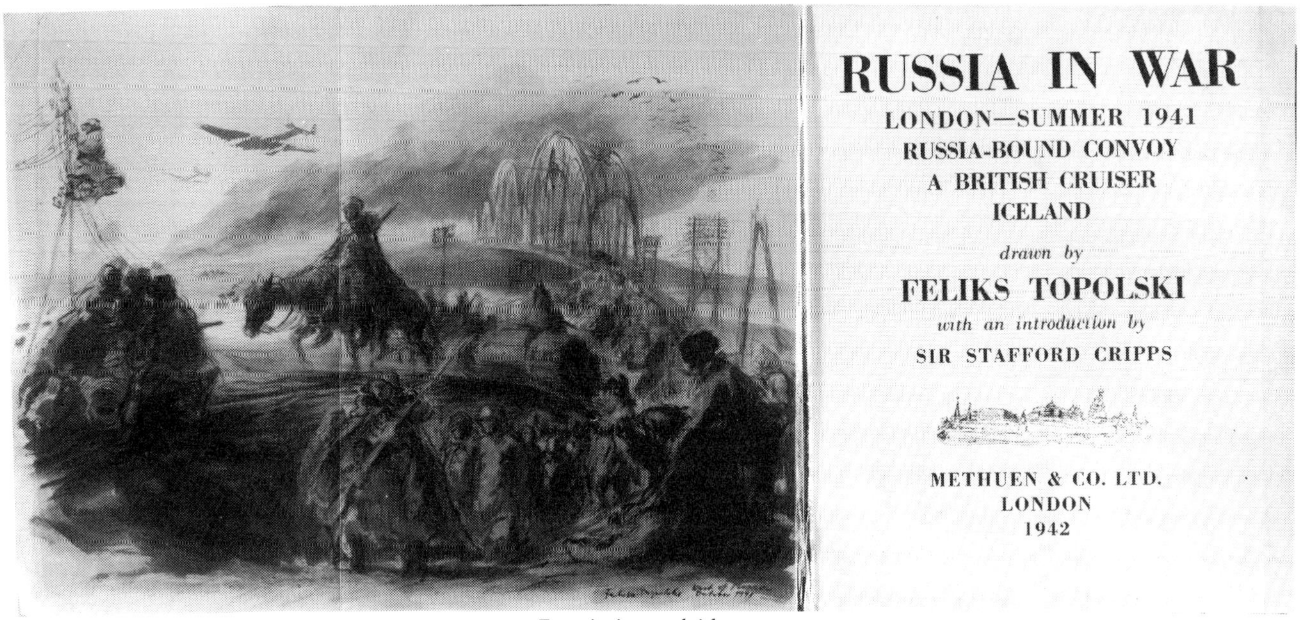

RUSSIA IN WAR

LONDON—SUMMER 1941
RUSSIA-BOUND CONVOY
A BRITISH CRUISER
ICELAND

drawn by

FELIKS TOPOLSKI

with an introduction by

SIR STAFFORD CRIPPS

METHUEN & CO. LTD.
LONDON
1942

Frontispiece and title page

My **Russia in War** (1942) had a formal foreword by Sir Stafford Cripps, then the British Ambassador in Moscow; and Tom Hopkinson, the editor of *Picture Post* – in which on my return my drawings, as the only pictorial reportage from Russia (photographers not admitted), covered many pages in several issues – wrote for it a long wise essay round his concept of me as an ideal spy, master at sinking into the background, thus watchful but not seen.

Miserably, my publishers and I could not accept it for the book – with the Russians' utmost alertness to the spy presence; with my drawing permits apathetically and insufficiently provided, thus most of the book drawn either from secret notes or from memory; with the Polish presence in Russia becoming vulnerable – his thesis could be taken literally, and . . .

It appeared, though, as a review (in, if I remember, *World Review*) and, dates pressing, I wrote my own piece.

First British War-Convoy to Russia: A Diary

Monday, 11 August, 1941

Euston station. Thick with Poles: '. . . madman, what are you going for . . .?' 'I envy you . . .' Pantomine of embraces with anybody handy for tradition-fulfilment. Marion: '. . . goodbye for ever . . .', her theme – our private separation, unaware of her words' grimmest implications: the dangers of this passage and Soviet Russia potentially an inescapable trap. The train starts and accelerates leaving behind review faces, familiar but newly revealed: pitying, shrewd, formal, Marion's finality-face; the last, Professor Kot, Ambassador designate to Moscow, completes the ritual with the ultimate hat-wave. It darkens and England flickers by, also 'revealed'. Smoke-framed, blackened, there rush by the architectural ranks of poverty and industry – pockmarked by bombing. Crewe – the same world, but arrested: the station platform rollicks with unbuttoned soldiery and white-calved girls; beyond, glazed over by steam and mist, the landscape of rails, signals and blowing chimneys, balloons dangling from above – England at war . . .

Tuesday, 12 August

Eight o'clock. The hotel window frames impressive blackness of Liverpool – tempts. Walk into the fierce after-battle-scape of every city in this country: the black classicisms of the George Hall and its columns, and the horse-riding statues wreathed round with shutter-clanking shops. A policeman traffic-crucified against the majestic ruin of commerce – 'Marks and Spencer Stores'.

Our ever-alert Polish Agency man reads out in today's paper that the Italian press calls upon the German fleet to turn their attention to the only sea route leading to the only open Soviet port, Archangel, along which the British will attempt to supply Russia with war materials. Just in time, since we are about to embark on such an undertaking – and one more piece of news tells that the *Tirpitz* has already sailed out of the Baltic.

——— *Castle*,* repainted in grey and colossal. But when, after the celebratory unmooring manoeuvres, she detaches herself from the shore – no concentration. Soldiers at the rail shout basic rudenesses at the Wrens below on the pier. The Wrens giggle, and so, to the sound of the boorish/squeaky disharmony, the 11,000 tons (says a steward) of aloofness turn, rocking waters separate us from the land, the huge wind blows. Details get lost. Liverpool becomes a 'panorama'; familiar squat figurines in khaki, already toy-like, busy at the shore guns. Nudged by the tugboats we fall on to our course and progress in truth.

I vainly attempt tensing myself for sense, drama or whatever one may try for on such occasions, but trivial trifles come to the fore. Even the alarm test-call, the first rehearsal of our modest tragicomedy, reduces the ill-boding drowning/rescuing instructions to triteness with Vernon Bartlett MP's head, served on the dish of a life-jacket, ceremonially

*The full name was censored then. Now I can't remember what it was, unless, perhaps, the *Llandudno Castle*.

exchanging bows with Mrs Haldane's.

Wednesday, 13 August
'Lovely morning,' says the steward. 'Fairly rough' – an RAF officer. On the 'promenade deck' there paddocks quite a fascinating cast: an American airman – bumptious freshness; the American United Press correspondent, Carroll – stability and a child's tongue; the British General Staff Colonel, Lovell – a hand-coloured folk-print: pink (cheeks) – black (perked-up moustache) – khaki with red patches; Charlotte Haldane – truculent costume of a leftist-suffragette gypsy. The diplomatic Czechs of both sexes, all façade, roll along medal-flashing and fur-swishing. Vernon Bartlett: Pickwickian – John Bullish – confident. A little medical Major strains upwards; and, the supreme matter – transporting an Air Force Wing (the airmen – frolicking) equipped to full fighting form. Plus one single married couple disrupting order with cries for a common cabin; plus an interlacement of Poles: each different – fine to provincial, 'well-bred' to the very raw; the 'Polish Diplomatic Cavalry' (our future Embassy's counsellors and attachées, still – and for a long time to come – in high boots, buttons shining, colour-accented emblems, tin eagle-mounted berets); plus one naval unit and one Royal Marine; plus military/naval/air experts.

Thursday, 14 August
My 34th birthday. Flabbiness in deckchairs; the Russian ABC; convoys glide; booming Hudsons amongst seagulls; the Hebrides landscape dull.

At dusk, on the rear deck, an improvised concert. I am made all soft sentimentally by the English populace's trashy sing-song. The music-halls taught me the real style of England in Rowlandson's tradition. With this people I would not mind living through revolution.

Will our prattle keep pace? – in two, three weeks we shall hate one another. Is my friend/cabin-mate (Ksawery Pruszyński, Press Attaché designate, the brightest/sanest/bravest political and travel writer in Poland – and, of course, in exile) sensible with his anti-leadership principle? Woken up by tea at 6.45 I torture him with counter-arguments. He replies from his bunk beneath – as if from my belly. An intensified dialogue with myself in two voices. My advice: begin by lifting your society upwards, and only then smash the props of prejudice. Mrs Davies, my London charwoman, an example: to assent to her attacks on 'things as they are' dangerous. Into the vacuum will sneak fascist propaganda, not 'good tidings'.

I squeeze my face into the port-hole – an island-cluttered bay loaded with a many-hued (pink, grey, green) fleet. Scapa Flow. Dazzling 'Naval Display'. Black rocks of aircraft carriers (field-glasses unfold fantastic camouflaging) press onward soundlessly. Tugs snort. We take something on board. Craft piled with invasion barges defile. Balloons and gulls thick under a marvellous sky.

In the largest saloon a lecture on Russia by the writer/RAF Adjutant. First of a series. Fine. Impartially but with sympathy Hubert Griffith prepares the non-commissioneds of the Wing (the officers and guests marginally) to assess the Soviet achievements not by the British measure, but by Tsarist pre-revolutionary standards. We journey to discover an unknown world. The gravity of it all is affecting, though the first question from a rating is 'Could you tell us something about their currency?' But immediately following: 'Why do we send a force to Finland against Russia one year, and the next to Russia against Finland?'

Saturday, 16 August
A shapely, jokey speech by Vernon on the European situation. Soldiers swing into ease and demonstrate (I always knew it) the fine level of social interests of the British masses; and a leftish tendency.

Questions:
- What about after the war? – return to the old order?
- Were there so many wretches after the First World War because there were so few rich? What about the Spanish credits?
- Perhaps already now, during the war, profits should be controlled?

Export/import; barring the unemployed from the colonies; more about burning grain and pouring coffee away; why the BBC did not play 'The Internationale'; friends of Hess; will it not end with an attack on Russia; why Churchill doesn't disclose the list of that Right Club; Finland?

The mounting talk on the Historical Occasion – ourselves. We attempt to pose grimly when around 5 pm our anchor screws creakingly out of the water and the ship heads from the bay into the sharp, drizzly storm. The convoy clarifies: a pink cruiser (sailors say 'light Fiji type'); destroyers shepherd the herd; trawlers see-saw at both flanks; gossip that the *King George V* and the *Furious* will be met soon; cargo boats carry enormous boxes – the friendly-gesture 'Hurricanes'. An occasion, all right.

The imposing hugeness of the ——— *Castle* – the troop ship clamours with Russian conjugations, arguments on fundamentals, Polish laments, flirty giggles of the Colonel and the Czech dame, the knocking of quoits.

Again a soldiery musical evening: after plenty of rocking black seas, of the hackneyed-by-now grand form of our ship wallowing in them, the steep descent into the light, song and drinking of the lower ranks' quarters 'harmonizes', while the diplomatic bar, where I dropped in on the way, was, exactly, diplomatic. And the other way round: the heaving hulk of the vessel, the populace below plainly panting with life, and, above, the insane intrigues of an assemblage of rulers, lackeys, Blimps and candidates for people's tribunes: this whole conglomeration shipped into the 'unknown' agonizes mightily and movingly with the almost-kitschy completeness of epic.

Sunday, 17 August
I open my port-hole. The dawn-pink cruiser winks/signals at me out of smothering wet fog. Sunday. The two of us, Ksawery and I, revolt, and do not get up for breakfast. Soldiers on the deck lazily stamp their morning routine, sergeants bellowing.

The compasses are giving trouble – we voyage godknowswhereto.

At noon the cacophony of cannons starts to bark and roar – they say: 'Cleansing of barrels.'

Again, a flood of questions after the 'Mother of British Revolution', Charlotte – agitator's gesturing – has delivered her commonplaces: what do they wear in Russia; education; how are the workers runged; have they conquered TB; and divorces?

Kennedy, part-Jamaican RAF officer: coquettish, he fishes for applause: 'Do women pay for themselves in bars?' Charlotte, provoked, offers a round punctually at 5.30.

And the guessing and analysing in groups and singly: WHO, WHAT and WHY to Russia?

Monday, 18 August

'Sea choppy.' Unsavoury rolling – again the race between us two: who'll be the last in crawling out of the bunks? – the joy of laxity. Yet our conversations never slacken below utter honesty of non-conformism; and he, Ksawery, has no peer as a fearless political/social thinker. I relish to the full this weeks-long intimacy given to our friendship.

A sleepy day. The cruiser no longer with us – we have left the 'danger area'.

In a series of 'lectures' Wallace Carroll of United Press speaks on America and the war. Again the pleasure and questions from the ranks; also a light on and a prognostic of young Britain's mind – and future voting:

– What's the Nazi propoganda like in the USA?
– What about the Federation of the States with Britain?
– Lindberg – a fascist?
– How's the post-war planning work going?
– How would voting for war come out in percentage terms?'

About strikes; propaganda; and debts – questions cover the ground, and – when a corporal asks for a comparison of the techniques of the British and the American governments – and Wallace answers, 'The English can act more quickly' – the room brays with good fulsome laughter.

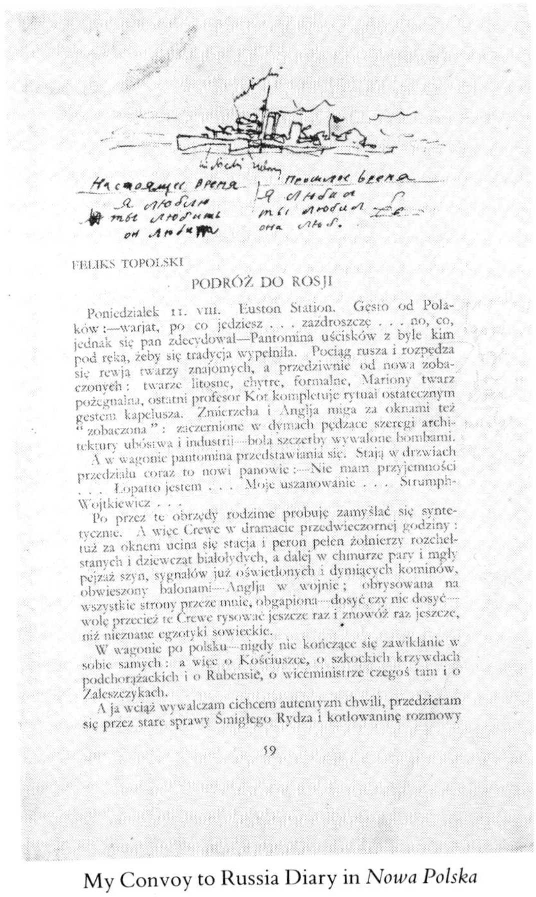

FELIKS TOPOLSKI

PODRÓŻ DO ROSJI

Poniedziałek 11. VIII. Euston Station. Gęsto od Polaków:—warjat, po co jedziesz . . . zazdroszczę . . . no, co, jednak się pan zdecydował—Pantomina uścisków z byle kim pod ręka, żeby się tradycja wypełniła. Pociąg rusza i rozpędza się rewja twarzy znajomych, a przedziwnie od nowa zobaczonych: twarze litosne, chytre, formalne, Mariony twarz pożegnalna, ostatni profesor Kot kompletuje rytuał ostatecznym gestem kapelusza. Zmierzcha i Anglja miga za oknami też "zobaczona": zaczernione w dymach pędzące szeregi architektury ubóstwa i industrii—bola szczerby wywalone bombami.

A w wagonie pantomina przedstawiania się. Stają w drzwiach przedziału coraz to nowi panowie:—Nie mam przyjemności . . . Łopatto jestem . . . Moje uszanowanie . . . Strumph-Wojtkiewicz . . .

Po przez te obrzędy rodzime probuję zamyślać się syntetycznie. A więc Crewe w dramacie przedwieczornej godziny: tuż za oknem ucina się stacja i peron pełen żołnierzy rozchełstanych i dziewcząt białołydych, a dalej w chmurze pary i mgły pejzaż szyn, sygnałów już oświetlonych i dymiących kominów, obwieszony balonami—Anglja w wojnie; obrysowana na wszystkie strony przeze mnie, obgapiona—dosyć czy nie dosyć—wolę przecież te Crewe rysować jeszcze raz i znowóż raz jeszcze, niż nieznane egzotyki sowieckie.

W wagonie po polsku—nigdy nie kończące się zawiklanie w sobie samych: a więc o Kościuszce, o szkockich krzywdach podchorążackich i o Rubensie, o wiceministrze czegoś tam i o Zaleszczykach.

A ja wciąż wywalczam cichcem autentyzm chwili, przedzieram się przez stare sprawy Śmigłego Rydza i kotłowaninę rozmowy

59

My Convoy to Russia Diary in *Nowa Polska*

The bar chatters: about Wells and Rebecca West, about Maugham and a Chinese consul's wife, the Finns, and Blackpool, the dictatorship of one party in the House of Commons, about a wound in the arse in a Warsaw suburb, about the *Book of Polish Cavalry*, about negresses and American aircraft gadgets. We drink gallons of dry Martini. I crawl on to the deck, but overawed by the surplus of the night's grandiosity I am swept down to my berth.

I dream about a good friend, Tony – who died in May in London – on a platform of a Warsaw tramway at night. (This never happened.) He smiles strangely – we ride together.

Tuesday, 19 August

Approaching Iceland. Kitchen boys' gossip says that we'll bypass Reykjavik – to keep secrecy.

Land. Snowy Mount Hector – the southern tip of Iceland. We lie about the decks, wrapped up. The MP disrupts our lethargy with his increasing drinking/leaping frenzy (somebody says 'He's going to pieces'). Whales spout gaily.

I write obediently/helplessly under dictation: **МЫ–ВЫ–ОНИ–Нас–Вас–ИХ**, and steal schoolboyish squints at the fantastic view 'on the starboard bow': rough-edged lilac hillocks under the pink-pearly sky above a grey-green sea. We progress along this pastel, distanced by 30 miles – apparently to dodge the mines.

Wednesday, 20 August

Moon-cum-map landscape. Aniline green of the shore stratifies upwards through bronzes to black cones stuck in clouds. Our field-glasses assess the anchored shipping (a medical Major knows: the British *Shropshire*, an American cruiser and battleship), fingers anxiously plot/trace routes on the northern map, expectations pile up.

A destroyer, dragonfly-tinted, dances/circles, disquieting – speaks through megaphones: 'Conference!' Our captain departs: surely because of bad news from the Soviet front: the northern ports are possibly cut off – hopelessness overhangs our drinking; the MP prances – falls apart. I draw the seamen – great fun. White night – 11 pm.

Thursday, 21 August

The aura of gravity. It begins. Commander/Captain secrets do not reach even the ship's officers.

The convoy fans out: the destroyer-dragonfly leads, trawlers smoke, cargo ships drag on in three rows; we are overtaken by the flock-formation of American hydroplanes buzzing ultra-seriously.

Perhaps, after all, we are 'first rate' and our prattly shameful sloth preserves us, gathers our strength for future trials.

Friday, 22 August

They say that we'll reach 75° latitude. We enter (the map tells) the Arctic, and lowering clouds hide the moony colourings. No doubt I've trodden into an Odyssey – and, sure enough, the whole lot of us are mere 'treaders in'. But surely this is the basis of an epic – little people entangled into grandeur and grandeur-bearing.

Ominous bustling in lifeboats – checking seaworthiness? counting the iron rations?

Saturday, 23 August
Am trying to persuade myself that the seascape is polar (400 miles north of the Arctic Circle), but only greyness and cold encompassed me. I play quoits for hours in the open. The radio at 3 squeaks in Attlee's voice non-committal Rooseveltian and Churchillian generalities. People grow 'redder' as we move east.

In the evening, betting on when the attack will come – 'heavy' betting on Wednesday to Friday. Deliberations over the lifeboats. I load sweaters into my haversack and neatly line up my boots.

Sunday, 24 August
FL Hodson chalks on a blackboard *Bolsheviki* and *Mensheviki*. He had been to Archangel in 1918 with the British Intervention Force.

Conversations circle self-consciously round getting drowned. The *Bismarck* was finished off in these waters. The *Tirpitz* – the radio says – is now in the northern seas. We keep guessing where we are and whether within the range of German planes. We try laboriously to be witty. The MP too gay ('wound up', says the 'matushka of British revolution'). At tea grimness descends. The Polish Consul produces a penknife and cuts out his approximate likenesses from my sketchbook – leaves square neat holes; a quarter Muslim, as he claims, he insists that a lot of artists who tried to picture his family died tragically. He says, straight-faced, that a 'special ceremonial' is needed; that, if I survive till 10.30 'when dusk will make white thread invisible', he will save poor me. A troublesome fellow. I fail with dozens of patiences – no, I don't get panicky, but weighed down: do not feel my return to England.

Churchill prattles teasingly. Little arguments spring up: a biting discussion amongst the Poles on the rights to wear uniform. At midnight – the deck. Bright (apparently night only between 3 and 5). We advance slowly within a ring of fog. The shipping huddles tightly.

Monday, 25 August
Leadlike water gluey – the sun beats/flashes on the ocean, soon leaked over by damp slushy fog – and then (in the clatter of quarrelsomeness: rainbow or **aurora borealis**?) the luminous glow, milky-colourful, embraces the convoy in a ring, whitely rests on the ships' edges.

Later, with Ksawery, we feel our way closer and closer towards A SENSE OF RESPONSIBILITY. Well into the night, in whispers, we debate Poland. And endlessly wonder what those Poles in Russia will be like – revengeful, communized – will they embrace us, or tear us to shreds?

Tuesday, 26 August
Our Major writes in his diary: 'First contact with the A/C Carrier and 2 County Class cruisers off Spitzbergen.' A tanker oils a destroyer through a giant hose. The horizon throngs with the multicoloured fleet. Something is coming. We are a huge armada. 'Pincer movement,' says our 'press commissar' Strumpf-Wojtkiewicz – 'over Persia from the south; and from the north by way of the White Sea: that is, us'.

Wednesday, 27 August
A great effort at scrambling out of my bunk. The Major wrote: 'Two most dangerous days.' Refreshed by the gun-deck and the snaps of a seaman's girlfriend Peggy from Nottingham. Peggy, simple, 'cute', shapely, willing – brings a strong, first nostalgic sniff of England. Peggy, not the hefty Missus, helmeted and shielded, is the true Britannia.

At breakfast, weighed down, my arguments extra-tangled; but the MP calls them, not disapprovingly, 'topolskiisms'.

Hellish mysteries – are we aiming at the White Sea or at Cheshkaya Bay? unless along the Novaya Zemlya? – to the left or the right of Jan Mayen Island? or from the north above 75° by Bear Island?; have we rubbed against Spitzbergen (Russian, Swedish, German?) or not? One knows only that we have covered over 3000 miles. Menace and bitterness. 'Matushka/babushka' excites herself by gossip, weaves theories, who with whom. Bored and panicky (I suspect an 'approach') I refuse to watch the sunset with her. Ksawery's talk to our countrymen on how to make rapprochements with the Russians. A great change from the early days' consular advice on resistance towards rapacious women spies. One hears the word 'Panslavism'. A weariness overpowers.

Thursday, 28 August
I lose at quoits repeatedly. Now our course is clearly east. The planes skid off the carrier and work on their morning gallops – diving. The associative prattle reaches its wary zenith. The sea ugly, but it gets warmer and, after the perpetual day, an evening arrives at last.

'Babushka' insists: I must declare whether I am an enemy or a Communist – for her, no middle way. Luckily a Czech Ambassador's wife interrupts with cooing in French. I tiptoe to Griffith, we down six dry Martinis each, and blissfully/warmly devote ourselves to the actresses of London. Fair, lofty Oriel Ross cements our friendship.

But 'duties' press. The fat cook attacks first: dressed, as he says, in his regalia (tattooed *décolleté*, starched apron), ready to pose. Everybody wants to be drawn. Souvenir profiles of joined-up good airmen; some 'crack pilot' or 'crack plumber' pushes at me the back of a menu and his profile; faces of stewards disgruntled because I haven't done them. My sketchbook passed on, mucked up – all quite harmful: I begin involuntarily to draw 'for scrutiny' and, because the enthusiasts go only for 'likenesses', collapse into trashiness.

Telegraph Operator Wallace, of the Canadian Navy, holds some magazine with my photograph, smiling knowingly; then the kitchen hand with *Picture Post*. The whole crew seems to know my name and drawings. Such pleasures contain, the devil knows why, a dash of bitterness and embarrassment.

Friday, 29 August
Notice: 'Passengers and crews are warned that they must not divulge the route or details of the escort to anyone. Remember we have to get back.'

Agitation on the bridge; telescopes point south: planes (impatient dots) start off the aircraft carrier stuck in distant mists, a few weak detonations flash-sparked over a cruiser on the horizon. The New Zealand Wing Commander drives, with some embarrassment, the slack crews to their guns; gallops down the companion way importantly – and returns on his short legs wearing an emphatic/wide-flung, completely new, gold-braided cap – now ready for anything. 'Second in Command,' he announces, 'Huns are about.' It darkens. We take pre-dinner drinks in the bar – significantly bare of talk about having been 'spotted'. Radio gossips give out that fifteen German planes flew – direction north – from Petsamo.

Punctually at 9 the farewell party starts.

The charms of soldiers' chorals ('Swing it!'); the spun-out song by a lance-corporal to an old Scots tune touches:

> It is of the Air Force I'm going to sing,
> Not of their exploits but a different thing,
> Of 81 Squadron and 151 Wing
> And 134 Squadron to finish the string.
> They're bound for a place the name I don't know,
> From what I have heard it is covered with snow.
> They'll keep the flag flying I bet you'll agree
> Where the Northlands of Russia jut out to the sea.

A Cockney sergeant dances a wooden puppet, plays on spoons – the heights of charm, of the comic's gestures; little legs – twisty/mincing, rhythmical; the bunched shoulderblades the wittiest; pursed lips narrowed/twisted cutely – a miracle of East End style. Then the RAF boys got up as bearded Volga *burlaks* (Hodson, in contrast, dances in the old Petersburg manner, one hand on the hip, the other in flourishes, a leap up) pull in on a long rope, acting weariness, a chamberpot. Now new Russia (from the trip's outset this had been in secret rehearsal): Hodson again, conducting the humming of the notorious tune of the Soviet Cavalry, all the effects (advances and retreats) provided. And the Poles. And choruses: 'Lambeth Walk', 'Boomps-a-Daisy!' And tossing up. And careering human chains. And ending with 'God Save the King', 'Jeszcze Polska', 'Kde domov moj' (the Poles support the Czechs).

With drunken meticulousness we line up gloves, haversacks, sweaters, lifejackets, before climbing up into our bunks – no one has forgotten that we are just now heading into the narrowness of the White Sea, that we have been tracked down, that at dawn we shall be attacked.

Saturday, 30 August

The ship is doing 4 knots. A fog, white and cutting, helped. The expectancy; but they will, as things are, not find us. Three minesweepers in front slowly drag the water and possible mines with splashing 'paravanes' marked red and green.

With Ksawery, sleepy conferring over how honestly and sacrificially we shall foster reconciliation between Poland and Russia, fight prejudices on both sides.

Around 6 – the Soviet land 'in sight'. Mists tear up on the waters' surface – disclose the surprising nearness of the shore.

Signals and lights begin to wink on all the shipping – 'Blackout off' – we are in safe waters. We have missed the pre-planned Soviet honorary escort – and so will hang about till tomorrow.

A lighthouse beacons from the darkness. 'Babushka of the British Revolution' quotes, the devout, Stalin – 'Russia – the lantern of the world.'

Sunday, 31 August

Sunday over the celebratory sea, with the swarming signal-flags, with the garish destroyer wave-sweeping, with the crew rolling the now superfluous lifeboats on to the decks – after their weeks of meaningful suspension. The flotilla hardly progresses, anticipating some welcome. Hours pass. The staff, the MP, the Navy, the Diplomacy, the Air Force, decorate in a monumental (looking up from below) bouquet the irregularities of the upper deck – binoculars, bellies.

Snorting modest little tug. A barrel-like rowing boat, six-oar-paddled, detaches itself. **The pilot**, a weighty blondie, hair lined/shaved neatly above the neck, brassy buttons, black greatcoat. The passengers – a gaping flock – trot in his footsteps. Kennedy crouches, aims his Leica, misses. **Russia.**

An explosion of protocol disputes: the British, that the pilot was not correctly greeted; the Poles: whether to disembark in uniform or in mufti; in formal square hats, or in forage caps; was there an instruction that only the members of the Embassy . . .? or only the Military Mission . . .? The lounge hums at tea-time.

The pilot rotates the ship. She anchors under the extensive skies. We listen to London more attentively than ever. With the Captain, in the bar, a *post-scriptum* to the voyage: still plenty of secrets, but one certainty: 'It was hazardous'; second – the compass played tricks close to the Pole; third: 'Yesterday's fog did its bit.'

At dinner the protocol again: *faux pas* or not, the pilot is fed at a separate little table in the corner – a bit like a chauffeur. 'Babushka' unnerved – terrifying and revenge-threatening (she has already tried to fraternize in dumb-show with the shy guest). Universal rattle-chatter.

At dusk, with the tide, we slowly cross the bar – and again anchor. The pomp will then commence tomorrow. Because we expect it: the first convoy and the first real 'help'.

I stare into the darkness. Emotions of adventure, of the unknown, culminate to a maximum. Russia, communism, the Poles, the war – close and most murderous. Threats and enticements and immensity.

The melodrama of the gigantic puzzle. Too much at once; and will the answer (already, tomorrow) be beyond my measure? Thus I fret and stare into the dark.

The solid fog-bank that saved us releases now our steely floating 'castle' fringed with mid-twentieth-century Britons, unveils prehistory – **the timber age**: flatly, below us, passes us hours-long and as far as the eye can see a pale-yellow lumberscape, fresh-yellow cut/sawn/chiselled/planed/joined pine; logs/beams/planks assembled/shaved/sliced/bent/scaffolded into mounting, thickly propped-up, skeletal-ribbed, ship-shapes (beneath, mushrooming wooden shacks). Horizon-deep – but hold on: there, at the sky-edge,

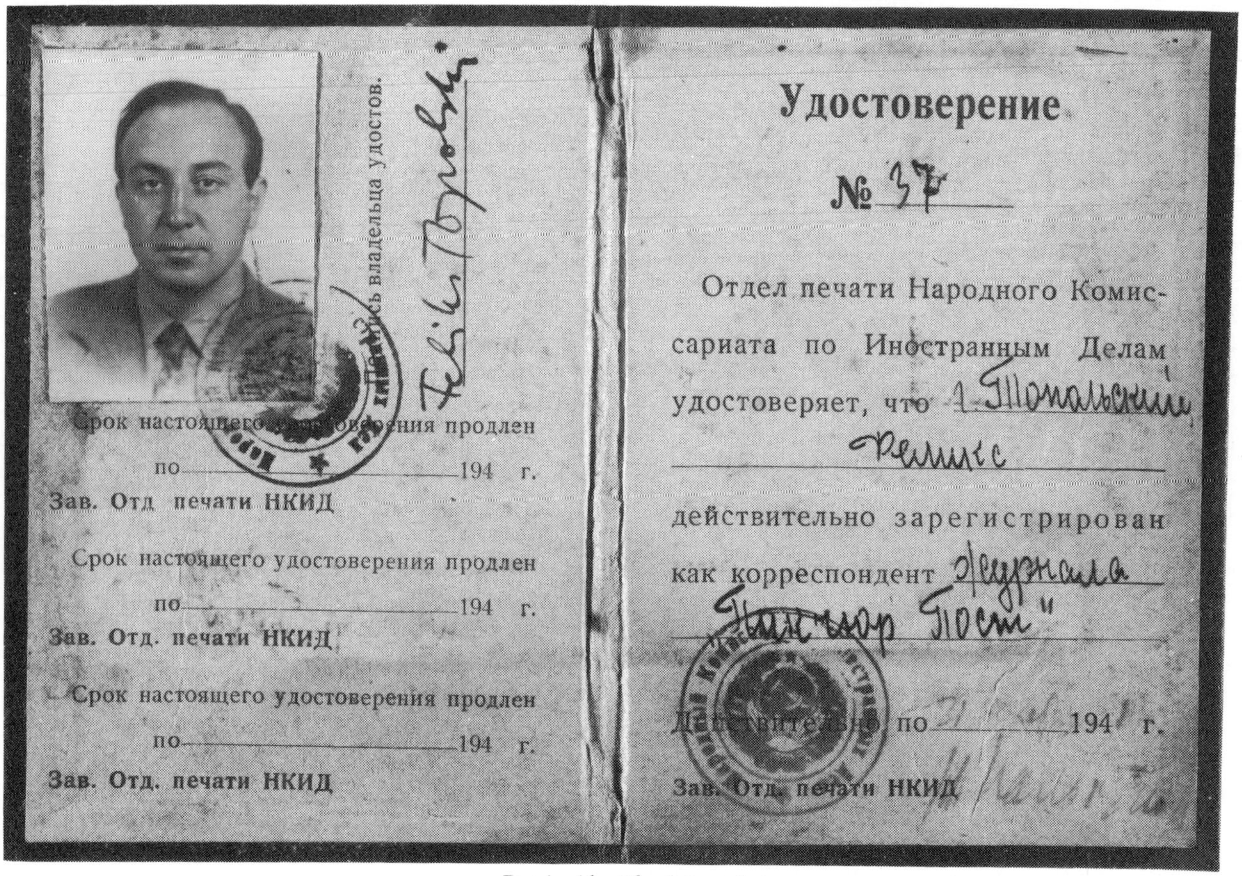

Подпись владельца удостов.

Срок настоящего удостоверения продлен
по ______ 194 г.
Зав. Отд. печати НКИД

Срок настоящего удостоверения продлен
по ______ 194 г.
Зав. Отд. печати НКИД

Срок настоящего удостоверения продлен
по ______ 194 г.
Зав. Отд. печати НКИД

Удостоверение

№ 37

Отдел печати Народного Комиссариата по Иностранным Делам удостоверяет, что Топольский Феликс

действительно зарегистрирован как корреспондент журнала "Пикчюр Пост"

Действительно по ______ 194 г.

Зав. Отд. печати НКИД

Russian identification card

taiga-flanked and raised up, a sinister secretive parade of **watch-towers** – not yet telling . . .

But close to the shore, accompanying us all along, small, padded, felt-booted, fur-hatted lumberjacks/cutters/soldiers/boatmen applaud/respond with a running steamy choir to our prolonged floating chants/cacophony.

Ancient, backward yet dynamic, low-flung but timber-rich; outlandish inadmissible barbarism yet smoke- and seagulls-whirling – and seemingly unafraid/uncowed.

The surprise and puzzlement of this evening at the Archangel moorings: **the Soviet Harbour Commander** invites on to his yacht for a formal feast only the Polish contingent – none of the select others. A narrow state cabin bears a long table hugely loaded. Most of us in uniform, many at ease with the language, with the hosts: the first – for me – eye-opener on the tight tradition links (educational and social/personal) between the two breeds; the Poles of a generation before mine fraternize happily – the Russians genuinely (instructed?) open up. Whichever – a promising inauguration.

Ksawery the Press Attaché of the Polish Embassy in the making and I (under the Embassy's wing but not on its staff; also a War Artist, a Polish officer, a *Picture Post* correspondent) – having been convoyed over the Arctic, almost caught by German planes – had it not been for a curtain of fog – flown over Russia from Archangel to Moscow, given quarters at the Hotel National (most of the night in its basement under an air-raid), and deprived of all our documents – taken for registering our presence and purposes in the Soviet Union – stepped out in the morning on to **Red Square** tensed with the act of entering and experiencing the Communist reality.

A crowded open-terrace café wedged into the Square seemed right for our needs: to absorb and, for me, to draw on the tiniest loose sheets of paper. At my initial briefing I had been informed that, on my submitting the list of subjects for my drawing, permits for each and assistance would be given.

But, in the face of this drawable abundance, it was impossible for me to wait – my habit of instant and unpredictable scribbling of action in the raw is not compatible with settling to pre-defined subjects; and so I began from the start noting furtively – the previous night in the basement shelter daring to put down only the irregular timber pattern of bunks and lairs, interesting but impossible to remember, with a future painting in mind.

Here, under this café's full impact of strangeness, the irresistible itch for drawing brought out the little pieces of paper, well shielded, we thought, and I started to put down the surrounding faces.

But, we, conspicuously strangers, must have upset the watchful Muscovites, alerted by the spies-from-the-skies official warnings – and very soon we grew aware of a tightening/trapping/falsely stilled mood enclosing us, thus sharpening our perception of the agitation outside the front entrance to the café's enclosure. We rose, made our way to the back exit, my new note slipped into my pocket together with the rest. My Russian hardly existent, Ksawery's perfect, we rapidly agreed to mine being nil – in case of need.

And, of course, two gun-carrying militiamen were there. Documents? None – a crime even in peace-time. On Ksawery's explanation, that we belong (even I) to the diplomatic sphere and that I (moreover, a famous artist) had been sketching (this was their information) only the people, nothing of the topographical or camouflage layout, came: 'Show!' I fingered out from my pocketful the last sheet, hopeful of this being the one I had just tucked in – and, the horror, it was last night's grid-like note, an urgently scribbled obvious situational plan, nothing else.

They took us between them and proceeded – 'Where to?' 'The Militia Station.' I had embarked for Russia conscious of the chance dangers lurking in the immensity of its entangled and ruthless conveyor belts of interminable punishments or untraceable disappearances – and this fearsome progress was to our certain and ugly Calvary. Once within the interrogatory procedure, our future would be dim – we knew it, and Ksawery's persuasive fluency (and my muteness) intensified with every step: we were soon to pass our hotel; why not, to save trouble, stop there (the most prestigious lodgings reserved then only for visitors of importance) and have us identified . . . and he gave them the irrefutable tale of our 'first convoy from Britain' tribulations, our Embassy's more-than-routine mission, the documents' absence falling in smoothly. He won. The two bright militiamen thought it unnecessary even to do the hotel check-up – but, before parting, there came a question, most reasonable by their scale of what matters, astonishing to the Western ear: 'Why does a great artist stoop to use his time/energy in the service of diplomacy?'

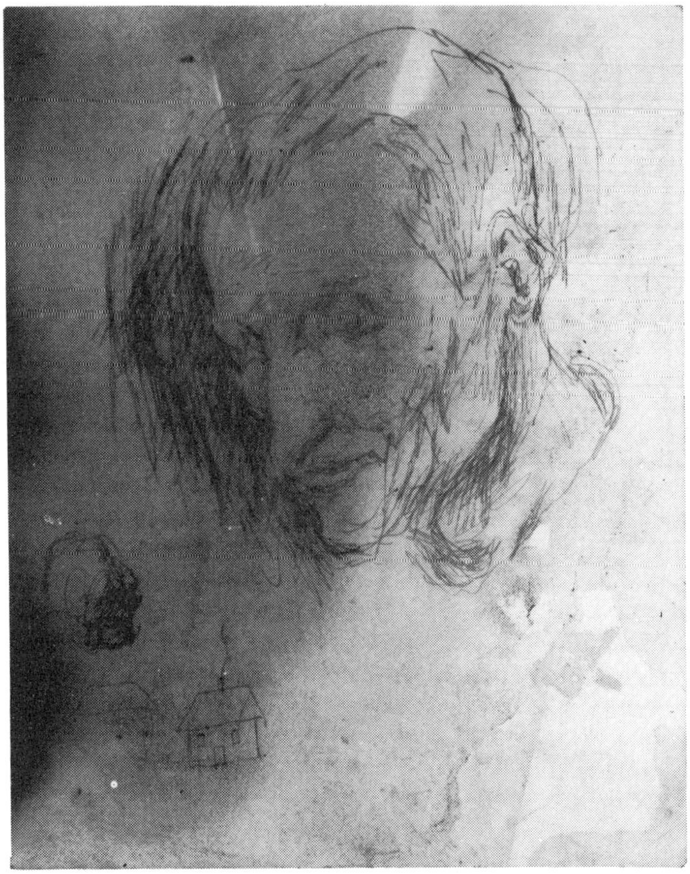

Victor Alter, leader of the Bund

With the Germans closing in, **Moscow** in September was in edge-of-the-precipice vigour. I plunged, as if in the nature of things, into this *mélange* of tensions, these out-of-my-depth whirlpools, in foolhardy ease.

Perhaps only later when out of it the full realization came of mortal dangers, of threatening and tragic paradoxes, when a restaurant table, an unruffled group round a samovar, a Hall of Columns rally for **La Passionaria** may have kept one only by a fraction free or alive.

Poles of punishable 'merit', that is, those locked up in Moscow prisons – masses of others liberated from labour camps and exile were moving south across Russia – now freed, stood out in any gathering purified/blessed, their gaunt faces/bodies given a spiritual nimbus. Not for long. I watched them daily, accumulating corruption in return to their old pursuits: greeds awaken, taking on flesh.

But **Alter and Erlich**, Polish-Jewish leaders of the Bund – angelic and undaunted over their not-yet-discharged mission – towered above the loosening up of other late prisoners. They sat once at our garrulous Polish table in the Metropole – silent.

Soon they were imprisoned again – condemned and executed. Their new crime: instantly when freed they began fulfilling their promises to political-prisoner colleagues of other nationalities left behind the bars, by sending abroad SOS telegrams from ordinary post offices on their behalf. But the shock rests in the false ordinariness of our socializing going on when aware of those saints' martyrdom – not indifferent, but also not made different.

General Anders, out of Lubianka Prison, poses for me in his Moscow rooms, faultlessly fitted in his new, British-cut uniform brought for him from London, all insignias/orders/medals correct; top-boots though respond to his cavalry past; a stick reflects the weakening inflicted by confinement. But young women's laughter in the next room establishes the present: two gentry girls extricated, like Anders, from imprisonment, and selected (of the finest cut, like the new uniform) by General Szyszko-Bohusz. He and Anders both handsome officers, matched well by these two handsome girls – a *ménage à la guerre*.

The Actors' Club. Beautifully groomed has-been Parisian Ilya Ehrenburg lectures preciously. Tairov (a skimpy hair-fringe) on the platform. Some uniforms – panachious *rubashki*, traditional peasant-belted side-buttoned blouses, still *de rigueur* as revolutionary style, they will disappear with the post-war imperial assurance. All is calm. In the **Writers' Club** round a bottle of Moskovskaya elderly Russian intelligentsia faces range: thin and bold, goatee, duck-nose, pince-nez-adorned; hefty short/wide-nosed, pig-eyed *moujik*; heavy-hairy (long beard, eyebrows, locks-over-collar) Tolstoyan. No agitation.

– **The University**: Major-General A. K. Kuzmin lectures on 'New Tactics in Contemporary Battle'.

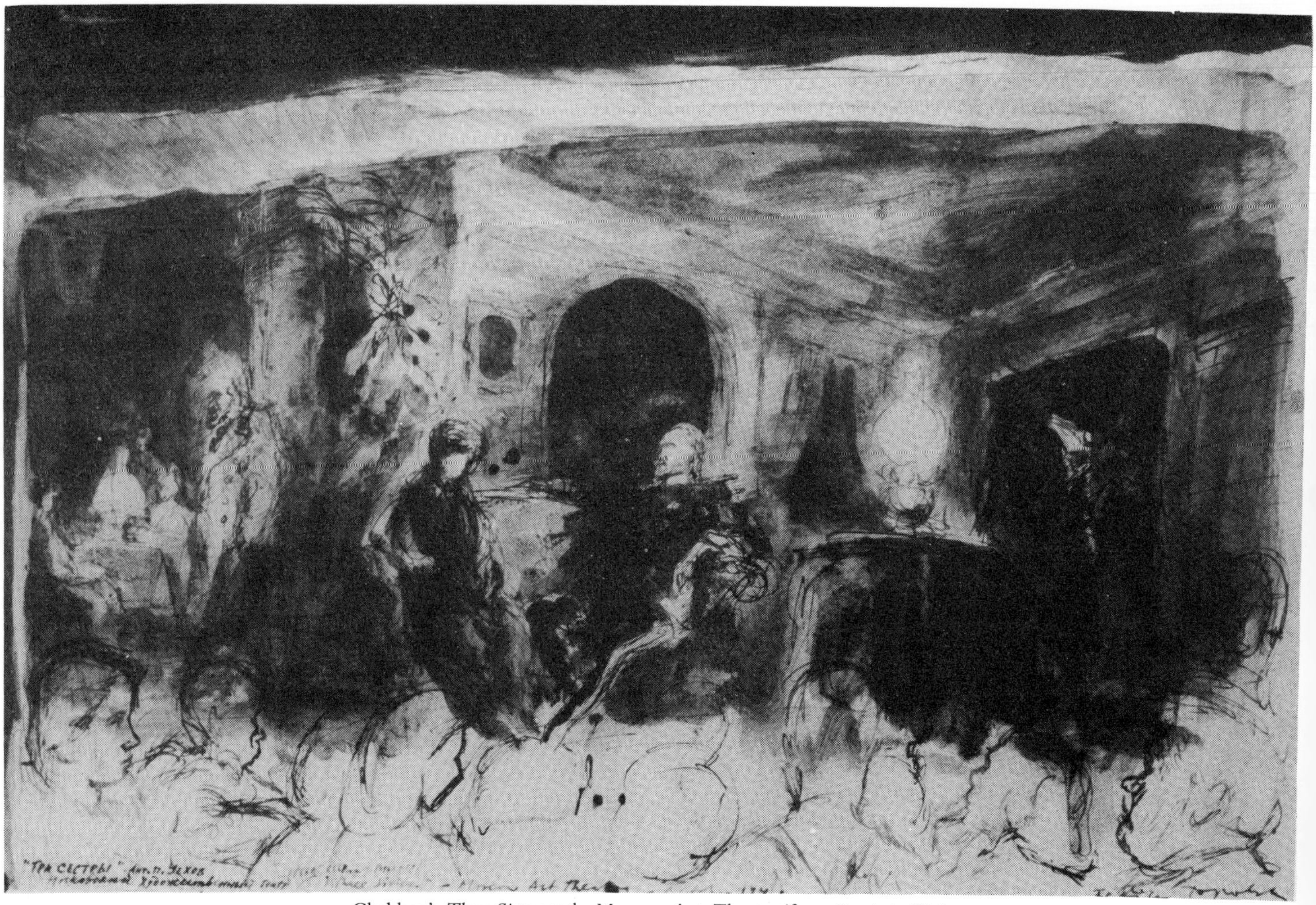

Chekhov's *Three Sisters* at the Moscow Arts Theatre (from *Russia in War*)

– At **the Moscow Conservatory**, Oborin's Chopin recital.

– At **the Pedagogical Institute**, a lecture on the history of Slavonic languages.

– **The Opera House**: painted-canvas-draped and fancifully reshaped, within its wide square's camouflaged paving, but it performs.

– **The Lenin Museum** is crowded.

– At **the Moscow Art Theatre** a truly convincing *Three Sisters*. This must be told: the low but widest stage so that (wings absent) one can perceive beyond the centre – a modest country-house salon, a sofa in mid-stage with a pair engrossed in each other – to the left, as if rounding a corner, the *enfilade* or rather the promise of the next, the dining, room; and to the right the entrance lobby with curtained doors leading out.

The dialogue: a timid woman in black and a bearded correct reserved-but-in-love officer, in the mood and dimmest lighting of the turn-of-the-century – slow, sparing, loaded with pauses. Then (but the sedately pregnant aura lasts and culminates towards the decisive with hardly any gesture) the complete stillness – of speech, and facial even – stillness of arrested life; the two turn puppets – but gently – and (a paining very long pause) the whole stage begins to turn; not far, but far enough to confirm the manipulatory theatricality of those two and of their interior, which was to us life itself a moment before; and far enough to bring closer the edge of the next room, into which they and some others will pass. This trick, because it has become so with over-use, of arrested action is nowadays no longer convincing; but it was not because the device was applied possibly for the first time, certainly for me, that it turned out to be my most moving theatrical occasion, but because of the profoundest directorial balancing (or unbalancing) of utmost stage reality at its highest (I hasten to say: not my preferential form, but this was Stanislavsky's theatre!) with the shock of the reminder (destiny revealed at work?!) of the artifice, of the mechanics of it all.

This contemplation of love's slow motion; while the invaders, a mere 90 kilometres away, advance. And Alter and Erlich . . .

– **Broniewski**, the favoured Communist poet of pre-war Warsaw high-*bohème*, puzzlingly imprisoned by the Soviets – now, out with everybody, he brings back his Legions past of a brave officer (he is nearer to my father's generation), but in the meantime settling his drunkard's/scrounger's charms of yesterday on me and my hotel bathroom and drink supplies. A charismatic unpredictably wild man, he joins me at dinner at the Moskva, which I chose on account of the most impressive Latvian waitress. The air-raid alarm sends us all to the hotel's basements, even the indispensable vodka-indulged brawlers – I masterfully settling with the girl, by then not disapproving of my advances – but Władysław: in no time he chain-recites in his booming lovely Russian Pushkin's poetry

– for her; and she yields predictably to the spell.

– They always forgather in the evenings, not unlike the Poles, for the sit-back endless talk. This is the **home of a prominent Party-member.** She is of Polish origin, but the room is filled with men, women and children of the Soviet élite plus one black, pipe-smoking friend. Boys wear Young Comsomol shawl-ties; there sits prominently and narrates a Hero of the Soviet Union – an officer on leave from the Front. The ease soaked in gravity; this is how they await calamities.

– At the Dom Sovietov in the filled-up-to-the-balconies Hall of Columns speaks **La Passionaria.** Huge spotlights, cameras, Stalin's vast plaster head behind the Praesidium, red-gold sloganned banners the length of the Hall, chandeliers. Noble-profiled, she is a bust above the multi-microphoned stand, emanating internationalist passion.

But the banners spell Defence of Mother Russia; but the war propaganda directed at the masses does not risk speaking of Communism, but calls for unfailing patriotism.

A distinction: **Simplicissimus** Feliks, the aggressive *peregrinatus* – from the Feliks held by his roots within his fences. The obvious often pondered: a child, while observed, is reforming itself into another.

There is a natural formation – the DNA (is it?): predictable inheritance. And, how very soon, longings for another, out-of-predestined, fate-shape begin to implant features, feathers, clobber, attitudes in imitation of one's heroes/models gathered on the way – play-acting in desperation to get out of/beyond oneself.

So the straight-backed bearing would be on hire from a gym teacher; the speech-intoning from several; the step-length and the foot-placing from so-and-so. This dressing up/make-up, known also as self-consciousness, cannot surpass nature's confinements; and these put up with/blend with the aspirational make-beliefs into a shaky, doubt-ridden, inconsistent and off-splitting whole.

A seductive thought: to present myself as a Simplicissimus Candide★ – that is a present times' version: a border-case moving along the border-lines, trying to negotiate multi-crossroads wilfully mis-signposted; not always an innocent but sometimes a shrewd/slippery survivor/dodger – now a helplessly buffeted pushover, next a zealot at witnessing. A half-baked sceptic/stoic – the other more-or-less half made of ill-focused play-acting greeds: of sophisticated simplicity, the non-voting member of opinion-forming/fawning 'social strata'. Never beaten by fate, because, being *simplicissimus*, he does not mount the barricades of many-coloured convictions: and this day does not waste its time much in thrashing under-bridge (or -roof) dossers.

Simplicissimus is an intermezzo performer within thunderous epics. He lives the human scale, pathetic but comic-smart, but participating in and minutely propelling events. Schweik – a cardboard clown; but this 'person' is funnier because aware and of 'our civilization'. So his anecdotes, pickled into history, mark truthfully, the events' fluctuations.

Respected War Artist, arrived from England in the Soviet Union at war to witness the Polish resurrection, now on a momentous flight from Moscow: the newly formed Polish **High Command under General Anders** (a few days out of prison), aided by the Soviet KGB General Zhukov, is on its way to take charge ceremonially of his future army, still growing – still a multitude of stragglers, who had made their way to a remoteness below the Urals from labour camps and prisons all over Russia.

Indeed, **history-in-the-making** to be recorded. The moulded-anew high-ranking Polish officers around me, dressed in semblances of their former uniforms, jibe at my single-pip second-lieutenant's (my proper rank) British-Polish battledress, the first and only one in Russia: for their high-boot-and-tight-tunic tradition, it is not military.

We land in the evening in **Kuibyshev**, a city on the Volga (soon to become the temporary capital after Moscow's evacuation under German pressure), at the end of an exhausting day which had started at dawn, followed by hours of delays.

The Grand Hotel. I am to share a room with the General's Adjutant. But there is no rest – a banquet has been prepared. The authorities of Kuibyshev live up to the significance of our visit: the vast U-shaped table, the immensity of *sovietskoye shampanskoye* and the full turn-out of the élite of the city, led by the governing personages, civilian and military, and the continuity of toasts in astonishing accord (many high-ranking Polish officers – pre-eminently General Anders – brought up in the Tsarist military schools) with the Soviet dignitaries. Even I, seated (but standing to toast) between two beribboned lesser civilian officials, sustain the appropriately dignified camaraderie. And even try to sketch.

But my hazy (weariness and drinking) concentration on the matter of this portentous rapprochment is disrupted. Simplicissimus spots, across the banquet in the farthest line of serving girls, a living symbol: a very **young Mother Russia** – monumental, yet not monstrous, the superhuman dimensions of a hoarding poster of peasant vigour of the land; the lapidary wide Slav/Asian features top this mighty edifice to perfection – the folklore accessories (a kerchief over plaited black hair, a long belted linen garment) right. The whole as if a portent of the invincibility of this country. Am I attracted? Rather elated at this acme of otherness. I try to scribble her into my notes between the blow-out dishes and stand-up cheers, but she becomes the focus; Simplicissimus is in danger of neglecting his higher purpose.

The end of the endless banquet, a late hour, the final clamorous shake-hands/hugs and optimistic declarations and, as I turn, there she is – curiosity about my drawing may have made her cross to my side. And how in my drink-food soddenness, tight involvement with my hosts and elementary Russian do I manage an invitation for her – keeping up

★*Simplicius Simplicissimus*, by Hans Jacob Christoffel von Grimmelshausen (1669); *Candide*, by Voltaire (1759).

pretences (cunning of a drunkard!) – to bring coffee to my room – assuming that the celebrations are ended and having been told that my ADC has moved to another room?

But I reckoned without Russian parochial stamina: the evening has only begun; a gala spectacle at the operetta comes next. And this is the only time in my life when I fall asleep at the theatre – seated between attentive local worthies. And there is more in store, since this is Russia: the interminable intervals are properly, for this most serious occasion, conducted as formalities; my Polish superiors seem to fall in naturally with these protocol requirements and we (with me at the end – the lowest rank), together with our hosts, **parade** circularly around a purpose-shaped lobby – an impressively grave uniformed cortège, a conscientious demonstration of indomitable revival, of **the returned Polish presence** on the stage of history, and of alliance, with the ordinary theatre-goers crowding in awe against the walls.

In fact, although enacted within a distant backwater town on the Volga (or perhaps because of it), a moving apotheosis. Well into the early hours, back in my room, collapsed in sleep – even though there are no blinds and across the street all the windows of the municipality hall glare in our honour. But then, a scratchy knock, and, the door opening, the Gogolian past of distant Tsarist garrison tradition unwinds: a dwarfish old night porter (I assume) enters in the cringingly appropriate dance of a procurer, the prologue to a pantomime of naughtiness: the world of officers' sordid fun in the *cabinets privés* of 'grand' hotels astonishingly revived, or surviving. There is no way to brush him off; the affair is 'institutionalized'. He circles round me till he has blotted the new 'dignity of labour' rules from my mind: I have not yet fulfilled my part of the *commedia* – the tip! He backs out bowing, but: will there be also the *shampanskoye* and the cakes? I chase him out.

A proper pause. The gentler knock and – fantasy: she fills the doorway. She is no longer disguised as a serving wench, but the symbol of alliance fulfilled and humanized by the betrothal theme: her hair unplaited, falling down, her white robe probably the same but now unbelted, reaching bare feet; she and her expectations tower above my panic and exhausted inadequacy.

I am somewhat touched – certainly not enticed. But the irreversible takes place. We perch on the high spare bed, and, convention's bidding, entangle in a tentative embrace while disbalancing towards horizontality.

At this point the door opens: the instant matter-of-fact entry of my lieutenant mumbling about a forgotten attaché case (Polish Staff Officers always distinguished by their blasted attaché cases); indeed, he drags it practically from under us and departs. Disaster.

The proud moment of recovery from the Polish martyrdom of this war, the 'face' of our elevated group honour-bound by our uniforms, our mission, under the watchfulness of yesterday's enemies – and I, this second lieutenant twerp, blemishing the momentousness by low whoring with, into the bargain, a 'Mother Russia'. These would be the thoughts of the world outside.

But the night takes the non-political course, fulfils itself on the simple level of tenderness. As the folk of Russia tend to be, and mostly so their women, she shows generosity of warmness, of confiding, of pluck and concern. And she has a child and was wronged and will manage . . .

My morning entry into the breakfast room. General Anders with his impressive entourage – he summons me. I make my regulation three hard steps/attention/'Second Lieutenant Topolski reports etc.' and 'Yes Sir' to this order: 'The Lieutenant' – when addressing this low rank there is the courtesy omission of 'Second' – 'will assist General Szarecki on the train journey to Bouzułuk with the baggage.' 'Yes Sir General', turnabout, three hard steps, move off to receive breakfast from the hands of **my serving lover**.

The immense plane with its vast capacity which had brought us to the Kuibyshev airport cannot land in that distant wilderness – hence a smaller plane with no room for the baggage. General Szarecki, the Chief Medical Officer and the oldest man on the staff, and I, the youngest in rank and age, were the obvious choice for assisting the land transport; and, thus, I was to miss the sole reason for my being there: the documentation in drawing of the great event, the epic solemnization of the arrival of the Commander to face the liberated men who will form his army.

I never learned whether this was the punishment for my having degraded the Moment of Pride; or whether, as I was warned, one pip on the shoulder, denoting a second lieutenant, made my superiors treat me only as such.

Long after the war General Anders lunched with me and my family, but I could not, in the circumstances, bring out and resolve the puzzle.

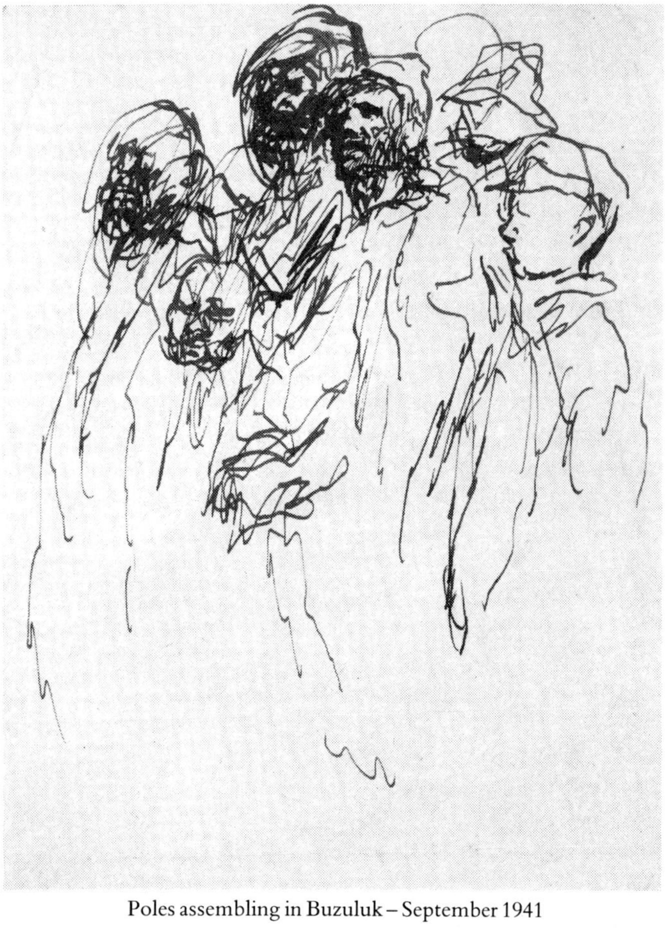

Poles assembling in Buzuluk – September 1941

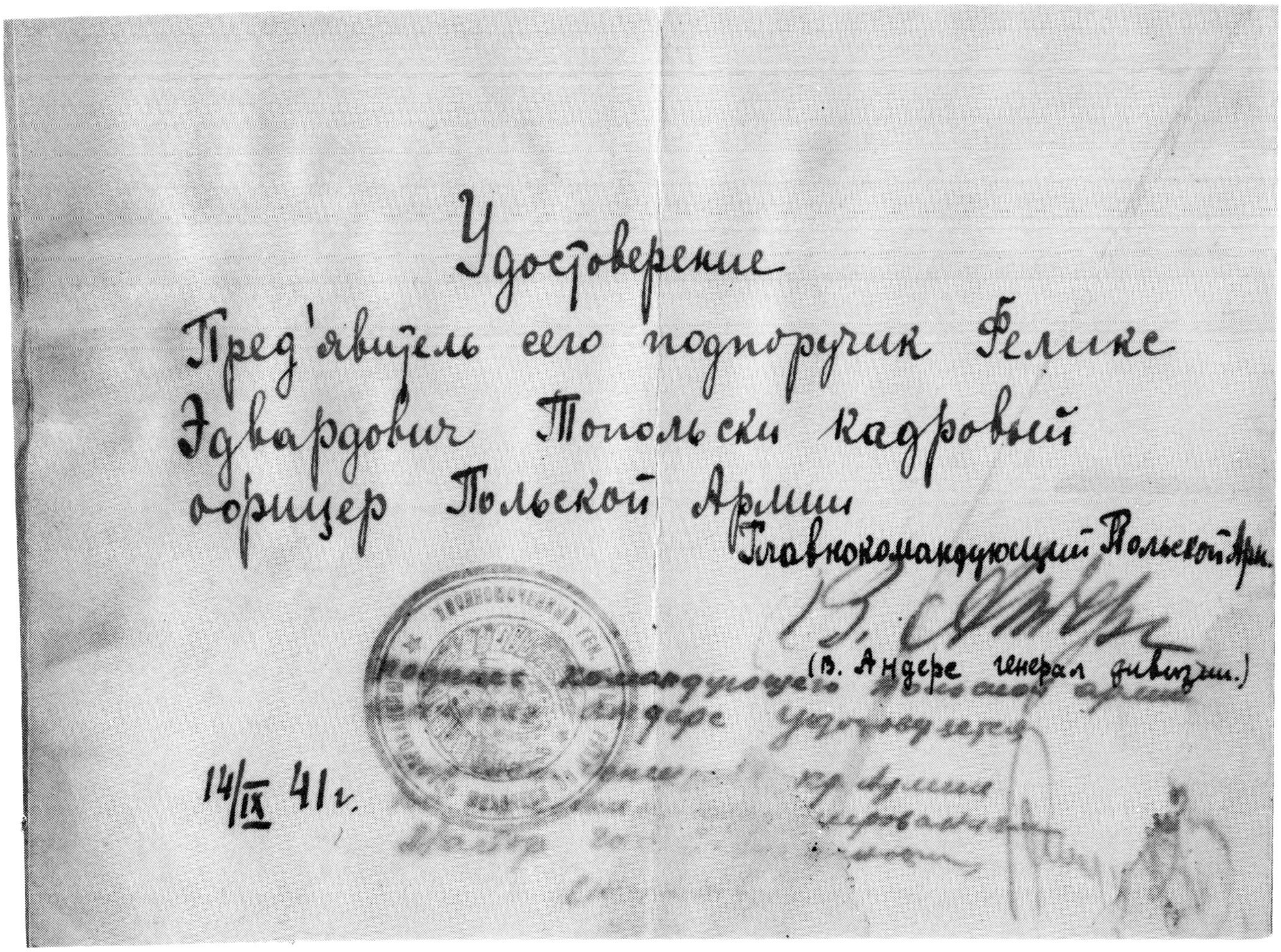

Удостоверение
Пред'явитель сего подпоручик Феликс
Эдвардович Топольски кадровый
офицер Польской Армии
Главнокомандующий Польской Арм.
(В. Андерс генерал дивизии.)
14/IX 41 г.

NKVD safe conduct pass back to Moscow

A link to eight (nine?) years earlier: a smartened-up cadet officer dotted with accessories (buttons/spurs/ribbons/epaulettes/badges) recalled from the bi-annual army exercises in the dull Ruthenian landscape postures by a hospital bed in Warsaw's officers' hospital. His **dying mother**: 'Save me, save me.' He is lost/embarrassed. He is not prepared (nor fitted?) for the ultimate, the tragic. Strangely, or consequently, his sheltered growth within the fiercest times had alloyed into impregnability.

Now, on an eastbound Russian train, this time in battledress, I face (both of us incarcerated for ages) **General Dr Szarecki**, who carved my mother, let her die. Placid conversation drags on, bypasses that matter.

The NKVD attached to the Polish command at Buzułuk gives me an inoffensive slip of paper which will do miracles. I walk the long wide dust-road, to the distant station. The flattest horizon – the highest hot sky, thickly bunched telegraph poles for longest distances. Already Mongol faces. Lenin found his way even to this humble pedestal. Great flocks of crowing crows. Kerchiefed village women posted hieratically at their fences buxom-laugh at me, '*Krasivyi Soldat*.' It will be some four days on this train – against the tide **back to Moscow**: we pass raggedly overloaded (doors and roofs) eastward transports of Poles – later of refugees.

'Hard Class' accommodating. Sleeping shapes shelved above the filled-up but room-making benches: an old peasant: beard and peaked hat; a Moldavian Member of the Supreme Soviet: banner-badged belted *rubashka*; opposite: a military Political Commissar – care-taking of his uniform (hammer-and-sickled red stars on sleeve and breast, red collar patches with romboidal badges – no epaulettes yet; greatcoat self-consciously hugging the shoulders) and brimming with envious curiosity about the West, almost entirely given to matters of manners, thus possible tips, as it were, for his – a careerist's – budding snobbery. And all over, the domino players. And in charge of the carriage, properly insignia-marked, a warm but firm little girl, and a good friend soon, also a tea-brewer.

The Kuibyshev station square – a limitless fires-dotted night display of the refugee/troops/Poles amassment/chaos with bursts of abandon into dance/music/love-fight-making; a great whirl of living at the extremity of survival.

Night also for Moscow station – there boom the anti-aircraft guns – exiting forbidden. My outlandish uniform, supported by force of my mini-Russian, and by my Commissar; but, above all, by my magic NKVD *propustka*, gets me out. I even manage to bed at the *Nationalny*.

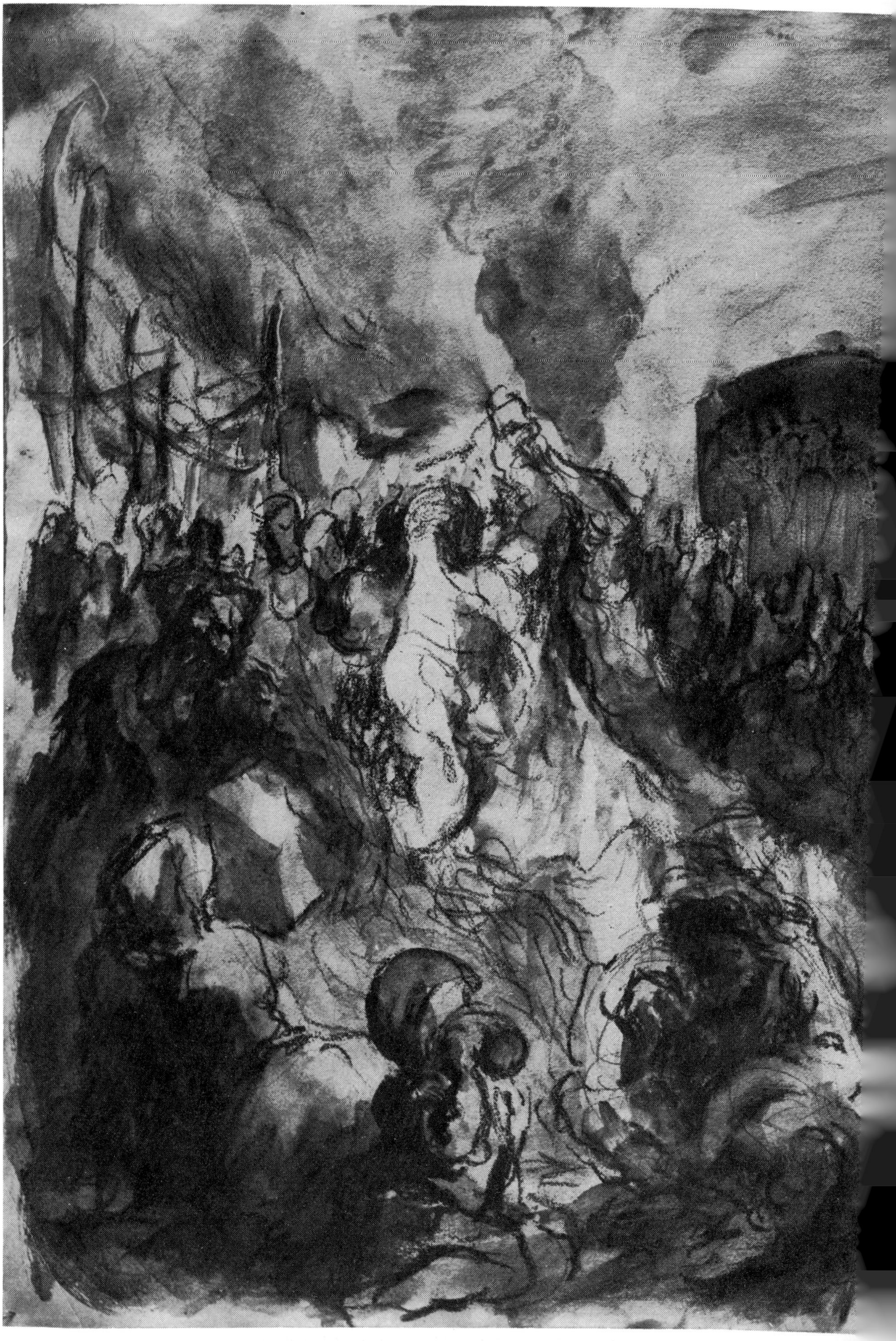

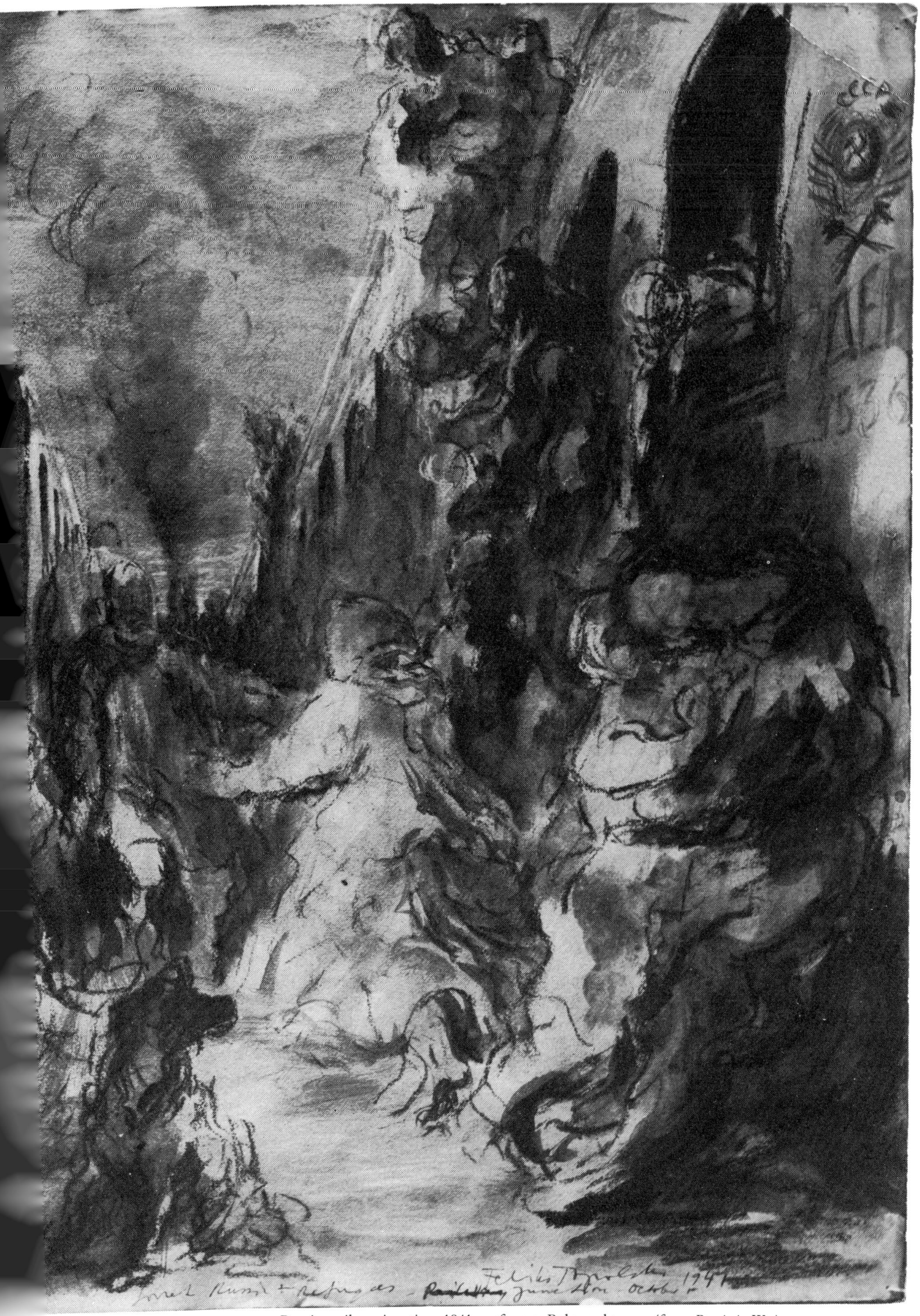

Russian railway junction, 1941 – refugees, Poles and troops (from *Russia in War*)

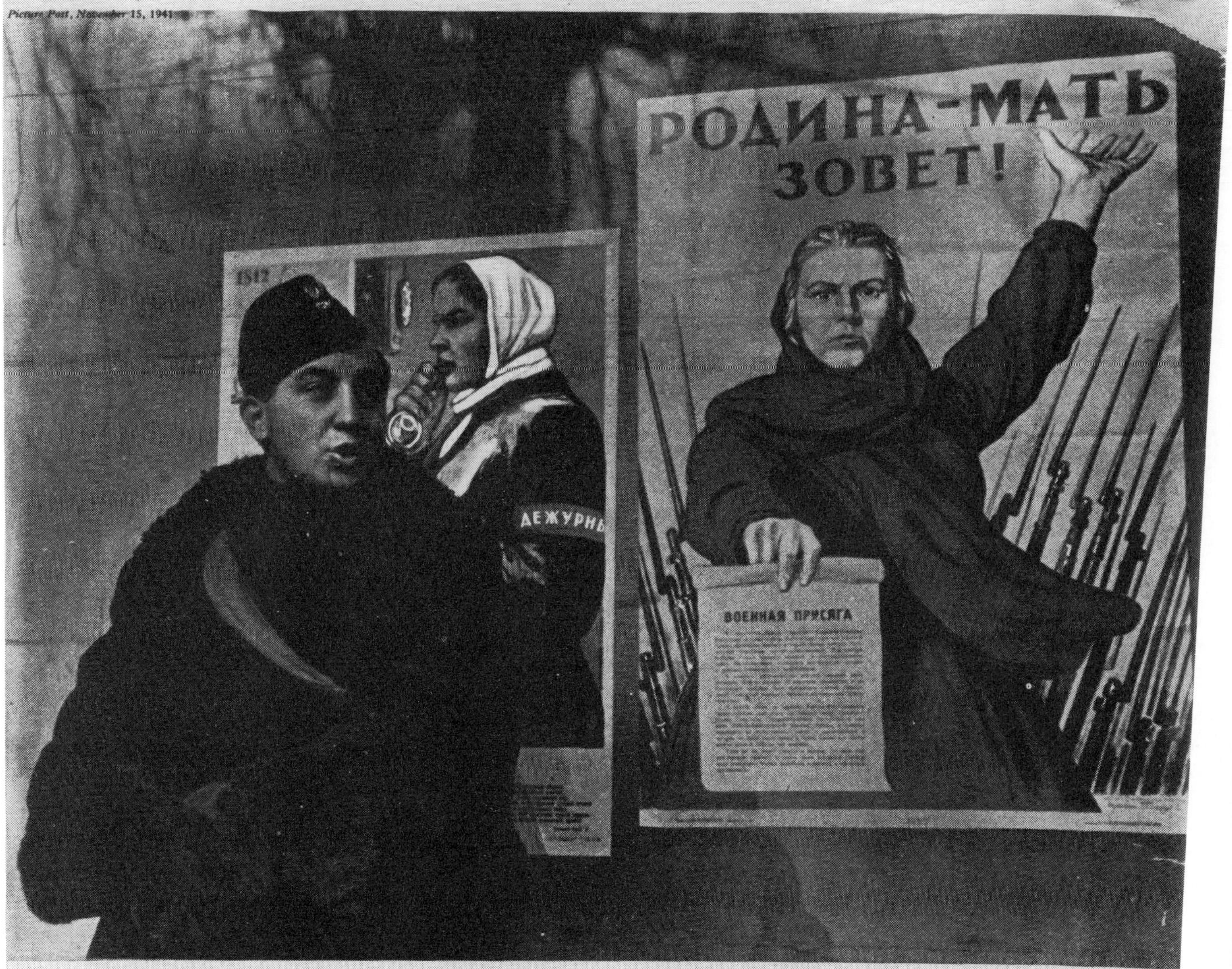

WE SEND AN ARTIST TO THE SOVIET UNION: *Feliks Topolski Sketches the War for PICTURE POST*

He goes to Russia to draw for PICTURE POST. He goes as official artist with the Polish Military Mission sent to help organise the Polish Army in Russia. His last big job in England was a series of drawings on the bombing of London, and he was wounded while he worked. Now he goes to the new front-line, to a country inspired by the message of the poster behind him—"Protect the Motherland!"

CONVOY TO RUSSIA

Vivid photographs of the Russian battle-front are few. The war moves at a great pace. The Russian censorship is strict. Many things are seen which may not be photographed. In such a war the artist has a big advantage. He can see, remember and record. We chose our artist, sent him to Russia. Here are his first drawings—part of the finest record yet made of the most prodigious war in history.

THROUGH the courtesy of a government department I managed to telephone to one of those rare specimens—a man who had returned from Moscow since the beginning of Hitler's attack on the Soviet Union. Could he tell me, I asked, what sort of place Moscow was? Faintly across some hundreds of miles came a hesitating reply, "Well," he said, "it's a large city." I explained that that was no news, but I wanted to know what sort of life people led there. Again there was a pause and then the voice said: "Well, one doesn't dress in the evening." So I shouted my thanks into the telephone, and hung up.

At the last minute they explained that there was no room in one of the very few aeroplanes, and that I should go by sea. Secretly I was delighted, for I loathe flying and I needed a few days of holiday. But I might have to fly home, and the problem of packing all the necessities for an unknown emergency into one small suitcase had still to be dealt with. I did not anticipate that, to reach Moscow from London, I should go far nearer the North Pole than many Arctic explorers, and with no warmer outer-garment than a Burberry, until I borrowed a British warm from Topolski.

We sailed from a Northern port in what an officer who met me there called "a lousy old tub." He was very wrong. Our ship had just returned from the tropics, and, with a deck still looking like a carpenter's shop, she was finishing a record refit in order to reach her farthest North. Her

Page from *Picture Post*

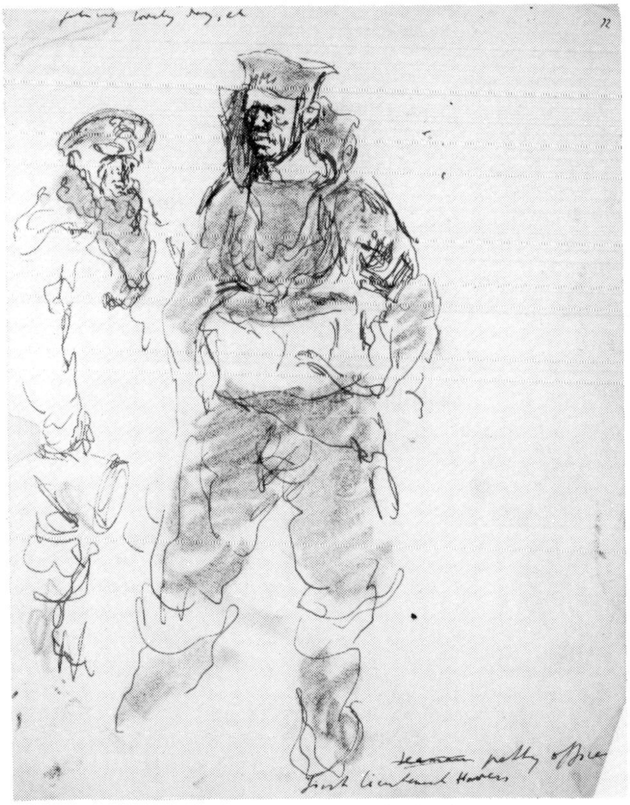

On a British cruiser in the Arctic

Sir Stafford Cripps, the amalgam of contrariness of English high-breeding cum rich Christian socialism, fitted handsomely into the Western palatial convention of the British Embassy across the Moscow river from the Byzantium of the Kremlin and St Basil's Cathedral.

Those ambassadorial figures/stage parts – are they given for the likely physique or do the chosen performers make up and enlarge to act fittingly with their décor? Whichever, Sir Stafford was unmatchable. And got me on to the Arctic out of Moscow, mere hours before the general evacuation eastward.

Wintry Archangel war-blotted. The wounded from the Leningrad front. Troopships. Girl soldiers frost-packaged. British-supplies-supervising Naval Commander monumentally above his Soviet recipients: pipe/stick/towering fur hat.

British minesweeper. The Captain: similar distinguishing ensemble – sartorial non-uniformality (pork-pie hat, beard, duffel coat) over his best-mannered length.

Transition to a **cruiser** (HMS *Suffolk*) at anchor: learning that this will not be a speedy passage to Britain but a full month's duty tour, with two destroyers in tow, criss-crossing the Arctic Seas.

The routine of club-like officers' messroom (old *Illustrated London News* abounding) interpolated by (even for me) stretches on the bridge – in other words hazards and the dozings of cosiness – most appealing. The ratings and the Marines hammocked thickly in any spare spaces and strictly undergoing their drills, always in appropriate formality. (Those on the destroyers prefer their ease.)

This unchallengeable ritual of a multifold hierarchy in control from the bridge to the bowels of the steely advance to the liquid horizons of frosty elements; in co-ordination with or enmity of other floating/flying fortresses; in unending alertness (catapulting the plane for air reconnaissances, signalling, firing 4-inch H.A. guns, sighting enemy aircraft, oiling destroyers for action); in ACTION, dispatching a landing party of Royal Marines, geared for battle, under our two destroyers' cross-protection, to the **Isle of Bear** (in rowing boats!) to subdue **a German post** there as reported. Or much more of an undertaking: a surprise night attack on **a German convoy** sheltering at **the North Cape of Norway.** For this, the previous night (and here my idea of secrecy went to pot) a spectacularly loud exercise was performed – over many sea miles: we, the cruiser, engaging at speed our two destroyers moving at us, in tremendous exchange of blank fire; indeed our presence in these waters revealed, thus shadowed/assisted next day by **German planes.** The following night, 'action stations' *et al.* We moved slowly into the narrowness of the fjord with the destroyers left guarding the entrance. The fullest cannonade from us at the assumed targets – and full-speed retreat back on to the wide seas to gain distance before the daylight and the chase from the air. At least, this was my understanding of the operation.

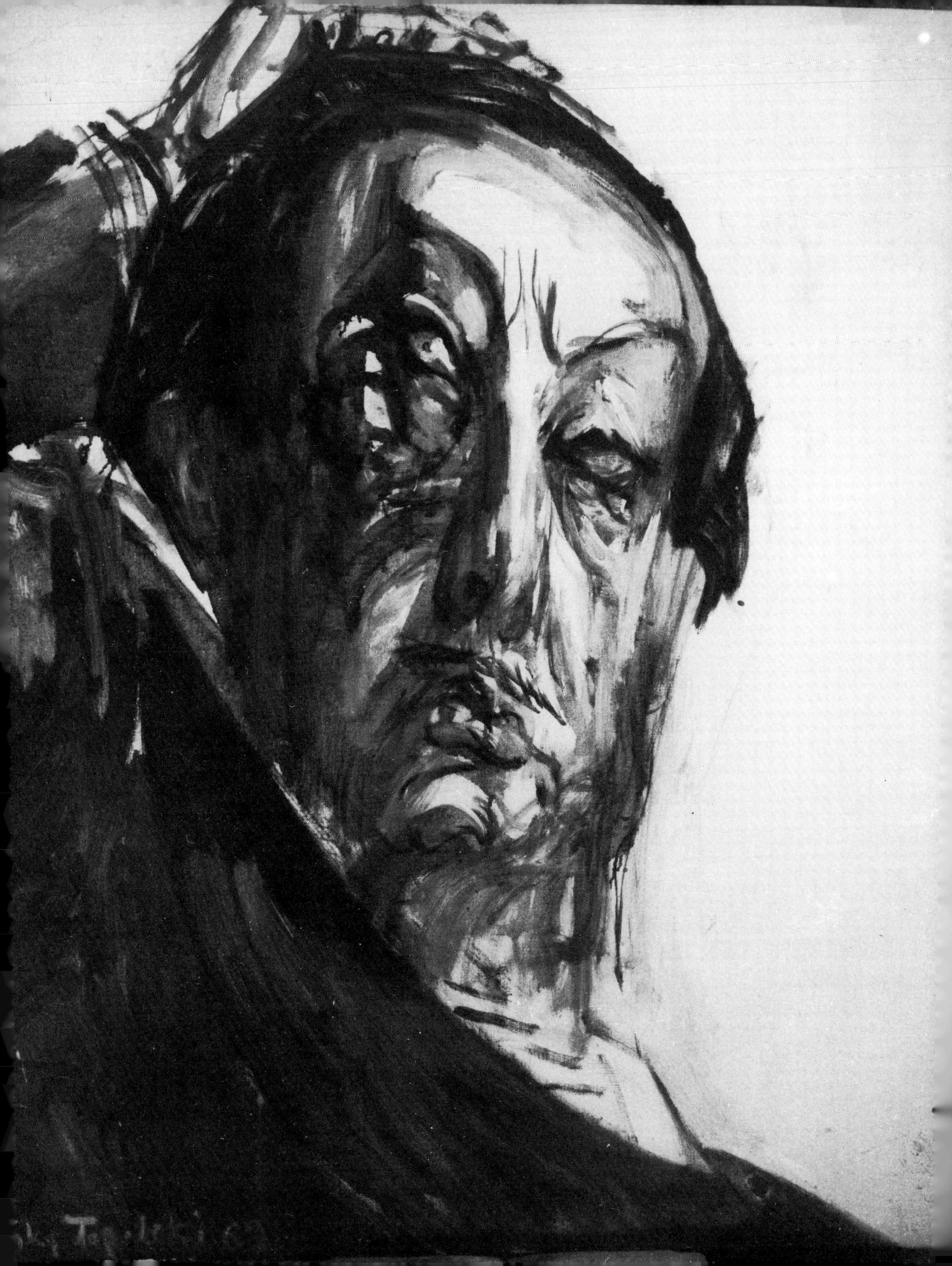

On a war **blackout evening at the Studio**, a batch of decorous ladies garlanded round **King George of Greece**; at the end of very private and unaffected pleasantries, when the farewelling clustered/paused at the door opening to the dark garden, a female voice ceremonially intoned/commanded: 'The King goes first!' A flicker of bafflement. But it was not a protocol matter – the King held the torch!

One war day (1944?): a young Free French Air Force officer of Latin good looks thin-moustache-underlined – this emphasis needed because **Lieutenant Romain Gary** addressed me in a rough Warsaw schoolboy's tongue (of the very school which used to fight it out with mine – they tough, we superior), having started his life as a Russian.

This lovely sensitive brute married **Lesley Blanch**, a supreme *précieuse*, in a harmony of extremes. She used to travel (between Turkey and France) with a very large trunk filled up with her 'home', so that any hotel room could be instantly converted (draperies, pictures, lacy nothings, books, *bijoux* – all Middle Eastern and Byzantine) into her ambiance; he entered her subtleties smoothly – under his man-of-action uniform a budding *littérateur*.

His inner gravity; his gift of concentration: evolved from loadfuls of drawings brought back from the Asian warfronts, I had painted, amongst many, a very small picture of the Yangtze River rapids pressing on a boatful of Chinese soldiers; but not really – this would be the flat reality of what I sketched at the time – the painting turned out to give the elemental struggle purified (by chance) of detailed associations. But I did not strain, while painting it, towards a 'higher' aim. It was Romain's doing to alert me to its strength. And he did it by silence.

The picture stood on an easel and Romain sat himself in front of it. The rest of us drifted to feed and drink in the other room assuming that he would follow. But, his absence prolonged, I went back: there he was, as motionless as when I left him, staring at the painting; and after a further length of time still engrossed. This lasted a long time – possibly as long as it took me to paint it. Indeed he embodied, as only a few can, the intensity of living and appraising.

A grand European (I think German) **art-dealer** at my studio, barely a few years after Romain's visit, sombrely selective until settled on a painting of a group of women, but beyond a factual portraiture, in my view the most successful of all, choosing impressively to be left alone with it. After a long while, curious, I peeped in: he held the work upside down, great concentration visible.

He left, non-communicative (our unmatching languages not helping), then and ever since; but I was clear that his sombre professionalism was checking on my overall worth as an artist – on his terms: excluding emotive/character content which might have disturbed his cold analysis of what – to him and the art values of the time – only mattered: the ability to

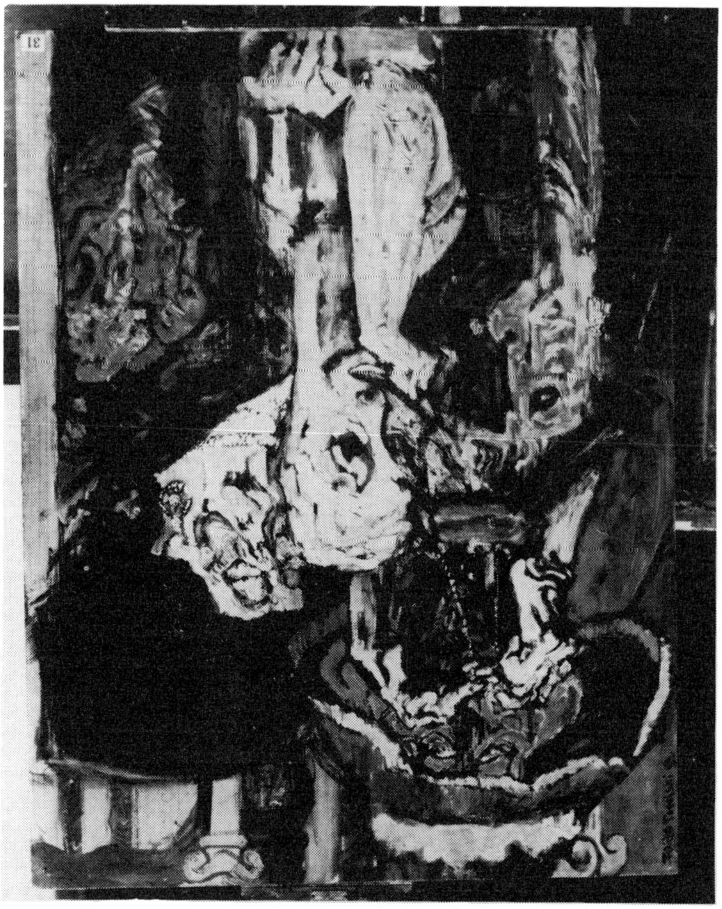

English women, as viewed upside down by a German dealer

handle the abstracts of colour/pattern/brushwork. This exclusion of the very motivation for painting it naturally demoted the picture (and my work in general) to being unworthy of his patronage. But it took him a long while to decide, since he must have been attracted to it, in spite of his rules; I did not bother to sort out whether I had witnessed a contest in him between dealer and 'collector'.

Today's top-gear mercantile propaganda hoists to the top of international sales-success a German painter of upside-down 'figurative' compositions. Is he (subconsciously or deliberately) an inheritor of that dealer's system of values? Have the intervening years devalued all measures of quality/assessment except for this mechanical device?

But a German woman, here a few days ago, had a pat analysis fitting in with her and overall German complexes: this painter, a serious man, suffers from the necessity of putting up with their upside-down immediate past – to him, as to her, this German madness continues – this **German upsidedownness** (her repetitions). In other words she claims that his funk stands for the whole of Germany's on-its-head apotheosis.

Much later, in 1956, I found Romain, now a prominent writer, in Los Angeles in the role of **French Consul**, wrapped in notoriety-legend as a uniquely stylish Californian ladies' man. And in an old Polish way he took it that I must be provided with female company, arranged a cocktail party for

Opposite: Romain Gary

THE SECOND A.E.F.

A PORTFOLIO

OUR FORWARD BASE FOR THE ASSAULT ON EUROPE IS THE BRITISH ISLES, CHIEFLY NORTHERN IRELAND. HERE A GREAT ARMY TRAINS FOR A HISTORIC TASK

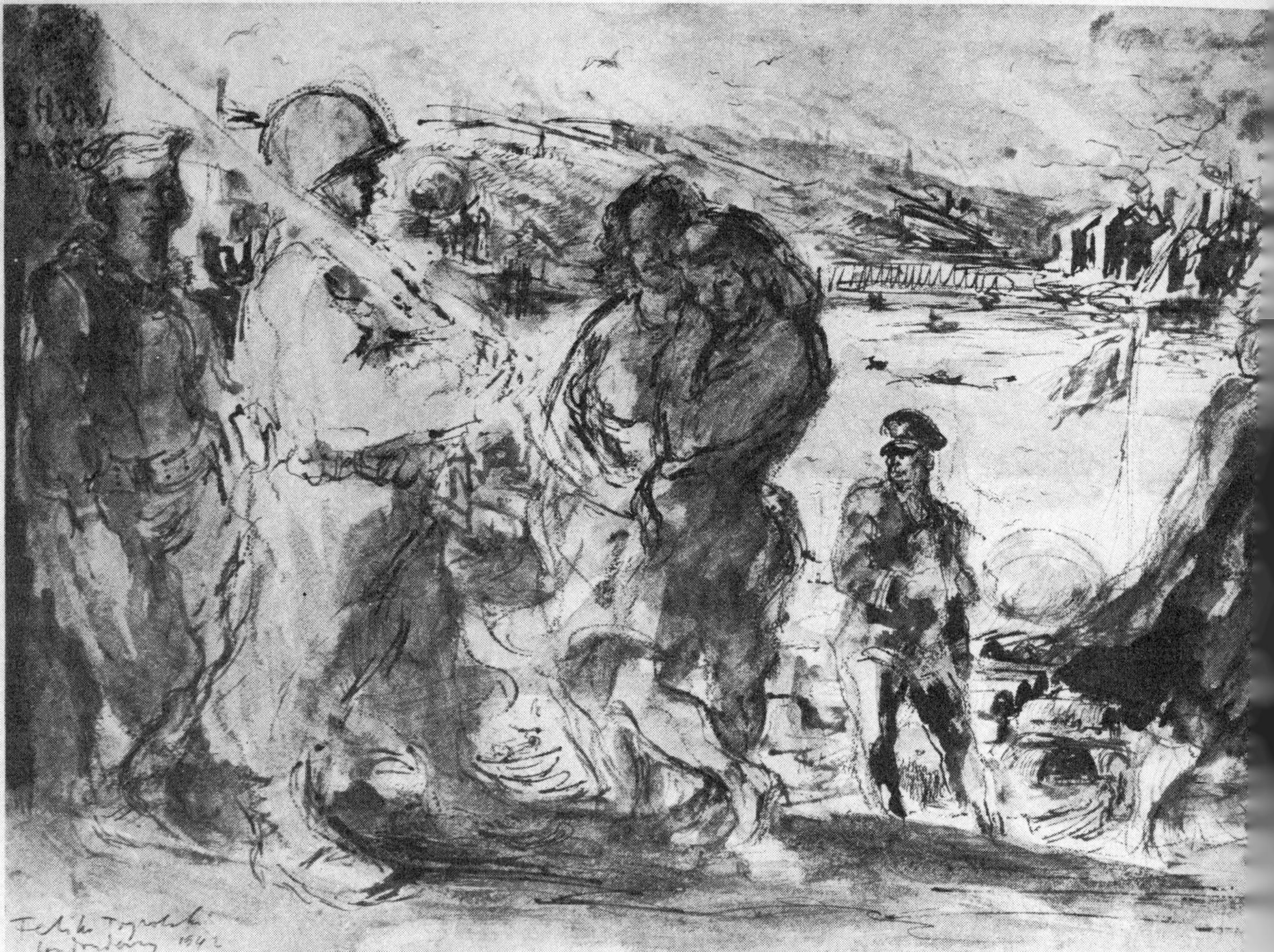

Feliks Topolski, who executed the accompanying portfolio for FORTUNE, was a caricaturist in his native Poland. In 1935 he went to England to sketch the Silver Jubilee, became so fascinated by the flavor and picturesque contrast of British life that he stayed. Thereafter in journals ranging from *Studio* to *Picture Post* he published his keen, satirical but sympathetic impressions of prewar British class formalisms. The war destroyed this subject matter but supplied him with the mood and material that have since made him a truly significant artist. Still essentially a genre painter, a descriptive draftsman in the great tradition of Rowlandson, Hogarth, and Daumier, he has expanded his scope to all mankind caught in the tragedy of war. With his Polish-English point of view he sees the American troops in a fresh way. The sketches here show vigorous and husky young men with heroism implicit in the almost classic arrangement of the figures.

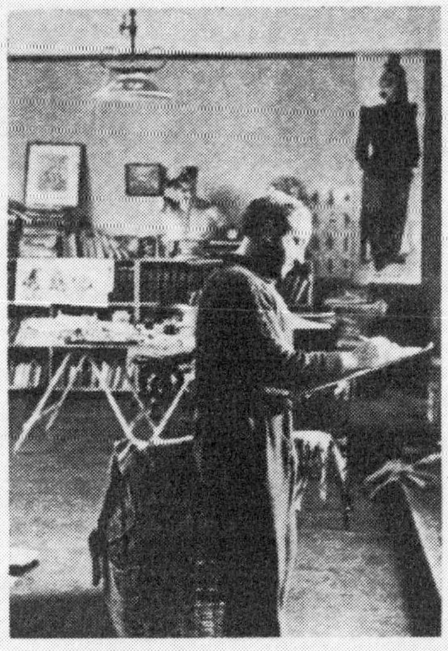

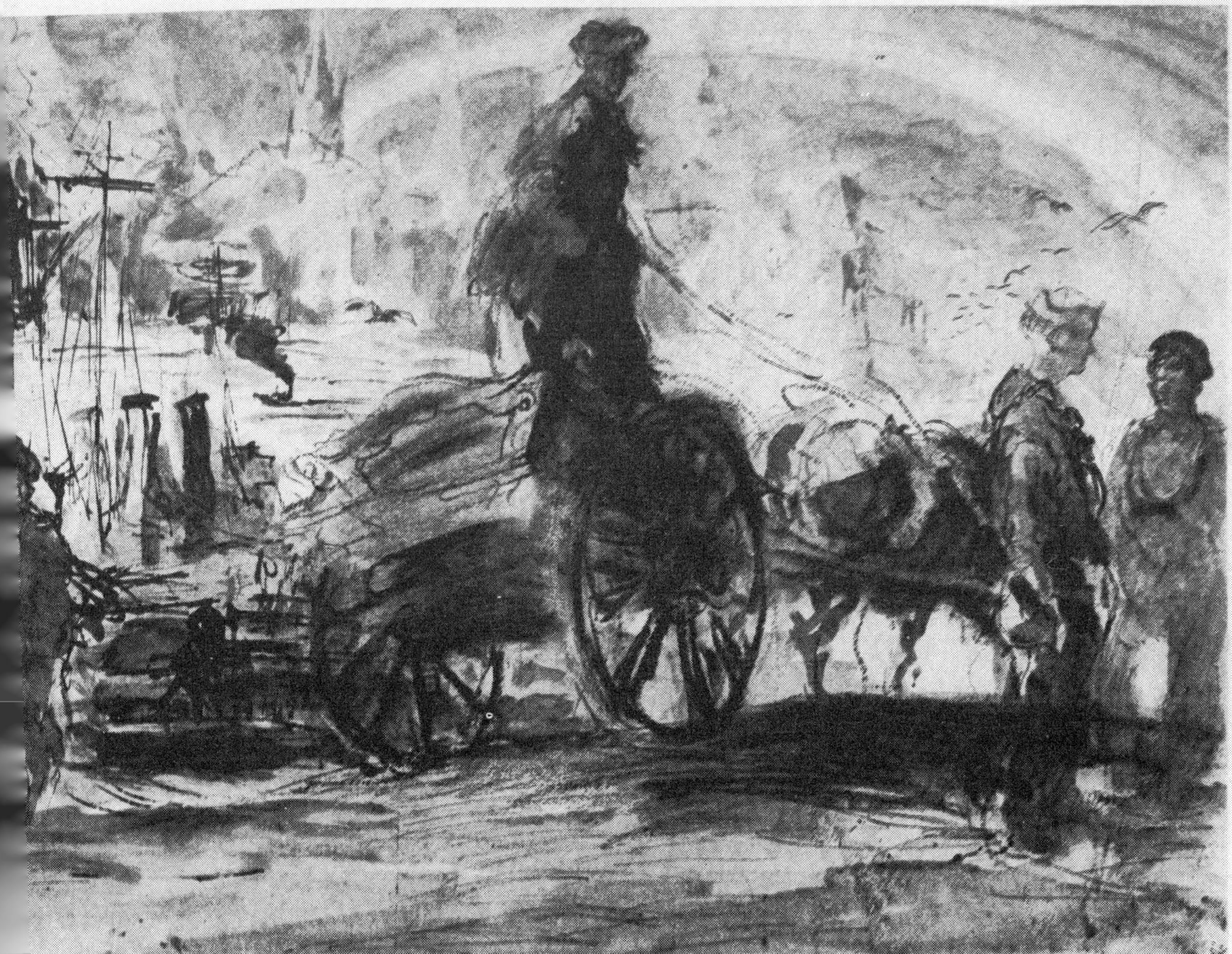

DONDERRY NAVAL BASE, 1942—SAILORS, MARINES, NURSE, BRITISH WREN OFFICER

Double spread from *Fortune* magazine, January 1943

the purpose, instructing me to give a secret sign if impressed, and ended by blessing my departure *à deux*.

On her recommendation, we two settle in a prestigious restaurant, where a first discord registers: I am genuinely curious about Californian wines, never tried; the wine waiter supports me but she is indignant – it must be French, in a well-moulded bottle. At her 'apartment' her status asserts itself: she designs clothes but is **a singer *manquée***, still hopeful – Hollywood of the aspiring and the achieved is not quite hers. And so, tiredness engulfing me, I am bound in the role of obligatorily appreciative audience, while she, in the centre of the room, legs solidly apart, stretches her arms and her voice in prolonged operatic arias.

Having drifted into the above it becomes irresistible to offer a counterpoint. Even in Los Angeles, as anywhere else, there functioned a jousting sphere – populated by the not-too-aspiring, keen on the moment not on the future. There could not be a more entire specimen of North American femininity than the girl (met the night before at a composer's house) who entered my ground-floor room at the Beverly Hills Hotel, rented for me by my CBS Television patrons of the day: her (frequently encountered then) naive pouting and swaying *à la* Marilyn apart, she was superior to her ideal, being 'natural' in gingery blondness, freckled whiteness, well-leggedness, and well-held small-bustness; and her complete devotion to **unadorned physicality.** One of my greatest lovelessly bacchic afternoons.

Later, in Romain's *Prix Goncourt* days, I drew and painted his giant head-portrait – possibly our last meeting.

Since then, one of the leading novelists of France, with his face, to match, given a beard, he slotted fully (this is only hearsay) into sternness – leading him to a chain of **ultimate tragedies**.

Was the early Romain, with his cynic's armour (or core) overcome by circumstances? Or did the marriage drama become a destructive force when welded to that very boyish pride? I have no right to toy any further with Romain Gary's last sombre years, distant from me.

The magic/rapture/exhilaration of entering othernesses. England was such. Russia was a different matter, *terra incognita*, an enigma to be cracked. The supremest elation came in 1944 when the Occident gave way, for the first time, to the Orient – not yet when convoyed through dangers round Iberia and the Mediterranean at the presences of Lascar seamen, though this was the proper overture – not even yet at the entry in squalls (was it Hamsim?) into the resplendently luminous, gull-resounding, ship-hooting, felucca/dhow/sail-dotted old-print panorama of the hue-and-cry port of **Alexandria** – a mounting promise – until: with the mooring, there rushed at the ship's hulk, inconceivably outlandish as reality yet wonderfully related to childhood's imaginings, a mob of thieves of Baghdad – their flowing ruggedness (rags streaming off their heads), their overstressed ruffian shapes and overtinted bearded masks, their gesture-

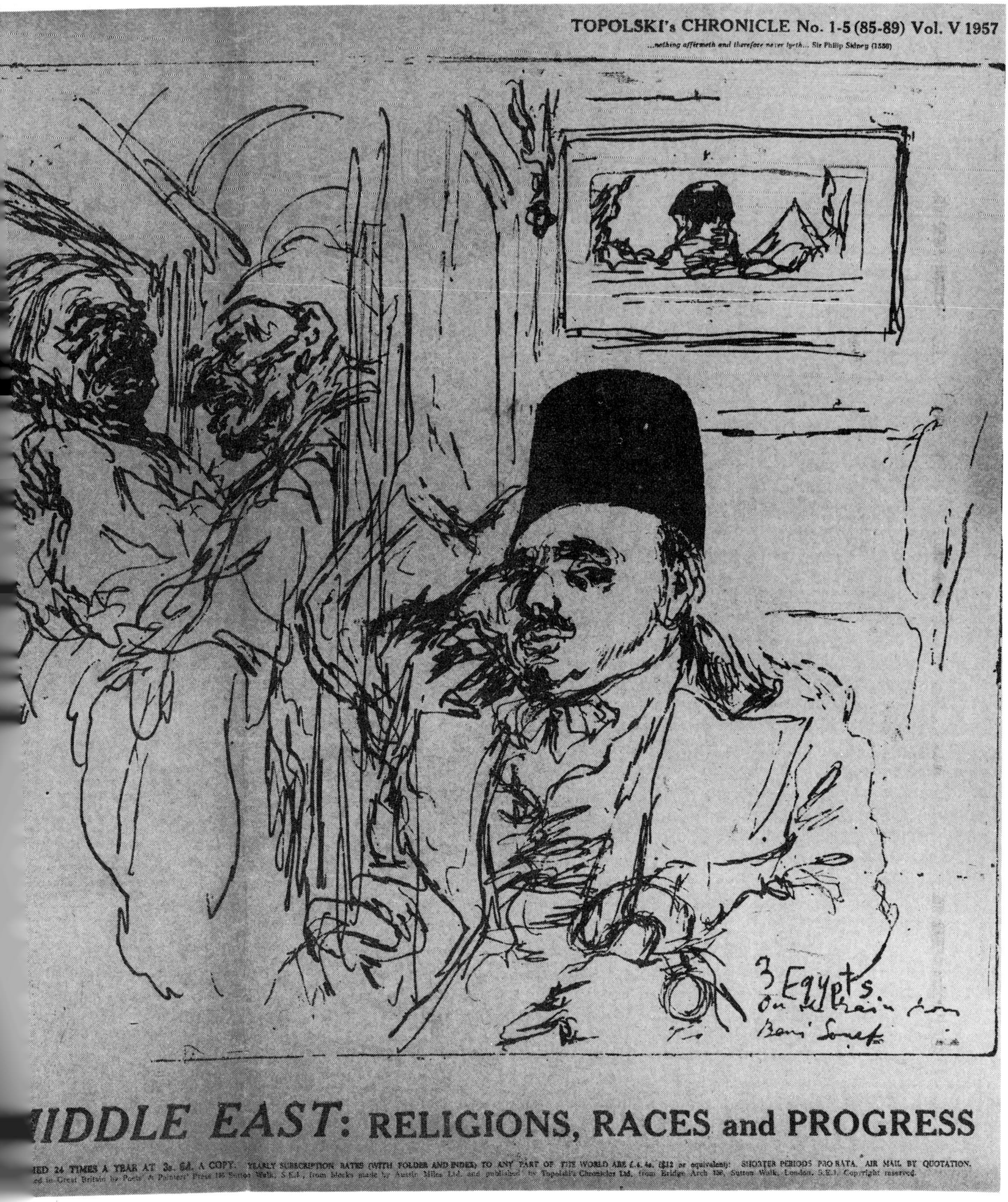

Cover of *Topolski's Chronicle*

and-talk agitation! Then the histrionic crawl of beggars; the gallop of small boys – selling and stealing; and in the centre rock-still police – black, hooded coats to the ground, tarbooshes.*

The short train journey to Cairo makes up **the fullness of Egypt**: Nile valley men-and-beasts dream-exotic rurality outside masses at small stations into multitudes of another era, another world, and emanates two sempiternal *fellahin* into the corridor outside our compartment. Inside, a photograph of the Sphinx and Pyramid above – seated opposite me – a round young narrow-moustached *élégante*-lawyer, a tarboosh, a velvet-collared *paletot*, a bow-tie, a gold-ringed stick . . .

There must be a hidden but overriding rhythm in humanity's hither and thither undulatory disorders. My routes led, between 'theatres' of conflicts, over lands of assured calm, which would flare up soon after in fiendish upheavals. A single African's or Arab's total repose, as if everlasting, would flash straight out into cat-like action; the sedative gentle tribes/cities/nations erupt, not a tremor predicting, murderously.

The Levant in 1944 lived, cosily and sardonically, oblivious towards our bumping over the war roads, united in its decorous pattern of tarbooshed, turbaned and burnoused Moslems, black-pot-hatted Maronite or Russian Orthodox priests, fur-hatted or black-trilbied Jews, brown-habited Catholic monks. Only **Jerusalem and Tel Aviv**, permeated by newcomers from Europe, exuded a promise, perhaps, of tensions. But **Syria and Lebanon** snoozed in relaxed conjunction – our khaki traffic eliminating the frontiers – of noble yellow landscape nobly populated by robed/kerchiefed elders, caryatid women, hand-holding puff-trousered youths, drape-floating mounted Bedouins at a gallop. Then waterwheel Tyre; then **Aleppo**'s elevated castle circled by leisure – uninterrupted by motors – of flowing styles, horses, donkeys, camels; then Homs's natural order of delightfully unthreatening confident brothels and singing ladies. In the Druzes' hills richly dressy weddings (the dowry sewn all over the bride). And the entry into **Damascus** sang with cascading/springing/streaming/spraying/jetting/welling-up water fantasia; the Omayyad Mosque, intimidating but also fatherly tender, murmuring with rows of Koran readers (white-wrapped tarbooshes, white beards) squatted in dwarf enclosures at their massive volumes; in the evening the darker hospitality of Dervishes: shadows evolve sombre turbaned heads – their all-ages secretive/emphatic faces (a bare-headed boy's from behind a white-beard's) set round the space on to which the devout dancers would glide to rotate, at first stately, then engulfed in their speedier and speedier orbiting white skirts (the high-coned white hats – serene pivots).

Harsh all-night passage, zigzagging roadlessly across desolation, brings **Baghdad** steaming supine at the Tigris's edge; but the opposite course along happier roads ascends **Ba'albek's Roman Acropolis**, still dominant, even though

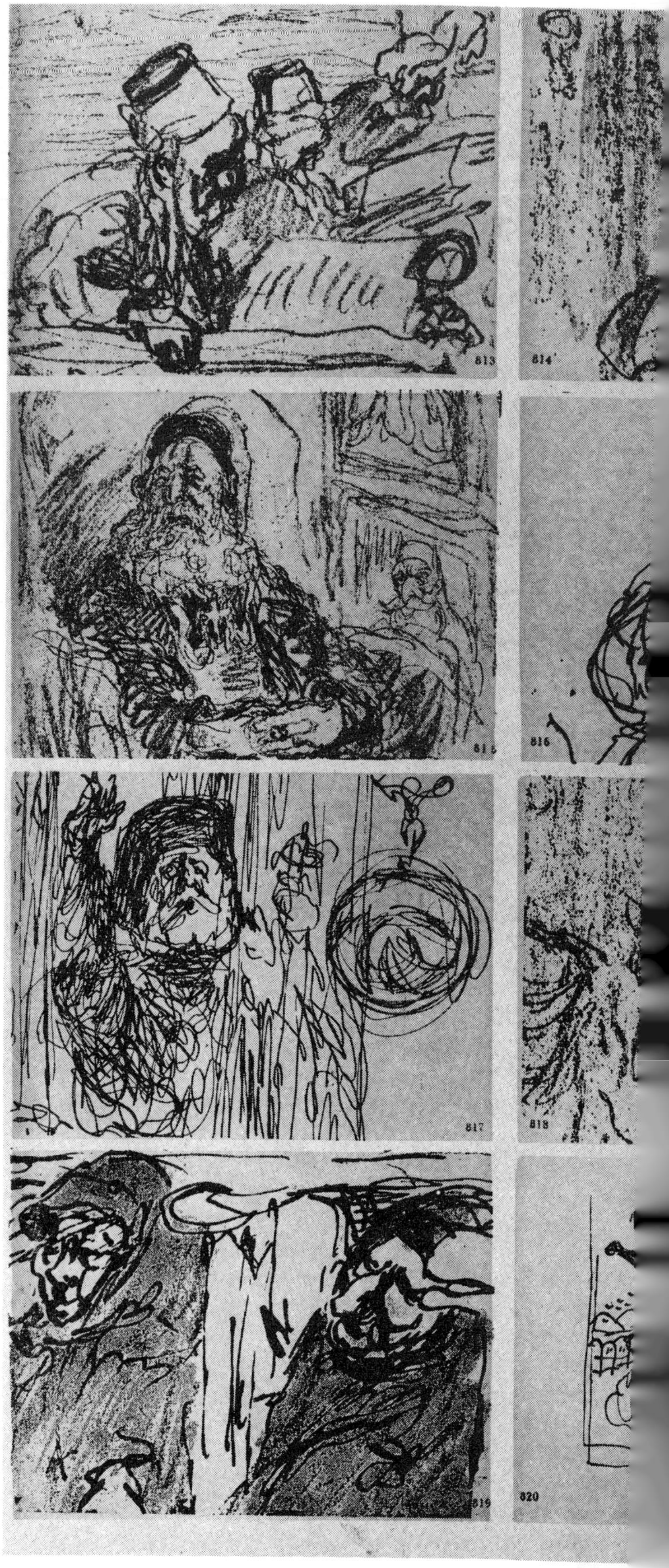

*The East fed well my predilection for a first-timer's unforeseen astonishments. A later minor feast on encountering **the Tropics**: landing in humid Calcutta on a flight from scorching-dry Delhi and, fetched at Dumdum airport by two dutiful British officers, riding in a jeep through sudden vegetal exuberance. Although the baobab trees carried rubber-condom adverts, enchantment at this first humble sample of the explosive Tropics descended on me and I tried to pass my joy to my companions: their deadened mute discomposure – disbelieving their ears and too mystified at my status to embark on jests – told me all about junior British officers posted in the Eden of Calcutta.

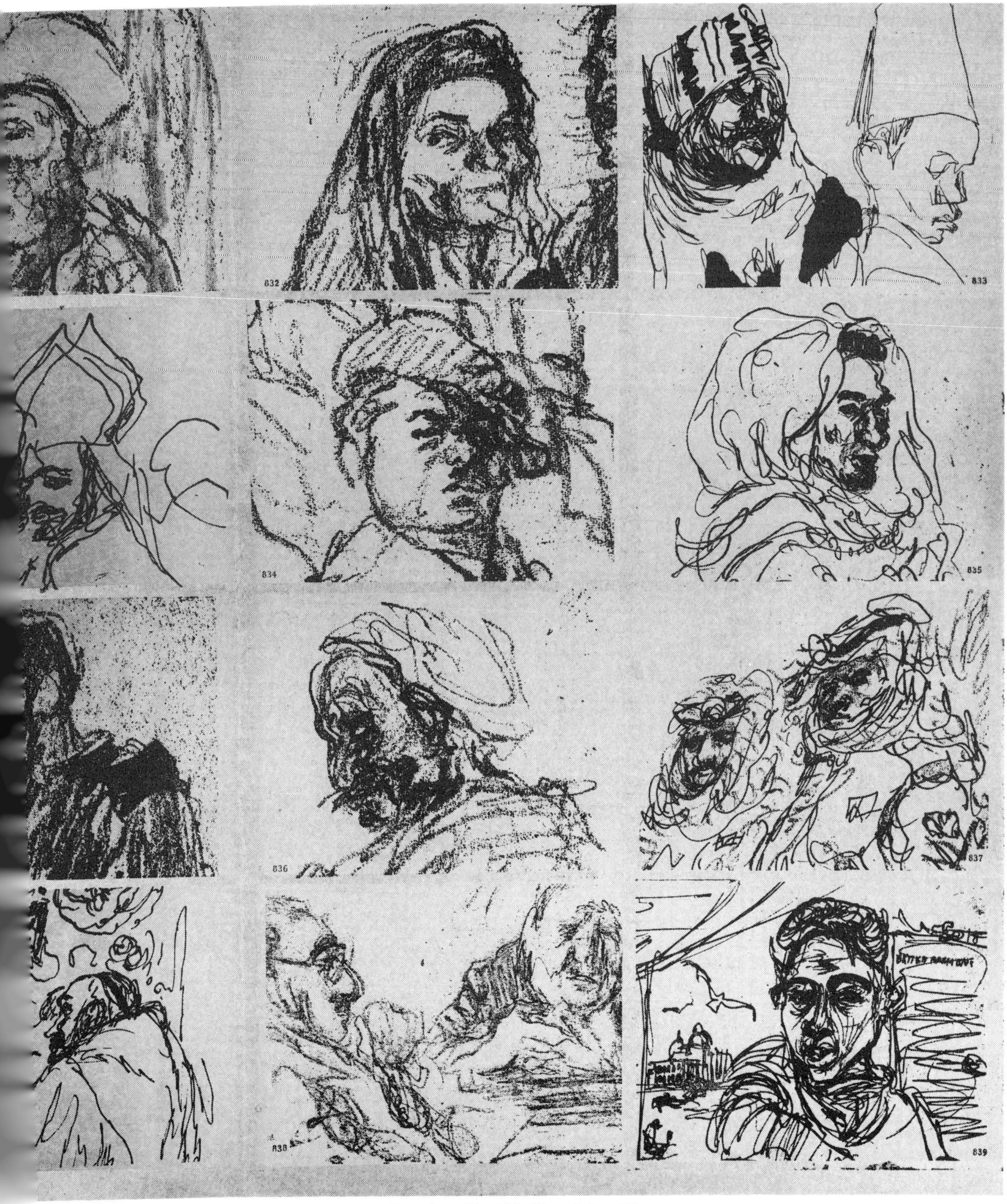

Pages from *Topolski's Chronicle* (as p. 93)

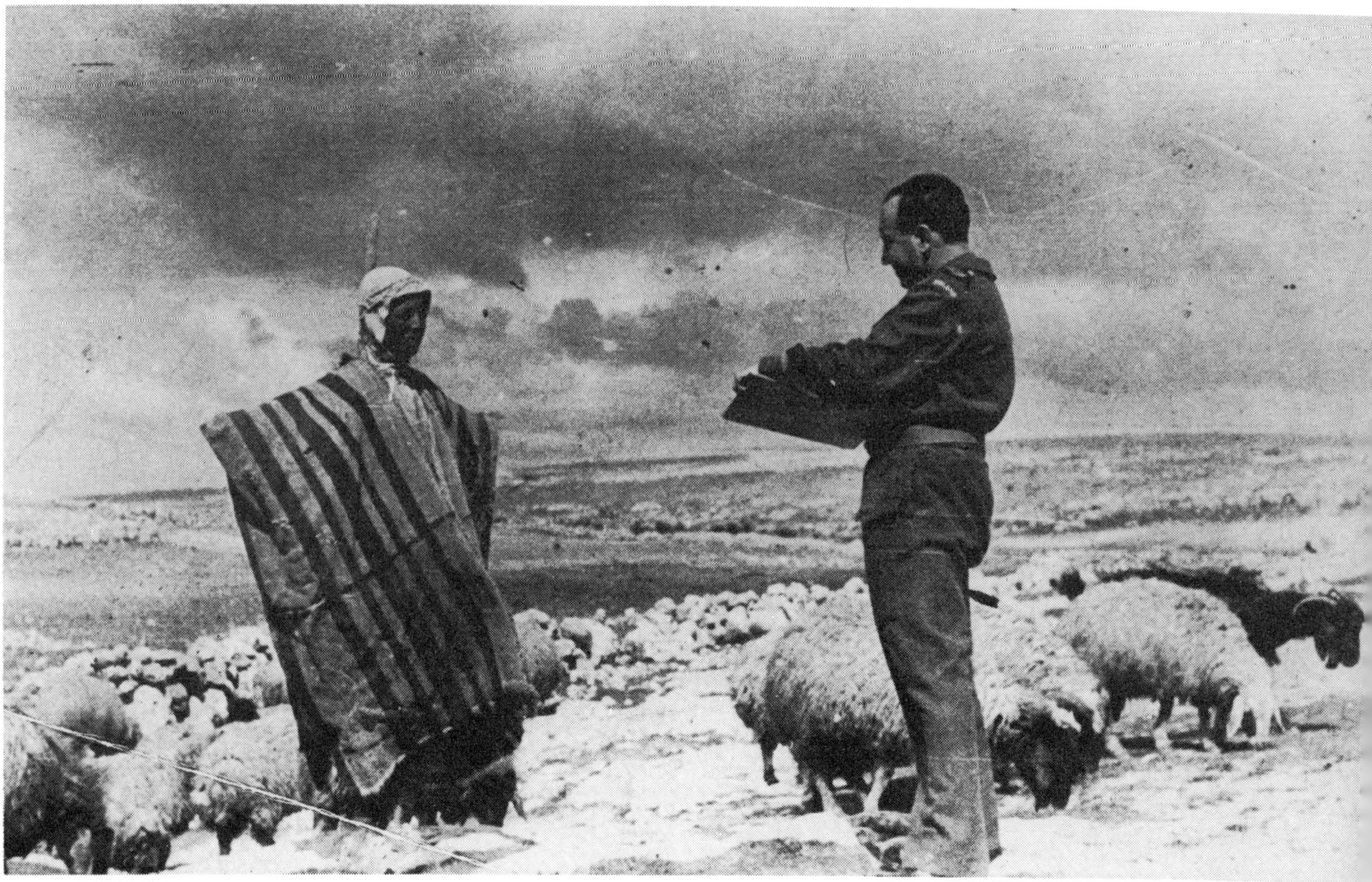

In Levant

used for its lion-headed pedestal by two seated, unlikely legionaries: below, a forage-capped, pensive British enlisted man – *Syria-Lebanon Guidebook* in hand; higher up a bereted Syrian soldier, attempting a pose of might. But the thorn and nettle clumps bristling out of ancient cracks mitigated these layers of recent history; and so, the batch of Ba'albek village worthies at roulette: the tarbooshed Mayor (calligraphic tatooage on his rolling-worrybeads-hand; Hadji Habibrahiv – also beads, an ancient topee and collar-tie; Jassem Farra – ringed fingers elegantly laid on a stick, well-trained moustache and well-bound headscarf.

Through a charmingly diverting village of **Alaouits** – their black dramatically shaped head-hoods, prolonged down their backs by wrapped-round ends, engulfing in shadows their moody faces – to the old and touching Basta quarter of **the Kurds**, with their women's indescribable folk elegance: they move on bare feet, bent backward – necks erect, under tilted-forward round flat headpieces, set atop wrappers playing hide-and-seek with their features; and their good height hung over by many-layered tabards (and of many fabrics, up to the top one of patterned homespun wool), ground-reaching and belted – and open to ankle-bound bloomers.

But then **Beirut** proper, a happy mixture – with the French accent (though besides de Gaulle, also Stalin on posters); the *Grand Sérail* military HQ with descending dandified **French officers** – an open tunic over coloured waistcoat, stick in hand, light blue kepi tilted – and Senegalese sentries presenting arms; *Le Quartier Sursock*: **the high society** hostess French-spoken, narghile-smoking, high-fashion-turbaned – that is, demonstratively *la Parisienne* stylized into native *je ne sais quoi* – within an interior oriental cum French-doubtful – *Louis-quelconque*; the Government House antechamber nicely adorned by finely turned-out clients, surveyed by a be-roped/aiguilletted adjutant: a group of white-over-red hatted, robed mullahs; a bearded Jesuit; tarbooshed but lounge-suited citizens in hands-awhirl converse; and, in the innermost sanctum, **the Cabinet meeting**, with the President (a long cigarette holder), the Prime Minister (the only tarboosh), the Vice-Premier, and Minister of Justice (small glass at his mouth and worrybeads fondled), Minister of Foreign Affairs (young and shaven) – sedate unperturbed rulers of an easygoing borde country growing rich, and sure of its 'civilized' East–West ever-richer future.

A complementary court: His Beatitude **the Moronite Patriarch** receives; plenty of velvet folds and holy oleographs backing the white-bearded threesome – another scene of permanency. And also, up in the hills, at **the Malula Monastery** presiding over a Christian village, Père Grégoire Abusama amongst his icons, high above and untroubled by th surrounding 'Western' worldwide turbulence; after some prayers, an Arab boy gracefully robed enters with a trayful of tiny coffee cups.

Even not so many years ago (**1964**), possibly still more confidently, Beirut stood out amongst the Middle Eastern uncertainties as the unshakeably reliable international trading/banking and pleasure post. Its opulence (social and hotel-transitory), its refinements (nightlife and the beaches), its all-permeating reasonableness (in the manner of Western hypocrisy crossbred with Eastern Allah-blessed marketing corruptions).

Yet that proven oasis of interacting correlations soon erupted with and feeds on unhinted unreconcilable hates.

Cairo – Bombay – Cairo

Official wartime trust was put in the patriotic loyalty of 'pedigree' girls: thus the 'war effort' recruited them for the British Embassies as **cipher clerks** to handle crucially secret messages. **Barbara** became one in Cairo and, when in 1944 I began to criss-cross Asia and Africa with Cairo as the junction, she prepared a room at **Shephard's Hotel** for our cosy reunions. But cosiness was soon challenged: after a short stay together in **Luxor** we sensed on our return in the evening enough unwelcoming tension in the Moorish reception area to send Barbara up the back stairs, for appearance's sake, her status being that of spinster. This turned into a slapstick chase – the horde of long-gallabiahed and tarbooshed *safragis* and Nubian porters racing up after her, and, finally, gathering outside the room with bangs and shouts: the room was single, not double, but also there was a rule about night visitors.

For my next return she reserved a double room and all was peaceful. This was after my longest absence – in India, Burma and China – during which Barbara was introduced to and entertained by **King Farouk**: for my last *thé dansant* in the garden at Shephard's before my departure had been routinely adorned by the bulk of the King attended by the stylish British liaison officer, his liaison concern being with English pulchritude. We danced, singled out for intense scrutiny, so we felt, by Farouk's party. And soon indeed the master of liaisons presented her with an invitation for a weekend at the King's summer palace; what followed was put down much later, and with precision, by Barbara in the first of her several comic novels. With all this going on, she found one morning on her desk at the Embassy a polite note suggesting that, in view of her duties, she might be associating too much with non-Britishers. Did it mean Farouk, myself, or others unknown to me?

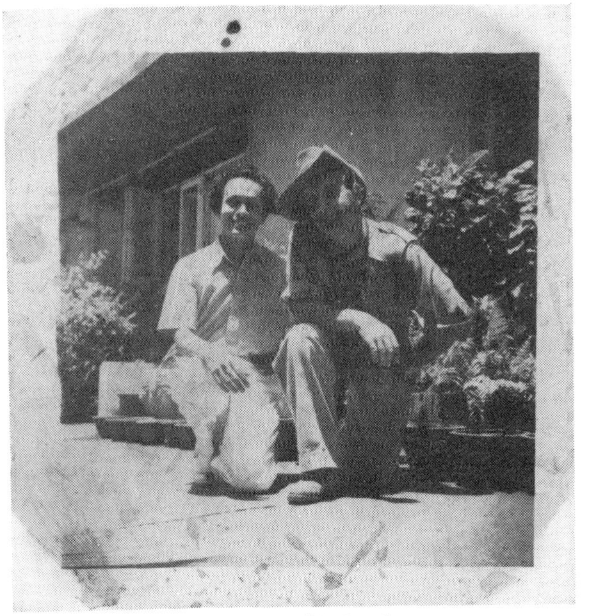

With Ram Gopal in Bombay

Now India. Or rather, my **last days in India** as the link with the return to Cairo's double room. As a youngish second lieutenant I was nothing, but as a dual War Artist, well introduced by friends in England and received by the Viceroy, the Governor of Bengal, the Congress Party worthies, also Mr Jinnah, the maharajas, the army, the universities and the artists, and a sort of celebrity in the Polish sphere, I must have mattered enough to deserve, when in Bombay, a drive out of the city for a day with **Mahatma Gandhi** (a noble Polish lady in a sari, his follower, and a gentle poet Mr Batha took me to meet him) and a reception in my honour given a few days later by the **Mayor of Bombay**.

Also, in between, came the joy of a night rendezvous with **Ram Gopal** at a railway station halfway between Bombay and Bangalore, the city of his dance gurus, to travel back together to Bombay, where he was keen to demonstrate his progress by dancing for me at the next evening's reception. This was a pre-war friendship begun with his triumphant season in London: the most beautiful enchanting creature, groomed by an amateur manager, a Polish poet and my old friend, Alexander Janta, who found Ram dancing with a travelling group in Tokyo, fell in love with him and lifted him from obscurity.

Marion, then a 'starlet' in Korda's publicity circus, insisted on taking Ram to the London Films studios in Denham, where *Elephant Boy* with Sabu was being shot: the film was well advanced and there was no room in it for the princely Ram Gopal. He faced there Sabu, a squat peasant boy subdued by this unmatchable grace. The railway reunion, five years later, and the journey in a compartment penetrated by the dust of the land, kept us blabbering all night long, so that on arrival in Bombay my voice was gone: gravelly whispers were all I could muster for my occasion at the Parsee Mayor's house. And there in the sumptuosity of the interior, flower-laden, lavish eatables, the multi-racial 'exclusive' crowd, stood out this **Botticelli blonde**, not just because in contrast to the rest, but because of her singularity – the Swedish wife of the brother of the host.

Impossible for me to give a factual tale of what went on. This was a stroke of infatuation I ought to have been incapable of, led throughout my life that far by self-conscious detachment. Here, with me being the centre of attention – and she, of course, as well, with her beauty, her social position and instant harmony with me – we disregarded our duties towards our public roles.

And how, handicapped horribly by my hoarse whisper, and within the crowd containing her watchful husband, did I convey to her my adoration and receive reciprocality? We were, I suppose, inapproachable in the magic circle of our instant love (because this is, indubitably, what it was) whispering, yes, of elopement – of life together ever after. Ram changed costumes for each dance, generously and meticulously partnered by his former girl pupil whom he had dug out in Bombay. I even tried to sketch flimsily in infrequent moments of pretence at justifying myself.

The end of the party: she leaves with her husband (an assignation for tomorrow fixed) and I with Ram. Now the utter change, the waking up or escape from passion (which had enwrapped-imprisoned my free-wheeling egotism) into levity. Ram, roguish trooper to the fore, gives his boyish mocking admiring resumé of my and Birgitte's behaviour. We walk along the seashore round **the Gate of India** under the star-infested sky in laughing *duetto*.

Without going back at this point to **a fraction of Cairo** it will be impossible to give full resonance to this tale. Cairo, for me, a leave-town of many layers, most often non-converging. There gathered a rather exclusive collection of my old homosexual friends elegantly transformed into officers of various allied nations (mostly English and one Greek) and denominations, entirely happy at the city's provisions for their pleasure: and, in my fresh enchantments with Exotics enhanced by the ever-prancing ballet of fetching urchins, I told these friends that, if ever, it is now and here for me to taste what they would be glad to provide.

The usual source of their satisfactions were **the Turkish baths.** I was instructed that, once in, I had to accept what came. One of my friends, the Greek, led me into the steaming penumbra, settled to wait through my ordeal, secure in the immaculateness of his uniform, while I, helpless in a cotton robe and clogs, found that I could not choose my partner/masseur, that they came in a rota and that, from amongst many charmers, there moved at me a man – not a boy – of square harsh shape and pockmarked angry face.

The rest was predictable pathos. A tattily curtained cubicle; the pantomime of danger and secrecy; I, laid naked on a high table and the monster busy soaping solely my penis, which raised mechanically, unassisted by com-passion. Time was passing, the man growing impatient, until (enough is enough) I shut my eyes, imagined being with a woman and by this device ended the experiment.

This camaraderie with lovely Ram unforgivably redirected that evening's earlier palpitations: the cold-blooded plan to use Africa–Asia for filling in this particular gap in my collection of experiences re-emerged, the touch of tipsiness helping.

We go to my room in the **Taj Mahal** – a tiny room with an oddly high bed and a tightly glued-to-it bathroom. Ram perches on the bed cross-legged and takes me aback by an instant switch of mood: he embarks on a romanticized tirade, stuffed thickly with calm seas, moons, swaying palm trees – all-in-all, nature and humans as sentimental cronies. I suppose that, the unspoken accord having been reached, his desiderium is for the atmospheric overture; yet some practical words percolate as well, while the flow of his purple fantasies grows in intensity, unobtrusively (in brackets so to speak): that he will stay on, that (coyly) he will take the bed and I the carpet.

But I could not wait any longer – I had to deal most urgently with my food-bloated belly. I excused myself, perhaps too abruptly; he caught in that little space (in front of the thin partition), my performance must have been coarsely assailing all his senses, and for a very long while.

When I emerged, Ram had already slid off the bed and now matter-of-factly announced he was leaving for his lodgings, instantly.

So much for my second and last attempt at enlightenment in that direction.

Having gone this far in self-disclosures, what comes next must not be omitted, as these inconsistencies may be a common condition but customarily concealed under current anathemas, lived or wistful.

Next morning I went to see the sculptures of a grand English girl, a friend of Birgitte, and did not try to tame my urge to pursue her amongst her impressive pieces. **The trinity**, interlocking and complemental: the sculptress provoked sexual urges, Ram presented uncharted territory, and the Swede materialized the dormant fabled ideal.

In the afternoon Birgitte and I met at a **Europeans Only** club – cunningly to be secure in our *tête-à-tête*. We were in harmony and, my vocal powers having returned, planned the future, though elopement had to be postponed, my marching-flying orders, as always via Cairo, being set (desertion would not be my style) for the early hours of the next day. This dialogue evolved with dignity in a quiet recess by the pool. And as the conclusive stamp on our treaty I clicked my old Roleiflex at her twice, after which we rode in one of those antique, jubilantly open and colourful Daimler taxis driven by a turbaned white-bearded Sikh to my hotel, my little room, our **consummation.** But as soon as we locked the door, there came a gentle knock: I had forgotten my popularity; palms clasped, Mr Batha enters with his gentle farewells and gifts; he and several others had waited outside the room for my return and, now, they all entered, smiles and hands supplicant, tender; Birgitte towers over us all, with sweetness and acceptance.

And there was to come another and yet another turn to the story. **In Cairo** Barbara, when told of my Bombay beauty, showed for the first time during our friendship some disquiet – and we both waited tensely for **the two little photographs**, now gaining major importance, to be printed. In a little shop* we confronted them – I in a shock of disbelief, she relieved: the miserably amateurish two-by-two prints presented an indifferently plain female. This was – more than bad photography – the absolute opposite to the radiant reality. Of course, her fascination transcended her beauty but was engendered by it. The photographs denied all, offered ordinariness.

To bypass the occupational soldier's oscillations between battling and wenching: was I then (circumstances breeding delusions) bewitched? 'The circumstances' – too meek a word for the pressure of the dwarfing absorption, at under-a-year's swoop, of **Asia's extreme severities**, cut through and erupting in war: the Levant, multi-India, the Japanese in the

*By the by, in that Cairo shop, as in many, my **Churchill Penguin print** was pinned on the wall, with the '. . . we shall never surrender' caption/quote supplanted in Arabic. I never bothered to clarify this mystery edition, which neatly bypassed my copyright.

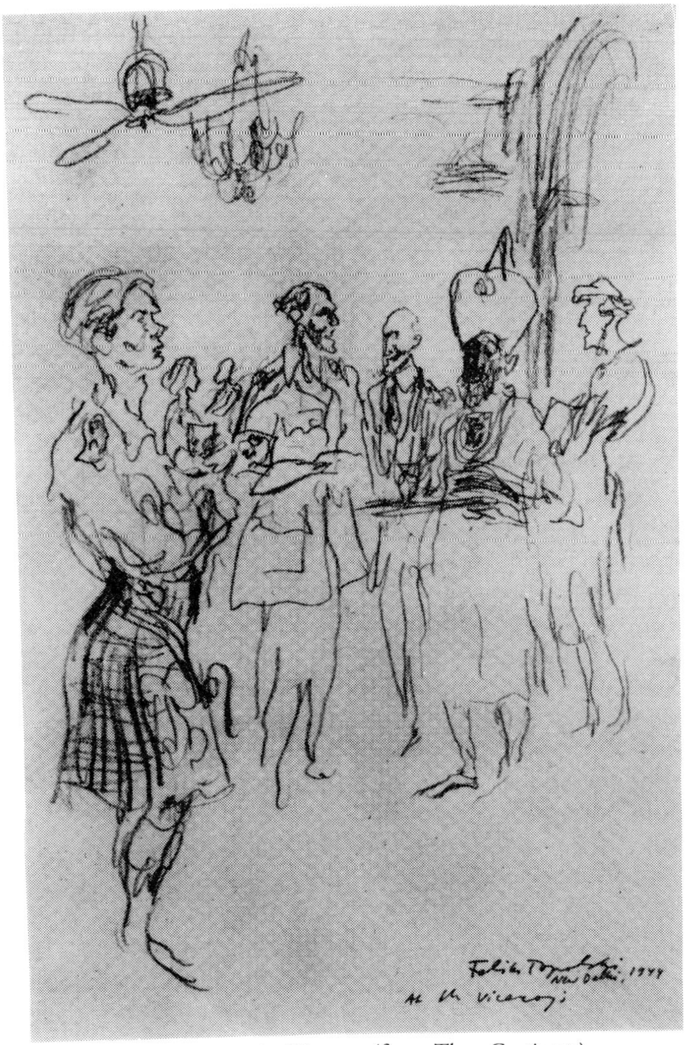

Luncheon at the Viceroys (from *Three Continents*)

Burmese jungle, the Americans as *Herrenvolk* over 'the Hump', Chiang Kai-shek's China in retreat.

This should have proved beyond endurance, yet I emerged unscathed on the surface, because tempered by the day-to-day **safety valve of trivialities** – but, surely in some measure, unhinged. Unhinged, hence open to nostalgic longings – hence this bewitchment?

And did the return to Cairo and to Barbara, a substitute homecoming, sober me? Yet further contacts with Birgitte's ambiance through her friends carried on her legend of beauty.

Then the news of Birgitte's grave illness – tuberculosis. Then a knock at my studio door: she, on the way to a Swedish sanatorium, unrecognizably wasted – neither the bewitching girl, nor her antagonist-replica recorded in the photographs, but a tragic figure. Soon after, she died in Sweden.

The Viceregal Lodge is an immense dusty-red-stone palace, up echelons of staircases, colonnaded domed beflagged, beringed with straining turbaned lance-holding warriors – but, penetrate the innerness of its antechambers: the customarily English '**conversation piece**' sprawls in languish-offering armchairs, inflated though: their love of costuming is indulged in a many-coloured range of regimental 'mess', 'undress', 'demi-dress' uniforms, their six-foot-something exuding narrow lengths of decorously crossed red/yellow widest-striped legs – the Mayfair pansy, now ADC to His Eminence, the Chelsea/Academy painter – now official portraitist, dressed as Major of the Royal Dragoons.

Their freckled generously boned women, chosen for size – the background. Drinks, name-tossing – as at home. To an alien – a 'native' outsider – however, this tall-stemmed **fashionplate selectivity** might seem the breed's superior standard – and intimidating.

But all this will spring to attention and recede, with the reception-interior taking over for a formal meal. The guests will enter – a mixed lot; and also **the Viceregal tribe**, substandard by the measure of those idealized subalterns, demonstrating the privilege of rulers and mirroring the rise of British meritocracy. But: the ever-celebratory *corps-de-*bearers, stiff-turbaned, bearded, sashed, emblazoned; the fans' whirl; the token fighting man: the young wounded (arm in a sling) Wavell son in a kilt . . .

I draw habitually through the stand/drink preliminaries and prop my sketchbook against my chair leg when we sit down – I on Lady Wavell's left – and, only in mechanical courtesy, ask her if she would mind my inconspicuous and intermittent drawing. She turns at me her whole upper bulk – 'Of course I should mind!'

Perhaps on the same day lone **Mr Jinnah**, the exquisite, white-suited/pressed patrician – his soporific eyes, his hawk-alert countenance, his outpourings at me alone (but this must go on in continuum) benumb, give inevitability to this Pakistan madness.

Then **Mrs Naidu**: she squats high on white linen and perorates, corraled – Congress people are never secluded – by acolytes in emotional chorus.

Or Congress leaders in conclave, dominated by the then young son of the Mahatma, **Devadas Gandhi**, who in a few years, as the editor of the *Hindustan Times*, will spread my drawings and written nothings on India over many pages and publish a book of my *Sketches of Gandhi*. They sit in a hieratic circle – another, saner, inevitability.

Other pools of haughtiness: the whites-only-club swimming pool in **Calcutta**, and later the **Bengal Governor's** supreme Residence. I could not resist placing in my *Memoir* (but also reshuffling the players to bring into one painted sequence the last of the British presence in India) this cosy incident: we, the guests, lined up, and the Caseys (I think they were still Mr and Mrs) reviewing us, as it were. **Mrs Casey**, to shake hands with me, stopped/stepped on to the up-blowing air-conditioning vent, all her skirts surging over her head.

But at the level of ordinary conveniences and graces, **Old Delhi's old Hotel Cecil** was imperturbably settled into the style/discipline of master versus mastered races.

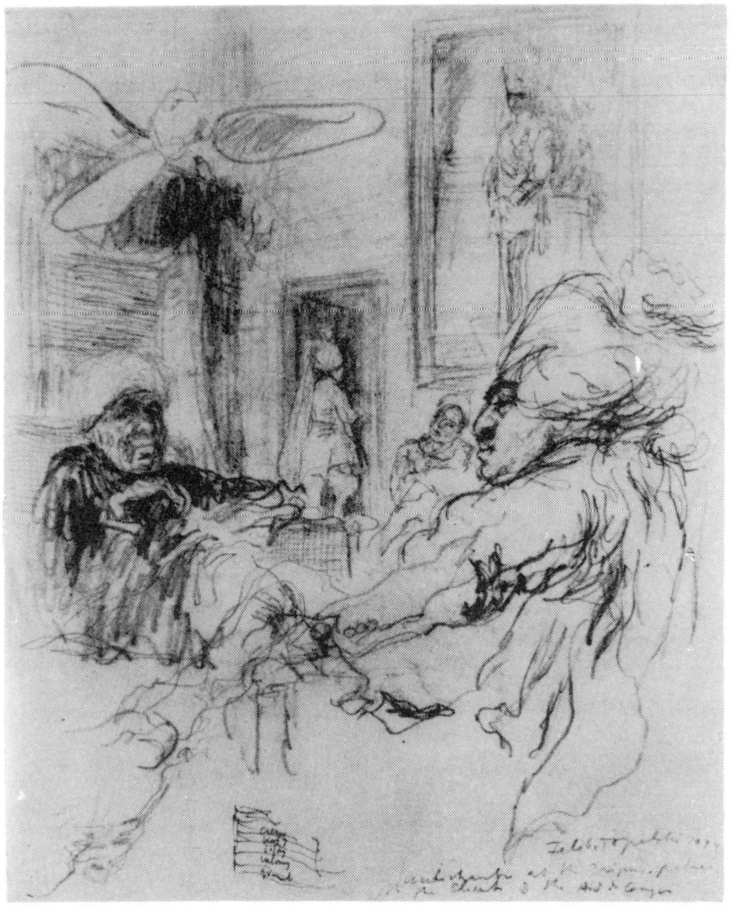

At the Maharajah's of Jaipur (from *Three Continents*)

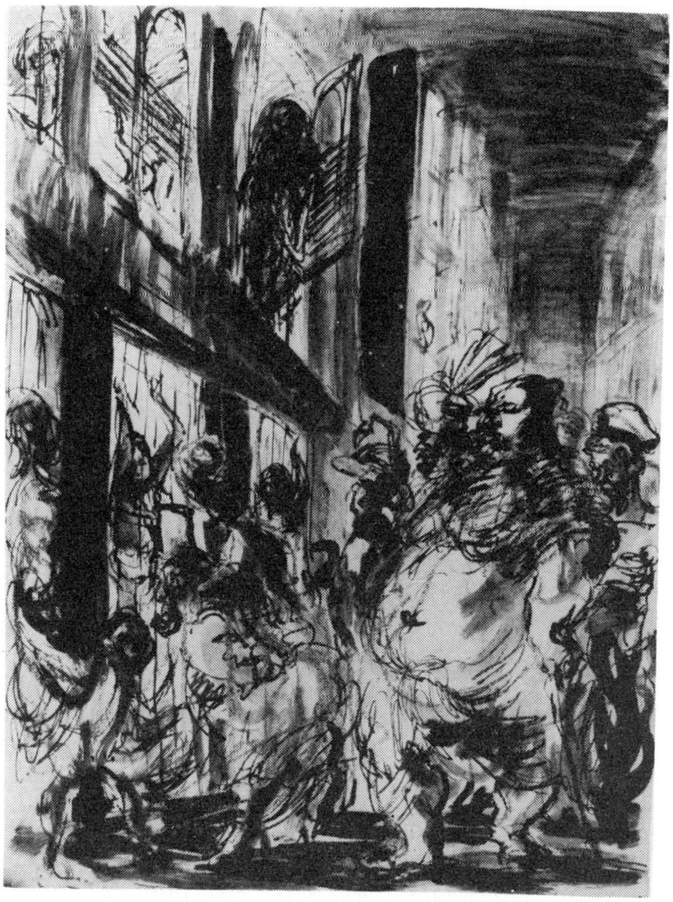

Out of bounds, Bombay (from *Three Continents*)

Old Delhi's agitated agglomeration gharry-transporting me to darkening threats – or to The Great Shahjahan Theatrical Company's ageless spectacle; or wedging through clusters of sadhus/fakirs into Mogul red granite wonders.

Such selective and neatly-framed 'scenes of India' do not reflect the onrush of immensity. Spaces: nature's and man-evolved; kaleidoscopic peoples: now in uncontrolled stampede, now tidal/pliant, but throwing forth singularities; the war: the **Indian Army** monumentally mounted on trucks, turbans fluttering, in westward convoys towards and across the Iraqi desert, responded to by the Bedouins' rearing horsemanship; or, in Meerut, the warrior-grimace **Punjabis** drilling for the East.

Then, this picture: trailing the caparisoned would-be-hasty buttocks of processional elephants into a pink walled city, amongst multicoloured crest-turbaned men and sari-flowing bare-backed jewelled women, the margins filled darkly by the indifference of sadhus and, in the blueness above, of vultures. But in the lead, the progress motivation: a violet-turbaned straight-necked youth, loin-clothed, hands tied at his back by **a long chain** held well behind, ceremonially and allegorically, by an equally straight (the Indian bearing proud, but denied by bent knees) white-clad red-turbaned sepoy, a long gun horizontal over his shoulder.

Sun-faded India thirsts for colour – and so the hamlets weave/print/dye cottons to frieze the scorched roads with the brightest cotton-wrapped **hardship-slimmed peasantry**; their betters, better fed, thus bellied, inferior; inferior-clothed in Westernized mass-makes.

The flatness of **Rajputana**, vulture-surveyed: the hunch-backed bullocks and camels, and horse-pulled painted carriages; the white-masked secret women; clusters of clients kowtowing to a topeed babu, fat conceits and thin servilities – all costumed for their roles; the aloof martial races, the Rajput chieftains equipped with a sword and an umbrella – all seductively true to themselves.

The **Maharaja of Jaipur**'s troops, choice in colouring/cut; his courtiers flabby under slow fans; he himself uniformed as a British Lifeguard high-ranker, whisky-soda in hand, ungladly staging for me a Nautch girls' performance.

Then. **Bombay**'s streets of **show-caged women** on sale.

Calcutta's crumbling vastness and China town and street-strewn down-and-outs – ultimately fearsome; also: the grimness of the **Hugli river** and the burning ghats; the blood-stench of the Kali temple; Tolly Gunge races; **the University** (studious girls in white blue-edged saris) and **Jamini Roy**; the aloof Government House; **the leave-town** feverishness – imposed on Calcutta's 'out-of-bounds' ordinariness, which was mass apathy. The nearest all-on-offer city to all Eastern war fronts has taken on the passing/amassing leave-greedy soldiers, airmen, sailors: British, American (white and black), Indian, Australian . . .

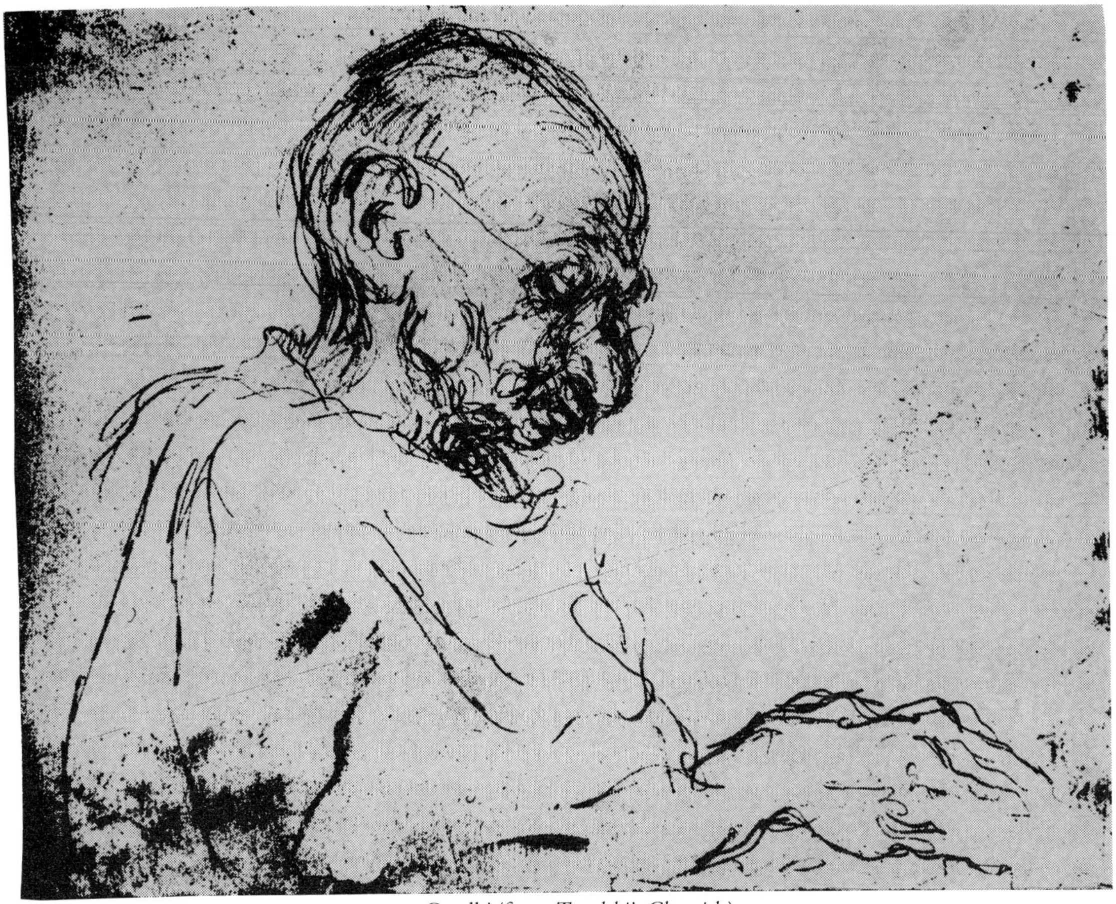

Gandhi (from *Topolski's Chronicle*)

The regulation-barred quarters of danger to life and health burst open, men brawl/drink/fuck in nightly abomination – child-women, roughly curtained/cubicled, or pickled up with babies and boy-pimps but still distinguishable: Bengali, Chinese, Burmese, Anglo-Indian, Tamil . . . **Frank Owen**, his London career abandoned to edit the Burma soldiers' paper *SEAC*, large and potent – American forage cap, khaki shirt open over mighty chest – refuses to join me, faithful to his two London ladies.

Leave cesspool of the Burma–Pacific war. '**Out-of-bounds/Off-limits**' in-out-pourings. Military Police patrol bang open cubicled whore-pen. Out of the shadows there jerk up panicked immense pig-pink rumps, fat backs curve up disclose underneath crablike minute bundlings: crumpled cottons, dark-skinned protrusions, terrified eye at the centre, feet foremost. In the torchlight the overgrown bulging dripping/drooping/shy – now at attention (round heads hit the rafters) – bodies: **America's task-force men**. A symbolic pointer – a comparable scale: against Asian minute fastidiousness, the otherness of the Americans' giant physique destines them for the *Herrenvolk* role of bungling rapers.

Above all this, **Gandhi**: the decorum-essence of India's white-draped nudity prolongs antiquity (the turbaned-martial sphere is Islamic; the British presence feebly pronounced); thus the Mahatma, within his saried circle, stands in continuity with the ancient sages. Precisely because there is in him no pomposity or enslavement to dogmatic rituals in the manner (and robes) of high Western religious hierarchies (a frequent cause of dismissiveness by Western witnesses), he must in his ease be matching his predecessors of old. My day with him happened on his release from prison, which he accented as a **day of silence**. And so it was contemplatory, and my only communication with him was by writing – including his signing one of my drawings of him in Hindi and in English. But, largely perhaps because of this condition, I was not exposed to his, derogatorily promised, political shrewdness – it was all beatific, as if a prediction fulfilled: the sun filtering through the mat canopy, the white mattress-linen and white-saried young girls in devout closeness, even his forthright unselfconsciously ugly-intelligent looks, rare in a land of beautiful people – the respectful visitors, such as I, at a distance.

Mountbatten flies to Burma front for the morale-boosting of his troops. I watch the formalities of his arrival and the briefing. The Supreme Commander in South East Asia supremely towers his manhood-dummy face above the campaign's **bush-hatted brass hats** – but discordant: against this jungle setting he appears as an extravagance-display of accumulated glories – his bush-blouse correct but given to an amassment of ribbons, surely deserved, but . . . And the Naval gold-braided cap – perhaps here *de trop*.

My stay is shamefully not much longer than his, but three

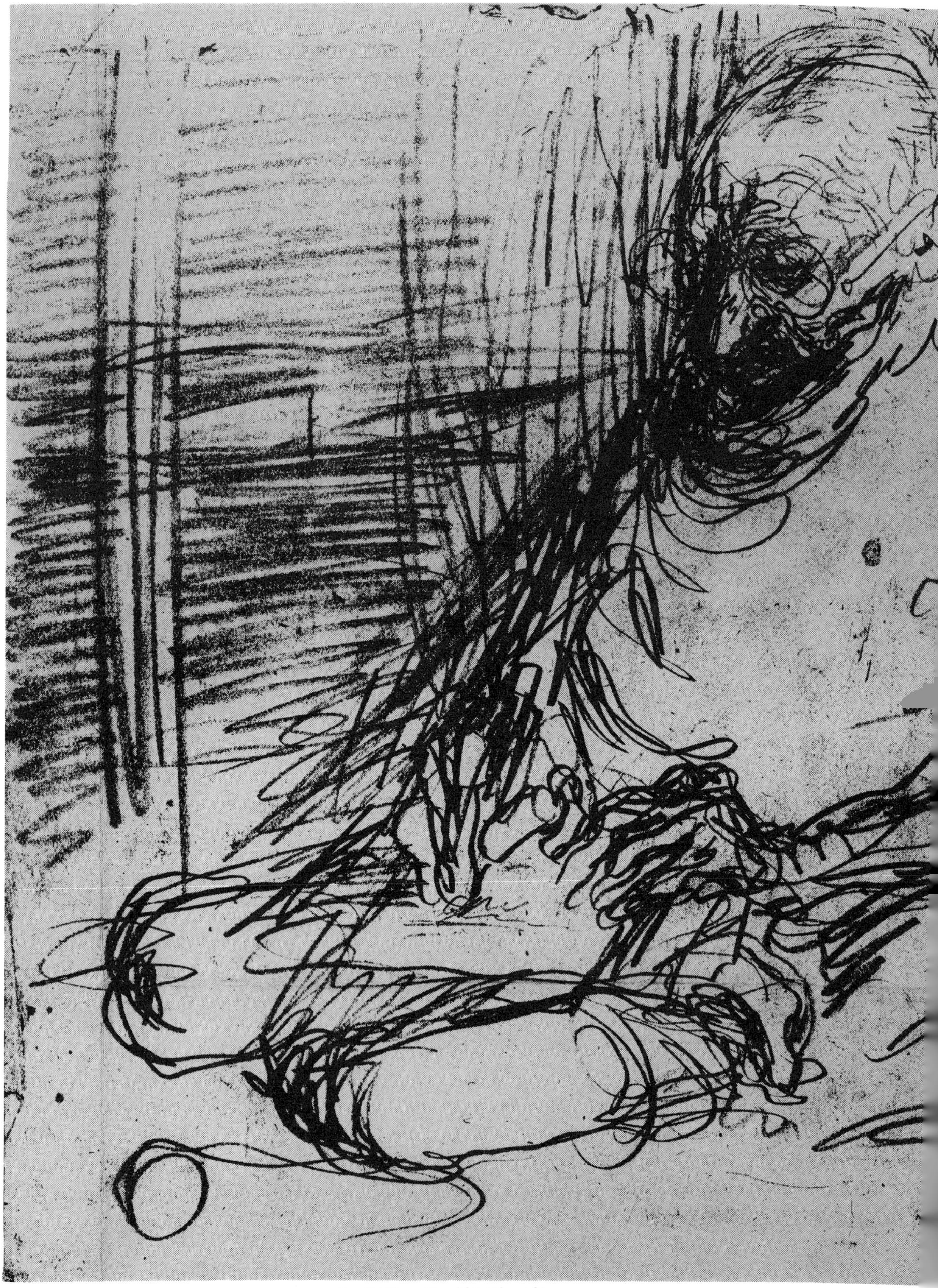

Gandhi (from *Topolski's Chronicle*)

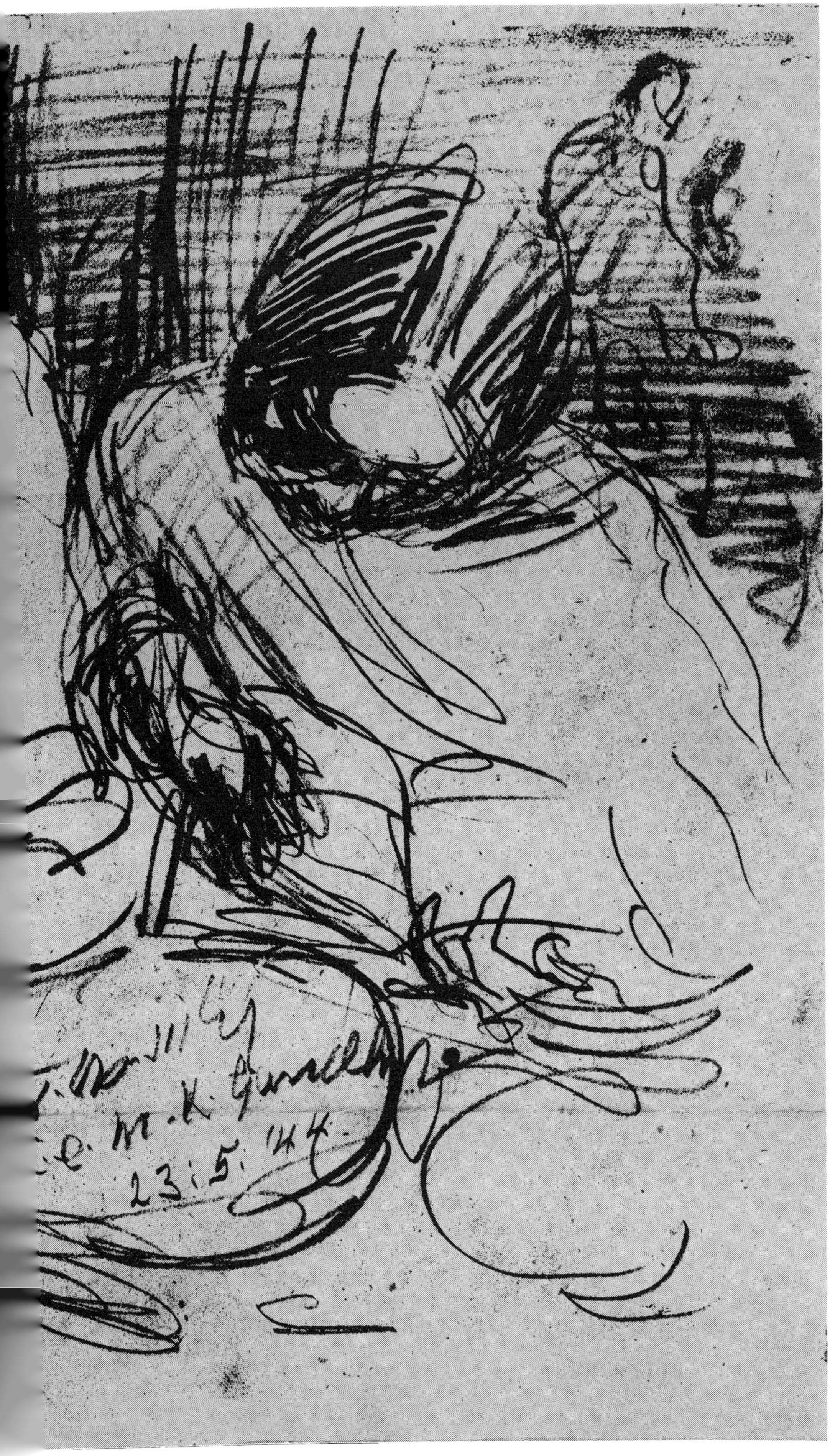
23.5.'44

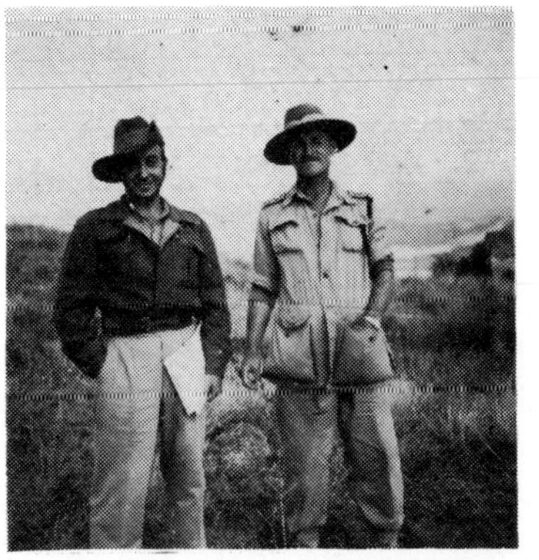

Burma campaign

forward forays into the front lines of **Taung Bazaar**, the **Western Tunnel** on the Maungdan Buthidaung Road and **Ngakyedauk Pass** give me a modicum of redemption.

Burma 1944. Arakan front. Flamboyant Sikhs at the cross-trails. Jungle war in Ngakyedauk Pass: **British troops' non-heroics** woven into steep damp greeneries: the emphatic class counterpoint: the soldiery officer-surmounted. English officer narcissistically continues his life-habit of dressing up rightly for an occasion (with all unerring felicities of individualism), parades for a '**good show**'; the English private soldier deflates/mocks/clowns his hazards – a Shakespearian intermezzo device – deliberately unbuttoned, a non-hero, gads about – joke–obscenity–repartee–joke – labourer/yokel making good-naturedly the best of a bad job. All and each bent/sustained not on loyalties to ideals but on not failing the others. These men in this manner put together a comparatively just uncruel empire – and never caved in. The complementary – officers and men – contradiction steeled into strength.

Americans seemed (only glimpsed then) utterly different: the strut of ostentatious manliness (in dress and manner) compulsive to all – always in 'combat', if not with the enemy, in competition to outdo one another (the English – at that time – relaxed within their station). Impressive, this ambition-drive, but relentless. Thus, tensions built up by battle strains never eased, they had to sustain themselves by building up resentments, hate–love abstractions – bending towards hysteria. These would be white Americans.

An interaction tableau at **Taung Bazaar**, with a trapped **sole Japanese** extricated from the jungle, still awesome, though cowed; still an alien enigma. The awesomeness of

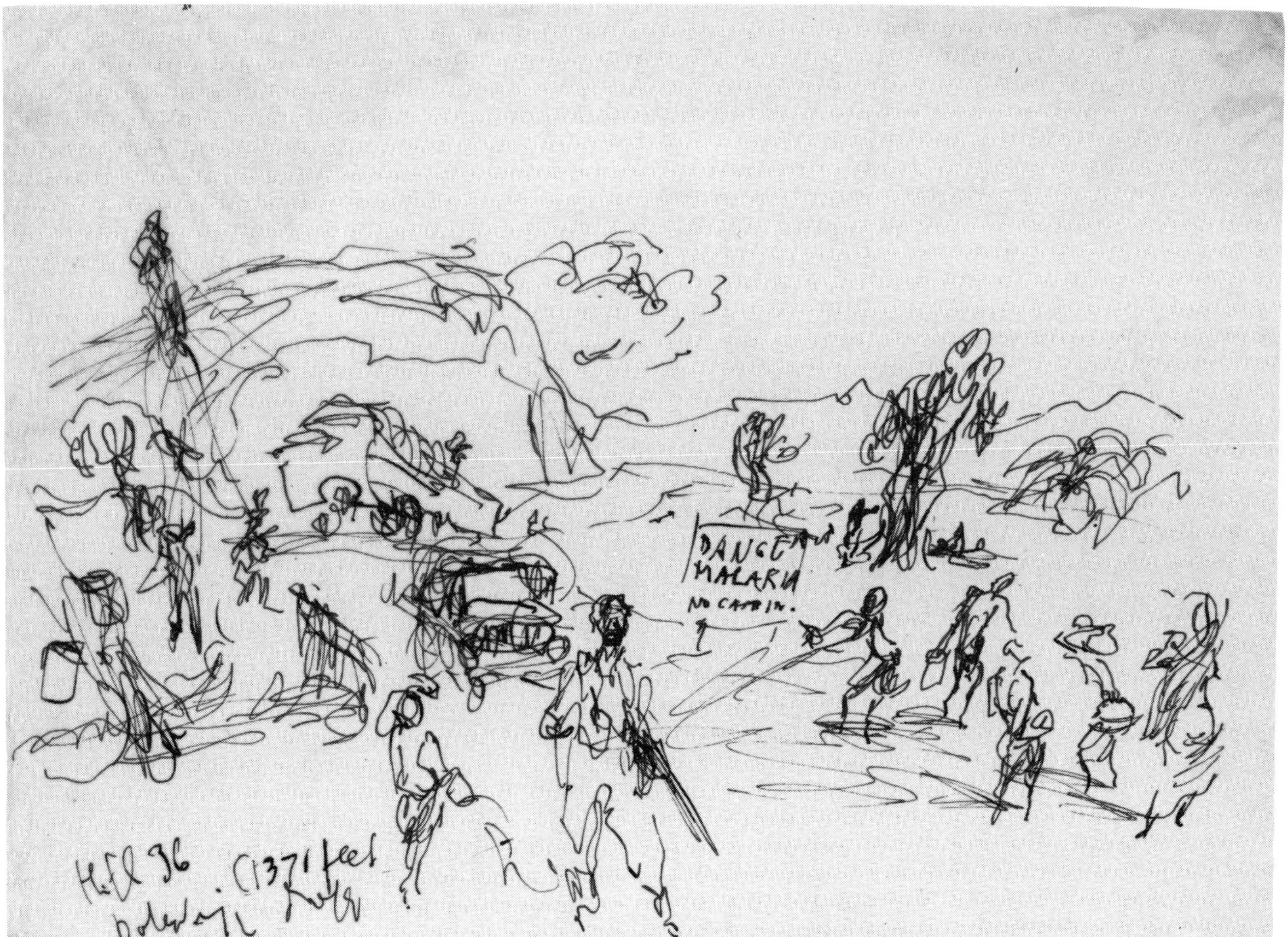

Burma campaign (from *Three Continents*)

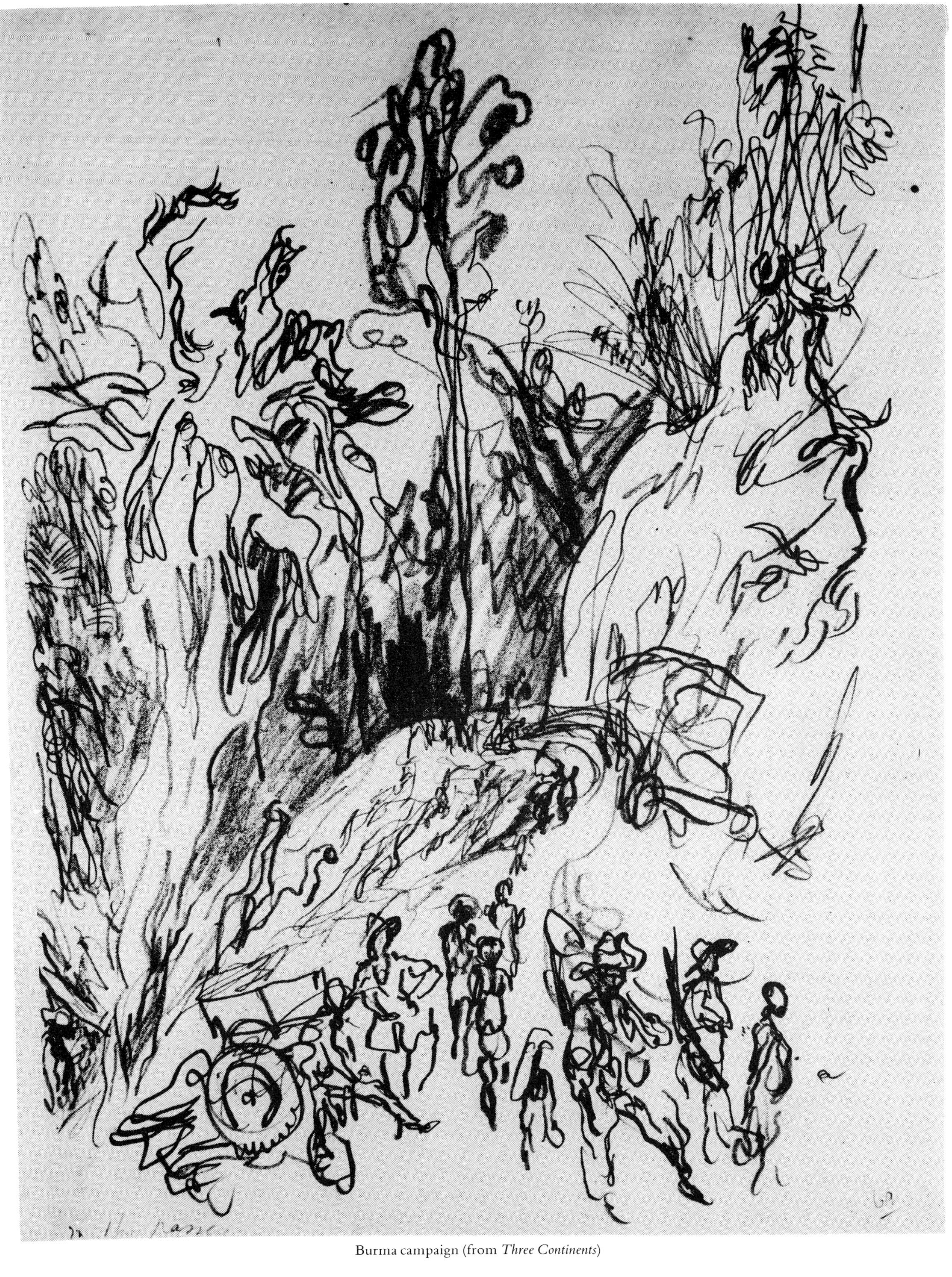

Burma campaign (from *Three Continents*)

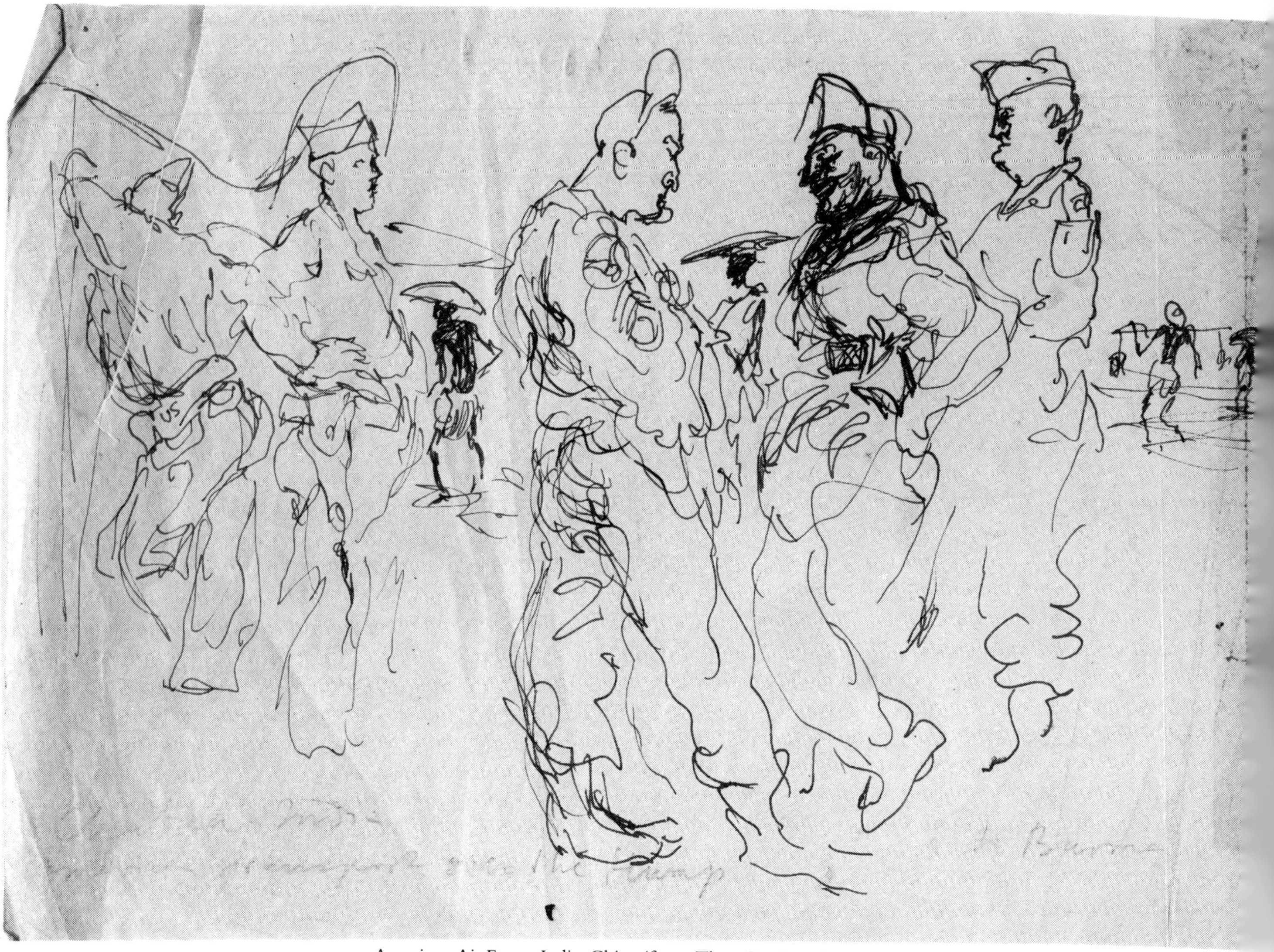

American Air Force, India–China (from *Three Continents*)

incomprehensible threatening nature becomes embodied in one creature almost approachable, yet stamped as part of the savage darkness. Conrad's 'there is simply darkness, there is no heart at all' does not annihilate '**the fascination with abomination**', and the mystery-shiver perpetuates in the face of an alien being emerged from the dark formidable green inimicality around. These reasonable pink-plump-fleshed officers in futile confrontation with the emaciated yellow-skinned materialization of the jungle's mystery, who will not, who cannot pronounce its meaning, because there is none.

Then **the Western Tunnel**, and in the lull stepping to its gaping opening held by Bengali soldiers – comprehensible death-frontier.

Polish junior officer, with fully documented marching orders **Calcutta–Chungking** (including a confirming telegram from the Commanding General of the United States Army forces, China–Burma–India Theater, **Joseph Warren Stilwell**), on a flight (Burma Road cut off) 'over the Hump'. But at the foot of the Himalayas (US outpost) taken off the plane. The reasons: red-tape tit-for-tat between themselves, here and in Chungking – I a pawn in the game.

My concept of footloose liberty-first America is shattered – it seems unbelievable that American officialdom when given rein surpasses all, wallows in the novelty of global/imperial/impersonal power tricks of bureaucracy. The vaster the more crushing the weight of the monolithic situation.

The tent camp is standard military; I am given a bed, food, outdoor films wrapped in clouds of mosquitoes – and no ear for my case. After a few days (with no action taken or promised by the command to resolve my 'arrest'), I go on a hunger strike – no one notices. I learn that there exists some miles away a British liaison officer, but transport is unavailable. I hitch a lift and the Englishman (swagger-stick and all) shows the humane tradition of imperialism: cup-of-tea and authentic concern. He does his utmost and, as a benevolent gesture, the American in charge puts me on a plane – back to Calcutta. My Chungking flights will be made on Chinese and RAF planes.

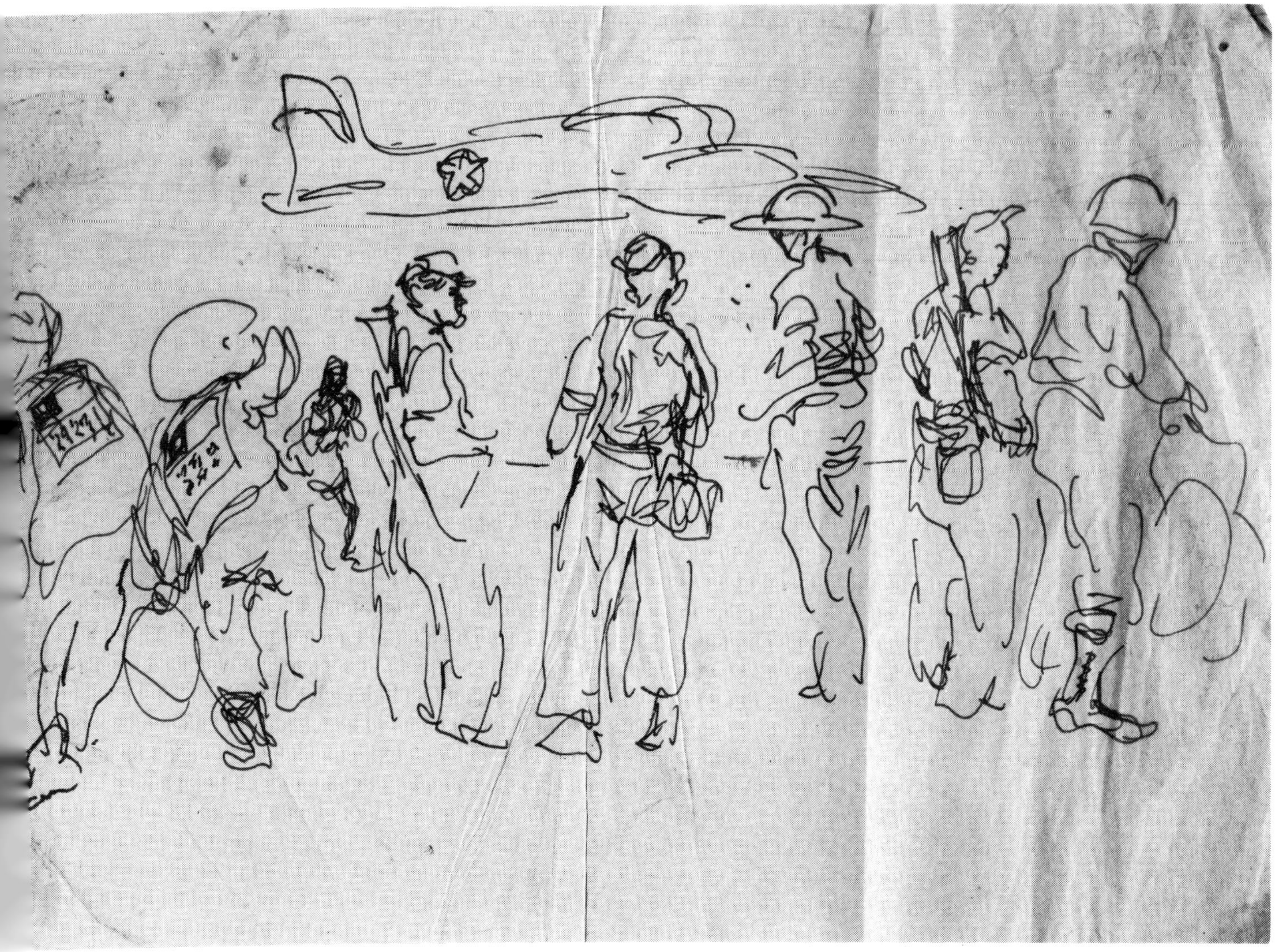

Matter-of-fact bearing within the myths unfolding/crashing: the Himalayan top-of-the-old-world skimmed over ramshackedly by already junky flying machines' age; the facile conquest of the racial barrier by 'travel document' non-heroes.

Lungs-explosion threatens – only one breathing apparatus between Fryling, the chargé d'affaires and me – I, younger, make him hold to it most of the time. **'Over the Hump'** sudden, and more, unimaginable singularity: this mist-edged rolling vastness is not a land of soil and water, but a formidable stratification contour map meticulously curvy-lined – explained by the planter-geographer's hand – thus the nature's recognized/approved/accepted mysteriousness eliminated by this Mandarin completeness of administering on her own terms, not by the leper sores malady-imposed – the breathtaking veritable human contribution; in fact merely a steep rice cultivation.

Down and out of harsh unconcerned imposition by the American tiger-emblazoned aeroplanes, there labour those **Yunnan-cultivators**: big-legged slender-able-bodied straw-hatted blue-patched. Beyond: the town of **Kunming**, the natural emanation/accent, ancient-patinaed, accommodating. We fly on, over ever-same ever-changing mirror-calligraphy of rice, until: flanked by two rivers' mists a colossus beehive, the veritable tumour. The plane drops screaming down to **Chungking**'s foundation on to the Yangtze river-dunes. A long tumultuous almost vertical **palankin-lift** upward, to the top.

In the morning, true to my military school *savoir-faire*, I dressed in the full worsted uniform – tailored in Savile Row, Sam Browne-belted – in readiness for my introduction as an officer to the Colonel, my sole superior, who lived below in town.*

The Embassy sits on the heights above Chungking close to the two-spheres-on-a-pole air-raid-warning system. The city slides down, thickly proliferating on the way – swarms of humans and steep steps accelerating the pace – to two

*Colonel Kędzior, the **Military Attaché** at the **Polish Embassy** in Chungking, is in fact banished. His unquenchable ambition and intelligence had set him up as the top intriguer within the contending factions around the **Polish Government in Exile** – in London. The Prime Minister, **General Sikorski**, had commanded him out of the way as far, and as far from any harm, as possible.

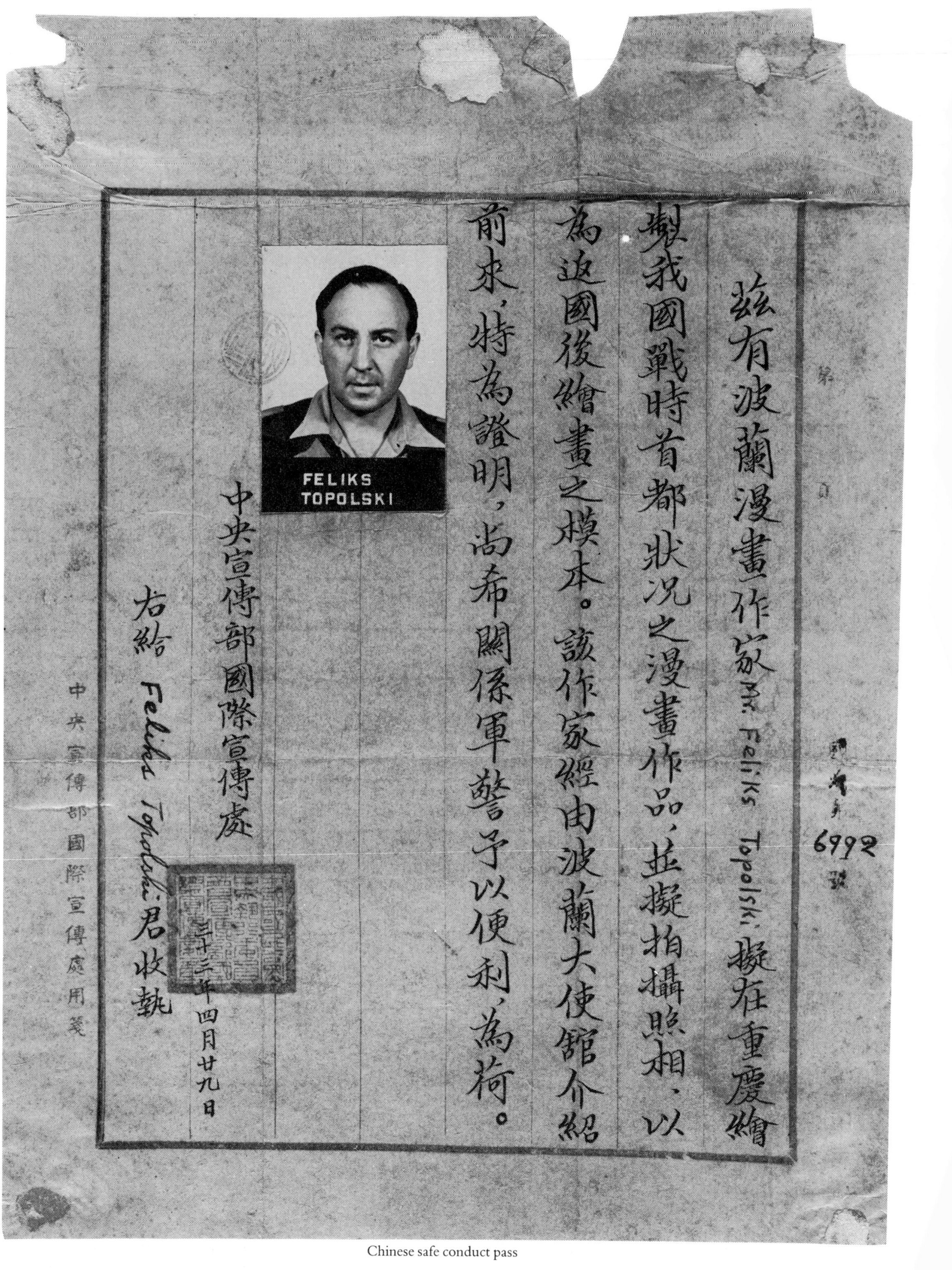

6992號

茲有波蘭漫畫作家Mr. Feliks Topolski擬在重慶繪製我國戰時首都狀況之漫畫作品，並擬拍攝照相，以為返國後繪畫之模本。該作家經由波蘭大使館介紹前來，特為證明，尚希關係軍警予以便利，為荷。

中央宣傳部國際宣傳處

右給 Feliks Topolski 君收執

三十三年四月廿九日

中央宣傳部國際宣傳處用箋

Chinese safe conduct pass

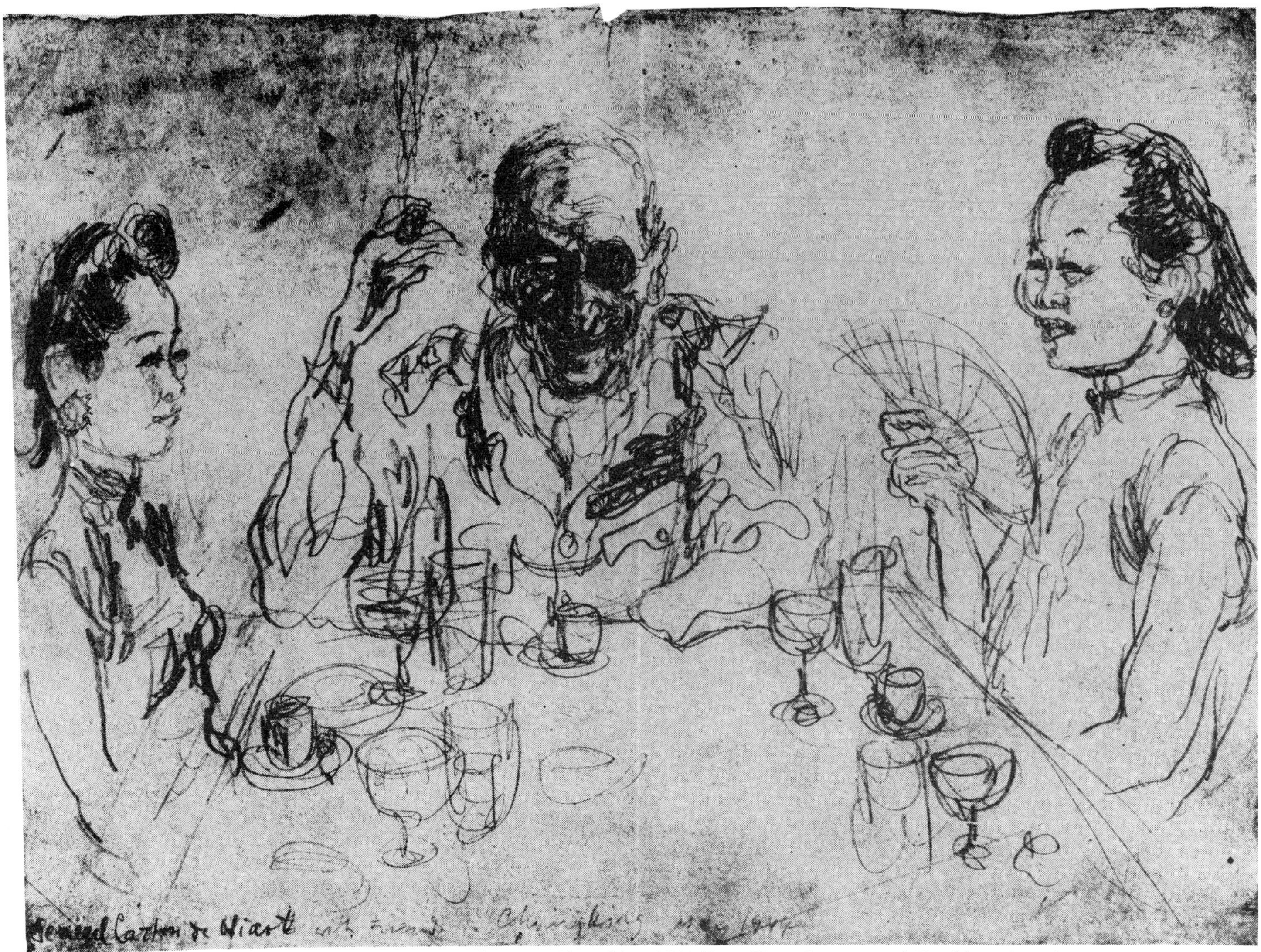

Luncheon with General Carton de Wiart, Chungking, 1944 (from *Three Continents* and *Topolski's Chronicle*)

different-coloured rivers below, which fetter this frenzy-hill. A climbing creature zigzaggedly enlarges into a full-scale military gallant, meticulously outfitted on the British Colonial model: open-necked bush-blouse, shorts, stick. And while the Second Lieutenant, foolishly at attention, declaims his formula, the Colonel cuts in: 'But why this thick wool outfit? Too hot – change instantly!'

General Carton de Wiart is the British Military Attaché, the key figure in the Allied war strategy in China. A marvellously stylized grandee cum dandy, he would have appeared exaggerated to the point of parody but for his truly knightly past: if the eye-patch, the empty sleeve, the decorations had not been marks of challenges met. He invited the War Artist cum Second Lieutenant to **a private lunch** – there was a minor flurry at the Polish Embassy over this distinction, not given before to any member of it. The reasons might be simple, it was argued: the artist was the one among them in some possession of the English language, also known to de Wiart from London.

The lunch was for four – the two others were purely personable young **Chinese ladies**; the conversation's essence was that the Polish guest should pass on to his chargé d'affaires the informal but serious warning that the Polish Military Attaché should stop throwing his weight around in Chungking, that he had no function there but to keep up appearances until the end of the war.

Next day, 3 May, a Mass in the French church to celebrate **Polish National Day**, with the Chinese government and the whole Diplomatic Corps present. This time Colonel Kędzior wears his full uniform and the Second Lieutenant likewise, acting as his ADC, a step behind.

Some, obligatory for her, attendance at drilled files of war orphans. At some point **Mme Chiang Kai-shek** and I face each other alone, a chance crack in protocol; and the frequent with me dud in confrontation with the luminaries: without preliminaries, in intimate agitation, she loud-whispers at me: 'I itch all over!'

Road to Chengtu. Navy-blue sleepy dawn. Squeezed into a puffing farting crush within a patched-up croak of a folksy stagecoach, machinery creaking, track-bumps bruising, stinky fuel dust and mud choking. Sidetracked by Mr Chi (the ever-dodging 'all-purpose'

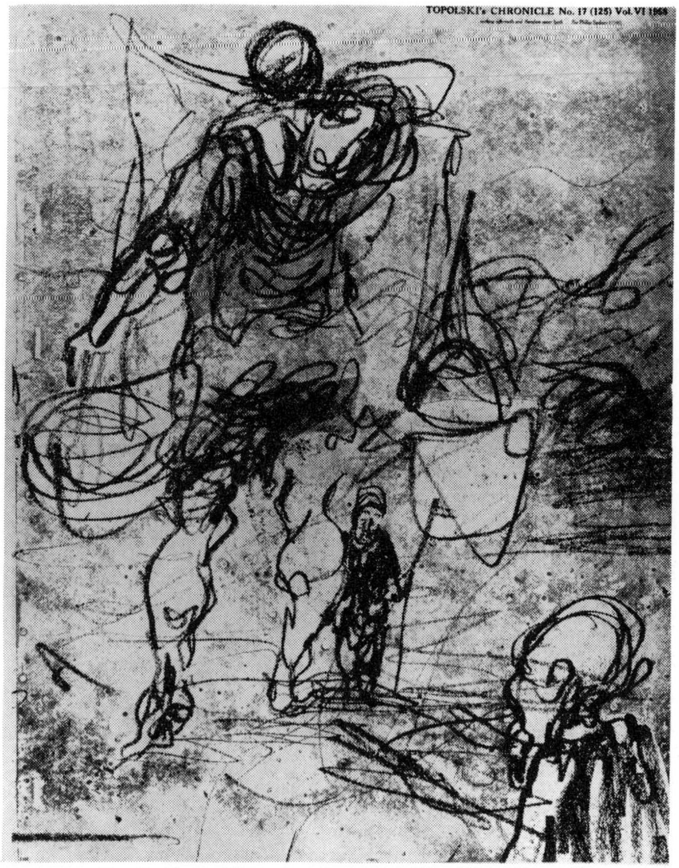

Coolie (from *Three Continents* and *Topolski's Chronicle*)

'English-speaking' go-between attached to the Polish Embassy) from the pursuit of war, but the rewards: the land, the multitudes sharpened up by the slowness of the bus – to reach fullness with the accumulation of frequent and prolonged punctures, when compensations of lazying amongst the hills or ricefields – or in roadside tea-rooms – consort with the country's rhythm – to gape straight unhampered at China:

Lung-Tang: slanting rain over eggy hillocks, dozen-tiered-pagoda-bordered; green-brush mirror-fields yellow-hat-spotted, dungy slush-dripping water-buffalo-circled.

Win-Tshang: bent blue backs over orange harvest. A chain of the blind (umbrellas under arms). Male friends hold hands. A woman lowering her breasts down to a babe. Rickshaw-man sprawl-napping, legs up. A piglet and a cat on a common string; hoofed old women load-weighted.

Tsu-Tsung: a black/yellow-walled house bearing the hugely calligraphed slogan CHING–CHEN–TUAN ('Charity–Honesty–Unity') and kids at play and in readiness: their pants square-open for their bare bottoms; and a hunch-backed pedlar; and fishes suspended/stuck/crammed on a stick by their mouths; and a pompous master heading a queue of pupils; and a calm pisser, an ancient woman on his back. Thus the **Szechuan** folklore panorama, man-made curve-contoured heights, drying washing-garlanded, bamboo-stick-traced, water-pedalling, and decaying cemeteries shrine-marked – the feel of this land's vastness clustered with ant-like diligence, breeding on shit, on layers and layers of crumbling ancestors, multiplying fourfold crops of rice cotton beans sugar cane tobacco wheat mulberries, paying taxes, yielding sons to be consumed by wars and unconcern. The bus's snail-like progress on patched-up wheels through this endless landscape over thousands of generations of assiduousness buried and turned into black soil – until, finally, the great breakdown in the thick of **Tui-Pin-Gou**.

Noon broils over the dust, over the clitter-clatter of daily doings. Black house-fronts; black sheets, shoved up by sticks, solicit streaks of shade. Behind me, already past, the curve of hutments towards the heat of openness, ricefields and the splashing of buffaloes; in front, beyond the patch of most modest shops, a bridge, ornately carved, curve-roofed – still unknown. Closer: grimacing gnomes mount the rotting roof of a polluted temple: **the Kuomintang sun-emblem** on the gate, soldiers sprawled all over consume, chortle, scratch, chafe – flabby simpletons but, drawing-alerted, heads up screwed brows eyes distance-gazing in the prop-poster semblance.

I sit in **the static bus**, village-surrounded, and travel through the day: the bus's stately move towards the evening and into the depth of local matters.

The sun turns brassy and catches now on to the right-hand hutments – colours the market square, which slackens and regroups for the evening ballet: **the return from the fields**. A handsome corps steps forth from the far perspective of the road and strides up the shadowed bridge towards me – the scythes the hoes catch the sun, straw hats thrown back gold-halo their heads – young and old in the wonder of patched blueness and brown limbs; the dogs' clamour, the geese's gaggle, the women emerge and advance to meet them.

They pass and the stage darkens, blurs the corners which breed hucksters, huddle gossip; the elders of the town settle in tea-rooms with a fan and a pipe, the children's chatter ceases, soldiers take the street corners. With the paper lanterns lit, **a flamboyant tramp** enters the village and places himself in a ring of light – which also reveals the mah-jong players, rattling their dice, hawking and spitting, well into the night.

Twittering **chirruping dawn**. Basics continue – monumentalized. Wives lean their flat faces out of the windows, patter on their hoofs round the stenchy stoves; water-carriers fill up their buckets. Soldiers warm up by choral mooings. The peasantry procession marches out to the fields. Doorsteps swept, kettles burble – the family at their table: a black interior – light falling in through a narrow yard opening confused by gallery steps and the coach-house – deep alien and faultless; father-baker swathed in a constellation of skirts and headscarves, thin scraggy and sexless, wife weedy ever-driven, a hive of children – that ranges from helplessness pity-imploring, through discovery-bumptiousness, to the intimidations and disquiets of the *début*.

I sit with them (a pig buffets my arse) for hours on end, drink teas, drive away gapers, commiserate . . . An antiquated old man, a relic, stately in black cap and silks, begs for help, pulls out a note: consultation, deliberations, and groaning deciphering by the 'literate' of the letter, perhaps from his son, perhaps from the war front.

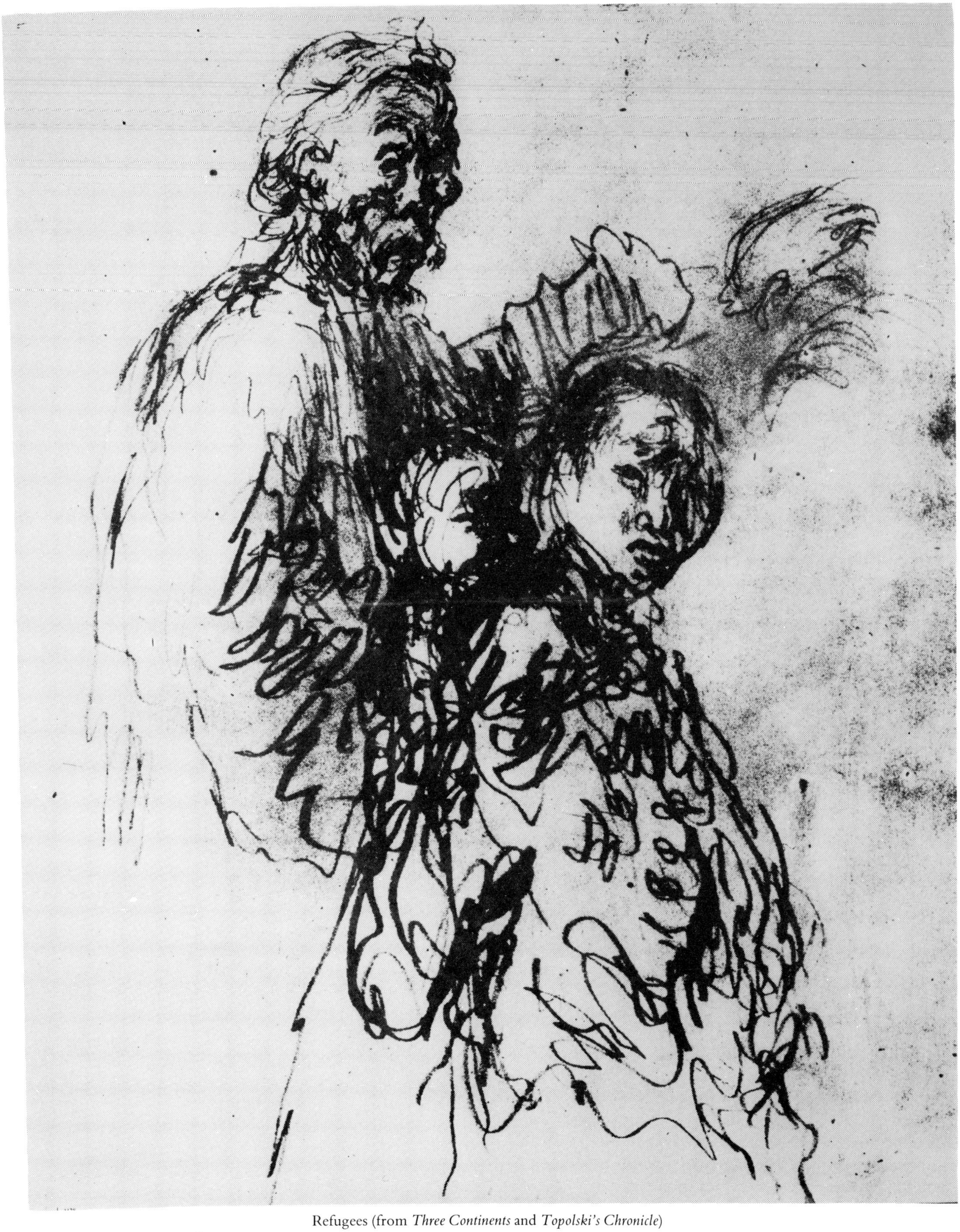

Refugees (from *Three Continents* and *Topolski's Chronicle*)

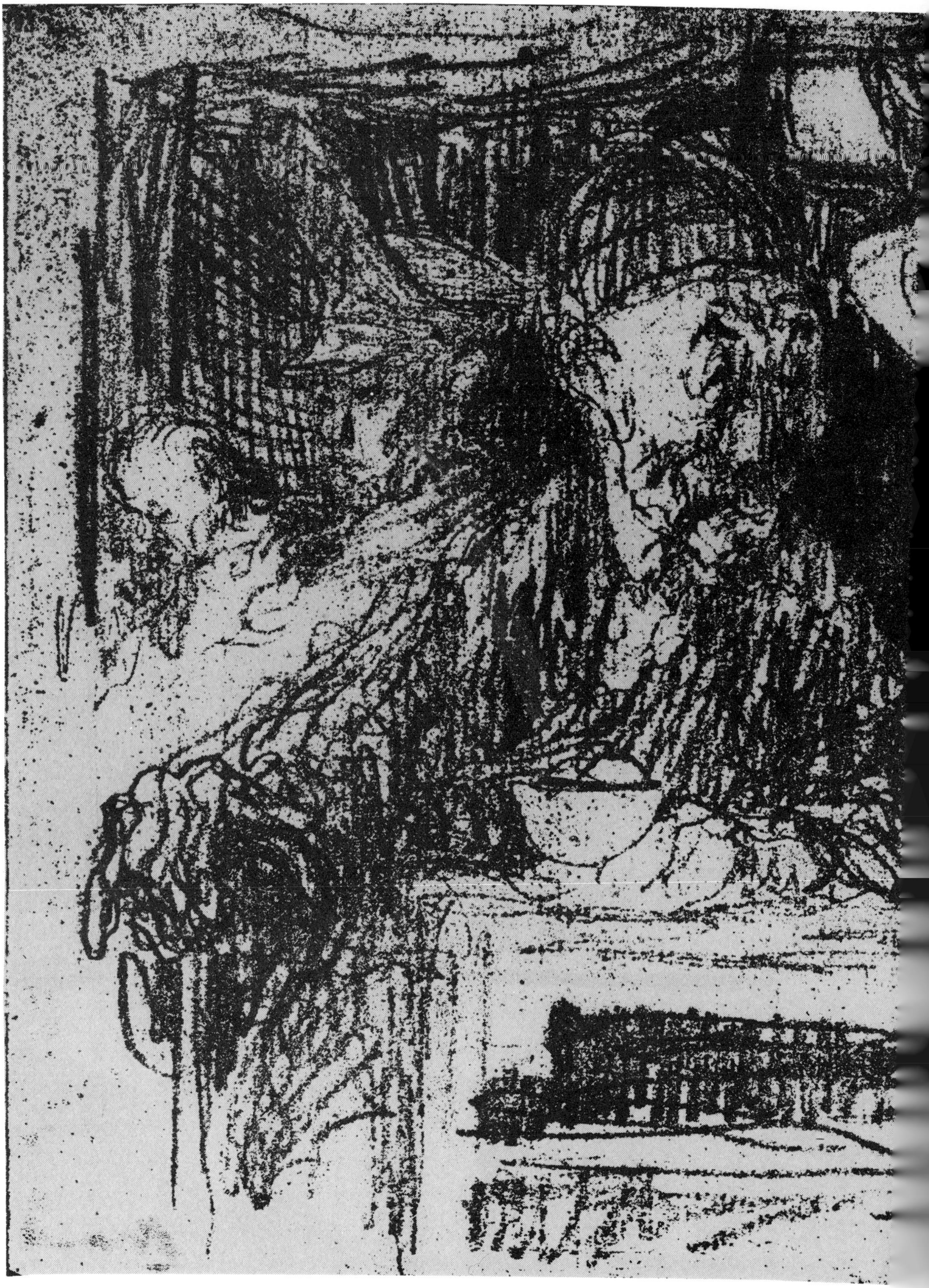

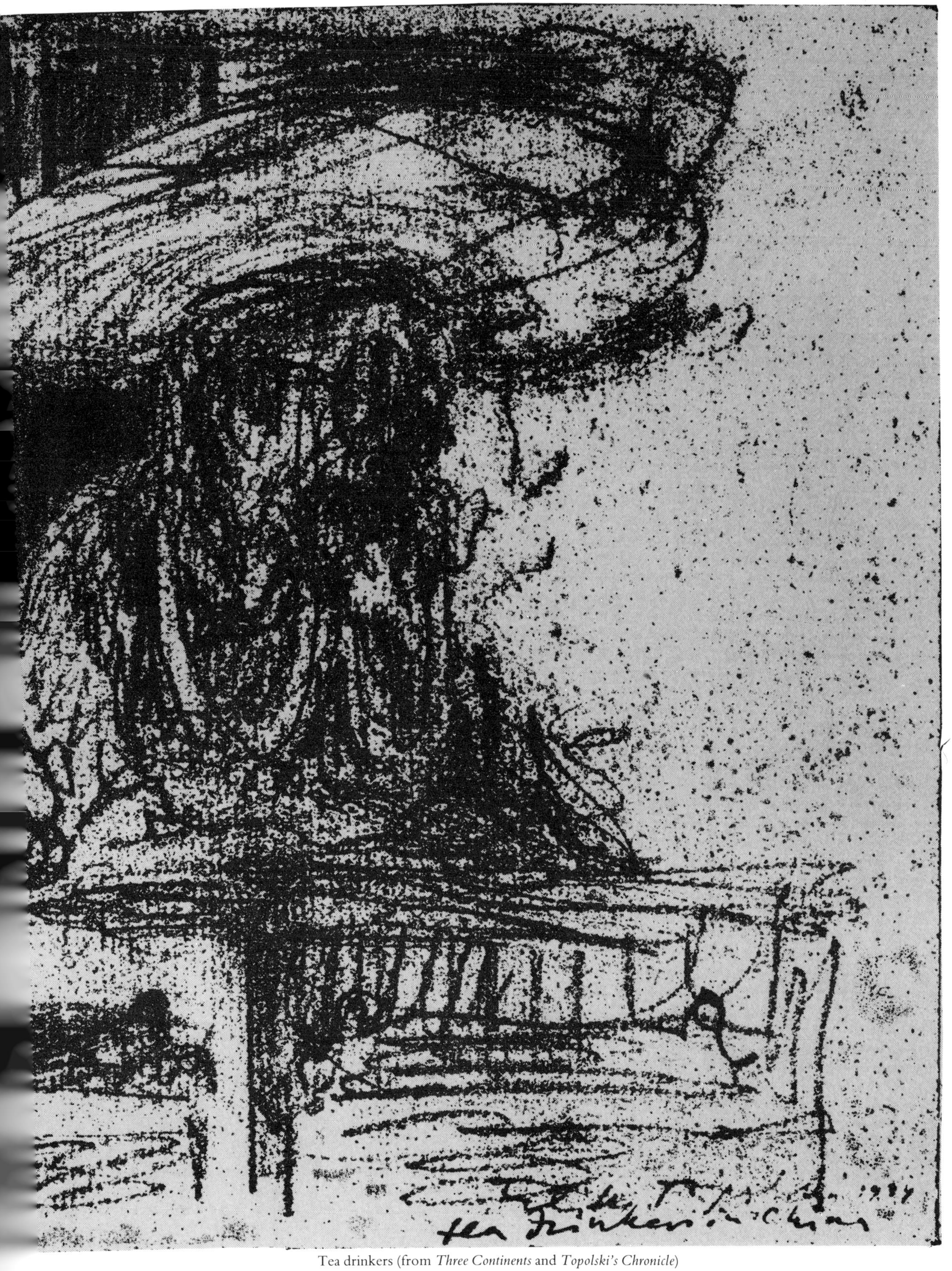

Tea drinkers (from *Three Continents* and *Topolski's Chronicle*)

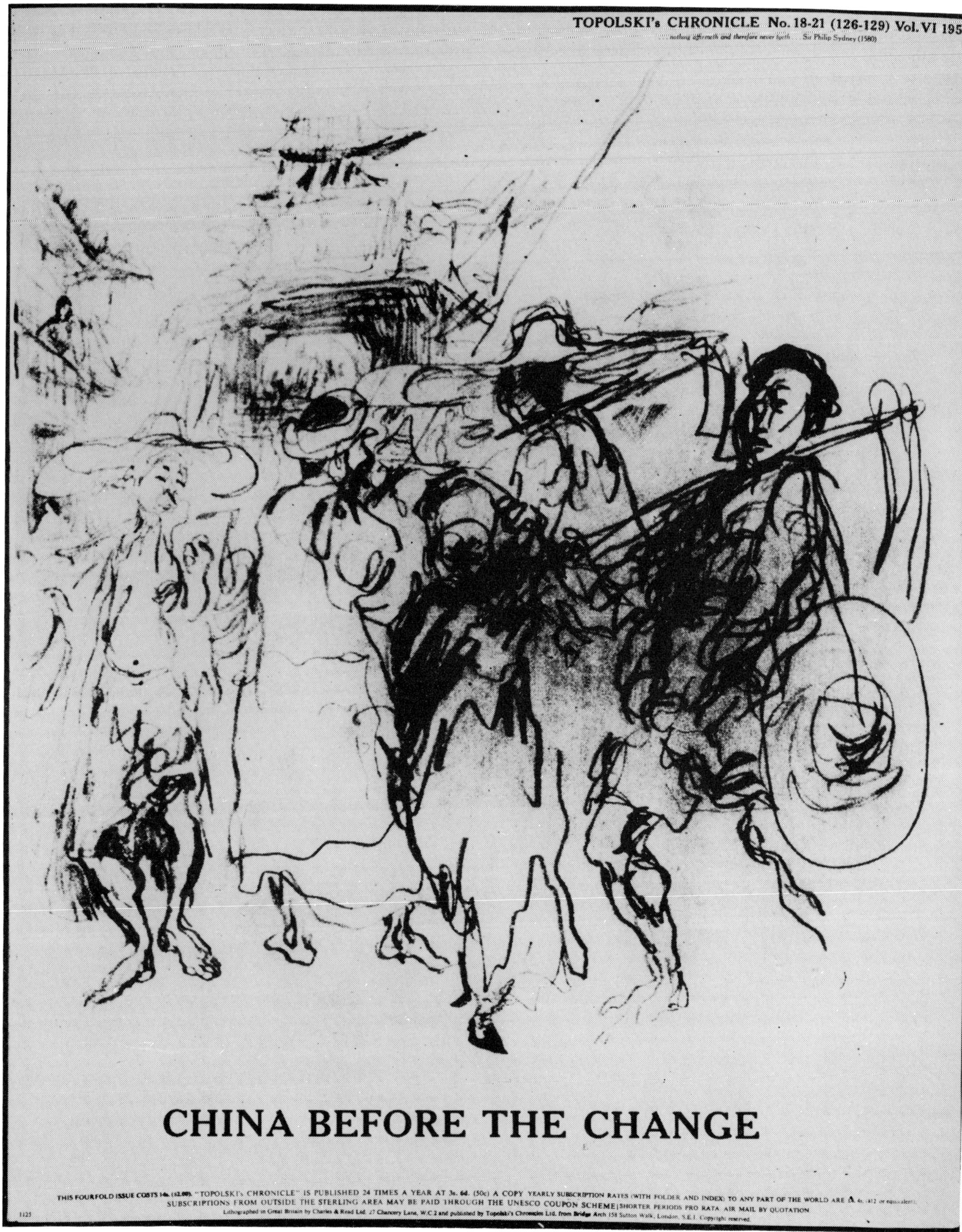

Szechuan village (from *Three Continents* and *Topolski's Chronicle*)

I stroll round the village, the tea-rooms, make noises, make acquaintance of the people and their homes, peep into barns, puzzle out eternal crafts, descend to the riverside ledge of overheated fields: the languid river perfectly fishing-fringed; a boat: birds on its bow, cattle and sedan-chair at its centre, boatmen in action. My village, at a distance now, braced by the swelling bridge, lingers on in slow pulsation.

Return by way of the backs and, beyond a ridge of excrements, there stand the stereotyped netball poles and the school chorally screeches under the Generalissimo's oleograph at the command of an angry-faced woman teacher.

And in **the afternoon**: a crowd swayed by laughter, by attentive but indifferent curiosity – and a man carting off, or tossing to the ground a screaming woman, dragging her in or throwing her out, revengeful or imploring – perhaps both playing out a familiar and customary act in a family drama, of loss? of faithlessness?

Trivial, maybe, but, dressed in mysteries of alien form and language, the simplicity of essentials turns epic – more so when set against the comicalities of imported modernity.

From netball and a regime official's watchfulness to the bizarre temple courtyard gallery-wound, with a ruined centre guarded by fearsome/threatening giants, cobweb-roped – the gamut. I circle, I fumble into the day of the poor – disentangle emotions, surface commiserations, musings.

The day ends. The ritual return from the fields passes; I am familiar with the place and its inhabitants – and, knowing who where and what for, I feel gratified when watching the expected deeds.

The long day had closed the gap: my explorations stamp the faces; I am included among them, and their vague curiosity, their passers-by vacant grins transform into contact, experience – drama. There tangles **an intrigue**. Within the tea-room nearest to the bus, heads gather in whispers. The motive – as it must be – a woman: last night I took notice of and stared at the painted face of a girl. This evening she settles again opposite me, legs-eyes-body movements denote the furtive pantomime of provocation; already she concentrates my attention; already draws out of me the response in the coarse role of a white barbarian – when, suddenly, a nearby group emits a blue coolie: he approaches her, argues, others come forth supporting? or in argument? then a young officer leads her out resisting. That's all. But after that there is no more indifference around me.

The street darkens ominously this time for, so I presume, a drama on the theme of hospitality abused by a Foreign Barbarian. In challenge I search out contact, idle about the backstreets – wonder over possible tactics and choose, a faithless fatalist, brazenness. I believe (schooled on films about the East) that there is danger. On my entering the tea-rooms invariably the tea-drinkers stiffen and look through me – their faces, I imagine, deadened by pitilessness. I tuck in on the bus, isolated; guilty, or a victim of circumstances. The Chinese forgather in the greyness outside, murmur, turn away. I lie down in the transparent-feeling bus, in dread and expectation of a night attack: unarmed yet not utterly submissive, yet not quite resolute – a white explorer. I fall asleep.

The dawn, a hangover from after-night tensions – and embarrassment. But the day floats along by now as if in immemorial routine – without surprises. I live in this village and will live here my whole life. The morning walk reconciles me with yesterday's adversaries – I collect new friends, gape, pity, admire, meditate.

The repaired wheel arrives in triumph – we depart between rows of farewells.

Some days later, Chengtu ever unreachable and dates pressing, an encountered military lorry tempts in Shihkiakia or Yiu Shan Chen, unless it was Tze Chung: I **turn back**. Frosty and magnificent ride on top of the back-load over the familiar landscape, through familiar hamlets and towns – and mounting expectations: Tui Pin Gou, where I lived, will appear at any turning and will bestow something special; Tui Pin Gou, where I lived for ages, anonymously flashes by in a second, turned in painful disappointment into **any hole**.

The outward ride was China's everythingness – the ride back focuses on the road; the amassing **soldiery** – trudging, sandaled, loaded; or chained (caught deserters, press-ganged villagers); or prone, wounded. There hunch up the heights; we climb up in serpentines mist-encircled – far vistas shoot left-right – huge waters pass by. The road thickens with stinks, chatter, haste – **Chungking**. A city bus; a rickshaw; a sedan chair swinging me up the steps. The Embassy like a family home.

Black Africa – then an immeasurable island of calm.

Sudan, Omdurman: the house of the Caliph, grey, rugged interiors of the warriors – turned into a fondled museum. Cut out in mahogany a furious Dervish with a spear. The rows of aged photographs of 'bad' angry men. After the sweet-sour Cairo, the bitterness of the desert.

Khartoum: the high voices at prayer time.

After Khartoum the desert; the pink sand edged by splotchiness of vegetation and flattened by the sun. The sky entwines with the land. The air travellers suspended over Africa, the many-coloured sphere (or rather hemisphere), yet wrapped cosily in habits of their northern little island, solemnize their civilization over the paper cups, plates, pepper and salt bags; over the scandal scoops and antique-dealer murders on the Sussex Downs, at the vicar's, or in the Albany rooms.

The immense pink and fuzzy expanse with the obese mounds floating over it. Giraffes bracket this formidable landscape, silhouetted – hence devoid of their clownish chequers – and primeval.

Juba, Sudan. The devil-like, jutting-out, curvilinear presences – the smile, half smirk, half somnambulist bliss – threaten unpredictability; fearful grotesqueness of peroxided thatch and of powdered faces; the eyes – attentive bloodshot umber eyes of predators; their rubber walk – the pendulum of immense phalli. Only the dress, part-dress (hat, uniform coat) comforts – indicates drollery. They hold sway over the flying machines – and do not bend their aloof heads when a

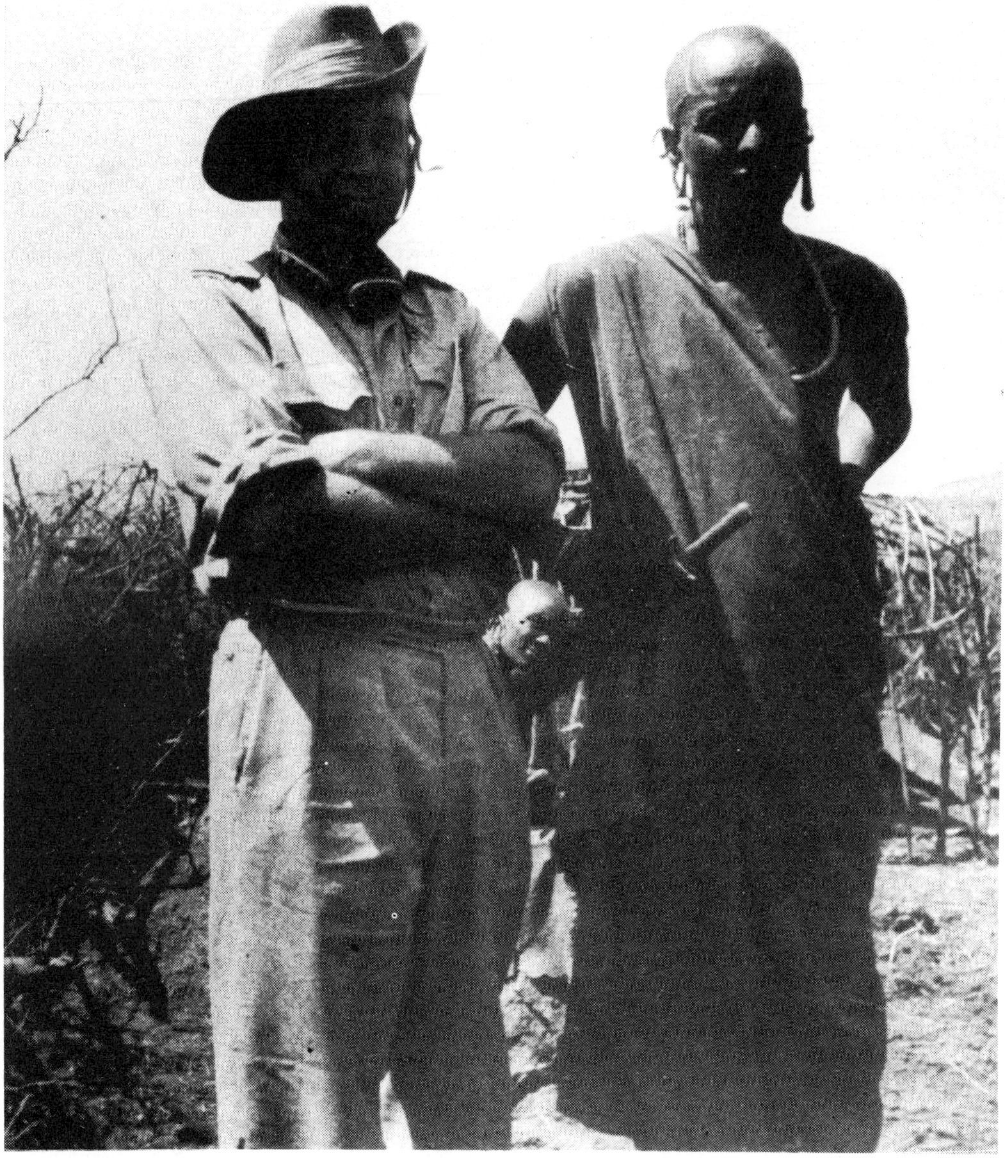

With Masai, 1944

metal sluggard roars down.

The Nile narrows and rusts – the flattest of lands, flyblown by clouds. We fall. Malakal, and there rise above and around us the stilted, awesome Dinka men. Again those disdainful heads, but humble ape-knees – they stride, they pause (carved-faced, jewelled-eared, yellow-eyed), always pensive. Their ominous suspense echoed and confirmed by the praying mantis in the foreground.

Tanganyika. Out of the bush move the satans – along the warpath in black-white warpaint – the Massai. Terrifyingly they step stealthily on bent knees, seemingly fixed on a cruel purpose. A motor-cyclist, helmeted and tommy-gunned, roars by – but they – more true. And then, a moment later, the shy boys under the paint pose for a snap, giggle, take shillings.

Light-generating green-blue-pink and russet patterns over the vast void, and black-white zebras cutting into it. Above, the vultures float. And old men, draped in camouflage brownness, transact amongst the large white flowers.

Uganda. In the hot-house landscape (light and vegetation), the queenly lady under a parasol, her entourage attending.

The road rolls along, red and embellished with black peasantry, hieratically weighed down with their tools and their fruit and prey.

The coital dance. The down-tug of the hand to close in: taking possession, or entering the erotic *carnet*. Then the next man and the next – the girl is uncoy, yet yielding, yet withstanding. Then the momentary attacks: to grab at the breast, at the waist, to fasten on to the buttocks, to glue the face to the belly. Then the most impressive circular run in pairs: huge, bosom-jostling maidens, drumming of the feet, the shouts, the roar of horns, men – great black spiders –

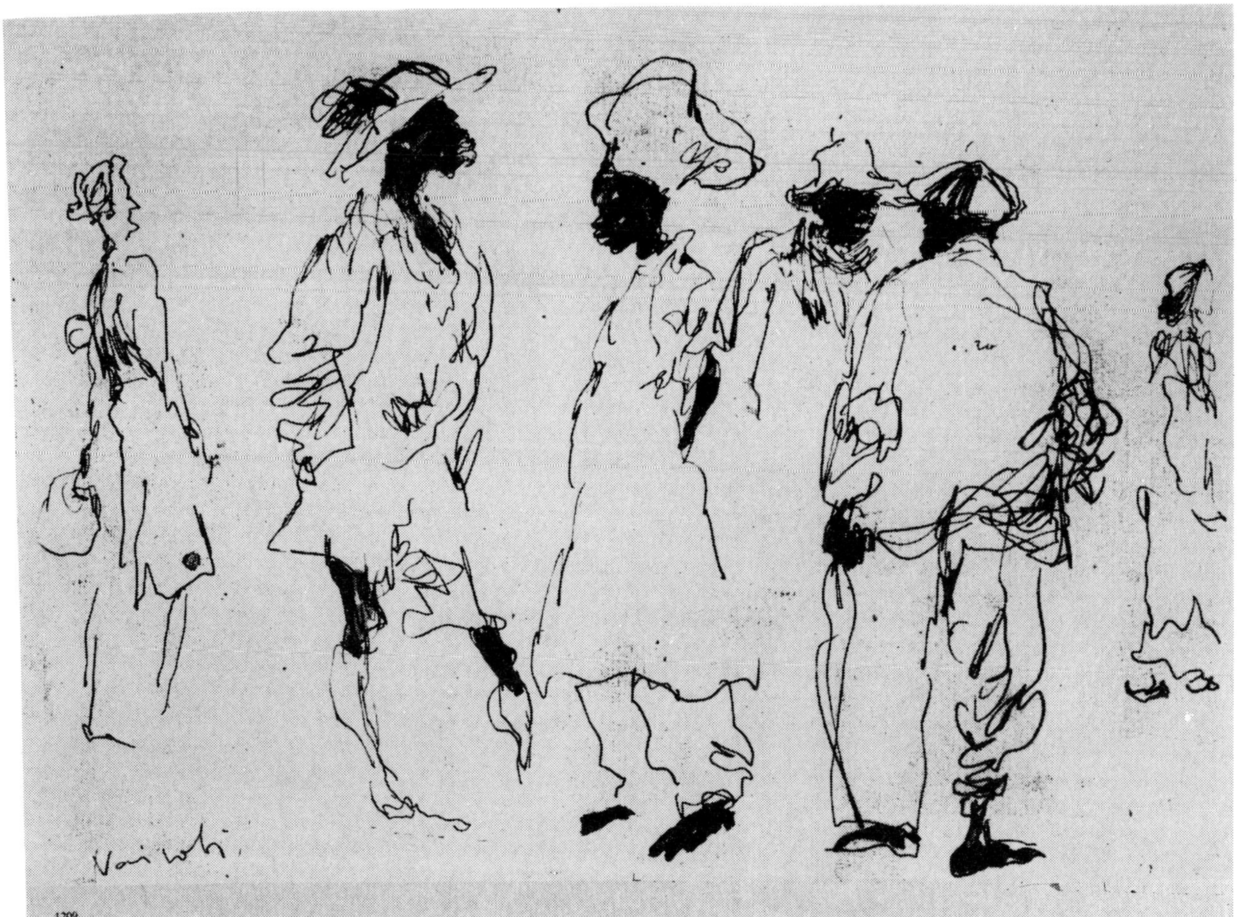

1209

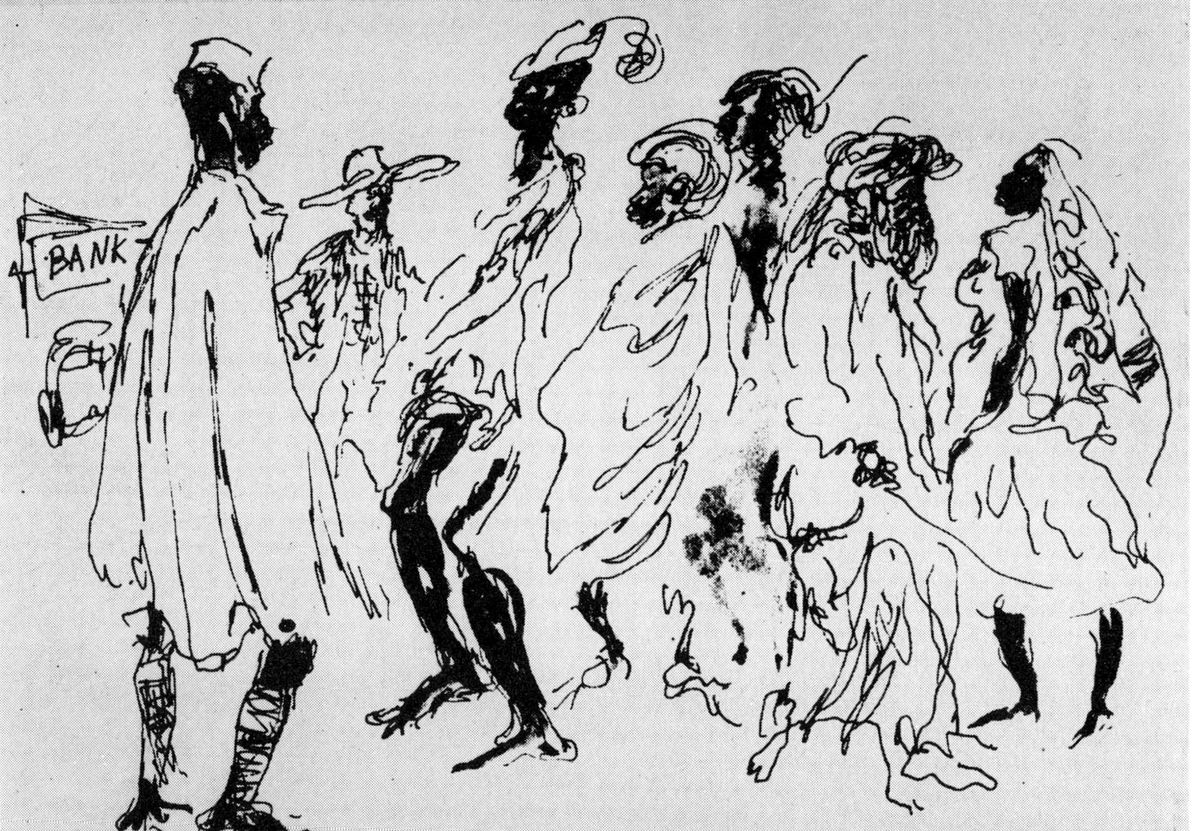

1212

Black Africa (from *Three Continents* and *Topolski's Chronicle*)

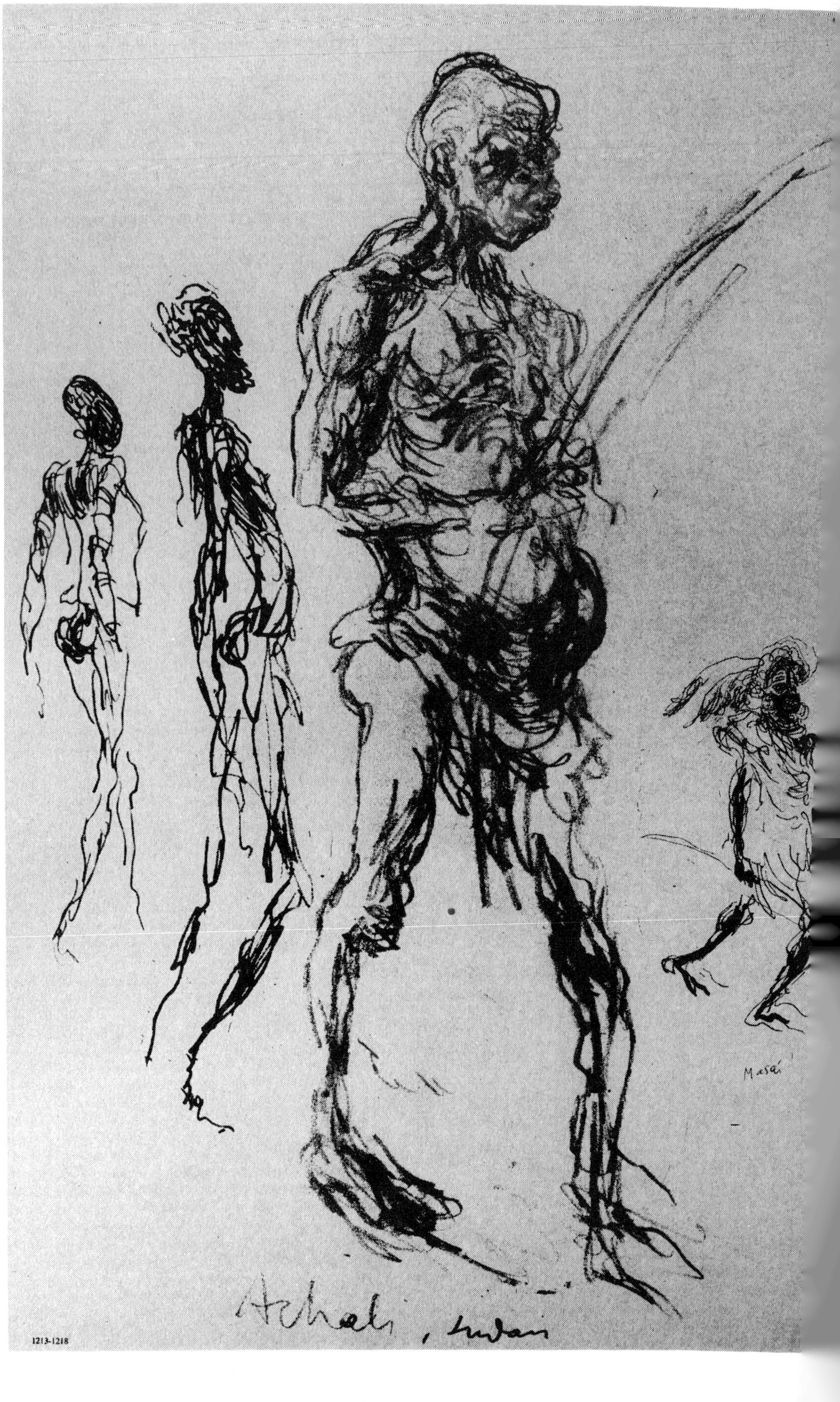

1213-1218

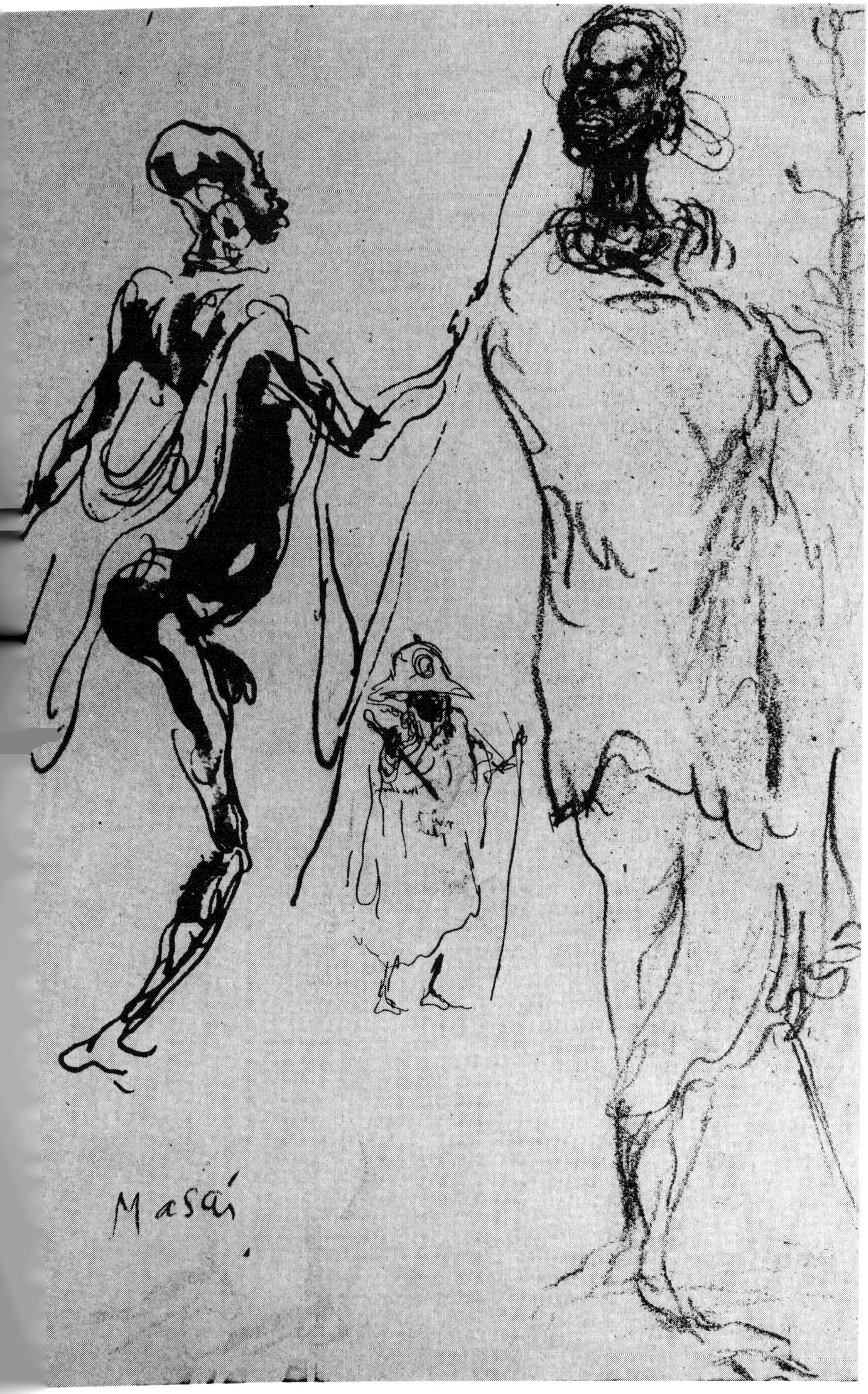

Black Africa (from *Three Continents* and *Topolski's Chronicle*)

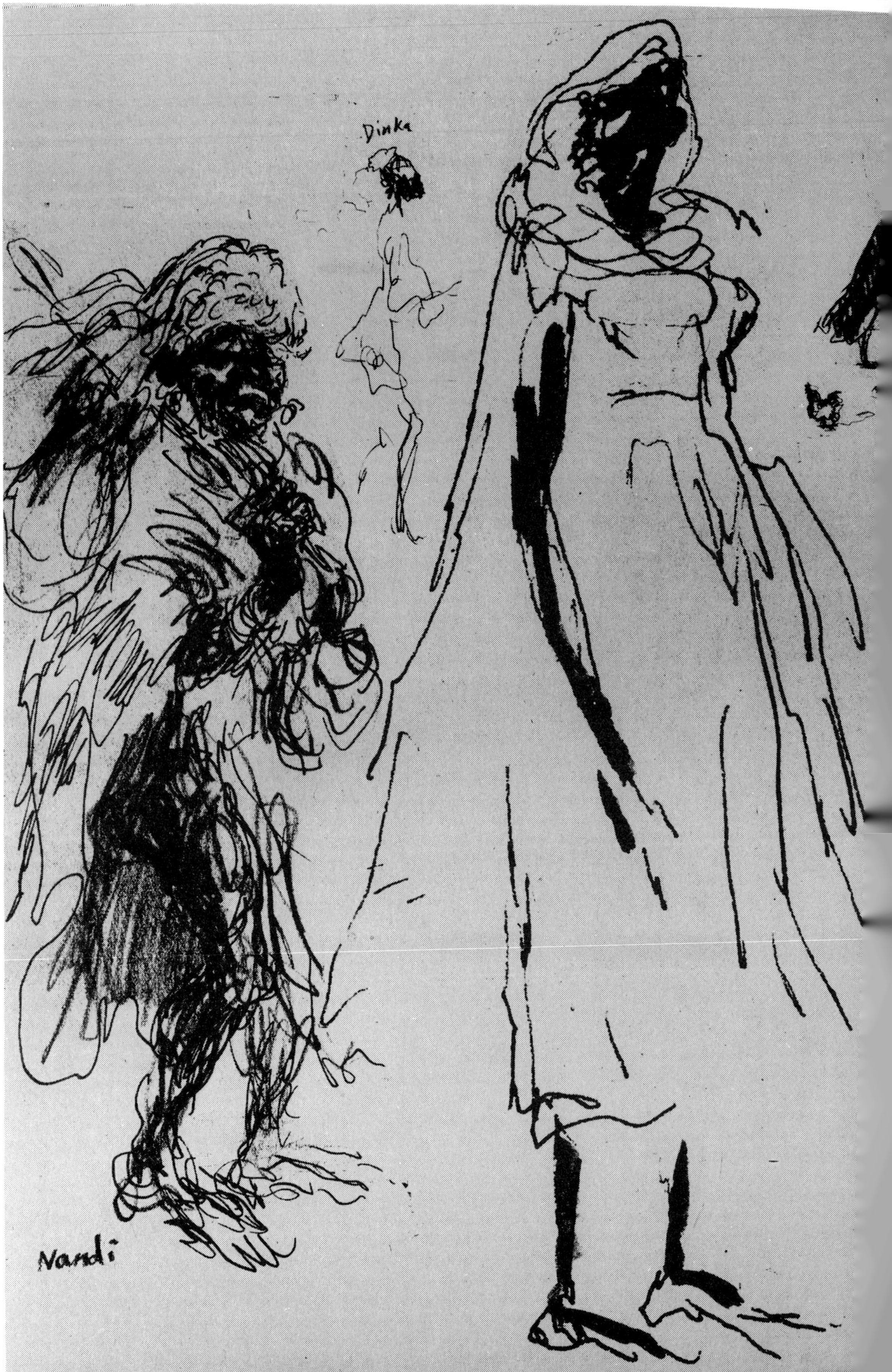

1219-1222

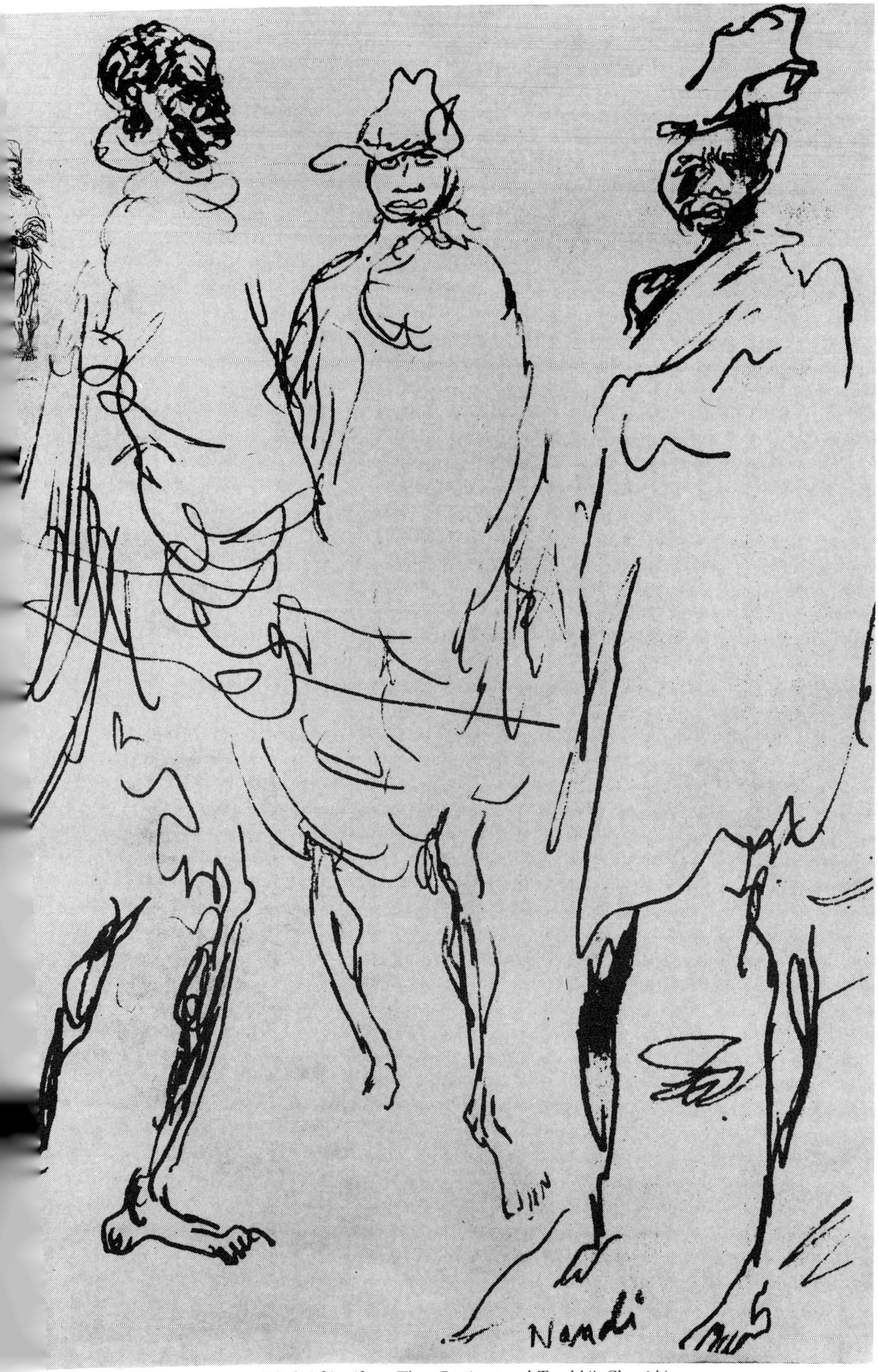

Black Africa (from *Three Continents* and *Topolski's Chronicle*)

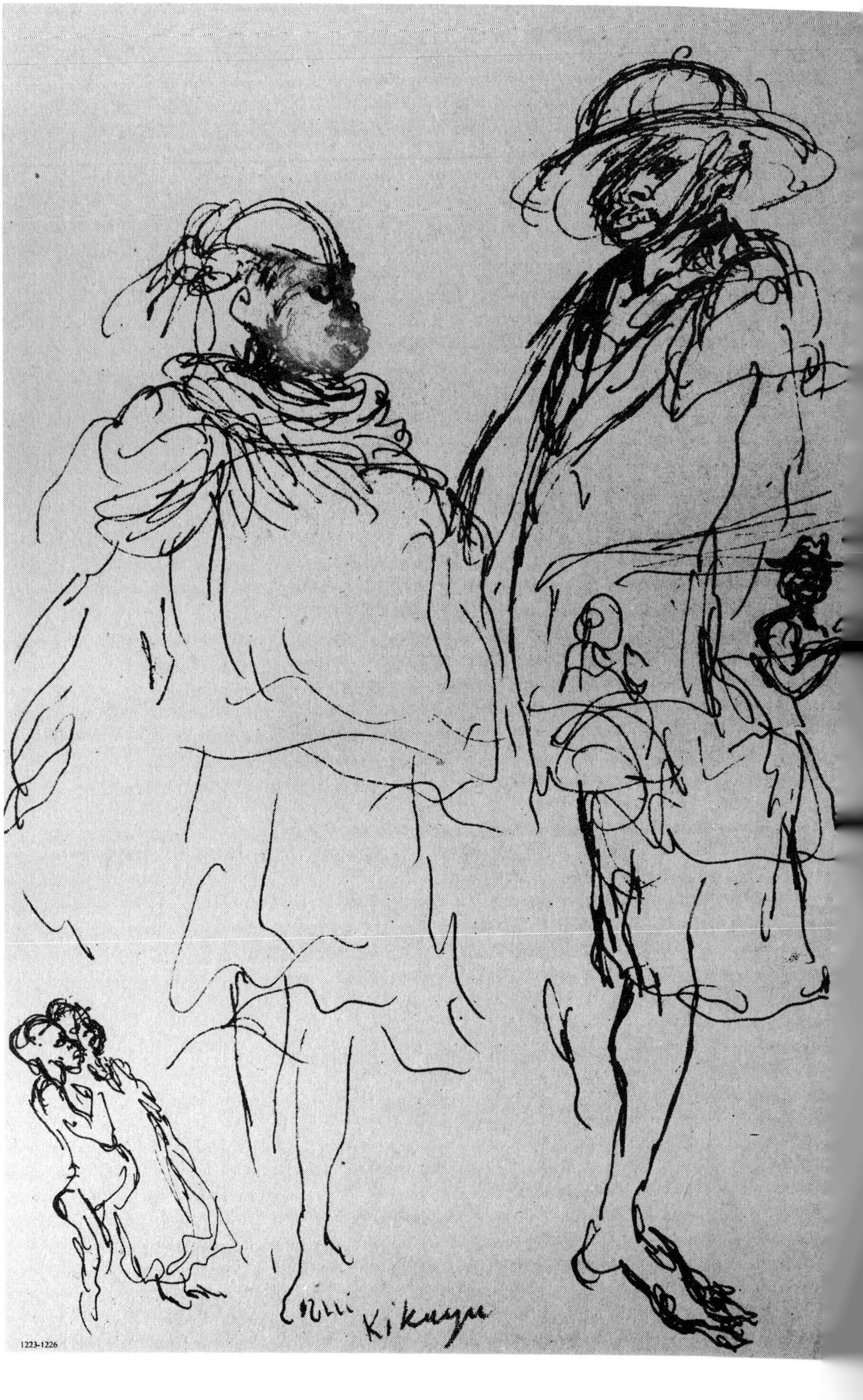

1223-1226

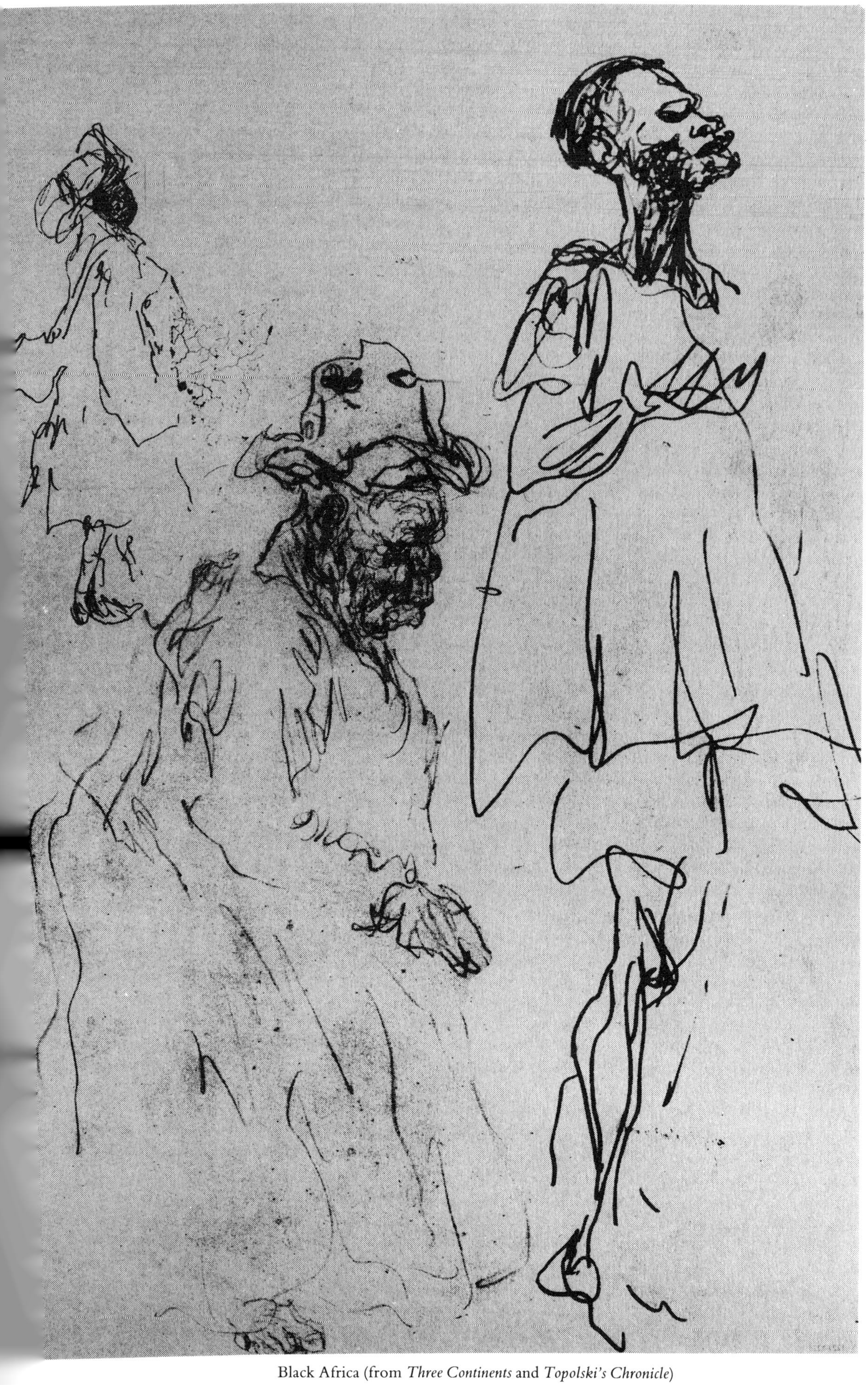

Black Africa (from *Three Continents* and *Topolski's Chronicle*)

rushing. And on the margin lively single sallies, pseudo-combats: to frighten with assault, almost clash with threatening raised weapons – and, instantly relaxing, trot back to the circle. It is not a vulgar mime, but a dance – wild creatures the masters of its sophistication. The distinguished Nubian ladies attend calmly at a distance, away from the hot vortex. The air is cool and transparent under low clouds.

Kenya. Nairobi's young female colonials carry on their faces the germ of old age – old Negresses preserve grace.

Before conveyancing to the white man's war, the King's African Riflemen frolic with bark-clothed maidens.

The majestic oleograph: between damp red earth and the reddish sky (squandering the purples) the village huts smoke bluishly. But driving up and beyond the hills almost brings back the sun. Time retreats through colour: the yellow-green jollities of an earlier hour return. The equator's conceits – the grand show on the edge of the earth.

The memory perches me on top of an open army truck amongst **Polish soldiers**, windblown and exulting in the fast panorama of **Apennine villages**' self-redressing gestures (the Germans have just retreated): the crowding piazzas with **the new mayors in judgement**, the division into the accusing and the cringing overthrown, the Allied convoys applauded, the banners – until, up on to the wilderness, against the backdrop of the peaks, **Italian guerrillas** prance forward in a buffoon parade, all got up as a gamut of Garibaldian, whiskered, feathered, bare-chested, ammunition-wrapped extras. After this, descent to the real business of the khaki and regular **Polish Second Corps**, engaged in pushing **the Germans** north along the Adriatic coast. The command tents are pitched on a green patch; surrounded by his staff, **General Anders** – stripped to the waist, and seated on a camp stool – has his chest shaved (his bare skull already dealt with), and directs the battle in progress. A message comes that the overall British command has two planes spare at the moment – any use? The shaving

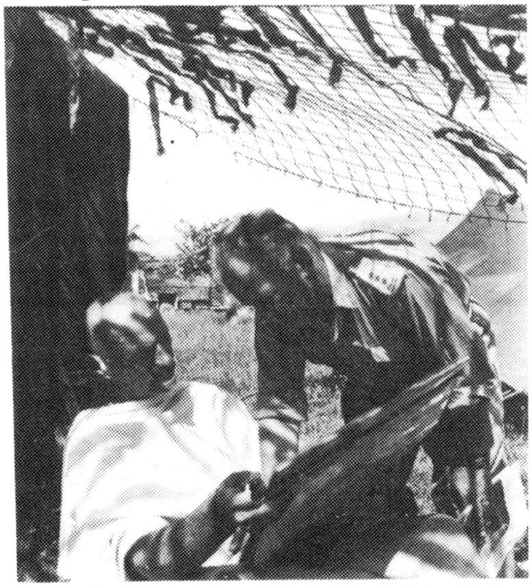

General Anders commanding action in Italy, 1944

goes on, teas are drunk, and random applications are vaguely suggested for the planes – the offer a not very welcome distraction.

Now I am rolling towards the battle line in a large vehicle amongst the literary camp-followers, led by the heavy old Melchior Wańkowicz, the official epic-writer of the campaign. All uniformed panachiously, tin eagles gleaming from their forage caps, all aglow with well-being as Culture in the service of the Cause. But, at a safe distance from Loreto which booms with gunfire, they encamp in a picnic mood.

And what follows must not seem a piece of self-laudation: compulsion, by then given gravity by wounds – a sort of annointment – in the London Blitz, lifted me out of meandering *bon-viveurism* into that 'holy war'. And the old mere appetite for being there, with a chronic unsureness, ever demanding that I measure myself against others, propelled me as well.

A tiny open **carrier** – a motorized-cavalry subaltern and I swaying above the driver – rushed into **the field of enemy fire** below Loreto in the wake of our advancing tanks. This was a rapid, bravado sweep offered by the young officer as a hospitable pleasantry, but it encountered plenty: a hit, **burning tank** – half-roasted, screaming, tossing men pulled out of its depth – Red Cross orderlies to their side; the rush under a blanket of noisy smokiness over the unprotected openness, passing a broken-up cottage, its black depth – framed by the doorway – revealing momentarily a static **petrified group** of peasant women.

The gesture completed, back and round the corner of cover given by DONNE and UOMINI, where **Loreto's worthies**, unstained by Fascism, are already grouping in a square to retake lawful possession; and the climb up to the attic of a narrow highest-placed house on the steep edge above the battle, the Corp's artillery observation post. And there, in the bawling of orders-giving and -receiving, in the concatenation of functions amidst the entanglement of watching/telephoning equipment, at the head of his supporting staff, concerting the whole Corp's artillery orchestration, is **General Ząbkowski** – out of retirement for this supreme fulfilment – once the Colonel heading the School of Officers of Artillery Reserve where I, as a cadet, had painted his formal portrait as CO. The General recognizes me, and, within all this urgency, we find a moment for **an embrace**.

Many years later, in London, the sketch made then, in that attic, is given to the General; but the final sequel – touching, but also uncomfortable – followed much later. That **old portrait**, pompous and smoothed out in the extreme, and embarrassing even at the time to the artist, who was glad of it probably being no more, surfaced in Poland and was brought with the utmost difficulty to England, and – by the General – to my studio, in the hope that I might touch it up to its original, intolerable glitter.

The massacred flesh of rocky ascents crowned far and high by, still fuming, broken stumps of **Monte Cassino Monastery**, less fearsome – the eye inured to ruins – than the

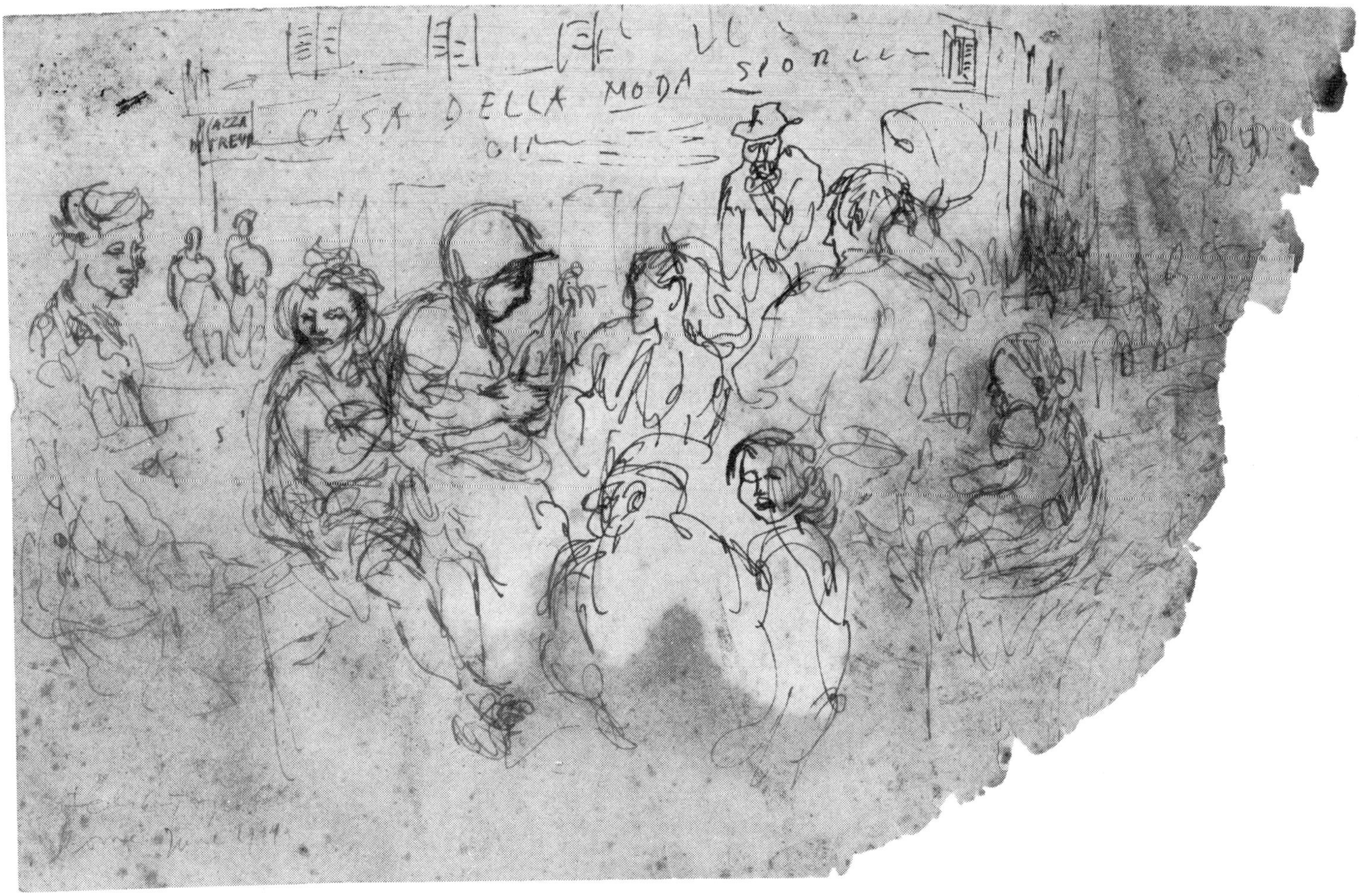

Allied soldiers with girls in Rome (from *Three Continents*)

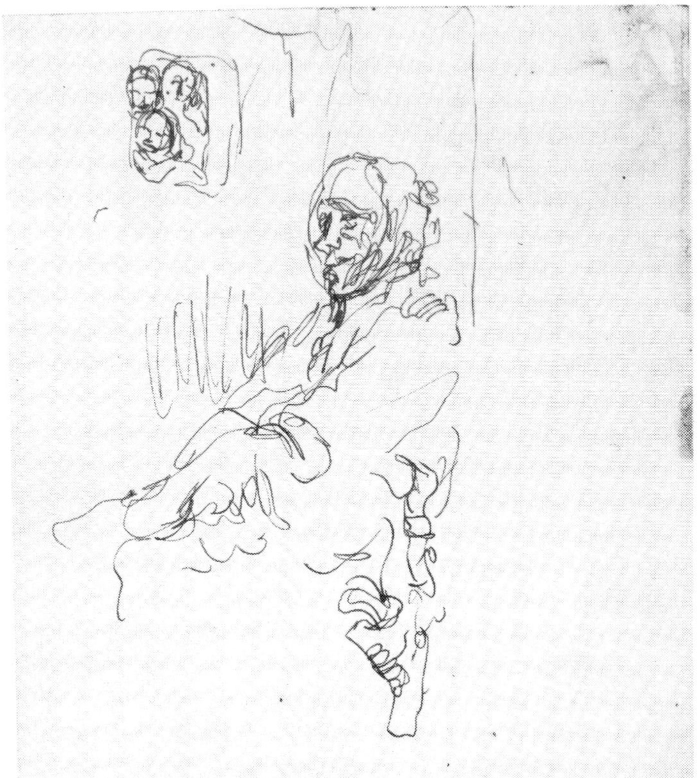

Wounded Polish soldier at Loreto (from *Three Continents*)

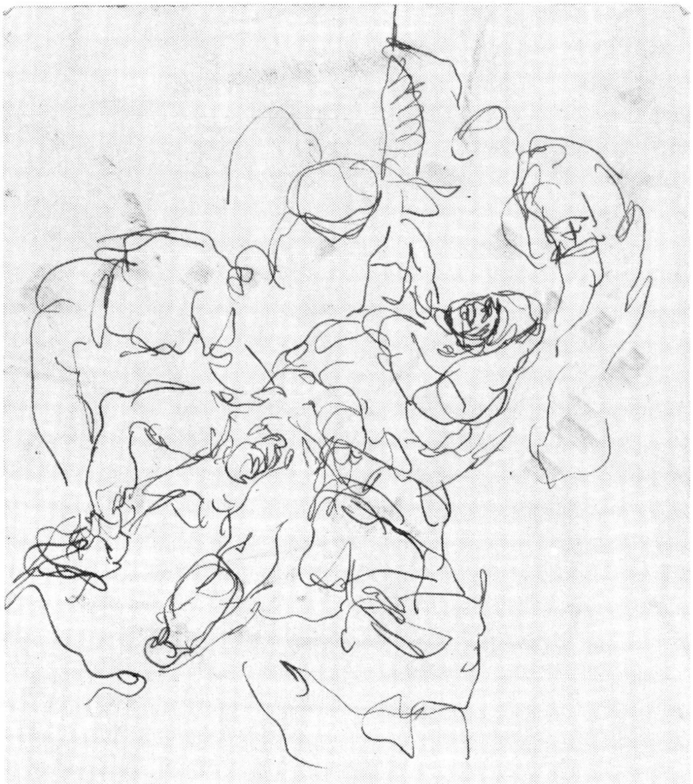

Out of a burning tank at Loreto (from *Three Continents*)

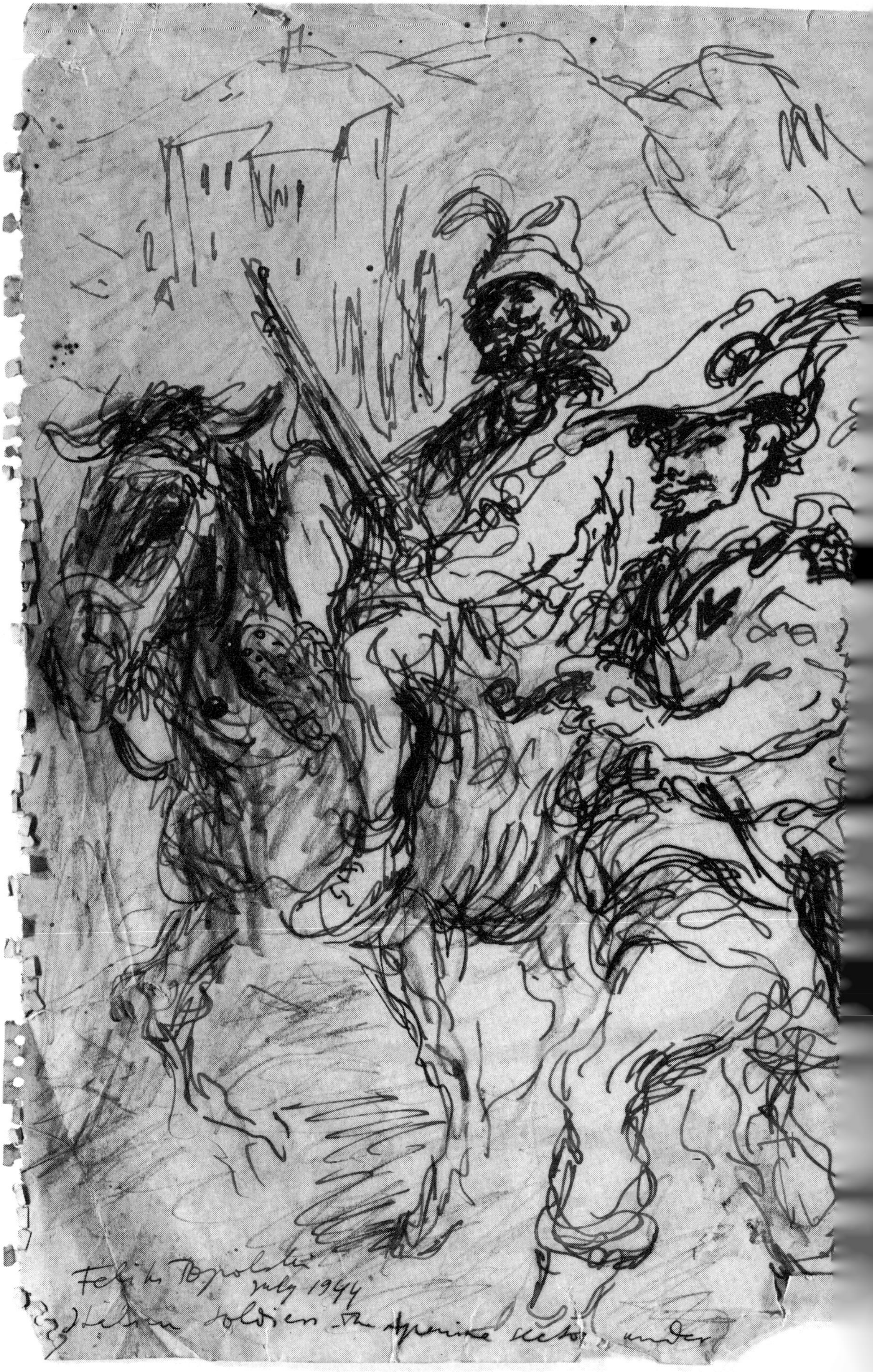

Feliks Topolski
July 1944

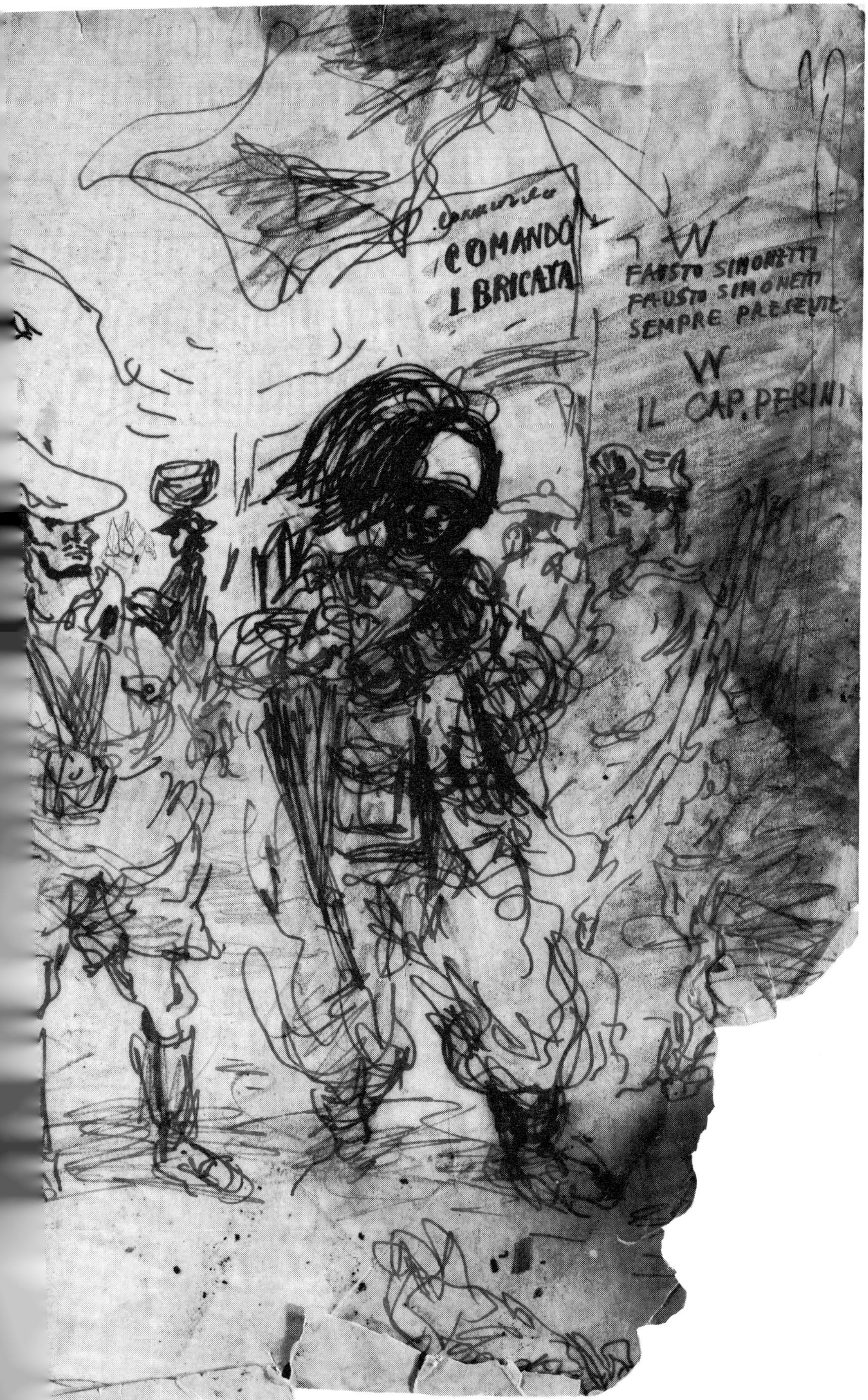

talian guerillas in the Apennines (from *Three Continents*)

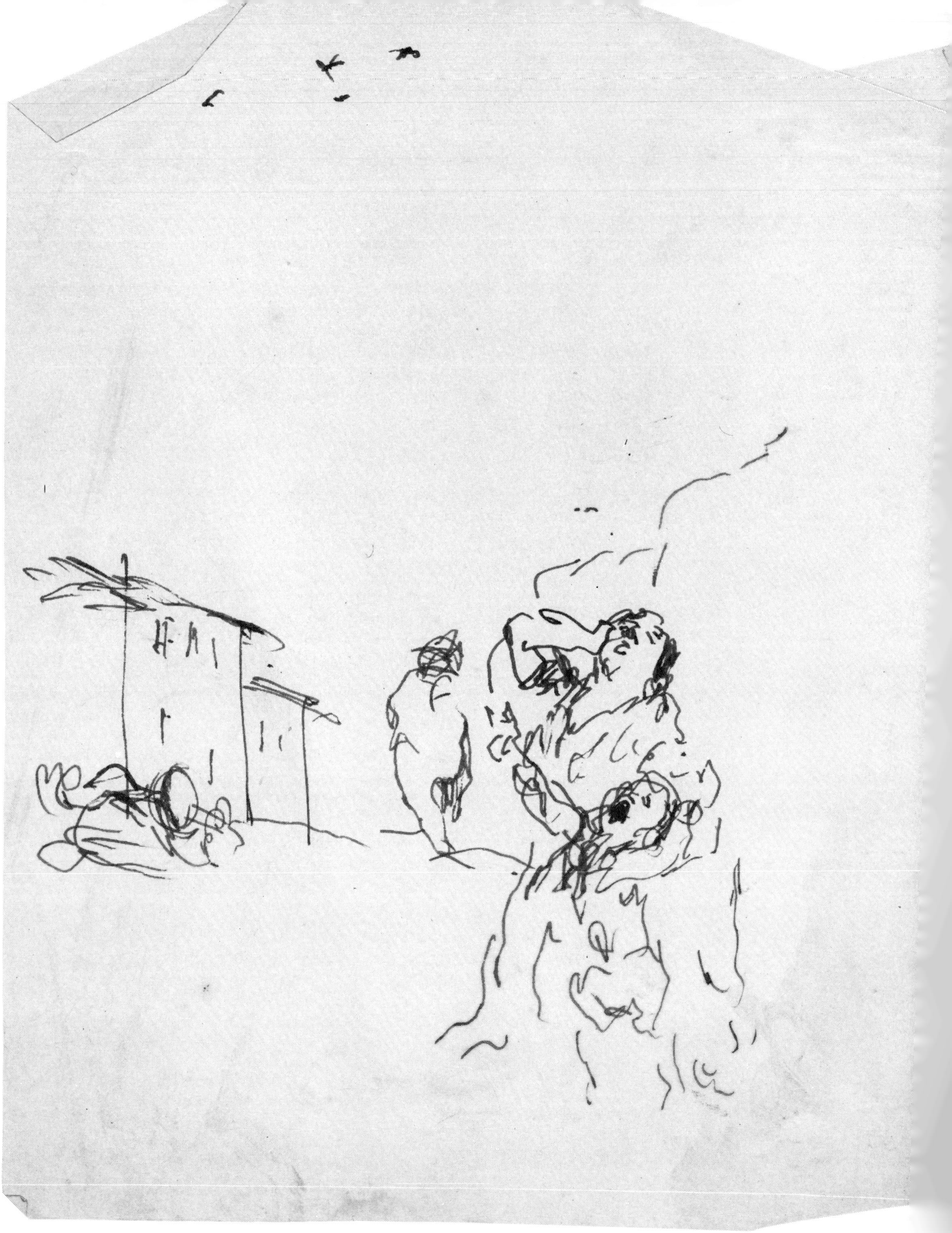

Air attack (from *Three Continents*)

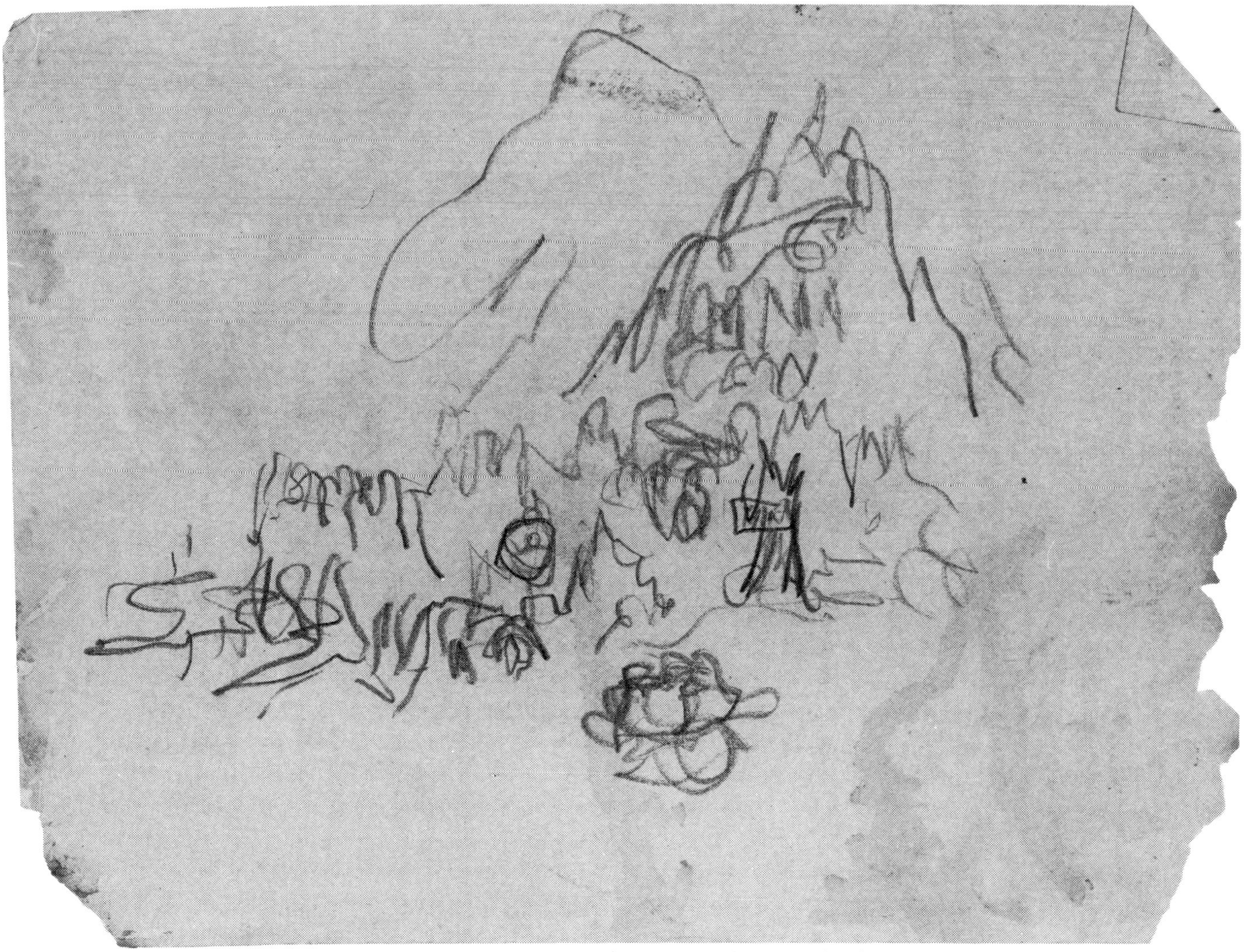

Monte Cassino after capture (from *Three Continents*)

assassinated nature leading to it. No stone spared – all crushed; vegetation and military junk (metal and of men) stamped into the mire.

The powdery grime and the deadening silence distance this only yesterday's battlefield, turn it into an object lesson in impossible history. Unimaginable that feebly armed men, friends, ever exposed under ceaseless fire, crawled, cowered, advanced up and conquered these steep defences.

Only at the edges of this landscape-mortuary our retreating jeep encounters piled-up shells, tangled armoury, burst machines, half-buried signs: MINES, INFERNO TRACK – and, unaccountably materializing out of the lifelessness, leisurely donkey-back-mounted, black-cassocked, black-umbrella-and black-glasses-shaded, a demoniac priestly rider.*

Night curtains over the snuffed-out inferno of Monte Cassino – the jeep rides on **to Rome**. Willy-nilly it becomes a 'back from the front lines' war-chariot: the ever-clamouring crowds, the swift – as if by assignation – leap of girls on to the jeep, the ride up to the dark gardens of (was it?) the Villa Borghese, the unearned privilege of Roman gratitude.

Wake up to the sound-kaleidoscopes: stamping clattering clacking pattering – echoing with resonant human/bird voices – holy day's sounds.

Outdoors: ochre breeze-swept architectural abundances – stages for crowd scenes of elation: Roman women in flocks, their shoe-straps undone, clicketing on high heels; men-at-arms of all colours all tongues all uniform-shapes wander, sway, strut, pair off; bivouac, nap, sing, entwine; groups interweave, advance banner-raised . . .

This holy day's, this **liberation's enchantment** orchestrates the whole in never nowadays allowed to be lived in reality, guessed only from old pictures – the purest marriage of the habitation with the inhabitants, not confused/polluted by the motor traffickery.

*Years later, the pathos of 'cosmetic' recovery: the 'landscaped' approaches to the freshness-gleaming monastery, and, below, long clean perspectives of crosses 'dignified' by a neatly/functionally designed *capella*.

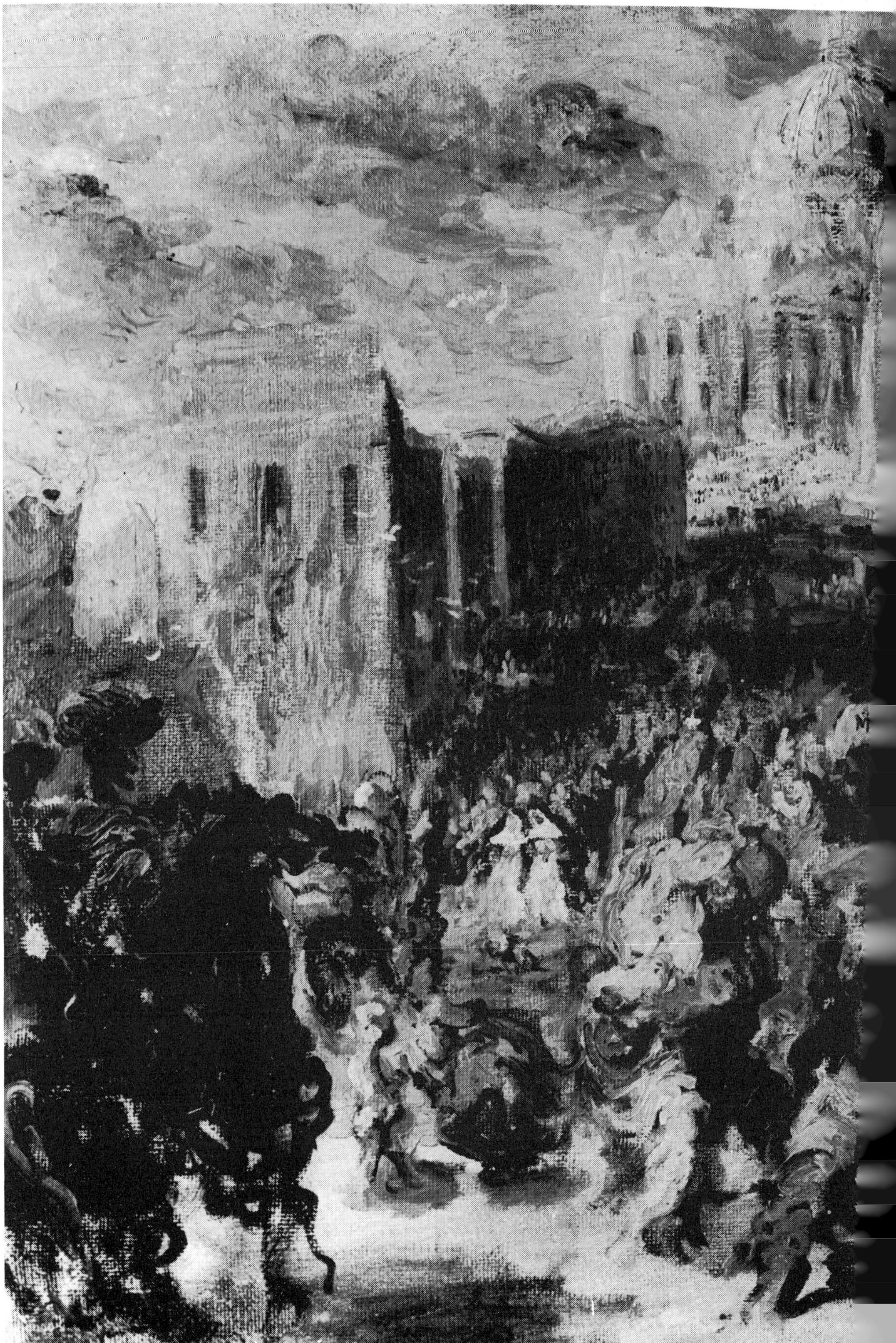

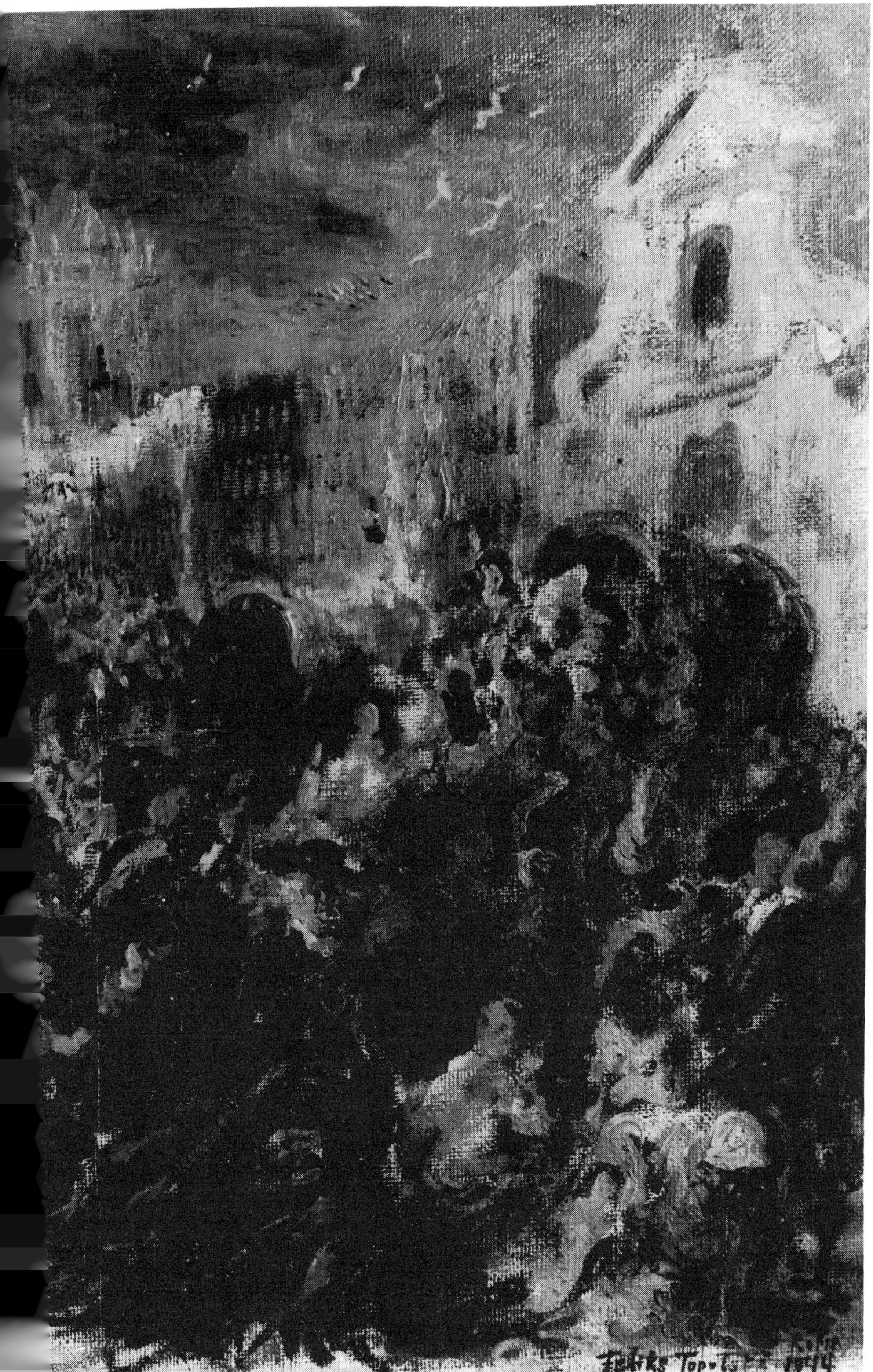

Rome liberated (from *Three Continents*)

Towards the end of the war or just after, an unlikely location for incubation of great art – the bare little top room of elegant narrow Park Lane house turned dormant offices of a banker-politician Edward Beddington-Behrens; or perhaps just right: **Oskar Kokoschka**, ever itinerant yet ever patronaged, hence ever precisely suited (Clement: 'These beautifully straight press-trousered legs'), so that ever ready to step from behind the easel into his collector's salon a floor below. A major European artist thoroughly ignored by the British Establishment of the time,* throughout the war years could rely on his private following.

But this unstained little room, enclosing this beautiful precise man working on a very small but ultra-feverish painting – astonished. Also this strange link with Jack Yeats: he proceeded to set unhurriedly into the same frame a series of identical in size small oils, one after another, on the easel – and explain!

His index finger would roam over a delightful crowded scene, exposing his cartooning naiveties, with a girl-England seated in the centre, swinging a shoe off her bare foot at a fleeing rat-spy, but falling back upset by a Churchill figure, black hat over its eyes, firing blindly upward a defensive shot cracking a hole in his own ceiling, the setting being a pub as symbolic no-shelter for the Londoners. Another picture: the demise of Imperial Britannia – fat Victoria just afloat on angry oceans.† They were cartoons in oils and I badly wanted to buy one. But Oskar's poverty did not disarm his eye-on-the-future confidence: he fobbed me off, making it gently clear that I couldn't afford his pictures.‡

This time, by the British art bosses still ignored, he received us in horribly neat furnished rooms, in which the Kokoschkas lived without a trace of domestication, within one of those well-off refugee-inhabited blocks on the main road towards Swiss Cottage – perhaps deliberate accent on refusal to settle on this London level. First time ever he embarked on try-out water-colour flowers.§ Again, one after another, they were propped up for us ceremonially at slow pace – an endless series, to me faultlessly routine studies, by the watered-down Kokoschka, while to Marion . . . she fell asleep: a dramatic *faux pas*. True, she was in the last weeks of pregnancy, and enough excuses were propounded to make our precipitated departure not quite ignoble.

Germany's defeat; 1945 Diary

Brussels. A 'leave-town' packed with the same soldiery, but devoid of the handsomeness of Rome, Calcutta's strangeness, Cairo's style. Europe of the north: hefty, dull, grey-stoned, in compensation adorned at the bottom of ravines of streets with friezes of white, cowlike, opulent she-creatures.

A prostitute says: '*Les Allemands étaient chic avec les femmes – les Americains . . . quels brutes*.' The stage is set, at last, for soldierly leave as it should be – without restrictions. Low dens, glossed over to seem streamlined, boom with populace and music ('Chocolate for b–a–a–aby and for me.'). At ten o'clock at night the human tide flows into the Avenue du Midi and whoring goes 'out of bounds'. Already here, in Flanders, the local hussy is turning 'cutie' – shines her platinum locks, gurgles an American curse, swings her arse, mills her jaws. By the Gare du Nord bargaining goes on till the curfew hour. Springtime barrows are filled with lilac, soldiers tease with part-time tarts ('Business – business, *cinq-cents francs!*').

Under the surface of LIBERATION the human comedy rolls on untouched: the women's over-embellished hats – the men (those who have black-marketed into opulence) fashioned by puffy tailoring – and the grimly impoverished mass. A young man, a publisher, tells all, as it was and as it is: 'We lived those years in *prosperité équitable*. The Germans behaved correctly. A letter and reply from Switzerland took only three days. One travelled to Paris without a passport. Now one cannot move anywhere. A letter takes ten days and the reply is held by the censor . . .' He checks himself and backs up a little: 'Oh, well, it was slavery, but . . .' – and again – 'Freedom? Now frankly personal freedom is curtailed, only the sense of freedom has returned.'

That ONLY defines his terms – where for him abstract truth touches the common day. 'One could play the hero', he says, 'but one needn't' – he is a socialist – 'Even the Jews were not condemned to martyrdom – they signed on for it.'

Peace settles thickly, greasily over Belgium. '*Pendant la guerre, monsieur*,' states the girl behind the posh counter (stockings 1000 francs). That is her war. A hotelier refugee from Germany in London expounded his: 'Why do you travel so much, expose yourself to danger? War is on, one should stay at home.' Men panting with haste and speculation, women frozen in *maquillage* and fashion. I goggle at this exhibit of wartime life – and after. Abomination.

I am seconded for the duration of my assignment a jeep manned by two: a mandatory 'conducting officer', Gerald; and a driver, Smith. Guidebook zigzagging over Belgium. Women, stilted by platforms and scaffold-hats, perform up to the outskirts of Brussels. Saturday – the day of weddings: carriages and top-hats jolt along village streets; nuns in pairs punctuate the landscape. Warlike, aloof from the life of the country, the British ironmongery clamours diagonally across it.

Ghent sweeps hurriedly by: the beauty of its cathedral, thronging of military lorries, conceited houses of the burghers, stuck with half-masted black–yellow–red flags – mourning for Roosevelt.

Entering Bruges through the old gate, through the

*The war ended, he was given instantly immense showings all over the Western world, and only then the London Tate Gallery bosses followed suit unabashed.

†His *My Life*, fallen into my hands recently, tells, 'During this period (1939–43) I painted a series of "political" pictures, not out of any political commitment but with the intention of opening others' eyes to the way I saw the war,' and proceeds to describe the pictures in the same confused way, strangely assured of the 'prophetic' value of one of them. This one he calls *Marianne-Maquis* and explains its contents as satirizing France, her field-marshals and the Maginot line. Yet my memory is clear on this score: his version for me, full of details, was of England not France. And to play on such commotions: in the other picture his Britannia 'rides on a shark'; but in the postscript to the book by another pen, 'Queen Victoria is riding on a whale.'

‡An unsuccessful transaction with Stanley Spencer at his Cookham tiny house, his large canvases pinned around the walls: his seductive-erotic pencil drawings (the cheapest paste-in cuttings books), my painful selection to buy one – at his accord; and his letter some weeks later going back on the sale.

§*My Life* lifts up these flower series to the level of an ideological proposition.

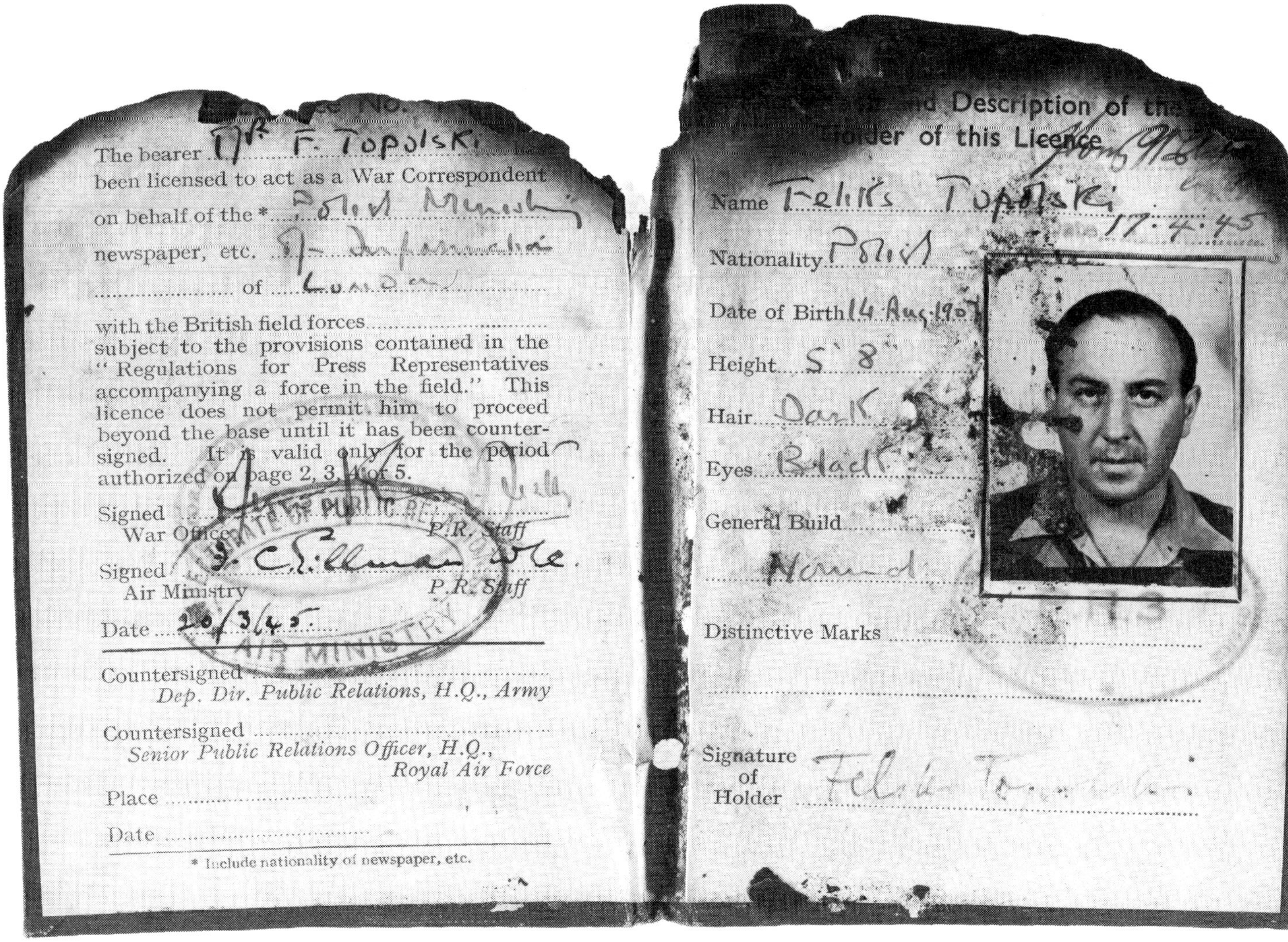

The bearer Dr F. Topolski has been licensed to act as a War Correspondent on behalf of the * Polish Ministry of Information newspaper, etc. of London with the British field forces subject to the provisions contained in the "Regulations for Press Representatives accompanying a force in the field." This licence does not permit him to proceed beyond the base until it has been countersigned. It is valid only for the period authorized on page 2, 3, 4 or 5.

Signed .... War Office P.R. Staff

Signed .... Air Ministry P.R. Staff

Date 20/3/45

Countersigned .... *Dep. Dir. Public Relations, H.Q., Army*

Countersigned .... *Senior Public Relations Officer, H.Q., Royal Air Force*

Place ....

Date ....

* Include nationality of newspaper, etc.

... and Description of the Holder of this Licence

Name Feliks Topolski

Nationality Polish

Date of Birth 14 Aug 1907

Height 5' 8"

Hair Dark

Eyes Black

General Build Normal

Distinctive Marks ....

Signature of Holder Feliks Topolski

commercial hubbub (the world where the dog does not earn his bread by love and charm, but struggles in a cart's harness) into beauties different from those I imagined: not a serpentined-streeted compact medieval fortress but a smooth town-museum. It is a relief that the Polish troopers swagger in hospital blue, that an English *élégante* offers Bruges the colour and style of the knightly costume of a parachutist.

Rushing into Antwerp, the only 'honorary' wound of Belgium. Smashed by flying-bombs, it looks heroic and dull.

Departure. Drippy, windy. Call in at POW Reception Centre – the freed prisoners already nestling into the boredom of an armchair, an old *Daily Express*, still try to dish out stories already paled (since yesterday evening) of suffering – grow tedious – give up – pay with the loss of a halo for homeliness ever after.

The warriors, returned to bourgeois cosiness, fall behind: we pursue the last days of the Heroic Time.

But the theatrical gestures of the MPs (sten-guns across their backs) point east. We clatter on – overtake the flat life (so we imagine) of Sunday-bored, redbricked villages, umbrellas, a chapel – and, nonsensically blocking the bicycle path, small mounds with crosses topped by Prussian helmets: a torpid landscape and the discreet tragicomedy of the German conquest and retreat.

Unsorrowfully we leave Belgium and (with no sense of frontier) bump into Holland (shutters painted into lace curtains). Eindhoven – Philips's spooky town-prison: by choice, slavery in comfort. Civilized, trimmed probity.

Scrupulously heaped gliders' skeletons – the approach to **Arnhem**. The Canadian Army's sphere of operations opens up with swarms of hoardings urging to buy 'Victory Bonds'; thus military might ricochets the post-war anxieties of how to survive the peace against the provident haste of the Dutch, exposes shamelessly the realism beneath the 'Citizens' Army' veneer – while a peasant galloping beautifully on a huge carthorse echoes the heroic past. Contradictions of our days. But these are the antics of behind-the-lines, and of the end of the war. Dutchmen hang out little flags on the gutted cottages, but look strangely well for a nation dying of starvation. 'In Amsterdam and The Hague' – they say – 'there is hunger.' Later those who travelled north will tell us of people hungry but dignified, of well-pressed destitution, small talk about a crust of bread, and death from hunger behind the starched net curtains of appearances.

An overture of awe opens up the landscape of Liberation. We clatter over the Rhine bridge loaded with history. 'Liberated fully', Arnhem breathes stench and massacre – an abattoir of bricks and mortar, not just a ruin. But smashed trees steal the show. A cinema poster juts out crookedly: *'Hab' Mich Lieb!'* Orange and tricolour flutter pitifully on the rubble. Booby-traps. Craters. Marking minefields white tapes outline, museum-like, the outstanding exhibits. The war traffic hoots on, carried by its own momentum.

The German frontier. Bang. 'Tortured' Dutchmen give way to the nation of torturers. I part without regret from the liberated and rush towards those who are tormented by our advance. 'Here ends the civilized world'; 'You are now in Germany – behave like conquerors' – slogans tested instantly by a youngster whining, '*Zigaretten für Papa.*' White tape (marking more minefields) encircles a bleak populace. The gestures are of the defeated as anticipated. Cringing, dog-like then grateful; servile, cap doffed, a craven giggle; but a hard boy stiffly staring, a heedless kid, a girl watchful.

Flat, flat, grey, grey; dirty-white flapping rags of surrender. The gloomy mindless nothingness of this northern corner explains their itch for conquest: surely it is the longing of the deprived to break towards the light – the provincial's dream to 'visit' Paris has to become (because he is too grey, too inferiority-ridden) a MARCHING into Paris. A tempting argument, though the handsomeness of southern Germany *gives it* the lie.

Roadscape of war – since fighting is highway-bound: rusting vehicles, tapes, wires, mud, ammunition and petrol tins; women tied to the carts, oldsters shovelling slushed tarmac. Entry to Lingen – and a beautifully stage-managed scene: shell-ploughed marketplace: a fragment of the *Rathaus* decorated with a signboard of the Military Government and Anglo-American flags; a bulldozer shows off – its steel nose kneading the remnants of the *Apotheke* in a roar and dust of collapsing storeys; the Germans cluster, subjugated into admiration; prisoners in convoy. A paddock of nations in the costume of beggar-soldiers, in the aura of brigandage, rowdiness and destitution. 'Displaced Persons'.

Lingen DP Camp. The roads-deluging masses are raked into crammed misery: cowshed, pigsty, stable nestle the human herd. Stinking vistas of shadowy interiors stacked with human pulp. UNRRA has not shown up in time and Civil Affairs in the person of a fussy British major segregate and feed. One distinguishes, disentangles single people. Warmed by attention received, they open up: a Polish 1939 soldier religiously attached to his clumsy uniform, a Yugoslav lad, and oversized red star of Tito on his cap, a Russian wench loaded offeringly with lewd flesh, a French prisoner already nearing home – and a British major gloats over his loot: SS daggers, Leicas, a faience jug gilt-glazed. By the doorstep a flattened body – a Ruthenian yokel drunk on spirit taken out of a lamp. A Polish mother (a newborn at her breast) wasted by child-bearing and infamy, propped against a wall painted with the pompous apotheosis of Wehrmacht soldiery and nordically joyful families gazing into the rising sun. A man with stupefied eyes, beating against the barbed wire, entreats (needle stuck in groove): '*Ich bin nicht Deutsch, ich bin Lothringer, ich bin nicht Deutsch.*' We move on – pursued by '*Ich bin nicht Deutsch.*'

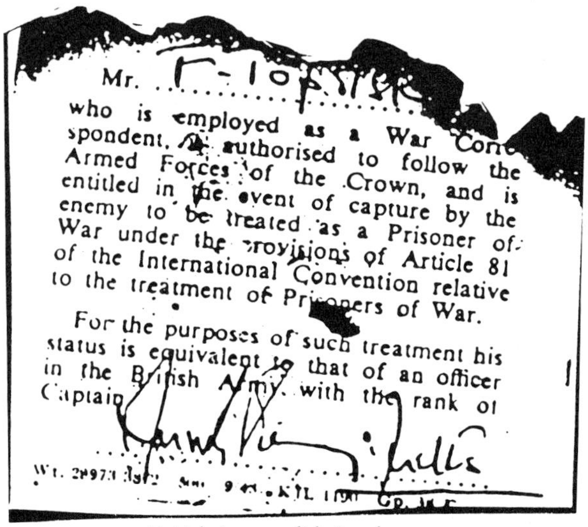
Mr. ..F-Topolski..........
who is employed as a War Corre-
spondent, is authorised to follow the
Armed Forces of the Crown, and is
entitled in the event of capture by the
enemy to be treated as a Prisoner of
War under the provisions of Article 81
of the International Convention relative
to the treatment of Prisoners of War.

For the purposes of such treatment his
status is equivalent to that of an officer
in the British Army with the rank of
Captain

British Army validation document

Now the roads ('always the roads!') swell with people. Mine-warning signs ('Road only checked') and trees, split open and gaping yellowly, bank the deluge of wanderers. The crowds on the Italian roads were different – weary and 'local'. Here are the delivered; here is privation, but also bluster, a mix of tribes and of fortunes. German prisoners roll past in trucks: Soviets, Poles, Frenchmen, Belgians, Yugoslavs, Dutchmen, Greeks, Ukranian crones, Asians: ex-prisoners, ex-slaves from factories and fields – all tramp on in small clusters. The triviality of everydayness and distances dilutes the drama. The speeding of the car through it detaches, but also accumulates, thickens. The car stops – and a different dimension envelops one – one is in the life of the road. Conversations disentangle nationalities, characters, gestures – wasted lives shape themselves out of awkward words.

A new group. We stop. Different from the others, unlike anyone else in the world; clowns' patchwork rags, skeletons eaten into by dirt and hunger – also nobler, through martyrdom. They stink of corpses. 'Where from?' '*Konzentrazionslager Schwagerl bei Papenburg.*' ***Konzentrazionslager*** for the first time heard, with that shivering shock, near faint, near spasm when facing the sinister, the beyond reason that cuts across, leaves shattered our world. They move on wings. But my 'conducting officer' Gerald does not believe, suspects they are disguised soldiers. And it is true – in a way. I shall learn later that theirs was a deserters' concentration camp.

Muscovites (dyed dark-green) present the full scale of their folklore – from the turbulent Ivans through the forlorn Mongol to the old *babushki i dievushki*. A stick under the arm, a lady's bike brand a robber. Polish soldiers rib-dig with the Russian *dievushki*, comfort *mamashe*: 'How's going, sister?' One says: '*Nu, harasho* – Fine, when are we for home?' Another: '*Vot*, now an American for me – to revel round New York.' Or another: 'What's Stalin to me – the world's big.' Just people. They do not embrace matters of politics and history. Soon they will be herded again, Political Expedience will reshuffle them. 'Order will be restored' – but now, for a flash, the fences of determinism of the West's 'civilized life', and equally of the Soviets' in the East, are down and vistas of adventure beckon.

Poles, however, tend to be Poland-stricken, their national over-sensitiveness bred on their country's crippled life. They incline to present in self-defence a pathetically haughty aura of

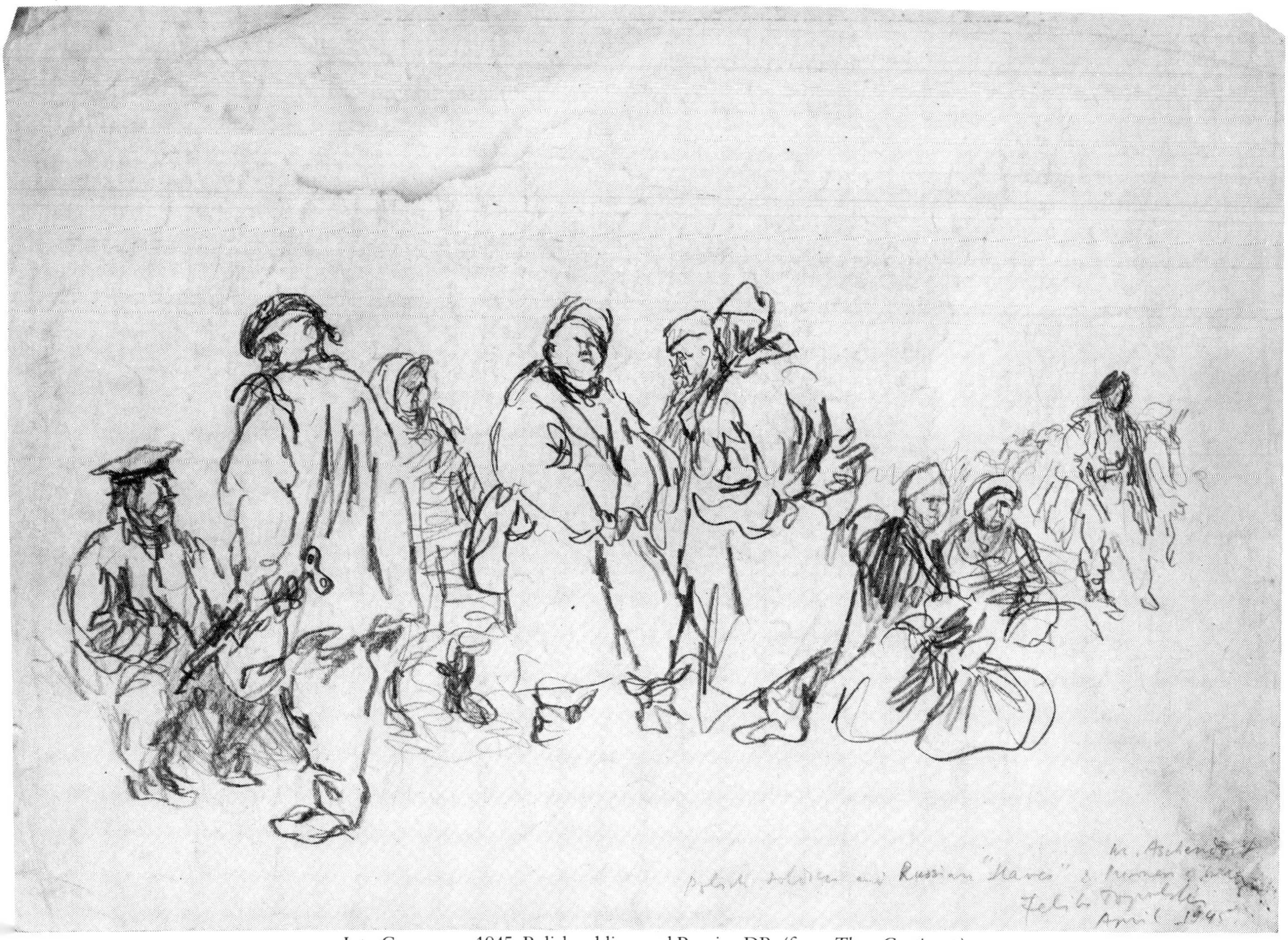

Into Germany – 1945: Polish soldiers and Russian DPs (from *Three Continents*)

superiority towards the neighbouring breeds. 'Sir, I shall not return to such a Poland.' 'Look at them, these Russians – savage rabble.' Or: 'We've volunteered already for the army' – shabby, exhausted prisoner-of-war of 1939. Yokel: 'There'll be trouble with the Ruskies and, if we must, we'll take up the cudgels.' Or others: 'Propaganda goes this way and that, but we're going back.' But prudent Polish peasants stay put in the villages of Westphalia and Hanover where they slave-laboured; they will not come out on to the roads and fall into the mangle of world balances: 'Better wait till the end, then we'll see – here the folk are good.'

Churlishness, verve, challenge, humility, grief, loneliness flow down the roads, united in rags and bundles in direction, but not in aim. Simplified progress of humanity: grotesque, pitiful, insipid, diluted in the vulgarity of daily needs, with only the reflexes of aspirations; trivial in humour, mean in wolfishness, slow in conquering mile after mile – but, for all that, a march; for all that a freedom march.

Nevertheless its greatness and monumental force are not conveyed by the sight alone. The image – when written into the catalogue of history: GERMANY DEFEATED – FREEDOM FOR MILLIONS OF SLAVES, APRIL 1945 – seizes one with the realization of history fulfilling itself here in the dust of the Oldenburg road in a frame of spring-flowering orchards and peasant compulsions (sowers, though panicky, step out into furrows) – with the machines bristling with arms (central motive of the picture) hooting over Bailey bridges, clattering through the iron and rubble of flattened cities, artillery-roaring, salvoes-crackling, with men's voices spitting blasphemies, crying out in pain, or in conquest.

A jeep swings from a side road: the khaki loadful hemming in a grey-green cap puffed up high with wired structure – a captured SS General. We are reaching towards the war, scattering swarms of *misérables*. Thickening of traffic, signs, soldiery, arms, white tape's calligraphic flourish, telephone wires – the bubbling of the 'tactical rear' opens on to the big lordly house: eighteenth-century muralled hall, staff officers, portable comforts of the Command, toadying lackey-cooks in uniform, and in the clipped park the General's caravan.

But, when Gerald loots and grabbles in the private rooms, and the hefty blonde permits herself to protest (and soon screams in panic when soldiers jab all over the garden with antennae and are almost on to her buried hoard), I know that the *Landrat* family are people of the regime, that they do not belong to this house; their hideous but costly lumber, the *Autobahn* maps, the cologne waters and rubbishy booklets (the old and dignified library in the loft), and albums of family-cum-party snapshots reveal to me the ugly boredom of the **nouveau-riche** life of Hitler's Germany.

'Prisoners of War Cage'. The threshold – the true abyss will follow.

A defiant scoundrel – the concentration camp head guard – who, throughout the night before the Polish entry, went on shooting camp inmates (150 of them), not quite managed to change into a civilian, caught, beaten, stands for some hours now, one boot on, 'at attention' (a naive punishment) in the centre of a meaningful scene: he in a cage among the prostrate guards of Konzentrazionslager Papenburg, on the left a crowd of their former victims, on the right the prisoners of war proper (miraculous luck for them to be not dead but freezing here, herded in dull fear).

The delivered martyrs open-uncross their arms, bare their fouled bashful torsos, shrivelled genitalia: the gesture of self-offering, of trust – also the narration of suffering. The white dust of disinfectants envelops their bareness. Thus should the Last Judgement look: they, the Innocents, stand in white clouds as if being admitted to heaven; the Angel-avengers – Polish soldiers; the Damned – the caged guards; in Purgatory – a grey pile of German soldiery. The meek shall be raised . . .

Later the arch-sinner – the CO of the camp. People, out of the routine of ordinariness, play parts learned from cinema melodramas. The sinner acts *hauteur*.

Interrogating sergeants try to penetrate the truth, but do not know how to. Amateurs. Being angels – simple, good boys – not for them to twirl through the routine of prosecutors, investigating judges and brutes. The Last Judgement will fail too. The Saints cannot voice murderous verdicts . . .

Konzentrazionslager. Shuddering confrontation with the inferno – just extinguished in more than one sense. Collapsed furnishings of guard-towers, barbed wire, swastika-painted sentry boxes. The Typhoons attacked the camp the day before the 'liberation', splattered bombs on the barracks, blasted, burned inmates; there they lie, fantastic object-bodies transmuted into roughed-out, multicoloured dummies, some with extremities rolled into ash-made reels. The prisoners ranged over the camp, flooded out to the fields, the guards volleyed salvoes.

A few still stupefied meander, devotedly cleave to the barracks – 'belong' to their cells. I crawl through a wrecked wall and watch: two human rags squeezed into a murky stall. One cadaverous, head tied up in a bloody cloth, flat on his back, eyes rigidly on me; the other picks his lice, busies himself in his tatters, suddenly stiffens agape. Another cage-cell: perched on the edge of his stinking lair in the submissive prisoner's pose (unchanged for years?), the shit bucket in the corner under the frail patch of light – ARREST over his open door. But the routines never seen, only imagined with effort, are (side by side with the dead and almost dead) shamefully trivial: the commonplace day shines, those who escaped on both counts circulate matter-of-factly, gossip composedly – in circumstances of madness.

Under artillery fire, lines of polite housing degutted of the abject possessions of our age: the whole civilization (wedding-group picture, wireless, funereal top-hat, electric iron, clock curved in mahogany) easily fits into the looter's sack. In dead village streets we barge into houses and shops. Gerald and Smith plunder, inspired. I meander behind in awkward embarrassment, grope in old letters, flee at the sight of a petrified woman taking shape behind a window, circling politely the garden beds (Smith, conquest conscious, tramples across). The artillery hots up, infantry defiles sluggishly, plunder-burdened, random ones on bicycles. Gerald,

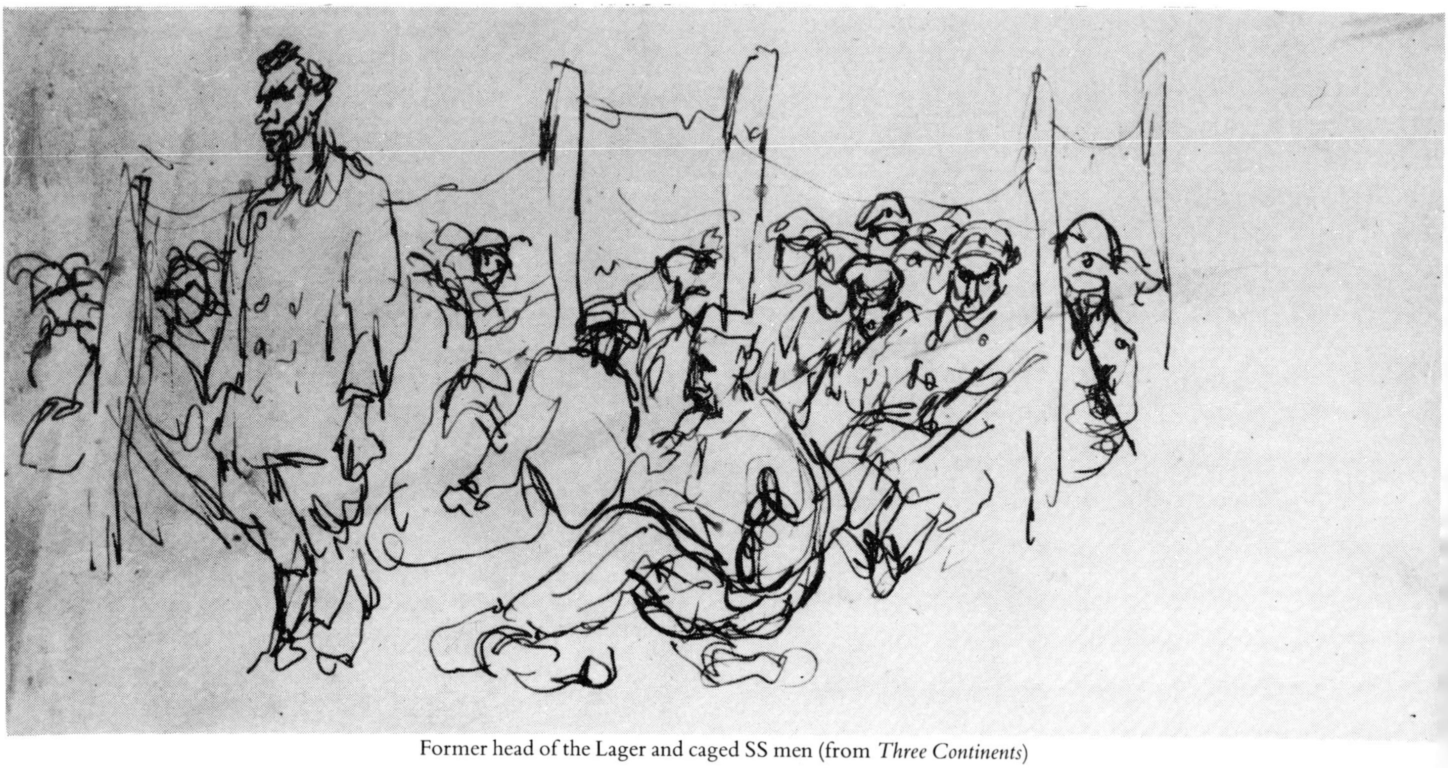

Former head of the Lager and caged SS men (from *Three Continents*)

mesmerized, overloads the car with hideous junk, furnishes his 'young life' with tattiness – weights himself down with ballast never to be shaken off. But we have driven too far forward.

We turn back and stop at the TAC of the brigade of Colonel Skibiński – the armoured knights grouped round a large windmill. 'My dear sir, we pass now as ***Herrenvolk*** – yet in days, a few weeks, we'll be again the paupers of Europe . . .'

But there is no time for politics – the fighting job uses the whole store of energy; Polish exiles' conversations on Poland, Russia, Yalta do not manage to cross from England, get drowned in *la Manche*.

Again prisoners; a pale youth clumsily bulgy in black – '*Panzerjaegerabteilung 20*' – is professionally respected: he belongs to the élite Panzer divisions, now crushed out of existence.

'Out of Bounds' is on the Asian sectors a refrain of miserable soldiers' leaves. But here, in this victorious campaign, with the backing of Brussels *cocottes*' hospitality and of Dutch gratitude, soldiering returned to tradition – the armoured regiments push forward, intoxicated with triumph, robbery, revenge.

'Framed in flames, we hurled ourselves on Papenburg, like Tartars,' says Colonel Dowbór. 'Men were leaping off tanks for hand-to-hand fights.' Battle-bivouac of the 24th Regiment. The regiment, indeed the whole division, crouches in the network of canals and the mud. Charges of tanks, bravuras of outflanking are cut short – Papenburg was the last of such gestures – now comes the time of laborious groping for the Germans and trudging through the quagmire. They fight back fiercely. The captured always announce: 'Americans are pushed back behind the Rhine and on us here in the north depends victory.' Tragic nonsense.

A labourer cycles up to us and in Polish gabbles a menacing story of a **wicked Nazi *Bürgermeister***, of denunciations, of internments – the repetitious saga. The penal expedition is marshalled: two soldiers with sten-guns – 'Where's your belt? Christ, what a patrol! Oh well, never mind' – one sergeant and an array of curious officers, we stride gravely forward, worked up with Grand Guignol expectations. But the mood gets confused as a dapper, moustached lieutenant joins in: 'What are you up to? I'm staying at this beggar's. Leave him alone. He just sits politely in the kitchen. Why make a scene?' But another voice: 'The swine buried his Nazi membership card. We found it.'

We, the Poles (though now in uniform and victorious) know the workings of the people's mind under conquest – the dread (after the fighting operation uninterested in civilians) of the first groping, denunciation directed. We know of fear held on by the nervous readiness of soldiers' weapons. We know that after this comes short-lived quiet – till the Gestapo arrives. Now we are this army – and we experience from under the helmets what the eyes see, what the thoughts are. *We* know though too (too well) what the blanched *Bürgermeister* feels. And this hinders horribly – the interrogator omits, uneasy, the denunciations – falls into the regulation routine: 'List down the members of *die Partei*, surrender arms.' Again one is struck by the youth (in contrast with the furrowed-in-sin old mug of the Hitlerite) and shyness of these boy soldiers – their shyness when free to administer the law of lawlessness. We return with embarrassing insipidity. 'His bloody face should've been smashed in.' 'Eh, you didn't know how to begin.' 'In our unit we'd have kicked the fucking bastard to pieces' – no one believes.

And still another **questioning of a Nazi** smudged monstrously with denunciation – and the same, how

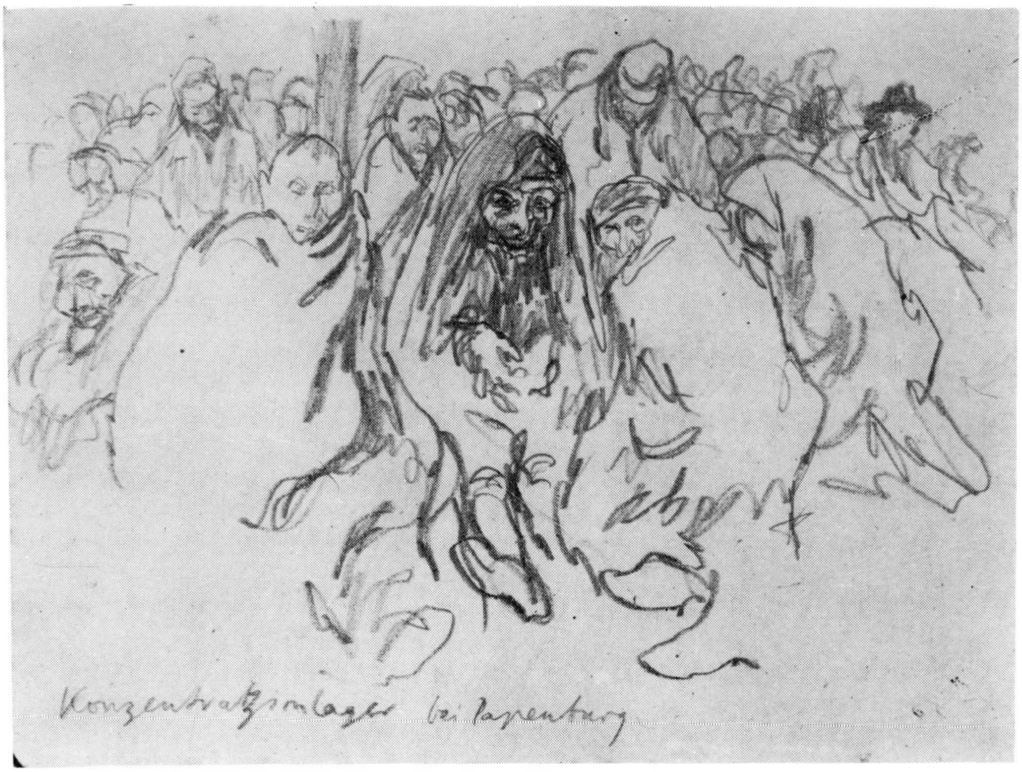

The liberated from concentration camp near Papenburg (from *Three Continents*)

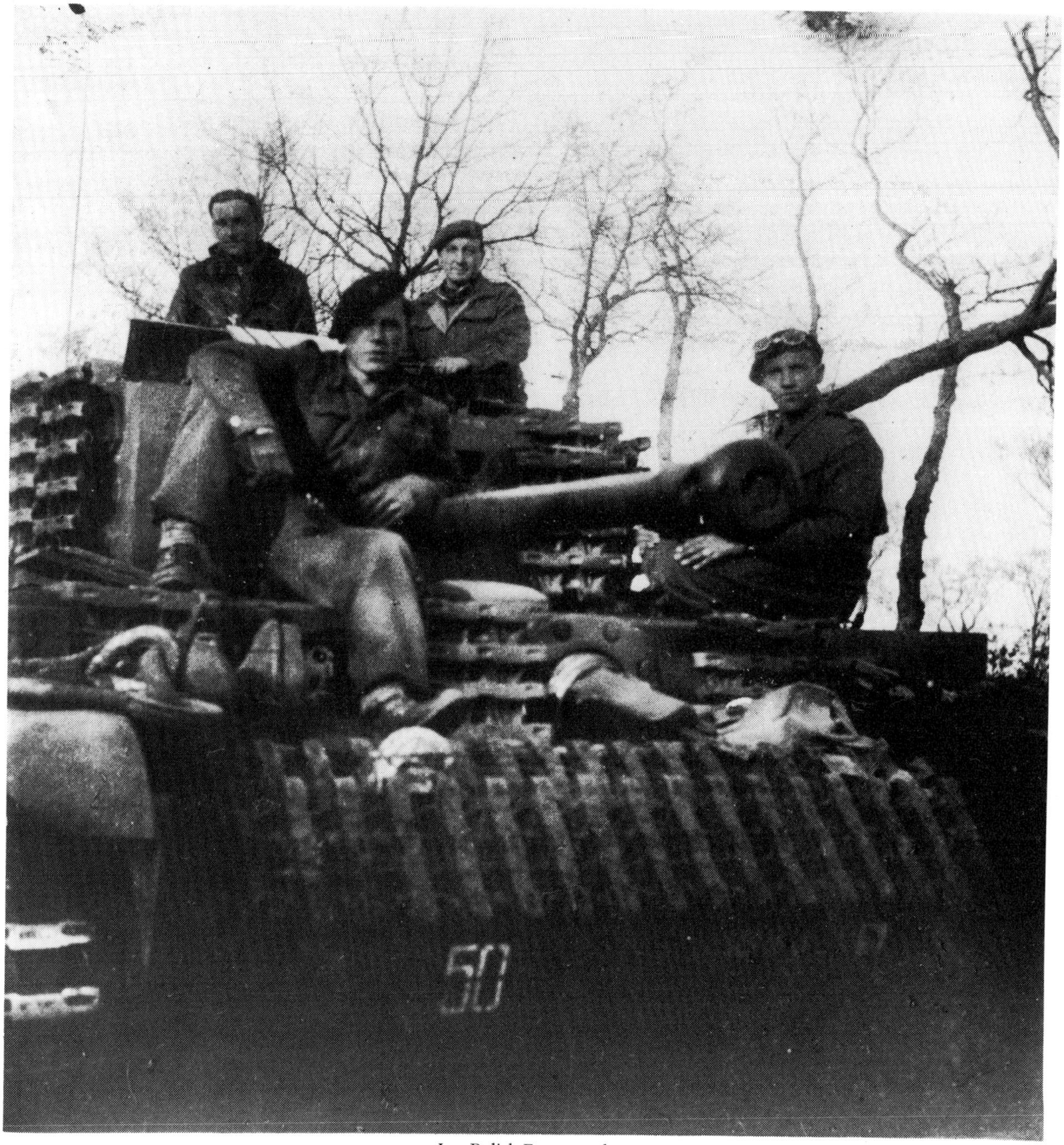

In a Polish Forces tank

touching, helplessness of good people. Outside, the singing. The Ukrainian Natashas and Katias wash the khaki shirts of the Polish Macieks. Giggles, assing about, cards and accordion – in the shadow of sleeping tanks. Blustering permeated again with charm of bashfulness.

Discourse on the faults of Shermans and the values of Cromwells. Cromwell – a fiery stallion; Sherman – an outsized cow. A rattling stallion drives up; I climb into its turret (Gerald and Smith left behind), we are to ride into the line. 'Staff car too soft,' they say.

Beautifully the Cromwell applies itself, slows for a turning, careers on, sails through the dry spattering of waves of black soil – strength and fieriness, sense of charge and fantasy, the armoured divisions emerged from cavalry.

Random thoughts – the 'just war' justifies attitudes perhaps not to arise again. We were brought up on pacifism, in an unshakeable belief in the stupidity, hideousness, criminality of the business of war. The intellectual taboos excluded almost any appreciation of fighting virility – it was more than heresy, it was bad taste. But here it is and it has to be recorded. Without prejudice, objectively, one watches the men of war, one spies for lowliness, selfishness, cruelty – the promised vices – and finds virtues instead. These men outgrew in stature their peace-designed destinies with their clean, knightly, military aura – exalting the elation and simplicity of their routine. There is nothing in them of the vulgarized modern glamour of the airmen with their armchairs, cocktails and publicity at the end of every few-hours-long performance of courage. Here is life in keeping with their deeds; in the incessant trial of male camaraderie virtues multiply (easily raised in the air of victory); the danger wraps the most trivial matters in singular happiness. The light wounds excite, the grave ones and the death match the whole – are a necessary tribulation – do not shame the survivors, but underline the sense of being alive.

We were brought up on a complete trust in the equality of men, but here the pleasure of giving orders and the complementary pleasure of obeying them rule: the simple peasant-like robustness of the soldiers sublimates naturally to the officers' decorative panache (even though it verges on pose and pretence, even if this besieges one more law of our time – the code of modest inconspicuousness). During manoeuvres with my old Officers' School one thought: 'A bit too much of this equestrian order – the noblemen and their serfs.' In action, regulated by the classical and natural laws, everything fits. Commonplaces of our day: 'War is a necessary evil'; 'War in defence' of this or that, but 'against our wishes' – disappear on the battlefield. Peace passes on to war a loadful of 'citizens' – 'soldiers' emerge.

Perhaps the 1914–18 war was staged on a patch of slaughter-bound swamp to fit in with the pacifist mentality. It was meant to be frightful. But this war gallops its armies all over the globe, raises them to a high pitch of emotions, gives them the communion of men and freedom from care, feeds their curiosity with a panorama of races, teaches them to fly and to swim underwater, to rule and to obey, to give life for a great cause, to prove themselves in a thousand ways. There will be trouble with those awakened men, when peace offers them as a prize the drudgery of wage-earning, and the security of tracing and retracing their bench-, office-bound footsteps for ever; even the daily fierce combats with their wives will not suffice to use them up. The business of soldiering is no longer just a slaughter, as we were persuaded – it knocks at all the elements of human emotion, and the tight clinch of fear and death sharpens the taste for life. They will pay, these men, with a restless lack of peace in the peacetime to come.

The Typhoons, splashed with salvoes of German A.A., draw rings – swoop hawk-like on a clutch of cottages. Smoke seethes up towards them, and higher. Our tank clatters in that direction, with me in the open turret. A ballooned-out cow, hoofs jutting widely up, strewn with paper swastikas. 'Fucking Kraut-cow.'

We sidle into the **fighting column**. Tanks, carriers packed with dragoons. As ever, the battle dramatizes, dresses the landscape with lights and shadows – farmsteads in fire and smoke. 'Action.' There swings over a mortar series. Across a footbridge gallops a little flock of mothers and children. Momentarily ditched dragoons dig themselves deeper. Bodies of men and cattle – the cows that survived ruminate heavily – the infantry files through and, flanking them, tanks jammed in the village dazzle with salvoes. In the tank earphones and on the ground the many-voiced jabber grinds in ceaseless waves – staccato-chopped and overclipping: warning/advising/sustaining/encouraging, hasty-slangy-coarse – this choral cacophony drowns crackle-and-blasts of 'action'. A close-range rattle – dragoon's helmet and skull shot through – the holes in his helmet interest his colleagues. We are a **target**. I slide from the turret to the ground. Soon two **German soldier-snipers** stumble, hands up, along the furrow, belts off, open greatcoats entangle their boots, into the field against the sun – the ugly crackle of a sten-gun – they drop like dummies – a scattered pack of sweetheart's snapshots spills on the soil the romance of a life.

The thinness of the borderline perplexes – a gesture, a word pulls the trigger and turns a human being into a comic object – or bestows the grace of a life-saving kick. I see now how the imprisoned of yesterday, squeezed in the misery of barbed wire, already somehow (by some turn of fate) have won – they stink with sweat, chew a crumb of bread, stumble into living on.

And the heaviest irony of these combats. The Nazi caricature of human exaltations, heroic myths, contorts them hideously – unlearns one's respect for the multicoloured soldiers of the past. Hitler may have harmed the world most when, with his ape-like grimace, he imitated gestures of greatness and pride. The path from Hitler's patch of moustache, perorating ludicrousnesses and swaying millions – to the disasters of war, culminating in grey much too young snipers dying with *Für Vaterland* on their lips. We learned in childhood to respect this cry in whatever language – we unlearn it now as the circus of German chauvinism stands on its head, and the besotted, faithful heroic *Trupper* repeats the faded gestures in the distorting mirror of the twentieth century. Or do we learn that it does not matter what serves to bring about the supreme orgasm of sacrifice?

Again shots. We drop on to the fresh-turned soil, cool and blithe, at the feet of the two Germans. Another volley. Urgently, but without losing dignity (the face matters), we back out from the open field – the shots go into the nearest cottage, develop into a fusillade – snipers aim from somewhere.

The Dragoons (soiled, casual) crouch along the hedges or, stuck in trenches, mechanically exchange jokes – attention really straining at the battle routine; they bite at sausages and eggs grabbed from broken shops, load machine-guns – one pulls up without haste trousers over his bare bottom – another, rooting in a battered cottage, throws on the road a ruffled Nazi flag, searches for treasure – still another, wide-stretched, snores. Soon they will go over the hedges across the canal.

From among the now calmed tanks, edging past the fires and sparks-whirling barns, I creep forth on to the churned, reverberating canal's edge: across, a Polish soldier, gun pointed, leads out of the fire and din a tragic group: two Germans, white with fear, hold up a third, sagging, with head all red, as if dipped in a bucket of paint.

Typhoons and tanks having silenced the *Wehrmacht*'s mortars, priest-like there step forward mine-ferreters and draw rings round Cromwells, Dragoons emerging from trenches, homes on fire: a gesture, mixed of blessing and listening to the earth's pulse – tender yet distrustful.

Slowly, with moments of breathless haste and drawn-out pauses, the battle's order of things works itself out.

Papenburg flutters white tatters, yawning with ruin, cross-cut by canals. Out of holes crawl the burghers, roll belongings back to safety, to stop helpless and disbelieving in front of their pulverized homes; cram into queues, give way

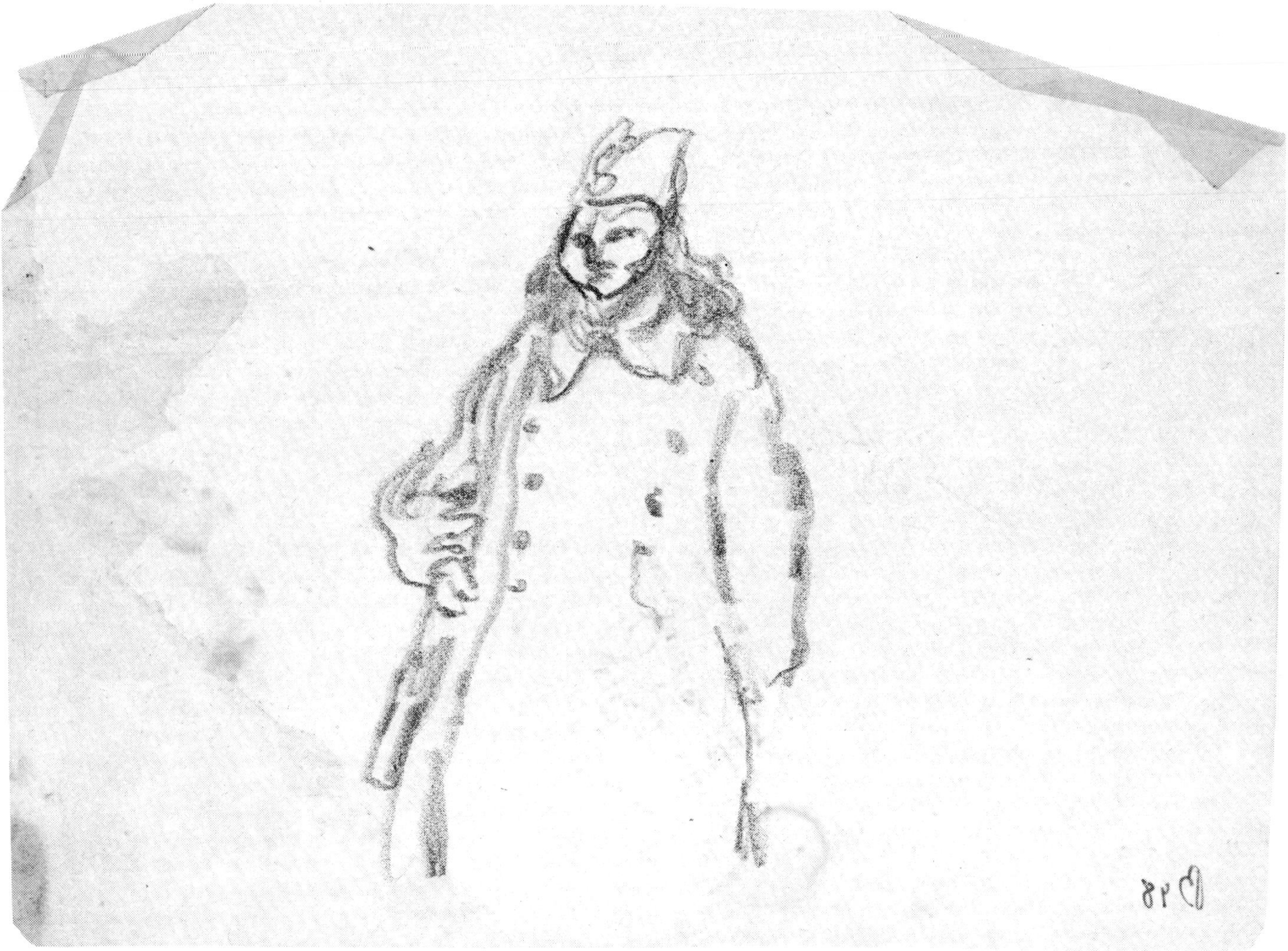

Polish woman soldier ex-prisoner from the Oberlangen Stalag

to the ceaseless procession of famished semi-cadavers, gaze slavishly at the pink hulks of Polish solders lolled out in the sun above the water; black-clad *Hausfrauen* tightrope across the broken gangways to shopping; a girl thinks of rape, panic and expectation tangling her bare red calves.

Our jeep launches out on to the country lanes rutted into furrows by tank tracks; having to stop, we look threateningly (as conquerors, and because of concentration camps) at the string of gay peasant women laying fascine over the surface – but a happy farmhand with a purple 'P' on a yellow rhomb appears and says in Polish peasant tongue: 'Sure, it's my village: these good people, can't complain' – another one of the vast number of Polish slave-workers, uprooted yet gratified. So we grow bashful, spatter kind words and, cheered, thawed and warmed by maidenly giggles and coynesses, drive on lost in thoughts: white flags – not only of capitulation, but also of innocence of the simple heart. The Polish easily got together with the German folk. The contagion of Nazism stopped somewhere here on these country fences. A German farmer lived in fear of God and cannot connect the 'original sin' of Fascism with the disaster of invasion. Robbing and rape transfer the guilt to us.

'Requisitioning receipts of sorts should be given, with a printed explanation that this or that was done as a punishment for Nazism and war – or what?' we say.

It is hard to hold to narrow tracks with mined flanks and huge convoys to pass. In a broken pine wood, we overtake a rural funeral with the pastor, the few mourners, the coffin on a farm cart and the white rag on a stick; the gallop of mechanized war, a factory of corpses and graves by the thousand – and now this of-the-past, on-foot, with squeaking axles, slow cortège over the death of one. Our jeep jogs on between horizons giving out smoky fires and a prattle of guns; Polish soldiery warming up on doorsteps with the ancient peasantry ('Fraternizing?' – 'They're Ukrainians, lieutenant sir!'), German battle graves – to reach the field menage of the 10th Chasseurs.

And so: the **major-zagończyk*** commanding the regiment, the chaplain who tank-rides scouting, the tank driver who broils chickens ('We save – we don't touch His Majesty's rations') and would rather paint.

Over 'Bloody Shirt Bridge', we pass (here, in the depth of the German mud) Polish soldiers shouldering sacks of booty,

**Zagończyk*, n. (pl. *Zagończycy*). One of the seventeenth-century freelance rough-riders, defending Poland's eastern borders from invading Tartars and rebellious Cossacks – matching them in fiercely unbridled tactics, but superior in their chivalry and patriotic motivation. The Thirty Years War lured some of them, as mercenaries, to western battlefields – one of them posing as a model for Rembrandt's *Polish Rider*.

promenading away for leave – in Scotland. We park in the line of stationary tanks – Captain Kłodziński, commanding the First Squadron, lounges on a sofa dragged out into the open, deep in a Polish literary magazine, February issue from London. Further forward – bivouacking and rollicking in 'liberated' top-hats, red scarves – strips of Nazi flags; the smoke billows over the canal's surface – carries the lilt of the polka, struck out on 'liberated' fiddles; peasant women who, stubborn, persisted in their homes, bring out pails of milk.

And still further, beyond the turn of the canal and of the hamlet – heavily weighing calm. The village ripples lightly (curtains, dust, open gate) but lifelessly – except for a cock sauntering across the street unmolested. The tanks lie in wait attending (crews in earphones) to the silence.

The jeep sweeps up and stays with Gerald and Smith in the shade and cover of a ruin – then on foot; somewhat self-consciously, a group of officers, we stride in the centre of the road, dismissing the exertion of stalking – the invisible enemy watches – with the sense of *noblesse oblige* up to the leading tank, present ourselves, exchange commonplaces. Then stillness, the pregnancy of street turnings, house corners, fences, tree-assemblies, of the perspective of the canal – **THE FRONT.**

The front at the end of April 1945, awaiting the command to press on – or to 'cease fire'.

The arrow on the road signs points down. We turned to the rear.

Haren, a hole mucked up by bombs. Squabble at the entrance to the Military Government – lamb-like *Polizei* and lionesses in too large uniforms thickly decorated with white and red – **Polish women** ex-prisoners from the Oberlangen-Stalag, **soldiers** of the Warsaw Rising. Again the ominous towers, no longer working floodlights overhanging barbed wires, lines of smoking barracks – but the springlike sun and the droll but spicy girls promenade with their heel-clicking Polish liberators, recline in pairs along the wooded road, stand sentry (huge rifles, curly hair-dos, jolly legs, extra-high American forage caps and oversized tunics) garlanded by Allied admirers. An operetta of charm and fanfaronading masquerade, strangely interwoven with the sombrer virtues of bravery, patriotism and sacrifice – also with inseparable human ignominy and smallness; a serene nineteen-year-old, in approximation of fighting attire, will tell in a few phrases of her Warsaw secret matriculation while officially one of the Gentile seamstresses at a uniform factory in the Ghetto – witnessing daily the heightening annihilation – and afterwards, in the evenings, underground art school classes.

Zofja, girl cadet officer, will narrate in schoolkids' cynical slang the routine of the Rising – of an excursion for parachuted ammunition on the roof of an apartment block, of an ambush, of hand-grenades, of an officer of the Home Army who covered her and slid off her, dead, and her forty scars counted by her colleagues in the bath yesterday. And there is the flapper's exclamation: 'The Rising was divine!'

But another will tell of chicanery towards those few **soldier-Jewesses** of the Rising (hidden, passing for a Slav, or escaped from the Ghetto) who persisted in Polish patriotism. A Jewess stares, her eyes in tearsome circles – the only sad face: she survived the war, her family, and still hides under a false name. Inconceivable, petrifying truth: the organic and degrading human need (even on the level of slavery) of still degrading another. The humble in need of the humbler still – to despise. You and I believe that this 'necessity' is not in us – but perhaps we do not even guess at our evil potential.

'People don't see their own baseness' – says a rediscovered old friend (also an inmate), Madame Pokrzywnicka – and she knows.

But the camp has passed through the dazzling emotions of liberation by the Polish Army – the morning roll-call hymn rises in great happiness.

Driving in **the Ruhr**. Factories gutted out (but not all), black landscape of industry, *Fräuleins* getting shapelier (nourished by the coal-riches) cycle, rather dressed up in the tight bodices and wide skirts of the all-European folklore. Paratroops convoy by in a string of cherry berets. Frenchmen flag-flutter in triumphant groups on the trucks 'Pour Paris' (while the German prisoners are sardined flatly and greyly). People ant over the kicked-open villages, drag out bits and pieces, crawl up the rubble – burghers who returned, or robbers still?

Crossroads – a sentry-box and within, spread commodiously, an extensive helmeted Negro (a circle of marvelling *Fräuleins*). We ask the way. He rises lazily and gigantically, fluttering eyelid, a perplexed eye coys and rolls: red and white mouth sings out (magnificent *andante basso*), 'I sure dunno, boss.' **The American Sector**.

Dursten. In a broken-up square stand shady chestnut trees and old bucks with pipes sit staidly in the quiet of the afternoon, kids seem to be already returning from school, girls pace about, signs in American, 'Road and shoulders cleared of mines', pleasant black cheeks swing by in jeeps. The sedate picture of an occupation a score of days old.

Crawling through Duisberg. The Rhine clasped by a pontoon bridge (massive stumps of steel-concrete jut out of the seething water) – sky strewn with balloons, A.A. batteries, horizons of chimney-stacks and pit-shafts, pulp of bog and post-battle scraps, with a thick stench of carcasses rising from the expanse of muck.

Homberg – murdered town emptied of life – an occasional GI napping in the desolation on orphaned plush furniture – one senses, one smells, the zone of monstrous slaughter.

After that, again an idyll. A bridge over the stream is named 'Love Bridge'. Nuns in twos interweave with pairs of challengeful girls, their slacks in discord with their bottoms, and doughboys mince cock-like in their footsteps (risking a $65 fine). 'Hitler kaput' scribbled here and there, and in Krefeld 'Adolf Hitler Strasse' hangs on one nail over the Pompeian landscape.

A Polish-American sergeant from Chicago, pointing to the barbed-wire Displaced Persons barracks, informs in halting Polish: 'Bosch are being murdered here.' But the Germans carry expressionless faces – their grievances sink deeper. People crawl about – giggle in subjugation – stare sideways in dog-like expectation of blows – they expect them, yet they are out and about – pushed into the open by their daily needs. In the same way the Jews moved around the Warsaw Ghetto.

Evening darkens Suchteln, a village untouched by war – British 21st Army's Groups' HQs. Curfew sweeps empty the streets – the patrols (old cockneys) stamp against the silence in time to any jazz tune seeping from the blacked-out window of the Sergeants' Mess party.

Again from square one. Once more violence and dread is being breeched by trivialities of everydayness, drizzle, humility, chiming bells, and the Catholic chants of the Cathedral; starch-minded *Hausfrauen* under umbrellas, *gemütlich* little girls – the people playing their devout part skilfully, in the hangover of crime.

The disorderly associations of the last days stumble against each other – I pass all this into memory's corner to clear space for tomorrow: shots and death in battle; Gerald's hideous treasures (clocks, radio sets, dresses, shoes, spoons, electric bed-warmers); 'Russkie – good' and 'I fear the Russians'; Germans – a forward hussy in the HQ kitchens, a grandma in obliging titters, murderer awaiting death, soldier humiliated, liberated skeleton cracking along the road flatly and meekly; tormentor and tormented propping one another up in the night that carries the unknown; barracks of the camp stinking with filth but bearing carefully calligraphed notices; manacles and chains undone by a polite little key on a string.

An American youngster at a crossroad muddles our directions but opens the day with a beautiful smile. Gerald clumsily 'feels' our way towards the Rhine through a panorama of the military rear. GIs rock on careless legs, stretch on requisitioned *chaises-longues* – offhandedly assist, support, belong to that loose but massive structure which rolls over the 'Roosevelt Rhine River Bridge' (while building it), grinds the enemy and organizes the Military Government.

Wesel. Crashed remnants of river-guarding bastions show through intricate camouflage. The games of the camouflage may serve against reconnoitring – but, when the offensive thundered, all of it collapsed under her giant and heedless fist. Force pushes on without finesse, and now the entrails of multicoloured netting hang stupidly from poplars lining the Schermbeck Road above the military 'rolling stock' turned junk. Slowly intensifies **the nearness of war**. The looter in morning coat or bowler hat again rules over the ruins – the *Wehrmacht*'s steel hats again crown the crosses, the stink of burning rot returns. 'This is 'ow I like to see Germany,' declares Smith mechanically, faithful to gutter-press commonplaces.

We are hungry – enter a cottage, stamping victor-like. Tension-bristling faces – grouped in a pose of terror, break down in minutes into recounting troubles; we pay in Guldens, morally endorsed by the Dutch boy with them – another ex-'forced labourer'; two city girls and a small boy, who lost their parents and home, are sheltered by the farmer.

It fills up with guests, swarthy churls. I drag out fractions of words, understand scraps. They would . . . something or other . . . Hitler (tone of anger and contempt). Big conversation on *Russen* who rob, rape and murder – Nazi propaganda has driven into their heads fear of Bolshevik barbarity – a *Russe* is perhaps to them every rampaging DP. Can they expect Allied protection? '*Nein*,' I say and draw a large 1933 to put before them **the 'original' guilt**. They do not see the connection. '*Sie haben Krieg angefangen – Konzentrazionslager gemacht, Polnische und Russische Slaven gefangen*' – I toil. No and no – they do not understand – cause and effect will not fit together in their heads. 'Let's get going.'

Walfen – mud and destruction. A huge slice of the land annexed by triple barbed wire – DPs stuck behind it gape torpidly. Order starts its defence against anarchy – the 'liberated' put behind wire – and, at liberty, the bowed *Schutzpolizei* confer with their weary people over self-defence, under the posters '*Sieg oder . . .*' – the rest torn off.

The road stretches out, twirls, forces through the rubble of cities, repeating the same elements, but gathered ever differently – drab kaleidoscope of wartime.

The Press Camp. The usual marginal atmosphere crammed with brandy and any chatter – gossip, shuffling of acquaintances, competing stories of transport cum facilities. Night in a German feather bed in plain but well-scrubbed provincialism – 'golden heads' of German children in the nursery bow courteously to the invaders.

Belsen, 29 September. Under a grizzly sky there smokes and moulders human refuse. There reel about, advance gripping-scratching at the barracks' walls, crouch in dysentery, drop to the ground, die – apparitions.

But life never offers uniformity: people are differentiated – by nation, class, age, 'status' and time-length of imprisonment. Next to the 'slow-motion' old-timers in martyrdom vibrates the instinct for self-perservation of those who were only a few months in the paws of the butchers or given 'functions'. Even the ultimate (masks of awe) monstrosities, seemingly beyond the unbridgeable chasm, when aware of an outsider, complain, explain, narrate tortures in ordinary human voices, divided, up to the communal end, by the accents of home.

Over the rag-strewn waste, women squat and jut out bare, shrivelled buttocks, corpses outrage with a half-laced boot, a diligently wrapped swollen thumb; emaciated skeletons drag a quivering-in-fever bogeyman to the hospital block. Set over intent brewing, the Jewesses let drop tales of torture, interpolated with 'You do look well' – in a bundle of voices; a girl from Kraków ordinarily: 'They took me for nothing – for Jewishness.'

A woman-shadow does not understand my questions – a Greek; but a ginger pupa of a wasted child informatively answers: 'I speak Polish – the dead are there.' Phlegmatically workmanlike, the SS – their turn to slave – unload lorries stuffed with human carrion, throw half-bare, half-trash carcasses into multi-layered pits – bellies sunk in and green (turnip fed).

Loudspeakers scream out jazzy croonings – a kindly British notion – there sway, out of rhythm, striving for survival – for a chip of wood, a potato, a lair – the Belsenites liberated ten days ago.

I gleaned before the elements of 'camps', men under guns, bound, patterned in barbed wire. 'Chain gangs' somewhere on the highways of Egypt, or an Arab caged by Palestinian

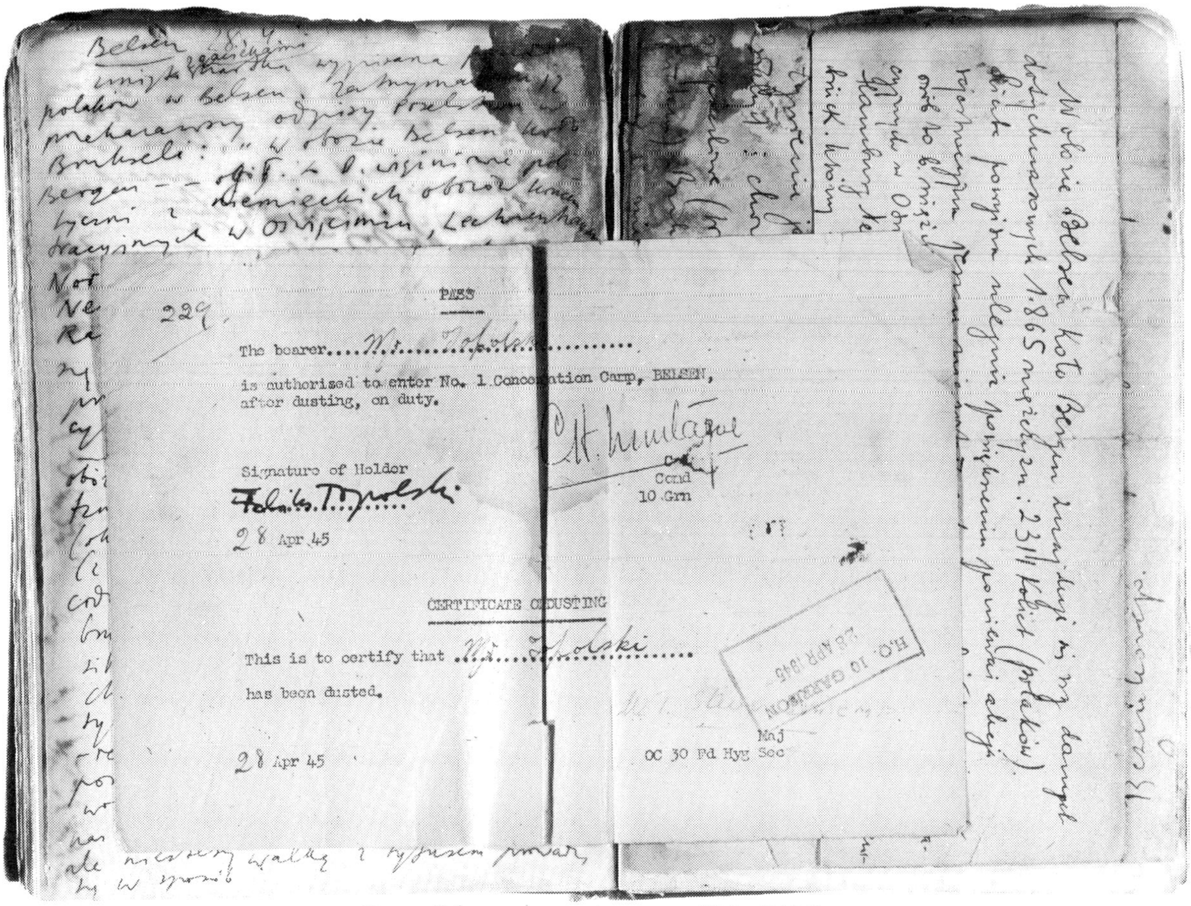

Pass to Belsen concentration camp – 28 April 1945

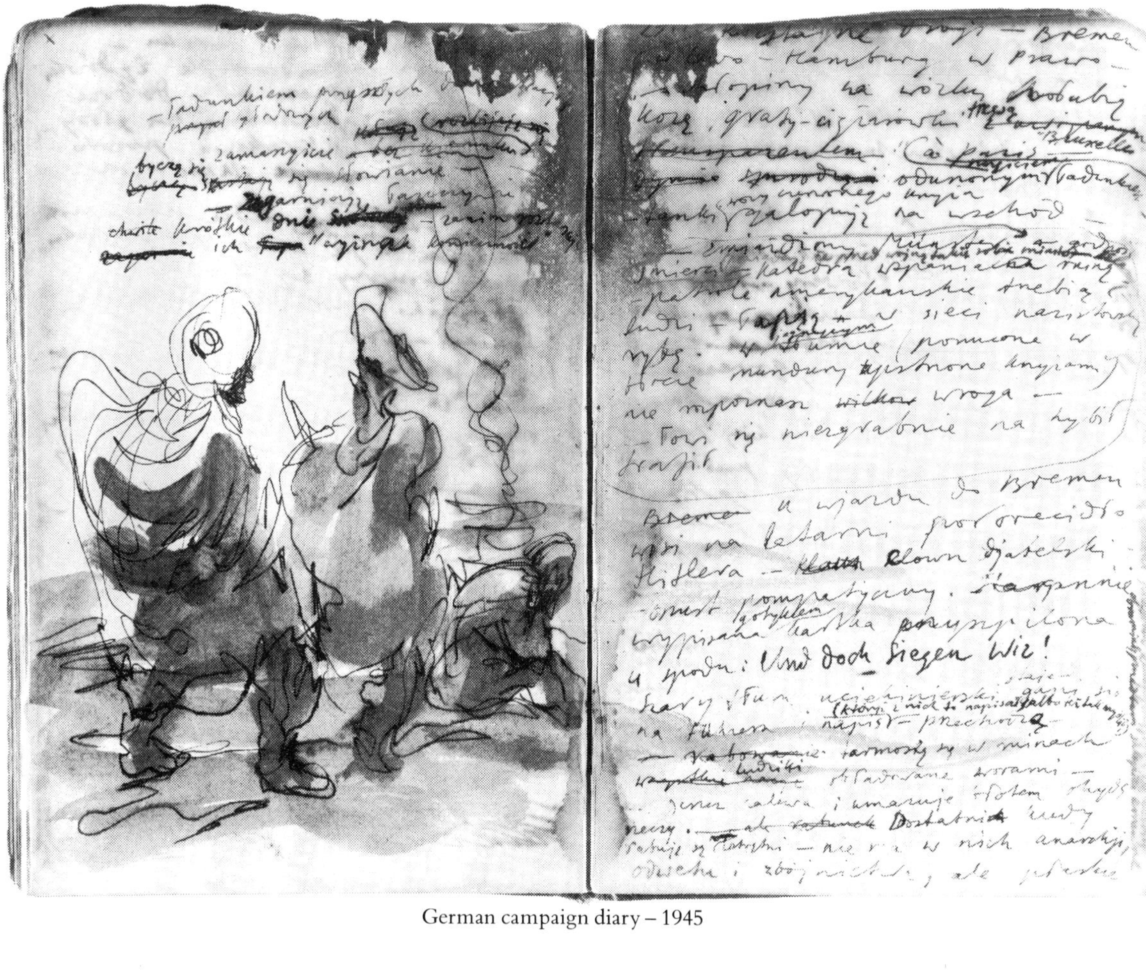

German campaign diary – 1945

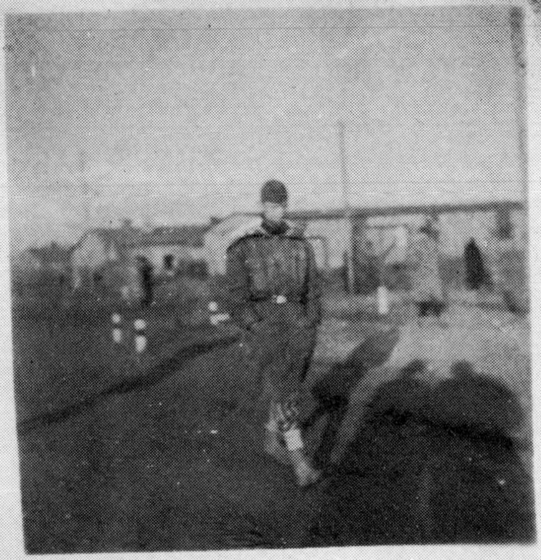
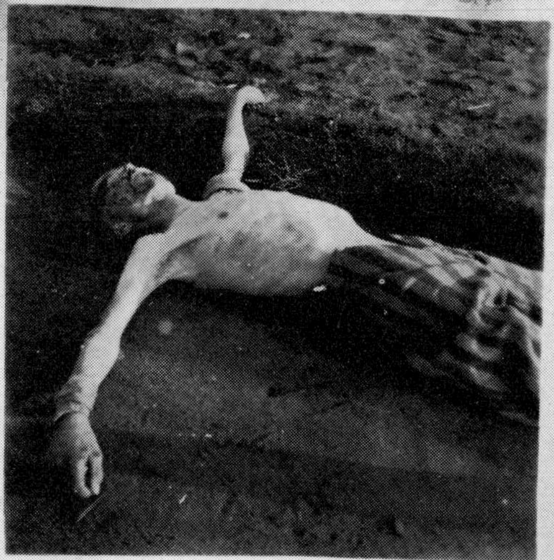
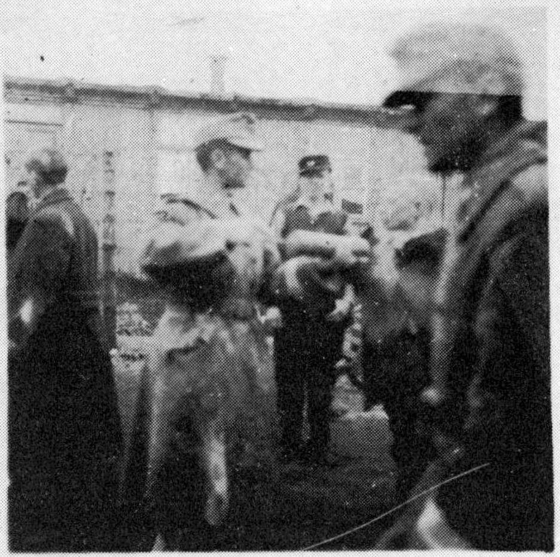
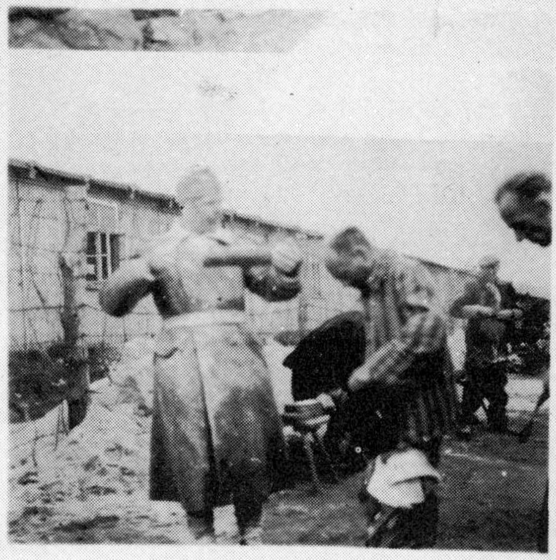
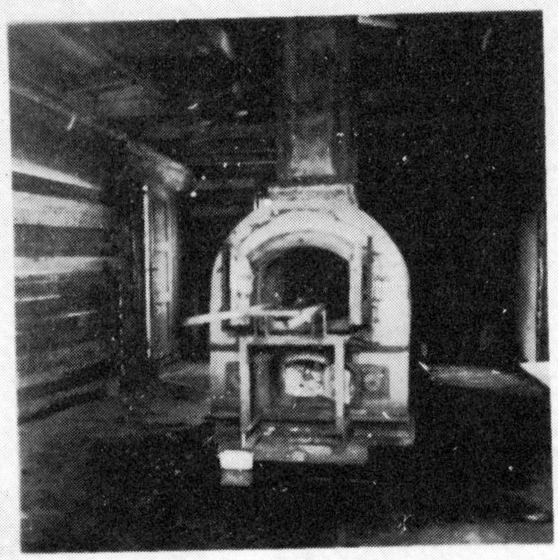
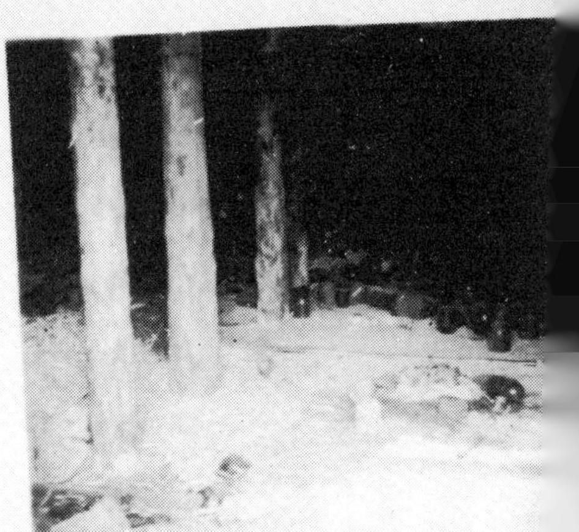

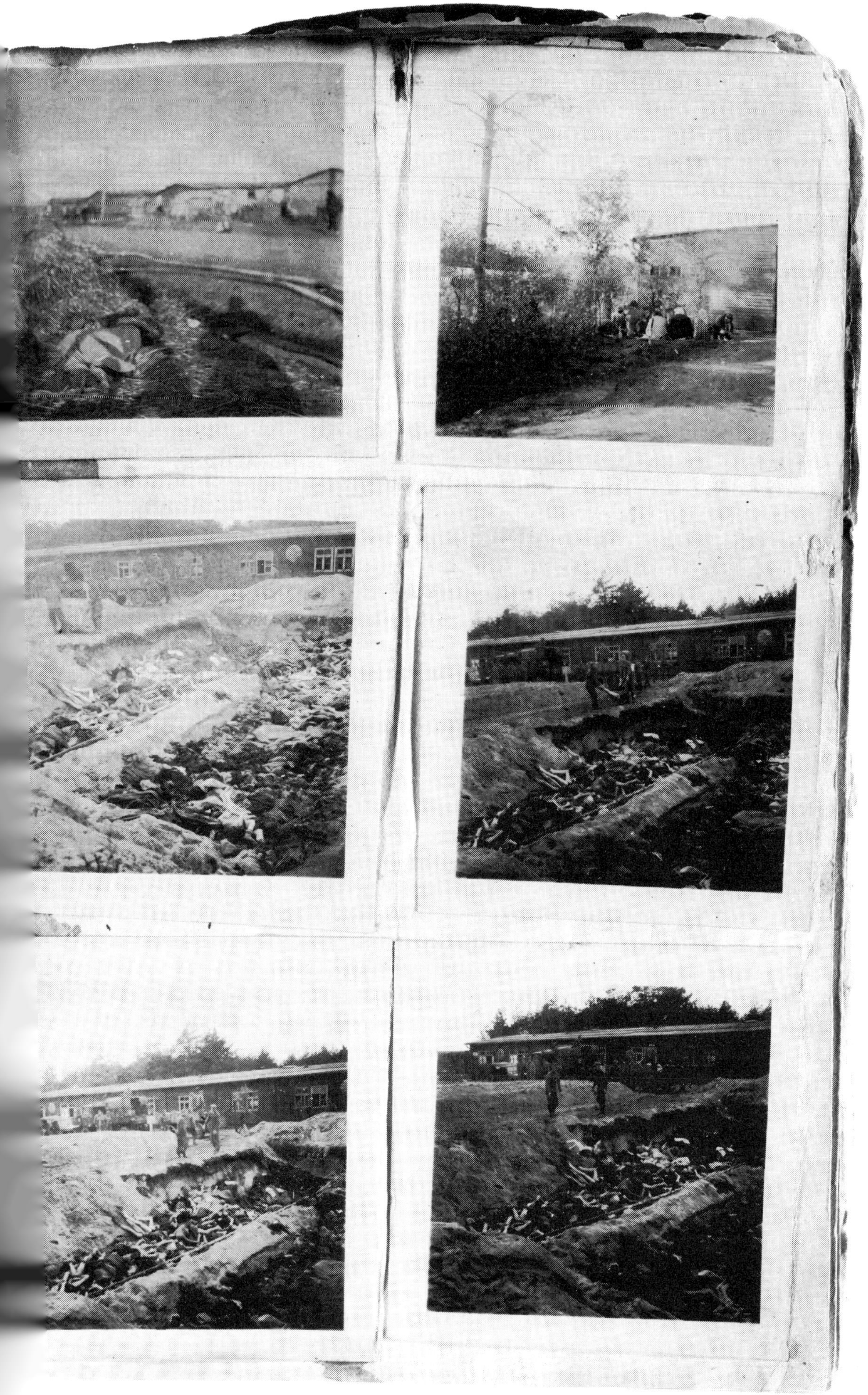

Diary pages with my photographs of Belsen

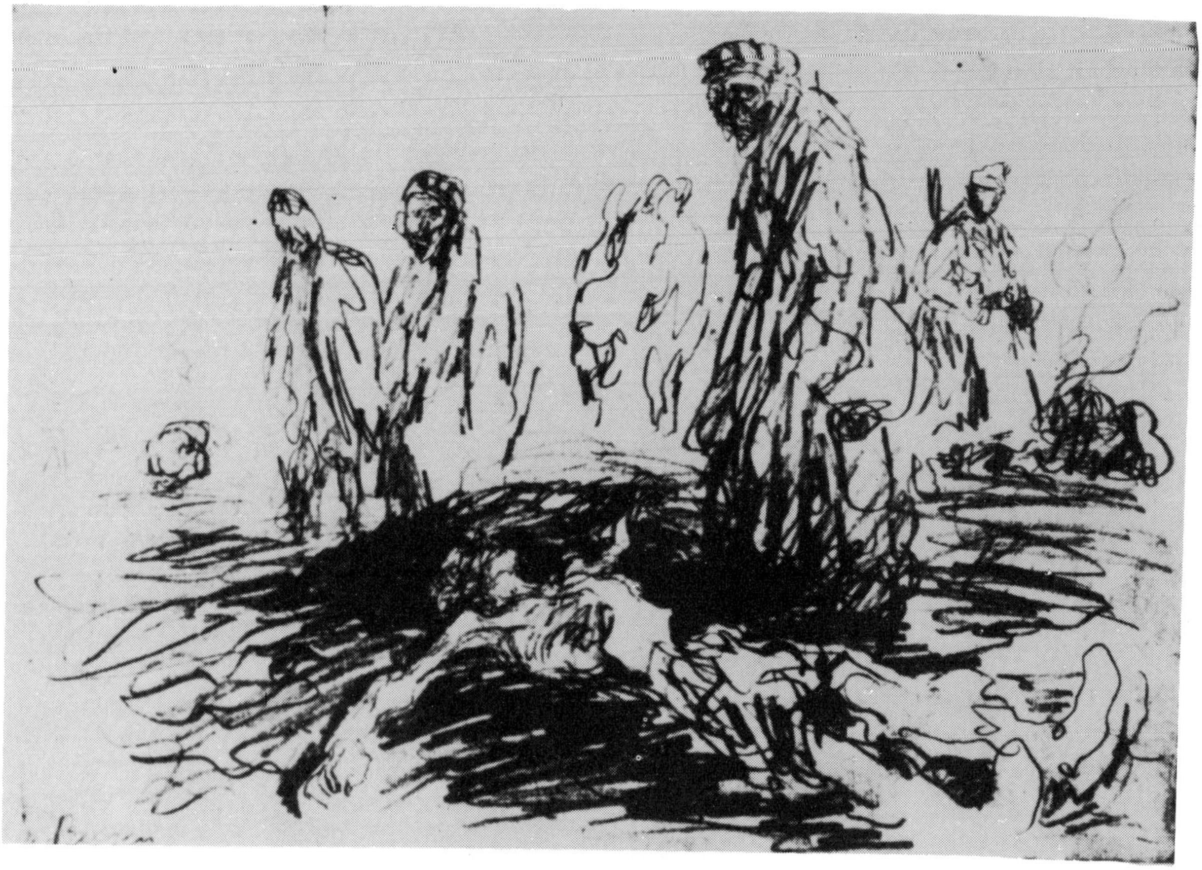

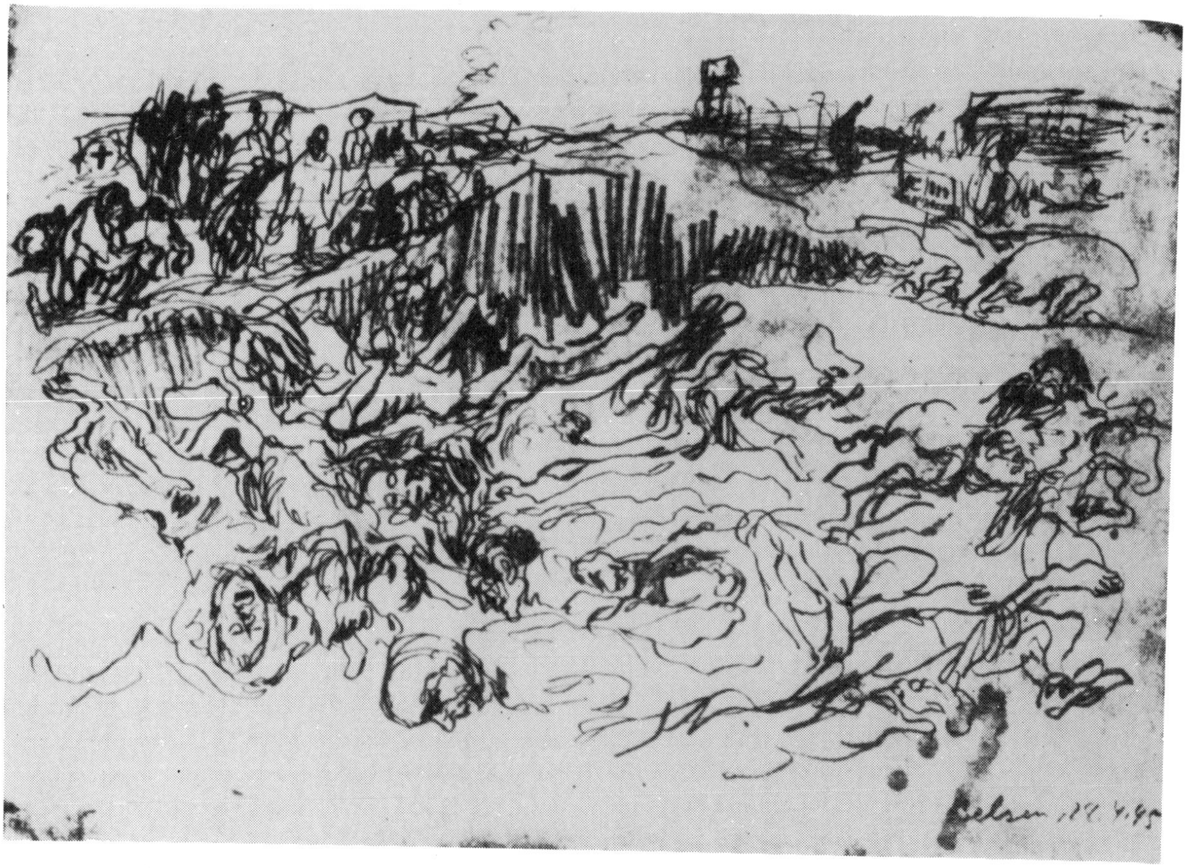

Belsen (from *Three Continents* and *Topolski's Chronicle*)

police, would hit with a panic at confrontation. And so too: a rope-led Hindu, or a Japanese captive shrunk in animal fear, Chinese forced-conscripts dropping with hunger on the roads, jabbed with gunbutts.

That world girded with barbed wire, forced into barracks and soup queues; the terror of interrogation, faces smashed, bones broken, reduction (in the crowd) to the solitariness of the drowning – all this I have been guessing at, and in down-weighing obtuse ruminations, I envied those subjected to it all. In addictive gathering of present history, or perhaps in a flesh-soul need to merge with the fulness of life, there was lacking in me, painfully and stupidly, a portion of the 'lower depth'. Fortunate or unlucky, I had none of these as yet. But in Germany I touched, again and again, the pulse of things dark – across a terrifyingly thin border.

These are probably the strongest reflexes when confronting the diabolical: fragility, the groundlessness of the margin between tortured helplessness and its spectator; the appalling nonsense of *chance*, which tears apart these two worlds so waveringly, mindlessly – without appeal. The same chance decides the crossing into the next dimension – death.

This could be me, *that* somebody close to me: thus I try to inject myself with responses. The piles of corpses, the multitude *in extremis*, are more than alien – horribly outside my equipment of susceptibilities. Indifference, ambushing behind the bend of consciousness, is driven away with great effort. And it no longer surprises that the RASC Lieutenant-Colonel a few miles from here does not believe (but vouches for the terror by ex-slaves, because he saw it). Indeed, one is hard pressed to believe one's senses – immersed in stench, stumbling over bodies pulled by the legs into the open, passing among living ghosts, molesting one or doubled up in excrement.

In spite of thickly piled reports, 'Black Books', photographs, the bag of associations passed on by upbringing still does not contain, so cannot convey, the reality of nightmare transferred as the waves from hell. Perhaps this is also why I stare at the martyrs with sinful envy: dormant faculties beg for a delivering shock.

But there is one more issue, less subjective, massively pregnant with warning – the most important. The gigantic amassment of suffering, millions perishing guiltless, the boundless lament – have no content. One would have thought (nothing being lost in nature) that, although most of the millions entered martyrdom without knowing why – passively – the accumulated energy of torturers and tortured should have born an Idea: faith-recompense. Nothing. People suffer, debase themselves, die, complain – flatly, abjectly, selfishly. One would have thought that for this mass-crucifixion there would descend on humanity redemption – renaissance through the birth of a mystical legend. There is no legend, no faith, no conception.

The early Christians went to martyrdom for something, offered themselves to torture for their faith, as later did heretics, revolutionaries, patriots. Patriots and revolutionaries still wing into the ecstasy of sacrifice. But the masses of passive martyrs, not moulded in heroic clay, passively fall – dust to dust. There was no energy in them to discharge. Precisely this mountebank terror's legacy – nullity of the liberation day, shreds accommodated in hopelessness, in ever-onward harrowed bustling, clamouring only in the language of the stomach (even the acrid taste of sex is no more), crush the beholder.

This is the true ignominy: a hideous game of mauling the little in spirit – aimless, sickening and bottomlessly stupid. Against all this, the astonishing singularity of those who held on to their humaneness within the mob cowed by mortal dread, at the price of going under . . .

Because out of the 'survival' tales a horrible certainty emerges: almost every one of THEM, who lives, escaped over the dying others – he pushed another in front of himself when the choice for the kill was made; he strangled another in a fight for food, or let the weaker die barring the way to air; he earned the barrack guard's status and retained it by bottom-licking, denouncements, cunning, viciousness and ruthlessness – the virtues for survival in the raw. The SS were high up and very few – the camps were run by the selected inmates (mostly criminals) – the Kapos who had to make the choice for the death chambers. And, before that, the school for vileness – the streets of any occupied town in Europe – the mob's instinct of chase and hatred of the underdog, thoughtfully provided plenty of training.

It is of a piece when from the depths, from the stenching huts, from the dung-hills, from the mortuaries, the victims come out and say that a dying woman begged her pals not to let 'those dirty Jewesses' (detailed to bury the dead) touch her cold body. Or that respect and admiration for Nazis exist among the captives.

Or that Jews, specialists in recognizing the undisclosed co-racialists, 'worked' in the concentration camps.

The flesh-coloured Christ on the roadside crosses of Germany seems not the Son of God, but one more murdered 'Yid'.

The rubble of Münster (not much of a town before the war, they say). How nobly rise the stumps of the classicist pilasters, which previously framed little grocers' shops – the dignity of death. American patrols weed out Nazis. Among the lamb-like crowds (in the mud, cast-away uniforms spattered with medals), how to recognize the foe? They work clumsily, hit or miss.

Crossroads: Bremen left – Hamburg right. At the entry to Bremen on a lamp-post hangs an image of Hitler – diabolical clown, pompous swindler. A scrap of paper carefully filled with Gothic script pinned underneath: *'Und doch siegen wir!'* A grim refugee group stops, stares at the Führer and the note (which of them could have written this, or would think so?) – they pass on. Figures loaded with loot clump about in the ruins – rain floods and smears with mud the hideousness of things. The prosperous, when **looting**, are disgusting – there is no anarchy in them, no revenge or brigandage, but the sneaking removal of goodies from strangers' firesides to their own.

Bremen – stinks cruelly of burnt rot. A Dutch sergeant tears bicycles from under Germans and presents them to DPs. *Rathaus* – Military Government thick with staff officers, supplicants, uniforms of German police. A hawk-faced British Colonel behind the *Bürgermeister*'s desk barks dispositions (through the interpreter) – a group of police-dignitaries contorts arrogant Teutonic snouts into ingratiation. The Colonel, grown shrill, culminates his instructions – rises – almost a dwarf (a hint-prognostic) – a huge revolver dangles to his knees, the bulging German ox-necks bend humbly. At the door the pushing, noisy salute by the *Schutzmann* (still on duty) obtrudes with a camaraderie of uniform and law-abidingness – uncomfortably, caught and perplexed, I return the salute.

A column of scout cars and carriers curves widely into the flattened vastness of dockland, under the rent bridges, around the basin (a breathless, ratty mob, sacks on their backs, flees at a trot from the giant warehouses); brakes screech at the edge of the quay – soldiers sweep off, crouch, arms forth – a perfect capture-drill. Huge trembling waters (crane and mast-framed – seagull-swung) open up.

The locusts of looting fall on the town – swarm to the staid gilded houses of the market square (slices of façades torn off, opulent stuffing of interiors gone). Smith and I tear into the wine-soaked darkness under the *Rathaus*, down spiral steps – matches crack, din, yells, trampling – a drunken voice roars in Russo-German: *'Ubiraisia svolotch – Deutsch nicht – verboten!'* 'Smith, Smith' – I lose him.

Bottles clatter, shine, splinter. But in a moment: 'Sir! Sir!' Here he is, strolling, boisterously cockneyish, among the gleams of match lights – two *Moujiks* devotedly pulling in his wake a huge load of Rhine-wine bottles. Confusion of feet mucking puddles of wine. Roused people struggle in the befugging aroma – German crones in abandon, boozed boors. Americans pile up their jeeps. The British load with feelings of guilt. Muscovites and Poles set bonfires, cook, drink, pinch girls among the ruins that stand grandly and Hanseatically around them – the whole throbbing with the urgency of the marauders' orgy. The image of war completed.

The evening smudges over the show. The unbridled rabble quietens down, melts away. Cold, darkness and downpour shrink them. They crowd darkly, shuffle in submissive queues at steaming cauldrons.

A light tank rattles by – the night patrol; on its rump perch two *Schutzpolitzisten* – wet bats; it turns the corner – German caps protrude unpropitiously over the silhouettes of the guns and the British berets.

'Dust means death – go slow' signs and rain. A German boy fills in a grave. **British infantrymen**, draped in brown-green raincapes, march along the verges towards Zeven; their boots spatter slush in file athwart the fields.

The last warlike gestures: soldier and officer, distinct species. Men clinging to armoured cars on the move. Men resting – leaning on rifles, lolling in ditch, on one knee over an undone anklet. Clusters of men off the carriers, moving flank-wise, bent stealthy – then sluggards. But infantrymen on the task of going forward: clumsy, clattering with equipment, they lope, and fall, and lope again – weariness, discomfort, bewilderment flush and pale their faces; their pathetic trot zigzags, there is more of the dispersed flock about them than of a disciplined aim and charge; their backs in action suggest preoccupations of working men in a sticky job, labouring, laden and uncomfortable, in haste to the next point of rest and safety; their rudimentary mateyness – the 'good show' compulsion – just about sustains their progress – voiced in cynical standard jocularity without any trace of patriotic fervour or hate for their adversaries.

Tanks stuck in the slush, entanglement of supply lines and stampeding refugee horses, old women howling in fear. Postures of command, of thrusting forth from the gun-turret to peer into a wall of smoke. Hooded (overalls) faces tied to the machines by earphones and binoculars – expectant; gestures under fire: lightning and frozen; faces of the wounded – resigned or putting on a 'show', or sucked in with pain, or unconscious. A bullet pierces a soldier – first, the body's revolt, then an instant withering.

For the last time perhaps I look at all this. Darkness spreads and the shapes grow hieratic, gain monumentality. 'Let's beat it,' says Gerald. We leave behind, in the night over Elbe, **the last day** of the epic of almost six years. A somewhat regretful and confused sensation: 'left before the end' muddles in my head. But also: 'Exactly so – without an ending' – night falls and shrouds the waging battle – this is most true and most menacing. Tomorrow, the day after tomorrow, I shall read in the papers of 'surrender', of 'victory'. But I, an eye witness, will not believe and will always remember that only darkness fell.

Germany closes with the defunct world of the night curfew – with heavy stench, with sinking into the ground the lumber of war. The highway, horribly ripped, melts into a timeless unbeaten track. Night, silence, void – a cataclysmic landscape; a twisted sign says '*Nach Holland*' – we cross the divide between two countries, among those which lifted 'European civilization' to its highest, as if in prehistory – in a complete wilderness.

Le Bourget sets a slovenly double line of a score of French soldiers – each different. The routine of the formal reception of *nos héros* air-transported from Germany. I trespass between the lines and board a bus for Scribe.

Panorama of the jumble and poverty of the outskirts; coaches, swinging with enthusiasm of return, carry tearsome repatriates, drive through still shabbier than remembered hungry ordinariness. Market women, blue workers. A poster: *A bas le vote des femmes!* Now the streets uppish with opulence, women perched up by platform soles and towering hats (as in Belgium, abhorrent fashions evolved under subjugation) – shops sneer with riches and prices. Poster *Berlin est tombé! Vive la France! Vive de Gaulle!* Crowds do not notice the returning men. And so, in the shaking bus, at the tail of the liberation convoy, I cut through the **Parisian strata.**

Métro. A raffish chap, hat tilted, yawns profoundly over *France Soir*, headlined hugely *Hitler est Mort.*

A brothel at Porte St-Denis. Helmeted GIs showing off at the bar and dejected tedium of women. In the corner a thick false brunette in a black bodice and transparent skirt (buttocks heavily hang above her old calves) haggles over something. The costume of a seductress, but the gestures of serious business transaction. I take a peep. Deep in discussion with a beggarly old man, she rummages meditatively among four loaves in a basket – gropes for crispness, fusses, selects – buys BREAD.

'Les Invalides'. Cupolas shine proudly, old cannons project over grandiose perspectives, the Eiffel peers from round a corner (tricolour flapping), young civilians swaggeringly mount a huge Sherman (on show in the square), bumptiously feel for gun-triggers, lounge in the turret. American fortresses roar over.

Boulevards, corner. A street *chanteuse* – accordion-backed – awakes old sentiments; she croons yearningly and from the guts – the admiring chorus mounts – it is all vernal and almost as it was 'before'. But to the left stands an eyesore wretch in the patched overcoat and striped pants of *Konzentrazionslager*, GIs paw gum-chewing *mademoiselles*, a beggar moans, cabmen at their jades quarrel over 500-franc fares.

'Le Théâtre de la Mode' – exhibition in Pavilion de Marsan: Paris attempts to regain the throne of the world's fashion industry. Preciosities and whimsies, *les goûts* of the Parisian-cum-voguish 'baroque' of the 1930s – and the goggling mass of dowdy women. Paris tries, strains to forget the years of shame and re-erects (with the hands of Bérards and Cocteaux) the arty screens, which were the background of life before the war, and now are meant to hid the ugly truth.

'Mouvement pour l'Indépendance Hongroise' opens an exhibition of 'Des Artistes Hongrois'. Yards of canvas worked on with brushes, dry of heart and energy. Galérie Beaux-Arts crowded with posturing, pretence, conceit, jealousies – a Hungarian dwarf-Parnassus – half-landing of Parisian *Bohème*, choked with the belchings of pre-war offerings. Over all this the confidence of a *marchand de tableaux* – with his policies-intrigues, his current exhibitions he despises but arranges to get free advertising write-ups for his backroom big sales of little green ('***Oh, quel merveille!***') Impressionists.

Picasso's studio presents a suspiciously orderly disorder. A disagreeable Spaniard bars the way – factotum or bodyguard – Picasso is not at home and the pat tidiness smacks of the cadaver – of the posthumous museum, not of a living workshop of living art.

Braque lives in the modern suburbia of Cité Universitaire. Derain (*collaborateur*?), neatly stylized giant, opens the door of a demonstration studio. We enter, led by an acquaintance of his, without appointment, but *le Maître* (and his interior) look as if they had waited for the tourists, arranged into *Derain chez soi*: untouched, prettily posing brushes, canvases, paints, pastels, marionettes' theatre, the white *lavallière*, the cocky workman's hat. At the bistro lunch (*la patronne* when press-buttoned proudly sings out her heroic story – of Maquis and husband killed on this very doorstep) we talk about Picasso. And old Derain, though irreversibly wreathed in fame, falls to the level of envy-mongering, lines up the same facile denigration props as my own generation at Du Dôme, or Paddington: 'Picasso, *mais voyons*, he's surely not a painter – only a *dessinateur* who fills the contours with colour.'

The painting *marché-noir* and scrambles for material blessings of Commercial Paris. Café Flore – the same out of breath, in haste elbowing to the fore of '***La Culture Française***'. There are vacancies – these got killed, those have not yet returned, others – *collaborateurs*. La Bourse of literary coteries, of art dignitaries – the race for culture hierarchy is on – till presently (after the strategic positions have been secured) it will ossify into authorities and eminences, unshakeable – for the next twenty years.

Conversations. Constant horrifying accounts of desperate hunts, of murders, of theatre- and café-going in the net of *rafles*, and mostly about the police, about the dehumanized Frenchmen. It becomes uneasy – Paris. One starts eyeing mistrustfully its beauty, its bistros' and its shopkeepers' charms. They fawn over us, but who did they fawn over yesterday, on whom did they inform? 'France – *la cocotte*,' says Irena. Old cliché. Reflection: 'But of course, the whole of Europe harloted itself – France is at least a gainly *cocotte*.'

Foul *marché-noir* bistro. Delight of the profiteers. Old wretch enters, lets fall her overcoat – a frivolous and crumpled frock, weary veined neck, creased elbows and palms – sings-shouts obscenities, yanks her hem up to her chin, pants (her face absently harassed), cavorts jerkily.

'Les Oubliettes'. Cosy interior, old jokes (we settle at **Table des Cocus Gascons**). Students' night. Starts with a refrain:

> Zut, merde, pine et Boxon
> Le père . . . something . . . est un cochon.

The cellar swells with youths and *cochonneries*. Hours pass filled with lavatory humour. Onanistic pantomine *Mister Jim* raises the crowd's enthusiasm. Boys abet a well-to-do brute, just arrived with a *poule*: '***Embrassez, embrassez***!' . . . and then: '***Pelottez, pelottez***!' Till exhilarated: '**A poil**' The brute pushes on to the platform and insolently undoes his flies. The phallus looms over ***La Jeune France***, frenzied in admiration.

'45 Club'. Champs-Élysées. Heights of mondainism. Chic *à la* pre-war dance-place. In sultry smoke, in the clink and rasp of jazz, preen, sit at their cognacs puffed-up people – a tight parcel of mincing women and men trots, wavers on a square of flooring. The rich and their pleasure-purveyors did not invent anything new in time – the costly interior seems ridiculously sham and unreal. The rites performed by dutiful puppets. But fun flew away with 1939.

3 May. The National Day at the Polish Embassy: rendezvous of ghosts. Conventionally gilded salon, reception-poses – but closer: patched pre-war uniforms, women torture-aged; a cavalry Colonel after years in a prison camp swaggers – a lady preens in response, interrupting the narrative of beating and night abduction; chit-chat, smiles, cocktails, gossips: 'My dear, surely there's Lusia – can you believe it? – during a night round-up and deportation her mother volunteered to replace her. Oh dear, hasn't she wasted, poor thing.' Such salons were not to be seen even after the French Revolution when the guillotined heads were counted up. All the Polands – Siberian and German-ruled, Middle Eastern and Italian, Scottish – separated for six years, are here matching, adding up, auctioneering experiences, agreeing on most points, catching up and spinning the threads of the yesteryears' sympathies; guardedly they stretch their antennae towards the strangers, back out (though unassuredly) into cool haughty tones in face of the potential supplicant, or the 'not-one-of-us': 'Mr Redski? No, I don't know where to find him – he does not frequent the Embassy'; 'I hardly know her – she's rather unattractive.' We are in one sphere – the salon *is* pre-war Poland: a diplomat from London, a journalist from America, a painter from the Near East, a high staff officer from the 1939 campaign, one higher still from the campaign in Italy, a subaltern from the Warsaw rising in 1944, another from the German front, 1945; a countess from Vichy France, one from Auschwitz, and another from Cairo, a woman writer from Siberian-taiga, and ladies from Uruguay and Uganda. These thunder-smashed hot-house plants try, in spite of the ominous skies, to straighten their stalks, to bristle with colours and shapes.

Tomorrow another Polish-American soldier will stop me in the street and tell me of another ceremony into which he blundered: 'It was fine – the table had been covered in *red*, but all the same it was very patriotic.' Next day, wandering round Vendôme Column, in the shade of Napoleon's glory, Jędrychowski, delegate of soon-to-be-in-power Lublin Government, will say that surely the tables are always covered in red at commemoration meetings.

And others still, helpless in the chronic lack of 'official support', will sit (the unfulfilled masonry of the world) in thousands of identical little cafés and will debate most intelligently about the necessity of 'an intellectual renaissance', about the defeat of 'systems' and the 'need' for faith, the desperate derailing of Europe.

The quays are lovely of an evening. Mattly stand the façades of Île St-Louis. Notre-Dame's black height of beauty humbles the present. The figures on the portico lean downward to appraise us. My cousin, Jadzia, when an emissary for the Maquis, went through (besides everything else) a cosmetic operation. She tells swiftly and simply of fear, torment, death and strength of character. She reported herself to the police 'for a Jewess' (although her Catholicism and name – Drutowska – assured safety) out of loyalty to a rounded-up Jewish girl friend and to the persecuted. She was already in the French transit camp on the way to death trains. She could endure the most difficult trials most heroically – but breaks down now at conflicts of peacetime dailiness. 'I could be strong in face of the Bosch and the police – now I am weak, terribly weak' – she cries and in turn laughs tearsomely at herself. Steadfastness in singleness of purpose, the white and black of good and bad enforced by war or oppression, as against the division of loyalties, confusion and 'each man for himself' of peacetime.*

As always, **the British Islands** are wrapped in a cotton-wool package of fog. The plane dips into the whiteness – and finds, in time, the tedious landscape of Croydon. Stuck in a lorry (returning soldiers) we thunder through black Sunday slums. Bomb-torn tranquillity. WELCOME HOME, MAC! WELCOME, JOHN! scrawls garlanded in paper Union Jacks brand the soldiers' nests. On the doorsteps stand broadened wives, waiting assuredly. Tomorrow: V-Day.

7 May and 'unofficial' **Victory Day**. The town packed with humanity booms, but pansy, tart, American break to the fore. Darkness dignifies the spectacle – symbolically rent by a lit-up SIMPSON'S OF PICCADILLY; the store focuses crowds – the shopkeepers' triumphant hope. I go home. A clear starlit sky, but (there are witnesses) the horizon groans – gathers a thunderstorm. Wide glow of bonfires, hiss and bang of squibs and crackers, firemen's bells – there accretes (illusory or in truth) the scene of war. The storm is already overhead.

On the table there lies a reprint of Dyson's cartoon from the *Daily Herald*, 1918: Versailles – Lloyd George, Clemenceau, Woodrow Wilson – in the corner a crying child, labelled '1940 Class'. Brutal title 'Peace and Future Cannon-Fodder'. Caption 'The Tiger: "Curious, I seem to hear a child weeping!" '

Behind the door bleats my newborn son.

A Berlin girl: 'Americans are Russians in pressed trousers.' **1946**

Nuremberg Trial. Eight months, six hours a day, in artificial dead air, under a ceiling of dead-white lamps, in the shadowless brightness sit twenty-one accused, surrounded by their mates in torture – the judges, counsels, prosecutors, secretaries, interpreters, pressmen, and the operetta-like US military policemen. And in still wider circles rotates the whole tremendous machinery of the Trial: the endless corridors serpentine throughout the enormous building – the wiring of the system which officiates, facilitates, promotes, records, administers, guards that unimpressive bunch of Nazi specimens. Swarms of men and women trot round the corridors, sway in their office chairs, giggle at the chocolate-and-gum counters of the Post Exchange, clash, unite, divide over forms, priorities, facilities and prestige of doubtful importance; gorge their meals in queues, gossip feebly over the artificial intercourse of their short lives on the smashed body of Nuremberg. The *contredanse* of canteens, rest rooms, dazed dashes in urgent jeeps across the awed streets, tiptoe entries into the court, bows to the tribunal and coy humour over its deadly proceedings. Quarrelsome interpreters' voices murmur from the glass cages – or brain one through the earphones. Russian chirping, French sing-song. American twanging, German throatiness. The mangle of a pressing, tense but sedative routine. The men in the dock yawn, ache for diversion, nudge one another over a peroxide-curled girl in the gallery. Only the public, always changing, gloats, searches for sensation; opera-glasses in the prettily gloved paws of plump wives and over-powdered girlfriends of the MG (Military Government) officials, German Jews gaping, recognizing,

*My old friend, Czesław Bobrowski, his credentials, his fearlessness, supported by a fictitious charity document, explored those first-stage camps bringing out to safety whomever he could, on whatever justification he could muster. Thus Jadzia and he met, fell in love. But she refused to abandon her friend – extricating Jadzia was easy – and the date of transporting the condemned nearing, Cesław's efforts, the tug-of-war against all odds with the 'authorities' must have been superhuman. He won, left with the two girls, and Jadzia and he married.

In liberated Paris he and I had long walks pondering their future. They returned to Poland – he to be one of a triumvirate of economic planners. A rare thing: he, never self-seeking, resigned when the Russian-imposed counterplan had to be accepted. He resigned, but respected as he was, the post of the Ambassador to Sweden brought for them a year of vacuosity, which they could not bear. They, again now in Paris, unlike most others who sought asylum, did not make political – thus material – capital out of their decampment but, penniless, tried to make a living by writing thrillers – unsuccessfully. She died of TB and undernourishment.

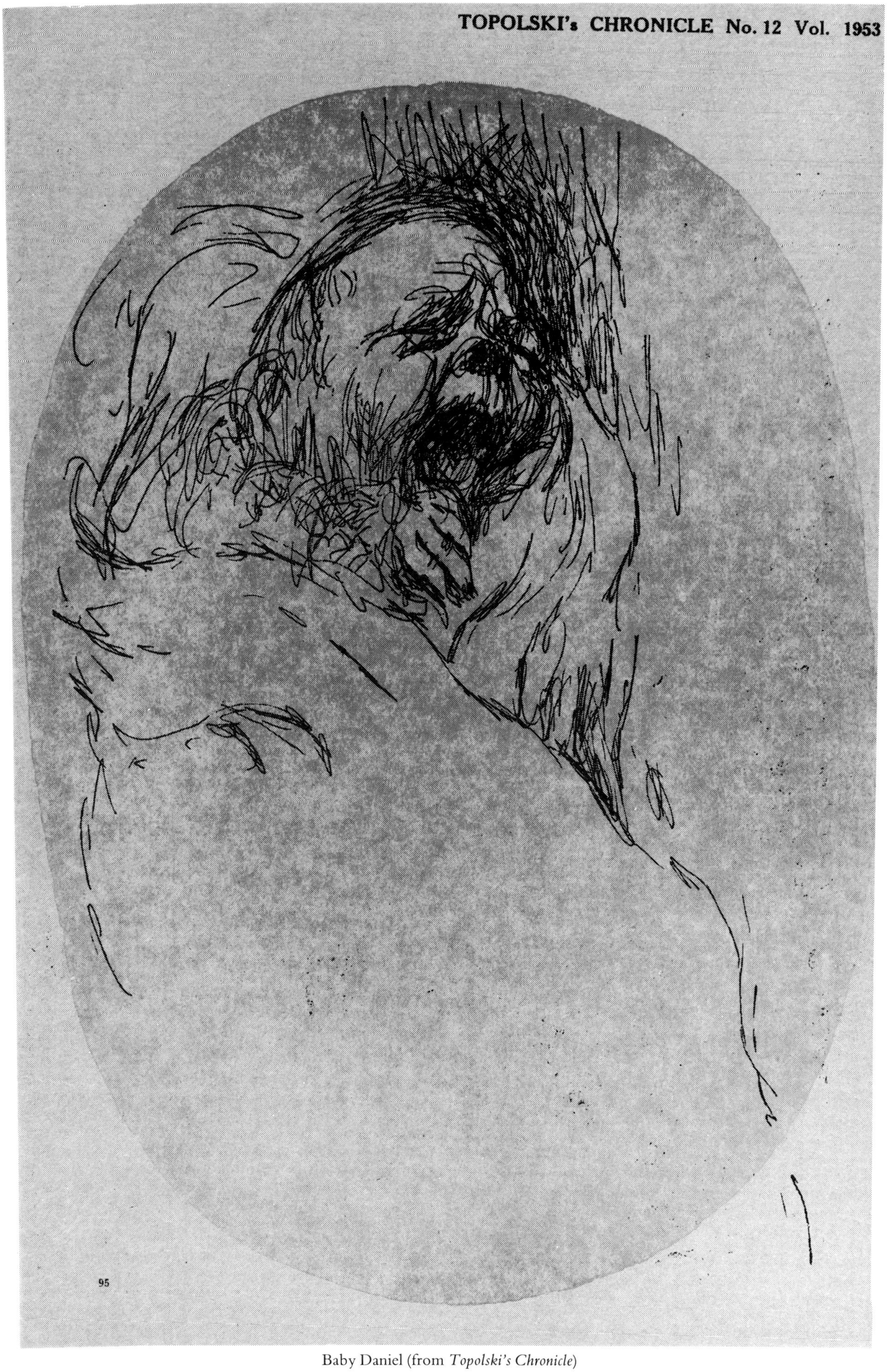

Baby Daniel (from *Topolski's Chronicle*)

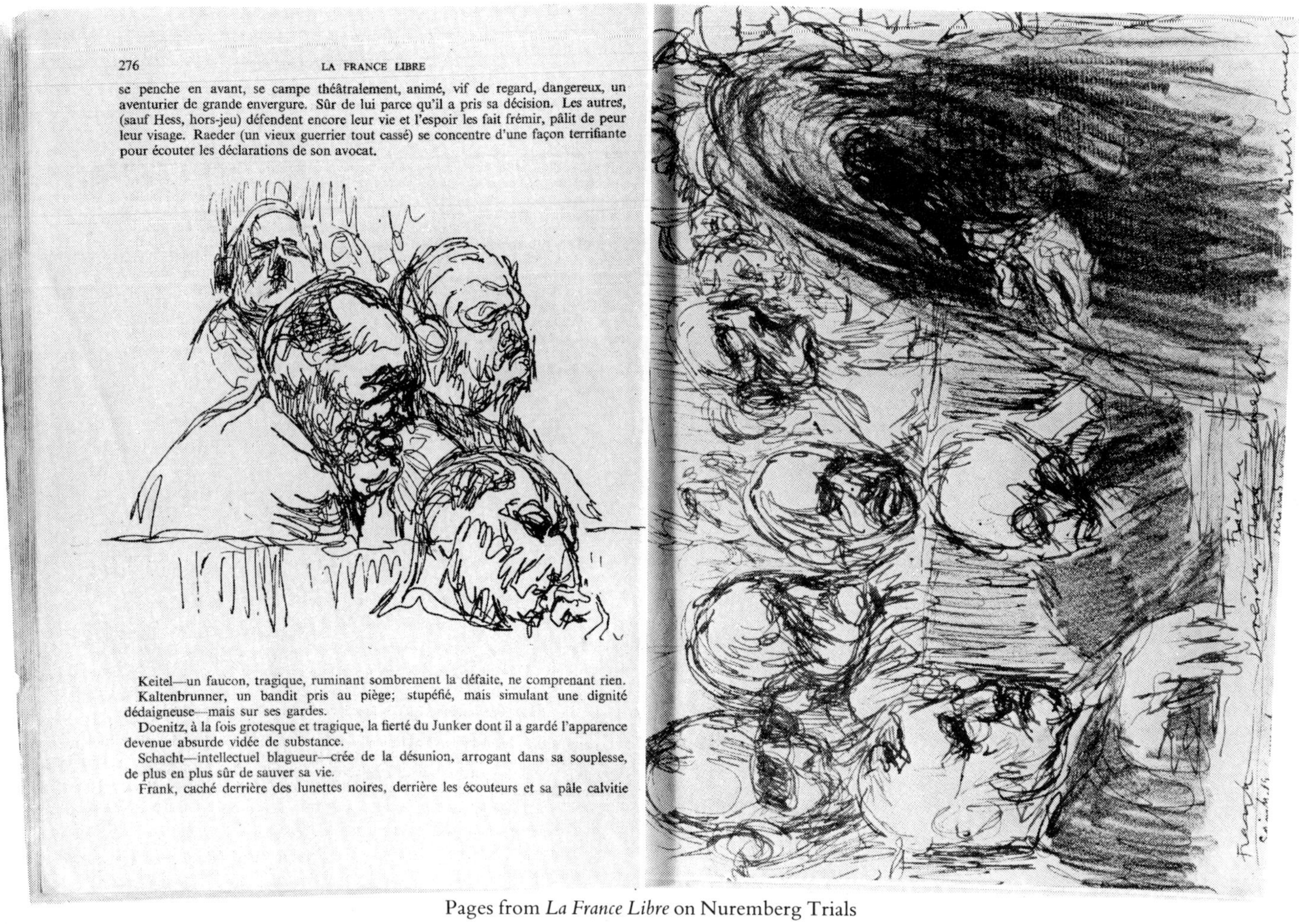
276 LA FRANCE LIBRE

se penche en avant, se campe théâtralement, animé, vif de regard, dangereux, un aventurier de grande envergure. Sûr de lui parce qu'il a pris sa décision. Les autres, (sauf Hess, hors-jeu) défendent encore leur vie et l'espoir les fait frémir, pâlit de peur leur visage. Raeder (un vieux guerrier tout cassé) se concentre d'une façon terrifiante pour écouter les déclarations de son avocat.

Keitel—un faucon, tragique, ruminant sombrement la défaite, ne comprenant rien.
Kaltenbrunner, un bandit pris au piège; stupéfié, mais simulant une dignité dédaigneuse—mais sur ses gardes.
Doenitz, à la fois grotesque et tragique, la fierté du Junker dont il a gardé l'apparence devenue absurde vidée de substance.
Schacht—intellectuel blagueur—crée de la désunion, arrogant dans sa souplesse, de plus en plus sûr de sauver sa vie.
Frank, caché derrière des lunettes noires, derrière les écouteurs et sa pâle calvitie

Pages from *La France Libre* on Nuremberg Trials

still implanted with dread . . .

One is amazed at first by the tame obedience of the prisoners to the rules of the game (they stand up for the entry of the tribunal). Do they recognize its lawfulness, and why?

Goering, at close quarters, petrifying: thinned, but his huge face (one's eyes travel over its stretches) truly lion-like; he yawns, chuckles, prattles, stretches, leans forward posed grandly, is lively, quick-sighted, dangerous – a large-dimension adventurer; confident, because he has made the decision.

The others (except the stunted **Hess**) still fight for life and hope troubles them, pales their faces with fear.

Roeder – an old broken man-at-arms, listens to his counsel's pronouncements with horrifying concentration;

Keitel – hawk-like, tragic, brooding on defeat, not understanding;

Kaltenbrunner – like a trapped bandit: stupefied but watchful, feigning indifferent dignity;

Doenitz – both tragic and grotesque, his *Junker* pride turned to absurdity, he still retains its bearing emptied now of content;

Schacht – the intellectual *blagueur*, creates discord, arrogant in his suppleness, more and more sure of his safety;

Frank – hidden behind dark glasses, earphones, pale tufty baldness, the shabby mask of a *kitsch* villain, who interwove ruthlessness with the sloppy romanticism of his love-life.

He and the next few surely look what was understood in Germany as non-Aryan: a tiny dark-bold attorney, furiously Nazi; **Streicher**, a broken cripple; **Funk**, **Sauckel** – the rabid victims of complexes, helplessly chasing after physical handsomeness, after Valhalla, climbing on stilts of anti-Jewish pure-blond-giant deeds, to cut themselves off from the dark and the tiny. These are the butchers of the regime. Many others simply yielded to temptation.

The accused men look at us with the faces of a soldier, careerist, aristocrat, intellectual, adventurer, brute, fool, swindler, degenerate – the most shattering are the faces that could be labelled 'normal', that could be replaced by anybody from the public gallery. Proofs of the everpresence of evil.

The men of the tribunal have the blank faces of the Law of England, France, America, Russia – abstract creatures moulded into the traditional shapes of Judges.

The court drains one's energy; the bedlam of little contacts, promises, drinks, 'who's whos', saps one's alertness.

The drama is performed against the constant interferences of whispers, smiles, diversions; the background weighs heavily on the show, shatters with its trivial comedy one's sense of Judgment and Retribution.

The men of the court are all united in an awkward dedication – they have their favourites across in the dock. 'Goering's in good form today,' gaily announces an Allied lawyer; 'Frick was suicidal again,' they worry; a woman journalist, writing Frank's story, talks of him with intimacy; a British prosecutor, Elwyn Jones, overheard at the *pissoir*,

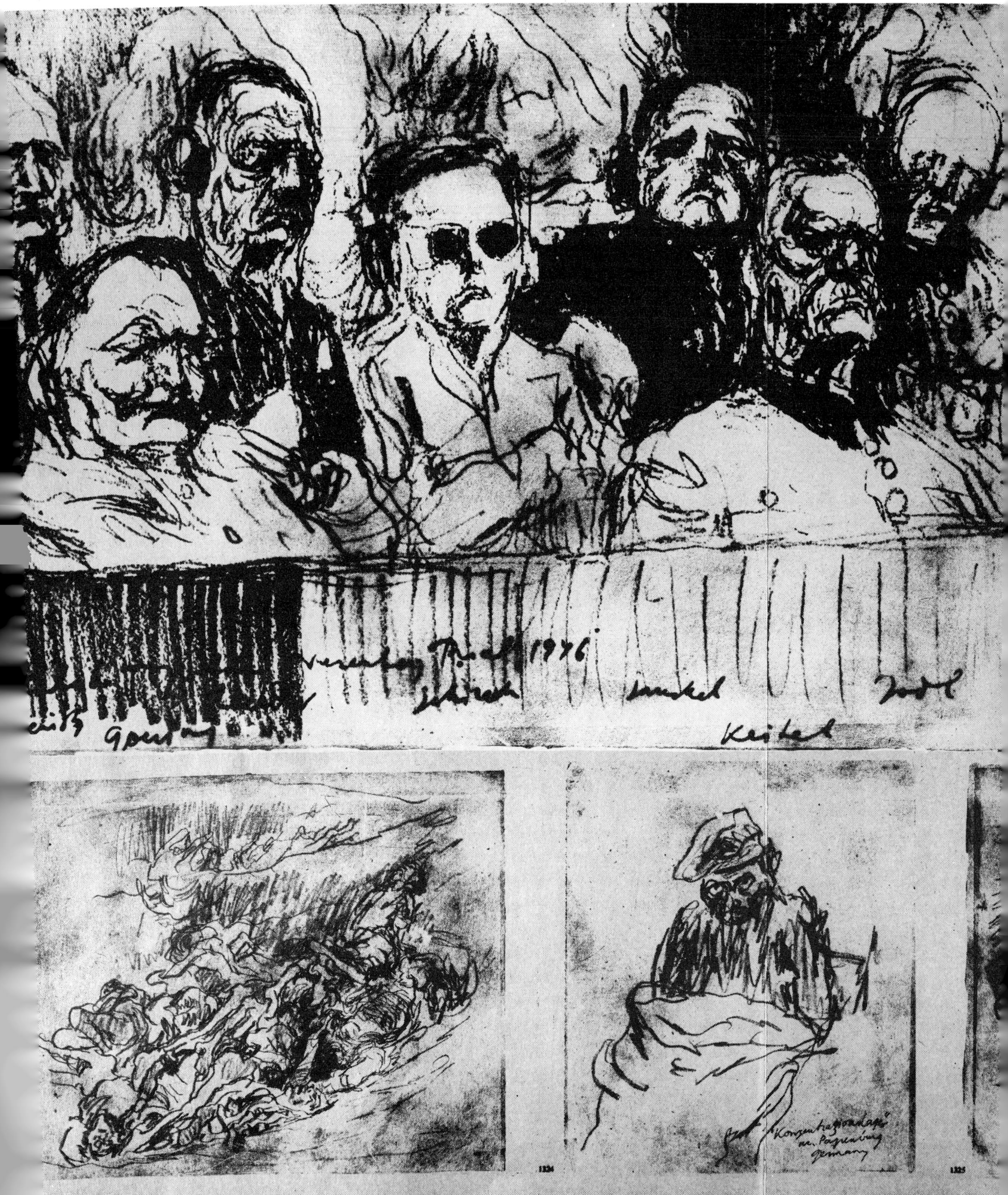

Nuremberg Trials: the accused (from *Topolski's Chronicle*)

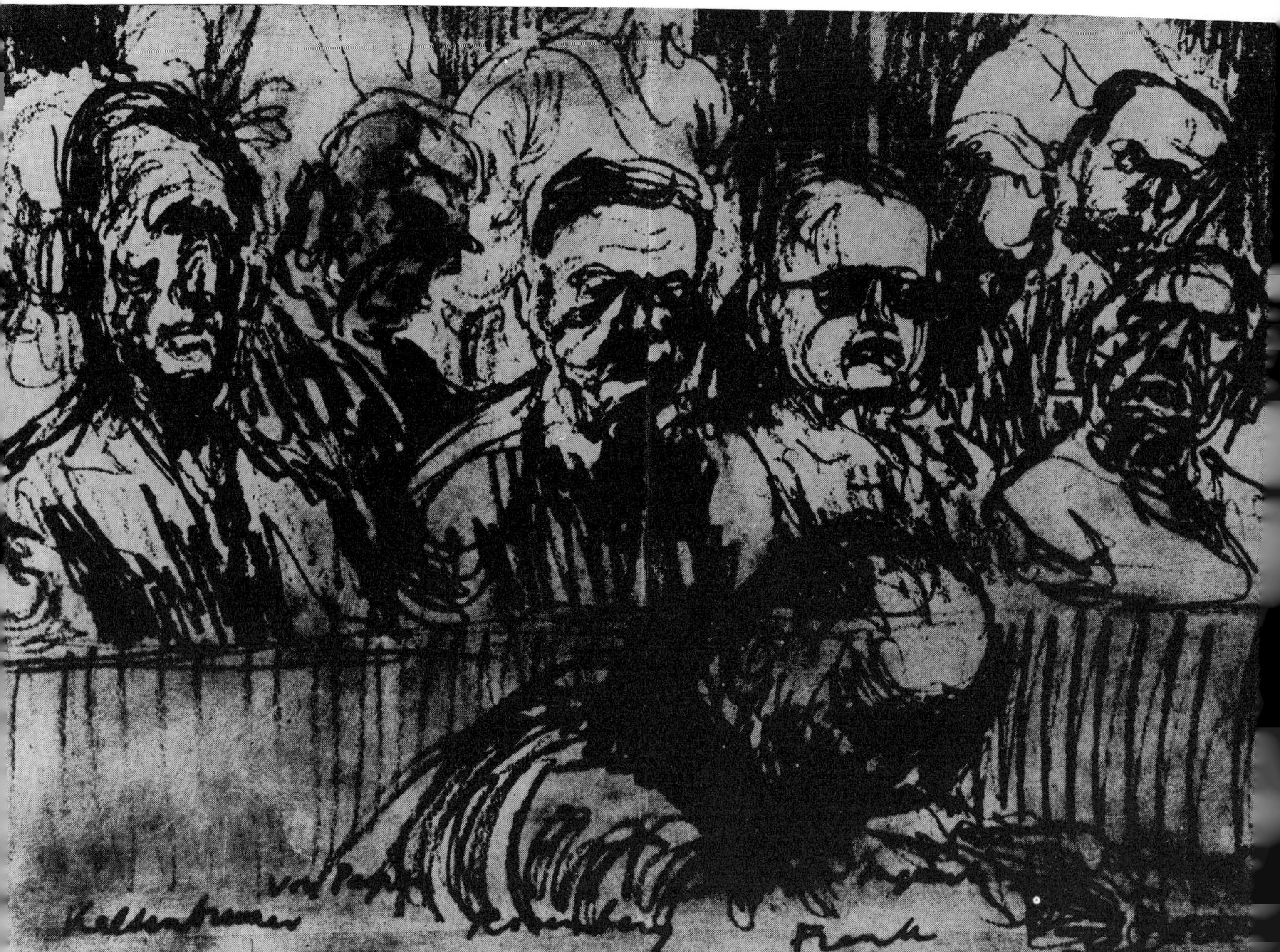

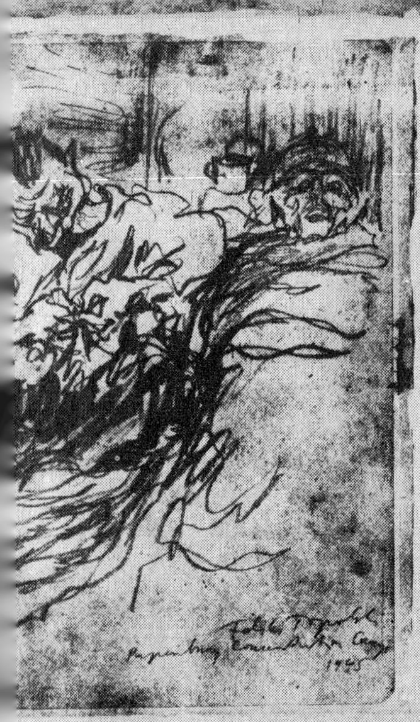

1326

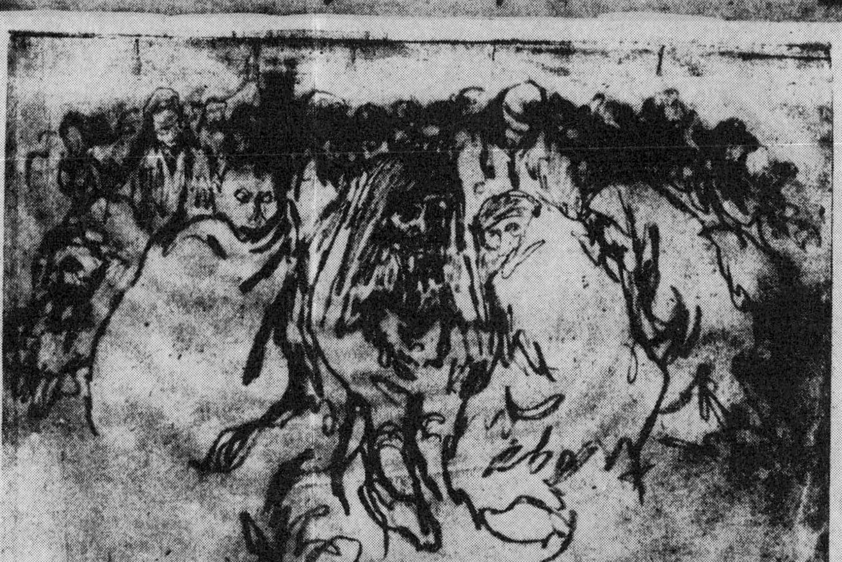

1327

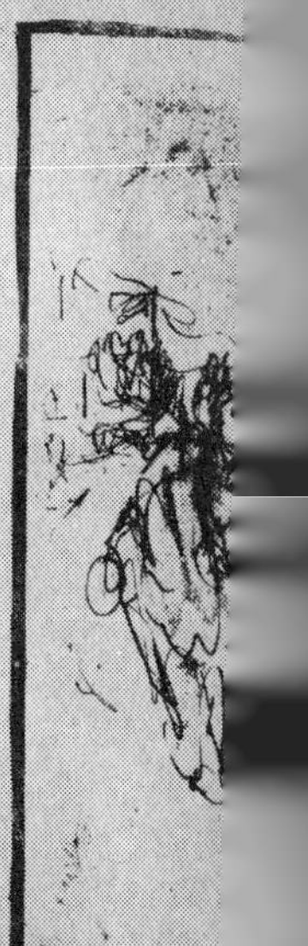

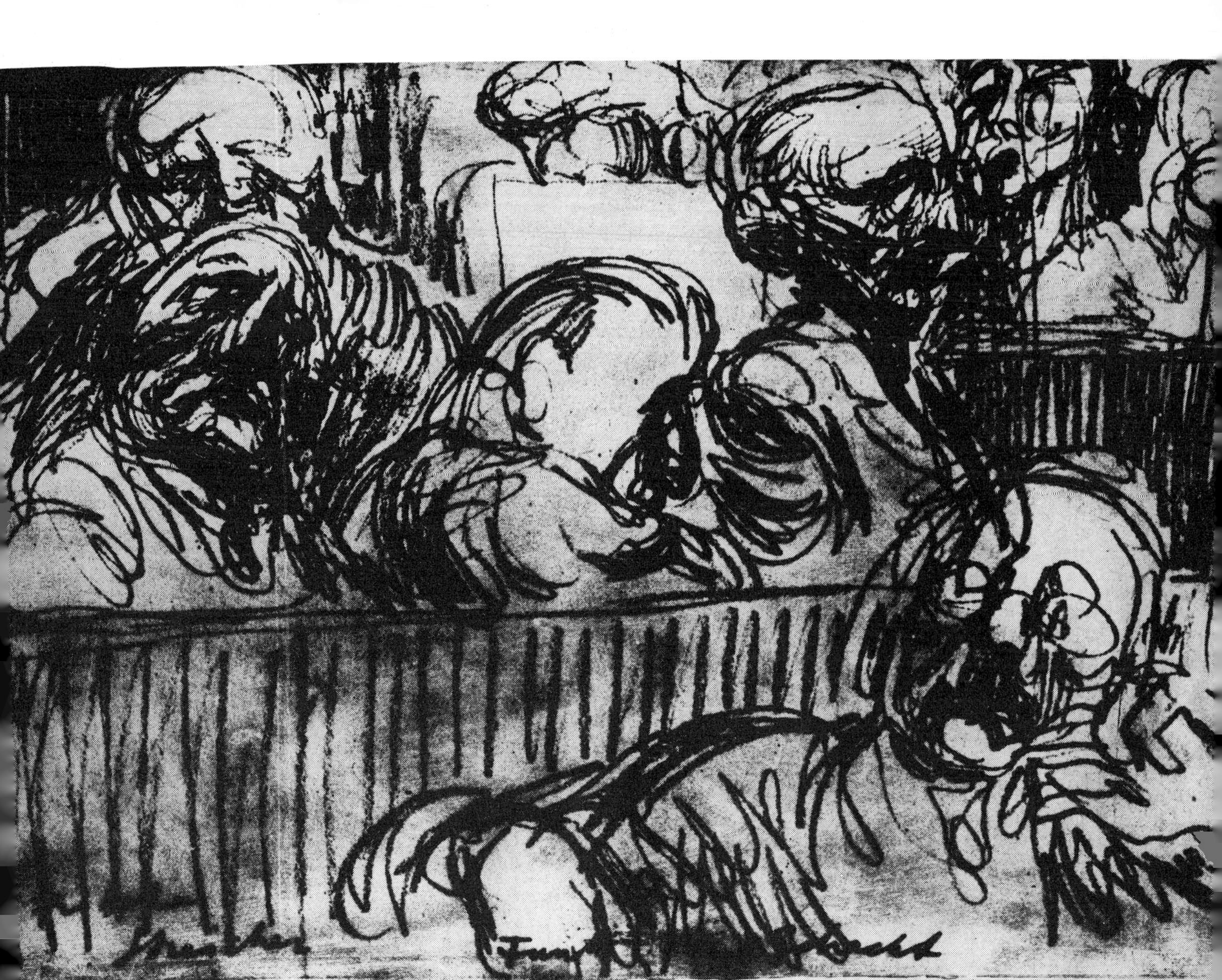

By courtesy of the Trustees of The Imperial War Museum

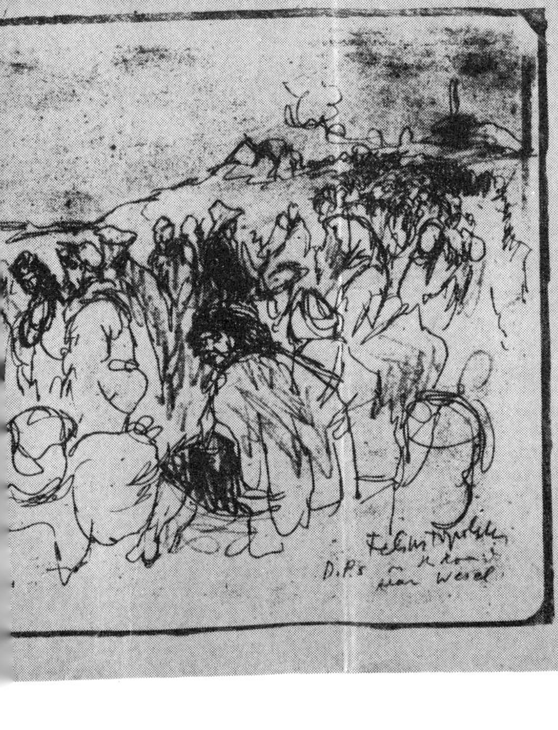

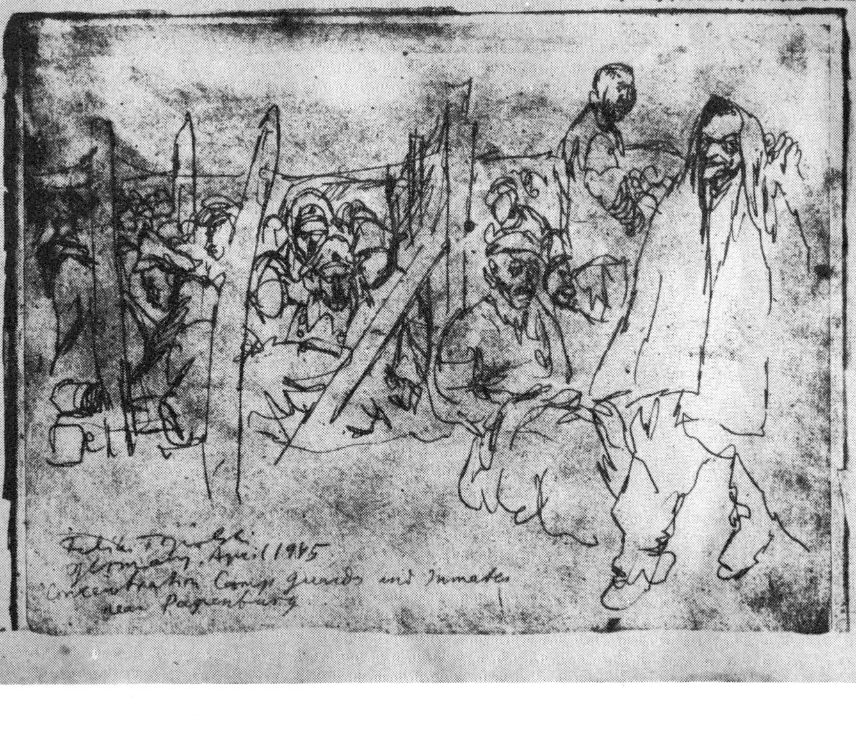

says to a German counsel: 'I enjoyed your excellent speech.'

Professionalism dominates the court. The lawyers took over the melodrama and turned it into the precise weighing of paragraphs against deeds.

Propped by the seemingly careless bored theologists of Law with rare outbursts of emotion diffused in endless speeches on military rulings, neutral seas and justified invasions, trickling drop by drop with history – the Trial wades its way towards Justice.

Ancient sailors, grouped over the Port-of-**Dublin** steps, bleakly stare at their ancient tidal past. At Jammet's private room an old, very old man, **Jack Yeats**, displays refined coquetry of a dreamy head out of loose low collar, of shy sureness in his craft and his great age which leave the young far behind; his ambiguous gusto not varying, his pictures' sophistication having reached naivety, he pours into them untrammelled poesies; as forlorn as his ageing country. He is it, and that shaky vision and brush conceal poverty and bring out purity. The dealer rubs his hands.

The old man Yeats 'explains' his pictures at his studio – as innocently as Kokoschka. He explains his nymphs and their absurd adventures with men on white horses. He points to blood on the grass and the knife in the white breast. But the painting beams over his black-coated shoulder, beckons to its own lustre seemingly unseen by its procreator.

He scribbled for me on the edge of the menu a prettily trembly drawing. I examined it later: a stormy sea and a shore with a lively horse upon it greeting a top-hatted flag-wagging upright figure in an approaching boat. So this is how the old man's mind works to turn out his enchanting images: I am John Bull with the Union Jack in hand visiting the white horse's island.

Drained, clinging to the gossamer of a legend, the Dubliners keep on replaying their short-lived outburst of heroics-revelations, sunk now into the past – the present bleak; **the Abbey Theatre** replays itself with *The Plough and the Stars*. The old curtain goes up on the lot: the crumbling redbrick Georgian slum, the cluster-chorus of black 'shawlees' – the tragic women's *pietà* round a bleeding hero, lovers' farewell in the doorway, the banner aloft. But young voices from the gallery: 'We protest' '. . . protest against Irish theatre' – meaning, 'We protest against ourselves!'

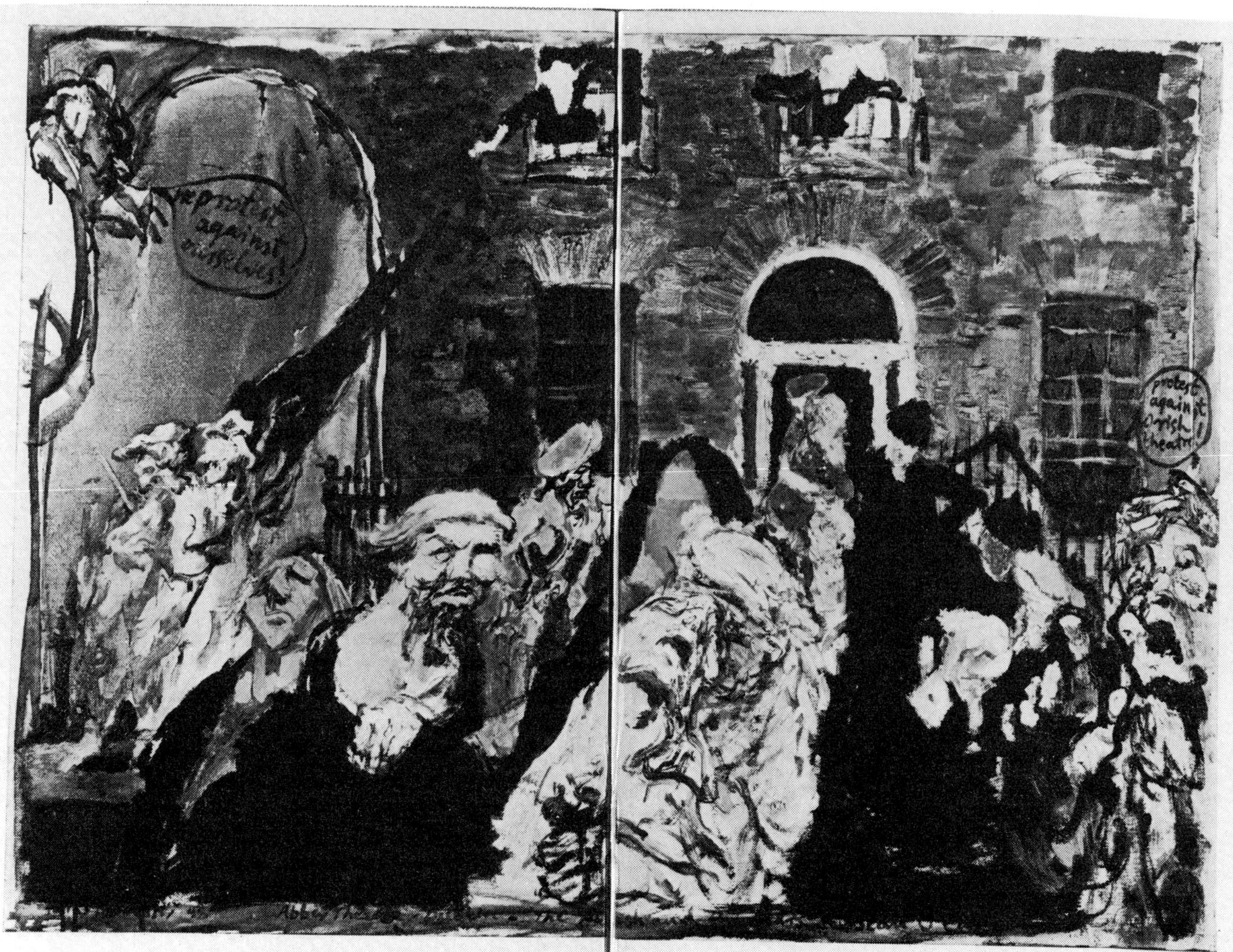

The Plough and the Stars at the Abbey Theatre, Dublin

TOPOLSKI's CHRONICLE No. 4-5 (64-65) Vol IV 1956
...nothing affirmeth and therefore never lyeth... Sir Philip Sidney (1580)

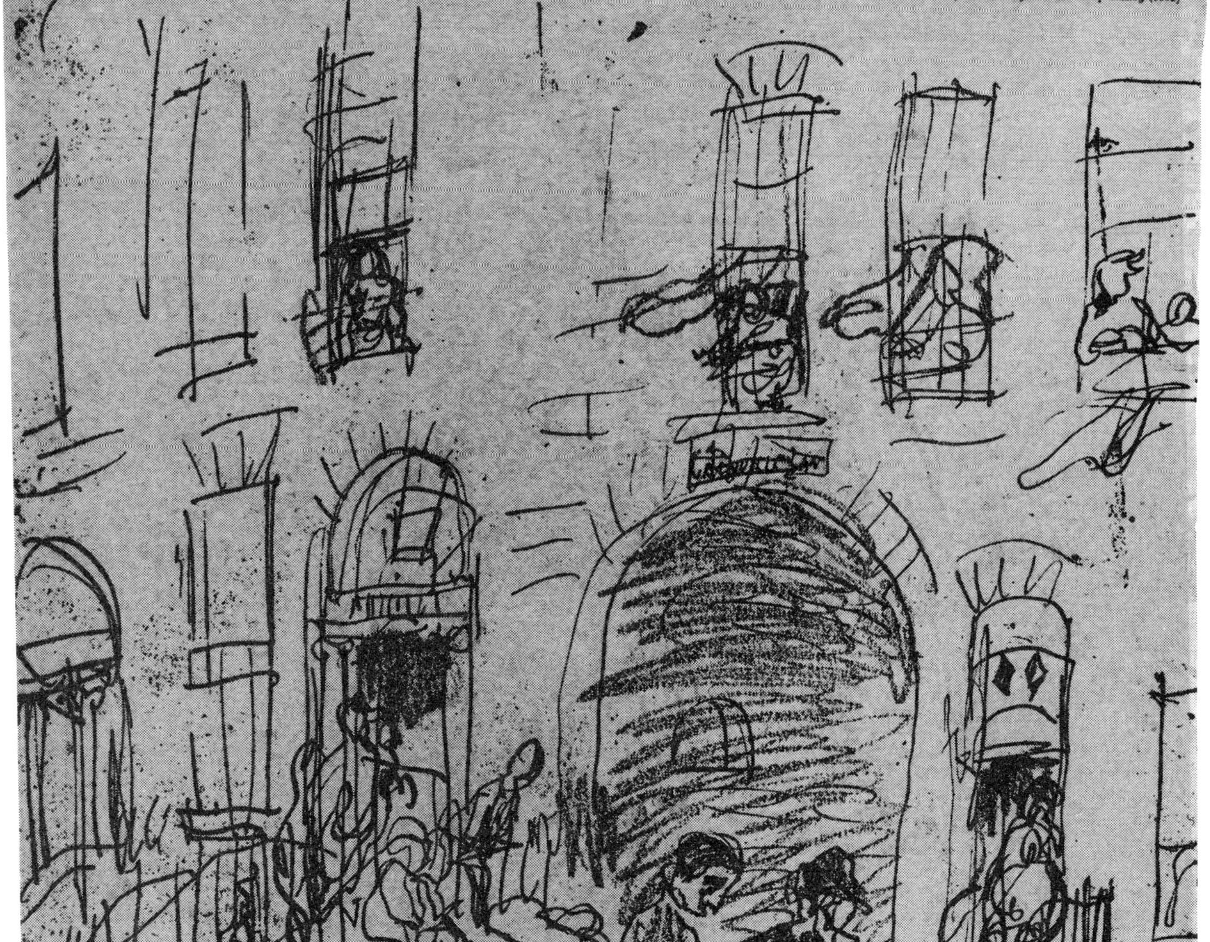

618

DUBLIN

In the wet-blown greenness, customarily lost in blue smears, the eccentrics in large numbers perch on their shooting sticks round the paddock of **Naas Races**. My hosts whisper in my ears the tales of mere womanizers and drunkards – as uniquely Irish display of conceits – the human orchids (immodest whiskers, noses of immoderate size, leafed and petalled in extravagantly coloured/shaped cloaks, boots, cravats, hoods); the human gibbons chatting away in their drunkards' swank: soldiering, gamble, sport, Mayfair girls, braggadocios.

Beyond the fences of the Enclosure, the coarser species carry on with folk-whimsies – a furthering of snobberies.

Connemara bogs, a horse, a cart, tinkers slogging along. The dazzling Atlantic, wave-propelled, beats/blows at this crushed land stone-walls-chequered. A cross among the boulders, the wind bedevils bends dark shapes rooting after the chime of bells – Sunday. The stony chapel is a crumbling battlement against the elements and dying, and its evensong choruses are as if the cries of drowning – hence the pub and whiskey and the camaraderie of those united in hardship.

The hardy **Kinmon Lushington-Tullochs** hold their Shanboolard Hall, an eighteenth-century Gothic fortress, garrisoned by their dogs and horses, the Anglo-Irish 'Norsemen', hoary with manly jokes, sieged/ringed by the Celtic natives.

North Wales. In the depth of Ffestiniog's slatiness **Koestler**'s alien-voiced apodictic chameleon-reasonableness tames us – unwilling; tiny Mamaine – subservient.

Back up on the mountain in the lone chalet we revert to our squabble: the morning wakes it up – the duetto's theme this time is about my delayed return from Dublin, thus her gypsy-carting on her own – just out of childbirth – the two babes, the no-language no-use Polish amateur nanny, the whole household's paraphernalia – up the unknown wilderness.

Booted, haversacked, stick in hand, I walk steeply out, up and into the early sun. Promptly stripped-naked (clothes dangling over the sack), but heavy-nailed soles crash confidently on the stony pathlessness.

No botanist/geologist/zoologist in me, my mounting mounts in generalized exhilaration (unhampered by detailing/naming stones-bushes-insects-fourleggeds) at the height, the silence, the aloneness.

Hours and distances up-and-onward; and, orbiting after the sun, full turn: this could not be elsewhere – grand summits and swift element-warped majestically congested steeps descend hastily, fall, plains omitted, into the immeasurability of the seas. And: I am a giant – this monumentality is carved in miniature; the Welsh Alpine grandeur – in itself true – is an accommodatingly graspable miracle, yet, or because of its unconcern with scale, achieving awesomeness: this was one of those very few illuminations which bring me to my knees. It is always nature; and, since I am sworn to clear-sightedness, I try to avoid such subjugations.

We called him Recio, Jusuf, Jusufek, Józek*. He was ceaselessly on the move not so much by the means of his limbs (tendons and muscles apparently absent), but by a sort of glissade, shuffling just just from armchair to taxi to restaurant table to lift to aeroplane – and we would say: he will live for ever – he doesn't use himself up! And when I stupidly repeated this, to give him heart, during his last day of consciousness, at the Westminster Hospital, he said 'Sure, that would be true, if I were not paralysed by that parachute jump.'

Once, long before the war, staying in my cottage on the Thames, struggling and bored by sweating out a book of his memories of Conrad (which was to relieve him from his current penury), he blurted out that he envied the red-coated guardsmen, spotty, twenty-year-old six-footers – envied them above all! Thus it was that this elderly intelligentsia-shelved softie enforced on himself, just once, a physical gesture – and chose the most testing: a parachute jump into the Nazi terror. This he did as the envoy of the Polish Government in London to the Underground network, and fulfilled his mission, though almost throughout wheeled about.

Various people prattled various tales about Recio: that he was an agent paid by someone or other, a Mason, an *éminence grise*, irresponsible. For me, he was a guardian angel, appearing from nowhere. Angel because – inhuman in this – he never looked in the mirror, never bothered about himself; instead he would give unlimited enthusiasm and devotion, straightforwardly (without sentimentalism), to his 'protégé' or to his 'leader'. The cardinal point: he 'gave', precisely, to a person, not to a 'cause' – to the aspirations of that person, to his minutest problems and anxieties – *au fond* people were his passion.

Those who knew him when he was swept away by one of his currents of dedication† might have taken him for an 'idealist', but having watched him over many years, I was clear that even his patriotism was the sum of his Polish friendships, not an abstract notion of Fatherland.

This alone perhaps explains the inexplicable: without bureaucratic promotions and without the shortcuts of nepotism he would, during the First World War, appear out of the blue at Asquith's side; or, later, as a confidant of the leaders of the Mexican revolution; and again, still later, close to Morell and the British Labour Party. And, on another plane, as the most intimate friend of Conrad; or, in a period of historical impasse, putting as much devotion into the small matters of an artist friend as, later, into the national/international ones of General Sikorski.

A 'man of action', it is known, wins by the force of

*From my chapter in *Hommage à un grand Européen, J. H. Retinger* (le numéro spécial du Bulletin du Centre Européen de la Culture, 1960–61), containing tributes by Prince Bernhard of the Netherlands, Pietro Quaroni, Lord Boothby, Denis de Rougemont, Major-General Sir Colin Gubbins, Geoffrey de Freitas and others.

†France invaded, the *ad hoc* Polish Forces and élite refugees attempted to filter with great losses across the Channel. Those days winged the meek Retinger: his long-dormant powers/connections awakened, he flew, with Churchill's accord, to immolated France to pluck out General Sikorski, the Polish Prime Minister in Exile, and his Ministers, to reinstate them in London and from then on to be their – constantly intrigued against – *éminence grise* and the almost-sole link with their mighty Allies.

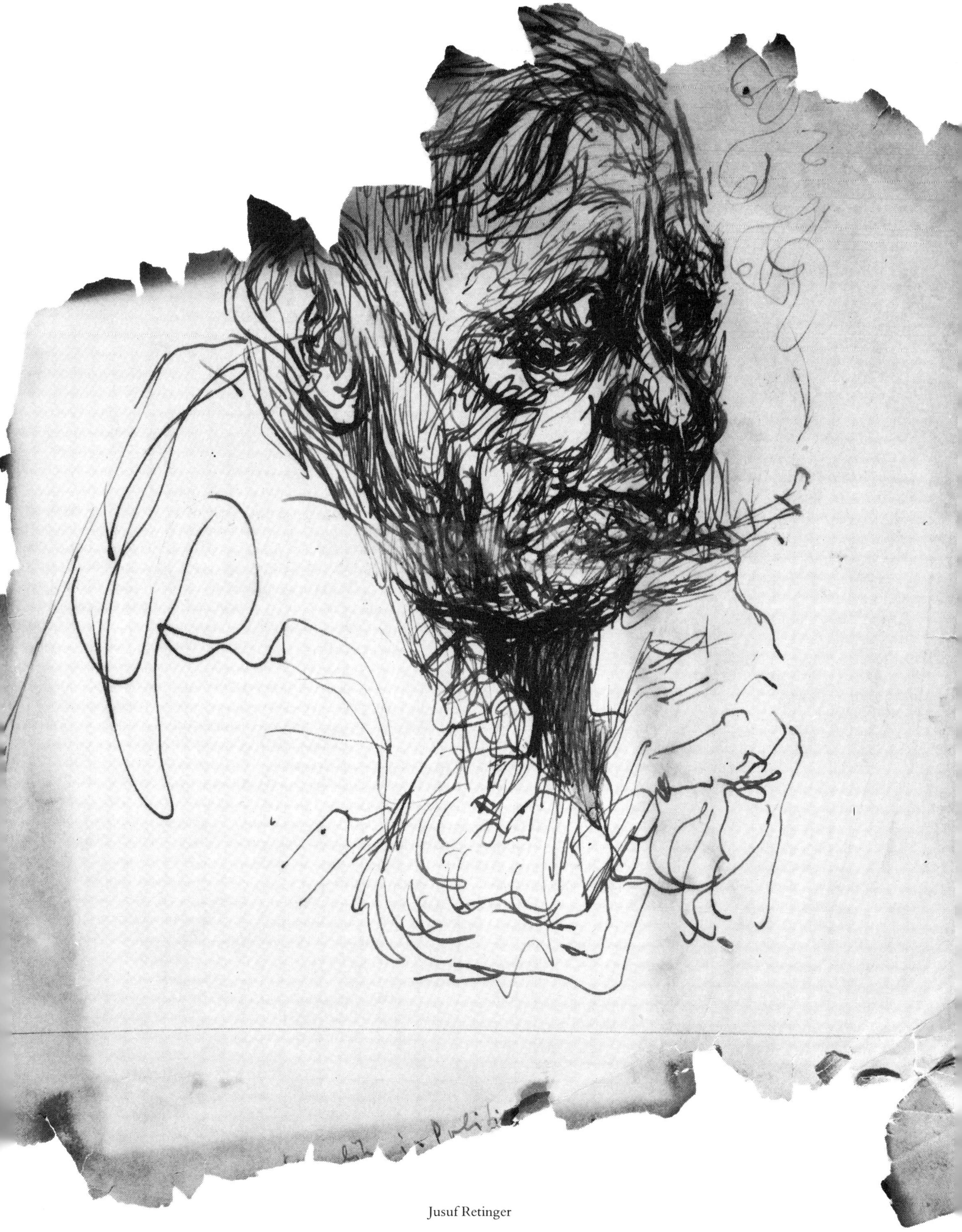

Jusuf Retinger

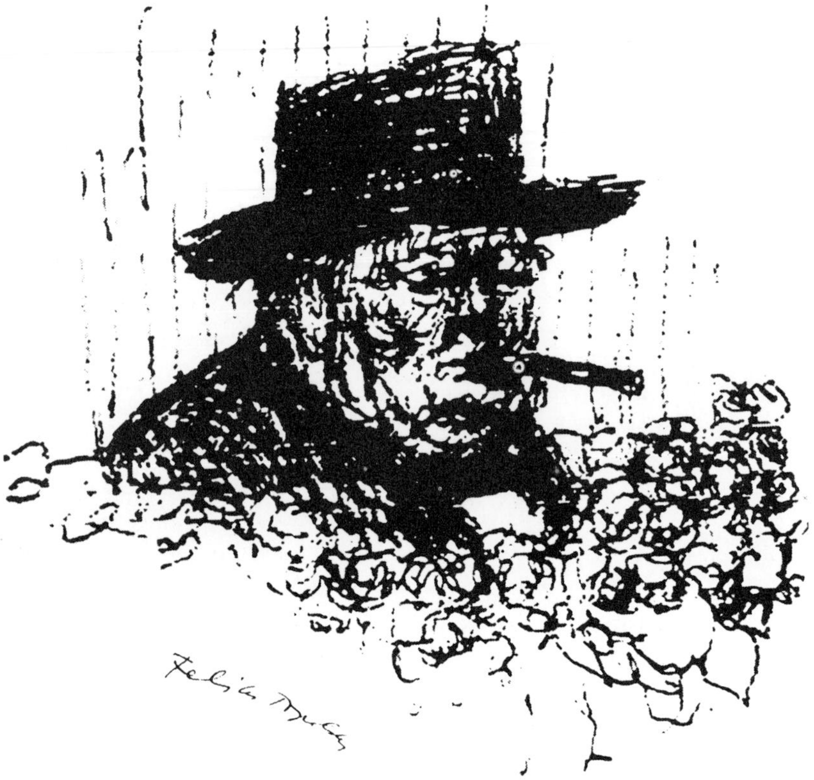

Winston Churchill (from American *Vogue* 'telexed' from the Hague)

conviction and decision – the results of single-mindedness. This is why, in the shadow of his gestures, there inevitably stands a complementary figure: the adviser weighing pros and cons with no subjectivity (thus powerless), sorting out the complicated material of motives and prognostications to be simplified for the leader.

Recio was an adviser by vocation, by inspiration, organically; the rarest and most precious because totally without personal *arrière-pensées*. Thus unavoidably all his vertiginous careers were to end catastrophically because he would never secure for himself official and pensionable appointments.

I think that in his last period he took to self-praise and to status-seeking, but only a little, and how clumsily. During the post-war years, when he put together Churchill's European Movement, or the Dutch Prince Bernhard's Euro-American Bilderberg Group deliberations, weighed down by politics and crowded by statesmen, he began to give in and to serve concepts rather than friendships. He was changing into a professional, into an 'animator' as he started to call himself.

Éminence grise? An astrologer refashioned into 'expert'? Ancient Jungian sage? Or perhaps all of these combined? One of the imperishable protagonists in humanity's spectacle, a character uncatalogueable but of astonishing presence, even in this epoque of the supposedly hermetic barriers of bureaucracy/democracy/totalitarianism.

But such a personage, conjured up with the help of clichés, seems inflated but hollow – he is not Retinger. Recio, shuffling from one hemisphere to the other, selflessly intertwined in the history of the twentieth century, was almost unnoticeable, yet indispensable . . .

The Congress of Europe at the Hague, 1948: Marginal comicalities: the poses of the American Voguess, fashion-swishing in the grandest hotel's grandest suite – her descent on the Congress solely to assist me (also gilt-chaired/bedded in that suite, but separately) and to put in motion the wirelessing of my drawings to New York (beautifully jerky they appeared on *Vogue*'s pages); but in the meantime making a social furore and impressing no end the veritably proverbial Englishman Auberon Herbert introduced by me (also only a hanger-on there) who, in the nature of things, impressed her too.

But the catalyst of this fussiness was my idea, set off perhaps by Retinger's readiness to ease me into the Congressional agendas – since this crowded gathering (momentous it seemed) containing all the great figures of the West – **headed by Churchill** – had as its conceiver/animator this very Retinger, edge-perched at a little table (a stick, a whisky and a phial of Benzodrine) in some lobby or other, by the bottom step of a towering staircase for the grandest delegates to ascend/descend.

There he would carry on his whispered parleys – with Ramadier, Daladier, Reynaud, ex-premiers of France; Van Zeeland, ex-premier, and Spaak, the premier, of Belgium; Count Coudenhove-Kalergi, de Madariaga and Bertrand Russell – prefacing the Congress Plenum for which Churchill rolled in. (I stood cheekily in mid-aisle, drawing while he orated – this was the nearest I have ever been to him.)

Finally came the open-air public apotheosis – again personified in Churchill: the monstrous rounded Holiness, the embodiment of imperishable faith in might upheld in well-ordered masterhood by the West.

I painted a largish picture with this Buddha-creature at the centre of symbols/banners/crowds/slogans, amongst the heads of his pantheon. If I remember, it was bought by a professional bodyguard-for-hire.

Confessions of a Congress Delegate.*

An account of the adventures of an artist-delegate to the International Congress of Intellectuals for Peace, held in Wrocław, Poland, in August 1948.

[This piece, written in 1948, is given unaltered. But unavoidably (and unpredictably!) thirty-some years have dismantled most of its assumptions. The division into two bellicose camps (East and West) is sustained now by power systems rather than by ideologies: the latter loosing/splitting their dogmatic force – the East permeated with the Western greeds, the West responding to the echoes of old Lenin – Trotsky slogans.

Again, time has altered this view, which might have held up in tight isolation. But the force of the other, the 'modern' culture's appeal, penetrated and created imitative (thus parochial) forms joining the end of the queue, confusing – rendering impossible – the 'ordained' progress. And to add to confusion: the early years of the Russian Revolution gave leading figures to all European arts.

Later doubts: the old guard – decimated, or cowed and turned into *aparatchiki* of the power system; while some younger Russians grew into sophisticated self-questioning.]

The reasons I had for accepting the invitation to go as a delegate to the Wrocław Congress were far from honest.

My political affinities are nil. I still claim, though with lessening assurance, that I am not of those who make, but of those who record history. The implications of that suspended-in-the-air standpoint, both pleasant and unpleasant, are well known to me. To be impartial does not free one from taking a decision, but prevents one from it; the lack of urge and conviction condemns one to a luke-warm life – the mental high-gymnastics of hatred and love are above one's prowess. And for the gift of objectivity one has to suffer sooner or later, when caught in no-man's-land between two lines of fire: the most pathetic martyrdom. But the expectation of it provides this clownish 'cause' with a smug halo.

However, it was to be a congress not of politicians, but presumably of men such as I. But I could find no justification for my presence even in such company. I do not believe in elation through unity of intellectuals and I rather expected this occasion to be a showdown of these supposed Magi of esoteric wisdom and moral integrity; their creative talents are mostly those of craftsmen, even when the craft is thought and word, and their present boosted prestige is often authorities-engineered for the idolatry of a public, turning away from religion, but in need of new gods. Only a few amongst them ever have the makings of a prophet or a leader – in a body they are sure to add up their weaknesses rather than their strengths and be swayed mob-like as any other human gathering.

With the political palisades drawn crudely athwart the world-encircling cleavage of ideas, their position is weakened further. The intellectual of the West (more strategically than geographically) still holds to the humanist ideas of the various liberties of man, still by inertia repeating, in the midst of the break-up of civilization, the weary platitudes on European values; the intellectual of the Eastern denomination has subscribed to his militant faith, but, born and bred in the nineteenth-century tradition, has not yet emerged from the embarrassing stage of transition.

And the peace. A few months ago I witnessed a Western European Congress, where, in search of flaming words, the speakers kept crying out: 'Security! Old women and children! Our homes! Tradition! Eternal values!' The deadening air of senility made one feel bellicose. Certainly, the self-assertion of young virility was not there. And, whenever it appears, it will not mean peacefulness. Perhaps, then, it is bloodshed this Wrocław Congress will try to avert and will propose not a fight, but a sporting match of ideas.

To tell the truth at last: with the growing pressure of political religiosity, I had lately become restless, and ready to take a stroll, maidenlike, along the Lovers' Lane of beliefs, and to expose myself to the dangers of seduction.

I wanted to visit my Old Country, Poland, which I had left thirteen years ago, to sound its 'new reality' – and, by the by, as most often with me, to watch, but not participate in, the laboratory experiment of the Congress.

I imagined that, merged in the crowd, I should be freer, not realizing in my naivety that the role of a delegate, and a British one in Poland at that, must bring me unavoidably to the point of commitment; even, if hiding at the crucial moment, to commitment of cowardice.

Or, worse still, that the edge of division might fall upon my unarmed self; that this operation would be painful or even mortal; that it might bare the bones of the matter and show that outsiderism means perhaps adolescence and dodging may be felony.

The massacred town of Wrocław, populated by toughened explorers, who dared or had no other choice but to wander West. The war still hangs over life here like a cloud of bomb-dust.

And then, against that alien-to-me background, the descending swarms of old friends. Their tender antics will not leave me for a moment. I am moved and bewildered. They hide and confuse the perspective of happenings; their vast numbers reproach me for the gluttony of my life, mixing my memories and feelings, bringing forth all at once my whole Polish past – childhood, school, the army, adult life all askew and incoherently shuffled in the wrong order. They all exhibit features of my past, but seen in the distorting glass of fifteen or twenty years. There is a melancholy air in the whole *contredanse* of recognitions and reunions, accentuated by a strangely cut-out quality of the circumstances of our meetings: greyed figures pirouette in a vacuum – the stage of Wrocław is false.

*London Gallery Editions, 1949.

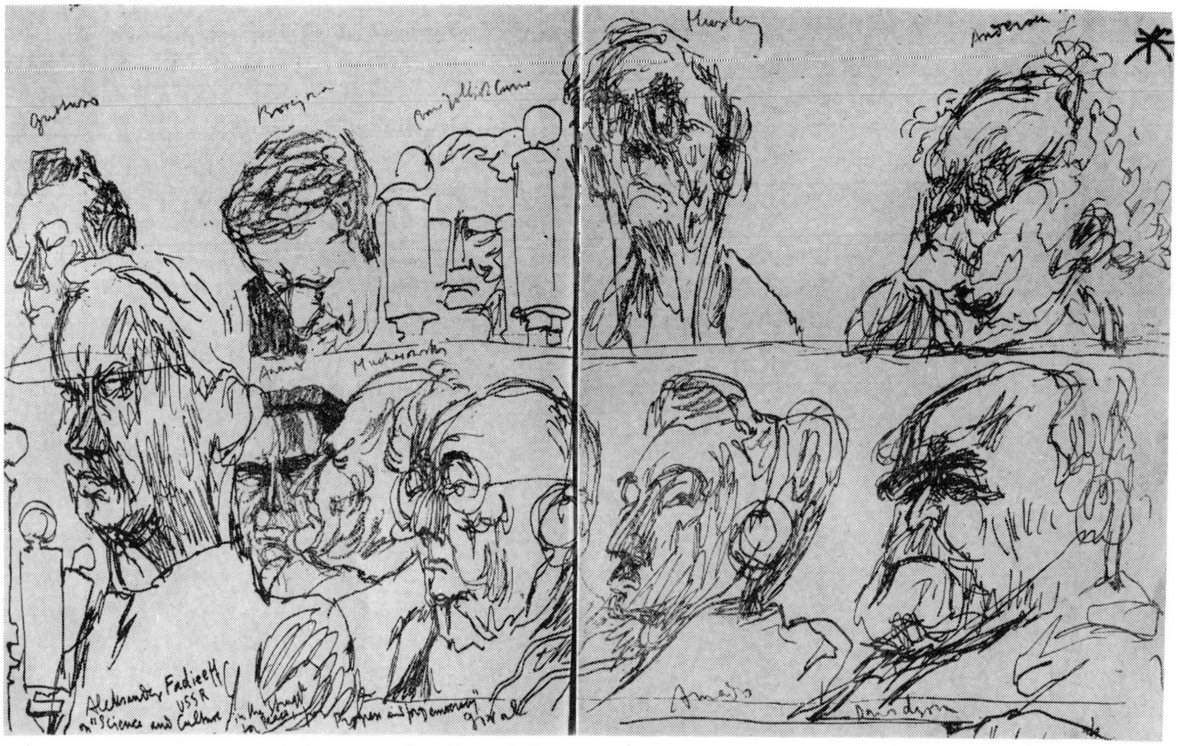

Presidium at the International Congress of Intellectuals for Peace in Wrocław, Poland (from *Confessions of a Congress delegate*)

But the producer of this spectacle throws in still another dissonance: the incongruous mob of foreigners (of which I am one) keeps loading and unloading in and out of the coaches, hotels and congress buildings, watched by the awed inhabitants, as if it were composed of superbeings.

Inside the congress hall they fit better. When, having been conducted, like made-up film extras, through the outside reality, they enter the camera-clustered interior, they come to life.

But, for me, the whole occasion will remain throughout an interplay of harassing clashes; an anguished and futile mental chase.

My old friends are here in a body, circle round my British table, whisper their discordant and divided views – weigh their bared lives against the hocus-pocus of the foreign delegate's mind.

And beyond the windows, behind the flapping kaleidoscope of flags, stares the battered face of late Germany – which was Poland 600 years ago.

While the churches become empty, the modern man builds gigantic civic structures and fills them with a multitude of 'delegates', subjected to a ceremonial hammered out in the forge of rational democracy.

There is a strange, concerted acceptance of the pious 'service' of congresses. The etiquette of oratory, the inevitable running out of time – each speaker set statue-like on a pedestal to assert his eloquence against the anxiety of the chairman. The mass of mute congressmen needed as numbers, who pass the wordy resolutions by voting almost unanimously, while their composition is entirely haphazard – the handsome wives and secretaries also recording their views in the excitement of the moment. The chairman, the presidents, below, the vice-presidents, the applause and the disapproval, the attendants' charms and the translators' mistakes, the boredom and the visual pomposity of 'the display' of emblems, the meal tickets, the showers of bulletins and the invitations to the functions, the journalists and photographers with their eye for the picturesque and the obvious; and above all, the organizers.

The Secretary-General of this Congress, Jerzy Borejsza, is said to be one of the mightiest men in Poland. There is a legend growing up round his political powers and his position as the boss of the newspaper and publishing world. The story goes that he sits at his desk twenty-two hours a day, driving on the most amazing venture of creating and supplying new readers by the million. Huge, heavy, but lightningly alert and supple-brained – an impressive figure of strength and ferocity lurking behind a seductive charm, which paws at you unconcernedly. Knotted hair and eyebrows, glasses, a circular nicotine stain round his mouth – a man possessed, but 'sane'. Some say that he behaves as the private proprietor of Poland; or that, if he worked less, more of his brilliant ideas would be realized. But even adversaries of the regime have been heard to say that he is one of a brilliant team which governs Poland.

The Secretary-General pads round the Congress room, here puts on his charm, there explodes; corrects, accelerates – navigates the proceedings in several languages. Agile, but mighty (jacket off and huge haunches) – the perfect 'man of action'.

I will pass by the early proceedings of the Congress – the expected prominence of showmanship over intellect, until the speech of a Russian Popular Writer, Alexander Fadieeff, banged the fist of Soviet self-righteousness and upset the precarious Polish-made structure of a fair exchange of views.

Although my attention is centred on the faces and gestures, the divergencies and comicalities of the gathering, the mood of the speeches penetrates and worries. Against the Russian fist-work a perky English Don, A. J. P. Taylor, thrusts with a liberal rapier in the hand of a corporal of the old guard; after him another Russian with a Parisian past, Ilya Ehrenburg, whose Montparnassian airs give a lie to his dogmatic conclusions; superficially the able speech of a learned man in the Western manner, but the core of it is of a different world. [. . .]

The Russians: their unexpected aura of venerableness jerks one to the realization that they are in the middle age of their fortunes, that they, in fact, have already settled down to decorum and stiffened hierarchy. With their senatorial airs, they are solid, faithful emissaries of their cause; there is about them a unity and readiness to repel any plea for compromise – they will accept only vassals of their idea. Yes, this aged but fiery political journalist Zaslavski is an old warrior of polemics – more of an expert than a fanatic; this sleepy chronicler of Talleyrand's doings mumbles his thoughts absent-mindedly; the writer with the Parisian past poses aloofly; a member of the Ukrainian Academy of Science, shaped into the Chekhovian convention of a provincial professor, seems to have a precise intelligence; that young writer has stubbornness; the author of the Don Epic, Sholohov, keeps disappearing – perhaps unedified; the creator of early film masterpieces, Pudovkin, looks back to the *Sturm-und-Drang Periode* of the Revolution. There they are – the Russians: varied but faithful.

It is not so with other delegations. The French appear uncoordinated, although the elegant Poet-Master of the Order (Eluard) officiates impressively among the brethren and sisters in Communism. *Soignée* women (Mesdames Recamiers in the making) play an important part in this group – their function may be that of herding together with emotional barking the professed individualists who tend to stray; a Famous Painter (Picasso) takes off his shirt at a banqueting table and thus cools off his volcanic Ego without straining the party line.* The Poles are more truly a gathering of intellectuals than of a united purpose and not all of them will be present at the final voting.† There are groups with picturesque value only, but also others which have shown a singular audacity in joining the Congress.

The English Chairman, Julian Huxley, declares the biological law of compromise. The Oxford Liberal (Taylor) demands love and states his readiness to hate. The American lawyer serves out psychoanalysis. But the majority 'see the light'. And, though the vocabulary in use is, by habit or hypocrisy, that of tolerance and justice, there is no chance for polite exchanges here. PROGRESS is a word which embraces a great many concepts, and, in their interpretation, in its way are the evil forces. The peace they claim to want is to be against these evil forces.

The strength of conviction, the readiness for crusading, the expectancy of an unavoidable and early triumph flood the hall again and again. It all tempts one, but, at the same time (seen too closely the crudeness of the stitching is accentuated), brings forth one's urge to march out of step.

To be clear about it: this avalanche of an idea, suspended as yet, but ready to descend on the globe, seems capable of sweeping together on its way all the subcurrents, rocks and vegetation of kindred beliefs and rolling them into its own power. Seen from this gathering, it forces itself on one as the direction of the century, with its opponents inevitably put on the defensive – their strength built on obstacles, traps of negation, trenches of *status quo*. Or does it only seem so, because at the Congress even the opposition is non-political or of the Left? It needs an effort to remember here that to the West, beyond Europe, stands not simply a Clique of Fascist Warmongers, but another force. And still more effort to think of a stubbornly empirical Labour socialism doing its 'job of work' in the British Isles.

The resolution is being drawn up and alarmist stories penetrate into the plenum. Some of the British may consider walking out. A separate resolution might be put forward in view of the projected voting by acclamation. The Secretary-General announces *ex praesidio* that the voting will be individual and tempers are calmed for a time.

The next wave of anxiety rises high above the paddling voices of speakers and interpreters, when the rough text of the resolution is brought in. There is a battle going on within the committee over the alterations, interpolations and style. The Unesco President is leaving the Congress. The Russians accept only so much and no more.

> We, men of culture, of science and art from forty-five different countries, gathered in the Polish city of Wrocław, address ourselves to the intellectuals of the world.
>
> We remind you of the deadly danger that only recently threatened the culture of mankind. We witnessed fascist barbarity, the destruction of historical and cultural monuments, the persecution and murder of intellectuals, the total suppression of all spiritual values, which constituted a threat to the very idea of conscience, reason and progress.
>
> The culture of mankind was saved at the price of unheard-of sacrifices and privations by the rallying to the full of all democratic forces – of the Soviet Union, of the peoples of Great Britain and of the United States, and of the heroic popular Resistance movements in countries invaded by fascism.
>
> And now, against the will and desires of the people of all countries, a handful of self-interested men in America and Europe who have inherited fascist ideas of racial superiority and the denial of progress, who have adopted fascist methods of solving all problems by force of arms, are once again making an attempt against the spiritual treasures of the peoples of the world.
>
> The culture of the countries of Europe, which contributed greatly to the total of human achievements, is being threatened with the loss of national individuality.
>
> In a number of countries – in Greece, Spain, Latin America – forces hostile to progress are not only safeguarding but are planting once again the seeds of fascism.
>
> Contrary to reason and conscience, the oppression of human

*In the lobby of Warsaw's Hotel Brystol, the Wrocław Congress having ended, I hold, just given to me, an advance copy of a Polish literary weekly, large-newspaper-shaped and multi-paged, its more than half-front page imposingly filled up with my vast and crowded painting *The East*.

Picasso, ringed by his followers, descends the staircase, and an impulse – conglomerate of homage to his greatness and pride in my most achieved painting – makes me spread it before him, stating that this is my most recent work. He, without a second's look at it, takes the paper out of my hands, flips rapidly through its pages, and, predictably, since all the papers are full of him – the star, opens it at a reproduction of one of his: 'Et ça, c'est la mienne.'

† Indeed, the Poles, the most insubordinate breed, brought up on *Liberum Veto*, will thrive on negation and Western temptations.

beings and of whole nations which are called coloured by the oppressors, is not only continuing but is actually being intensified.

Within their countries men who have adopted fascist methods are practising racial discrimination and persecuting progressive scientists and artists.

Scientific discoveries, which might be a blessing to mankind, are being used for the secret production of instruments of destruction, a fact which discredits and perverts the sublime mission of science.

In the hands of these men human expression and art are being used not to enlighten people and bring them closer together but to excite base passions, to preach hatred for men and to prepare for war.

Firmly believing in the necessity of the free development and diffusion of the achievements of progressive culture throughout the world, for peace, for progress and the future of humanity, we protest against all interference with that freedom and stress the need in the interest of world civilization for mutual comprehension between cultures and peoples.

Realizing that modern science has released great new powers which will inevitably be used by mankind, either for good or for ill, the Congress protests against the use of science for destruction, and calls upon you to do your utmost to spread knowledge throughout the world and to apply science to the rapid reduction of the poverty, ignorance, ill-health and misery which afflict the majority of mankind, and to collaborate in reducing restrictions on the free circulation of persons who serve the cause of peace and progress, and on the free publication and circulation of books, results of research and all scientific and cultural achievement which serve the same ends.

The peoples of the world do not want war, and they possess sufficient strength to defend peace and culture from a new fascism.

Intellectuals of the world!

We bear a high responsibility to our peoples, to mankind, and to history.

We raise our voices in defence of peace, and for the free cultural development of nations, for their national independence and close friendship.

We call upon all intellectuals in every country to discuss our proposals.

We propose that national cultural congresses for peace be convened in all countries, that national committees for peace be formed everywhere, that international ties between men of culture of all countries be strengthened in the interest of peace.

An innocent conversation takes place at lunchtime. We read the draft of the proposed resolution and, all other factors apart, the intellectual muddle of it is pointed out: it looks for the guilty, while the sober fact is that two coexisting and contradictory concepts of living are at grips. The job of the intellectual, if anxious for peace, should be to probe for a means of solving the conflict without war. This is apparently what everybody at our table feels. We disperse – I entirely ready to avoid the final session.

But first comes a public meeting in an immense hall in the centre of an imposing exhibition of the 'Recovered Territories'. On to the platform in the steel-bound interior the Congress delegates climb in a string. I sit below and watch with the eyes of the crowd the sudden growth of my colleagues: as soon as they step into the arclight and the concentrated attention of 15,000 people, they become the high priests of this secular service for peace – the hieratic English Dean (of Canterbury) blends the Church with the materialist worship in a masterful act.

The sincere prayers of the populace, intoned by the stentorian slogan-criers, beg for peace – the delegates on the platform are likely to be as unreliable as intermediaries to Fate as the ministers or religions are to the gods.

It is announced that the Congressmen will leave now to continue their good work – the hopeful crowd applauds them as they file out, while I still wrestle within myself: to follow them, or to stay on here and miss the resolution? The temptation to dodge the issue, against not so much a brave preparedness for it, as perhaps (prodded by my ever-present curiosity) the pull of the predetermined – and of my flock, the tail of which is just departing.

I follow.

And in the anteroom an agitated British group bars my way. They are collecting signatures for a provisional declaration, developed on the lunchtime idea. It is shown to a Prominent British Communist, the Hon. Ivor Montague, and, with his compliance, its uses are to be decided on at the coming pre-resolution meeting of the British delegation, preferably as an additional statement. It expounds my point of view; it does not separate itself from the peace-call of the Congress, but, as it were, corrects its simplifications; it seems to need some re-editing, but in principle . . .

I sign it with many others.

We, the undersigned members of the British group, state with regret that we are not able to accept the resolution as the whole truth. We deplore its oversimplification. The first duty of intellectuals is to be intelligent and the duty of this Congress should have been to examine impartially the germs of a future war rather than to recapitulate the causes of the war which is finished. Two ways of life and of thought are in conflict throughout the world and it should be the task of intellectuals to resolve that conflict by peaceful means. We feel the implication of this resolution that one side alone is to blame to be a waste of a great opportunity. We believe that though we are in a minority at this conference, we represent the majority of men and women throughout the world.

Some of the undersigned have also signed the resolution, some have not.

The paper circulates openly among our delegates. There are already some fifteen signatures on it, when we are called for the meeting.

The matter is broached, but the document is missing together with one of the delegates.

Somebody (is it the lady secretary of the organizer of the British delegation?) rises and gives an intelligence that it is almost certain that the missing gentleman is passing it for publication to the American press.

And pandemonium starts. A sense of utter disaster paralyses me. The brave attempts of some of us to justify a completely legitimate statement of opinion are smashed by the obviousness of the malevolent ending. The accusations of secrecy and trickery are flung freely by the above lady and a ready chorus. There takes place a general flight from the declaration under the concentrated fire of 'shame, shame' by the Communists. They form instantly a magnificently co-ordinated phalanx and attack from the four corners of the room – the Red Dean in the Last Judgement gesture in the centre. Those who dared to differ on certain points of the resolution are now cowed and branded as traitors. One after another, clumsily, the signatories rebuke their missing colleague's action. In a moment it will be my turn . . .

The Missing Delegate appears, confesses his crime and, pale and guilty-looking, is chased out by the big voice of the whole meeting, ordering him to recall the document.

A very uneasy pause indeed.

And time to meditate – how, against the singleness of purpose of the Communists, any divergency will appear as treason (most of the signatories are near fellow-travellers); their faith demands, like Catholicism, a complete surrender, without argument, by the act of grace;

–and what motivated the culprit's deed, which destroyed a serious and effective gesture, giving in return nothing but a sense of foul play.

Defeated, he returns – the document went to the press and cannot be recovered. The meeting breaks up.

Shame. Indeed, the feeling of shame overcomes me. This is the gravest catastrophe, which, through no fault of mine, involves me in a bare half-hour in a very definite move, terribly far from my professed detachment.

Action, even involuntary, breeds action. I am surprised at the swiftness with which I lead an agitated detachment to the General-Secretary's room. More surprised still at finding there ahead of us the Editor of a London political weekly (Kingsley Martin).

The Secretary-General singles me out for the charge and proceeds, in the silent ring of Englishmen, to abuse me in Polish. But time is pressing. We want his help in recovering the document. He sees our distress, categorically states that it is too late and leaves to open the final session.

Only one road is left. The Editor of the weekly escapes, but a less nimble Novelist (Richard Hughes) consents to deliver a public recantation. Now completely given to action, I dash to the platform and pass our decision to the Secretary-General. The Novelist is announced, while I, exposed to the full assembly, involve myself moth-like in the cables and lights of the cameramen preparing to record the triumphant end of the Congress. I collapse on the nearest empty chair within the Indian and Ceylon delegation, listen through the statement that a document has been passed to press by mistake, though the essence of its meaning is correct, and get up to return, dutifully, to my British seat.

The Secretary-General begins his final oration. My chair is taken by a Polish cartoonist (Jerzy Zaruba) and I must settle to decide on the supreme matter: with the possible amendment turned into a gift for the Red-baiters in America, should I, or should I not, sign the resolution?

The lines of tables, crowded with the busts of the delegates, roll in restless perspectives. I struggle along the British delegation from the Dean depthwards in a maze of centrifugal-like motion: rejected, rejected, rejected. The dull machinery of the proceedings revolves – the faces, hypnotized and united, are passing me, the outsider, as on a roundabout; but it is I who push along the static rows in a symbolic search for an inviting chair, a copy of the resolution in hand, desperately alone, unable to find comfort in decision. This is Purgatory. This punishment. This demand. The despair of the lost black sheep. The guilt. The human pitilessness round me – the only moving figure in this vastness under the General-Secretary's resounding, potent, inviting, threatening voice: 'We men of culture . . .' A desperate dash across the room. A chair. I slide into it awkwardly, head bent over the document – seeing sentences, but not taking them in any more.

Voices around startle me, I look up – I am sitting amongst the Russian delegation.

So sheltered, I consider chaotically, across the booming words from the rostrum: indeed, the resolution is given to possibly tendentious simplifications; but, if anything, I am more in support of the idea of this Congress than against it. That statement-become-letter, which will most certainly be used to destroy the prestige of this demonstration, can only be contradicted by signing the resolution as well. In fact, the resolution can be signed with the statement serving as a corrective. And again, surely, my only true stand would have been to abstain all along – but this I have refuted already.

Voting! Back, back. I cannot go on hiding with the Russians – my cross must be borne to the end. I find that the majority of the signatories of the 'document' are now signing the resolution – prompted by the same argument as mine – or, perhaps, by mass psychosis. I sign.

There follows a scene of enthusiasm, unity, emotions of the highest uplift, I am sure – but for me this is deflation.

And it can be still worse.

On leaving the session we learn with a gasp that 'the letter' was stopped after all. The whole torture starts anew: now there remains only the fact of having signed the resolution, which by itself is unacceptable.

The Oxford Liberal and the Mishap Colleague step forward. Heated and determined, like two Homeric fighters, they push grimly through the resolution-enraptured crowd – copies of the declaration their shields, fountain-pens their spears. They urge their earlier allies to send 'the letter' now – their arguments are indeed aggressive – I demand time to collect my thoughts and allow myself to be carried off by ever-ready old friends.

This is great theatre, but, alas, I am an untrained actor in a leading part: the celebrating crowd of delegates; two oppositionists in pursuit of the dwindling waverers and my multi-faced personal drama of lost detachment, wrong commitments, divided loyalties; and now this scene – the display of friendly trivialities, while watching the ominous approach of the General-Secretary.

He is most violent. He knew all the time, well provided with information as he is, that I, mainly I, have been secretly intriguing for the sabotage of the Congress. What vileness on my part.

The force of his attack covers the feebleness of his argument. I am amazed and, in my affronted innocence, raised to fury. I shout down a Polish literary friend, Antoni Słonimski, who leaps to my defence, and loudly demand the Secretary-General's attention for my statement of facts.

But he turns about and disappears darkly into the jubilant crowd.

And without respite, I find myself once more surrounded by the letter-writers. The Oxonian is, by now, like a little fast-firing tank: 'Even if alone, I shall send this to the American Press!'

The whole business grows out of hand. I pull myself together and, with some authority, say that what they propose is sabotaging the Congress (happily remembered phrase), that I am in principle in sympathy with its aims and that now, after the resolution, when the opportunity to read out the statement to the assembly has been lost, there is no hurry in choosing the appropriate action – but that I stand for dignity and not for scandal-mongering. A little shapely speech like this gives pleasure in the thick of adversities. It impresses a few others and only three are left at it.

The melodrama goes on, however.

'The letter' is again and again proposed and, at the end, I find myself in the emptying *couloirs* writing a copy of its text, at the dictation of the pretty American lady journalist (perhaps the villain of the piece), who holds the only draft, under the probing spectacles of the Secretary-General's henchmen. I am copying it, because I and some others will pass it for publication in the London political weekly (its Editor has already left, presumably for Warsaw). I clearly tell the American lady (who appears to act now as a secretary to the absent chief letter-writers) that I refuse to have my name in any other paper. It is proposed to re-examine the text in the peace of Warsaw and to rally its supporters there with less agitation.

I discover also that the last line of the original draft is missing from the present text and the Novelist, who actually composed that line, dictates it to me and to the Lady who inserts it faithfully: 'Some of the undersigned have also signed the resolution, some have not.'*

It grows dark and the place is almost empty. I have the acute feeling of an onlooker brushed aside by a vast army marching with the clangour of machines, shouts of command, with men's heavy gaiety and angry impatience. The column has passed and the onlooker feels alone and regrets momentarily that he is not a soldier.

What is the force which urges me to go on blatantly? It is perhaps the exultancy of the battle, when coming up against a truly conflicting adversary: the meek versus the mighty.

Fatalistically I enter the Secretary-General's office.

It would be untrue to say that the welcome is cooler than during my former visits. No. But it may be recorded that an unknown receptionist faces me and I have slight difficulties in sending in a note: 'I consider it essential to iron out your misconceptions – preferably now – or please suggest appointment in Warsaw.'

I am let in, as usual with him, into the bedlam of other matters.

Triumphant, his torso towering above the desk, he receives benevolently, surrounded by spectacled courtiers.

A rare gesture – he dismisses everybody, but, disappointingly, restarts his attack on my supposed misconduct. I demand a hearing and, after an introductory statement on the authentic goodwill of the whole of the British delegation and on our readiness to defy the unpopularity of this excursion and to go a long way towards the aims of the Congress, I narrate most faithfully the tale of dissension, concluding with an obvious, but clearly needed moral on the usefulness of variations of views in an individualist gathering.

He has listened silently throughout, but, when I expect understanding, he states briefly, almost mechanically, unaffected by my tale, the same story of my secret plot – perhaps his dogma requires the presence of evil. And then, at length, he returns to accusations strangely personal, concerned with his own disappointment in me, which, oddly (perhaps, because of the illogical, childlike sense of injury emerging from this massive man), contain a more dangerous threat than if one could grasp his solemn motive.

In front of this display of unreason, I puzzle whether I am facing fanaticism, or an inner anxiety which deviates into a paroxysm of anger against the handy objective.

I thank him for sparing his time, regret that we do not understand each other and depart.

The courtiers, spread over sofas in the outer room, put on their glasses.

I emerge into the night curious, confused and emptied. I give up the idea of a leisurely car-trip (advised against as unsafe), pack in no time and join the Congress-sleeper to Warsaw.

The puffed-up, asleep face of the Editor of a bi-monthly (Weidenfeld) on the opposite bunk becomes the Secretary-General's.

There follow weeks of high-pitched experience. My old country opens up to me with its ruins and graves; of its smashed past remain only some aged faces – the cut-short world of my generation.

On the first day in Warsaw I make a sombre pilgrimage, faithfully retracing my steps – guessing my familiar way amongst the rubble. I enter the courtyards which do not exist any more and lean against the homely doorways that have no interiors behind them.†

I give my attention to the present and the future:

In front of me the broad town-river, half-braced by broken viaducts, banked with scaffolded ruins – the pontoon-bridge throws forward the hurrying populace. I stand at its base and watch closely the throng marching at me: these are the people of Warsaw, holding secrets unknown to me of five years' terror; of utter self-sacrifice side by side with the lowest debasement; of the spasm of the armed rising and the reaction when driven out of the crashing city; of their mind now.

*The Editor of the weekly never came to Warsaw. A new draft was composed there and several names collected at leisure, but, when the text arrived in London, the original letter had already appeared in the leading provincial daily and in the aforesaid weekly, with the last phrase omitted. Hence the further letter to counteract the inaccuracies of proceedings and of text.

However pleasant it was to find my signature under it, this final letter was entirely different from our Warsaw draft.

I was still in Poland when the copies of the British papers containing this chain-correspondence arrived, one by one, creating quite a stir.

†Private diversions:

Among the mountainous rubble, pigeon-dotted, Próźna 12, my schoolchild/boy to departure habitation, stood – a propped-up rotting cadaver, seemingly in its wholeness. But inside its bruised/filthy courtyard, eyes up to my expected sixth floor found nothing: it was sliced off, at the top of the fifth, out of existence.

Leszno 75 (or was it 71?), where I was born on the fourth floor, was marked solely by its turn-of-the-century fancy-topped gate and bits of scorched ground-level brickery with: 'Lila Silly' and 'Midwife' chalked on. Yes, the overhead wires dangled randomly and tall lamp-posts tottered in perspective; a rucksacked schoolboy passed by, two girl guides at a run improvised hoops and two dogs circled at a loss.

The soldiers, workers, marketeers, officials, schoolboys, priests, devouts – they return after the day's deeds amid the ruins. From a distance they look as they did long ago, when servants of the old system.

But this march, their stamping feet, the hardness which has entered their faces, more of one kind now that the Jews are weeded out. How has it come about that they build and live a different life, learn a different content, defend a different law?

Cross the bridge. The bitterness of the rubble stretching down to the flattened Ghetto throws into sharp relief the fierce activity of this people in the act of resurrection.

The present makes ready for the future. And, as to the future, it is uncertain. The rapid change and the intense urgency; the wit and the rivers of talk; the breach and readjustment; the shadows of anxieties and lights of optimism at the slightest excuse, like the ups and downs of neurasthenia – the deep and fast flow of life keyed up as in a war.

I am immersed in it. My personal encounter at the Congress and hence my precarious position, imagined or real, precipitates me into the mood of this land. Yet, confused and lost in a world populated by familiar shapes and voices but organized in an unknown pattern, I stray hopelessly from my quest.

Among dearest friends the pathetic, gauche gaiety copes helplessly with the nearing parting. The saddest thing of all: chained by the despotism of politics, people, who have met warmly, separate miserably to wait for what is to come.

I look back to the Congress and, now, seen from within the pulsating, living organism of Poland, it dissolves, like a makeshift troupe of performers, who have packed up their props and costumes, and, leaving behind a dead-trodden patch of grass, stroll away into the distance.

This is a bad time (in life and in congresses) for those who, surveyor-like, try to measure and map the landscape of the human ordeal. They are welcome nowhere. Not even in their own professions.

With the growing vehemence of the struggle, the brutality and lack of sentiment in life, an odd strain appears in the arts and letters: the critics become increasingly unforgiving to a writer who shows no compassion. The Voltairian ruthlessness, when operating on man, would now be called betrayal. Even a satirist must be a lover of humanity to be applauded, while the humanity he pictures does not obey the rule. What a strange discord – can it be another self-deception of the intellectual, an escape into the mild mist of generalized pity, when unable to hate or love. But he who is not good at loving and hating and less still at sentimentalizing, might, while trying to understand, take to contempt.

Autumn, 1948. Kazimierz, Poland.

The Vistula slaps against the flat bottom of the fisherman's punt. I push upstream against the current and steer it by the iron-pronged oar-pole towards the wind-blown clumps. The sky drifts high, the quarries rattle to the left – I am wet after my swim. Thus I attempt to navigate against the current of time – back 15–20 years. The obedient oar casts the boat, as it used to, on to the bank, legs splash through the water, hands pull the bow over the white sand, plait the chain in the thicket – automatically, I spread myself in the granular softness, stare at the far shore: **Kazimierz** . . . I shut my eyes (sun scorches and the sandbank blows) and let half-thoughts, shreds of associations flit about. Here I am on the pilgrimage of an egoist – back towards the beginning. A review of memories knots disjointedly. I open my eyes: A round-eyed creature sticks up before me – we stare at each other; Vistula, birds in the sky, bells from the village – thus the commonplace of unchanging vitality. I scare away the creature and float down to Kazimierz.

And already on the shore the talk of the fishing folk cuts off the past – narrations of terror, of partisans, of the Tartar-like Russian advance, of anxieties and hopes. Already on the dusty monastery-edging highway and at the bridges – unease. Then in the marketplace, grief beyond measure and impotent outrage.

The out-of-the-way village, war-invalid, wretchedly and shabbily hobbles through the afternoon. Once most beautiful, now debased, in vain it colours with the sun – it only repels. Because friends tell about wrongs and betrayals; because along with the Jews, their humble architecture was also murdered and the jagged gaps hit the eye with monstrous meaning – the altars of human sacrifice, while the goy houses that remain stand as if in pillory; because the homespun fabric of Polishness interwoven with black Jewish thread has ceased to exist. Because in the pokiness of the tiny familiarity of a village the tragedy is contained within the human compass and it smashes at the face, kicks at the crotch, wrings out the tongue, flays alive – tortures physically, while in Belsen or Warsaw the onlooker's senses could not cope.

I climb over wires on to the old synagogue half dismantled ('by the locals and only now – after the Germans', informs an old colleague); I enter the weed-choked, shit-befouled ruin – already antique; I stare at incomprehensible inscriptions, at obscure patterns, at the traces of exoticism that once existed close by my side, yet carelessly slighted, and rubbed off the surface of the earth irretrievably. How terrible to stand on the wreckage of a world that has been erased in my time and to know that there is no putting right my past indifference; to stand in face of an end more ultimate than death.

I visit the few old painter friends who held out – little canvases, easels in little shadowy rooms, but their 'truth' putrid. People and landscape of my time in ruins – bad bad. I climb the Mount of the Three Crosses; I look down at the defiled charms and at the river that has backed away and shrunk as if pained. I run an eye over the map of memories, stumbling on the rubble.

I turn away from the smashed past. Tormented, I look about for solace. The day cowers towards slumber, but still warms and with dry fragrances soothes.

The seven-year-old son of a friend, long pale locks, bare feet and bare torso, leaps, a bizarre and graceful faun, above the wide panorama, the arch of his jumps embracing yet unhealed wreckage and the romantic décor of the view – the ruins of the Castle and its Tower – the remains of a forgotten tragedy of before yesterday; and also bracketed into his jumps there fit the Three Crosses – the established memento of torture and salvation.

Postscript, 1984
The ending on a note of renewal, merely 'seasonal' – a new child following the murderous nightmare – after almost forty years seems hollow. Not because of the apocalyptic crimes, for which there is no balancing consolation to be found so conveniently, but because that particular 'seasonality' has declined. The child is no more a promise, his father is dead. The village of Kazimierz is tidied up as a tourists' item, without memories. Oscillation optimism-pessimism is inevitable.

The flight from Warsaw casts me harshly back into the English autumn. A handful of formalities and transport jerks and I am in **Kent**, back in Cliff's **the Earl of Darnley's, Cobham Hall**, our home for a year while waiting for our London house to be ready.

'Taking a walk' is a legitimate country palliative: I take a walk, further afield than usual – as it turns out, a truly cross-country walk.

At first the primeval motif: under the forest's basketwork roof, I make my lowly way through the giant ferns, soaking and rusted.

The shooting-stick – which was attempting to swagger – and my left foot hook me in the undergrowth. Thus immobilized, I send my eyes reconnoitring: the soft undulation of the ferny waste loses itself in the ring of dead-bare wintry bushes become-firewood; the trees, welded above, slide beyond the horizon; grey, soggy tranquillity – cut by squirrels. I pull myself free and walk on, seemingly the sole man – hence somewhat self-conscious, but also elated.

Suddenly mangled vegetation: human footprints. And so I yield unavoidably and with devotion to the power of the Path, let myself be led, circled round the fallen trees, until there comes the conflict of junctions, rapidly multiplying criss-crosses of trails – pointing, tempting in all directions, destroying the aloofness of the forest and my pretence at exploration.

And already the rot of human poverty and smouldering rubbish shuffle their stinks in with nature's. A few paces more and there stretch rows of long iron-black barrel-shapes – the left-over army huts; window pricked and smoke billowing out of the multitude of chimney pipes; barbed-wired cabbage patches; little rheumatic people blotting the abused landscape; a scraggy car; old gossiping women shaped in the off-the-peg shabbiness of townsfolk. The 'squatters'' camp.

'How goes it?' I ask a man with a bucket. 'Good or bad – as you make it.' The pioneer. He points a finger at his plot and then shakes it mockingly over the wilderness – he believes that he wrenches the land from nature. But, nearby, a kiosk: chocolates, lavatory paper, razor blades, tinned food and a peroxided girl behind the counter. But, just beyond, a vast highway, rumbling monster lorries, symbols of 'Nationalization' and 'Export' coastward. But a mouldy board guards this very wilderness forbidding this and that by order of the Earl of Darnley. The nomad (his tents made of corrugated iron) – The Socialist Welfare State – The feudal lord: contemporaries in today's England.

Under the arcaded gate (FINEM RESPICE over it), then, side-tracking the grand drive, I scatter the hens and creep over the 'no entry' stile into the expiring park.

The decorative urns crumble at the turnings of the lane, moss-green pavilions tinkle like pagodas with broken window-panes. Creepers, having penetrated the loosened walls of a Gothic 'folly', crawl, as if in claustrophobic panic, across the rotting floors (lifting the frightened whitened faces of their leaves) towards the narrow windows and, in a rush, fall softly into the entanglements of freedom; further down, in full attack, they strangle and overthrow the old oaks (Laocoön like, the tragic bare branches stretched high), the mighty trunks. Piously I go by these mortal but soundless struggles and – following my habit – enter the Swiss Pavilion (brought here by an earlier Darnley) in which Dickens used to write: the tiny interior takes my breath away, as always. Though the windows, open in four directions, let in the green-yellow light, the walls enclose me tightly like the skull the brain. The room for a fiction weaver. It is odd to think that the pinewood surfaces were, I am told, covered for him with mirrors; that perhaps Dickens used to make faces, perhaps to enact for himself his characters.

Now, I rustle along the leaf-strewn and shadowy avenue, while on my left (outside the railings) there spreads in full light the wide greenness belted by trees, dotted with the distant strutting and synthetically puffed up figures of golfers (the clatter of flying balls).

My avenue sinks now into the darkness of the pebble-lined fancy tunnel. Listlessly I beat with my stick the tempo of the echo and listlessly I emerge on the other side into the day (by now departing, blown away by the wind and clouds) – and into a change of scenery. The huge carpet of lawns. The massive bracket of the mansion screwed to the landscape by

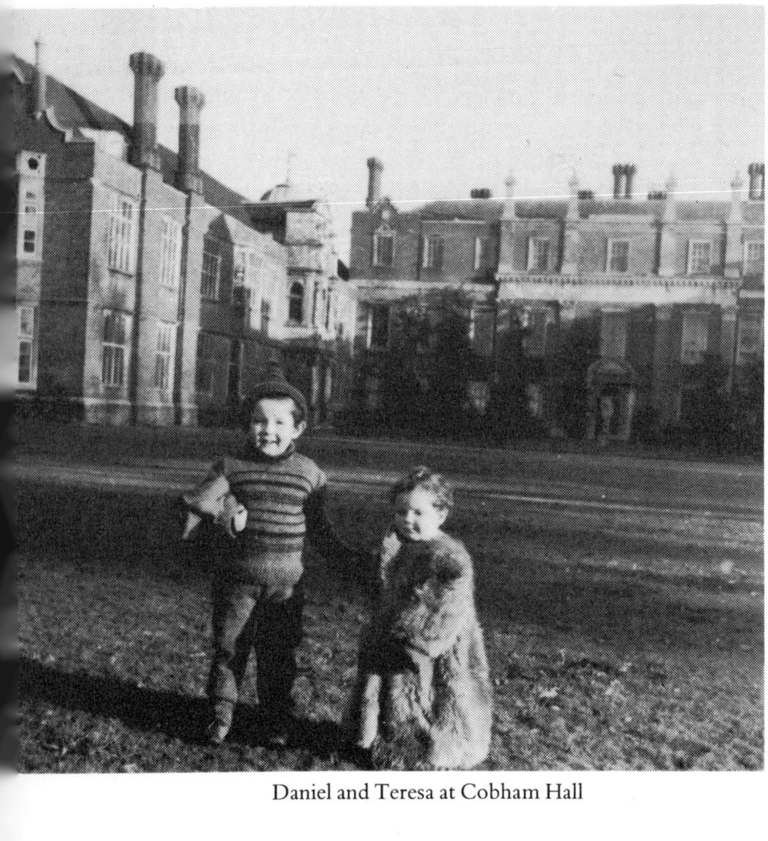

Daniel and Teresa at Cobham Hall

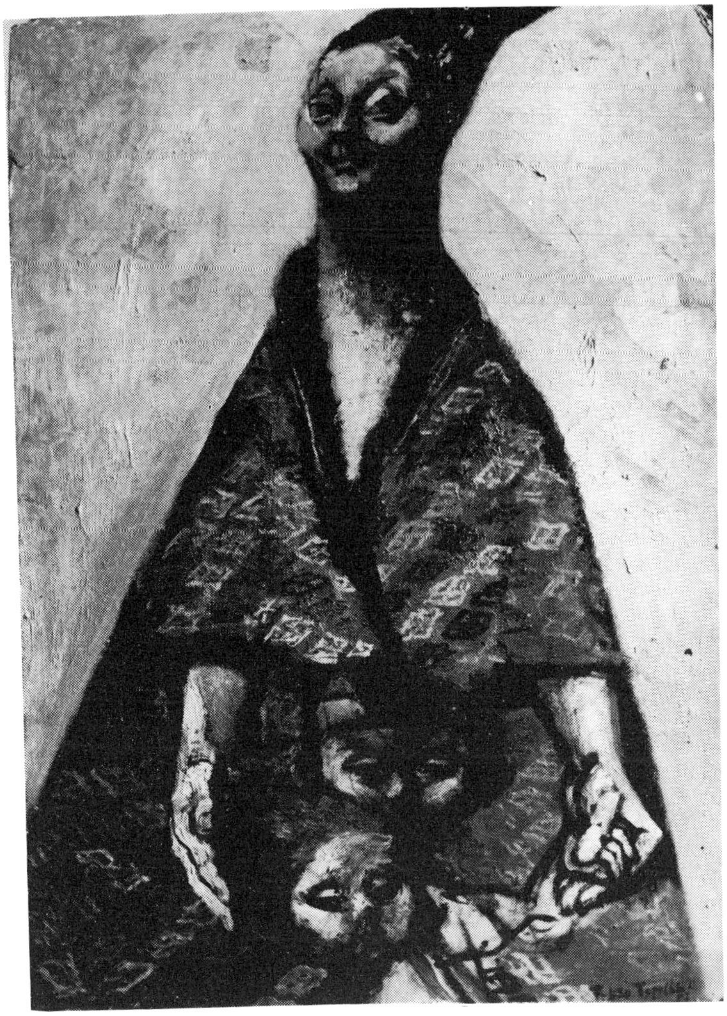

Marion with children

four slim towers. The left wing (Elizabethan mellow brick) is ringed by a slow-moving procession of cripples on their way to a miraculous cure: Mrs Gilbert, a faithhealer, revives by touch and prayers every Sunday at 3 p.m. in the portrait gallery, under the patronage of Her Ladyship.

To the right (the lovely architecture his background), with the manuscript of his yearly pacifist speech in hand, stands my choleric host: of immeasurable tallness, in dark coat and black hat (as if on the point of departure for the House of Lords), but leaning on a long shepherd's crook. He is on the look-out for me, I know, to try out his speech.

I dodge towards the centre (our family domain) – the dark-vermilion Wren façade – scurrying amongst shiny smudges of starting rain; gallop through the colonnade of the freezing hall (our dining room) and the faded, patched dignities of the library; hop up the service staircase (nowadays empty of servants) over the cat's daydreams, get involved in the double doors of the extinguished picture gallery and pop into our bedroom (hand-painted Chinese wallpaper and canopied but weary bed). I search for my family.

Until I find in the Victorian drawing room grouped round the fire: Marion with Daniel, Teresa in the arms of the Polish nanny, Lady Rosemary stylishly expectant amongst her children. I enter and settle self-consciously into this scene – calm deliberations, newspapers, dignified acceptance of children's antics.

I perform, we all perform (for a while) sedate and untroubled family life, acting characters in a 'conversation piece' picture of the nineteenth century.

A father-of-the-family, within somebody else's mansion, in the socialist era: Rosemary looks after her children, Marion feeds her brood, I carry the logs. Then we have guests, Darnleys' and ours: they all bear themselves with airs appropriate to the place. The drudgery having been done by ourselves, we, the hosts, also fall into the manner of ease and graces. To Rosemary highest praise: she is truly at ease. Polly Peabody and the 'blonde' Mrs Biddle stay for a while as 'paying guests' and their inability to cope with the buckets in the mornings sets off nicely their party bearing of the evenings. Clarissa Churchill's drawling inattentiveness is a masterpiece. Cruikshank seems what he is – an old warrior of Toryism, but his entourage (his daughter married a Persian, a pink and plump Iranian diplomat) is confusing. Kingsley Martin turns in the park into an irrepressible wild and leaping man of nature.

Periodically in London, I would muddle neurasthenically in front of the easel at my studio. Within the sluggish post-war London emptied of vigour, cautious, living on the provincial's hearsay of Paris, I am an odd-painter-out – the cognoscenti are uncomfortable: nothing here matches their current 'appreciation'. But the act of turning away and the display of discomfort are also pleasurable to them. They crowd my studio. The social atmosphere there is different from the weekends at Cobham Hall. The poseurs are more flamboyant and the eccentricities more expected, though often more riotous.

But, with all this the Polish experience is heavy upon me. I write a pamphlet to throw off the burden: it attempts to describe with the utmost truthfulness, not the Congress, but the pathos of an artist-innocent caught unprepared by Politics.

The generous goodness of those old wise men. **H. G. Wells** had me without haste at 13 Hanover Terrace, talked to me, crediting me with equality, though perhaps by then less buoyant and with a touch of melancholy; took me to the end of his garden to guide me over a graffiti-strip painted by him on the walls of an open alcove carved out in his mews cottage; the theme 'the lords of the world' and their subjects, beginning with dinosaurs and ending with humans.*

His generosity emerged in the following instance, undimmed by the most usual territorial caution prompting other tribes to stay at a distance. He and Moura Budberg came to lunch at my studio at the time when, the family taking shape, our approach to the Crown Commissioners for a house in the Regent's Park terraces (our ideal) was rejected: no house available and long waiting lists. HG, on being told

*Sadly this 'mural' was whitewashed by the next tenant.

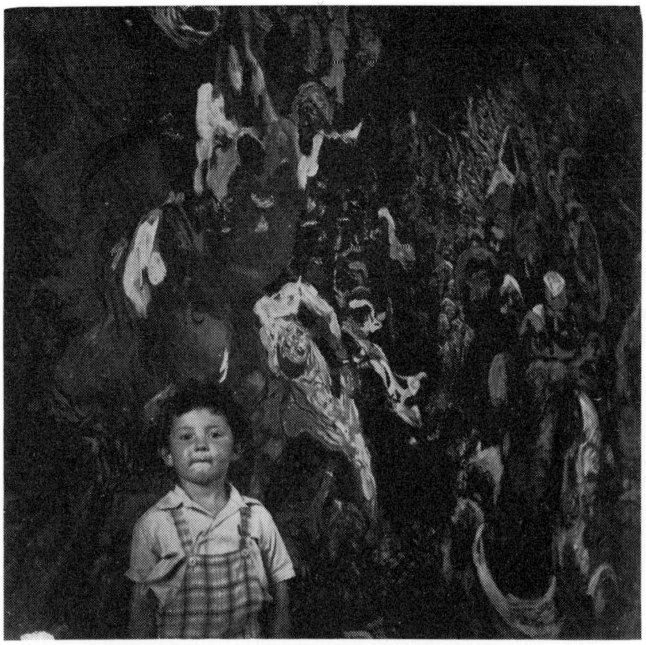

Daniel in front of '*The East*' (Photograph by Baron)

this, offered help – and, indeed, a few days later the Crown telephoned proposing the choice of three houses. We chose No. 14, next to his (garage, cottage, view of the lake), but costly bomb-blast repairs and earlier hesitations delayed our occupation until, miserably, after his death.

Wells's last slim book-pamphlet *The Mind at the End of its Tether* bewildered the followers of his optimism. Perhaps facile saving grace for them was to assess his new prophet-of-doom stance as old man's identification of his own deterioration with the world's. However, soon he was reaching his end with Moura memorably saying to me, 'Tragic to see a great mind going.'

There was a momentous gathering at the **Royal Institution** in his, but seemingly also his time's, memory. In this temple of the age of science and reason, faultlessly darkly rotunded downwards towards the lecture/altar of certainties, there crowded the still faithful, depleted by atrocious years – far from certain of holding the future. No surprise that the voices, commemorative of H. G. Wells's life-long preachings, have suppressed his clashing disquieting turn to despair – a heresy.

The ritual nears the end – the temple of the nineteenth-century faith sinks into sleepy boredom. A bowler-hat rolls/jumps down the steps of the amphitheatre – the offering of a napping devotee.

A miracle.

An Indian boat, under an Irish captain, with Indian officers and Lascar crew, takes me and my painting 'The East'* to **Bombay**. Being an official guest, I am given a grand pilot's cabin on the exclusive officers' deck; and, after the initial fun and games with the first-class crowd below, I withdraw and settle, with weeks going by, for becoming a recluse, perched each long day on this deserted deck-space high above the passengers' scramble.

The books strewn over me concern aloof Hinduism, Gandhi's utopia – crossed with London sectarianism, Nehru's reasonableness from behind British bars.† All through those long days, half musing over the Holy Trinity – Brahma, Vishnu, Shiva – and the God-is-love of Gandhi, half intoxicated with the sea, the sky and the passing line of biblical lands, I must be moving into a state similar to that of a contemplative hermit in mountain isolation.

The sun is ever more eager, the sea moves with waves ever more hieratic. On the port side there rises the significant Old Testament rockiness: in harsh steepness from the yellowness of the desert at the sea edge, and higher into grey solidity, hidden and embraced at the peak by a massive cloud thrown down vertically from the heavenly ceiling – like a tarpaulined shaft-descent, set for a visitation.

I guess the name of the mountain, but shout up to the Indian officer on the bridge: 'What is that mountain?' Obligingly he dashes off to the chart room, and returns with: '**Sinai. 7,450 feet**. It'll be alongside punctually at 3 p.m.' Heathen that he is, he is not aware of the resonance of his information.

I tread around my deck. The starboard burns under the furious sun and moves along the Egyptian shore. Below, a sari and white calves romp in deck-tennis competition. Back on the port side now a white sail glides in front of the mountains and momentarily damages the effect of monumentality.

I return to reading. I question languorously Gandhi's egalitarian concepts which hit at the caste system – the *raison d'être* of Hinduism. Whatever the theme, it soon dissolves and my state of calm is re-established.

Three o'clock. I rise from my corner and scan the whole horizon. The sun, its ginger face just visible from behind a wall of clouds, discharges its rays over the multi-waved, multi-planed purple of the Egyptian land, over the alloyed waters, over the deeper violet of Arabia – and, dispelling their awesomeness, blesses the mountains of the other side with a benign rosy tone.

And then the miracle: on the sheer flank of Sinai there lights up a cyclopean eye of rainbow-coloured fire. It glows with splendour. Created in this instant yet there and unflinching, it holds me, the doubting Thomas, confounded and rapt. And its stare, unrelenting, makes me eventually mumble hesitantly in my childhood's language, 'Our Father, which art in heaven' (an embarrassed formality drawn out of meagre equipment) . . .

The voices from below return, and a Sikh, a co-passenger, comes up (against the rules) to lean at my side, casually commending the view as my Burning Bush vanishes. The prickly and hurried flicker from a destroyer over there under

*'East' acquired by Nehru for India.

†Was Gandhi's vision of a **home-spun India** fundamentally in opposition to world progress?

With his holy grasp on his nation, with the subcontinent still rural, surviving on handfuls of rice and on faith, with the potential of this immensity to be carved away from global greeds – he could have upset and eventually reversed humanity's seemingly inevitable certainties – inevitable as they now appear.

And if this was his master plan and the feeblest possibility existed of its being set in motion then his inheritor's unflinching Western-model 'progressiveness' was treachery.

TOPOLSKI's CHRONICLE No. 1 (13) Vol.II 1954

of a voyage round the world (a)

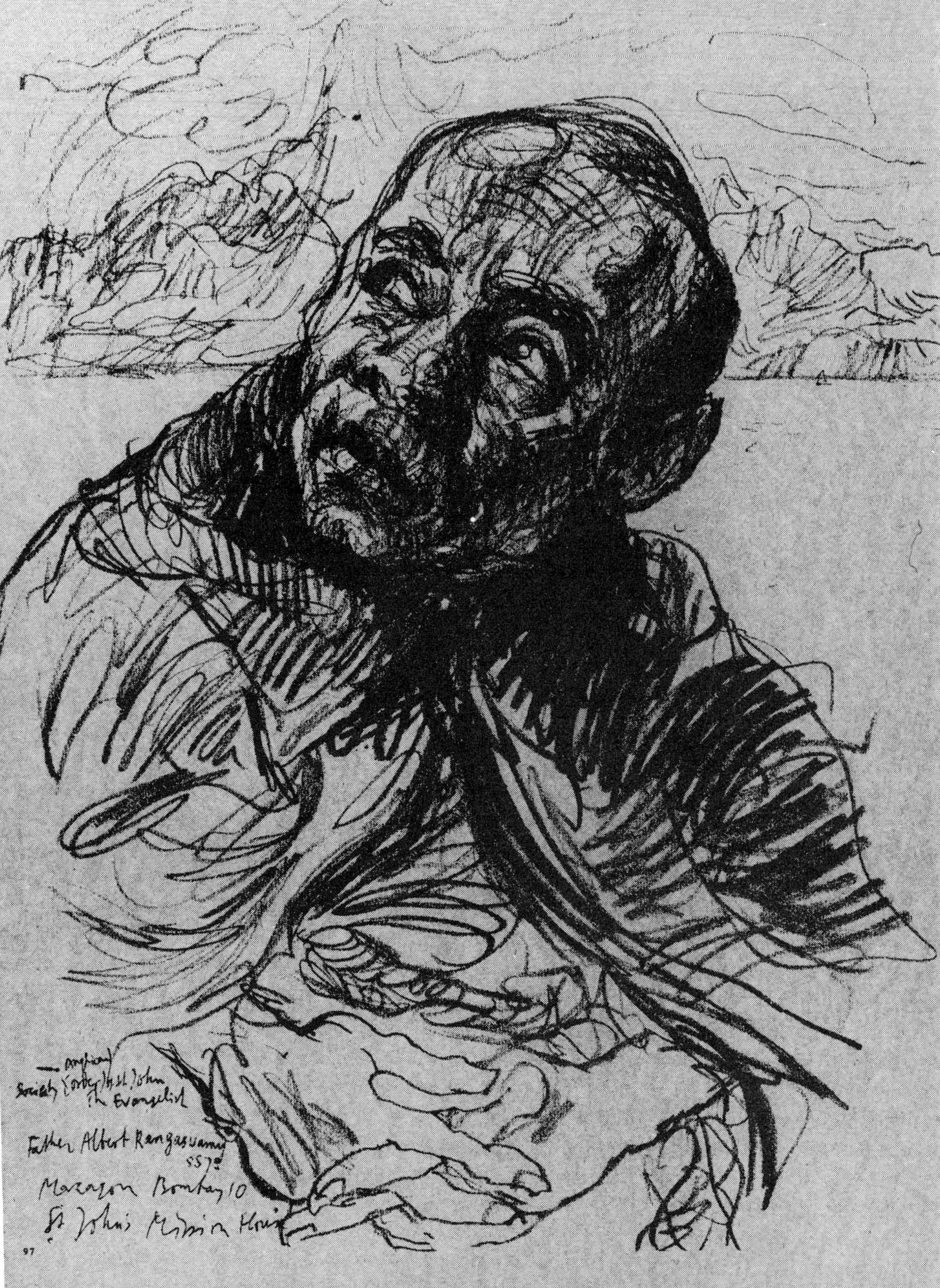

97

LONDON—BOMBAY

. . . My cabin immediately under the bridge, looks ahead onto our course. The rising sun fires at me with a red glow straight over the bows of the ship, renders burning the foremast and its riggings. We travel east . . . An Indian ship carries me eastwards, amongst the New Asians, to NEW ASIA. The eastern wind gathers strength; we sail stolidly against it, carrying the seeds of the west: there is a meeting held on the poop to exchange ideas, the speakers—an Indian member of an Anglican Order, who travels back to his Mission in Bombay; a doctor from Lucknow, who has gathered in England the latest in the field of serums and vaccinations; a nuclear physicist going back to Mysore and a genetician from Madras; a young man from the U.P. who has studied in Birmingham the economy of agriculture; and an English lady, who taught in Bombay for 20 years and felt like returning . . . The ship is officered and manned by Indians, but captained by an Irishman. And it contains a number of German technicians and British businessmen. A collection of "English brides" on their way to join their Indian husbands completes the cargo of western influences . . .

London–Bombay, by sea (from *Topolski's Chronicle*)

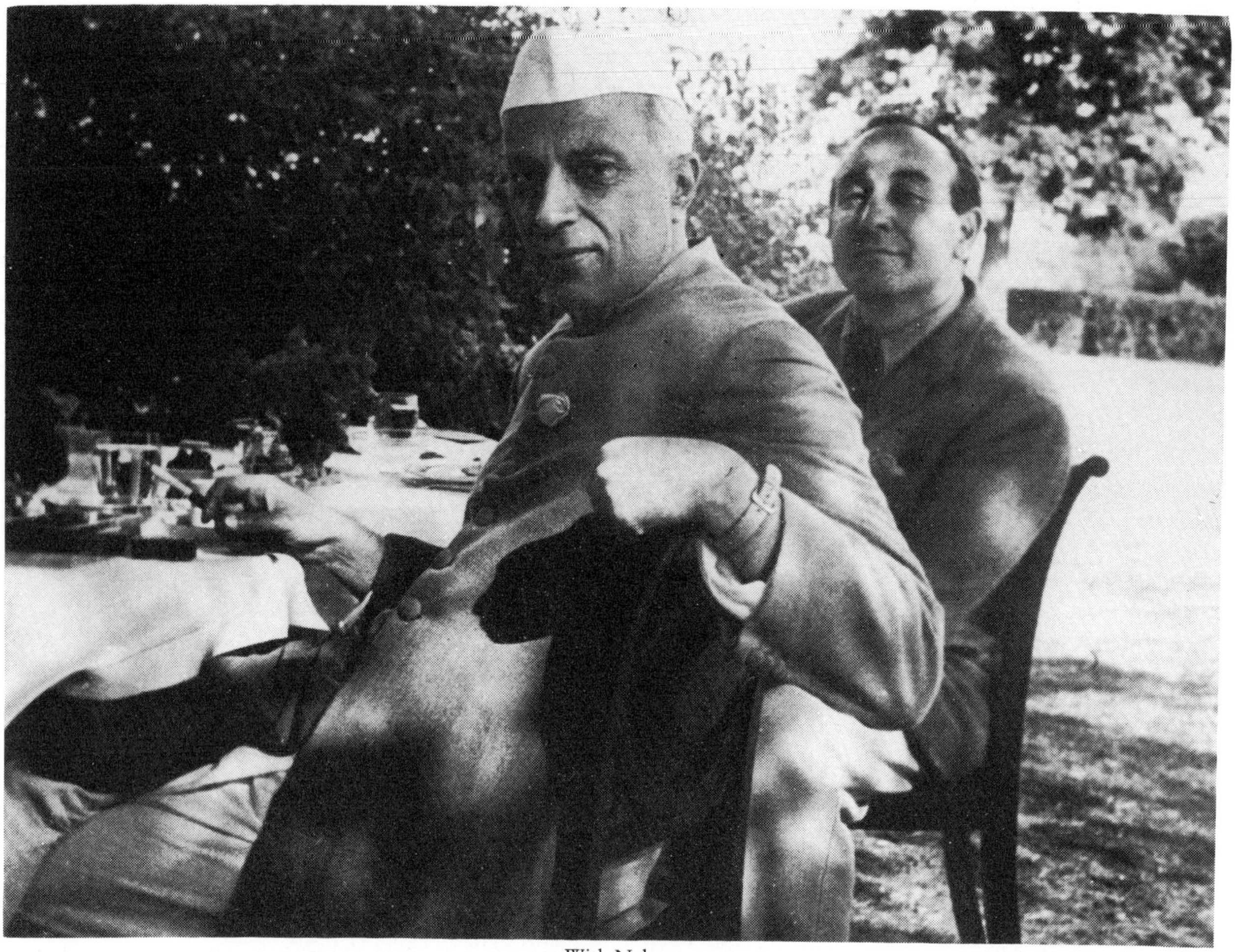

With Nehru

Sinai has begun to sent martial signals.

But the peace of the consummation remains for a time. The huge captain, propped sideways on the bridge's railings above, a human barrel silhouetted against the sky – silent and contained. The Lascar seamen are static and gaze into the distances of devotional colours, the landscape which breeds religions.

The reasonable explanations go rolling through my head. Yet I should like this to be the sign, and seek out a shipboard acquaintance, an Indian Anglican monk, to tell him all. Cautious and suspicious, he parries with the language of science: atmospheric phenomena and so forth, the land not of grace but of phantasmagoria.

On my own I ponder that it is true, that the miracles of the Bible may have happened yet can be explained on the level of physics. But because they coincided with particular circumstances and influenced men, they were indeed miraculous.

This corner is rich in mirages, and hence perhaps its religious fertility; but its God, having conquered the world, became Truth indeed, Revelation indeed, for thousands of years.

The final night-round of the deck. Over the point where the sun hid its cooling head, there hangs the crescent of the moon and a couple of stars, brighter than the rest of the sky. In the slowest of motions, the moon and its accompanying star slide down defeated. The other star holds on alone . . .

Thus gazing around, I watch *that* day and *that* night from my vantage point the cosmic contest, and though uninitiated, seem almost able to interpret its message. The feeling of nearness is around. At midnight there descends on our ship a sudden squall. Stretched in my confinement I listen to the heavenly roars and explosions until I fall asleep.

With all these celestial weapons used, the most stubborn Saul would have turned Paul. But the anger of Nature is no more a trial to man – in the well-engineered ship he stays unperturbed. I do not make the grade.

Having passed through the tribulations set by the angry and demanding Jehovah, I sail regretfully out of the Red Sea along the Middle Path, comfortably bypassing fulfilment and mystery.

Seven days later the ship is anchored in the waters of **Bombay**. An uncanny odour comes from the land – the votive suppuration of burned flesh and rags and incense; of heat; of decay. It is the stink of the East – of man's living sweat heedlessly borne upon the loins of death.

An anointed ruler would do better to hold aloof, separated from the ordinary by ritualized protocol and by the awe-inspiring stagecraft of towering rostra and thrones, lights, music and costume. Whoever is made a ruler (whether by vote, putsch or inheritance, it does not matter) becomes a Ruler. His subjects wish upon him a larger dimension – the myth dimension of their hopeful expectations, and he ineluctably grows up to this legend of himself.

The supreme hypocrisy of the contemporary leader's pose of appearing to be like anyone else, of mixing on the common level, distracts, creates difficulties, and is plainly unfair to everyone. Indeed, it seemed unfair that **Pandit Nehru** should be exposed to my sharing of his privacy. The man is great. Or at least greatness is his role. Yet at breakfast, lunch and dinner, in his home routine, in his appetites, playfulness, flirtations, tiredness, impatience, he was displaying to a curious stranger himself disrobed.

Nehru sat for me for some days after breakfast. I painted or drew while, at my suggestion, Lady Nye, the wife of the British High Commissioner, took on the role of a conversational stool-pigeon. I work better when my models are alerted by an outsider, thus being prevented from weighing me down with their attempts at 'best face' alternated with sleepiness, even though they are not still.

Lady Nye possessed the frame and aura of a romantic woman of Destiny. Given the circumstances, she had in her a Madame de Pompadour, a Lady Hester Stanhope or an Empress Dowager Tzu Hai. She spreads the possessive nets of a courtly *intriguante* or a favourite. Hers is ambition and vitality, but also subterfuges, dodges, and flatteries – all ideal qualities.

I watch her and learn my history lesson about 'great' court ladies. She shimmers with the outer garment of culture, to which the master responds. They understand each other wholly: both relishers in weighing up people mercilessly/inexorably, in shaping dilettante-fluid opinions and judgements – joyful at themselves, she reached this facile mastery in the sham brilliance of English society, he by self-instructed Westernization.

Our sittings were gay and stimulating, often tense with history in the making – the mood of imminent political decisions, the adjectives to define and direct personages, were all subtly modelled in small talk.

She and I had our multi-faced model. Nehru had fun. Now letting himself be drawn into grave deliberations – then, cutting them short by leaping down to kneel on the floor and show us how to keep a double chin at bay: straining his tongue out of his mouth so that he trembled with the effort, his eyes bulging, blood rushing up, ears and cheeks sucked in.

If, tempted, I were to go on putting down such minute descriptions and indiscretions – the sum of Nehru's weaknesses, or at best the 'also human' evidence – I would not add an iota to the great theme.

A group of members of **Nehru's household**, gathered on a freezing winter morning for breakfast, may seem impressive from the outside; the familiarity of sitting day after day, morning and evening, at Nehru's right opposite **Indira**, may be envy-inspiring; the *al fresco* lunches with the passing show of Distinguished Guests, the late hours in his drawing room, should be the apex of intimacy.

But the household-only meals were generally homely. The elated guests self-conscious and cliché-bound, Nehru tired, eager to relax in pranks or catching the news on the radio.

These were not the circumstances to do him justice. The colonial/imperial Lutyens plan was to erect New Delhi away from the restive native quarters. Still at some distance from the Viceregal Lodge (now the President's residence) and spaced widely, there stretch the 'suburbia' of high officials; and Nehru's house, within it, distances him from his nation.

But the nature of things cannot bear such dry devising – the 'communal' riots of 1947 brought refugees on to the empty stretches of New Delhi, with their tents/shacks, the chants of the Sikh rites, the hubbub of natural growth of life; perhaps a 'fill-in' promise for a living city.

I pleaded for this future New Delhi in the *Hindustan Times*, but already then the tidy planners began to uproot the campers.

But I was lucky also to be close to him at different times when he was truly Nehru the leader of India.

Tour of the Prime Minister

Saturday, 31 December, 1949. 07.00 Departure: New Delhi–Palam by RIAF plane.

Anne, the saried Danish housekeeper, this time definitely pleasant. When she chided me over the threadbare seat of my trousers disclosing the pink shirt (I had deliberately packed my oldest suit, meant to dissolve on this journey of unpredictable sartorial changes), I took it for disdain, but when this morning she commented on the shreds in the seams of my new suit (made of a cotton chosen for its texture not reliability) and followed with an anxious gaze a lump of sugar in tongs carried towards an empty eggshell, having bypassed the cup of tea; and then pondered over my manner of walking ('a certain Hungarian sculptress moved identically, but she had bad feet and one eye') and my head side-inclining ('perhaps because of painting'), I saw an old nanny's concern. Was I already fossilizing into a type and a maniac?

Nehru speedy and mood-tossed – now suspended in the silence of a statesman caught in a worldwide crisis, then, his eye striking a pomegranate sliced by me, single-mindedly holding forth, explaining my mistake: that the cutting should be done an instant before eating it, because of the dust, the flies . . .

Sandy tight overcoat, the stick of a dandy; without ceremony we bundle into the limousine in the last of the darkness. India's pennant, tremulous in the headlights, masks saluting shapes at the road's turns. In the front seat a new-to-me hefty figure – later apparent as a bodyguard.

Palam airport. The sun clambers up redly from its lair of black earth and, without coquetry, begins its work like an electric heater. Unromantic land revealed – the empty stage.

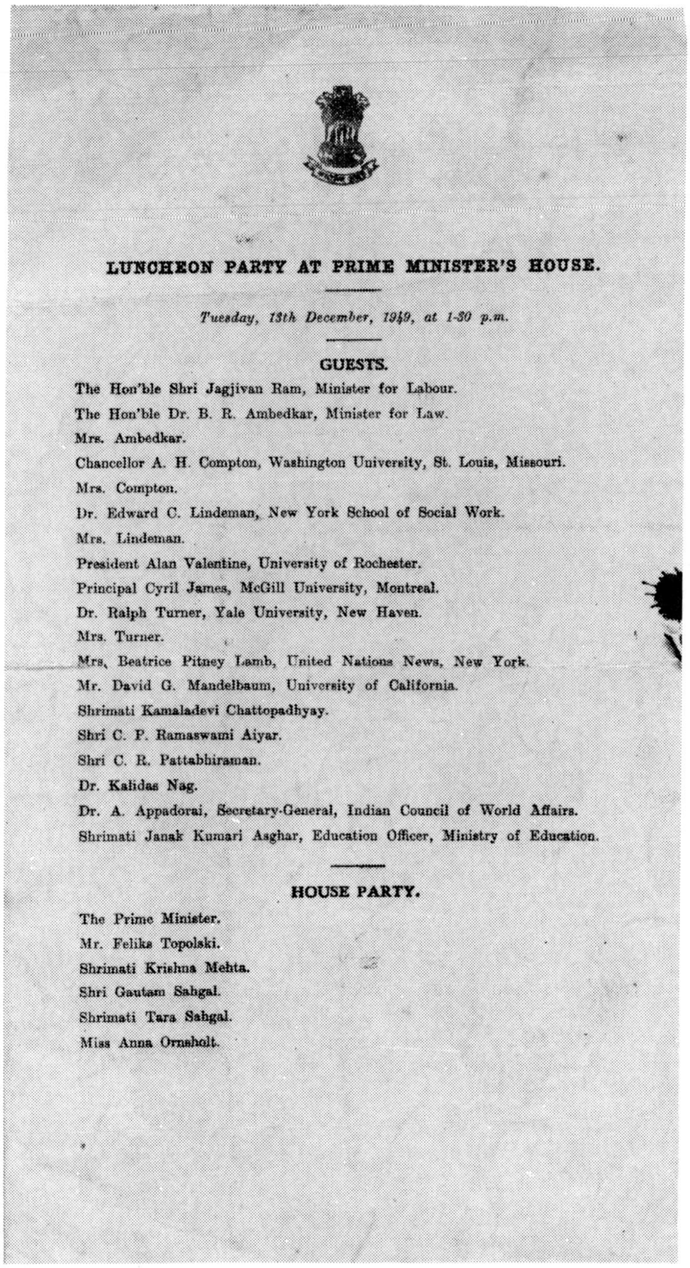

LUNCHEON PARTY AT PRIME MINISTER'S HOUSE.

Tuesday, 13th December, 1949, at 1-30 p.m.

GUESTS.

The Hon'ble Shri Jagjivan Ram, Minister for Labour.
The Hon'ble Dr. B. R. Ambedkar, Minister for Law.
Mrs. Ambedkar.
Chancellor A. H. Compton, Washington University, St. Louis, Missouri.
Mrs. Compton.
Dr. Edward C. Lindeman, New York School of Social Work.
Mrs. Lindeman.
President Alan Valentine, University of Rochester.
Principal Cyril James, McGill University, Montreal.
Dr. Ralph Turner, Yale University, New Haven.
Mrs. Turner.
Mrs. Beatrice Pitney Lamb, United Nations News, New York.
Mr. David G. Mandelbaum, University of California.
Shrimati Kamaladevi Chattopadhyay.
Shri C. P. Ramaswami Aiyar.
Shri C. R. Pattabhiraman.
Dr. Kalidas Nag.
Dr. A. Appadorai, Secretary-General, Indian Council of World Affairs.
Shrimati Janak Kumari Asghar, Education Officer, Ministry of Education.

HOUSE PARTY.

The Prime Minister.
Mr. Feliks Topolski.
Shrimati Krishna Mehta.
Shri Gautam Sahgal.
Shrimati Tara Sahgal.
Miss Anna Ornsholt.

10.15 The Honourable The Prime Minister will arrive at the Sonegoan Airport and proceed to Sevagram.

The customarily repetitious ceremonials: ranks of dignitaries, National-Anthem-led Guard of Honour by the Jodphur Regiment, the garlands round our necks, the arches and bunting/streamers. Then the running enthusiasm thins out, but there remain, far-spaced along the road, bewhiskered massifs – turban-ends floating. We dust-erase uncaring carts conducted by blissful floppy bullocks, and high-necked barefoot women, basket-caryatids; the horizon-pressing flat earth, here and there scratched by a lazy hand, prays for events. We travel to the World's Pacifists, symbolically dug in at the subcontinent's centre in Sevagram, Gandhi's Ashram. But on the way Nehru commands a detour, challenging the tight-fitting programme, to **the saintly Vinoba Bhave** – once Gandhi's closest. All of a sudden we are squatted sedately round a very frail old man in a rustic interior, gnawing sadly at some resolves perhaps no longer of avail or enthusiasms that have turned brittle with the passing of time; and there are young disciples standing in the background who may mean the future. This is a moving scene, grown into significance by its immobility, the two men facing each other in the long silence of parted ways . . .

Sevagram Pacifists: for a 'visual' man, having been surrounded for a length of time almost exclusively by Indians – their features glazed by a touch of idealized conformity – this tight grouping of emphatically discordant middle-to-old mostly Western faces queers its intention; blotchy colouring pushing into comic or vicious masks those exaggerations of protrusive noses/chins, and liplessness and bloatedness and hairlessness (or many-coloured frizziness) – underlined by the ultimate distortions of framed/coloured/magnifying eye-glasses. And this is the most benevolent selection of the whitish race, yet even a Japanese pair (perhaps we are too close to the end of the war and the concept of Japanese inhumanity) seem false, and so does a white devotee squatted barefoot, spinning a Gandhi wheel in front of the final gathering, at which Nehru declares, 'I am not a pacifist.'

Sunday, 1 January 1950, 08.30 Arrival at the Convocation of the Nagpur University.
British-modelled gold-edged robes and mortar-boards under the colour sway of canopies and fans, the young turbaned mace-carriers, the Rajas (their tight gold-embroidered turbans, chest-crossing shawls, hair-effects, ornate sticks, limp bejewelled hands) – and Nehru's aloof beauty.

16.00 – 17.00 Public meeting at Kasturchand Park.
Nehru's stand-up back (in his open car in front of mine) rides – **JAI HIND!** – through folksy patterns of arches, folksy masses in elation. Nehru inserted high up within the canopied folksy frame – a folksy market print come to life – and the immense *maidan*-full turns brown: raised arms: 'PANDIT NEHRU KI JAI!'

Poona Airport
As ever: a little platform for Nehru. We, his party, lined up behind. Facing us a guard of honour and again and again the band-whine of this endless droning timid Anthem stretched out resignedly. His open-car stand-up ride, but within the homogenous crowds, a remarkable memento: an invalid-chair given the prestige of a seat of honour by a decoratively arranged **relic of British India**: bush-blouse, shorts and one hose (one leg only), white squarely trimmed beard, old-time topee; a most presentable bearer behind, a finely spread (as often) vulture above.

18.00 – 19.00 Municipal Address.
When, for a change, seated below at the front amongst the public, there is no awareness of the amassment behind – all attention goes to the apotheosis soaring above: the flower-fragrant lovely/touching taste bypassing naivities glued together into a fretted altar-offering, outlined by the unlikely accord of chains of coloured bulbs and neons holding halfway up a chorus of white-saried black-tressed maidens, backed by giant likenesses of Gandhi and Nehru. And Nehru in person, under the topmost dome, fulfils expectations in the endless speech in Hindi – perhaps the verbiage strays into justification

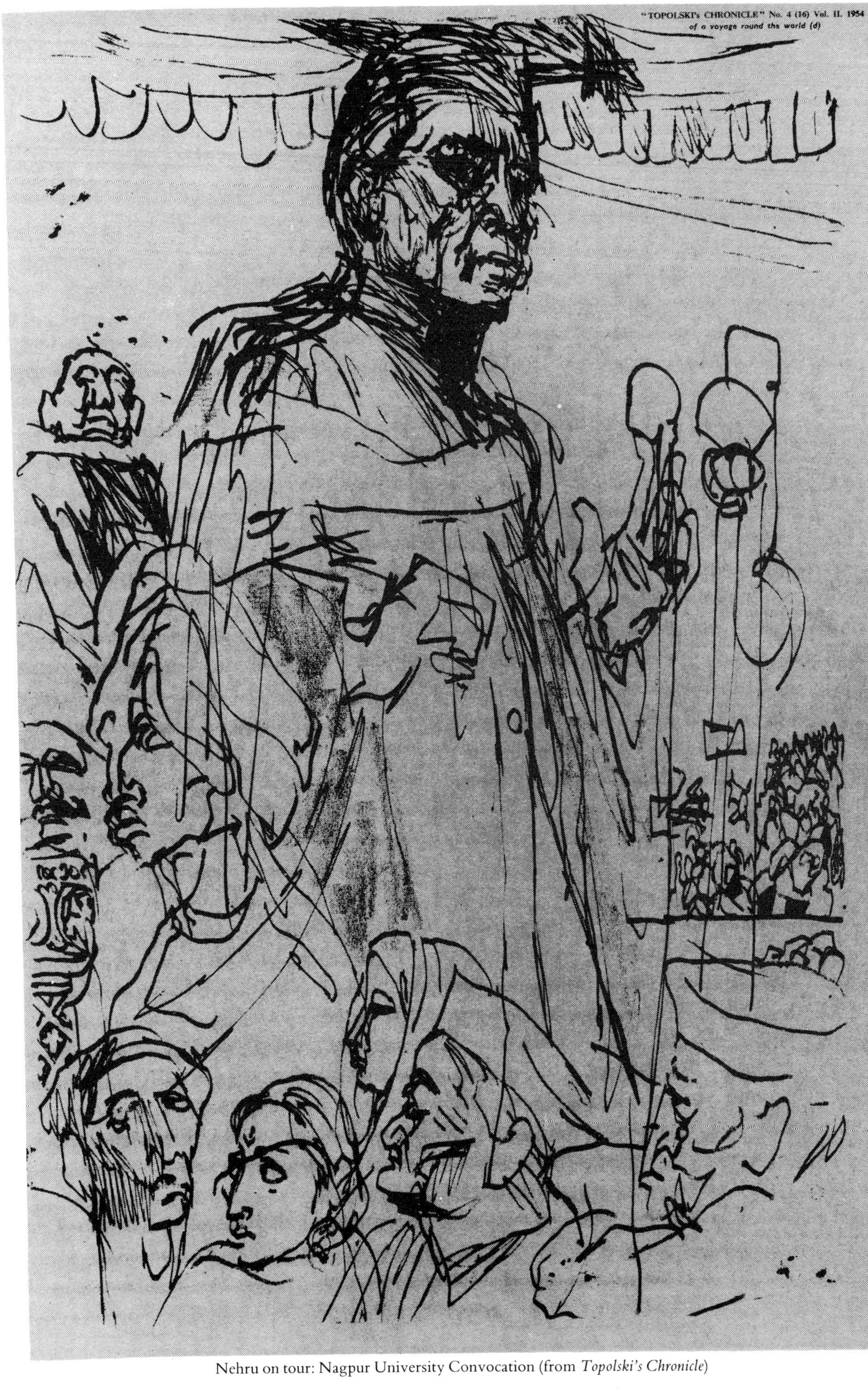

Nehru on tour: Nagpur University Convocation (from *Topolski's Chronicle*)

of his elevation by the confession of self-doubt. The exhausted adorers suffer for him.

Massive limousines take us across dusty desert (helpless, shelterless people stand in the heat; barbed wire round soldiers in bedraggled hats; some steel masts and NO THOROUGHFARE) to the climax of our and the country's progress: **The Science Congress.**

Human figurines shuffle mechanically into programmed schemes. My bustling athwart India becomes a chain of exercises in statistics, shifting through tens of thousands of subjects at each stop.

For example, we bird-fall on Poona: the band inaugurates tediousness with the national-military rhythm presenting a line of nameless puppets. Throughout the few hours they come to life, perform their foreshortened Poona existences, line up again at the airport for our departure but now, shallowly unveiled. The Anthem. The conditioning of those on the plane to summary disregard.

We fly above milky see-through spaces, lit aslant – with the earth as if at the waters' depth – as if examined by Noah's dove prematurely despatched over the Floods, over the catastrophic quiet of the end. And ourselves, as in my recent painting, the ill-boding and inattentive observers – another cloud above the earth, immune to its attractions.

We shall ferret out a consecutive city in the shallows of indifferent water-mists, we shall fall on it carelessly, the mournful hymn will brass up and figurines will form a welcoming line.

And I return a second time to Nehru's family welcome: the daughter **Indira**, her two boys and grandfatherly games – in the car, I tacked tightly within this alien, simple family – which ought to be seen from afar as a sacrarium – trivial intimacies, unfairly for them, disclose/demonstrate their ordinariness to a stranger. I begin to respect the distancing ceremonials of the anointed. Don't familiarize with those below you, because they will espy plain humanity in you and will peeve at your not being more than themselves.

Two hoopoes belabour the lawn outside my french window (Mohican crests, spiky beaks, but short of leg), then, summoned by the sun, scamper colourfully. It is noontime, but today I miss out the far-end distant garden-lunch, as usual garnished with foreign dignitaries, because I have with me, smuggled into the quiet of my room, the Anglo-Saxon star of my India war-days, ginger, freckled, and generously boned. No one, I thought, had seen this attempt of mine at privacy. The verbal preliminaries on the past, the hand holding, the bodies, the embrace, **the kiss**. We stand tightly in the narrowness of the little room, but into the corner of my upper eye enters, horror-of-horrors, a large group, in the act of placing themselves – the faces turned at us – a bare few yards from my window: Nehru at the centre, Indira, the Naidu sisters, Krishna Menon, General Cariappa, Philip Noel Baker, Sir Archibald and Lady Nye, Rajkumari Amrit Kaur and some other Ministers, Maharaja Dalipsinhji; and a batch of American luminaries, pillars of the American state; obviously a unique unpredictable Pandiji initiative to lead all his guests from their tables over the length of the gardens to show them the planted-just-here patch of some corn for change-of-eating-habits publicity.

We pull apart and, within this instant, I glimpse Nehru back out and precipitate alone and away, shaking off, with impatient hands, Anna who attempts to follow.

Indeed horror-of-horrors. We two, shaken, gather ourselves into composure-of-sorts and escape on foot, over the never-walked-in-by-anyone Lutyensian grandiose landscape cum monumentalities. She was in my room as it were incognito, and so hopefully unharmed, thus this being my catastrophe solely, her loyal assistance welcome.

We analyse – calmed by then by mere physical exertions of conquering up-and-down ponderous and numerous staircases round the Presidential Residence – the possibilities: to begin with – were we seen? or, the bright noon outside, contrasting with the unlit interior . . .? But Nehru's speeding away in agitation? anger? embarrassment?

This unsolved, yet, in any case, demanding of me to be prepared for disgrace – or, in the knightly samurai manner, to make the first move – meaning not suicide, an outdated honourable exit – but instantly packing up and departing, with a letter of apologies left behind . . . But perhaps less evasive (thus less cowardly) would be to face the wrath and bear the humiliation of expulsion from favour and from his home.

I walk back alone, the grimmest expectations and shame weighing me down – and enter the lobby, under the passive uncommitted gaze of the amassed *chaprasis*, still at a loss, meaning to sneak into my room for inspiration to descend on me.

And a shock: as never before, Pandit and Indira step out through the centre inner door towards me – smiling, gesturing invitingly: 'We have decided to go to the cinema: come with us!'

Next afternoon, my accomplice brings her husband to my room – to see some particular drawings. We have tea, oddly and brusquely (without a knock) cut in by Anna. She claims a mistake and withdraws. But, at our next collision with each other (the same evening? in a corridor?), she exclaims: 'I don't understand, I don't understand anything any more . . .'

So did only Anna Ornsholt, with her housekeeper's eye, see us? Or . . .?

The **farewell flight** south of **the first Indian Governor-General** after Mountbatten, **Sri Rajagopalachari**, who refused the Presidency, a wonderful ancient. Colonel Chatterjee announces: the desert (hillocks swell and the horizon's edges turn up), but close to Visakhapatnam will come the thickest jungle in India. To the right, he goes on, Jobbulpur, a famed river, marble-paved.

Further east big oceanic waters are revealed out of the mystery of far-distance-recoiling light, the continent ending solidly as if in finality. But because I know that within those (rosy now) ethereal farnesses there lurk further lands, an indefinable allurement beckons.

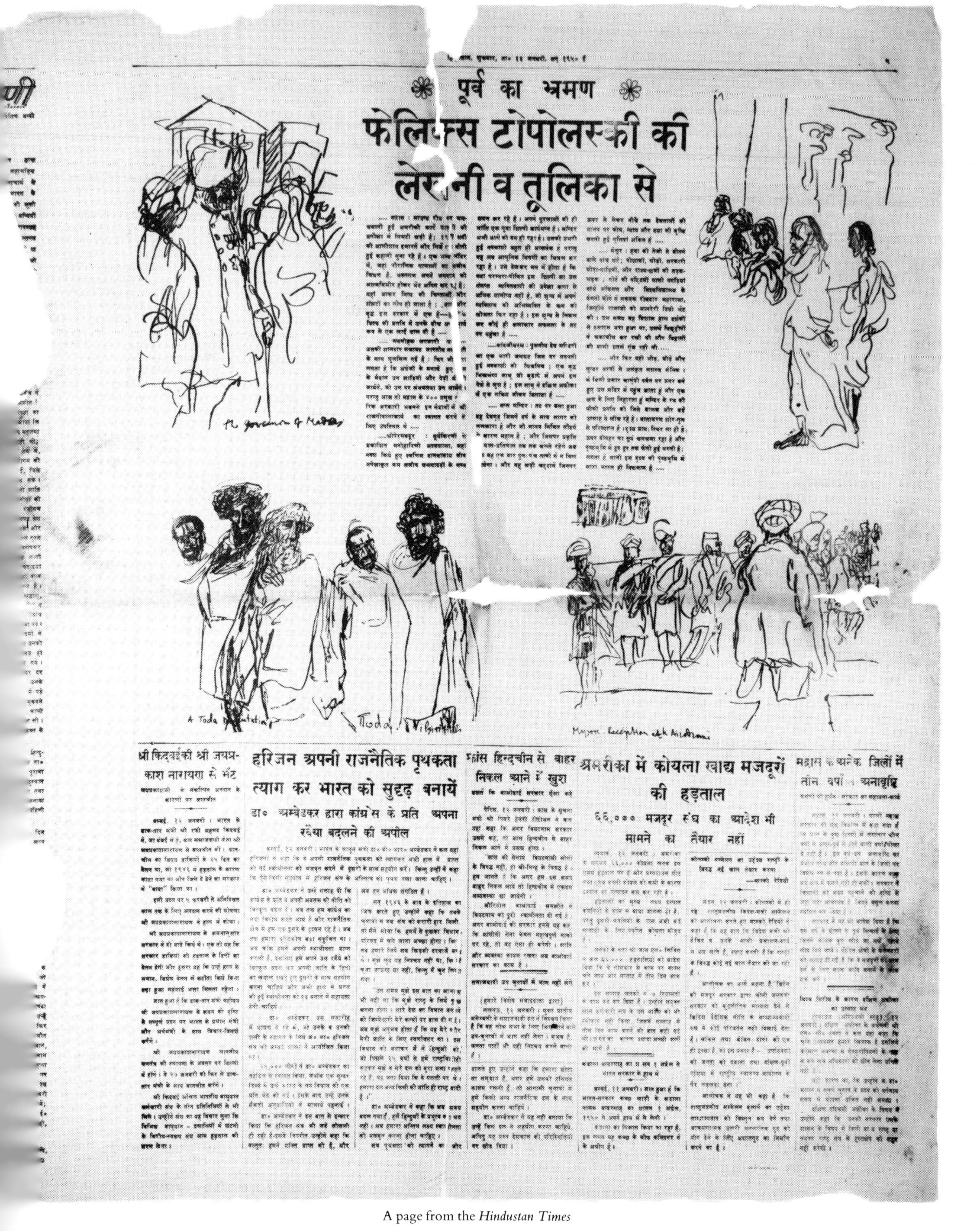

पूर्व का भ्रमण

फेलिक्स टोपोलस्की की लेखनी व तूलिका से

श्री किदवईकी श्री जयप्रकाश नारायण से भेंट

हरिजन अपनी राजनैतिक पृथकता त्याग कर भारत को सुदृढ़ बनायें

डा० अम्बेडकर द्वारा कांग्रेस के प्रति अपना रवैया बदलने की अपील

फ्रांस हिन्दचीन से बाहर निकल आने में खुश

अमरीका में कोयला खान मजदूरों की हड़ताल

६६,००० मजदूर संघ का आदेश भी मानने को तैयार नहीं

मद्रास के अनेक जिलों में तीन वर्षों से अनावृष्टि

A page from the *Hindustan Times*

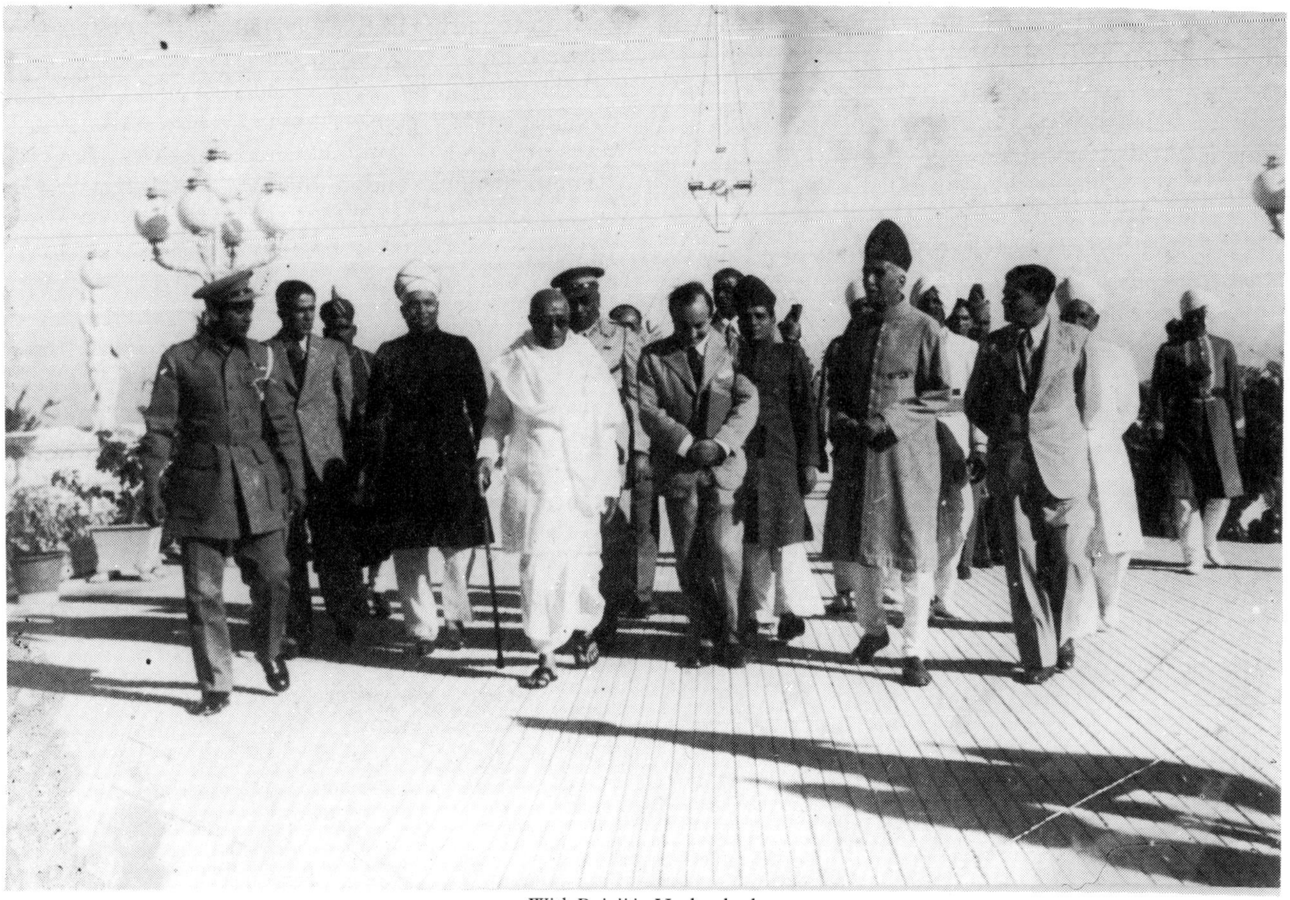

With Rajaji in Hyderabad

Rajaji whitely wrapped (cleanest/pressed dhoti). His Excellency, **the Governor of Madras**. Naval white and Madras green uniforms, foot-tappings to prescribed music; Englishmen command this martial ballet, bare swords upright. Hot; and pleasant – mainly because of the policemen's high turbans – red and coconut-shaped.

The landscape now a hothouse. The galloping review of palm trees filing along like herons. The sea-azure seeps through. Women in undulating/enchanting wrappings magnificently press forward under their head-baskets; or – statues, bareness classically part veiled, round a well – gossip biblically; loin-clothed male groups: return to pre-original-sin innocence.

But already the guest house and the adjutants and programme-problems. And so, elude it all and, led by a naked child, enter the rolling waves ('dangerous drifts') and let the hurling booming waters pitch-and-toss me.

Detached from Rajaji's cortège, roll away **on a train** within the heat-passive vegetation: against the well-being of fields and cattle and banana-abundance begging hands and hungry gestures – children given the role of wretches amongst the indifference.

The hot day held in balance until the early afternoon, long-spun diffusedly and considerately – now, at five, suddenly in great haste the sun tears away from contemplation and scurries downwards. In accord, the land flattens out – while, since the morning, it has been shooting up high hillocks – and lays itself for the night.

A random stop. Small boys hastily/resonantly smack their napes – to earn *bakhshish*? Banyans led by their own huge bellies over the station's platform. Sessions of vultures fill up the widest stretched mango tree. By now the sun is rapidly tumbling/rolling on the horizon's edge – misses to make sport with colours – sinks.

In the darkened distant criss-cross of cultivation a planter's bungalow and veranda – Englishmen sit under a light and netting (tiny figurines) with glasses in hand. The train stop's name – Rajahmundry. With the night the compartment window frames, cotton-coiled like Lazarus, an albino. The cows confident, but the dogs wretched/unloved demonstrate by their debased manner the truth about unequal opportunities.

Enter *cosy temples* modelled out of twisted figurines, whitewashed and then painted coyly/rurally; whitely draped white-beards, naked brown youth, orange-red-wrapped criss-cross-daubed holinesses – animals participating plentifully (clouds of bats around). My bare soles softly receive the cool and the warm – friendly mementoes of the just departed day. Now, the neons, the yellows of electric bulbs, the minute reds of oil-flames diversify the intricacies of interiors. The crowd presses/sways towards the stable of godly monsters, colour-accented, with offerings/garlands. The whispering silence – people at ease with godliness: all painted foreheads, a young brahmin offers on a tray a flame to touch. Darkness gathers and I feel the humble sorrows and solaces surrounding me – the communal blisses, the harmony of young and old – always discordant in the worlds of progress – here in immutable concord.

A young anonymous stonemason faultlessly chops out of

granite the ever-same old gods ('living tradition'), but trips up on Gandhi's – emblems? symbols? – glasses, watch, sandals.

A high-relief: animals aimless yet wilful; humans passionate yet phlegmatic. And that compact temple carved into a battling sea and an undefeated *lingam*.

Then in wide unmarked uncharted space two strolling ancients, whiskers, orange rags, adornments a-blow, sticks and vast conches for alms – wild, elemental. But: born, having lived and retired in South Africa, they transported themselves to India to take to the road – the seventh age of man.

Prince Peter of Greece with his veritable *Russkaja* wife in an air-conditioned caravan – car-pulled and another for the luggage; and, a French cook thrown in, gadding about from the Malabar jungle to Himalayan villages to governmental palaces – with nonchalance, untidiness and charm. An evening with them refreshing, though our Russo-European attachments and accords, sharpened by the Eastern background, perhaps led me on. I like them, I open to them and, when they ask me about Nehru, I confess timorousness towards him. Also possibly confess to myself: I have never – in the hubbub of Nehru's household – before this moment paused to assess myself *vis-à-vis* the great man.

They take me to a popular noisy inn – the top-floor door opening on to a roomful of antiquity incarnate: five **Todas elders**, erect – a string of beards and brown nudities held majestically in white folds with black/red edges: the Prince to be their grievances' advocate.

Madras again. The streets are dominated by fattened-up brahmins, ambition-driven shopkeepers, massive officials wrapped in the muslins/silks of botherations; but in the slender black bodies of the coolies – both straining and merry-making – poverty shoots up high and with grace. But I can't lose myself, my liveried chauffeur returns me to the handsome **Government House**'s British psuedo-classicism laced with Indian ornaments – its elongated lawns lapped by distant forestation, extirpated of palm trees and tropicalities: an English-nostalgia park. The Mogul-costumed servants belong to the nostalgia.

Mysore still a private state – the ministers lined up along the carpet, the master of ceremonies bearing a huge mace, the serving staff, their diagonal- and waist-sashes, turbans of great colour refinement, all leading up to **the Maharajah**, an ultra-supreme immeasurable mountain of purple folds over white, ear-ring, watch-chain, his turban an unmatchable coil of gold and blue. And the lancer escort – a still more blinding colour scheme of red-green-white – round the landaus. The emphatic give-away faces round me at the official banquet. The farewell (to us and soon to his rule) sight of the outsized Maharajah set on the red-carpet perspective against the sumptuous tentful of his grandees, bordered by his private army lowering their standards.

Hyderabad. Another shape of a court masterfully defined by fantasy-reaching sugar-loaf head-dresses above avid faces as the background to His Exalted Highness the **Nizam**'s miserly littleness, emphatically countering 'the richest man on earth' with the abnegations of elastic-sided boots under clumsily too-short white pyjama-pants, an ill-fitting crumpled tunic, a weary suspicious droopy face. And the crowd's defiant cry.

Another banquet and another and yet another – as ever in the East and as it may have been in Europe of earlier centuries, and more so here in Hyderabad: under their sugar-loaf hats there is no *politesse* to mask their greedy-featured intentions.

White-shawled Rajaji and his gentle goodly – and tragic – speech – and the inescapable tears-come-to-my-eyes: the dreamy idealist, not a politician, caught in ruthlessness, reaches back to his earlier simple encounters, and deplores the use of police force now – nostalgia and defeat. But he charms with irony: speaks of the architecture of this fine open-arched 'folly' and the constraining 'architecture' of public meetings – would rather get himself killed than . . . The populace held back at street exits howls with hate; the Colonel at my side whispers that the Government will be offended.

Am I staying at **Falaknuma Castle** or another guest palace? Whichever, this shoots far beyond ostentation: Victorianism, the brashest-ever performance of world-dominating abundance, is transferred here and brought to the heights of parody by the naive (but victorious) device of scale gone awry. Some already-extravagant English pile is faithfully copied but in inhuman enlargement – the building inside-and-out and then every item of the interiors, from chairs to vases and marble busts. The English craftsmen produced and equipped this abode for giants – and we, the Nizam's guests, knock about in it, meant to feel small, but merely astounded and amused.

The stylishly shabby Nizam is slavishly/tightly grouped round – **a true court**, whether at garden parties under masterly massive canopies, or at banqueting tables backed by many-filed servants, or at carpeted bannered lancer-on-foot-lined academic or public functions.

A slim twisting path carved in a sheer precipice carries the cortège: sedan-chaired Sri Rajagopalachari lifted on four shoulders followed by the train of his courtiers, servants, soldiers (turbans, umbrellas, weapons) – I, bare-headed, close amongst them. We extend and bring to twentieth-century life the painted cortèges, peeling/fading – the same people, same gestures of respect, awe, agitation – progressing from rock-hewn cave to cave of **Ajanta**, one after another – over thirty of them.

India's most sublime offering to me – the Ajanta cave-paintings (and their tabernacle-statuaries) – the closest to my ideal in imagery, and in their setting. The unwavering continuum worked on in the early centuries of this era and before by five-six generations of nameless anchorites: along the shadowy and ravaged walls there are born, feed, battle, worship, love, multiply, age and die the people of India, punished/led by the giant Buddhas towering over their subjects – while the amazed animals look on.

This art has nothing to do with our contemporary art theories. It gives the lie to most of its aesthetic commandments. And it has not been shown justly in reproduction (except for the costly Oxford University Press survey), because modern European taste finds comfort in turning all art into 'detail', as if in fear of the large sweep. The well-known Ajanta details are of a charming group of ladies, or of a Bodhisattva torso, but never of the crowding continuity of it. Thus the Ajanta one knew about had been reduced to fit into the mean measure of today's aesthetics, and its overwhelming reality, stretched out beyond the reach of human range into nature's phenomena, came upon me when already moving towards panoramic solutions to my life-long accumulations of our time's globality. And so in one way Ajanta confirmed/ encouraged, but also threatened insurmountable obstacles.

The processional pilgrimage in attendance on this highest-in-the-land successor to past rulers, along the same path: the modest Rajaji is making the last formal tour of his Southern India before stepping down – with me in the background, the only European invited by him to accompany him. The Ajanta and Ellora Caves are a detour at his request – I can guess to gratify me.

In celebration of the Inauguration of the Republic of India a series of 'requests the pleasure' of my company at functions such as a performance of *Kumara Sambhava* or the Ceremonial Parade to commemorate the Republic Day, 26 January 1950 ('the Guests requested to stand' at its many climaxes).

The inimitable blend of Victorian-Imperial with Indian martial drills/attires – fossilized into unchanging rituals. I felt then that Gandhi's India should have stripped the trimmings of the past for home-spun humility. But no more now: the past must, like the rows of medals, be added to, not cut away from the present; the ceremonial wear *commémoratif* of the whole great story of India – now marked by the shape/colour of a tunic/turban, then a single button or feather.

However, to quote what I wrote at the time for the *Hindustan Times* or/and *Yomiuri Shimbun* of Tokyo:*

DECLARATION OF THE REPUBLIC OF INDIA
Celebration on 26 and 27 January 1950

The swearing-in Ceremony was held at the Durbar Hall of Government House. The Viceregal interior, almost viceregal protocol – its whole design being not of the popular Congress mould, but of the Imperial order – failed to reflect the meaning of the occasion.

The flag-hoisting ceremony moved smartly to the rhythm of the bagpipes. The Garden Party was held in the grip of the Western pattern of the Mogul gardens.

The vast body of the Diplomatic Corps formed throughout the celebrations the solid background to the elated personalities of India – with its deep, closed ranks, top-hats and women's formidable feathers, it seemed to perform grimly the functions of an indifferent chorus for the much-in-the-picture Guardian of the new Republic. The people of India, kept well back, were hardly included into the procedure . . .

Benares Airport cameo: peripatetic congressional global-circuit academics/delegates backed by a plane, at their repetitious pantomime of greetings/farewells, costumed in parody of Edwardian-colonial Panama-hatted styles, oblivious of the Holy City (merely another conferential stop).

The rackety tumultuous shadowy tightness of Benares-town lanes unlocks to sublimity: high-edged by Rajas' dreamy exotica-rococco palaces, the wide sun-whitened steep steps carry a vociferous frieze of the ritualized life–death span – all included, all dignified – to and into the **Ganges**, which – beyond ablutions and the floating ashes of the dead – dissolves into unremarkable distances, lost in light.

Viewed from the river: pink kites and black-winged vultures above white palaces laced and horizontally red-striped, and vertically striped temples; steps, protrusion- or niche-accented – each a relief-frieze of agitation or repose under a sunshade, or occupied by a painted Ganesh; steps ascended/descended by multitudes, stilled by the stretched colours of drying saris, exhibiting nakedness glorified then river humbled then in worship – the vigorous monumentality of young bodies: male bare but for the loins, female wetly draped; wrapping/unwrapping modesty-ruled; the stately aged grouped in the coolness of *chattris*, contemplative, as it

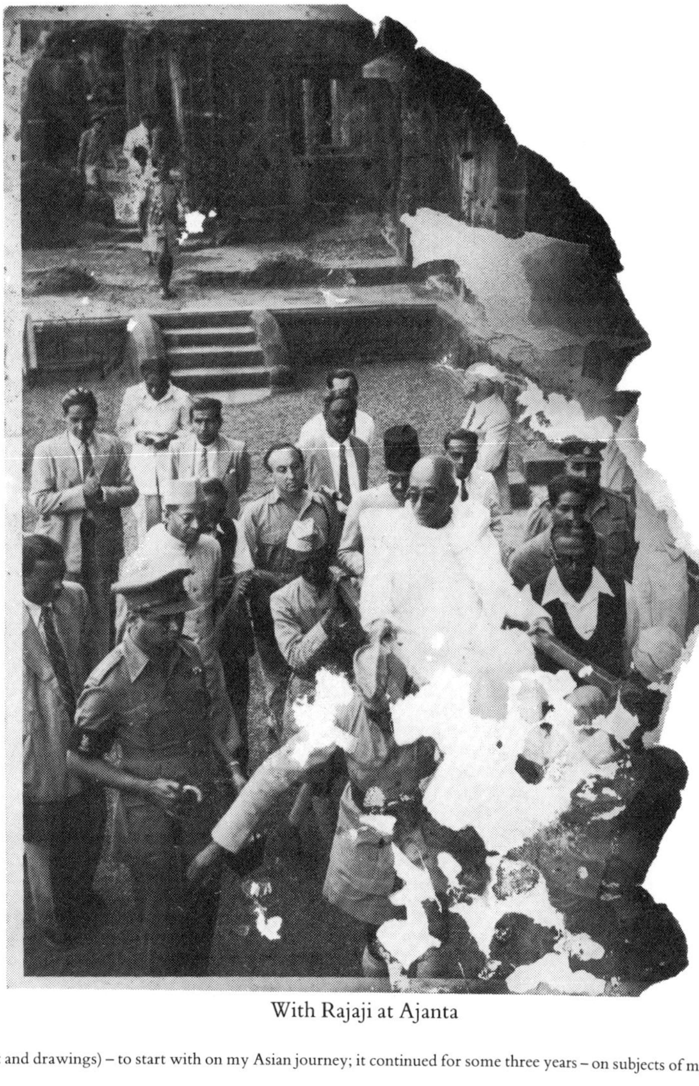

With Rajaji at Ajanta

**Yomiuri Shimbun*, one of the leading dailies, proposed on my arrival in Japan to carry my 'column' (text and drawings) – to start with on my Asian journey; it continued for some three years – on subjects of my fancy.

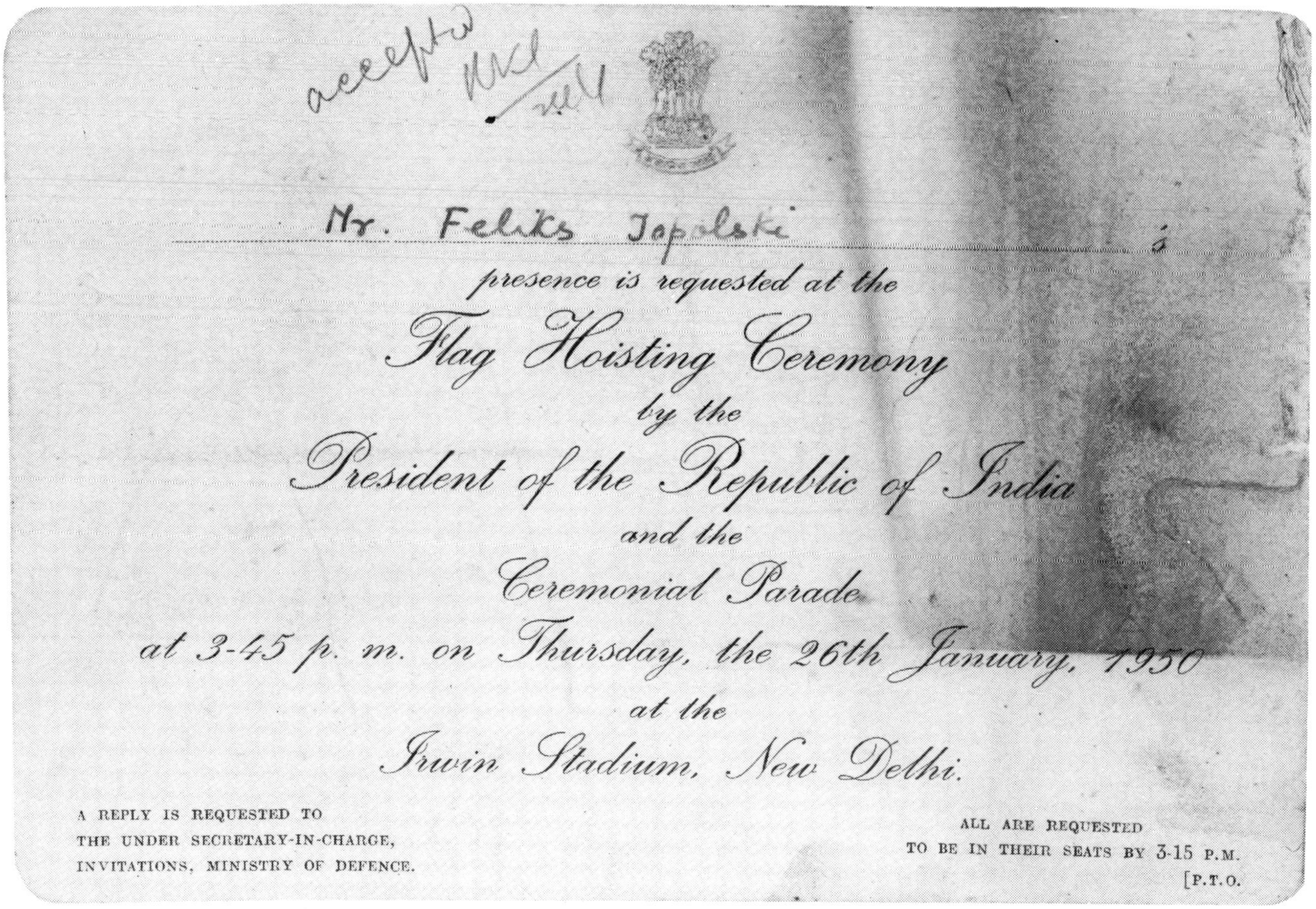

accepted
Mr. Feliks Topolski
presence is requested at the
Flag Hoisting Ceremony
by the
President of the Republic of India
and the
Ceremonial Parade
at 3-45 p. m. on Thursday, the 26th January, 1950
at the
Irwin Stadium, New Delhi.

A REPLY IS REQUESTED TO
THE UNDER SECRETARY-IN-CHARGE,
INVITATIONS, MINISTRY OF DEFENCE.

ALL ARE REQUESTED
TO BE IN THEIR SEATS BY 3-15 P.M.

[P.T.O.

should be, clasped palms, eyes closed or widest open to enlightenment. These steep riches of levels culminate in the descending carriers of wrapped and beflagged bodies, in the business of **burning ghats**.

Not a physical but a 'cultural' queer, my tastes harmonize with those of the 'beaux' of the genre. It was all harmony to stay in one of the palaces overhanging the ghats' holy business – refurbished and revived by my Franco-Swiss musical hosts to India's old graces: the unforced unblemished gatherings always in princes' courtly tradition, ancient instruments fingered by decorative players, servants and food in accord.

Out of these 'reproduction' exclusivities, whether down to or on to the river, or up to the temples and markets, enchantment, and much more – the complete transposition to the past – held.

Close by my friends' palace, reachable by a winding path along the high edge, **Sri Ma Anandamayi** held her holy festivities. On my first night, guided by drumming music, I walked alone (the moon, the Ganges, the silent ghats – all there to my right) in the elation of merging with a most distant world, alert to my feet grinding ground not only alien but not of my time, yet pacing this unreal path in assured intimacy. Such bridgings – between myself and uttermost otherness – all too rare, and more and more so – happened to me mostly in those years – perhaps my only brushes with the 'mystery of enlightenment'.

And this solitariness along the elusive path, aiming at the rising rhythms and chants from the shades, with the unknown ahead – the faith-charged scene itself and what reception would be meted out to an interfering stranger – evolved, oddly, into closeness. Soon I entered hospitality and predictable, though highest-pitched, fervour.

I drew incessantly, then and throughout my stay in Benares, and, on my return, painted conglomerations up to 20 feet high of holy men and women, worshippers at their feet, or in circular praying sway-processions led by long-haired ecstatic bandsmen, or immobile in contemplation, or immersed in the River; storytellers, yogi; the fat and the thin united (their ever-emphatic faces/gestures/shapes in everlasting draperies); elders or women in concordant groups; the bedecked dead on the way to burning – my images, however crowded, always inadequate to this amassed upsurge, differentiated yet blended.* But there must exist in some writing (I don't see it in Rushdie's) a text worthy of this magnificence. Not for me to attempt it.

That night of Ma Anandamayi's enshrined splendour (yet also accessibility of flesh), of her circling congregation, of homages paid to her by garlanded ancients – a cortège for

*Association: at my old studio, on the easel, one of these large paintings – of an entanglement of adorers round a possessed Holy Man elevated under a canopy; unbroken dark green backs and throws forward this restlessness – clashing with the prevailing textured paint application of the fifties. There are guests crowding in the other room (it may be the Picasso reception), but, entering this one for some reason, I glimpse Rothenstein, with Sutherland, waving his hand derogatorily at the background: a tableau of Art Inquisitors excommunicating heretic art with unsteady dogma.

each, all encompassed by the procedural beat – the whole (mixed spheres they seemed, mixed ages) of nature's congress. That led to days' diversities, however mischievous, of holiness: an interior heavily flavoured with indolent sexuality, as if momentarily pausing, wearied – the vast reclining bulk of saintliness, a shrewd eye out of a wrapped head, bare belly overhanging his couch, thick legs devotedly massaged by one or two of the surrounding proselytes; another – a bony, garlanded, story-teller; or a canopied den embracing a yellow-wrapped and squatted taciturnity – round him, in respectful postures, shaven-headed, also in yellow folds, their high-lifted staffs with begging bowls (their right) attached – pilgrims; the ashy/hairy saddhus and fakirs; even the shiny wrestlers exuded religious grandeur.

There is a boat for me and we proceed to float along the ghats. But first: the heat. My river-loving past and perhaps a touch of **the Holy Ganges**'s magnetism obliterate warnings, and at my request we move a few hundred yards up the current (a pitiful precaution) for me to dive in. Thereafter the day passes in blissful painting of the grandest panorama of living religion.

A Babel of agitation: turreted/balconied/canopied narrownesses; shadows-slashed holy nakednesses; women of consequence saried within garries; an aloof Raja in a horse-drawn carriage – turbaned *chapassi* perched at the back; and a two-domed ornamented curtained palanquin; camels ridden; white cows erratic – all of it monkey-sprinkled from pavings to roof tiles – vultures unfailingly above. Shiva and Kali Temple: monkeys monkeys.

I am led on foot by **a young Hindu protégé** of my hosts who, impressed by my athletic and painterly deeds on the River and having gone away for a day, inflict on me the gift of this probably willing courtier of theirs. He is sweetly gentle, the day is bright and any illicit thought is far from me, not to speak of having to summon extra courage to embark on the unknown; and, without a common language, my discomfort is furthered by not knowing whether he had been briefed for submission, thus expectant – and puzzled. Because I procrastinate and thereby, somewhat upset, dissipate the sharpness of my acquisitive eye by hanging about amongst inquisitive monkeys, scantily taking in the blind beggar children, the gravity of the fakir and the sacrificial stench. Then a long tarrying walk back to the palace to bring us, continuously exposed, to the time limit of our tête-à-tête, with the return of my generous hosts.

A drive some miles out of Benares for a moment of silence under a handsome baobab purporting to be a successor to the one under which Buddha . . .

A few years later there materialized an epistolary connection with **Swami Agehananda Bharati**, a Hindu sage cum monk and a professorial personage at the University of Benares, rounding up my links with the Holy City. Along with the arrival of his erudite and wise dissertation on Indian mysticism, *A Mystic's Epistle*, written for my *Chronicle* issue on Benares, came the news that he, a high-ranking yellow-robed member of a monastic order, had been expelled from the University for being seen applying his tongue to the clitoris of one of his girl students; then it came out that banishment from India had followed, that he had failed at establishing himself in Thailand, that (this after a stretch of time, but not very long) he had settled to a professorship of Eastern Religions at the University of Buffalo, USA.

Further passage of time: the Swami visited me in London, accompanied by a handsome English girl disciple; he, not an Indian monk, but an elephant of a man – an immense and immensely brilliant Viennese in a three-piece suit and a tie. As an appendix to my probably unrelievedly romanticized assumptions about Benares (even my European hosts moulded themselves into Indian princes, though they returned not much later to careers in Paris and Geneva), the tale of my Swami will give a glimmer of India's less declared contents, but also place him in my treasured list of rogues – whom I collect and admire, sadly not having it in me to be one of them.

Before the war this giant teenage Austrian had put his overflowing gifts into learning Sanskrit and his duties with the Hitler *Jugend*. The war, progressing, deposited him in German-occupied France, so my imprecise information tells, attached because of his Sanskrit and India-centred studies to

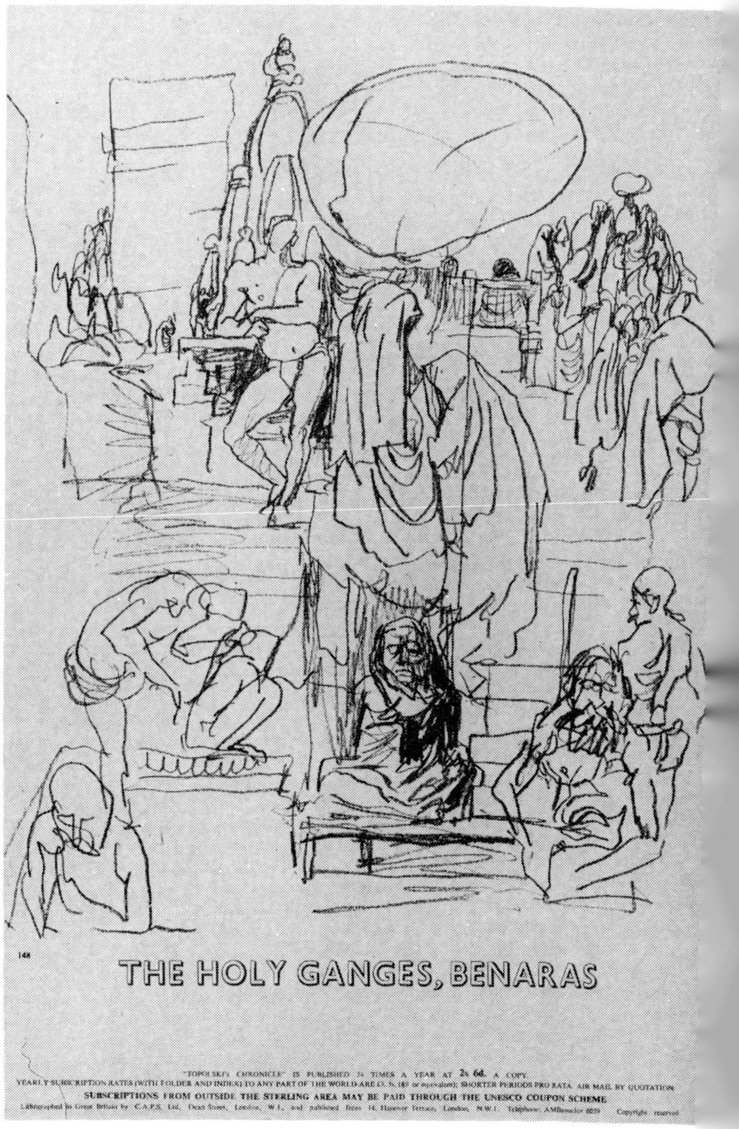

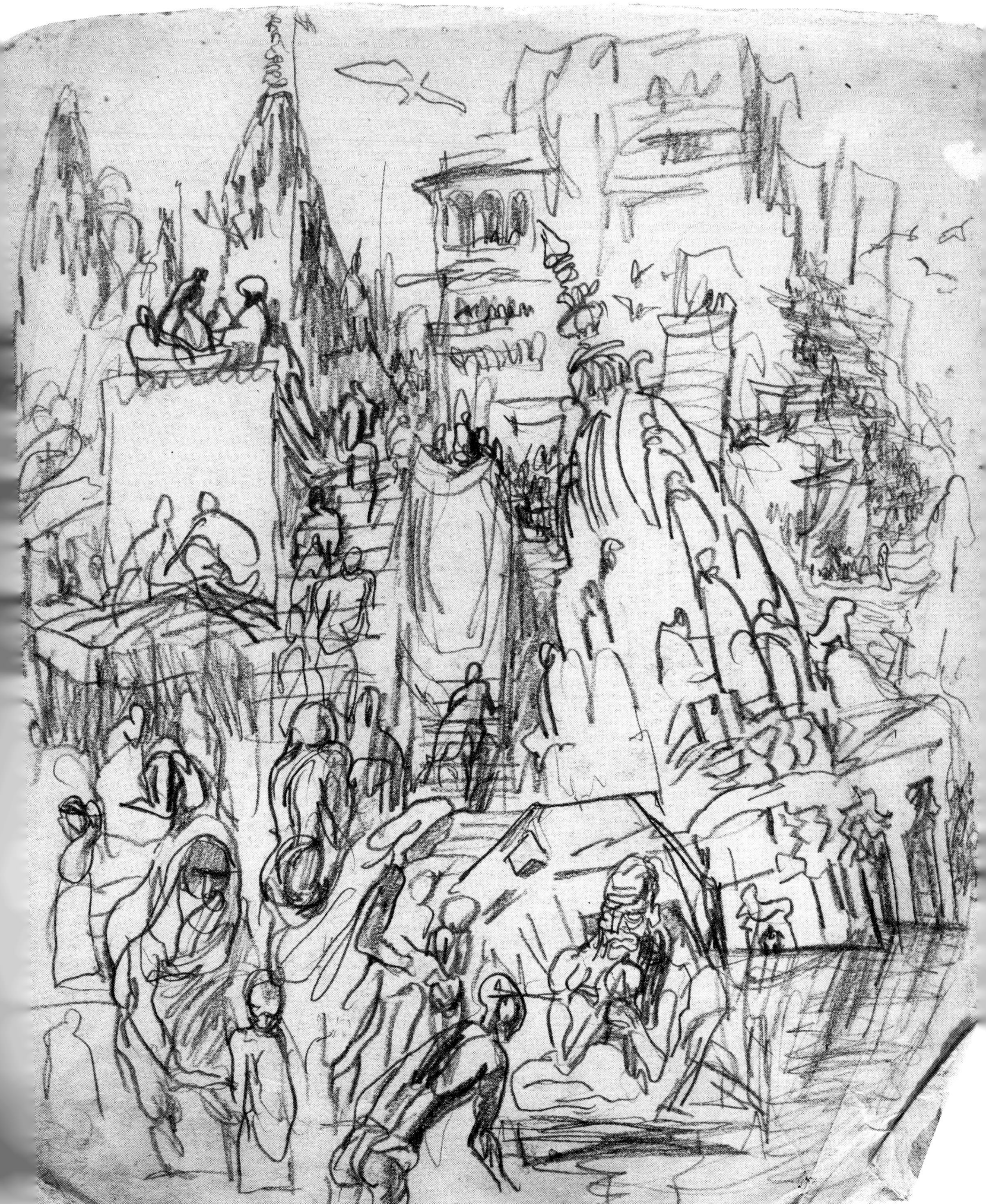

The Holy Ganges, Benares (from *Topolski's Chronicle*)

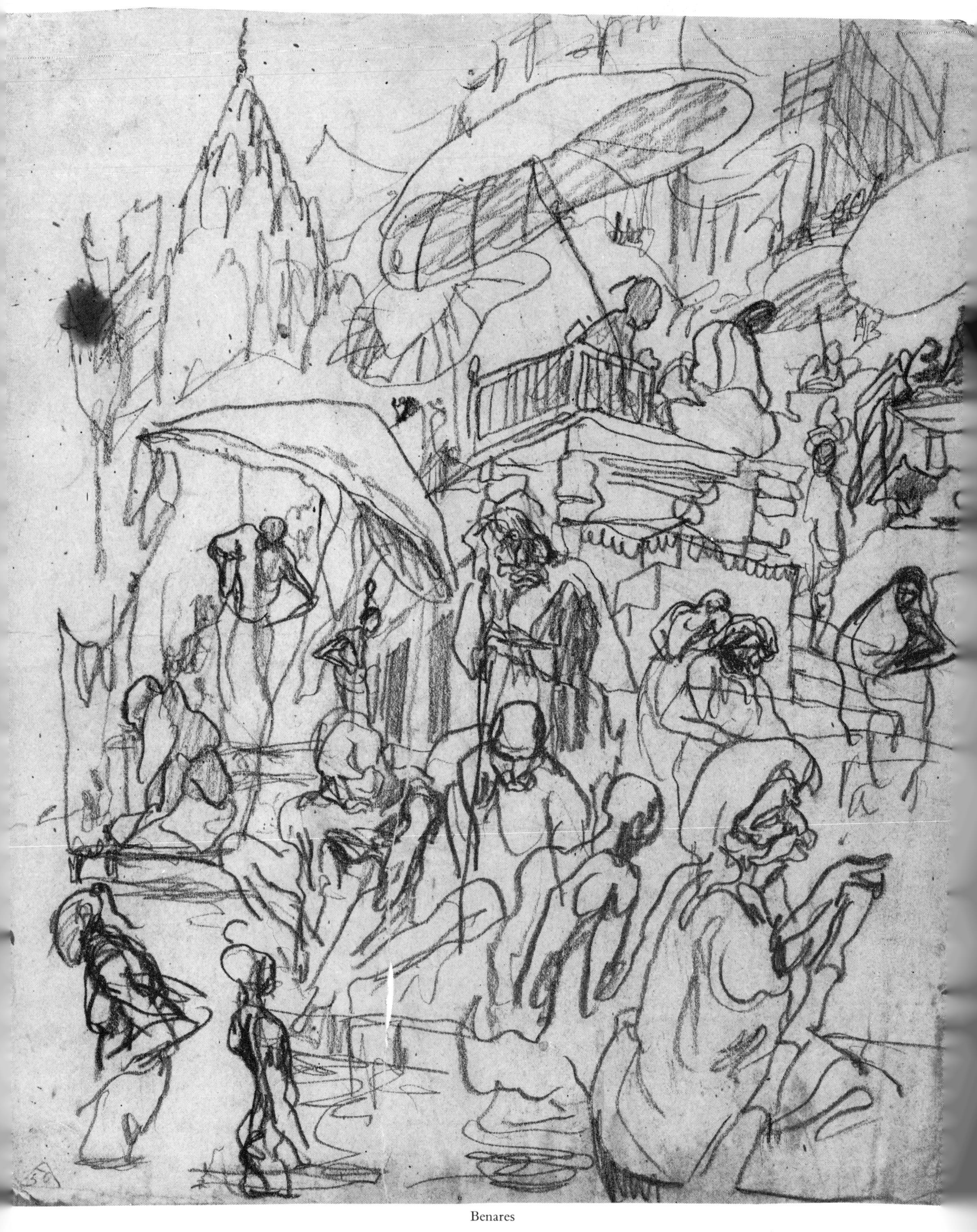

Benares

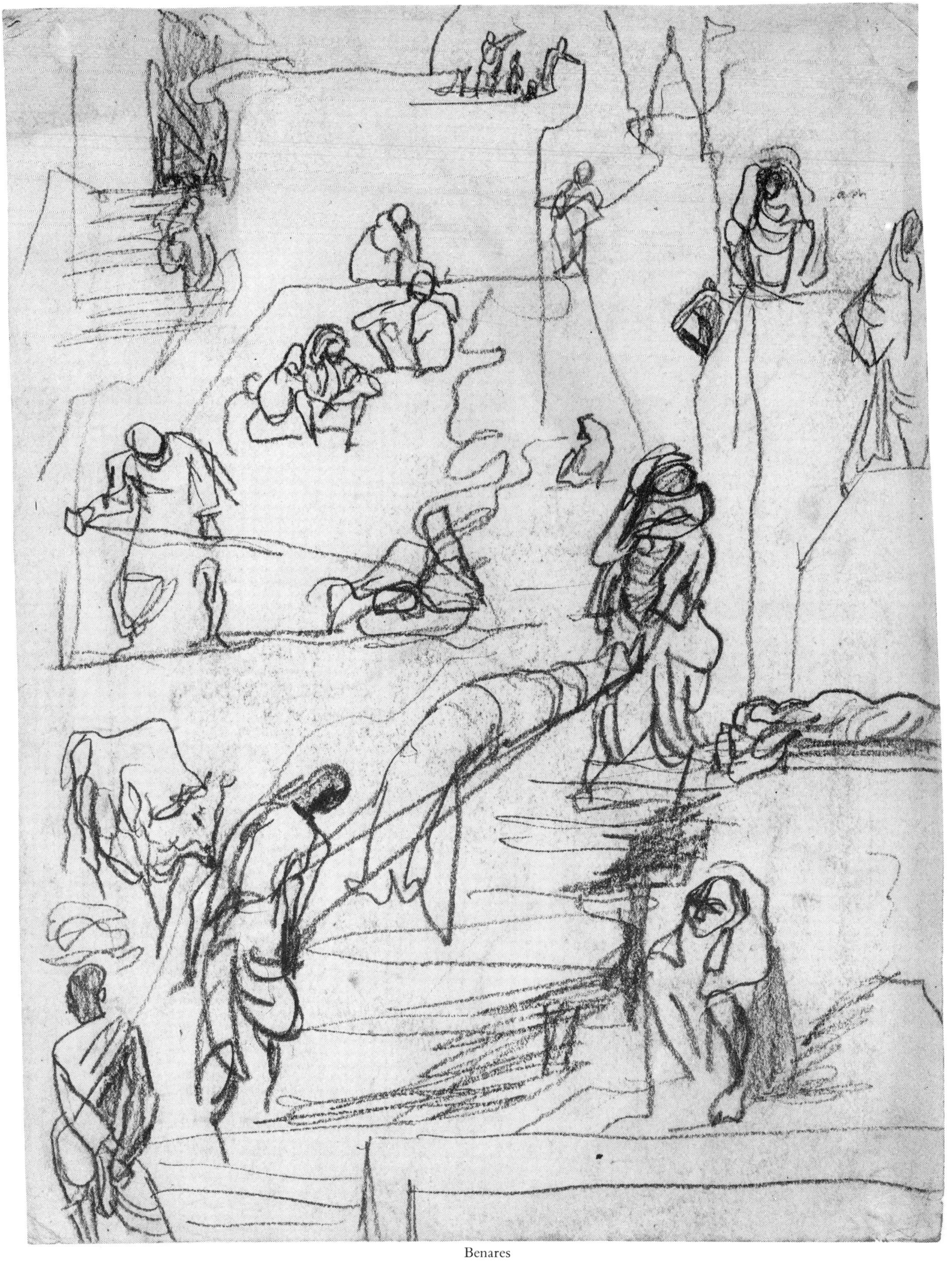

Benares

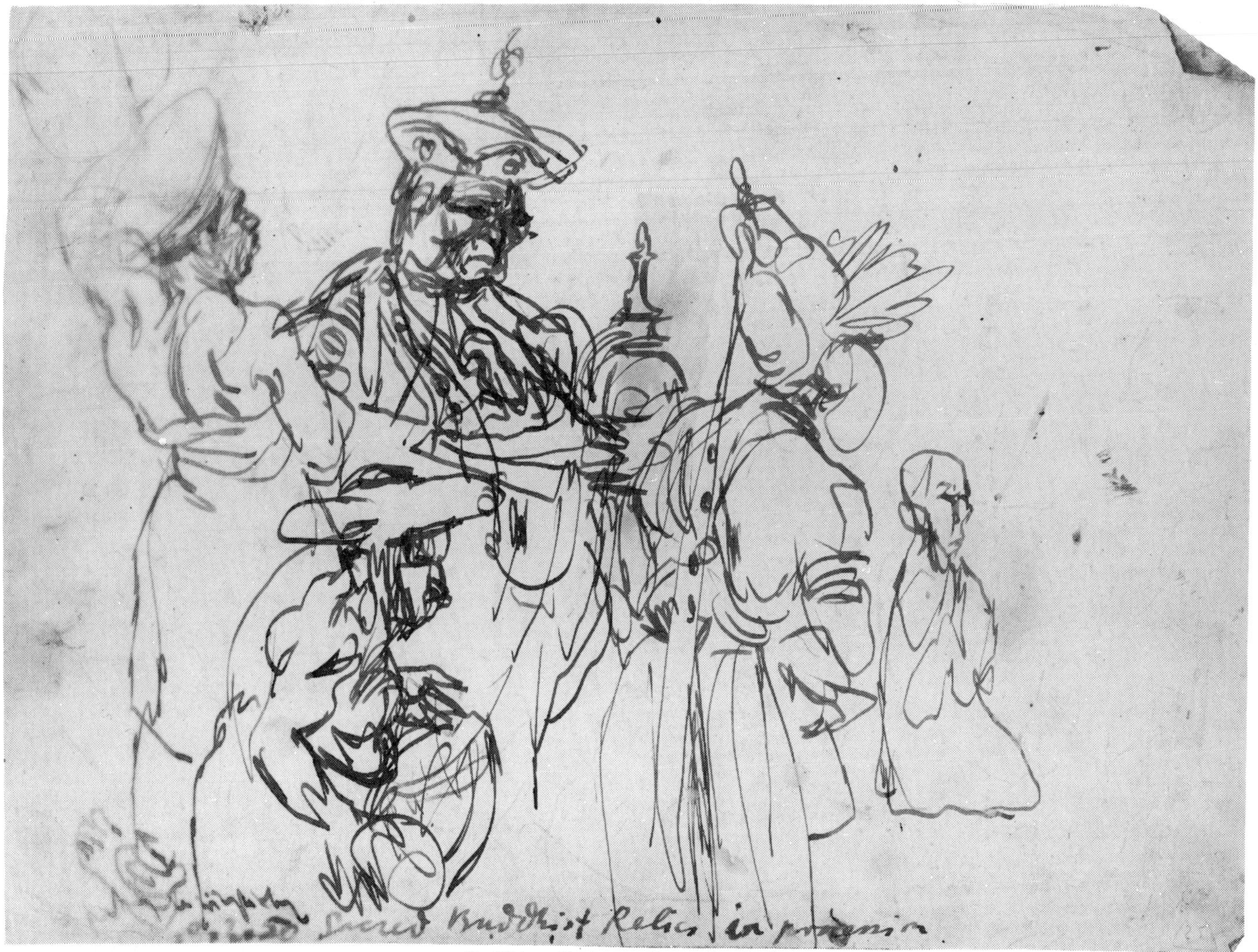

Buddhist relics lent to Burma by Ceylon

training units for the potential (or already partly active?) anti-British Indian force under Subhas Chandra Bose. The inevitable followed: the victory of the Allies directed his escape consequently to India, where in no time, with his worldly cynicism, he metamorphosed into a worthy Hindu monk – so worthy and devout that, his blatant Western shape and colouring notwithstanding, all honours came his way; without him relinquishing, however, his private ways.

He visited London as an American professor, not a Swami. but his bag contained (I was sure it would) his yellow robe (just in case the reverse change might be needed?); and he posed in it for the initiation of my try-out canvas nailed along some 40 feet of damp wall in the future *Memoir* arches; I painted at his side Teresa – small as she is, much reduced – to emphasize the Swami's monumentality.

Further east: into the lands of the jagged peninsula, only a few years back barred by battle-jungles.

First **Burma** put on for me a mainly **diplomatic/political** *performance-monstre* set on Rangoon's landing stage:

A Sacred Buddhist Relic – **the Buddha's Tooth** – arrives in Rangoon aboard a British Cruiser, attended by priests, temple dancers and drummers – the heaviest weapon against Communism.* The clashing yet united ceremonials/ demonstrations of *status-quo* defenders: there shuffle in single file summarily summoned cockade-scarfed Burmese civil servants – paper windmills a-whirl. To face them and to lead in the Tooth there dance off the battleship the Sinhalese temple-performers/musicians – but there cuts in the unsubtle ally: the booming British guns' measured salvoes introduce the Royal Marines' brass in 'God Save the King'. And only then the majestically hatted High Priests of Ceylon carry down the glowing casket – the Tooth – to process triumphantly.

Within **the Shwe Dagon** (Golden) **Pagoda**, up high steps, bare feet soothed by watered courtyard tiles, amongst the stupas – concretized whirlwinds amongst the yellow-robed shaven-headed parasoled monks, with the grace of it all the Tooth seems superfluous.

But at Rangoon's gates, barbed-wire fences – and only a plane over rebel territory takes one to Mandalay.

Burma's civil war. Rebels hold mid-country, **Mandalay** is

*'. . . the threat of Communism has stimulated interest in the Buddhist way of life as the basis of national recovery . . .' (from *Buddhism*, by Christmas Humphreys).

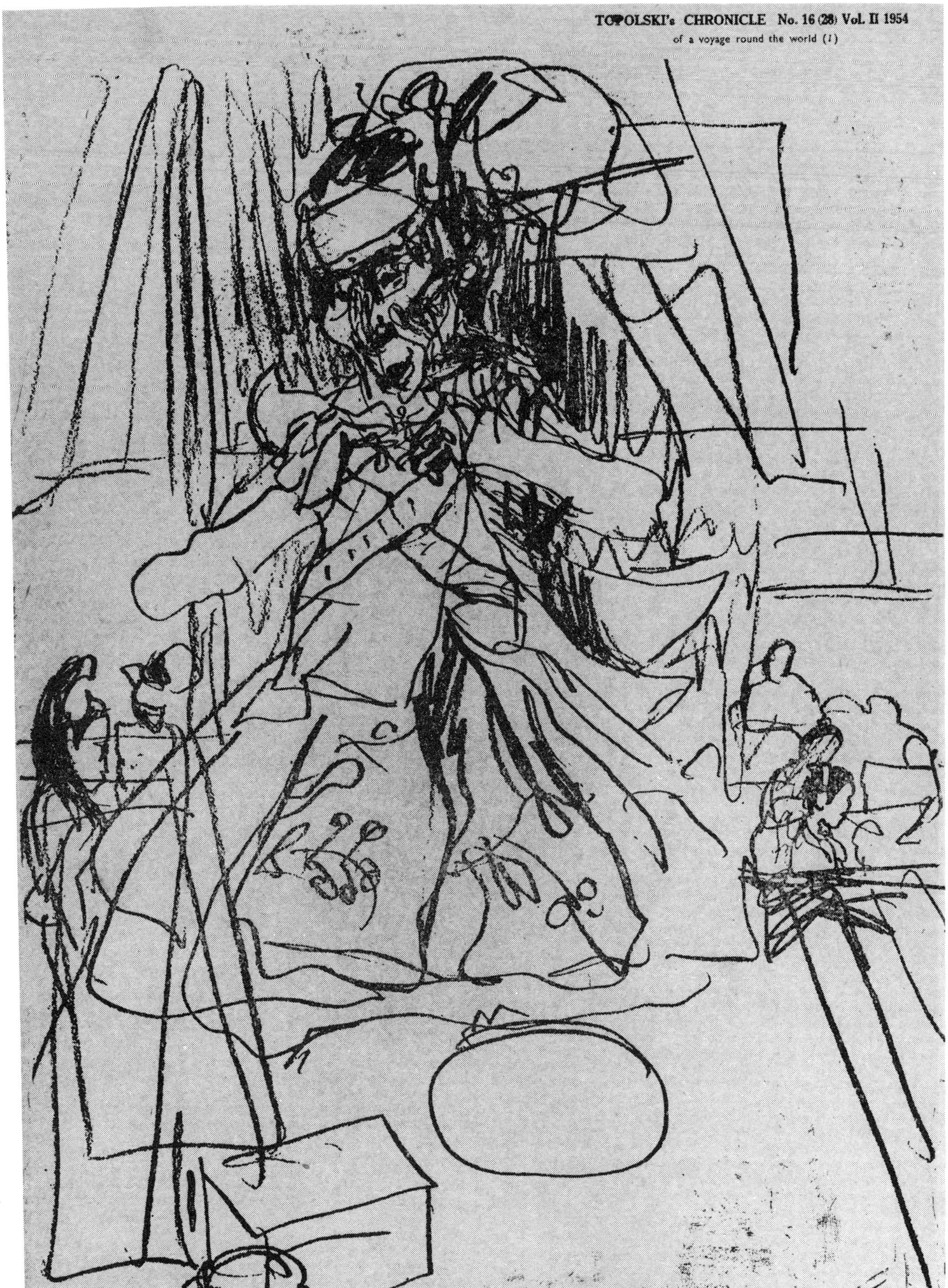

Burma – The great dancer U Po Sein (from *Topolski's Chronicle*)

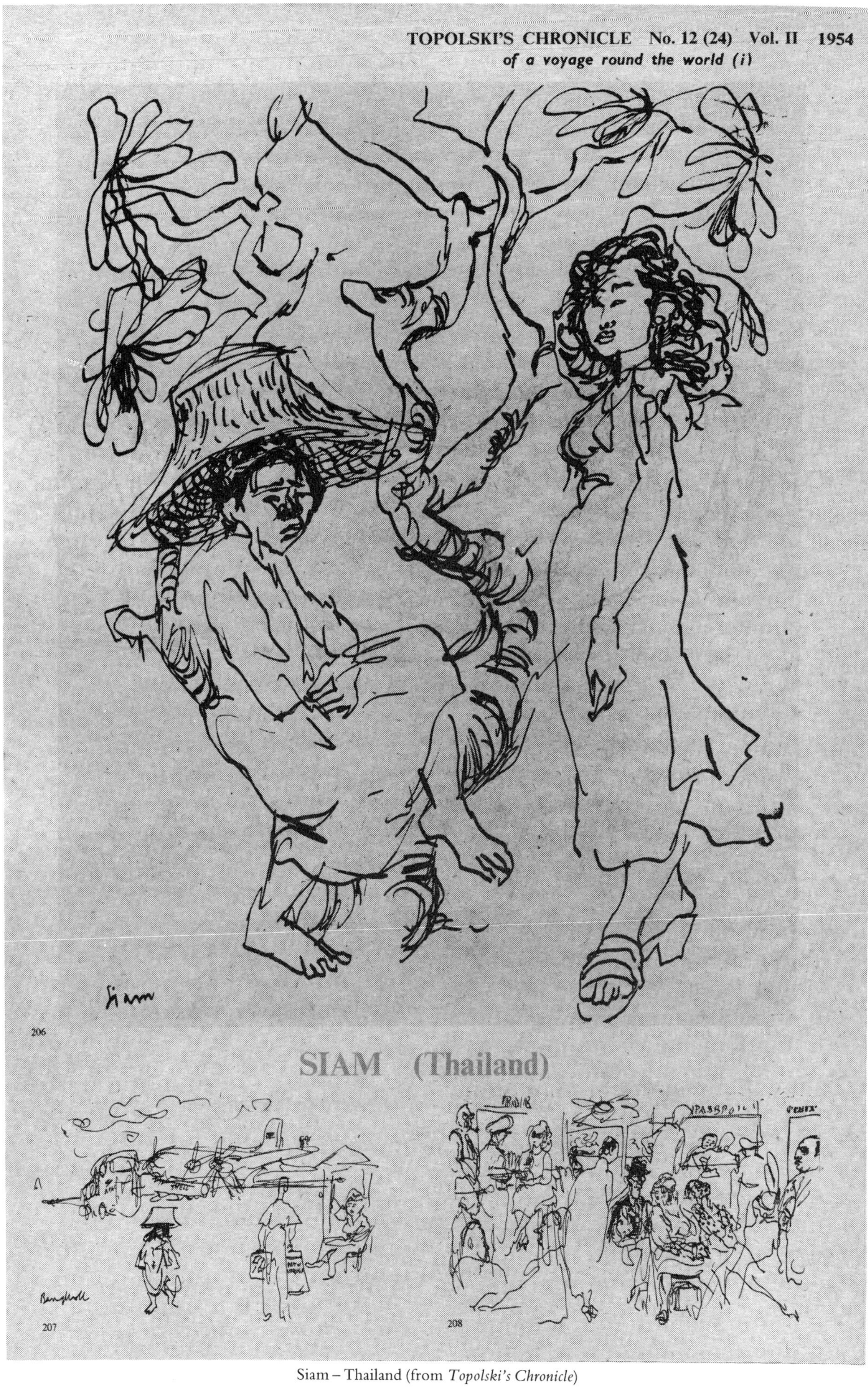

Siam – Thailand (from *Topolski's Chronicle*)

atrociously taken, freed and retaken. Heroes – it seems the coming post-colonial unarmed expansion will choose the match-making Swedes. They fly me in a trading plane to their Mandalay factory over rebel land. The factory functions although only the other day its Swedish bosses/foremen were interrupted by a recurring wave of guerrillas and nearly shot. In the plane's rudimentary interior I spread over bales of dark-blue paper: inner matchboxes must, from time immemorial, be lined in blue – and traditionally Sweden alone produces this paper; so it is shipped across the globe to Rangoon and at its last lap (fighting raging on the ground, communications cut) is flown for the glory of Viking steadfastness.

But no, this scheme cannot deny time. In a shack at the Mandalay air-strip there sits alone, coke in hand, an out-of-the-blue young American. His fierce lost face, his undaunted purpose, his mission . . . There he is, the pathetic Herculean pioneer – a revived Conrad character – Colonialist for the next season.

In **Siam/Thailand**, I had a taste for, and tested, another kind of climax – moving out of the bounds of rigid protocol into the well-being of the multi-national/international **business network**; I deliberately chose the friendly Polish Calcutta 'Bata'-chain representative's introduction to his Bangkok 'Bata' link, the right guide over that city.

I am told it is now quite different – streamlined and dangerous; then in 1950 it was, besides its Buddhist and palatial elements, a steaming cobbled near-village, but underlined with emphatic pleasures.

After damp/hot days, mostly spent under the cold hotel shower, but lyrically punctuated by the floating market and Tachin River life of basket-hatted boating peasantry and their mooning bullocks, or by the bright yellow-robed monks circling round the charming frosted Buddhist edifices, their whole surface textured endearingly with pale-coloured light-scintillating fragmented porcelain,* came the all-important evenings. A chorus of plump, Western *bonhomie* – the big-business representatives – the twentieth-century's gallery of international (white) privileged *roués* – ciceroned me and formed the benevolent background to my comparatively youthful probings.

Their unhurried erotic gourmandise progressed through a night over several dishes.

A China-town striptease theatre, then (regrettably no more) of the naive art *par excellence*, might start the evening. Afterwards perhaps a number of establishments where the shows in the flesh and on small screens belonged to the fullest to the naive strain, while the bellied/unbuttoned executives spread on cushions round me (gradually reddening in the face but expertly rationing their gluttony) would be 'attended' by beautiful boys made up/dressed as girls. And there was, in between, foods and beverages.

The happy orgiasts, declaring their lives in the East *non plus ultra*, would in their fullness be generous: when at the final establishment, sumptuous in comparison with the others, both in décor and pulchritude of the ladies, I, by then befuddled, displayed desire for the company of the more ornamental offering than the one placed at my side, given to one of my hosts – he unconcernedly accorded her to me. And truly this was luxury – the procedure opened with the blissful obligatory cold shower, palatially spacy, hand in hand with the prize I had as it were battled for.

French Indochina. Precisely costumed Annamite matron (black robe slit all the way to the armpits over wide, white trousers), her face an offering of hieratic expanses of paleness formalized by the hair shaven back and made to serve as a black halo, stands calm and impressive against the airport's white-man drab fussiness. But, in Saigon, this dignity will not be sustained by the younger women on view.

French Saigon is chopped into French *colon* divisions, blended in the Rue Catinat: French provincial parade – tree-shadowed, Le Continental-terraced, *pâtisserie*-dotted (one called 'Ismael Fils') – of *outre-mer*-attired ageing dandies bowing hat-sweeping to *mesdames* with children at their coffee-and-cakes tables; *mesdemoiselles* striking poses in swift *pousse-pousses*; and also on wheels: Annamite and Chinese *élégantes*, suave but accessible, on exhibition cycling to and fro or in rickshaws, circled by also-*fauteuil*ed US sailors – one, cycling, floats the back of her split dress behind her, her left hand (coy wrist) steadies her straw cone; supreme ancients under their straw hats; the sin-and-bliss grace of beggar children weaving through the pre-Judgement Days.

Less in harmony, the soldiers: a slovenly sergeant on leave, *Légion Entrangère*, kepi off forehead; Cambodian priests in pairs: French topees, spectacles and cravats. But opulent Saigon personages recumbent in rolling armchairs – behind their stately backs the intent, diligently spinning bare legs, in common rhythm with the swirling fans, wheeling jeeps and all kinds of *moteurs*.

I sit on '*Le Continental*'s' veranda – blue walls hung over with swarms of lizards – under the brutal neon as if inside a reptile house – their heads, stiffly raised, throw shadows towards me, perhaps attempting hypnosis on me as on that fly which, still free, struggles but holds to the spot and doesn't slip away.

Round the corner, over the *Hôtel de Ville*, two-storeys-high Emperor Bao Dai (head cum collar-and-tie), above one-legged veterans of earlier encounters.

As a preliminary to the instant justice of the field of battle, the *Palais de Justice*. I penetrate: my old military bush-blouse gets me through the sentries to **a Court Martial** closed to the public; alone in its empty benches I concentrate on the secrecy of my drawing, not on the case, but even without knowing its substance, which must nevertheless be military, am astonished at the judicial languor at no distance from harried field-brutality. The passive line of officer judges (their high-ranking

*Amazement, when closing on those exotically glittering walls and fingering them, at finding them tightly and all-over embedded with crushed English-looking cups and saucers. I never confirmed authoritatively the informal information that the Siamese at one time imported shipfuls of the cheapest broken English china to enrich their not-so-old temples. The present day's favourite American Saachi-formula artist Schnabel who loads his surfaces similarly, charging a fortune for each, cannot (like a lot of contemporary artists who try to compete with nature's – or man's – realities) match the sweep and effect of this earlier 'coup'.

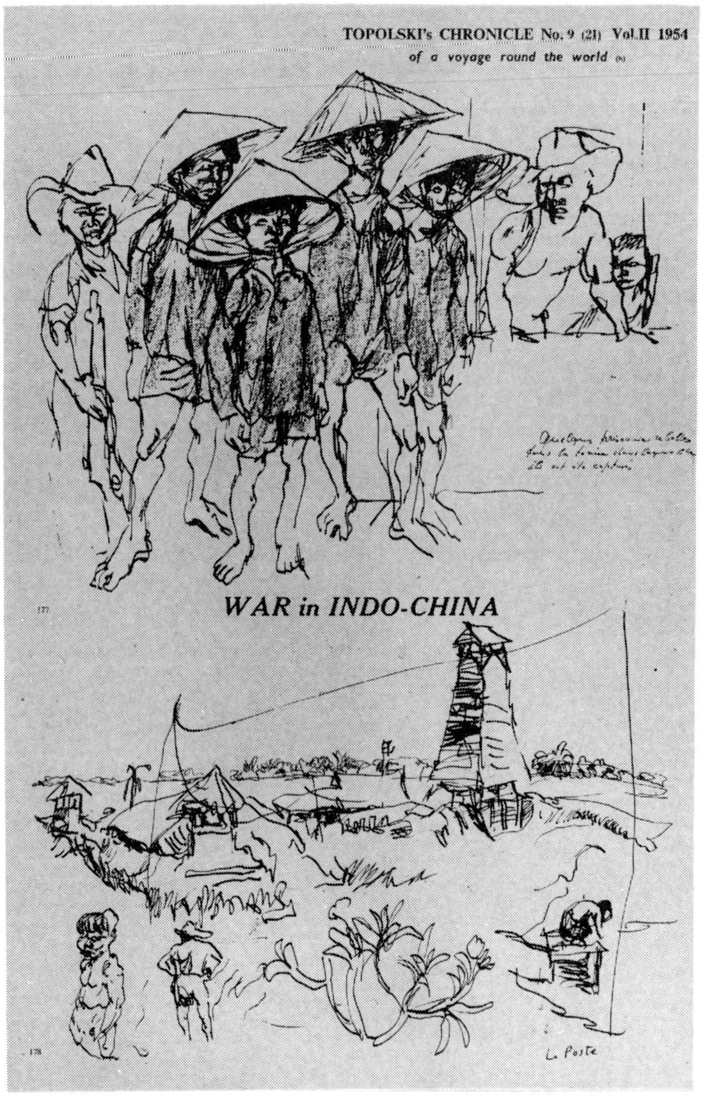

kepis lined up in front of them, some symbolic plaster bust above them); the witnesses: bare-headed soldiers; and the accused: a mere black-pyjamaed young peasant given an interpreter; the armed guards (one, his back to the proceedings, leans out of an open window); and, oddly, black-robed civilian lawyers given to the customary French-oratory vocalities and gestures (bare arm, signifying a short-sleeved shirt under his formal garment, waving at his legal adversary: '*Ne jugez pas, Messieurs, par la sécheresse du fait . . .!*) And, outside in the corridor, ever-waiting (for the accused?), the ever-present ornamentality of young women of Annam, sandals off and feet up on the seats.

Still further penetrations: into the presence of *M. le Haut Commissaire de France en Indochine*, Léon Pignon, *au Palais du Haut Commissariat* where *il tient une conférence de presse*: his civilian entourage, including a Vietnamese, all tie-adorned, ditto a uniformed and bespectacled General at his side, and all strangely un-French; but M. Pignon fashions an open-necked short-sleeved white *blouson-sportif* – without shedding a *débauché* bloatedness, a weary-watchful bruised eye, an upper lip curving askew up-left – *le colon par excellence*.

Quite a distance away, in Saigon's outlying China-town, **Chalon**, *Le Grand Monde*, the routine gambling palace. And halfway back to Saigon, on *Le Boulevard Gallieni* (I think), the vast night-club becomes in the daytime a **military bordel**. Again my semi-military blouse gets me in. An open, sun-sizzling, slumbering-dogs-infested quadrangle packed with men of all the breeds that form the French colonial might: the Foreign Legionaries, French sailors, the Senegalese, the Moroccans, crawled over, driven (hands, knees, feet enclosing, exploring) by temptresses of all of South East Asia.

The surrounding low-roofed wall contains multi-partitioned cubicles open to the centre – a packed bar, fans swishing, amongst them, but all the rest, say fifty of them, roughly curtained for momentary communions/confessionals. To exit, every customer must line up for compulsory expiation/purification with sacred rites of anti-VD injections – I managed to bypass this.

The usual officer-corps *savoir-vivre*: a commandeered country house as **regimental** (or was it battalion?) **headquarters** of the *Infanterie Coloniale* within the hostilities. We, the officers and I, glasses of cognac in hand *après le déjeuner*, stepped on to the veranda to inspect '**quelques prisonniers rebelles**'; below, at its foot, stood five meagre peasant boys – black pyjamas, bare legs (the left leg of one of them bandaged and bloody), conical straw hats – guarded by armed *auxiliaires cambodgiens*.

The stab of outrage in me at this reversal, never imagined possible, from identifying only a few years earlier with my countrymen '*rebelles capturés*' by the Nazis, to being placed among the oppressors. I drew, though; that is, instinctively escaped into my *métier* – witnessing and recording, my justification.

Now into the depths of it. The plantation land has been grafted/dotted with '**Postes**' – rough bamboo stockades (barbed wire and earthworks added) – all locked by *chevaux de frise*. A French device, *Les Postes*, spreading forward as a mode of advance/retreat/defence, but unnervingly vulnerable to being wiped out by the Vietminh, attacking at night.

La Poste de Ba-thou-Cochinchine was a three-towered triangle, a messy patch, tangled with shacks, thick with congested domesticity, transitory in the extreme: the warriors (white, black, brown and yellow) awaiting most probably extinction: the armed men in a besieged defensive-offensive flimsy encampment, the tension rising from night to night – unbearable had it not been for the soothing protection given them by the peasant fatalism of their *congaies* – wives for a while – given by the humble observance of their way of life: the serene (or impassive?) rounds of clothes-mending, clothes- and dish-washing at the stream, loving, baby-bearing and -caring, goat-milking, cooking – always squatted.

The heat of the day, slow-motioned business of anticipating the night: the French and the Legionaries – all stripped to the waist, sandalled, except for the heavily booted *Chef du Poste et son Adjoint*; *le Chef* tiny, thickly haired narrow chest, but his facial growth elaborately trimmed into a martial pattern, all topped by the highest well-looked-after insignia-marked forage-cap; his second-in-command – another breed: large, fat

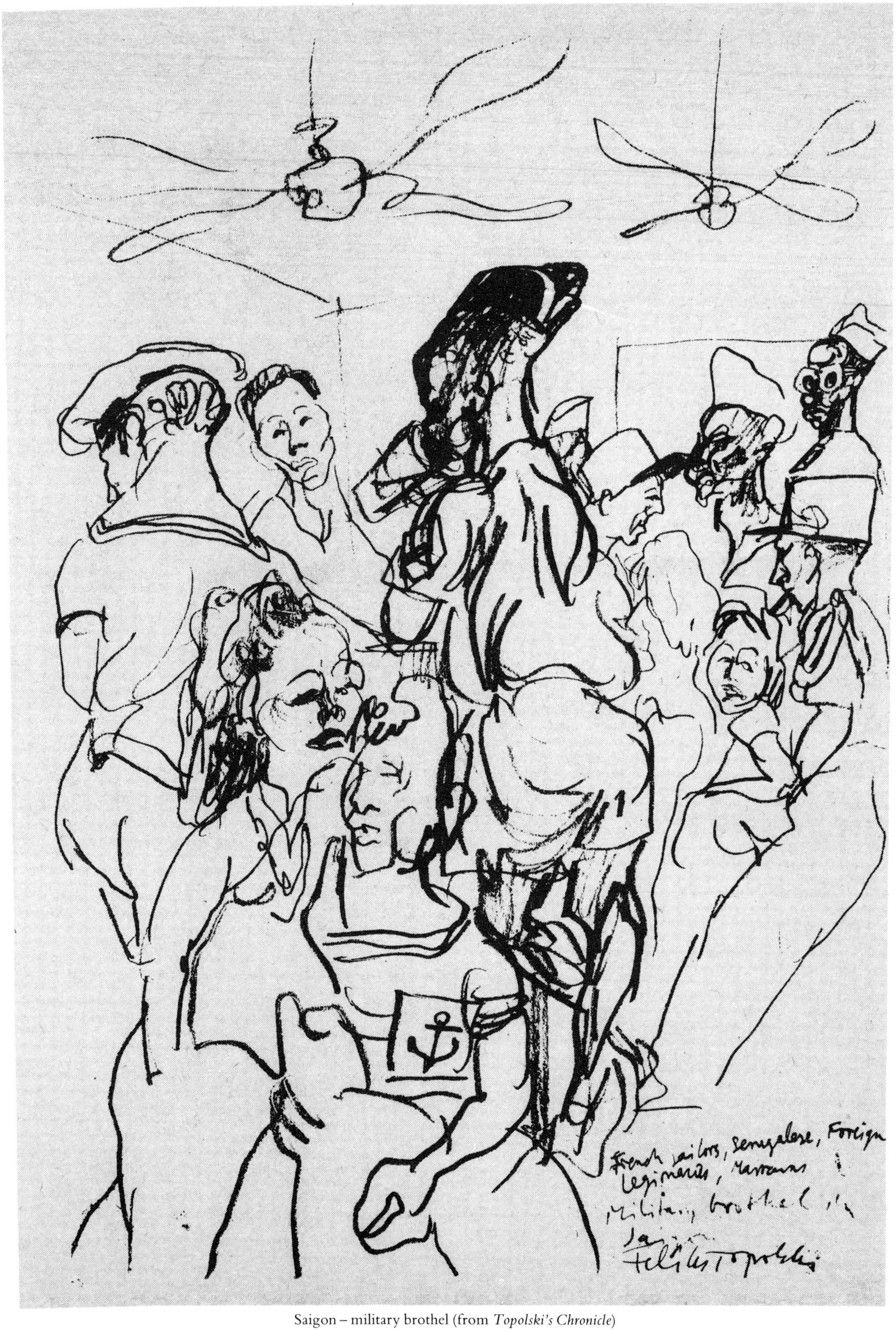

Saigon – military brothel (from *Topolski's Chronicle*)

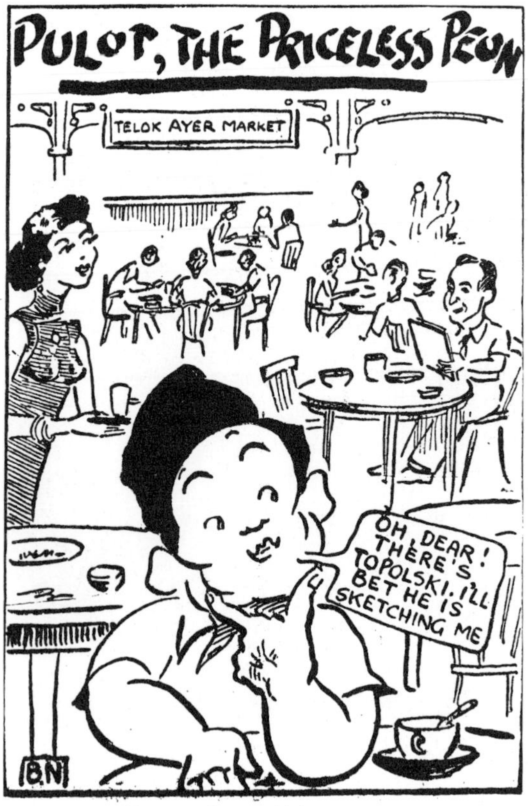

Cartoon from a Singapore paper

and pipe-embellished. '*Le Soldat Grosset*' calligraphed over a doorway announces a thin, pensive blond boy under a wide-brimmed regulation hat, faithfully attended by *sa poponne cambodgienne*. *Les Tirailleurs Cambodgiens* and *les Sénégalais* labour over the barbed trenches, their weapons perched at readiness against a tree trunk.

But *La Bande Noire*, an auxiliary élite, dark glasses their mark, bristle with weapons and hellishness when embarking on a mission, killers and robbers that they are, thus fearless and merciless – exude abomination.

The '**Malaya Emergency**' – and again, the recorder's dilemma after the years on the side of clean war: before, the just cause and glorification of the European underground against German terror-occupation; now, the issue at least confused when the guerrillas of Malaya, called officially 'CT' (Communist Terrorists), face the colonial troops. But to witness, one has to fall in with the situation.

The long-boned **Scots Guards**, stylishly variegated in dress, sportingly and off-handedly – the last imperial stand. They tower above the **7th Gurkha regiment** – whose jeep patrol, led by the armoured car of the 4th Hussars, carries me along a jungle road, guns bristling; they halt/run/file out into the bush . . .

Other guardians – the **Police Field Force**, detailed for my safety – get me into a kampong's interrogations and in front of a prison-cage of 'detained suspects'. And this does not end my eye-witness's private purgatory: a large, turbaned Sikh MP presents to me '**surrendered Enemy Personnel**' in the rudimentary shape of a single 'Chinaman', vigilant but resigned under a roughed-out military cap held by his ears, red star sewn in front: its top – all my disturbing associations bursting out anew – squared in the manner of centuries of Poland's tradition.*

At the end of the trek of danger, **Kuala Lumpur** in 1950: still a jungle slum village except, as everywhere, for the botanic gardens, and the sedative, faultless King's House, the residence of the High Commissioner. **Sir Henry Gurney**, an unperturbed British Empire Pro-Consul, a richly providing host: within the Residence, a presentation Honours ceremony gathering the worthies of both worlds (His Highness the Sultan of Selangor and wife amid hatted Englishwomen) and their defenders (the Subedar Jaibahadur Lumbu of Gurkhas obtaining an MBE) – all costumed (their wardrobes extensive) as prescribed; he, his Anglo-Saxon moustachioed length mid-bulging gently over narrow legs, carrying impressively the white ceremonial topee, ribboned decorations and sword.

But in the daily mufti and defying safety, he would take his house guests, myself included, to an evening meal in the town market's Chinese stalls, or, true to the eternal tradition of patronage (none of today's bureaucratic stiffening), would cosset me to sketch out lifesize full-length images of the country's beauties (Malayan, Chinese, Indian) on the wall of his formal study – to be hidden or disclosed by curtains at the pull of a string.

The ending seems repetitious: soon, Gurney was killed in a jungle-road ambush.

Still **the Crown Colony of Singapore**, it had in residence His Excellency the Rt. Hon. Malcolm Macdonald as **The Commissioner-General for the UK in South-East Asia**. My introduction was to him and so I stayed at the Bukit Serene Johore Bahru Palace of the Sultan, his for the duration. And so on my first evening I sat at the dinner table, amongst such (men only) company, starting on my left: the Hon. Mr Jumabhoy of India, the Hon. Dato Wan Idris – Prime Minister of Johore, Mr Lee Wee Nam – Singapore millionaire, the Hon. Justice Laville, Dr Warlick, Dato S. Q. Wong – member of Johore State Council, Sir John Kotelawala of Ceylon, Malcolm Macdonald, Mr Saravanamuttu.

Exhilarating ride over the Causeway to Singapore port: the vessels of all times, West-East, wobbling/flapping/puffing/bouncing against the sea-front – exhibit of all Asia, of all its races; of vigour/lethargy, of deeds/misdeeds – through (as expected) Chinese application, Malay repose, Sikh surveillance – to the Chartered Bank gathering thick-waisted calf-displaying whites, to Raffles's revolving door at which, faced with the entering **Lady Mountbatten**, I embark on

*One more confrontation on the side of the victors – years later in a lull early in Israel's tensions.

Marion in a chic St Laurent safari blouson and I in my usual old bush-blouse led by our guides, some military, into a rural Catholic Convent during our tourist-reportage explorations.

The entry – and this theatrical confrontation: an old nun (the prioress?) bars our way in an 'Over my dead body' stance, eyes blazing, arms outstretched, as if in anticipation of crucifixion – the tableau of desperate saintliness, unchanged for centuries in the Holy Land's clashes of creeds and conquests, and of martyrdoms at the hands of infidel soldiery.

Our group, led by the obviously high-ranking Marion and I, appeared as fitfully – ever-anticipated takeover – expulsion – rape: the end of their bastion. But to us, then, the Israeli uniform was of the forces of good, and we – the people of the sixth decade of the century – laughed and calmed the nun.

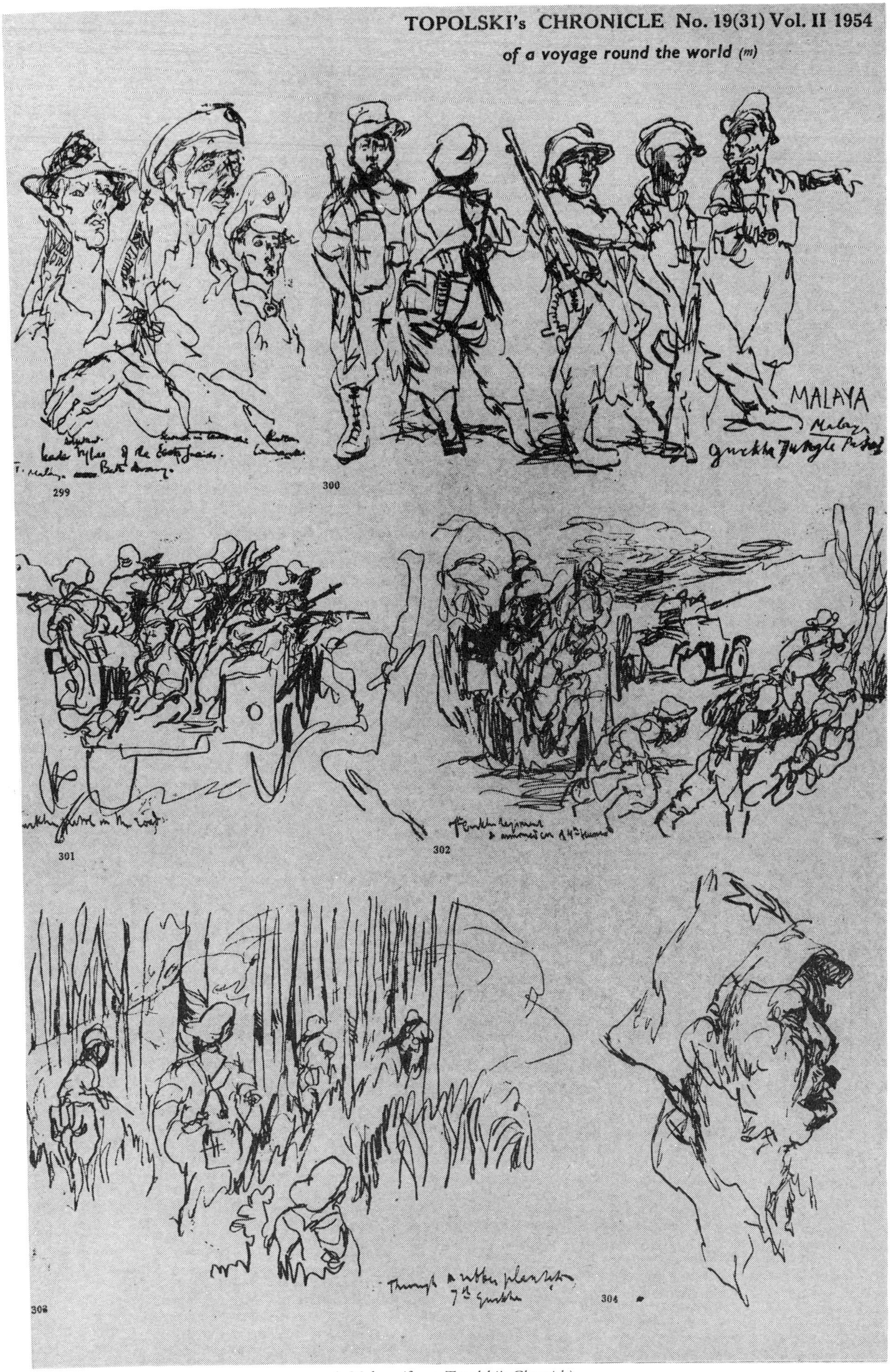

Malaya (from *Topolski's Chronicle*)

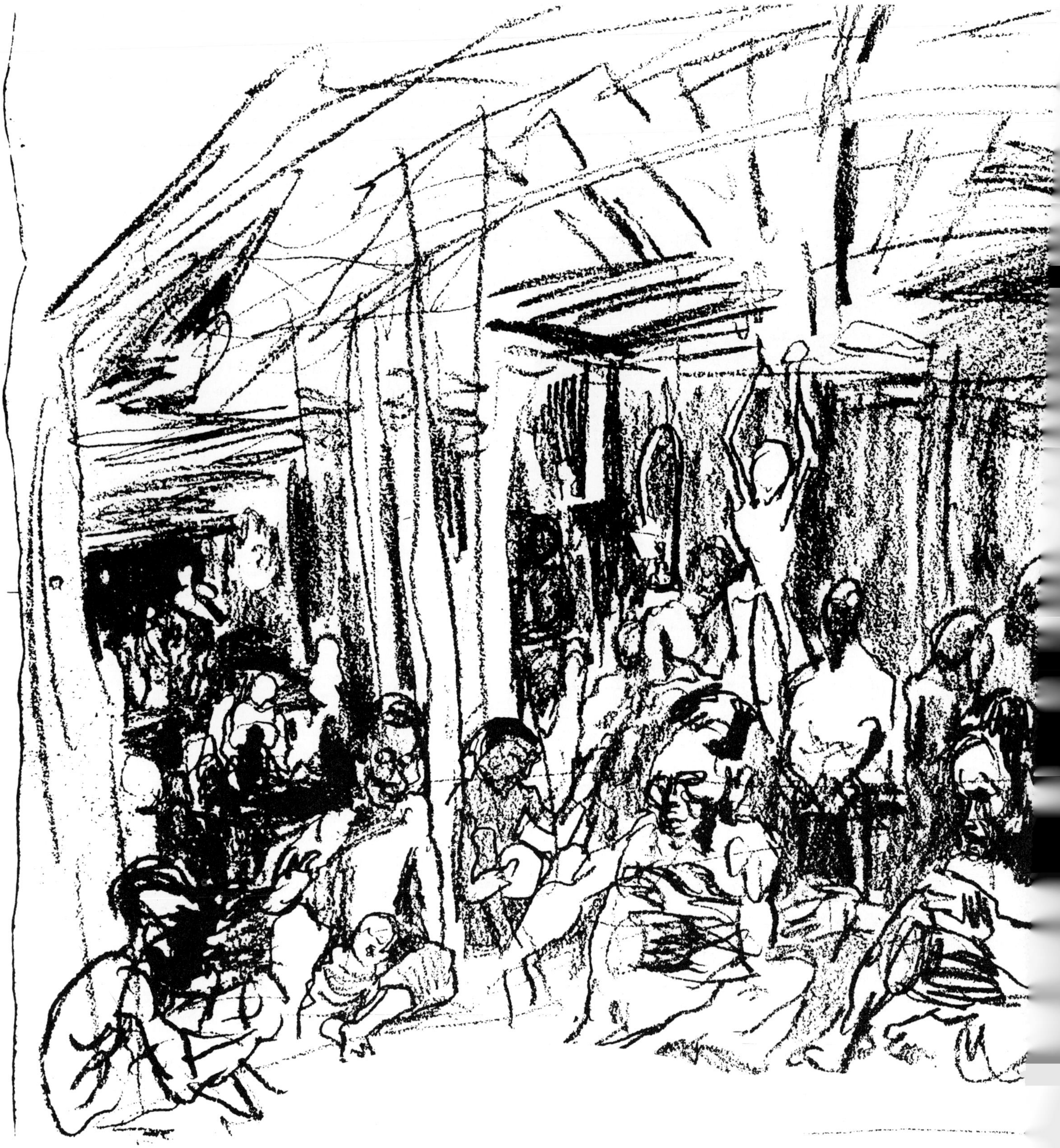

Sarawak – Long House (from *Topolski's Chronicle*)

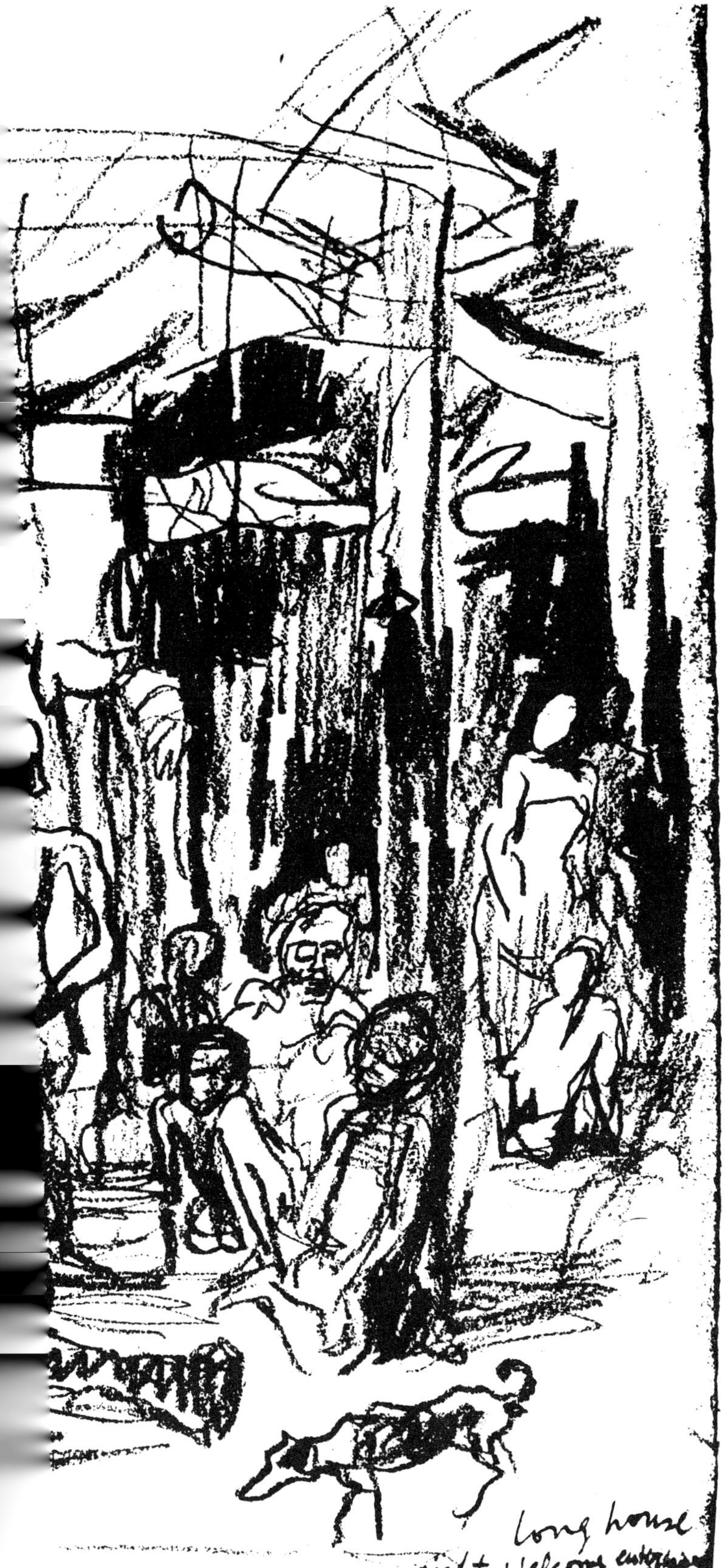

joyful greetings, oblivious to her being the spearhead for an attending pack of notables.

With the dark, the lace- and sarong-draped Malay beauties recede, to be replaced by still more beautiful transvestites Chinese-robed slimly/tightly to mould their manhood; these parades lead into purely Chinese mute/sinister passages, with, on their doorsteps – classically paired – cowering old protectresses/duennas in black (single long black plait) and their bright-pyjamaed merchandise. But round the corner, a Chinese baby-ridden family – under a carbide lantern, crumbling stairs for the mounting young; the old, the very old, in the circle by right.

But Malcolm's range was wide – further evenings with him, his conversation and company, unpredictable. And later, after the Festival of Britain, when most of its artists' contributions were dustbinned, he had my *Cavalcade of the Commonwealth*, all of its 60 feet by 20 feet, placed in Singapore's **Victoria Memorial Hall**, its governing assembly room.

With Independence the painting was taken down, supposedly only for cleaning, but there was a rumour that it may have seemed to Singapore's new rulers too 'imperial' in character. This counter-balanced a London paper's outcry when the Festival opened that, as it detected, the tone of my painting was 'derogatory to Britain': their reporter pointed to a 'torturing the natives' sequence – this was a group of Dyak children on a jetty, diving off it, based on sketches drawn in Sarawak; and to 'symbolic gravestones of British Colonialism' – again elements from my sketches, drawn in the Free Territory of Kowloon, of China/Hong Kong borderstones.

Among the few remaining pockets of the wilds – **Sarawak**. In the roadless depth of the jungle – there may even flash through the orang-ginger – on a narrowly winding river, the Batang Lupar (the only means of communication between Kuching and inland **long-houses**), a tiny motor boat manned by two Malays, perched on by two reddened flabby torsos, **Tom Harrison**★ and myself. The jungle around and above screams, sings, echoes – and we two argue quarrelsome/gossipy over girls and unresolved jealousies in Café Royal and Soho circles.

But days of inaccessibility emerge at the river's bend with a trading compound (first shirt and first bottle of 'arak' for a Dyak) – Chinese. The Chinese have created their business empire embracing Asia, and slices of the West – without armed conquest.

Back in Kuching Tom, a lot of whisky in him, swings his stationwagon between his museum, the Club, the Government House, with two Dyak-girls slavishly bundled/hidden on the floor of the vehicle – in reserve.

For protocol reasons I move for the rest of my stay on to the hospitality of the Governor. **The Government House**: yet another lovely/modest colonial structure, in which still

★Tom, dropped on the Japanese-occupied swampy bush, raised a loose head-hunter Dyak force; now, barefooted *persona grata* in **long-houses**, is welcomed ceremonially in one after another: customs costumes war-paint sword-dances unaffected yet by 'civilization'.

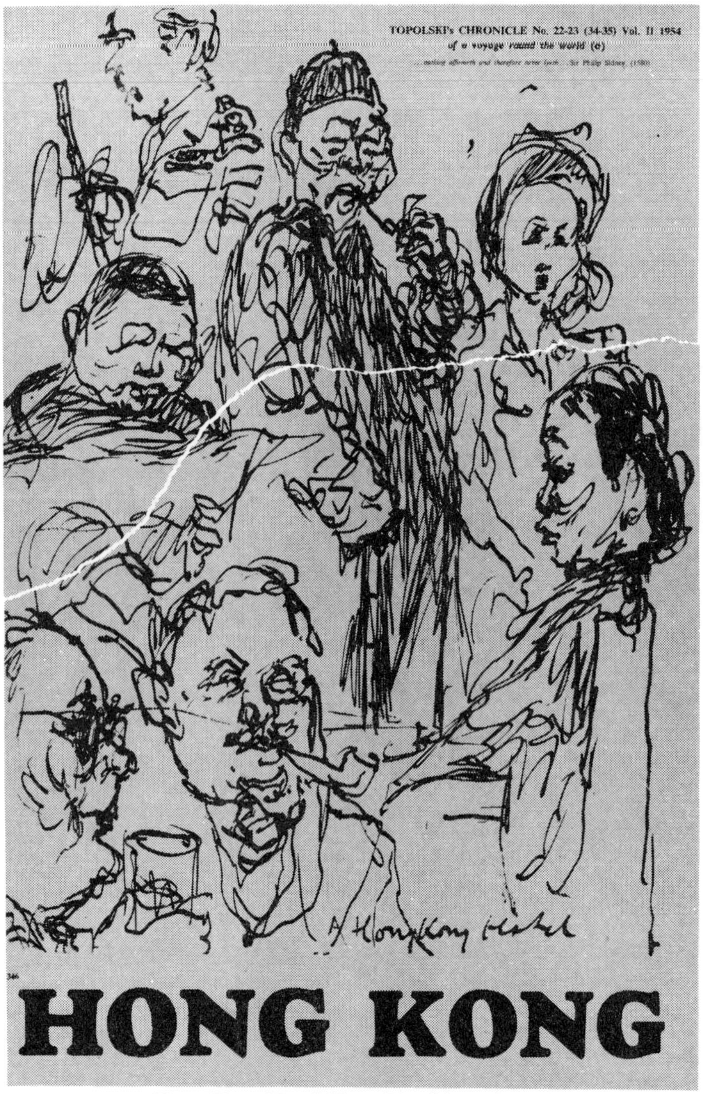

Hong Kong Hotel (from *Topolski's Chronicle*)

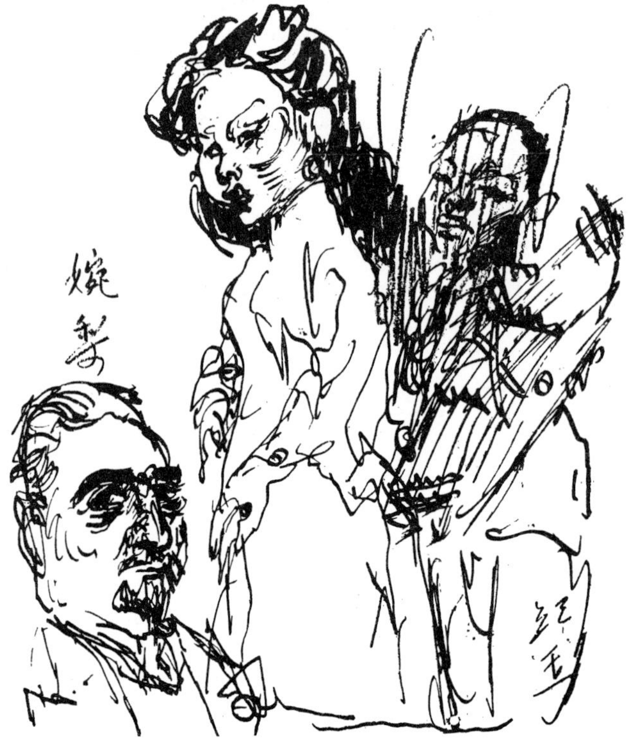

Macao: Herman Machado and singsong girl (from *Topolski's Chronicle*)

hang portraits of the three White Rajas. Three generations and a complete tale: Sir James the romantic **conqueror** (loose cravat, flowing hair), Sir Charles the hard-headed **consolidator** (stiff high collar, buttoned-up suit), the third a spent ceremonial **figurehead** (droopy-eyed, flabby-featured over gaudily decorated uniform).

Histrionics at the expensive purchase of a head-hunter's weapon and the troublesome dispatch of it home. The London junk shops, full then – on my return – of exotic souvenirs including those swords costing next to nothing – overflowing with objects gathered by generations of colonials now reduced in circumstances and in space, sweated out on to the uncurious market. I concluded that my traveller's collections should be made only back in London.

This tight air-hop on to rocky precipices massed and soaring from the seas, seemingly perilous, presages the chaotic discordances of **Hong Kong** island.

Han Suyin, a hospital doctor then, and Morrison, Far Eastern correspondent of *The Times* (prototypes for her novel *A Many-splendoured Thing*) invite me to dinner and get angry when, given a lift by a young lieutenant from Kowloon New Territories, I feel bound to bring him to our table.

There abound: Chinese magnates and European ladies repatriated from Shanghai; British administrative, garrison, press and business gentlemen; international adventurers; American sailors. Also **General Morris 'two gun' Cohen**, the late Sun Yat Sen's bodyguard and an original member of the Kuomintang. Also Sikh policemen searching travellers from Macao; gaming and 'ill-repute' houses; exhibitions of Chinese art; floating restaurants; Russian *émigrés*; junks; feverish crowds; landscapes of Hakka women shaded by their black-cloth-fringed hats.

On the mainland's edge, marked by stones proclaiming 'Anglo-Chinese Boundary 1898', **His Excellency the Governor** of Hong Kong, standing upright in a jeep, receives/reviews the Ceremonial Parade of the 40th Infantry Division. There are a Scottish brass band, 'official guests' and the usual awkward, outlandish (for the Asians, I am sure) drill. At the ensuing Reception one hears all round: '**A show of strength** all right – it'll give "them" something to think about . . .'

Macao: the worldly and hospitable editor of *Noticias de Macau*, Hermann Machado Monteiro, dines me – a sing-song girl, Pui-Cheng, with her servant assisting – demonstrates gambling, opium-smokers, young toughs, the faithful in the Cathedral, the classical theatre and the *Beco da Felicidade*.

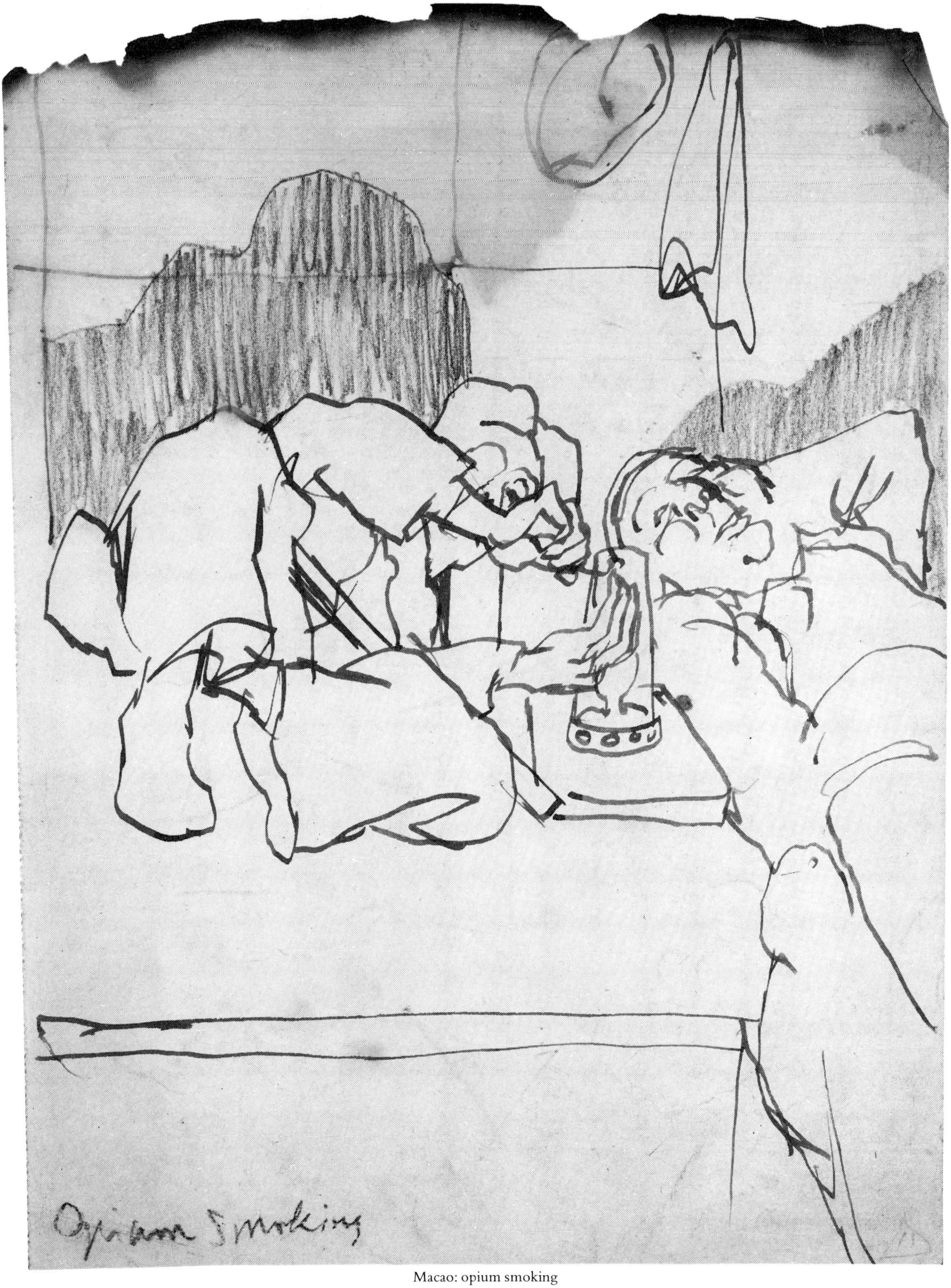

Macao: opium smoking

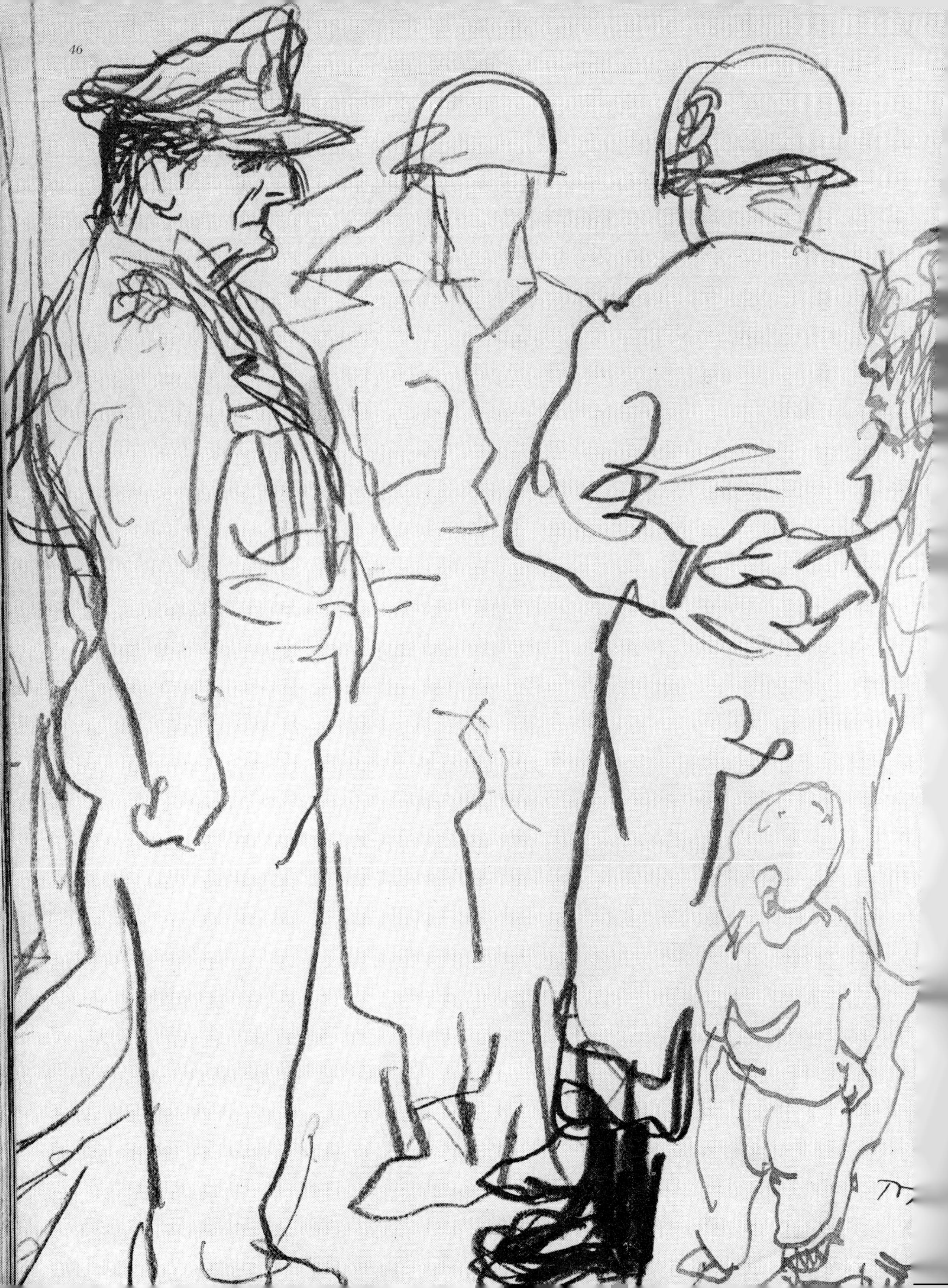

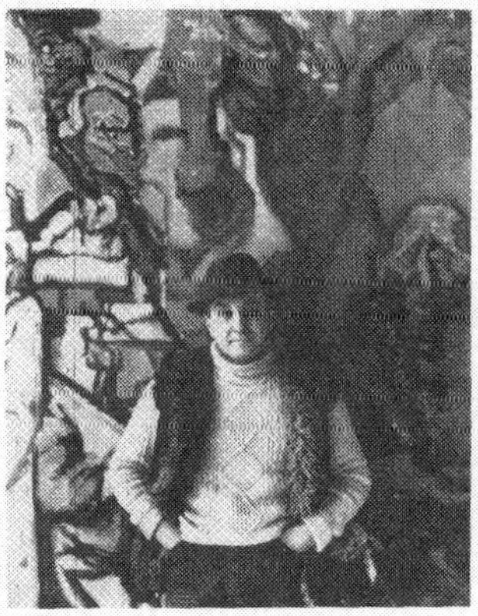

トポースキー

Of Topolski

トポースキーのこと

by Kobayashi

小　林　雄　一

一九五〇年の四月だった。当時イギリス労働党の機関紙デイリー・ヘラルドの特派員だったヘッスル・ティルトマンから"よろしく"たのまれてトポースキーをむかえた。なるほど、ちょっと変っている。ネズミ色フラノのシングルに茶色の皮チョッキ、半編み上げの黒靴で、アメリカ人新聞記者の多いプレス・クラブに現われたのだから、そう思ったのもムリではありますまい。

表通りの東京見物は外務省のある若い人が案内した。たまたま、この二人がこれから出かけるところに行きあって驚いたね。トポースキーは白いズダ袋——あの水夫や水兵などが自分の持ち物を入れてかつぐやつに似て少し小ぶりなの——を重そうにひっさげていた。たずねると、スケッチ用の道具一式と写真機やフィルムが入っているという。画家はスケッチ帳小わきにブラリ出かけるものとばかり思ってたわたしはちょっと面くらった。写真機のことをきくと彼はスケッチと同時に必ず写真をとっておき、あとで画にするときこの写真と照合するということだった。その後わたしは彼の画がすべてこうしたスケッチからテーマごとに選ばれた材料を組み立てたものであることを知った。

夜の生活、京都見物、特殊な美術品の鑑賞など厄介な方の案内をわたしが引受けさせられた。夜の見物にぜひ近藤日出造君の同行をねがいたいと思ったのだが、どうしても連絡がつかないでそれができなかった。近藤君を彼にひき合すこともできなくて残念だった。そうした案内の一つのときこんなことがあった。彼が着いてからまだ三日目ぐらいだったかな。ある実業家の秘蔵する漆器をみせてもらうというので夕方の五時にプレス・クラブで落合うことになっていた。ところが、トポースキーが現れないのである。六時が過ぎたのでとうとうその実業家にあやまって、日をかえてもらうことにした。それからしばらくして彼は大へんなご機嫌で帰ってきた。話の模様だと、時間待つ間にぶらり近所かいわいの見物にと有楽町の新興街に出たところ、おでんとカストリがひどく気に入って約束をすっかり忘れてしまったらしい。似た様な話はティルトマンが桜見物かたがた箱根へ彼を案内したときにもある。ティルトマンは勝手のちがう日本旅館に泊りたくなかったのか、日帰りのつもりでいた。ところが箱根をまわって熱海へ出るとトポースキーはどうしても日本旅館へ泊るというので彼を残して帰ってきた。彼はあくる日の真昼間、ヒゲもあたらない顔を満足そうにほころばせて帰ってきた。

浮世画風のストリップに出た女の姿、とくにえりあしを非常にきれいだと感心していた。二日間の京都旅行も"まるでイタリアへ一週間の休暇に行けるくらいかかった"と高

23

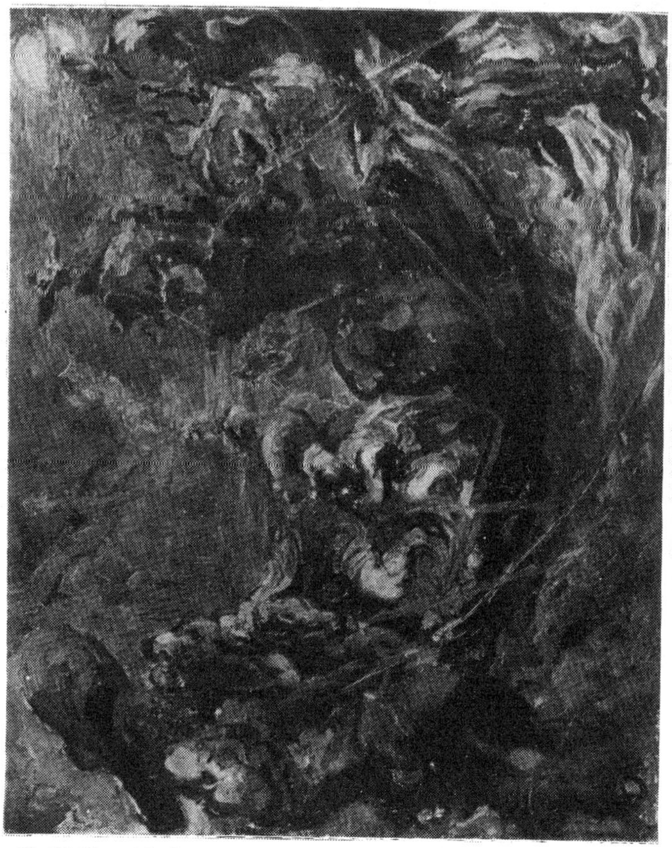

Pages from a Japanese art paper

Tokyo 1950. The city/the country brought to its knees. Women, stricken, plentiful; old men all uniformal: black Inverness cape/hat/cap; below, dingy bedraggled khaki hosts of war-veterans, war-crippled, war-lost, a-begging; close to the ground: a trapping/tripping web on the move of crawling, searching, pouncing mucky war-orphans; head-and-shoulders above: girth-astounding, the US occupation men.

Jaunty-hatted **General MacArthur** makes his daily appearance (tanks- and baseball-supported) – his Nippon democracy, black lounge-suit/tie/collar/spectacles, applying itself in a circle at the new House of Councillors.

At **Yoshiwara**, not yet struck out by US puritanism, protracted undressing–dressing in symmetrical (obi – kimonos, kimonos – obi) demonstrations carry on throughout the nights.

But: Ginza palpitates with many-storeyed commerce. But: Mr **Yuichi Kobaiashi** of the *Yomiuri Shimbun* newspaper waits for me, first thing on the first morning (how? why?) with an engagement for a series of written and drawn pieces. But: an exhibition of Westernized paintings – even the nudes are blonde and round-eyed. But: schoolboys in black brass-buttoned uniforms play baseball, yet bend down at the Yasokuni Shrine to their war dead. But: Hugh Hessell-Tiltman, the most senior foreign correspondent in Japan, is back and sits with me at the Western-style Tokyo night-club.

When in 1950 in Tokyo
under beau MacArthur's course in democracy
on the first of May
defiant bunched **Nippon Marxists**
red flags flapping
sang (in Japanese) the *Internationale*
the Imperial Palace in the background
short in black drab
so many Prometheuses and Chirons
challengers – meek but standing their ground,
I felt the dampness in my eyes
(caused by the ducts having conducted tears from tear-glands
caused by emotion triggered off habitually when in the face of
a stand against odds
caused by my outsider's deficiency in side-taking
resulting in the side of the stands being immaterial),

while
the US sub-pro-consuls

Opposite: Japan: General MacArthur (from American *Vogue*)

★ （第三種郵便物認可）　昭和27年9月23日　夕刊　讀賣

アフリカの王様とイギリス

狂わぬ民主主義の心情

えと文　フェーリークス・トポースキー

保護領ベチュアナランドの統治者で追立てをくったセレツェ・カーマが、自分の相続権と英国政府の法的侵害について名調子の弁舌を揮う。ベチュアナランド諸種族の長老たちの代表団は

ーフェビアン主義か、あるいは自由党的伝統ないしは分派キリスト教の古強者連、ただの労働者と左派知識人。色とりどりの英連邦人たちだ。彼らの気分には思いやりがあり—みんなほとんどあけすけに首長の地位に対するセレツェ・カーマの要求を支持する。しかし彼自身はおきまりのデマ演説の誘惑に負けない。彼は、よし受け入れられたとしても、どんな悪感も、民主的改革もあるいは共和国の樹立も約束しない。西方風の「開化」（それがどんなものであるにせよ）を身につけ、それを人民に及ぼすだろうと人から見られているとはいえ、彼自身の人柄がにじみ出る。そして質問が政策にふれてくると、一人の上品で、いんぎんなイギリスの弁護士（高慢ちきな夫人といっしょの）がいち早く立上って、外交的で、なだめるような陳述

を占めて自国のセレツェ・カーマへの忠誠を誇示する。堂々たる男子である。彼は大きな、黒い体躯を胸ともたせて前の方へ乗り出し、聴き手をおだて、魅了し、楽しませ、思うままに操る。彼は金髪、顎ヒゲの眉目うるわしい青年で、セレツェ・カーマとその金髪のイギリス出の妻との間に座っている。この妻は物静かで、美しくはないが完全な北欧型だ。それはちょうどその主人が典型的なアフリカ人であるのと同じ

わたしに並んで座

問題にされない　イギリスの世論に味方にセレツェ・カーマに同情しており、民主的だと称する英国植民省に反対する一封建君主に味方するものであることを意に介さない。

「進歩人たち」は、もし彼らの女王がイギリスで似たような要求をせまったならば街に飛び出して革命を起すだろうに、自分自身にもまたセレツェ・カーマにも満足して天使のように微笑むのだ。恵まれたイギリス人だ。彼らはただ首長罷免の仮定的（だが決して公表されたことのない）理由すなわち白い婦人との結婚という理由に憤慨しているのだ。彼らは自国の憲法上の王が一離婚婦人と結婚したがったために廃せられたとき全然その感情をあらわさなかった。

皮膚の色の問題は道徳問題であり、イギリス人は道徳的だ。英民主主義の頭は混乱するかもしれないが、しかし心情に狂いはない。

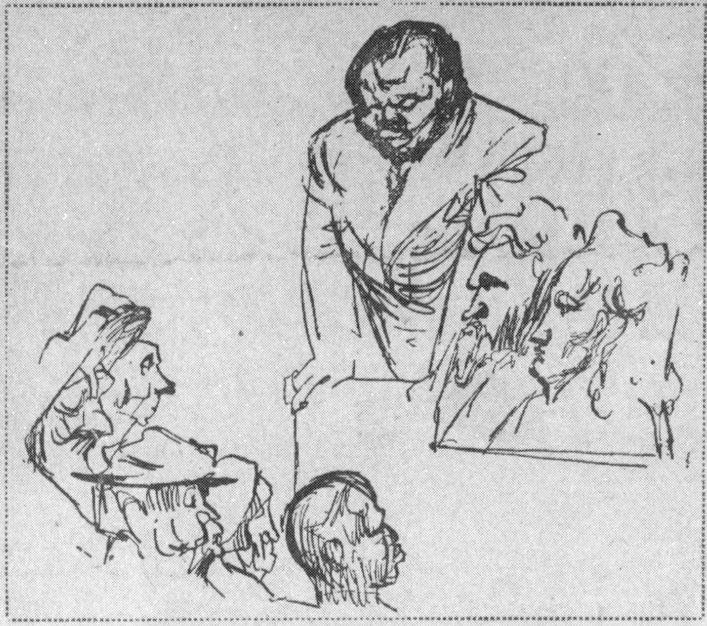

トポースキー氏略歴

フェリクス・トポースキー氏は四十代、働き盛りのイギリス画家でブラック・アンド・ホワイトでは欧州一ときえいわれる。故バーナード・ショウは彼のことを自分の相棒と呼ぶほどに買っていたし、彼にだけその作品に挿絵をかかせたものだ。戦後五冊の画集を出版、昨年の大英国祭には「英連邦の行進」という大壁画をものして飾った。一昨年春東京を訪れたときその印象記を本紙によせたことがある。今後月二回絵入り通信を送って来る。

Feature by me in *Yomiuri Shimbun*

security/press/CIA/Photo News/MPs
milling around and above from their tallness
subpoenaing their dwarf-opponents
for the open (f)air court of democratic justice
by the means of
survey/black-listing/recording/threatening
through PHOTOGRAPHY,
this occurred to me in uncommitted sympathy:
the uniformed encircling tracking men
camera-pointing/clicking
were the Holy Office Inquisitors
SHOOTING
flash-burning click-killing the COMMIES
their gods' enemies, doing
their coming religious wars' war-dance, pursuing
their cold hotting-up war.

Then a country inn (**Fuji** in view) in which the semi-militar
two of us act our kind's mannerless coarseness: a cosy girl fo
each, we gaily go native (so we think) in the communal batl

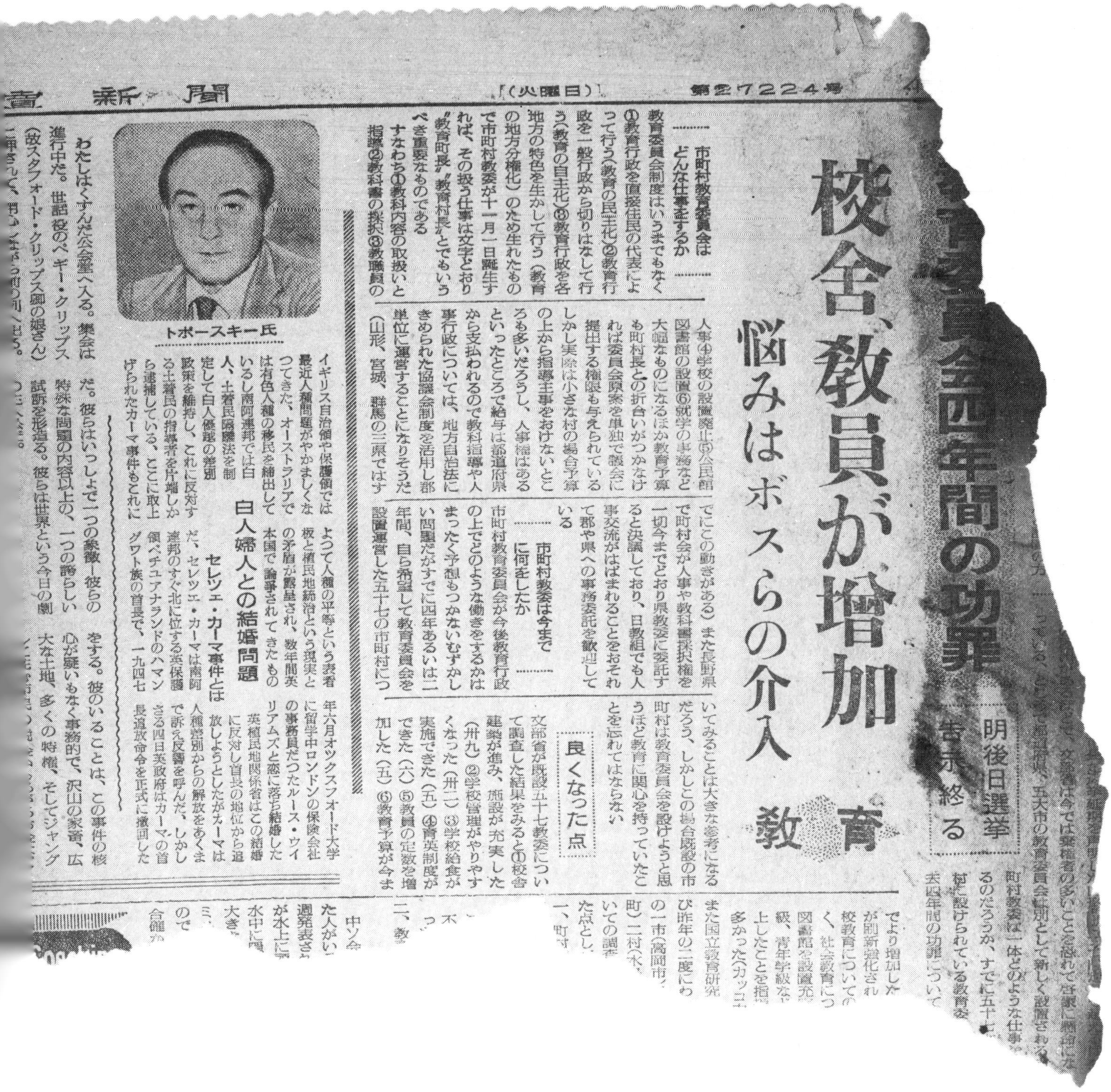
讀賣新聞 （火曜日） 第27224号

教育委員会四年間の功罪

明後日選挙 告示終る

校舎、教員が増加

悩みはボスらの介入

教育

市町村教育委員会は どんな仕事をするか

教育委員会制度はいうまでもなく①教育行政を直接住民の代表によって行う（教育の民主化）②教育行政を一般行政から切りはなして行う（教育の自主化）③教育行政を各地方の特色を生かして行う（教育の地方分権化）のため生れたもので市町村教委が十一月一日誕生すれば、その扱う仕事は文字どおり〝教育町長〟〝教育村長〟とでもいうべき重要なものである すなわち①教科内容の取扱いと指導②教科書の採択③教職員の人事④学校の設置廃止⑤公民館図書館の設置⑥就学の事務など大幅なものになるほか教育予算も町村長との折合いがつかなければ委員会原案を単独で議会に提出する権限も与えられている しかし実際は小さな村の場合予算の上から指導主事をおけないところも多いだろうし、人事権はあるといったところで給与は都道府県から支払われるので教科指導や人事行政については、地方自治法にきめられた協議会制度を活用し郡単位に運営することになりそうだ（山形、宮城、群馬の三県ではすでにこの動きがある）また長野県で町村会が人事や教科書採択権を一切今までどおり県教委に委託すると決議しており、日教組でも人事交流がはばまれることをおそれて郡や県への事務委託を歓迎している

市町村教委は今までに何をしたか

市町村教育委員会が今後教育行政の上でどのような働きをするかはまったく予想もつかないむずかしい問題だがすでに四年あるいは二年間、自ら希望して教育委員会を設置運営した五十七の市町村についてみることは大きな参考になるだろう、しかしこの場合既設の市町村は教育委員会を設けようと思うほど教育に関心を持っていたことを忘れてはならない

良くなった点

文部省が既設五十七教委について調査した結果をみると①校舎建築が進み、施設が充実した（卅九）②学校管理がやりやすくなった（卅二）③学校給食が実施できた（五）④育英制度ができた（六）⑤教員の定数を増加した（五）⑥教育予算が今ま

トポースキー氏

白人婦人との結婚問題

セレッツェ・カーマ事件とは

イギリス自治領や保護領では最近人種問題がやかましくなってきた、オーストラリアでは有色人種の移民を締出しているし南阿連邦では白人、土着民隔離法を制定して白人優越の差別政策を維持し、これに反対する土着民の指導者を片端しから逮捕している、ここに取上げられたカーマ事件もこれによって人種の平等という表看板と植民地統治という現実との矛盾が暴露され、数年間英本国で論争されてきたものだ、セレッツェ・カーマは南阿連邦のすぐ北に位する英保護領ベチュアナランドのハマングワト族の首長で、一九四七年六月オックスフォード大学に留学中ロンドンの保険会社の事務員だったルース・ウイリアムズと恋に落ち結婚した 英植民地関係省はこの結婚に反対し首長の地位から追放しようとしたがカーマは人種差別からの解放をあくまで訴え反響を呼んだ、しかしさる四日英政府はカーマの首長追放命令を正式に撤回した

わたしはくすんだ公会堂へ入る。集会は進行中だ。世話役のペギー・クリップス（故スタフォード・クリップス卿の娘さん）……だ。彼らはいっしょで一つの象徴―彼らの特殊な問題の内容以上の、一つの誇らしい試断を形造る。彼らは世界という今日の劇をする。彼のいることは、この事件の核心が疑いもなく事務的で、沢山の家畜、広大な土地、多くの特権、そしてジャング

the girls scrub us squatted at the edge, pour water over us; and in laughter/frolicking all four of us plunge in. There are, of course, other naked bathers of both sexes, but somewhat apart – and, only years later, I was told that we had behaved shockingly: decorousness is expected in the bath as well.

Kyoto overpowers with decorousness. It makes clear the rurality of old Nippon. The temples and palaces may be reconstructions, but assuredly most faithful – and all is timber, all comes, however enlarged, from the shape of a peasant hut. But the long passage floors squeak feudally underfoot – a device against creeping assassins.

In **Yokohama**, I board a Norwegian ship for San Francisco: out of Asia. One of my co-passengers, the Reverend J. T. Takuda, belongs to Tokyo's Society of St John the Evangelist, the same Anglican order of which Father Albert Rangaswamy of Bombay, who patronized the opening stage of my voyage east from London, is a member. A mere chance?

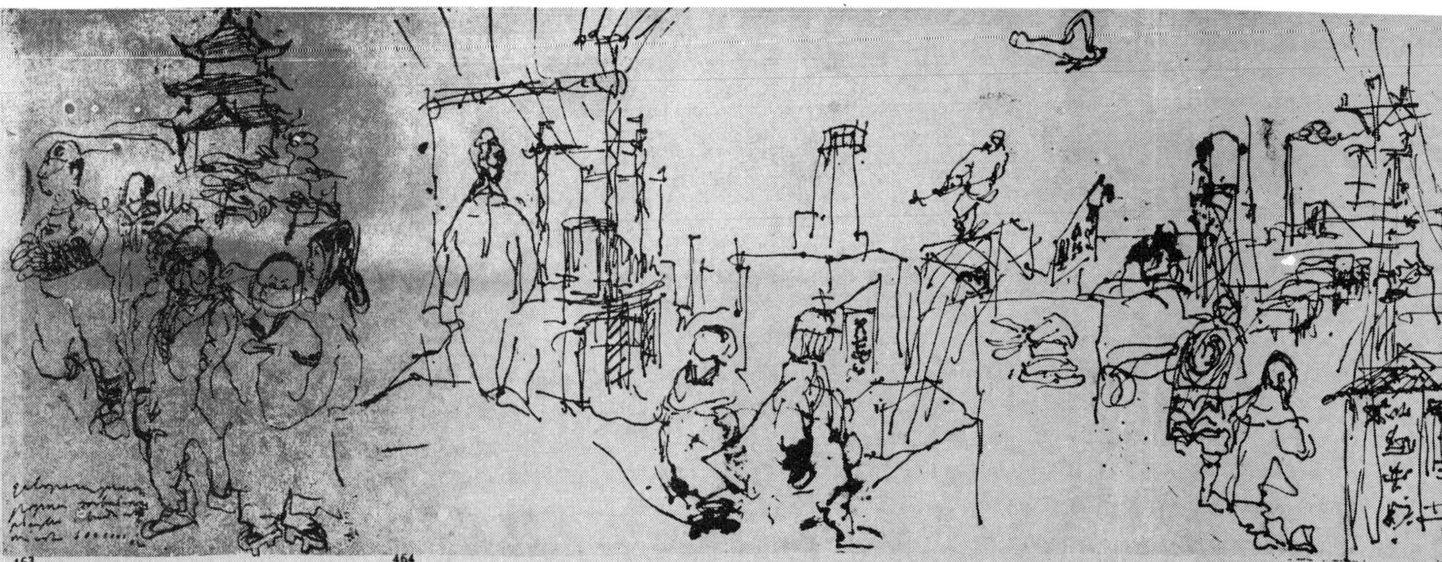

463 **TOKYO - FUJI** 464

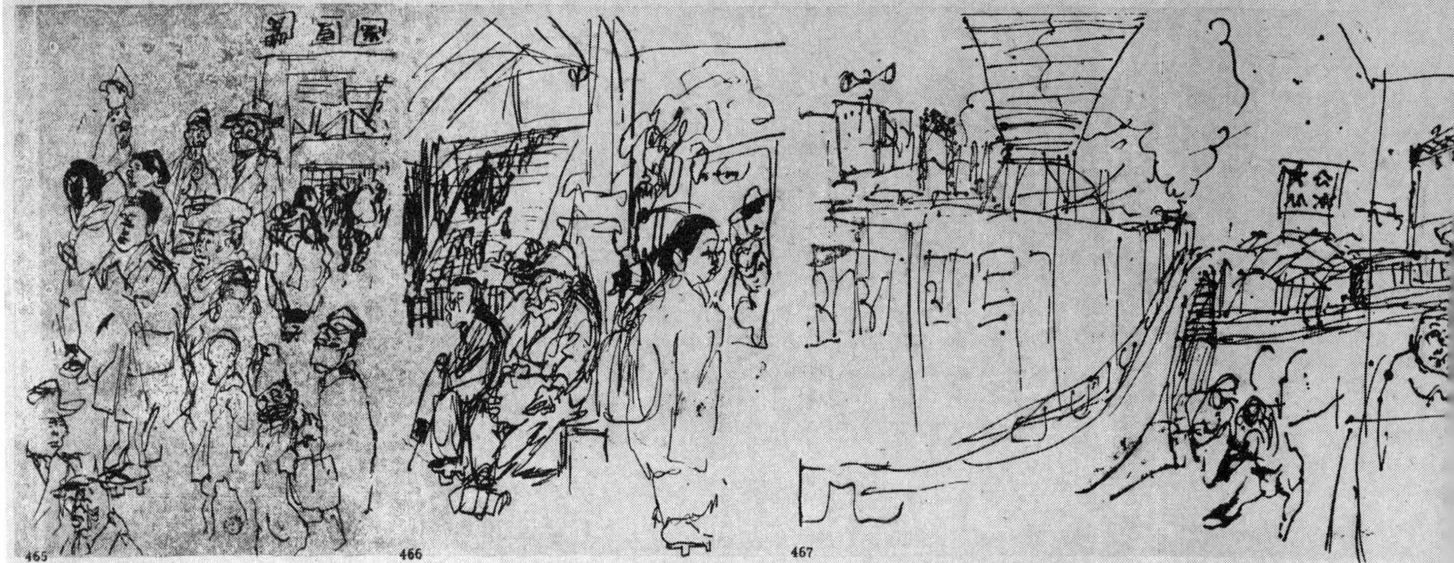

465 **TOKYO - KYOTO** 466 467

Japan. Train journey from Tokyo to Kyoto (from *Topolski's Chronicle*)

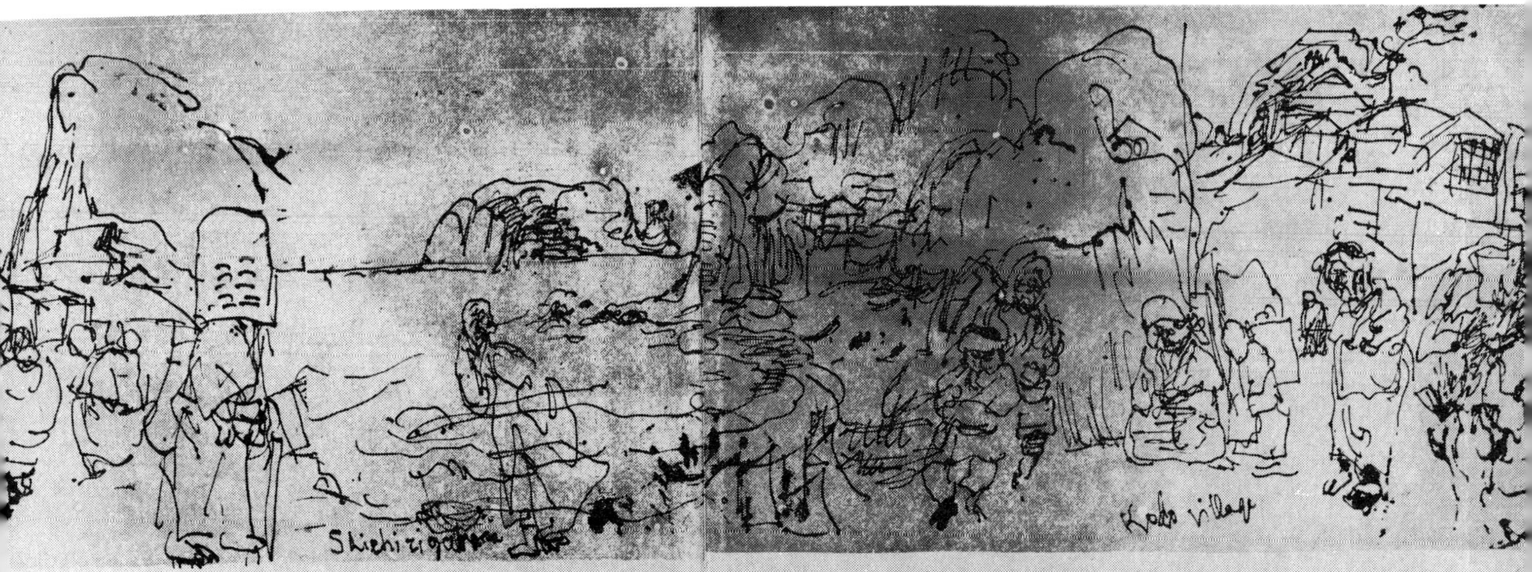

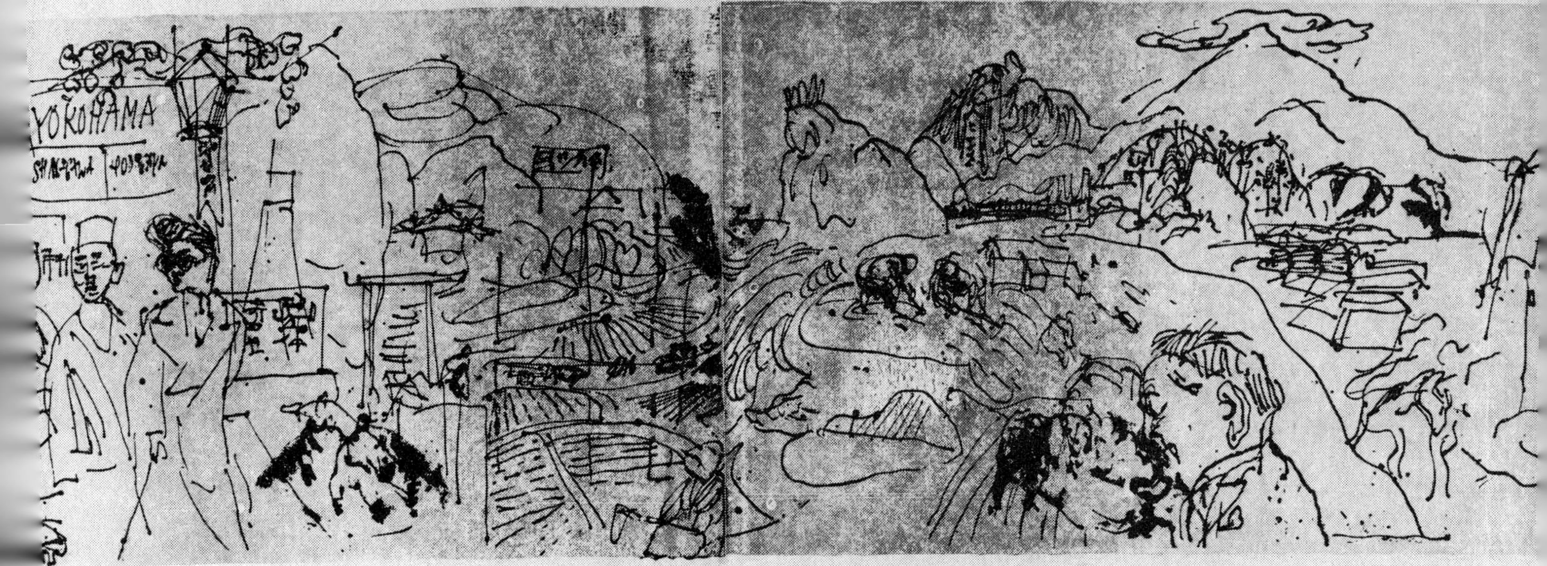
YOKOHAMA

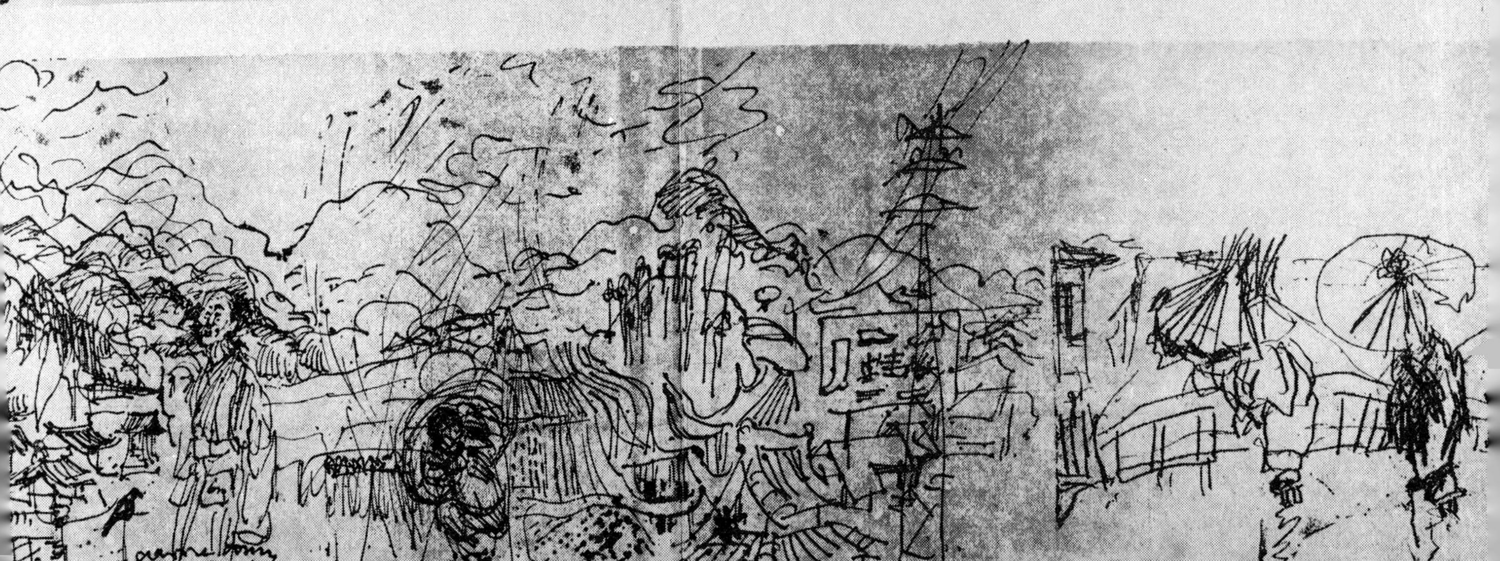

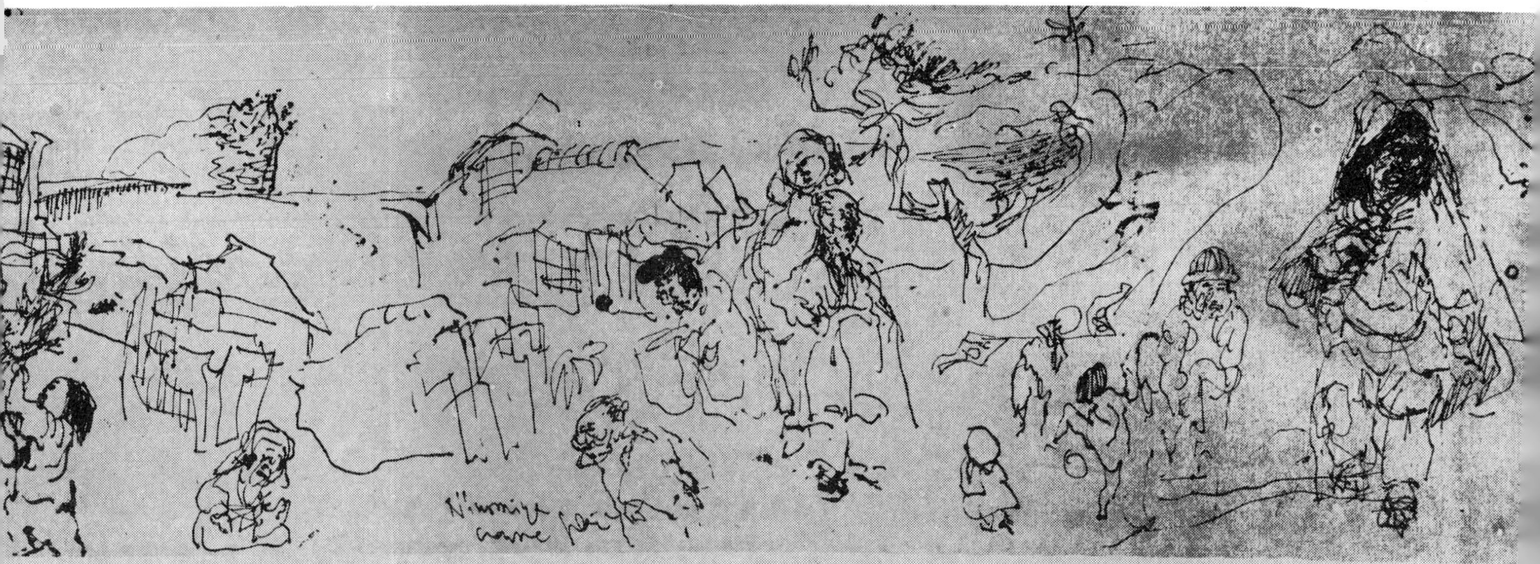

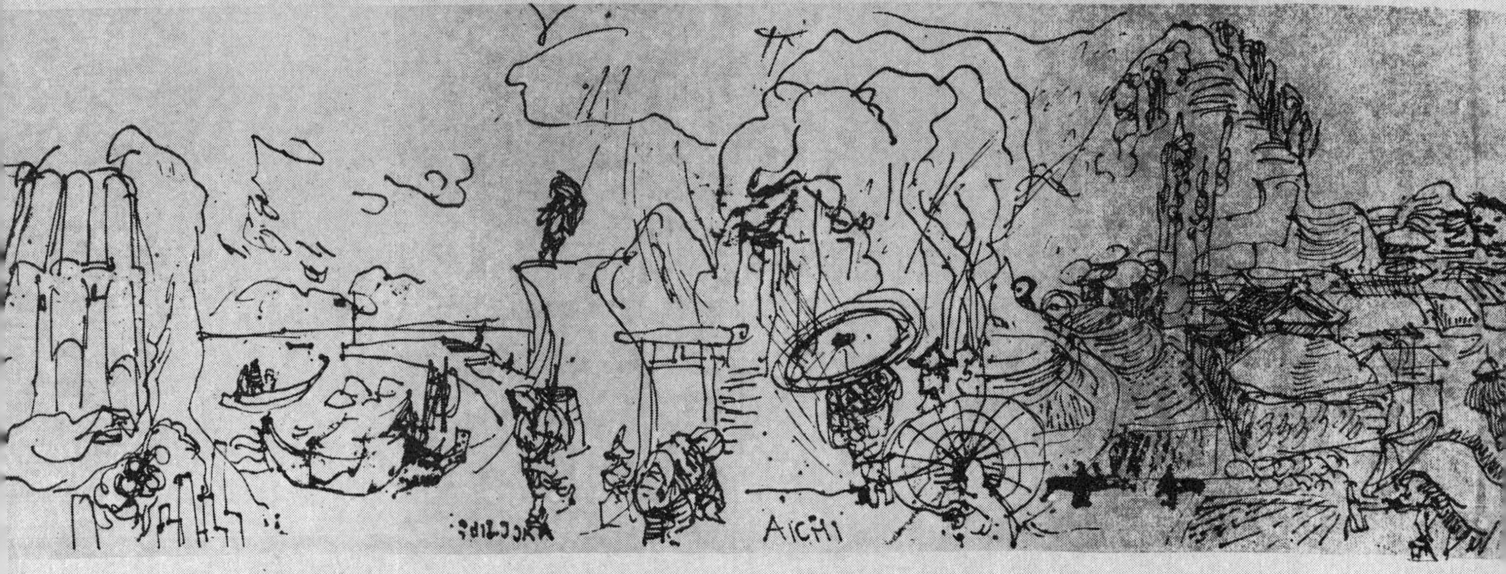

469 470 471 472

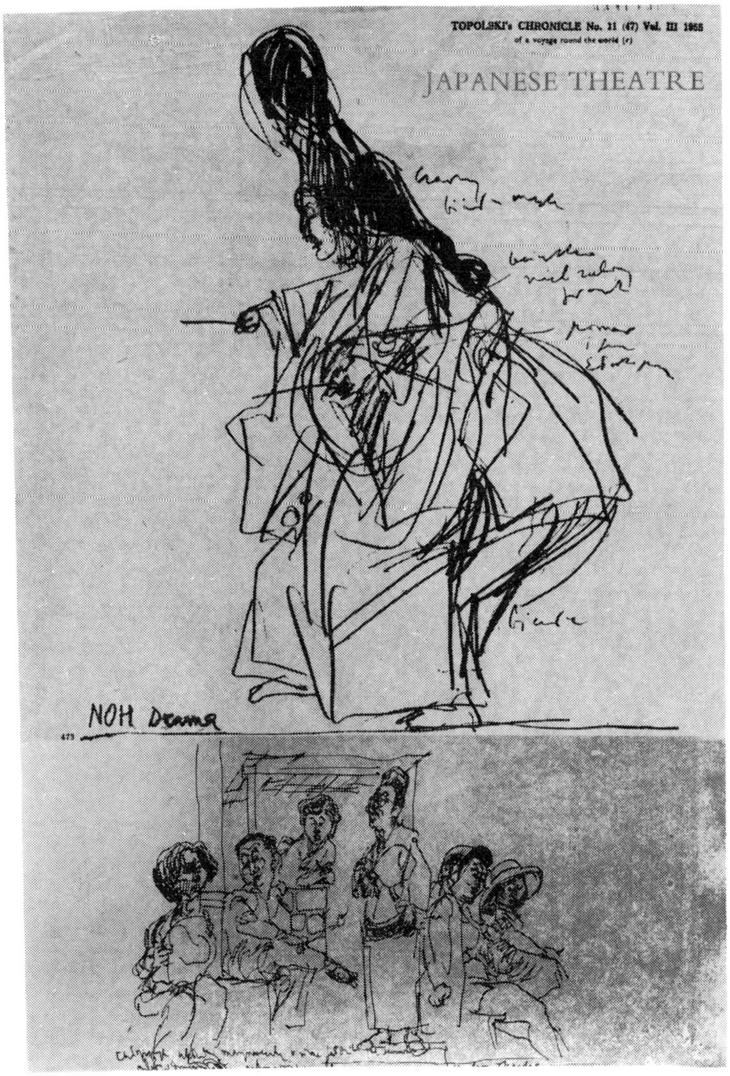

Japanese Theatre (from *Topolski's Chronicle*)

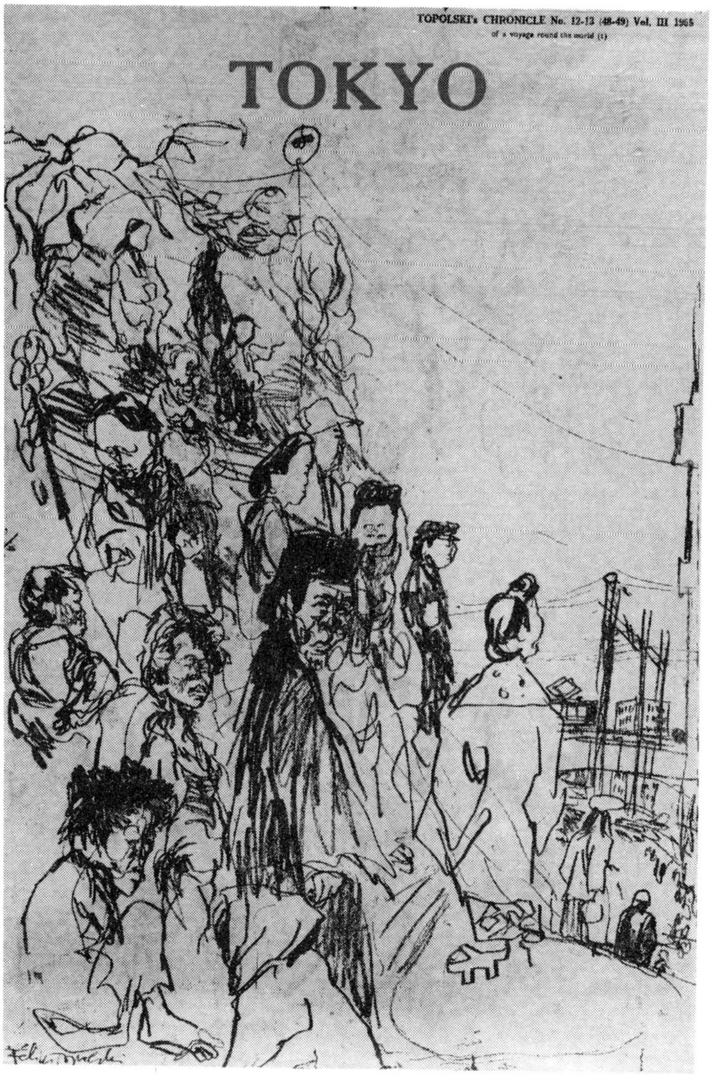

Tokyo (from *Topolski's Chronicle*)

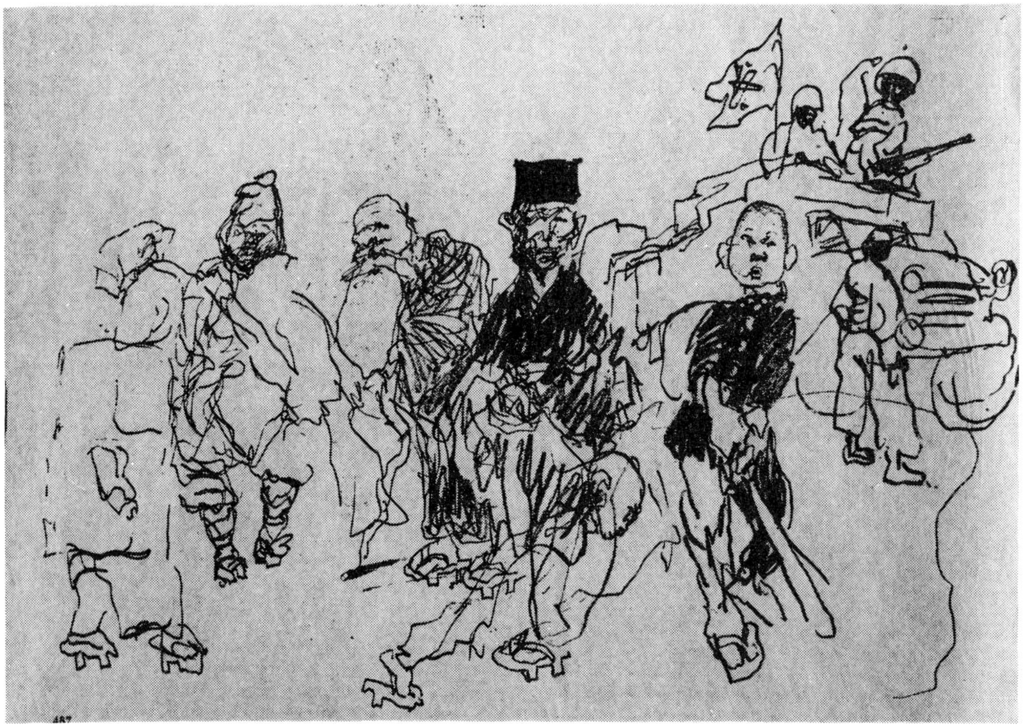

Americans in Tokyo (from *Topolski's Chronicle*)

The United States of America gathers into one language the children of Noah's three sons and attempts to build again the tower that may reach unto heaven, so that nothing will be restrained from them, which they have imagined to do. Yet again some Lord seems to be disturbed and going to confound them so that they may not understand one another and so be unable to carry on their conceits.

1950 Diary
Yokohama, Japan – San Francisco, California, USA
The ocean-birds, steel-winged and fierce, pass their escort duties to the plump land-gulls of the American shore. Dollars emerge; somewhat self-consciously traditional banknotes, not unlike testimonials of a Free Masonic Lodge – the stern, thin-lipped images on them reassure.

A gentle sailing boat brings the pilot – and marks the pace of **San Francisco**. The least expected America: cosy and mellow. 'The American Tempo', taken up by its imitators, now jerks along in distant lands, the States themselves seemingly settling into their 'Victorianism' . . .*

San Francisco Art School peep: amphilades of abstractions and one student left behind washing brushes in front of one more canvas/amassment of abstract emotions – deflated crazy-eyed, with an aura of worn-out scraped-out 'inner sources'.

All across the continent the schools and galleries, by the order of the day, raise perspectives of introvert inspirations – all good, all vital, all drying up . . .

There is one godhead and He is the Abstract Art-Head. A total conversion of the Continent for oneness of adoration – other directions condemned. The response of the Americans (upper bracket and artists in their service) is this time more than conformist fashion – it is a communion, a comforting confirmation – the religious art of/for Materialist Western Faith materialized: art (a spiritual domain) anointing canonizing sanctifying enshrining it in glory.

An abstract painting stated to be an object in itself, associative/symbolic/pictorial meanings (dangerously loaded with heretical secrets) eliminated, is/remains for ever a reassuring piece of property, tangible/displayable and above all excluding the lowly – the very symbol, the orthodox icon of Plutocratic materialism, US model.

Its opposite pole – USSR materialism, being populist, created its religious art along the line of 'lives of Christ/Saints' story-telling strip cartoons – but naturally in pictures understandable to contemporary masses, *ergo* 'life of Lenin' in POP-socialist-realism.†

Immensities of smooth speedways luminous with giant bridges. The rush amongst the unexpectedly mixed flock of motorcars . . . Round Los Angeles – not so much film as other industries – blunt-headed oil-pumps ceaselessly suck the seemingly barren earth . . . The one lap rail-ride across the States bypasses the 'fabulous nature beauties', shows only glimpses of handsomeness, steals at night through some, and concentrates on viewing the linings. Old Californan farmers hug languidly the cornices of small stations, huge pumpkins at their feet. Soon rocky desert – high and mighty. And astride the mountains step out, rise, aggress the monsters – steel skeletons; empty of volume and therefore filled with anger. They throw forward arrows of wires – the 'robot' army, serving or threatening the USA man. They circle round the train, change expressions – I cannot draw their message. In this many-houred landscape they outnumber men . . . Morning becomes New Mexico: empty and undesirable. The passengers, swelling into an air-conditioned coma, sprawl isolated and stupefied in 'duplex roomette' comfort, write picture postcards from New Mexico to be effortlessly stamped and non-stop posted . . . The desert, patched with crippled bushes and meagre whirlwinds of dust, cut through with flat roads of dried-out rivers – lies vast and voidal. Here and there sheen, with pathetic attempt at attraction, rubbish heaps (tins and bottles) grown from mean shacks that hang out the blowing lines of washing, as if signalling distress. The lonely posts are marked thus – statistical illustrations – the height of the pile of refuse shows the number of years . . . On the train: sandwiches in a paper bag with the freshness diagram: date, place, conditions and ingredients – all duly perforated; most efficient, but the perforated day is Saturday, while it is Friday only . . . Colorado: a wall of mist meets the train and is a sandstorm. The rubbish heaps come to life and rise high, sheets of tin-roofing roll along screeching, the roads are swept of dust, trees wrestle clumsily – weakening . . . the winds gain power. The emptyish train howls in the night of storm. A stop. I lift the window blind in the dark and gaze through the rain-crisscrossed window into the face of a Kansas village perhaps; perhaps its name is Syracuse. It yawns a bleak yawn, toothy with the shining shapes of the parked motor cars, and the eye reaches easily down its entrails lighted with neon thriftiness. The town stares back, anchored against adversities by the chapel and the movie-house. It does not suggest any secrets . . . Huge brown-grey water glues athwart the land – snails against the sand-walls: the Mississippi River. Miserable cottages uglify the shores. There reappears – scouting, spying – a single giant aggressor of the same steel breed as in California; it stands widely astride the damp fieldlets of Illinois – then a whole army marches over the battered, machine-conquered land; it gets rottener, and the 'rubbish multiplies over the wastelands in misty smoke, amongst the cupolas of industry. The giant towers were surely begotten here . . . Hudson River is greying – the tugs appear pushing the barges with their noses – but the empty horizon returns. One hour and a half from New York – yet foresty and riversidey and light-heartedly rustic. Then, on the other bank, there starts a line of industrial fortresses. Now the waters flow widely – we rush along a narrow dam. Rust-red bulks of ships huddle in flocks at the riverbanks. Stores of

*Next the San Francisco of the Republican Convention 1956 nominating Eisenhower and Nixon – a very short formality, although crowded with folklore, fun, little elephants, and processions/cavalcades. But the town was still napping in the background, a few bohemian outsiders snugly settled in ramshackle boat-houses.

†Next, decadence sliding in, US POP slid back 'figurativeness' through the back door of self-doubt/self mockery – US religious imagery: the apotheosis of cartoon-superman cum sex-strip and tin-can food; imagination in supermarket chains. 'Trends' rush in-out fast: 'minimals' serving – anti-arts in revolt. The white world (and Japan) prostrate in unquestioning imitation. But abstract-action-expressionism may have been the art-leading-life augury – a paradoxical twist: from the shrines of collectors to the New Left's war cry, 'action for action's sake'. And next: the see-saw brings violent echoes of German expressionism, but its protest missing.

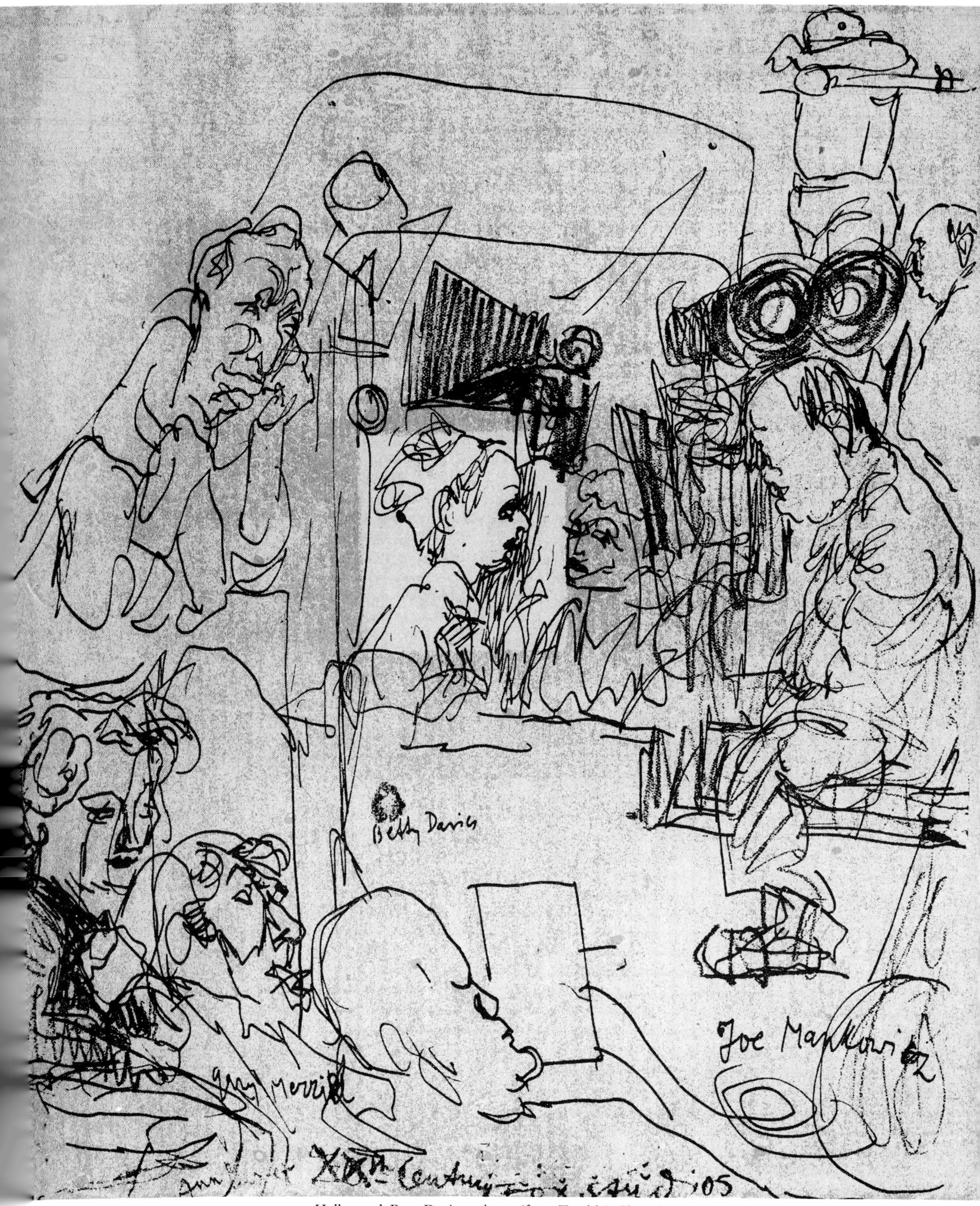

Hollywood: Bette Davis on the set (from *Topolski's Chronicle*)

junk – leftovers of the sea and land. A tunnel hits blackly – and again water – now vast. But the rusticity returns fully. Most surprisingly, New York leans against nature . . .

Harlem's blackbrick backs: perch high–narrow; the in-between slits: belch out rubbish; the upper storeys strain forward: window-framed shapes-portraits of dark female loneliness; the lower: males, children overhanging signalling as if for get-aways . . . This grimness was monumental and countered the grand canyons of skyscrapers.

New York, confined to the routine of my limitations, somehow ended for me then at: West-5th Ave, North – The Plaza, East – the Elevated, with dashing blind subway/taxi excursions-leaps into incalculable depths. It was oddly an old sedative city centre, mystery edged, but, in this explored area, familiar. People transplanted from the Old Continent, pursuits/plans recognizable and easy to join, interspersed thickly with the continuity of one's old European ways, even more so – to the level of ostentatious indulgence; a dispersal of those weeks into personal/anecdotal details. New York, being reached (from the back as it were) after a long journey round the world and across the American continent, offered itself to a nostalgic traveller as the Westernmost city of Europe – and did not stand apart from it as the New World.

My many visits to the States need forewording. **I did not go to America as a painter's Aladdin's cave**, a breathless, blinkered, self-centred race. My life-devouring appetite turned outward my fortunes, my preoccupation with globe- (and history-) trotting in drawing-becoming-painting was fortified/sacramentalized by publishers of books, by *Fortune*'s, by *Life*'s, *Harper's Bazaar* and *Vogue*'s pages given to my unrestricted portfolios, and by my own *Topolski's Chronicle*; thus, already in the war years, *Fortune* gave my many pages' coverage of the American Expeditionary Force (and so did *Life* with my East–West fronts drawings), and my first entry into America through the back door of San Francisco, and onward, was guided by *Vogue* ladies and Alex Liberman on the level of 'consequence' (loopholes for diversions plentiful), so that the 'career' was there – a carpet laid *a priori* for parading my indulgences, that is on-the-spot investigations.

– The shortness of each stay condenses these participatory surveys into a VIEW. First, 1950 – a mere passage across the Pacific to complete the round-the-world circle – contained the upper strata and houseboats of San Francisco, Hollywood stars' partyings, train across the continent; Washington Maiden's Choice Dance, and all obvious elements: the Senate, the House of Representatives and the Supreme Court, but also the Negro University's head and Eunice Kennedy, and New York's great many aspects . . .

– Second, 1956, much more: San Francisco Republican Convention bring forth Eisenhower, and Adlai Stephenson's Chicago; fuller Hollywood and New York.

– Third, 1957: a formalized view, when tailing the Queen's visit. But also private games.

A weary block of studios on the corner of Sixth Avenue and 57th Street – a lovely/messy one on the fourth floor, lent to share by my senior colleague at the Warsaw Academy of Art, Eljasz Kanarek; he, when rarely in New York, in a chair collapsed into a fitting shell for his snoozes, but mostly away on portrait commissions.

Shamelessly, I pinned up sheets over his paintings and threw a party – a summing up of that longish stay. Besides the varied cluster of my Poles – mostly pretty ladies who had 'made it' in the States (Kriendler of the 21 Club possessed by one of them) – there was handsome Kay Kendall (whom I drew then, courted once at a London occasion, turning my back on Rita Hayworth and her professed charms, not knowing who she was or of her attachment to Rex Harrison) and of the English stage Michael Redgrave and Eileen Hurlie, Maggie Smith – then a breathtaking solo comic in *New Faces*, sadly imprisoned later in 'straight'-jacketing theatre, Julie Andrews and her designer husband. There made their entries large teams from CBS Television, from *Vogue* (Alex and Tatiana Liberman) and from *Fortune*; also Philadelphian and Washington tall squads.

At some point, the place packed, there appeared on the edge (the impressed observer's stance) Alistair Cooke with the Edwardian-by-choice Ben Sonnenberg,* the supremo and creator of PR glories, who, a few days earlier at that studio, had to rush to the phone to clarify his yearly one million dollars' profits.

This was, to overflowing, my New York at that time: my current conceits sated, I watched the fooleries of High Art marketing from my perch, not tempted to step down into the rough and tumble of it.

A cluster of expeditions, 1960–66: beyond the witnessed events and formalized history of the UN sittings, the net took in the social antics: the stilted exclusivity, the 'alternative society', and many facets in between, slaves of sugar plantations in Florida and Harlem included. An odd domicile in a suite of rooms at a snob St Regis Hotel, while painting a set of large panels for their 'Maisonette' night-club, brought in more or less *tout le monde* (feminine) of the day, led by Robin Butler, Marion Javits, Vrena Van Allen, a star of a musical success, Catherine Milinaire and the Mortimers, to feature in the paintings. Baby Jane Holzer's essential inclusion failed. She came for lunch and there was an instant lack of rapport: this fluffily false blonde, the very synthesis of a New York Jewishness masquerading as an Anglo-Saxon, was made solely for frontal presentation; sitting on her left during the lunch in my rooms, I began drawing; but she flew into panic-rage, objecting (in defence of her precarious celebrity – the whole of a miserable falsification); her cultivated image clearly did not include her profile.

But there were also such gate-crashing callers as Jerzy

*His Rolls the oldest in New York, his Churchillian square bowler, his Gremaercy Park beauty of a period house (outside and in), and his incomparably stylish receptions, the most decorative and the most 'in-view' people contesting their perches; Arthur Rubinstein clutching at women and simultaneously managing to slight me – I suppose sensing competitive similarity of looks and background in a bit younger compatriot. Sonnenberg suffered, though, at the peak of his castle-in-air achievement, the usual fate of a lonely fantasy: his son, so he conveyed to me, had turned away from PR accumulations towards the 'alternative' denials – the whole collecting, preciousizing life to be negated, swept away.

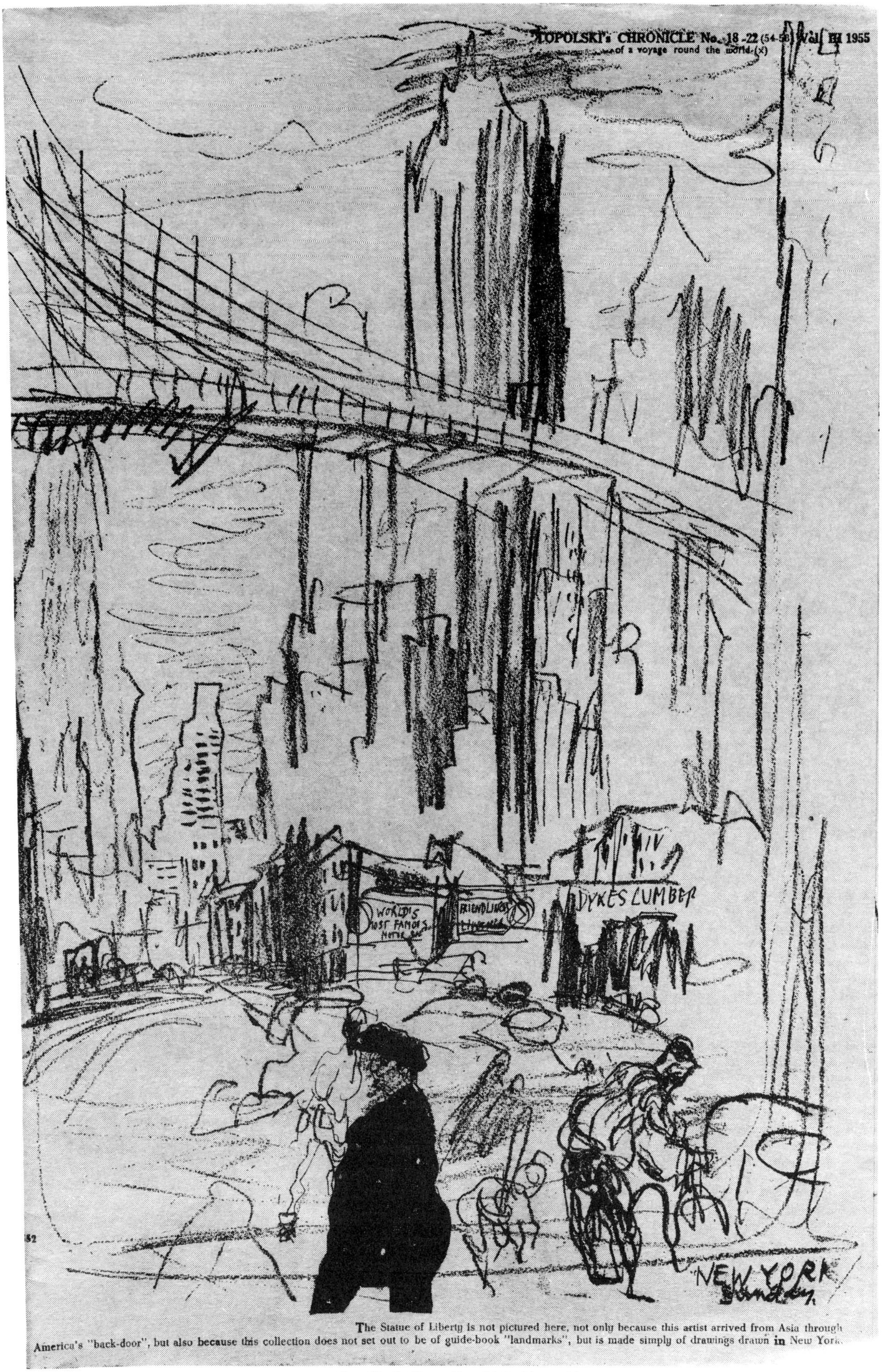

New York (from *Topolski's Chronicle*)

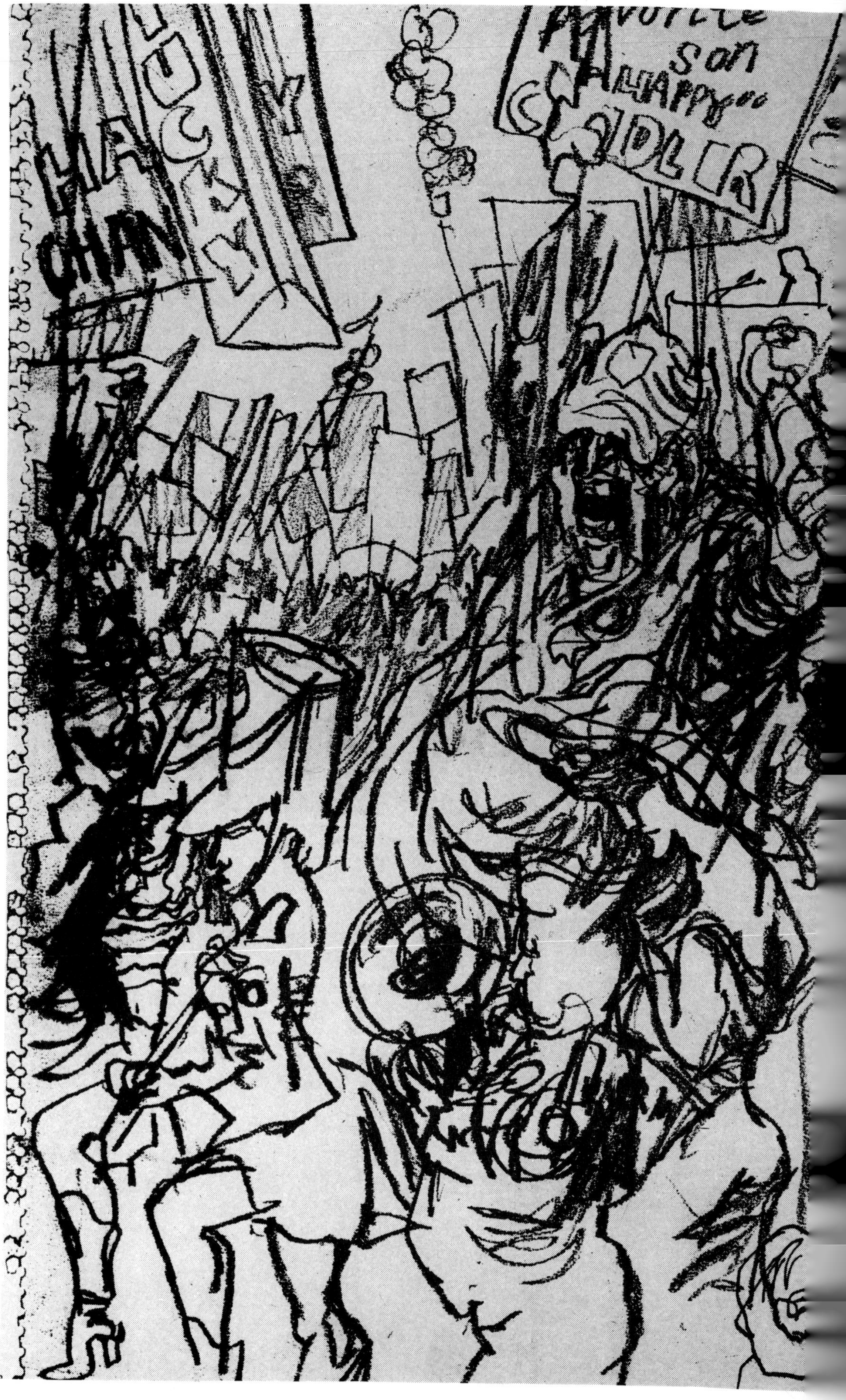
son

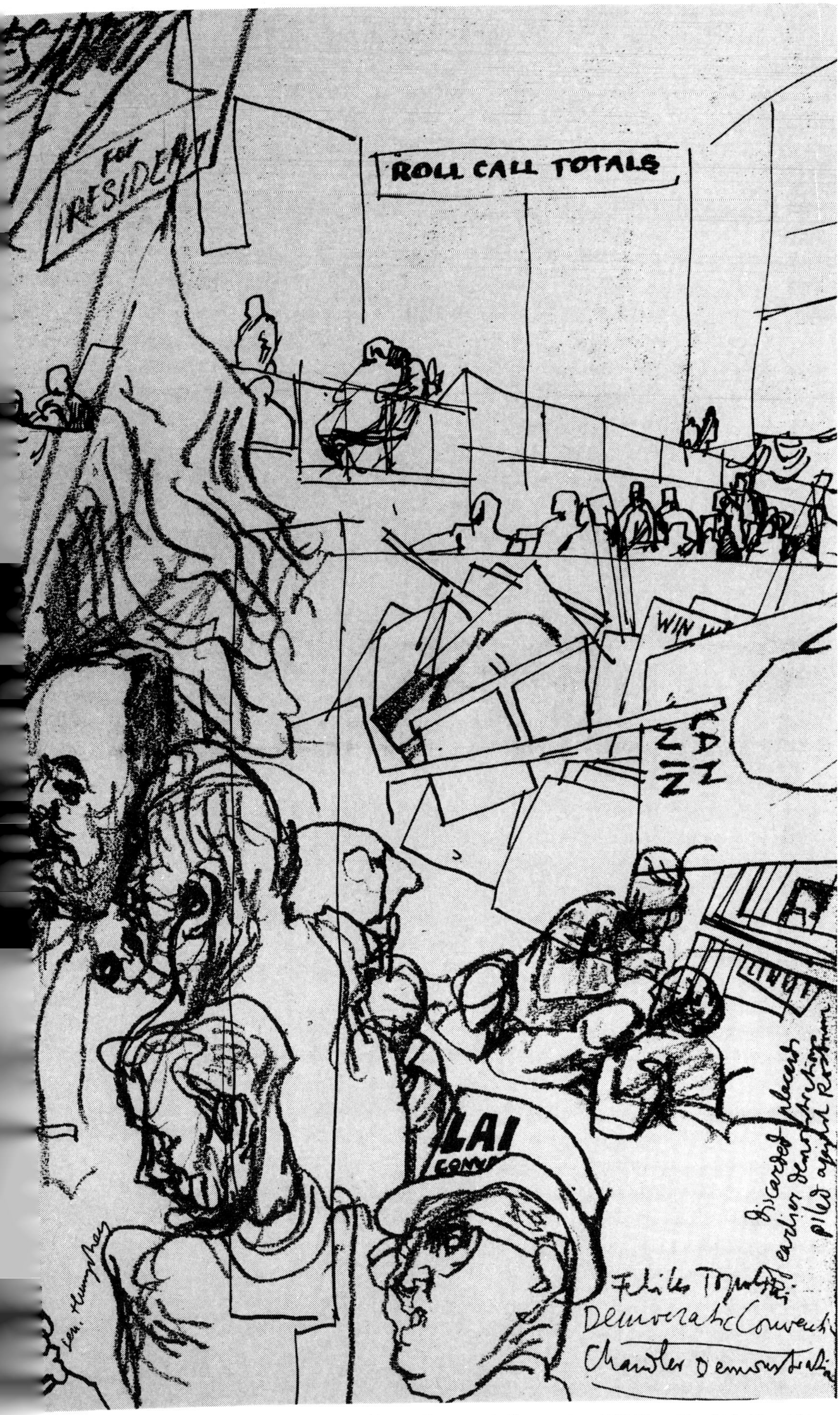

Chicago, Democratic Convention, 1956 (from *Topolski's Chronicle*)

TOPOLSKI's CHRONICLE No. 16-21 (76-81) Vol. IV 1956

. . . nothing affirmeth and therefore never lyeth . . . Sir Philip Sidney (1580)

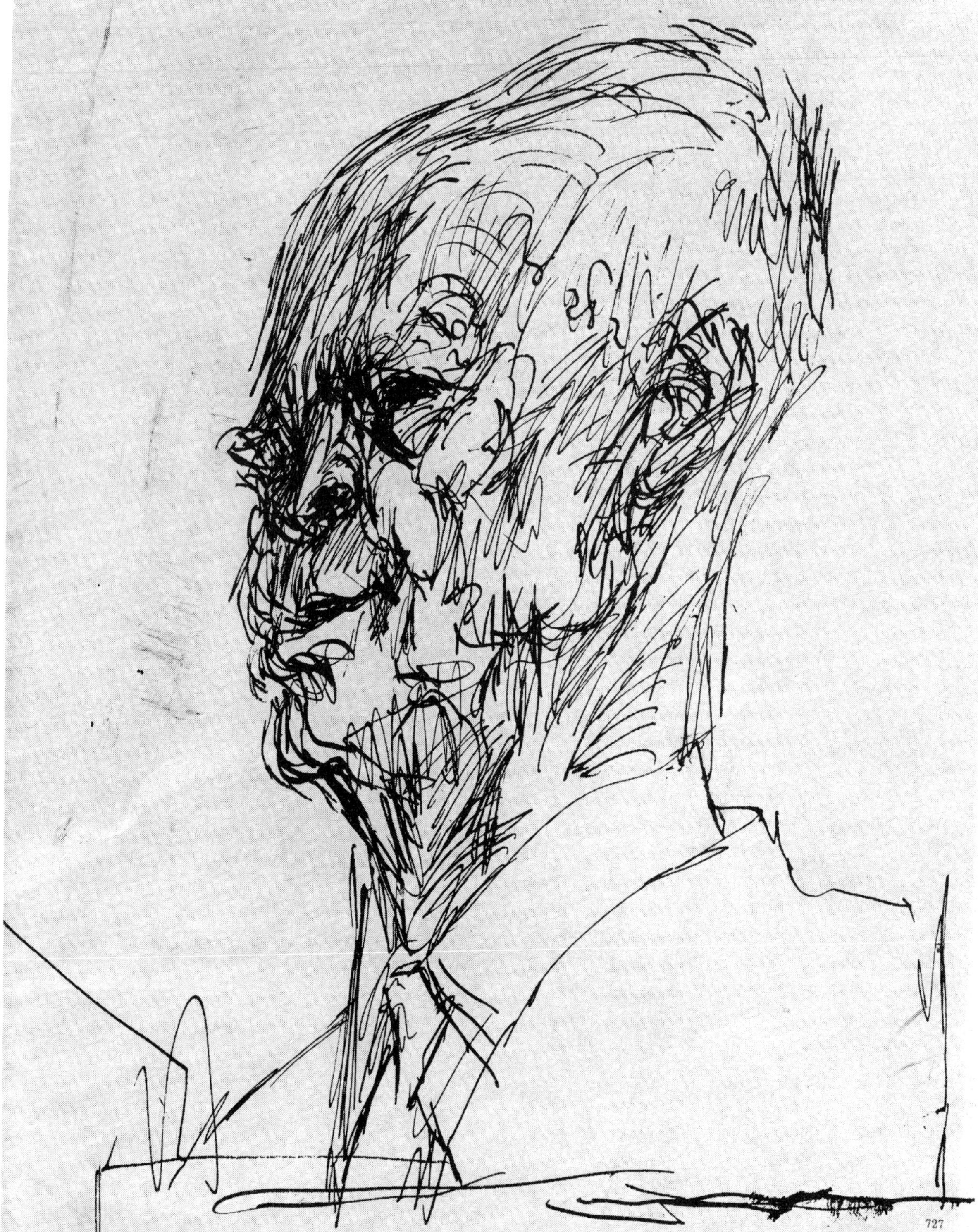

727

U.S.A. ELECTS PRESIDENT

The drawings in this issue were made possible by the invitation of CBS TELEVISION to attend the PRESIDENTIAL CONVENTIONS in Chicago and San Francisco

General Eisenhower at the San Francisco, Republican Convention, 1956 (from *Topolski's Chronicle*)

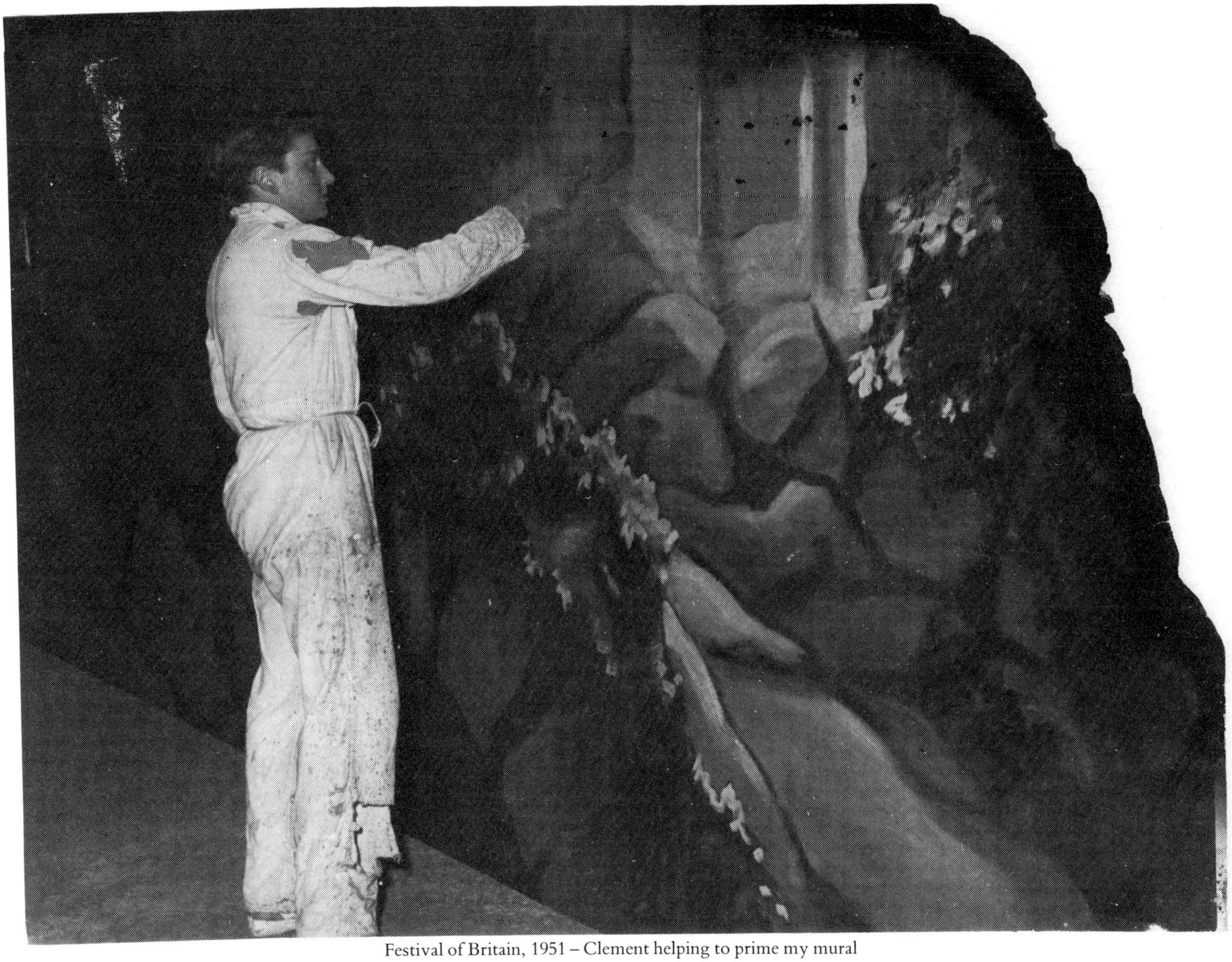

Festival of Britain, 1951 – Clement helping to prime my mural

Skolimowski, who presented his early films at the first New York film festival; or my son Daniel, with his school pal at the end of a trek across the land, stinking with sweat and dirt and settling to camp on my quarter's floor, bizarrely clashing with the hotel's pretensions; or my newly formed links with LSD – Milbrook, Timothy Leary and Hollingshead culture.

And, somewhat separately, my *Chronicle*'s exhibition *monstre* in Madison Avenue, decorated by fourteen and a half thousand visitors, *New Yorker* leading article, breakfast television interviews and a gossip piece syndicated throughout a chain of newspapers, which stated my views on American women's underwear.

In 1956 Saul Steinberg dashed at me at a Central Park South party of well-selected expatriate Europeans (he, René Bouché, Anthony West, with their prizes – American top-college six-foot beauties), 'Why do you stay in England, forever a second-class citizen? Europe's no more, only America – utter equality of chance/recognition.' I feebly protested – never unequal and liking Englishness, but he remained puzzled at my countering that period's truism.

Tides have a habit of receding. Then the Atlantic flooded the US with Europe's little Columbuses – New York was lifted highest on the Westward waves, Europe drying up in world esteem. A few years later (the moon directs the tides? Politics rules the waves?) the movement reversed, the Americans began to float to Europe and further. The same worldly conversationalists began to talk of the States having lost the post-war prestige/credit for world leadership in South America, Europe, Asia . . .

Out of a sea of mud arose the **Festival of Britain in 1951.** I perched for some months on a high scaffold painting **Cavalcade of the Commonwealth** in the open square arch of the Hungerford viaduct over Belvedere Road – a fierce wintry wind-tunnel, without any premonitions that in the second arch from there I would, soon after, continue – for about thirty-five years by now – and probably conclude my working life.

The panels assembled over this vast surface of 60 by 20 feet (the largest painting of all there) and the colour pattern

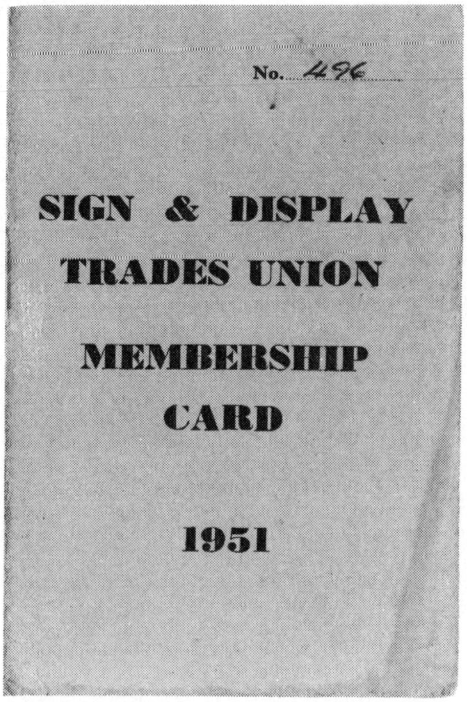

No. 496

SIGN & DISPLAY TRADES UNION

MEMBERSHIP CARD

1951

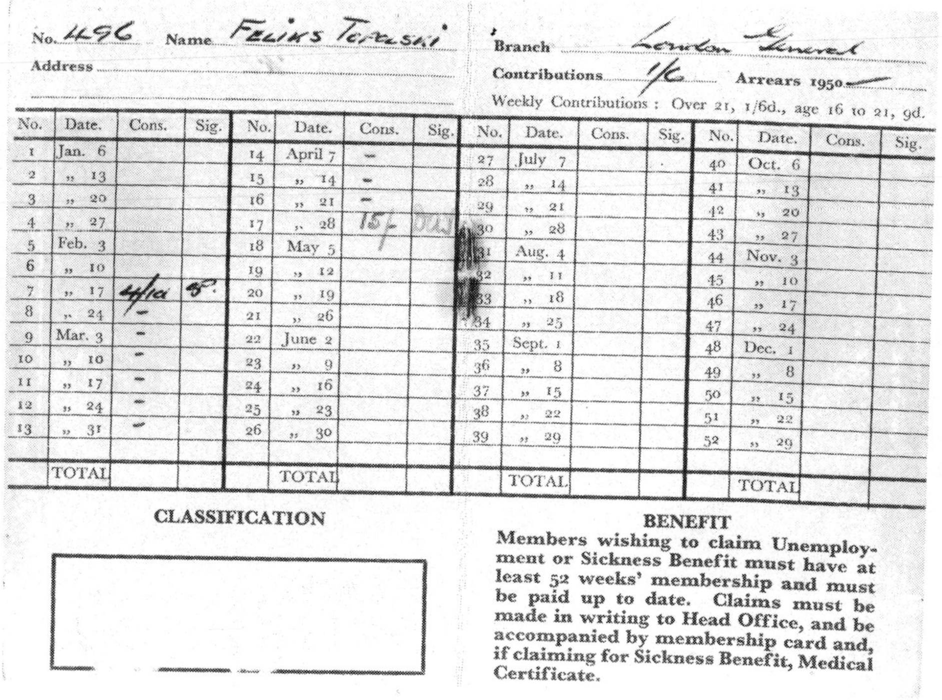

No. 496 Name Feliks Topolski

Address

Branch London General

Contributions 1/6 Arrears 1950 —

Weekly Contributions: Over 21, 1/6d., age 16 to 21, 9d.

No.	Date.	Cons.	Sig.	No.	Date.	Cons.	Sig.	No.	Date.	Cons.	Sig.	No.	Date.	Cons.	Sig.
1	Jan. 6			14	April 7	–		27	July 7			40	Oct. 6		
2	" 13			15	" 14	–		28	" 14			41	" 13		
3	" 20			16	" 21	–		29	" 21			42	" 20		
4	" 27			17	" 28	15/-	[illegible]	30	" 28			43	" 27		
5	Feb. 3			18	May 5			31	Aug. 4			44	Nov. 3		
6	" 10			19	" 12			32	" 11			45	" 10		
7	" 17	4/10	[illegible]	20	" 19			33	" 18			46	" 17		
8	" 24	–		21	" 26			34	" 25			47	" 24		
9	Mar. 3	–		22	June 2			35	Sept. 1			48	Dec. 1		
10	" 10	–		23	" 9			36	" 8			49	" 8		
11	" 17	–		24	" 16			37	" 15			50	" 15		
12	" 24	–		25	" 23			38	" 22			51	" 22		
13	" 31	–		26	" 30			39	" 29			52	" 29		
	TOTAL				TOTAL				TOTAL				TOTAL		

CLASSIFICATION

BENEFIT

Members wishing to claim Unemployment or Sickness Benefit must have at least 52 weeks' membership and must be paid up to date. Claims must be made in writing to Head Office, and be accompanied by membership card and, if claiming for Sickness Benefit, Medical Certificate.

roughed out on a criss-crossed piece of paper – **Clement** stepped forward. In my earliest Café Royal days a two-abreast dual friendship arose: the twin-sisters Clement and Robin, noble Forbes-Robertson featured, grandly cast in Amazonian mould and heroic of character. They gave me their closeness unreservedly and lastingly yet alternating in relay since, somehow, only one of them would be in London at a time. And once Robin delegated for me, impressively, in Poland. Clement, later, back from America with John Davenport, her massive thunderous husband, resettled with William Glock and condensed her manifold gifts into running the scenery painting at the Covent Garden Opera – her physicality and modesty satisfied.

And so, in a loving gesture of loyalty towards me at this major challenge, she climbed my scaffold with me on the first morning, and, together, we laid out the colour base.*

This length of 60 feet and the scaffold climbing to 20 feet did not trouble; the content abundantly overflowed out of drawings, loose and in sketchbooks, brought only weeks before from Asia; having lapidarily positioned the spaces for the hooked-together themes my confidence was such that composition cartoons for single sequences were only roughed out, so as not to consume 'creative' energy: the act of painting itself, 'on the spot' drawings in hand, was to give the muscle.

This was the patronage of dreams: the governmental Paint Research Centre was seconded to concoct paints for my demanding conditions: the part-open huge draught-sucking/blowing space needed strong lasting materials, and indeed the paint lives on – never since have I dipped my brush into anything so individually prepared. The arch-surfaces behind the painting panels sweated dampness – and, in a matter of days, the whole mural was transported to my studio and re-created in huge slices, turning horizontal under its lower ceilings, so that my work would not be interrupted during the wall treatment. Even the constant din and mobbing of my scaffolds (my wall in Belvedere Road lined the main traffic route between the east and west areas of the Festival) added to the overall urgency. And this participatory paradox: it was demanded that I, a worker amongst others, sign into the membership of the nearest to my occupation, the Sign-Painters' and Something-or-other Union, to be followed a few days later by a Union order to stop work – a strike being declared.

Even after the ignominiously speedy smashing up of the Festival my mural survived honourably: **the Colony of Singapore** had it re-erected in its **Victoria Memorial Hall** for some ten years; with the Independence it was taken down, supposedly for cleaning, but then happily returned to me (I paying the cost). It participates now, in parts and some disarray, in my *Memoir*.

Yes – vote-winning thus consumerism and all the adjoining sins of averageness may have snuffed out the burst of vitality in 1951 Britain, led (a rare instance) by the arts, with Labour's accord.

But that same Labour, perhaps greatly influenced (certainly at its low-brow fringes) by their ensuing election fiasco, moved to caution; and the same **Tory Minister Eccles** who rushed the wiping out of the memory of the Festival's undoubted triumph, proved, in a minor incident concerning myself, his side's humaneness: expelled against reason and morality from my old studio, I was offered by him, as the Minister of Works, but also moved as a private person, the assistance of his Ministry's surveyors in finding me a new workshop. They did so: after a series of Crown-owned

*Clement, at the peak of her forceful beauty and ever at the centre of a coterie of her choice, was stricken by a brain haemorrhage and died within days. Robin, a commanding and eccentric figure now, descends on me at long intervals – every time steeped in a novel other-worldly passion. Their children, all somewhat cut to the measure of new times, scattered away from that past concentration of blessings.

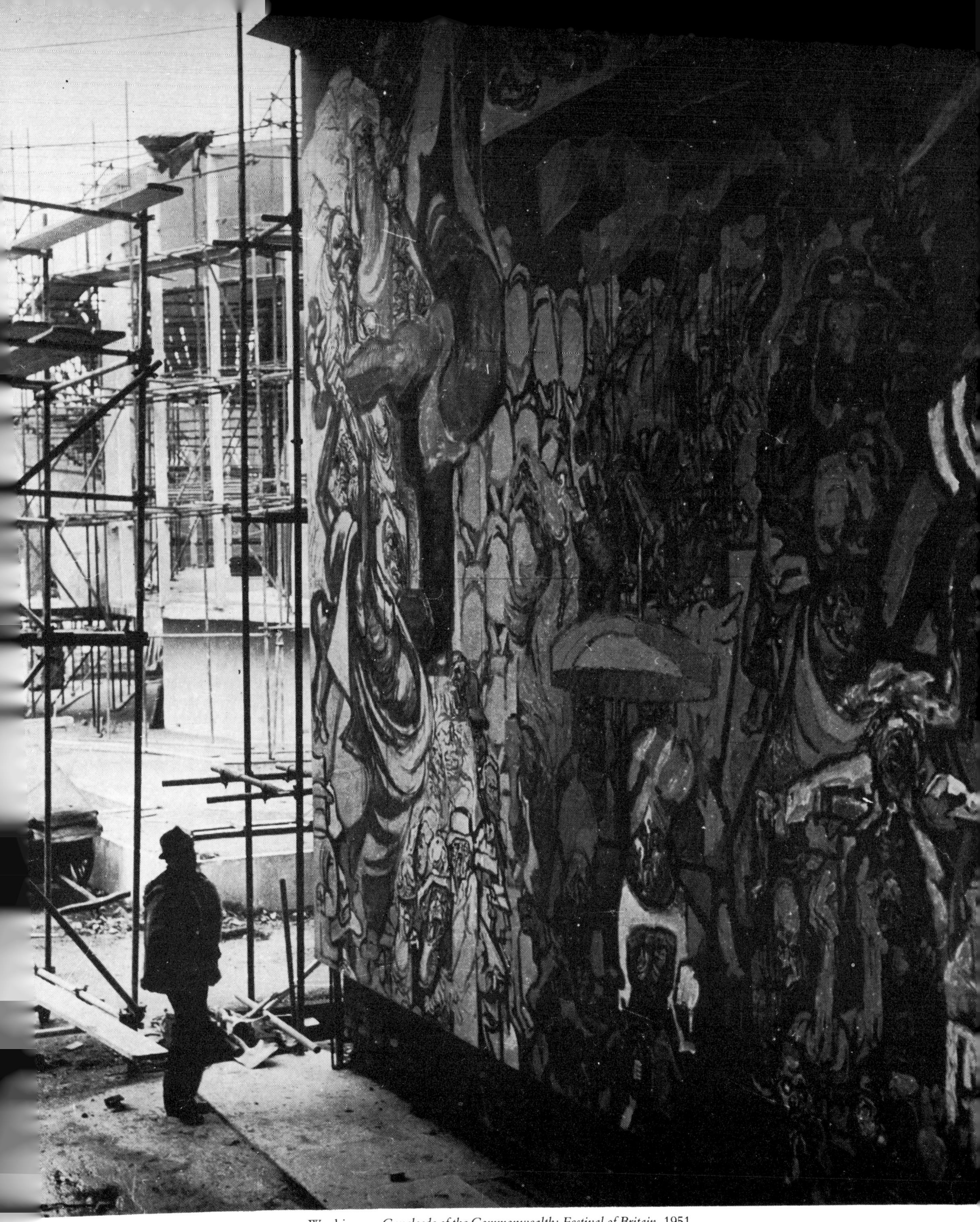

Working on *Cavalcade of the Commonwealth: Festival of Britain*, 1951

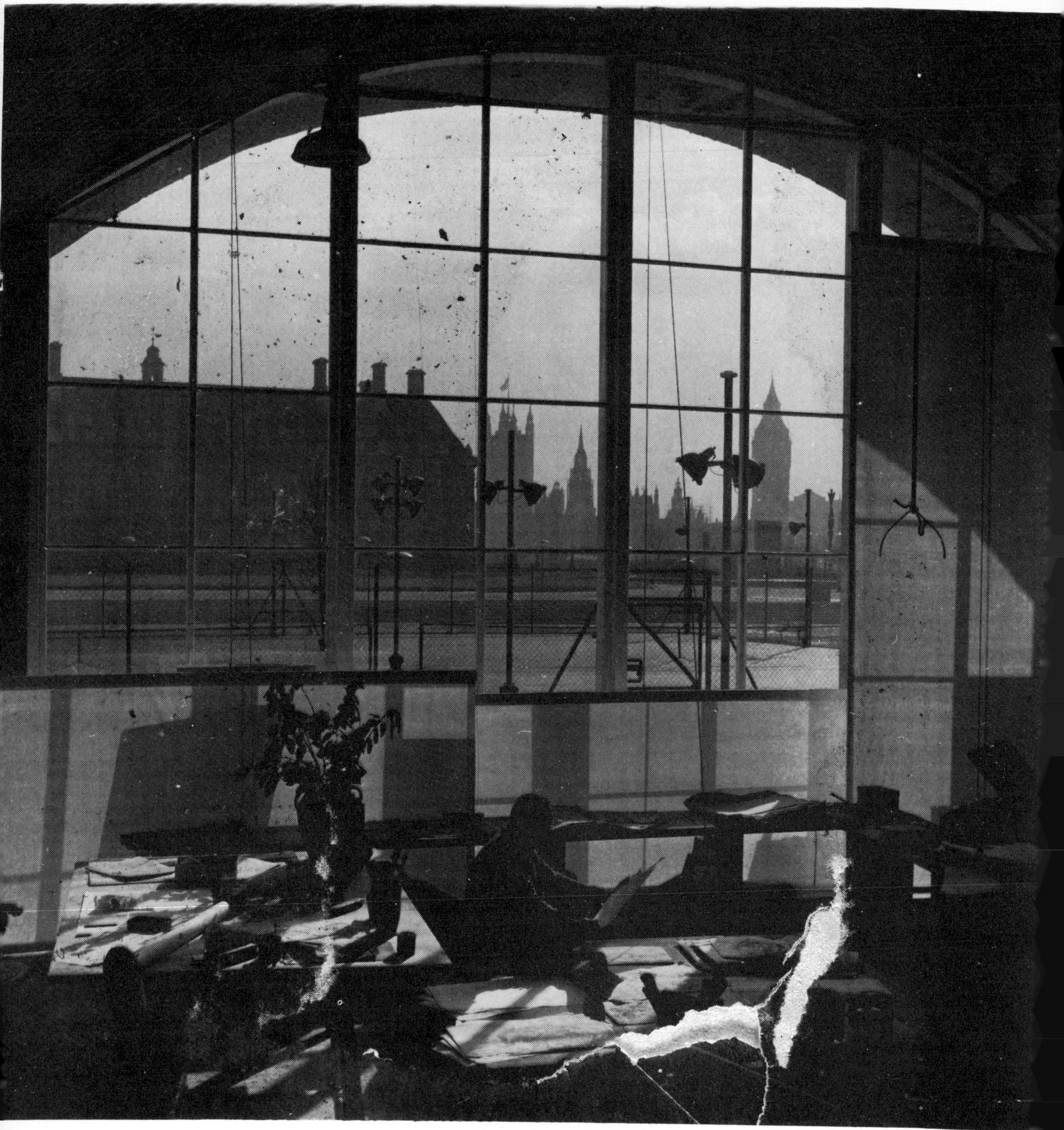

New Studio, 1953

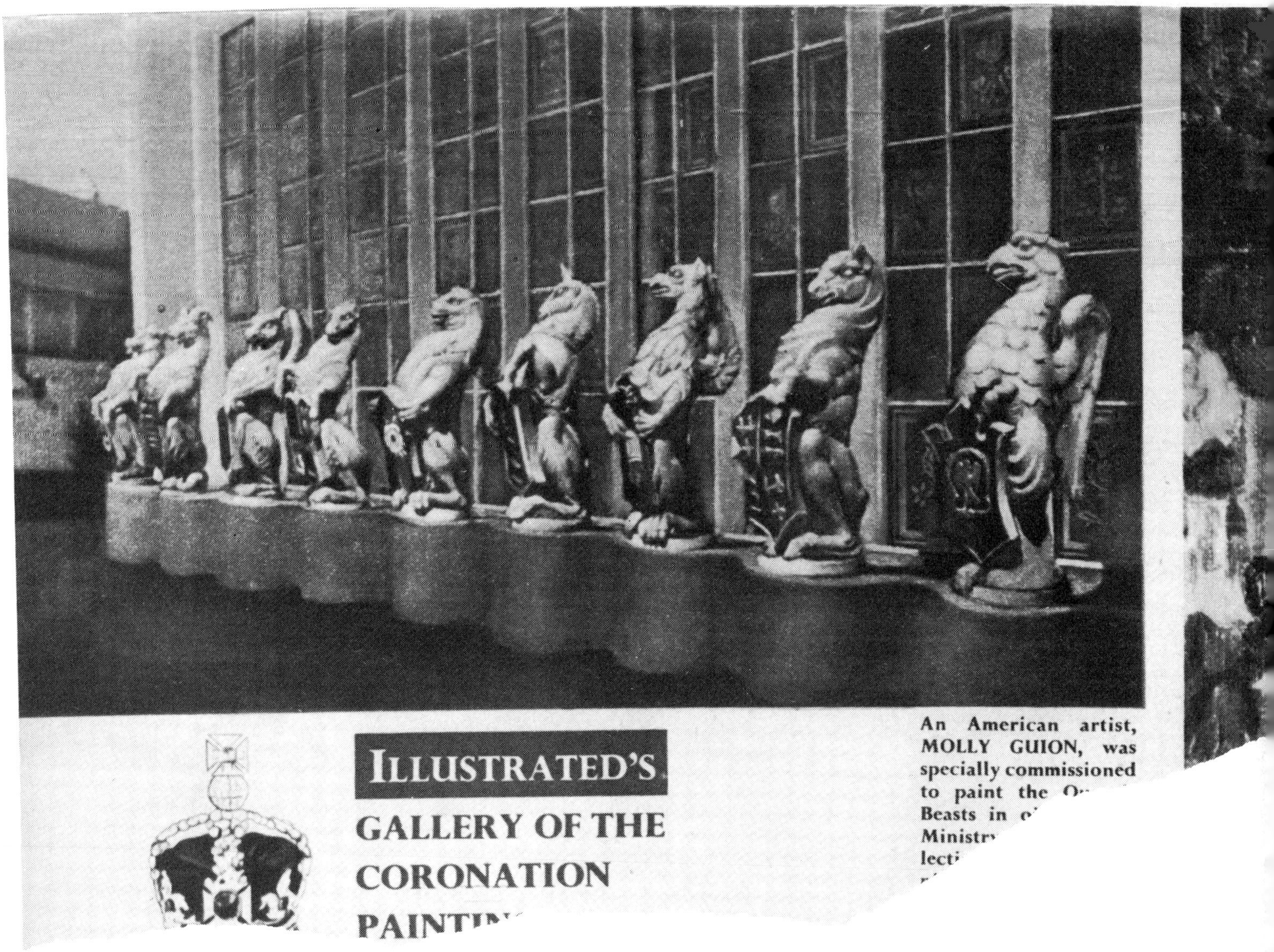

Coronation Abbey Annexe (from *Illustrated*)

garages, a bridge arch was proposed and, in spite of train noises overhead and water drips all over, accepted for its spectacular size.

But (this is now 1953, the Coronation over and my series of recording drawings on the theme, made at his orders, being examined by him at my house) to his question how my studio-arch is progressing, my answer has to be negative: both ends of the arch needed immense windows beyond my means, without which the place would be an unusable damp/dark horror. And then his on-the-spot offer of the 60-foot window, about to be dismantled, which had enclosed the Annexe to the Abbey built temporarily for the Coronation, for a nominal sum and the cost of transport. This was done, the halved window sufficing, with the addition of vertical louvres, to fill up each end of my arch. And this reflection: Eccles acted single-handedly, prompted by my hardship and his spontaneous squire-instinct: the issue was just and the response within his power. A Labour Minister, however sympathetic, would in such a case not even have imagined the possibility of out-stepping procedures, but would have referred the matter to the departments/counsellors/committees concerned, thus activating the cautious machinery over private favours – and assuredly loosing the window for me.

Celebrating the future annihilated, it had to be replaced by the return to reliable traditions: the Coronation. Although it carried the aura of the Imperial finale, its ceremonials – the forte of this country – were magnificient. Not a sycophant but merely now a breadwinner, this hireling painter drew/painted, and watched the new Old England emerging, re-emerging in a somewhat pauperized imitation of its former self.

France–Spain. *1951 Diary*

Under spreadeagled sun Canterbury silhouettes as if for Chaucer's Pilgrims. In Dover, the motor cars fly pantomime-like on wires over crinkly waters – hopeful ascension. Officializing officials – devils grounding these aspirants of heaven: machines' judgement day.

In the last few days (as always before departure) the sizzling of Edgware Road folklore pleased unexpectedly: grimy grimy vistas, selling-shopping slimy; overfecund, overgrown – the

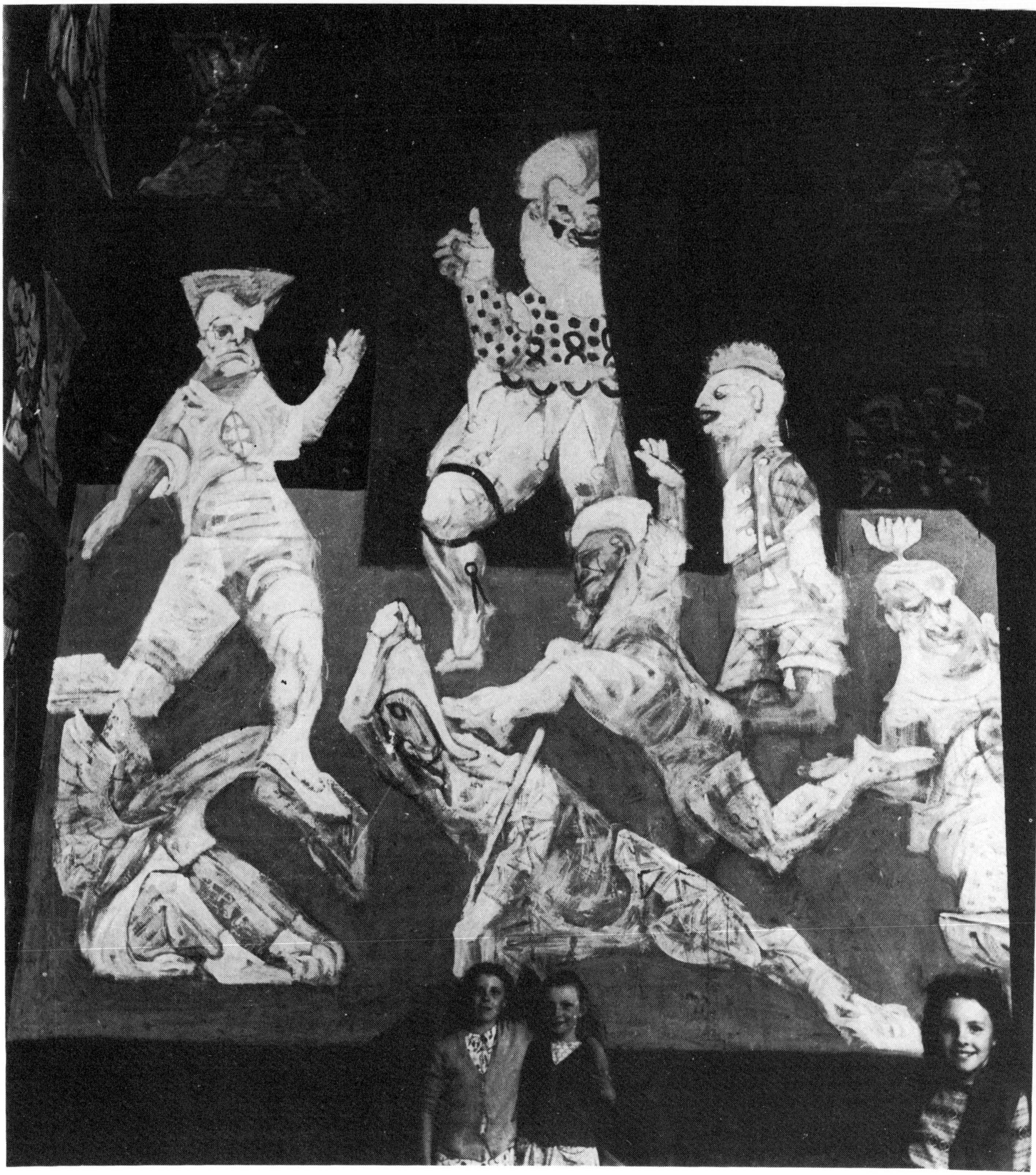

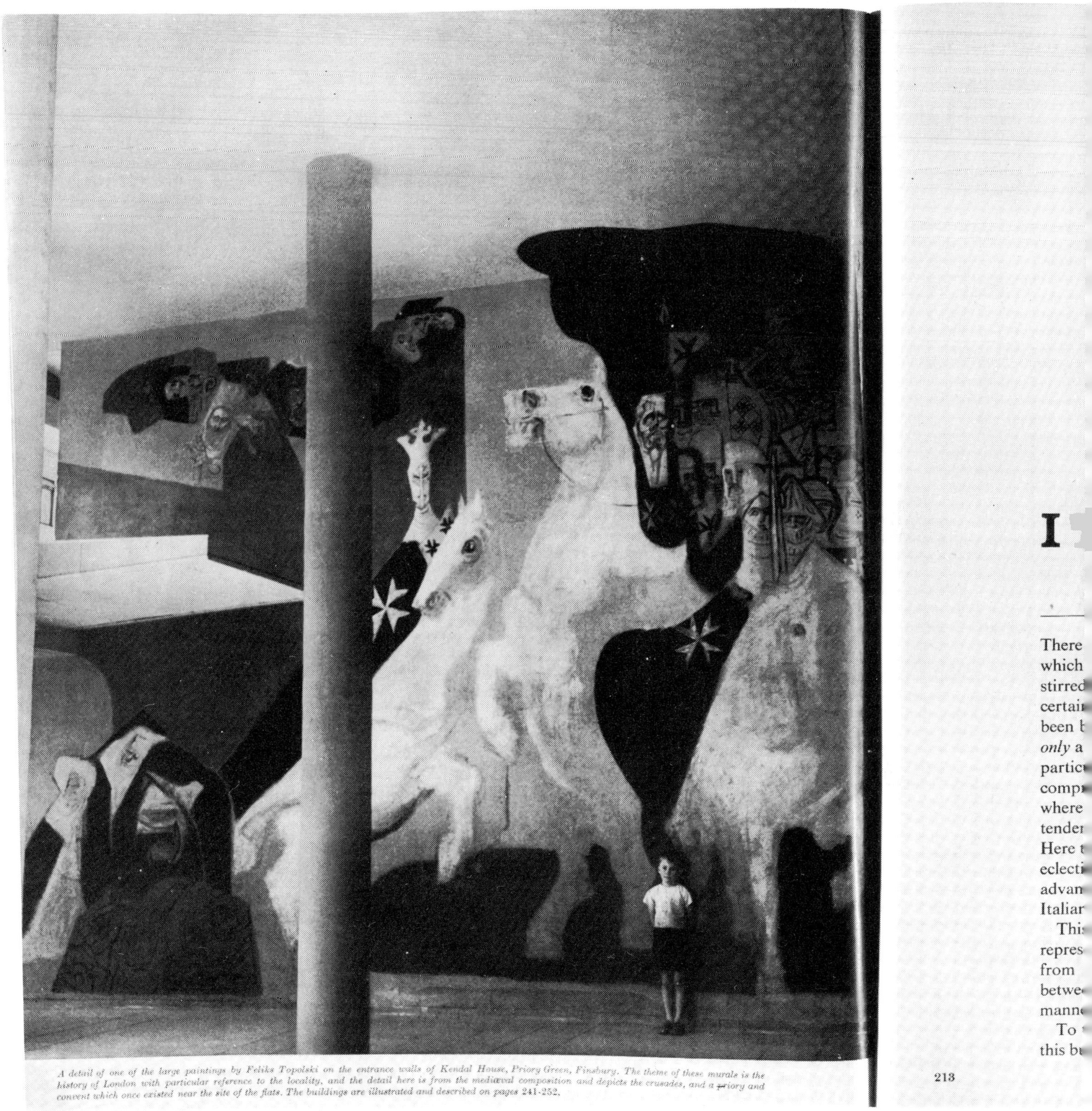

The Finsbury murals, as featured in *Architectural Review*

populace boils over, takes over. The gusty frieze of the people moves on – coarseness of the background reflects in their large-nosed, thin-lipped, bony squattiness. The bawdy intermezzo-faces occupy the whole stage – the pathos of human comedy without the tragic princes. Yet this ungainly inundation carries on its bosom young females of tender beauty – the inexplicable messengers of hope – unrequited. Yet a high wind chases vast clouds over the roofs. And the high and low momentum seem to send the island afloat – a mock-heroic ship of doubtful discovery.

But the Channel steamer contains a different – propertied – kind. Fixedly staring at their chained cars, though really on the move, they seem static.

Les gendarmes step aside. Past the lifesize Jesus twisting on a cross; past the walls chalked with 'Algérie Française' and 'Paix en Algérie'; past the still-heaped-up rubble of architecture – life returns in nasty shapes – spreading herpetic trash. But Boulogne encloses momentarily within sleepy baroque shadows, with dark people in blue, heavy on doorsteps.

The English are picnicking along the road and signal 'GB' loyalties. Our charabanc carries the FAMILY: frenzy of the children, Marion suffers and I – the cross on which she is nailed and which endures her weight. Incubator on wheels, hatching emotions energy anger moves, as yet detached, athwart lazy and sleepy France: feathery-green, cattle-and-widows infested. At petrol pumps the yokels watch unruffled our stop-exposed squabbles.

A strange long-tailed bird flutters across the growing view of Chartres – heralds sublimity. We enter the cathedral, divided. The marvel of stark glory; and when the swallow-nested organ tears the silence, there is no holding back elation. We leave arm-in-arm, Marion in tears. But Teresa's red hair burns for an instant, under the stained-glass beam of light, falsely and satanically. And I see my mistake: Marion's tears are not of peace between us, but of wider protestation – her moral sense is always lurking – no 'pure aesthetic pleasures' for her – and so, when confronted with man's soaring genius, she cries at his simultaneous baseness. The magnificence of the one makes for her the other more of an unbearable enormity. Thus she is condemned to unhappiness.

Either France has no temptations, or the spices of the East spoiled me for more subtle dishes. Coaches filled with tourist-pilgrims rush on along highways, framed by the natives languishing along the roadside – each breed jealous of the other. Limoges pores over aperitifs, suspended in the oblique present, leaning back on 1900 grandioseness. Now the roads narrow into rusticity; yet 'Liberez Martin' on the walls ('a Communist saboteur' some say; others, 'the resistance hero') show the way back to prehistory – to Montignac and Lascaux caves.

Detoured to a garage, I return alone through the night to my family. A pause at a turnpike, where my car's lights create a living village scene or extinguish it at will.

Back in Montignac the shops' illuminations hang out along a street modest genre-pictures – a gallery of tableaux vivants: the sports goods and clothing shops (patined by yellow light) with a group of melancholy women round a young man who holds his bicycle-Pegasus – a symbol of impending escape; next an old man trapped by shadowy junk; next in purply light of neon the provincial *précieuses* of a *salon de beauté*. But it is a shallow tradition of genre, nourished only by the shopkeeper's hoard of mass-produced inheritance.

On the bridge I lean in the darkness over the parapet. The black Vézère alive below – the other parapet ornamented by young men, silent but restless against it: the Vézère booms, impatient, through the village, through their senses and, by the by, saddens me in my pretence at belonging. At the Hôtel du Soleil d'Or a boy leads me through the blackened garden to one of many doors, as if chosen at random, into the dark interior – light – bedding crowded with slumberers – another 'genre'; a scrutiny – yes, these are mine.

'Cissy cavemen,' says Marion. Commodious grottoes lit theatrically. Comely little cattle, smugly drawn in sepia and black, trot over the shadowy roughness. Charming, almost too charming to be true. The dead corner of France in need of tourism-injection – could these chic *grisailles* be faked? There is also a secret piece: I win my way down a ladder and, under the guide's stern eye, squat respectfully in front of a small gently obscene scribble, an artist's clumsier afterthought that supposedly suggests magic. A religious aura: the tourists – the sophisticated pilgrims; their ritual – to circle in the grotto's centre with the preacher intoning false data, perching here and there on the rocky steepness; to crawl deeper and deeper into the caves, printed archaeological mementoes in hand, in a symbolic worship-search of the pre-beginning. The Western agnostic reached the end of his tether – he retreats, refusing to admit defeat, lecturing, reasoning (a rearguard action), hoping to rebound from the bottom. He climbs humbly the steep pinewood under the rain, gives alms, is admitted, descends underground – his catacombs – and expects to gain, through contemplation of the calligraphic bullocks and the mumblings of 'facts', the communion with the PRIMITIVE and to KNOW.

The drowsy land of Garonne droops under dripping skies; the villages decay; generation upon generation in stagnant layers within the mustiness of the Café du Commerce. The shutters half closed over the shops displaying anti-mosquito concoctions. Torpid devout females in black, sluggish against the forgotten valley, bring the climax through monstrosity – one of them, unobtrusively one of them, wears a long black beard. The freak mushrooms out of vacuum. Vacuum, hence expectancy.

And soon, on the vacant horizon, scouts, skirmishers appear, guns at the ready. The landsman, not the landlord, is the huntsman in this bareness. Crawling over the landscape, purposeful, they could be the avant-garde of an invader, but are still part of some RETREAT. Their flat immediate purpose in this bareness is the search for prey.

One of them cycles away towards the cluster of road signs; gun across the shoulders, a dog in the basket tied at the back, and a wooden leg – a musty laggard. In an instant his track is crossed, joined and overtaken by the hullabaloo of massed cyclists at speed, multicoloured, goggled, marked with numbers, fierce. They swish into the suburbs of St Livrade

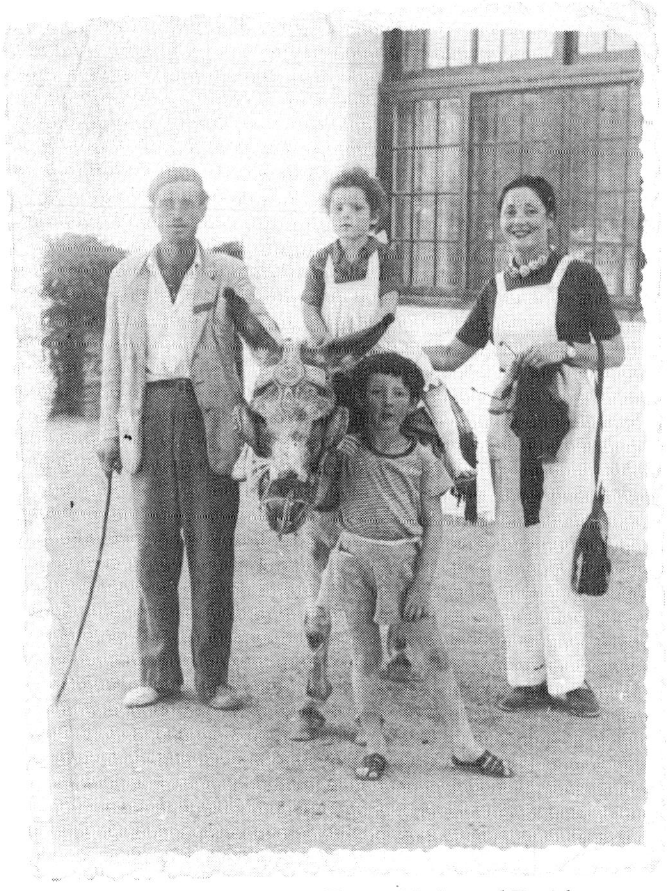

Spanish donkey man, Teresa, Marion and Daniel

through accumulating roaring spectators; they encircle the packed town, revolve endlessly, broil round and round the ecstatic rain-beaten multitude.

An evening gala at the Hôtel du Siècle. Humble room. Humble dishes. Humble wine. Damp urine odours at the door. Young men intent, but passive, boisterous fat woman holds her obscene own at the bar – young timid girls play and sing rumbas, flock of dogs crowds the floor. There is no key to this noisy congested room – sex seems to be the aberration of the middle-aged, the young women – pensive geishas; the men, perhaps the heroes of the earlier contest, are they spent, or their gravity means forebodings or purpose? or stunned, having raced into a blank wall?

The morning fusses on, naggy and mordacious. Over the posters of presentations (*'Non! La France ne sera pas un pays colonisé!'*) the government pastes orders. The bourgeois emerge, immersed in newspapers, tiny dogs at their feet. They talk 'la patrie' talk.

From one cave to another: from the altar of data at Lascaux to its complementary – at Lourdes. Utter change. The land grows in pulchritude, yields gently to tending by sharp-edged, solemn people. Blessedness seems near, but forfeited it must be. Expected and accepted *a priori*, the polypus-town of miracle-mongers and holiness-vendors appears. '*Embêtissez vous! Embêtissez vous!*' said Pascal. We propose to pass the markets, join processions, fall on our knees and abandon ourselves to the Grotto and the sacred springs.

Under the lolling Basilica an immense French platter with a tastily arranged dish of piousness: the meaty centre – a red cardinal within the chopped mixture of violet-black bishops and prelates, whitened by the amassment of nuns' wimples; the garnish – the thousand invalids on stretchers (courteous and lifted on elbows – who can; the others flattened in infirmity); a huge camera busily operated from high ladders documents all this.

The faithful crowd hungrily into the Grotto. The wheeled invalids exchange politenesses. An unpleasant, hence doubly moving, bourgeois, propelled by a fickle daughter, crosses himself painfully and trembling-tense drinks THE WATER, given by his wife's impatient hands.

An American girl waves a rosary – a souvenir. The proprietary aloofness of the clergy: healthy in spirit and body. Hustled, a blind and twisted being hurries to the Grotto – jingles a bell for self-announcing. A good woman perspiring in sacred agitation in the crowded queue at the Grotto thrusts quickly into our hands toffees – good deeds, earns indulgences. Men kneel – arms spread. Each for himself. Human perplexity and grief at oneself; the appalling confrontation with solitariness – and unashamed howlings for mercy.

Marion shields the children and, unable to bear all those self-supplications, overcome and in tears of readiness to give, forgets her own pains. Yet urged, she washes not her, but Teresa's left leg (mosquito-bitten, it swelled a bit since yesterday at Montignac) in the holy water.

In the mountains, on the headland between the crossing roads, above the railway and the river, we eat our supper. The vast, noble now, Basilica far below. Before us the sunset and the clamour of children.

Lestelle-Betharram. The storming river and the transparent climatic handsomeness. But afterwards tragedy. In a garage in Pau a huge lorry-wheel falls on Teresa and breaks horribly her left leg. The garage-hand holds and compares her two legs tenderly. The terrors. The compassion. The waiting. The child-invalid emerging from the operation room. Daniel's diary says: 'Bad day. **Mamusia** cried in her mind.' Teresa's twisted leg. Two bad worlds: sickness and 'grand' hotel. Marion says: 'She didn't like me, the saint of the Grotto,' and later: 'I washed this leg (it itched a bit) in the holy water.' Sad.

Pau has charms. It slides down from a higher level, helped by a little fair-like steep tramway. It hums and whistles with criss-crossing trains. It has old squares and – the Hôtel de France. Daniel's diary item: 'I pressed the lift button by myself in the biggest hotel in Pau.' The lackeys in and out of our rooms. Grand dishes feed the pains. Curtains are drawn. Curtains are opened. The bills are presented. Hired Good Samaritans.

Teresa's punishment. Lourdes. The irresistible musings: Christ's afflictions were incomplete – bachelorship eases martyrdom. The complete Golgotha should be ascended in a family group, in torments of compassion, in taking on oneself others' toil, in temptations to escape and in returns to loyalty; the dragging hither and thither Laocoöns – the threat upon all of them. Thus fared the families of the Jews under Hitler –

their road to sacrifice, though unwanted, brought on them such hells of conflicts and such self-denials that their sacramental powers must pale the myth of the Celibate.

Our humble touristic golgotha is a pedestrian matter. But it has some pathos. The everyday family routine put into the moving charabanc, involved and shaped by the outside, yet enveloped in itself.

The unbeliever's heroism is unmatchable. He does not fear premonitions, signs of the gods' displeasure, nor bargains for eternity. No props. He leans on little guidances, and poorly equipped as he is he has little to lose. Unpropitious signs we had plenty and then merciless punishment. But we move on, Teresa, prostrated on a makeshift litter, and when, a few miles beyond Pau flames shoot out from under the car's bonnet, we quench them and do not think ourselves defeated. The musty farmyard close by, where I seek help, grasps at me like witchcraft. Gulpy bogginess of nature overpowers the silent tattered house. The shutters are blocked, not a domestic beast nor a bird in a tree. And there, within the doorway, that just now squeaks open by itself, there shadows forth immobilely an old mad malevolent face; bat-like and unresponsive – but mocking.

Shall we ever escape France? But on our side, appropriately, are the men of the roads; a brisk lorry driver amputates a knot of wiring and gives us heart: '*Montez vous en route!*'

The landscape climbs up, children are joyous (still the beasts of instinct, or already punch-happy humans?), goodly mechanics pass us onwards.

The mountains are around us and the evening upon us. In Montory, a frontier village, out-of-content young emerge from nowhere, ask unusual questions, are gone – to nobody's surprise. The borderland yet the hinterland – the yokels' awkwardness touches the bizarre, mingles with the adventurous and the secretive. The bells and tic-tac of the cattle's hoofs. Black shady berets – an eccentric leads the blind. Hôtel de Pyrénées. A pale boy, perched high behind the counter among the drinkers, casts shadows over an aged book, *On se bat sur mer* by Paul Chack. High rustic wardrobes and beds; Teresa in pain and play – a Basque doll in impatient caressing tyrannizing hands – a prolonged performance of dominance and envy. Downstrairs the Basque boy mumbles in the corners: '*Mes contes.*' And at dinner, under a bare investigatory bulb, four solitary inexplicable men bend left and right in ever so slow unison, watching gravely the combat of two cats. Daniel at night: screams half-asleep, mumbles of pain, battles uncannily – wins his mother's company and calms down.

Vaguely, doubtfully I trace a thread through this voyage: Canterbury opens the Family's Progress. Cars in flight, 'Algérie Française' and cindery towns. And altercations to reflect the outside aura. The English hikers and the wandering poor – a parabola in passing. Two religions: Chartres and the golden giant. Marion's illness – Limoges, its banks and apothecaries. Lascaux and Sarlat's decay. Hunters and cyclists. The gala evening – the Family's downfall. The posters. Lourdes, The Supper – and Teresa's martyrdom: in the garage, nursing home, hotel. And Family reunited. The fire and the witch. The angel-mechanics and then entry into the mountains – with the last combat: the cats, the boy-poet and Daniel's night struggle. An ordinary travelogue – or a string of messages, a lesson straying among the incidents, evasive but essential and URGENT?

A few days accumulated enough oppression, clashes, stabs, stuff of life in fact, to furnish the frontier post at Valcarlos, even though of a tyranny, with the customary magic of escape and hope. Daniel's entry: 'We are in Spain and we touch the sky.'

Mountains unite but divide – harsher now under the red–yellow–red banner. And the different people: 'Pasionaria' faces and untidy clusters of truly simple soldiers-peasants, dangling tassels on their forage caps but without panache. Yet stratification confirmed by the split between those angular, hard-edged folk and their fattened commanders.

Architecture grows high and manly, majestically descended to by nature's amphitheatres. And our private tale loses itself in this domination. Soldiers on foot, soldiers and their mules, squat across the road; women settled, their backs to the road, sewing: the donkeys close-staring at the walls. Daniel and I taste and ponder a mountain stream after a stroll, a fruit in hand, taking in the vastness of heights against the cuddled-by-them hamlets; mountains – raw-fallow yet rearing fallow huts in fallow destinies – the old static world ribbons by, but also shelters; the world more truly blessed than by the hands of priests, though they – the priests – multiply.

In Pamplona's roadside inn, cheese and fruit – but accumulated tensions/signs demand: has this a meaning too? No message yet as people amass: black-clothed old women, waitresses, nuns, clergy, black shiny hats of the Guardia Civil.

Again on wheels, but the rusty station-wagon breaks down for us to review an enduring gypsy cavalcade; and to explore the roadside forest brimming with voices: from behind the bushes we watch this shallow pale stage-clearing filled with prancing playful hundreds of young clerics (black, black crown-shaped hats).

This, and the gypsies' unconcerned passage, may bracket our Spanish meaning; also, following, Logroño and its *paseo*: perhaps this cyclic promenading fills in: personages emerge, define themselves momentarily – that's all. In Logroño night-tombola, loudspeakers and unemphatic parade – but two little ice-cream girls dance under a lamp-post.

Majera: the mountains, now pink, permeate the pink houses, the pink soil offsets green cultivation. And Burgos, a show city – dense ogling our martyred baby Teresa, her plastered leg cushioned on a chic café terrace, ice-cream in hand, against the Cathdral, baroque-swollen into ostentation. But inside it, the pietist traffic to and fro of coiffed/veiled nuns makes the maze of immensities seem a roofed/colonnaded city within with its own purpose.

It is already dark, but quarter-mooned, when **Segovia**! The shock entry under the measureless viaduct into a tenebrous, thus secret, vastness, lit by a multitude of candles on the move, thus disquieting yet adductive – the vastness carousing with a mass of humanity, clamour of lungs and music; all this hitting at/on/in the simultaneous patined cacophony of all senses – all brought into one volley by the richest multiplicity of LIGHT – the flicker-lights (and shadows) of the past, pre-gas, pre-electricity.

And so Segovia (within Spain) stands as culmination of living nearness to – or glimpse of – the past, as France stood as the present.

But this enchantment did not last. Segovia's electricity repaired, the full illumination turned on swept away the mystery-pregnancy into the shame of Muzak-driven street-foxtrotting and tin-footballing side-shows, *Salones de los Deportes*.

The Cathedral squats in the sleepy morning heat, entwined by beggars. Women's black-accented black-swathed white faces and worshipful deportments; the swash of clergy in processions, lifted by the littleness of boy acolytes to the fore, but reduced by the murky heights, wind through gold–red–white paraphernalia of their idling business, their impious features, drowsier replicas of their merciless predecessors.

Over the rocky heights, and the steepest miraculous descent (measured by crosses on pedestals of piled-up boulders) into deep gigantic lowland within staggering immeasurable horizons; then the ride into **Madrid** between the walls still bullet-scarred by Franco's army's assault – a city grand, sprawling, thronging, throbbing, bumptious. The tenth-floor hotel – a view of the royal palace and open distances – maybe this posting will carry on the quest, with the children over the precipice on the hotel's balcony and our financial ruin borne upon us by this luxury of John Marks's choice.

My plan of action: to find d'Ors, *toros*, *gitanas*, low life, social occasions, official occasions, Caudillo day, military pomp, the Prado. But for a time, hellish quarrels with Marks, his own various quarrels (also with the waiters), his theme: a bad friend. Another theme in this travelogue into the heart of grief: Carmen Amaya's stamping, trailing her train, stylized anger.

A drawing (possibly a future painting) formed itself out of my tenth-floor view – the city and the plains beyond and three street passers-by: a tasselled soldier, a thick bespectacled señor and a bereted, shrivelled proletarian. The Prado and Goya's cul-de-sac of final Satanism and despair; also detected in a back passage, *La Decollación de San Juan Batista* by Anonimo Flamenco, a fine courtly scene encircling the yokel rustic head – a startling irrelevance, hence anonymous.

Then the religious service of the Corrida de Toros, fossilized; the failing matadors in face of a resisting bull show impatience – abominable; the affected enthusiasm for it of England's sophisticates – a facile conceit of expertise-exclusivity. At night a den with private rooms: a self-praising guitarist and fiery aged *gitana* entertain us for 150 pesos. West-East: the most westerly brink overhangs the western ocean and fastens to eastern geisha houses.

After the initial passage through the unfailing blessedness of peasants, Madrid's mean-streets parade of harsh Iberian features (those out-of-the-shadows girls in the railed windows included) wakes up a punishing thought: the folly of rolling this charabanc, overloaded with the whole lot of us (our own conflicts seizing in it), into the unpredictable unknown *mañana*, the grieving land of decline, hence thinly blanketed tensions; of getting-stale repression, hence the shifting land; us utterly at the mercy of it.

Madrid tires, but Goya recompenses though El Greco too repetitious. Then the President of the Philippines visits Franco: the tin-helmeted but grubby soldiers under drizzle, then the downpour-driven Moorish cavalry (turbaned in red–gold–white) trot (their Arabs tasselled) on the road to Toledo,

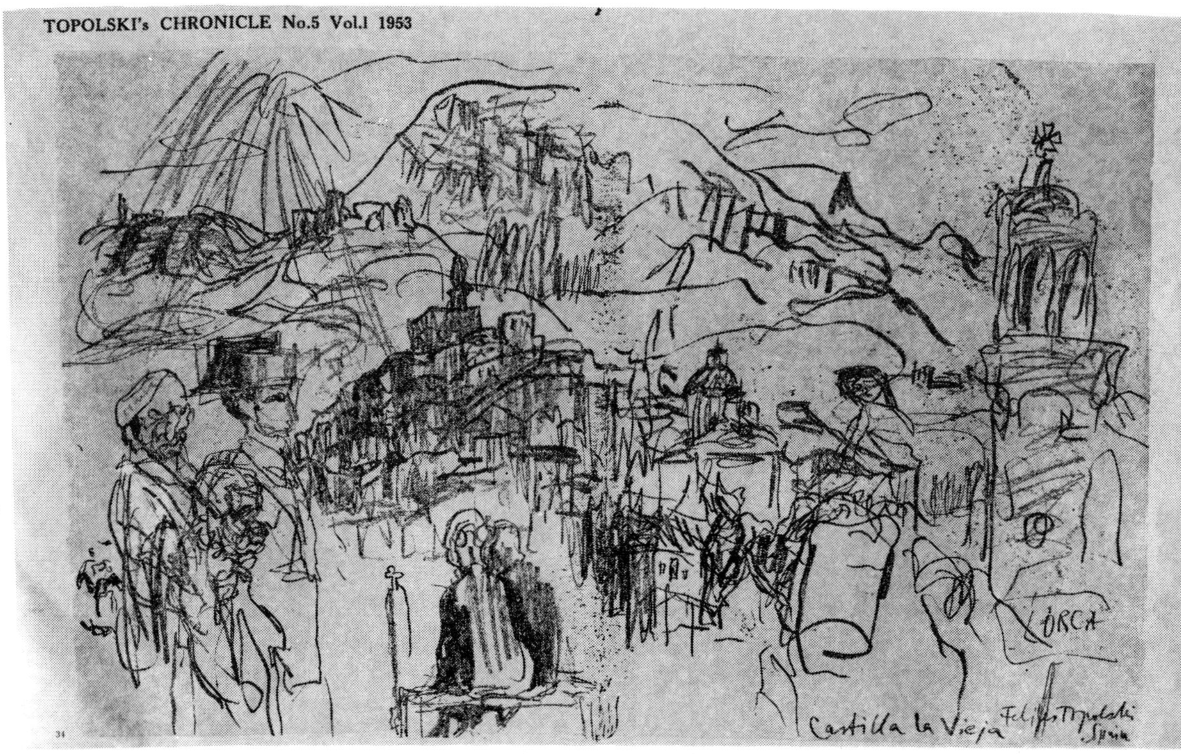

Spain (from *Topolski's Chronicle*)

with us tailing. Wide-brim-hatted, massive priests; brown monks; black-shawled, bigot women; soldiers contrasting with their officers' swagger; the Guardia Civil's sinister headgear; street-cleaners at it, and humble fathers carrying their small sons; and banners – the roadside range; one does not detect opponents unless it is *Ketman**-ingrained pseudo-tameness, the plastic-wrapped girls with paper flags in hand maybe bearing hidden thoughts. The ceremonials (dictatorial West and East) united in turn-of-the-century riggings of power (feathers, cockades, tarbooshes, ribbons, gold) jell this monstrous Spanish cake with put-on awesomeness – parallel to Chinese opera warlords.

Toledo Cathedral, overgrown with centuries of wonderfully discordant litter of styles. Up and down I trot under the rain, knocking at wrong doors, entering tender *casa privada patios*, to find a little room – El Greco's work room, the Funeral of Count Orgaz, Toledo map-panorama; through the *plazas*, colonnaded *galerías*, infested with cripples, blind men, dwarfs, tourists and traders, to the synagogue's scruffy but latticed Arabia; and away by a by-road into the late-hour Sierra and Ciudad Real.

Next day along the way – the dirt-tracks – to the car's destruction, beginning with a burst tyre, when traversing a road-gap (the earth befouled and the men coated with dust and toil) and a hamlet-burrow; emerging to totter over jagged rocks until the radiator lets go, cracks, water and petrol seeping out. But I tie it all up with strings and the car responds, climbs up mighty mountains – away and above from humanity, valleys below yawn from great depths, but usher us, spiralling, into the prettiness of Montoro, suspended above a river under the reddening sun, to fall into eternal friendship with mechanics, who replace the string with wires – and catch the radiator, at the last moment, from falling out.

Montoro counters mighty steepnesses above with olive groves patterned on rusty soil – twisty midget treelets, doubled in loving embraces, stand gracefully (move-dance for us) in long romancing ranks: the arboreal Cupid's roll-call tattoo. We race the sun-setting to arrive at Cordoba in daylight.

At last Cordoba: a bit of industrial stink under matador's-cape sky and endless lines of little homes back-turned to the narrow streets.

The cathedral cushioned/nested in this modesty like an alien elephant – Moorish colonnades very, very . . . And within them Chinese-boxed a Christian structure – buzzbuzz of the clergy and blackened women among gilt – the innermost box stuck in grey heights. But the priests are restless with a problem that sways them in their stalls towards one another, hands at gossiping, prattling lips; sends them in hurried relay-race clusters to pass on this gossip in gesticulating murmurings.

And these cadences serve as accompaniment for the disjointed quarrelsome interiors that got glued together not in communion but by parasitism and conquest.

Repairs delay the start until six. Speeding over precipices, thankful for the remains of daylight, but in the vast valley the new moon emerges (behind glass!) with the next massive chain and next – night growing out of them; and now in terror of abysmal twists the clutch fails, and braking-stopping at each abyss, the moon leaping from behind gully after gully (seen always through the windscreen!) encores the threat of disaster. The loathsome immensities, the dark passage in the whining heroic-broken old four-wheeler, prayers barred, as they brought at Lourdes Teresa's tragedy (so Marion says), solitariness of family's elementary contest-errantry – verily purgatory. And so I conquer (the manly hand and will – as it should be), rush through Malaga's sinking anthill to darkened **Torremolinos** – and the last trial: the house locked, unattended; and victory: my climb up the façade on to the first-floor balcony, crashing open the door, our (temporary) HOME, over the humming sea, achieved.

Morning reveals at our windows a lovely close *plaza* (white and grey, a black stately cross backed by a modest church), filed through by fishermen returning with the night's catch, tattered-brown-heavy – different.

Teresa and Daniel already settled: thunders over food swelling on their plates, set by the servily helper – heavily in black, tooth-gap grinning – Maria, who fries heaps of fish, white rustic wine plentifully chased. The eye travels further: the hot *plaza* ends on a view of the sea, bordered by bluish creepers. The ear receives voices: own, near and far – from the neighbourhood, the sea – *shoo-shoo-froom-shoo*, scratchings, knockings, traders' calls; all raised to clamour when the dog-catcher's cart enters with a cortège of uniformed men and swarming kids. And again women to the fore, high-pitched cackling in shops and doorways at their daily rounds – all is silence in the afternoon, to wake up by the shrieking radio for the evening.

The smell of poverty, of shops in the heat, of, stepping down to the sea, cave-dwellers' mouldiness and of grey sandbank fishermen's leavings. Daniel in raptures; Teresa, carried by four hands in a towel or pick-a-backed, plastered leg a sceptre, wise and stately.

Second day slower but fluid. Watching the day's curve dimming, cooling, into a *paseo* round the lingering and trivial little square.

Sunday. The church, prettily decked out with people, disappoints by prattle, lack of music, collection throughout the monstrancial gestures.

But the idyll is hollow, too hung on to a big city, too holidayish – Torremolinos, not enough a simple village, and we only the holiday-trippers, in spite of the black cross and our private *pietà*-in-plaster, squealing with joy.

The smeared sun hangs some two yards above the mooing, droning sea; on the now brown beach ant-humans align themselves in two slanting rows, pull assiduously and slowly, shove into a single streak along the waves – then regroup into a circle, with a few two-legged ants trotting towards them, their small ones at their side; they tug the minute boats over half the

*A Persian word, going back centuries, defining double-facedness (commendable) as private camouflage against oppressions.

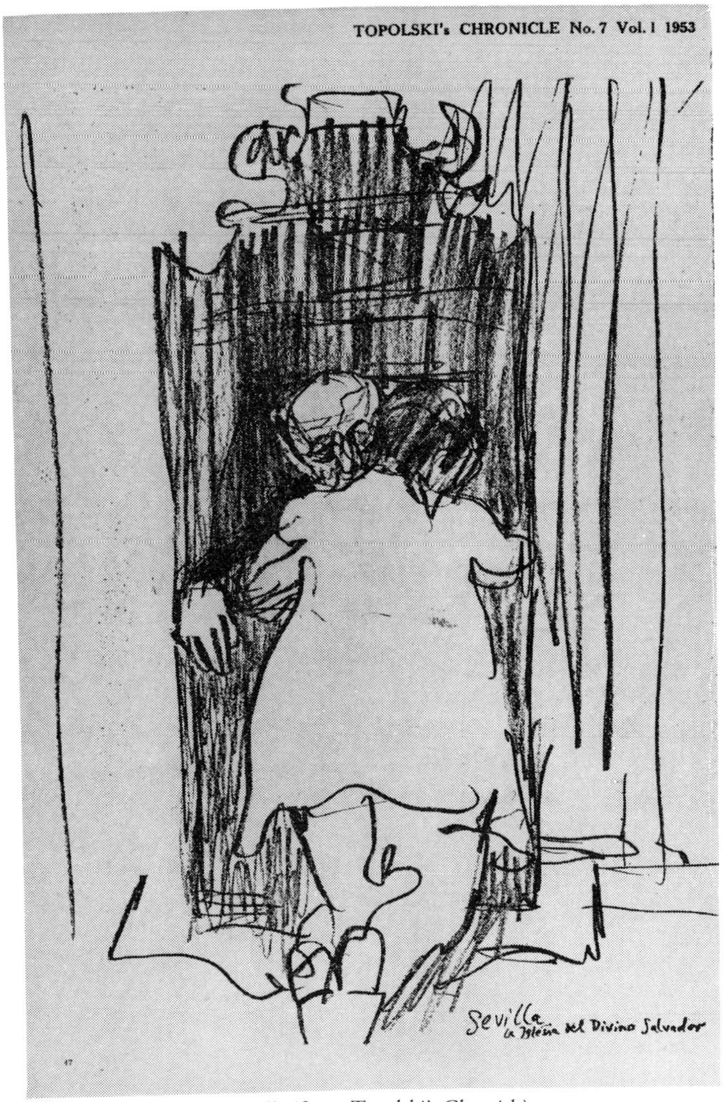

Sevilla (from *Topolski's Chronicle*)

sea, hooked in by the vague sickle of mountains. Watched from on high, all this disquiets by its strangeness and acrid thriftiness – one does not receive the message of benediction and fishing, but of indifferent mechanical and irrevocable ant-like exertions in routine biological murder.

This Sunday mass: pride of old women at settling in pews, having dragged themselves there on tormenting legs; also the crippled hunchback lording it with dark shades and black moustache, trimmed squarely. But the horrid priest with borrowed side hair brushed over the top (who clashed with me at the post office) carries in his physiognomy, cunning and dogged, a potential of enmity.

Enough enough of Spain, of the family-voyage, of Spain-loving friends. A bore, lift-taking in the car, prattles about smugglers and the Guardia Civil (a gesture of bribery) and comments on a large house we pass (the same gesture, but now it means riches) – enough enough. Will settle on my balcony, eyes on the sea, will dampen in the sea, eyes on the sky. But a telegram from the Rothensteins: tomorrow, in Seville, there will be a ticket for the *toros* and a hotel room.

Thus on the 11th I force into gallop the dripping-water-and-petrol jalopy, lonesome into the by now loathsome landscape – I battle the miles hatefully, and, when the heights mount and the **Ronda** fork unfurls rocky jaggedness, I swear and madden and regret and, omitting today, aim at the day of return.

Give a lift to a group of slouching peasants – only later learn of the brigands (*maquis*?) infesting these parts – and good men they prove to be when, after some kilometres, a tyre bursts. On and on, the mountains turn from earthy olive-bearing to white cragginess. Equally shaky half-thoughts on the ancient Moors' conquests over this fearsomeness, ambushes-mounted, with knowing not whether it is the doorstep to Hades, or does it bar the way to treasures? Those breeds of super manhood, while I, motorized, on a treacherous, but mapped, road leading to towns open by hotels and trodden by the old maidenish foot of Rose Macaulay, indulge in self-pity. But the drama continues hidden: the *maquis* of a lost revolution hide in these rocks and attack.

I change my 'crew' and enter Ronda in bottom gear – an unstuck miserable led in narrowness by a black funeral over the spectacular bridge. The homely townhall bears the red batch of Fascist arrows and '*Viva Franco*', '*Arriba España*' – the bust of a forgotten hero in front.

Then **Sevilla** and night brings *La Terraza* – a throwback to vigorous 1900: emphatic (bulging) tarts gravely weighing prospects or flaunting auguries and grim pre-caresses for ancient *roués*; and flamenco swamped in smoke and in entirety the style of noble, truest vulgarity. Detached from the Rothensteins, I drew my *de rigueur La Maja Desnuda* . . .

The Sevillan day of wonders. In a pretty Plaza del Salvador, mantillas/high combs out of a horse-pulled, rolled-in equipage (yellow wheels, green frockcoat and top-hat of the coachman) in *vanitas* round the newlywed – deep bowings and hats sweep-lifted and cocky personages and clergymen out-in shady porticos; and inside La Iglesia del Divino Salvador, the Virgin Mary flesh-colour glazed for real, real crowned, real starched- and lace-chemised; and in the manifold church-business, split into lights and dark turnings, folk choose themselves their favoured ways to God; and assiduously approach confessionals frontally, mouth to mouth.

Now the Cathedral: lined-up Guardia Civil – the Latins (as the Asians) stretch from bony rank-and-file to the fatter and portliest in grades of command. Ceremonial red-hatted, sashed, high-ranking replicas of Franco accumulate; Cardinal Segura, robes-buttressed/borne glides/floats through the hand-kissing genuflections of the human mass, leads the generals' ostentation to the altar – and a military trumpet will signal the monstrance elevation of the Host.

All this by common assent – no 'security measures'. And the mighty grandees stroll insouciant (when just then Henry Gurney, the British Pro-Consul, is shot dead in Malaya) to feast under bulls' stuffed heads (belatedly defiant) now changed into English flannels – before later receiving obeisances of the great matadors, present and past. This, and the yellow ochre arena and the ritual breaking into it of an amateur-boy, focus my attention (omit the picadors' horses squelching when banged). The bulls bite the sand pitiably.

I motor back (bringing the Rothensteins), leaking and

smoking, notching up my catastrophes, one after another thronged with folksy goodness and help, yet exposed to my American she-passenger's disreputable drivel, if I hear rightly: as a convert to Catholicism she cherishes (this perverse sham bigotry pronounced with idiot's ardour!) Spain, because of the presence of poverty, its great numbers of poor, enables the well-off Christians to have the advantageous chance to perform good deeds. Estepa: blackened women among whitened houses. At last Torremolinos, 'home', and piquancies of Marion's regency: sign-language propelled, she entered the village, established secret anti-fascist whispery accord with the garage mechanic, and impressively mounts every day a cortège: she at the head, a picturesque bereted villager leading a caped/saddled donkey ridden high by Teresa, her plastered leg pointing forth, with Daniel rummaging at the rear. A harmonious culmination. But the Spanish quest dilutes, submerged in beach-swim-gabble-sundown drinks of vacational dronery, accentuated by touristy bother arising from our guests, the Rothensteins, having lost their passports.

And the string of futilities of Malaga: the junk of the commercial centre (only the Cathedral, warmed by a ring of squares, cradled securely) leads to the doctor's waiting room, to ungainly souvenir shops, to a compensatorily pleasing restaurant: a serving girl's flowering – a she-dove jutting-bosomed and round shouldered – held up only for a short while, to slump/plump into womanhood's shapelessness.

And more of Torremolinos: above the cemetery – a packed chest of drawers for the dead; from the gypsies' cages below issues a dirt-patined, barefooted, burning-eyed urchin – an outsized sack on his back – purposeful; another in tatters, settled on the beach – grim side-glances – at the edge of daily non-deeds by non-people: local and holidaying pederasts, Americans on the make, riches-branded kids attended by a *niñera sirvienta*, starched, but skirts/aprons lifted above wading calves; Marion's devoted donkey-keeper stretched/napping with his saddled animal and a boy assistant close by circumscribe with Spanishness our outlandish enclave.

The journey back was not easier. The car, owing to the Spanish roads, a total invalid now, funds exhausted (owing to the currency regulations) and winter upon us, it took eight days to reach the frontier at Irun.

The Customs passed, we were stopped by the frontier police, who consulted their files. Told to unpack the whole most complicated load, I showed impatience. And only, when a scrap of paper thrown carelessly away was pounced on eagerly and examined minutely, and when the chief of the post bullied me to drag into his shed singlehanded every piece of luggage, as he was 'under no obligation to help me', I realized that this was to be something 'special'.

And indeed, for two hours the search went on, at first unpleasant, later hesitant, when letters and notes, meticulously read by an interpreter, revealed rather respectable connections.

But, when my Spanish sketchbooks were opened, the tension returned. My drawings were never examined with such devotion by friends or connoisseurs; never before had they raised such response. The policemen were adamant.

They proposed to arrest the sketches as unfair to their regime. They pointed to the predominance of soldiers, policemen (Guardia Civil) and clergy in them.

I saw red. My wife blazed. Her theme was Goya and the policeman's qualifications as art critic. Mine, that I shall not leave Irun and will call upon all the authors of the letters they read for help. Their determination subsided. And there were some messengers going back-and-forth before the invitation, now most polite, was given to proceed. The French, at the other end of the bridge, waited in agitated anticipation: 'What were we searched for?' We could not say. The Spaniards would not tell us.

The detached life of a tourist, hoisted along by the ever-ready help and kindness of the people; the barrier of language; the marvel of the country; the current argument of foreign Franco-fellow-travellers that this system is nothing like Nazism and it suits this virile nation. All this lured one into smug comfort.

But this frontier incident jerked one to the reality of fascism – the rule of the policeman and the informer.

While the search continued I tried to list in my mind those who may have held against us – and counted at least a dozen. Within one month in a small village we managed to gather a bunch composed of – an abandoned shopkeeper, a bypassed beach-trader, a cheating cook, the priest and the postmaster who disapproved of my drawing in the church, even the police still searching for the Rothensteins' passports, a mechanic who took liberties with the car and that one who had plotted with Marion . . . any of these may have been guilty. How many such adversaries a native could count. And how far their whole life is lived in the network of fear and 'strike before you are struck' mentality.

Explanations do not diminish the force of this finale. My obsessive reading into the journey of a minor tourist calvary-parable was given another accent by a thundering storm over Châtellrault and its Boulevard d'Estreen in which on the corner of Rue de Colombien *vis-à-vis* No. 96 at 4.27 p.m. a man flew spread-eagled over our advancing station-wagon; by instantly afterwards the sky-conquest by the angelic light of departing aureolan sun above the purified land. The obvious: the sacrifice and the blessing.

Night – headlamps, half torn off by the blow, half dying – sends us onward now with one light-eye pitifully swinging left–right (the weakened bull that rocks its lowered head in defeat), till settled wedged skyward.

The direction lost – off the Versailles highway on to rural and deserted distances; a path of wilderness carries us, feebly SOS up-signalling amongst deadened blind-windowed stony silences – for hours. Horizons of busy lights, but we circle in medieval stillness – it must be less than 20 kilometres to **Paris**, yet cobblestones, shutters closed – absence of café canopies, bicycles, humans. We seem led (a punishment) back into other centuries, never to emerge/arrive . . .

But there appears a man – offers a turn: and the huge highway of rushing cars – worse for light-twisted us, more devilish than those bizarrenesses of emptiness – 1 kilometre to Paris. Then, no transition, shock, crammed Parisian boulevard conformity. The ill-disposed slackening in us: Paris laid bare, caught unawares. People squeezed into lit glass-boxes (Boul'

Mich', St Germain des Prés), each labelled but each in flurry of singularities – for gathered grubby existentialisms.

Turns in foul dampness throw out the Eiffel, Champs-Élysées, Louvre – in the crush of cars, fury of the crowd and of *agents*. Miriam a sudden widow: Gilou killed by another driver arguing in the street out of their cars – the killer (with his bare hands), a returned Indo-China Army man. Dinner table sex-frivolities ('*Nehru, voilà c'est mon homme.*') Myself, torn out of bed and brought down at a horrible cold early hour (the odious parking left–right regulation), and pushed by a sadist *agent* into an ugly wrestling bout.

But later at Dior's couture parade a thick throng on the staircase parts, applauding, for Teresa: about 2½ foot high, crinkly red hair mounted high with a white patterned stocking, a frilled white poncho, striped scarf wrapped at the neck – ends hanging low behind, just visible checked trousers tucked into high boots (plaster had been taken off in Malaga) – she steals the show.

The car expires at the entry into the ferry boat. Rain, rocks and bony people. My studio meanly robbed of lead roofing, downpour-flooded, bedraggled, execrable; on the doorstep, a council man with a menacing note threatens banishment.

In 1952 Elizabeth Spriggs, a civilized witch, saw in the cards the pit awaiting me. The gravity of her prognostication was such that she would not tell what was coming; and, a year or so later, she was amazed at seeing me alive, not even damaged.

But already that evening when we sat over the cards, **my old studio** was stripped of its charms – **a stage for disasters.** While I was abroad the thieves had torn the lead from the roof and the November rains had soaked, crumpled and soiled the interior. And these were the last stages of a long campaign.

I saw my old studio as the symbolic bulwark of old ways. Having been overrun by enemies and flattened to the ground, it freed me to move ahead – therefore I like to think the portent did not prove wholly true.

I fought for my workshop fanatically, though not unaware of the hopelessness of my case. This being so, perhaps such a combat was just and inescapable for a solitary artist claiming his place in the Welfare sun.

In the early days of the war my studio had been in coalescence with the world. It bowed tenderly to the fauna and flora of the canal and of the gardens, and held open its doors and windows to the passing bargee-gypsy, the child and the trader; a patina-faced bargee on the towpath, his elbows on the ledge of my huge Victorian window, unhurriedly evolves his home-philosophy. It was at one with the trusting and trusted life round; everyone within his own calm boundaries.

The war embalmed all this for five years. But when it ended and the too-long-held solidity dissolved, the change and decay of the last years oozed into view. Harmony upset, the issues had to be battled out.

The first skirmishes were gay enough: it happened that Eric Linklater, the evolver of incongruous adventures, was with me at my studio, his high-domed bald head craned forward to watch the strangest scene – a slapstick chase: a deserter and policemen on his trail swimming the canal, rushing in and out through my open windows and doors, wet through and dripping.

The onrush and swelling of **barbarity** was quite rapid. The studio stood between two Blitz-blasted houses and on a stretch of neglected canal bank – shaded enough from the streetlights to bring more and more attacks. It was broken into regularly. Imperceptibly it turned into **a fortress.** The window shutters were smashed and had to be replaced by iron bars and grates.

There is a feeling of **pollution** and untouchability in one's own rooms when found outraged. An assault by Martians would give the same shudder at the slimy unknown. THEY, when unseen, become creatures of fearful imagination. They are from the other side, across the gulf of social conventions; they repel yet fascinate the stolid citizen, such as I became (my bohemianism child's play) when treated by them like any other man with a key to a piece of property in his pocket.

The clues left behind suggested at one time rough and ruthless destroyers, at another soft-footed cup-o'-tea-brewing professionals, or more fervently smash than grab youngsters. The litter of glass, the old and musty papers and clothes flooding the floors, the footmark and the tear across the long-preserved photograph, a table and a sculpture thrown to the ground and smashed as an afterthought. This happened all the time.

When every remaining object was so polluted and many gone (the pleasures of dusty accumulation rudely upset), it was impossible to sustain the earlier mood of cosiness. I went on with my life in the studio no longer at ease, but in defiance. The police were more and more reluctant to engage themselves. At night in my garden, menacing with its ruins – their ambushes, traps and pitfalls – the policemen would file in exaggerated caution, each behind his shaky circle of torchlight, again with slapstick associations. Yet once caught, a man held down would more often than not turn instantly from a threatening monster to a squealing whitened vomiting coward.

One of the tie-ups of those **decay-nights**:

An early-hours telephone call, pressing. I obligingly drive to a Westbourne Grove address – an impersonally partitioned house; led in by a naked woman I knew, I enter a darkened bed-bottles-smoke-filled room with another one stretched in a posture of expectation. They have used up their erotic repertory and are in need of topping it. It is all majestically wordless – the two women are indefatigably generous to one another in the entanglements which service/involve all three of us (a sample: they lie on their backs on top of one another, the lower one's lower body protrudes between the other's wide open legs and receives my erection, while my face explores the whole of the upper offering). Having done I leave.

Returning in the darkness at 3 a.m., I found the door glass smashed and bundled loot on the floor. I walked tense into the lightless room on the left, switched on the lights: no one. I went into the other room, switched on the lights: no one. It was not fear but a sort of submissive and hollow anticipation of nastiness. I paused, unsure. And, then, he stood in the connecting doorway. A ridiculous scene followed. We both acted the **cliché behaviour** ingrained by the cinema. There was the 'manly' calm and abrupt clipped phrases and – utter sloppiness. 'Call the police!' he said. 'I will,' I said. I reached (slowly) for the receiver; dialled the number; it began ringing. And only then: 'Unless you let me go.' So the receiver goes down and the *schmaltz* starts. When he realized that it was my studio he did not mean to take anything. He wanted to be an artist, but could not make a living. A young cripple in a soiled battledress jacket. A muddle of yearnings and shortcomings. I advise. I comfort him. He comforts me – his hand on my shoulder. I lead him through the broken door and he hobbles away.

And then a tearsome misery overcomes me when I stand alone under my roof. A sharp desire to get him back. The feeling of unbridgeable gap and of being left on the wrong side.

The pathos of the *condition humaine*, indefinable yet sharply shown as in a simple parable. And the unbearable cafard.

Next day I had iron sheetings installed over the doors and some of the windows, together with more formidable locks. One window, left accessible to continue the pleasure of the undisturbed nearness of water, made me sleep with my wartime lead-loaded swagger-stick by my side; yet, when woken again and again by shapes with one leg inside, I had to bar this one too.

But, before then, a contrast, also significant of that time: in the early daylight two figures bending into the studio from the canal footpath wake me up and declare *good* intentions: they are a London *Vogue*-girl guiding Penn, the American photographer, in search of me to include me, as instructed by New York, in his series of portraits.

A Polish girl (also significant since a rare example of 'collaboration' with German officers in occupied Poland – unembarrassedly self-confessed and entertainingly relating incongruous fun tales of the kind censored out by the Polish pride in the united anti-Nazi stand) left under my mosquito-net, I, dishevelled in dressing gown, posed for Irving.

Then the next attack came through the skylight – vain youngsters, obviously, who took war souvenirs, my prized army trousers made in Cairo, my bush-hat, and indulged in polishing a line of shoes before taking their choice. The quieter stretches were punctuated by the smashing of the window-panes.

The studio grew grim and grimy. The armies of lawlessness were rising round the stretch of wasteland, and the studio was under **a relentless siege**. They were there at night on my doorstep prowling, testing my defences, ever ready.

The neighbouring Fulthorp House ceased to be a romantic ruin and crawled with tarts and vagrants. When one slept there in the Blitz – the studio's huge skylights trembling and ringing too ominously with bangs and shrapnel – the house had an airy solidity. Later it was a thrilling nature-invaded dereliction to be explored. Now on entering (the human rats having scattered for the day) one met the sickly stench of human degradation. The tatters of clothing, the stained disgorging mattresses, the detritus of food – all had a repulsive greasiness and near-warmness surpassing by far a monkey's cage.

The constant night communings with the lower depth and after-the-shock collapses required the chemical neutralization of being submerged in a crowd; then the ugliness could be turned into a facetious story.

My work routine was challenged by the bellicose purpose of the others: I was in their path and they invaded my world. Most of my vitality was engaged in that war, while a lot of my energy was taken, as if between the rounds, with recovery exercises – that is, lightweight, even if somewhat sinister, amusements.

Because there were other night invasions: the illicit mobs of **libertinism** recruited from all strata of society (those *comme-il-faut* by day in predominance) reinforced by anybody who qualified by anti-conventional urge, brazenness, and stamina.

My defeat of Germany diary gives at length the ultimate degradation of 'displaced' masses herded at the southern edge of Germany – decomposing into a hardly alive sub-human plasma, thus perhaps the potential incubator of a New Message. Similarly I think of my night enemies and friends: their 'evil' doings were the swellings of social energies ready to explode – they were the matter of change. There was no change – these symptoms, when smoothed over, could turn poisonous under the surface.

Events, episodes, entanglements that mark life's pilgrimage, that is chronology; but the ever-beating pulses of bodily existence, starved or nourished, Bacchic or suppressed – even by age – must not be left out. Sins obscured by virtues: here an appropriate slot for a few carnal improprieties webbed in memory, but names/times blurred.

This Simplicissimus's late-night walk back to his New York studio on West 57th from a posh occasion for which, according to his 'merge with the background' routine, he wore in that era a black Lock Homburg, a Savile Row suit and a bow-tie made to right length-width by Turnbull & Asser of Jermyn Street – and, yes, a Brigg umbrella and a sketchbook in hand. In narrow West 58th at the side of the Plaza, two mackintoshed black girls, ruffian amateur tarts on a risky for them foray from Harlem, pass him, they and he stop and turn and in a moment they are within a concave shop-front cavity: there is no hesitation – the girl who raised him, skinny nakedness under the mac, surges (his foreign decorum blends for her perhaps with the forbidden territory into an aphrodisiac), meets his far above his average readiness to take on her spinning, whirling rapacity, now front, now back. The other girl stands guard, holding his sketchbook and umbrella (hat still on his head); taxis deposit, at intervals, opulent parties to the side entrance of the Plaza just across the narrow street from their danger-loaded, exhilarating *duetto*.

Summoned and extricated late one evening, from among his

routine, into a Chelsea tastiness, her husband away; she atremble, yet takes time precising the verbal contract of discretion, and only then unfussily strips, and the memory climaxes on the back-view bareness purposefully flopflop marching into the bedroom and her taking off the corners of the bed, one by one, the four, shakily perched, decorator's upright whimsies – to put them safely away in anticipation of abandon.

A Copenhagen art-world banquet in celebration of my and two other draughtsmen's official visit – each representing a different country.* The majestic editress of a women's periodical departs with me at the end, without much discretion. There is a gay applauding send off from a group of local male worthies. 'What do they shout?' I ask. 'For Fatherland!'

The pair of musty ancients in the cold daylight bleakness, within roofless squat-ruin stand bent and glued dog-fashion, rags-frilled mid-bareness and, on top, two panic-eyed faces squint/turn – but on and on the see-saw of these braves.

Or this unparalleled nature *in urbis* apotheosis: Hyde Park skirting over the dusk rush hour – first, I trace among the bushes a rotating ring of timid stalkers – its pivot a mighty tree; an upright woman – her bare trunk embedded in its trunk, upper flimsinesses of tart-hood erased by shadows, only the white immensities of breasts/belly/thighs glisten forward, encompass (not yield to) a spidery male-form clinging from below – dark folds-draped but for articulatory pale buttock-doubleness.

Post-coital confidences in his bed. Lady So-and-so (indeed her spouse concurrently tucked away in the House of Lords) lays out her dilemma: her demanding leading beau had her exposed (truly) to maltreatment by a whore (only then willing/able to mount her) – and wants more of it. But, with the mutual preference for spontaneity, and the dangers of blackmail, she, in her overwhelming desire to please him, invented a reliable potential partneress, to be soon available; warmed up the tale gradually until, delays exhausted, the non-existent creature must be produced. Milady pleads for help, and, obligingly, Simplicissimus searches out an idiotic *Ladies Directory*, given to him a long time before in a Soho joint by its compiler (he was imprisoned for it), and they proceed to turn the pages for likely candidates, since, hidden from her beloved as it must be, the only instant one, and removed beyond possible indiscretions, must be a low professional. A few phone calls buzz unobtainable – the *Directory* tends to be out of date – but one boorish/suspicious voice (I explaining my intermediary function) agrees to confront them at her place for the preliminary parley. A murky street, not even within Soho; a daunting door and the descent into a semi-basement – and, halfway down, the ladyship halts, grabs his sleeve (as thrill-convention dictates): 'I've been here! This MUST be the same tart I went with him to!' and backs up. 'Oh no,' he says, curiosity/amusement raised, 'Now we'll face it.' There is even an old maid to let them in; then the two women face to face, pretend, he assumes, not to recognize each other – a long silence and the puzzled fury of a truly ugly middle-aged wretch measures against the towering blonde's perfumed and minked panic. His role of an outsider is again proclaimed by him, supposedly unaware, of course, of the juxtaposition, and the proposal elaborated for a session with the proper protagonist. The whore obviously does not believe all this, but, details of personalities not bothering her, states the price. And the visibly shaken, silent till now, aristocrat pipes up: 'That's twice as much as it was last time!'

A risky punting expedition upstream flood-rushing Vistula with one of the two shapely sisters from Lublin aboard. The heavy fishermen's boat's heavily oar fighting/skirting the bushes overrunning mad current, until away from the humans and well into wilderness, he threw in a little anchor – its straining chain many yards long. They dilly-dallied to their hearts' content, but, when ready for returning, the anchor refused to budge, entangled in the secrets of inundated thickets.

The fearsome conditions and the girl watching: he took the deepest breath, dived in, holding to the chain (otherwise to be swept away at great speed) and, hand-over-hand working the fastest, pulled himself into the depths. Luckily the underwater bushes did not clutch at him and he freed the anchor easily and surfaced – the boat already whirling back to Kazimierz.

In a tiny car at 3 or so a.m., returning with his hosts (the host driving, she in the back seat cramped with the Simplicissimus) from a prolonged heavy drinking and advanced necking at the neighbours – (the neighbour emphasizes his high status manliness by two days' growth of beard) – they swapped and he, an appendix throughout. And so in the car his crutch tends to bulge. And the slack conversation's theme being exhaustion, his hostess undoes his flies announcing, 'But you seem quite alert.' Later she enters his room and climbs on to the high bed.

The next morning only the two men at breakfast. And the host's confessional musings that he would truly rather not indulge in last night's cross-fondlings – one woman's man. Not long after, they part and the very neighbour-lady marries him for a happy life ever after.

The road to Wilanów from Warsaw cuts through a forest and so in the empty darkness the car swerved on to a sandy path amongst the trees to a stop, safely hidden. The back-seat conventional love-making soon interrupted: the torchlight, the commanding knock and voice, the shine of the uniformal weaponry paraphernalia.

The hasty half-dressing – but PANIC. The formal visitor (and his well-known partneress) revealed in dishonour on every possible count. A feeble blank-minded argument with the gun-in-hand militiaman – prolonged by half-thoughts (a bribe, if refused and reported, would sink the guilt deeper; retreat on to VIP level may aggravate matters as well . . .) – concentrated pathetically on pointing out that there was no impediment to the traffic.

This lasted unnervingly long – eventually the guardian-of-

*Saul Steinberg, the USA – a Romanian; Vertès, France – a Hungarian; myself, England – a Pole.

the-law withdrawing with 'move away'. But, notwithstanding the shock of a catastrophe barely averted, there was still the obligation left for a modicum of an honourable ending: 'the act' was resumed and completed, rather formally. The militiaman's hesitation and withdrawal: the posh 'GB' car must have meant, on his side of the encounter, possible conflict between his simple duty and uncomfortable consequences, if (as he must have imagined) the pair were of a high order, besides the involved procedure to be embarked on . . .

A telephone call proposes a commission of a large drawing of the unknown her in the nude. A young and shapely person arrives and is duly drawn in full horizontal length, payment overlooked.

After a time, some acquaintance tells me that a call-girl he visited in a Sloane Avenue flat receives prone beneath my picture of her reclining self.

This gratified and also turned profitable, since she posed again and again now with her Chinese neighbour and night-club 'dancer' blessed with unmatchable physique.

A mighty, wide-reaching (legs and arms) night-club solo dancer – 'dancer' would reduce her to precision of averageness – while this seems a rather unprecedented ritual act, given her bodily perfection, unleashed in the vulgar night-club space turned temple, thus amplified.

Fierce female in a monumental argument with an equally impressive man – conducted on an ascending tube escalator: she, recognized as that dancer – but put into a human-scale triviality – hence suddenly of one piece and desirable.

Walking from the Savoy bar I spotted a group of men with her at the centre, now almost accessible, although not at all aware of my existence and her place in my fantasies. This remote chance had to be pinned down. A call from a telephone box asking the Savoy porter to extricate from the bar the carefully described lady. She responded. Next day at my studio my attempts at pursuing the demi-goddness in her were dissolved in bed – and, soon, in ordinariness.

A Blitzy beginning of a nice studio evening with a declared, but inconsistent Lesbian. Then, the glass roof a bit disquieting, we move out for a roving hunt round the pubs – she the bait – a miniature soldier girl extricated and taken back to the studio. But the soldier takes command: yes, stripped bare – but solely to demonstrate her remarkable head-stands and voltas, well dramatized from above.

Ronnie Duncan's minute-gypsy captivating looks provoked and illuminated the unknown London: busy daytime Queensway. Ronnie carries a tidily packaged purchase: a pound of mushrooms. An immaculate English matron blocks his path and says: 'What a pretty parcel you're carrying.' He, taken aback, says, 'I just bought some mushrooms.' She, pointing at his crotch: 'Oh no, I mean there, the other one . . .'

But at his blessed Devon rurality, with the grace all round (the green land heaving to the sea, the rustic farm, the hospitality), the most touching erotics declare purity: in the stable a breathtakingly beautiful sixteen-months-old Arab, pale bay white-marked, advances for caresses: only a few strokes on his pink nostrils needed for him to respond, how justly, in harmony with nature's rulings – the youthful erection foremost.

The crowded unpredictability of the Canal-bank studio. There were the worthy Thursdays, Marion-presided. There were some, not less stately but consistently young evenings (somewhat without Marion – perhaps punctuating our frequent and short-lived separations), unaccountably and inexplicably of one piece socially. I cannot recollect why, for instance, one of those gatherings had the line-up of socialite beauties of the day – Clifford sisters – one of them the future Lady Norwich, pre-Lolita June – to be the future Mrs Randolph Churchill, Lady Masserene and Ferrard, Lady Rose Maclaren – conducted, as it were, by (the only male there I remember) Klaus von Bülow.

But, entirely unconnected with the above and unselective sessions, gate-crashers confused, would assemble by chance. The male in memory was Stephen Ward* leading in his female devotees. More than their performance, the impressive daring of these lanky girls, diving into the murky rancid, spiky rubbish-filled canal outside my windows (Stephen dived with them) – I never would have dreamed of doing it even in the daylight – and back, wet and muddy to the wordless business. In somewhat more exclusive sphere, on different but equally unrestrained occasions, the females would talk about, 'one *has* to have good feet' – and assess trooper-like tragic decimations of their ranks.

Movie-watching dries out action.

Still in Warsaw, and youthfully confident, I felt, seated in the cinema, a fetching girl's (glimpsed earlier attended by a boyfriend) foot pressing my buttocks from behind. I wrote my telephone number on a scrap of paper and pushed it into her highish winter bootie. She rang next day and we met. No, she wouldn't go straight to my place – first, a cinema.

Never given to furtive petting, I devote my attention to the film. We emerge – she furious, refusing to follow our agreed *tête-à-tête*, leaves me with 'You didn't warm me up!' I proved not to be her kind of man.

Potem kutas jest taki czyściutki – 'Afterwards the prick is so spruce' – why this remembered, thrown out in passing, while pissing at the Café Royal's *pissoir* surrounded by a group of Polish fighter pilots, happily fulfilled – I (in mufti) lined up with them, but not disclosing my Polishness. Remember this *czyściutki*, spruce/dainty, because perhaps this silliness, this awkwardness, contained those days' extremes: of men's post-coital gratification (those generous good English women left behind!), of their uniforms and winged badges commanding them to death maybe the same autumnal night of the year 1940.

Recommended call-girl proved her validity (bedding almost forgotten) as ceaseless raconteuse (and diary writer!). Her

*'Topolski's view was that . . . Ward, of course, had to do with women, he himself had in his possession a drawing of him having intercourse with a woman . . .' Maurice Collis, *Diaries 1949–1969* (Heinemann, 1977).

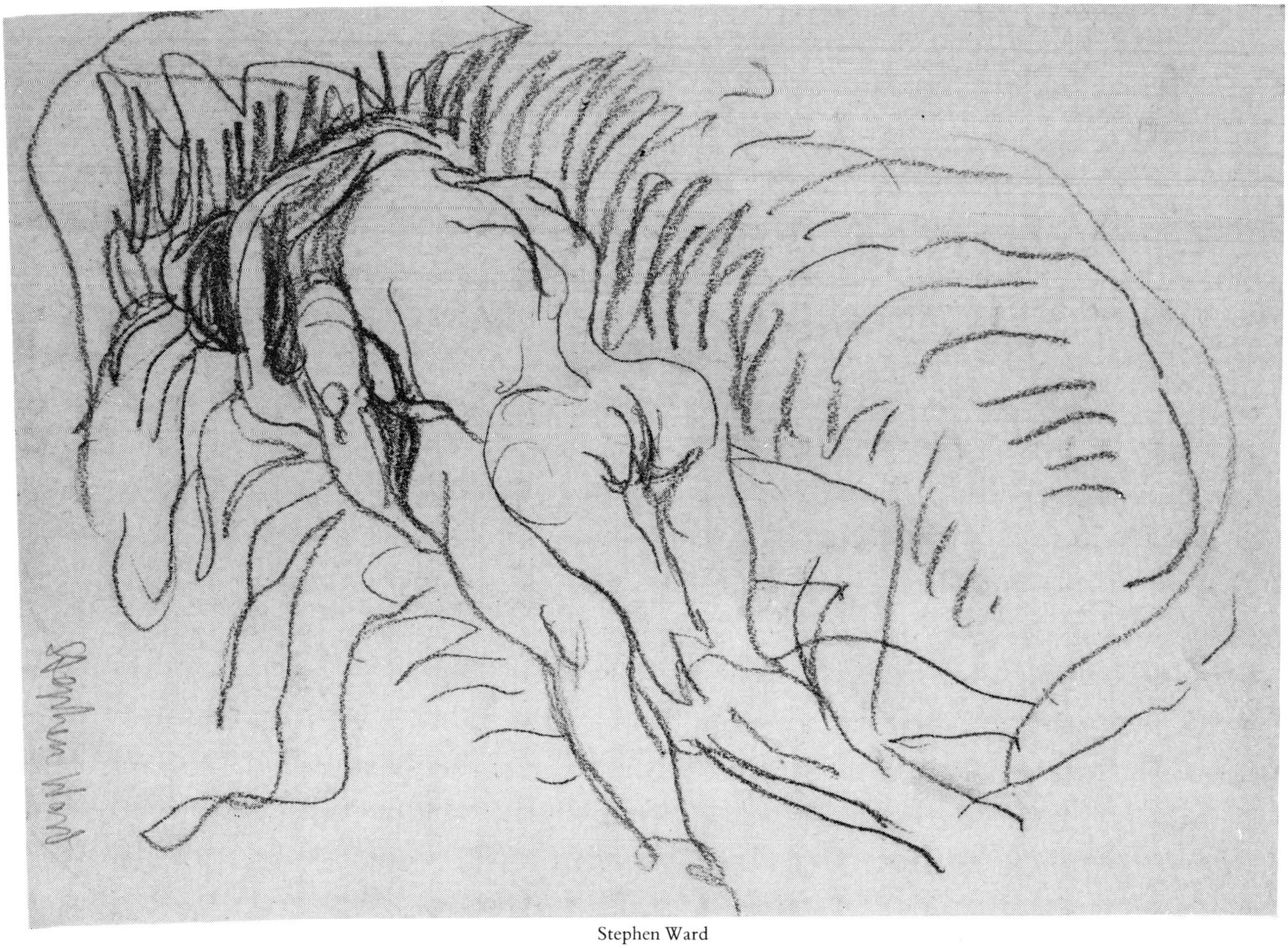

Stephen Ward

chain-tales of always bizarre encounters with men of prominence faded away, except for one: I truly forgot the name but he was an imposing Labour Party Minister, with Oxbridge background, as so often; she, my narrator, watched through the fanlight her colleague and him at a periodical deed: he, laid down (tied?) naked, and sacredly ringed with lighted candles, the girl threading needle-cotton through his nipples – to tear it all off with one mighty pull, bloodily, on his order and for his gratification.

The nostalgia-infected media of the eighties accelerate their phone calls: How well I knew and what can I say about Melanie Klein? about Bronowski? about David Low? about **Stephen Ward**?

Stephen, a smooth-featured well-English-shaped and -clothed debonair osteopathic medic of successful practice, with two manias in one: through knowing everybody, hence being indispensable as a go-between, to climb up. His attraction for and to women – the demi-monde was his main arena – went with his assembling men of consequence. Not an unusual recipe in snob society, with appetite for clandestine sex – but, in the early fifties he was far from being a sinister manipulator – there was not such a role in a widely mushrooming sphere of untrammelled sexuality, with many rogues (male and female) his betters. For some this was only the overflow of their other preoccupations; but for others – mostly females – the crucial test: thus men tended to enter this playtime and exit at will, while for a lot of women it may have been the gravest end-of-the-tether struggle, all their defences shed off, even punctuated in suicides.

I witnessed only his earlier feats – but, although the later ones, out of my reach, brought catastrophe of the highest order, I held on to my belief that his was, after all, not a sinister, merely any hostess's passion, when making up lists of her salon's guests, for along with social/mixed status the most important ingredient would be the male–female balance.

In my days of Stephen, he was in a way at the centre of naughtiness, because, precisely, his joy at netting good-time – that is non-commercial – girls and matching them out. Most men, even in the fun-and-games sphere, tend to be possessive, but sharing thus generosity (in both sexes) must have been/was/is a *sine qua non* for 'the Swinger's' way of life. And, in that loose circle, there was no dearth of similarly gifted enthusiasts: one, for example, would, on the way to a party, drop in at a pub and shortly emerge with two or three new and keen companions (never professionals) far from bound by loyalty to him in the following hours.

I saw Stephen after a long interval only once: he came to my studio to make a drawing of me for inclusion in his exhibition of likenesses (flat, spiritless, but in support of his 'celebrities'-chase) he planned – this was not long before the scandal.

But there took place about that time a ludicrously linked little conflict, which has to be prefaced lengthily. Quite another, innocently gambolling, loose 'circle' – its spread and density giving it the status of more or less the icing on London's limpiness, went under the name of **the Chelsea Set**: its seasonal fulfilment the fancy-dress New Year's Eve balls – proud of their themes and out-of-the-way locations. To give the claim some substance: one of these sessions filled up my studio with 'somebodies', had a page in Tony Armstrong-Jones's photographic album on London, and, in the early hours, newsvendors burst in bringing morning tabloids with front pages carrying headlines and pics of our party still in progress – naturally set on snob-cum-sensation accents: Lord Milford Haven and film actress Eva Bartok in cheek-to-cheek reconciliation.

Bronwyn Pugh, a prominently stylish model, impressively hatted at that party, posed for me a few days later for the fun of it. And when, soon after, I painted some twenty tall compositions on the theme of my 'Chelsea set' lady friends for the Chelsea Room at the newly built Carlton Tower Hotel, I naturally included her.

But by then she was Lady Astor, and Bill Astor, with whom I lunched now and again in the past, became incensed – no one else thought of objecting, but he, in his aristo-American pomposity, proposed that it would tarnish his noble name to have a picture of his wife displayed in a hotel (or was it a restaurant or both). Bronwyn, greatly embarrassed and dissociating herself emphatically, passed to me his objections. I found them mockable, and so he arrived at my studio to plead, to vaguely dangle some carrot or other, to claim his right – an abominable performance.

And then followed **the Profumo case.** Astor's central involvement in it as the permissive landlord of Stephen – and his ignoble silence, amounting to the sacrifice of Stephen. Truly defamed, Astor rapidly declined and died. But Stephen Ward: his suicide's motive is obvious and pathetically cleansing: his social climber's 'ideology', nothing else, crushed – his patron-friends having disallowed him.

The Citizen-Artist.*

In 1945, at the time of 'Labour for Ever', I wrote in *Tribune* on Planning for Art. In 1946, when the optimism of that period was marked by the inauguration of the Third Programme, I held forth in it about my artistic creed. One of my calmer phrases was: 'The airless studios grow stifling. Kick the door open – the hum of life turns into a roar.' An artist may be excused for taking his own urges as universal; I spoke of 'an art of synthesis – painting fed on reality – the reality of today, which is that of the awareness of multitudes on the move, of global oneness torn by conflicts – and achieved, not by retrogression into 'realism', but through the formal liberty won by modern art. An EPIC art, to match our time.' I ended with such passages: 'This is the right moment to help the new life springing up in visual art. The yielding of the walls of public buildings for mural painting will most certainly draw the artists from their shells, forcing the growth of likely talents up and away from drawing-room canvases. Michelangelo's vision, had it been squashed into the easel pictures of today, would never have expanded into the miracle it is. How unfulfilled he would have been without the Sistine Chapel.'

This call fell on the deaf ears of the esoterists, placed strategically in positions of advice and responsibility, at that time uncompromisingly seekers of 'Recent Trends in Abstraction'; the critic of the *New Statesman* mocked my ungentlemanly show of emotion, the critic of the *Evening Standard* my accent, and I was never asked again to speak on the Third Programme. [. . .]

Music, ballet, theatre, are given straight subsidies; it means plainly that these activities cannot exist on their own, but, their desirability established without doubt, it is worthwhile for the State to pay the musicians, dancers, conductors, singers, doormen, stage-hands, producers, paint-room staff for their professional services. [. . .]

A wide concern was shown by the country over the MPs' insufficient salaries – concern, because it is accepted that the MPs are needed. It seems by now accepted that the arts are needed and therefore (there is no way out of it) the makers of art; and it is obvious that they cannot support themselves independently, that is, their products are not a commodity, but belong to the spiritual foodstuffs along with those of the clergy, university dons, ballet dancers, bluemantle pursuivants, and MPs; and with these, they should be taken into the bosom of the nation.

Perhaps the simplest solution would be, therefore, if the artist and the official merged into one: let them both be civil servants, for better or worse. Nobody will dare, then, to complain about this 'unnecessary luxury'. With the arts nationalized, an artist would be a regular government employee, as the Court artists, or the War Artists, were. I assure you that I am not facetious.

It could be all rather simple; a large number of legitimate jobs for the artists could be listed, with more *raison d'être* than many which custom has made respectable. [. . .]

The popularization of art, and the museum worship, with the attached multitude of high priests (given tremendous prestige out of all proportions) can be, without much loss, reduced in rank and numbers, while the living art would spread over walls, flower in popular festivals, replace Dodos in misused, vast museums, come out in the workshop-art-centres. [. . .]

A major exhibition palace (perhaps the Imperial War Museum, renamed the War and Peace Museum) would be given to current shows, at present reduced to the measure of commercial galleries. Commissions and employment

*Extracts from a paper read at the invitation of The Arts and Amenities Group of the Parliamentary Labour Party at the House of Commons, on 23 February 1954.

schemes for the artist would be planned on a permanent basis, to include: the documentation of our time; designing for public festivals and processions; executing series of portraits; designing interiors (furniture, hangings, lighting) for public halls, government offices and embassies, hospitals, endless waiting and reception rooms; designing uniforms . . .

Art centres should be provided which would bring artists' workshops into the orbit of the community.

And:

– permanent appointments by local authorities for artists to look after and design the colour schemes of the townscape – planning the juxtaposition of colours of the façades of the houses, shop fronts and street furniture;

– creating an opulent library (not designed solely on sales prospects) of pictorial surveys of the lands of the Commonwealth;

– to include the artists in town-planning bodies, and co-operating with the architects on the plans of new public buildings. This is tried in America, and rightly so – the modern architect conceives mainly the plan and function of the building – he is, in fact, an engineer who needs a partner trained in visual aspects. [. . .]

I did not speak here of the inner core of art which is the flame of an idea in communion with life. Bernard Shaw wrote once that only the assertion of conviction can produce heat powerful enough to fire the shape of true art. Indeed, all the organizing in the world may not rekindle the creative fire. But this would be more likely to happen if the opportunites matched the time's immense aspirations. Ours *is* the golden age.

The 'social' period did not dwindle away, but ended in an apotheosis; **a party for Picasso**.

Two issues clashed. There was to be a Peace Congress in Sheffield, and Picasso was to be a delegate; the Arts Council's important London exhibition of Picasso's work had been conveniently dated so as to be grandly opened by the master himself. But the Labour Government, anticipating the Congress's political bias, and their embarrassment therefrom, sabotaged it by refusing key delegates entry to this country.

My Wrocław Peace Congress experience persuaded me that my medium of expression was painting and drawing, not the platform, and ever since I have rejected tempting invitations to travel on the 'delegate' ticket, both Left and Right. I was invited in 1950 to the first Congress for Cultural Freedom to be staged in Berlin. This was the West's 'cultural' answer to the 'intellectual' congresses initiated by the East; it was marked by Koestler's oratory, and developed later into the solid patronage of the committed, such as Stephen Spender and Denis de Rougemont. I refused to attend, giving my anti-congress-of-any-kind argument. The swift reply suggested an exhibition of my work in Berlin at the time of the Congress. I replied that I should be delighted with an exhibition a bit later. This received no answer – the exhibition as such was of no interest. And my work as such is of little interest to the patrons of 'free culture'. Similarly, I said no to the other side's later invitations to Vienna, to Helsinki – and to Sheffield.

All this has to be declared: the contemporary ablution-ritual – the act of uncovering the respectable inner vacuum, before one is accepted as a *bona-fide* celebrant of TRUTH.

So in this mid-twentieth century year of 1952 the Congress in Sheffield which propounded (not necessarily performed) a free exchange of ideas, was quashed by the socialist Government of freedom-loving Britain. However, a few foreign delegates, less dangerous than the others (that is, nearer the vacuum ideal) were admitted; also Picasso as there was an official use for him: free speech-delivering and ceremonializing at the Government-sponsored exhibition.

Most understandably Picasso refused to oblige and it occurred to some people, made uncomfortable by our rulers, that it would be right to stage an act of hospitality cum sympathy for the master. It fell to me to invite Picasso to meet the angels of London.

It was a mammoth occasion, starting in the early evening with the eager Henry Moore, Graham Sutherland and James Laver who all arrived an hour too early; continuing for hours in thrilling suspense before Picasso descended and started to plough through the field of two or three hundred tight-fitting hommagers; and expanding into the early hours of the morning with the arrival of some late-sitting Members of Parliament.

We were told that the Arts Council's opening reception was a sorry and depopulated sight. 'Everybody' was at my studio, and the rare spirit of a righteous and near-daring cause lifted the usual gathering of egocentrics to the level of elated camaraderie. Perhaps this was the last united stand of the culture-crust.

I encountered many unfamiliar faces. With an easily assimilated prejudice, I was inclined to take them for political

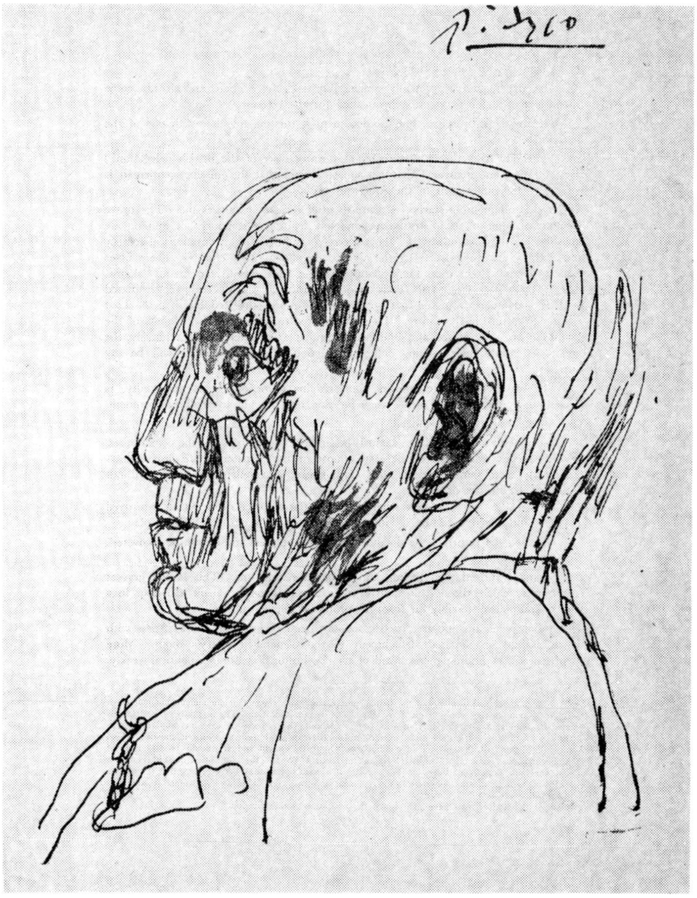

Picasso (from '*Confessions of a Congress Delegate*')

gate-crashers till a square and bumptious Latin type, sneering at the unavoidable presence of my 'work in progress' – and myself – was explained to me as a Glaswegian with an Italian name, a rising abstractionist.

The gate-crashers, then, were also artistic.

But most of my guests I knew: Epstein with his ladies, and Rothenstein unburdened, all the artists, even some patrons, all the critics (Eric Newton gathering support for his claim as an indispensable feature in Art – his Sunday paper having dismissed him from the Olympian post of the dozen-line art reviewer), many writers and journalistic pundits, several managerial personages and – ministers of the Crown: Nye Bevan and George Strauss.

Picasso moved around, with me bubbling in my clumsy French the congested *Who's Who*. A veritable *dago* he (silks and elaborately cut suit, the narrow multi-buttoned sleeve revealing the deliberate length of the jewelled shirt cuff) – dashing, neat and little; a veritable monkey he, with his brown ball of a head and nippy plastic-black eyes; a veritable child genius – vain, ageless, naughty, energy-loaded and never wrong.

There were a few who even in this atmosphere looked for an 'opening'. Incorrigible Freda pursued him to assure herself that he would remember her and receive her in Valauris and perhaps let her sculpt him; loyal Frederica chanted into his ear the name of Sir Francis, her husband . . . But on the whole the mood was that of a noble demonstration received regally.

The reporters and the photographers laid siege outside. I kept them out, but a young woman friend, who was working on an evening paper, came, naively invited by me. She described the occasion truthfully for her column, but, the paper being of the opposition, the editors rehashed the story into an attack on one of the Ministers, who had attended the Picasso reception.

The girl reporter, being a General's daughter, was prone to honourable reactions. She resigned her job and collected a number of impressive signatories from amongst the guests for a letter denouncing the paper's action as ignoble. This was printed in the *New Statesman*. But when the girl began to look for a new engagement by approaching its editor, Kingsley Martin (also one of the guests), she got a reply which indicated that her behaviour had been unprofessional and that neither he nor anyone else in Fleet Street was likely to employ her. Though gifted and well equipped for such work, she searched in vain for two or three years and finally in desperation got herself married to a very rich and handsome young man.

The last war-action, as it were, of the united mass was the vote for Labour. The Welfare State unleashed the monster of bureaucracy and of little mighty local bosses. These were my subsequent enemies/conquerors.

The post-war years were not, as is now commonly assumed, dissolved in greyness – I, for one, moved onwards.

A painting reflecting my wartime traversing of three continents, **The East** – congested into the limitations of my studio after failed searches for panoramic spaces – took me round the world: Nehru bought it for India (parliamentary protestations!), invited me to stay with him in Delhi, which set me on explorations through Asia and America. On my return Gerald Barry's 'Festival of Britain 1951' commissioned me to paint its largest mural, perspicaciously exploiting my new materials but – to conform with the Festival's theme – embracing only **Calvalcade of the Commonwealth**.

The impetus gained then seemed unstoppable.

Then the thunderbolt – by the soulless contemporary equivalent of Fate, the **Planning Authorities**. The unanimous outcry by the prominent in my and the studios' defence hardened (one never learns) the power-holding nobody-councillors; they, secure as the elected voice of the majority, evicted us, the artists, to turn the little patch into one more municipal squarelet with a public lavatory and a few benches.

The last of the studio came.

The boards of the **demolition** contractors went up over my gate, and, left and right, on the expiring houses. The dull rumble of falling masonry, the white clouds of dust, started to close in upon the studio. The black-hatted and spectacled officials replaced the gulls, gone with the winter, in the business of circling round the studio in flocks; excited by their triumph, watchful, feast-ready, yet, to hold on to the democratic proprieties, mumbling commonplaces about the good of the community, and the fine gesture of staying the execution of my studio till the last.

In the midst of this overpowering onslaught, my fort surrounded, I staged my finale. The whole vast wall-space of the two studios was given to an *exhibition monstre* – almost a retrospective – impossible to hold within the confines of an art dealer's gallery. A symbolic sale of the household chattels was added.

This became a valedictory demonstration. Christopher Fry, who lived across our lagoon, wrote:

FOR FELIKS TOPOLSKI
The mornings and the evenings go.
Remember how, often in this studio,
Among the visions exploring colour and line,
Talk and a happy hospitality
(Felix felicity)
Were as vivid as the flash of gulls and the sun.
But now we have seen the window's light
Hang its last lamp on the sleeping water.
Serenely sliding, the narrow-boats will pass
Only what falls and shines in the memory's glass.

This poem was included in the catalogue, arranged dramatically to indicate sorrow over the destruction inflicted by *force majeure*.

The exhibition lasted three weeks – till the last – and drew a continuous procession of visitors. It was charming of Harold Macmillan to make his way, black-coated and immaculate, through the rubble, to shake my hand in funereal commiseration, to assure me that he, the Minister who had signed the verdict, was powerless – and to buy a picture for

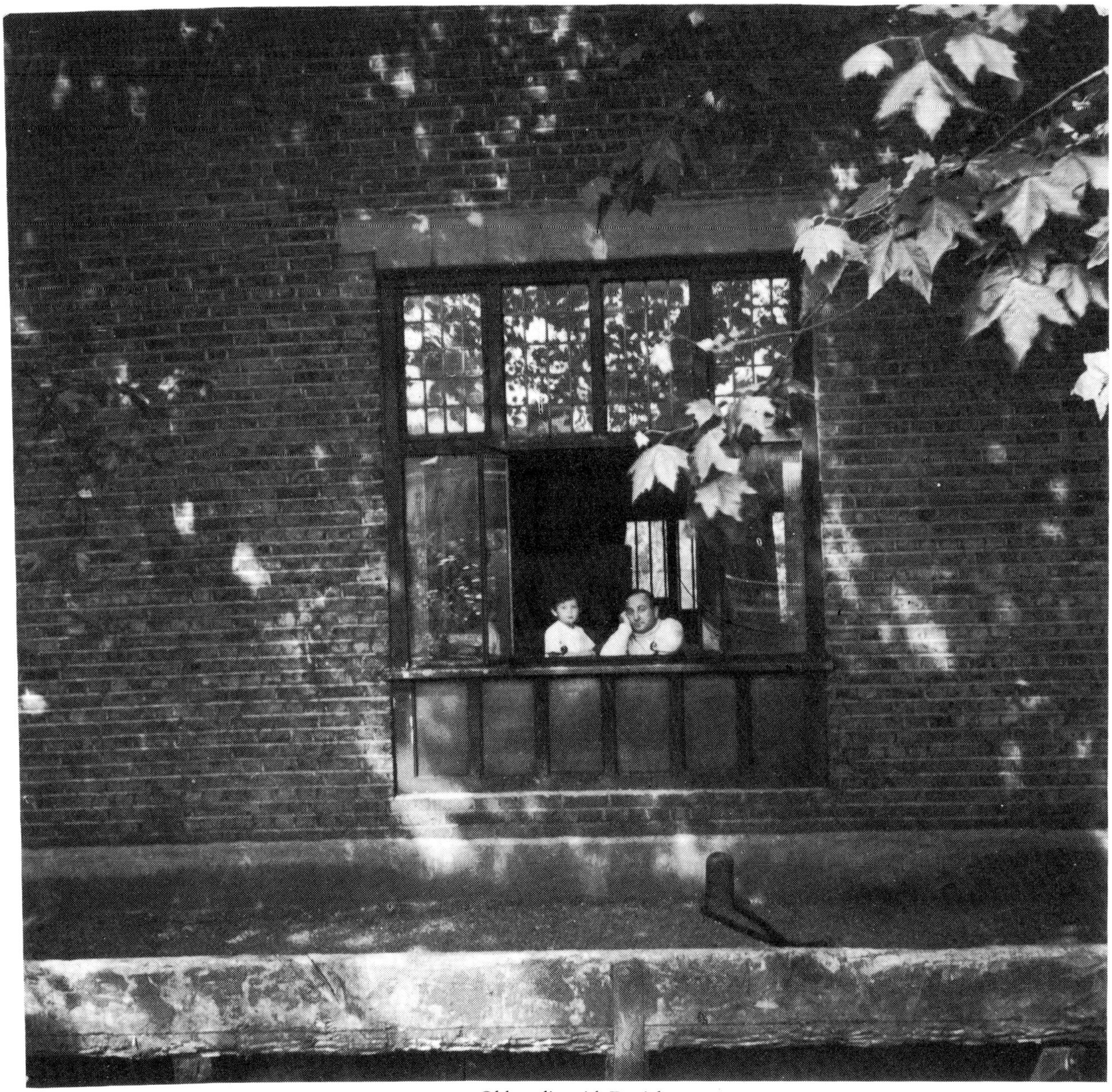

Old studio with Daniel

his Ministry. It was nice to watch the local officials back away in consternation when the Duke of Edinburgh arrived with the regal condolences. It seemed that all those who came, high and low, the Ministers and the men of opposition, the journalists, actors, writers and art students, the Guards officers and foreign tourists, the curious locals and the very workers about to demolish my workshop, wished to dissociate themselves from the Olympic councillors.

The line of the demolishers was moving on. Fulthorpe House was revealing one after another its secret lairs. As I held to the last, so did the homeless scum. And they were being truly dug out, forced like bats into the open. The filthy wasteland that was now my garden became the stage for the daylight visitations of nightmares.

One dirty day evolved an accumulation of contrasting symbols: the climax and the true finale – perhaps the finale of an epoch. The studio, calm and visited by a continuous trickle of polite individualists (Herbert Read silhouetting on the path, Malcolm Muggeridge and Hugh Casson discoursing in front of a picture); the dust and the din/crash round it – the labourers' assault. Then a sudden hubbub of animation and the men clustering in the gaping ruins. I follow into the crumbling ceilingless interior. In the corner, still shadowy, a stinking coal cupboard, and in its tightness, extricated by the torchlight, squatted yet prostrate, a woman, in rags, unconscious or dead, a bottle of 'red biddy' at her side, face and hair patchily painted, oddly grimacing. A stubborn wretch, defying the welfare amenities, holding to her right to independence and vice. A symbol indeed. And now, my eviction kicks me into camaraderie with her; our common plights sum up the social paradox.

The afternoon: my exhibition hours are over and I, dressed in my best, come out of my studio, on my way, of all places, to an appointment with the Lord Chancellor at **the House of Lords.** It is still light. The workers are gone, and I stop outside my door to assess the day's losses. To my right are the transparent remnants of the next-door studio and there (the pathos of it), a man and woman, elderly and shabby – the breed of the ruins – copulate standing; the woman's bare buttocks cling to the man. He is upright, on guard. His alert and tortured face. His animal eye when it catches mine . . .

Half an hour later I bow to the procession of the Lord Chancellor – my Mace-carrying friend Charles Rankin (black-stockinged, sword-and-lace) winks at me in passing: I follow and in the Lord Chancellor's room exchange leisurely pleasantries with this imposing dignitary, bewigged and berobed.

There should be a moral here. (All this does not just happen in London under democracy.) Perhaps the no-man's-land where roams the criminal, the vagrant, the prostitute, the artist and the bully – however official – has to remain as society's safety valve.

My defeat became a prestigious success. But the bureaucrats had cut short the most promising flow of my progress – studioless, I was undone.

But then the **Coronation** . . .

Subdued pent-up graces of 'before-the-war', only tentatively picking up the threads – and suddenly this burst into a glamorous allegory – real enough, yet more: sharper in focus and colour, fuller in emotion, since staged against the changed, greyer normality.

This parade (bracketed by the populace) gathered round the pivot of English hierarchy the utmost of the period's harmonies and contradictions, established prides and aspirations, the West and the East, the Left and the Right, the Two – and the Third World, and sent it all in a moving frieze (personified and haute-coutured for their roles of the manifest masters and the masterful) to pass in selective metaphors in front of me (as if solely for my wishfulfilment) – the grand curtain-taking by protagonists of the multi-spectacle I had to circle the globe to watch in sequences. A miraculous gratuity.

The Coronation brought my old themes to a marvellous climax. The pomp worked once more, because of the circumstance of victory; and the Commonwealth prestige seemed vital *ad infinitum*.

The glut of notes – all contain promptings (being pinned-down memories) for compositional inventions, even the detailed 'records' that turned kitschy. So I dare not destroy the failures, as most artists do with an eye on their stature.

Nevertheless, the selection imposes itself and some drawings seem to merit standing on their own, not solely as 'materials'. But, in my case, they are not 'beautiful'; they seem to strike *en masse* and are in need of a 'platform'. Today's newspapers forget the uses of draughtsmen, books and exhibitions are too 'precious' and too selective – my ***Chronicle***, its rough-and-ready character, its immediacy and flexible format had to be invented – indeed, invented, because even the last century's broadsheet was not quite a precedent.

At the height of the triumphantly 'logical' sweep of abstraction the obvious argument was that photography has wiped out the IMAGE in visual arts.

The counters to this:

One: the urge to make images cannot be extinguished – the 'hundred flowers' of talent will 'blossom'; anyway, figurativeness is 'on' . . . The photograph, even in the hands of Cartier Bresson, is a hunter's weapon: he has to 'catch' reality, however abrasively confused, blotted by non-essentials. My drawing 'in terrain' (because my painting is another matter) is of a seismographic inspiration: my hand/eye react instinctively and selectively and knit together the elements which may be gathered while I move/travel through or take part in an action; the page receives and accumulates the visual messages, and if the 'high' of tension and the response of the hand are inexplicably right, the notes (best if in batches) 'come off'. Movement/character, not form, seem their *raison d'être*. I seldom draw a static scene; I draw badly when posed for – but, even when working on a sitter, I try to make it an encounter; and I have several 'goes' circling round.

Two: I tried to use the camera in the war for rushed recording of details, but have found that the slightest scribble proves 'nourishing' while a photograph bogs me down. It seems that my 'on-the-spot' drawing is a personal, naturally evolved process, concerned with linear stimulation by, say, a crowded 'demo' – nothing to do with photography, and everything with *picturing*, that is, creating images in concord with a given surface – that is making art.

Three: my painting moves, of course, still further into the creative (away from re-creative) process: I never set myself to enlarge and copy a sketch in painting; I paint crowded (over-crowded to those conditioned by castrated one-element aesthetics) IMAGES, fed on the essences squeezed out of numerous drawings – raw material; on memory, fantasies, politics, lurid news . . .

And four: the art schools in this country began to send off a new breed of draughtsmen, equipped well with the ability to draw static/posing subjects; they descend on themes of vigorous action, but are able to draw only the repose in-betweens – thus serving the argument for photography's superiority. Pity this, because they confuse my specific singular gift (and of those few like me) as a scribbler of character/crowd in movement seen in the round, thus unrestricted by the life-class upbringing but free to throw the line about adventurously. No tailing a photographer here.

All in all, I would not have felt it merited the dedication to become a painter if my supposed gift for painting – image-making – was to be limited to 'pure painting', or inventing conceptual/esoteric games or any other compartmentalization, instead of being the means to give out one's totality.

Yet the creative gap had to be filled in a major way, and my toyed-with idea of *Topolski's Chronicle* became fact in **1953.** I don't regret having given to it most of my energies in the following twenty/thirty years. But the fact remains that the heavy authoritarian hand arrested my natural progress and redirected my course.

In 1953, *Topolski's Chronicle*, No. 1, Vol. 1 (the first of a great many) came into existence – printed on an old pedal

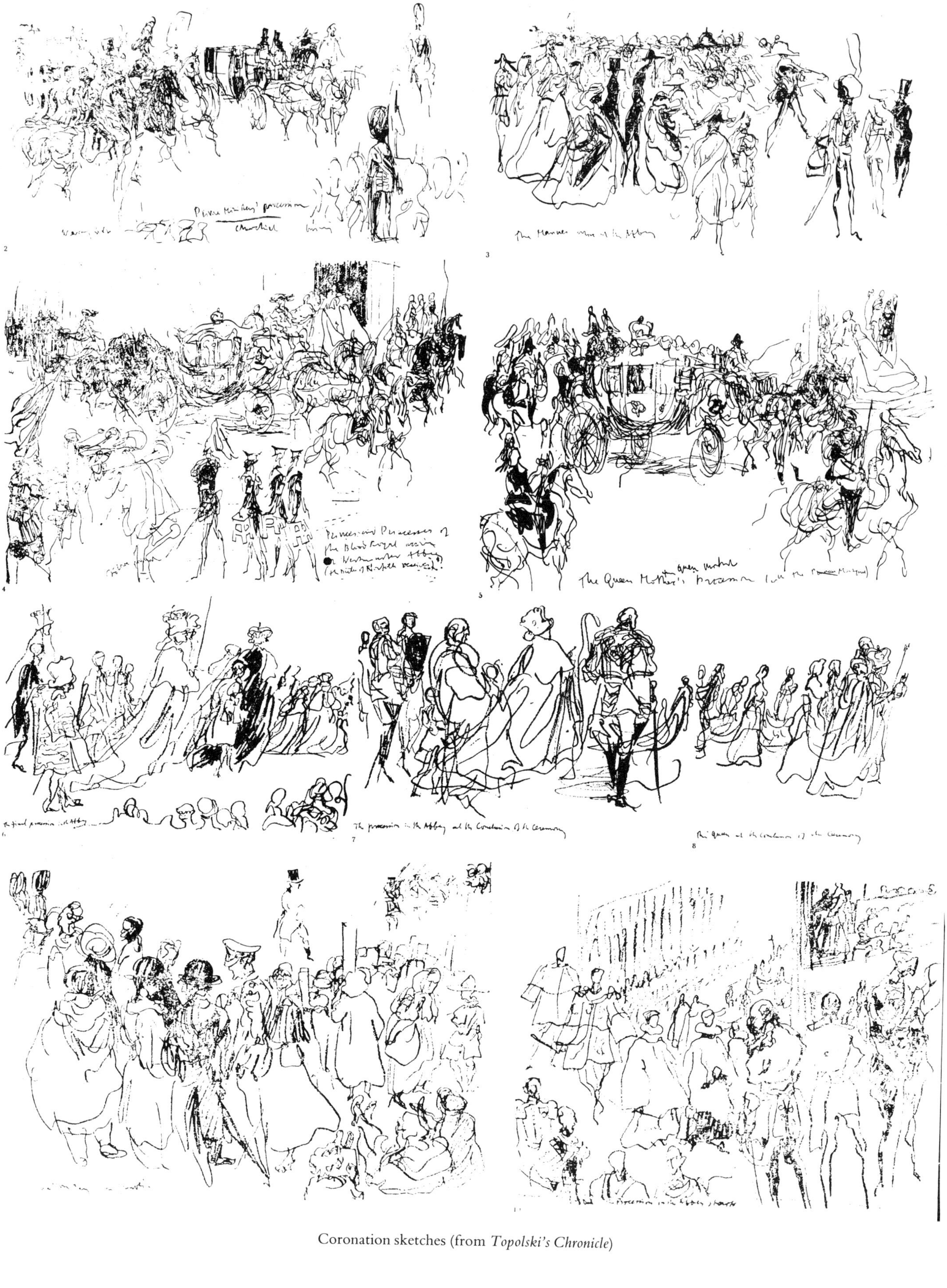

Coronation sketches (from *Topolski's Chronicle*)

machine by a young Polish couple in a gatehouse to the grounds of the Polish mental hospital at Mabledon, where the husband worked as a gardener.

They came to my studio like many other Poles.

The most tempestuous separate roads merged to bring **Krystyna and Czesław Bednarczyk** to my studio door in 1952 – the latest in the Polish diaspora.

Czesław, a young agriculturalist, mobilized as Second Lieutenant of the Polish Reserve, fought against the Germans in the doomed retreat, at the eastern border dodged Soviet imprisonment for a time, to be deported from his house in a provincial town to a labour camp in the furthest north, his guilt unrevealed. Fleeing on foot; hiding at strangers' mercy; sub-human horrors/terrors and brute routines – summarily related by many *ad infinitum* and *ad tedium*, but all this his real lot. Then the '**amnesty**' for Poles, freed to make it across Russia to the south where the rebanded Polish Forces, but also families and the old, were being assembled. The wintry-by-then passage, the assistance almost nil, though the desperation of the masses on the move evolved life-saving devices: aged and hefty Russian peasant women would, for a few *kopiejek*, let strangers cling to them at night for warmth.

Czesław proved to be a good soldier and, raised to Lieutenancy (a rarity for a Reserve man) was given responsible functions – to find himself, a low-ranker, at the centre of a momentous divide, probably decisive to Europe's fate.

The Polish Command was falling out with the Russians. History and cultural longings bent the nation's sentiments towards the West. The Soviets at first it seemed set on redeeming the recent past, hardened their demands: the Polish Army to be put speedily into fighting order and dispatched against the Germans. This would have led them, if victorious, straight into Poland, a considerable force. But accumulated imponderabilia (perhaps even the nation's memories of the Legions of General Dąbrowski, which campaigned with Bonaparte in Italy; and grew into larger forces faithful to the last to the by-then Napoleon), Western promises, the dominant distrust of their hosts and, conclusively, the discovery of the murder of Polish officers imprisoned at Katyń, decided a bizarre exodus via Persia to **the Middle East** – and, soon, to the **Italian Campaign**.

Czesław's superior, General Boruta-Spiechowicz, inclined towards the first solution, was (in a way unclear to Czesław) removed, and found himself in England with futile promises of another post; shortly, after the war he returned to Poland. But (Czesław's version), Colonel Berling, given command of the Polish embarkation post for Persia at Krasnovodzk on the Caspian Sea, declared, 'I'm not going to end up herding sheep in Australia', stayed on in Russia and, as General, formed the Kościuszko Division, which entered Poland – and Berlin – along with the Russians.

Czesław dutifully crossed with the whole of General Anders's Second Corps, camped in Persia, the Lebanon, Palestine, and Egypt, until in 1944 his Battalion 14, with him commanding its 4th Company, landed in Italy and began battling northwards.

At **Monte Cassino** the company dug in under ceaseless fire, went into series of forward manoeuvres interchanging with Companies 1 and 3. This lasted two days and nights. They dug in again shallowly on the rocky bareness for their major attack – the enemy's fire intensified – he twice wounded, carried down the slope, hospitalized, promoted to the rank of Captain and given the Cross for Bravery. Back in the advance, as Deputy Commander of the battalion; at Palazzo del Canone before Bologna takes full command – wounded lightly – continues into Bologna assisted by two artillery regiments, air support, a squadron of tanks. Ends as a **Major** decorated with the **Virtuti Militari**.

Krystyna, a Warsaw teenager under the German terror, falling in with one of the heroic breed of emissaries parachuted into Poland to liaise with the Underground Army; then a **secret courier** at the time of the continuing struggle between the elements under the orders of the Polish Government in London and those of the Government in power in Lublin.

Eventually she was smuggled out of the country on an under-cover mission to the Polish 'Army in Waiting' in Italy.

But it is time for clarification: the Second Corps commanded by General Anders was made up of Poles dispersed/exiled/imprisoned all over Russia. The bulk of the army (besides the professionals) were volunteers, reinforced in Italy by captured Poles forced into the German army. And a massive body of men and women too old and too young for the service followed the Corps onward to the Middle East, dropping out for a time into far-flung camps in Palestine, India and East Africa. And this whole vast civilian trampage meant to reassemble and to trail – tailing the Corps – back to Poland on this colossal curve of a trek home.

But the superpowers' political opportunism withdrew support from the Polish Government-in-Exile (this made easy by the Anders-led Poles absenting themselves from straight battling into their country), the praised combatants of yesterday, now disarmed, were held, futureless, stranded under their tents and in their billets of passage. Later they were given the choice between returning to Poland, glory denied; or entering Britain as refugees.

But Krystyna arrived in their camps before then, at the hour of bitter suspense. However, for those amassed men in uniform whose Poland had ended in 1939, she was, six years later, the first and only flesh-and-blood Polishness stepping into their midst straight from THERE: and with her impressive exterior, her impact must have created a legend – and a distance. She must have personified their longings.

Thus the most withdrawn, melancholy and poetry-writing agriculturalist-Major stood with her at my door, both of them demobilized and pauperized.

The *Chronicle*'s motivation: my mania for drawing 'in action' (never redrawing) – drawings accumulating in vast numbers, but denied a proper 'stage': books and exhibitions too precious and selective for their numerosity-impact; the contemporary periodicals jealous of their spaces. Hence the natural conclusion: a paper/broadsheet of my own,

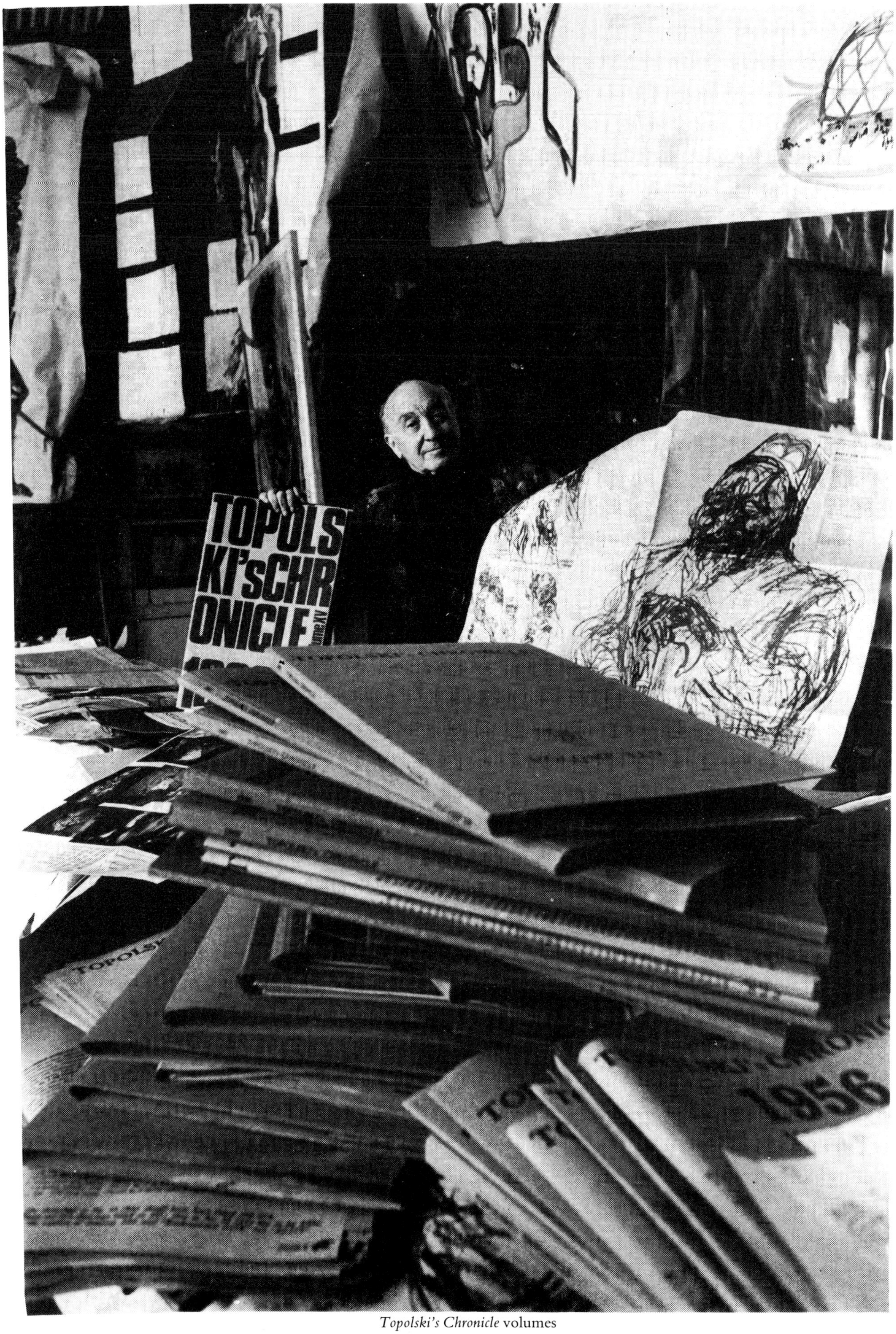

Topolski's Chronicle volumes

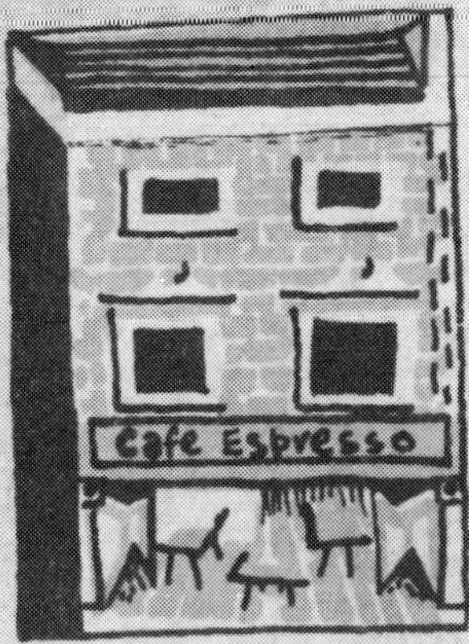

Price sixpence.

THE BROADSHEET

A weekly magazine of art and epicurianism

No. 1 OCTOBER 23 1954

EDITORIAL

" The Broadsheet " is not a pastiche of the publications of the eighteenth and nineteenth century; it is designed as a service for the Cafephile and those in search of entertainment. The first edition is published at the same time as the opening of MR. FELIKS TOPOLSKI'S exhibition of " Historical and Contemporary Broadsheets," and this issue is devoted to the reproduction of some of the exhibits.

Topolski, in his fortnightly " Chronicle," has revived the manner of retaining the simple and direct expression of the artist, by controlling the print production of his drawings himself, without being hampered by the vestigial conventions of the print technologist, with his *Valhalla* of facsimile reproduction and the layout man's typographical hoohaa.

The Chronicle is a graphic survey of the current way of life. Topolski, having been persuaded that he was good at trapping the spirit and shape of our time, assumed that such a continuous panorama, when collected and preserved over the years would become a unique document. The content is not subdued by any rules and swings from a number of issues given to one theme to single " omnibus " issues, with serial features, textual decorations and round the world experiences included. Folders are made for the 24 broadsheets which appear yearly to form a handsome line on the bookshelves; and each year is closed with a list of drawings and an index of the people, places and events recorded.

We devote part of THE BROADSHEET every week to reproducing a reduced in size version of the Chronicle—not as a collector's piece, but as a topographical statement to a wider audience than can be met by the limited and more expensive editions of the " originals."

In subsequent issues THE BROADSHEET will publish critical surveys on entertainment, epicurianism, exhibitions and fashion, and will include sectional maps in colour of London streets, showing the location of the coffee houses, restaurants and places of entertainment in fashion.

BROADSHEET EXHIBITION

On Tuesday, Topolski opened his exhibition of historical and contemporary broadsheets, his own being sold by street literature sellers dressed in early nineteenth century costume loaned by the Players Theatre.

Although millions of these sheets were sold by the flying " stationers " in Georgian and Victorian days few have survived, for during subsequent generations, which experienced so great a change in printing design and technique and frowned on this crude ephemera, such things quickly disappeared. Further, their flimsy nature and awkward size made their survival in domestic hands very difficult. They are of interest today from a social point of view and also

Photo. by courtesy of Keystone

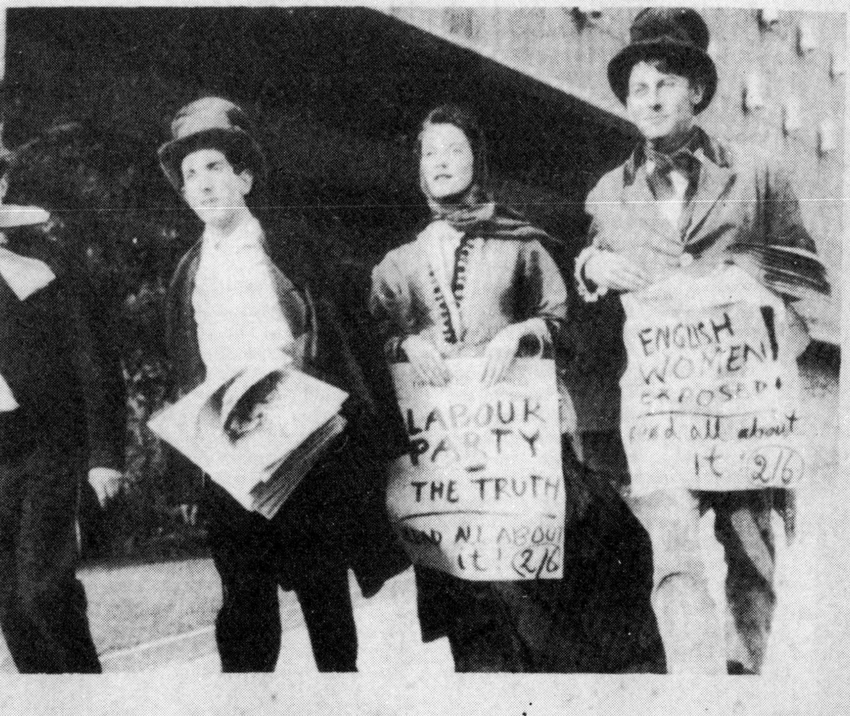

Hawking first issue of *Topolski's Chronicle*

TOPOLSKI the CHRONICLER

1953-1967

Original Paintings and Drawings for "Topolski's Chronicle"

Grosvenor Gallery

28 February - 23 March 1968

Daily 10 - 6   Sats 10 - 1

30 Davies Street London W1
telephone 01-629 0891
telegrams Sevenartz London

showing the best of them and accumulating into a singular record of our time.

My Polish poet-printers could at the outset print at one go only the space of 11½ by 18 inches, a half of my spread-open sheets, so that the blocks of some larger pictures had to be cut in two and, with our pleasurable play of colour, may have needed four or six patient runs through their little machine.

These were morale-contributions: Ronnie Duncan's words put on a poster: 'The Best Paper to Read'; Marion's fanatical peddling of leaflets, posters, copies, ideas for presentation: she won an open window at Foyle's and another at Hatchard's – in the manner of last century's print shops; and, crucial, the instant subscriptions – in response to the first issue sent out widely as an appetizer – from friends and 'casuals' ranging from the States to Japan. Then came the Americanized stunt-style ardour of young and powerful Philip Singer. He, a complete stranger, chance-descended on my farewell exhibition in Little Venice, bought a number of wisely selected pictures to the accompaniment of praises ever hoped for by an artist, and – his pennilessness disclosed – offered his devoted services in lieu of payment. Indeed with *Chronicle*'s advent he worked hard, although our combined brains tended to be over-daring – or ahead of the time.

My antipathy towards the false exclusivity of the print market – graphic techniques, having been a hundred and fifty years earlier a pedestrian reproduction-means, now taking the middle position of tasty semi-originals with an abracadabra of numbered/limited/signed/costly editions – underlined the opposite character of the *Chronicle*: its rough-and-ready packing paper, its deliberately inelegant typeface, its harsh line reproductions* contrarily printed on both sides of the sheets, its ludicrous price. I meant it to propose itself over the heads of tastefulness and, in the manner of old broadsheets, sent out into Piccadilly Circus a wave of youngsters, dressed in Victorian leftovers given us by the Players' Theatre, to sell copies from the kerb.

The hurried commuters turned their heads away in embarrassment – although a bare few years later the hippy mood filled up the Circus with pavement and stall salesmen of oddities, well received by then, as against the precocious assault of the *Chronicle* which had to retreat into the stolidity of subscribers' support.

Single sheets soon proved, with larger drawings and wider coverage, too binding and I had to move from the pleasures of almost-hand-printing with my Polish friends to a more impersonal, larger scale with offset printers – but with effective compensations.

The 353 editions and 2123 drawings so far embrace a large slice of global history, every line drawn 'on the spot' and never touched up. But the function of these drawings being primarily that of a seismographic record for the ultimate stage within my self-designed progress – synthesis through painting – this emphasis began to dominate, eventually tending to chronicle my inner advance rather than being solely a drawing-diary.

The hugeness of my new studio-arch, besides serving as the Chronicle's headquarters and, at times, its printing shop, consolidated my animosity towards **the mercantile 'art world'** by distancing myself from the dealers' network in a declared return to the earlier, healthier status of a craftsman who worked in the back and showed in the front.

There, in my rash confidence, I was satisfied with my name and work existing outside the registers of the all-powerful rule of auctioneers/art-dealers/museum-directors/art historians/

*A shock of my earliest days in London: at the Victoria and Albert Museum, the breathless hand-laying on a box of Doré's original drawings – and disappointment; these of London, known and admired in his book in their woodcut rendering, are palely hard-pencilled and gutless. Thus forceful woodcuts, a reproduction technique of the day, translated drawings to book pages. I decided to use the line-block of my time in the same way: deliberately brutalizing my drawings to fit my broadsheets, in preference to the polite usage of soft pseudo-facsimile half-tones.

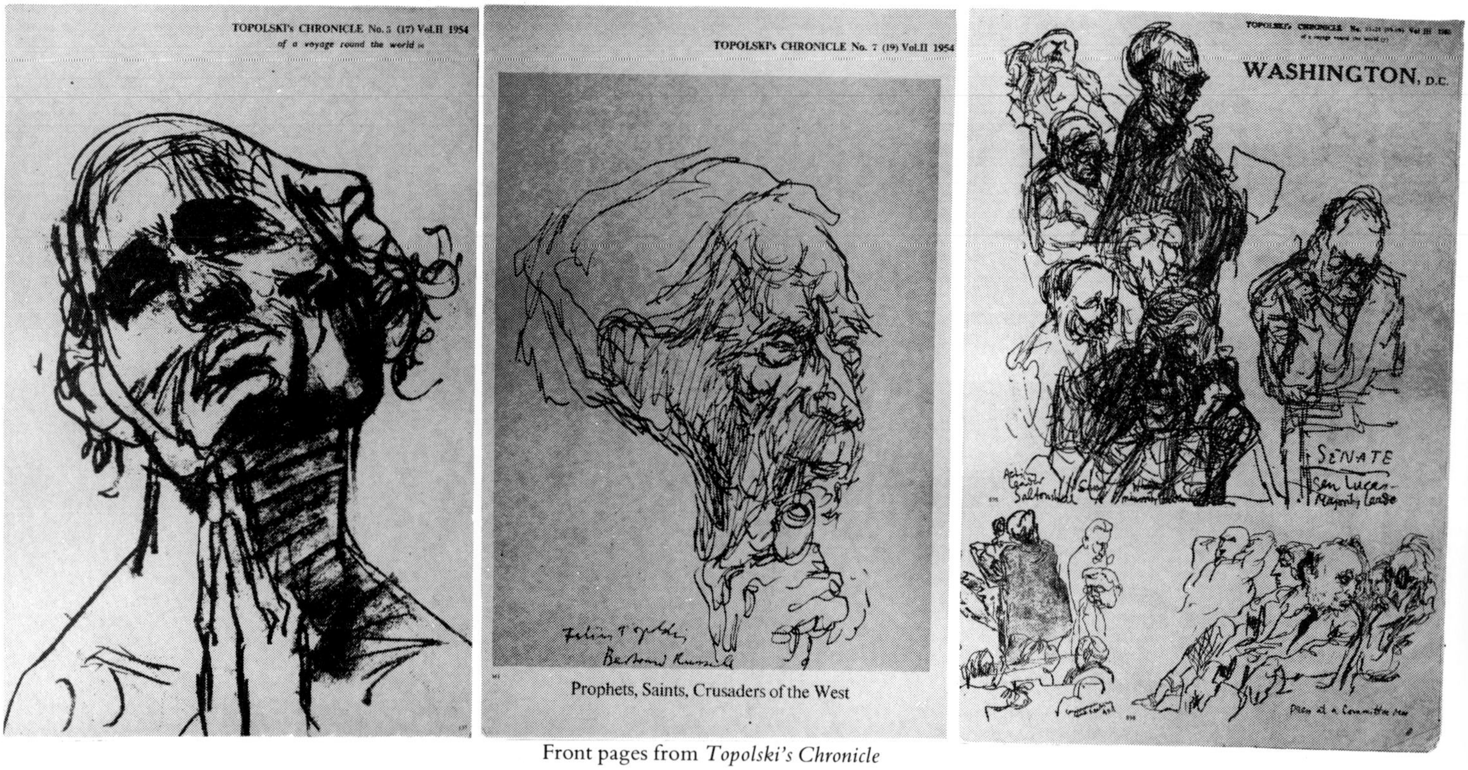

Front pages from *Topolski's Chronicle*

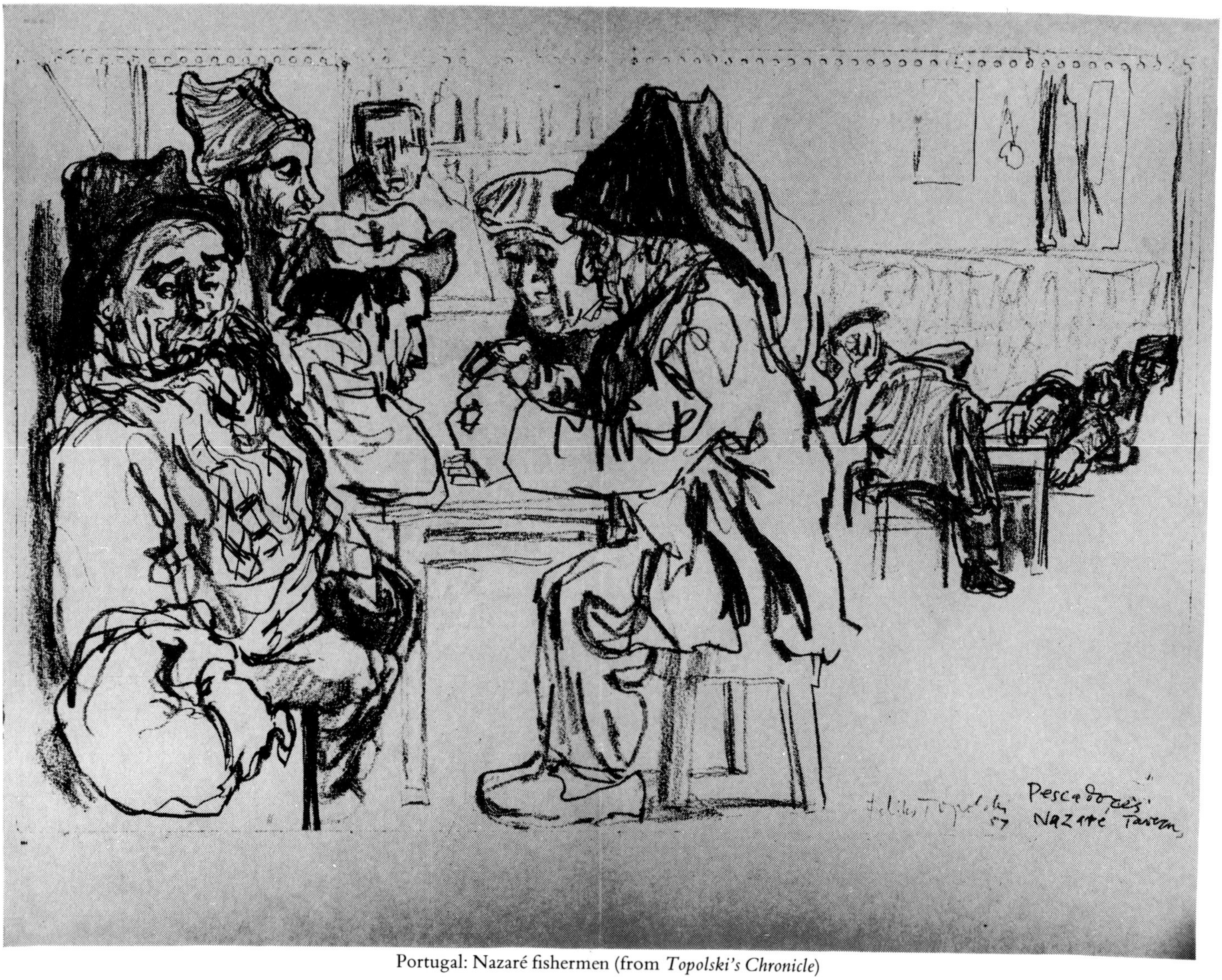

Portugal: Nazaré fishermen (from *Topolski's Chronicle*)

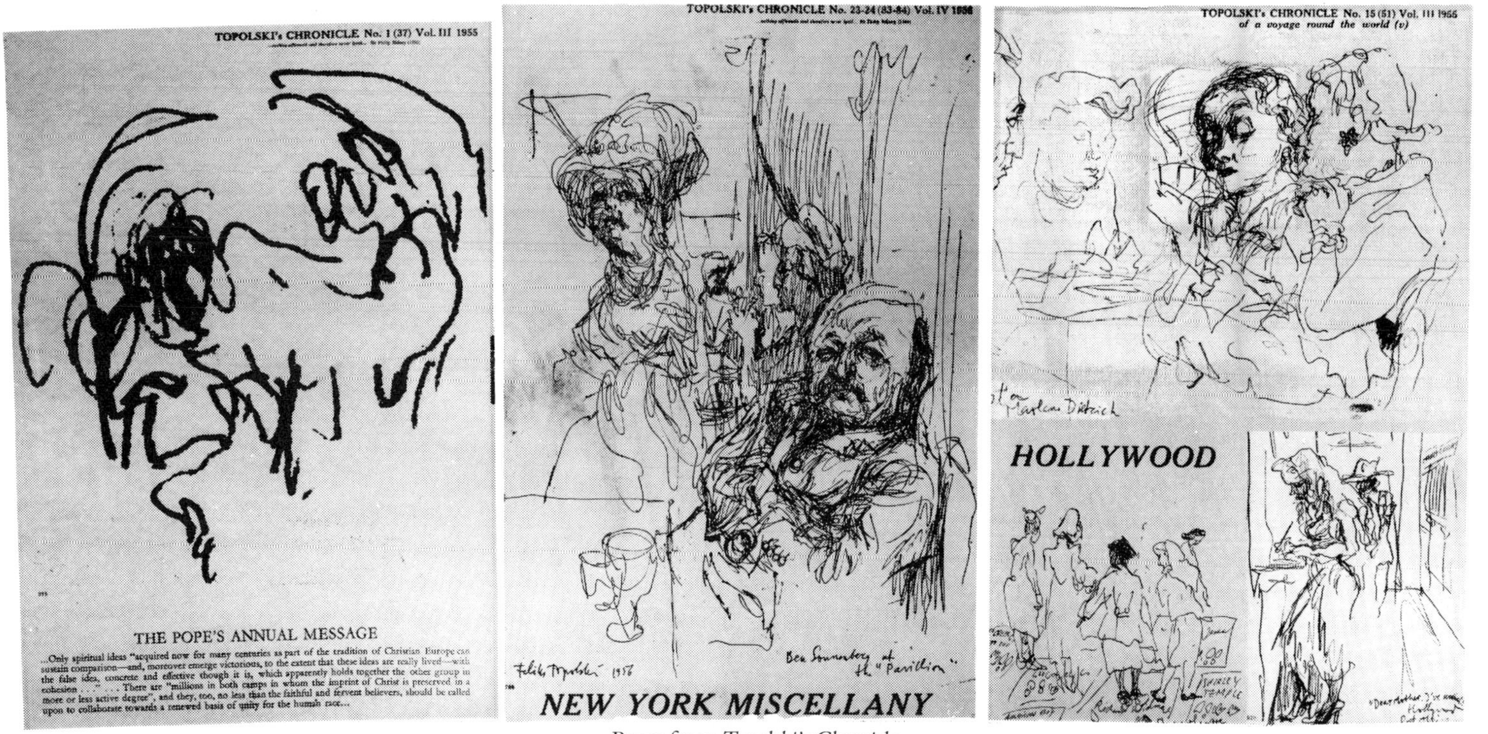

TOPOLSKI's CHRONICLE No. 1 (37) Vol. III 1955

THE POPE'S ANNUAL MESSAGE

...Only spiritual ideas "acquired now for many centuries as part of the tradition of Christian Europe can sustain comparison—and, moreover emerge victorious, to the extent that these ideas are really lived—with the false idea, concrete and effective though it is, which apparently holds together the other group in cohesion . . ." . . . There are "millions in both camps in whom the imprint of Christ is preserved in a more or less active degree", and they, too, no less than the faithful and fervent believers, should be called upon to collaborate towards a renewed basis of unity for the human race...

TOPOLSKI's CHRONICLE No. 23-24 (83-84) Vol. IV 1956

NEW YORK MISCELLANY

TOPOLSKI's CHRONICLE No. 15 (51) Vol. III 1955
of a voyage round the world (v)

HOLLYWOOD

Pages from *Topolski's Chronicle*

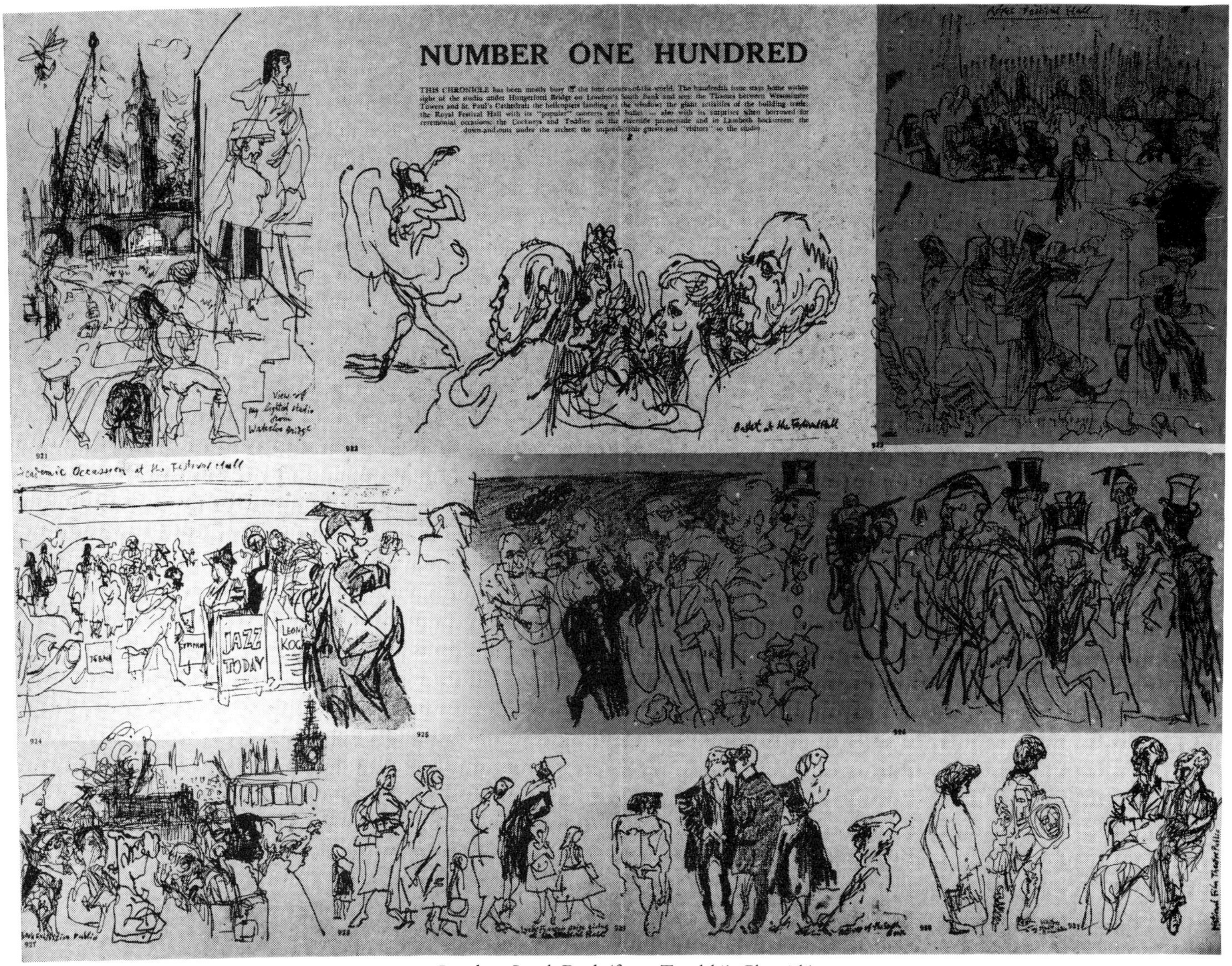

NUMBER ONE HUNDRED

THIS CHRONICLE has been mostly busy at the four-corners-of-the-world. The hundredth issue stays home within sight of the studio under Hungerford Bridge on London's South Bank and sees: the Thames between Westminster Towers and St. Paul's Cathedral; the helicopters landing at the window; the giant activities of the building trade; the Royal Festival Hall with its "popular" concerts and ballet — also with its surprises when borrowed for ceremonial occasions; the Cockneys and Teddies on the riverside promenade and in Lambeth backstreets; the down-and-outs under the arches; the unpredictable guests and "visitors" to the studio...

London: South Bank (from *Topolski's Chronicle*)

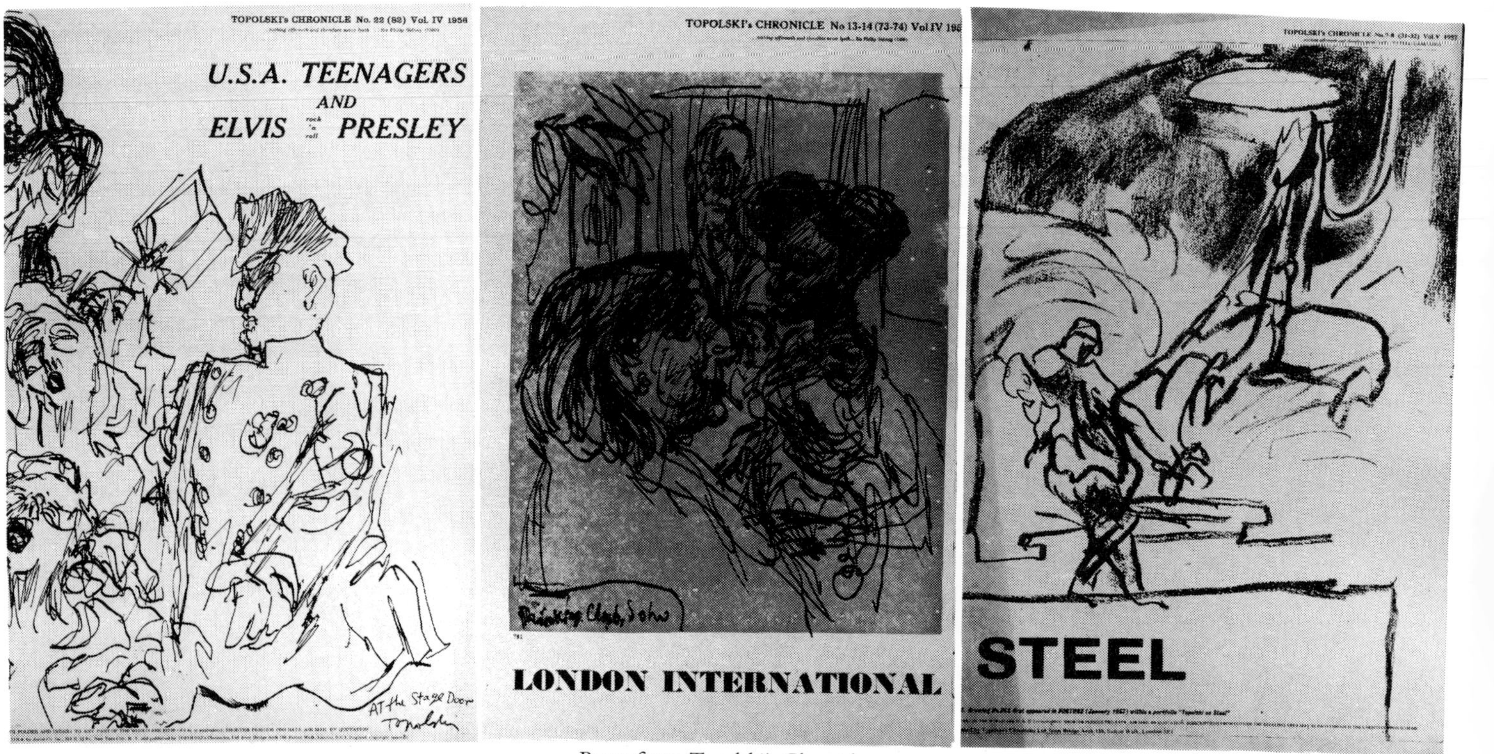

Pages from *Topolski's Chronicle*

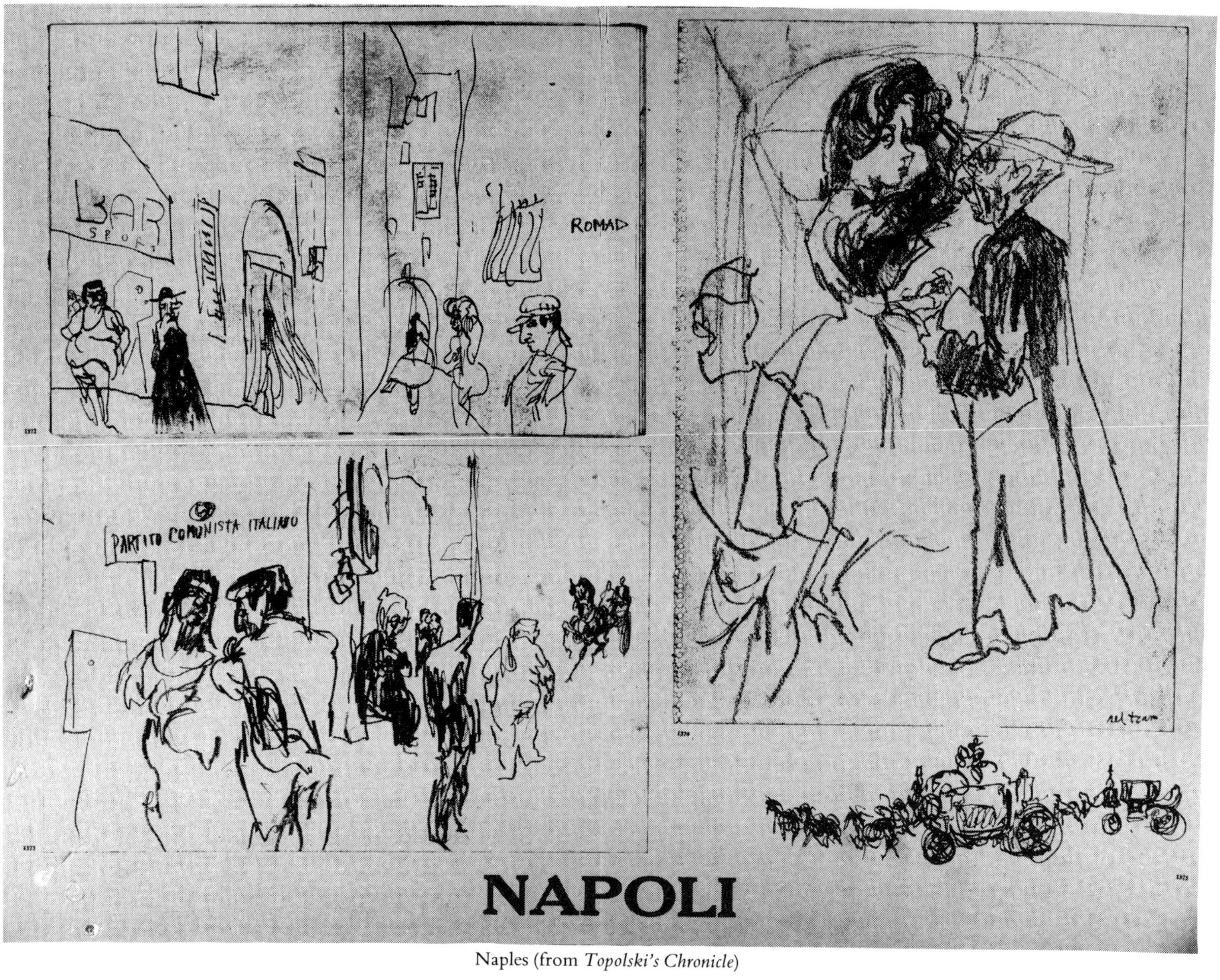

Naples (from *Topolski's Chronicle*)

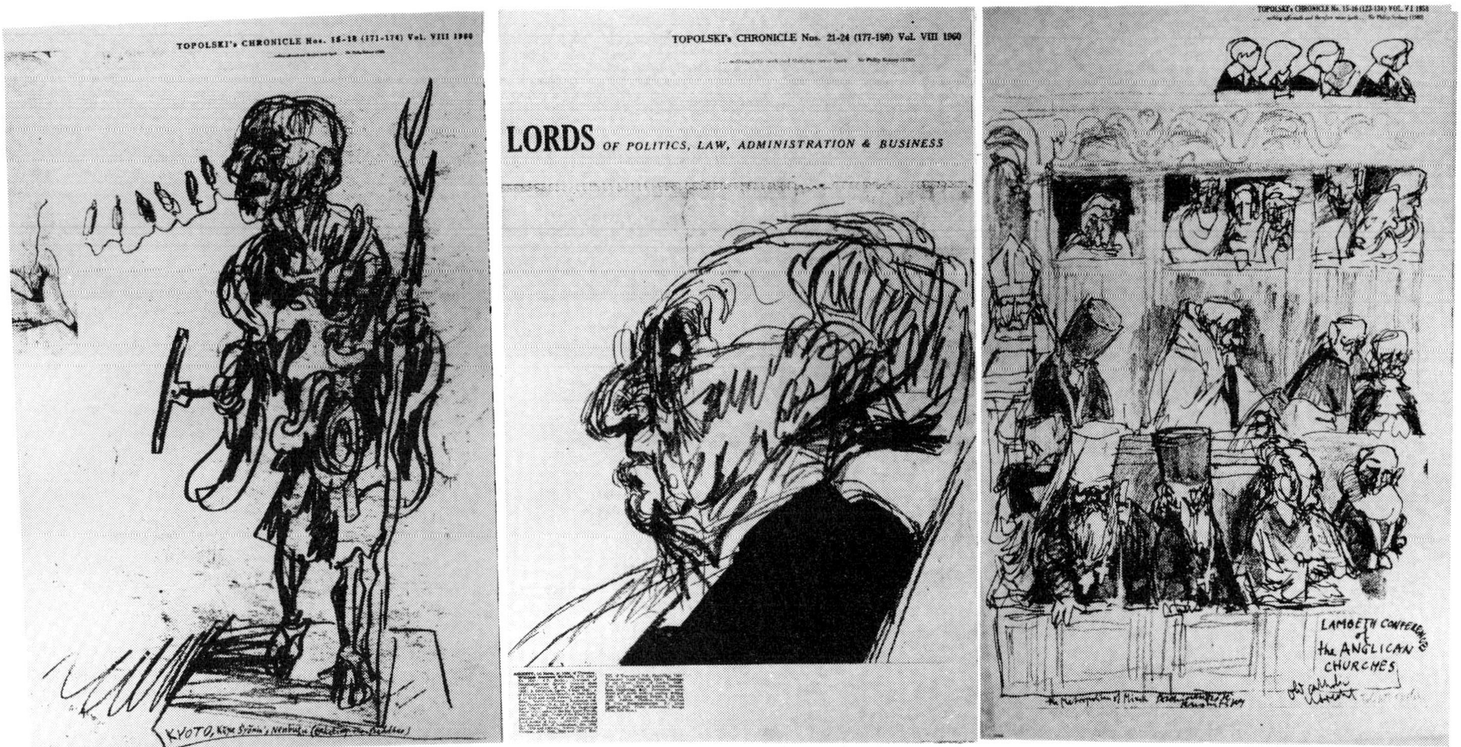

Pages from *Topolski's Chronicle*

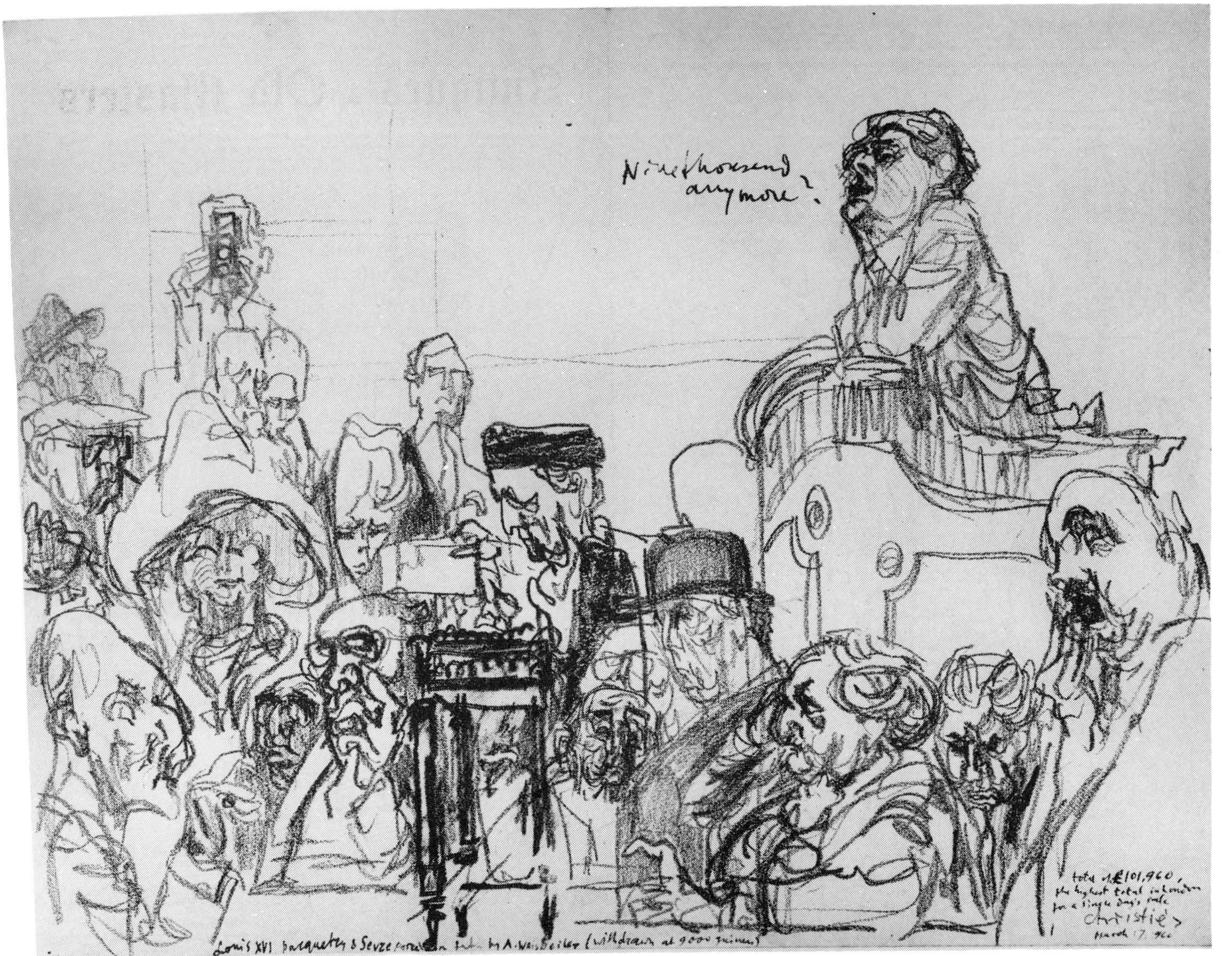

London Auction Rooms (from *Topolski's Chronicle*)

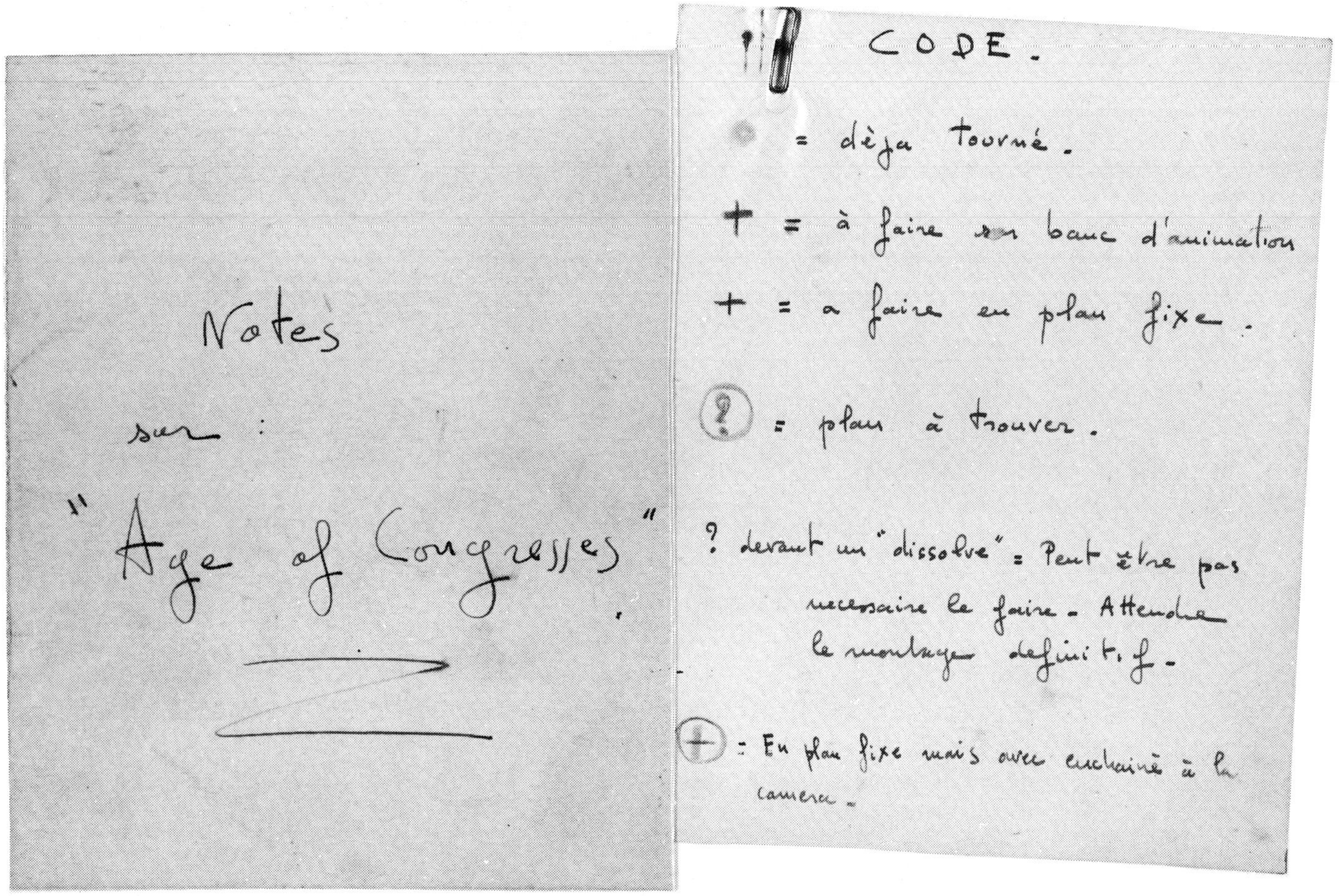
Notes

sur :

"Age of Congresses"

CODE.

● = déja tourné.

✚ = à faire sur banc d'animation

+ = a faire en plan fixe.

(?) = plan à trouver.

? devant un "dissolve" = Peut être pas necessaire le faire. Attendre le montage definitif.

(+) = En plan fixe mais avec enchainé à la camera.

Alain Resnais's shooting script

art bureaucrats. It could of course be argued that I never deserved inclusion therein – a handy and useful argument in the sphere of ephemeral (yet ruthlessly binding while they last) judgements; but there is no lack helpfully of less conformist but still 'legitimate' supporters of my work . . .

However: not having a dealer detailing his underlings to the auction rooms discreetly to boost up the prices of his stable's work renders my market values ridiculous; official collections, international showings, 'authoritative' books/ catalogues on the art of the day derive not from artists' studios, but through the dealers'/critics'/collections' cause-and-effect chain – the middleman being, in art as in all aspects of consumerism, the key figure. In other words, selling/ buying is the supreme criterion, thus only conveniently movable products are considered, not art bound to its locality.

I was and am aware of the foolhardiness of my Don Quixotic aloneness, though of late reconciled to my defeat in the 'marketplace' – which, *ipso facto*, confirms the rightness of my stand.

Closeness with **John Whiting** was most precious; a noble, graceful, youthful person, beautifully evolving his audaciously contemporary morality plays – resentfully kept down by the critics. 'Success' arrived with (was it Peter Hall's prescription?) *The Devils*, a thrilling play, but devoid of his authentic purpose. Then the shock of his death – unjustly early.

This lovely gentle-inspired-man-boy John wrote the commentary-poem to go with a film of my drawings. The two of us worked hard sieving out and matching into his poem-script drawings which would dramatize/satirize the flow of our theme.

However complete seemed our prolonged effort, it was considered necessary to put it through professional scrutiny. The producer, working between England and France, summoned **Alain Resnais** for the job: he had become then highly appreciated for his shorts – particularly the one on Auschwitz – but was still to move on to his great feature films. Thus, in this pause, our project fitted and he arrived to stay at my house and to tighten up **'The Age of Congresses'** into a precise shooting script. Poised, calm in his assured, it seemed, direction, he was a good guest and a marvellous worker – though John and I were pained now and again at his 'professional' ruthlessness towards our more adventurous montage ideas. Yes, his script did reduce/cut our explorations of the drawings down to conventions of camera cum cutting room; and we accepted that the test of his undoubted dogmatism was to come with the shooting . . .

But, even in this small venture, capitalist censorship struck – money the ruler: at this late juncture, after much devoted labour, the project was cancelled.

John's cudgels of satire and warnings emerge from over thirty years ago almost too tame for now: World War III is held back less by talk than by armaments race, or replaced by

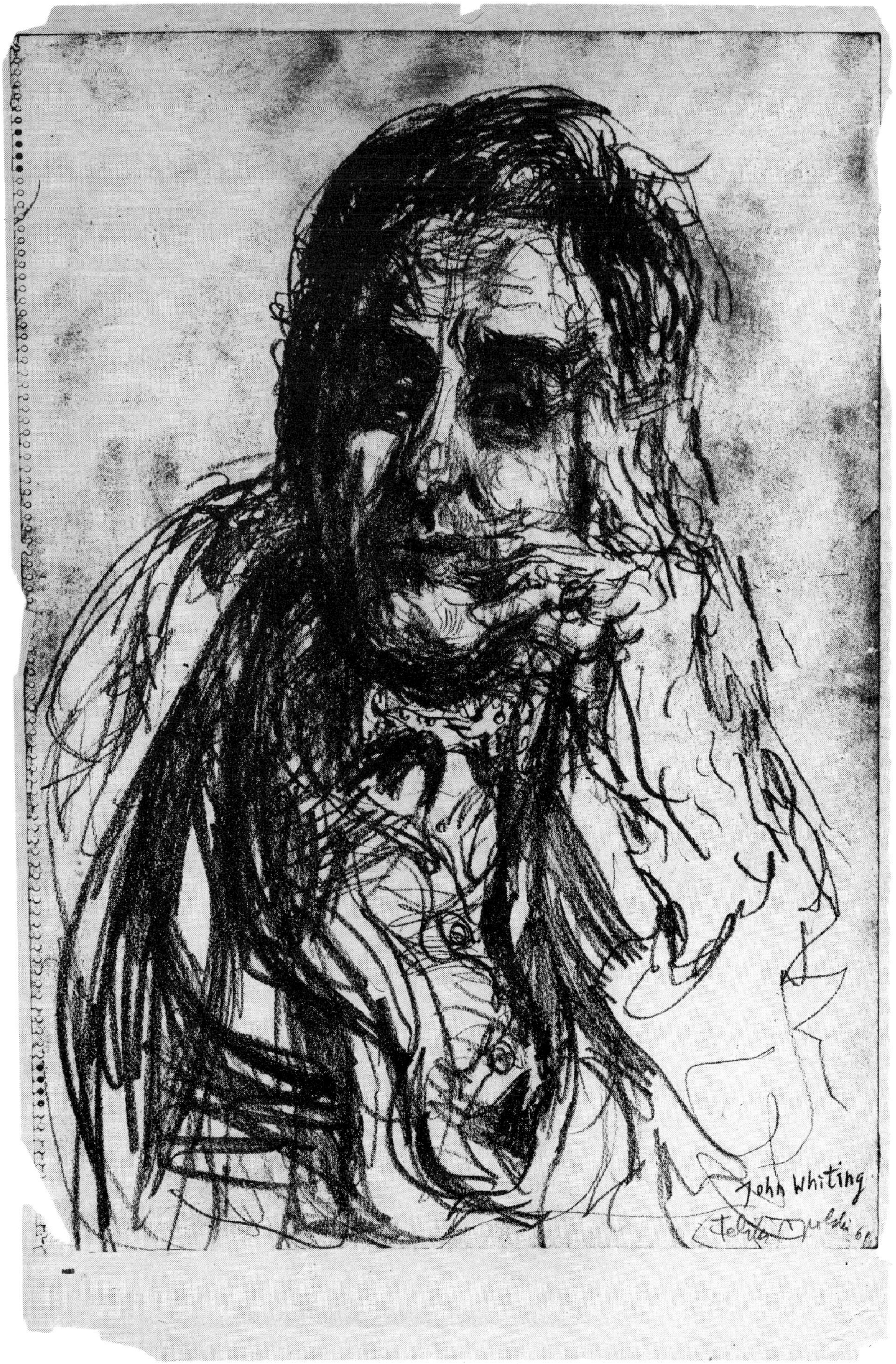

John Whiting (from *Topolski's Chronicle*)

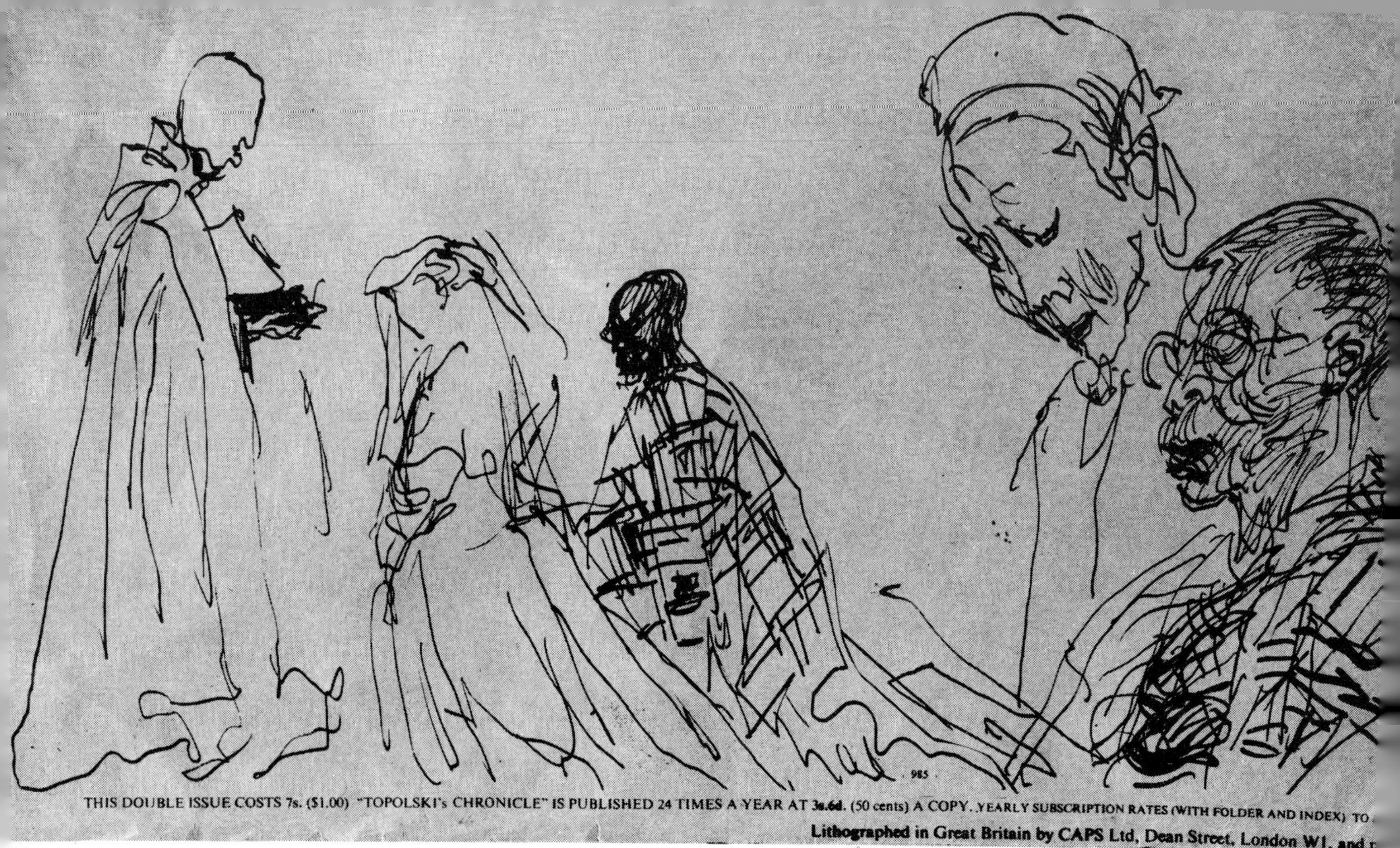

Wedding of Peggy Cripps and Joe Appiah (from *Topolski's Chronicle*)

gang strategies disregarding frontiers. And the drawings: I have 'covered' since then quite a few new themes (Vietnam; Congo, Ulster, and Chicago civil wars; Greenham Common – London – Rome – South America protests/clashes), but the global and multiplying spill of wars, guerrillas, assassinations, ambushes, single-handed kamikaze, fifth columns Left and Right, hijacks, spreads beyond my reach.

Less the age of congresses, more the worldwide weapon-testing grounds – in earnest.

Peggy Cripps settled in our cottage at the back of the house. A large protrusive girl, honest-unlovely-faced, Peggy waited. And, in the meantime, the family tradition practised on her *massif* the scales of Puritan thrift and God-fearing socialism, of mellow service to good causes of the old Liberty/Equality/Fraternity variety – this time, according to the day, applied mainly to the coloured races. But her robustness was impatient for the tune proper. And, when it came, it struck a grand chord; all the *études* blended handsomely.

She confided one day to me, when back from her first trip to the Gold Coast: 'Marvellous country; you know, at last I've come across a people who admire me for my looks and my figure: to them I am a handsome woman.'

Joe Appiah was then often at her elbow – a head shorter, spectacled, very black and very bright. Joe made his way to her from the opposite direction in a not unsimilar vein. But he was also, *malgré lui*, a Western neophyte and a man of high ambitions. And his joy at himself was endless: his hobby-horse, proving the Westerners a bad lot and himself their ever-mocking uncoverer.

Peggy insisted that I draw Joe for her wedding present: wrapped in the orangey zigzag-patterned tribal cloth, spectacles dismissed and commanding posture struck, he was unrecognizable. Indeed, he was to become such a man in the land of the Ashantis, though at the press conference called by Peggy in our drawing room, dapper and glittering (watch, glasses, rings, handkerchief), he lacked that dignity, dominated instead by his snobberies and evocations of his chieftainship. And Peggy joined in: 'Of course, we have a lot in common; we come really from the same kind of family.'

But while they stood there, questioned and camera-flashed-at, the comedy of motives and idiosyncrasies subsided. Olive and Roy, our Jamaican servants, were a-wonder: 'She has pluck!' The world was a-wonder. This was the wedding of our time, Old Non-conformist England in Peggy's hands had yet another symbolic lead.

At St John's Wood Church the English county aunts passed hymn books to the fat black cousins from Accra; the top hats and morning coats together with the bared shoulders, patterned togas and sandals . . . I looked round over the chessboard of faces and they were all remarkable and beautiful through this act of grace: the faces attending a holy deed – that will pass into the Book.

Marion's face next to me blessed with tears and with the presence of its two replicas: Daniel's and Teresa's; negro faces – as if reaching the Grail; and the stony bony and moustached faces of the Britons – not defeated, only conquered by piety; the noble face of Lady Cripps – as if listening to her voices.

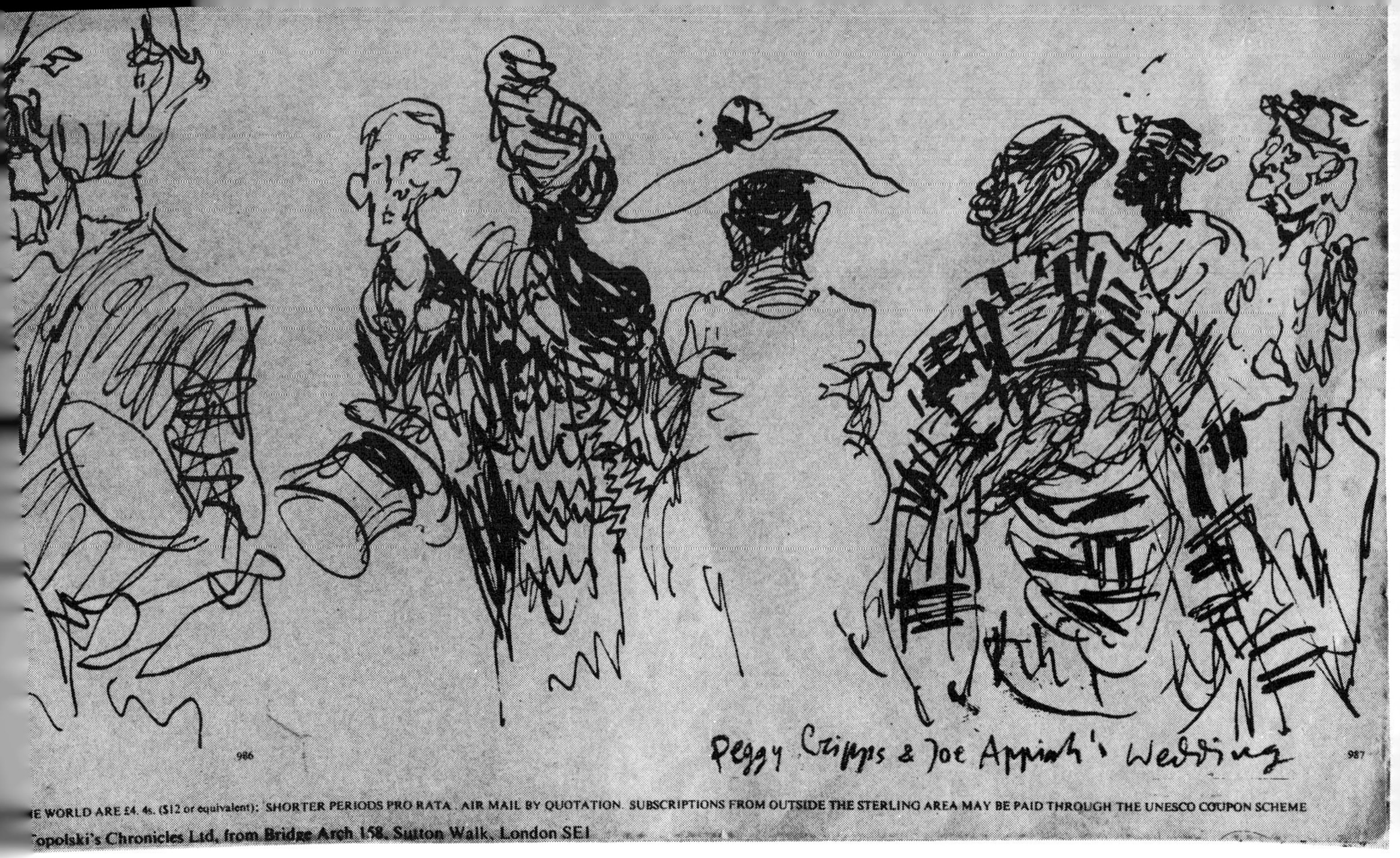

The clumsy big freckled girl, towering over the Ashantis – her people – was beautiful and majestic when turning from the altar of the little church.

My versifications, self-consciously knitted together and leaning upon the hope of reassurance, only once found it from a 'professional': **Cyril Connolly**, caught at the studio, read the African ones with great care, commented, found a point of adjustment – and praised *The Retreat in Ghana*, consequently incorporated in the next *Chronicle*.

Connolly 'caught'? In a Molièrish triangle-comedy, but *à la* twentieth-century *mode*, being enacted with a large eavesdropper audience spread over two continents.

Barbara, the pivotal heroine of those days – her allure relying on the sphinxish muteness of her never-unriddled unpredictability married to an appropriate physique – stood between her wronged husband Cyril and **George** the Viennese wizard. And I sat at my studio – the seat of arbitration: my all-round intimacy with the three protagonists, yet disinterestedness at the centre of the triangle, destining me for the role.

My days/weeks were stolen by the trio demanding my attention one after another for the display of their ego-desired remedies.

The most interesting contender, George, deserves an introductory parable-fable. In unworthy outline:

George, a planner-in-totality of his climb from zero, having

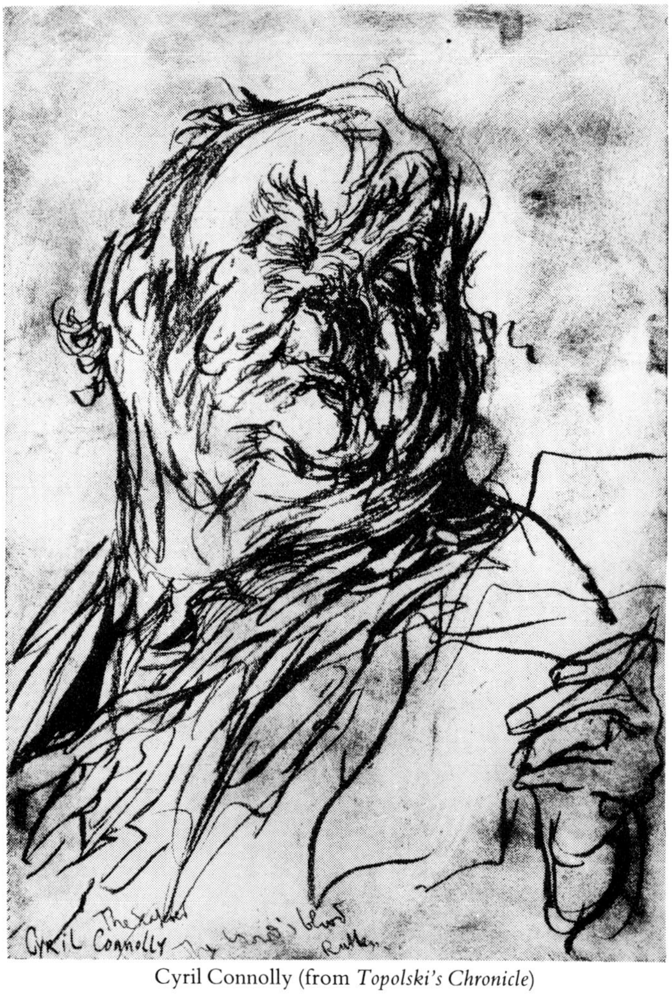

Cyril Connolly (from *Topolski's Chronicle*)

installed himself in our house (our Thursday hosting at that time embracing a rich variety of strata and George perhaps calculating on this), said: 'The English despise foreigners who attempt Anglification – they appreciate a Jew being ultra-so, better still exotically-so.' George could not do otherwise – his bloated cheeks/eyes/nose/shape enforced a manner of multi-concupiscence, of such over-the-top self-exaggerations of comic-cum-distasteful Jewishness that there was no room left for taking the mickey. The acceptance of this bizarre Jewamoor-come-to-life was his first victory, rapidly built up through his sweeping progress in serviceability – a genius omnipotent go-between – into his recognition (this age of knight-errantry of business, pen – the lance; bankcard – the shield) as the hero and eventually the master, with all, from the Duchess of Westminster to Marcia Williams, serving him – his court.

Already grandly located in Chester Square decorator-designed rooms, supposedly anxious for advice, he deliberately (on principle), against the rules of Gentile England, put about the double gaffe – that of his despicable tactlessness, and of his power- and/or riches-prospects (because up to then his were bluff fortunes, not a fortune) – to unroll the carpets of rumour.

His love of option-collecting (also in character) expressed itself thus: he announced that he had three potential marriages on his roster: Clarissa Churchill – a beauty of the highest Debrett echelon; a very lovely daughter of one of the leading members of the Israeli Government – her majestic aura would pair well with his own standing as Weitzman's intimate; an equally impressive daughter of the Marks & Spencer empire – an unlimited network of riches.

And his neat analysis on reaching this pinnacle of signposts: that within high-birth-regulated society he would be a pariah; that Israel could give him its highest but was a small ominous cul-de-sac; that the Jewish business empire would place him, with his equipment, as an equal or a leader in handling their riches – and this was what he chose.

An addendum is needed to give some sense of his attractions: George could charm. And his 'charm', a switched-on-and-off device, went in step with his all-revealing – thus disarming – ostentation.

But his computerized ascent was UNpredictably brought to a chastening halt. The Marks & Spencer clan proved to be exclusive of their morganatic penetrators; George, not admitted to the family conclaves, and barred from the coffers, found himself for the first time not in the Chair, not even round the table, but at the door handle.

He had chosen publishing as a short cut to influence and gentility; as a publisher-editor, judiciously playing on the hunger-to-be-in-print and vanities of authors, on the choice of his well-born staff by their snobbery-appeal, and also on the gentleman-publisher tradition by establishing a *soi-disant* salon which brought together the upper classes and 'the world of art', he gained an eminence of sorts.

And so, Marks & Spencer's utmost deed of cutting him down to size: they underlined publishing's midget status within consumer society (and his within their empire) by admitting him to their fold only as the supplier of a set of children's books for Christmas. This order – tiny for them – would give financial security (unattained till then) to his whole 'prestigious' publishing *raison d'être*, but amount to one one-yard-long shelf for Christmas sales only, to be cleared for more marketable goods the following week.

The onset of marriage produced a child but – reasons abound and he told the tale with relish – soon marital impotence set in, his body succumbing to his failed calculations.

His erotic appetites were – not surprisingly in an avaricious muncher of alien pickings – not raised by a girl of his own breed (however well endowed), set on a bed of humiliation, but by conquest of the less-in-reach Anglo-Saxon.

And such a female, to precipitate his epic downfall, came within his reach, setting off the boomerang or recoil or contrariness or whatever motions confuse and enrich the obvious in natural selection. Barbara, perfectly boned/proportioned, irresistible in her disregard of 'deportment' but also imperious – in all, veritably English – had a penchant for male-beasts, hairy and excessive in bulk (there was a string of these – King Farouk and others – ruthlessly fictionalized in her comic novels); Cyril, no mean specimen; George, a desirability. The Connollys were invited to stay with George when in London, and, indeed, the inevitable was pounced on *in flagrante* by Cyril.

The studio negotiations turned into 'stations' in a medieval conversion: what may have begun as a tourney, into which Knight George rode to win the maiden and to unseat the notable adversary, miraculously became a road to redemption. The unscrupulous self-seeker, now blessed or blinded, shed his life's cool villainy for loving need of Barbara: the undoubted negation of his hitherto purpose.

I conducted the closing stages of this transfiguration into George-the-good and the undoing of George-on-the-make with respect for the momentousness of it all, however dressed 'in modern clothes'.

A gossip had become the fable of our time: George, the supreme embodiment of the manipulator-errant, assumed to be destined for the highest trophies on account of his steely soullessness, had emerged now at his sexual Grail, a fanatic – ready to shed his Purpose – of Barbara-worship. A *dégringolade* was to be the price; he knew it and he fought – for once so to speak idealistically, hence heroically – the aforenamed triangular contest to gain her hand in marriage – thus marking his redemption as a man and blotting out as a meteor.

But in no time, he himself (unwisely, or as a challenge?) set the scene for the showdown of split-George. His attempt at persevering with the 'salon' was dismally destroyed by his wife-by-then Barbara disdainfully cutting through the assembled opinion-mongering worthies, flaunting prescribed pleasantries and walking out on her (after all) guests.

Happily for George, sadly for the parable's neatness, and amazingly his fatal fascination shed, his garish *primum mobile* returned to hold his undivided fortitude. Having retreated and entrenched himself to perfection within the minor princedom of publishing prestige (spread internationally over politics/society/academia cum literature – complexes/old loyalties/daydreams kept out) he speedily brought all he – and perhaps his old Viennese mother – may have imagined, beyond attainability, desirable: mansions in the *contredanse* of marriage and divorce with an American WASP princessmillionairess, Harold *nomen omen* Wilson's knighthood, and a Life Peerage in rapid succession.

The deeper into the rings of birthright-prerogatives, the tighter the diameters/restrictions. At the very centre, the ease re-enters, but it takes the shape of nursery naughtiness.

The icon-monarchy of today, without ruling/threatening power, magnifies its stilted theatricality – a meek compensation for making history – and the world populace, starved of life-confirming accents, gives the vast 'claque' to the make-believe performance. This sumptuous masquerade and its circumstantial and pomp-mixed ironies set my pencils dancing.

When the ruling ladies of Monaco enter their functions cinematically chosen for their princely parts, it is laughable; but **Queen Elizabeth**, her historical territory the richest, enters modestly and dumpily – thus redeeming the show.

'**A visita da Rainha de Inglaterra a Portugal** 1957'. From the official programme, '. . . visiting *Nazaré* en route . . .': in the wintry landscape the uncoy village dug in grimly against the bulging furious ocean to solid purpose; the fishing boats lining the beach were harsh and primeval; the men sturdy and panachious – they once manned the world-exploring ships; the women blackly draped – right for their sombre routine and ever-recurrent tragedies. Men who live by their manly virtues with their women serving them and, when the time comes, weeping for them. One seldom sees nowadays such unblotted purity and it is impossible not to feel humble before this harmony.

But next day awaited the Queen and the Duke.

The art-craft-tourism-wise organizers and the photo-telecine operators and reporters from both hemispheres fluttered in the rain, shaping the 'local colour' displays. The fishing crews, self-consciously seated in their boats, yesterday tossed high on the surf, now placed neatly on the pavement of the market square, were photographed by the dozen; a platform was set for the dancers and orchestra; several pairs costumed in a variety of Sunday full-dress strutted up and down; and strategically placed groups were arranged into *tableaux-vivants*, well spattered with nets, pots, carts, spinning wheels, babes and dogs. The one-legged and bemedalled veteran life-saver was summoned to his allotted position. The dignity of these people, when turned exhibits, suffered.

Nevertheless, the overwhelming aura of this proud occasion (proud because the humble fishing village was considered worthy of a long detour by the Royal Visitors) lifted the whole – the reality and the farce – to the level of a happy and folksy *Levée*. And EXPECTATION mounted to the extreme with the Arrival somewhat delayed.

At long last they were there: the band struck up and the dancers started to rotate and leap, the crews in the landed boats to perform their pantomimes, the pairs to strut, the art-and-craft groups to weave – all, as planned, well spread over the marketplace – all ready to engage the interest of the

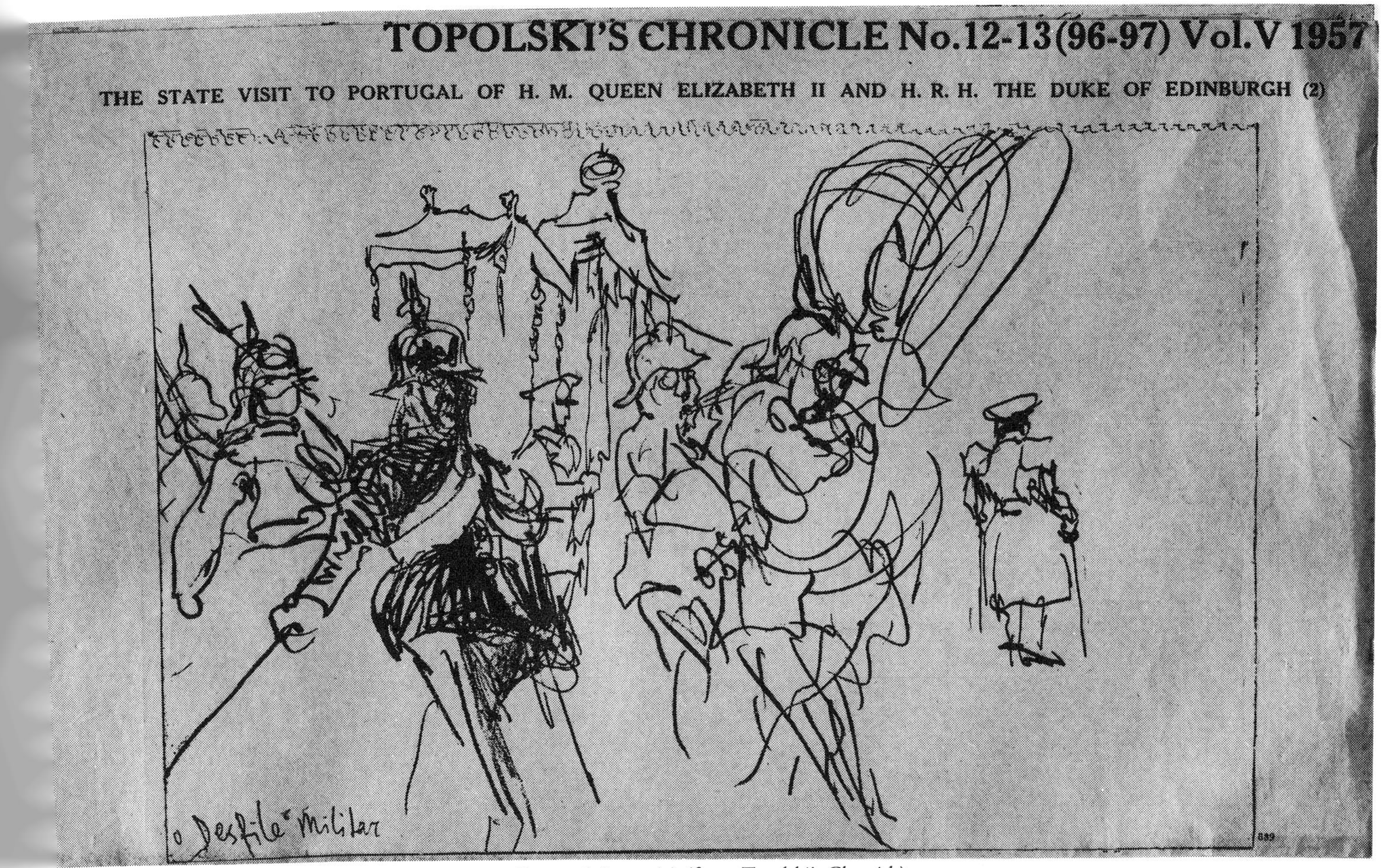

Portugal: State visit (from *Topolski's Chronicle*)

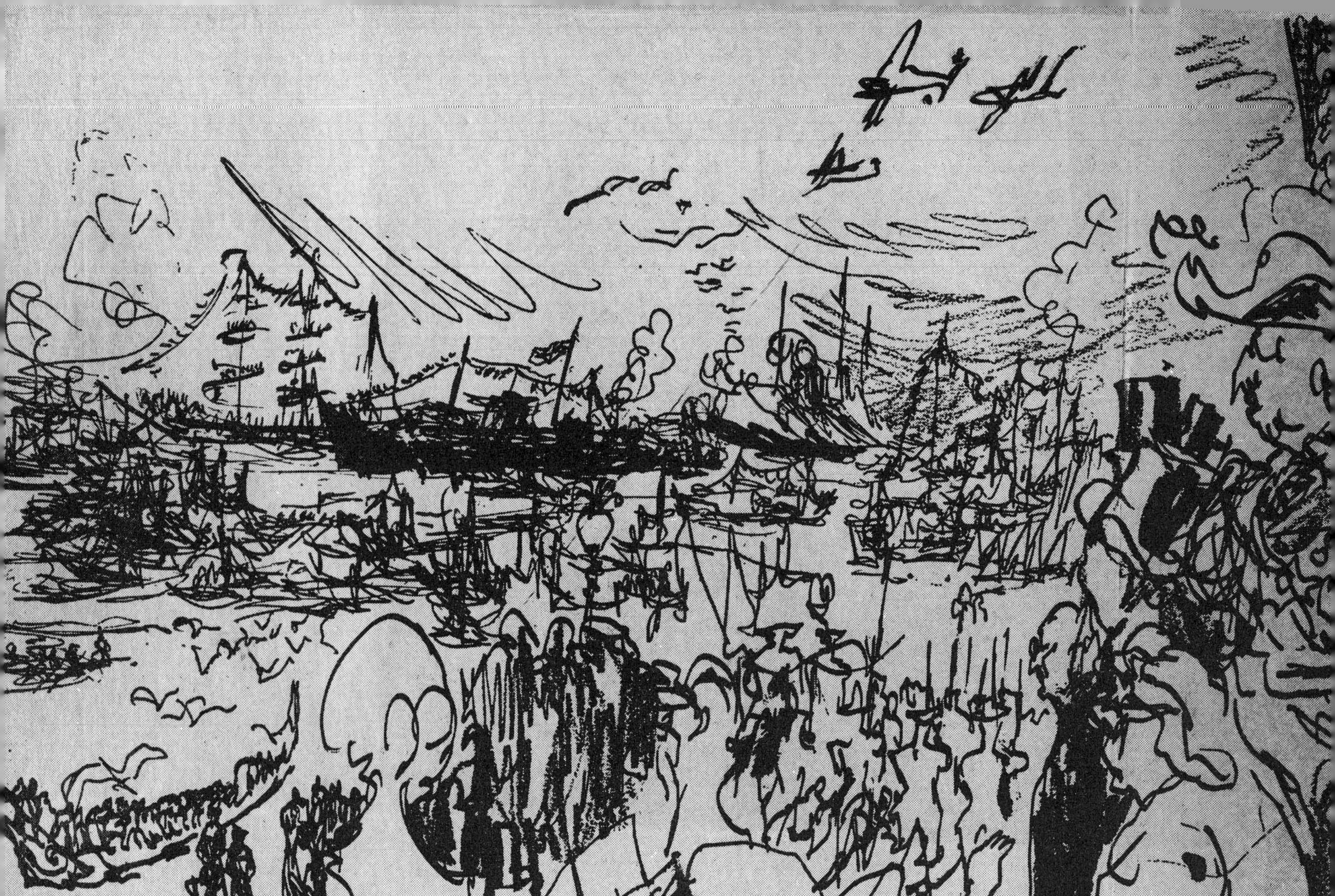
magnífico
O bergantim do século XVIII, conduzindo S.M. a Rainha da Grã Bretanha e S.A.R. o Duque de Edimburgo aproxima-se do Cais das Colunas

893

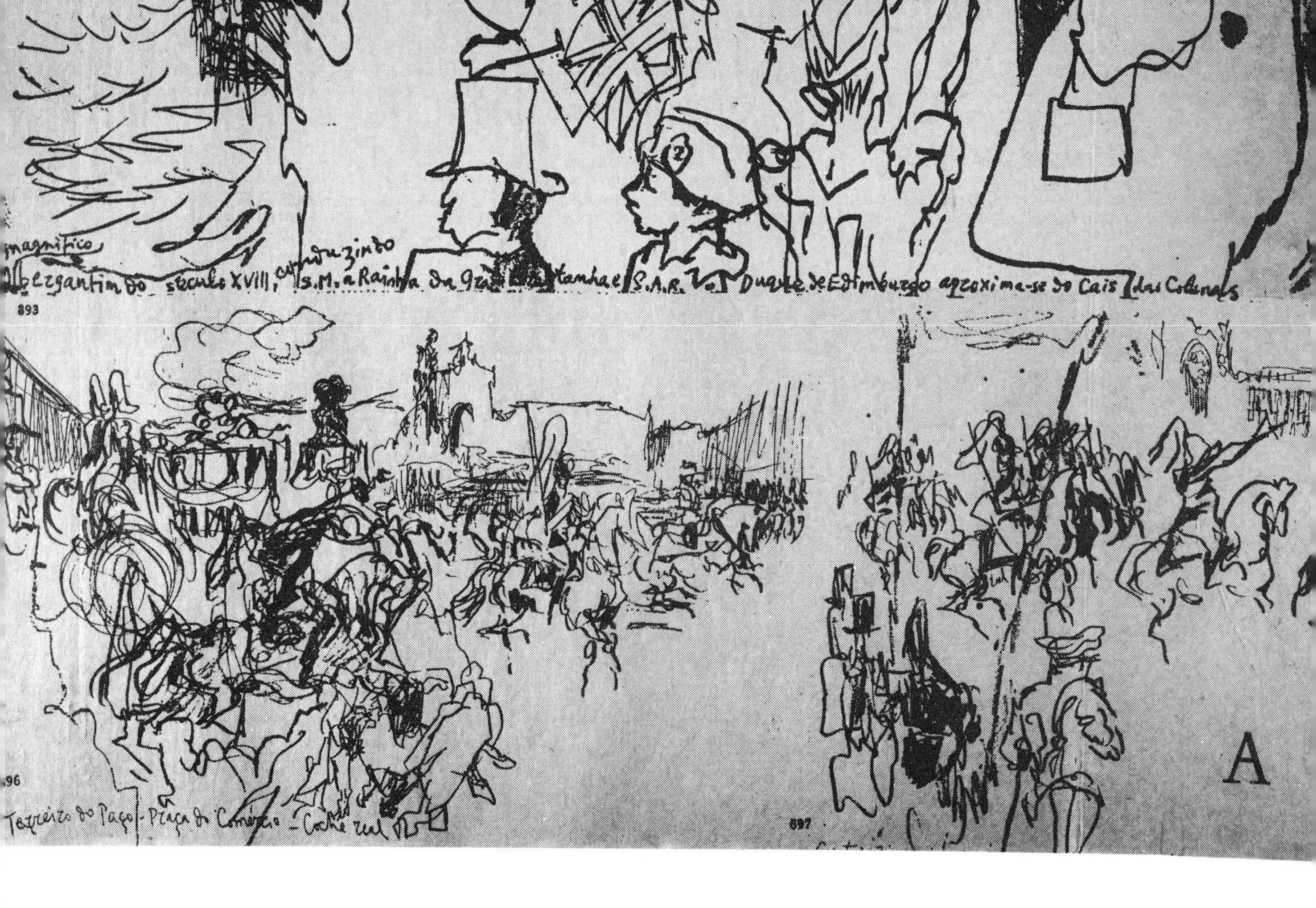
Terreiro do Paço - Praça do Comércio - Coche real
A

896

897

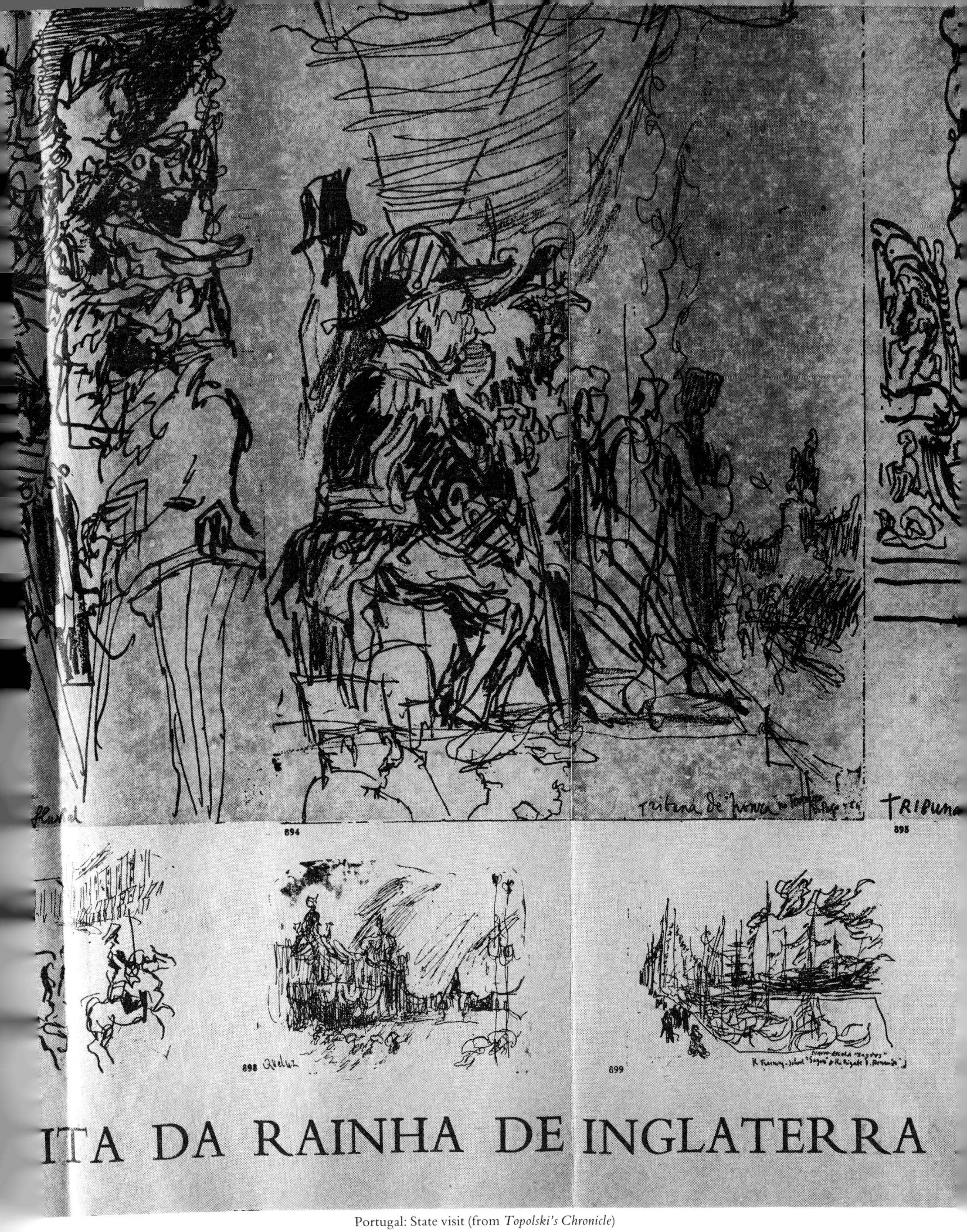

Portugal: State visit (from *Topolski's Chronicle*)

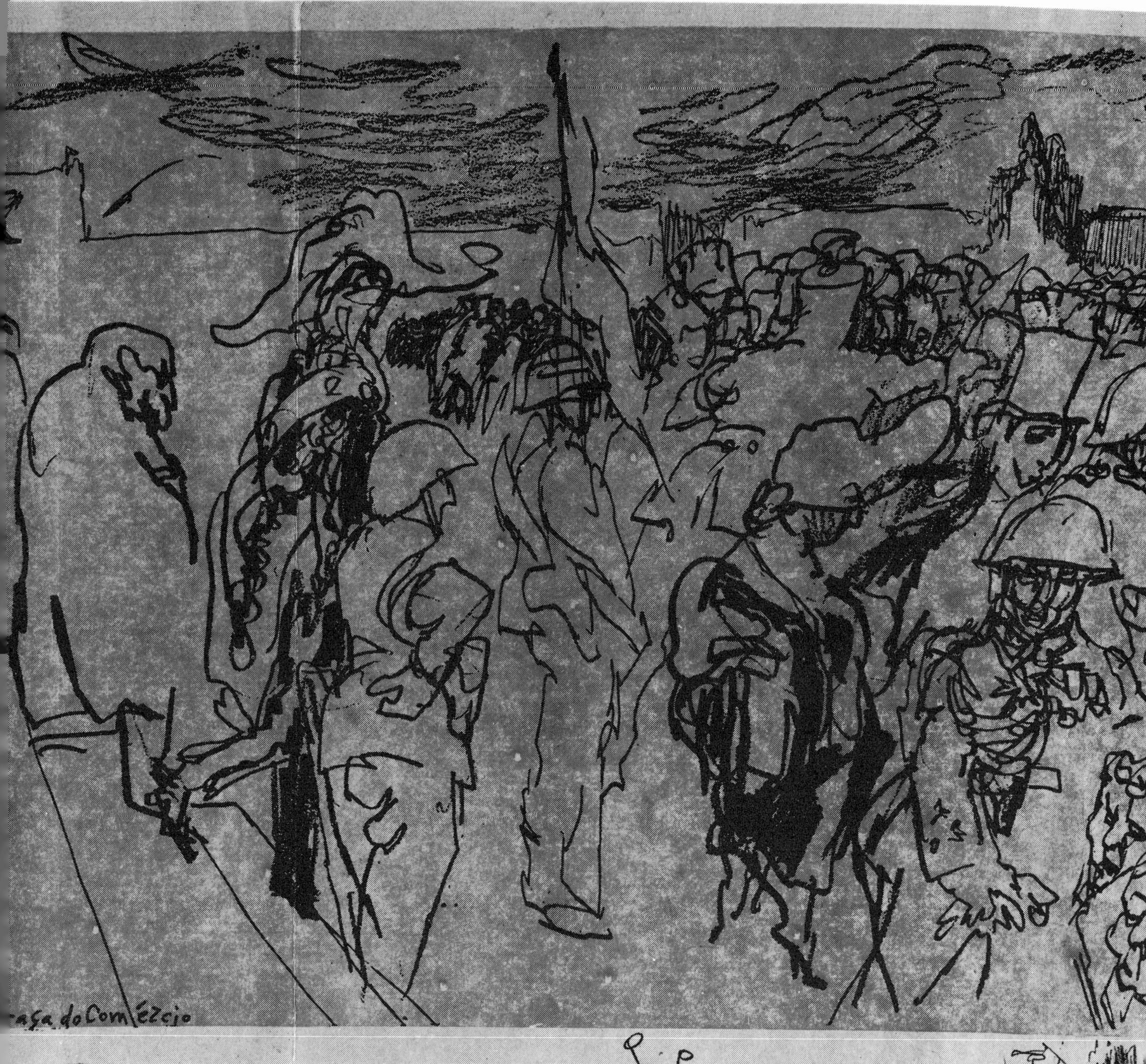

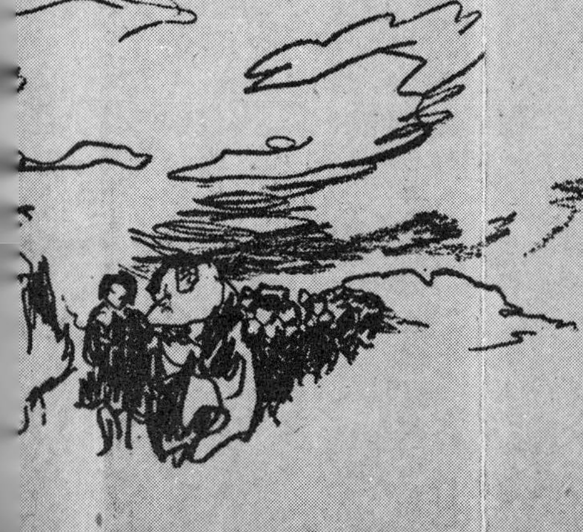

RTUGAL

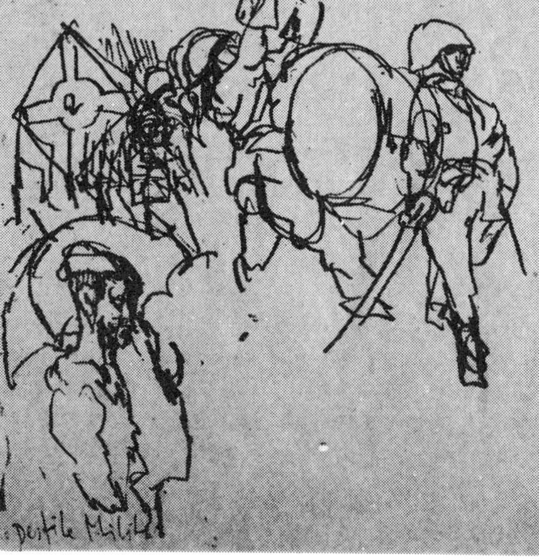

301

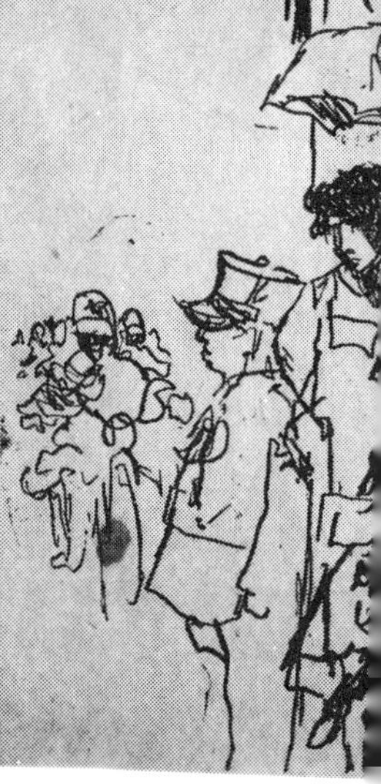

302

Queen and the Duke. The line of limousines rolled slowly round the square, but the Queen's head happened to be turned towards the public-lined houses and shop fronts, and away from the ambitious display. And it was all over. The backs of the motor-cycling guards were disappearing up the street leading to a longer engagement: the laying of a wreath on the Tomb of the Unknown Portuguese Warrior.

Lisboa. The well-positioned plinth of the stone staircase ascending from the ocean supports/erects, with me, too many gapers. The welcome-ritual must contain a sacrifice: a young man at the back – an insignificant thud but ugly as if of a falling soft/heavy sack – he is no more. But heads do not turn – **the Royals** have landed in the commotion of the bannered/pennanted/flagged *Cortejo Fluvial*, and upstepping from the echoing shimmer enter this grandest, now over-adorned, architecture-bound space, the *Tribuna de Honra* embedded in it, under the blue indifferent until gun-firing sends planes and gulls crashing through it.

It is the imprecision/tears in the man-made protocolar fabric of society which catch my mind's eye – my eye's mind; in other words, I am not for adoration/admiration, but thrive on discord. My patron – Doubting Thomas, because slyly 'doubt' is my motor; therefore the *Desfile Militar* pleases me, since led by plump bandsmen in *pickelhauben* marching past tricorned admirals and ambassadors – all *ancien régime* but for their ladies lost in presentday styleless fashions. But the gold *Coche Real* and its escort ride impervious to inconsistencies.

And next day's programmed *Festa em Vila Franca* canters its surviving *cavaleiros e campinos* triumphantly.

Private explorations with **Thomás de Mello** to rich feeding over *fados'* melancholy, or, with **a young Tyszkiewicz**, into Alfama of the poor beflagged with washing. Or the restlessly cloaked *estudantes* and sturdy beshawled old women against the backdrop of the *Mosteiro dos Jeronimos* enact in harmony the parabola of living.

So it is: past conquests erupted once and then entombed in architectural testimonials crossed with the present reduced and restricting circumstances.

Geneva* sheds orange-coloured leaves over very green lawns on the shores of the lake. The steel-helmeted soldiers lurk, guns at the ready, behind the trees of the pretty Parc de la Grange, round a villa where an official luncheon takes place. At the Maison de la Presse the journalists race to the information counter for the hand-outs or over the stairs and corridors to listen in turn to the simultaneous 'briefings' – that is the interpretation and the daily report of the real thing – by the four lesser spokesmen: the Soviet, the French, the British and the American. They differ in character but from these summaries and the hand-out speeches, the uniform impression is that of recriminations, uncompromising and harsh statements, declarations of almost pained dismissals of the adversary's point of view. Particularly

*Extract from *Chronicle* No. 3 (63), Vol. IV, 1956.

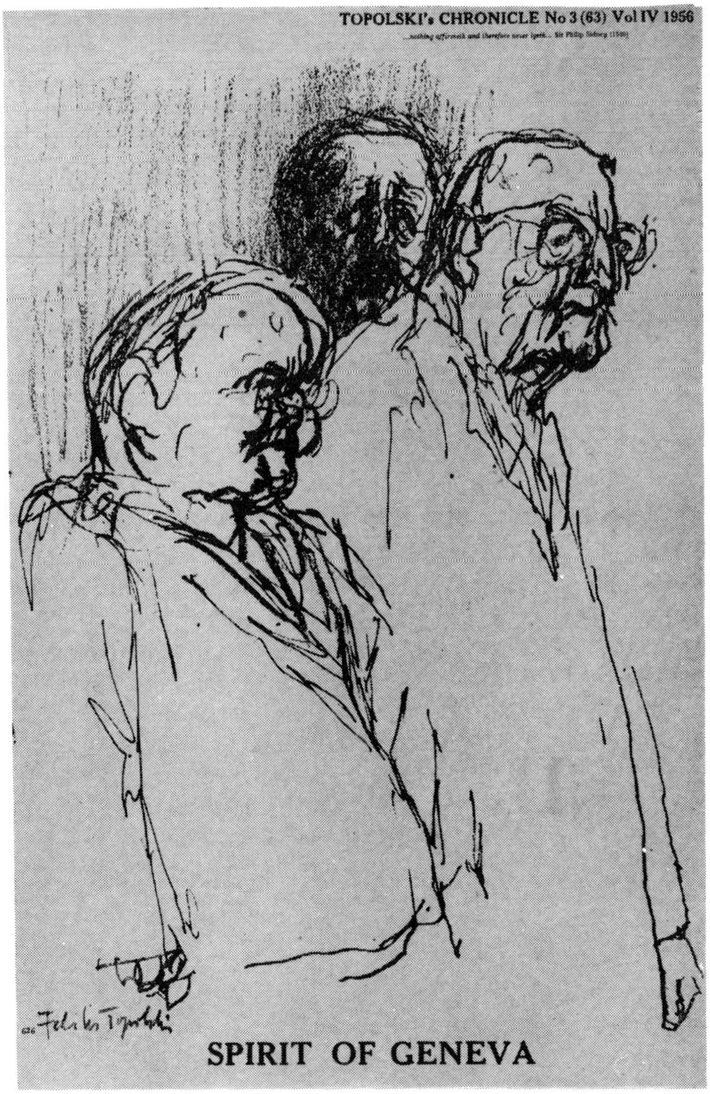

Geneva: Foreign Ministers' Conference (from *Topolski's Chronicle*)

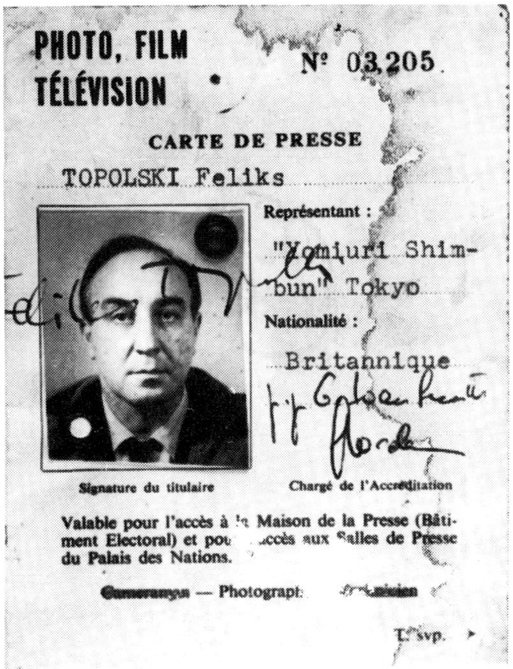

PHOTO, FILM
TÉLÉVISION

Nº 03,205

CARTE DE PRESSE

TOPOLSKI Feliks

Représentant :
"Yomiuri Shimbun" Tokyo

Nationalité :
Britannique

Signature du titulaire

Chargé de l'Accréditation

Valable pour l'accès à la Maison de la Presse (Bâtiment Electoral) et pou… accès aux Salles de Presse du Palais des Nations.

Cameraman — Photograph…

T. svp.

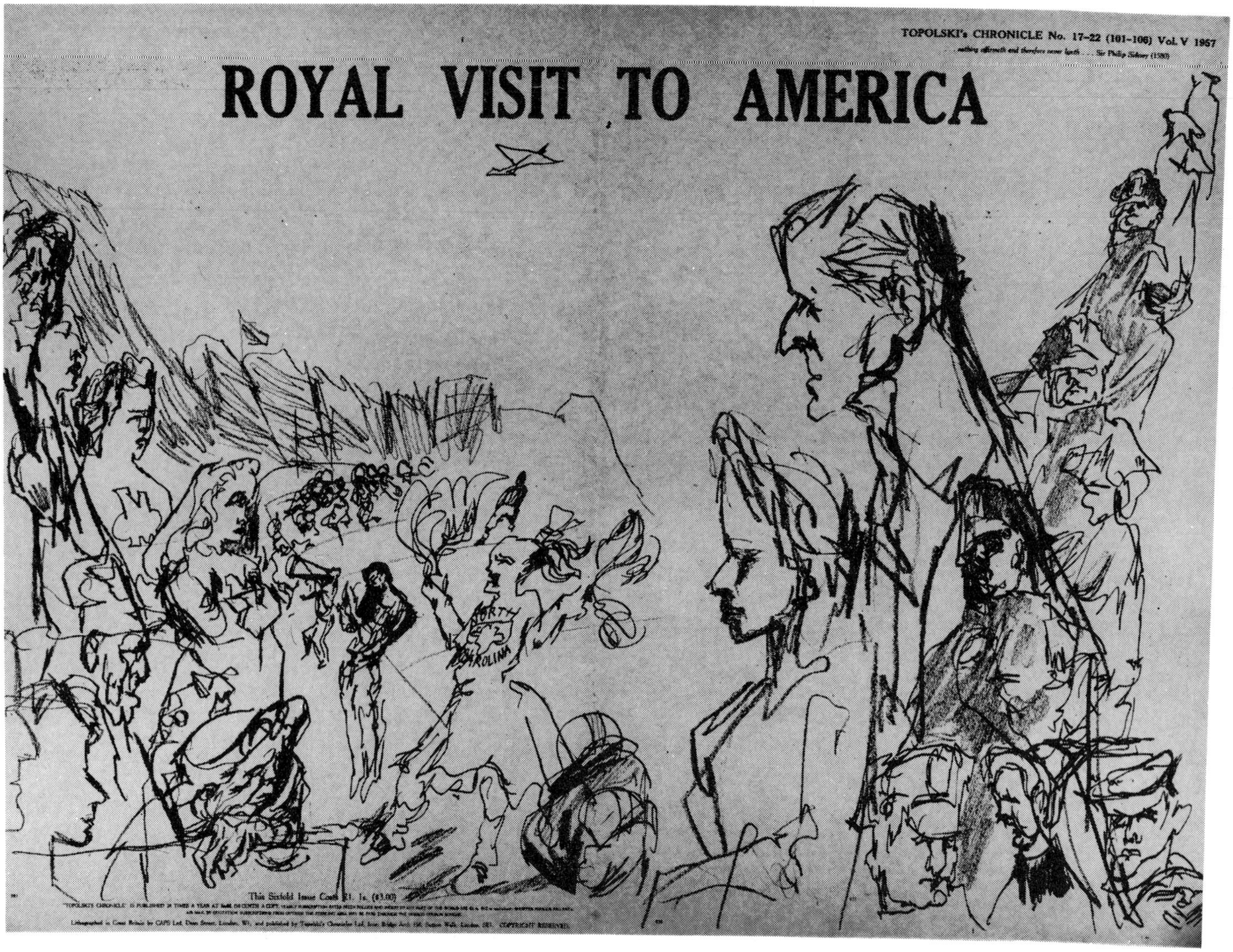

so in the case of the British Foreign Secretary.

Yet, later in the evening, in Hotel Beau Rivage (the residence of the British Delegation) I watch Mr Harold Macmillan lead Mr Molotov to after-dinner coffee and liqueurs with such a display of bonhomie and of gestures and smiles suggesting the most attentive camaraderie, that Mr Dulles, less nimble perhaps, seemed to be positively left out.

Royal Visit to America

The mishmash of America's nostalgias/conceits/stirrings:
the stuck-up hamburger's strain to un-hamburg itself,
the obsequious choc-ice-shake's strain
to upheave into milk-'n'-honey,
the vainglorious dollars' strain to turn into golden crowns,
the strait-laced WASPS (the usurpers of the baronial/heraldic claims)
straining to be sanctioned by divine right
in snob catalytic fervour 'By Appointment to HM THE QUEEN'.

17 October, 11.15 a.m. Washington, The Military Air Transport Service Terminal

Queen-awaiting – Drum-Major, a 'musical'-clad (traditions overshot) eight-foot-high bearskinned/feathered/tasselled and next an old Negro plain good soldier/corporal ropes in top enclosure, excluding a makeshift 'folly' with COLOURED on it.

12.00 noon. Procession along Parade Route to the White House

Carefree fifties: sharp-shooters' vintage not yet matured, nevertheless the limousined bullet-proof bubble-immunized Iconic Heads, escorted by lancers updated, gaily motor-farting pennon-aerializing, and by perched/crouched/poised on mudguards sinister/familiar large-brim-hatted unflexible heavy-plainweights.

5.00 p.m. Reception in Honour of The Queen and Prince Philip at the Statler Hotel

A hand-shake line – a strait-laced female falls out/faints – the line closes ranks, grimly: loyalists to the last.

19 October, 2.15 p.m. The Football Game between the University of Maryland and the University of North Carolina

Boys-padded-into-supermen, up-down majorettes, bobby-soxers cheer-leading New World multitudes, but in the honoured segregation, supremely puffed-up stuck-up (seen from below) the WASPy democr/aristos bouquetted round a

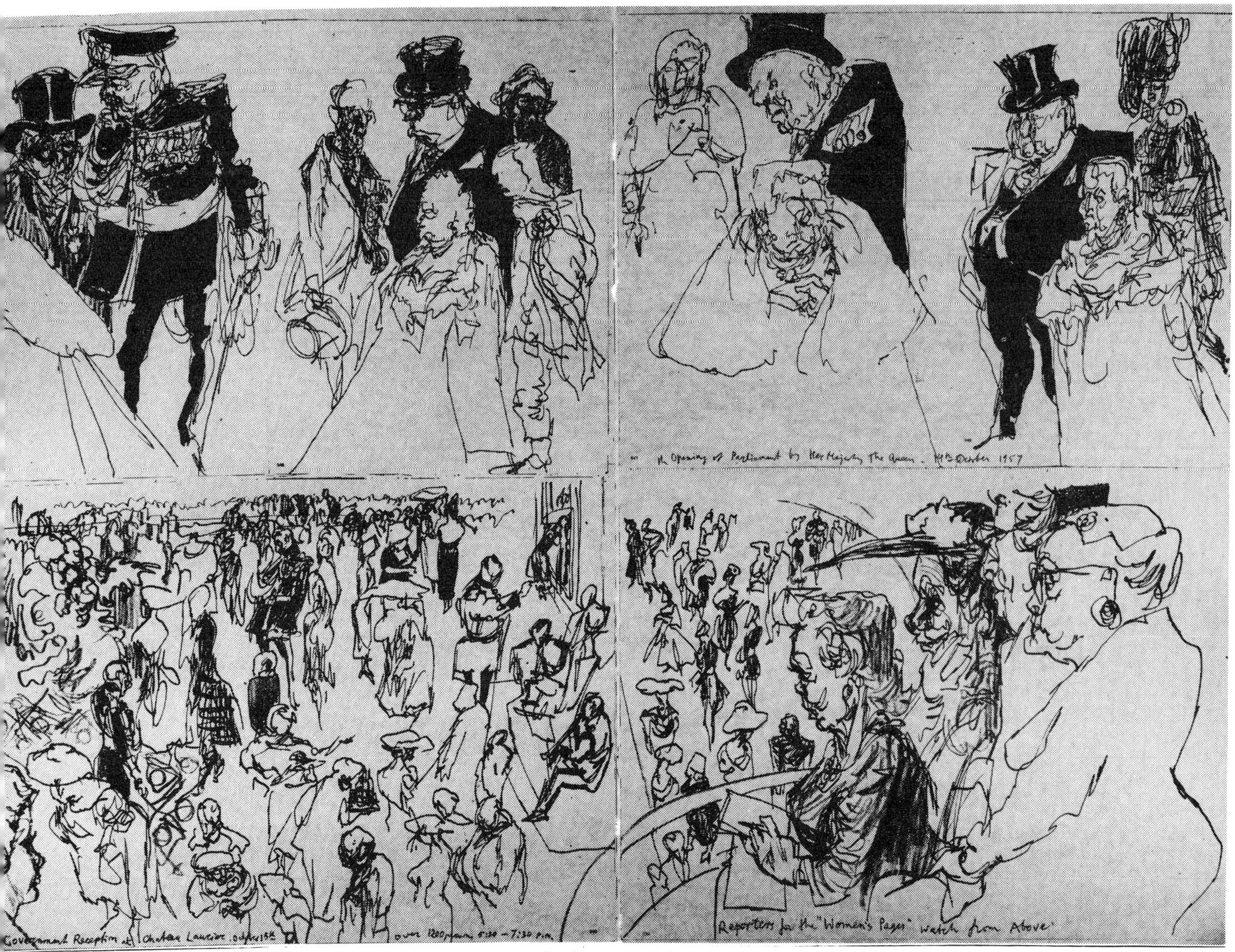

In Canada (from *Topolski's Chronicle*)

divine-right' *fleur-de-lys.*

21 October, 10.35 a.m. Departure from Staten Island aboard US Army Ferry for the Battery Manhattan New York City

The sumptuous ocean-harbour-metropolis-scape Glory Be! For elements Glory Be! For senses (salt-sprays ozone sirens vessels sea-and-air She-Liberty gulls towers buntings wails towers TOWERS) immeasurable Glory Be! Women's-page ladies (packaged and ablow) pencil down Queenly assumed/supposed common touch responses to THIS Majesty.

11.30 a.m. The motorcade proceeds to City Hall

To enter the dark stony solids of narrow canyons, heights jettisoning tickertape/roar/human vastness and humans minimal – humans enlarged and reduced; to 'motorcade', however perched/tacked into this mammoth happening – indeed THE METROPOLIS of this century IS visited and IS greeting, at once total/multi-various/mighty/coarse/western/exotic/contradictory/stately/ruthless/laughably touching. The eye shoots fast up up to banners up up up to heights of window faces and fast down down and ahead moving into brightness – draws along Police Barriers, West Point red-feathered white-crossed cadets, police horses starting to rear – because old-time field-guns fire the first of twenty-one diagonal grunts and billows, as if in *pro-forma* defence of the many-tiered red–white–blue fortress (review stand packed with the neatest selection of Plymouth Rockers) about to surrender back to

Hanoverian dalliance
frippery/foppery *ex officio*
puppet-queenhood;
bubble-proofed motorcade wheels
blazons forth
triumphant return (by *vox* US *populi*)
to recapture
Caliban grown giant
hence *amour-propre* swelling
– hence obsequious to be knighted.

3.15 p.m. The Queen and Prince Philip at the United Nations

The Royals here, extra-mural to America's complexes, a couple of quaint exhibits stiffly perched on chairs set askew at the Platform's corner – the Assembly (although in fact a market of patriotisms-merchants in 'independences') seems a learned studious gathering at the fossils-examination. Outside, salesmen of bi-establishments' dual-home patriotism badges/banners/icons/reliquaries and of those

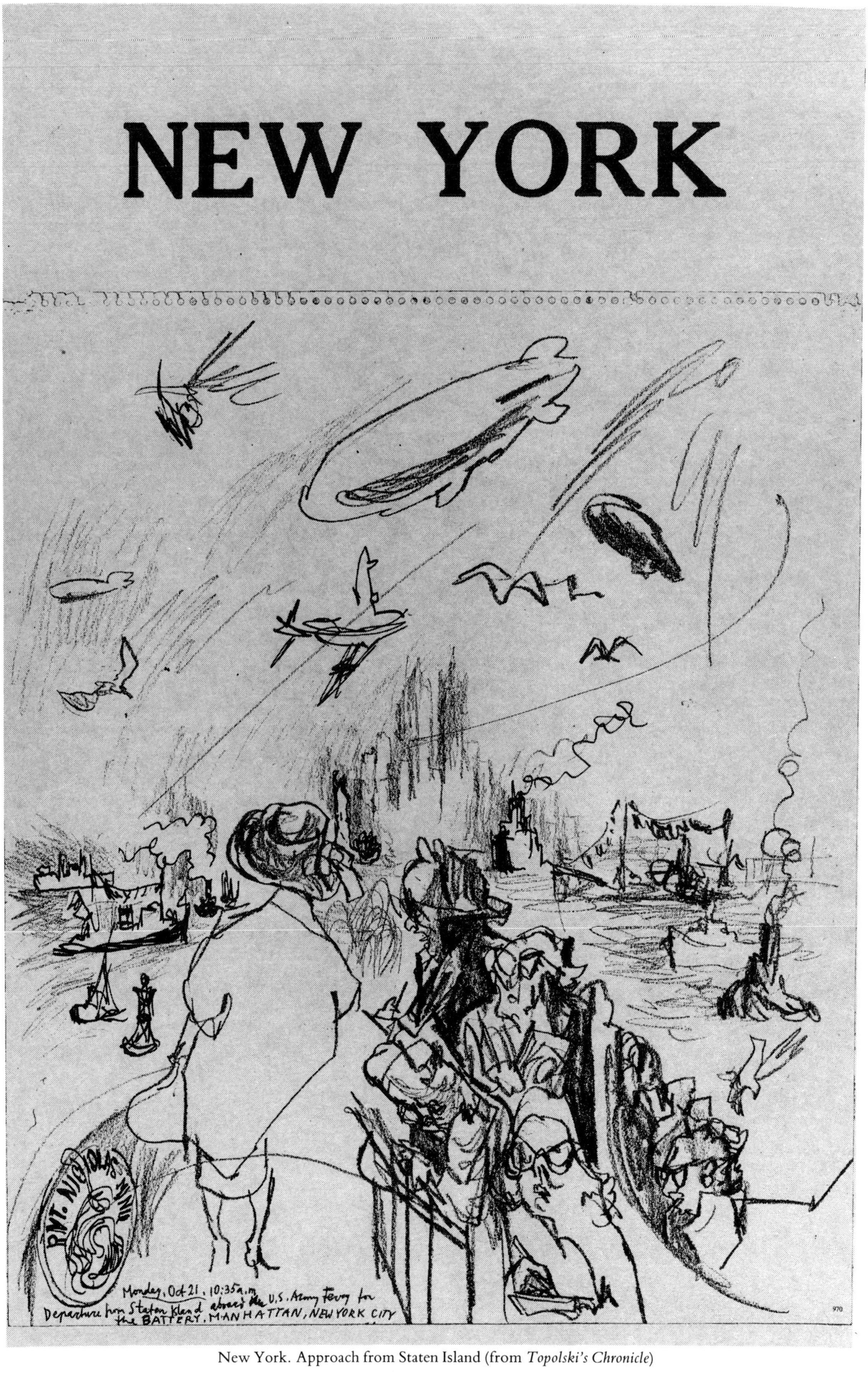

New York. Approach from Staten Island (from *Topolski's Chronicle*)

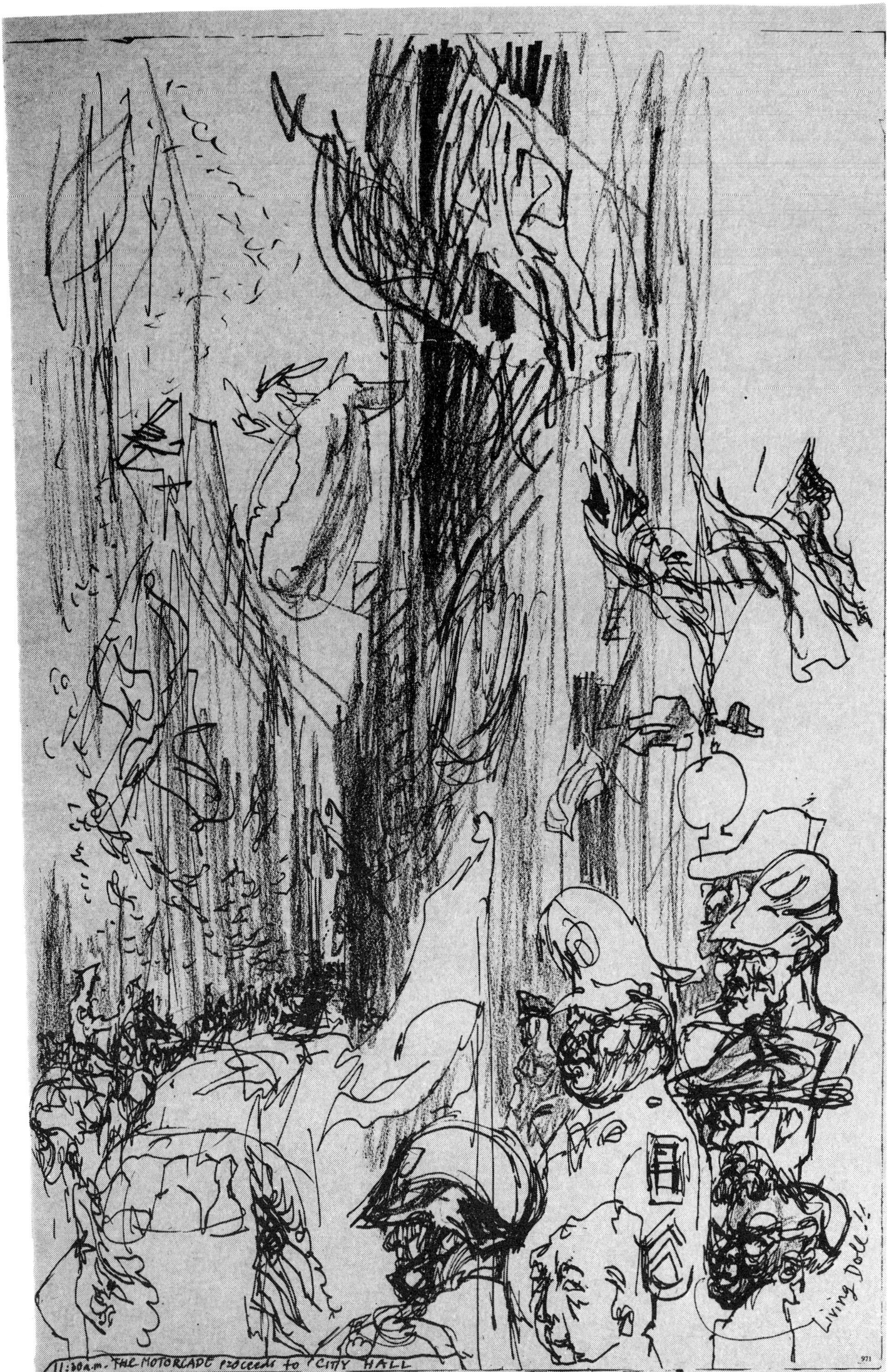

New York: Motorcade through city (from *Topolski's Chronicle*)

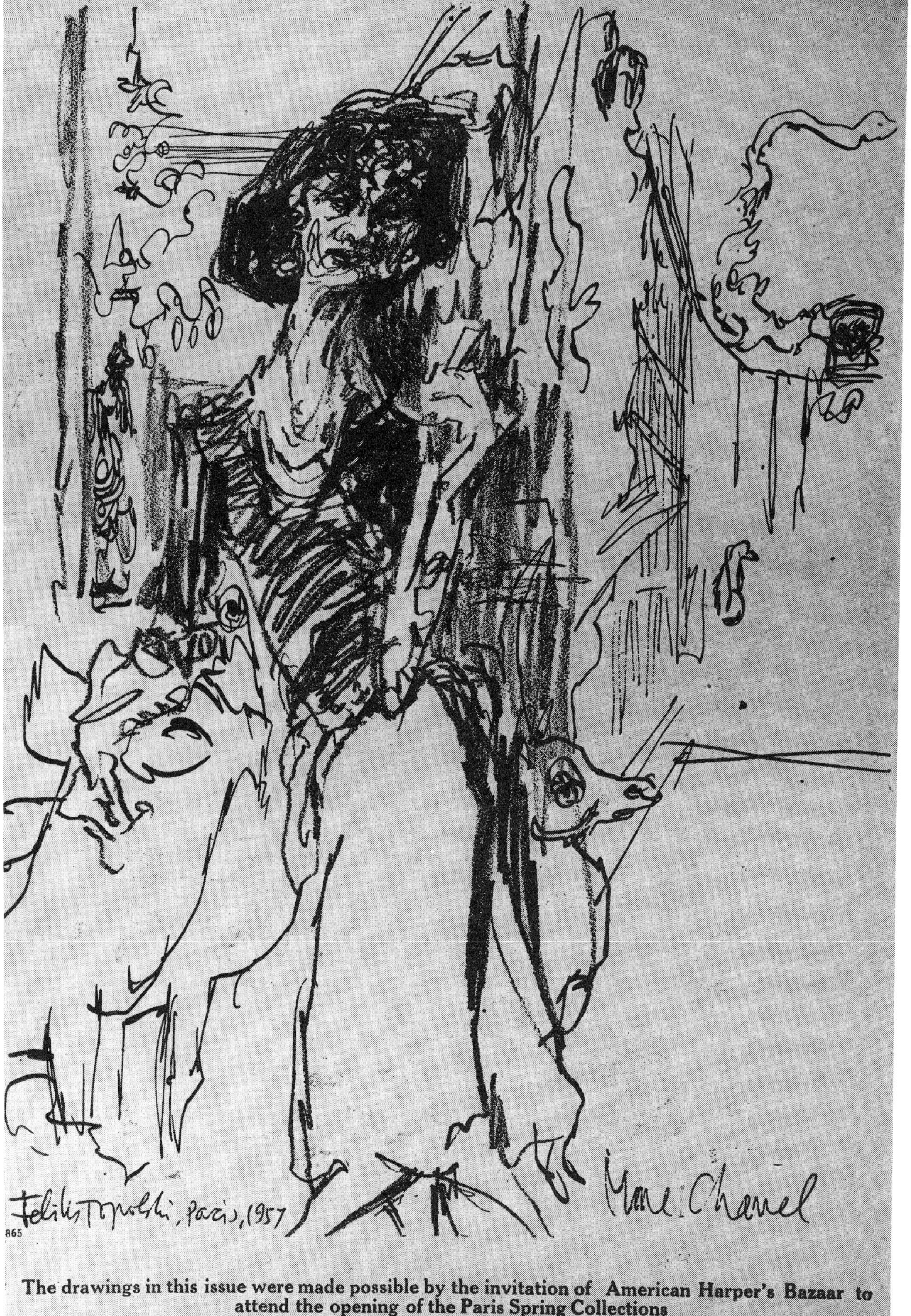

The drawings in this issue were made possible by the invitation of American Harper's Bazaar to attend the opening of the Paris Spring Collections

"TOPOLSKI's CHRONICLE" IS PUBLISHED 24 TIMES A YEAR AT **3s. 6d.** (50c) A COPY.
YEARLY SUBSCRIPTION RATES (WITH FOLDER AND INDEX) TO ANY PART OF THE WORLD ARE £4. 4s. ($12 or equivalent); SHORTER PERIODS PRO RATA. AIR MAIL BY QUOTATION.
SUBSCRIPTIONS FROM OUTSIDE THE STERLING AREA MAY BE PAID THROUGH THE UNESCO COUPON SCHEME

Handprinted in Great Britain by Poets' & Painters' Press from blocks made by Austin Miles Ltd and published by Topolski's Chronicles Ltd. from Bridge Arch 158, Sutton Walk, London, S.E.1. Copyright reserved.

Madame Chanel: Paris, 1957 (from *Topolski's Chronicle*)

others on the way 'Free Kenya from European rule!' 'Northern Ireland. . .!'

8.00 p.m. The Pilgrims and the English Speaking Union of US Give a Dinner in Honour of HM and HRH at the Waldorf Astoria

But the ceremonial dearth: hotel-pluto-palaciality for hire; a showless amphitheatre up to the girandoles of table-bound/ graded exclusives face-to-face with also tabled top-rankers on the stage (tables – the shields? the bulwarks?) eat out-eat eat-to-eat eye-to-mouth-to-two thousand eyes, divided by two (per personage) mouths eating, mouths chewing, mouths mouthing pre-digested words, watch peach melba turn on ELIZABETH's dizzy/languid smile; the sounds of banqueting ritual – interlude bells/organ replaced between the courses by a pandemonium in crescendo of the change of dishes – crockery/ cutlery clatter – servants' heels stampede.

Out: lack of parade-ground perspectives for flounces/ acknowledgements/slights; conceits, thwarted into passages elevators back-stairs, unfulfilled – without a murmur. Only the entries/exits of invitation-holders canopied carpeted over narrow strips of sidewalks are lifted momentarily on the envy of the crowd of outsiders who may imagine that miraculous pontifications and climaxes of pleasure took place behind the closed doors.
To be on the inside –
the joy is in record not in experience.

Past imperial robbers of exotic fortunes
carried their own filth/faith
on a par with enslaved infidels – thus immune;
but a clean all-American
hygiene-caressed-sealed-conditioned-disinfected-disinsected-
canned-pilled-capsuled and hygiene-clad
thus non-immune (soul/spirit have not found their Pasteur)
infection-prone he threads the areas of
Zen contagion
Ho pestilence
Guru pollution
Kama Sutra pox
Beggar bowl defilement
Yogi vermin
Mao indoctrination
VC leprosy
Mau Mau undergrowth putrescence
Grass dross
Elephant memories
Mushroom taint
Noble Savage *redivivus* –
– and (quarantines being what they are) brings them all
back home

Was it 1957? '**Les Collections** *de Haute Couture Printemps–Été*', in **Paris**. New York, bidding for domination, pressed for ostentatious conquests in the pushing manner of eternal *nouveaux-riches*, say of medieval vassals, well-muscled brutes enriched with booty, boosted

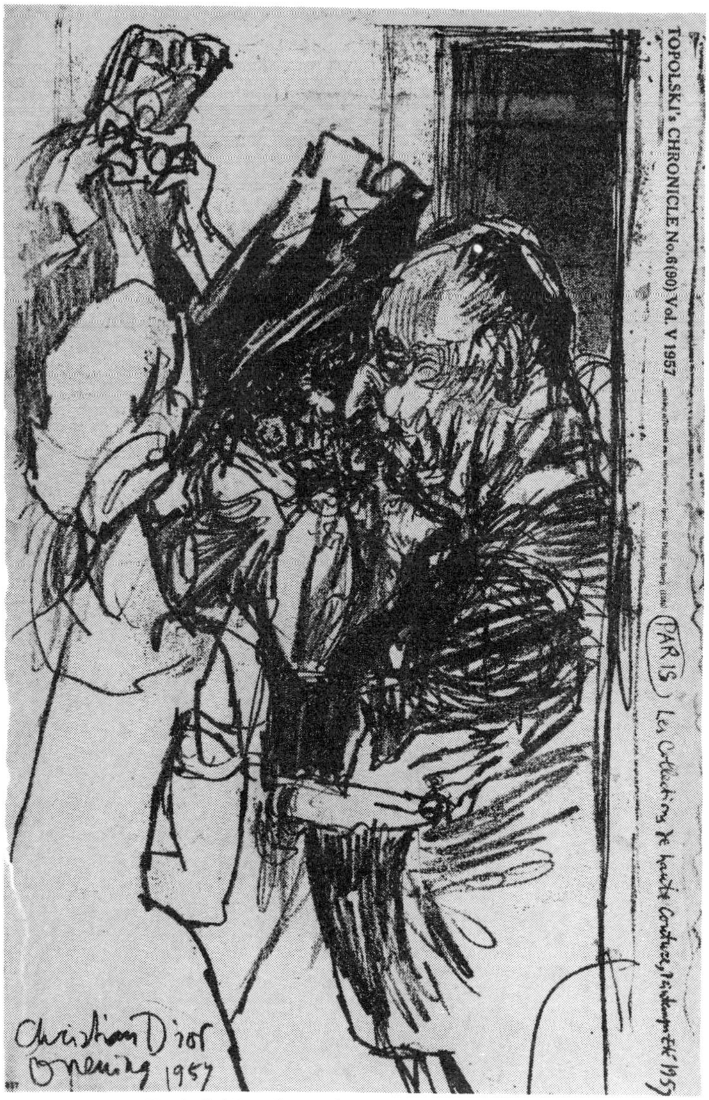

Paris fashion show (from *Topolski's Chronicle*)

with land and honours by their equally crude kings and princes, hence, vanity-and-power-propelled, plotting/grabbing and draping themselves in decorous aggrandizement.

Thus the self-annointed Great Lady of glossy US culture, at the time **Carmel Snow** of *Harper's Bazaar* (in later years the crown taken by Diana Vreeland of *Vogue*), would demand and get at every first showing in Paris the imperial treatment. Within the suffocating tumultuous gilt-interiors' perch-manipulation of those already selected (therefore the fiercest) the front seats and the starting of the shows were always kept for the measured late entry of Carmel's cortège. I, summoned from London to be of her court, held another unheard-of privilege: *Les Maisons de Haute Couture* waived for me their exclusivity-conscious ban on 'taking pictures', as it was understood that I was after the atmosphere, not stealing dress designs.

But all this is told only to justify (ever-dutiful towards my observer's inconspicuosity, thus merging with the scene) my attire on that occasion: my Savile Row three-piece suit and black (velvet-collared) overcoat, Anderson and Sheppard bow-tie, black Lock hat, Brigg's umbrella; and to lead to the probable impression I may have made one of those afternoons when I entered the **Musée d'Art Moderne**, mistakenly assuming it to be the opening day of a major exhibition. The

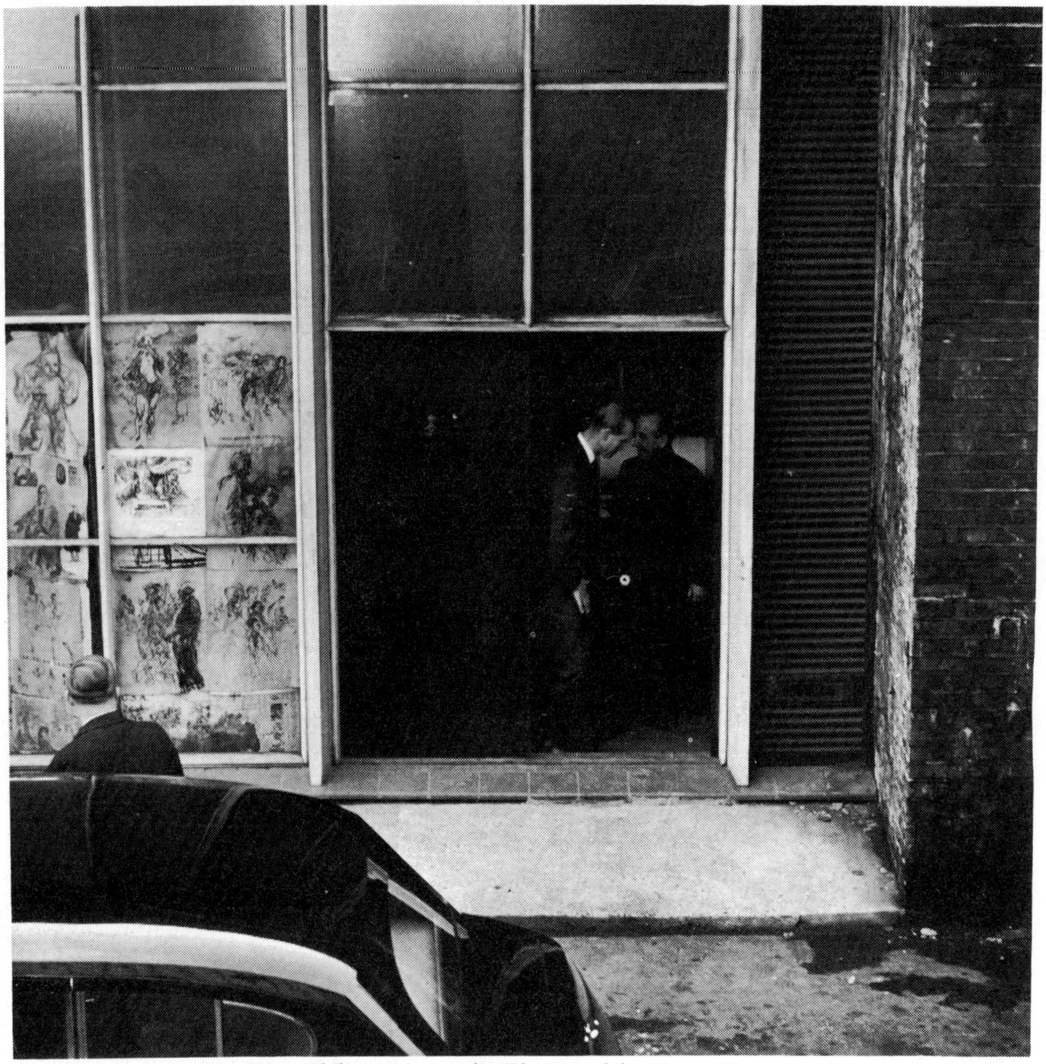

Prince Philip visiting studio (Photograph by Marcus Harrison)

pictures were still being hung and the artists fussed around them, but cutting through the *mêlée* I went round.

Yet not for long: a young couple accosted me and cajoled me indomitably to confront **Yves Klein**'s laundress-blue modest-in-size canvases; they were Mr and Mrs Klein: he, averageness in size/shape/features, she, averageness in prettiness – but for their intensely eloquent *duetto*, clearly multi-recited, on the theme of his work: its ultimate philosophy was laid out at speed and, in conclusion, I was pulled to an inch from the paintings to attest to the proud achievement of utter evenness of blue surfaces, without the blemishes of brushmarks (yet another unexpected horror was revealed: those plain blue rectangles triumphed in such a mixed show – the painterly subtleties of the neighbouring pictures rendered timid).

Their concentrated and prolonged surge upon this stranger would be puzzling, if not for this – that, in the midst of the assault, it dawned on me that my grand costume marked me not as a mere 'colleague', but as a foreign collector, museum curator, dealer or critic – and the momentary reversal of roles, the seductive sampling of haughty superiority as one of the powerful beings bathing in artists' sycophantism made me play up my pseudo-status to their probings by letting it be known only that I came from London.

Both exhilarating and distressingly humiliating – this taste of elevation to hollow object-of-worship pressed (but instantly/smoothly absorbed as due) on an anonymous impersonator by his cringing betters.

I, in full detachment, watched my own response to the Kleins' kowtowings swelling into the not-quite-attentive cliché-queries of a royal walkabout; my step, even when freed from them, springier; my umbrella-arm firmer, swingier – the hat angled on my head.

The later upsurge by the art writers in placing Klein's antics within the sign-posting acropolis of modernity demonstrates that the young couple's indiscriminately, but persistently, machine-gunned verbiage reached the right targets.

The turn for the summing up of my preoccupations with the British ceremonials had to come – the 'full-dress' Britishness. . .

One day in 1959 Prince Philip arrived at my studio on one of his sporadic visits and made a proposal: might my Coronation sketches not serve as a basis for a large-scale painting at Buckingham Palace?

Instantly we drove, I still dressed for a day at the studio in paint-daubed sweater, to the Palace to inspect the site Philip suggested.

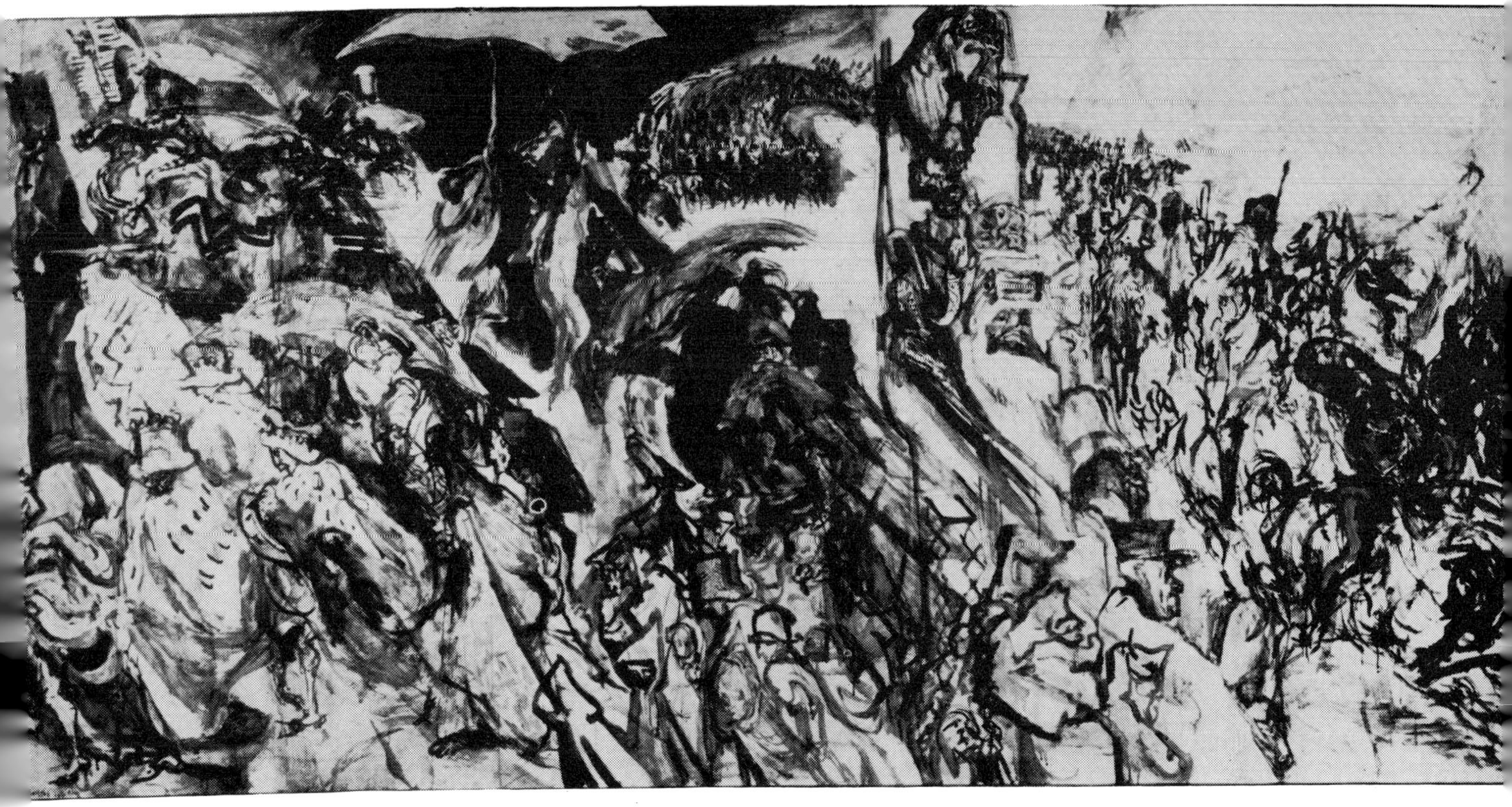

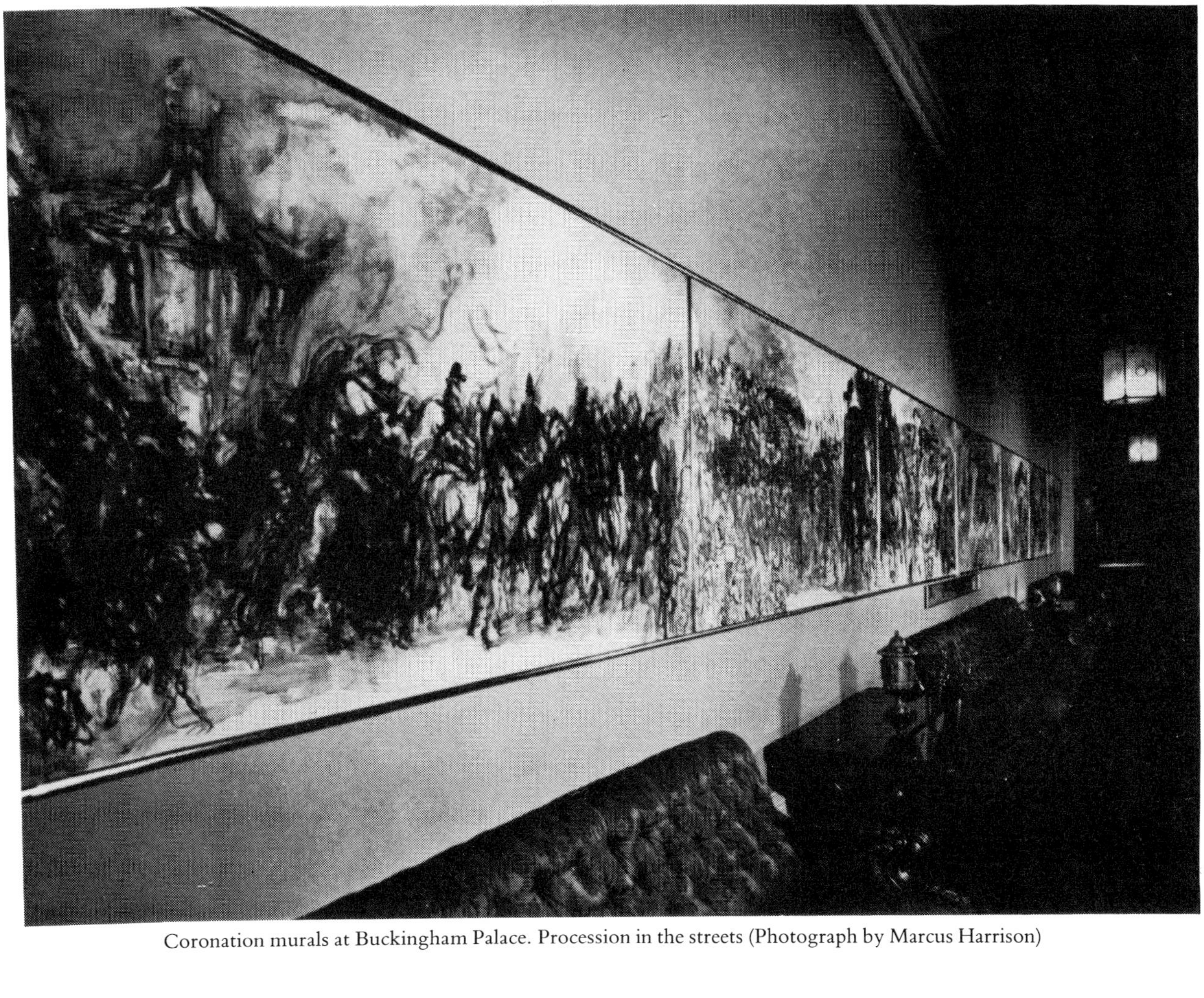

Coronation murals at Buckingham Palace. Procession in the streets (Photograph by Marcus Harrison)

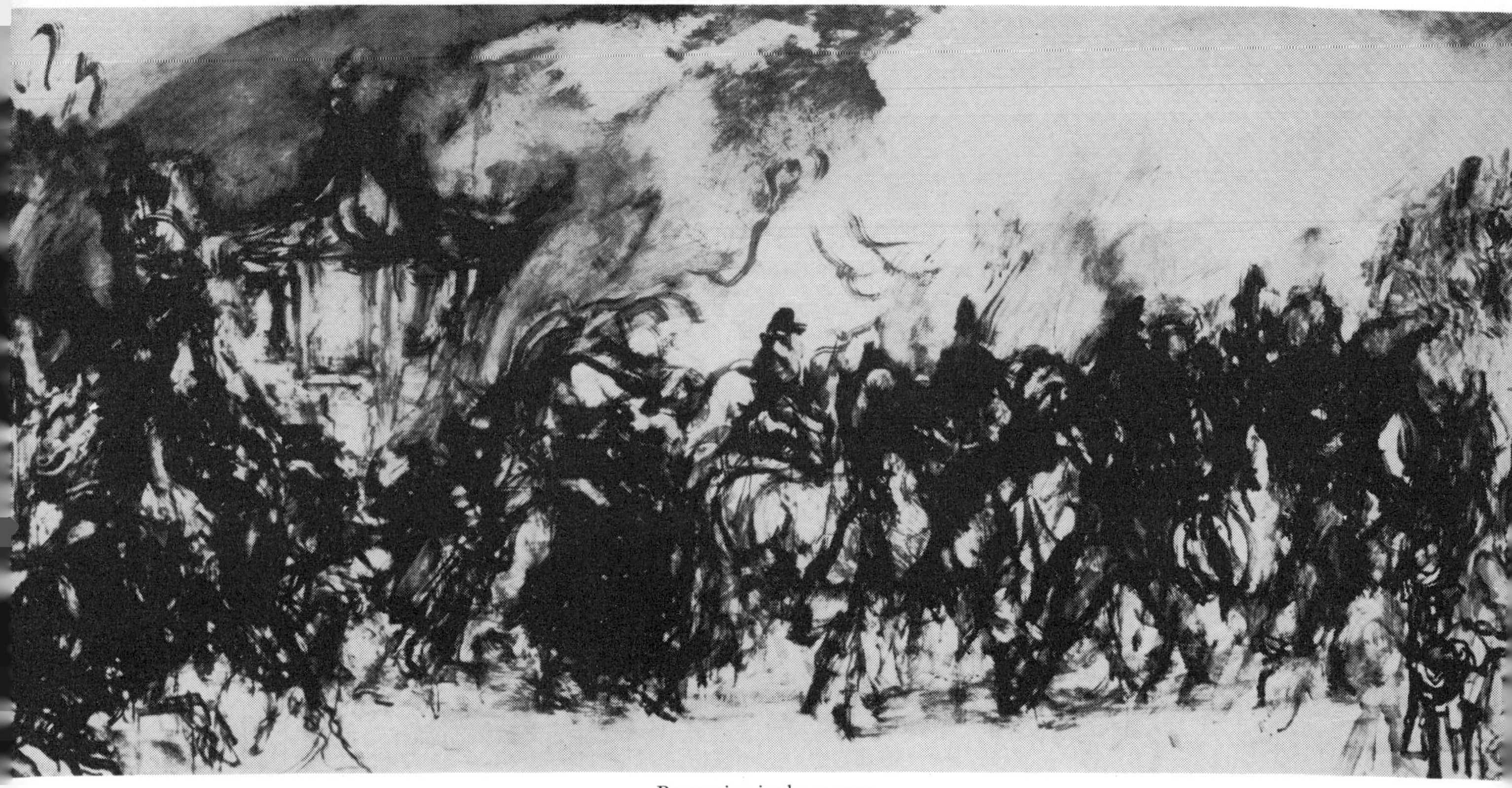

Procession in the streets

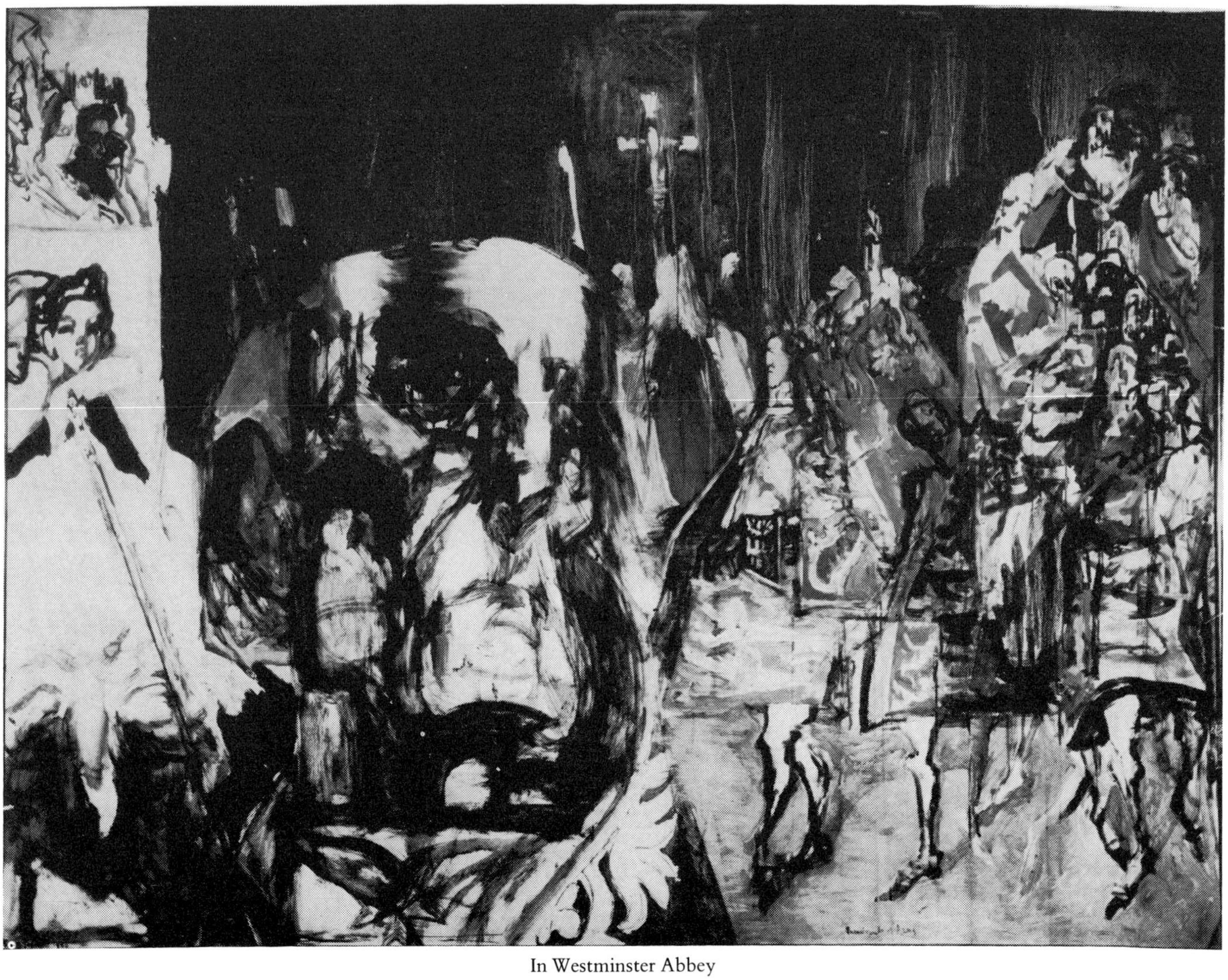

In Westminster Abbey

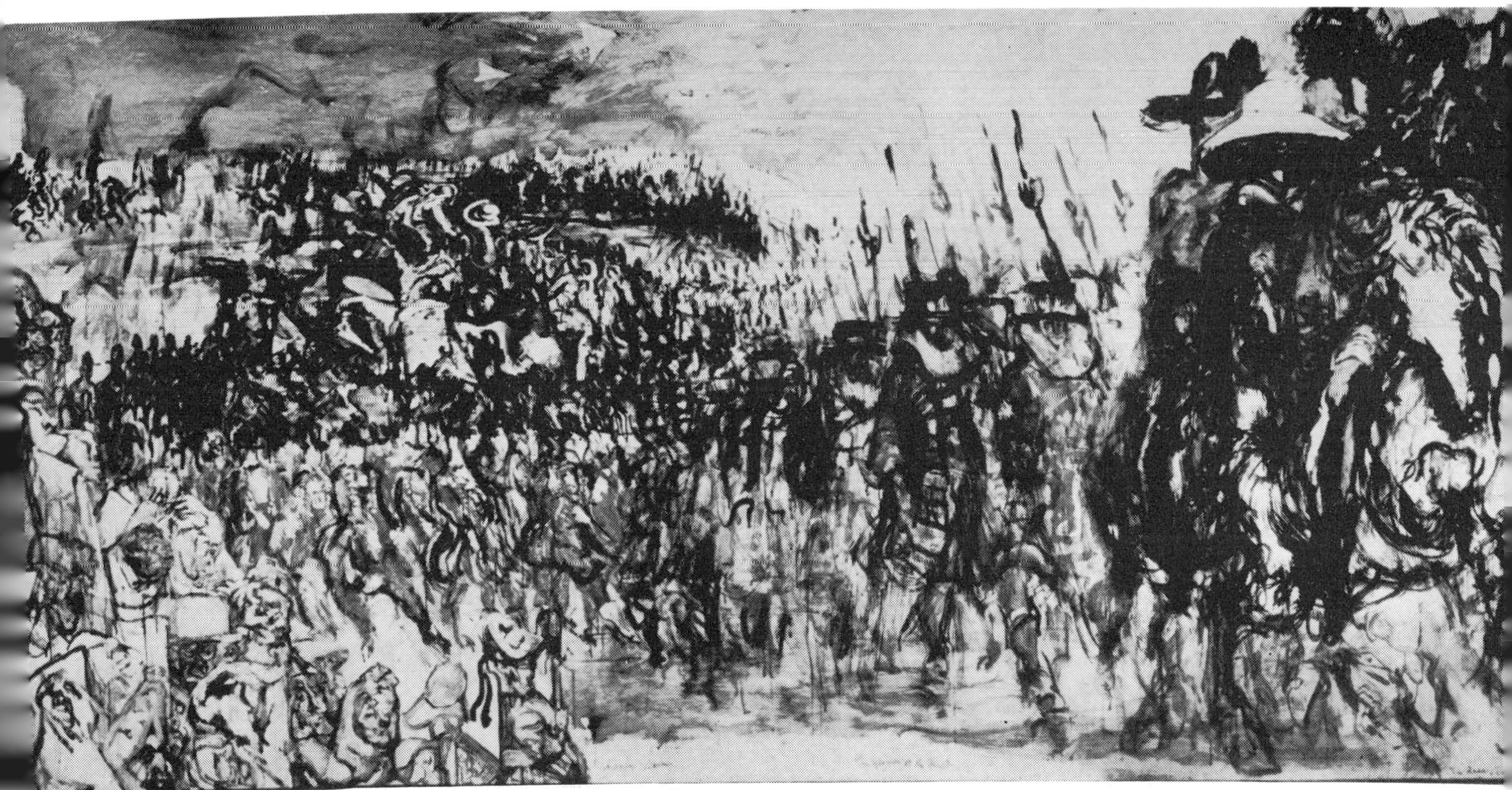

Procession in the streets

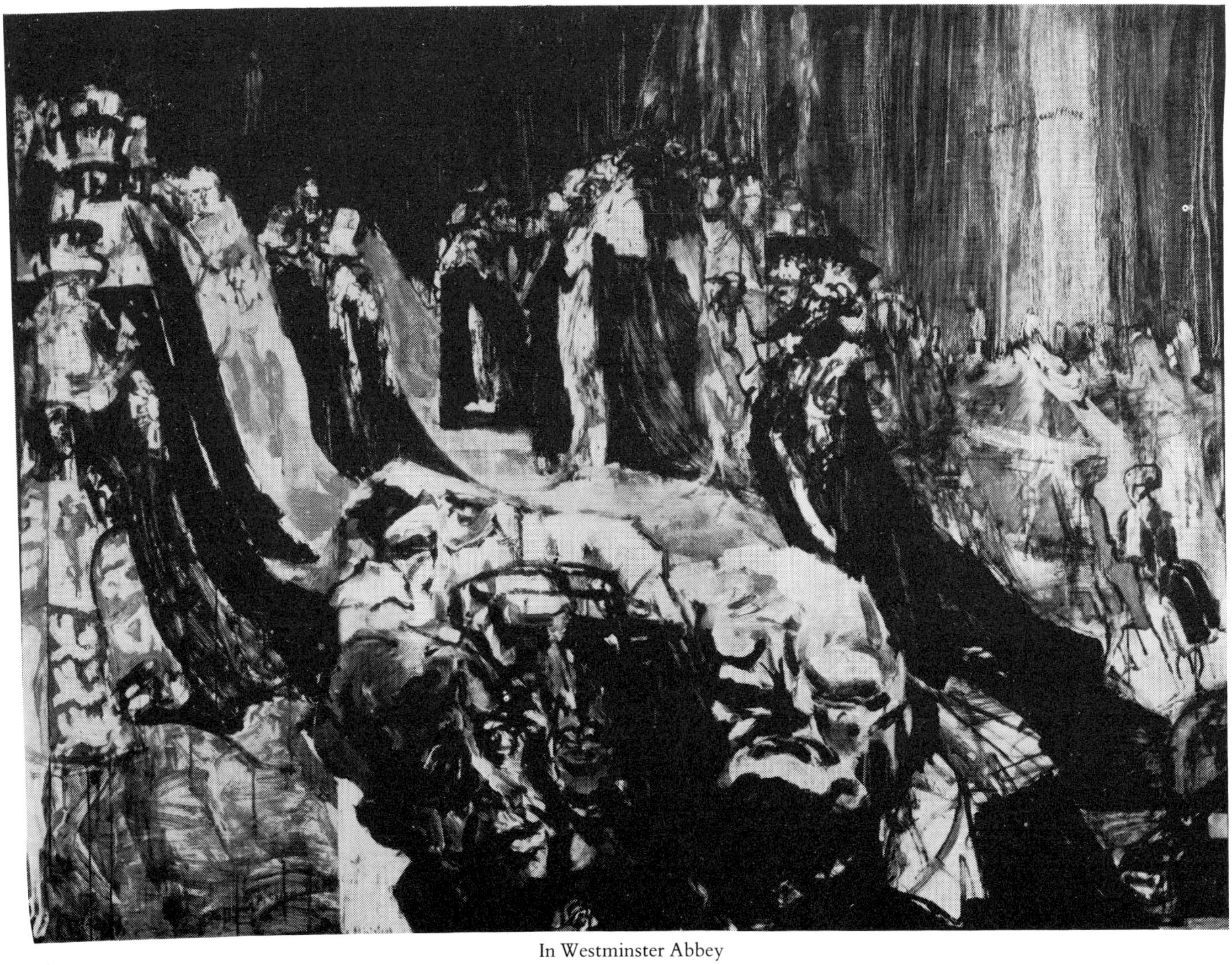

In Westminster Abbey

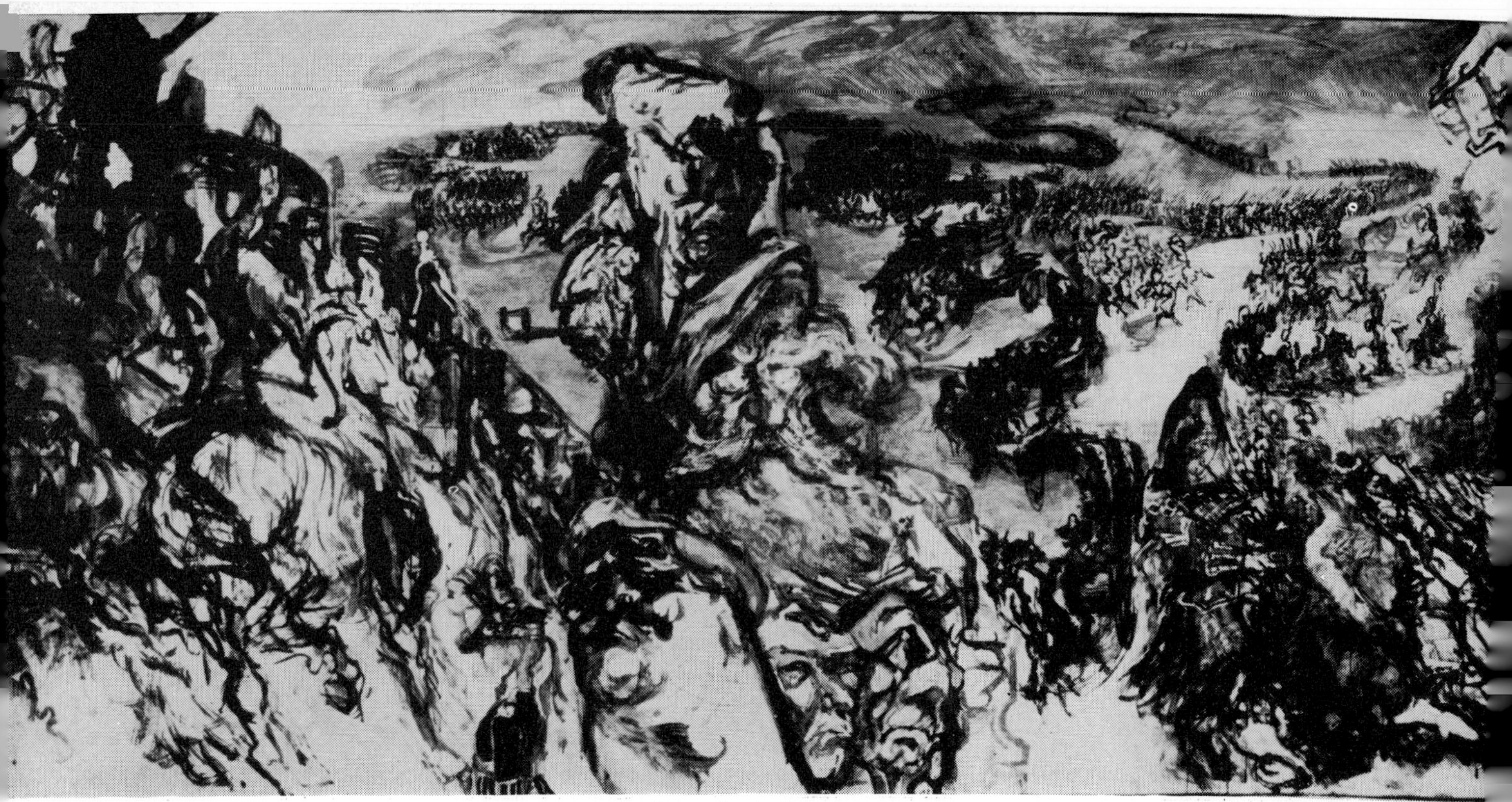

Procession in the streets

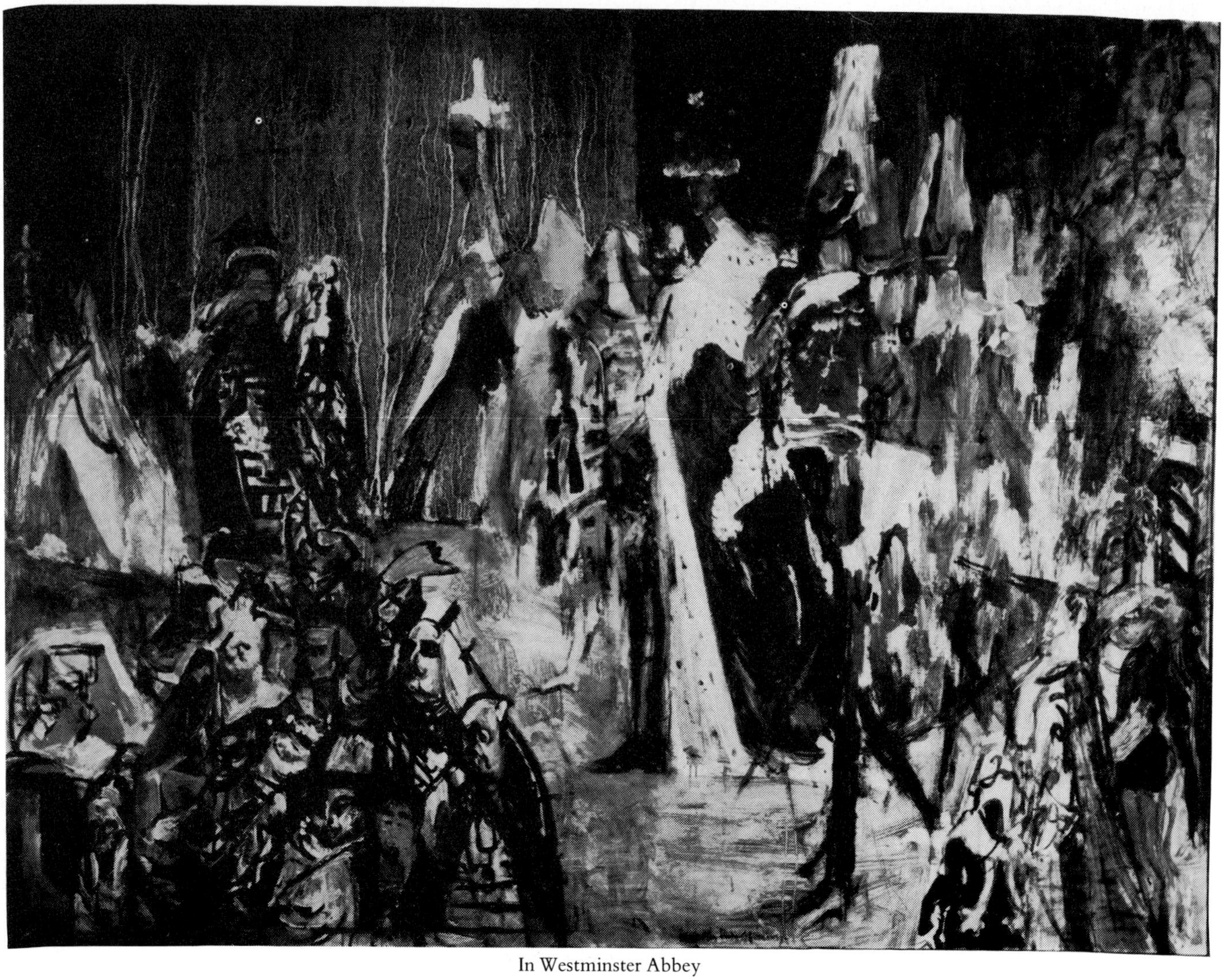

In Westminster Abbey

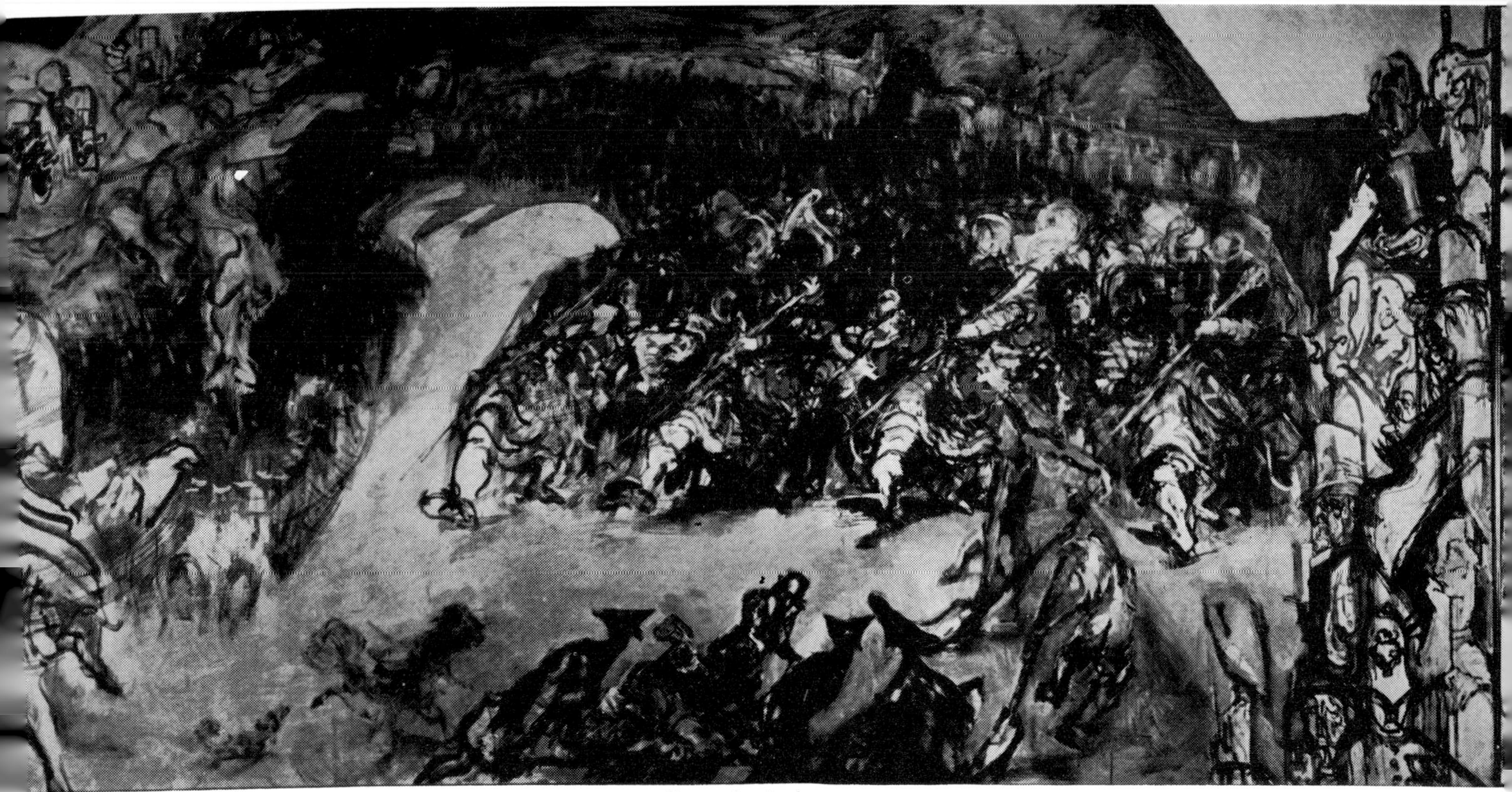
Procession in the streets

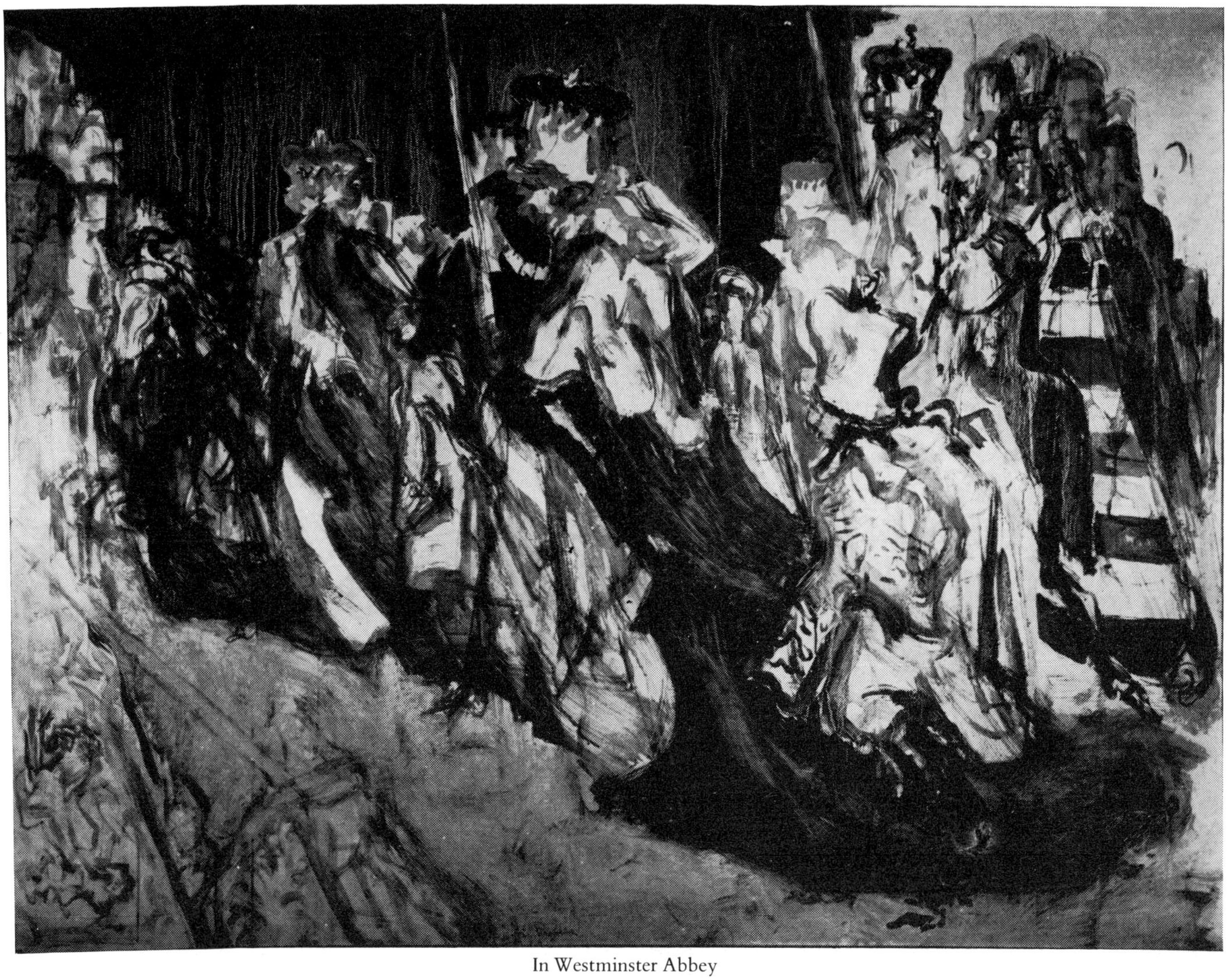
In Westminster Abbey

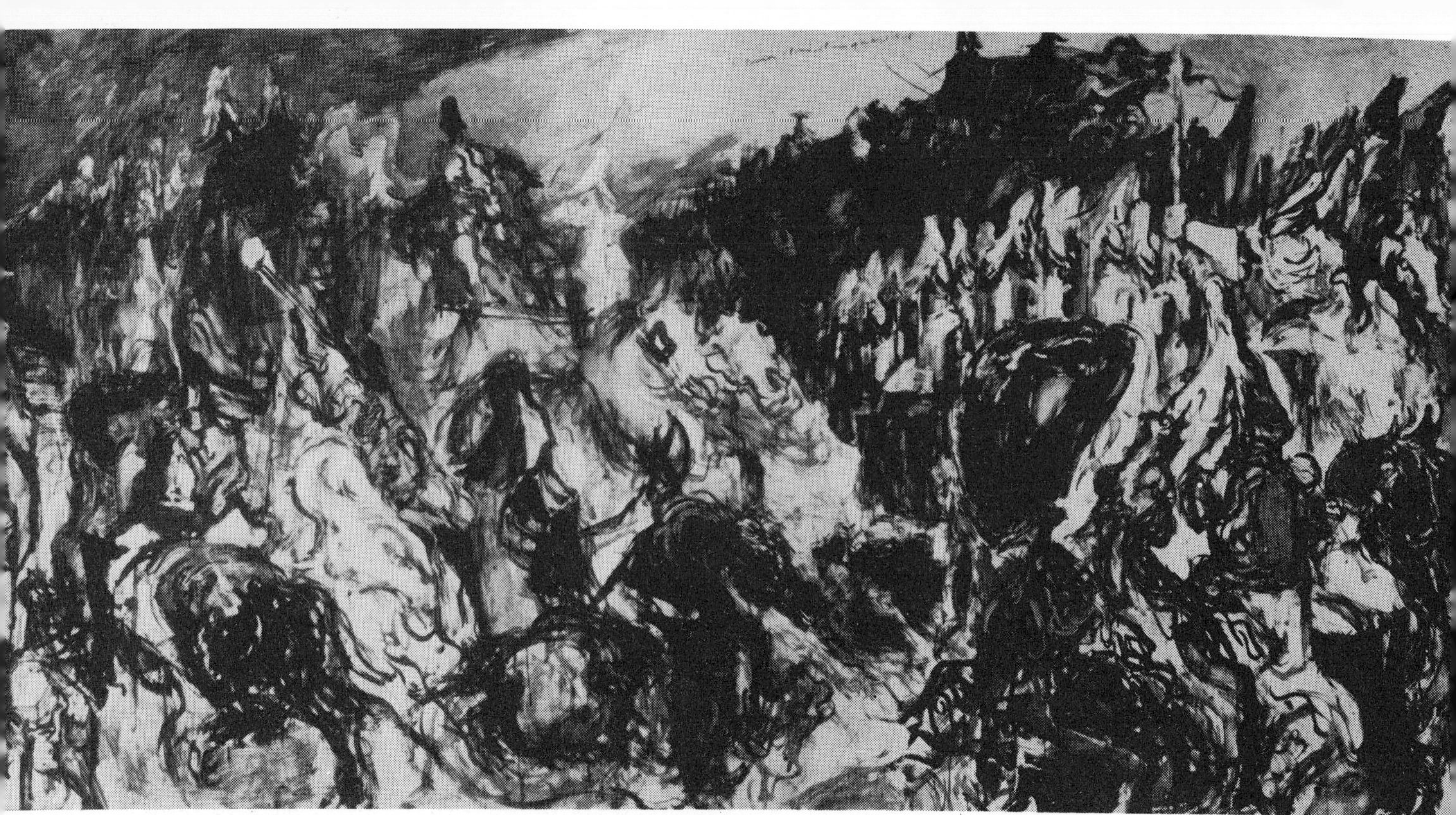

Procession in the streets

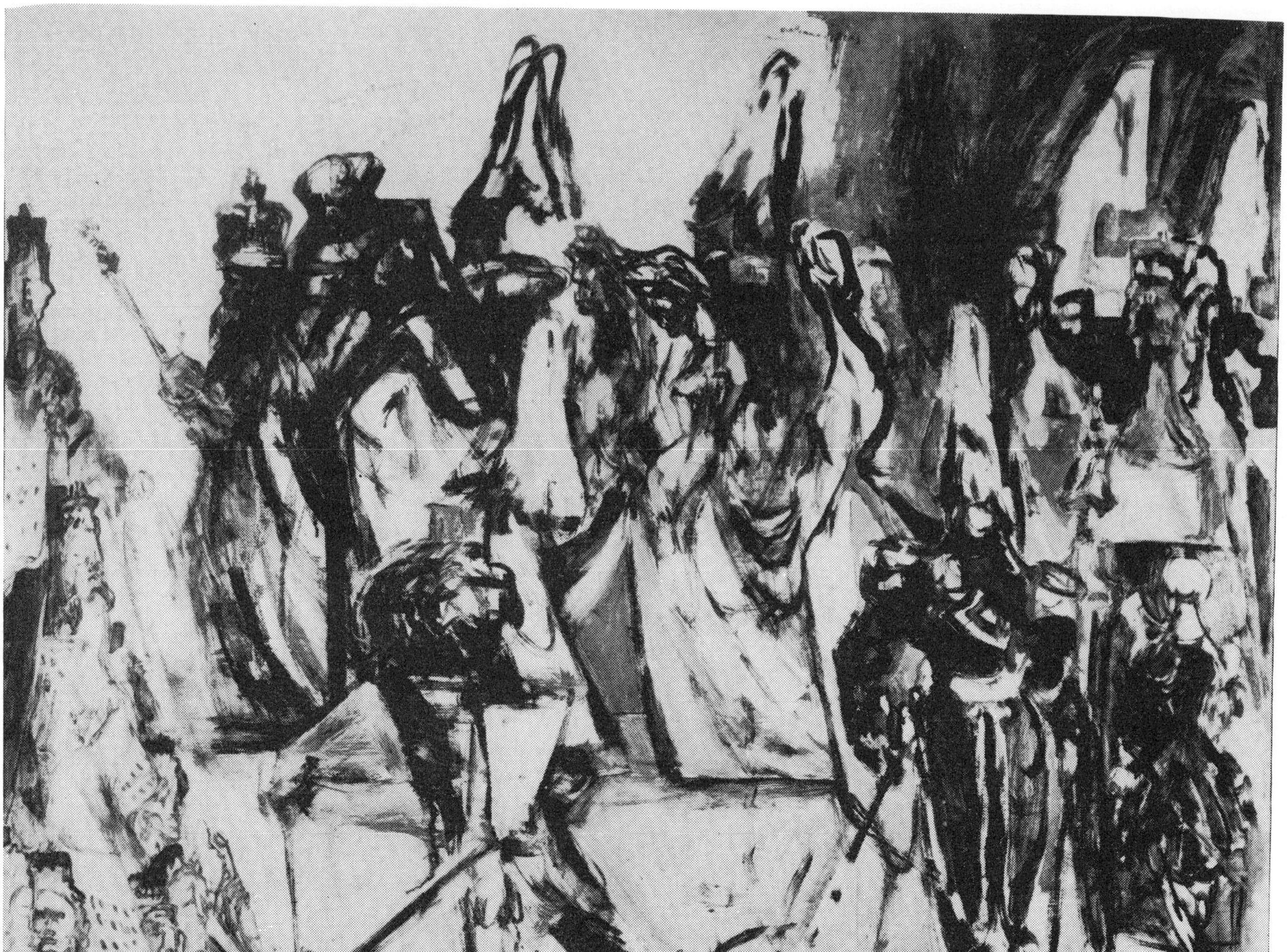

In Westminster Abbey

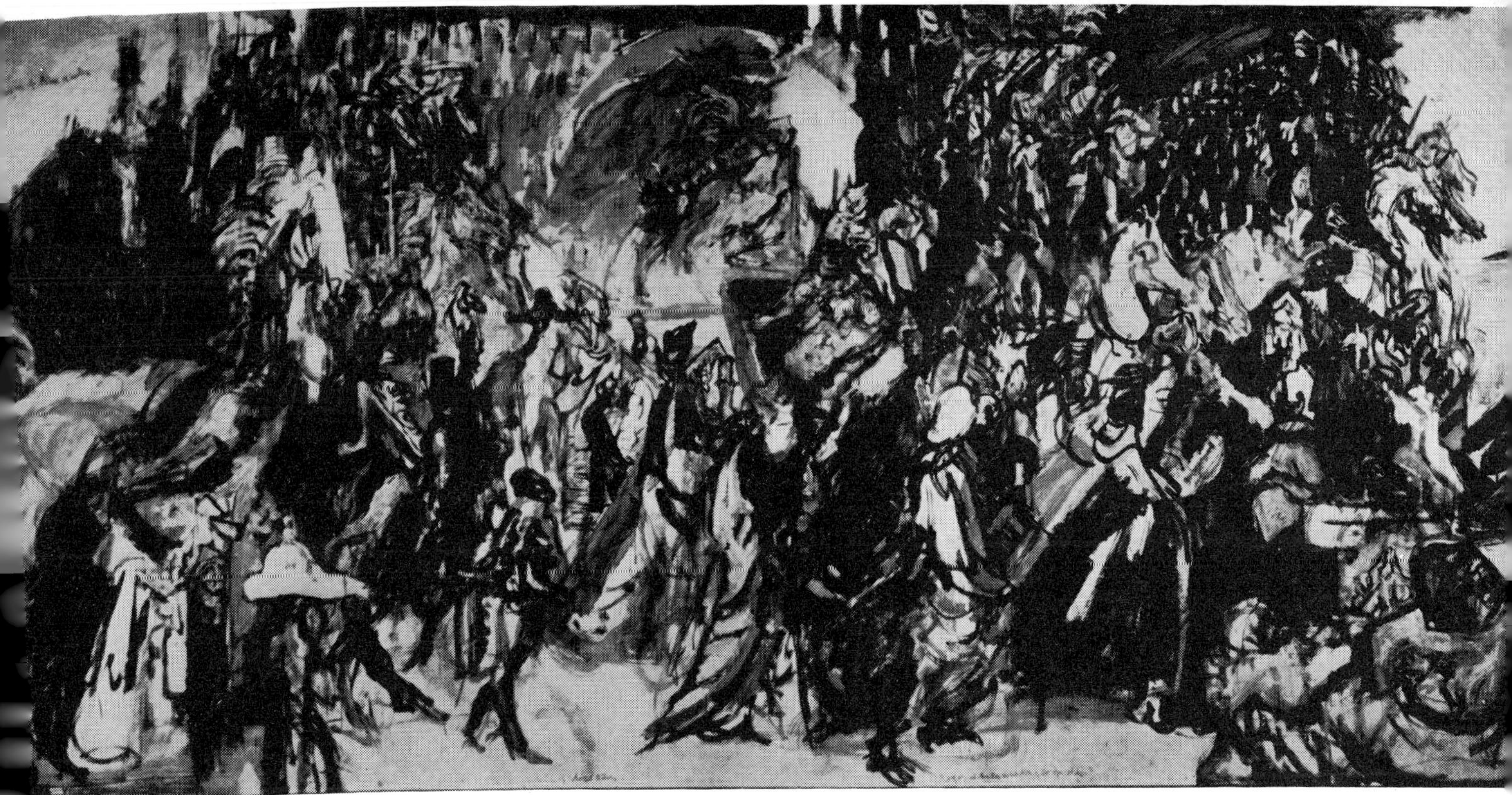

Procession in the streets

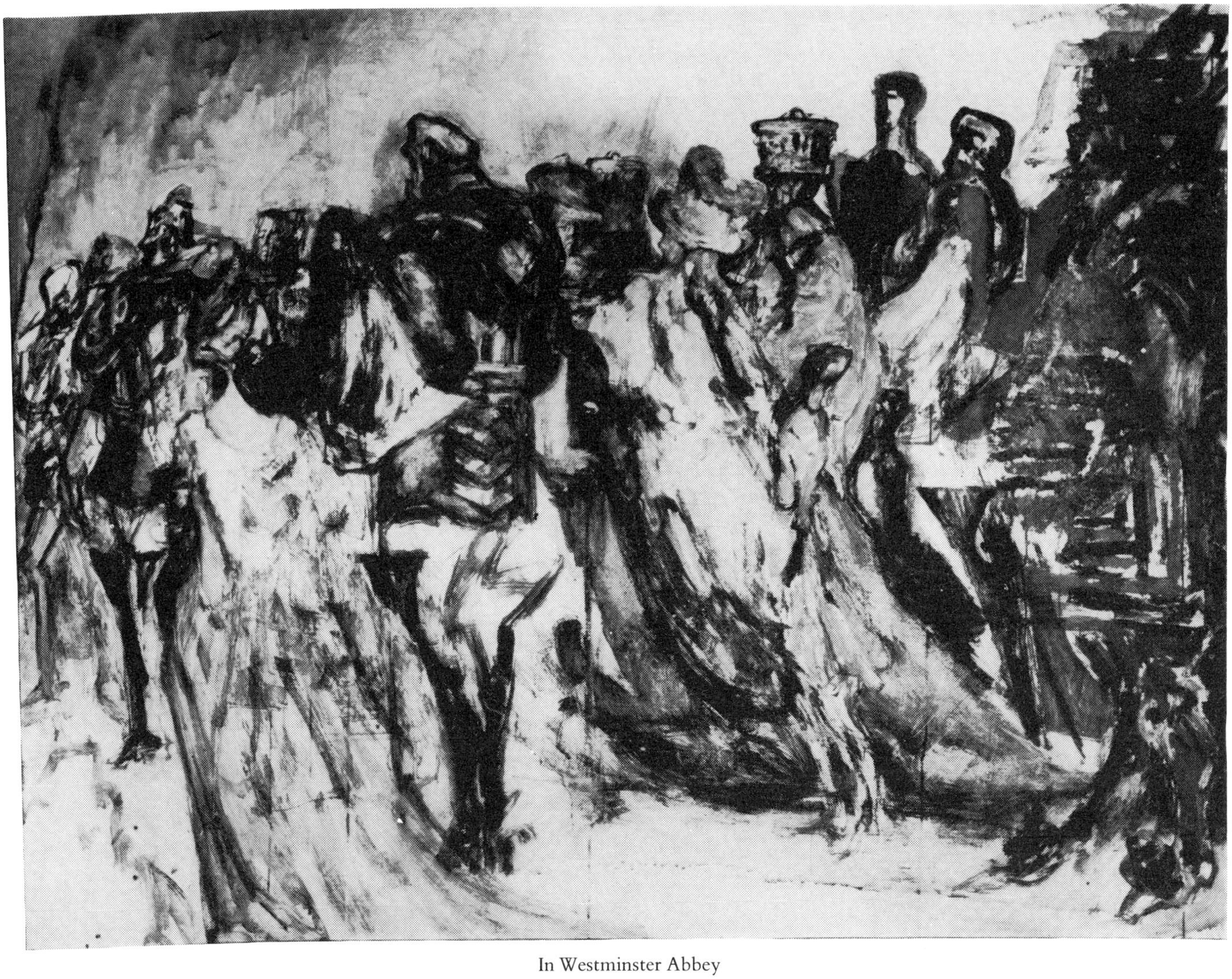

In Westminster Abbey

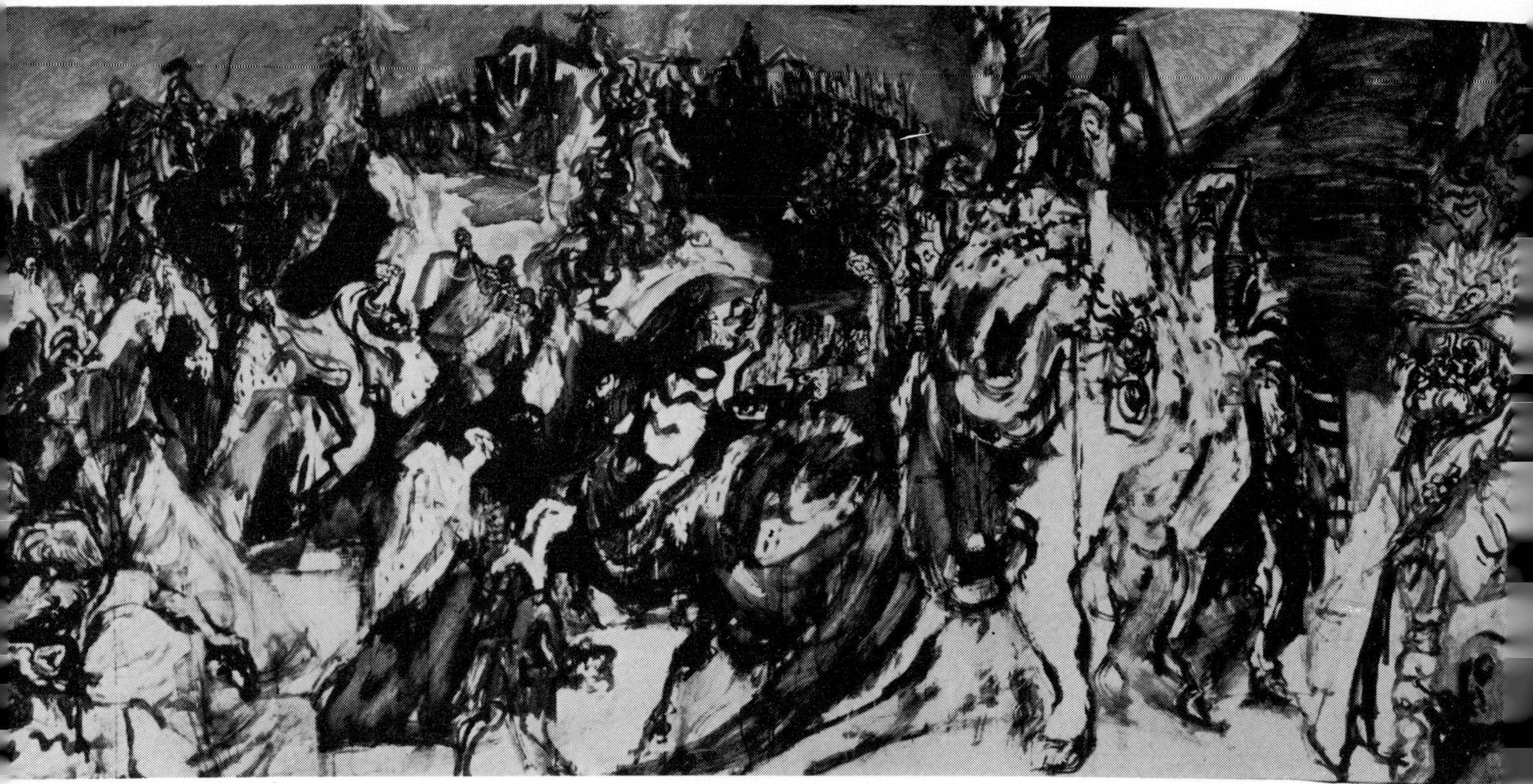

Procession in the streets

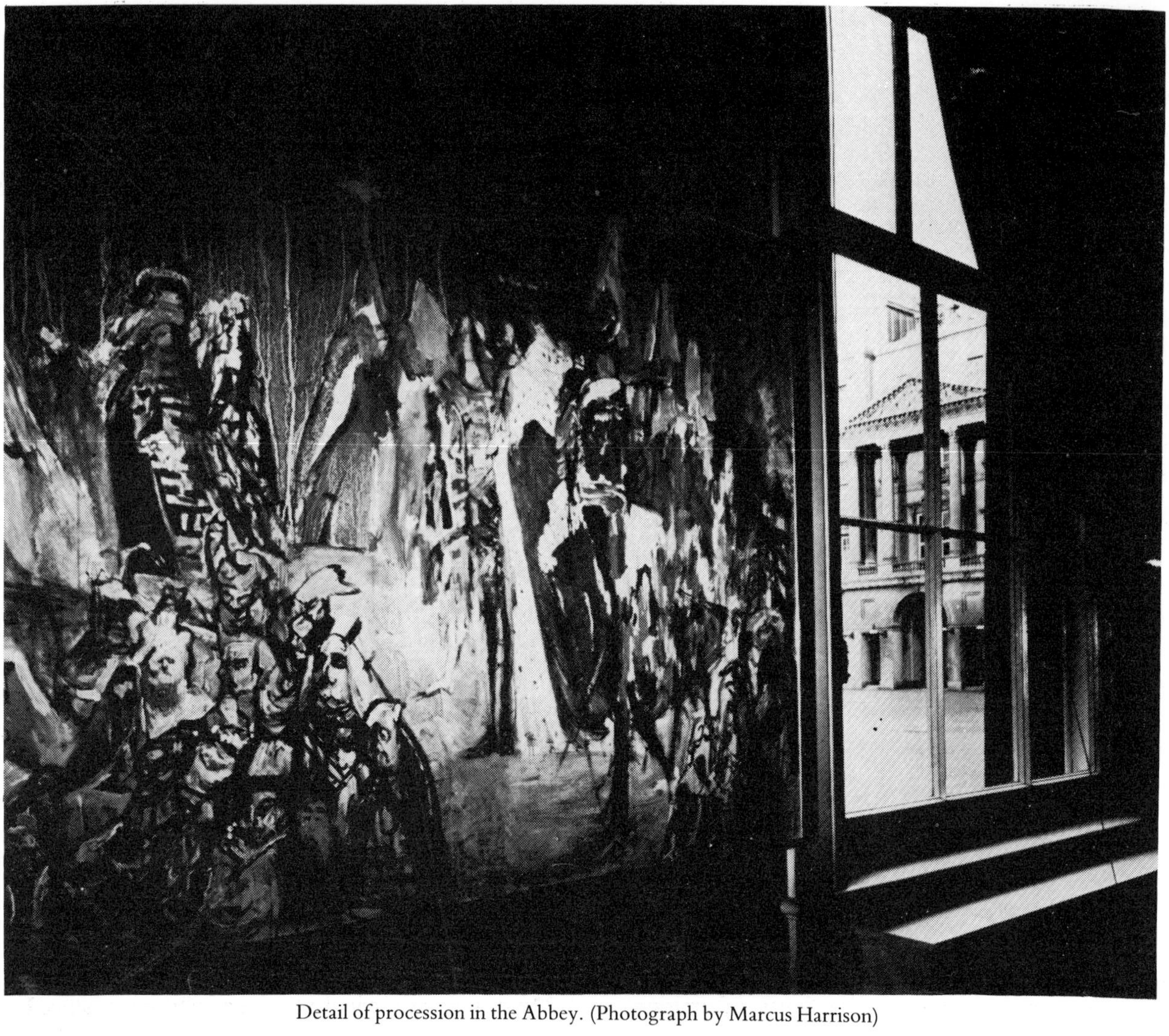

Detail of procession in the Abbey. (Photograph by Marcus Harrison)

Callot, like others in those centuries, dedicated his work as produce of his 'barren talent' to his patrons, 'humbly kissing their robes'. The 'free' artist in our seemingly equalized society falls into more humble genuflections/prostration: to the committee-cum-bureaucracy-cum-dealer.

And, in supreme contrast, this open-handed squire patronage: an instant idea marrying a painter's potential to the specific space, instantly commanded into realization, the enthusiasm not allowed to cool off.

No house, continuously and long-lived-in castle, palace, stayed arrested at some date, as some conservationists would wish and, given a chance, proceed to chop off 'additions', eliminate objects which go beyond their chosen period. In a living house, each generation added/adjusted/made changes. But just the same: this is a Palace-cum-cultural revolution: the entry of unruly contemporary paintings into the preserve of static formalities (limited, since more or less the beginning of this century, to past works of art) demonstrates the vitality of its present inhabitants.

The paintings aim at a flow, united-in-discord. But it is all meant to be seen in two ways (always in progressing survey) – as movement in colour and large forms; and in close 'reading' of details . . . There are no mistakes in order of processions, in costume the on-the-spot notation and research were meticulous, but documentation was not the uppermost aim. . .

The gallery is narrow – the paintings deliberately demand that the onlooker moves along – they are panoramic/processional and the conventional stepping back to take the whole in does not apply. Jokingly Prince Philip said, when first time seeing the work installed, 'Best to look at it from the courtyard through the windows.'

The point at which the lead/initiative is wrenched from the painter – when the work gains momentum of inevitability, takes over . . . the leap up of aspirations (no levitation this) brought down by the gravitational pull of his own limited ground. . .

. . . not the whole story though.

The Pompeiian clumsy/lovely pictures set within assured geometry of colour: the image-making brush-strokes are everlasting – millennia did not alter the 'natural' way of painting, whether a master's or itinerant jobber's; formalized stylizations come and go, yet serve to embrace the unruly sensitivities – even, paradoxically, to transcend them: formalities and their logical continuum – *ergo* 'abstractions' – reach towards limitless nirvanas.

In practice: first, all-is-possible untouched surfaces; then the spaces of colour in their anarchy seemingly resolving all – their decisive divisions, presumptuous of a higher sense, tempt to stay put – a happy abstractionist. The entry of sensibilities – the first image-suggesting stroke over these intense purities – appear to be polluting impositions: subliminal colour retreats, muddy life's barbarities invade . . . But (as in nature) it does not need to be a 'battle of attrition' (the living shapes will evolve/accommodate within the formality): there shall emerge (if courage lasts, if the idea-vision leads onward, if luck holds) the alliance! Miraculously, the image will submerge in the general, and then surface, strengthened by contradiction; or colour will transform into the linear non-formulations, from which will filter our declared messages – thus the threads lost/merged in non-figurativeness' (!) and picked up somewhere along the way may carry my work further. . .

Every creative kick-off is legitimate, whether it is Braque's table-full of junk, the later Picasso's flesh-adoring impotence, the colour-texture rainmaking hysteria of Pollock, the commercial art's revenge of 'Pop'. Almost all these are obsessions of the modern city-dweller locked indoors, turning the pages of the 'glossies', tantalized by his deep-frieze, perhaps peering through a microscope at his 'identity', or her 'genitalia'. I claim equal rights for the opposite: my ever-shifting territory – the modern globality: the demanding/impossible subject of the simultaneousness and diversity of humanity's palpitations: in fact a simple matter of wide-horizon accumulation, rather than a laboratory isolation.

The four of us driving to Poland caught in mid-Berlin by barb-wired obstacles erected unpredictably that day – 13 August 1961. At Brandenburger Tor, East German uniformed boys green-faced with fear yet guns at the trembling-ready – for perhaps deadly uncertainties, seen in our outlandish car advancing at them over a vapid no-man's land as some half-expected cunning ruse-move by the adversaries. But Marion acted unerringly to cover, and gain time for, my incessant drawing in the front seat: she, the driver, jumped out to close on with those soldiers and produced a flow of English, meant to be explanatory/pacifying, yet ascending to the non-linguist imperious tone. They, naturally, lost their aggressive posture; I scribbled a lot; and we moved on in search of the only remaining open passage to the East.

We got through in a fierce storm, enlightened on the way by a comment from a British press correspondent in East Berlin: the West Germans learned nothing and retained their arrogance, helped into well-being by the Americans; the East Germans, tamed by the deserved punishment, acknowledge the guilt and the defeat.

Warsaw was quite neat by then: its old city prettily re-erected, culture-busy; its theatres ambitious – but painful on the level of its West-imitations. An embarrassing evening at a miserable nightclub-cabaret, shared and suffered (at the next table) with President Kennedy's sisters. His wife Jackie's sister was married to a Polish Prince Radziwiłł and these two came to Poland surely only to trace the former magnate's former magnificence. I knew one of them, Eunice, from Washington, as an effective often tipsy fun-girl, so could be sure that her Polish visit did not carry grave (political?) momentum. But the awed Communist rulers of Poland strained at official hospitality.

My stay that time had a touch of VIP status since I brought

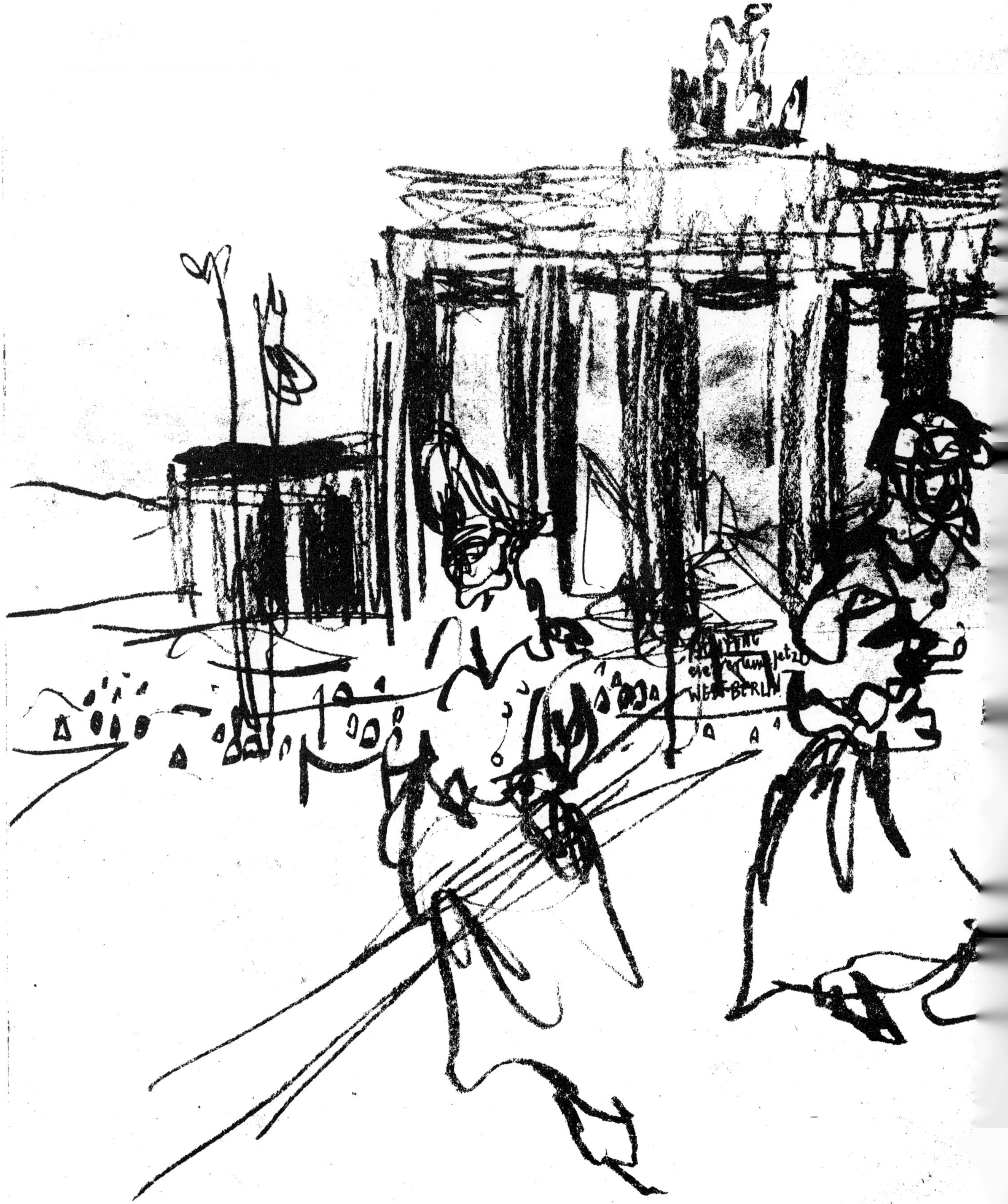

Brandenburger Tor

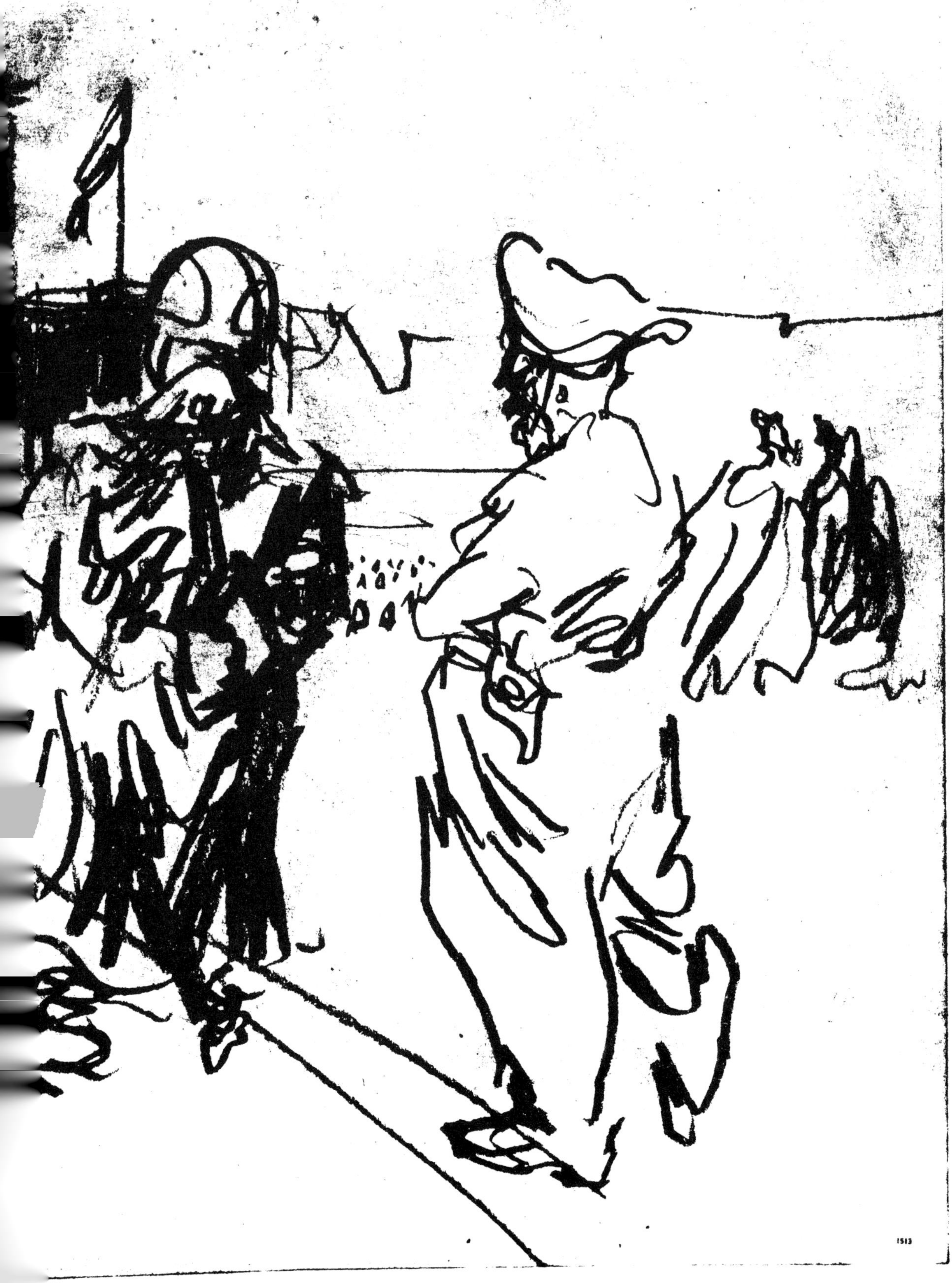

West Berlin, 13 August 1961 – Division Day (from *Topolski's Chronicle*)

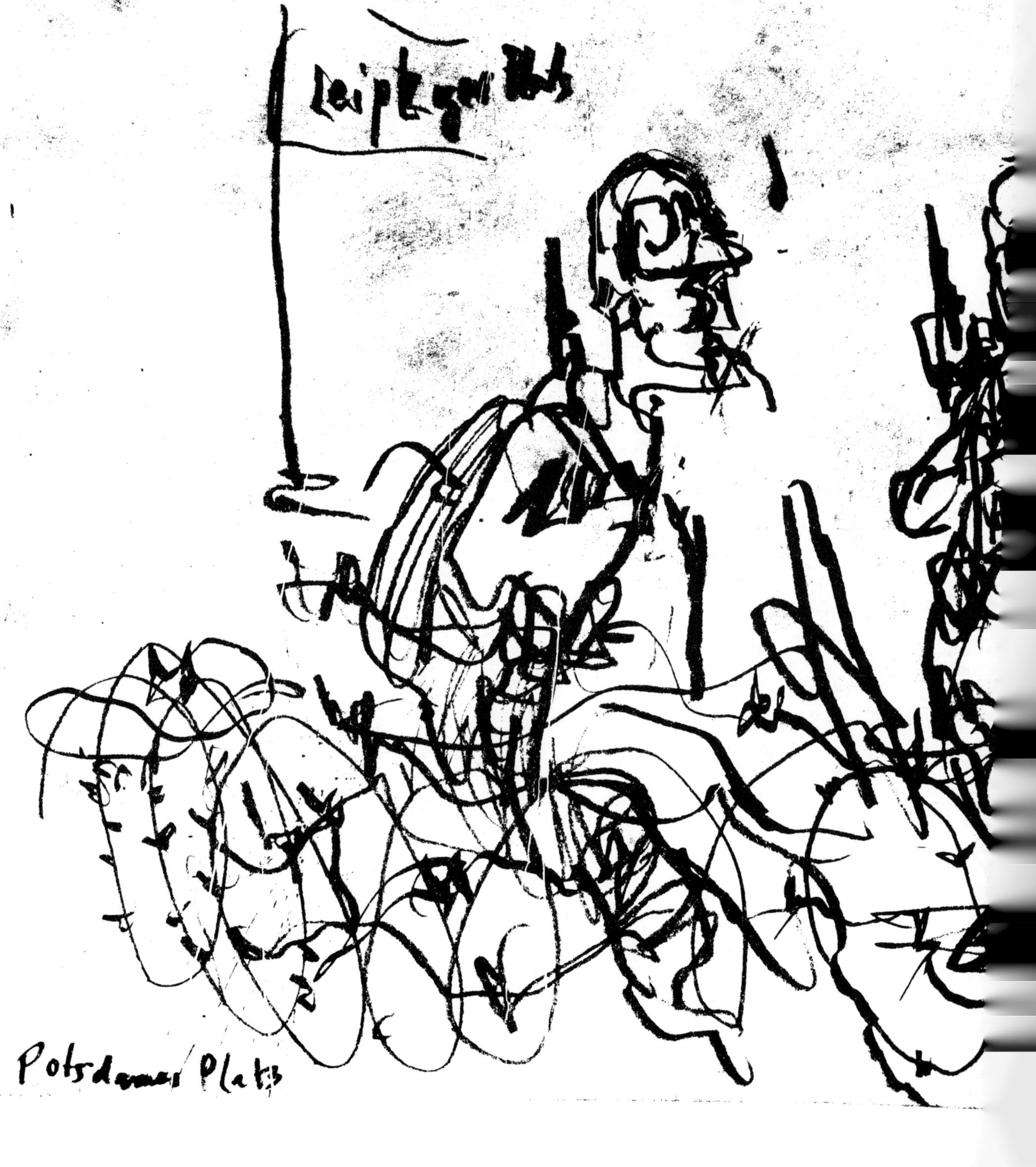

Potsdamer Platz

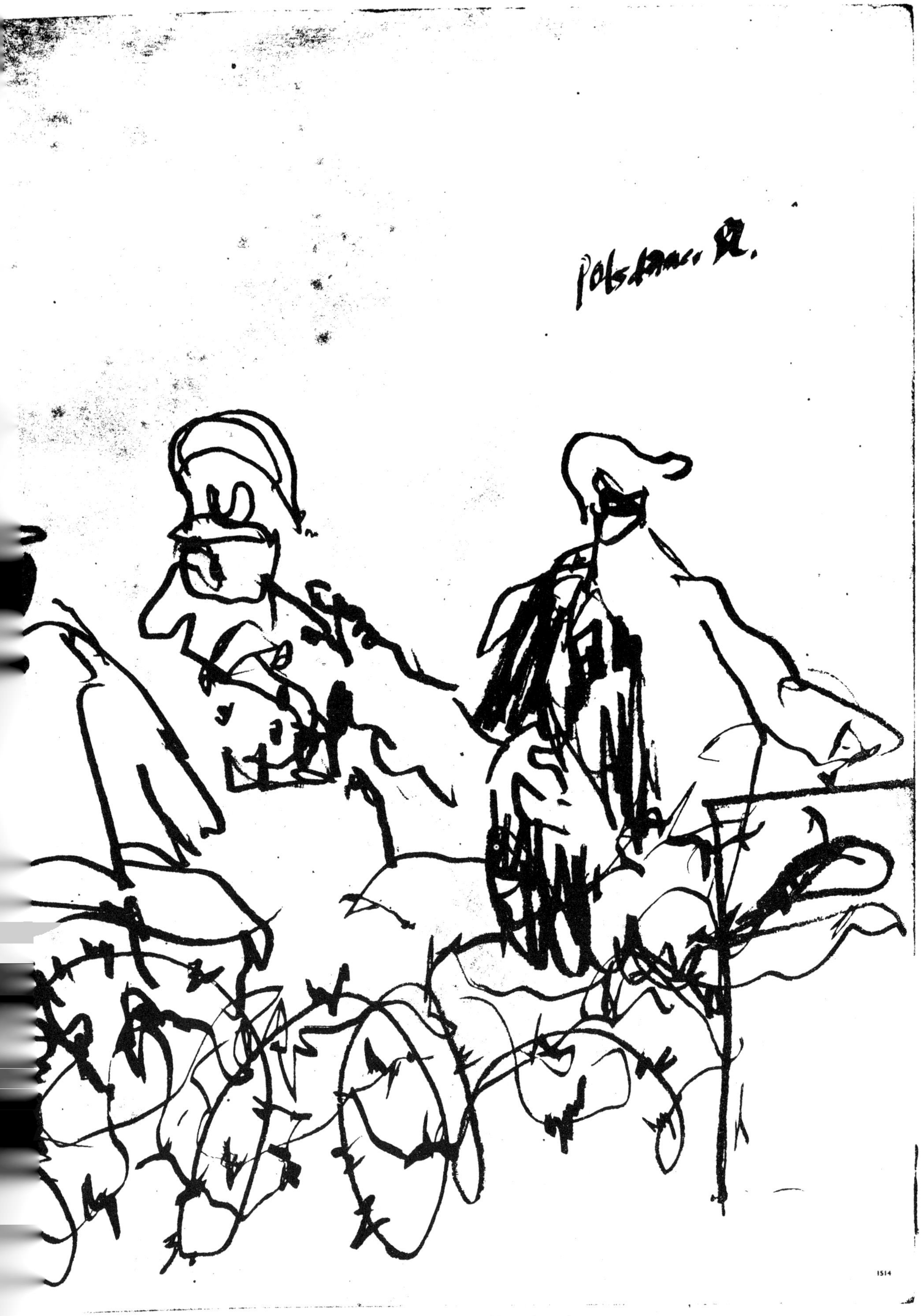

East Berlin – Division Day (from *Topolski's Chronicle*)

as an offering for the National Museum in Warsaw a hundred drawings done in action amongst Polish forces in world-wide War dispersal. We were received grandly and given a state-suite at the old Hotel Brystol – but, after a short trip to the country,* found on return our rooms occupied by the Kennedy girls.

And so it continued. They obviously had their aim, bet, or whatever, which demanded a visit at Nieborów (the old Radziwiłł seat), by then the established country abode of 'creative' (literary mostly) worthies. We were invited there – as a matter of convention – to a formal lunch but, some confusion having arisen, it proved to be the same date, when the American sisters were to be also treated to a meal. The official hosts settled the problem simply: we (my family and friends) were served in the modest semi-basement quarters of the custodian of the place, and the two girls surrounded by a large assemblage of Polish courtiers passed us on the way down ascending the imposing tiled staircase to the main dining room.

Heading their party, and guiding them throughout their stay, was my old/young aristocratic friend – the only English-speaking and the only worldy *élégante* amongst them, worthy of this protocol-directed function.

He was, during the war, a dashing and spoiled *aide-de-camp* of the Polish Prime Minister in England, General Sikorski, but, sadly, with the sudden change of political fortunes, could not find his feet in the abject shuffling of a civilian reject. Clumsily he got encompassed into minor dishonesties, sentenced, and given a choice of British prison or deportation to Poland under a Communist regime – he a Count with a criminal conviction. He chose Poland and soon, with his adjutant/linguist past, became most useful on the stately staircases, linking opposing yet cohabiting systems.

And, one way or another, the facts and the motives of the Kennedy sisters' excursion – emphatically to Nieborów into the past of the Radziwiłłs crystallized: they triumphantly carried away to Washington their trophies: a few pieces of silver cutlery marked with Radziwiłł initials and coat of arms.

The 'upstairs–downstairs' structure goes up all the way. A dinner party at the courtly home of **the Queen's Equerry** within Buckingham Palace – some years ago. We all perform the confident observances of the upper strata, until (the meal almost ended) the hostess (a message having reached her) announces, **'The Queen will come DOWN.'** Her tone, a fraction intoning, puts an end to the top-of-the-ladder simplicity, snobberies withered away at this height; now the gathering becomes muted, bewitched into *downstairs*, subservient to the lady of the house about to grace it by her descent.

And this astonishing transformation of privacy into a ceremonious protocol charade: we are lined up round the cosy drawing room, an unbecoming wait – and the Queen, the only homely accent in accord with the interior, enters, but does not move forward. And we are named, one by one, or couple by couple, and have to walk up to her – my wife and I, for some reason, the first.

The Queen brightens at my name, says that, yes, she knows it – her husband has some of my pictures; and asks if I DO MUCH OF IT? or OF THAT? Her phrase may have been differently shaped, but this was the sense of the question, to which I answered, 'But, Madam, it is my profession.' Back into line and the next person is called.

A thought: perhaps her intention was to put me at my ease; the caste system, and its impenetrable divisions make it axiomatic that the guests at her Equerry's could be nothing else but ladies and gentlemen of breeding, thus dabbling, but never working of vocational necessity.

Indeed, about that time it reached me that the 'celebrated' Cecil Beaton was received at the Palace as a **photographer**, that is as a back-stairs professional. His grandiose gentlemanly posturings would be reassumed on re-entering his domain – outside the gates of Buckingham Palace.

The weight (children are growing) of the family becomes immense – and all dangles on my art's corruption.

1962. Old Dublin as rotting as before but without redemption of black-shawled women. On the roads **the Irish folklore murdered/vanished.** Improvements. The driver's feet stink – so these are the changes; horse-pulled carts gone, a rare tinker mucky and embarrassed. Am here to draw-illustrate, for money, the optimism of waking-up Ireland – hate my *paterfamilias* harness more and more. Dragged by Tim my guide over progress-schemes: those state training centres seem 'con'; somebody fools some others – bureaucracies impregnate with paper forms and breed further bureaucrats.

Now **Wexford** and the chatelaine of 2 million shipping kingdom and their haughty Georgian up-many-steps-entered house – yet, into it, the vast hall, ungainly but costly objects-filled: obvious Regency to obvious Epstein.

No preliminary graces; the three of us, our hostess, Tim and I, have reached the evening's target: Jameson whiskeys line up, the single-minded drinking begins – with pathetic proviso; wet glasses to be kept clear of the treasured mahoganies. At my initiative we slide down on to the wall-to-wall carpeted floor and concentrate on this foolishness. The side-foolishness of her come-hitherness with the husband asleep overhead. Foolishness of dialogues' attempt at rumbustiousness yet slack yet way-losing between halting laughter and lachrymoseness, yet, unmolested by feeding, but sustained by continuity of relentless brimful whiskeys, the brutality of it. I am here in the heart of Irish whiskey-land, locked with those two maniacs at the nightly nationwide contest.

Yes, I drank well in my youth and a par with others, but many years elapsed since and here, putting on a pretence of being adept at this assininity, I watch and sink into the grossness closing over the three of us – no escape in prospect.

Hours and dozens of glasses go by . . . a purgatorial daze; in

*That was to Kazimierz – the first time for the children, initially uncurious/blasé – crowded with their alert, handsome Polish contemporaries; and, as Daniel claims, the crucial turning pointer in his outlook and direction, away from the British islander's narrowness.

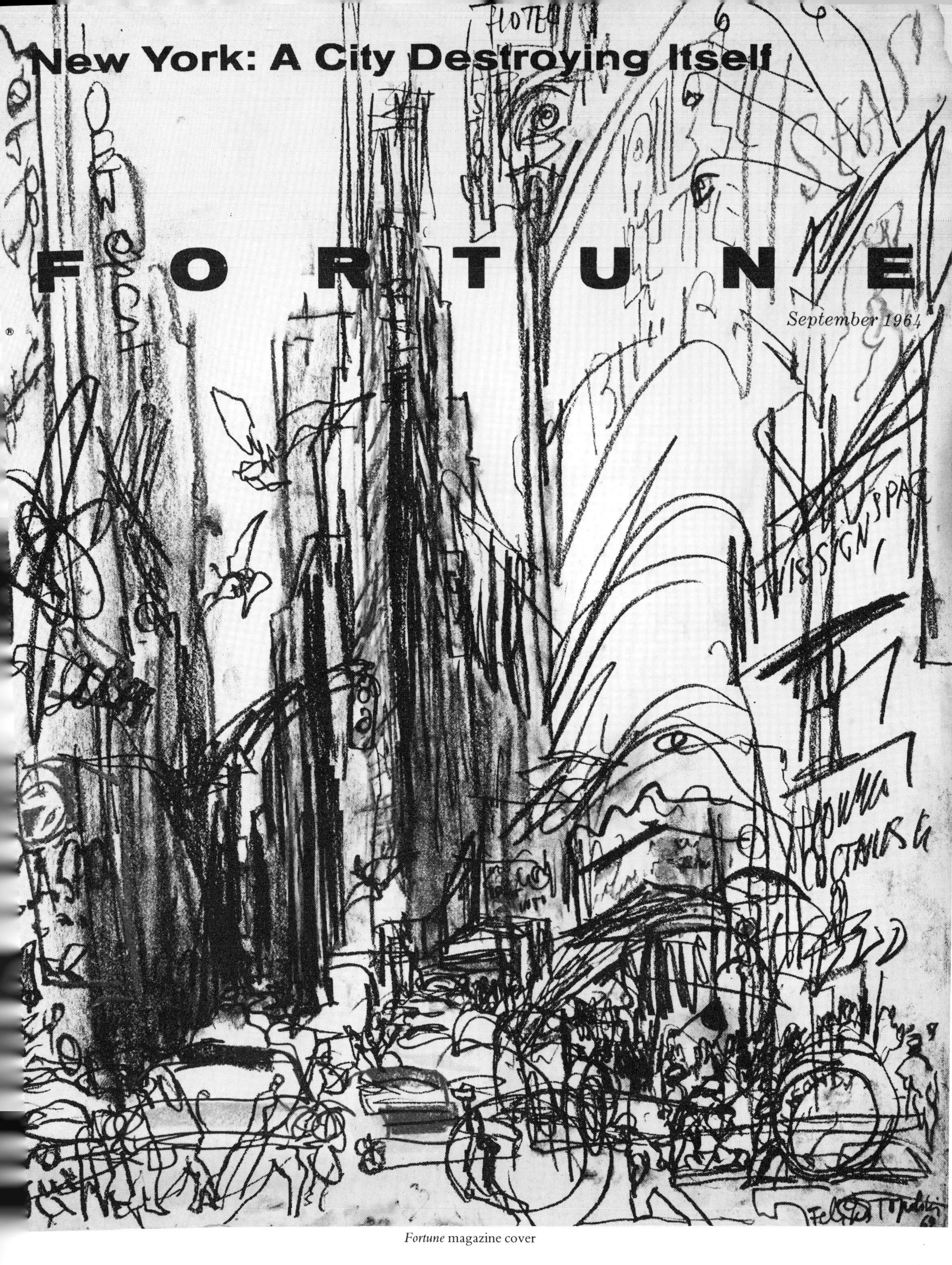

Fortune magazine cover

threesome mis-embraces rolling under the tables/chairs; then Tim flattens out, dissolves. Then my dissipating declarations of duty (echoes from my past of such necessities) to extricate/ drag out the two of us men – to achieve after prolonged trials and errors a reeling uprightness – the muddled exit – the faithful Mercedes – the hotel. Thus the last of Irishness and three hours' slumber.

The 1960s. **New York**, a city in a state of siege – no-man's-land: Central Park. **Fear** of Harlem, no more a teasing item in an evening's outing – horny white men retreat, black phalanxes pressing. Fear enters advances on all sides: from the Lower East Side, from the Village, from the Hudson's edge. And **guerrilla penetrations** into the East 50s 60s 70s. Business types panic when in the subway a group of Puerto Rican youths file through. Ferocious tales of assassins at the turnings of carpeted tenth-floor corridors in secure apartment blocks.

The little editor cries doom – the editorial conference planning *Fortune*'s issue, entitled **City Destroying Itself** – from above the pulsating spiky depths. I, a contributor, secretly exhilarated at the mammoth confusion/clash/ diversity/growth. The expansive riches strangle Manhattan from within: skyscrapers knuckle under and higher towers push up – ruthlessness carried by the helmeted half-naked multicoloured brute armies. They invade blockade turn streets into dusty roaring battlefields – opposing hordes of cars at a standstill glowering, thin trickles of ransomed inhabitants, grotesquely out of place in their fastidious clothing, gingerly navigating scaffolded-planked passages on the way to their appointments with 'civilized' routines – to plot further and further upheavals upon themselves.

The centre goes development beserk
while the circle of slums unremembered breathes fury.
And echoes of clashes/marches across the country breed zealots.

In July 1964 **Harlem riots**.

Harlem's is a running riot
those who run towards
and these away mark the shifting spots hither and thither
in West one-two-five at 7th fury flowers –
unpredictably out of the bubbling swamp
– upwards
opens in red petals
on an instant
withers falls apart is brushed away;
long loud post-mortem in women's voices follows
on a red-splashed pavement.
The shout the bang by the Bible School
this time a crouching low hitting heaving centipede is formed.
At Lennox and one-two-five the guts-goods belch out of a
cracked bargain store's belly
maggots crawl in.
Along West one-three-five – fire engines.
The Palm Café – helmeted cops give the bouncers a holiday.
Outside Law Office over liquor store
lazy hands-in-pockets boys in-wait to pounce
when the through traffic lights turn red.

But for a 'New Yorker' all this naturally is always some blocks away. The social paddock buzzes unperturbed within its own high fences – the all-preoccupying snakes-and-ladders of snobbery-success – the ever-tense litmus-paper on which invitations are printed. American society (**New Victorians**) breathless at stabilizing the upper-class *status quo*, at formalizing plutocracy into aristocracy.

The outdated (for Old Victorians) rules of etiquette are obeyed and serve to assess. Divisions, on whatever basis, created and solidified by exclusions. No alliance between the groups – each assumes itself to be superior. This is why (conveniently outside, therefore preferable) freakish jokers serve the periodical sorting out of preferences: their lists of invitees become *Debretts* of the (American) day – only one day.

For every outstanding achievement elsewhere, there has to be an American counterpart; more, it has to be **the greatest** – the machinery for trumpeting it is the most efficient/ sumptuous in the world and it must be fed. Some thin art/ theatre/writing gets on to the conveyor belt of Great Americana each day. But also the ceaseless pandemonium of communication/display/sale/patronage sucks up the inspirational juices – the last ounce of them – from the very spine of straining creators, bubbles them up to elephantine bursting – and, behold, arts grow; arts metabolize out of control, challenge/threaten the parent/patron himself.

Herzog – the *ne plus ultra* of the Jewish-American culture explosion: this intentional epic-scale view of America omits Gentiles; its academics are all Jews, even the picked-up girl is Jewish – race-compartmental **unmelting-pot** America. This has passed – within a few years the cultural revolution of the young, though perhaps given its fever by out-of-the-ghetto pressures/yearnings, has begun the mixing job, in earnest.

Ennobled in destruction murky Roman columns raising arches suspended symbolically over the falling bricks/walls of Penn Station, over the rush-mob disunited clashing rebounding bundle-laden out to scream (into taxiless desolation) for succour, streaming underground accelerating avalanching into the makeshift timber palisades their compulsive directions – their near-panic their varied congeniality their common separatedness.

Closer – their faces – their FACE.

The FACE is moronic – made so through drifting in harassment; the faces declare the denseness of their ghettos their stubborn yokeldom arrested in Europe's backwardness of that day, when the cord was broken by their emigration, when they stuck in the old mind/mud not to lose themselves in the fearsome ungiving quicksands of the New World. How do these still bewildered (but shallowly cunning) peasants craftsmen workers parochials, with world-backwaters' minds of tiny loyalties non-comprehensive of global/technological demands, make up, sum up into the immense power of the United States of America. Her power-men, her inventors, her Jeremiahs – are they in (and of) this crowd?

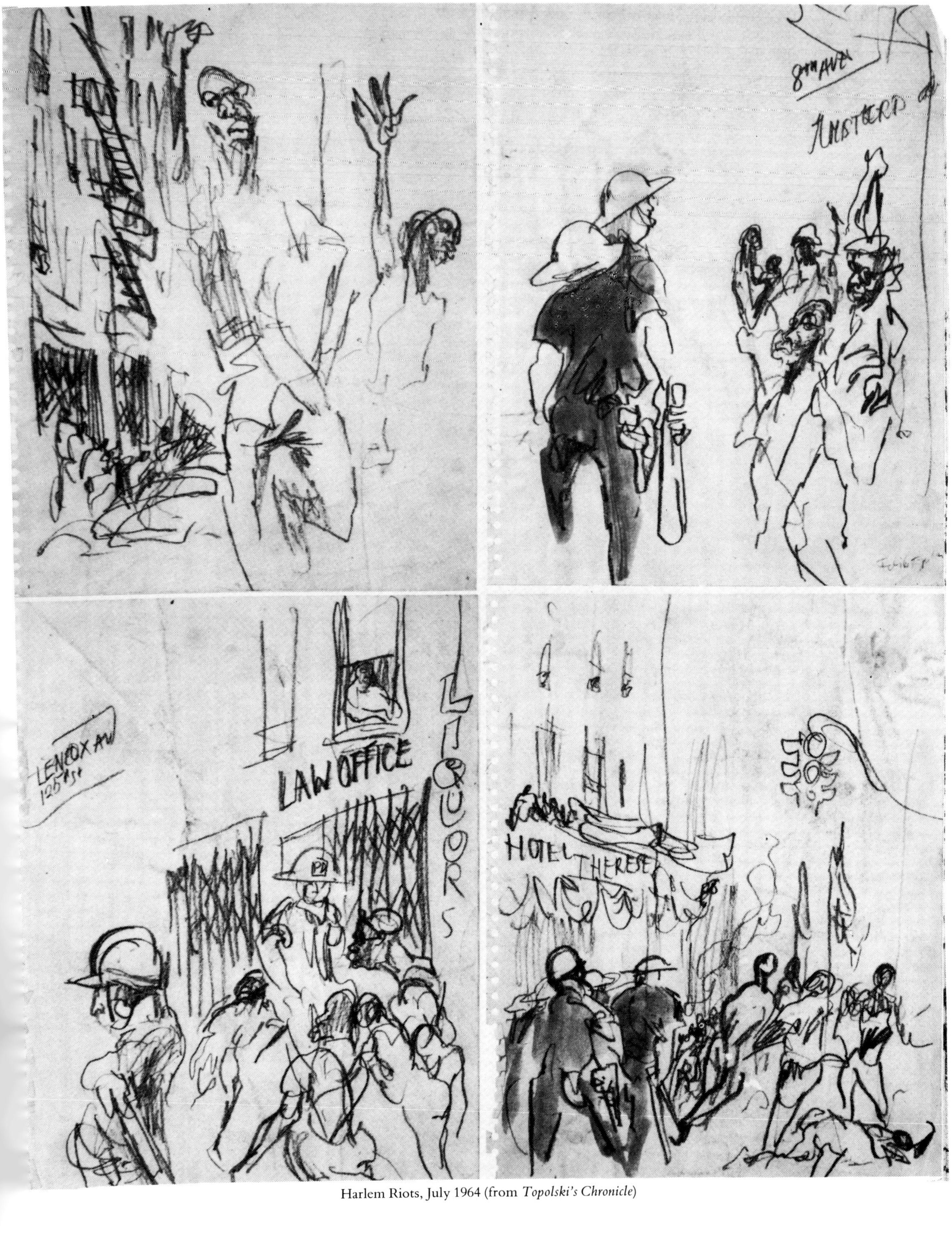

Harlem Riots, July 1964 (from *Topolski's Chronicle*)

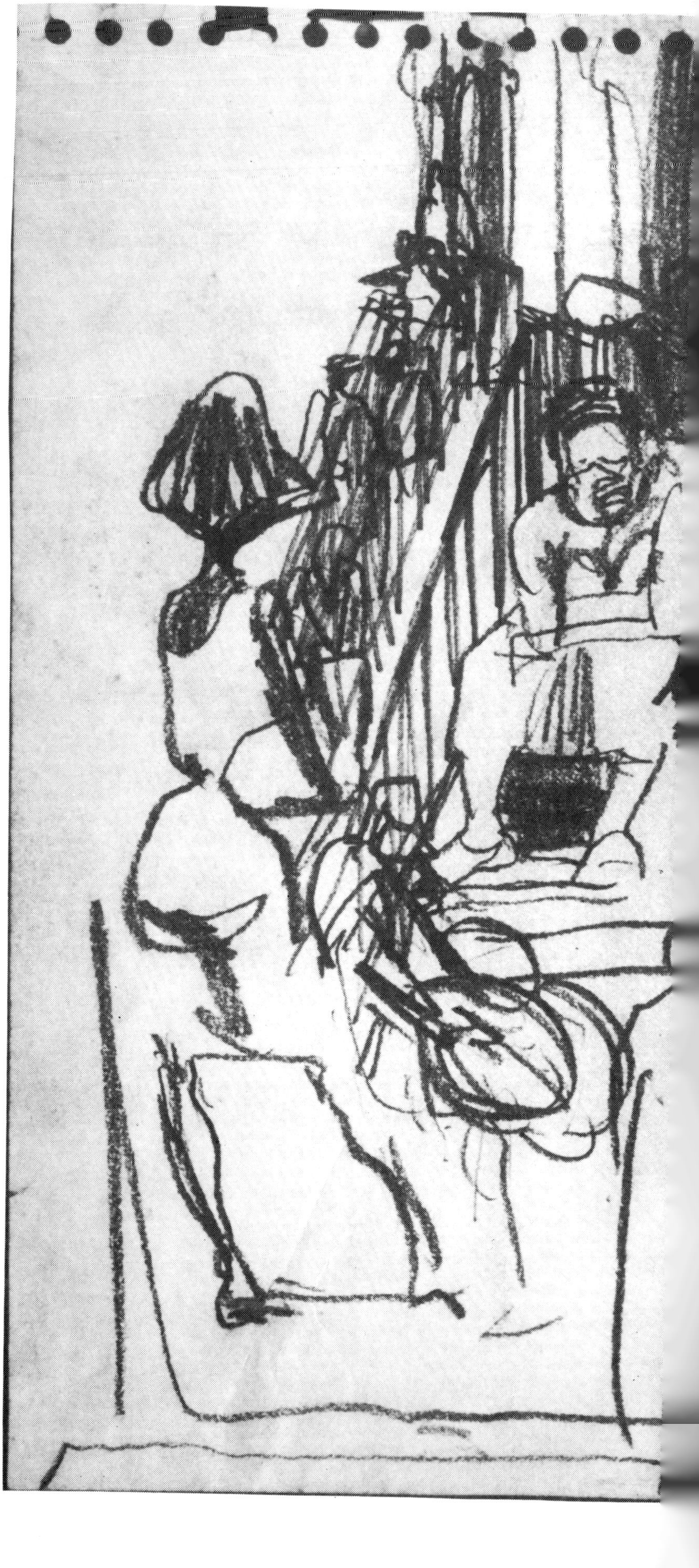

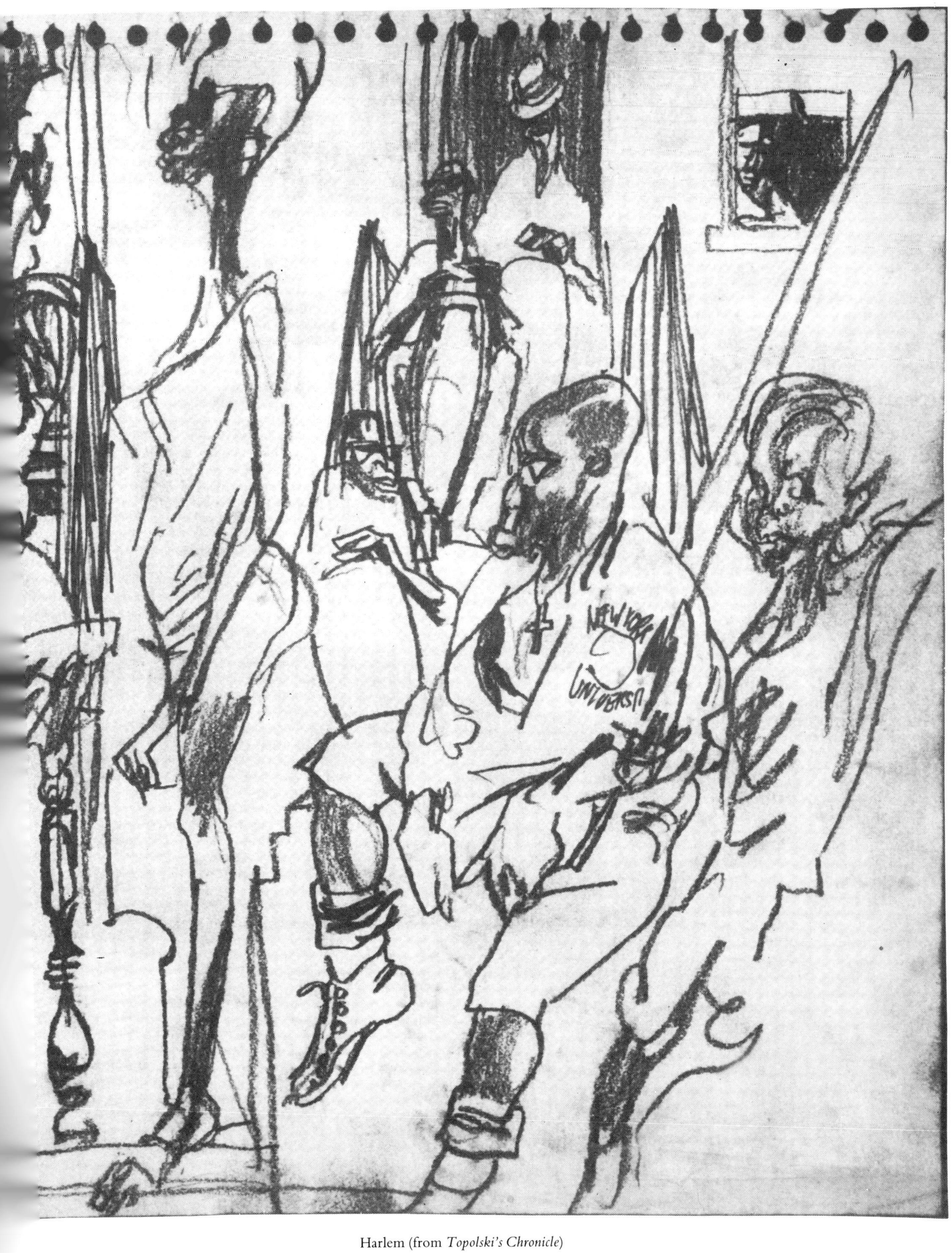

Harlem (from *Topolski's Chronicle*)

Pop and rock Liverpool beat puzzlingly beats 1965 America to its knees: discothèques ('Ondine' first) imitate London. But my very young arty/contrary sympathizers lead me – a treat – to their latest clever-clever fad: a pre-war model 'cosy' drink club, a jazz-band platform, refined fat-neck black-tie black players – and the climax: an ample Negress (one of the great of the past dug out) enthroned (folds overflowing) chain-sings 'nostalgic' blues. My friends chorus in adoration – the lady comes graciously to our table to receive our prolonged prostrations, smart connoisseurship blossoming. Passé to me, I sink in boredom and exhaustion – stumble out into the rain, a lucky taxi – and instant revival: the driver has the radio piercing the latest POP – sound stridence stressed by windscreen wipers' beat swinging/fanning: spray and lights-cacophony and Manhattan's rush, beat left–right–left–right in announcing/heading for the change, uncharted.

My *Chronicle*'s retrospective exhibition in New York furnished with PR services: their achievements – my torture; they count happily items (for quantity) and rush me to Radio/Television studios, dawn appointments at a commuter-bungalow of a breakfast-chat interviewer, puzzling assignments cum photographers at the World Fair and way-out collisions with press reporters which culminate in a flood of continent-wide paragraphs devoted to my views on American women's dress accessories. The exhibition is visited – an outstanding success – by 14,500 patrons.

A chorale for forty thousand voices:

Rally for *Kenyatta**

Forty miles north of Nairobi
forty thousand roars:

U-**HU**-RU! U-**HU**-RU! U**HU**RU-NA-KANU!
U**HU**RU: Freedom!
U**HU**RU-NA-USHINDI: Freedom and Victory!
U**HU**-RUral rustics gay
U**HU**-Roost fatly draped women
U**HU**-RUthless rustics black
U**HU**-Rooted in tribal land
U**HU**-RUmours of revenge and spoils
U**HU**-rain over spears and parasols
U**HU**-ritual of politics
U-**HU**-RU!
U**HU**RU-NA-KENYATTA!

High up Jomo Kenyatta is robed black-and-green and capped gold and given symbols of sovereignty and charms and offerings, ringed by frilled umbrellas, white plumes, red-black zigzags, leopard skins over the London waistcoat; Kikuyu Masai Wakamba elders, politicians, trade unionists, large gestures, big men, joy – JOY upon the forty thousand roars:

U-**HU**-RU!
U**HU**RU-NA-UMOJA: Freedom and unity!
U-**HU**-RU!
U**HU**RU-NA-KANU!
U-**HU**-RU!
U**HU**RU-NA-USHINDI!
U**HU**-RUde roar of BLACK AFRICA
U**HU**-RUlers of tomorrow
U**HU**-RUination for the settler
U**HU**-RUination for the Asian
U**HU**-RUination for the Arab
U**HU**-RUby turn the sky and the slush
U**HU**-Ruby swells the Negro blood
U**HU**-RUeful range the white policemen
U**HU**-RUral rally in Machakos.

Muddy dark **Mombasa**: a vast puddle bars the way of our massive limousine – but my host, **the Hon. T. M. C. Chokwe,** MLC, the dashing wide-moustachioed local MP, rushes it to applause, in and outside the car, swings us over the town in an overjoyed gallop – a cavalier, a loved hero, a triumphant prince: if on horseback, this would be a cavalcade of the politics of exuberance as lived in Poland in untrammelled times. We halt, we enter-swagger (flamboyance carried on) the packed Majengo Town Hall pre-election rally; even I serve, being introduced from the platform and roaringly approved as some sort of celebrity/friend; his speech and its reception manifest festivity whipped up into elation. Back in the streets, the mood is precipitated

Jomo Kenyatta, 1961 (from *Topolski's Chronicle*)

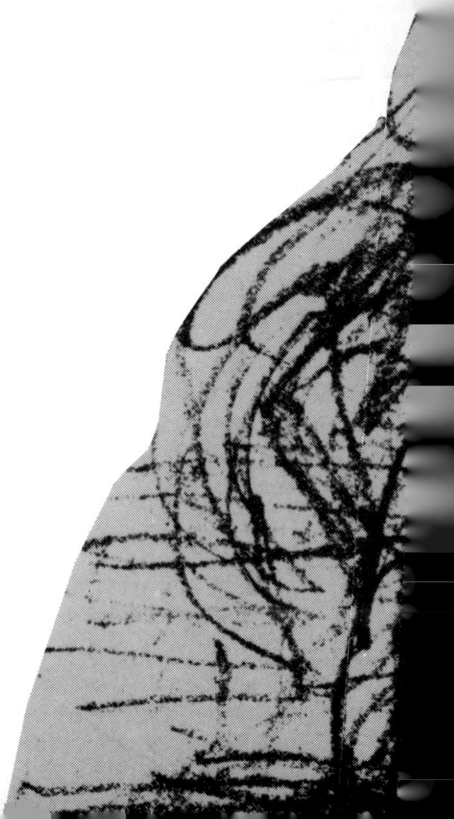

**Chronicle* nos. 4–7 (208–221), Vol. X, 1962.

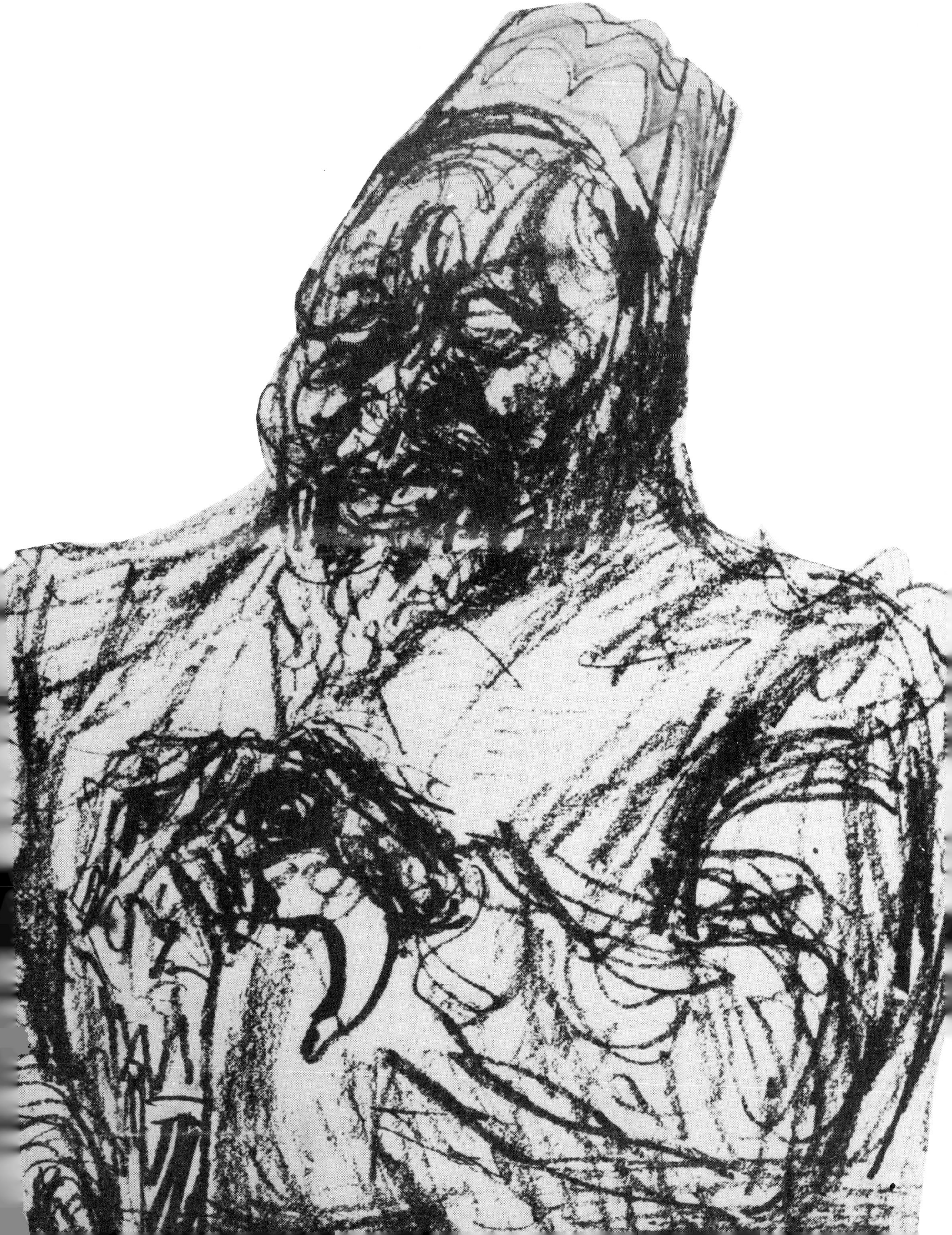

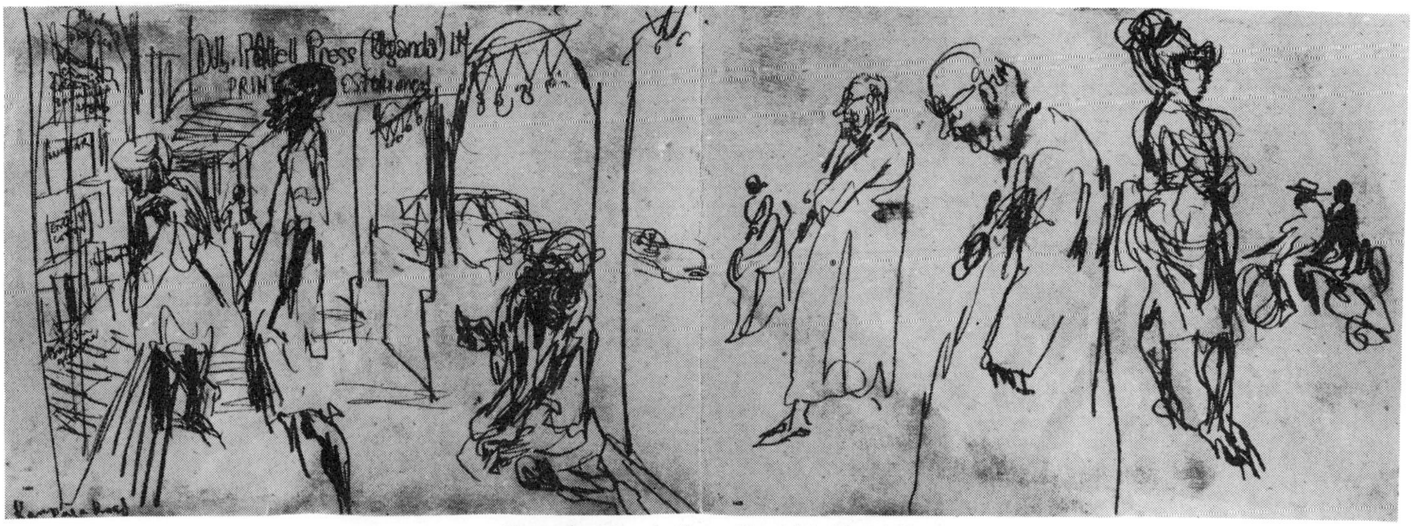

Kampala, Uganda (from *Topolski's Chronicle*)

by mud-sprays and the screech of tyres to stopping and unceremoniously collecting out of the shadows, as if at random, a batch of bare-footed beauties – now on the way, in the time-honoured order of things, to the celebratory climax, the Dance. This 'community' spirit, this effervescence of loving as emanating from, and in concord between the elect and his people/tribe – candid, against – experienced a few days earlier – the **Legislative Council's (LEGCO)** pomposity set on the British model, demanding gravity and refusing my entry without a tie.

Kampala, almost-post-British, proposes to continue being gentle – for a time.

Ever-graceful and Pharaoh-featured (a black version) **His Highness the Kabaka of Buganda** rests gently yet regally, courtier-ringed, advisers bending to his ear, a nowadays obligatory sample of English comeliness at his feet replacing the cluster of black wives of the past. Obligatory, because the Commonwealth independencies awaken young ruling-class appetites, hitherto suppressed, for the preciously unobtainable Anglo-Saxon Venuses – who now in their new world-encircling adventurousness make themselves available, perhaps fulfilling an equal curiosity. Over the years the Kabaka has established a light-hearted prerogative for me: now again, with mock formality, I am given a roll of Uganda's earth-tinted **bark-cloth**. The colour of the land is burnt sienna and this enchanting fabric serves as the ceremonial toga of rulers and priests, as well as the cloaks of shepherds. The tradition of my 'right' to receive the gift began nearly twenty years earlier, when I lunched at the Residency. A significantly still-imperial assembly of equilibrium: the Englishness of the host – an assured Pro-Consul; the massive presence-support of the Armenian Mr Moses, the richest man in the country; and the figurehead boy-king HH Kabaka (neat suit and tie) tutored in the prep-school vein. The conversation dealt with the subtly essential matter of state stability: should the Kabaka continue his education at home, with British tutors of course, or go to a public school in England?

But my delight in bark-cloth and the impossibility of tracing it in the markets and shops filled a conversational break – and resulted in a huge package being dispatched by post to reach London before me. Some years later the grown-up Kabaka visited my home – approved of my bark-cloth curtains, announcing my 'traveller's room', though by then in shreds – and the gift of a new roll soon arrived. I do not remember now whether he was then already exiled from his country (to Britain!) by the British Government – his 'secure' education, as with a great many other colonial and dominion choice young men, taught him British democracy's dogma of opposition. But my established 'prerogative' operated once again, the new curtain having disintegrated with the passage of years. A happy farewell at the Dorchester (Tony Armstrong Jones, the future Lord Snowdon, found his way into my sketchbook as typical of the young set then close to the Kabaka) and my last visit at his Uganda home – and my last bark-cloth roll. Soon he was dead and my paradisical Uganda metamorphosed into viciousness.

For **Uganda** in the forties seemed unique even within the whole East African impact – an enchanted Eden-of-a garden, circumambulated by pastoral angelic white-gowned black males and Victorian-bustled black females, straight-backed and neat-headed. That rhythm, that harmoniousness (perhaps only to the careless eye) under the never-setting British sun was by 1962 upset by inroads of Westernization: Kampala's young men fed their vanity on shorts and hanging-out shirts patterned in Düsseldorf or Utah, and their spiritual hunger at D. L. Patel Press (Uganda) Ltd on books on *Brighter Grammar, Shorthand, Elementary Chemistry*. In Kampala Road: American missionaries ('Adventists' church'), decorative sun-glassed *élégantes* on foot and on motor bikes, but also grey-bearded Sikhs and, in the shaded arcades, the beggars; all this pushed back by the triumphant procession of open trucks, filled up with slogan-blaring, bare-pink-fleshed, high-heeled, fancy-hatted, yellow-curled girlies hung with 'The Refreshment of Friendship Pepsi-Cola' banners. The dark crowds stopped watchful at this changed persona of the former master race.

At the Imperial Hotel the old balances still lingered under old fans: the robed waiters serving now modern-chic black couples alongside – oddly in full bemedalled 'blues' – the British military.

TOPOLSKI's CHRONICLE No. 8 (212) Vol. X 1962

...nothing affirmeth and therefore never lyeth ... Sir Philip Sidney (1580)

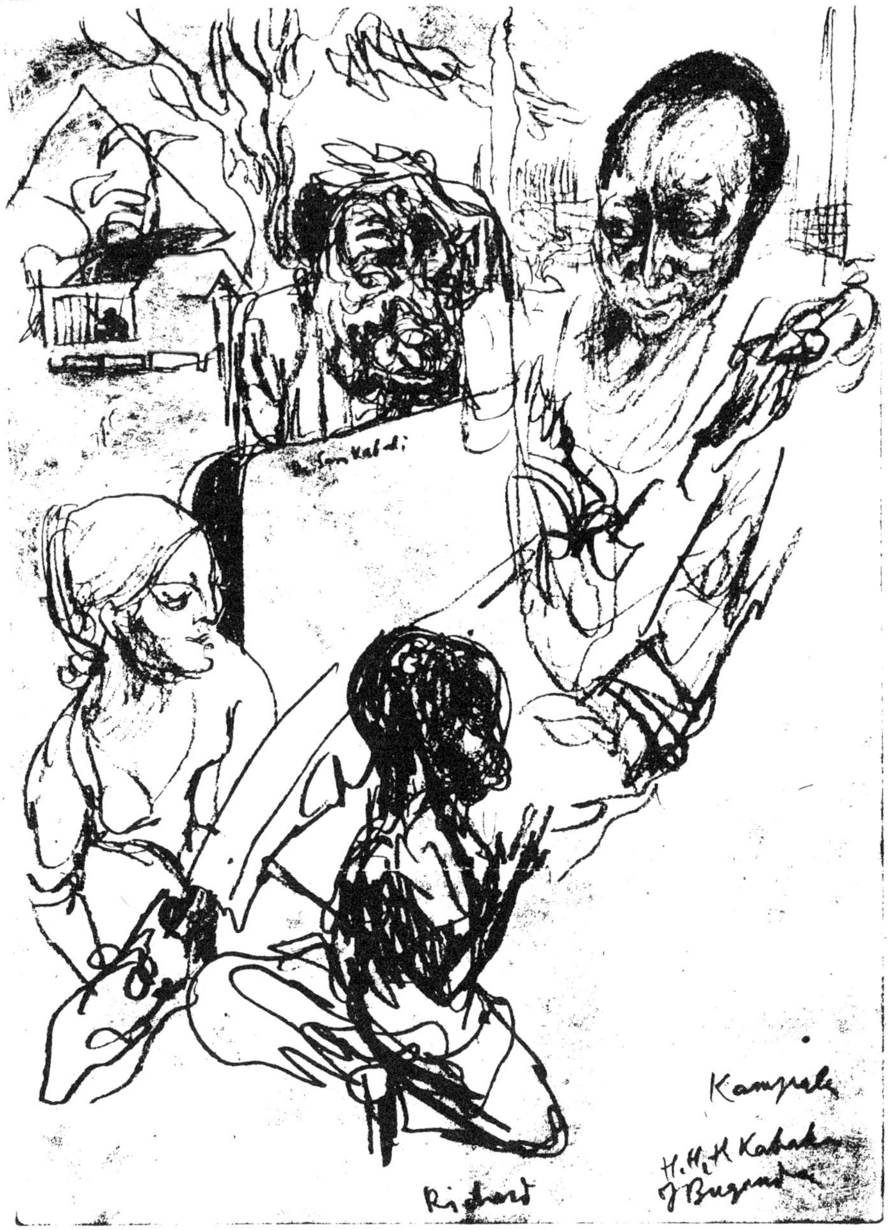

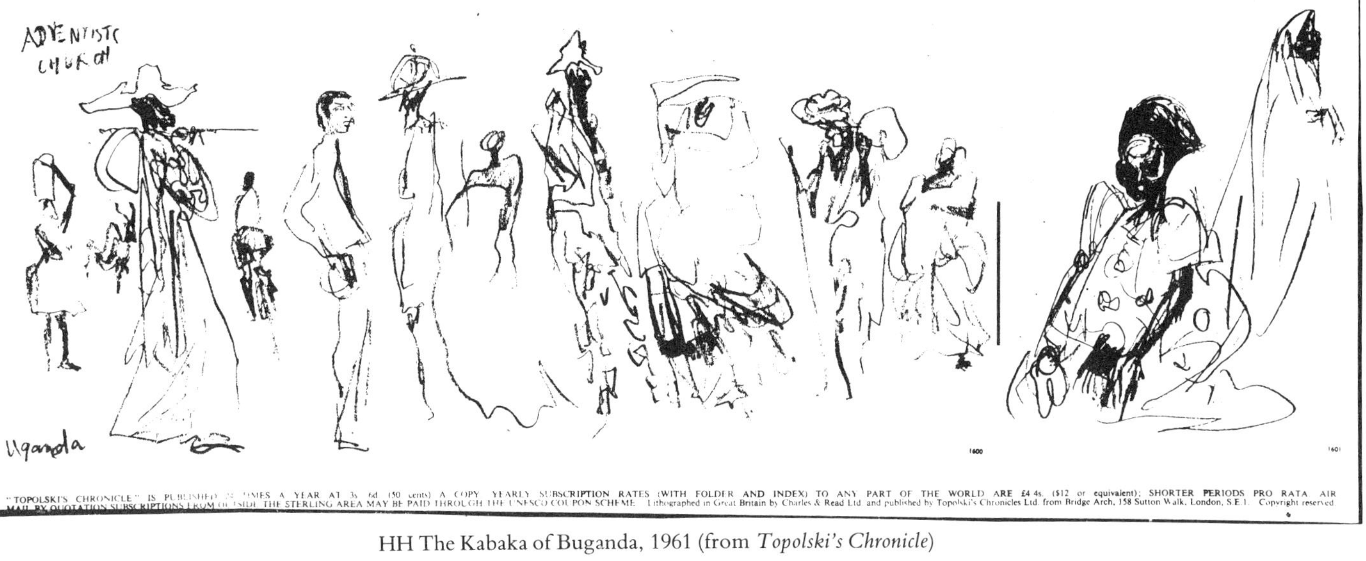

"TOPOLSKI'S CHRONICLE" IS PUBLISHED 24 TIMES A YEAR AT 3s 6d (50 cents) A COPY. YEARLY SUBSCRIPTION RATES (WITH FOLDER AND INDEX) TO ANY PART OF THE WORLD ARE £4 4s. ($12 or equivalent); SHORTER PERIODS PRO RATA. AIR MAIL BY QUOTATION. SUBSCRIPTIONS FROM OUTSIDE THE STERLING AREA MAY BE PAID THROUGH THE UNESCO COUPON SCHEME. Lithographed in Great Britain by Charles & Read Ltd. and published by Topolski's Chronicles Ltd. from Bridge Arch, 158 Sutton Walk, London, S.E.1. Copyright reserved

HH The Kabaka of Buganda, 1961 (from *Topolski's Chronicle*)

A few passengers, heroes and victors of today; **German and American salesmen,** muscling out the British goods. **Congo at civil war** is not on their import/export list, but our plane is forced to land.

My obsessively poised pencil at the port-hole window scans the landing field, ominously panic-swept empty. As a scheduled passenger for Ghana, thus upset and scared, one would not leave the plane and wait to fly on, but the notorious eye-witness is gratified by being ordered out.

Inside **the airport**, locked in chaos and near-terror: the Congolese soldiers battle-armed (dangling hand-grenades, bayonets, watches, assorted guns) on the loose – seemingly beyond the control of their officers – dominate, threaten equally the whites and refugee women/children in back-country rags, clustered/cowering amongst their chattels – the worldwide refrain. The black warriors are close around me and all this I ache to draw, but their fierce masks – heightened by dark glasses – of savage unpredictability (unlike the more-or-less decipherable reactions of whites-in-uniform) do not tell me how they would act instinctively (that is crucially) at the unexpectedness of my pulling out the sketchbook – shots on the spot?

This is, I considered later, the real trial of my dedication. All those scraps of thoughts in my head, my sketchbook comes out of my haversack and I begin to draw; and apparently the magic of evolving images works worldwide (these soldiers are not even subject to a possible abhorrence, forgotten by me, of being thieved of their likeness): they laugh, they accept my dare.

From then on I draw ceaselessly – the Congolese in their ruptured actions, the floored captives, the United Nations troops' manoeuvrings outside – the Belgians, the Ethiopians, the Indians, the Canadians, up to a Canadian Brigadier-General impressively conferring with the plumper Ethiopian Colonel Teshome; the interplay of ill-at-ease Congolese officers with their men and, above all, the tremendous analogy with earlier European centuries of the soldiery in tumbling wenching drunken accord with female 'camp followers'. The airport accumulates the clashing extremes of the civil war.

The exploration of the city of **Leopoldville** gives the usual lining of battlefields. UN armoured convoys pass friezes of humble unhurried doings, a siesta-bound man in the crook of a tree under VENTES PUBLIQUES with a leisurely policeman directing traffic of stately head-carrier women – their long many-coloured robes develop, nearer to the city's centre, vagaries of fashion, set well against white nuns' white coifs and habits. Yet, rounding a street corner: a shouting, fist-waving mob (against UN interference?) emerges, but easily contained by policemen – as if an ordered orderly illustration of a riot; an obligatory burnt-out car with COCA COLA CHEZ NOUS above; a single rags-shedding man seemingly escaping – running by a wall, which gives a glimpse of a palmy garden with a calm Belgian (surely) priest in white, holding his breviary. A chic café terrace culminates: the leisurely postures over the drinks of mostly white clientèle (the blacks distinguished by their full tie-and-collar attire) – moustaches, pipes, blue droopy sideways eyes under false blondness; and a Swedish UN officer to highlight the precariousness of the

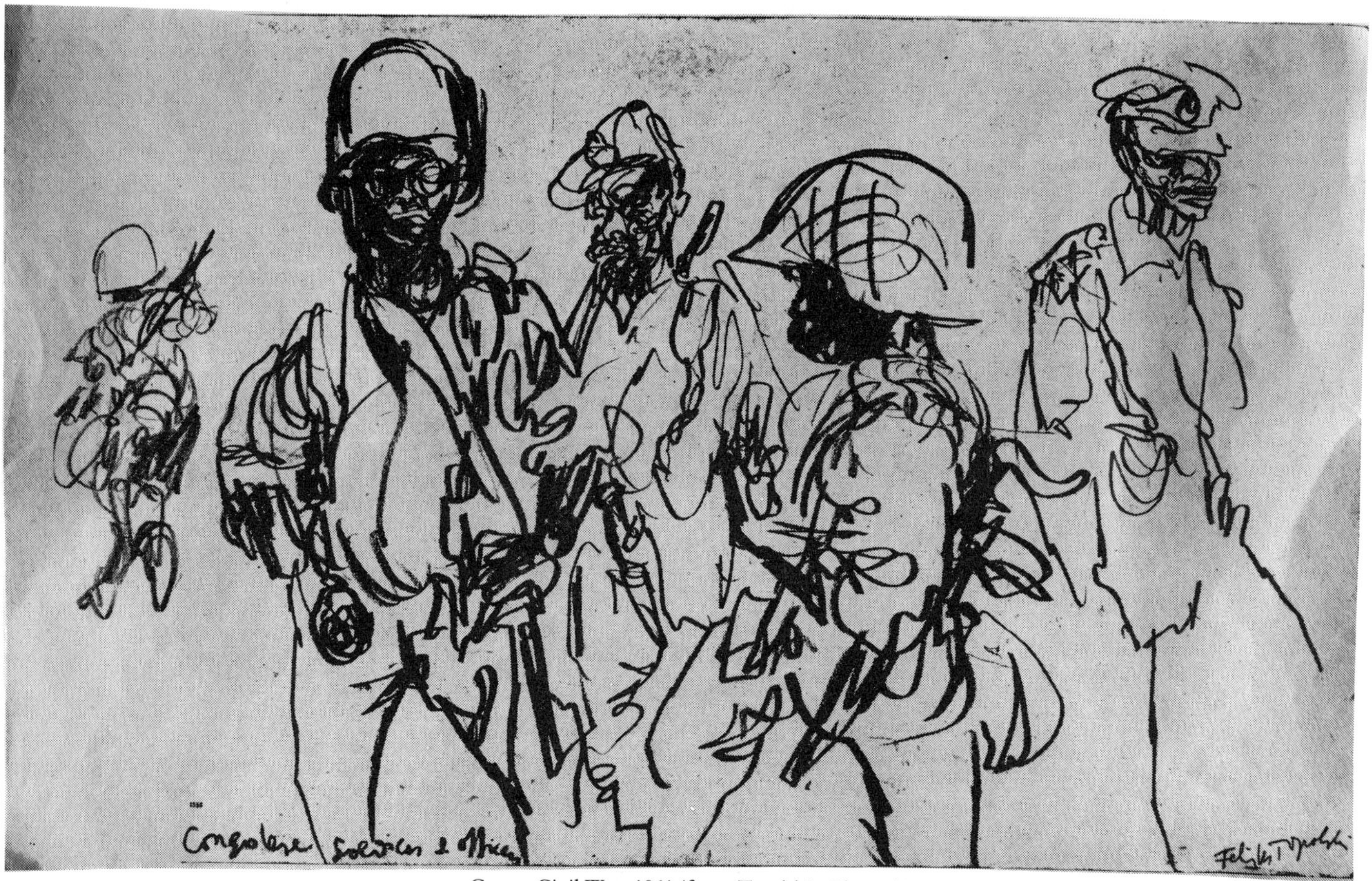

Congo Civil War, 1961 (from *Topolski's Chronicle*)

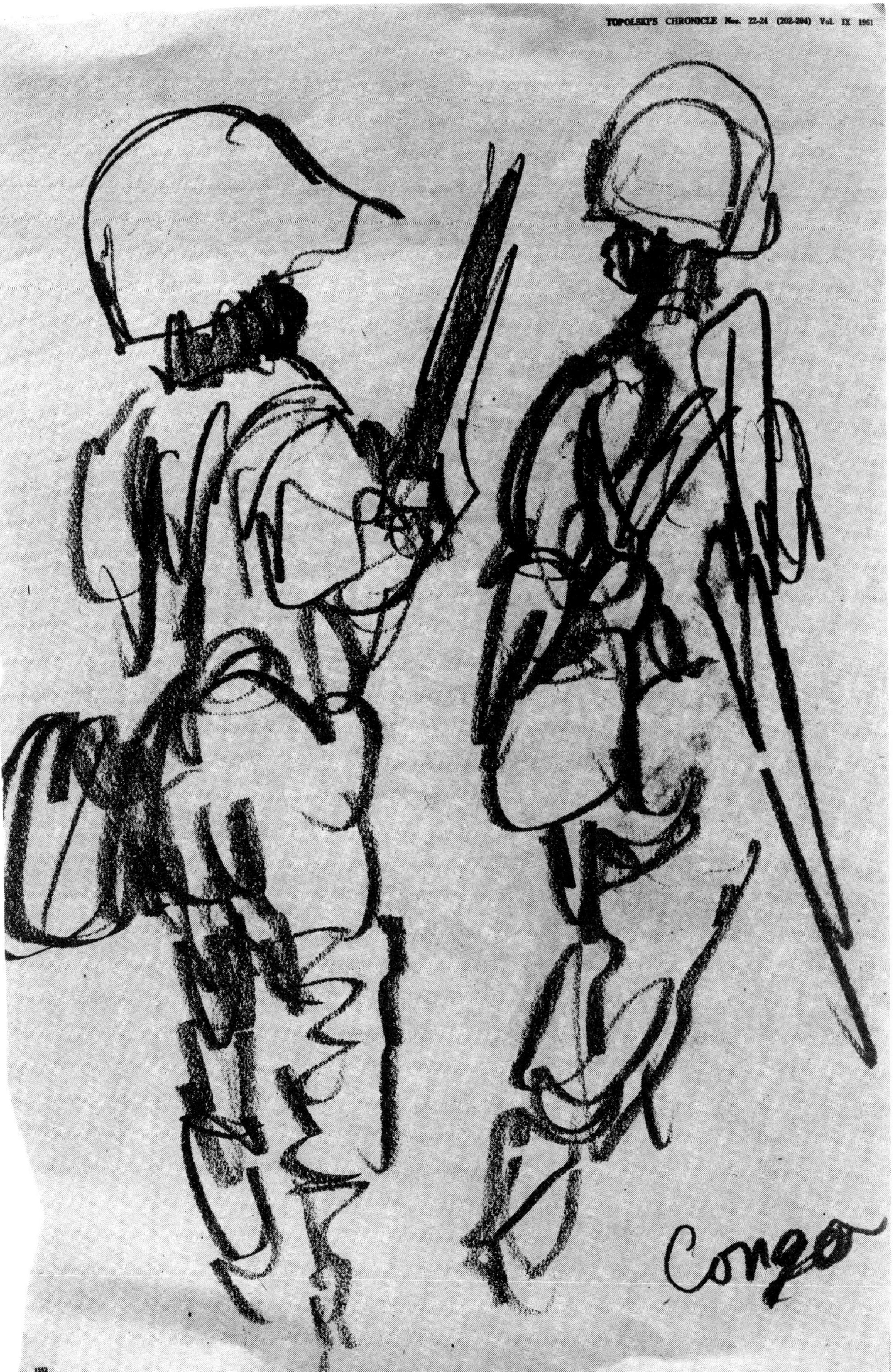

Congo Civil War, 1961 (from *Topolski's Chronicle*)

tableau, perhaps their last such day snatched out of the false calm.

Rwanda Burundi, Sumbura Airport. The urgency of the murderous Congo border. The privileged refugees first to reach safety – they look the part: a flesh-bursting black has-been beauty, dangling costliness from *bijouterie* (including glittering sun-glasses set as a tiara above her forehead), to *recherché* luggage and puffed-up kids; her mohair/silk-clad menfolk; the hatted and priestly whites – all (except the fatty) in pleading attitudes at the high official desks, against the ominous background movement of **the Katangan troops** being exchanged for **UN Irish troops** and the **Belgian paratroopers** being evacuated by plane. But a spotlessly uniformed black air hostess marshals all, as if on an ordinary passenger flight.

My *Chronicle's* three issues will later be filled with these Congo notes; but uncomfortable for me will be the double spread in American *Vogue*, given to my single drawing of a frightened young mother and child squatting on ground strewn with sub-machine guns, captioned *African Madonna*.

In some pseudo-wise exchanges at the outset of Africa's independencies it was said (besides puzzling over the British moving out without assured commercial priorities, thus losing the markets to others) that the preservation of the colonially roughed-out 'national' pattern would turn this continent into a long-lasting blood-bath; there was no anticipation of the initial unstoppable wave of throw-back tribal civil wars – sweeping epidemics from country to country. Thus at that time **Nigeria** basked in imperturbable well-being, above any predictability of later upsets, while, behind the Eastern border, Congo. . .

The law courts in Lagos were still faithful to the British legacy of wigs robes striped trousers and decorous procedures assured by Victoria's plaster bust.

But beyond that: a gathering of **the rulers** advancing to the fore under state umbrellas, their unmatchable shaping-costuming for their parts: the old, bent but awe-inspiring, His Highness Ewi of Adoctiti and His Highness Esezu II, The Orodje of Okpe under his chain-helmet, his garlanding necklaces, his ceremonial fly-whisk, his favourite turbaned lady close by; and the Arabic, tall and wolf-faced North Nigerians in white burnooses; then, fitting in well, the new men: Mr Foncha, leader of the Opposition in the Southern Cameroon (a singularly shaped cloth round the fez and voluminous layers of multi-patterned robes) and the Attorney-General of Ibadan, a giant in height and breadth, tall cap and white wide pyjamas under a brown sleeveless monumentally draped garment. All grouped in high theatre's tenseness of concord or discord. None of the West's gentlemanly understatement – in their flamboyance they challenge one another: they are competing princes once more.

But also, the sumptuously modern villas in **Queen's Drive**, built by top Western architects in lined-up competitive

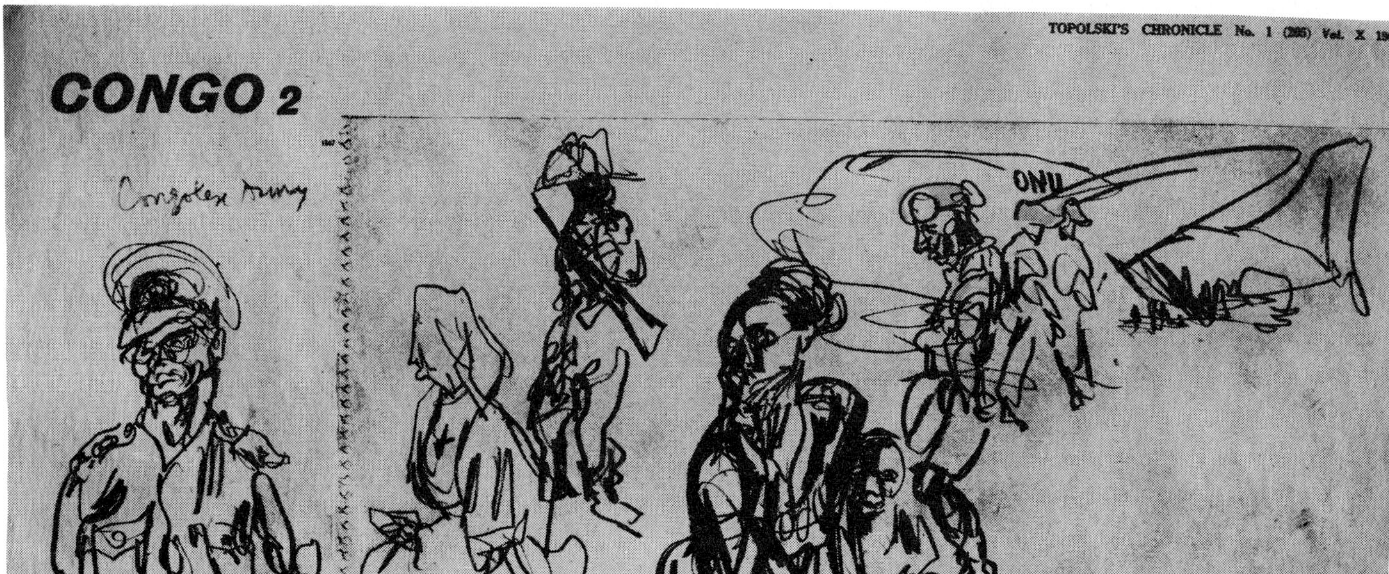

Stanleyville, Congo, 1961 (from *Topolski's Chronicle*)

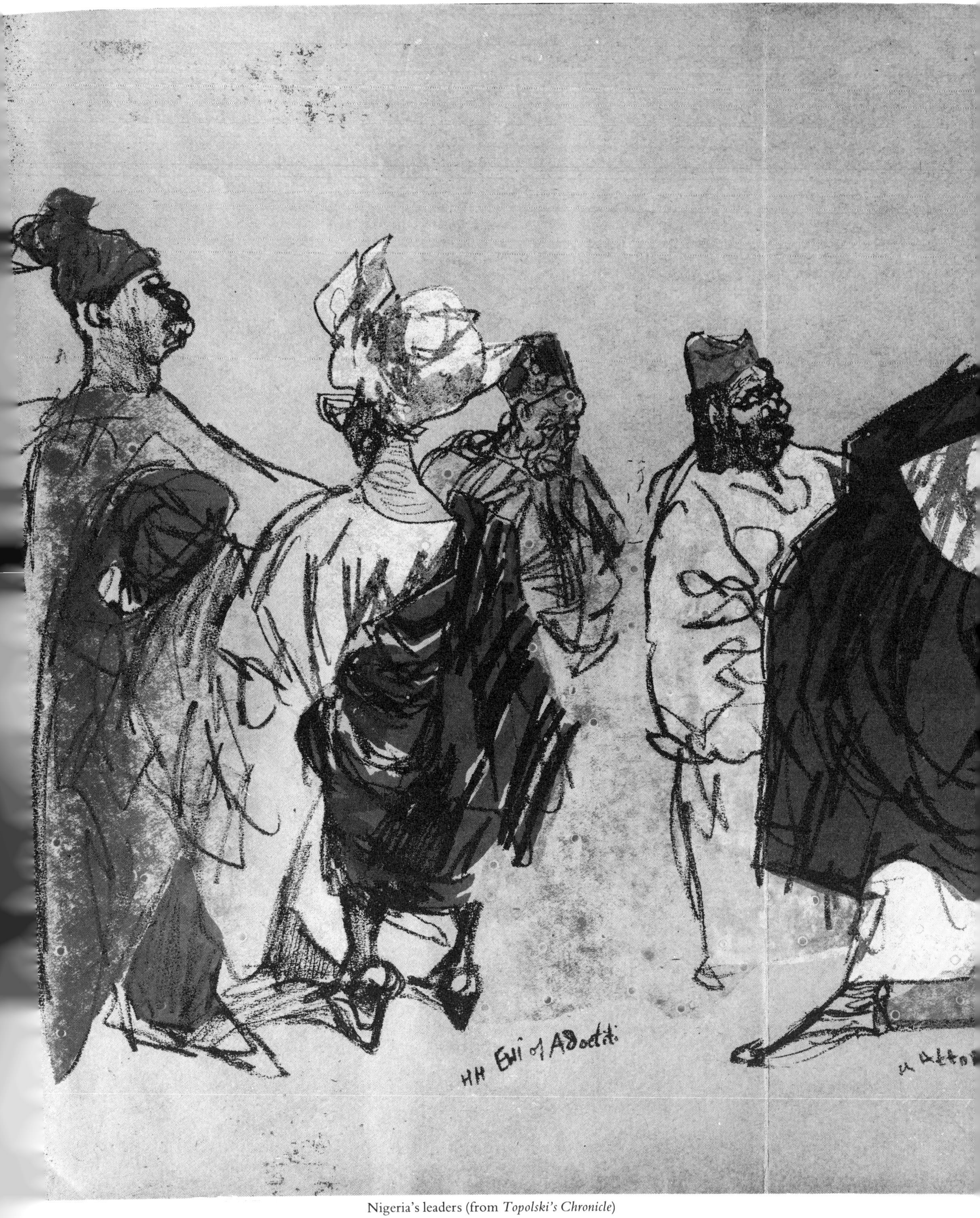

Nigeria's leaders (from *Topolski's Chronicle*)

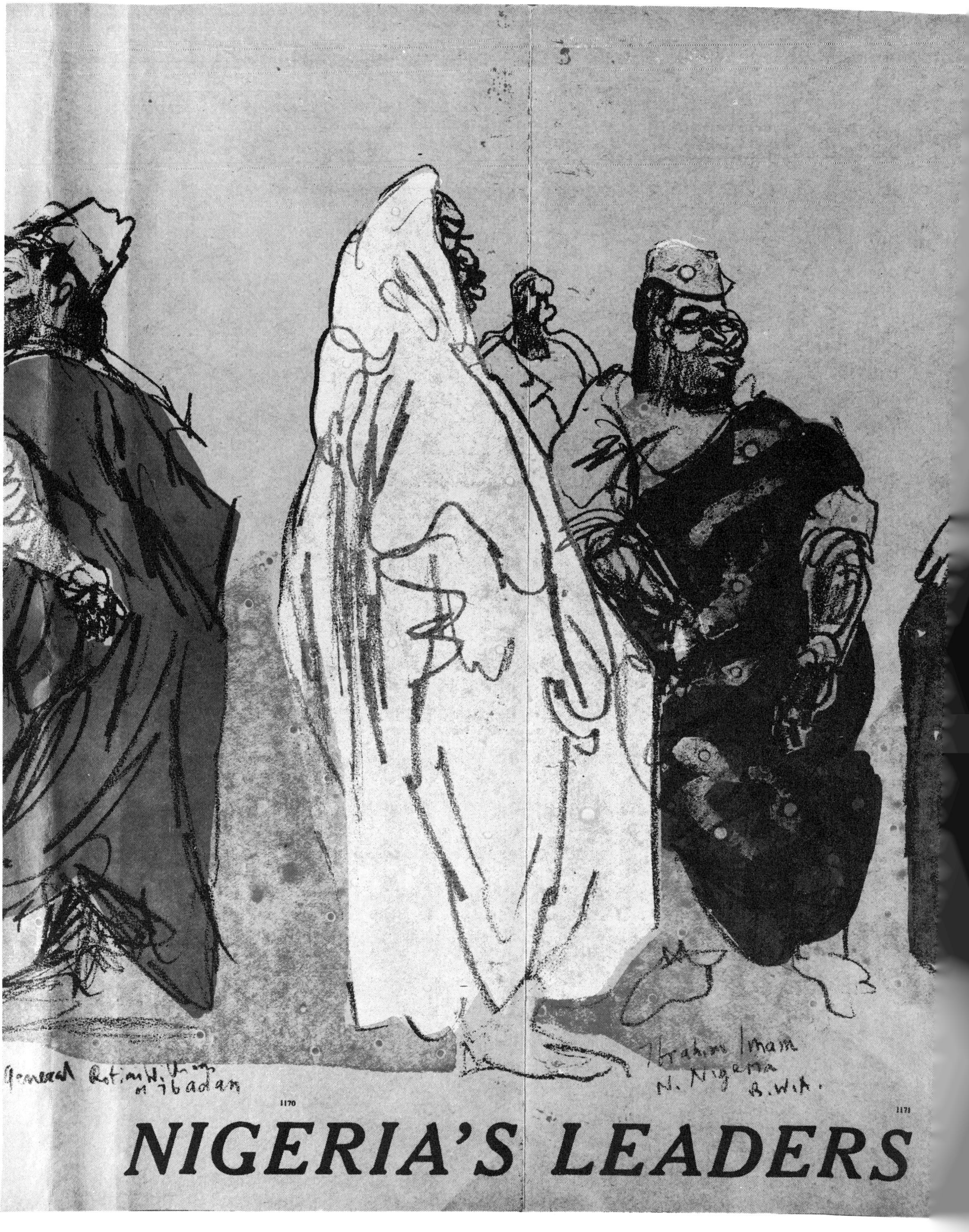

NIGERIA'S LEADERS

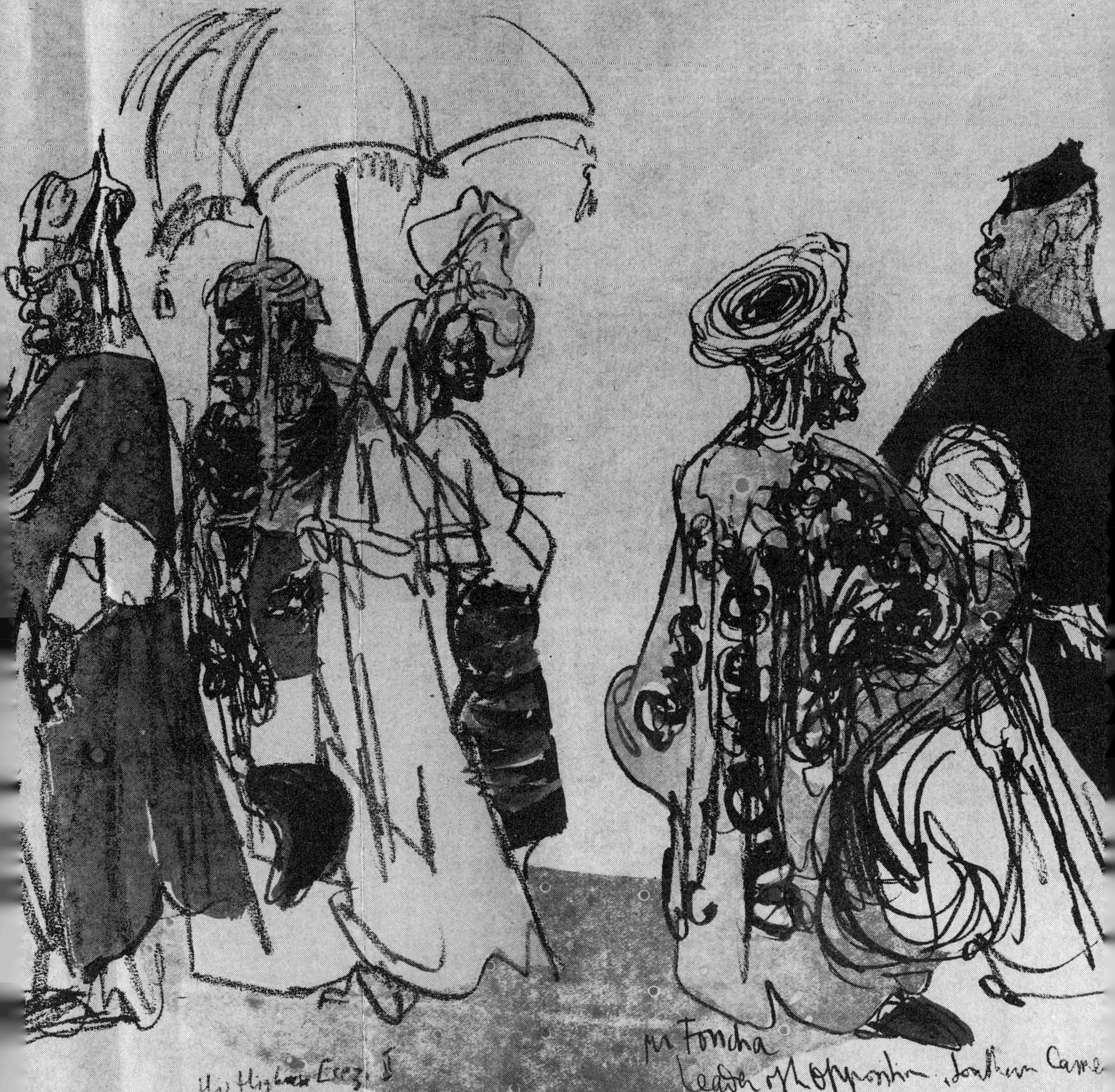

His Highness Esezi II
The ORODJE of OKPE
Mr Foncha
Leader of the Opposition, Southern Came

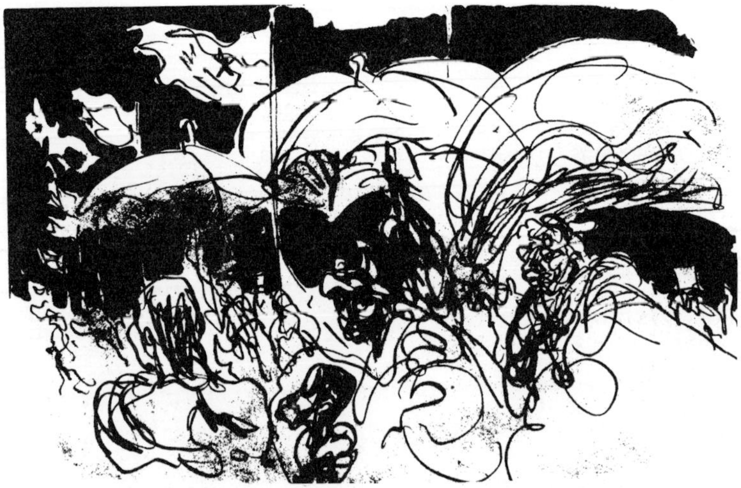

The Retreat in Ghana (from *Topolski's Chronicle*)

display for the rich and those in political power, that is enriching themselves Ministers of State – baroque American limousines serving the appropriately robed potentates. And, at the populace level, the most vigorous **Highlife** dancing at night. Lagos – the stage prologue for the drama to follow: market women and grandees, day and night dressed flamboyantly and proudly underlining their roles and shapes, in their flowing turbaned swish of colours-folds, performing their joyful musical *commedia* – seemingly for ever. Yet they will take their parts in the civil 'epidemic'.

The Retreat in Ghana*

When at **the Garden Party for HM the Queen** the time came to beat THE RETREAT,
the evening darkened the sky
so that the formal palmy greenery tightened round the lawns
in a rough imitation of the menacing jungle.
Then the posturing worthies and ambassadors of THE WEST
were swept off the centre of the stage
by the line of BLACK lancers
and held back as if under guard.
Thus, with significance lavishly provided,
the dusky expectancy set some seconds of silence for History to move a fraction. . .

The bugle. Burst of drums and platitudinous rhythms
of the British Brass cut the suspense with false comfort,
as there marched forward,
under this camouflage of reassuring tunes,
a jerky, BLACK-faced ten-deep column of IMPOSTORS –

– which they must have been,
Since their British drill had
swingier the strut
brasher the sound } than need be;
triumph-surer the advance
since their British-shaped uniforms signalled
not red-&-blue
but BLACK-&-silver purpose;
since their Drum-Major (more of a peacock than need be) was led
by the blackest midget, his emphatic miniature, for irony? Or symbol?

And while the weavers of the RETREAT paraded up-&-down,
HM The White Queen and HE The Black President leant forward
under their State Umbrellas.

Why?
Because the circle of western and westernized
diplomats plutocrats chiefs bishops judges QCs CMGs OBEs PhDs BScs
was being swallowed by the shadows under the equatorial skyline?
Because, this Imperial Farewell going on and on and on,
they could discern History advance another step?

That was only a *comme-il-faut* service:
Beating of The Retreat, still provided by Whitehall-designed protocol,
possibly the last,
fittingly provoking melancholy and obvious reflections.
But out of the polite calm of the Castle Gardens:
THE RETREAT!

The – snap! – darkness, howling gale – thunder-dishevelled, the
perspectives of tearing banners
over 2000 worthies struggling to car-parks,
turned into a panic-mob on the run –
roaming lights spotting insignias of late glory:
Top-hats wagging – dignity lost;
the jewelled Chiefs, scattered
(their umbrellas – sails in the storm),
hastily setting spectacles on their noses to stalk their limousines;
the Bishops – skirts up;
the ladies – ceremonial hats in the air, heels broken;
photographers (their weapons no more pointed) – disarmed.

The populace, still awed,
not quite daring yet to laugh,
but narrowing the path,
pressing . . .

**Chronicle* nos. 2–3 (206–207), Vol. X, 1962.

TOPOLSKI's CHRONICLE Nos. 2-3 (206-207) Vol. X 1962

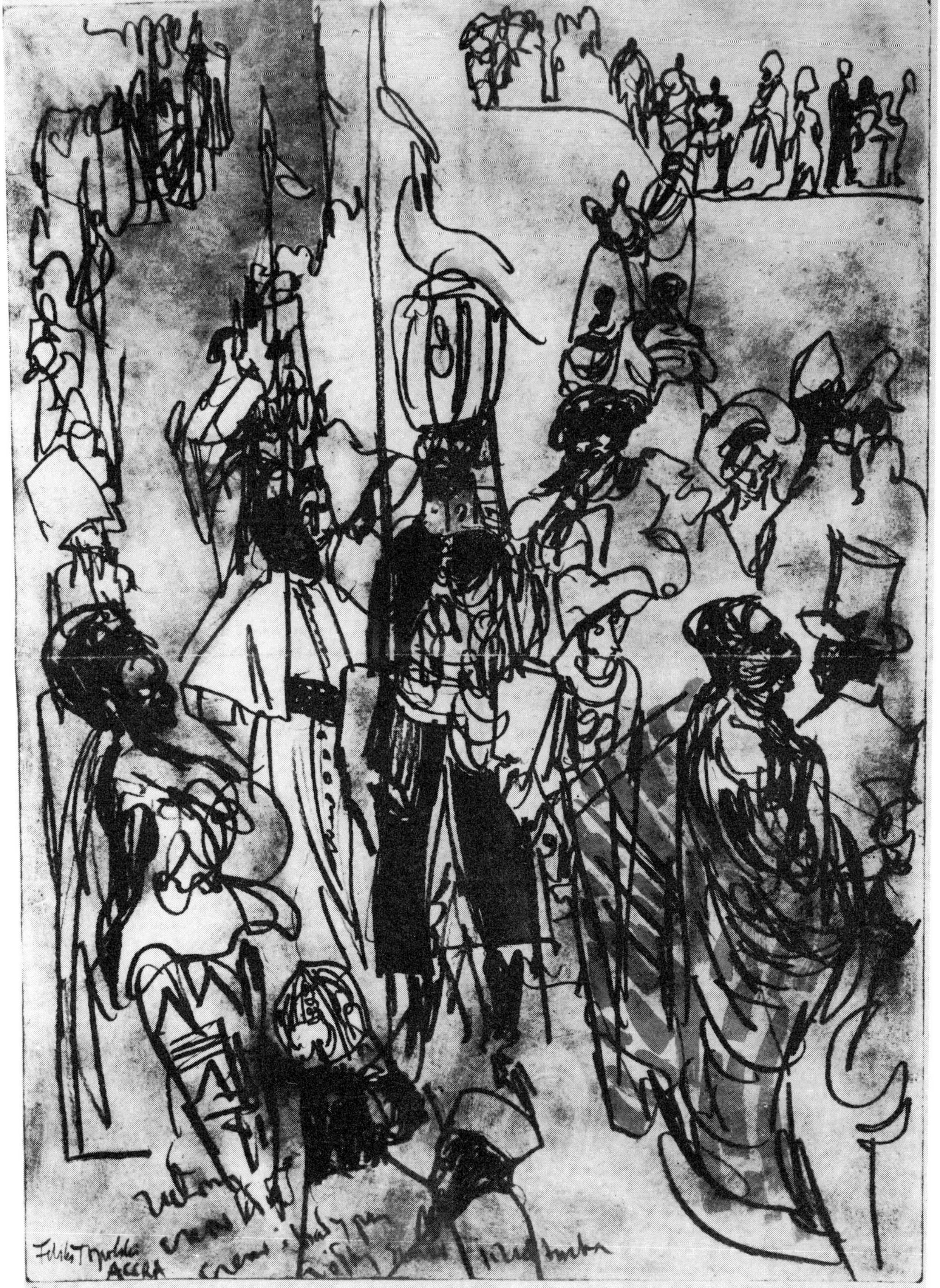

THE GOVERNMENT OF GHANA'S GARDEN PARTY FOR H.M. QUEEN ELIZABETH

THIS DOUBLE ISSUE COSTS [illegible] "TOPOLSKI'S CHRONICLE" IS PUBLISHED 24 TIMES A YEAR AT [illegible] A COPY. YEARLY SUBSCRIPTION RATES (WITH FOLDER AND INDEX) TO ANY PART OF THE WORLD ARE [illegible] SHORTER PERIODS PRO RATA. AIR MAIL BY QUOTATION. SUBSCRIPTIONS FROM OUTSIDE THE STERLING AREA MAY BE PAID THROUGH THE UNESCO COUPON SCHEME. [illegible] Copyright reserved.

The Government of Ghana's Garden Party for HM Queen Elizabeth, 1961 (from *Topolski's Chronicle*)

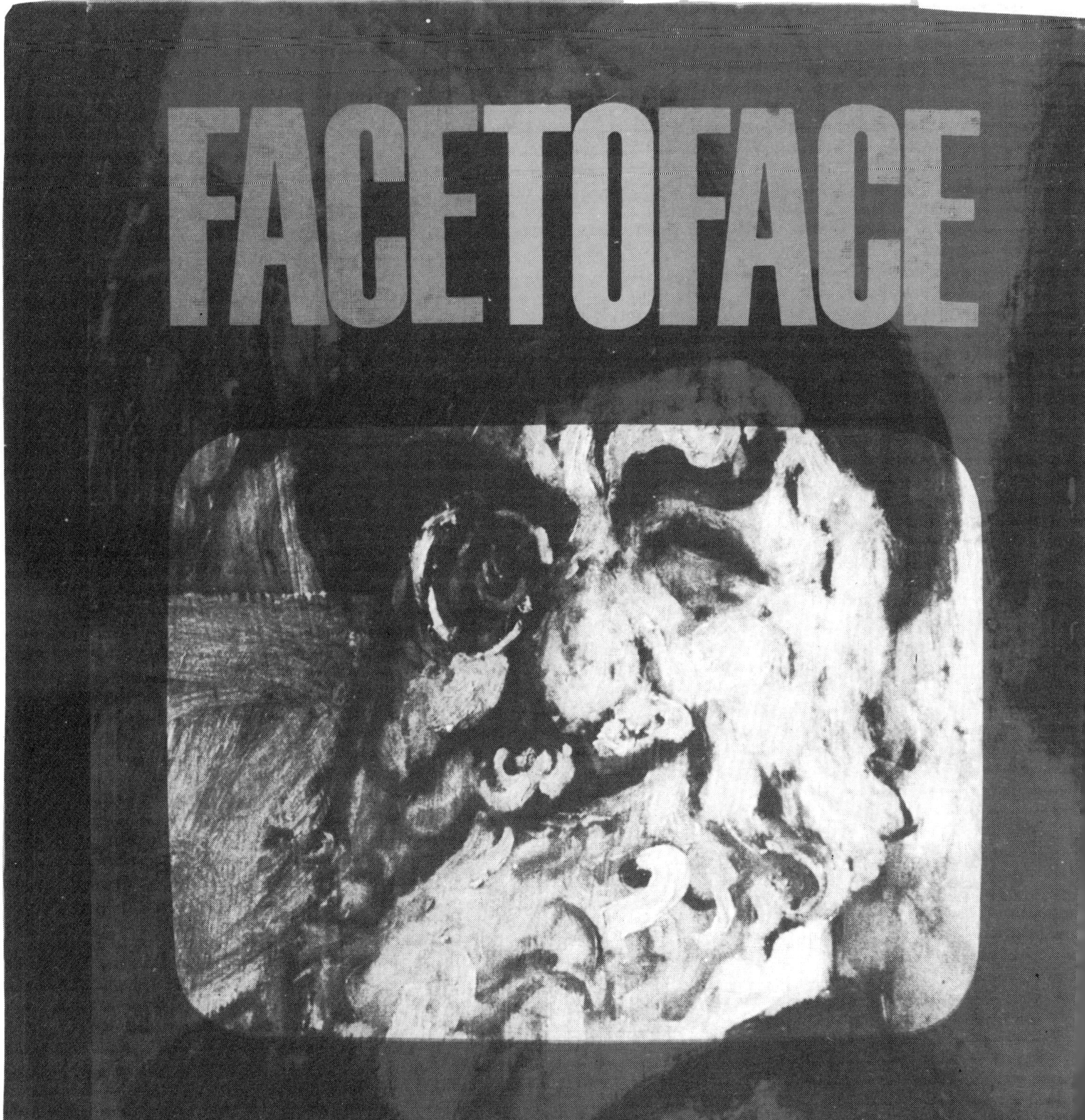

Nubar Gulbenkian: *Face to Face* TV Programme, (book cover)

BBC Television's ***Face to Face*** programme streams 'personages' to my studio. In my habitual way, I draw each, circling round, several times – drawings are hastily whisked away and shown one after the other to open and to end each interview. Over thirty people of one or another prominence sat thus without much impact either way: it was for me concentrated work – for them a self-conscious preliminary to the next day's grilling by the interviewer. Here they are, little more than listed:

Nubar Gulbenkian, having arrived in his glamourized taxi-cab, projected the supreme personification of the paradox of sun-never-setting yester-time imperial civilization: this extravagantly made-up/curl-bearded/over-tailored/over-jewelled Eastern potentate-dummy articulating (in speech and manner) the faultlessly English public-school breeding of predictable and understated deference.

King Hussein of Jordan had to be found in his suite at the Dorchester Hotel. Another England-shaped Easterner – this one, marked for life by the clipped Sandhurst pattern, would be indistinguishable (even it seems in his mind-processes) but for his demi-stature.

Jomo Kenyatta had to be found in Kenya – literally 'found', because of the obvious pleasure he derived from not being easily available. A grand decorative icon-of-a-ruler differently gilt-draped/gilt-hatted for each appearance, modelled on distant-past usurpers. Eventually he posed for me devotedly.

Sir Compton MacKenzie in Edinburgh, settled in his self-designed machine-for-writing chair – a generously styled romantic, an entertaining gentlemanly host, fine to draw – underlining somewhat his role of master writer, as if in need of reassurance. He responds gracefully to the story of my panel-stealing from the bomb-shattered canal-bank room in which his *Sinister Street* came to loving conclusion.

Gilbert Harding: for me the very acme of a media-hype paper-tiger.

Martin Luther King arrived in London on the morning of his late afternoon programme, was taken to my house (not the studio), went to sleep in Daniel's bed, had lunch with us – and I drew him on until he was fetched. There was plenty of easily flowing simple talk; however, with such a singular anointed gospeller, it never left his apostolic theme.

Danny Blanchflower, Sterling Moss, Adam Faith, Albert Finney, Tony Hancock: the last with a comic's melancholy; Finney, powerful and progressing; the others, nice people – Faith possibly less so, anxious since barely afloat: the slimmest gift painstakingly kept up by the hot air of vested interests.

Otto Klemperer, at my suggestion, let me sit facing him within the orchestra at a rehearsal for a radio concert (or recording?). His baffling vanity was probably inherited by his daughter, who, after his death, barred my painting of him, I was told, from the Festival Hall.

Lord Boothby: a poised – thus perfectly at ease, thus not driven by ambition – English political gentleman, inside and out.

Henry Moore: benevolent, concentrated – grave. Daring his Everestian-solid reputation, I feel like probing the idea that he personifies ideally, within British class-society, the

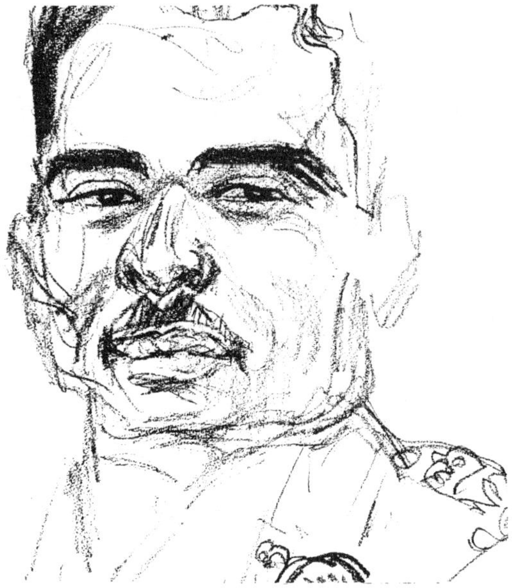

King Hussein of Jordan (from *Face to Face*)

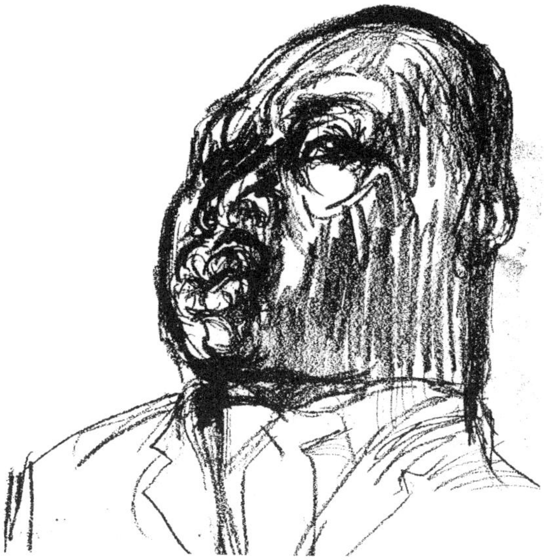

Martin Luther King (from *Face to Face*)

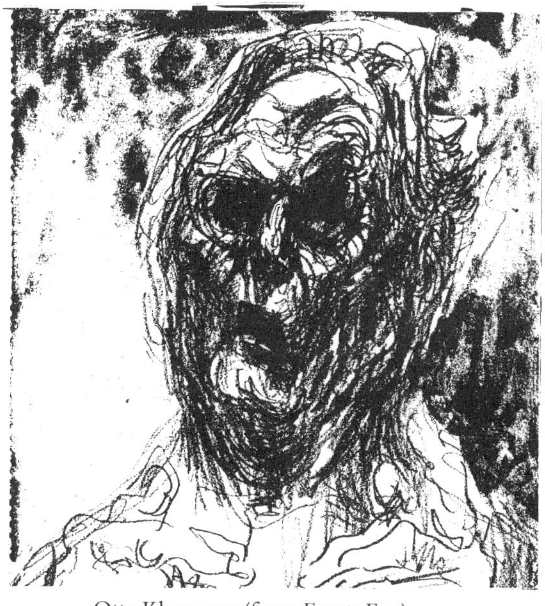

Otto Klemperer (from *Face to Face*)

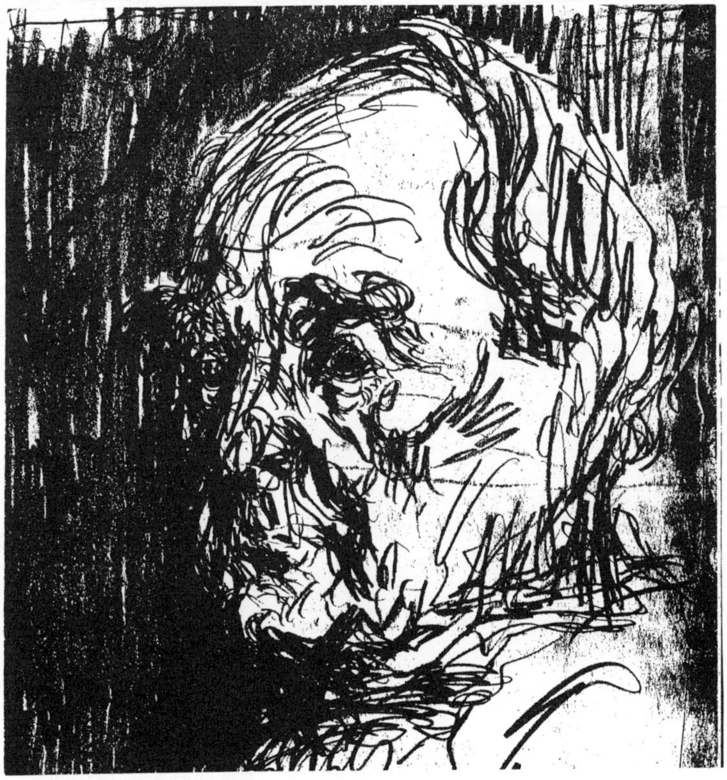

Henry Moore (from *Face to Face*)

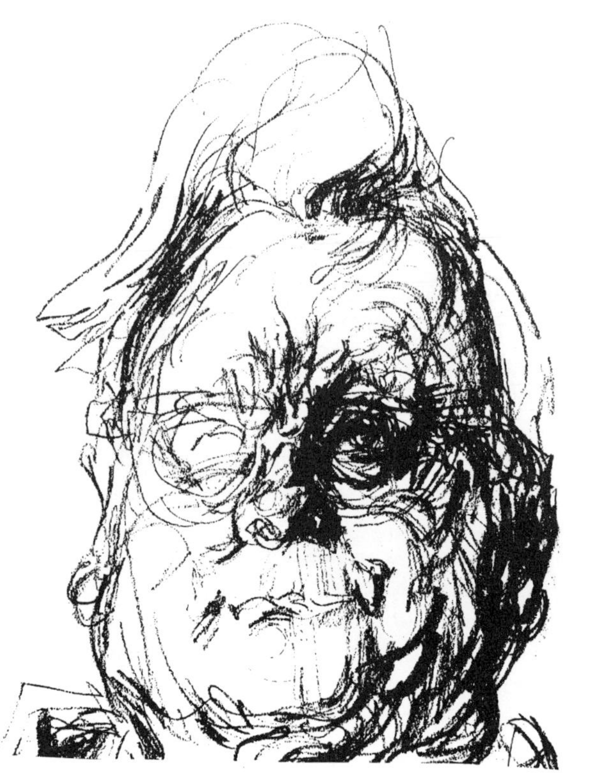

Herbert Morrison (from *Face to Face*)

artist-craftsman class; that is: to be looked down on – but with the satisfying self-congratulation of appreciative patronage by those securely above; that is, 'knowing his place'; that is, easily enough assessed not to upset his protectors' (collectors, art officials) comfortable sense of superiority as an artist not so classified might. Thus, like say a secluded Flemish painter at the first trip out of his parish, the first sight of the unusual – in his case a single hole in a single Aztec carving – shaped his whole life's *oeuvre* – with, for good measure, scratches/blots of pseudo-old patina; all-in-all accessible modernity roughened up by association with the past – by a securely non-revolutionary peasant-craftsman, and older retainer, not a jumper-above-his-station.

Victor Gollancz: his leftism went hand-in-hand with publishing/selling. I have never been clear about my antipathy towards Mammonite profit-counting socialism; or to his self-conscious self-styling into a hair-flowing idealist.

Sir Cecil Beaton: still in Poland, and, as ever (then and still), not a career-plotter, I half-listened to a gifted caricaturist, friend Czermański's – returned from years in France, England and the States – advice: 'First you'll have to dislodge Beaton from his ruling plank . . .'

I met him only under the *Face to Face* aegis at my studio. Enjoyable subject, not enjoyable company. His elaborately worked-out posturing gentleman eccentric, his dressiness – with the elaborate hat battling against baldness – above all, his posing for me in full knowledge of my inability to flatter, so transparently building up a store of negatives: these confirmed in 'friendly' reports.

But not only confirmed – he felt obliged, well before the sitting, to minimize my status (the reversal of my Polish friend's advice). His reputation (and rewards) shot up greatly on the basis of his designs for *My Fair Lady*. My drawings for Penguin's *Pygmalion*, done years earlier, and 'popular', must have counted in the film producers' deliberations over the appointment of a designer; they must also have stood – and served or annoyed, or both – at Beaton's designing elbow. And he must have detested me for it.

Lord Shawcross: Boothby's counter-balance on the Left – which he abandoned later. His handsomeness and celebratory manner – and elegant wisdom – made him seem almost a speaking dummy of English decency; until, one completely unusual day for me, I found myself descending the back staircase of the Savoy after a banquet lunch and crossing with Shawcross, ascending with the air of a usual-for-him routine. I assumed his presence there (since I have never before or since been there – no, maybe once or twice.) as being his life, as it were, hence he the grandee of convention.

Lord Reith: a daunting tower of a man filled my doorway – the face to match. He must be the model of the breed listed as material for high appointments; that is, not meritoriously promoted, but nominated according to the strange duality in the democratic machinery: it declares a shaky four-year rule by majority vote, yet acts, yes, through promotive hierarchies (the Civil Service, the Forces, the Police) and – yes, yes – hugely supported by institutional bosses, given their near-uncontrollable power-for-life by arbitrary selection. These people come from nowhere – they seem to be kept on ice in readiness for their supreme nonresponsibility-to-society. The essential request is that they look and dress right. Lord Reith had these prerequisites in abundance.

Adlai Stevenson: I had followed and drawn him throughout the 1956 Democratic Convention in Chicago – at the smallest gatherings, in the Convention Hall, on the rostrum, in the grill room of the Sheraton-Blackstone Hotel with Mr Truman, at his and Mrs Roosevelt's reception at the Prudential Building. His 'chamber' charm and lecture-room intelligence could not vote him into a mass-elected office.

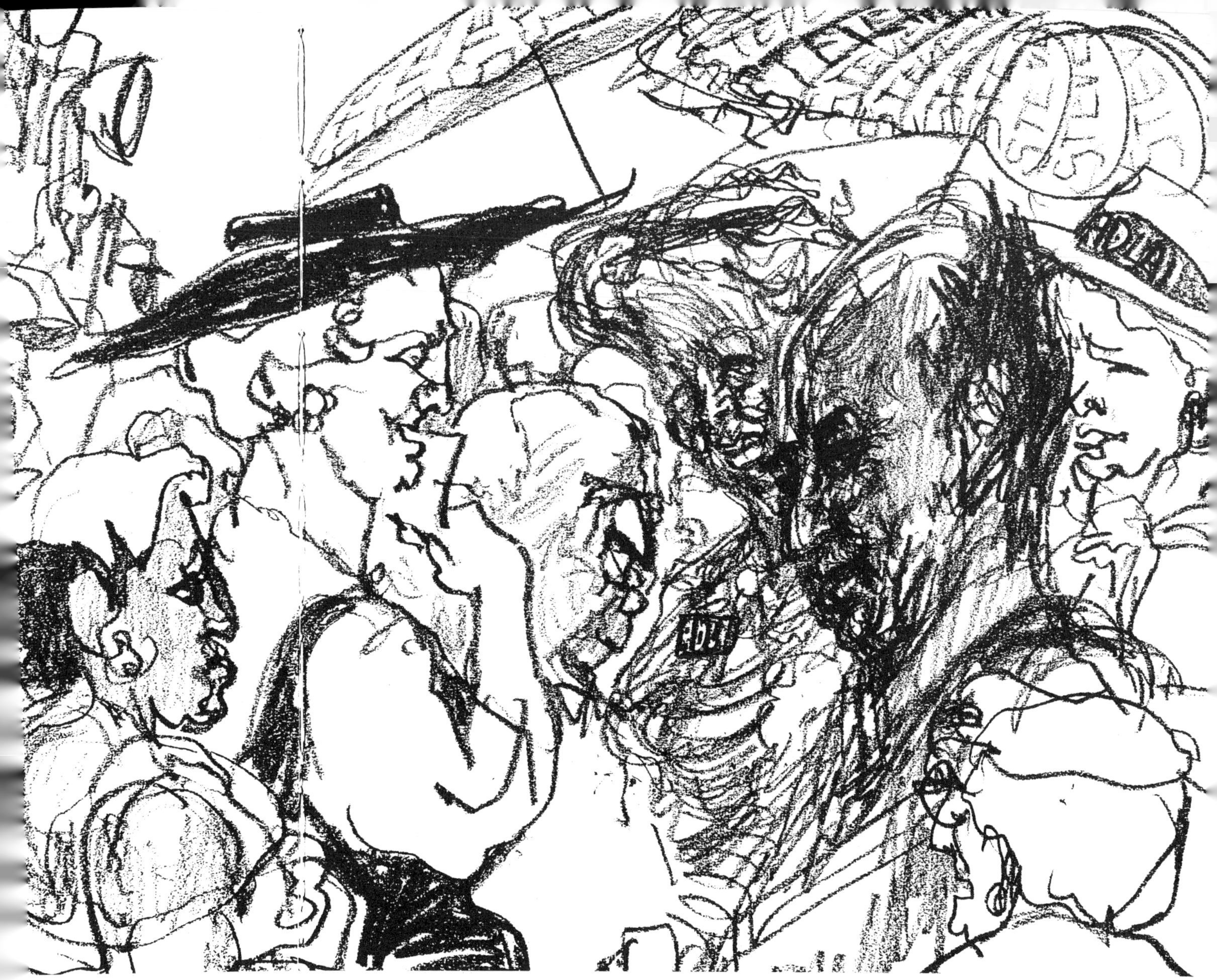

Adlai Stevenson (from *Face to Face*)

Lord Morrison of Lambeth: fun to draw, touching to encounter – the relic, he seemed, of the single-minded populist vigour and astuteness which surged to the surface of old England.

Frank Cousins: physically the other was a midget rider on the wave of early optimism, he a giant of crusading passion, also single-minded, but angry – having come up against latterday pragmatism. His great potential was shoved (the frequent fate of ideologues) by party politics into oblivion. An impressive Dantonesque figure and fate.

Carl Gustav Jung refused to be drawn. There were some reasonable explanations for this, but I was certain that this shrewdest shaman, who gladly faced photographers confident in his nimbleness at turning to them his best cheek, would have felt defenceless if exposed to an artist's circling and perhaps penetrating gaze.

Augustus John: in the late thirties this fable went about, smuggled out of a secret Tate Gallery meeting: somebody opposed the purchase of my three mere wash drawings with: 'We must draw the line somewhere', to which Augustus retorted: 'But can you draw the line like Topolski?' and got the picture in.

Later he charmingly cultivated me, brought the spectacular Marchesa Casati to my studio, and insisted that, in Sir John Squire's *Festschrift*, I should picture him on the page meant for his own contribution. I drew and painted him plentifully and hung about with his coterie at the Antelope pub. It was warming to have Barbara (close friend of his daughter) tell how in a taxi this shaggy/bearded hulk threw himself at her – not really an act of rape, but an obligatory *comme-il-faut*ism. 'How did it feel?' 'Like an immense warm teddy-bear, easily put back on his seat.'

Much later, he had to be reached at his country house, sedate – Dorelia hostessing and some girls-in-waiting in a neighbouring cottage; the studio-annexe housing the never-to-be-completed monumental canvas pronouncing idyllic optimism.

Surrounded by the downy landscape, and part of it, there stands erect this legend: rough-barked thick trunk, the streaming hair-leafery – an arboreal crown; oak-like, he deserves to endure. A singularly pernicious trick of nature to cut down Augustus.

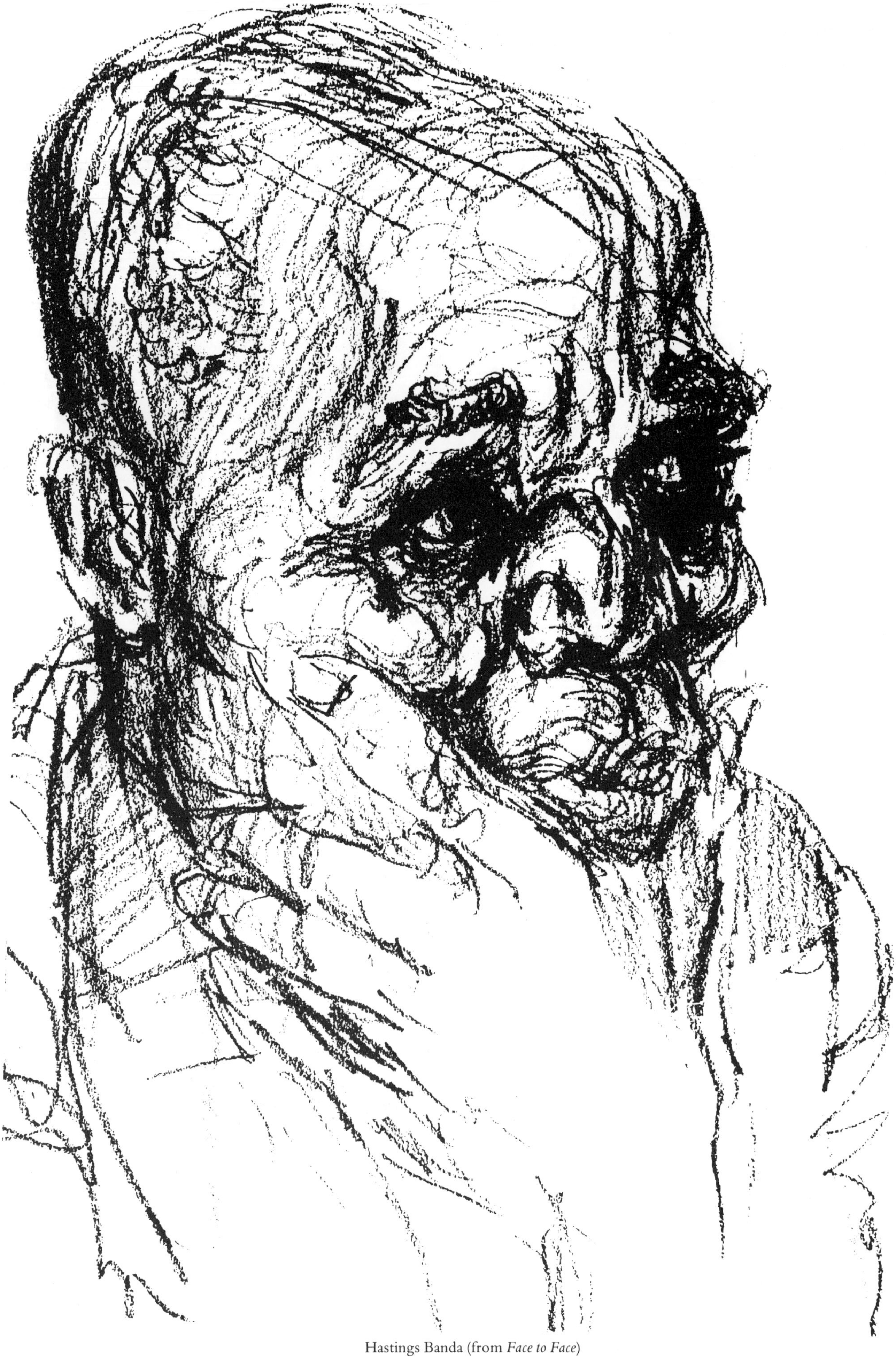

Hastings Banda (from *Face to Face*)

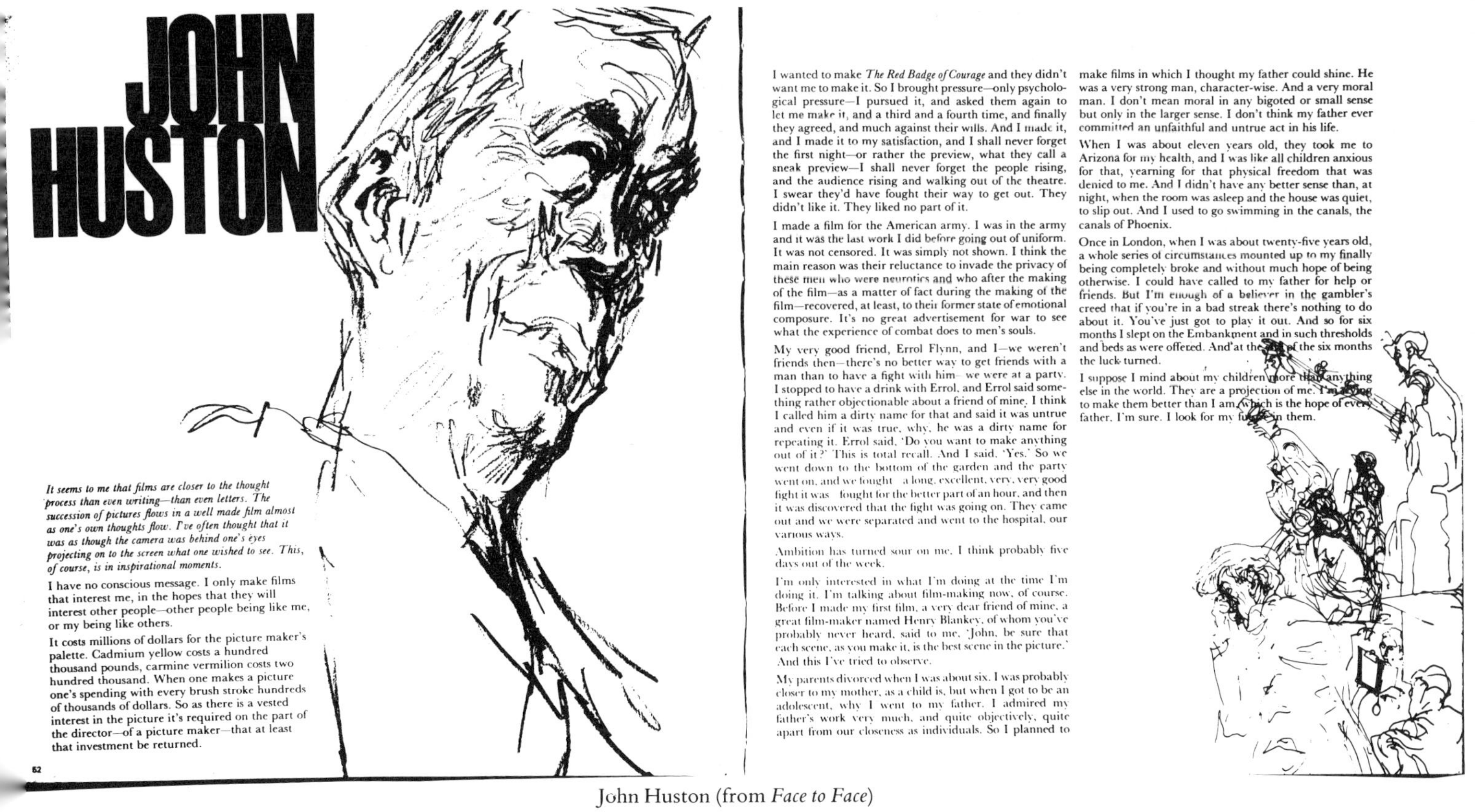

JOHN HUSTON

It seems to me that films are closer to the thought process than even writing—than even letters. The succession of pictures flows in a well made film almost as one's own thoughts flow. I've often thought that it was as though the camera was behind one's eyes projecting on to the screen what one wished to see. This, of course, is in inspirational moments.

I have no conscious message. I only make films that interest me, in the hopes that they will interest other people—other people being like me, or my being like others.

It costs millions of dollars for the picture maker's palette. Cadmium yellow costs a hundred thousand pounds, carmine vermilion costs two hundred thousand. When one makes a picture one's spending with every brush stroke hundreds of thousands of dollars. So as there is a vested interest in the picture it's required on the part of the director—of a picture maker—that at least that investment be returned.

62

I wanted to make *The Red Badge of Courage* and they didn't want me to make it. So I brought pressure—only psychological pressure—I pursued it, and asked them again to let me make it, and a third and a fourth time, and finally they agreed, and much against their wills. And I made it, and I made it to my satisfaction, and I shall never forget the first night—or rather the preview, what they call a sneak preview—I shall never forget the people rising, and the audience rising and walking out of the theatre. I swear they'd have fought their way to get out. They didn't like it. They liked no part of it.

I made a film for the American army. I was in the army and it was the last work I did before going out of uniform. It was not censored. It was simply not shown. I think the main reason was their reluctance to invade the privacy of these men who were neurotics and who after the making of the film—as a matter of fact during the making of the film—recovered, at least, to their former state of emotional composure. It's no great advertisement for war to see what the experience of combat does to men's souls.

My very good friend, Errol Flynn, and I—we weren't friends then—there's no better way to get friends with a man than to have a fight with him—we were at a party. I stopped to have a drink with Errol, and Errol said something rather objectionable about a friend of mine. I think I called him a dirty name for that and said it was untrue and even if it was true, why, he was a dirty name for repeating it. Errol said, 'Do you want to make anything out of it?' This is total recall. And I said, 'Yes.' So we went down to the bottom of the garden and the party went on, and we fought—a long, excellent, very, very good fight it was—fought for the better part of an hour, and then it was discovered that the fight was going on. They came out and we were separated and went to the hospital, our various ways.

Ambition has turned sour on me. I think probably five days out of the week.

I'm only interested in what I'm doing at the time I'm doing it. I'm talking about film-making now, of course. Before I made my first film, a very dear friend of mine, a great film-maker named Henry Blankey, of whom you've probably never heard, said to me, 'John, be sure that each scene, as you make it, is the best scene in the picture.' And this I've tried to observe.

My parents divorced when I was about six. I was probably closer to my mother, as a child is, but when I got to be an adolescent, why I went to my father. I admired my father's work very much, and quite objectively, quite apart from our closeness as individuals. So I planned to make films in which I thought my father could shine. He was a very strong man, character-wise. And a very moral man. I don't mean moral in any bigoted or small sense but only in the larger sense. I don't think my father ever committed an unfaithful and untrue act in his life.

When I was about eleven years old, they took me to Arizona for my health, and I was like all children anxious for that, yearning for that physical freedom that was denied to me. And I didn't have any better sense than, at night, when the room was asleep and the house was quiet, to slip out. And I used to go swimming in the canals, the canals of Phoenix.

Once in London, when I was about twenty-five years old, a whole series of circumstances mounted up to my finally being completely broke and without much hope of being otherwise. I could have called to my father for help or friends. But I'm enough of a believer in the gambler's creed that if you're in a bad streak there's nothing to do about it. You've just got to play it out. And so for six months I slept on the Embankment and in such thresholds and beds as were offered. And at the end of the six months the luck turned.

I suppose I mind about my children more than anything else in the world. They are a projection of me. I'm trying to make them better than I am, which is the hope of every father, I'm sure. I look for my future in them.

John Huston (from *Face to Face*)

Hastings Banda sat for me (and talked) at my studio, and we moved to continue over a lunch – such was his conversational hold. A reasonable, warm, alert and dedicated man – in a fitting office, thanks to having bypassed political wrangles.

Viscount Hailsham: difficult but endearing to draw with his aged/plumped baby features. I did masses of drawings against the odds. And a lot of conversation which I fuelled but failed to recall, having been battling for my drawing to come off. The gentlemanly charmer at ease with the world, unshakeable views exuding from his standing. I find it impossible to comprehend (or maybe I've forgotten) why the premiership evaded him.

Simone Signoret: she confuses me – having first seen her in a film as the embodiment of young *fin-de-siècle* femininity – when, seemingly soon after, reshaped into motherliness. A visit to her rooms in Paris made my peace with this new embodiment, enhanced by her love of mass-justness. But, soon after, I fell victim to her social claws.

Sidney Lumet, the worthy young American film director, held, when filming in London, a dinner party for his cast and myself. As sometimes happens with me (and with everybody?) halfway through the drink/food stultifications my alertness switched off for a few instants, to revive when *The Pawnbroker* was the theme. And so I moved in with my mixed views of the film: yes, its high level granted, thus provoking the highest demands on it – several elements of it troubled me, which I lengthily enumerated.

Simone drew me on – others, particularly James Mason, attempting to digress – and I was by then aware of my almost exemplary textbook clanger: *The Pawnbroker* was Lumet's film. Of course, a dinner party is not the time for a guest to chastise his host, yet my critique was honest, not mischievous, and I attempted to emphasize my overall appreciation of the film's high quality; but relentless Simone rejoiced at my gaffe, orbiting the rest of the evening round my execution by her laughter.

Roy Thomson and I, only the two of us, hired a car in Nairobi for a trip to Tree-Tops, a shacky hotel put together in a tree overhanging a wild-life reserve watering-hole. An old thing, transparently shrewd in self-advancement, he came out during our ride with a great desire to appear in the *Face to Face* series; he knew of my involvement in it and pressed for help without subtlety, imagining, apparently correctly, that a prestigious television inclusion would serve as a stepping-stone towards the Honours List – our conversation otherwise basic. And basically vapid it remained throughout our stay, except for his enthusiastic millionaire-arithmetic over the fifty–fifty sharing of our bill.

I did let his name drop – and there he was at my studio, more puffed up than before – perhaps already assured that his peerage was on the way.

John Huston: a faithful subscriber to my *Chronicle*, a stylish host: at his *Moby Dick* filming, at a garden supper in Les Ambassadeurs Club.

On the whole, film-makers tend to be certain of the height of privileged pleasure their invitees derive from foot-to-footing far behind the cameras over endless reshoots and preparation-pauses; but this was full of oddities. And a luncheon at which Orson Welles's conversation truly shone.

After the garden supper, I drove a Guinness to her home, mildly pestering her – her little son asleep in the vicinity. Could the Gareth Browne of the seventies, the rumbustious balding ginger-pony-tailed Irish squire, be he? He came my way through Farida Majid, a Bengali-Bangladesh poetess who, yes!, got me to picture seventeen poets for the

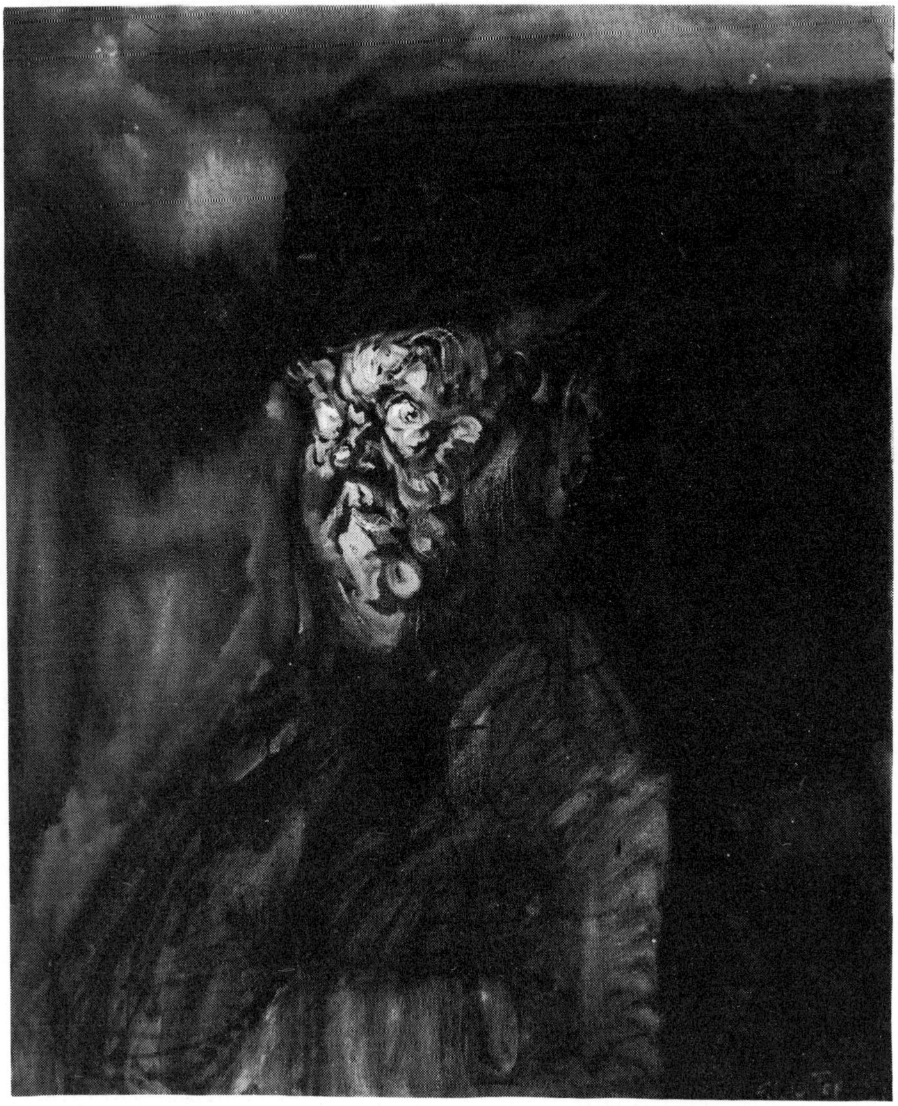

Evelyn Waugh (from Collection at University of Texas, Austin)

anthology of her London Thursdays; and did I not bring to her Miss Yamoto, a Japanese poetess, and Lisa St Aubin de Teran, daughter of Jan Carew, a Guyanese novelist and Afro-American academic, and herself now rapidly to the fore of British fiction. And I drew/painted them all – with (since I am now dealing with writers), recently, William Golding, Iris Murdoch, Jerzy Kosinski, Howard Barker. . .

This enlightening *Face to Face* variety was followed by another eye-opener – the Labour Party Shadow Cabinet – but first it overlapped with **a commission from the University of Texas for twenty portraits of living English writers** – the listing dictated by the University – three of them belonging to the above collection:

Evelyn Waugh: his reputedly undiversified rudeness did not materialize. On the contrary, he invited me alone to lunch before the sitting at his Wiltshire home but, bound in my loyalty to Hugh Burnett (the producer of this series) and belaboured by him with Waugh's shock-treatment on his previous visit, I declined, explaining a fraction tactlessly that I would come in the afternoon with Hugh. In spite of this I was received genially, apparently privileged by our pre-war camaraderie on *Night and Day*. And in an equally genial mood, we met again in London. In consequence no razor-sharp incidents spice my memory; only helpfulness: doffing his bowler-hat on-off for my drawing – the result, two largish paintings into which his sanguinariness possibly seeped with a lot of red-in-the-face.

Dame Edith Sitwell: while at it, I don't show my portrait drawings to my sitters, so that I draw unhampered by clogging restraints; and the same rules my portrait painting, whether it be done from drawings-and-memory or straight at sittings.

With *Face to Face* they would see the results on the screen, myself out of their reach, as it were; but, with portraits proper, one way or another the fateful confrontation would have to come.

The University of Texas planned a book of my portraits, and presumably following some code of academic publishing chivalry, sent out smallish black-and-white photographs

Opposite: Dame Edith Sitwell (from Collection at University of Texas, Austin)

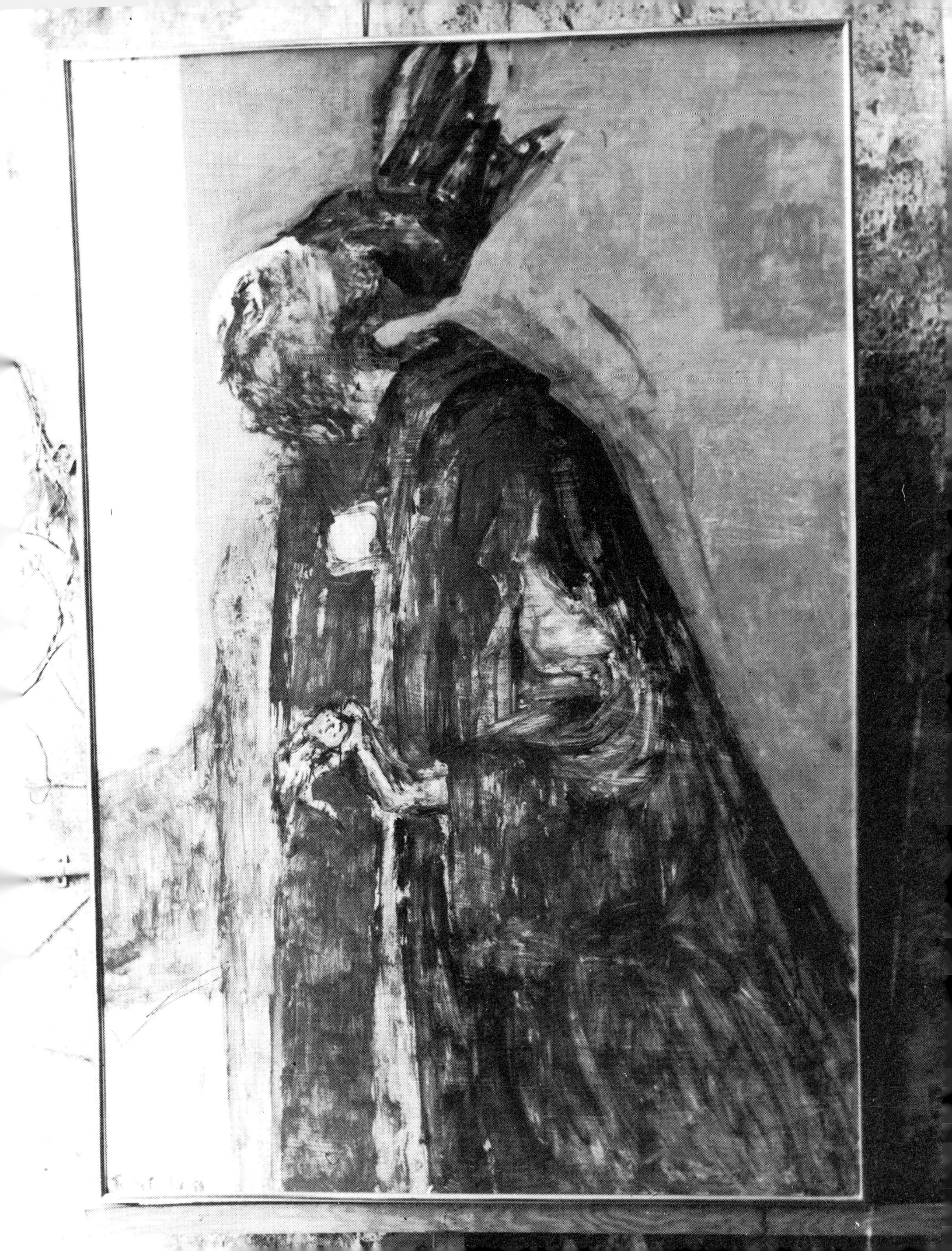

COPY

29 August 1963

Dear Dame Edith:

I hear in a round about way that you firmly dislike my paintings and drawings of you - although you saw only some of them and only fleetingly.

I am saddened by your attitude, which means that somehow my work (my kind of "gift" and my way of embodying it) must seem to you grossly offensive in intention. To presume any other reason for your reaction would be beneath my respect for you.

In consequence, it seemed to me important and urgent to put before you - a person I admire and would hate to distress - the argument which must make you see your mistake.

My argument is based on and resolved in this simple statement: as an artist, I am utterly SERIOUS in my work. My intentions are never those of a satirist, caricaturist or even a gentle mocker; and they can be clumsily summed up thus:

I yield to my instinctive "bent" and I "let go" towards an unpremeditated completion, which signals itself rather cajolingly and hesitantly, appealing to my often puzzled consciousness from "below", as it were; I paint (and draw) with tentative guidance of something undefined, which may be crudely called the theme's character; and I cut my exploratory path (I repeat without any derogatory or idealising preconceptions) until my instinct tells me that I arrived (or failed).

I do not need to tell you about this: how contemporary art has left the "portrait" behind and how common "academic" flatteries, or painting of "pattern and colour", embarrassed by the presence of a face within it, cannot claim the term. In my work, whether a composition or a portrait, I try, in contemporary terms and in utter gravity of purpose, to reinstate the human shape. And not because I persuaded myself this as a private or

-2-

fashionable "ideology", but because this is my "VOCATION" impossible to resist.

One more point. I draw many drawings from a model and paint my "portraits" out of these and of my memory of the person, on my own. Thus I can work on painting as such, free from the bounds of overpowering reality.

And so I painted my paintings of you - I assure you my only prompting to do them was a sort of elation at this marvellous theme - yourself. The sufficient testimonial of this is in the number of my attempts - first painting having started the very day after your visit.

Never, never any slightest notion of disparagement (or that these paintings can be taken as such) entered my head. In fact, the paintings and drawin s are liked, respected and often held in awe!

Yours sincerely,

My letter to Dame Edith Sitwell

42 GREENHILL
HAMPSTEAD
LONDON, N.W.3

7 September: 1963

Dear Mr. Topolski,

I was much moved by your very generous letter.

I should have answered it immediately I received it, but only the day before, I emerged from hospital after a very serious attack of pneumonia.

It is quite untrue that I do not admire and sympathise with your work (I had seen a great deal of this long before I came to your studio,) I sympathise with it, and I understand, I think I may say, the ethics of it.

The one exception (and that is neither your fault nor mine) was your portrait of me — and that was for personal reasons. When I was nine years old, my extremely tiresome parents got it into their [illegible] noddles that I am deformed (I have a slight curvature of the spine, which makes me stoop, and have extremely

2

delicate bones,) They incarcerated me, therefore, in a sort of Bastille of iron, from my shoulders to the soles of my feet. Even my nose did not escape their attentions. Only my hands did, for some unexplainable reason.

This imprisonment of my spine and ankles, made me accident-prone, apart from everything else.

One never recovers from the experiences of such a childhood, (lasting from nine to seventeen years old) therefore I am super-sensitive in some matters.

It would be a very great pleasure to me to see you again, if you can stand seeing a crippled old lady. (Owing to my Bastille-experiences, I cannot, at this time, move without being lifted.)

You must, please, forgive me. I now realise exactly what you were doing.

3

42 GREENHILL
HAMPSTEAD
LONDON, N.W.3

I know how busy you must be. But it would be such a great pleasure to me if you could find time to ring up and suggest an evening (5.30–6h) to come and have a glass of sherry with me.

I shall hope very much to see you.

Incidentally, I believe you know my young nephew Francis, — a great admirer of yours.

Thank you again for your generous letter.

With my best wishes
Yours sincerely,
Edith Sitwell

Reply from Dame Edith

(entirely false as visual information) to each of the 'subjects'. A few reacted quite violently: but only from amongst the oldest (similarly to GBS some years earlier); a reaction caused, plainly, not by vanity, but by a preserved/treasured mirror-view of themselves, still existing with the help of grimaces and wishful memory – challenged by what to me was a living face, but to them the kept-at-bay face of disaster – in short, the feared evocation of death.

I heard of Edith's discomfort and, upset, I wrote to her.

And her reply cleared the air, friendly invitations following.

John Osborne still partly an actor – thus clean-shaven: his restless intelligence badly served by prim baby mouth and inadequate chin. With actor's skill, he eventually and permanently corrected these deficiencies and made himself up into a handsome bearded 'character', an author.

Aldous Huxley: seldom in London, an apparition – stretching from floor-to-ceiling in this indifferent Kensington room – of idealized Englishness: contrived (not of current reality) by an overseas imagination; in other words he, as most often with transplanted Englishmen (though none equalling his grade of flamboyance), must have grown overstated in the Californian sun.

The framework was given: extreme length, down to his fingertips, the handsomeness of the facial set-up; but: an amalgam of postures/gestures, cross-leggednesses, clad in a miraculously cut white flannel suit cum very male jewellery cum a thick-knotted, clearly made-for-him, Union Jack-crossed necktie.

He sits loosely, with wrists/ankles performing miracles (as if never done before in any London clubroom) of gentlemanly harmonious ease.

But all this is not yet the essence of the Aldous Huxley of today: he is *old* – his clothing's effect merely faultless, but his head/face wrought to perfection: only the innocuous-English-young-male looks have this ability to reach a senescent beauty. His, again, is beyond imaginings: the near-mummified bone-stretched features present a purified disincarnation.

And this visual epitome of fleeting-away English-led civilization speaks beautifully out of that near-past. There is a conversation but I, engrossed in what I see, draw by the dozen, barely involved.

He died not long after. And soon, at some gathering, Lady Huxley, the wife of Julian his brother, rushed at me distressed and almost accusing: that ill-informing black-and-white photograph of my painting of him sent routinely by Texas University had shaken him terribly, and – she insisted – had contributed to his demise. I could see that this uniquely imaginative mind- (not eye-) stretching man, knowing himself to be exceptionally endowed physically, might have reacted violently to my way of reflecting his purified-by-age beauty – a blow to his habit-settled self-view.

Stephen Spender's political see-sawing – yet always with an aura of self-righteousness (supported by his convincing looks), particularly when at some point seeming in step with the US Department of State – was alien to me, never given to 'convictions', unable by nature to follow a dogma. Political converts' mentalities, that is, the mentalities of those who must be propped up by fearsome always earnestly reasoned beliefs, their former ones as well as those arrived at by *volte-face*: they (Koestler prominent amongst them) are demonstratively of fluent intelligence; and so their 'disappointments', leading them to the enemy camp, do not sound convincing: being 'contracted' they should have anticipated and been prepared to step into revolutionary power-fields.

Rebecca West: I respected her high-journalism, she in her country house was impressive; and I felt that I could show her the final portrait with impunity.

But at my studio, facing it, she exploded; astonished and perplexed I could not grasp the source of her reaction. Possibly, if I had known more, as every reader of her son Anthony West does now, that 'scene' might have developed further; as it was, I silently received what came, stunned and in consequence still puzzled. My guesses rested then on a perverse cause of her disapproval: she resented, I decided, a certain pedestalization, the move from straight 'naturalness'

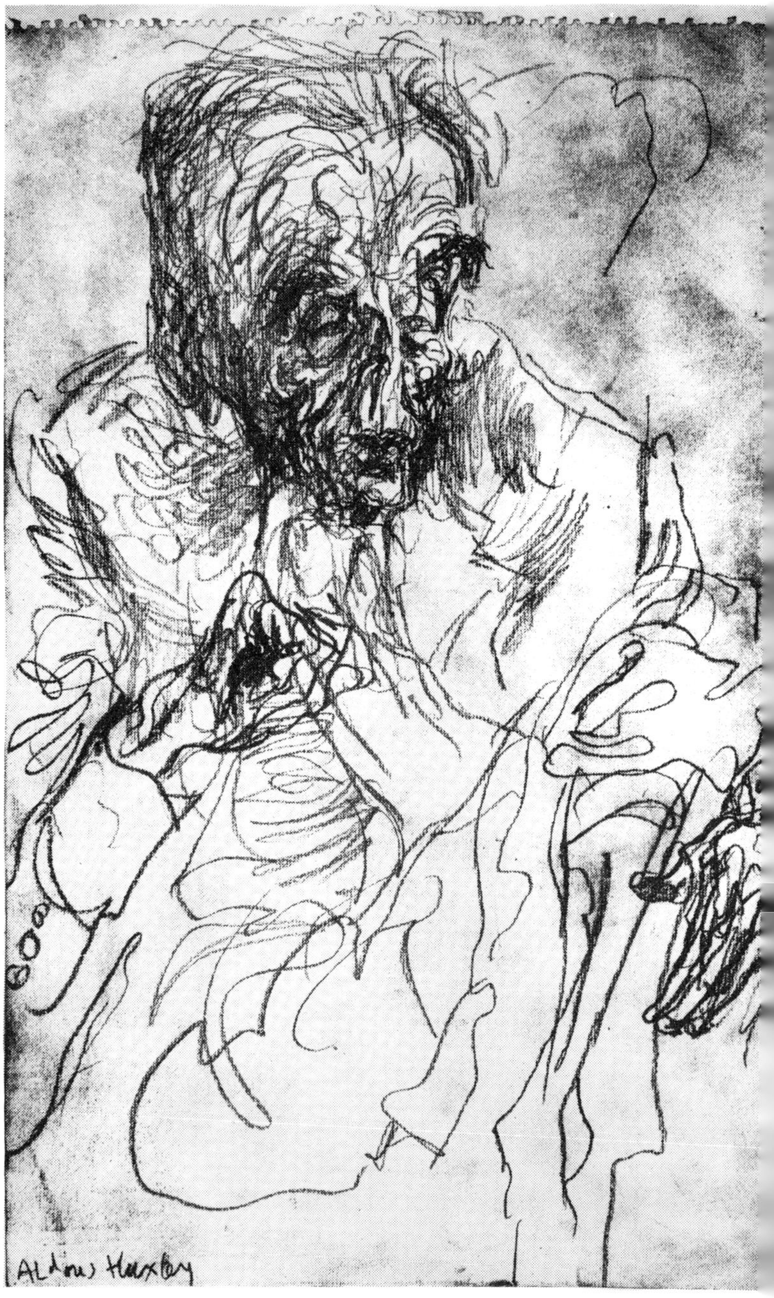

Aldous Huxley (from *Topolski's Chronicle*)

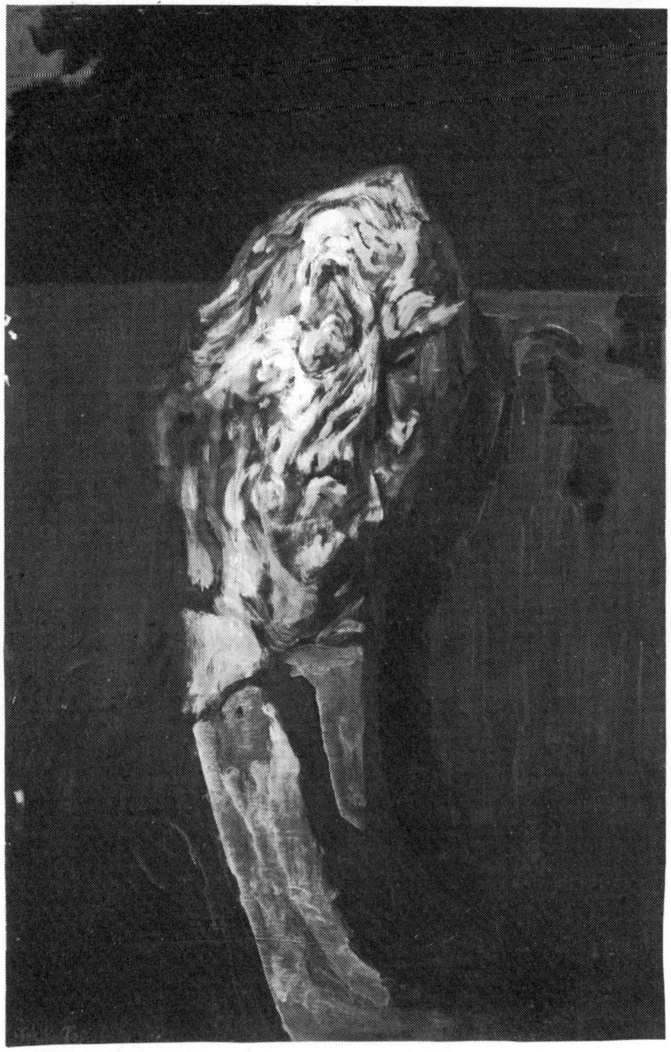

Graham Greene

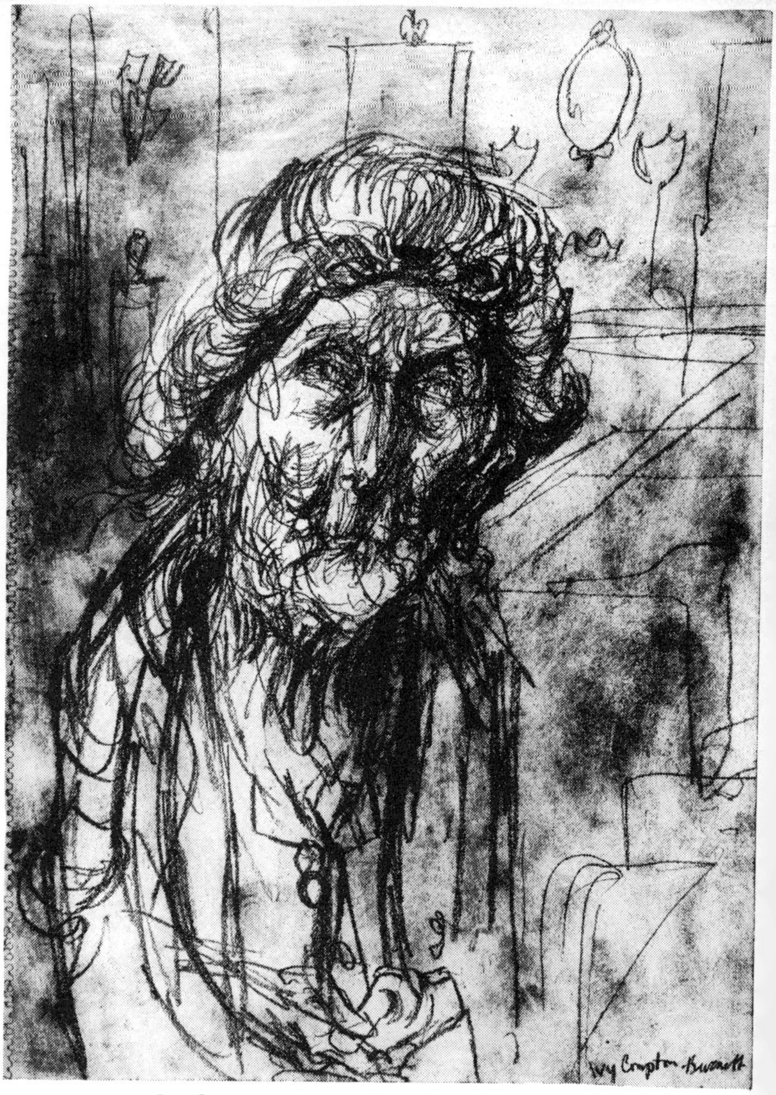

Ivy Compton Burnett (from *Topolski's Chronicle*)

in my portrait to allegory-tainted panegiricism, nothing to do with making her ugly or old . . . Could this be it?

Graham Greene, in friendly relations since my early days in England, was drawn by me more than once – but every time I was made to feel indebted at the exceptionality of the privilege.

Ivy Compton-Burnett predictably treated me to high tea amongst her velvets and laces.

C. P. Snow's steep bulk, round the corner from her.

Cyril Connolly's impatient bulldog's intelligence. But he was anyway woven into my London life. And, gratifyingly, approving of my version of him.

J. B. Priestley – tired, spent.

E. M. Forster: never met but sketched at his prelection, without him knowing it, at the Aldeburgh Festival.

Robert Graves: drawn during a reading of his. He was impossible to pin down at his rare stays in London, but once we bumped into each other at Regent's Park gates: hesitant almost-recognition, almost-acknowledgement. But, tripped by surprise – his must have been a similar predicament – we paused face-to-face but walked off. His formidable presence, appropriately costumed, daunted me as well, without doubt.

T. S. Eliot: almost as awed as the rest of the youngsters round him I once sat with him at Bertorelli's in Charlotte Street – a focal locality of pre-war Bohemia (eating as against the Café Royal's beer – or coffee-sipping) – but, not a worshipper, somewhat distanced from the master-disciples' aura. I chanced on him in the fifties on an underground train and began to sketch at a distance even before realizing who was this uncharming, haughty, black-homburged, black-coated city gent, attracted by his obvious rush-hour contrast with the subordinate and indifferent secretarial breed round him. This resulted in a largish painting-invention of a ceremonially red-robed Eliot in an honour-giving scene.

Herbert Read came, sat, gave out a smooth appreciation, groomed, anointed as he was for the inquisitorial papacy of the modernist art-church triumphant.

W. H. Auden: unyielding to me, posing from behind the exclusivity barrier, highly familiar to me but never experienced so blatantly before, of the English assumption, unassailable through parochial ignorance, of superiority to most of the foreign breeds and most layers of their own.

John Betjeman: in his little old crumbling nest stuck persistently into the concretions of markets and offices.

William Empson: I never even tried to follow his rapid academy-cum-wit pronouncements – I accepted on hearsay

Opposite: J. B. Priestley

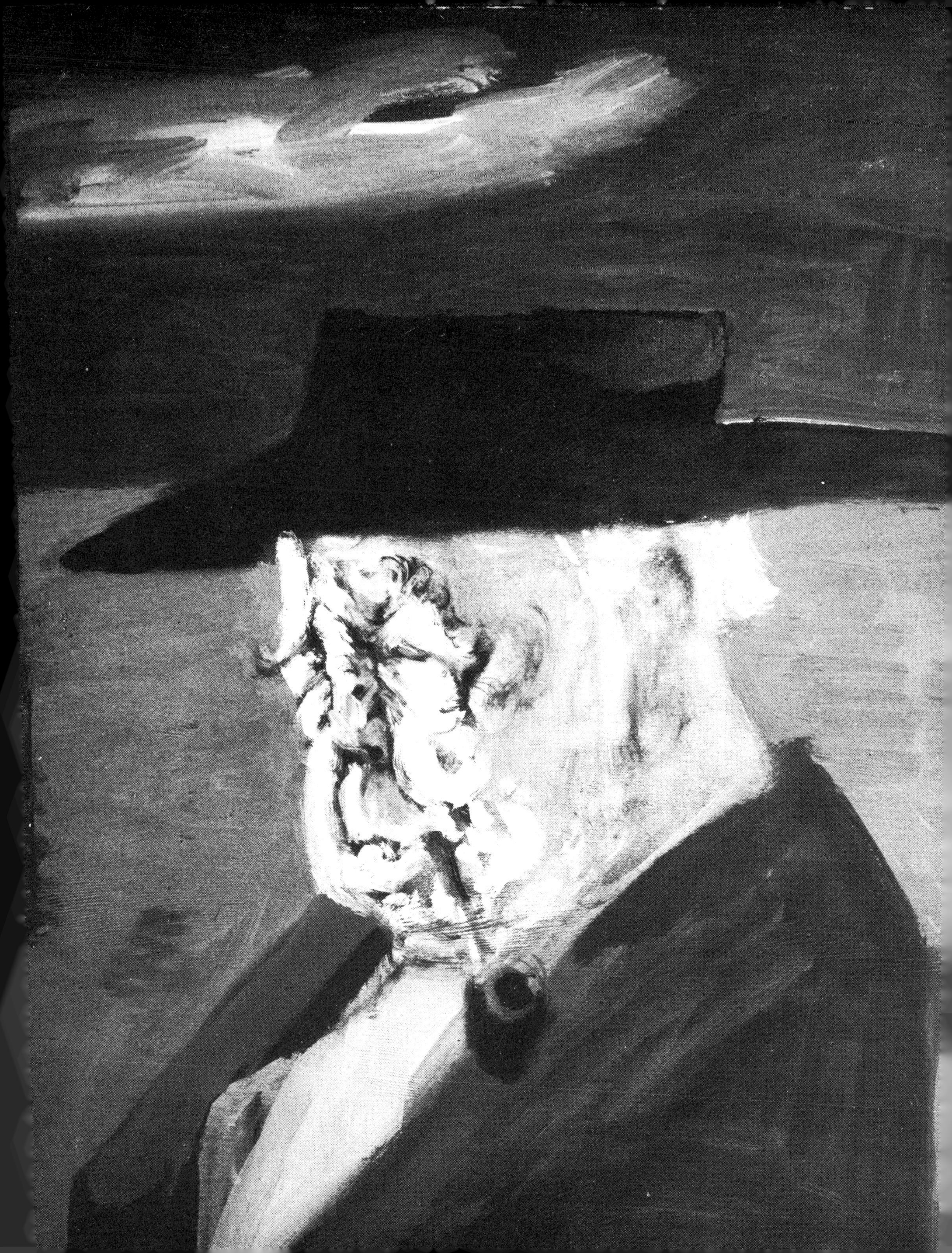

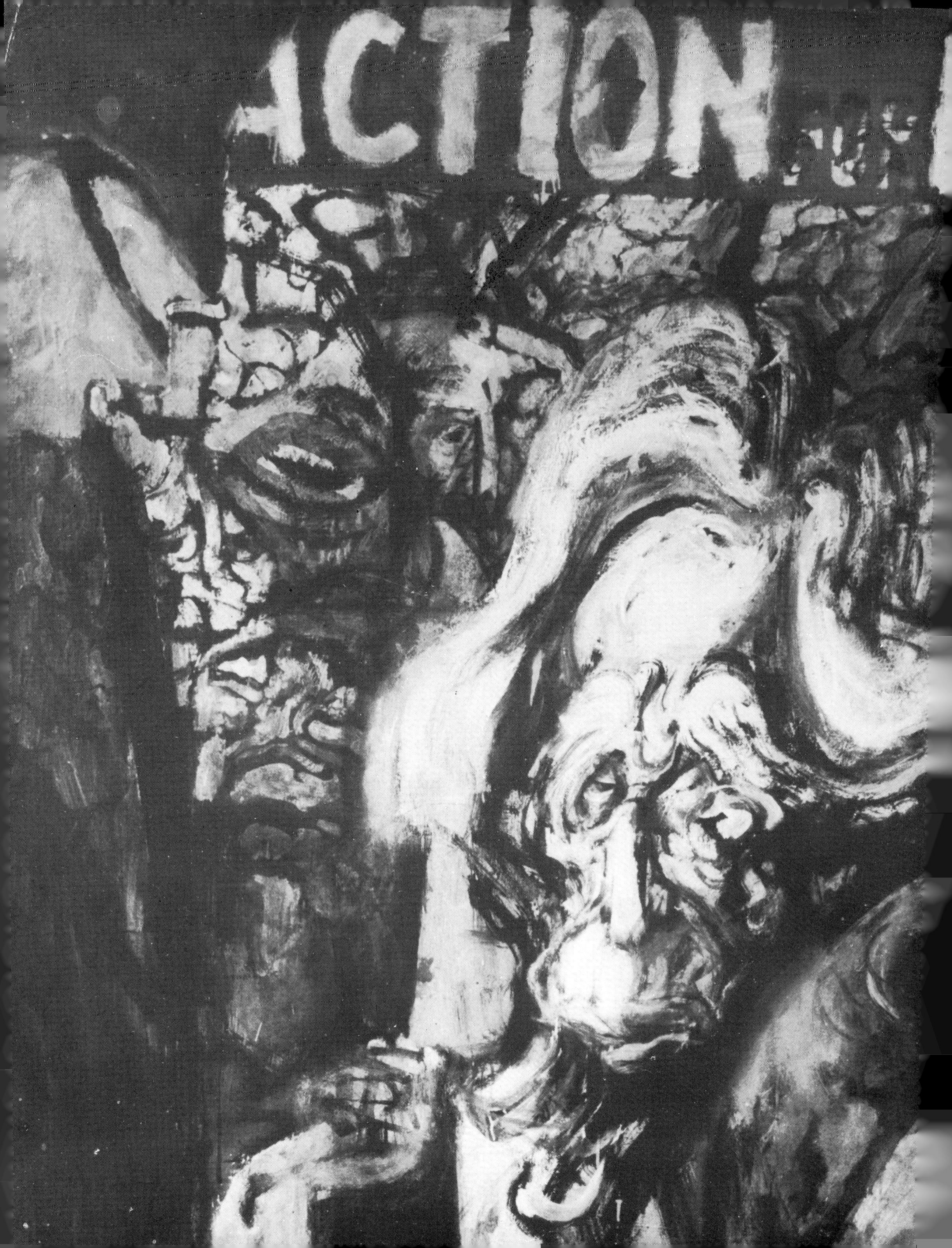
ACTION

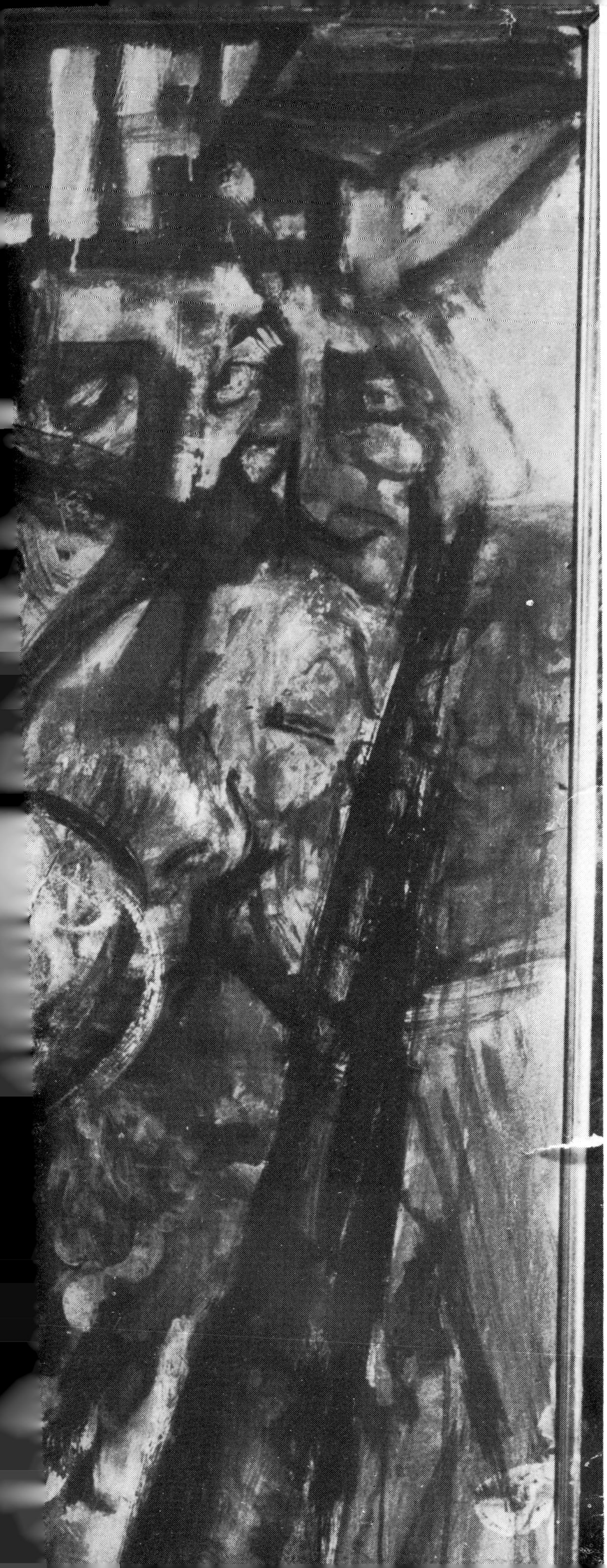

From: The Earl Russell, O.M., F.R.S.
PLAS PENRHYN.
PENRHYNDEUDRAETH.
MERIONETH.
TEL. PENRHYNDEUDRAETH 242.
25 September 1960

Felix Topolski,
Arch 158 Sutton Walk,
London, S.E.1.

Dear Felix Topolski,

The rapidity with which we are moving towards a nuclear calamity convinces me that events are moving too quickly for the present policy of our Campaign. It is my conviction that the effectiveness of our Campaign is becoming dependent upon its endorsing a programme of civil disobedience.

I am going to make a statement at the first suitable opportunity expressing the hope that the Campaign will become convinced of the necessity of such a programme.

I should like to ask your support in carrying this into action. A group of one hundred persons called "The Committee of 100" - for civil disobedience against nuclear warfare - is being formed and I should be grateful if you would join me on it. Could you favour me with an early reply?

Yours sincerely,

Bertrand Russell

Bertrand Russell

Letter from Bertrand Russell

COPY

14 Hanover Terrace,
Regent's Park,
London, N.W.1.

10th October 1960

The Earl of Russell, OM.,FRS.,
Plas Penrhyn,
Penrhyndeudraeth,
Merioneth.

Dear Lord Russell,

I apologise for the delay, due to my absence from London, in replying to your letter.

You will perceive from the enclosed broadsheet, which I published recently, and from the earlier 'Confessions', that I am a side-liner; a pictorial recorder of history made by others.

My instinctive need, supported by life-long practice, to watch and DRAW has withered away my action-urge potential. Being in the thick of 'it' would force me to drop the pencil to free my hands for weapons or banners - this, I must not do.

I am a professional by vocation, by which I mean that there is no citizen or revolutionary reformer above my artist self, and that I have no leisure. I assure you that I find no smug satisfaction in this confinement.

I hope you will not file my refusal amongst the mental dodgers and physical cowards.

Yours sincerely,

Feliks Topolski

Reply to Bertrand Russell

Opposite: Bertrand Russell: detail
(from collection at University of Texas, Austin)

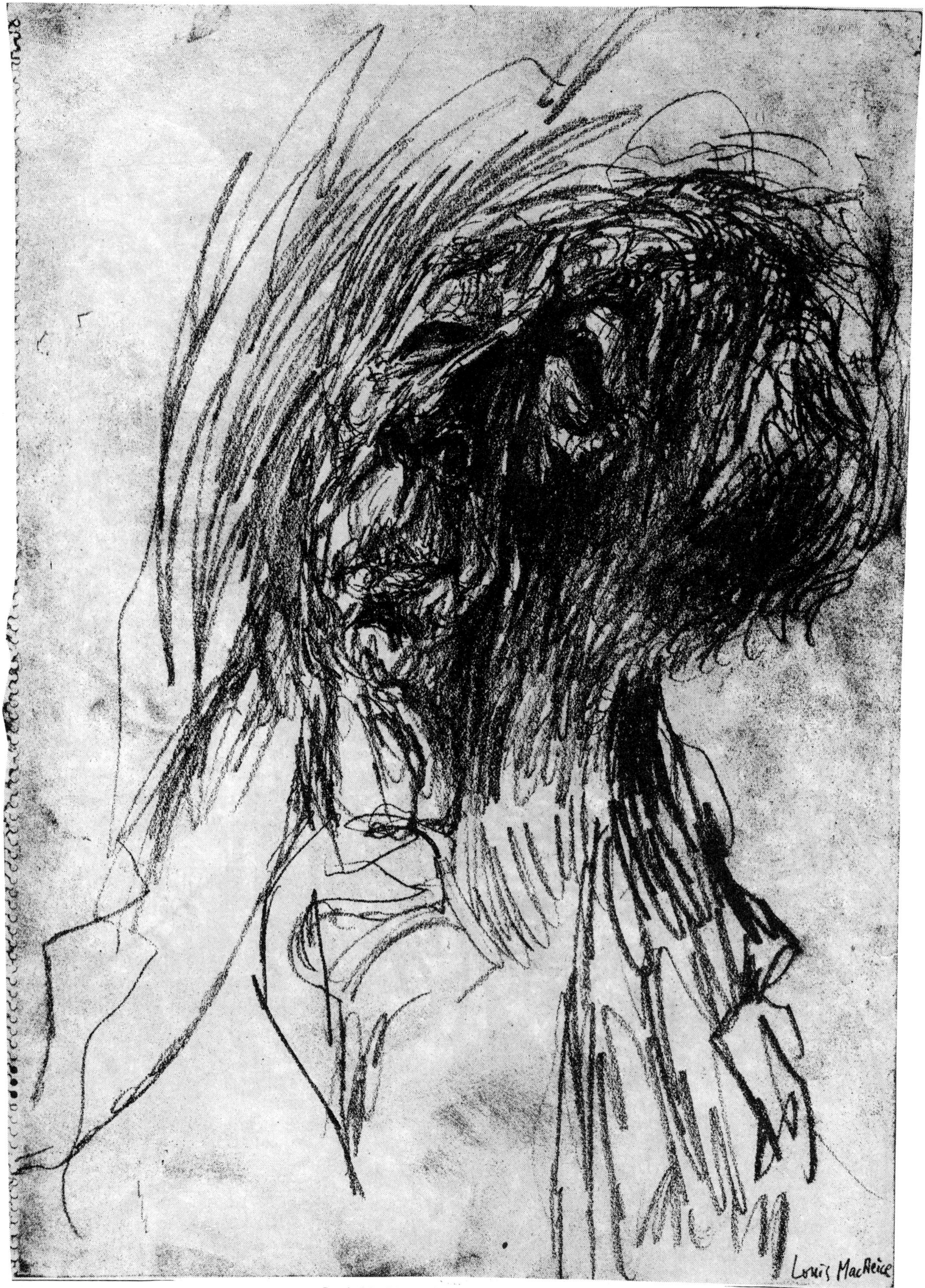

Louis MacNeice (from *Topolski's Chronicle*)

their profundity cum humour. When he posed for me my eye was not on his performing lips but aimed below at his then mandarin beard, springing from under his jaw, acquired in Peking whence just back. I felt fully comfortable with Hetta his wife, and the boys.

Hetta, soon after the war, posed in the nude at my studio for Clement Davenport and me: Clement's idea that we should refresh our draughtsmanship. Hetta, having never done this before, trembled all over reclination at first, thus implanting flesh-awareness on to her remarkable South Africa-moulded monumentality. With the years she developed her innate dominance – an impressive stomping far from motherly personage. Thus the boys, engulfed between these two originals, had to take command, aiming at normalness.

Louis MacNeice: my friendship bridged over into the next generation: he (his poetic Irish face and containment), Hedli Anderson (his wife – a *chanteuse* of reddest hair and whitest shoulders, bared by the Victorian dresses of the Players' Theatre) – and their daughter Corinna, of the tiniest hardest bottom on a girl.

Two homely anecdotes, as usually here far separated in time: in the early fifties Hedli asked me to draw her for a poster to announce her 'evening'. In the midst of this not-easy request (it has to 'please' her public) Andrzej Zamoyski broke in: he disturbed us – and more. He was a strong tall man; once, long before the war at his Kidlington farm outside Oxford, we playfully wrestled and once again, as puzzlingly often in my schooldays, I, smallish, got the bigger man down on his shoulders, thus winning – an episode which stayed in our respective memories. By this time he had moved far into what was to me lovable eccentricity, to his relations insanity – soon after certified; and so, my impatience with the interruption produced an unprecedented thus unexpected attack: from behind he twisted my right arm painfully backwards. I still held my charcoal, anxious to get on with the drawing rather than to have my hand dislocated; this would have happened if I had tried to break his by then very determined grip, I bearing in my mind but not disclosing a belief that his action echoed the not-quite-buried grudge.

I was never given to bottom-smacking but, when Corinna with a few other colleagues from the Slade (including the daughter of Gorky, the painter, now the wife of Stephen Spender's son) helped me at my studio with a complicated pasting-together of 36-foot-long prints of harmonica-drawings of a continuous train journey through China for my *Chronicle*, this one time, simultaneously with shame, I could not resist the challenge of this uniqueness.

I presume that we are friends now: recently we even did a picture together (in it I painted her in the hippy outfit of the day; and also, in the nude, leaping/flying; she hieroglyphically filling the in-between); and I possess one of her large part-self-portraits.

But Louis? A lot of drawings and a painting (all romantic, unusually for me) came out of his sitting for me.

I persuaded Texas to give the twentieth painting to a group of younger writers of my choice: John Osborne, John Whiting, Arnold Wesker, Shelagh Delaney.

Shelagh Delaney: then a hope-feeding impressive 'natural' from the North – a plain attractively shaped and explicit girl. She was at my studio, with several people present (my open day), being drawn, when Brendan Behan entered (door open) – large, shapeless, drink-sodden – claimed brusquely his right, and walked out – she wordlessly in tow.

Now to the Labour Party Shadow Cabinet.

Anthony Greenwood: a contemporary and a friend since my early England, charming, well-meaning, but (or because of this) dominated by his Ministry's departmental officials – as I experienced when pleading for the saving of an enchanting mid-nineteenth-century departure-for-overseas inn, unlike any other, overhanging the river at Gravesend.

George Brown, Deputy Leader: at his desk, irritable, self-centred, ungracious power-man.

Herbert Bowden, Chief Opposition Whip: probably an efficiently cold executor-professional.

Ray Gunter, Shadow Minister of Labour: he seemed to me a compromise trade-unionist choice: that is not because outstanding/wise/courageous, but the safest fit into the obligatory TUC pigeon-hole.

James Callaghan, Shadow Chancellor of the Exchequer: courteous and alert; but at this height and period, the career politician to the fore.

Patrick Gordon-Walker, Shadow Foreign Secretary: an endearing person – wise and seeming driven by convictions, not ambition; thus another of those best equipped to be entrusted with power, yet soon muscled out.

Denis Healey, Shadow Minister of Defence: to me, in possession of all the virtues required. After Gordon-Walker the best man of them all to converse with.

Harold Wilson, Leader of the Opposition: his rooms on some decisive day: the anteroom filled with secretarial ladies – Marcia Williams, a dominant posture and good tall blonde looks; the inner battle-command room agitation (messages by phone/mouth come in at speed – why don't I remember the exact issue?). Yet he manages to deal with me as well, though with, as I think, a usual-for-him haste and divided attention. Then there is an explosion of triumph – the 'vibes' that reach me are not comparable to the joy of a sporting/war victory, but rather to the coming-off of a calculated banking (or Mafia?) transaction, with a touch of bluff just kept under cover.

Tony Benn: He was not on my list then and unkindly gossip passed on his disapproval of my portraits, contributing to their dismissal.*

But recently, in 1984, he was brought to my studio and I drew – not well (his good looks and energetic discourse fuelled by Teresa unhelpful) and so, in some exasperation,

*To this request from **the Labour Party** to draw portraits of **the Shadow Cabinet** to accompany their pre-election television broadcasts modelled on the *Face to Face* programmes I objected with the warning that my portrait drawings tend to overcharacterize, thus would not be useful as propaganda; however, they insisted, and I liked the chance of having lined up in close-up the probable rulers of the country: and so I offered to do it free of charge, the drawings remaining my property.

As I predicted, the results were not used – such pathetic criticisms seeping through to me as Wilson's complaining about his eyes 'drawn too close' – and worse: when *The Sunday Times* wanted to reproduce some of them, there came a refusal on the basis of the Party's ownership of the publication rights, though there was no monetary transaction involved.

However, on the eve of the next election *The Sunday Times* supplement featured the story and the selection of portraits. And, of course, my *Chronicle* did this too.

TOO CLOSE FOR COMFORT

How Yesterday's Men (vintage 1963) commissioned drawings of themselves by Feliks Topolski which proved not quite beautiful enough. For the full story, see page 19

Ray Gunter

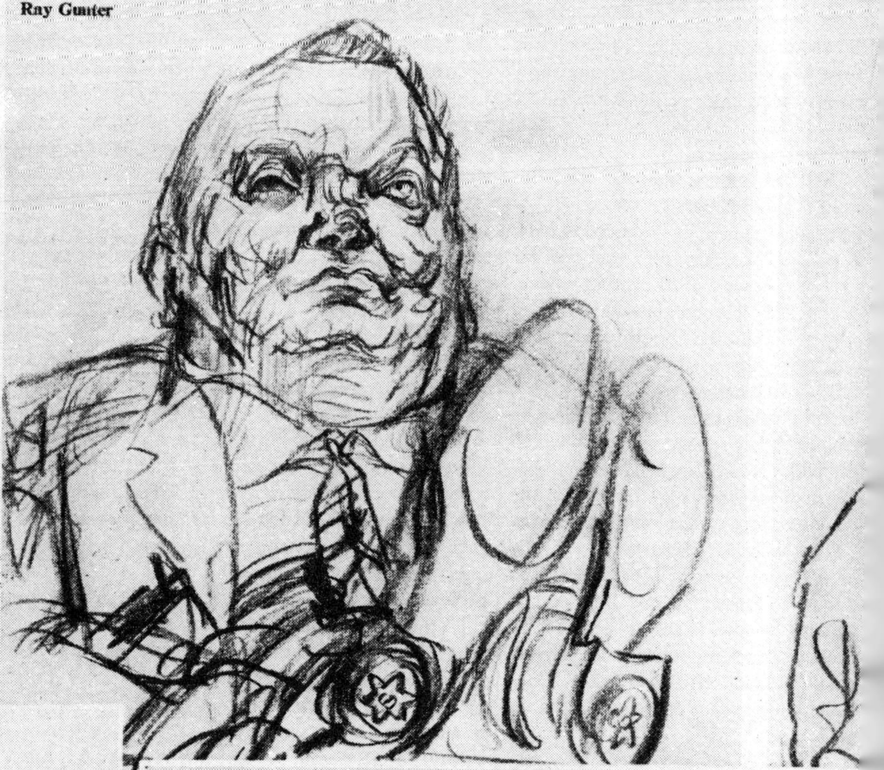

Harold Wilson

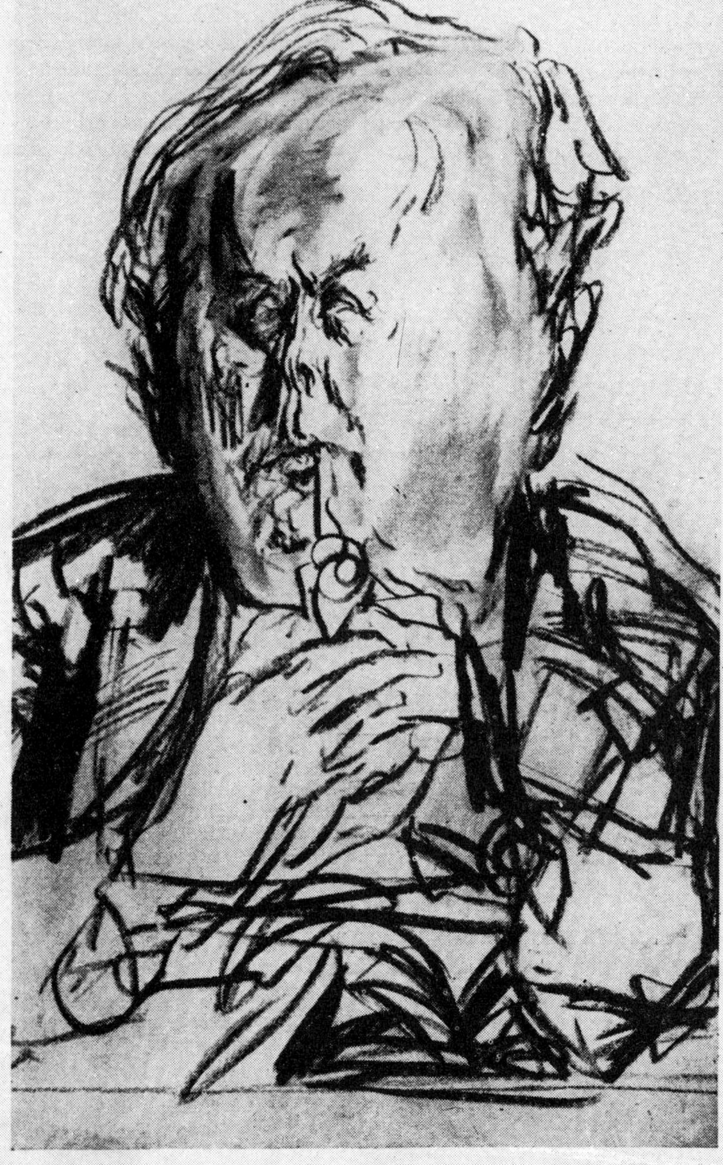

Herbert Bowd

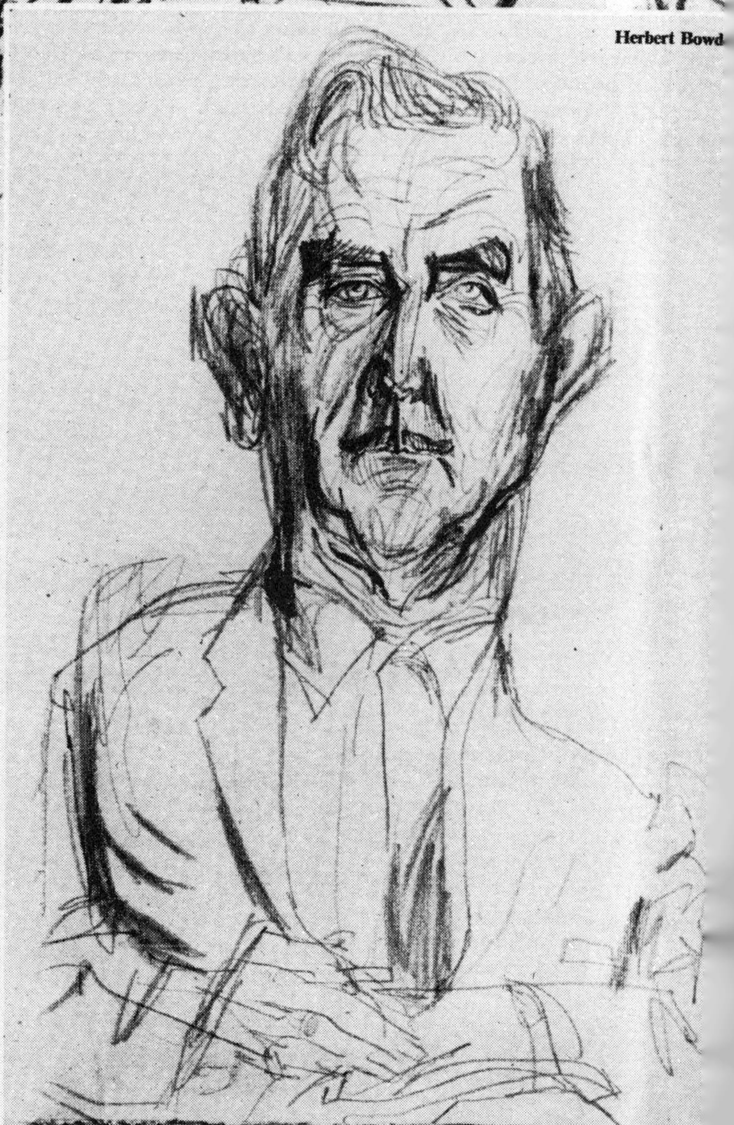

Denis Healey

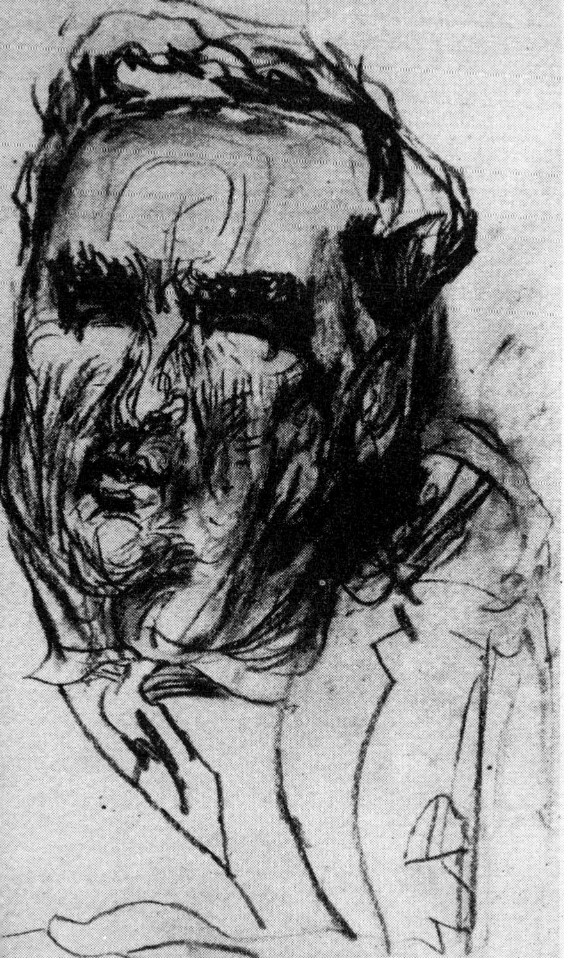

James Callaghan

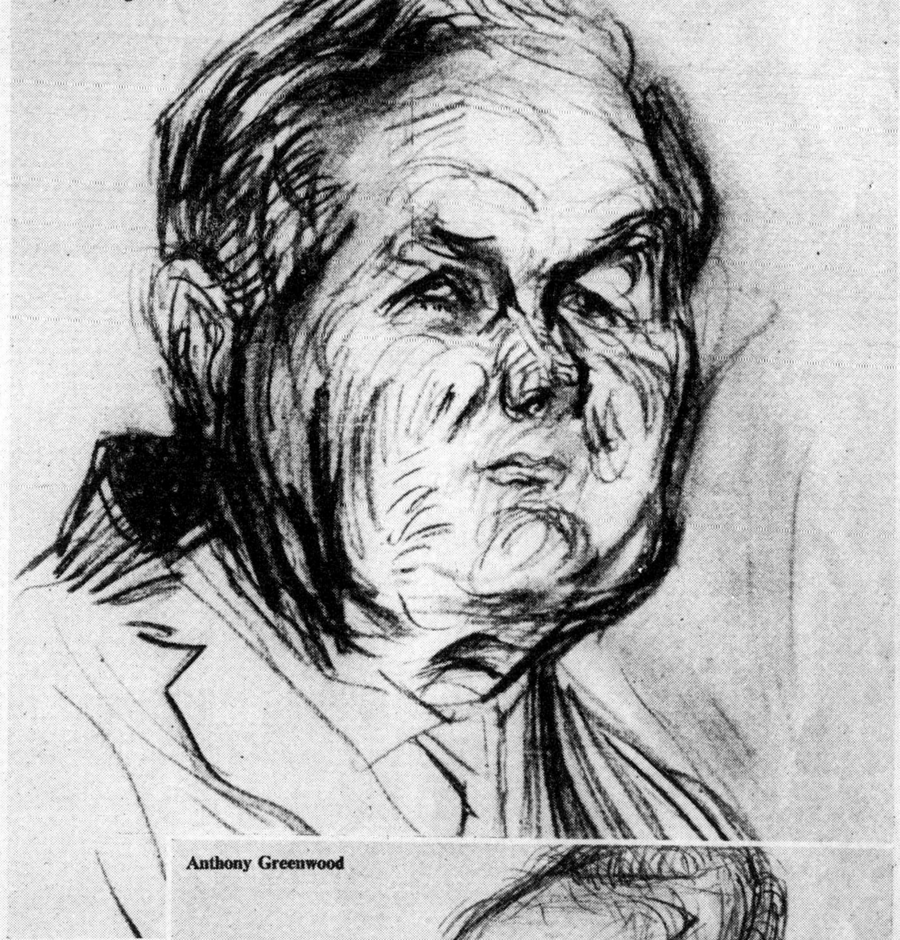

Anthony Greenwood

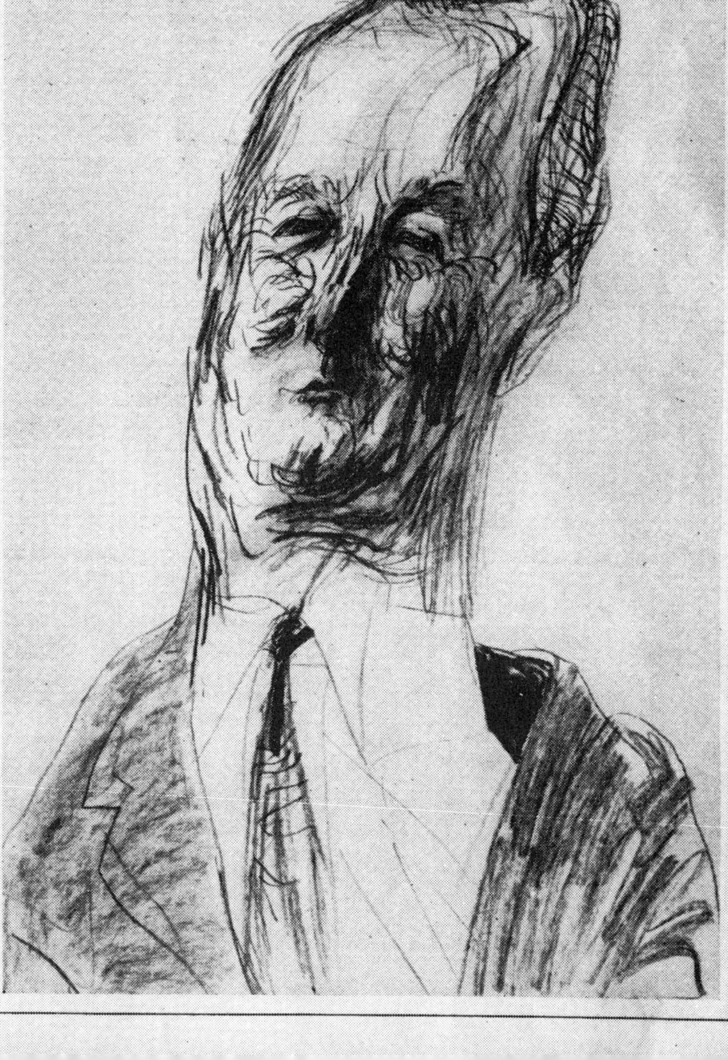

George Brown

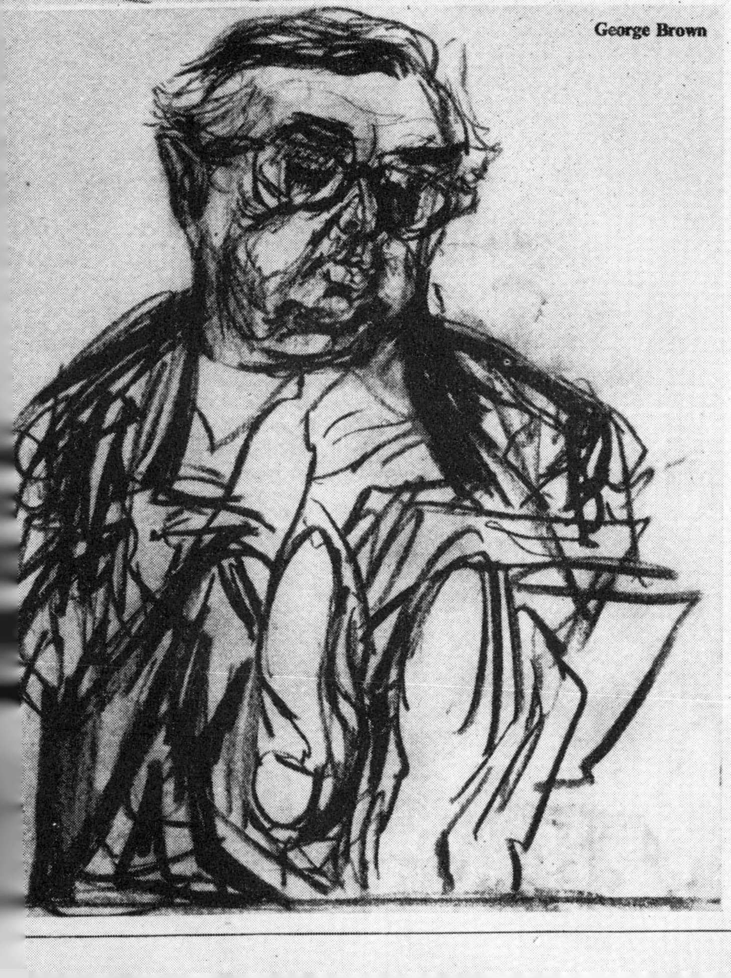

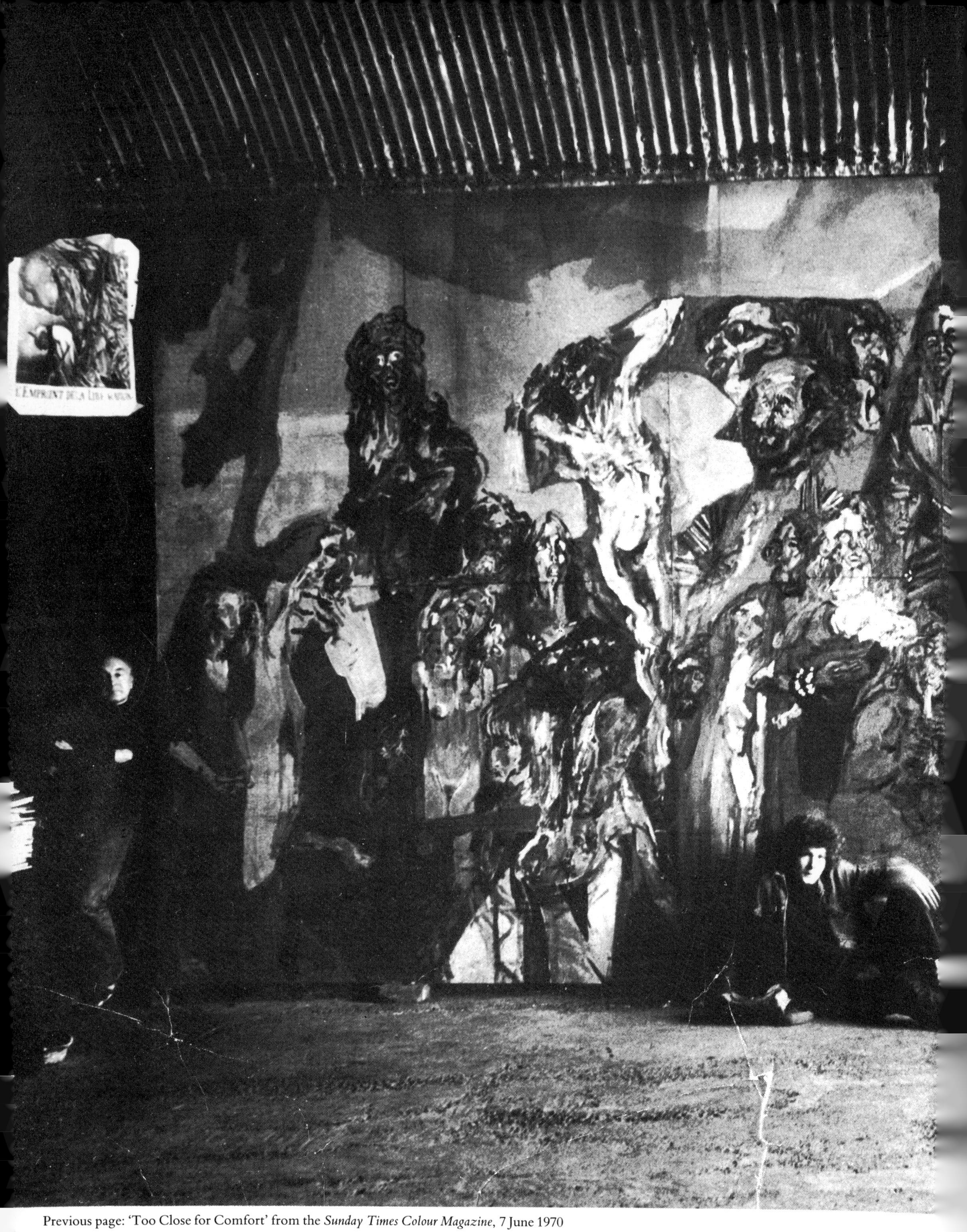

Previous page: 'Too Close for Comfort' from the *Sunday Times Colour Magazine*, 7 June 1970

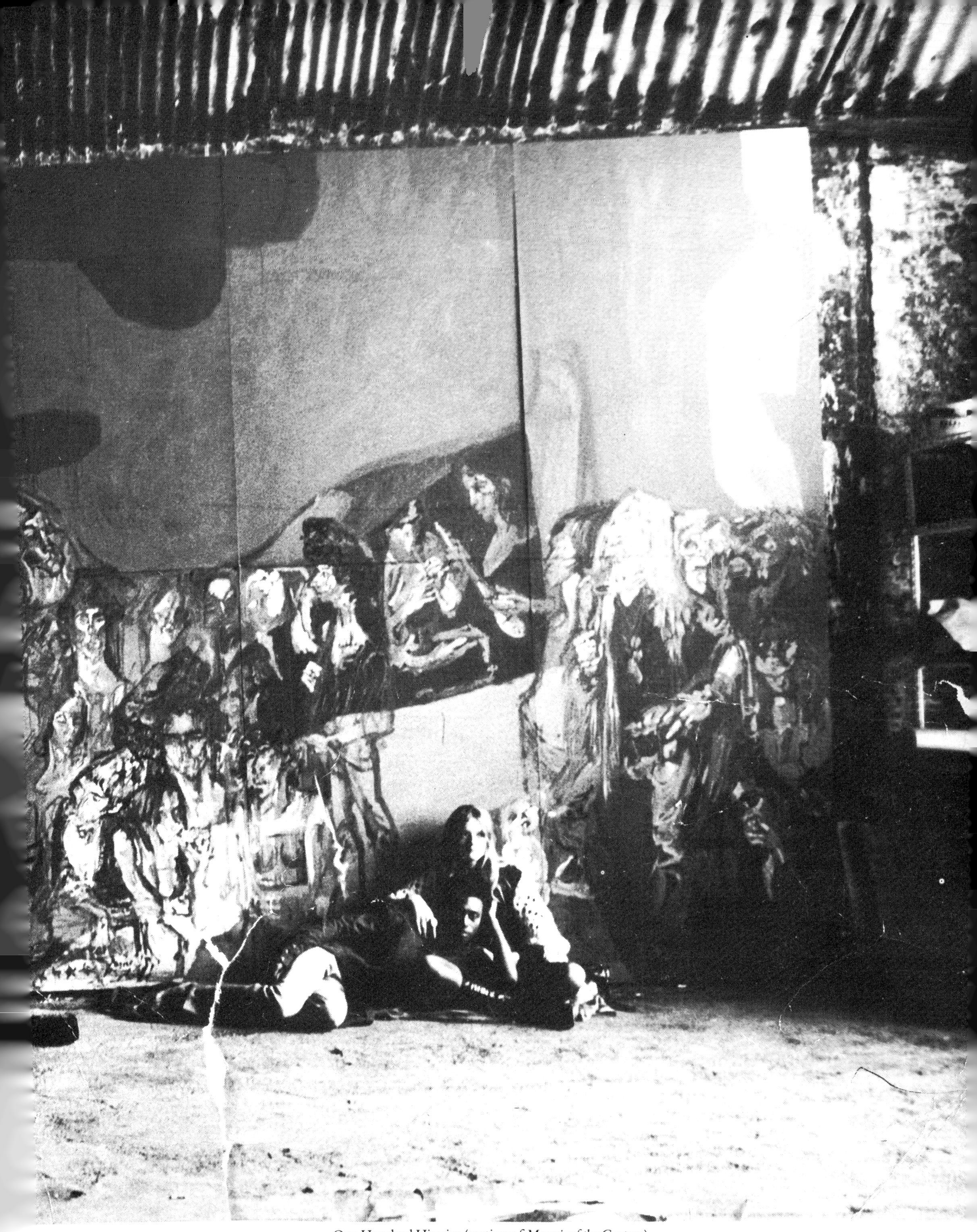

One Hundred Hippies (section of *Memoir of the Century*)

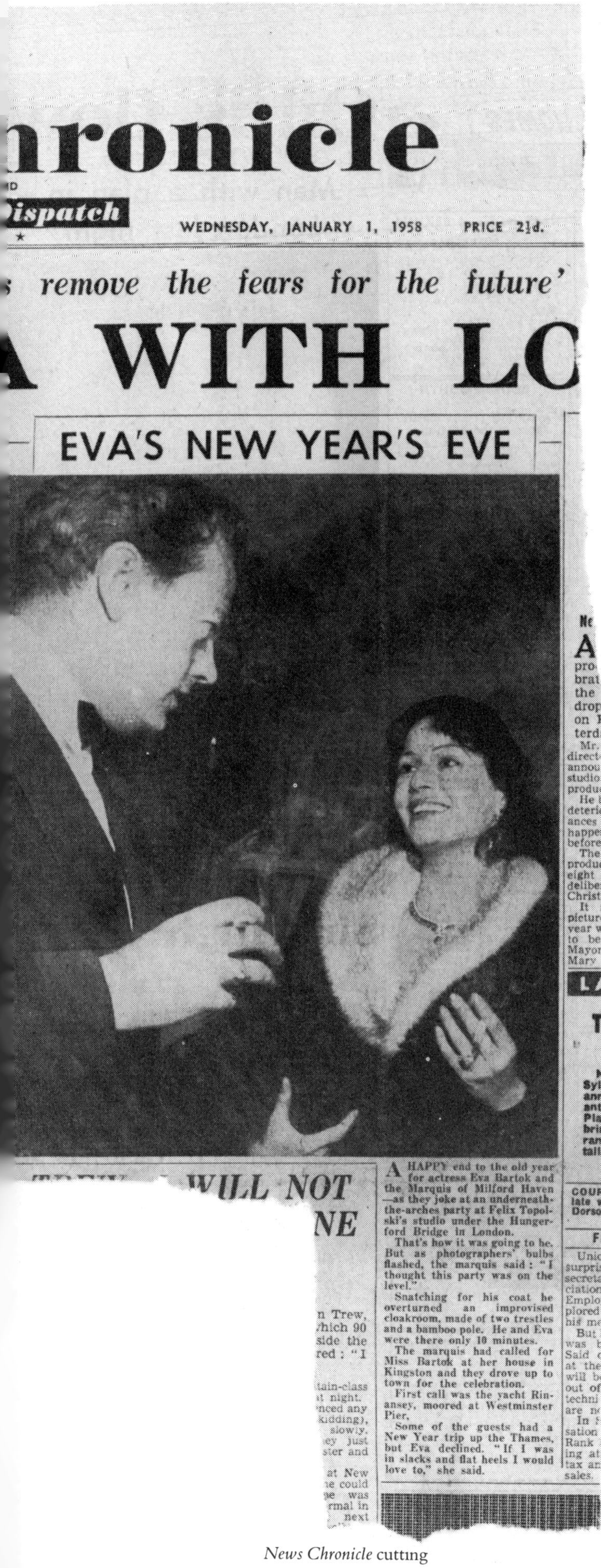
ronicle

Dispatch

WEDNESDAY, JANUARY 1, 1958 PRICE 2½d.

remove the fears for the future'

A WITH LO

EVA'S NEW YEAR'S EVE

WILL NOT

NE

A HAPPY end to the old year for actress Eva Bartok and the Marquis of Milford Haven—as they joke at an underneath-the-arches party at Felix Topolski's studio under the Hungerford Bridge in London.

That's how it was going to be. But as photographers' bulbs flashed, the marquis said: "I thought this party was on the level."

Snatching for his coat he overturned an improvised cloakroom, made of two trestles and a bamboo pole. He and Eva were there only 10 minutes.

The marquis had called for Miss Bartok at her house in Kingston and they drove up to town for the celebration.

First call was the yacht Rinansey, moored at Westminster Pier.

Some of the guests had a New Year trip up the Thames, but Eva declined. "If I was in slacks and flat heels I would love to," she said.

News Chronicle cutting

moved to painting, which worked. And his conversation was of the highest (and most honest) order. Is he going the way of other good men?

I gave the drawings and painting for his and Tony Banks's disposal and Banks (the initiator of the matter) presented the painting to the National Portrait Gallery, who promptly rejected it. And so a fuss ensued: papers, high and low, played up the story – next day *The Times* gave it a front-page mention, one of the leaders and an illustrated article on the court page. The Directors of the Gallery responded by declaring that Tony Benn, but not this painting, deserved inclusion in their collection.

Contradictory to Benn politically, yet a sort of parallel figure, outstandingly so in crusading spirit and intellectual alertness – Enoch Powell happened to pose for me not long before. Paradoxically, counter to socialist Benn's seigneurial aura, his blue conservatism is dressed classlessly (the colour/cut of his suit/shirt/tie featureless), as if deliberately to conceal what his face betrays: a fighter, perhaps self-suppressed.

There is no small talk: he is engaged to the full depth on each issue – and one is impressed by the range and the reasoning he masters, but applying a questionable pragmatism to his own 'platform' as if it were superimposed on an otherwise almost academic mind. Probed over his potential role as a 'patriotic' leader, he emerges again impressively, though unexpectedly this time, as a fanatical parliamentary democrat. And this must be honest, as the sole explanation why he has held back whenever tempted by short cuts. A dual figure? This most gifted and incorruptible member of Britain's parliament, yet also apostle to dangerous heresies, may be another incapacitated by his virtues.

Since, single head-and-shoulders portrait painting/drawing has thinned out, or has spread into group painting, the largest, *One Hundred Hippies*, growing over a period – of full-length (actually larger than life-size: seven to eight feet tall) 'characters'. Perhaps it was a play-marginality, stretching/gathering energies for the assault on the labyrinthian enormity to come. These images have never stopped materializing – new, most often nameless, personages appearing.

But having been enmeshed by the rigour of portraiture convention, I hasten to claim my independence of it: my galloping drawing always deals with people, trapping in, coincidentally, hundreds of shapes/faces, some of which may carry notoriety of sorts – and, even if not, certainly by my standards not in a lesser category: they have in them a latent potential for inclusion into my synthesizing works. As in my painting, so generally in my writing, but these 'celebrities' smuggled themselves on to these pages through the false-to-me prestigiousness of the term 'portrait'. In accord with my ingrained *alla-prima* ways, thus inability to rework my painting, I let these 'descriptive' passages of text stay.

Chelsea/Belgravia periodically spews cliquey 'sets'. **'The Chelsea Set'** of the end of the fifties carried on some impetus fed by the participation of one of the bridesmaids at the Queen's wedding, and culminating yearly in meticulous preparations crowned by a thematically costumed New Year's Eve festivity – each staged in a different challengingly unusual ambience, 'daringly' away from the dull convention of hotel ballrooms.

One was held at my studio-arch packed with people of so-called distinction dancing on my working tables, Tony, then Armstrong Jones, photographing, some Lambeth boys breaking in, and – with the party still bouncing on – the sellers of 'popular' papers bringing the morning editions carrying on front pages the occasion's apparent sensation, not even noticed by me in the crowd: headlines and photographs of the Marquis of Milford Haven in dance embraces of reconciliation with his errant Hungarian cinema star girlfriend.

This gallivanting is recorded here only to introduce another commission round 1959–60 involving further dabbling in portraiture: a new hotel, **the Carlton Tower**, its interiors 'glowing' in the American sumptuousness of the day, borne to giant measure in its Rib Room in the English pub convention of walls tightly covered with drawings/prints – my *Chronicle*'s ironed out/framed pages, and also originals, these mostly on theatrical themes: all in all some 200 pictures.

The entrance lobby's main wall was made of my horrid mural on painted glass, as demanded: the minor lobbies, corridors, suites, bars carried the overflows of my paintings/drawings/prints; but the hotel's more refined Chelsea Room restaurant was designed round a series painted for it of full-length compositions roughly on the theme of Chelsea ladies – most of the models belonging to the New Year's Eve balls 'set'. But not only: to round up the needed twenty, I added friends from other spheres.

A few of the twenty Chelsea Room subjects:

Two imposingly structured sisters – Sonia Melchett and Bunty Kinsman – the undisputed activators/arbiters of the Chelsea Set.

Recruited into the series as accessible friends from outside 'the set':

Lady Massereene and Ferrard, for her exemplary white-complexioned Nordicity of detailing; Lady Astor for her inventive elegance, the upturned nose emergent from a wide-brimmed hat's shadows; Labour Party Minister Anthony Greenwood's teenage daughter – a protest-marcher slogan-board-holding; Princess Radziwiłł, Jacqueline Kennedy's sister, a smaller but equal version; Lady Lewisham (then), an eighteenth-century powder-pastel strikingly embossed on to the drabness of twentieth-century Sotheby-bidders; Lady Peek then (now Mrs Peter Quennell) representing to perfection society's Bahamian outposts; Suna Portman, later my rarity-model for a pile of nude drawings, almost all burnt in the studio's fire; Mrs Rosenthal, the English wife of the German porcelain-magnate – another conquest of foreign territories by British females, armed with well-boned eccentricities, well-mannered vices.

The whole Chelsea-set episode non-habit-forming. But there were also dancers, a horsey girl, anonymous King's Roaders – and *hors concours*, Vanessa Redgrave. She was then in her first modern West End play with her father Michael, but we decided on a Shakespearian persona, for which we rummaged Berman's.

I drew and painted Vanessa, unposing but circling over the studio podium and, self-consciousness dismissed, mouthing some song or other. Those 'professional' sessions over, we moved to friendship.

The Carlton Tower sets a dinner of compromises for **my seventieth birthday**. Within the Rib Roomful of my *Chronicles* – no one lifts the eyes or mentions them – an enormous table for twenty-four and authentically celebratory waiters. Perhaps the best of it, the initial drink with arrivals trickling in, somewhat in the silly/touching convention of *This is Your Life:* at random, figures of my time; but ingrained? valid?

Over the table hangs the hotel's PR anxiety: the *Times Diary* gentleman and his wife who studied art, the strapping chic Hicky vulgarian, the embittered *New York Times* has-been-pretty old girl, the two PR girls and the 'must', my Arab publisher, and wife; and my conditioned choices: Arabella Churchill, because she personifies my hippy period (but proves to be the warmest guest) and there is Daniel's fading dolly, and Jonathan Stone, my erratic patron*. But compromises lead to a pocket of warmth: Caryl at my side; my no more children: Teresa agitated, and fleetingly happy; and Daniel; Marek Żuławski who (though ever anxious and scribbling addresses) reaches back to our art-school past and is important to me as a sort of ambivalent reflection; George Galitzine, a Russian prince – my initial English tutor, his first lesson: a vocabulary of rudenesses; Ram Gopal – the ever-recurring ever-falling star; Cedric Price, my almost *alter ego* in frustrated projects; Pierre Rouve, an equivocal case; and compulsions: saried Farida – getting tipsy in her frustrations – the bare belly swaying in a mini-scandal; and Irène Yamato – exotic, minus scandal: both girls perhaps another compromise – for a bouquet of colour. And I – an old frog, phonily brooding.

However, the Baked Alaska with seventy candles arrives and Caryl is at ease.

*Art politics at their most bellicose: their only, but central, figure invited – and significantly the only brutally without-excuses absentee – was **Jennie Lee**, the Minister for Arts then, included here as a representative of my early post-war friendships.

Her absence may have been more than an oversight. Nye Bevan and she were most respected friends – he having commended me for British citizenship – and frequent guests at Hanover Terrace. When nominated for the Arts, Jennie phoned and invited herself to pick my 'expert' brains, confessing to the vaguest notions about the field.

I prepared, conscious of her commendable humility and the seriousness of this opportunity, a longish list of reformatory ideas gathered for years. But Jennie, a parliamentarian uppermost, speechified as if at a populous campaign meeting, non-commital generalities a-juggle – my responsibly thought-out proposals (not helped by my lacking the negotiator's technique) facilely brushed out of the way, without being heard out, in the practised manner of a professional politician.

And it was not surprising to see her afterwards either seated smugly at some gala between the large legal shapes of a Birk and a Goodman, or guided/guarded, happy, by a cluster of handsomely groomed dark-tailored art dignitaries – since her rule reflected manipulatory institutionalism, not concern for the individual practitioners of the arts.

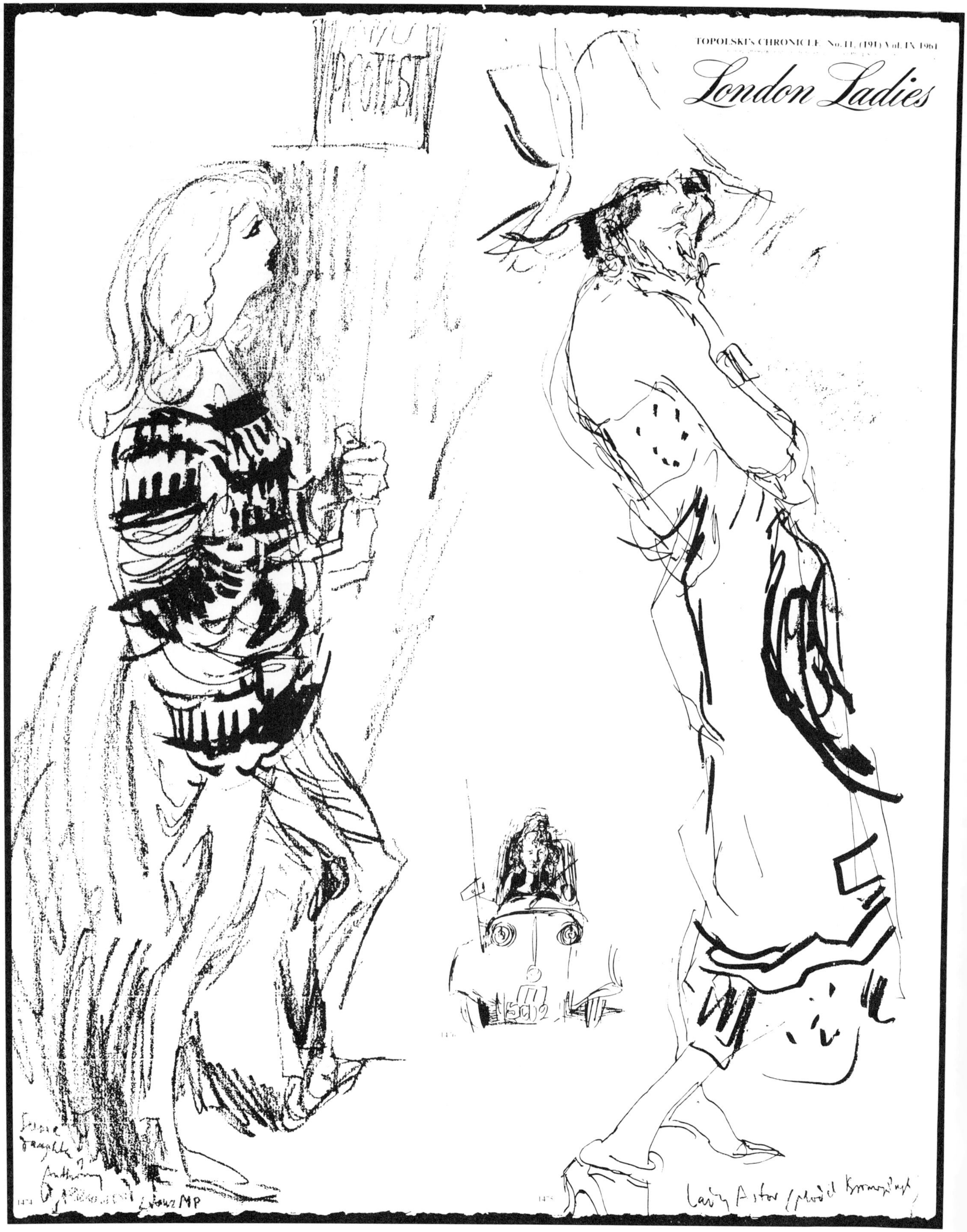
TOPOLSKI's CHRONICLE No. 11, (191) Vol. IX 1961
London Ladies
PROTEST
Lady Astor

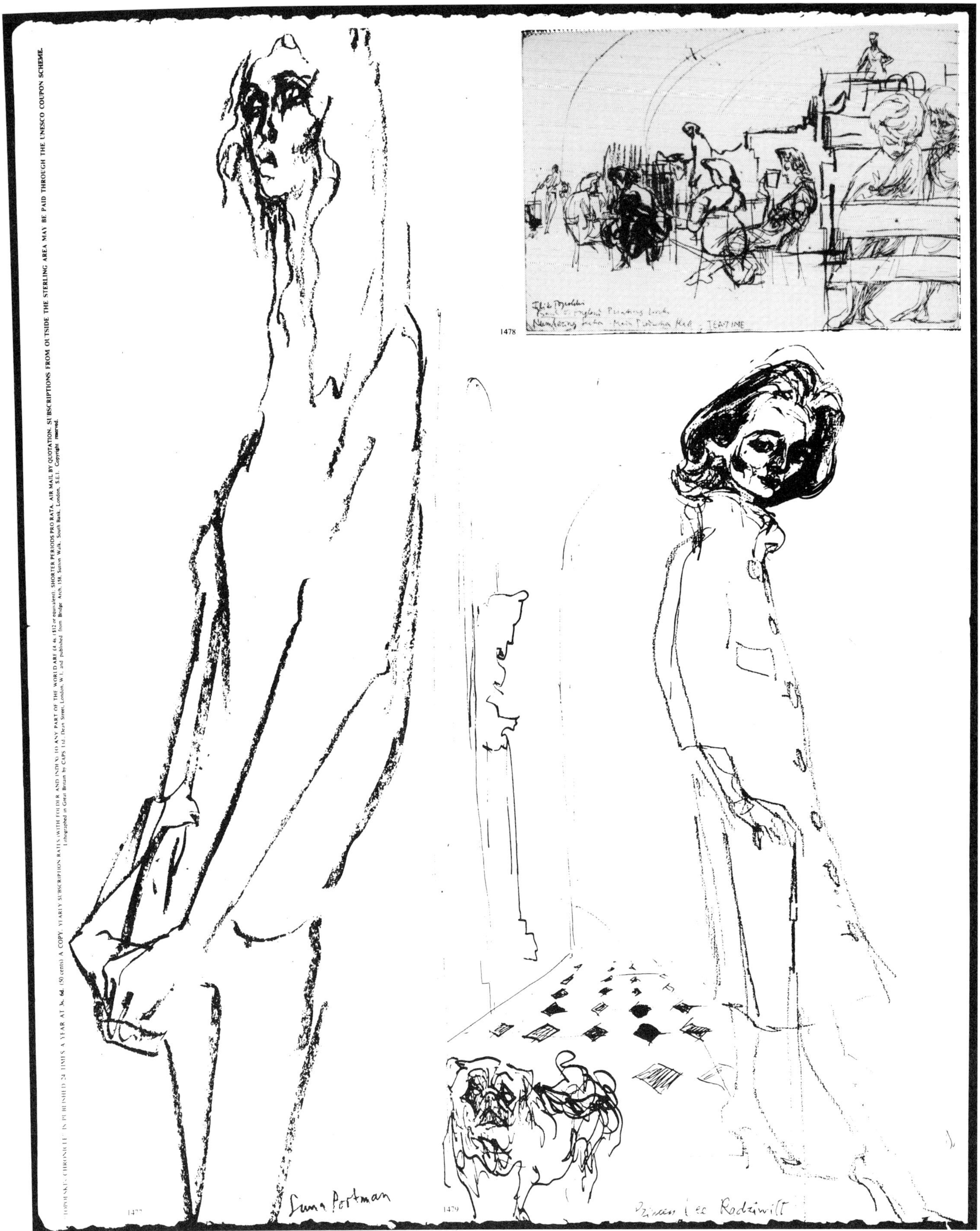

'London Ladies' (from *Topolski's Chronicle*)

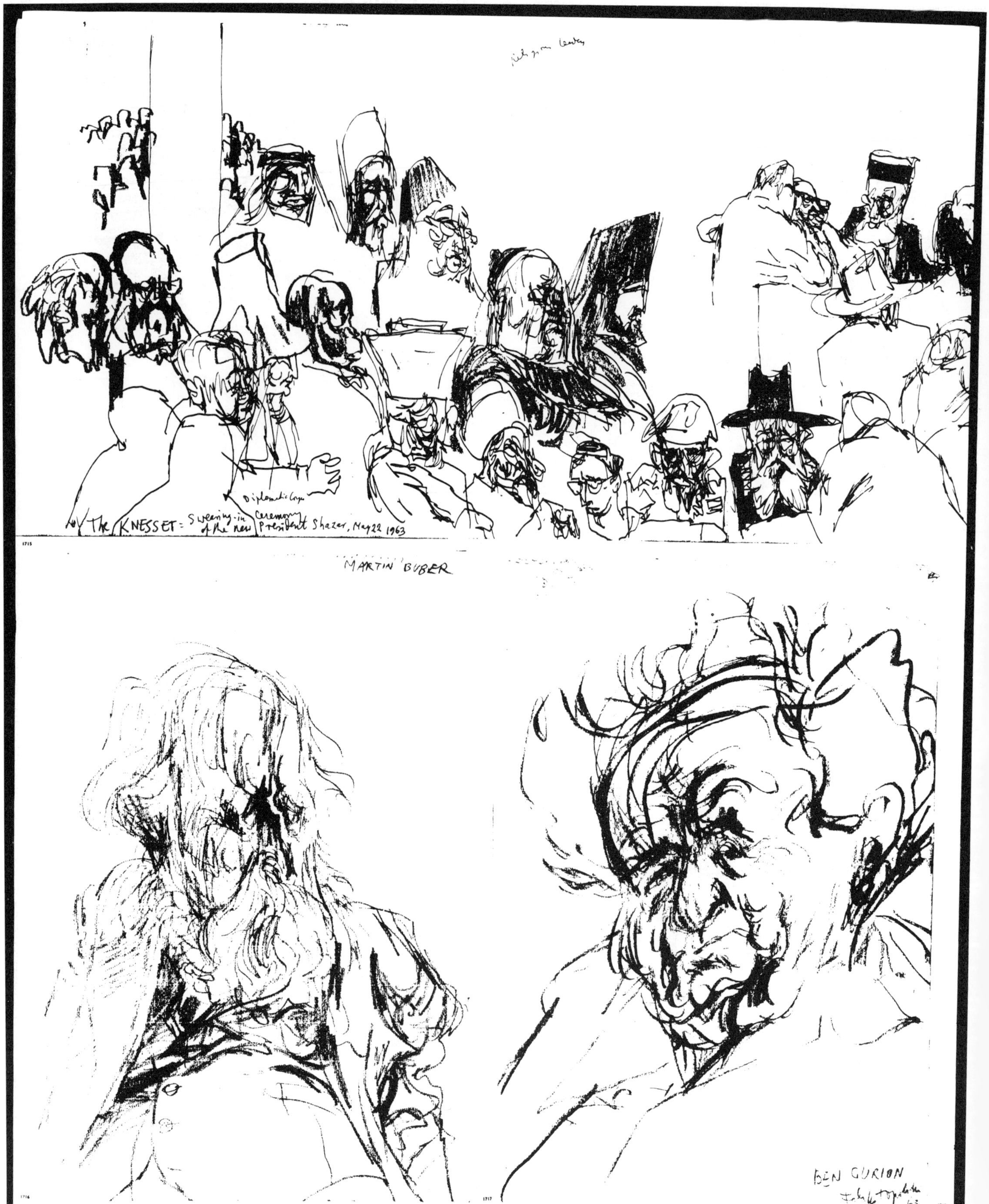

Israel, 1963: The Knesset and Martin Buber and Ben Gurion (from *Topolski's Chronicle*)

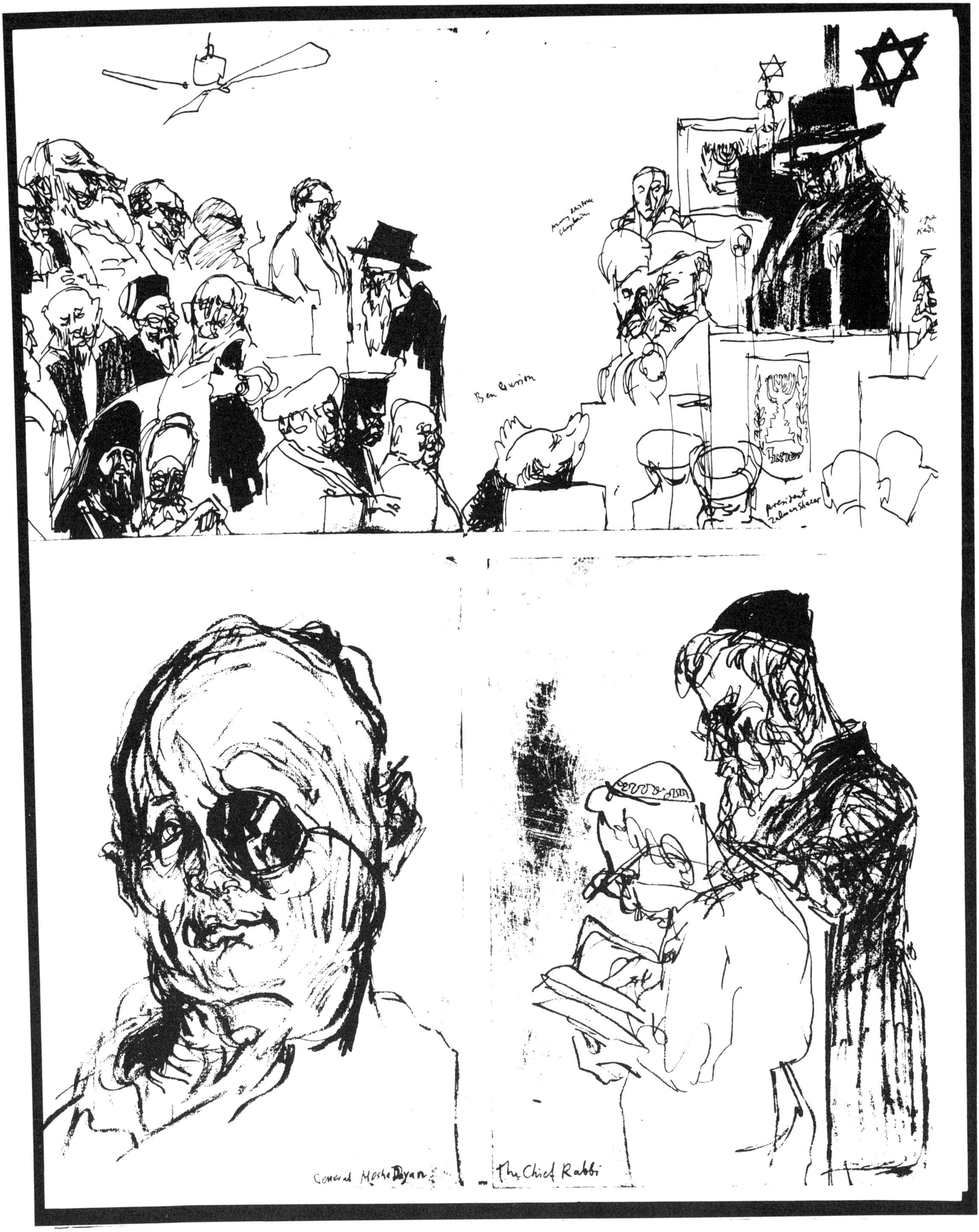

The Knesset, General Moshe Dayan, the Chief Rabbi (from *Topolski's Chronicle*)

War-time Palestine was for me (the Arabs an exotic background) dominated by the Poles in transit; and the Jews in their early-earthy ecstasies: the leader of a kibbutz, raised on adverse soil, stretching his open palm at me with an ordinary tomato nesting in it, triumphant in this ideological conquest.

Israel in 1962–3: to me a retrogressive step, the Jews in their diaspora, though almost brought to extinction, having been forerunners of internationalism as the positive future. However, this truly new state, scripted on *carte blanche* by enlightened progressives from the West, ought at least to have turned out a model utopia.

This is not a hindview from recent soured years; we saw Israel then at its most optimistic, yet were disturbed – greatly, because the Israelites were blank to our queries.

From the start, ungenerous divisions/strata set to last, the Asian and African Jews kept down together with the Arabs at manual services, and their children, by some statutory fluke I couldn't understand (paid schooling?), barred from the educational ladder. And the 'tribal' rifts among the up-to-date cultivated *immigrés* from Europe and America: the *Herrenvolk* stance of those from Germany, the pull of moneyed Americans. A Polish-educated architect and his Gentile Polish wife virtually ostracized – his winning project never to be executed, until forced to leave – for Canada. And this links with orthodoxy, rampant and enforcing racial prejudices against mixed marriages.

Yet there was the holy awesomeness of its rocky deserts, and plenty of enchantment, not least in the Arabic rusticity, which insisted on being drawn – possibly a reason why the idea of Israel backing the publication of hundreds of my drawings as a portfolio was ignored.

This emblematic hugeness, green fatigues, beret, revolver at the belt, face – massive-black-forested in unmatchable arrangement. The crowds round him, be it at ceremonial tree-plantings, or at the *celebración* in Plaza de la Revolución José Marti (he rostrum-raised and backed by undulating flags), are dwarfed by **Fidel Castro!** The length of his speechifying conforms to his extra size – even the Chinese Generals round him (sturdy listeners), as well as the other non-Spanish-speaking delegates, are stunned into submission (the contemporary endlessness of procedures at rallies academies conferences replacing religious rituals – I survive them by concentrating on drawing, but I am always amazed at the endurance of the 'distinguished' participants around me). The invariable entourage of *El Comandante* – **Che Guevara**, Raul Castro in battle-readiness – backed by 'BIENVENIDO FIDEL!' The ever-perpetual triumph.

But the hero's presence in everydayness: 'Floridita' of Hemingway legend, where his 'place' at the bar is kept honoured, presents the apathy (probably unchanged) of only two stooled and apart drinkers (one heavy, cigar-munching; the other, a hatted flabby *mestizo*) and a propped mindless barman. Yet this stupor is giantly countered by the new presence of the backcloth painting: Fidel (even bigger than in reality) leading his revolutionaries into battle – straight at the bar clients' indifference.

And at random:

The terrace of **the Habana Libre Hotel.** A blonde-locked-to-the-waist soldier girl, sun-glasses of latest eccentricity, in a sentry-post gun-holding attitude – ringed by photographers.

'Abstracto 1963' artists at the 'Writers' and Artists' Union' – solemn-faced, solemn-speaking on their social mission, but also on the correlation between their work and the Western trends of the day; and on the subsidies due to them.

Taken to a new settlement: a little cubby-hole three gods' altar: Christ, Fidel, and a candle for voodoo.

Open-air Aires Libres Café in the main square at the foot of the American-built Habana Libre skyscraper, its full frontage bearing a star made up of light-bulbs with the peace-pigeon inserted; a little folk band, fine black girls: the special one at our table – the star of the sumptuous nightly cabaret – will reappear a few years later in London, set on a career in Europe.

Graham Greene happens to be **in Havana**. He, the solo master traveller, master at keeping clear of the turmoil of phony 'delegates', British MPs with their 'priorities', profiteers of new regimes, fillers-in of gaps in invitee-lists, which tosses me about; I am for him outside all this as an old pal of *Night and Day*, but, having met in my room, we go to dine burdened with a Danish *réporteuse* who was there with me.

I incorrigibly trot to the next table for a clarifying chat with the black girl (escorted by a black friend) who, befriended on the first day, was stopped by the hotel porter from going upstairs with me.

Within the proclaimed Cuban racial harmony, I tend to sniff out divisions:

> On my Sunday arrival at La Habana Riviera Hotel – late temple to The American Way of Life – I watched, in the gaudy lobby, a procession of sumptuous and sumptuously dressed young Negresses on their way to banqueting and night-clubbing indifferently pass a photographic exhibition of the Revolution: groups of leaders, battle scenes, dead heroes . . . I knew most of these photographs, but here, because of the contrast with this vanity parade, I was struck by a sudden realization that the faces in the photographs were almost all WHITE. . .

I wrote this in my *Chronicle* on Cuba, introducing a piece by **Jan Carew*** – a writer friend, who had been to Havana for the *Observer* a year before; as a man of colour he mixed easily with the blacks of the country. He quotes Pepe, a Negro from the Oriente Province:

> . . . we are still black and a minority and the Revolution does not invent soap to wash you white . . . they free us on paper but there

*Jan is now an honoured academic at a leading American university – the head of Afro-American Studies: 'calming' departments introduced in consequence of black upheavals in the sixties.

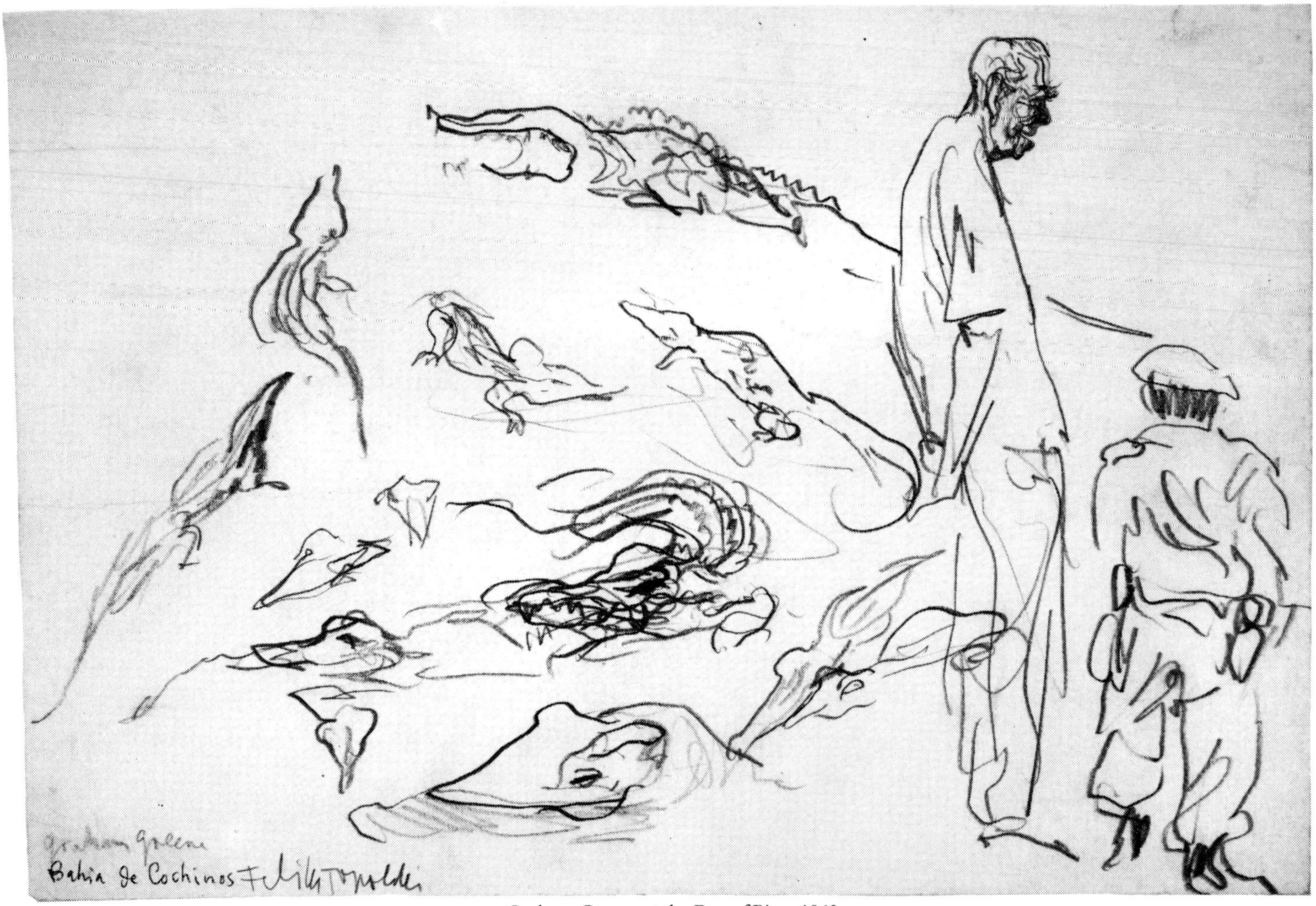

Graham Greene at the Bay of Pigs, 1963

is a lot of separateness in our lives still . . . and we're not like the Yankee Negro, we're not trying to be like the white Cuban . . . the white Cuban is one of the most boring human beings God ever made, they're heroic, extreme, they will defy the whole world and you will applaud and admire them but, try as you may, you'll never like them . . . my daughter goes to the university . . . she's nineteen . . . she doesn't go out with white Cubans . . . their law says it's all right but it still doesn't happen . . . now I wouldn't want her to get involved with one of those dull, sanctimonious, bearded white idiots, but I'm just telling you that it doesn't happen. The law says we can go anywhere, do anything but that law is a bitch when it comes to making things work. . .

Black Cubans, prompted by the supreme irony of their breed, tended to hold back and take their time before stepping in for the Revolution's pleasanter offerings, glorifying in their 'ideology' of opportunism.

Back at our table – the first dish just arrived – shambles: Graham stands up and leaves – a refrain from my past. Next morning he explains: he knows well the Dane's kind of simmering hysteria – about to erupt; and he wished to absent himself from the prospect.

But for the two of us he arranged a drive: he was determined to see the Bay of Pigs and there we go.

There had been many years between the last encounter and this one – and so for most of the long drive we toss about, not the time-bomb of now – vocation toilers of plots and images as we are, not power-plotters – but distant incidents and friends. Professionally, as it were, I respectfully acknowledge his superiority in collecting the world, alone and leaping at will over no-man's-lands, while most of my journeys have strings attached – obstructions of time and frontiers. He will move now to Mexico and, if my recollection is right, cross then to Haiti; I, a member of an invitee unit, will go back to England the same ludicrous, politically signposted and tiring way as I came – via Gander (Newfoundland!), Czechoslovakia, and Shannon.

Yet, his free choice may prove more binding than a prescribed trail's proneness to ambushes – often gratifying to me: the 'delegates'' return plane is mysteriously delayed at Havana for twenty-four hours – and next morning at the airport we face Castro, Che Guevara *et al.* lined up for double-kiss farewelling of **Colonel Boumédienne** – and an added diversion to Algeria. I spent a great part of the immense flight in the VIP compartment drawing him endlessly while conversing – I wouldn't know how to interview a man on the eve of becoming the ruler of a country with a drastic future – about women.

Now Graham and I are at the Bay of Pigs: he watches, I draw. The place is essentially a dull and basic resort with attached 'attractions', such as a crocodile pool. Graham's great length ponders the crocodiles – I draw the confrontation. Then the Cubans, accommodating in their

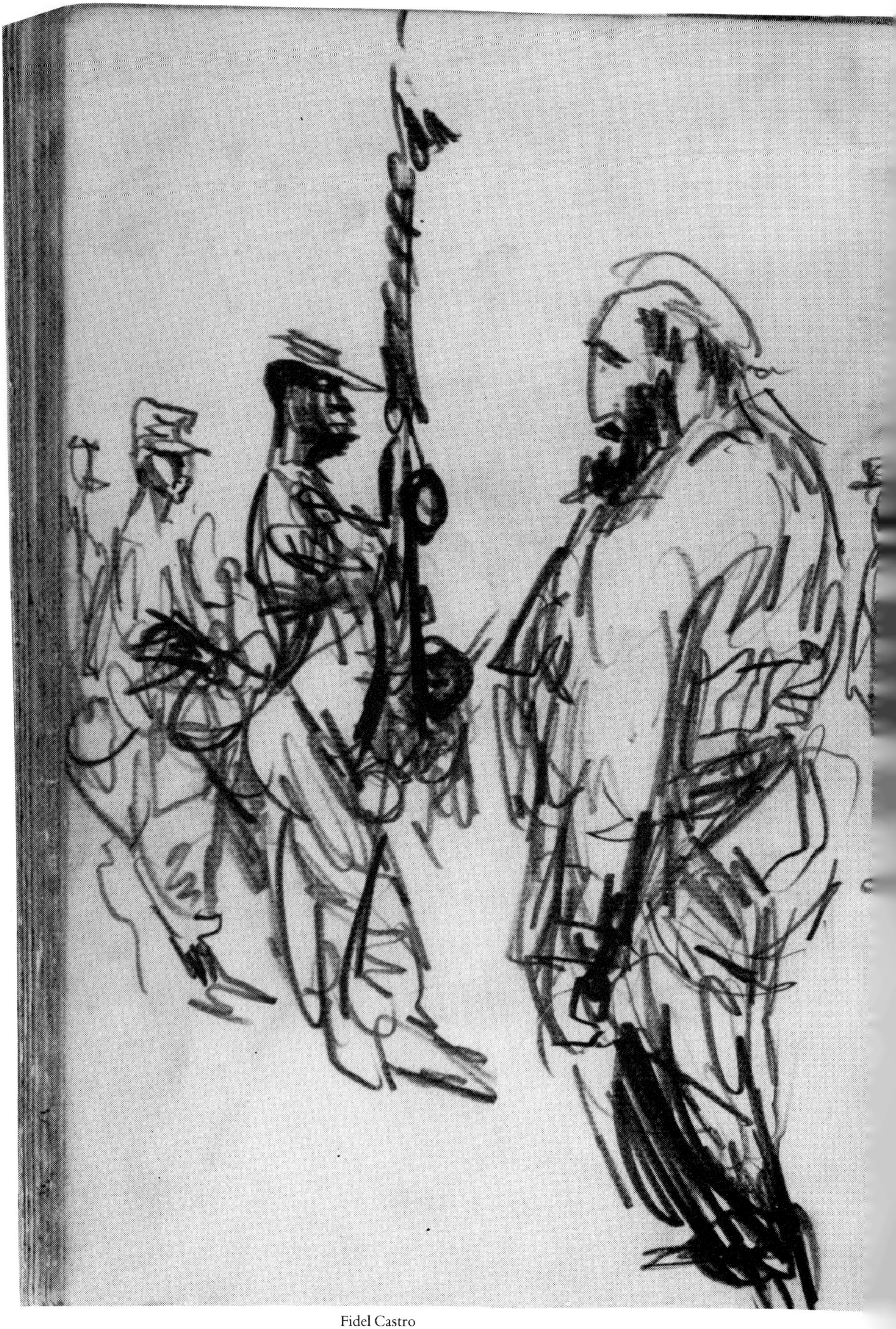

Fidel Castro

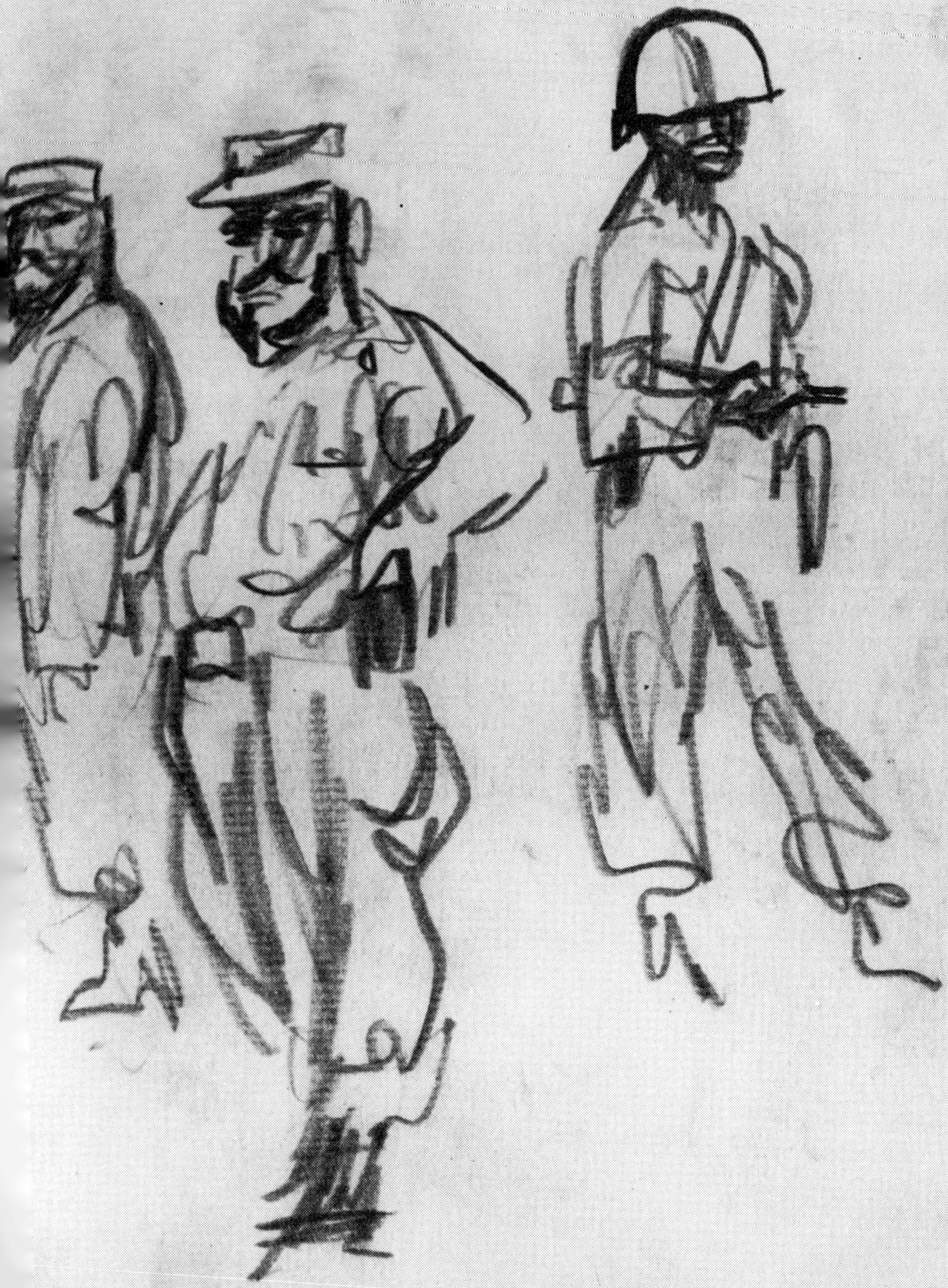

pride, put us – Graham, ever prepared, dons a beret – on a patrolling coaster (no Negroes in the crew): the fluttering of their flag over the cracked foamy trail circles-reviews the tracery of their victory.

Some years later **Amanda**, Graham's niece, a generous photographer of the progress of my *Memoir*, brought him along to my studio. We ended in Caryl's and my tower round the kitchen table, and this will stay in my memory as one of the tenderest moments of my life: two young women in devoted accompaniment to two aged men's unhurried revels over their past, with me, just that much his inferior in achievement and age, recapturing the long-lost state of gratification at looking up, being the younger companion, yet of the highest promise.

The Pilgrimage of His Holiness Pope Paul VI to the Holy Land

Still in the dark, **the Dome of the Rock – the Mosque of Omar** sings with men's voices. Can the sound come all the way across Gethsemane up to my window on the Mount of Olives? Or is it 'relayed'?

At daybreak, before the sun takes over, Old Jerusalem, wall-ribboned like an offering, emanates the rosy glow of daily regeneration – becomes New Jerusalem.

The desert of bulging rocks, dust-whirling. Armed sentries, perched high, quiver in the gale. The billboards (immense fountain pen in a giant hand, a blond angel at a typewriter) shuttle and shuffle with the Dead Sea and Jericho. The humble arches of welcome (Jordan River, Refugee Camps) banner forth their calculated greetings, each trimmed with a bouquet of the choicest locals.

Amman Airport. Nature stages its protest: the great wind freezes sways flounders the Diplomatic Corps and the press-tele- and cine-men; balloons the veils and skirts of Their Eminences the Cardinals and Their Beatitudes the Patriarchs, of the Bishops, Heads of Religious Orders, the Religious Justices and the Mufti of Jerusalem; baffles carpet-layers; upsets the stately pomp of the *parvenu* Hashemite Kingdom of Jordan.

Although He was to be received by the passes-holding elect,* not by the poor, the desert elements battered them into a modicum of humility apt for **His Holiness**'s arrival.

The MOMENT came when the giant whale-shark from the heavens settled on the tarmac and, Jordanian guns firing, began to wheel its way *rallentando* and determinedly towards the edge of the red carpet, shattering the scale of assembled dignity (now lilliputian), disquieting with the closeness of the irrational.

Mid-way down the steps of the white plane, a white Jonah spreads his white arms, and there it is: humanity's ever-luring hope of the Healer's advent seems to corporealize; rub out the ironmongery, and even the miracle of **descent from above** applies. Pope Paul is the only one who can and surely does bring conciliation to this patch, source of hate.

Then he stepped down amongst the 'well-wishers', placed His red hat on top of His skull-cap, and lined up to attend to the Vatican and Jordanian anthems 'as per protocol'.

The Church of the Holy Sepulchre, surrounded by handsome soldiery. Inside, hours of crafty skirmishes and humiliations over vantage points. My vantage point: held up by a friend-for-ever Arab *légionnaire*; left foot on a column's high rim and left arm round it; the other leg in the air – the lifted knee supports a sketchbook, and the drawing hand. The cameras with their lights, justly privileged, form a halo round the Holy of Holies, multiply the Apostolic message, *are* robot-missionaries.

The procession is crowd-entangled in **Via Dolorosa** – the Pope, off his feet, floats – they enter.

The surge within the church verges on battle and the Mass on a field Mass, in the *galimatias* of rasping shouts and the convergence of confusing clashes.

But His Holiness, having been brought in on the crest of the mob, emerges dominant within the circle of officiating priests. His face is better than expected, overdrawn beyond the retouchings of the official oleographs; the bombasticity of Rome's costumes left behind.

The Patriarchs, interspersed with interlopers and futile Knights of the Holy Sepulchre, have roughly assembled; the Franciscans function round the quiet centre of the whirlpool.

An indefinable significance fulfils itself – chaotic and diffused in conflicting details, as ever for a close eye-witness: tragicomic, hence epic, perhaps meek in intention, but raised by the strong arms of yearnings and triteness towards History.

The huge, shocking-pink Patriarch of the Maronites, Boulus Maa'ouchi, renders himself humble in solemn attendance at the Papal vesting in order to be elevated above the others. Most of the other Beatitudes are merely *present*: 'chosen' – and so, transfixed – not to rule but to be icons.

Humility, though, is here too. The modest Arab legionary at my side in his goodness advises me in the scramble: 'Push him hard!', because true goodness, like any other activity, must be directional. Also good is the anonymous plain dark suit who, in the emergency of sudden fire, comes forward alone, climbs up the scaffold and pokes at the flames eating up the electric cables.

The camera lights confuse, shoot flashes, vulgarize the rite. And only now, when extinguished, there is revealed under the crackling of the fire above the tense unity of the scene given by the candle-light and by the now-quiet crowd bent towards the Pope's Mass. The red headscarf thrown up by a soldier (to smother the fire! a second helping hand!) floats momentarily. Another deed of a legend in the making.

Afterwards, again, noise and searchlights and the Pope bending into the *Sanctissimum Sepulchrum*. And a sermon on peace, but in rather theological terms, with the Jordan legionaries in close assemblage – more appropriate to the occasion than the Swiss Guards of the Vatican would have been as a *memento bello*.

*The Jordanian web of obstacles in the way of the 'passes' was matched by our duo of supremely co-ordinated performers: Norman St John-Stevas and I – the former perhaps the greatest doors-opening master ever. He was then serving as *The Economist*'s representative.

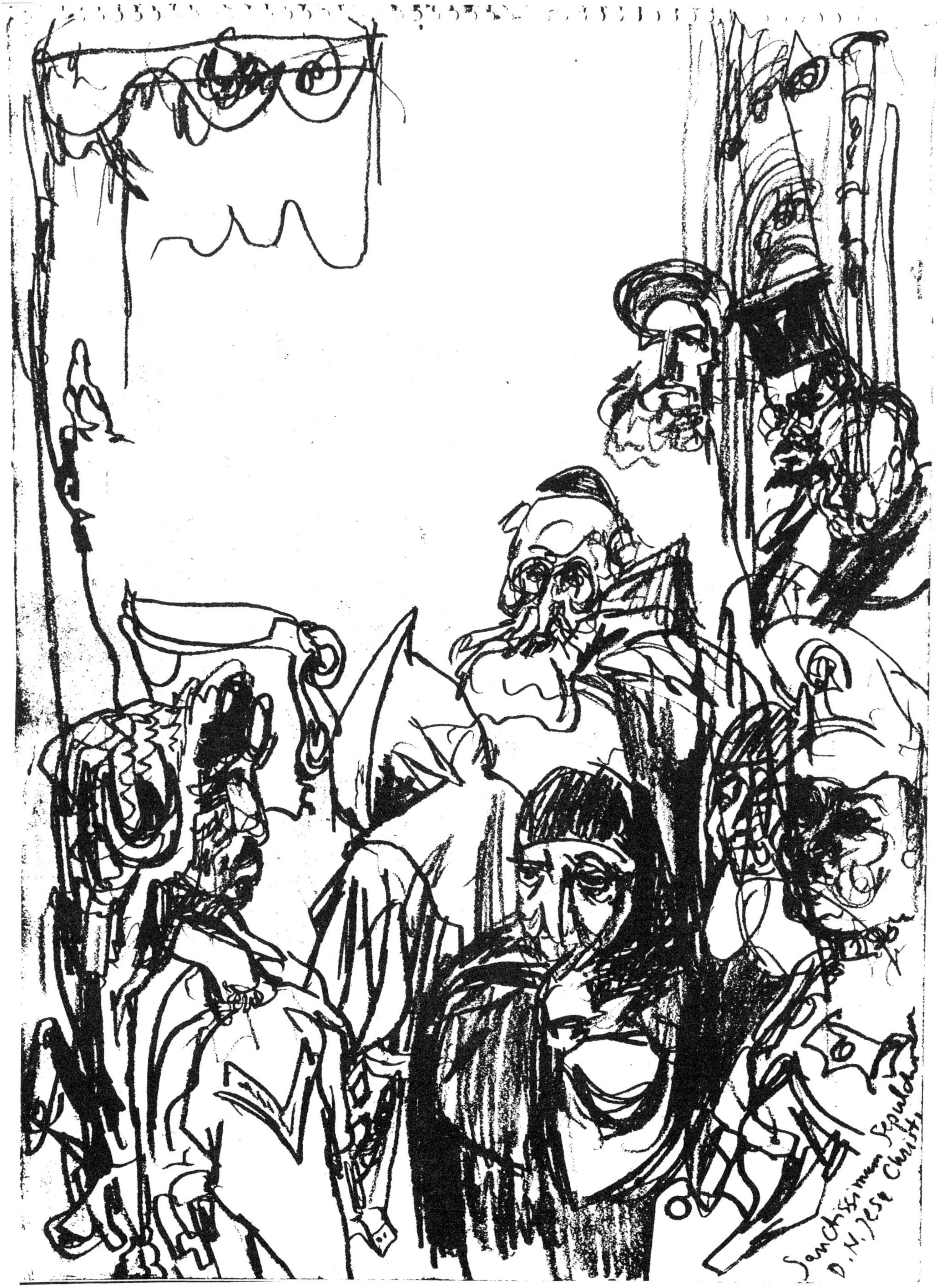

The Pilgrimage of His Holiness Pope Paul VI to the Holy Land, Jordan – Israel (from *Topolski's Chronicle*)

Departure seems unduly hasty: the cross, the palm-leaves, the tumult of Eminencies amongst the plain-clothes bodyguards – as if signifying retreat, a flight from this spot of fulfilment through martyrdom. . .

Israel's Jerusalem. The Mandelbaum Gate farewell. British-style battledress and drill. The drums lead into position the line of standard-bearers – some nordic, some not.

The stark tableau: the young soldiers, edged by the darkness of no-man's-land, presenting arms to the Israeli worthies (black hats and well-cut top-coats) who cannot rise above The Nation, and to this 'Pilgrim' (worldly in the carmine silk cape, scarlet velvet dalmatic, lace tunicle and white soutane) who will not transcend The Church.

In face of the murky threat, there is no word or gesture of peace, deliberate or spilled, to shield the youngsters bred for the 'tournaments' of the future.

I walk alone through the gate into the night and, halfway to the opposite frontier post, stop and urinate, while changing the Israeli for the Jordanian badge.

Bethlehem repeats the pattern of harassed rites, but also underlines this, that the Pope has progressed in these three days (for Christ's three score years) in reverse: he began with the Crucifixion and ended in the womb-like little underground Grotto of the Church of Nativity with the Pontifical Call: Pontifical indeed, hence doctrinal, hence, in the circumstances of his bestriding both sides of the belligerent frontier – both of them (and the whole world) expecting the WORD from him and not receiving it – shrinking back pathetically into the posture of the Vatican State and its nineteenth-century diplomatic manoeuvres:

> . . . O Roman Christ!. . . The door of the fold is open.
> We wait . . . we . . . have all the divine guarantees of
> truth . . . we believe that the salvation we offer is
> necessary for it (the world). . .

And so this has been a crusading 'pilgrimage' to take the Child Jesus at his very birth into the Roman fold.

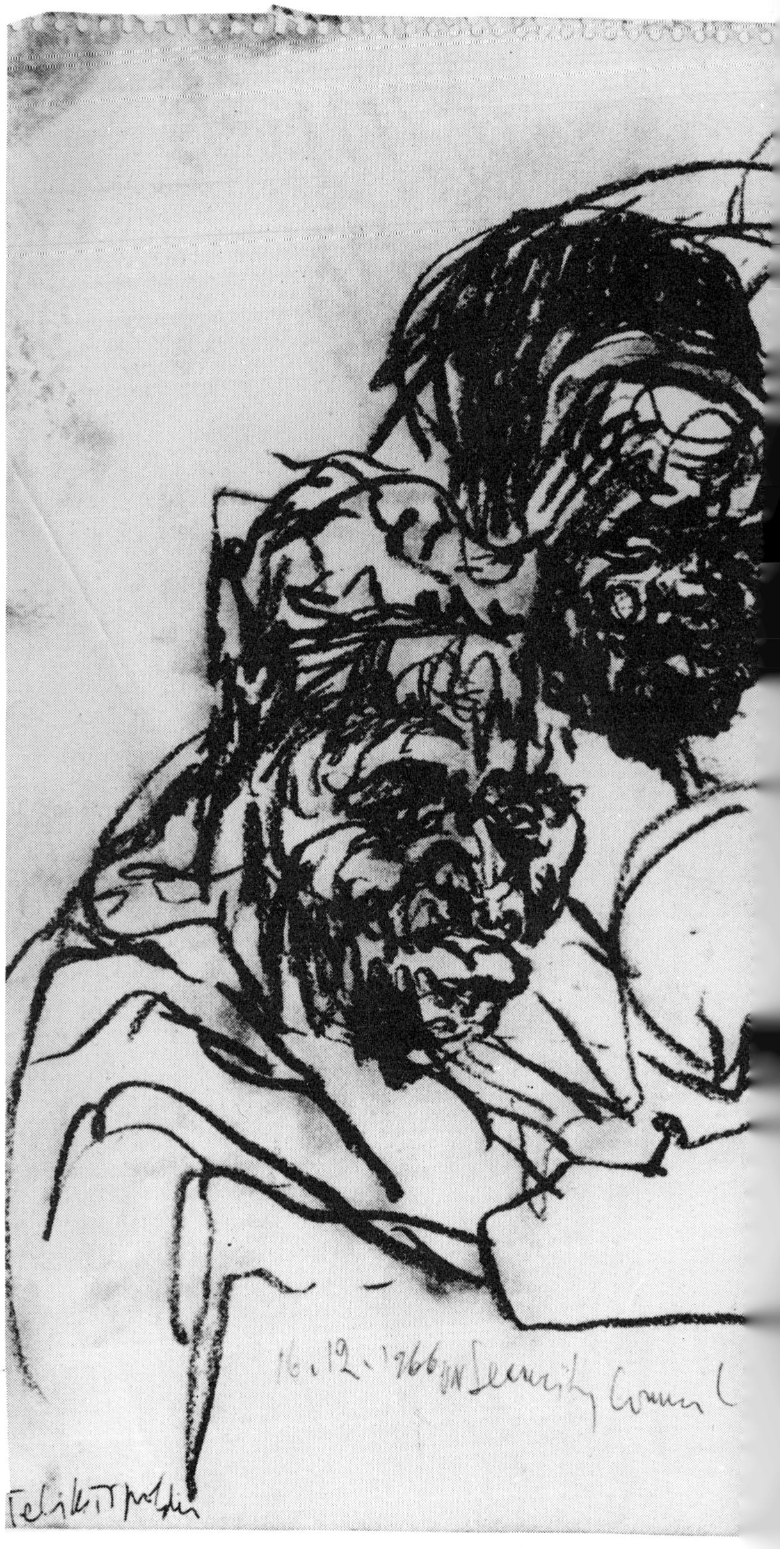

U----- Nations

(Solo recitative against an ad lib *cacophony of 120 national anthems for wind band)*

'. . . *the end of the road of tyranny in* **South Africa** is not in sight. . .'
a **West African** voice
at Special Political Committee 540th Meeting
Conference Room Two, United Nations Headquarters, New York City.
New flag (a commercial designer's adequate job) goes up
new anthem (so so) – one more black voice
(and limousines offices typewriters secretaries residences wives receptions travel-contact expenses)
added to the independence phantasmagoria
of one vote one nation
an odd axiom – nineteenth-century antinomy: national = human
– to found a faith on to give the lie to power

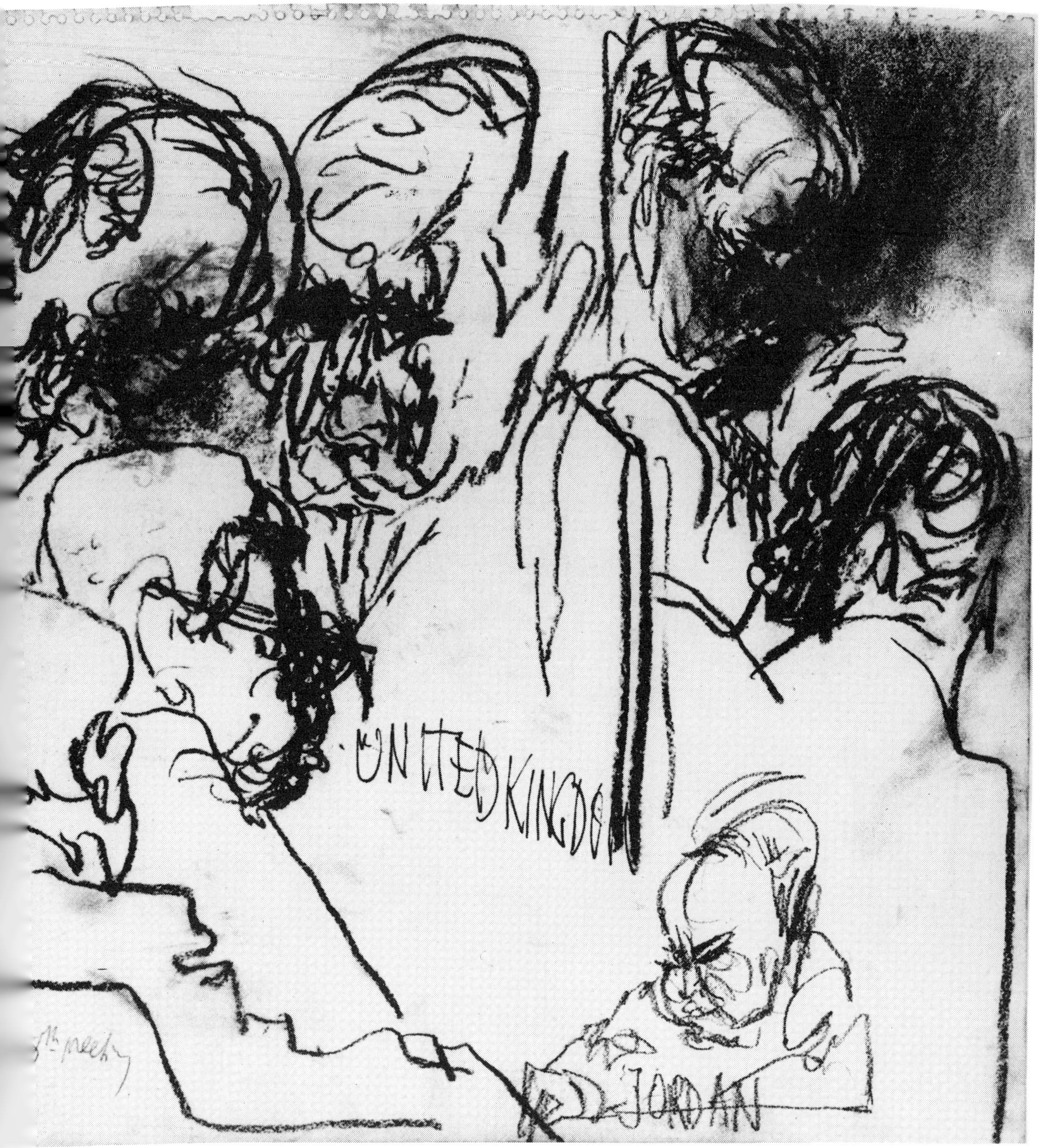

UN Security Council, 16 December 1966 (from *The United Nations: Sacred Drama* with Conor Cruise O'Brien)

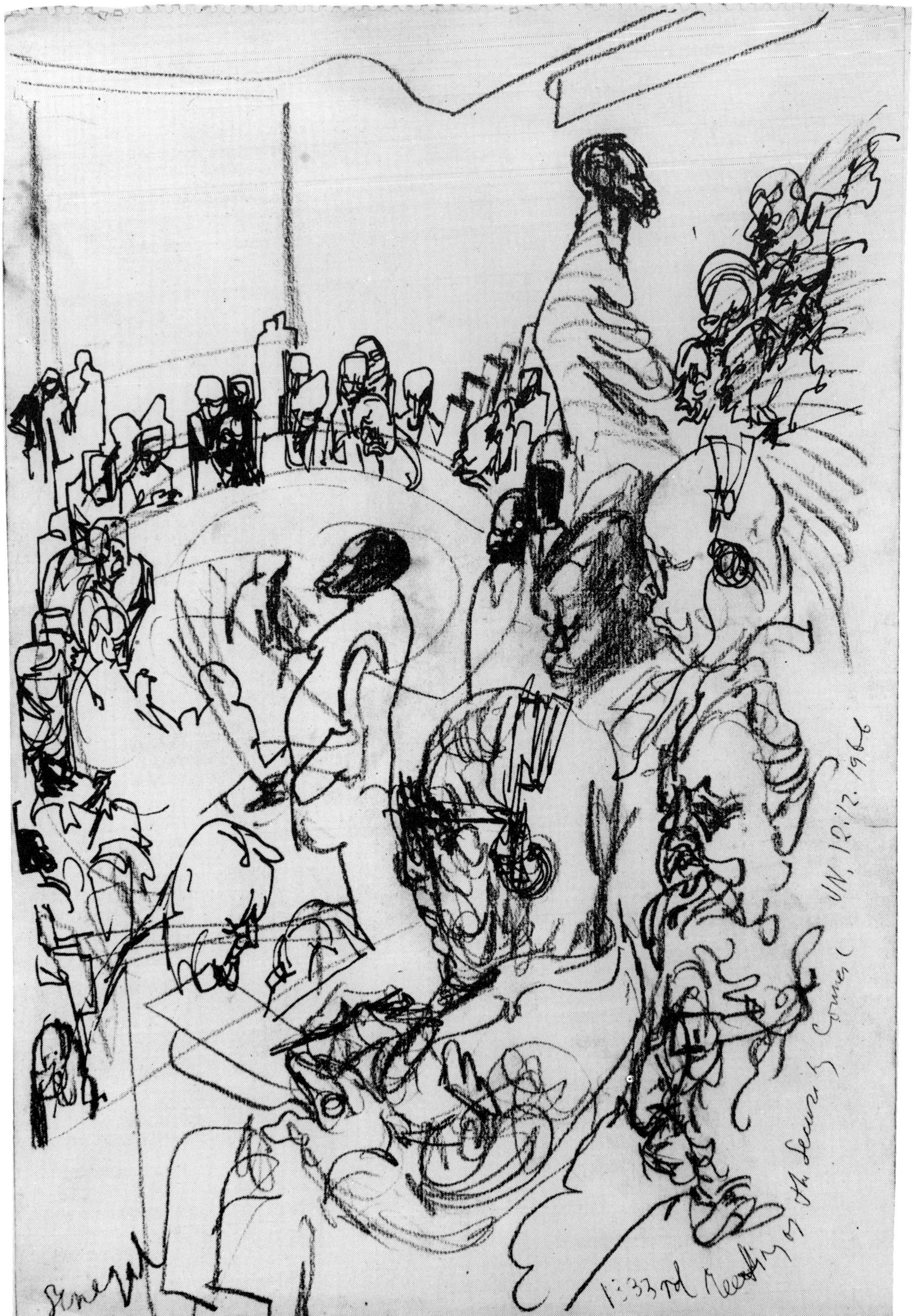

UN Security Council, 12 December 1966 (from *The United Nations: Sacred Drama* with Conor Cruise O'Brien)

so that the way to it belied with good intentions.
All sumptuously templed:
horizontal for supplicants and customary campanile
upright symbol of aspirations –
– the unseen bureaucratic manufacture of un-balances
– the Secretariat.

First Committee 1492nd Meeting. '. . . the treaty on
Outer Space comes before us . . .' intones old **United Kingdom**
'. . . the moon and other celestial bodies . . .' earphone translations
from the Orthodox liturgy of the **Union of the Soviets**
'. . . *y compris la lune* . . .' congregationally from **France**
(the fossil language of late diplomatic liturgy)
'. . . flight of space-objects . . .' factually and conclusively by **the United States.**
. . .

The black world takes the spectacular vote-centre of the stage, but
the elder and the wiser:
'I now call upon the distinguished delegate of **Japan**' –
– click-tap of well-shod heels.
'. . . all these endeavours . . . if I may express
my personal opinion – as regards the war in **Vietnam** . . .
. . . and I waive my right for consecutive interpretation'.
'. . . professions of peace if not followed by deeds.'
'. . . *ce triomphe de la révolution . . . représente La Chine*'
from the **Albanian** delegate.
A passive line of nordic walruses. The one-woman (*French*-bright)
Moroccan fashion parade. **English** prayer-folded hands
eyes hidden ear lent to the whisper of **US** neighbours.
Votes (writing on the wall) blink: YES – 78,9; NO – 0; ABSTAIN – 4;
blessed unanimity.
'. . . London is trying to push the United Nations into
a deliberately false cause . . .' the **Russian** delegate
white elegant ringed hands about a long-holdered cigarette
bow at the neck (spies say on elastic band) undulating hair-do
effect-in-all of Tsar Alexander at the 1815 Congress and
'. . . false diplomatic manoeuvres designed to cover the essence. . .'
(whisper '. . . the **Russians** daren't bring **Vietnam** up – out-voted
would lose face. . .')
This at Security Council.
Viewed from the **Chinese** interpreters' booth:
The curved array of bleak faces,
grotesquely overdrawn – bulging noses lipless –
moulded into them optical and smoking appliances –
busts in fact: heads supported on starched white halters
with silk-strips (different colour-scheme to each man) knotted
dangling down under festooning chins, metal and stone trinkets
sparkle at hands and chests – not at ears and noses.
Ambassadors for the power holders of the day –
their disdainful slick but *au ralenti* manner – a bizarre model
for the imitators from Asia and the rest.
But **Zambia** is about to protest:
We are in the tents of ancient captains –
(the Council elders on the defensive, therefore
watchful for irregularities – in procedure and in manners –
against the codes and decorum
as set by themselves) –
. . .

S. M. Kapwepwe: '. . . it is racialist of you, it is tribal of you
to bring a war between black and white. . .'
(speedily to succour his own side a liberal Labour-lord '. . . no government
has a monopoly in morality in this matter.') and
'. . . even here in **America** they butcher people in the streets. . .'
The Guinea delegate at Fourth Committee 1670th meeting
echoes '. . . *BRUN ET BLANC!*. . .'
Now the day ending, excluding the Reverend Michael Scott's desolate wanderings
round the corridors on behalf, this time, of action
for **South West Africa**
and the greed-anxious
utterly Seljukian un-UN Sheikh Suleiman
bin Himyar King of **the Green Mountain**,
for the most it's party-time.
But the Black delegates and their elegant entourage
dally-loiter in this palace-of-PASS cards,
loath to be parted from their daydream oasis.
Outside, New York – for them a predatory swamp.

An evening at **Gloria Vanderbilt's** and her then husband Sidney Lumet's. Her airs disclosed their vicious lining of the millionaire-classy-privacy code when she raised a law-threatening hell over the possibility of using on a printed page one of my habitual off-hand scribbles.

But the memorable core of the occasion: **Truman Capote**. We were only five – I must have been a New York novelty brought for his examination/acceptance/dismissal, and indeed Capote, a duellist and performer, exercised his talents on me, at once seductive and inquisitional – my resistance, having surfaced, unquestionably brought negative conclusions.

This abhorrent gnome held anxiety-driven malice: his overdressed dwarfishness battled upwards with subtlety – for instance, not resorting to high heels but, in challenge, the opposite, he would kick off his convenient-for-such-routines pumps and leap pseudo-unconcernedly into uncalled-for dancing, his head resting against the waist of his partner; on a drawing-room sofa he would train his curvaceous embraces on accommodating upper-crust patronesses. The whole of his functioning/costuming – obviously detailed to his physique – was stimulated to the maximum by my presence as (in his view, no doubt) a possible social adversary, only a fraction nearer to normal measurements than he.

Indeed the American WASP exclusivity, impenetrable and composed *de rigueur* of the tall breed, appointed as their animators/leaders/geniuses a dwarfish lot: Truman Capote, Andy Warhol, the Metropolitan Museum's Geldzahler, even Mailer.

What about such a brisk (perhaps untenable) proposition?: the millenia-ingrained protocol of emperors and princes demanded the presence of cheeky jesters, unpunishable for their trespasses. Our time with its democracy, its vote-sycophantism and institutionalized hierarchies censors out the jester but, the need of him undiminished, he returns by the freedom-through-art back door, still not a true equal to the multiple top people, but promoted to the function of an inspirer – an entertainer dismissable, as of old, if he oversteps his cues.

My school, universally assumed to be one of the best in Poland, was founded by the Evangelic-Augsburgian community and attached to its circular church. Chance had it that my son's school, Westminster, was furnished with similar attributes.

The practice of formal religion was never upheld in our household but, as in my schooldays, our children had to be written into the appropriate rubric, following Marion's and my register-enforced classification, to proceed along the prescribed routine of godliness, accepted as an inescapable necessity, with the meek justification that the children should be given a choice.

Yet for me among a few recollections of their schooling years those derived from enforced formalities stand out. My one single great effort: to sneak into the proceedings in Westminster Abbey in time for **Westminster School's morning prayers.** The nave greyly filled up with the boys, the Gothic light over the congregation of young heads. And there, submerged in beauty and picked up by dust rays, Daniel (by then a school prefect) raised in the high pulpit, reading out the day's lesson with a gravity unknown to his father; a gravity of conformity, or, as the father was then, of being affected? He was never asked.

And this, no lesser, indoctrinatory school routine – in nationalist-military vein – as with myself seemingly not successful, though similarly touching on sympathetic nerve-ends: **the Westminster School Officer's Training Corps parade:** the confident platform-raised harmony of loyalties – a brass-hat dominant, supported by a bishop and the public-school governing body; and the faithful parental following.

The boys, fully armed and uniformed, some military some naval, reach the ceremony's 'march past'. The army band plays the usual and from a distance they march at and by us blocked in ranks of eight; a salute-command and, as prescribed, eyes/heads sharply turned right, feet beating the ground. Daniel in the front eight, his sterling fidelity-profile under the emblemed khaki beret (as never before), intent (according to the drill's compulsion) on DUTY – his full-growth stamping in subordinate allegiance makes me melt in sorrows: another enforced yielding to 'systems' and the sacrificial preparedness; my marching thirty years earlier in an earlier 'readiness', under orders now clasping at my son and forcing him into step.

We talked of it today and I learned (or had forgotten) that this parade was perhaps his first, that later he began to sabotage the OTC, refused to be promoted to officer's rank and caused consternation by drilling as a private, older and the *princeps oppidanorum,* under his juniors, until let off altogether.

Teresa's confirmation – Queen's College (generally criticized by parents as fossilized and lacking in stimulation) routinely staged the ceremony in a little Marylebone Road church.

Our atheistic-liberalized life, unpunctuated by calendar-

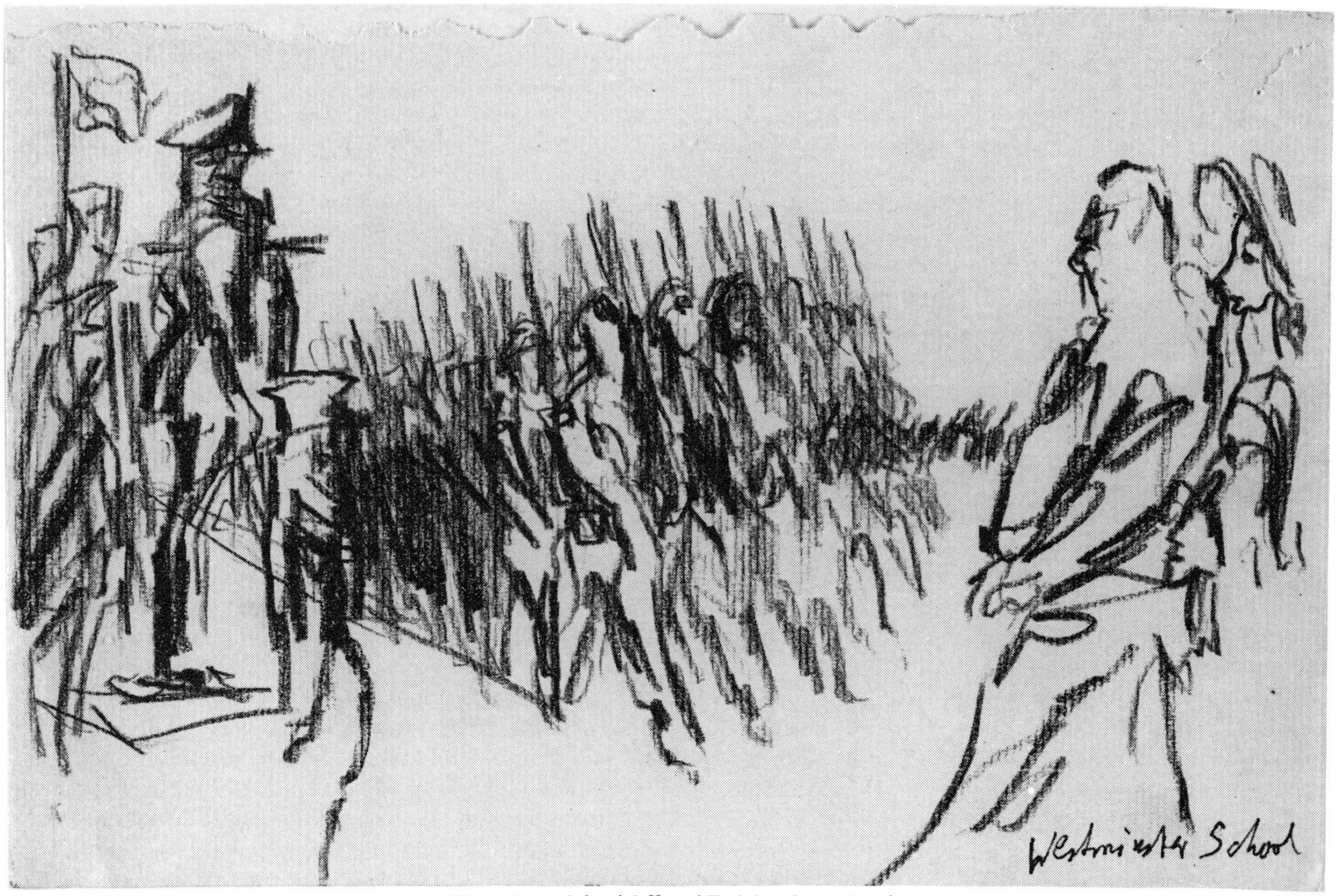

Westminster School Officers' Training Corps Parade

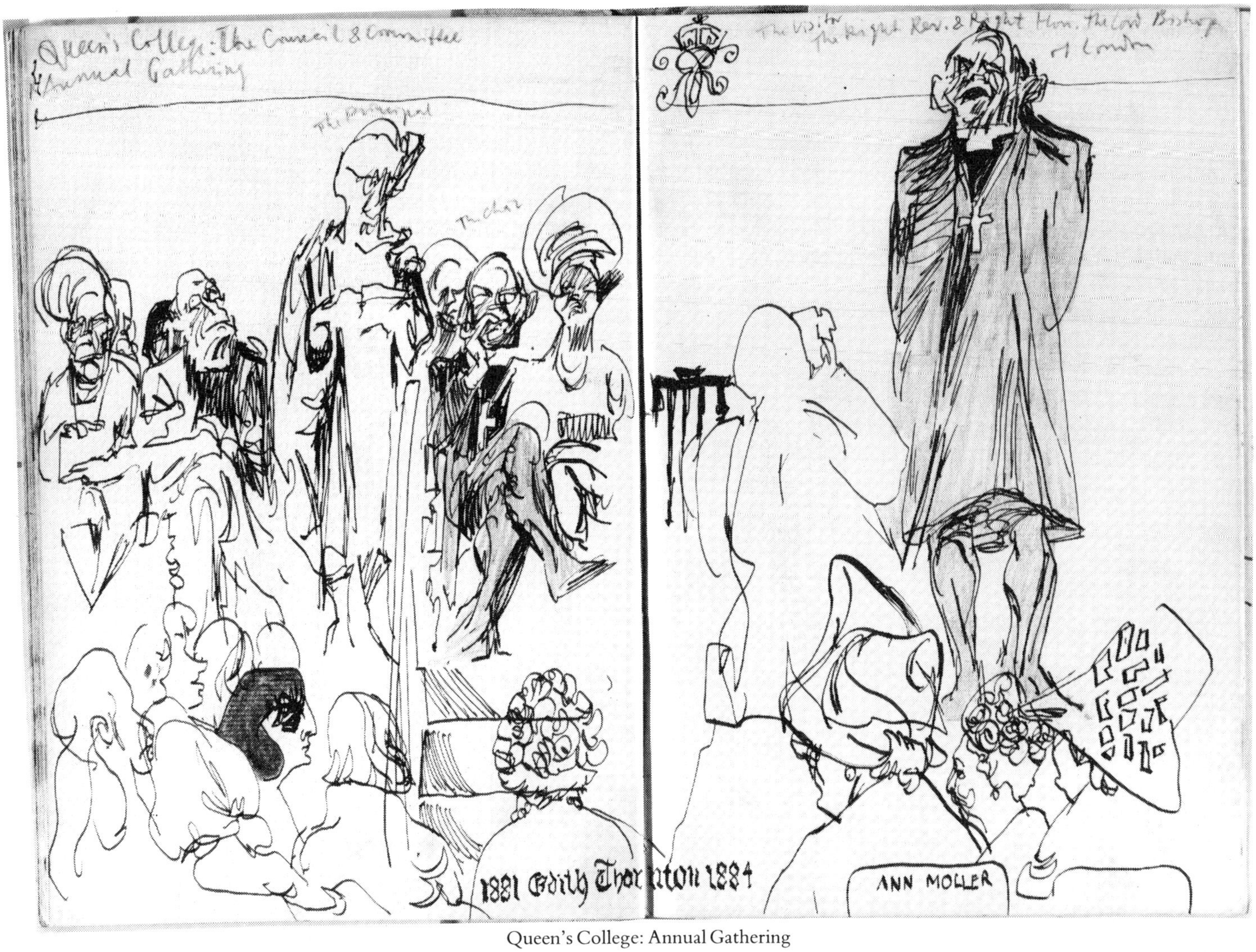

Queen's College: Annual Gathering

ordained celebrations, did not prepare for the surge of tenderness and the undefined, but valid, meditative state when we parents found ourselves facing the cluster of adolescent girls in white – ensconced within a rather indifferent interior, but also within ritual and choir music – and including, precisely as one amongst many, our Teresa, solemnized, beribboned, berobed and making ready for the next step.

But Teresa remembers the occasion only from my drawing of it. Yet, now, they both constituted Marion's entombment, led by a young clergyman of St John's Wood church, both having responded though outside any dogmatic religion to the need raised in them for help to retain her closeness – Teresa adding, 'Rigid negation is a mistake.'

In my foolhardy confidence it did not occur to me deliberately to pursue influential channels and personages. Only when my progress met with an adverse tide did I become alerted to surrounding games, to those selective friendships cultivated by prominent artists almost exclusively with rich collectors, museum and institutional directors, critics and dealers. I must establish my *bona fides*. My Little Venice 'Thursdays' contained random representatives of art-power, but they were participants in the usual social gravitations, not lured – and not meant to be used; the best proof being that, with John Rothenstein's regular 'Thursday' attendances, none of my paintings entered the Tate in those years.

So, with the erratic and chancy progress, I am now inexplicably close to the top of the 'pop' list in art, but, without Establishment backing, am an unlabellable outsider without 'market' legitimacy.

Benedict Nicolson once wittily arranged (was it in the fifties?) a large exhibition of art prominent in the public's eye – without separating high from low. I sent a large painting, perhaps the nearest I made to the demands of 'modernity' but, just the same, out of step with both the Tate of the day and the Academy conventions; it had for a theme defeated Japan and carried intentionally a then unfashionable tension in its imagery. The exhibition was almost ignored by art reviewers: the challenge to commit themselves over border cases scared them. Thus my position remained ambiguous until many years later a confrontation was at long last forced on me, belated, trivial, but blatant.

A friendly couple, not of the 'art world', produced a long-ahead invitation for dinner at a Spanish restaurant. Only closer to the date I learnt that it would be a dinner for four and that my hosts' cousin would be the fourth – **Peggy Guggenheim**.

This was obviously to be an occasion of some importance for them, and they, mistakenly as it turned out, but in the best of faith, thought of me, I imagine, as an artist of prominence, yet possibly and paradoxically fit to be 'discovered' by Peggy. Such a reading of the composition of the party came to me afterwards; it may sound implausible, but, being an artist outside the international patronage entanglements, I had a hazy idea of Peggy Guggenheim as simply a rich collector of works of art, and thus (why not?) a potential buyer of a painting by myself. This lead to a minor humiliation, but also to a major enlightenment on the nature of hidden (but perhaps decisive) undercurrents of art manipulations. Not bothered *then*, to my loss, with homework on Peggy and her period, I appended it only afterwards, but now must prefix it before completing the tale.

The art-greed of patron Popes and Rulers of earlier Europe was set on snatching the best of tested talent; 'modern art', anarchic at first, was soon conducted by middlemen and, much more, by a manipulatory out-of-control profit-race, reputations (and prices) overtaking the production of the works themselves; hence validity (and values) became greatly assisted – as in all branches of human commerce – by private appetites.

Peggy Guggenheim entered Paris at the right moment for modern art – when it settled down as respectable merchandise – and for herself in her life – when her riches matched her erotic demands – (it is all by now fully dealt with in print – even by herself); perhaps those demands were only then woken and fanned in a basically timid and conventional Jewish-American woman. Whatever the starting point her artists-in-waiting and her growing collection accumulated in unison.

It is a grand and lovingly assembled collection and it is complete (as she has declared herself, the later modernity was only a repetitious blunder); so is her parallel achievement as an *amoureuse*. She could not proceed beyond that wholeness.

Having reported my researches, there is not much more to be said. At our dinner table sat an old plain woman, and next to her I – an elderly artist.* The evening was charmingly sustained by our hosts and by the dancers who later joined us and whom I had, customarily for me, drawn in action. But, when I had driven Peggy to her lodgings, my unbriefed clumsiness made me unsure whether to suggest that she come next day to my studio, or to send her some pictorial 'data'. I did the latter; and she promptly returned them. I had pushed myself into the unpractised role of a pedlar, a salesman – one doomed to fail, unaware that her 'collecting' in every sense had ended. . .

Indeed the experience, only transitorily embarrassing, and my later grasp of the Peggy theme were worthwhile, making it sharply clear that my '*oeuvre*', whatever its worth, could not dangle at the tail end of her era.

The Next Decade†

We assume that movement is life, whether it is the movement of a pendulum or linear progression of a serpentine climb, ever returning and ever changing. Seen from a great distance of time vast slices of the past may seem static, but the ferment, the making and smashing, the wrestling of forces, never came to rest; never has a harmonious, ideal republic stayed without throwing up a tyrant or succumbing to a barbarian. Each empire, culture, academy in turn has become, at the peak of its security, a besieged fortress, and then a tomb to be dug out centuries later during a lesser period which needed to boost up its lack of assurance and restore its flagging momentum with an antiquarian pill. One is apt in *this* period, obsessed with the idea of the sempiternal, to see longevity in the past; yet at one end Napoleon's epic lasted a shorter time than Hitler's – a dozen or so years; at the other one learns (and it seems to be knowledge rather kept down by anthropologists) that the jungle tribes change the whole gamut of their ritual lore within a few years, the rhythm of generations being probably much more important in human history than tradition's continuity. So life is movement. And here comes the biological function of the artist. I see a sort of dull-witted, hesitant and sluggish multi-monster, a human tribe, society, civilization or whatever – always resisting, always slowing down and eager to settle into the slumber of the *status quo*, into permanency, and hence into death, then rapid decomposition. And at the head of this hesitant process, pulling, sniffing out direction, foraging, restless, are nature's scouts: the doubters, nonconformists, explorers, pioneers, researchers, challengers, prophets (false and true), the out-of-step breed – and the true artists prominent amongst them. They blazon new paths, they are mocked, they turn out heroes or martyrs eventually to be followed, at first reluctantly, by the modish, the band-waggoners, then by the exploiters and cultivators, until the whole tribal monster is vitalized. Yet again the adventure and the daring burn themselves out into academies, churches and establishments, the pace slows down to accommodate the dignitaries in their robes of office, until the sweet decadence breeds restlessness once more.

A strange somersault of priorities is performed in our lifespan and never challenged. At school and university the young who unravel a vocation, that is a gift in a professional direction, are hailed and move to the fore. At the instant of stepping out they find that the front line of initiative, the monopoly of opportunities, dignities and rewards, is occupied by the managers (whether of politics, administration or business) recruited from amongst those lacking vocations and therefore freer to roam and to choose. The professional, and most particularly the artist, is held down to his job, not admitted into the echelons of the bosses who direct and co-ordinate. The artist is diminished to the stature of a harnessed performer and the impresario-patron-society deprived of a most invigorating contribution: the non-opportunist adventure of inspiration.

The word 'communication' has conflicting connotations. What we communicate to our own young we call education. What those beyond the Iron Curtain communicate we call indoctrination. We cherish the fallacy that the public wants this

*Quite some years earlier (in 1956?) before my Peggy Guggenheim researches, on a boat to the States, a shrewd New York woman art dealer seemed impressed with photographs of my *Festival* mural and other paintings, impressed enough to ask my age: I told her – forty-nine; 'Too old' she said matter-of-factly. I was puzzled; how, supposing I meant to try to enter New York as a painter, could the top-form middle age be in my disfavour, if, as she declared, my work was impressive? But I did not, as she probably did, take into account the young gladiatorial fitness and appeal also required in that art-arena.

†Extracts from a paper read at the Tenth Annual Visual Communications Conference arranged by the Art Directors Club of New York in April 1965.

or that and the communication mediums oblige. But of course the public is also conditioned by what it is offered – the traffic moves both ways. Until somewhat round the beginning of this century the ideal of the communication mediums was to inform and uplift; and there is no justification for the current cliché that the public wants to be pampered and not instructed. One can imagine a conference like this in the Egypt of the Pharaohs, in the early Buddhist days in Asia, or in Christian Byzantium, devoting itself to sorting out the 'communication visuals' – the imagery officially approved as the most effective for buying obedience to a dynasty or for selling the new faith. The story of 'engaged' art, that is art engaged in communication, that is commissioned art, is *the history of art*.

Two hundred years ago there were no museums, no art dealers, and no art for art's sake with strings attached. A short-lived attempt of the artist to create in freedom instantly resulted in the most severe repressive dogmas (and consequently anathemas), then enslavement to fluctuations of fashion, hence eventually of markets. The liberated artist hammered out his own chains.

In fact the artist's revolt was a mere incident, completely conformist, in the multiform repercussions of early twentieth-century social revolutions, West or East. And so the art of the liberal era, pure art, finds its economic home and its dependence within the free enterprise of art dealers, creates a new big business, and is mainly engaged in satisfying the demand for handy and proud objects for the collector (this great figure in today's prestige arena) to put on his mantelpiece. The polite anguish of the artist beckons feverishly from opulent frames; ferocities of anti-art are tidily cut down to the size of the elegancies of the 57th Street dealers, haughtily aloof from the neighbouring Madison Avenue. They claim a closed shop of high art well above the commissioned art, but commercialized it is with vengeance. Even more vulgarly so when paraded as competing 'samples' and misused as market pointers placarded along the steepest walls of new museums.

Art is one. The entrenchment in prominence of art made portable for convenience of purchase has been too prolonged. The dominance of bibelot art has worked too long to the exclusion of traditional concert of murals, sculpture and stained glass within architecture. The pathos of these limitations must end. We look hopefully to the future for their integration in a unified structure of co-operating arts and for a renewal of the communal aspirations of the past.

We must combat too the falsifying inquisitions of *taste* which suppress in advance the heresies of reality. I think of recent exhibitions of Indian art. India is the world of overflooding humanity, overflooding, overcrowding on to the walls of temples and holy caves in the vast stream of humans, gods and animals, sculptured and painted in breathtaking *massement*. How different when they are presented by the contemporary taste of the Western *cognoscenti*! Torn from their awe-inspiring crowding, from being gods and from communicating high meaning, now reduced to single titbits of sculpture, set against coy and calming plushes and subtly lit to isolate them further into the gallery convention of art pieces, saleable and cataloguable! A deliberate truncation of the majestic truth. The same pretence that the sweep of art does not exist is enforced by the emphasis on detail in art books; they cut down the reality of all-embracing art to the measure of an art dealer's shop.

And the incomplete museums of today, conceits of possession, may be replaced by educationally valid, encyclopaedic collections of life-size replicas of the best in the world's art. . .

As it is, often the more talented, more versatile artist is tempted into the supposedly corrupting life of the communicating arts. And it is the same artist who may equally have been a star of 57th Street. Corruption, or perhaps plain waste, is engendered by the limitation of contemporary communications fields; by focusing mainly on pampering the passive-participation audience, appropriately called captive – the sit-down, endless perspective of consumers, each for himself.

Quite different to this was the inspiration of the Italian primitive to communicate and sell religion to an actively receptive public. Still another matter was the selling of Napoleon's glory by his chroniclers, painters, designers, architects or more recently the selling of Hitler by his paid planners of mass rallies and racial myths. And today, but still more so tomorrow, when production and distribution are almost the sole constructive forces for peace-on-earth and the bellicose instincts of humanity descend dangerously to the lowest depths of the *white* versus the *coloured*, it would seem desirable to coerce, nay conscript, the whole body of the communication media and their mighty sponsors into concentrated campaigning for such issues as the communal ideas rather than personal appetites; participation rather than seclusion; the spiritual rather than the material: in short, Humanism – and on a global scale. . .

A few years ago an American stage director came to see me in London. His was a heartening request. He was planning to put on the stage an adaptation of a famous book and not satisfied with pedestrian efforts at turning the book into a play, he thought of starting from the opposite end: to ask me as an artist to create a visual concept and structure for staging it and then proceed backwards, as it were, towards the *words*. The theme, the martyrdom of the Jews, took me a long way beyond the limits of a Broadway production. My fourteen-page promise of a fuller memorandum to follow contained such concepts as writing new chapters into the Bible, creating a modern version of Redemption and setting it into a ritual of a rationalist and international Holy Week, world pilgrimages and makeshift theatre-temples culminating in a modern Passion Play to progress like the church service through the liturgical enactment of the Stations of Martyrdom, engaging the greatest creative and performing talents into this all-arts cavalcade, activating a world movement . . . I filled it up with tangible proposals and assured him that: 'You must not think that I am getting out of hand. I repeat that everyone is free to aim at anything, and that one need not lose in the act any of one's sense of humour and reality.' In reply I received a feeble cable; later I learned that another director and another producer put on still another version on Broadway and that it faded away – a second-rate, naturalistic playlet. And until now my director, when visiting London, keeps well away from running into me.

I must hasten to clear myself of the possible suspicion that I am a crank, peddling frustrated rounds of mad fantasies. I mostly work, and also play a bit, and I am relating here, I presume for your benefit, my rare encounters with the future and my lessons derived from them. And comedy, naturally, goes with failures.

Recently, when queried by Britain's new Minister of Art, Jennie Lee, on my conception of the future of art, I vaguely formulated some ideas based on my devotion to the impermanent, the makeshift; my indifference to projects for 'housing the arts' while the artist is left unhoused; my anti-monumental, anti-antiquarian, floating, mobile bent for the all-in spectacle of collaborating arts, for bringing the citizenry into participation. I showered her with, and made recoil from, my list of the social 'incitement elements': the ritualized humanism and play cum creation of festivals, processions, tournaments and debates converging on the true Forum located on the ruins of ceremonially demolished cultural centres.

Yet more recently my tilt of mind proved to be very close to the 'Fun Palaces' project of the anti-theatre Joan Littlewood. And so we had numerous meetings in my studio on the South Bank, the possible location of the project – Joan, her young anti-architecture architect Cedric Price, and an anti-literature writer, Alexander Trocchi, who vaguely plans a sort of worldwide Mafia of the agin-it lone-wolves of arts and sciences. I feel that we hold at least the immediate future. My *Chronicle* (indeed the very essence of a makeshift anti-periodical) is to publish a large issue on the project, which, I am sure, will be realized. The Fun Palace will not be a building 'housing arts' in the *passé* manner, but a short-life plaything, an entertainment kit of immense dimensions set as an expandable, shape-changing structure of service towers, lifting-gantries and building components. It will emphasize 'do-it-yourself' participation of the public and will contain potential setting for adult toys, star-gazing, science-gadgetry, hide-aways, rallies, *kunst*-dabbling, theatre-clownery, dancing, and *no* doors or walls. The *New Statesman* said of it: 'It is all a wild, mod dream, no mistake about it, and this is precisely what gives it its meaning.' An enlightened reaction!

But to end on the solider argument of my own work and the changes it involves – I have been filling up my studio in the last few years with a huge, 12- to 16-feet high, and roughly continuous painting, patched up and overlapping, punctuated by three-dimensional relief accents, which forces on me as it creeps on, encompassing my workshop, the idea of an environment of painting – ceiling included; not in a tidy interior design, but a sort of Ajanta caves run riot. And there are architect friends helpfully suggesting labyrinthian and makeshift structures which would accommodate this growing panorama – proposals ultra-organic, untidy, assertive and muscular – and I think of the future, which will reject the pyramid-complex of monumentality and opt to live in the adaptability of flux.

I mean to go on painting this visual diary for as many yards or curving, twisting miles as I shall last. It will be well in character to have it not elegantly ended, but – I trust not too soon – interrupted in the middle of a brush stroke. [. . .]

Yet I know now, having begun to work my *Chronicle* drawings and my paintings into the film-form, that the painting need not be the end in itself. The urge comes to push the painting into movement through the mill of film; not cartoon movement which fails by its limitations, but the *eye* movement of the camera wandering over the expanses of painting, zooming in, playing on the drama of close-ups against vast sweeps, embracing sound and rhythm and, above all, blowing it up to any dimension when projected on huge screens, domes, skyscrapers' walls, skies; so that the painting is turned into a spectacle, its very colour changing in mood by varying intensity of camera exposure, fired by light to gain the blinding force fiercer than the stained glass of the past. The veritable visual explosion.

This is visual communication indeed. And more! The painter's brush raised to a size matching our time's scale and his gifts at last put to uses more challenging than ever before – technique and all other arts in alliance! To quote another earlier plea of mine published in the *London Tribune* under the heading 'Planning for Art'; 'Michelangelo's vision, had it been squashed into the easel pictures of today, would never have expanded into the miracle it was. How unfulfilled he would have been without the Sistine Chapel.'

We feel, and are, dwarfs in face of that giant, but given majestic opportunities the artists will grow in strength to match them.

But urban penetration was stunning/grim
cohorts turned on
abortive of direction
tossed about by cops
carousing over murky musty streets
(avenues clear for fast moving lawful go-getters)
bleating herded for Tim now-Messiah
tuned in through discothèques' blaring
Fug's Fuck-totems campaigning
and underground vacuous
non-procedures,
culture-as-we-know-it began splitting becoming
a laughing matter
and the Negro voices,
Broadway amplified,
cracked abysses under civilization-as-we-knew-it.

New York's Village Theatre – coronation chamber for **Black America's Leroi.** His *Ubu Roi* pomp-circumstance ceremonial mucks-you-Lady-Bird fucks-your-white-mother drums for Negro in-out-up rising. The ablest latest tongue – the bestest costumed showmanship amongst the world's reserve-leaders. His swagger falls into beat with the march of time. Virile st$^{a}_{u}$ff.

Hippy
dialectics
of de-liberation.
These sectarian devouts
self-assuring

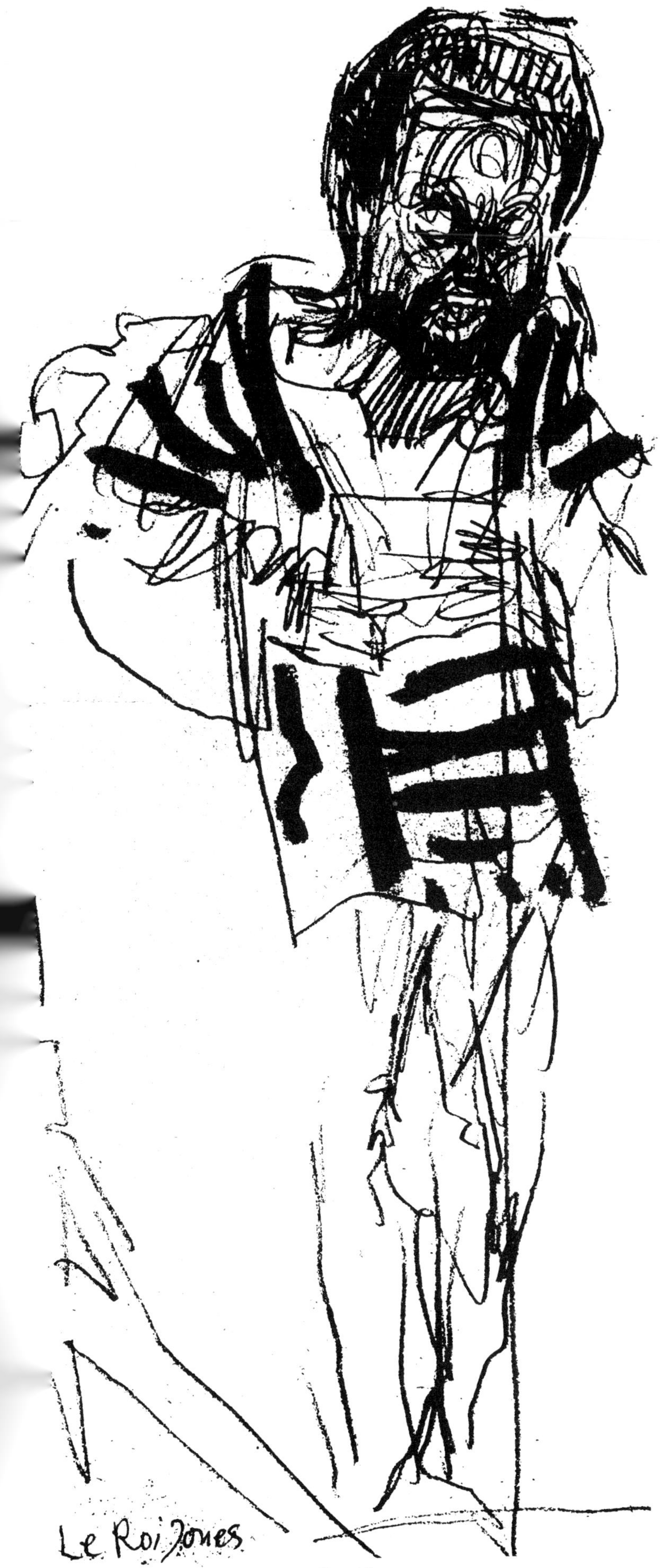

Leroi Jones

by solemn murmurs of persecution,
by their litanies,
their scholastic gossip,
their dreamful time-beading
and clinging tight
in the faith-warming togetherness.
And their
injured unbelieving grimaces
in those panics
when
Burroughs
(whisper whisper goes global rounds)
denies/denounces
dope.
London passes it over, Tonga
summons missionaries, California
formulates excommunications –
the blow
convulses the whole Holy body
of the Psychedelic Churchdom;
when
Stokely
pushes up his polaroids
in a vain-furtive gesture and,
in front of a thousand youths
(and cameras and reporters), says
'What's great about turning on!?'
See
the guru-poet's
shocked-hurt-stultified
priestly outsized eye –
the devil spoke, let us chant

In the dark, up the thickly forested grounds to a Swiss-chalet shape and to a moody interior at the top. A fine opening. But hospitable **'guide' Michael Hollingshead** upset the purity by over-staging: the candles/the log fire/the scents/the overlapping Eastern and rock sounds and projections – 'hospitable', or obeying the manuals, but also possibly anxious for assured effects, unsure of the psychedelia-workings, thus forcing his 'taste' upon my, in reaction, now resisting/sorting out bewareness.

Yet another obstruction – perhaps upsetting the yielding/emptying ('clear the consciousness of irrelevancies') as instructed by the masters of LSD – the habitual advance, within the shadows, of agressive sexuality towards several flatly laid bodies – Michael perched above conducting his 'effects'. As promised, venoms/acids strike and unhinge in waves – but after a prolonged attack, begin to serve the senses: he (I) plots and acts in a haze, but unshackled and callous: he slithers ruthlessly across the nearest woman-bulk to reach the anaemic mid-back bareness: the vest crumped up – buttocks half-jutting out from the dip of the jeans; he falls upon it and glues to it – and immensity/endlessness of copulative abandon, ecstatically fulfilling yet inconclusive, loosing itself in memory. Then, on cue, the storm – real, but its might surging to cataclysmic force.

He sways his way shakily on to the terrace – 'awareness' indeed 'expanded' – elements in concerted exertions at and through him culminate in cascading floods from above; he, still marginally fractious, contributes, beneath, a modest stream of urine.

Back, stretched out on the floor palpitating fast – and no respite: the last of the heavenly rumpus seems to crash open the door at his back, exuding a threateningly towering cortège of giant protagonists: flamboyantly costumed and posturing, their features strained and marked into masks of hate/disdain; they settle close to and high above his slave-become body – a regal tyrant's court: his up-gaze assesses the emphatic kitschiness of the group (probably his (my) own super-imposed aesthetics), thus convincingly and immaculately corrupt; the ruler bending his ear to a confidant (he (I) does recognize, but inconsequentially on his 'increased perceptions', **Tim Leary**); the mimicry/rivalry of queenly women at the ruler's knees – all heartless, all in fateful judgement over him.

But again, though intimidated, he rolls (a ruffian and a bad psychedelic novice) over and ventures some whispered asides to the nearest and grandest of the queens – which ruptures the sequence: they depart and, later, I shall be told that Leary was at fault in breaking into our session ciceroning (apparently) his mighty patrons – hence perhaps the evil aura of the intrusion.

Hours of intoxication (because, in essence, this it was) holding our prostrate group powerless, began to wear out into passivity – the physical oddities, such as the invisible cobwebbing blocking one's mouth, moving to the fore – the night paling. And yet another invasion, preluded by a shocking crescendo of machine-racket outside, sustains the elusive suspect significance of the rite: a pair of undoubted devils jerk/dance in, as if to collect their dues at the finale; their faunish fiends' grins, their tattooed (painted?) nakedness, dangling hair-nested swollen sexes; dangling cymbals drums and whatever brings forth coarse piercing rhythms. They are abominable, yet necessary, hence alluring. They shout and sing and stamp, their thin merciless energy hurting/offending to the core my (his) spent 'egolessness'.

Driven away at dawn, I glimpse, neatly set on the grass against a tree, alongside a man, the anaemic girl. She turns her head and blankly, composed or indifferent, follows – with her eyes – my departure. Michael, her boyfriend and my 'guide' drives me back and discloses an accord with me: his LSD-commitment is not of a fanatic, but of an experimenter – drifting into an opportune climate.

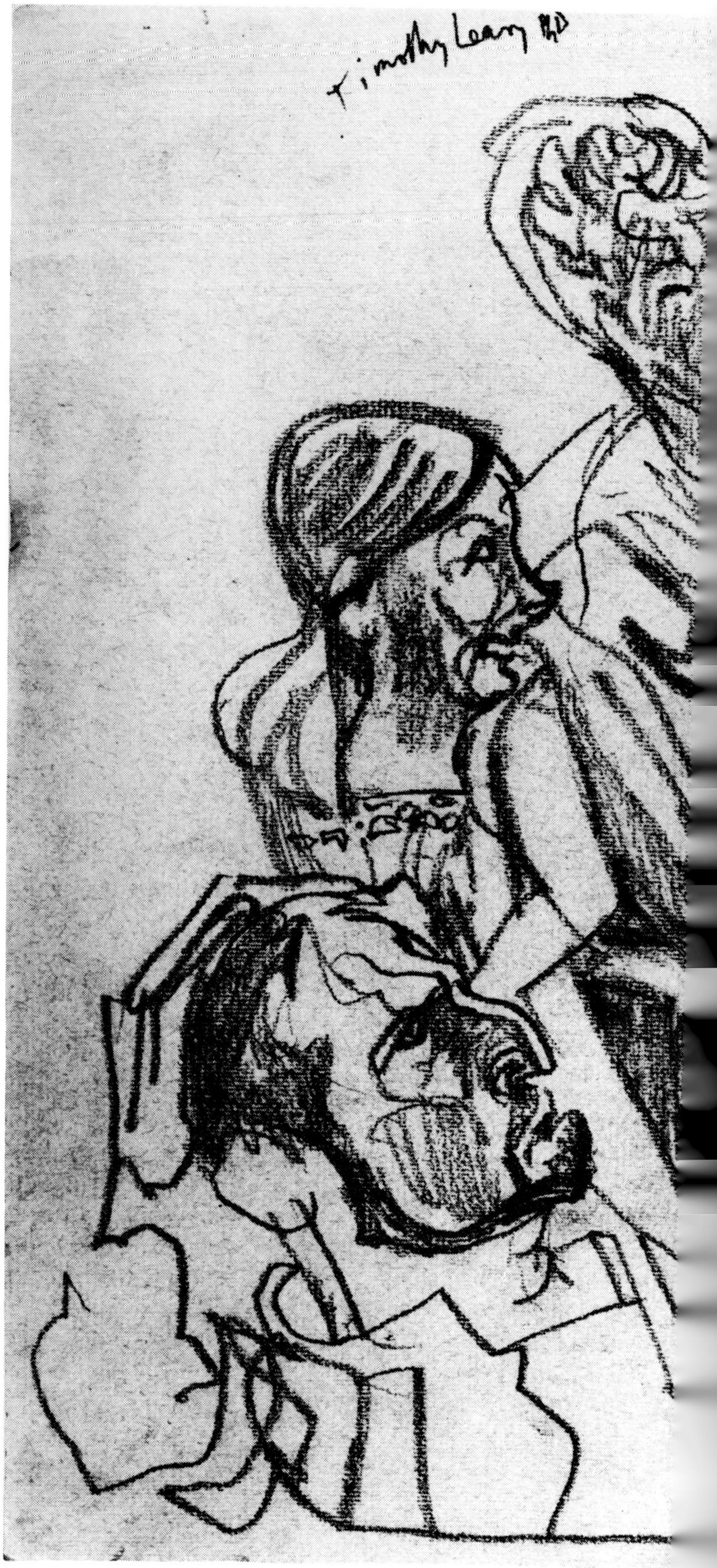

It is only 5 or 6 in the morning. My hosts **Mortimers' mansion** is locked, and, though not quite out of 'psychedelia', I have to climb up the vine to my room's balcony on the first floor. There a mini-*post-scriptum* for the maxi-night: a larger-than-life naked man blocks my entry, seems to square up with the window – merely a newly arrived guest to share the room with.

A day of convalescence for the hero of the moment. Wrapped in blankets, flat in a veranda-chair, I relate my adventure to impressed **Caterine**, who, with all the others, had begged me two days earlier not to go and undergo the 'experience', dismissive with haughty disdain of the hippy-bedraggled Michael and his girl who had come to fetch me. I did not now tell Caterine that the heroine of my LSD night was that one.

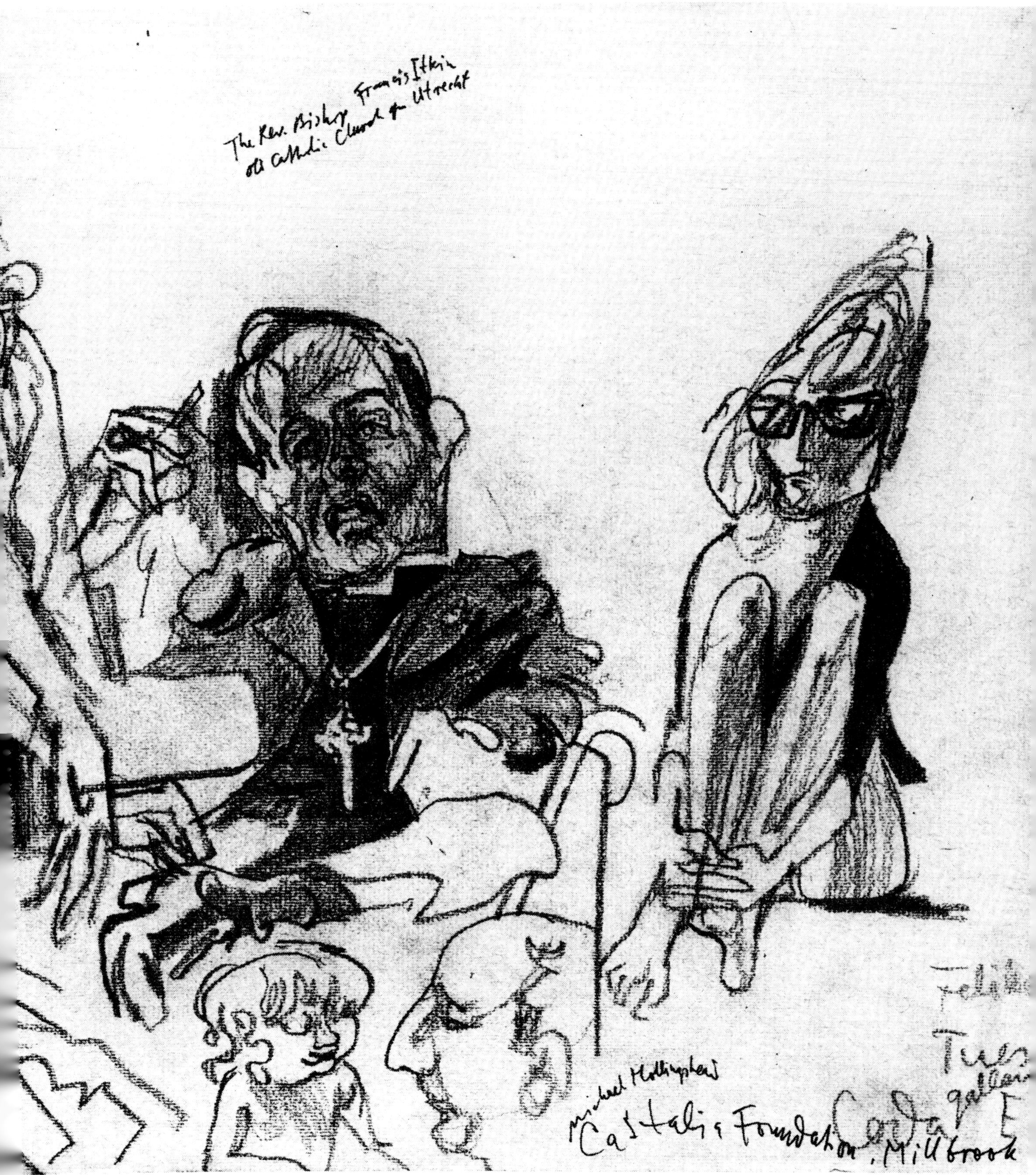

Timothy Leary and followers at Millbrook, 1967 (from *Shem, Ham & Japheth Inc.*)

Later, in New York, the 'court' scene of my LSD session, re-enacted in the comedy of reality: Leary – a sub-squire by the generosity of a grandee-millionaire – pseudo-ruling over the Castalia Foundation in the cluster of Swiss chalet follies at Millbrook, Connecticut.

But soon after, the LSD culture having been challenged by the law, he, the most supple con, manoeuvred an unabashed complete turn, the first of many that followed.

1966. The tatty Village Theatre every other day by now a temple to **Messiah Timothy**. With scientific mumbo-jumbo opaqueness discredited he dispenses, wrapped whitely, showbiz East-tinged faith, backed by prancing maidens and projected kitsch-psychedelia – all this to claim immunity as a religious leader. Thus staged the message made threadbare – another worn-torn Western banner.

Yet again – my urge to test not yet drained – this time at Christmas in London.

The acid-cooked visual glories are not that emphatic for me; the thought comes that Huxley's enchantments/eulogies over the palpitating beauty of a kitchen chair were dictated by his semi-blindness: for him it was miraculous enough to see it at all. And on the whole it is laymen, not professionals, who extol psychedelic colours; a painter in residence at Millbrook, obligatorily executing rather handsome mandalas, told me that he could work only in between, not under LSD. In short: LSD a compensatory gift for the ordinary, not for the 'creative visualizers'!

So, from this rather *comme-il-faut* session, I, 'high' all right, tiptoe away into the next room where a psychedelic groupie has gone for a nap. . .

And only now comes the hazard: having had enough LSD compulsions, yet full of the poison, I start in my jeep (in Belgravia) for my house in Regent's Park; tensed for vestiges of alertness, conscious of my reeling precariousness and of possible encounters with the police, I emerge into Hyde Park Corner. It is Christmas Eve night's crowded and racing traffic – a **'mindblowing' menace** to me: the circular swirl of machines and dazzle of headlights become a whipped-up cosmos of cometic fitfulness; I cut into this velocity-nightmare; travel, I am convinced, as a planetary element of the whirlpool, yet pushing my will to concentrate on the driving-wheel over the turmoil of the night's addiction – and arrive enigmatically unscathed.

The late dark hour: but small lights narrowly spill from Marion's room and, a floor above, Teresa's; and their unhurried low-voiced duet graces the height of the house. No longer watchful and so un-held, I stumble to Marion's door, fall on my knees clutching/grasping at her, whimper for forgiveness – for what? Yet contrariness, ever close to the surface, sniggers a thought at this, staged-by-myself hence maybe innate, melodrama; and another: a true penance, or self-exorcism/cleansing of accumulated devilishnesses?

This is **my last** – and unwittingly: when, in the crowded room, I realized that the stuff had gone into me, the pathos of anticipating dreary hours of its predictabilities working through my system infuriated, while the American girl I had brought lighted up with elated anticipation – an addict.

The surreal boredom. I fail to find seclusion: the back-room bizarre performance solely for me by Alexander Trocchi's teenage friend: bared to the waist, she sways upright on the bed and then stiffly falls back, head crashing against the wall; undamaged, again on her feet, she begins to intone: 'A–lex–Troc–chi–Fe–liks–To–pol–ski–A–lex–Troc–chi–Fe–liks. . .' to crash, to rant, to scramble up, to crash again, and again – faster and louder: 'To–pol–ski–A–lex–Troc–chi–Fe–liks. . .' I sally out of this tight space – a cluster of familiar faces expectantly outside in the corridor – pirouetting through them pursued by, now highest-pitched: 'Troc–chi–Fe–liks–To–pol–ski–A–lex–Troc–chi. . .' In the commotion, Michael blocks my escape. Face to face, I examine with my psychedelically sharpened eyes this visage disclosed/revealed/laid bare/manifested/explained/unconcealed stark naked: its pleading twist, its smile of friendship pitifully marred by the seen-through surfaces of usage – wasted, coarsened, signalling hitherto hidden secrets. My face must be just the same in his eyes. I run away, get again into my jeep, aware as before of my psychedelic headful and my risks – and drive away for good – this time a less trying space-trip.

Soon after this Michael's rooms were raided and he gaoled for a year. Freed, in a halo of martyrdom, he wrote the 'definitive' book *The Man who turned on the World*, to close the tale, but declaring, '**We won**. . .' And indeed the 'Atlantic' world bears permanent marks of the hippy revolution-in-manners.

But Michael himself died a few months ago in New York.

Haywire fates of parental resolutions. Children's initial gulping curiosity for knowing submitted to the conscientiously selected 'progressive' Hampstead heights **Burgess Hill School's** methodical-ideological pounding into them of the virtue of self-determined aversion to learning.

To save them, the obvious escape was into the strictures of Continental curriculums – **the French Lycée.** But this solution must have occurred at that time to too many parents, the Lycée's size swelled up, teachers of quality too few supplemented by (one suspected) *au-pair* girls swept from all over London untrained and without English – the educational standard tumbling down – perhaps to be recovered much later, but after our children have left.

Daniel, by then, could move to his reserved-at-birth slot within the 'safe conduct' of the **public school** system – out of parental experimentations. An oarsman of distinction, got to **Oxford** and Geography, the disdained but 'easy' subject; the rowing blue, stayed a year longer ('Social Anthropology' an excuse) to double his blue – and continue as the legendary Oxford coach.

But Teresa, now as adept at obstinacy, landed in a girls' school, old-time Protestant progressive turned retrogressive

4—EVENING STANDARD, SATURDAY, MARCH 31, 1973

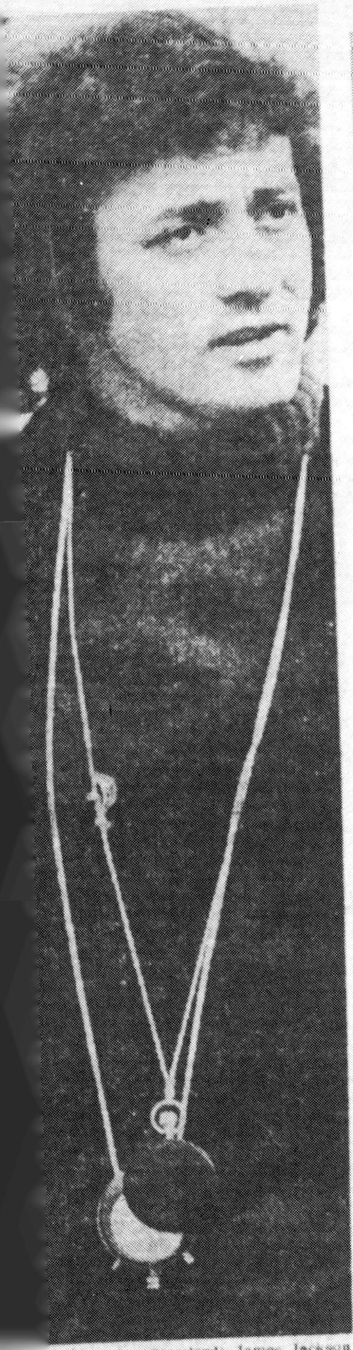

Evening Standard: James Jackson

DAN TOPOLSKI . . . desperate to end Oxford's losing run.

Desperate Dan aims to turn the tide for Oxford

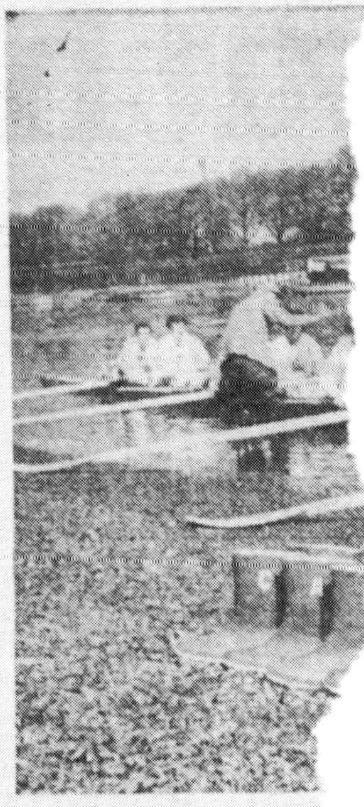

BEST FOOT forwa

BARRY NEWCOMBE dis Boat Race is alive and v very much afloat on the

THE SUN was glinting on the black patent boots of Dan Topolski. His blue velvet trousers crumpled and the shoulders under his red sweater heaved as he held the rope that connected him and the Oxford Boat Race crew.

Topolski narrowed his eyes and looked at his men.

"Are you ready—row," he commanded and eight glistening blades bit into the tideway and Oxford hauled themselves off downstream.

Topolski made them row flat out for three minutes and then came the instructions to ease off.

"You've had a hard day," he smiled. "That will do."

Topolski is the finishing coach for Oxford for next Saturday's 119th Boat Race against Cambridge, to be rowed over the Putney to Mortlake course.

Artist

It is his first year and, at 27, he is a young breakaway from tradition for the Dark Blue boat.

Son of the well-known artist Feliks Topolski, he works in administration for BBC TV.

He was a Blue in the Oxford Crew in 1967 and 1968. He has coached Westminster School, and, for three years, coached the Oxford second boat, Isis.

Last year he was one of the senior coaches and, this, year, the last demanding days are his alone.

Attitude

"When Adrian Hall, the President, asked me if I would coach, I was delighted," he said. "This is a challenge to me and all I want to do is break five years of depression for Oxford.

"We go into the race having lost the last five. We want a new look and a new attitude and I hope we have them both.

"From now on, it is all in the heart and the head. The physical work is over and ambition and the sheer desire to succ must count.

"I am so fortunate in havin a stroke to whom defeat an defeatism just do not exist. He is hungry for victory."

The stroke is America Olympic oarsman David Sawyier, a 22-year-old from Chicago who really adds some kick to the Oxford effort.

He has a gear-change technique that is quite staggering in operation and pushes the rate up and down with ruthless skill.

All hands

If Oxford are to break the Light Blue grip on the race, Sawyier is the man to lift them.

But old hands on the Tideway are wondering if Oxford have sufficient quality with him for the endurance test.

in an wh cont It

PERSONAL

., I need you. Please phone orge and Carolyn.
LEY, I love you. Bernard.
NEMARIE chou-chou perdonne n pom-pom.
RRY from Esher please contact athleen from Catford.
ACE DETECTIVE AGENCY, 437 5000. 734 5606.
ACADEMY KARATE course ndon Karate Club, 352 7716.
massage in your own suite. lection of massage. Large staff. 0 7558/9850. Ron Indoe.
CONFIDENTIAL PREGNANCY ST £2. RING or CALL CLINI- AL FACILITIES. 255a Grays

LED ZEPPELIN No. 5 L.P. £1·99. Ring 228 1399.
LONDON ESCORT AGENCY. Super girls. 836 9044.
MASSAGE sauna Aquarius 837 0846
MASSAGE Herbal Bath. Edgware area. Sharp. 952 9262.
MASSAGE (Poptant). 734 9208.
MEET HIM. Friendship, love and marriage through Dateline Computer Dating. Call 01-937 0102. 24 hours.
PHOTODATE for immediate results. 01-722 7930. 24 hrs.
PREGNANCY ADVISORY SERVICE K.A.S., 275a Kensington High-st., W.8. 602 6859 day, 727 3351, eve.
PREGNANCY TESTING Contraceptive advice, non profit making. Brook Advisory Centre, 233 Tottenham Crt. Rd., W.1. 580 2991.
TESTING CENTRE

CLASSIFI

DIRECT LINE TO SUCCESS

Monday–Friday 9 a.m.–6.30 p.m. Saturdays 9 a.m.

Daniel

conformist, and emerged an accomplished outsider. She made a bad showing (deliberately?) in front of Oxford and Sussex admission boards, refused to try elsewhere in England, or in France, agreed with the idea of the United States (reluctantly), but only as New York (parental enthusiasm: the dual education, academic and in living); rejected by Columbia, she woke up to welcome the **NYU** since it had, as the Visiting Professor for the Schweitzer Chair, Conor Cruise O'Brien with his distinguished invitees.

But, her academic dodginess aside, her moral and intellectual force prevailed, cut unscathed through the 'drug scene'; established her rapport and friendship with Conor and his guest lecturers the Ardens, Peter Nettl, George Steiner; she caused his and my book, *The United Nations: Sacred Drama*, assessed/rejected my New York friends; and seeded my American book, *Shem, Ham and Japheth Inc.*, by a telegram: 'The scene is here come and record.' This was 1968, the year of hippies exploding into yippies round the presidential election.

When/where to place the hatching of friendship between me and **Teresa**? It is firmly unsentimental and outside or even in spite of father–offspring ties (I have persisted since my adolescence in choosing my intimates, not having them imposed by kinship); it has not developed from them, but must have begun almost abruptly.

The clues should be in the painted *Memoir*, in its uncalculating selectivity interweaving essence beneath the story's hazards. So I enter my cave-arches and move along their labyrinthian imagery-assemblages as if a *homo novus* archaeologist deciphering hieroglyphic mysteries – leading to Teresa.

This manner of decoding illuminations topples over succession: there is '68 Chicago and San Francisco Black Panthers and New York's rise of revolt; much further follows the thronging of all-the-West's hippies overflowing on to the floor in flat cut-outs. And, only after two turnings, darkened stretches allude to intimate thus wider matters: illness and the closeness of death, young aspirations (Daniel as model), generations diverging or fused – and, at last, backed by the mustering of the outcasts or rather arising from their wretchedness, rueful, yet advancing/edging to the void, the end of the *Memoir* thus the gate to the present – Teresa.

That dark, and brooding area issues the maturing Daniel and Teresa, oddly evokes their father's tardy germination alongside.

There is the painting, and – submerged in paint – the message-answer surfaces, at the moment of writing, resolves the when/where: the friendship sprang up at Teresa's transplant into New York as an integral self-reliant student.

This was preceded by precursory signs though, which seem necessary here – in parallel with my panoramic painting in which mere routines aspire to roll into a saga – if this discovery of friendship is to be taken as cardinal within that teeming time.

Perhaps the earliest (was she sixteen?): only the two of us (I delegated to shake her out of an anorexic – not yet named – tendency) booked into tiny rooms behind **St Tropez** harbour. Whatever her slimming excesses she was at her best, and the bikini boutique *vendeuses* went a-twitter over this classic performance of a Lolita stripteasing for her sugar-daddy; we bought two bikinis, white and multi-coloured in expectation of contrasting demands. And indeed, at the Tahiti *plage*, we were instantly enveloped by a Franco-American group of the currently ruling arbiters of *bon goût* within the *Vogue*-cum-vogueishness sphere (my New York associates and others) and over Teresa, stretched redheadedly whitely and freckly on her back under a parasol, there began to circle a refrain, '*Regardez, regardez, la belle petite Anglaise.*'

Inconsequentially, the order-less fragments are of New York – of several New Yorks, but some, perhaps, subconscious-control-suppressed, because I notice that earlier memories – of the fifties – are not included, having been to some extent written down already.

So; the modern model-design interior cutting through the width of a brownstone house, with, glossy-advert armchaired: Robin Butler, an *élégante* if ever there was one (now London's Mrs Hambro); Jan Carew, my demi-godly Guyanese – top-of-the-Third-World-weaver; the boss of the Grove Press, Richard Seaver; and I – all sort of waiting for my daughter Teresa, reluctant student at the New York University and proposed researcher-editress for the Grove Press's *Erotic Art* Part Two.

The bell rings, I open the door and there enters the unobtrusive small-scale enchantment – Teresa at her still better: waify narrow-jeaned wise-child, virginal face – the neatest – under copper up-gathered hair. One senses the publisher's raptness – the virginal Teresa will compose the erotic-wisdom encyclopaedia.

Some time in the sixties I stayed at the **Paris Ritz**, not my lifestyle's predilection but packaged with a portrait-series commission for a Canadian whisky's publicity: such is nowadays the 'exclusivity'-clientèle.

That time in Paris was crowded with contrasting encounters: **Menotti** rehearsing one of his operas was my main preoccupation. He, as his orientation's network operates, occupied a sumptuous house lent to him by a generous Parisian. Otherwise there was a sweep of brash elegancies under the guidance of the painter Corbassière, an *habitué* of debonair spheres.

Corbassière, a puzzling charlatan-meteor of art: his St Tropez factory of paintings identical in size/character, sprayed/dripped by the dozen within a respect-inspiring little *château*, his seasons accurately following the world-cycles of the rich: Paris, Palm Beach, St Moritz – at every one of these his mucky workshop, furiously productive, he emerging unkempt, club-footed, aggressive and conquering. His vitality's scope: society, 'the' places, women, 24-hour days; his ravenous circling of the St Tropez beaches, understandably never undressed, shabby-ugly-limping yet doubtlessly hyponotic to his prey.

I phoned him on the afternoon of my arrival and that same

Opposite: Teresa (Photographs by Richard Avedon)

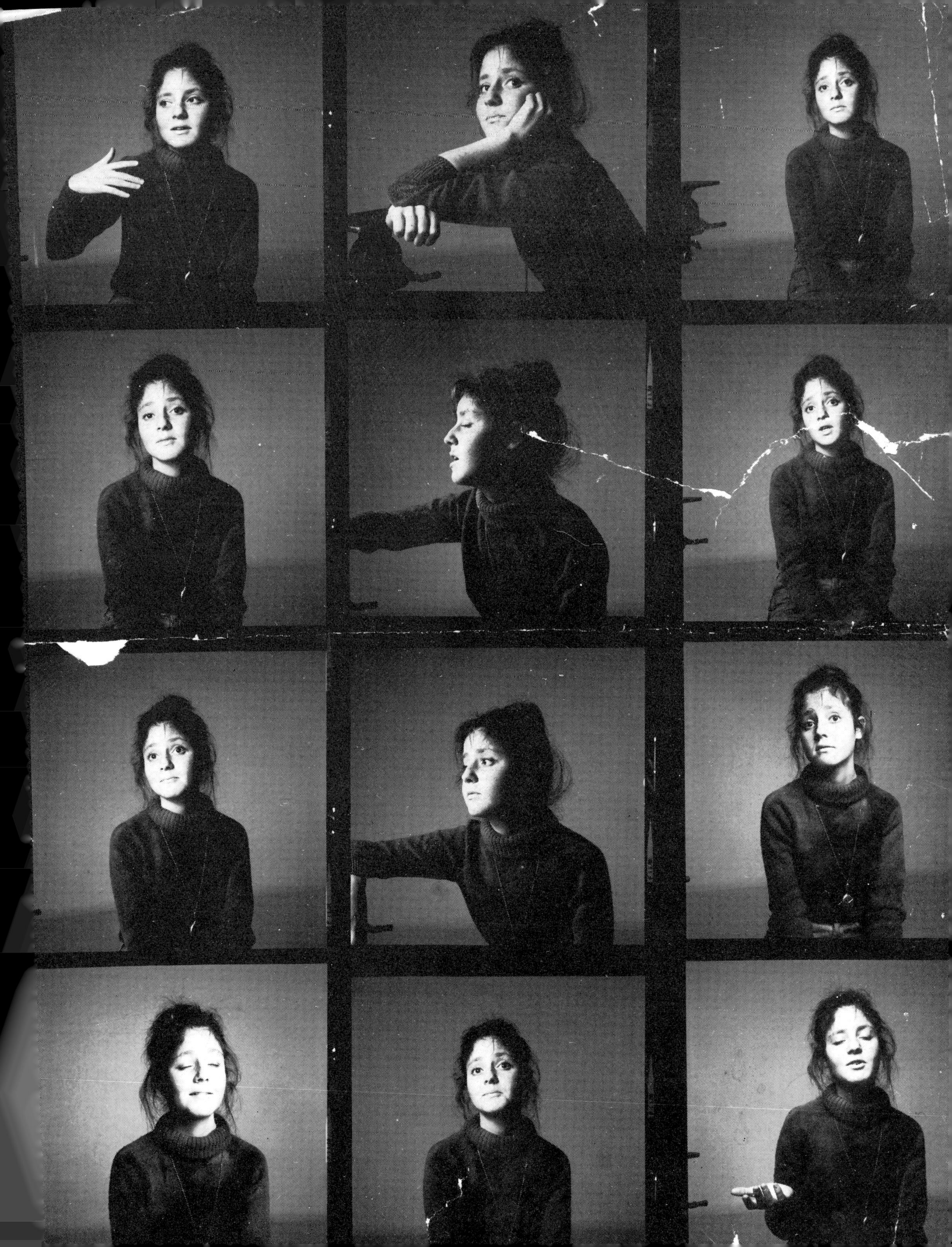

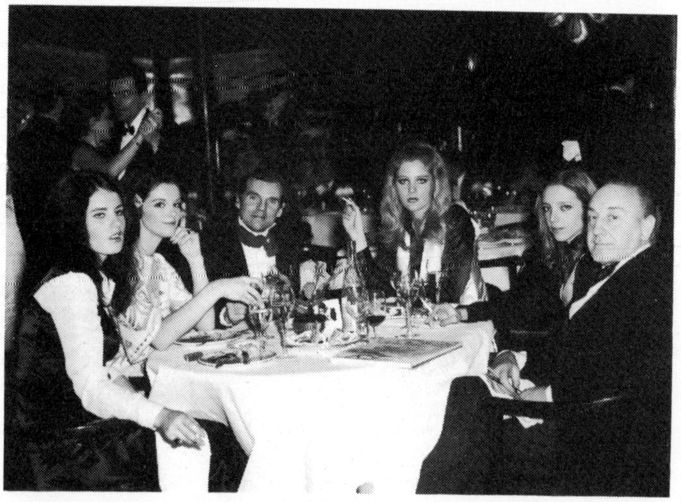

At Maxim's

evening the two of us sat down to a most subtle meal in a bistro *à la mode*, he in the widest of berets, in the company of five decorative young women, of various nationalities, mostly unknown to one another: this must have been his nightly mode of life – he could not have improvised the elaborate occasion at such short notice. The meal was, in the nature of things, followed by the crowded opening of a night-club of the highest mark. And, two evenings later, he led me to a large centre table at **Maxim**'s, again the two of us and a bevy of lovely ladies, the menu's heading printed with my name as guest of honour, and taking most of the floor, each dancing with two or more partners – he club-footed eccentric (though this time formalized by black tie) and I, a jot embarrassed *vieillard*.

Then, thrown in, a chance meeting with **James Mason** (a constant subscriber to my *Chronicle*) and the pleasure of revisiting the homely/snob Hôtel Régence off the Champs-Élysées to see him. Also, all charming stylization, hazily I see Lady Mosley and me in an innocuous dialogue in Paris (was it a hotel suite?) over tea, with no recollection of how it came about; bar-propping with Sam White at the Crillon . . .

But, in contrast to all this, the finale: booking out of the Ritz, made aware belatedly that my patrons were to pay my expenses later, I (rather dressy for the part of a Ritz guest) began emptying my pockets at the lobby counter of the pathetic remnants of cash – most uncomfortably not enough of it to meet the bill. But in the background there stood, ill-fitting the gilded interior, **two young hippies** (worldwide-fashioned in hair and fantasy attire) – my faithful young Polish friends and companions outside my more formal engagements who had come to give me a lift in their old Mini to the airport; and this incongruous scene: I beckoned to them, they approached, produced a cheque-book and paid my bill matter-of-factly, the liveried staff and buttoned-up *habitués* agog.

One of the two (both Krzysztofs, both having emerged recently from Poland, both precariously tight-roping their existences) was a nephew of my master Pruszkowski, he a master at dodging frontier-and-diploma fences – now half an architect, half a fashion photographer; the other was a brother of the leading Polish film actress Beata Tyszkiewicz, their upper-class origins not handicapping her career – and their mother having bartered their land and mansion with the Communist Government for rooms in the Castle Square of Warsaw, the windows framing the newly-built-out-of-the-ruins Canaletto-like view. And, through Beata's first marriage to Andrzej Wajda, back to a country mansion – where a party was held for me, composed of old surviving and new friends: the ease and well-being blending into the culture-élite of the egalitarian new Poland.

Black Notting Hill. In the routine terrace shabbiness, those upper rooms: mangled beds beneath sprawling ochre-to-black dishevelled half-naked men, sweating in the solid gas-fire heat. Bare feet overhang many days' layers of let-fall projects, emptied bags of crisps, Coke, beer cans – joints' smoke, silences and the slowest of language, all backed by wireless garrulity. Headquarters.

The leader summons.

And the rapidity of the change. Now ready: black-clad, buttoned high, black shades over dark faces, beards, one or two shiny shaven heads, all packed into a bursting van for the **Round House.** The ritualized fearsome ENTRY: vanguards hush-creating; the leader erect, chief's stick in hand, aloof, supremely unfocused – and the tight, shadowy group slick, grave, but also tensed, also threatening. The Round House psychedelia-crowd cracks open a wide straight path.

But this suspense, this cutting edge, this promise of a sequel, is only momentary – without issue. It gets submerged: rotating, flashing lights, roaring pop percussions, the plasmatic multitude press on. The whole non-climax, non-happening encompasses – splits – corrupts the group – the leader halted four-square by a barefoot junkie blonde.

A year has passed: **Michael X**'s prison year: his over-contrived black jingo-bluster having carried him there. Now, body draped loosely in prophet's kaftan, head still more richly decorated with hair, he talks against the gun-mentality of American Panthers, which would sweep his flock here into

Opposite: Michael X

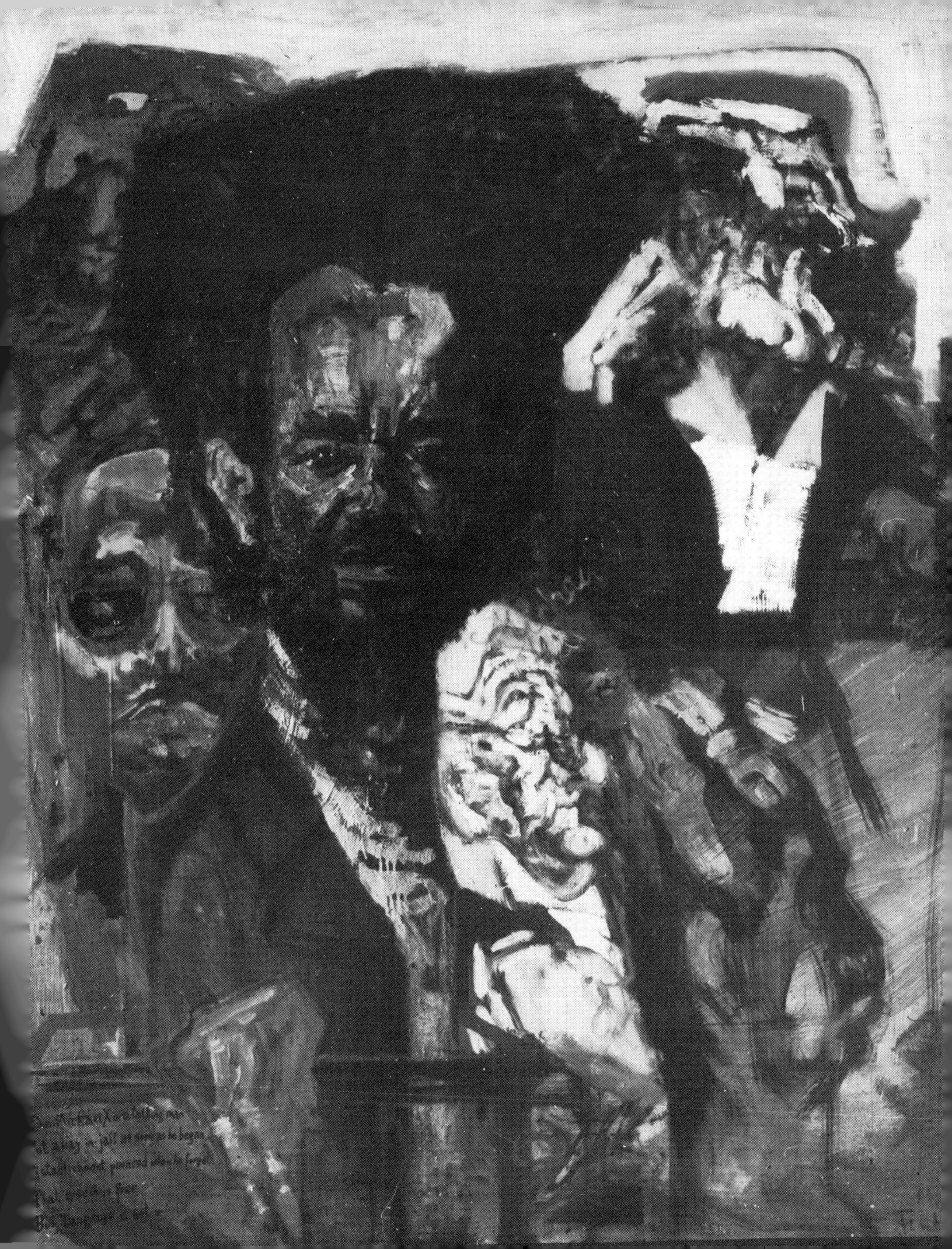
Michael X was a talking man
put away in jail as soon as he began
stablishment pounced when he forgot
That speech is free
But language is not

oblivion, and FOR 'the system' – his concept of superior, laughing Negro society coincidentally infecting the West with its bliss.

Thus he falls into the sophisticated stratagems of power in democracies. Leeway, as a mark of liberty, is given to cumbersome groups – this far, quite far, until a key personage is winnowed unerringly in an unostentatious, gently legal elimination: the collapse of another mini-revolt. Hence revolution – split into revolts, each rubbed out in turn by being rendered fuseless – does not explode beyond tiny localized riots.

After all, Michael was a hot-air merchant, a politician. Of course, he was a charmer – without charm a non-starter – ever keeping up his wide sphere of connections, ever masterly and elastic in plotting new schemes, bouncing into strength from failures.

He would phone often, assuring of no purpose but to keep the hot line of friendship going, and then come and be delightful and roguish. His memorable answer to my plain question about his Rachmanite past: 'To make it here, to equal the whites, a black has to move by short cuts.'

Michael X's foothold in this country shrank to nothing and he was made to sail **back to his Trinidad**. He saw his return to Trinidad as a triumph-to-be. His legend, and the saviour's aura, were to sweep those in power out of the way and take him – so he daydreamed rather than plotted – to the top; and to turn his island into a utopia beaming the Word and the Example out on to the world.

The word '**Alternative**' was to be made flesh by gathering there the academics and practisers of the love-cult **Society**, led by the Western sages he had befriended – from Ronny Laing to Alex Trocchi to Bill Burroughs to myself – in conditions of plenty.

At our last ever meeting in London, as I was about to go to the States contracted for a book and needing an entry into the secretive and embattled world of the Black Panthers, Michael composed a rather equivocal (as betrayals and ambushes were lurking) **safe-conduct letter** for me – and, half mockingly, half solemnly, pricked his thumb with a knife and signed it in blood.

The horrific end: the legal hanging in spite of worldwide protestations over the blatant tendentiousness of the proceedings and gaps in evidence; and appallingly wrong to those who knew him in London because murder, which would lead inevitably to the death cell, was not in his character of astute survivor. (His flaming speeches and even his excursions into selective bullying in England were showpieces.) This was not Michael, unless Trinidad changed him inexplicably. A flood of insinuating press reports and a melodramatized fiction-falsity by Naipaul drowned the **demonic**, secrets-loaded **verdict.**

Caryl's impromptu **calypso** written at the bottom of my painting on the theme of his trial when Michael was imprisoned in England:

The Michael X is a talking man
Put away in gaol as soon as he began
Establishment pounced when he forgot
That speech is free
But language is not.

The calypso written by **Heathcote Williams** on **Michael's execution** in Port of Spain and published with Caryl's in *IT* in a protest double-page:

The Michael XXX
Was a Revolution Man,
Fitted up with a Murder Rap
as soon as he began
His Muther Kuntry fucked
him right up the ass
and all he wanted
was
LIFE TO THE RAS!

Moscow-Irkutsk-Ulan Bator 'Aeroflots' four orange Lamas – Mongolia's gales float horsemen over the Gobi desert and stop at the plate-glass doors of the Ulan Bator Hotel.

The *sine qua non* of this journey was the stop in **Mongolia – Tartarland.** Over the horizon-wide flatness dotted with *jurtas* they galloped swept circled in loose cohorts, hollered; unchanged, fierce-faced in their winged fur-hats – boots and side-knotted kaftans, untidily high over their minute, unchanged ponies' necks – that is unchanged from my childhood's pre-vision.

Then another, complementary thrill. The Buddhist Monastery of Gandantegchinlin gongs/beckons me from the depth of this steppe. **The four Lamas**, my friends of the two-day flight, step forward and engage me in the eternal ritual of reuniting welcome. It is not, as with us, deterioration into formality: I fall instantly and blissfully into its import and its true joy.

Simple: we, the West, are barbarians, communal harmony and its rhythm forfeited or rather lost in our overcrowded chaos (substitutes: 'individualism' and a nuclear family). Truly civilized societies proceed within ancient modes, certainties grown from nature and gods, each minutest occurrence enmeshed in responses felt/acted to the full, no doubts entering; thus this classical encounter of 'old' friends is one of the richest. Correspondingly, our valedictions were profoundly acted – and felt.

Perhaps not quite so but I felt uniquely accepted and, in consequence the outsider's sharp inquisitiveness and cataloguing fervour blurred, I *lived* those monastic hours, thus remember little.

– For the eyes: shadow-held brown/gold depths and candlelight-pooled and -abandoned outlandishly 'different' orange shapes.

– The sounds: brassy, tinkling; but, dominant and everywhere, not only when among the low-planted orange ranks bent over the open vastnesses of parchment volumes, the deepest/strangest scansion-murmur/hum/drone.

– And the darkest hollows: the library – an unending perspective of those volumes – the intimidating over-a-thousand years' countlessness of, surely, the **Answers** – our edge-nibbling historians and antiquarians rendered ridiculous.

Even the meal amongst them (at ease, laughing, gentle) seemed a privilege.

My last China was of 1966, hence the need for an introductory piece now in 1986:

A grotesquely predictable crudity of history's cog-wheels/rotations: the revolutionary **Eastern** leaps tantalizingly ahead of plodding capitalist stabilities – often disturbing, but exploring – come to a halt; worse, their leadership forfeited to cultural-material **surrenders** by joining the **tail-end** of the Western-orientation queue, with humiliating poor-relation's imitations, in 'small stabilizations'. This circularity, observed in Soviet Russia and its satellites, is now enforcing itself on post-Maoist China. My *Holy China* becomes unholy under the grinding of dogmatically erratic reverses.

But these open crudities suddenly embrace the globe: my conclusions on the States of 1968–70 in *Shem, Ham & Japheth Inc.* are turned nonsense by new generations of Americans.

But more has to be said:

Mao and China by Stanley Karnow propounds the ultimate view of the West and China's present leadership on 'the Great Proletarian Cultural Revolution'. Yet he entered China for the first time only following Nixon in 1972 ('I was unfamiliar with the area before my arrival there . . .' '. . . fresher perspective . . .' '. . . while I relied heavily on the experts for assistance, my purpose was to tell a story as clearly and as impartially as possible . . .') – but then, he throws in the next line: 'The specialists were no better informed.' And soon enumerates the appalling disasters, with '. . . I relied mostly on documents and interviews with refugees, since they were the only sources available to a "China Watcher"' though 'wary of the Chinese tendency to exaggerate'. Yet again, 'Most of this material was compiled by the United States Consulate General in Hong Kong . . . upon which I have relied heavily . . . also depended for information on extensive interviews with refugees from China . . . information I was able to confirm during a visit to the People's Republic of China in February 1972.' Finally he quotes 'financial support, intellectual guidance and the inspiration by the East Asian Research Center of Harvard University' and 'the help of the Institute of Politics of the John F. Kennedy School of Government at Harvard University'.

I was still in China when the Cultural Revolution began and my son Daniel travelled too, and moved unassisted and unmolested around Canton some two months later, conversing and photographing the 'big-character posters'. I was taken aback by the anti-Mao self-righteous confidence of the middle class with the Western/missionary background: aged Mao's fear of party/apparatchiks standstill, or even of losing China, urging him to kindle the 'permanent revolution' fervour seemed (within his precepts) justified. Karnow writes of 'their tendency to exaggerate' – 'they' meaning his sole informants 'the refugees'. My China of the masses (both Chiang Kai-shek's and Mao's) maintained ingrained uniformity within its borders while, when dispersed abroad, desiring more than any other breed to conform with the local order. And so they, the refugees, 'exaggerate' in

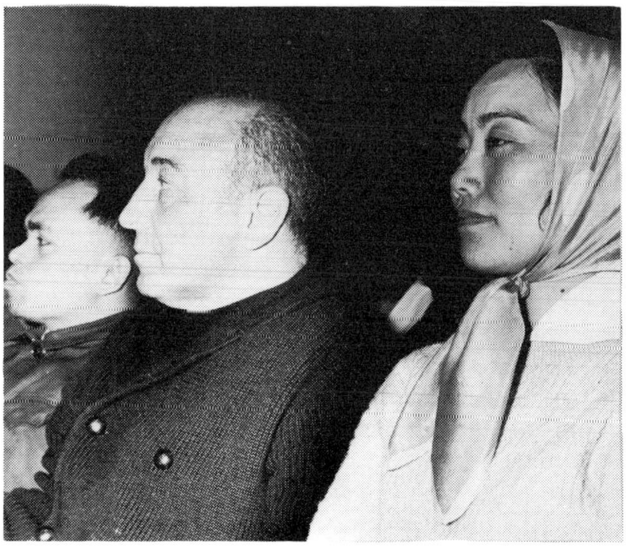

With Mrs Jack Chen in Peking

response to what they imagine is hoped to be heard from them. All this does not contradict the Western-bourgeois and 'revisionist' influences: they cut into narrow but dominant power spheres – the conceits of the West/progress pressures proving irresistible. But this abundant peasant nation sounds one common universal chord – in accord with the holders of power.

Conspiracies of silence, of obeisance, of sacrificing four scapegoats as a gang of villains – are the result; are consolidated, exported, exaggerated by the refugees and formulated in convenient myths by the 'China watchers'.

I only presume. The black/white record of recent and present China, formulated now, reads as if a dubiously deciphered hieroglyphic tale cut into archaic stones excavated from the murky distant past.

May Day: Old Guard dignitaries are led, supported by young assistants because of their fragility, under umbrellas because of the rain – or, ceremonially, out of youth's respect for achievement and age.

The haphazard procession on the way to mount the stands: the Minorities Delegations preening in their folklore for the celebrations – each breathtakingly scooped out from my childhood images of the Mongol invader, but now a tame line of provincial representatives, reduced to ethnological exhibits.

The Peihai Park turned into a milling fun-culture-cult fair. An unconcerned backstage mood amongst the rockeries and covered painted passages – boys and girls, faces thickly made up, costumed as soldiers, peasants, workers, and Vietnamese jungle fighters. They push through the crowd for their turn into clearings or on to rough platforms, and become set pieces: scythe crossed with hammer, banners raised, guns pointed and martial stare. Next the dancers, then a soldier girls' choir.

Ping Chu, local Peking Opera, set on a makeshift stage – clowning, in modern costumes but within the traditional convention, to a percussion band.

The platform of the soldiers' theatre: clown-acrobats, Sin-kiang pipe-smoking dancers, harvesting groups from East, North and West, Vietnam versus America.

A tremendous flurry of action, the rush-leap of dancer-fighters, faces fierce, necks strained, highest swing of weapons-banners, mighty legs lift these light torsos easily – the swiftness to vanquish.

Casually somewhere in the park – a lion's dance: two two-man lions stand on hind legs, roll, gallop, fuss, tease a dancer with the shining ball which symbolizes the pearl of happiness. Performance ended, the papier-mâché head off, out of a floppy costume the lovely head of a boy.

Today's Western Art, the artist's revolt of the nineteenth century become luxury merchandise and a snob plaything of the twentieth, begins to show longings for a reconciliation, however vulgar, with the masses and therefore to be contemporary – that is, to break away from the art dealers' and museum officials' stale routine of owned objects by creating a multi-branching art of all the senses. It is entertaining to watch how this strain is physically held down to the gilt-frame limitation of the plush art dealer's galleries; how more explosive attempts are ignored since they do not fit the market (even official socialist patronage in England obeys the orders of convention-bound art 'patrons' in disguise of committee men); how art accommodates itself by the anti-art label to the collector's need for the titillation of exclusiveness.

In **Tien An Men Square**, the POP realization, the all-arts performance erupts limitlessly. The overlapping sights and sounds, bursting out from a million sources under an immense pyrotechnic sky, could reach such a pitch only as a ritual of devotion. I am sadly outside it all, but aware of the magnitude and made humble. Their banners, their posters, their 40-foot-high paintings of the four-headed Saint (Marx–Engels–Lenin–Mao) *are* POP ART. It is all aesthetically shocking to the Westerner, who melts in front of a Warhol. The great difference is this, that Western pop is afraid of, or rather empty of, meaning – Chinese POP is as forthcoming as any religious art: it preaches.

Art in the West is regulated by art markets. An artist who does not sell is ostracized. True, he can make endless rounds until a merchant-publisher takes notice, but the capricious reality of commerce is a harsh master. The assessing words are 'success' or 'failure'.

In Communist China, the measure is social usefulness as defined by the rulers, restricted and unbending. The artist is a tool of propaganda as in medieval Christianity, or even in the service of Napoleon's Empire; the nonconformist is left to perish. But the arts are high on the list, dignified by the ever-urgent need of them. The eyes of the rulers and the masses are on them.

The act of creative expression demands reaction. One wonders which is more organic: the universal, but curbed, acceptance, practised for millennia, with the arts a necessity; or the erratic, exclusive-market bound, response – with the majority of society, including governments, indifferent.

The West is guiltily conscious of its need for cultural dissemination, but only when justified by the gods of commerce. Festivals multiply throughout Europe and America as tourism-spinners, pathetically prancing on the surface to the embarrassment of the locals. China provides the best soil for the fulfilment of the Festivity idea. And far beyond.

In Germany and Italy, Fascism tried to use *circenses* as a 'turning on' mass-accumulator, but in militarized formations and for short-sighted and short-lived concepts. Lourdes, Fatima, Mecca, Benares – the mass-ignitions of a receding era; the latest jamborees of the Western young attempt and fail to evolve a ritual without content; and, significantly, their only crusading contents are negative – of protest. In China one senses an eruptive force.

Tien An Men Square, on the first May night, bursts at the seams with amateur folklore groups from all over the country performing for a million of themselves: a giant open-air square mile of a HAPPENING. Ten thousand bands, choirs, dancing feet, whirling, flag-banners hoisting, slogans roaring, applause: light-sound movement assemblages of discord on a mammoth scale. This is the realization of an unmatchable, all-in-happening, a cacophony of the truest ultra-modernity. And much more: humanity gathered in one congested spot by an idea, accumulating single-minded force and, fully charged, exploding, leaping, unaided by supermachines, into new space dimensions. This pandemonium, this label of all the senses, is today's symphony of art-faith-will. Puny 'observers' from the West, Russians included, their assertive instincts at work, react piecemeal, get at and examine details to fit their own measure: their dwarfed art and 'good taste', their sectarianisms and their 'freedoms'. Thus, measure by false measure, they recover confidence and even attempt patronizing irony. But the whole: the whole answers well for China. Simpler, and therefore less boneheaded, 'delegates' from Africa and Asia are perhaps able to perceive the Majesty and Miracle.

Fierce wind raises screens of dust. Down into the crowd: the immense abstraction splits into man-scale stages, framed by tight circles of spectators, parting, clapping at the sight of a guest, leading him to the front row, laying coats, rugs for him to sit on. There, in the ear-bursting rhythms, with cold winds swaying, blurring the scene, one after another dancing groups rush in, the more obviously amateur the better, since the greater the fury of their ever-the-same, every-varying apotheosis, of labour, harvest and battle and victory over invaders. Close-up confrontation, and then the return up to the aloof stand for the elemental spectacle, misted-overblown with dust, swaying, spilling over the brim of Tien An Men Square – the foreigners, diplomats and delegates having fled the cold in their limousines.

The **modern opera** of Peking. The hero, tortured and bleeding but undaunted, a chained martyr about to die at the hands of the Japanese, sings his swansong in stylish treble, posturing classically.

The Westerners lament the passing of classical Chinese Opera and deride its modernization – an early deed of the cultural revolution. Those, who go for the 'living theatre' at home, prefer their exotics at an antiquarian standstill. It reassures their sense of superiority and keeps oriental tourism spicy.

We have a horror of official interference in the arts because it implies retardation. But throughout history, the artist served the power establishments, spiritual, and temporal, and developed to heights beyond the possibilities of an artist

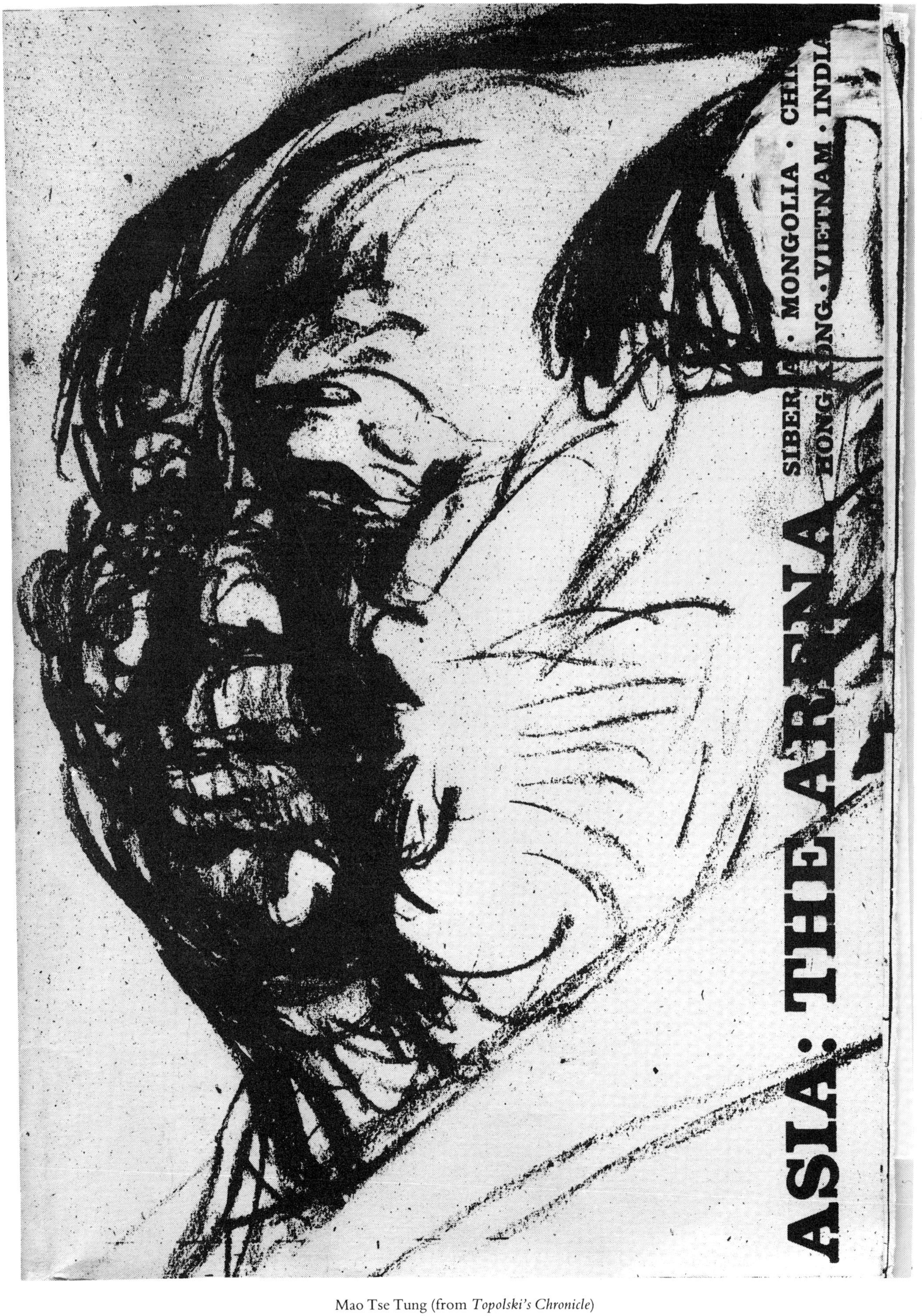

Mao Tse Tung (from *Topolski's Chronicle*)

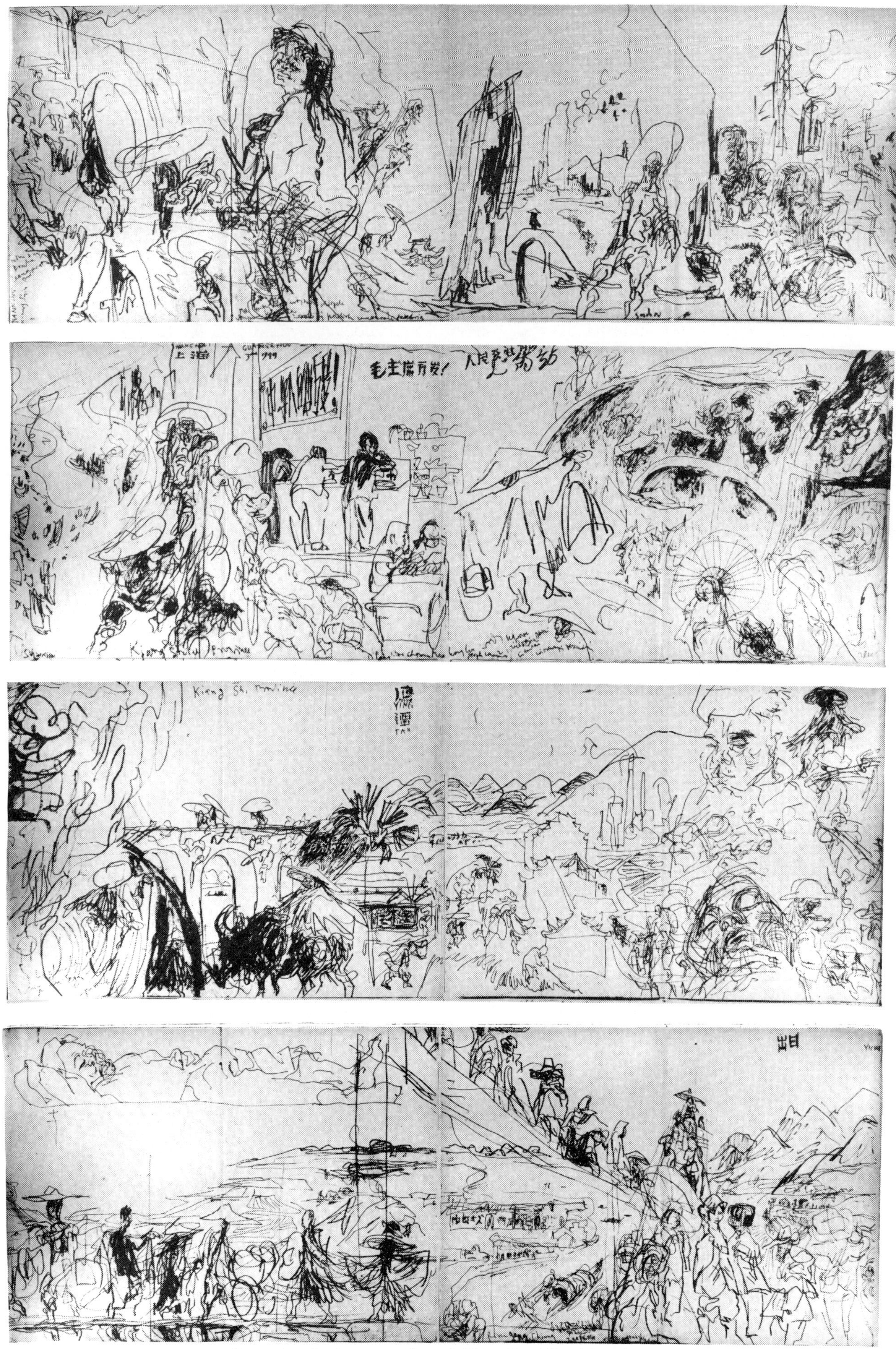

Concertinaed train-passage through China (from *Topolski's Chronicle*)

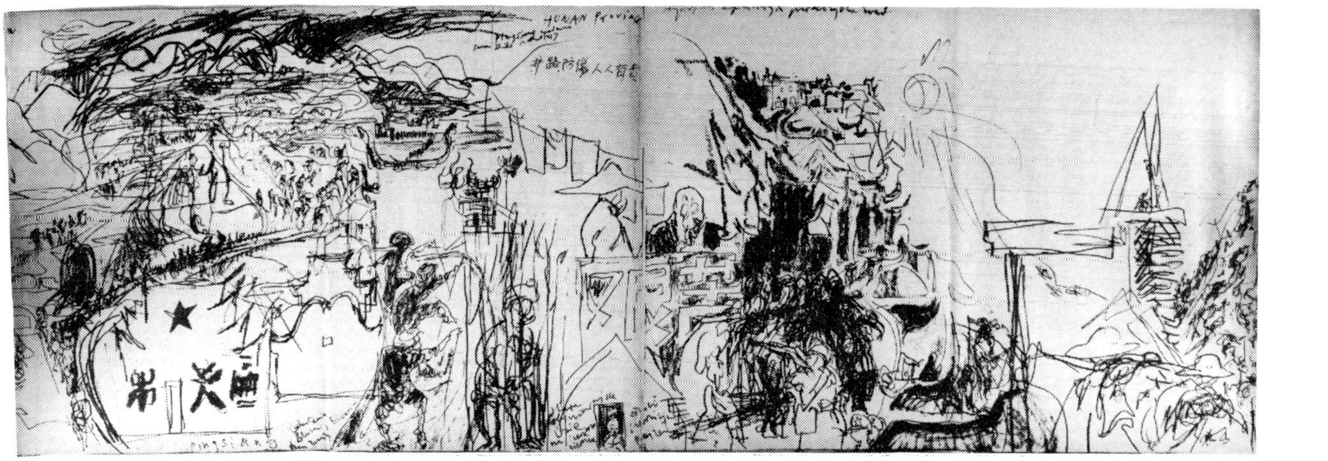
HUNAN Province

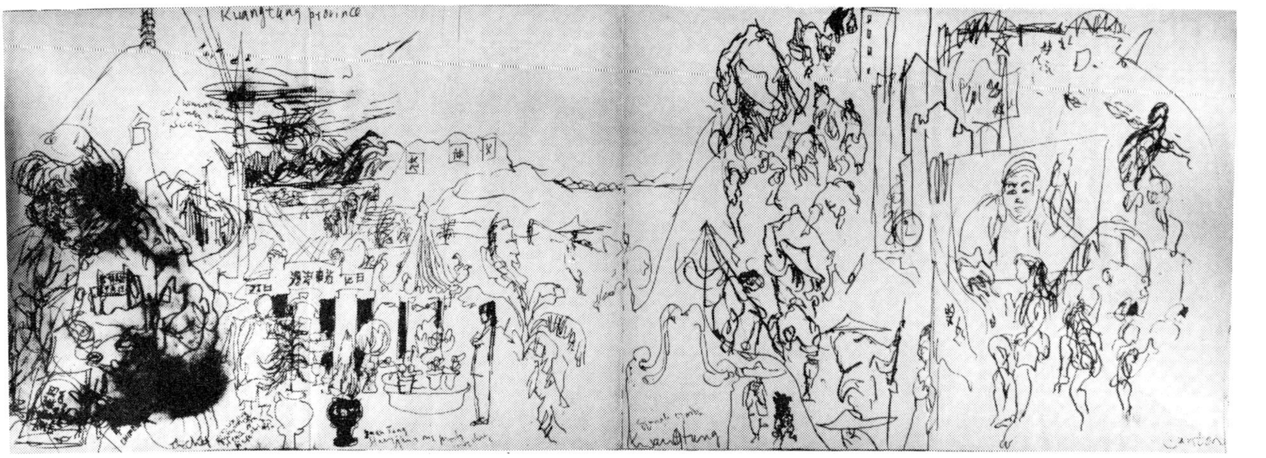
Kwangtung province
Canton

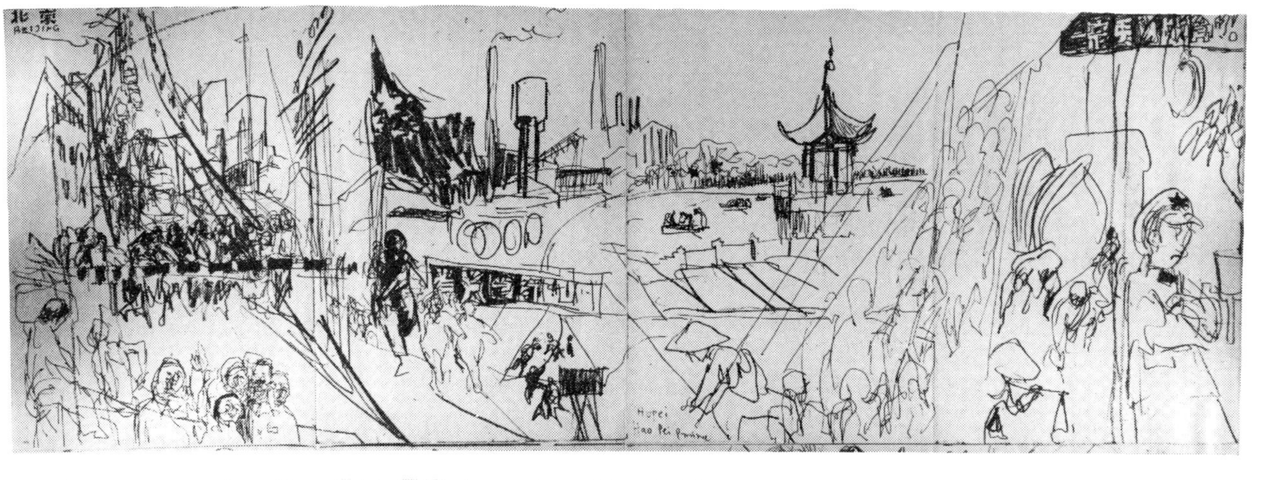
北京
BEIJING

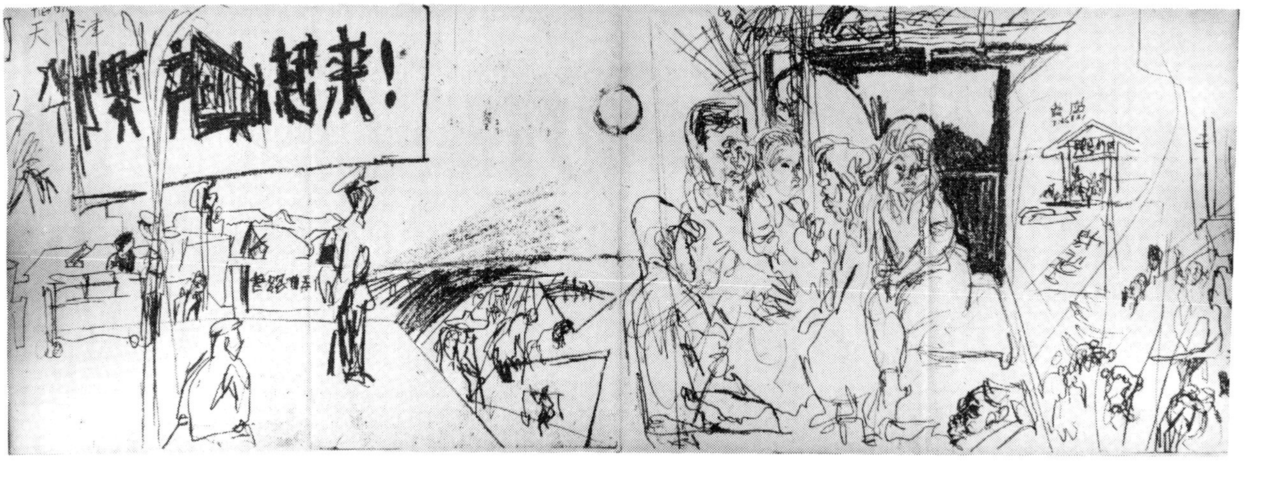

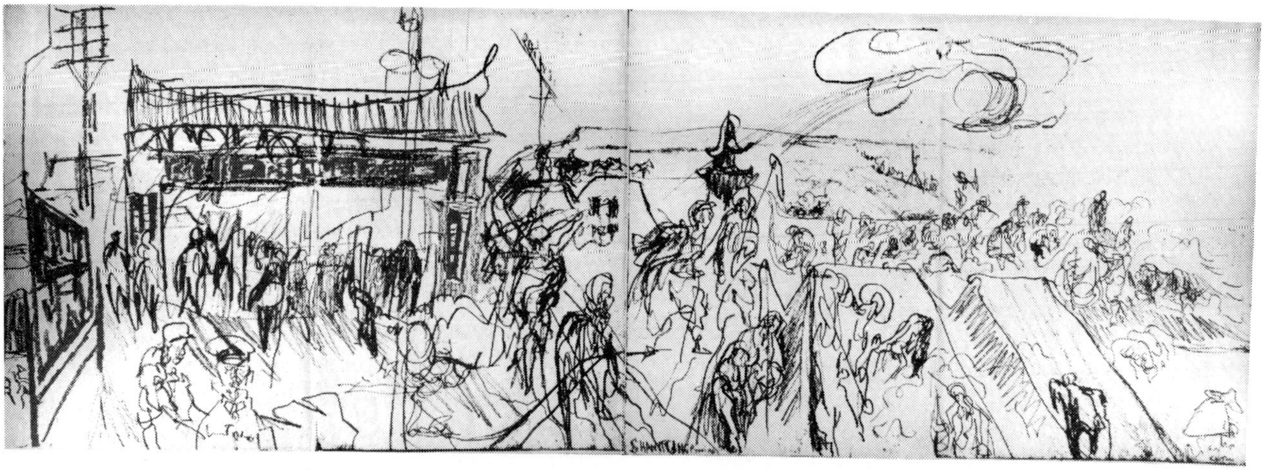

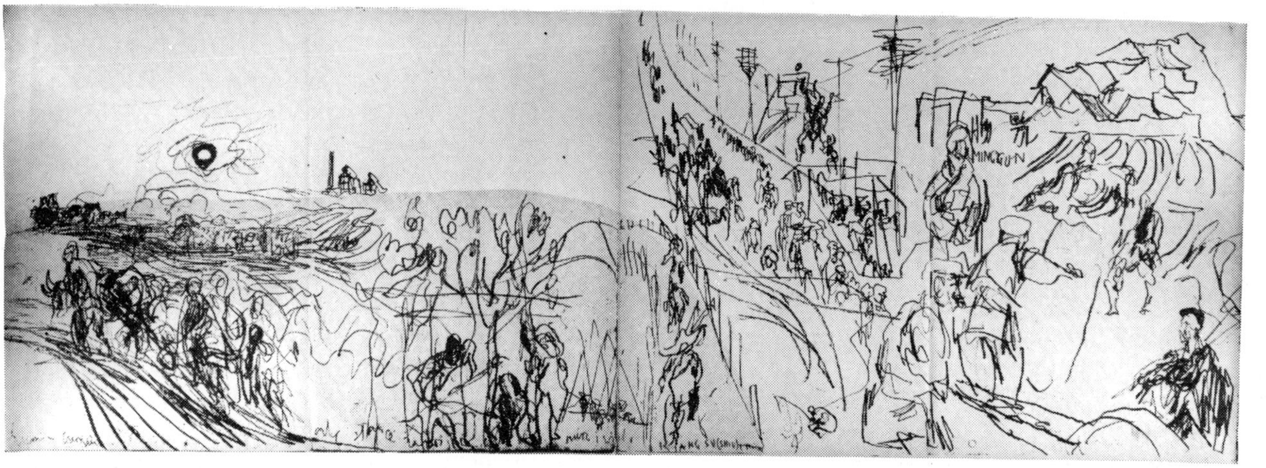

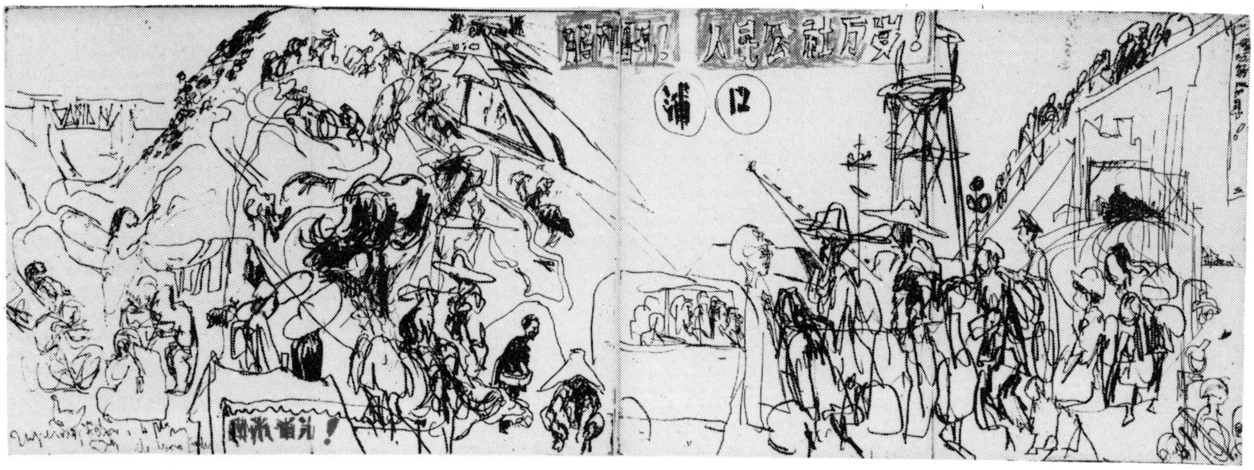
人民公社万岁!
浦 口

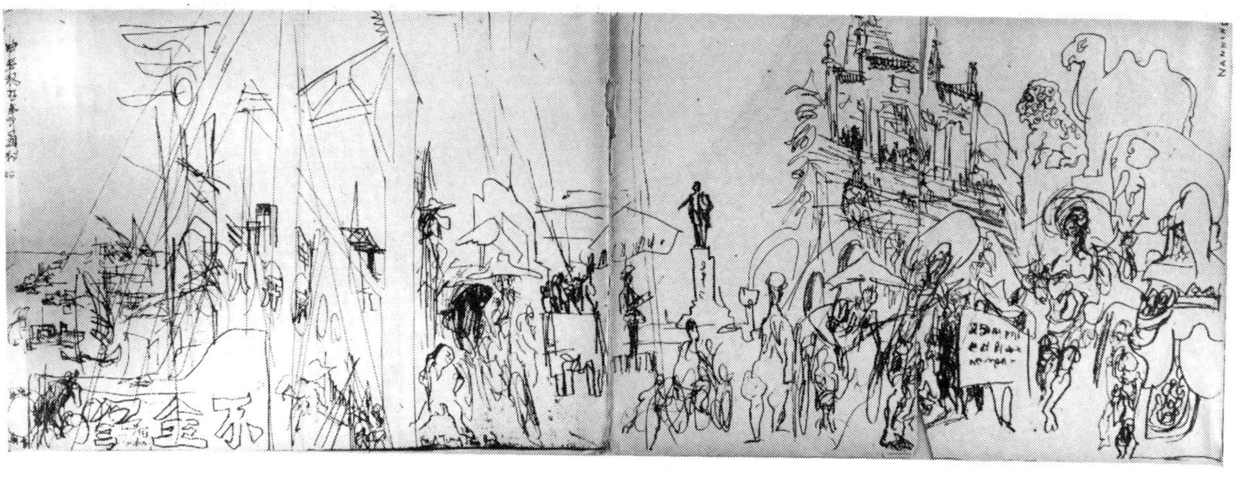

within our liberal-commercial society, who has persuaded himself that his isolation is a creative loneliness, and thus a virtue.

Nanking. The city's facelessness made worthy by the ever-moving friezes of 'transport' workers' (sempiternal coolie) harnessed to impossible loads on wheels, men and, still stauncher, women, singly, in twos, in large teams, pulling-pushing uphill, holding back downhill, ever straining in buoyant unity, hefty legs and arms, weary and laughing, sweat and flesh in flamboyant rags. Thrilled expectation at the approach of each tight-knit group, heads and limbs of all ages in the uniting heave, and odd regret at their noisy passing.

A castigating young companion challenged me on my preoccupation with strained muscles, calves and patched draperies – he implied a falsifying by a baroque-conditioned eye of the China of today.

Mao Chio People's Commune in Kangsu Province. Old man, old-China skirted, along the furrow by the spray-tackled field. A student operates a bottom-scraping contraption from a boat on a narrow stream. Another fusses in the piggery, side by side with a local man. In the crowded field, a member notes the work-points scored by each peasant; a medical graduate from Shanghai, who volunteered to work in the Commune, gets off his bicycle for a consultation.

The back-bent peasantry over the whole face of China are ennobled, given pride and faith; their former betters join them, court them, consort with them, their young move up and out. This is not merely progress like anywhere else – it must be truly liberation. The humble live the fable of Glad Tidings. And elementary possessions help.

Our habit tells of the peasant's conservative instincts; but in China they have risen from the depth on 'the wings of faith'. Their Maoist morale seems high.

Four girl school-leavers from Shanghai won, from amongst many competitiors, their assignment to the commune. They have moved into a new cottage and one of their first duties is to be dinner hostesses to my whimsy of staying the evening in the Commune to attend a meeting. Gentle, gay, composed – the girls. Facetiously, I propose that I should send them my handsome young son. The reply: 'Looks don't matter, but brains and idealism.' A cliché, possibly made so by translation. But clichés are truths, even if only of society's aspirations. And these aspire well.

The Shu family recently bought a vast, carved and canopied bed in Shanghai, cosily modelled on the imperial concubines' sumptuosity and Mr and Mrs Shu receive, proudly seated on it; but the grandmother opens a solid coffer and lovingly runs her fingers through her treasure – the rice.

Outside, a lamp lights up a cluster of people around charts of the day's scores, pinned on a board. The meeting has the shape of a morality allegory, of any 'early' earnestness. Old and young speak haltingly but at length. The scene is pure and stately.

Shanghai. Seeping rain and the customary ride to the roof with a view, and the obligatory commentary on before-and-now. But: in shifting sheets of mist, rain and clouds, there overflow below, and fold over the horizons, two-coloured waters, Wang Po River and Suchow Creek, studded thickly, far and wide, with the bulkily jostling rush-drift of junks, battered bat-sailed, shabby and tender, cut into by steaming, hooting craft hauling strings of barges – all this as expected, all legend-laden – but, above all, the junks: sails filled by millennia – the Easternest, the most alien shapes in the world.

The Bund: the old 'extraterritorial' promenade, edging the waterfront and narrowing upwards, halted by the Customs Spike, bordered by the banking now municipal edifices, once British this-and-that, Sassoon before but now Peace Hotel. Story-telling voices at my side spin later legends of mass executions, of American soldatesque molestations of women down in those Bund Gardens, and their murderous jeep rides. But after 1949 . . .

Posters of vast torsos reflect but dwarf the humans – repeat the icon device of large and small in one. Apologetic, on edge, posture of the pedicab passengers as against their pre-revolutionary sprawl in the old rickshaws. Gay dogs on bicycles, laughing at the girls.

Alone, along Nanking Road: the sports shop, an amphilade of interiors, crowded with fine gadgetry; chemist up the steps, art shop, elegant and meticulous. A delight – theatrical props and costumes shop for pros and amateurs; a flood of temptations – lovely folklore clothing (non-silkified for tourists, and not corrupted by Russians arty-crafts), masks, boots, whiskers, fireworks, wooden-prop armoury, uniforms of tyrants and heroes. The Friendship Department Store (Harrods' top floor in London) for overseas visitors, where under-equipped Albanians and Russians replenish their vanities; even now, 'on the road to bourgeoisie', Moscow is not as rich in the variety and display of consumer goods.

Outside my window murmurings and measured clapping: a close side-wall of an office building, one floor below, a crowded room across two windows, a meeting.

Mr Wang, one of the leading traditional artists daintily paints an elegant water-colour for me. He is utterly elegant himself. The mechanical reports of China's drab uniformity of costume are given the lie by his fastidiousness. Our reporters' eyes are blinded to our own drab, ridiculously outlandish, male outfit; lapelled and built-in padding, with the odd rigid device of collar and tie, a mark of some sort of pretence of respectability; to the universalized bathos of settling, as if for ever, our costumological conceits just at this point. The standard shape of the Chinese male costume, although another Western – this time Soviet – corruption, is at least more functional and lends itself well to refinements. Mr Wang plays charmingly on touches of tradition. The sleeves of his tunic are wide and folded over as if absent-mindedly; quality and colour of material are the choicest; the cut and tailoring are obviously planned to the smallest detail. There is a universal, less admirable detail: the top of the left pocket-flap has an opening for the insertion of a collection of Parker-like pens.

Canton Pearl River, from my eleventh-floor corner room: the river day is laid out before me in one circular sweep. Sun-glow in a mighty cascade rushes at me in the straightest line from the eastern horizon, pours forth a multitude of shipping; flows below in an uninterrupted view – but morning blaze turns to midday waters. Junks, junks, junks, sails against the light, with the light, full-face, sideways. I lean out of the window to the right and there, skirting my post, leaving me behind, the colossal flotilla speeds to the west, sinks in, overtakes the retreating darkness, presses the time onward.

From the shore, and from among the land-bound shufflings, the river's awesome purposefulness, propelling, yet harried by, the superior water-people.

The Bridge asserts land's supremacy; leads to a neat housing estate for the river people. Nostalgic regrets, perhaps only in the 'reactionary' imagination of the laughable folklore collector. And, driving on in our curtained car, pointing at the unconcerned zigzaggings of motorized ferries, Mr Chu: 'Junks are obsolete and will soon be discarded.'

My two ladies of the river – middle and aged graces: lovely parched textures, lovely brave old bare legs, lovely creature-dignity and gaiety; should like them both for keeps.

A blissful whirlpool of 'many simples'. The tides of Si Kiang command and all obey. Water against wood. Wind against sails. The rowers – set pieces high astern the junks – men and women pair face-to-face to pull–push, feet alternately raised, back–forth. They wrestle harmoniously in symbolic concord-contest: the family; tethered babies on strings, babies fed, flowerpots, fancy roofings, chickens, washing, drying – on the move. They come at us high above, alongside, go by, legs, chests, high necks, narrow boys, sturdy girls, slim oldsters, their backs: all beauty.

All this and Mr Chu voicing from under the sampan canopy his and China's stand, demanding answers: Tsesi Tse Li (INDIVIDUALISM) is discouraged, the cultural revolution encourages Ge Hsien (INDIVIDUALITY). Former China–India frontiers, arbitrary and British-made, are revised in detail. Russia's treachery and Krushchev's bossiness defined. Tibet always belonged to China; MacMahon's Line . . .

We tie up at a colony of water-people, at a *gallimatias* of paddling, women's cackle, modest girls splashing in their cottons. A policeman rows from the shore in jolly investigation.

Mr Chu, most eloquent. Incongruously at the heart of all this physical grace, we dialogue stiltedly about pride-in-

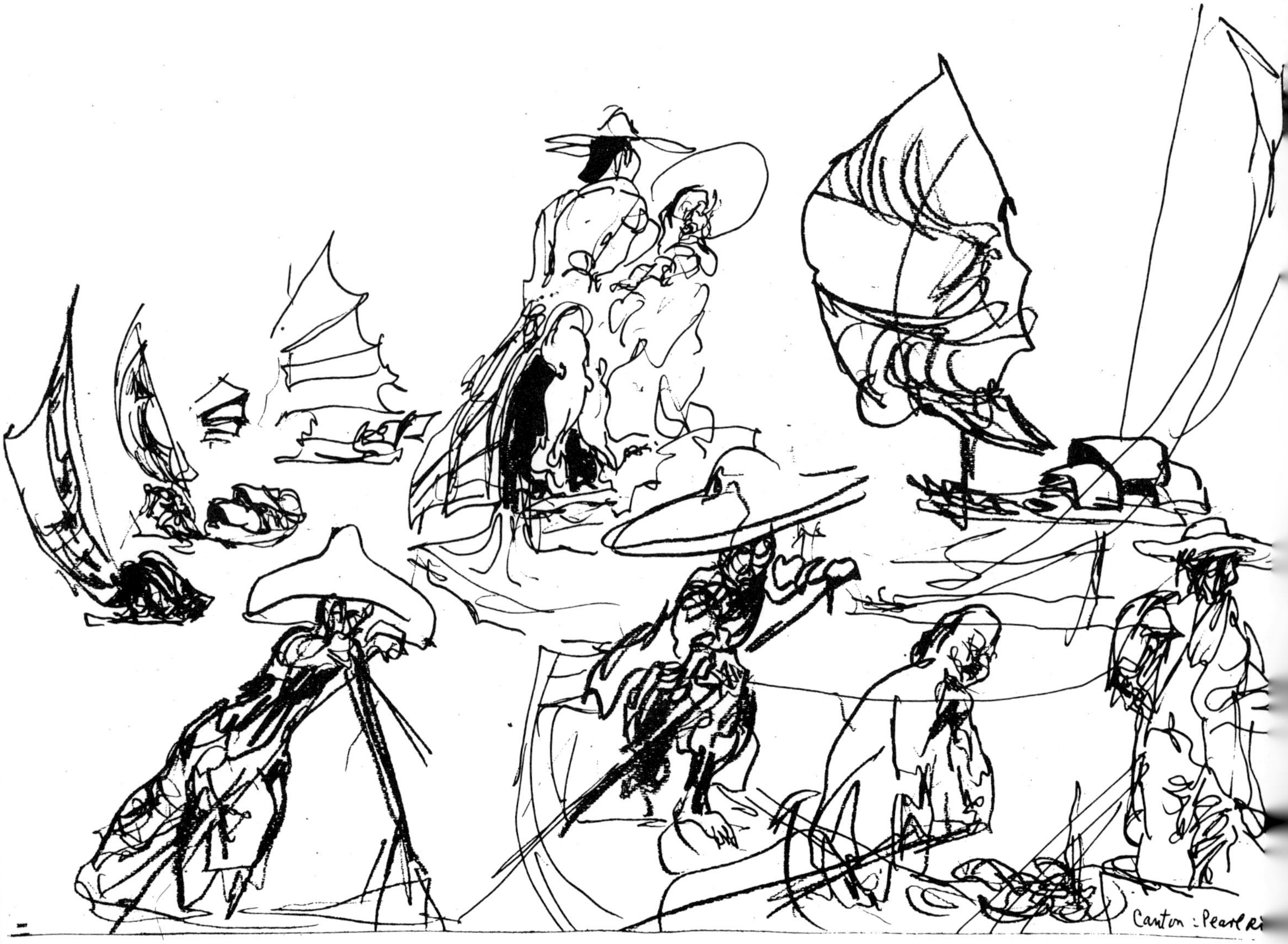

On a Junk – Pearl River, 1966 (from *Topolski's Chronicle*)

labour, with me falling back on the ever-useful gambit of the street cleaner; about bourgeois diversions and Communism's capitalists, about Picasso . . .

And a lot more. About the educational establishments being closed for rethinking the system within the cultural revolution. Yet the pupils are not dispersing on vacationeering sprees while old committee men reshuffle curricula, but have already begun to do it themselves – reshuffling professors as well. Soon the whole of China's curriculum would have begun to be revised – Red Guards at the head. And, this being a nation on the march, the youth would not be protesting but crusading, as they often have in the past elsewhere.

My Western out-of-stepism – a self-indulgent, sprawling blot against the clear mapping of Mr Chu's world. It helps, though, as an antidote against my world's prejudice.

Within the archaic flow of junks with New China's voice at my side, an elusive pivotal feeling is brought to a pitch. My contradictory sentiments (not unusual in the West, having been born of our contemporary inadequacies) – of patinaed nostalgia for the weathered ways, and for the opposite – the Promethean drive for change – are both evoked by this confrontation. And then, in this land's immensity, the scriptural, homely manner in which the natural cycle of life enmeshes the new creed.

It cannot be subdued by the march of Western panaceas, as was Gandhi's ideal of India the rural, Israel's equalitarianism, or African tribal divisions. A destructive holocaust may, if forceful and cunning, upset the devout masses, and perhaps even damage the structure of their worship, but this would be through an imposition.

Christianity did not flower in Judea but in transplantation, having acquired the grasping, expanding force of Europe. China, resurrected in Marxism, is churning it into her own image; the vastness, the pliability of the masses, their comparative innocence of Western ideas, and their isolation assure salutary conditions for travail – if unhampered. It will not serve OUR world's safety; but safety is a static term.

China's cultural revolution proceeds to the accompaniment of the world's jeers. The eternal antagonism of the stabilized therefore conventionalized powers, once themselves on the move, Soviet Russia alongside shocked to the core of her revolutionary conventions, is spurred by the cultural, more than by the initial revolution.

But there are fifth-column voices behind the front of power. Mao's child crusaders may be labelled naive or irresponsible by the simple 'voters' of the West, but would not seem so to the general and multiplying run of frustrated young Frenchmen – victims of 'prosperity', young Poles denied heroism, Dutch provos, German schoolboys – mute under their elders, English protesters and, above all, American escapesters. China's Red Guards canalize the unpredictable cyclical rhythm of the generations – shrugged off in the West as a nuisance.

And, besides the phenomenon of youth, the West is undergoing its own, possibly no less momentous cultural revolution. Its prophets have moved from liberal scepticism to a re-examination of its values – and desperation. 'Our alienation goes to the roots.' 'We are bemused and crazed creatures, strangers to our true selves, to one another, and to the spiritual-material world,' they say.

Also: at a Malcolm X meeting in Harlem I gatecrashed, China was upheld as a leader of the coloured world. In counterpoint, China-baiting may be a defensive instinct rampant: the closing-of-the-ranks from Seattle to Omsk – the blind exhilaration at ganging together in self-deluding superiority over the 'lesser' races.

Thus China – the Utopia, the Purgatory, the land of robots or of cynics, Yellow Peril or passive absorber; the focus of personal and group idiosyncrasies, the target for prejudices – moves on transcending contemporary Western criteria.

The return in the crush-dash of the turning tide. The Junks. The cocky sampans. Now the sails, greys to black, patched, shredded, battered, all lean to the water's surface in unison and speed-retrace the earlier course: a flight from tomorrow.

To end the Chinese journey, black-frilled hats, seen sixteen years ago on the other side of the border, expectedly reappear in the landscape.

Mr Yu waves me over the bridge to **the British** side.

Western travellers demonstrate expansiveness, light cigars, order whiskies. Slogans turn adverts; calls for public virtues and public hates become cajolings of private appetities. The Chinese grow very fat or very thin; Europeans act their customary role of superior purpose, accompanied by the brass band of the Queen's Own Fusiliers.

On my departure, my friends' *amah*, comfortable in her service to the rich, sweeps her hand over the magnificence of **Hong Kong Bay**, packed and active, the US aircraft-carrier a centrepiece, and in her utility English actually says this obviousness: 'Very poor hungry people down, very rich up; not so in China.'

The cultural revolution and its Red Guards still draw condescending smirks from Western 'observers'. But already the young of the entire West are marching, taking over universities and manning barricades under pop-portraits of Mao, their declared revolutionary aim being the destruction of 'mindless possession-bound civilization' to be replaced by the selfless 'society of continuous change'.

In 1966 a paying tourist in China, but, in Peking, given unexpectedly a sort of demi-guest status, I attempted to pull an admission to North Vietnam – almost achieved, but, by the time I reached Canton, revoked, as Hanoi had become for a time, with the American air offensive intensified, 'unsafe' for visitors; my arguments, that as a reporter I am precisely after action, did not work, And so, unable to wait (this was proposed), I switched to Saigon.

The descent on **Saigon** – the largest visible slice of airfield, overflowing with US-starred aircraft – an instant illustration: unlike the French Viet Minh earthbound war, this is the stragegy of assured supremacy. Other changes will be noticed. The grand old lady at the airport in 1950 now replaced by a glamourized come-hither version: the costume is still there, but the winged dark glasses, high coiffure, tightened waist and surely siliconed bosom, blatantly invite.

This is an illicit entry. Again my veteran bush-blouse and pretence at assured mien get me through the airport's confusion, to be stopped outside at gunpoint by a weedy Vietnamese sentry – his basic blankness, bare of associative reactions (on which I counted for my breakthrough) and no spoken argument possible, make him impregnable – the feeble obstruction fit to destroy, single-handed, my Vietnam. This sends me flying into roaring fury, winged by my not having any right to be there – which works as the certain proof for him of my importance: he lets me through. A moment later, it occurs to me that he may have been – not an armed innocent, but a cunning ruffian – provoking bribery, though my blind impulse forced the right choice – I am in Saigon.

American Saigon: soiled and uglified, corruption oozing out – with hindsight, French Saigon, even in war leave-town pollution, seemed graceful in comparison.

And so the beggars on crutches multiply. And the Yankees: men-boys back home – cogs in whatever provinciality. Soldiering boys dress up, become transformed, act the conqueror: enacting their uniform-given manhood – camouflage their homely pipelines; their seeming celibate inhumanity terror-inspiring to the *en pantoufles* locals.

And it helps that they had all (from young to old and, particularly, those pink middle-ageds) rehearsed in perpetuity for (not anticipating) such a call: this role of he-man is now hammed away, performed in the ricefields and in front of the Continental in Saigon – swaying hips, shoulders impossibly high-and-back lifted, necks bull-horizontal and crotch forward, elbows out and limp palms in, face martial-grim, dark-spectacled. Steel helmets weapons webbings fall in well with such a shape. But the naive deliberation of it all suggests weakness, shows momma's boys beneath.

Saigon. '**Bar Eve**' pros
in combat-ambush of sexes
sisters of their brothers;
ballet-panto seen in Peking
the classic of this war:
Vietcong temptress bottle in hand lures
GIs into a trap
'Bar Eve' enacts it:
Viet-Annamite-Chinese 'hostesses' bottles
and GIs in mufti, flaccid malleable;
I, high-ranking age, highly attended – a catch;
Black giants left out. Asian racism?
Or the legend of might scares the tiny cunts?
Observer's dilemma.

A tip about a **Buddhist demonstration.** The jeep's assorted American correspondents and a photographer. Darkened streets, a long ride, coming to a stop in Tran Quoc Toan Street, close to the barbed-wired Free World Military Assistance Post and a safe distance from **Viên Hóa Dao Pagoda.** Earlier, there had been an 'incident' close to the Pagoda, in which a Military Police jeep was overturned and burned: the Buddhists in that period had grown into a major force within anti-American resistance, with self-immolations by fire staged daily, and wave after wave of manifestations bred in and emerging from the Pagoda. And, at that very moment: the clamouring, heaving movement in the distance.

We disembarked in the dark, and instantly there was nobody around me and no jeep. But, flushed by this chance of entering the core of events within an hour of my arrival, I made my way towards the Pagoda's gate, still far away but defined by the glare of torches, now disgorging a multi-voiced multitude, banners-unfolding. Compulsively I moved forward, scribbling madly, though half blindly, hardly able to see my sketchbook.

The procession moved at me, filling up the wide street. And it is almost impossible for me to accept now that this was the way it happened – the only rational explanation being that I could not, the movement borne upon me swiftly, back out or to the sides of the street: so I stood, leaning against that burnt-out overturned jeep in the centre of the road, pencilling, face to moving-at-me faces, the marchers divided by the wreckage of the jeep (and by me) and – this was the culmination – the sloganed banners (some painted with comic Johnson profiles) passing, stretched, over my head, the pole-carriers to the left and right of me. In the magnetism of their rapture, in their united cried-out fervour, in their swiftness, in the flickering of torches and the flutter of banners – the anomaly of my presence; they may not even have seen me.

Next day, having cadged a lift, I gravitated irresistibly back to the gates of the Pagoda, its name, Viên Hóa Dao, translated as 'United Buddhist Church's Institute for the Execution of Dharma', or by some others as 'Buddhist Institute for Secular Affairs', or else as 'Vietnamese National Pagoda'.

No Europeans in sight and free movement in and out seduces. My tentative attempts at formalizing my presence are slighted by young monks settled at the entrance, writing, reading, sandals off. The large enclosure, a tall structure in the centre, its top bristling with beflagged protrusions, and the Pagoda at the back, overflows: the monks and nuns (shaven heads) in orange and brown; soldiers; all ages; traders in holy mementoes (I buy a Buddhist flaglet and a rosary); good-natured circling, squatting, conversing. Inside the pagoda, individual prostrations in front of gaudy modern Buddhas. A helpful translation of a banner text on the edge of a drawing, 'We must fight against the policies of the government', reflects the softer tendencies of the Buddhists as against the fighting Vietcong; also my engrossment in conversations, which result in a young 'modern' man giving me a lift back on his motor-bicycle with, on the way, a visit to his family. Mr Nguyen Luong Hung, the head, an elegant man (his trimly moustachioed face modern, but draped in a patterned robe), within the well-to-do, spacious but bleak interiors of a household of Asian-model nymphs and cherubs; he, a former member of the Legislative National Council and Vice Secretary-General of the Committee preparing electoral laws. They were all charmingly hospitable; and tranquil – entrusting their élite status implicitly, one imagined, to the might of the United States.

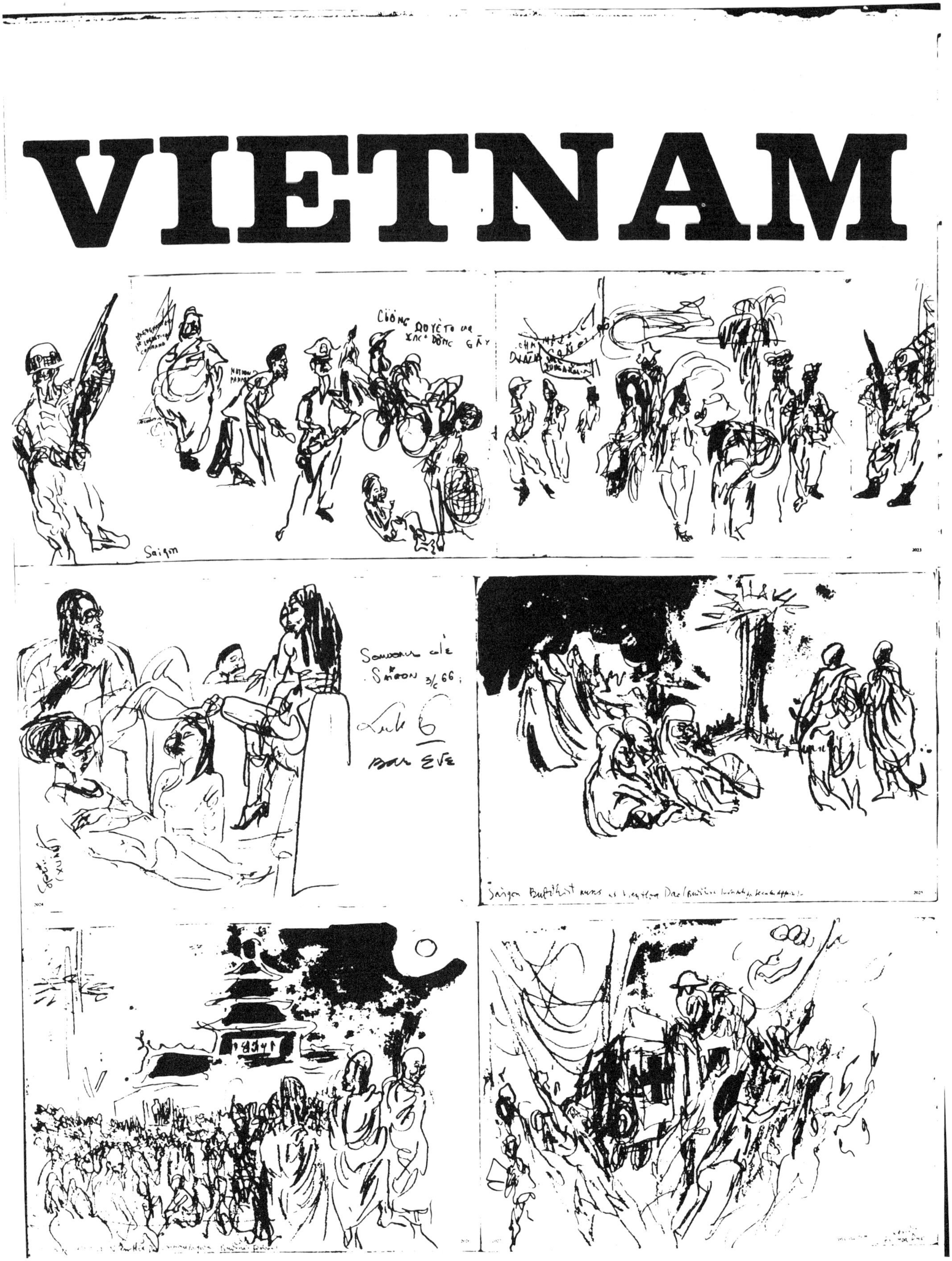

Vietnam (from *Topolski's Chronicle*)

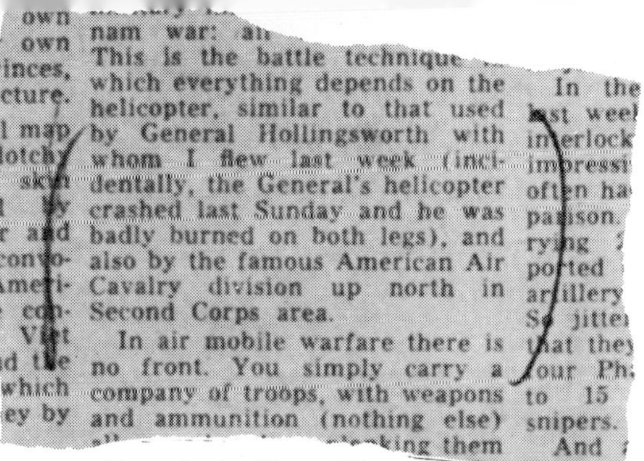

nam war: ...
This is the battle technique ... which everything depends on the helicopter, similar to that used by General Hollingsworth with whom I flew last week (incidentally, the General's helicopter crashed last Sunday and he was badly burned on both legs), and also by the famous American Air Cavalry division up north in Second Corps area.

In air mobile warfare there is no front. You simply carry a company of troops, with weapons and ammunition (nothing else) ... king them

(From *Sunday Times*, 12 June, 1966)

Having to descend at random on to enemy-held territory became, with Poland overrun by the Germans, the deed most dreaded by me. One became conditioned to 'frontal' clashes, but the unpredictable and hidden presence of adversaries would be, I thought, beyond me.

And so, I went on formulating the idea – as I was driven (the escort perched behind me, guns at the ready) through an ever-active area (indeed, on the way a cluster of huts sprung flames and peasants in panic trotted through the fields), and stated conclusively, having reached the **Di An Headquarters of the 1st Infantry Division** that I would rather not give trouble beyond having a few soldiers pose for me done up in full battle gear.

But then the officer-corps gallantry, perhaps even extra-expansive since formed on the mystique of British tradition, swept me into their hosting: the mess drinks, the luncheon, with me seated on the right of the two-star **General De Puy** and opposite **Brigadier General James Hollingsworth.** The conversation round the tableful of officers was that of happy hunters comparing their successes (**'haven't had my VC yet today'**), all keen on their safari, furnished with the richest gadgetry. I ventured to pronounce on their supremacy over the prey. For this they had ready a many-voiced answer: 'No, no, on the ground VC's superior!'

And then (I must have proved myself somehow, or my prickly challenge asked for a riposte) came Hollingsworth's utmost gesture of inviting me to his command helicopter for the routine afternoon '**mission**' within their 'Air Mobile Warfare'.

Triviality underlines the bathos of my inescapable predicament: it is declared that my all-purpose bush-blouse will do, but my own boots are no good for the marshy jungle; and, with my extra-tiny feet, their smallest size, still far too large, will, I know, incapacitate me. The lowest morale-moment comes with me bending down, lacing on those huge army boots – the irrevocable finality-sentence on all counts: with the boot-fetters in hostile terrain – and, again, sided with the invaders.

But, as one can guess, this rush and clamour of jeeps, men, dust-whirling choppers; this racket of flight over the under-foot lush-scapes (green – shade of Eden, thatches of innocence); those men, dressed into space-monsters, General James Hollingsworth swarthy/sporting hovering his binoculars for the occasional prey, **'haven't had my VC yet today'** – all this must be (an enlightening thought), more often than not, a routine show-off, a make-believe pie-in-the-sky masquerade play-acting a myth, which has to be regulation-booked each afternoon in this vicious quixotry-action aimed at this or that random rusticity for the watching world. Only now-and-again provoking, or unravelling the adversary. Indeed, we flew, we circled, we landed – repeatedly; we found no VCs.

Yet, about a week later, already back in London, I read in *The Sunday Times*'s dispatch from Nicholas Tomalin that General Hollingsworth had had both his legs badly burned, when his command helicopter was brought down on a mission.

Back from Red China, and concerned. And passing on, modestly but with urgency, the ultra objective views of, at that time, the British Chargé d'Affaires in Peking to an important liberal left Republican politician in his New York drawing room over after-lunch coffee-brandy, amongst some high-powered political academic finance worthies, their ladies – and single worthy ladies. He had just returned, flushed with success, from a duel on TV – reasonable and respected knight errant of good causes.

My British expert's line on China: their aggressive noises – a defensive smoke-screen to cover fear of imminent invasion by USA; admission to UN essential and urgent – both sides would learn plenty from one another. But this disputable message, meriting attention at least as a rarity brought by an eye-witness from an all-important but inaccessible (to the Americans) sphere, was not assessed/sifted out but used by the host only as a foil for an amazing display of bellicosity fed on customary clichés, America's own foibles lost in self-righteous indignation at Barbary-China's bestiality, of such shop-soiled turgidity – a language of such monstrous prejudice in this always calm and debonair creature of reason – that it seemed an act, not unlike the Communist recitatives of loyalties; blind or wilful – a passable oratorical performance for the electorate but surely out of place in an intimate gathering.* Yet precisely – this tame circle of civilized citizens of consequence (one or two tentative voices trying not so much to support my concept as to tone down the thundering castigatory performance at my expense) was even more disturbing. In an instant, free-wheeling conversation, a luke-warm 'free world' occasion shifted into an inquisitorial holy wrath directed no more at China but at my person. I sat cosily between two neat ladies, but condemned for the crime of nonconformism of the day, and more – for stepping booted unbent into the magic circle of American Sacred Ideology.*

But no, it is said often of the Americans, 'He's changed his views.'* This politician changed (partly) his views by now on the matter of his bygone stand – within (although it must be said in justice somewhat in the forward lines) the general

*George Kennan: 'The question becomes not: how effective is what I am doing in terms of the impact it makes on our world environment? But rather, how do I look, in the mirror of democratic American opinion, as I do it? Do I look shrewd, determined, defiantly patriotic, imbued with the necessary vigilance before the wiles of foreign governments?' Alexis Charles Henri Maurice Clezel de Tocqueville: 'I know of no country in which there is so little independence of mind and real freedom of discussion as in America.'

But why American? Why now? La Bruyère (*Les Characteurs ou les Moeurs de ce Siècle*, 1688)! 'Une chose folle et qui découvre bien notre petitesse, c'est l'assujettissement aux modes quand on l'etend à ce qui concerne le goût, le vivre, le santé et la conscience.' 'The folly which exposes well our smallness: our subjugations to fashions in the matters of discernment, conduct, health, conscience.'

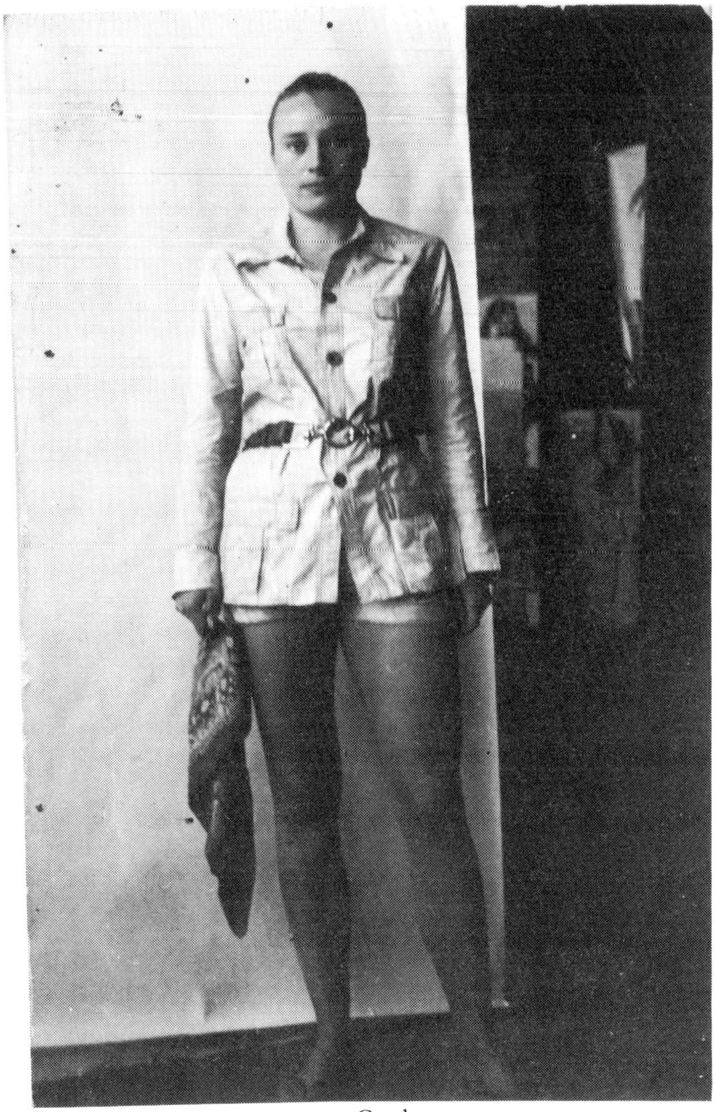

Caryl

Built-in absolescence conformisms chase/replace one another, never last, but have their day – no quarter given.* But why conformism in the land of ghettos? Perhaps the low level of averageness conducts vulgar novelties best; perhaps, what is happening now is beyond this routine of changes – a major *crise de conscience* – the final ridge beyond the continuum.

Caryl. First sight: Green hillock, water-edged, topped by this Saxon-flesh-coloured horizontal allure, without correlations: thus seemingly of Parnassian magnitude – a vision.

Second: face-to-face (sprawled) – features, a masterpiece of purist selection; beyond, imposingly receding longitudes.

Third, years and upheavals later: face-upon-face.

This height, overwhelming at first, becomes with time comfortingly proper – feminine superiority gladly confirmed; and, when watched from my doorstep, her advancing at me, the ever-recurring wonder of the small head setting her long movement into the floating proportions of the female idols in European antiquity and the Renaissance, not met with before.† Because – it must be made clear – there is nothing in her of a fashion model, none of their posturing or facial coquetry, nor mock-disdain: lofty gravity is the dominant mood, relying on the purposeful strength of generously sculptured legs.

No need to dwell on Caryl's inner qualities: they fill in well her form.

Two difficulties arise:

Domestication with such an ideal turns the husband-artist inward, thus reduces his outward curiosity – a hitherto propelling force.

Another lies in the expectations of sempiternal bestness in such a *ménage* – making tiny disappointments inflate hugely.

Her 'Phidian mould' matched with inner valour, with dedication. Involuntary trials reveal the singularity of her modesty-enwrapped fortitude; or, if brought to the extremity of anger (twice within twenty years), turning upon herself, not her adversary. Yet all this falls beneath her immeasurability – because she retains, even with me, an undisclosed sphere.

trend. Yet this CHANGE within, and of, conformity must have its scouting dare-devils? In such a society, with its 'universal ideology', there is a temptation for each four-years'-emperor to set dams on change by suppressing the restless avant-guards – the witch-hunt, a natural social bent, accommodating.* But then such bottling in of pressing younger energies manufactures explosives of revolt.

Joe MacCarthy's era came and went between two visits – news from darkened America blended with Stalinist tales from behind the Iron Curtain (yes, character assassination is a civilized weapon – not so physical assassination); but then perhaps the camp of brotherhood utopia was less criminal than extermination by super-race utopia – the twentieth century poses many novel problems. All Americans, even the victims, became stained – somewhat damaged and though shamefacedly apologetic – conceding.

Conformism served the devil. Conformism holds the sway over political prejudices and culture fashions. Dissent-resistance – as new conformism– well? save America, and the rest?

Sunday, 25 August, 1968

Kennedy Airport. Air conditioning reconstructs heat-shattered automatons and they parade: freckled boy indoctrinates himself on Captain America; soldiers-sailors-airmen – razor-sharp clothes dummies; fat white woman, a cosmetic patchwork, grip on her loaded handbag unrelaxed, manages to tint the old lips and to hold up a mirror; fat grand silky black middle-class family.

Fat teenage girls fill up Chicago plane – back from two months at an $800–$900 (not sure) slimming sanatorium. My

†Maureen Duffy, watching her cross the studio: 'a centurion's back'.

fourteen-year-old neighbour lost out of 211 pounds 33 – still monstrous. US affliction – the troubled rich youth. These winged fat-troubled youths; this airborne quacking on diets-and-trivialities – a preamble-warning, counter-poise to Chicago of the Lean.

Chicago old convention style blares at airport with song-jazz and candy-striped jovialities – childish clean-fun greeting the delegates – ye olde optimistic noises, AD-world welcomes: 'Welcome' straw hats; 'Welcome delegates! Mayor Richard Daley's Chicago Host Committees'. Turreting the horizon, bunched architectural samplings lure, then slide out of sight as the 'limousine' greases into the shadowy innards; and, out to windy watery 'Welcome to Chicago' Lakeside Drive, down Michigan Avenue abruptly blocked by the ultimate giantest PEPSI, patrolled by butcher-breed police, bellies lolling, fiercely bloated under their helmets – under flowery symbols of hospitality, voluntary ambulancers-in-waiting framed by 'Police Lines' and 'Chicago Police' barriers. Convention-time Hilton lobby as in '56 but grimmer more brutal. Out-of-hand hysteria mounting, as Reception holds up the privileged turned mob, punch-machines delay, multi-vouchers get lost and strikes of this and that cut VIPs to crowd measure.

The natty lollipop 'Daley Hostesses' have no chance to coo here – the overflowing mass flooding soiled lobbies-corridors-counters, storming in vain the elevators, hunting 'facilities' – all on edge.

Monday, 26 August: First Day of Chicago Convention
From my hotel window over the grubby backs, parking lots and strip-joints: a line of waggers of Hubert's smile multiples files below – a noisy open bus-relic, filled with Humphreyite amplified shouts/slogans-banners/brass-drums, detaches makes for the curb opposite (in front of car-hire office) unloads/strips. But soon gets dressed up again and topped with another (same?) enthusiastic loadful – this time for McCarthy.

I announce myself on the crest, instantly on the bullhorn 'a guy from London wants Jerry', and in a flash, from the milling below, the Commander with entourage unravel, rush uphill (hair cloaks banners expectations floating) at me, for succour(?), messages(?) – a forlorn hope, a false envoy, I am not the answer.

Jerry Rubin compact swift – the cunning hero and: the black rock-faithful, the Nike, the betrayer (later unmasked) – they, the fatal prototypes in this desperate elated group (the wise old tutelary counsel missing) pre-ordained for selfless sacrifice – for rebirth; their preparatory years, beatnik/hippy, shaped their ritual and costume for this initiation and they look timelessly right in their panachious varieform battledress.

The privileged extricate their drivers and cars
nested in parking lots, call offices to check business calls homes to check families have cocktails
and drop in at the Convention (correct badges for correct slots),
dine at Chicago Tavern Club or slum it in Wells Street while outside the thudding of
chase and nightsticks on sculls,

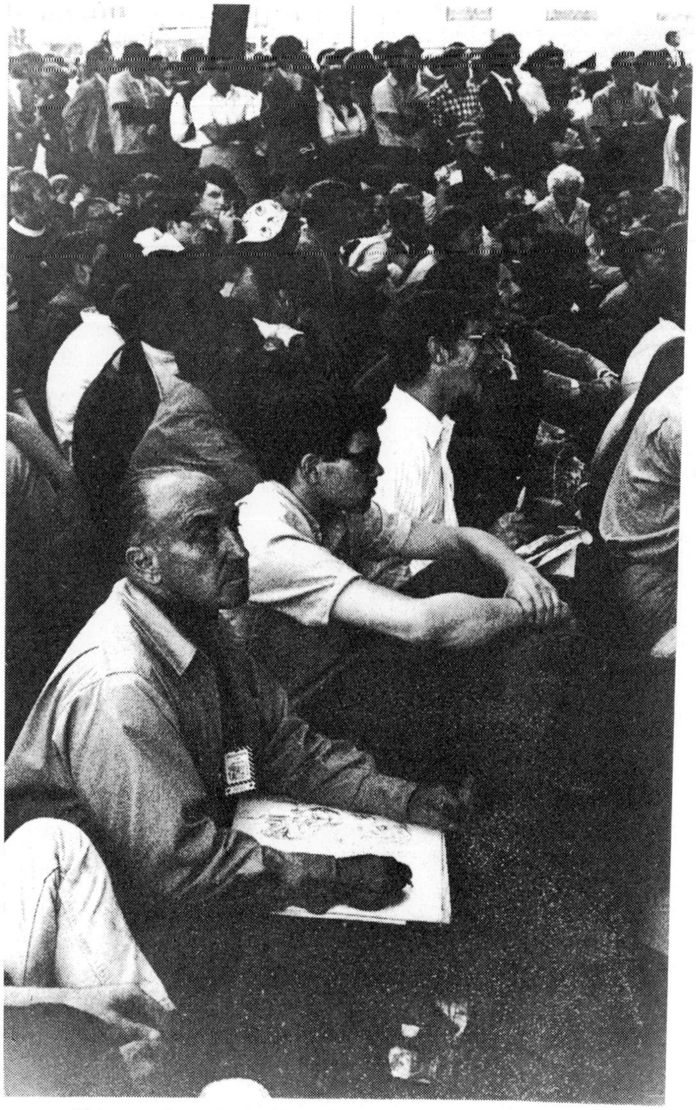

Chicago: Grant Park, 1968 (from *Shem, Ham & Japheth Inc.*)

change and after midnight 'drop in at Heffner's'
(Heffner's Mansion then begins receiving).
The have-it-both-ways, have it and eat it – the celebrity 'stoics'
are there: Feiffer ping-pongs with off-duty bunny
Mary star protest folk-singer at love/play in the steam-massage vaults.
In the Knightly Hall above (and later)
Mary the thoughtful lady in concord with influential
Senators and men of consequence.
Warren Beatty ever so modest.
Heffner agitated proud of a nightstick smack on his bottom –
this history-making for publicity boys.
Bunnies, strange affectation,
their duty-corseted breasts freed now in their 'salon' mufti,
drop under dresses to the waist and lower.

Tuesday, 27 August: Second Day of Chicago Convention
Bill G's car is brought by large young man – cropped under hat glasses – The Square.

Lincoln Park: he takes off his hat Brooks Brotherhood jacket tie but still does not pass – I order him to keep away.

The scene is enchanting.

Top of the hill held by the command: Jerry Rubin and his

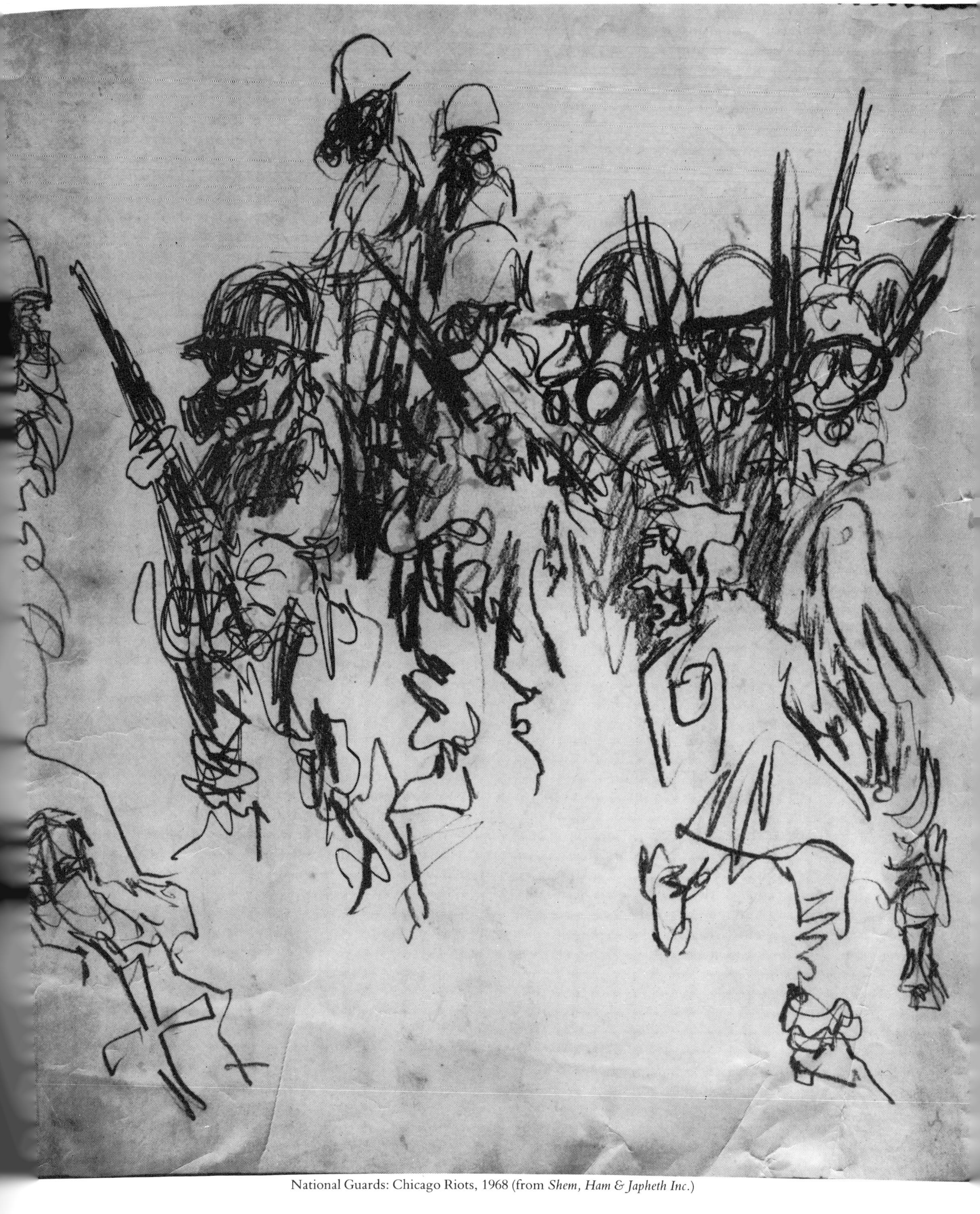

National Guards: Chicago Riots, 1968 (from *Shem, Ham & Japheth Inc.*)

retinue – also Ginsberg as guru, Feiffer a participatory jester – all miming to the tune of the (naked weedy pastoral torso) flutist. Down and up the gently landscaped crowd – an anarchistic bivouac held by, now thickened, helmeted lines – scouting helicopters above. Plottings and languor. And haunched circles – pot-peace-pipe passed around. And comic interludes and old-time eccentrics with their own idiosyncrasies/placards and elderly argumentative 'liberals' in shorts and OM-OM-OM-atic chants. The phalanx training – merely an endearing war-dance.

Across the street from the Hilton the strip of grass and trees banked by a low bed of railways bridged over by traffic, but easily a trap, now crowd-boiling held by a rim (at the kerb) of lined-up helmeted tough-posturing heavies. Oddly this is all arbitrary since, at both ends, marked by traffic lights, the lines of adversaries end. Perhaps back in the days of knighthood, in a field marked thus, the two armies met for combat without stooping to tactical shrewdness of outflanking and containment.

Night lays some, mostly in pairs, on the ground – for challenge at the cops' feet – mostly to sleep; others form lines to face the enemy or pyramid in monumental groupings (searchlights heightening their gestures) capped by bullhorn speeches (wide applause for fist shaking at the Establishment fortress – the Hilton).

Songs slogan-choirs harangues accumulate into cacophonous *fortissimo* – groups focalize, become the swell/sway lava – and then miraculously in response the whole towering façade of the hotel begins to blink, blink (conquest? recruitment? electronic gadgetry?), blink – masses of windows – one third? half? blink in response, a fifth column within the convention-ality fortress.

This is a supreme happening/birth of fact; long-rehearsed erratic attitudes, tentative gestures suddenly given common content/word – word-into-flesh.* Chicago – open stage-reality gives/grooves the old and the unprecendented drama elements on an unprecedented mammoth scale. Conflict: uniform force v. anarchistic plasma; staging: yielding nature v. Babel Towers, gashed by ever-streaming chorus of traffic – reminder of continuity of trivia. Then the amplifiers' demigod voices raised to heaven but nabbed apprehended, collared, by flying spy-machines. And that high flamboyant act of aid by electric multi-signalling from behind the enemy lines – the art-play of visuals/kinetics given scale/soul of the act of solidarity; the unplotted rampage – this Revolution.

And all intensified by non-action: the confrontation business – the fears the threats the brinks the taboos the media-replacing-action the unnerving-talking-waiting-without-parleys, for, when action comes, it deflates, reduces the scale to ye olde bashings. The bathos – the scale of a cudgel, of a brawl, not even of the turn-of-the-century revolutions because the lines of fighters do not fire or charge with sabres. It is all, that night, a war of hot nerves – 'cold war'. And when at some hour of the night the military manoeuvre is sprung at us, there is vast astonishment rather than fear. The incongruity of clattering armour pronounced in left/right drill and formalized manned weaponry – comic yokels' entry.

The lines of police (all poorly choreographed: their conspicuous whispers from ear to ear) turn right and quick march off, while the khaki cordon, guns at the ready, clumsily moves at us. This attack is intended to terrify into panic – it rivets with disbelief: helmeted gunned National Guardsmen against this playful crowd of protesters? It cannot be. And so a General bullhorns from the top of a jeep an ultimatum and gas canisters and gas masks are demonstrably manipulated, barbed-wired threatening vehicles to the fore. The crowd mocks. And with the night wearing out the mockery individualizes, clowns at, challenges the line of pathetic, shy, scared, armed/dangerous mutes.

Some New Un-conventional Weapons:

(match Column A with Column B or vice versa)

Column A	*Column B*
against military-industrial complex	– buffoonery
,, Un-American Activities Committee	– toy gun
,, Rotary clubs	– communes (also freak out)
,, two-car society	– squat
,, National Guards	– pot
,, law and order	– justice
,, pigs	– groupies
,, revisionism	– way out
,, US defence of freedom in Vietnam	– Swedish trip
,, Communist Party	– mind-blowing
,, vigilantes	– lead them a dance
,, image-makers	– the same
,, principles/hypocrisy	– whack off
,, age-old rules and taboos	– take off
,, American imperialism as international order and aid for development	– love-in
,, brotherly help to Czechoslovakia	– Westmoreland
,, Yellow Peril	– tribulation
,, backlash	– acid-head
,, Party Apparatus	– head-stand
,, scientists' } prostitution in service to politics	– travestites
,, intellectuals' }	– Simplicissimus
,, over-kill	– over-Spock
,, Outer Space	– spaced

Cybernetics-evolved guerrillas
by Hustling and Myth Making for the hell of it.
Fortitude: surplus-clad (dash of longing).
Valour: of unbuttoned vulnerability.
Daring: to merit mock-medals and mock-promotions.

*RITUAL BEFORE CONTENT. Ritual is the current WORD. As THE WORD should, it has the power (for a while) to contain the mysteries of the day. The young tend to dress and, in consequence, posture and frown romantically (in spite of the cheap readymades available) to gather in dark cellars for 'cultic' dances and 'skiffle' (in spite of the telly and the neon). It may all be animal energy. But one observes there is this exclusively youth-world set against the present vacuum a curious aura of subconscious anticipation and preparedness. Their plotting groups seem to be expecting a lead. Their sing-song rites seem made ready for the potential arrival of their prophet-poets, though meanwhile uncouthly willed in with American cowboy ballads. And so it can be said that a ritual is forming before our eyes in waiting for a content.
'Topolski's Chronicle' Nos. 1–2 (109–110) Vol VI 1958

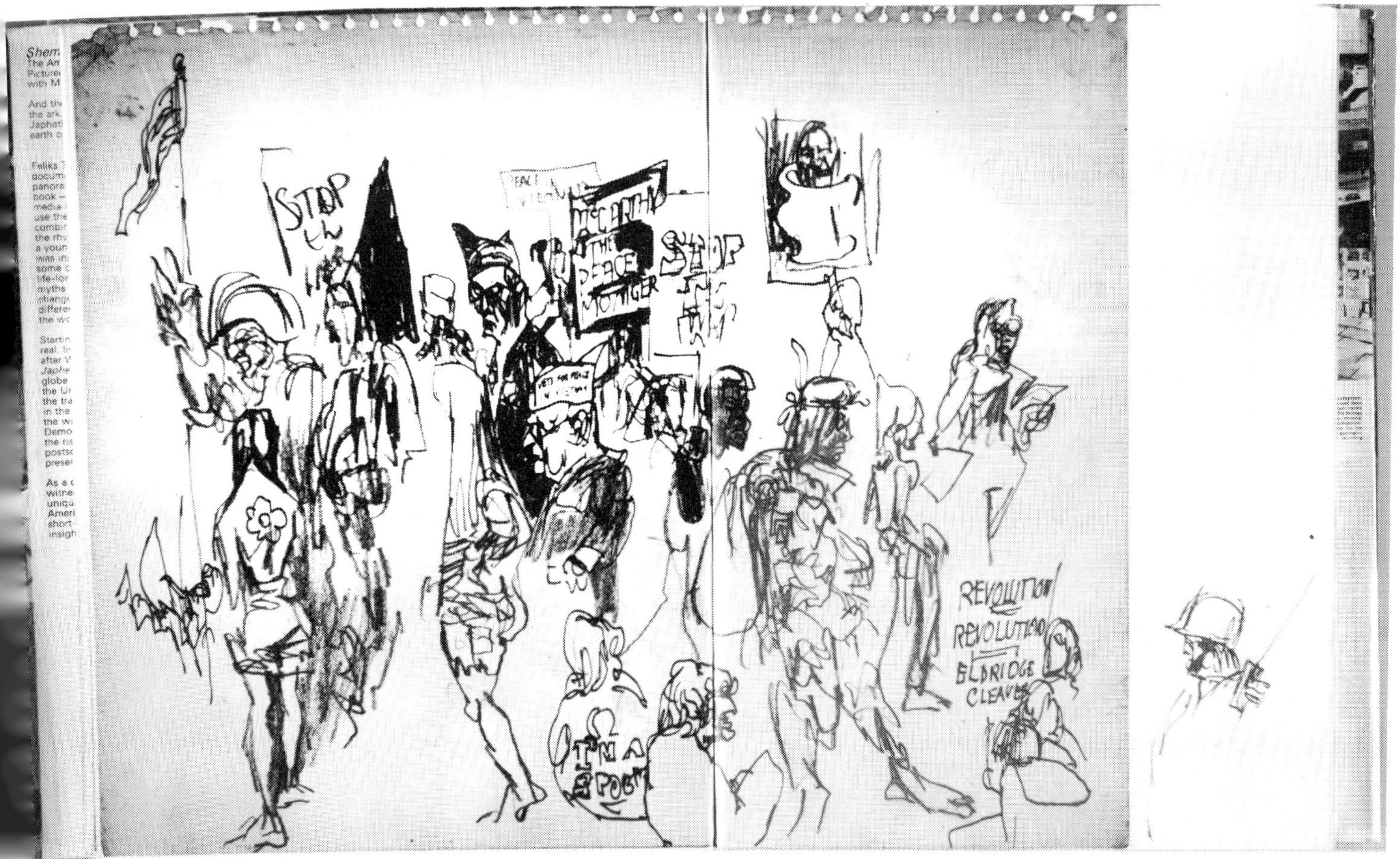

Chicago: Protesters' Rally, 1968 (from *Shem, Ham & Japheth Inc.*)

Semantic/ballistic logistics: adversary soldiers' private obscenities
writ large on own banners – ricochet.
Escalating confrontation: confrontation: self-mock-heroes/
dignataries – bare-chest bare-foot war-painted-feathered brass-
hatted (back-to-front) cloaked (tattered) –&– daggered (rusted)
decorated/ribboned (un-merited) tail-coated (bare-bottom) –
measure against
real weapons/costumes of might –
senatorial judicial naval-army-spacemissile federal mayorial
proprieties –
thus distort-mirroring infecting affecting contamination
de-foliating
rendering the ELDERS impotent –
the stooges of the knock-about
Stoop to Conquer – a morality play
Permissive draft strategy: alliance of warriors and amazons
breeds minority into MAJORITY'S NEMESIS.

Wednesday, 28 August – Third Day of Chicago Convention

clatters in on
the Mule Train
black peasants
in the Loop of power
a breath of innocent pastures
congests the traffic
holds cops
in reverence

'Rally in Grant Park' bullhorn orders. The strolling motley lines across the bridges zig over lawns zag amongst trees – again again the medieval memories the Breughel memories the memories of 1944 campers-stragglers-armies straying all over liberated Rome, of 1945 anarchic rollicking freedom-drunk marchers across defeated Germany – the breaking of the rules, the flood of disorder.

But this American revolt/display outwardly magnificent in promise, is still bridled by ingrained civic orderliness; however flamboyant and banner-dotted, they only rally to an appointed spot.

The regular bandstand formal flags flanked, faced with a landscape of benches – filling up with picturesque but lawfully gathering citizens – unharassed at last, this time protected by a ring of blue armies. Indeed single cops (black for charm) move through the rows distributing leaflets announcing from Chicago Police Department that '. . . you are permitted to conduct this assembly and rally and will be protected . . .'

And so the rally begins its guitar interpolated ('next song is dedicated to Hubert Horatio Hog') routine of speeches

(Dick Gregory, flower in hand, a charming comic battledress and hat to match 'since the Mayor failed the opportunity to welcome you to my town . . . this government, this convention every bit as controlled as the puppet government in Saigon . . .'. Far and high, beyond helicopters, 'STANDARD' 'YMCA' and armed men on the roofs. Down here placards 'Get troops out of Chicago' 'Black Amnesty NOW' 'Bring the GIs Home Now' 'Fuck the Draft' 'Prague same as Chicago', regulation forage caps 'VETS for Peace in Vietnam', on a girl's bare back 'I'm a Spock Baby', badges 'Fuck You'. Andy Haynes (who worked with the caucus of black delegates), Oregon, neat suit-tie, very black '. . . may be based on your blood'. Next, in eclectic hero-costume, a burner of his 'delinquency-notice')

but
A GREAT SHOUT
from the left
mounts me up on a bench
and there
in the wide greenness
the tumult
shapes, in a whirlwind of dust,
a vast Napoleonic battlefield picture.
The banners
black-red-Vietcong-Cuban-Old Glory
the Battle of the Standard
takes place
in the green of the field of the battle-blue
the enemy's blue cordons
thrust/whack at speed
fold back into running retreat
the darker panic-stricken mass
press toward my position.
Helicopters clutter/circle tightly, swoop to survey,
and up to assess
radio-coordinate –
officers armchaired within staff-cars
telephone orders encouragements
'advance to the charge! forward!'
to the second assault column.
Now pale blue centipede wedges at a stamping jog-trot
bellicose back-forth sharp truncheon probings
– a new technique. The wedge goes in fast.
No machine age, no Macedonian phalanx, but homoid formation,
these thick-waisted men
cudgel jerking at mid-man
rapid horizontal ramming – unexpected – at the guts.
The centuries fall back:
not the battle of conventional weapons
not the hard-edge battle –
the cudgel era battle.
But our life-respecting age
aims at mere balls-smashing, maiming
(Abraham's sacrificial murder of his son;
Oedipus and his father
both knowing their blood-ties).
Many feathered flamboyance
irresolute, still law-abiding (defence orders 'sit! sit! sit down!')
but the cops labour on
until the charge of these mercenary sloggers unopposed
spends itself before reaching the platform – and me.

Not a modern battle at all:
tricks of tracking/dodging forgotten
this is body-bold bludgeoning, vulgar and primeval.
The blue cohorts, oafs in blue, comic in their hot drill,
unisonous jerk of clubs
their adversaries – a soft fanaticism
yielding going under giving ground yet cohesive.

This is not a battle at all
but: a) sacrificial block for the young
b) Roman arena for new religiantes
c) mass-persecution
since they
unarmed (a few slingers of stones, shit-in-plastic-bags,
abuses, buffoneries)
and indoctrinated in Civil Disobedience rules.

Not unlike
the Russian Decembrists' uprising, 1825
described by historians H. Tyrrell and Henry A. Haukeil, 1891
'. . . the insurgents were assailed both in front and flank . . .'
But CS Gas Canisters play a tactical part this time:
'GAS'!
cometic parabolas (white vapours) wriggle fast
explode deep into the confusion
(could as well be cannons, muskets, fire-arrows out of cross-bows)
over the open field – packed and swooning.

Bloodied heads out of the *mêlée*
encircled by medic-priests
held up by red-crossed arms
for testimony:
crusaders undrilled unarmed
marytred
for resurrection/inclusion into
the twentieth-century gospels
by the communication-industry.

It will be said 'they were provoked'
'outraged at the FLAG dishonoured'.

An unacceptable evasion:
the 'law-&-order' policeman must be by definition emotion-blindfolded; and this assembly and rally was declared permitted and protected by the Chicago Police Department. But, if quibbles are sought, much preferable Pier Paolo Pasolini the Italian Communist poet ('. . . *vi odio come odio i vostri papa* . . .' '. . . I hate you as I hate your fathers . . .') upholding police as outraged proletarians against well-to-do-class students: legitimate envy of the upper estate, respect/ambition germinating, unbalanced by hobo-clad hobo-spoken hobo-nigger-loving educated – they double offend and double provoke to resentment the upping prole in power's livery, angry at confusion – personal insult – the
cop hits harder at the unfathomable.

The Notables Turn to Speak

Here – because commissioned
paid – therefore privileged
(photo-reporters claim rights by being on the job)
the anarchy pen-stars
foment the events
and write them up
the four-day massacre of innocents
sustained by the presence
of prophets
press-hired to be there, dangling badges of immunity:
Prophet Burroughs, Esq., '. . . the system – it is simply unworkable'
Star Genet, Esq., '. . . *il a fallu beaucoup des morts à Hanoi pour que*

cette 'happening' ait lieu'
these have and give it both ways ready for bruises and fees
a legitimate double hazard within message-media ethics
though another squire has the plainness
to exhort with battle-cries, lead on to the slaughter yards,
but without him in the lead
as he cannot afford arrest or hurt
having a copy date-line
thus earning wages-of-violence-on-others.

Publicity communicates
secret plots – rebels against democratyrants
Underground Conspirators dress up to stand out
stand up and are counted
on the off-chance that the voter/the great American viewer
will buy
Revolutions-happenings
at a fixed date and hour
and there gather
players extras film-makers commentators documentators
historians sociologists and gapers;
tactics victory – no matter
'the play's the thing' with some cracked heads
'the medium is the message'
'Liberty, let others despair of you'.

At the nearest statue of a legitimized American Civil-Warrior the illegitimate determined gather. The media line up. Some blond-bearded Hellenistic pensive heroes crap in the doorless latrines crouched/lined for purging before battle. Tradition upheld but adapted: the warming-up orations, skirmishes, final meditations and offerings. But encircled, the march – a non-starter.

Motorized for push across barriers, I drive into National Guard lines (flourishes of shouts guns bayonets pointed) on the bridge (over the railway-routine below) – out of the rout two boys beg a smuggle – lift them through the armour and gun-wagging siege.

Car-dash to the power-house of the Convention ('Hello Democrats! Welcome to Chicago!'). Here, in the hubbub of the female side of the coin, ball-having high-coiffed pastel-coloured trinkets-dangling, girlfriends families taking position of ranked prerogatives and the floor thick to a standstill with phonies gate-crashers and nepotism stooges, I, barricaded out, get boorish 'noes' from office-officious Chicagoans barricaded in behind desks; they love cutting down and my pleading of a 'special case' infuriates this fenced-in structure of privilege in reverse – the numbers, mass (media, supporters) exclude a single claimant.

The chairman '. . . the Johnson years have truly been the golden age of the American consumer . . .'. From a high-up gallery (nearly pushed out by a uniformed youth 'who are you taking a message to?' – my messenger's badge envied by still lesser creatures) my spy-glass runs over this bowl of vibrations, pans this Westernized Ajanta fresco of faces – this partaking act being only the sum total of the rows of seated provincials benumbed by state-patriotism speeches – the floor agitates in pockets nurtured by the holy eye of television godheads, reverently processioned in slow motion by burdened priestly exposure-dedicated men, light-sound auxiliaries in attendance, guarding/extending votive cords of Curiosity.

The televison eye sees/shows also this time's true Rubicon; tempts back.

The driver drops me at this Rubicon (Balbo bridge), reverses and flees. Out of the dark the Metropolitan siege light-flooded, afloat in billowing smoke, undulating with scattering crawling clustering plasma – humans against the machines and the armed and masked fearsome monsters. This non-battle livens up only in short bursts and then lulls. Into it – mostly a tear-blinded eyeball-to-visor closeness. Then the troopers, ferocious from afar, are revealed as clumsy misfits in shape/size, missing buttons or misholed hooks, minute inaccuracies of arms holding/holstering, a paradoxical and unexpected local militia diversity – in spite of the proud pretences of the US Army uniform.

The eruption comes to an end. The bridge is blocked, the dark depths of the Grant Park strip received the battered and the exhausted. Some in front gallivant with turned-on talk, over and across the heads of the now unmasked silent as if humble doughboys; on the damnedness of being a soldier, on the shame of it, some sit mid-bridge doodling fantasies on white traffic lines. Above all, overwhelmingly, they demonstrate/prove that they are The People – given the advantage of the popular insurgency in having their womenfolk ever at their side and in their embrace.

Thursday, 29 August: Fourth Day of Chicago

festooned with youths
afloat afruit
on branches,
squatter-paved,
outlined in blue and khaki
this trodden hate/love acre
lets itself for speaker's
ploughing/furrowing/partitioning
into partisan plots, sub-plots
of discord/dissent.
The sleep-out sit-around speak-in
on this trampled patch
battle-battered motley foot-volunteers
stir, wounds lick
the other cheek the other bandaged head
victors in self-immolatory tactics war
but steadfastly irresolute
but bellicosity surfaces shoals up
against linear authority –
pig-sticking
pig-cursing, belly-underbelly-cursing
cursing:
obscenely dangling assertions,
assorted aggressive armoury
cudgels for swinging
handcuffs for subjection
whistles for courage
keys for housekeeping
guns for twiddling
bullets for earnest.

There were promises, hand-outs leaflets were sent out widely about rallying the biggest ever display of the best 'underground' art – of lifting high the protest on the riches of pop culture. This could not have failed, yet strangely it did not happen. Only small voices in a trickle: a few weak star-turns, a solo pop-singer and Lowell's echo-less elegancies. Puzzling yet significant that this unique opportunity this very pop apotheosis perhaps made the pedlars of art-ifice for its own sake recoil from exposing their antics to reality – or were they simply dissuaded by their agents? or stopped on the way by the FBI?

> commercial successoiled
> made-good folk
> singer
> limousined to the site of the day's demo
> (for her a short charity appearance, each day
> a different costume – 'casual' but *haute-couture*)
> for a well-tailored umpha umpha protest –
> in this reality –
> a flat false note.

Speakers. John Birchard, a Vietnam veteran, 'I suggest a truly revolutionary slogan: not "Pig" but "Join Us".' Dick Gregory flourishes in his siren-suit. The blonde SDS boy is shouted down for moderation, but counted out candidate McCarthy is loved, perhaps mostly because these youths after three days battering feel orphaned and ache for a father. McCarthy descends from the hotel into the crowd (poster 'McCarthy the Peace Monger') for an appropriate speech but meaningfully is obscured by a tight square of dark-spectacled security men and forward shoving camera-and-recording crews. Thus the shapely words, sieved through these massive contradictions, of the prophet descending amongst the meek, loose their impact; or perhaps gain authority (obstacles – transformers) by the attention of the two Estates: State and Press.

Eugene (American polite culture) calls upon poet Robert Lowell to cover his retreat with precious New England word arabesques. This naive interpolation of élitarian sophistication – prolonged apologia cum modest and studiedly hesitant explanations preceding 'occasional panegyrics' for Columbia and The March on the Pentagon – is received with polite boredom by the crowd, arrested in its progress.

The progress begins: the march on the Amphitheatre is announced, warnings and loopholes are offered to the feeble-hearted and hesitantly the movement accumulates along Michigan Avenue. Banners placards lift up ('Chicago The Land of The Free and The Home of The Brave' 'Kill for Peace' 'It's Up Against the Wall Mother Fuckers' 'WASP for Peace in Vietnam and Chicago' '卐 Daley' 'Fuck you LBJ' 'Huburd How Absurd', posters of Johnson's head in the john) decisions are taken – Committee of Returned Soldiers step forward, boys with numbered sweatshirts move in, a touching group: neat elderly women and a priest, as I pass, make up their minds and start raising placards ('I am a

Suburban Square

and Protest Police Brutality'). All unobtrusive, all neatly moving along both pavements, traffic respecting – truly law-abiding citizens within their constitutional rights.

Motors diverted, the march spreads in width now passing through warehouse poverty – the locals, indifferent, gaping, amused; it does not occur to them (in their otherness) that they are part of the drama. Thus the demonstrators are isolated, forced outside the dreadful reality through which they merely pass. Thus – when this march between two walls of miserable acceptance is halted at 16th (or is it 18th) Street, under a railway bridge by ('A Tank!' marchers shout in disbelief) an armoured gun-turreted machine piled high with helmeted men and towering over the weapon-bristling foot formation which thickly fill up the width of the arch – the demonstrators, coldly watched on three sides, cease to lead a revolution, become invaders. The confrontation lacks the elation of the earlier ones which had only armed mercenaries opposite, but the Hilton signalled support. Here the working class – the body-America – stands unconcerned. And so the leaders call retreat 'We'll find another pass, that's all!'

There was a good quarter of an hour during which the National Guardsmen were faced, with the pressure mounting behind. Irresolute? Sensible? The marchers did not expect free passage, nor in truth could they find one around the corner; a fearsome clash, or at least a symbolic attempt to pass must have been anticipated – otherwise why march with a declared aim? And therefore fear, reasonable tactics (opposing faction voiceless without bullhorn) and relief at retreat orders – not all the elements of withdrawal. The indifference around – worse than animosity – contributed.

The retreat, triumphant with survival, spreads over the full width of the road.

> A unique incident (not broadly reported pictured though seen by hundreds): a police car halted and drowned in the thick of the turned-back marchers, a heavy policeman by it, helmet under arm, shakes hands, throws up the two-fingered sign, cries out/exchanges slogans, falls into shoulder patting, embraces, girls' kisses; the crowd relaxed, mills on; and one or two policemen stand, boulders in the stream, and watch this colleague of theirs stonily.

A modicum of moral support comes from other spheres. Now the oncoming motor traffic, rejoined, tries to make its way, honks in grand cacophony a tune of sympathy for these near-children of theirs – or to save their limousines, or even themselves. They are caught – the bourgeois at the mercy of perhaps (they do not know what happened ahead) an achieved revolution.

The exuberance of survival sweeps the retreating demonstrators into Grant Park, they climb up the equestrian statue; thickly covered from giant horse's tail to the top of the tricorn hat, flags of revolutions afloat round the raised sword of John A. Logan, Commander-in-Chief of the Grand Army of the Republic, the tableau is achieved – for climax and for the 'media'. Green slopes thicken with recumbent couples, guitars begin to twang, transistors – to deliver Convention speeches. TV vans advance.

Then there is the second march (by lawful invitation, in

lawful threesomes, to Gregory's home – 'legality' despised by some); considered, led – conscientious Convention delegates in front – therefore carried to conclusion – rifle butts, tear-gas, arrests. This march is also heightened because, not indifference, but opposition and contrast come on the way: sad – the decision to be lawful holds gentle fighters in threes clinging to the walls of one sidewalk so that at 18th and State Street they file along into the hands of the foe; young proletarians lined along the opposite side screaming abuses at them, thumbs down – while the centre is taken by the traffic-rush-hour traffic.

And at the Convention. Delay steals public time for a privately staged pre-prepared demonstration, galleries filled up (passes!) by his dependants with pre-printed posters 'We Love Mayor Daley!' and mini-American flags. This unspiced baloney averageness this loud pat meaninglessness – this *déjà-vu* HH – a dummy / mummy he must be by now, with twelve years unchanged (colouring-shape-gestures) 'public image' – this family around and supporters behind and lines left-right of top-average loyalists' boxes and names names names – averageness-distinguished biographies beckoning from people's lapels – and low-average liegemen's placards 'I'm for Albert! 'Daley is for Law! Order!' down to the audial climaxes of crass music, up to the visual crescendos of stripes stripes stripes.

This parody of worship: the crowded averageness of the consumer society on the altar – genuflecting before it a congregation of one: the chosen representative, the incarnation of aggressive averageness which he has to prove by thousands of stale incantations, thousands of apologies, patchwork rhetoric – to the bottomless pit of democratic *non sequitur*.

Humphrey begins his average acceptance speech with a heavy-handed quote to dispose of Chicago violence '. . . those few immortal words . . . a prayer of St Francis of Assisi. . .'

Then vice-presidential candidate Muskie drones on '. . . to God as a dispenser of justice' – applause and trumpets – '. . . exploitation by militants whose motives are suspect!' – bravoes and trumpets. Jules Feiffer, here a delegate, pantomimes (in my spy-glass) displeasure. A young German journalist next to me – an enthusiast for Daley – grows silent at my Polishness ('When did you leave?'), begins to be obstructive – places himself in my view, ignores admonitions. A German backlash.

Outside the Amphitheatre Muskie's voice from the loudspeakers over the slaughter-houses follows me rumbling on, stentorian, and on over my car radio, on and on . . . from protesters' transistors.

The last stand of Grant Park. The pre-dawn inventory: shadows float over flower-beds. Moon-sized lighted clock faraway out of darkness 5.04 am. Groups squatted at orange fires in rubbish baskets. Pervading sounds of dragging/tearing branches and fire-crackling. Vertical groups ungroup. Groups *couchant*. High lamps – blue. Conrad Hilton lighted ochre; and white arc-lights, still on, throw long shadows through the trees over the sleep-laden veterans. Sagging/stiff line of sad soldiers. Traffic begins.

I go back to the 11th floor, not knowing that a loose pack of policemen are now invading (or had a half-hour ago) the 15th floor and beating bloody the mild McCarthy volunteers.

The whole initiated by the American dream
and made possible by the American way
not by pre-Americus Vespucius grass-roots
when the earth was green
and the young grew out of the old like boughs.

30 August
Dispersal. Brashness takes over. The revolutionary folk-singing Mary is now a two-car multi-luggage 'star' – camaraderie stored away for agent's contracts.

San Francisco. My two-days' calls rejected cajoled, voices blurred with background secrets – his (Eldridge Cleaver's) gruff, unyielding yet evaporative. She (Kathleen Cleaver), tough-sane, supports tenuous connection. 8 pm no, meeting held (background murmurs) – tomorrow. I whine. 'Nine too soon – phone 10.30, maybe.' 10.30, some mumbles. 'What what did you say (panting not to upset the possibly propitious humour). 'Uh, come on.' Commotion as friends' cars not willing (radio says state-of-siege in Berkeley) – taxi, alone in the night space-travel towards black spheres. 2777 Pine Street. Questions from behind the high-up door. My name grotesque in this. Many locks clatter. And: the familiar head-quarters of Black power anywhere: stairs hall piled with disorder of many minds/ hands in a hurry – room loud smoke.

I stand within a crowded circle of watchful silence – again the play of legends of balladish kings warriors, courts of tyrants – this may have been part of a contemporary pattern in the States – I knew only the harmonies of the fifties, not the gangsters, mafias, subterranean ruler-boss and his slum-castles – but no, the Blacks rather, probably willynilly, enact – move into the heroic mould, although having invented-carved their hieratic imagery also out of the same squalidity. This deliberate ideal of tribal combat sets the scene back, say, in the Dark Ages of Europe and so reinvokes the gestures true to the circumstances of glory, loyalty, challenge, women and their heroes lovers brothers and sons. Then the dusty situation of old tales: I stand in the silent, expectant circle and have to make the first step – that is to recognize and revere the leader. And this to all practical purposes is an ordeal – I am here in face of a fearsome grave group of the committed, possibly at the mercy, as a White stranger, of their mood. Play the scene one must: I step forward and, though not knowing his face, approach the right man and declare him my host. To enter into conversation would distract my drawing, possibly strain their tolerance (perhaps wrongly, I feel that an unpredictable caprice may stop me or invite me out), and in front of this supreme theme I say that I shall concentrate on my work.

And so I draw while all round me the talk bounces about in short cuts, with bursts of gaiety, silences, subjects spread and played upon – the 'sky's the limit' refrain jazzed on, thrown about, once anecdotal, discursive, comic, threatening – it

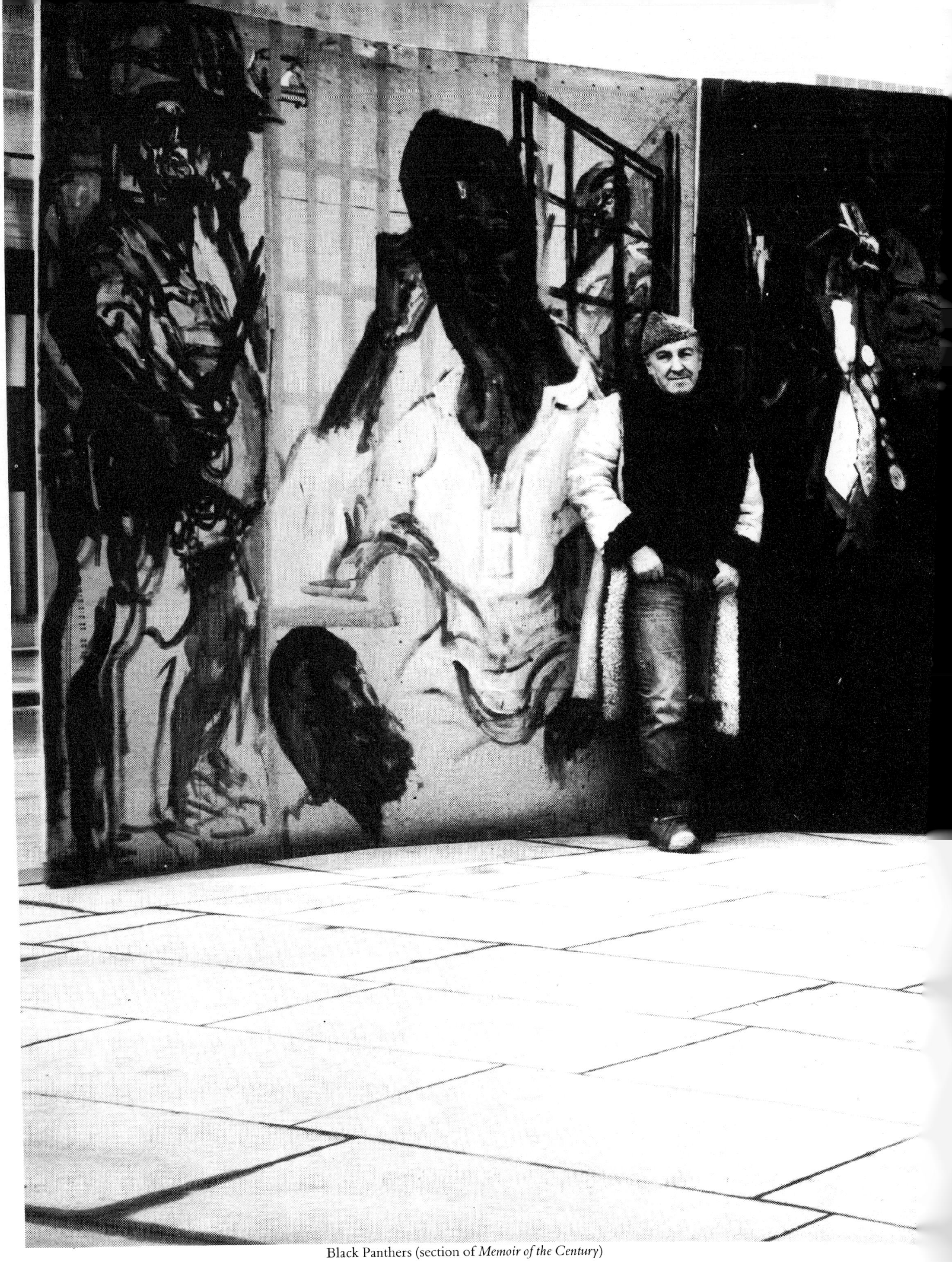

Black Panthers (section of *Memoir of the Century*)

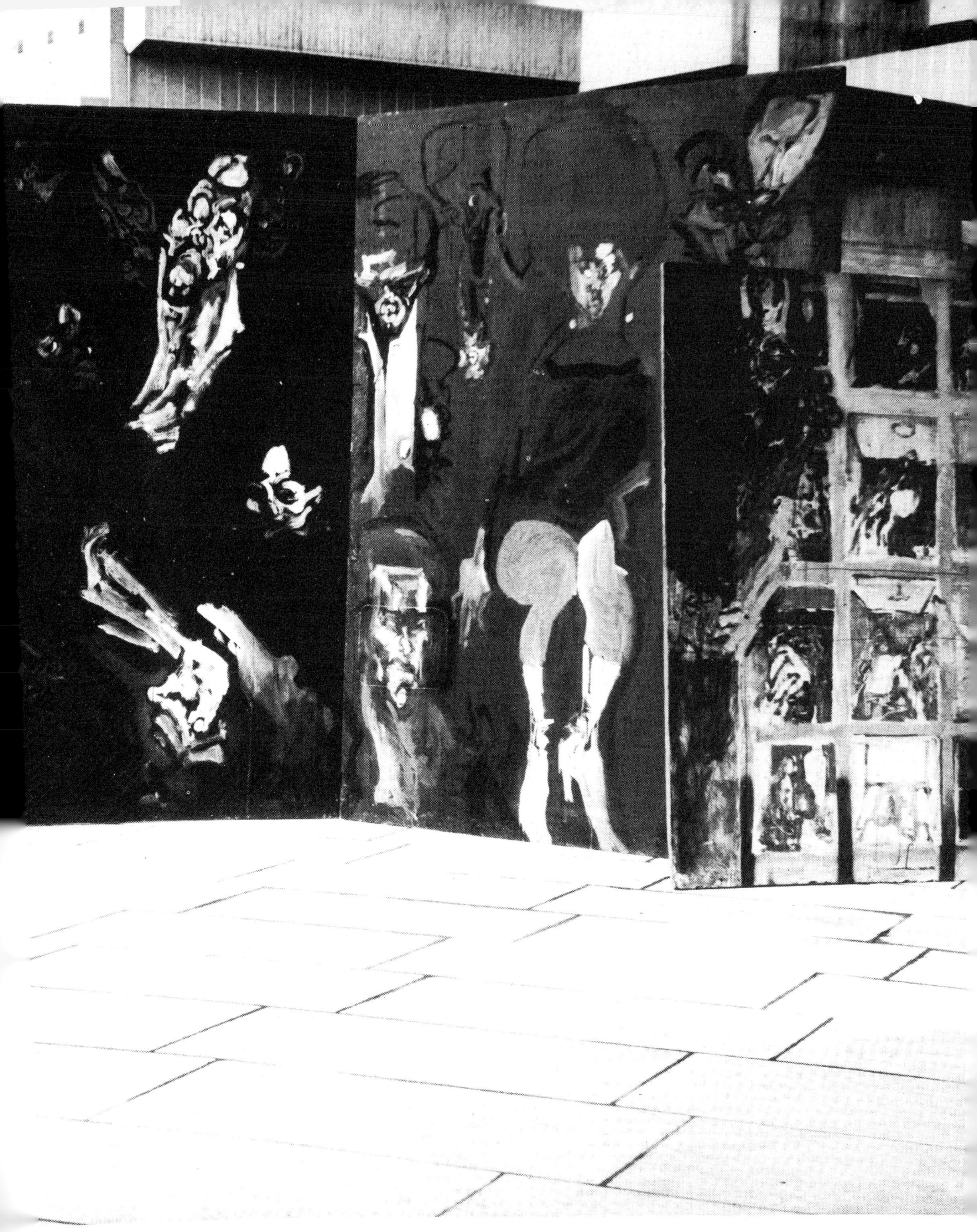

comes to me a musical thing, as the idiom bypasses me often and talk blurs – 'the group' seeming high (pot is supposedly banned in the Black Panther command; but drinking, all hours vigilance, stylisations of cool – turn on). This is the black dialogue, drum-jazz, counter-heat.

The talk-music flares up with repetitions, blares with laughter, gives room for solos – not only because the tongue is strange or I only half listen but because it has a motif of ancient themes: battles arenas mocking the enemy plots revengers commiserations with the fallen or taken prisoner enemy women. The talk may have been (and the whole aloof behaviour) conditioned by my presence: they were aware of me surely and they not so much acted in accord with my wanting to draw as in the unavoidable reflex (of such a group) to exclude Whitie, to ignore him (drinks were passed and cigarettes, omitting me) and to put him down. Or, more flatly, a court-painter/jester would not be, in the ancient tradition, an equal.

A Black stranger enters (behind me as I sit with my back to the door), and again a fantastic in its reality harsh modern-dress enactment of the Homeric tales medieval ballads. He declares himself a courier from Chicago and Bobby Seale engages him into a rich rapid rhetoric, almost ready-made challenge and password discourse of bona fides – of principles (articles of faith); this is crescendo – fast impromptu – yet as if life's at stake (as it well may be), painfully engrossing. This voicing of dissent fighting for acceptance, those challenges thrusting at his vulnerability – this ritual of a trial for the deviation of Chicago; the watchful many around the room, under the surface the acidity of effort of keyed-up cats, however languid the postures and hooded eyes of the protagonists.

And then Kathleen, an extraordinary *élégante* of the Vogues of the future (they say she gets her hair crinkled). She flutters, she offers repartee and gaiety to all; she complements, enlarges, rounds up, reassures the circle. I go on drawing while the room empties – it must be well after 2 am. Eldridge addresses himself to me: 'Hey, man, finish up, I'm sleepy, wanna go to bed.' Kathleen calls a taxi for me, then he engages the telephone in code-like endlessness. After nearly an hour of further drawing (Kathleen's small-talk bridging the gap), I decide that I shall walk; she affirms 'they don't come to the Black areas.' Eldridge protests 'this is not a Black district 'OK, half only' she says. I walk back miles in emptiness. . .

He writes the language of *Soul on Ice*.

He speaks American – look up any printed/recorded interview (Evergreen October 1988).

He speaks in a Black language, strung on rhythms-laughter-pauses, which I witnessed but could not join.

He does not speak at all, if he chooses – as some compilers of books on the American predicament unluckily experienced.

All this reflects elusiveness, but does not imply a deficiency in 'personality integration'. The Black American has to be born cunning, and imbibes early the art of camouflage, of dodging/stalking, of smoke-screen retreats and advances – a survival training for the ghetto jungle. 'Ketman', a word apparently of Persian origin, means the technique of living under oppression: acting/talking simultaneously to please the ruler, but adversely between the lines opposing him – erecting a façade of respectability/sycophancy/obeisance for hidden subversion; to trick – a virtue to be cultivated and refined.

Perhaps from that basis and, with the clearer view given by the twentieth century's shifting grounds, came this: the Black American (and so the Black Caribbean) kept his 'face' by taking the posture of a cynic who mocked his masters', the White Americans' (and Spaniards') drama of ideals; and preferred (as survival-gambits) the comedy of masks, the chameleon's way of life.

The European evolved a readiness to self-sacrifice for abstractions, on-the-barricade stances – bared chest and banner floating in the face of guns. The primeval instinct aims at outwitting and outhunting the adversary – and remaining alive.

But the white man may partly owe his worldly success to his readiness to lay down his life and so the Black Panthers fell at first into the imitation trap of exposed uniformality, when they marched into the open in step under new Afro-American banners; thus they reached out, on Western terms, to bridge the transition towards their own tribalism. But soon, proved unequal in strength and resources, they tend to use 'cover' and to be less easily trackable targets. Eldridge Cleaver – the past master of many speeches, many plots, many put-ons – their prototype.

Los Angeles. Round the Paramount Studios grounds nomadic Roman Polański rides his hired Mustang, in cowboy-imitation bravado of turns rearings dust-raising roars screams twists, through those empty backless Wild-Western façades.

Across the city: his exaltation at being here and conquering; tries to adventurize/to flourish his Hollywood, or clamours for the attention of the vacant roads and the indifference.

Race/wind up Beverly Hills. The house – borrowed and easy glory. Dogs – hugest and smallest. Sharon Tate *à la houri*. Eva *à la garçonne*. Super-karate instructor from Hong Kong. Sycophants. Hurried vehemence chopped-up whipped up to a rhythm by ever-pounding amplifiers, pressed on by ever-self-tending girls.

Beverly Hills as ever follows Sunset Boulevard. But Sunset Strip has 'Ye Olde Psychedelic Body Shop', 'Scum Restaurant'. On the side-walks young grotesques, in file and horizontal, and propped-up diagonal policemen. Serpentined non-valid breakneck drive to Mia Farrow's (her mother identical but of different make-up period). In-valid words ('What are you?' 'Leo?' conversations). In-valid gestures. In-valid smoke-screen. Posturings for long shots – close-ups out of focus. Barbecue joys: prettily cooked – some nice (something to do) roasting man-star. The hair stylists and photographers and PRs and climbers rather haughty, but those *arrivé* ones sweet in-validly vacant. Ado-for-nothing party.

In **1950** this was the Movie-Athens – seemingly for infinity. Its uncouth moneyed knights, producers/agents would hire craftsmen (like their medieval progenitors) to build their

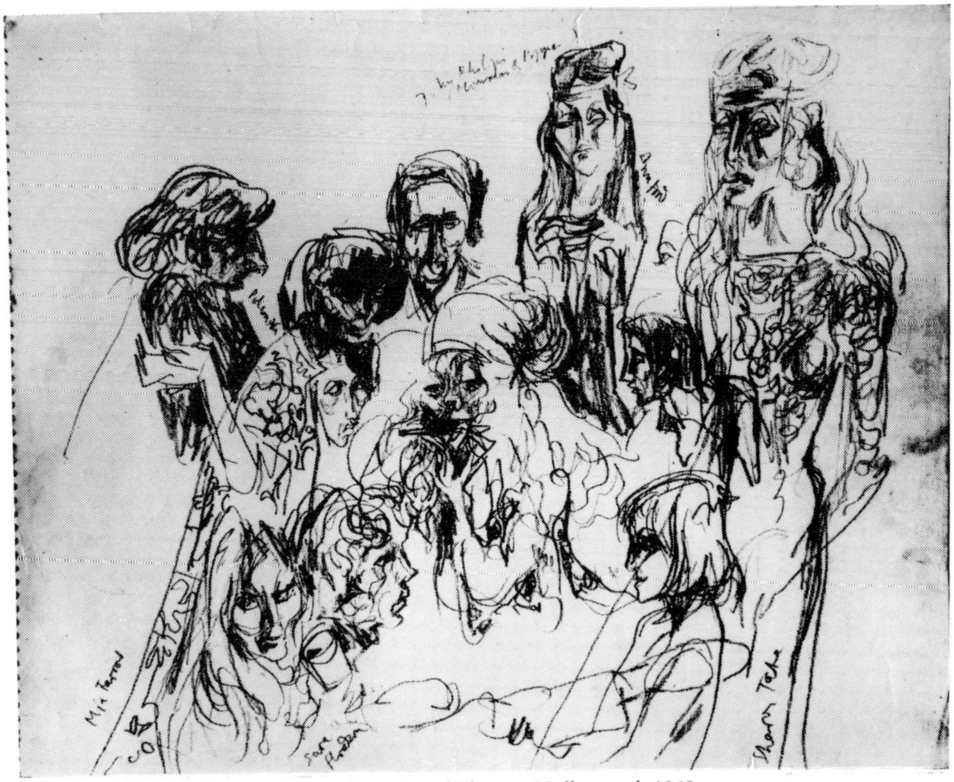

Polański, Mia and Sharon. Hollywood, 1968

minor castles, and interior decorators to fill them up with precious collections of Tanagra figurines or what you will (to make these appear as a life-time work of connoisseurship); would buy players writers directors women to be served and entertained.

A comparable party then (swarms of uniformed chauffeurs buzzing at limousines, uniformed flunkeys serving grand manner evening dresses sleek coiffures and dinner jackets) was dominated by proverbial cigar-smoking *seigneurs*, the romantics of the time, competing, running feuds over honour and women – their transactions the outcome of pride and jealousies rather than calculations, their actions reflecting fluctuations of bully temperaments – basic and transparent. Actors flamboyant but in subjugation. Very much a Rabelaisian court scene, underlined below by intrigues, above by humours to be soothed and directed – taken upstairs.

And downstairs (rooms dotted with pairing and repairing: Clark Gable-Lady Stanley. Hedy Lamarr-Charles Boyer, Joan Bennett-Dorothy Malone, Gloria Swanson-?, and euphoric father Kennedy) a Paramount chief, Harry Goodman (Ginsburg?), egged on by flattery, making a fool of himself (frustrated/driven by envy of the beautiful performers ever around him) by going on with a dreadful chain-singing, Nero-like, of ditties to subdued guests. After a good half-hour of it a grand English actor of unchallengable standing, Reginald Gardiner, pleaded 'End it, Harry, end it!' – it may have meant what it said; also it could be assumed, by his intonation, that he proposed a pointed couplet for the finale. But touchy Goodman in authoritarian fury hit out mercilessly and on target: 'You're getting fat, Reggie, watch it.' Reggie, an imposing man, paled speechless. Those were the days.

Now, the cultural-cum-underground revolution having upset box office certainties, the old hands' assurance recedes – and the dominant partyscene reflects it: it is young or youngish, in costume and manner – globe-leaping silkified trendified hippie, cocksure (the bosses and their ways swept into murky night clubs).

Roman's ambience again: retrograded by provincial Polishness which demands fulfilment of their Hollywood dream, several little gifted Polish gnomes had to make this pilgrimage and thus helped to bring declining Hollywood back to life as the film capital; but also to the high life of pot-chic hippyism: posturing hair 'stylists', PR men – and she-herds of all variations of Caucasian breeds (indentical girl-anxies) – faces made up/reduced to one – 'vulnerable' child's narrowness, blonde heads banded and feathered and the whole on sturdy (toes gripping carpet) bare feet.

Houses on heights. Pride in the night's spread of lights (like everywhere – this abstract contextless non-committal display, of whatever city, satisfies the need for some gesture towards the infinite): they lead one to parapets and rejoice over the phoney underfoot firmaments – by day a flat molecular 'dig'. By night smog-puddles wet seats wet grass – no outdoors (the sacramental swimming pool stands empty through the day of sleep or studio or office); again, as the night before, empty dark rooms scream from four corners with amplified rock. Ladies take baths upstairs, work themselves out of their private faces – and, at long last, again identical blondes come down ostentatious staircases, in the wake of their stardom predecessors. Another drive – another neat designer's feat (pool and view squeezed miraculously into a few feet) contains a lost Polish film-music composer boy and his Israeli mini-girl (his escape into a near familiarity) – but again the hairdressers photographers discothequers PRs crowd in, take the stage, pass puffs round, spread – purposeful (though all haze and giggles) girls after big game flitting through the cool-acting peacocks, unsure (as they well may be) of their valuations; and the host, on the edge of the crowd, grouped with his European cronies over sad maniacal Polish/French/German passport-permit worries. One goes through all this at a trot, as it were, and begs for a lift out.

Federico García Lorca:

¡Oh salvaje Norteamérica ¡oh impúdica! oh salvaje

The rite of passage
should end in Recognition.
My American Journey
failed
to unravel a new myth at its centre
to answer the quest
as it curves upon itself
(straight ways mislead)
from New York to New York.
Perhaps not terrible enough
or painful, or hopeful
though symbols-billposted, too smooth an air-free-way.
The tumult (a happening) – the desert (neon oasis) –
the campus (a term-break then another term) – the ghetto
(gagged and chained) –
the golden calf – the Power and the Wild East –
the stations – not of the cross,
but of the resumed building of THE old TOWER
the old returned Totem Pole the lingam
the wagging phallus
the grotesque triumph/defeat
the oldest myth's latest lurch:
Prometheus (still chained down) –
pseudo-named Apollo for Parnassian deceit –
wills
to join the orgy
of celestial creation
to reach/penetrate/rape
the body-godship,
wrenches – pops
its erection out of the roots (deafening *éclat*)
it shoots upwards
soars
but a seedless trip

¡Oué ola de fango y luciernaga sobre Nueva York!

Slime and firefly in wave upon wave in New York!
the firmanent – horizon – macrocosm
the spinning eye
selects/plunges on to fireflies' nest
nest whirls explodes up-out-ward
converges on La Guardia
turns slime-bound microcosm
Queensbury Bridge invades the mirage
Avenues unmask the Streets
give grime
growl
whimper
single flicker
singly

¡la augustia imperfecta de Nueva York!

New York's imperfect anguish!
Shem Ham Japheth in apartheid conclaves on the buses/subways
brought together in the frustration of uprooting
by poverty/migration – not curiosity.
Oblique Latin/Jewish pavements – murk of doorways
lighted with the Young emerging.
Rides over fetid
(as if already sacked/abandoned after street-by-street battle)
City's Lower East – the plucked out mind-less shantiness
will not be bulldozed out
East 29th and Park – people-garbage on the brink of 'all
comforts' –
'Eddie's Cut Rate Cigars', pleading flower-pots, 'Drugs'
– patriarchs enstooled on the corners
guard cave-era dignities of the slum.
Then a change
proclaimed by a large man in silks
hand raised
announces entry into the garment-district –
hails a get-away get-along grudging taxi.
Under neons secretaries reflect
business-bosses' world-weary down-gracings.
Corner shop's Yiddish cosiness.
Housewives' zigzag escalation – from basement bargains to
heavens of top-prices.
'Doctor Doolittle' receives goody White teachers
leading by hand Black children from a 'Neighbourhood Day
Camp'
over smoking man-holes (hackneyed collage this).
Banks furl stars-'n'-stripes – closing time.
New York cops
the keenest darkest blue
their night-sticks dictate their manner: twiddling, resting on
a shoulder, circular juggling, under the armpit, front: both hands
across thighs body-rolling –
summer-swarthy hip-trousered cops
block low East–West slit-horizons of circum-navigating flotillas.
But taxis ride up North–South sky-aiming perspectives
elating pseudo-escapes out of humbuggeries
(symbolic intermezzos within intermezzos
standstill-clusters of jams/red lights enhance
shattering breakaways)
cutting through the exposed (stilled by speed into waxworks)
'still-lifes' of the trapped –
the farer momentarily superior/detached
although on the way to another dwarf/crawl triviality
however high elevator-lifted,
evening coming lights mixing – seeps in proverbial hope
– night rushes rescue pace.
Into the darkest West 16th
crashed-in doorways broken-down staircases
in narrow squeeze against warehousing sheerness
a crowded Tanzanian (of all peoples!) *ménage*
brought and held here by the feeblest strings of politics
cum western-culture-theatre conceits (in particular:
the Stony Point Summer Theatre) and nightly
at Casa Di Pré in Greenwich Avenue
spaghetti-administered by hieratic vestals. Time to move on.
Mini-teenified Sutton Place-dignified hostess 'everybody's

mini now'.
Out of limousines desperate ladies dance self-conscious
round giant 'Picasso' *objet d'art* thin all ways –
within a waste-acre and chic soaring habitation
(from the windows peep private gilded rococos)
the Village pushed back for this.

But when the Village regained and the door to the evening found,
the promise of the straightest/steepest/highest stairs opens on to
old tinted-gravure poster-protest
boneless bodies –
pop-on-tape
stench-of-pot –
flat-out bodies.

'The vehement shadows'
ooze Streets
usurp power from the Avenues
dupe the 'time-space syndrome'
of the solitary night-walker
by breathing death down his neck
at each crossing
as he counts the blocks:
each – another escape.

'Art Establishment travels uptown to inaugural fête' (*New York Times*). **The Studio Museum Harlem** Fifth Avenue between 125th and 126th. Narrow stairs and what fantasy this hot 'pink-toe' revival tight-packed airless steam-pot of through-culture-to-hope: perverse farce, once more, of intellectual antics on the brink. The whites came with some bravery but act feebly their exclusive buffooneries; the blacks costumed in accord with principles (integrated opulence, Negritude, hip, highbrow-arty), act ditto. And this thrashing out this steaming in sweat (nature back-lashed and smothered air-conditioning) dissolve all into a procreation miasma to remould it for the theme – the last chance get together on this one of the few remaining bridges, the feebly signalling highbrow fairground: kinetic-electronic, as elsewhere and as good, art – smart blinking unnoticeable. If this works, the date of this Turkish- (Muslim) -bath will be memorable – the turning point; but the thinned-out universality of today's art blatantly reflects the vacuous élite. They, the artists, come at me and blackly (and kinetically) clown-mock (a performing group) pose for my 'on-the-spot' drawing – they are doubly mean and bitter – on both issues – three issues: this social 'pink-toe' pathos, their art's pretentiousness, their art's shaky Uncle Tomism. Little, shirts off black sweat, half-naked boys gallop, twist, squeeze amongst the crowd's legs – turn glass-clinking arties' lower parts into a wild forest. Ed Bullins promised black bourgeoisie – so it is and more.

There are downstairs at the door outside riotous mob-push goings-on; a large matriarchal Negress denounces pride and prejudice of the whole and calls upon the street-crowd to witness. Placed now in it I watch grotesque *élégants* of both colours emerge jostled askew and humbled . . .

I **walk back** from Black Harlem – gloom of the streets countered by buoyant spades in heraldic dasheki and embroidered caps, 'Army and Navy' 'Salvation Army' – through the '**Mueblería Gran Venta**' '**Boneparthe**' Puerto Rican grimness – to the bus-stop escape along 2nd Avenue (at 115th Street 'Macedonian Church of the Assemblies of God'). Forever shall treasure the bus-voyagings athwart New York's nations – a rotating kaleidoscope of shapes names hoardings – folklores, ever changing from race to race; all marked/soiled/sooted by the temporariness of the dorm/barrack city; the rigid sequence: run-down high class run-down.

Forever shall thrill at tramping/browsing through library-tight New York.

Cantonments line up Avenues, but because of this, because of the utter lack of cosiness of scape and architecture, this buffer-to-buffer estranged makeshift populace, shallowly fitted in, emerges stage-like emphatic.

And also: these strait-jacketing stretches of architectural non-domesticity, bleak-blank now but transplanted from England where conceived for the English home organisms, its family-blood circulation: solitary, but in tight concord with others, for a small island's loyalties – same of height breadth habit purpose – even of waiting for sailor's returns (English sailors); these brownstone harmonies become in New York's expanses (though patted by the cognoscenti in the centre and in the Village) neutral and less: perspectives of ill-fitting despicable alien shells when newer Americans are forced into them (the ground-level peasants, the world over, one level East European burghers cosy in court-yarded small blocks, the shady piazza conglomerating Southerners) – poverty/crowding perhaps least encumberant. Hence the revengeful (or unable to cope with) massacre of interiors: mess, subdivisions, spites of cuckoo nesting – the unfriendly doorstep – the slum.

Yet there is magnificence in this impermanence. As if the epic trek, the makeshift camping before the next erratic unpredictable move, has never ended. These migratory ever-striving ever-refugees/prospectors perpetuate the never-spent tradition of progression.

In the cities all over the continent there are the ghettos, criss-crossed huddled glowering at one another – the whole planet's backwoods, with the WASPs the overlords, confident – by the right of conquest and long history. They retain power and nobler privileges, though seeming stealthily outflanked. But in fact permissive of ineffectual impositions by the ambitious of the lesser breeds within the serving fields: professions, arts, commerce – as feudal tradition has it – serving as salesmen, entertainers and men of skills – even politicians. It all does not alter the roll of birth/right/birth, however profits may spill about.

The supposed ultimate Utopia-Land of Liberty for all breeds, this answer to racial-nationalist ills – by crowding, by fencing them in one giant camp – came out with reversal: all breeds heave back into tight compounds of belonging. The borders cease to be friendly (or never were). Neighbourly crises more than re-enact conflicts of the old continents: by casual unorganic displacements the accidental next door tribes clash full-face without root-security.

The young-named protesters are, as expected, intermixing curiosity attraction – united leaves of grass. Yet perhaps because they are apart from the silent mass (either as young or as privileged-in-education-and-marginality) the counter mood in all the components of the nation gnaws on all fronts – the generation clash, the race/nationality clash, the class clash, the urban-suburban-parochial clash – and claims all-American patriotism.

Nevertheless, the young are straining to turn the parochial and oligarchic Americas into the United States ideal, with the help, astonishingly, of the Mao/Jesus cultural revolution against selfhood. One does not know how deep and far the young become united people – at Alabama University, in the workshops, in slaughter-houses, at automation controls, in the graperies of California there is no sign of change; yet equalizing ferment eats at protrusions.

'Best book will be . . .' – booksellers' questionnaire in a culture-paper leaves out 'selling' and is the ultimate of the consumer society. The anxious **salesman's judgement** decisive – the best because sells most. The cooling manner the obnoxious gaze of an art dealer a publisher (the power-holders) when 'success' is not forthcoming.

'Protest' naturally rejects this scale of values – tends to stand on its head – from no-commerce underground press to no-value flaming content. But set afloat in all pervading gravy the purist becomes dissolved into yet another spicy ingredient. 'Hair' 'Voice' 'Chelsea Girls' 'Pop-Strip' 'drop-out gear' 'non-art' join the 'best' of the sellers vocabulary. A grotesque cause-effect. This side of the world's 'Permanent Revolution' translated incoporated into – nay helping to accelerate – the inbuilt obsoleteness, the consumer society's 'trendiness' becomes the West's 'Cultural Revolution'. The fashion then this year is for the inconclusive for the tentative forms in cinema-writing-painting – chopping of sequences. Yippy politics: non-policy – any action sets off reactions and provokes next steps. Black: unpredictability.

Bloomingdale's top floor propagates/displays an acre of 'novelty' furniture. New York Senator Jacob Javits and his wife Marion at one end promote an undistinguished bedroom suite under the arc-lights and cameras – at another London interior decorator David Hicks talks sales-talk – without reducing their status. Pre-Columbian monstruous mannikins are 'in' at Bloomingdale's and shower interior décor their ever-repeated rendering of the business of survival; primitiveness as a luxury gimmick now pushed into mass-consumption. The salesman-touted-polished sumptuosity – garish and dated instantly. 'Distinguished' 'Civilized' 'Whiter than White' 'Deep Down Clean' 'Gracious Living' 'Beautiful People'. But unwashedness is splendid – it patines into beauty.

2nd Avenue at night in early hours dark bizarre threatening groupings spilled out of doorways block the sidewalk – brigands, yet pilot Teresa through as if fog.

The scene at Dick Avedon's: topmost model – **photography** – hair – posery – all fan-switched awind; the dance of fashion-makebelieve which needs above all the artist of our time – the fluttering dandy-hairdresser. A girl extraordinary who ordinarily goes back each evening to husband-caring as she cannot sustain this artiness in life; and so, with Dick, there also has to be a holy family behind the scenes; and in view of the stresses, black-fringed Nippon youths have to assist with their supreme cool and stamina, so that the whole house of cards, the puppeteering, momentarily exists in a vacuum, as reality will later prove. Because first will come the lunch break and this pally-round-the-table, progressive-politics-talking, salad-cum-chickening, but nice; and of course, the supreme puppet-girl-model speaks out with the most human simplicity and is straight – and this is why neither such as she nor any of these at this table will be invited (expect for me – an impostor masquerading) to the party later that evening of plainer people who exist by evoking – exalting – and claiming it the norm, this shadow-play. Strictly flippant they are, the evening ones, rather the courtiers-intermediaries than the 'beautiful-Register-people' themselves; they balance between propelling speciousness but also beholding staidness of exclusivity; hence the gleeful declarations 'The whole of New York now wears pyjamas!' at that crowning moment of conformity when Diana Vreeland, the venerable Mistress-in-Chief of *Vogue*, enters, pantalooned out of recognition.

Exclusivenesses exclude one another. Thus the ultimate un-American/true American voice: the large blonde Philadelphian lazy predatoress, a WASP Statue of Liberty come to life, sprawled youthfully in her nordicity, queenly in her flesh-marriage-marketing, still dominant through birthright assurance, says, '**she'll never make it**' about an ambitious hostess – she is Jewish.

We stay on Broadway – tired and cannot respond fully to the vile vastness, to the vulgar mass of this all-in procession which can be read for all the answers. The Mid-Western brutes jostle – the false blind beggars touching with the hired dogs 'God bless the cheerful giver' – Sardi's *habitués* promoting themselves – the vanities of the parading Jewesses – the bum Cockney with no regrets – the freaks amass. Souvenir shops run riot, TV screens (for the reason of abundance) overflow into the pavement with a life-size ever-ready gun-hand shooting-it-out with the placidly perambulating all-and-sundry. A pyramid of icons: 'NIXON' immense, tops 'Canadian Club Imported Whiskey', whirling 'Coca-Cola' and, at the bottom, whatever that may mean, 'CASTRO'. But it isn't very late when the mob's majority non-committed to the night's business filters away.

Andy Warhol's '**factory**': unexpected shallow empty – a managerial genius amongst mirrors, glass desks, white telephones and pansy adjutants. Below, Union Square through the window 'for Peace and Justice in the World Humphrey Muskie' – slogans special for the Village. Inside,

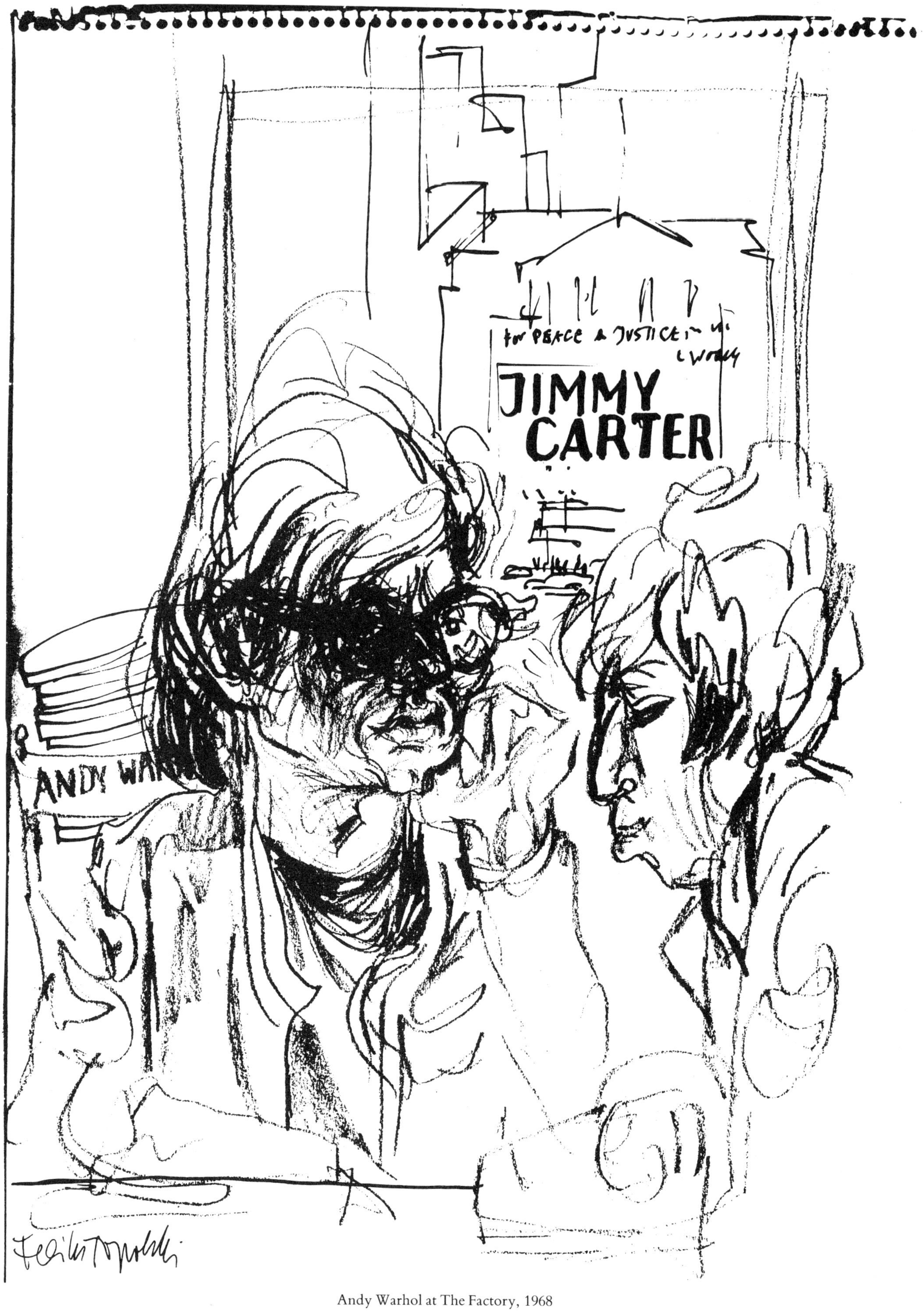

Andy Warhol at The Factory, 1968

agitation and action over gossip press TV titbits pasting-in-cuttings. Hoity-toity woman – fighting-off-age Ultra Violet arrives and we pack (eleven of us) into a limousine – some nice husky boy kept on the scent (her soiled thumb up his nostrils) of ever in/on heat ever-straining Ultra – Andy as if behind a multiple mask yet an innocent. Dash to East 59th poshness, filled up with ad-administrators: ballooning men and their balloon but laced women – and we, fancy troop of entertainers, walk into it and perform for TV and press cameras 'release': Andy, shyly determined, draws with many coloured marker-pens a butterfly on the bared thigh of homely pretty Leigh Taylor-Young – one of the essential moves to solidify her movie stardom. Dullness of champagne and caviare on promotional expenses.

Museum of Modern Art **private view** overflows. The US culture apotheosis. The ultimate concord of opposites: Dubuffet pictures play on vulgarity – and then the display crowns it by gilt frames and 'sensitivities' of background; this prestigious exclusivity makes the strivers, in their finery, coo over rectangles (conveniently modest-sized) of real muck – turned by the miracle of snob-commerce into gold.

Fine night setting. Courtyard closed in by the heights. Dressed-up crowd circulates over split levels. A meeting ground of the solid, the smart, and the *bohème*. Four costume tendencies point culture's indecisions: long gowns, pants, minis, psychedelic exotics. Directors chirpy-tipsy and *sans-souci*. Professionals glide demure/sedulous as if in a slave market – their physique a shop window for their ware. Games of power.

'. . . Because the time is just becoming ripe for a reaction against the 1960s' norm – nicely timed exhibition . . .' from a critic built up on a foundation of small review paragraphs into an authority amongst those who 'create' public taste – thus ruthless trend-mongering against artists known for their creative longevity – on the basis of a **rapid turnover** in the manipulation of art validity into values at the service of dealers, hence museums and hence Parnassus.

Commercial 'no hand' art's revenge/triumph over the 'sensitive hand', 'fine art'; art of participation, concept, not execution: the MOMAs, spoon-feeders of the rich and the snob, *volte-face* and retain power. And this is why 'the cultural revolutionaries' begin to invade them.

Central Park this time. Clouds – foamy scour-pads scrape the towers. Rocks elevate monumentalize old bums dosing – same men, same posture as twelve years ago in this statuary display of sempiternity. But, since then (one may say the classical period), there arose a twofold invasion: in the nooks of this pedestal rockery (proper Baroque embellishments) the softly lie-in-wait girl-nymphs – and the prance-round fawnishly pretty black boys (one of them in urgent high-step through the bush, beats his rhythm-call with a thin stick freshly stripped of leaves, bent forward, throwing rapid hunter's glances left-right). Less visual pleasure from ugly vicious other 'minority' youths – they grab. And the customary weirdies in new shapes: a bearded boy (Spanish hat, hair tied at the back, woodsman's lumber jacket checked black-red) hurriedly tops the rock-mound with a huge valise in hand, settles business-like. A yarmulkaed teenager. Waves of peacock pansies. Christly boys against the breezes, hair afloat. Soldiers clipped, revealed ugly, as one. Now clusters of variate, yet the same breed, men with dogs. Men down on their luck carrying old model transistors with very long aerials. Asians grinning loud-shouting. Now oddly unconnected but in close continuity lame females – and young. And the fountain hippies. Then in wave upon wave under the rocks the show-stealing bicycle parade – horse-cabs building up the carefree throwback nostalgia. Outside, Park South – benches of oddities and, deep down out of view, couples. Above, the Cuban Liberator's, José Marti, 'Apostle of Cuban Independence', unnoticed statue.

Descent at Gimbel's into the heat of subterraneity for Newark – change at Jersey City (Journal Square); empty train except for a Jewish whiskery boy *NY Times*-laden – crossed with black nun and horizontal black boy asleep ('Immigrant Savings Bank. Will You be a Burden to Your Children?') and dirty Hudson views. Hotel Robert Treat and a roomful of placard framed ('It Takes Courage! Wallace Has It! Do You? Stand up for America!') stolids – not sinister but somewhat emphatic citizens – these heavies are the backbone and they speak for Wallace. I wangle my badge for tomorrow and walk away (infiltrator's jitters and uplift) through windy foreboding police-studded everydayness (Private Armies no doubt stand by) – town as if shifting/retreating; those boarded-up bookshops 'moved' elsewhere – this often-met (augural?) aura of aftermath. But (change at Journal Square) the train has this eerie ballet girl – *emigrée* from Jersey City to New York 'Russian I am – Russian-American'. What promise is her instep.

Broadway – static heat; Avenue of the Americas – blowing heat. An old cowboy-beatnik fisherman (hookline) of sewers – aloof to crowds and traffic. Sanity-mad discordance with room for any social perversion, casually brutal (but indifferent mostly) only if confronted.

Next morning once more the subway, 33rd Street – Journal Square – Jersey City train does not carry the rally men or protesters. A Jewish man of affairs; a girl spotted (this rash on girls' faces – many with those oddly dark-dotted cheeks as if soot-branded by their cities), sad; a bum newspaper-bedded; a house- or career-wife; asleep black ample lady; a haughty Black Panther boy: rows of empty seats and worlds amongst/between them – shoved along the industrial contamination. Taxi man cares for Wallace, will come to the rally, Blacks, whom he knows, will also. Vietnam has to be won.

'Jersey City Welcomes Wallace'. A mean playground and a handful of placarded people: 'It's not a mirage Wallace!' 'Wallace in The White House', **'For God and Country Wallace'** 'Mercer County Wants Wallace & Le May', 'I Love Wallace'. A mean vituperative but minor affair. Yet police

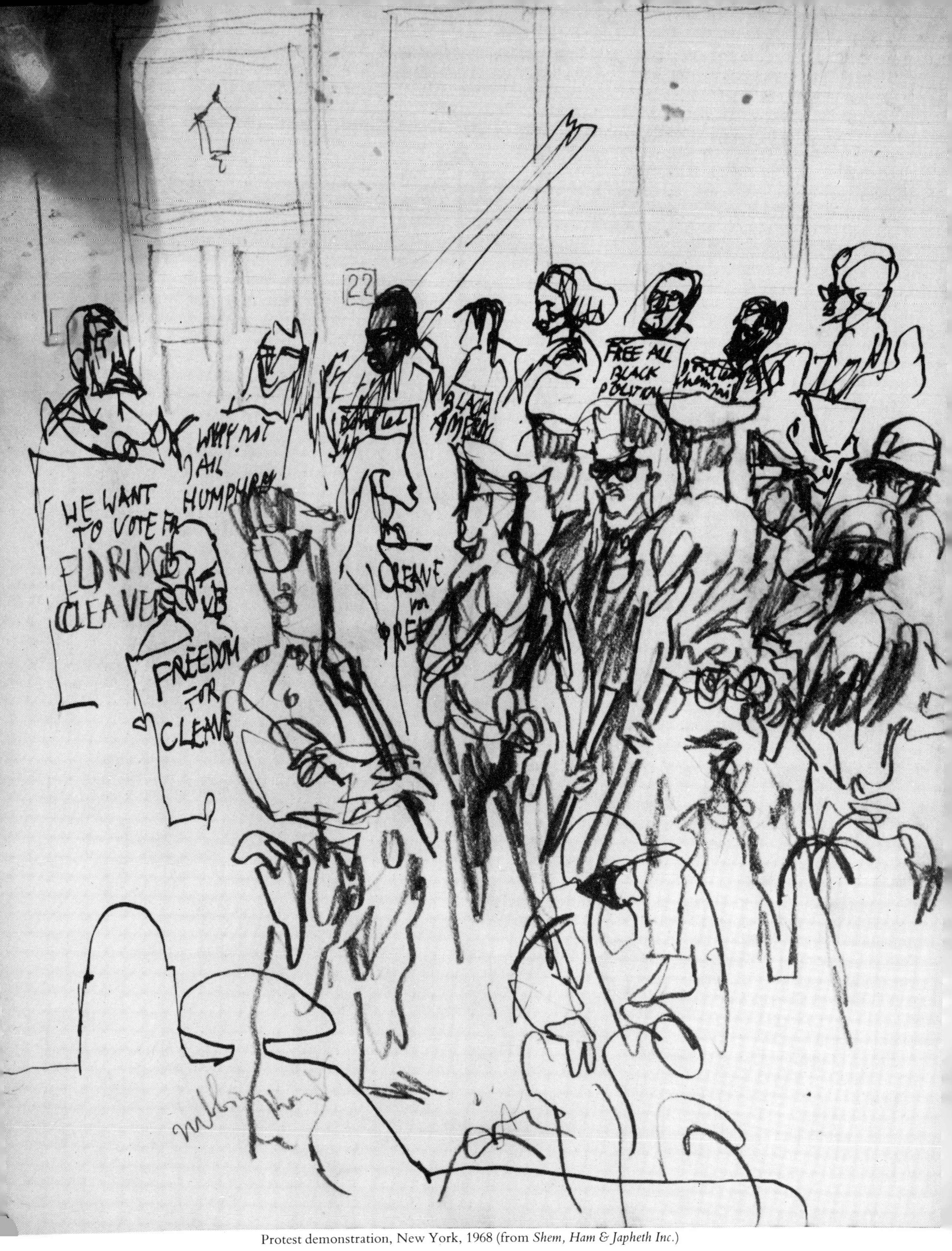

Protest demonstration, New York, 1968 (from *Shem, Ham & Japheth Inc.*)

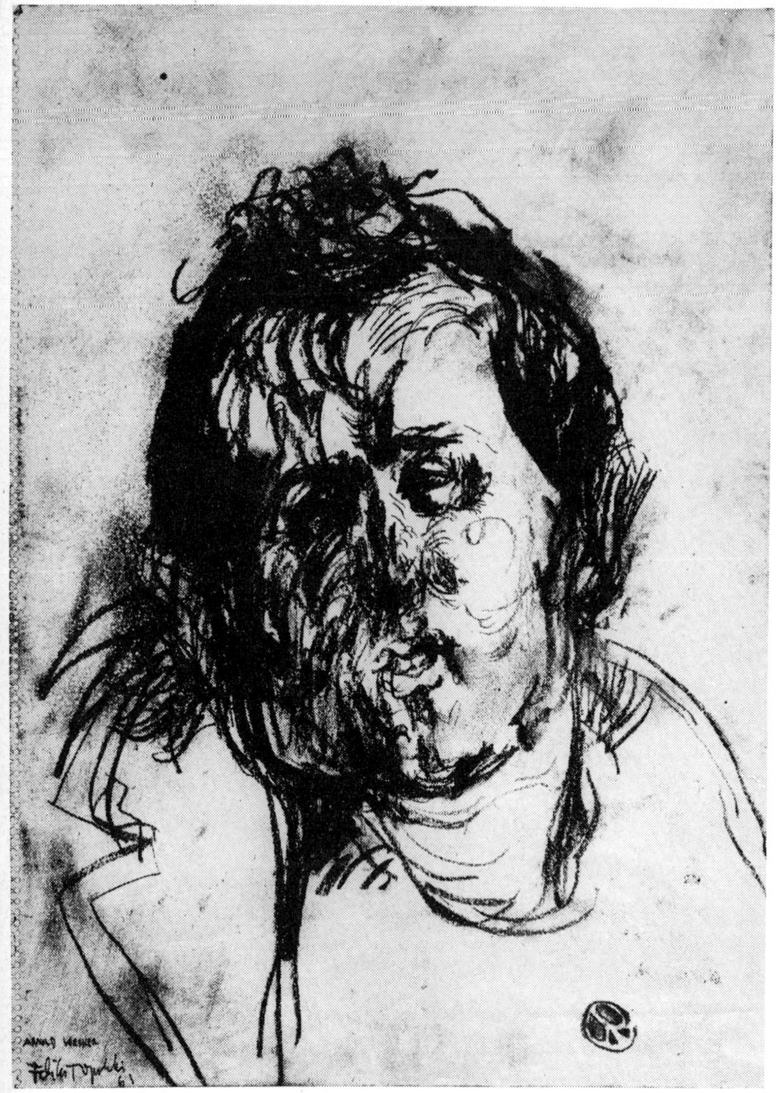

Arnold Wesker (from *Topolski's Chronicle*)

mighty of many shapes. And the vast communication machinery will blow up and spin round the globe this boring innocuousness. The baddy Gov. George Wallace makes no effort, jerks out clichés, all tested before – Retd Air Force Gen. Curtis E. Le May a fat retired dummy at his side and those prominents of the locality, thus displayed, seem over-fat, over-vain, depraved.

The General's rearguard volley – 'a lot of us spent time fighting these "Sieg Heil" boys . . . and it looks like we're going to be fighting them again' – implies Black 'Stormtroopers'? Yippie 'Red Indians'? SDS unarmed volunteers? 'It's not a mirage – Wallace!'

Noticeable: the excavated and revived Yankee bulldog – overall thick/wide (cigar neck spectacles hat-brim padded shoulders belly).

Down from the platform: how tiny, a miniature man twisted-mouthed fancy-tinted hair outlined at the edge perhaps by make-up – a street-parformer.

Plain rancid day. A Negro bunches up star-striped banners. Kids begin to kick dust.

Arnold Wesker wished me to see his great discovery – an assured fruition of his theatrical Messianism. A majestically Piranesian rotunda, shadowy and smoked over in its unfathomable height and spread, loftily balconied round still deeper recesses lost to the eye. The great imperial cum machine age structured such generosities – this, prosaically, a railway-engine turning shed – to be nowadays abandoned or flattened out; and Arnold had persuaded its leftish owners to let him use it as his Centre 42, a fantasy on the theme of the coming utopia with the Trade Unions and Arts in communion.

Enchanted by this blackened relic, by its wholeness, not tampered with (Arnold mumbling about time and money, about necessary adaptations/partitions/fire regulations), I implored him to begin at once (in variance with safety and other rules): performances torch-lit, audiences squatted on their own cushions/rugs – loosely knit productions, free to spread, to file out, to disperse behind the iron columns, to file in and cluster tightly – action using the depths of the full circle. True theatrical riches!

But no, no, it all had to be regulation-bound, to be converted into the proper thing. Waiting, struggling over self-imposed obstacles, over the Trade Unions' indifference, ate up Wesker's passion, though he managed to present one Centre 42 medley. Stealthily infiltrated by today's 'amenities' and 'entrepreneurs', the **Round House** gave some random showings, and muscled Arnold out (a manoeuvre never explained to me, perhaps too painful to him), but its dominant notoriety for some time came strangely with the unparalleled expression of Hippydom in its colossal space, still uncluttered, yielding weekly to many-thousands-strong stamping/deafening/spot-rotating rock-pop sessions.

Much later the relentless modernizers predictably shrank the unique giant interior to the more-or-less convention of an average theatre in-the-sketchily-round by walling in the area within the colonnade and suspending a low ceiling overhead for the disputable acoustic needs.

Only shortly before, an **Anti-Vietnam rally** managed to hang down from above the gallery the unhampered 30 feet of my allegory painted for it. Afterwards I had it rolled up in my Arches, but, a minor mystery, it disappeared.

These imposing **Round House hippy rites** I attended often. On one such Teresa and I (was Daniel there too?) spotted, within the whirlwinds of the avidly exultant, a lone poseur, languidly propping his top-to-toe beauty against a pillar. His studied detachment, his glittering ultra-clothing, his dark-accented Raphaelian profile, long-black-hair-adorned – invited (surely his calculation) our advance. We admired the creature and the act from a distance for a while and, then approached. He was a Parisian; his name: **Philippe**.

He proved not to be a loner at all – his outsider's posture to be rather that of a shepherd – surveying/guarding his flock amassed on the floor: a veritable proto-protagonist, or agonist. He positively commanded the hippy 'scene' in London, he

Opposite: Philippe

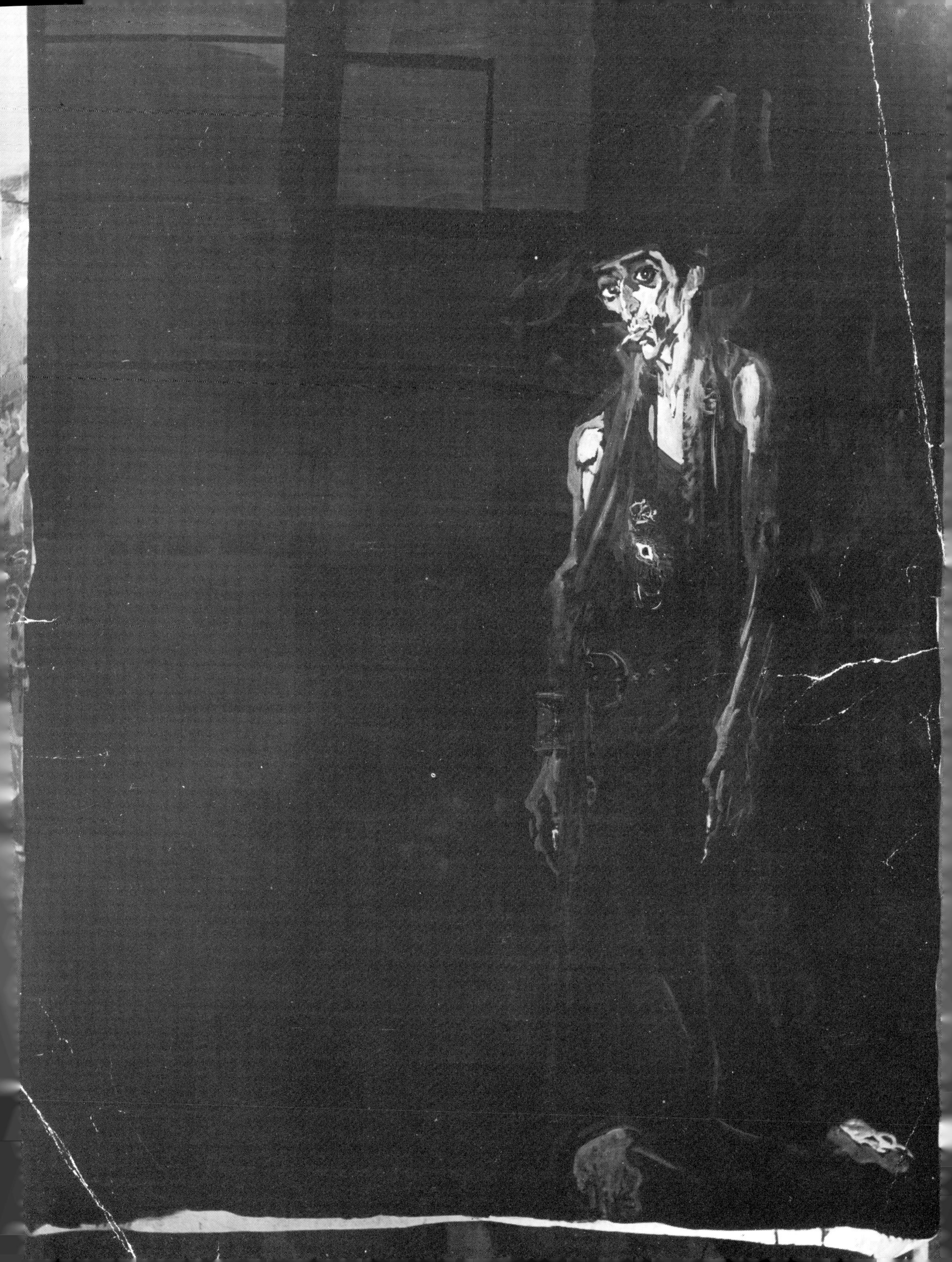

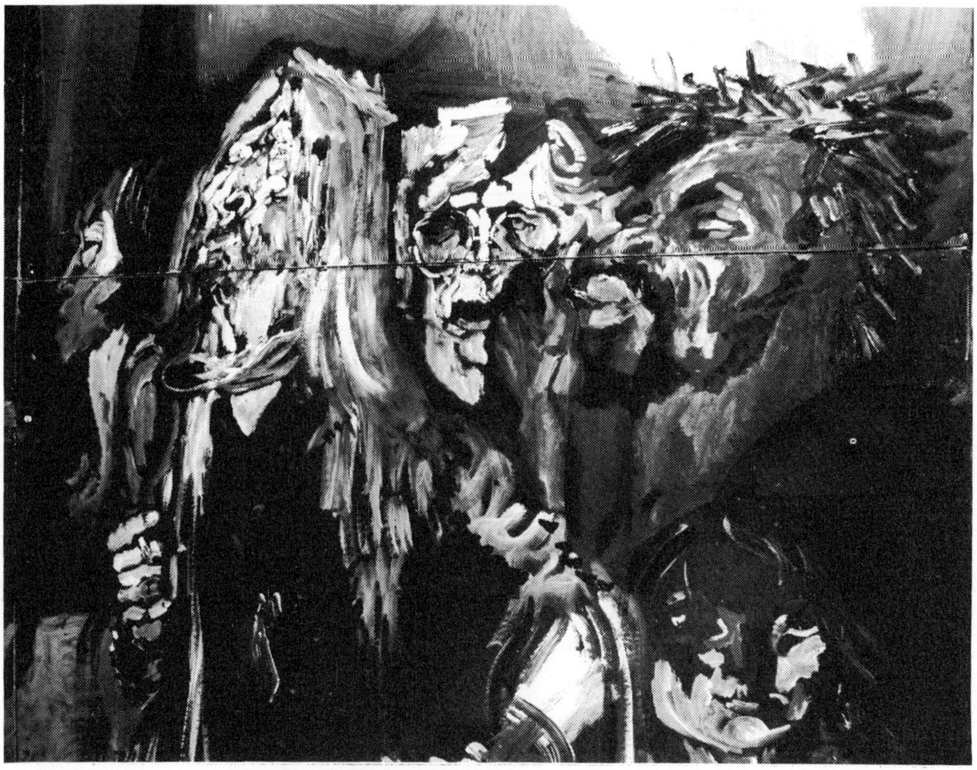

One Hundred Hippies (detail from *Memoir of the Century*)

could will/cajole their erratic meanderings on to unanimous targets. They all knew and loved him. And then his leadership was real, because sustained and ever renewed by prancing/ disreputable ingenuity in daring anarchy – never ceasing to astonish, never intimidated, even in prison.

He would conduct **the King's Road hippydom** from mid-road, cars respectfully dodging him; he would lead me into the lining of respectable Chelsea to collapsed hide-outs of joint-stilled haze, half disclosing shapes/features of meditation; there would be a casually kept rendezvous in a distant-field rock-festivity – he always awander; or at an island commune; or he would tow along to my studio fancy visitors: a San Francisco group, who the day before had dominated the Hyde Park free concert, led by **General Waste-more-land**, toy planes on his shoulders and peaked cap, mock medals on stretchable ribbons; a Portuguese deserter; French freak-film-makers; upper-class-turned-hippy flamboyants; but they would be amongst a hundred, two hundred originals who at his bidding would file in and camp dutifully, on Fridays, to disperse gently (but not timidly) at his (always loyal to me) command – except for one whole night's reverie rhythm-drummed by two alternating bands, the late-coming skinheads and Hell's Angels surprisingly blending in.

I was swept then to paint throughout over huge surfaces, while the central harmony-in-rhythms was countered at peripheries: some dogged hacking at my hoard of Chinese tins in the kitchen corner, and less stoned and less holy guests stealing away, with discrimination, my favourite possessions: a Japanese Noh mask carted all the way from Tokyo, a Polish hunting prince's sheepskin coat, cut with traditional peasant/ nobleman generosity, brought from Poland. But no matter. I rejoiced in these invasions – the studio mirroring the 'epoch' (so one felt), with me casting away my working inhibitions and painting 'in public', picking out one marvel after another from the sprawled heaps. Handily, one whole (30 x 12 feet) wall was panelled for some unfulfilled project, and now it rapidly filled up with entangled larger-than-life full-length portraits to become **One Hundred Hippies** and to be, later, beneficially incorporated into my *Memoir* – already an image of the past.

The gravitational field of the studio spread beyond Philippe's circles. On the one hand my devotion to Alexander Trocchi, the early guru of anarchy, carried me to **Ronnie Laing's Kingley House**, to murky acid and heroin dead-ends; on the other adventurous girls – Arabella Churchill, the Lambton sisters, all hippy-recruited, also served my painting gluttony. I composed a dummy for a book to follow the tradition of transitory fashion albums of the French Revolution (**sans culottes**, for instance), marking history through changes in manners/costumes, to be called *Manners and Costumes of the Western Cultural Revolution*.

No publisher here or in the States wanted it, though photographic surveys abounded.

But Philippe. His entries into the studio, ever more enchanting: besides his *vêtements* inventions, always assembled by stealing, there would be, more often than not, a companion girl: from Caroline Coone of Release to Vivienne of World's End – to the power-exuding American Chrissie Hynd, later a pop-star – to teenage Danuta of Polish descent, dressed lavishly and lovingly by him into a flower-nymph.

His thieving was 'principled': he challenged conventions at every confrontation; and imprisonments followed. He arrived one day, freed, with his long hair chopped off (pretext – hygiene) in a woman's long dress – a spectacular presence. His was not homosexual transvestism, but of vanity living its beauty to the full.

Time was passing, punctuated by more prison and

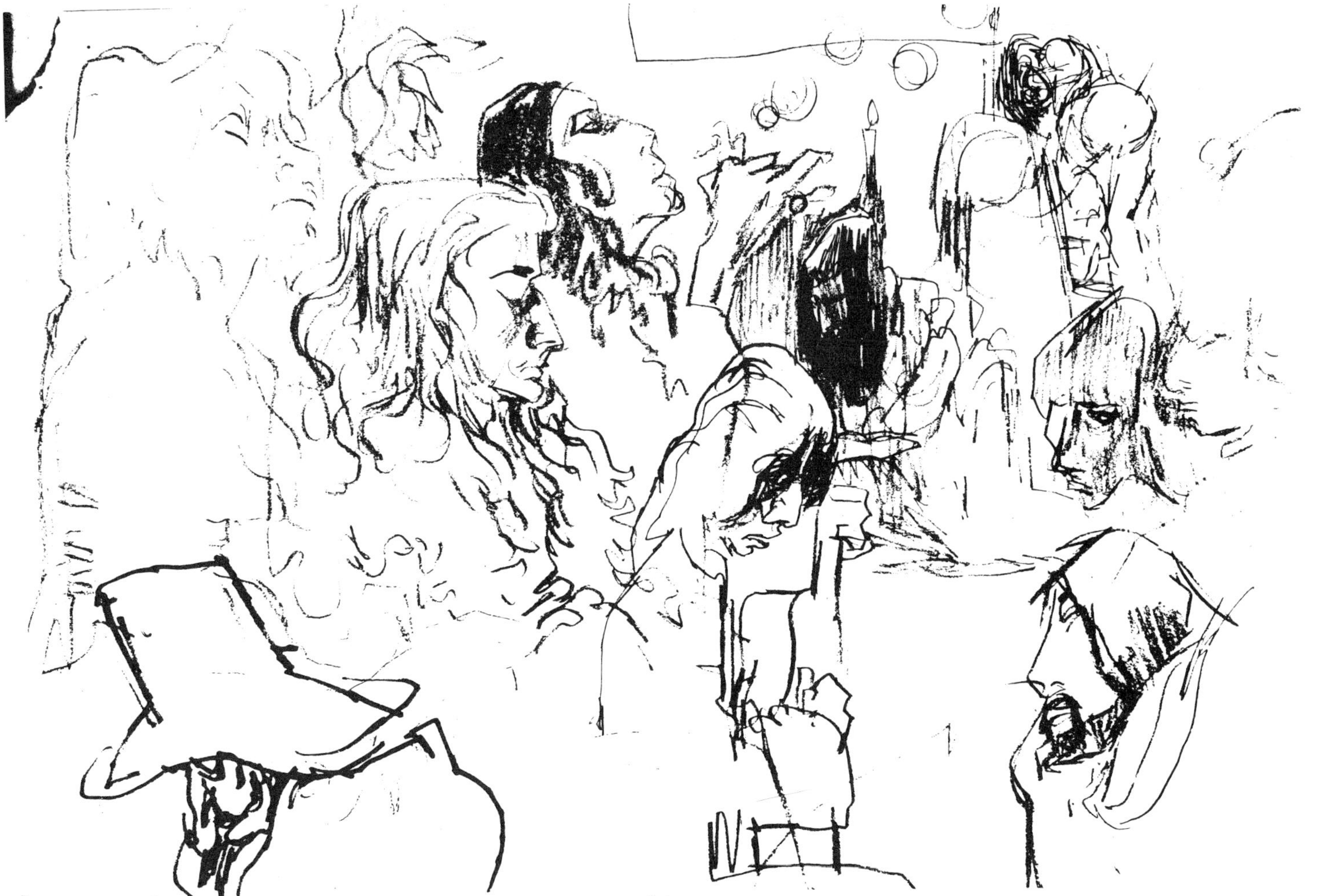

Joints

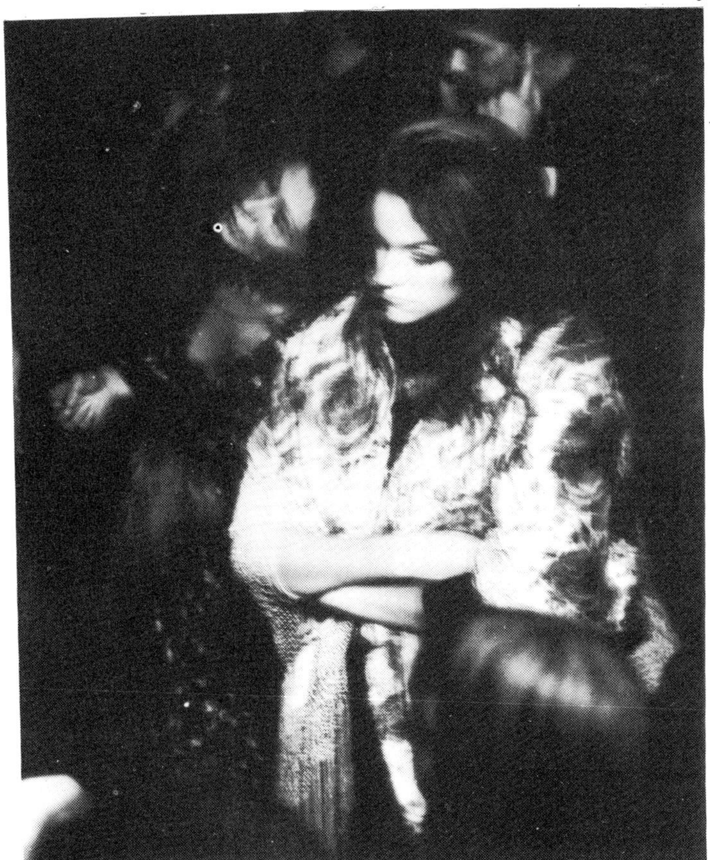

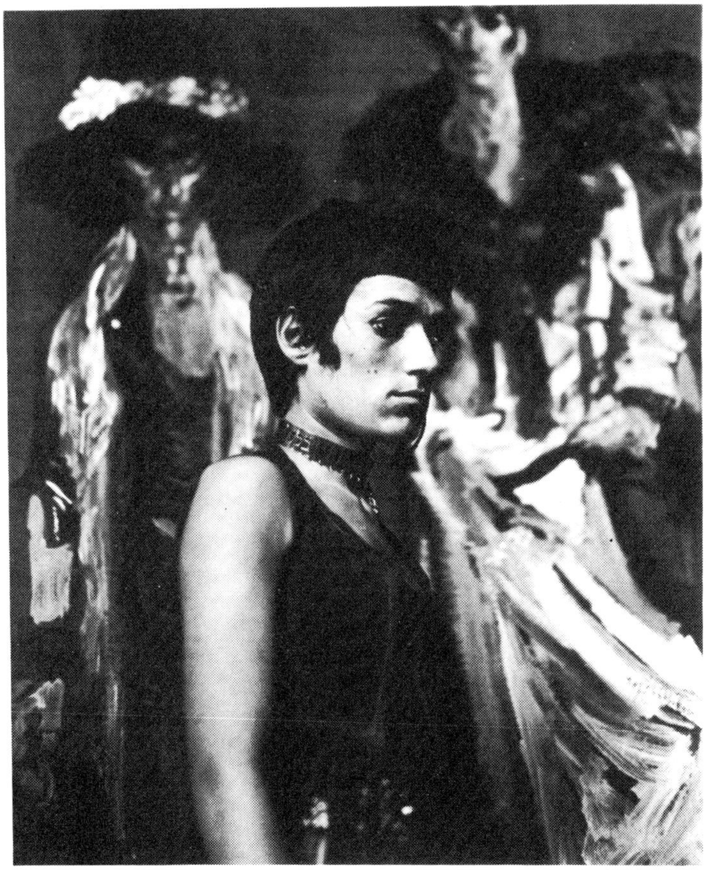

Hippies at the studio (Photographs by Gaby)

deportations to France – my role in many rescues useful but accepted without cringing as subsidiary.

His period's appeal and his own personal panache began to dilute. A pair of once-lovely drapery-floating communers from the Eel Pie Island of some two years earlier knocked at my door – she: in a Woolworth dress, he: a jacket and tie – now devouts (and employees with pamphlets in hand) of Jajaji.

Philippe, now almost alone – suddenly a **veteran**: or a mere young-old eccentric.

He is still a one-man procession. One hears his approach: one day a flute, another cymbals, another a drum; he is his own beadle: first enters the long stick wound round with mementoes of latest encounters and the aroma-cloud of freedom (mushrooms, rags, decomposition); he himself: the long-distance stride, unmitigated by the indoors, but abruptly transformed into a squat – his bundles/bags set, open – turned cornucopias cascading out trophies/plunders, his numerous coats hats shoes peeled off piled up – now a weary repose, feet blackened blistered stretched out; bent and grim-eyed, noble nose protruding out of falling hair – for a while.

Because he has to move on; because he, faithful to hip-anarchy, is battling on, alone – a minuscule hero.

There he recedes down the South Bank's concretes, somewhat bent/round-shouldered (the posture of a future old eccentric) but jaunty on neat thin legs, paraphernalia (badges, feathers, ribbons, scarves, bracelets, necklaces, sacks) dangling, the garnished stick high in the air – the knight errant unlauded, his challenges pathetic: the danger he courts is reduced to trinket-stealing.

My *Chronicle*'s confidence, in its rough-and-ready ways in disregard of arty commerce in harmony with printers and postal charges, turned quixotic at the end of the sixties. Repelled by any categorizing, dominantly so by the spread of uniting characteristics, insinuating decade-serializations – but how else . . . The growth of limited/signed edition prints industry, its falsity triumphantly wielding high prices showed up my *Chronicle*'s anti-market values (and the costs rising exorbitantly) as a folly, rather than a stand. Also the diverting, but impossible to avoid, book proposals, bore gaps in chronicling continuity.

And so I fell in with the 'demand' for limited and made-precious editions, thus forfeiting the impetus and betraying the *raison d'être* of it; thus the *Chronicle* slowed down, so that the arty corrupted elaborate volume XV accumulated not within one year but over nine years.

Later attempt at the revival through linking with a literary paper, *Quarto*, at volume XVI and contracted for a full year's twenty-four issues, produced five numbers to be brutally discontinued, with the whole publication, by its owner, a capricious oil-magnate.

Abandoning my independence lasting fifteen and one-fifth volumes, 353 numbers and 2,123 pictures and by entrusting it to 'patronage' provided yet another parable of Decline.

But, my pen-and-pencil curiosity ever active, I accumulated since vast new materials without an outlet worthy of the *Chronicle* at its most expansive: the United Nations 1966, Hippydom, and its Chicago 1968 supreme moments, Celebratory Moscow 1969, South Africa and Ethiopia, International Court of Justice at The Hague: the Session over Western Sahara, Bahamas and Jamaica, crucial Polish Journey (a compensatory film), nostalgic Paris (a film), **Ulster's Belfast** battlefield, South America's five countries (a film), and explosive/demonstrative England of now: its punks drawn and painted massively but buried unshown, its Greenham Common ditto. . .*

In a short space of time Pasolini and **Feltrinelli** were murdered – one in Rome and the other outside Milan. Pasolini I did not know – but with Giangiacomo Feltrinelli I was close friends I thought, and so his death puzzles. He was found in March 1972 torn to pieces under an exploded pylon.

Why? Why? belongs to docile Englanders running rigidly to type: answers, categories predictable ('And what do *you* do?'). Even their intellectuals get their whys fully covered, the *Concise Oxford Dictionary* their precedence bible. And my life-habit in England shamefully permits me to suppose full friendship with Giangiacomo – hence my puzzlement at his stepping out of the narrowness of our dialogue.

A Renaissance man, I presumed, at ease and to the full a rich patron-aristocrat: imaginative publisher (his functional marvel of a library given to Milan) and theatre supporter, *crème-de-la-crème* party-giver, thorough *bon viveur*, the Castello Villadeati thrown in. I stayed with him in Milan, in Rome, at the Castello; mingled with his friends from Monica Vitti to the Viscontis and the Medicis . . . Anna Olivetti, Contessa Beatrice Monti Della Corte, Contessa Brandolini, Anna Proclemer, Giorgio Albertazzi; he and Inge came to London, he published – a fantasy gesture – a volume of my Italian *Chronicles*. And, a participant in those packed timetables, I was naturally aware of his simultaneous left-wing commitments: his closeness with Castro, his activities having barred him from returning to Italy so that he settled to conduct his Italian affairs from across the Swiss border. The debonair presence never diminished – the sheer adventure of living seeming the orbit to this surface-friend of his, aware of Giangiacomo's deadly, as they proved to be, engagements but never to be admitted or even tested to that measure of manhood.

An Italian, I presume, encounters – does not pass by. He may be foolhardy, but is not a fool; though possibly fooled by the Nordic's apathy standing for haughty composure into accepting them as his equals? superiors? Their to-the-rule conformism framed in stoical-seeming, generous-in-inches structure promises secret reserves, which tend to be not strength but mulish stubbornness; or, in such cases as mine, of *faux* northernness – a transparent masquerade. The Romans, the Princes, the *condottieri*, the *Fascisti*, the *Brigate Rosse* – Italy should not puzzle; it progresses flamboyantly – abundant of gifts. Feltrinelli should make me humble.

Thus these two possibles:

– he crossed the border, treachery-lured; murdered; and his body set up in an imitation of a failed terrorist act;

*Yet, yet, a few days ago (March–April 1986) I began and continue working with young (and devoted) computer boys at their lab, manipulating buttons-screens – colour audacities, on the next *Chronicle* to continue this time not on paper, but as cassettes, or a feature on television. The first – transferring (indeed enriching/dramatizing) scribbles done at Greenham Common.

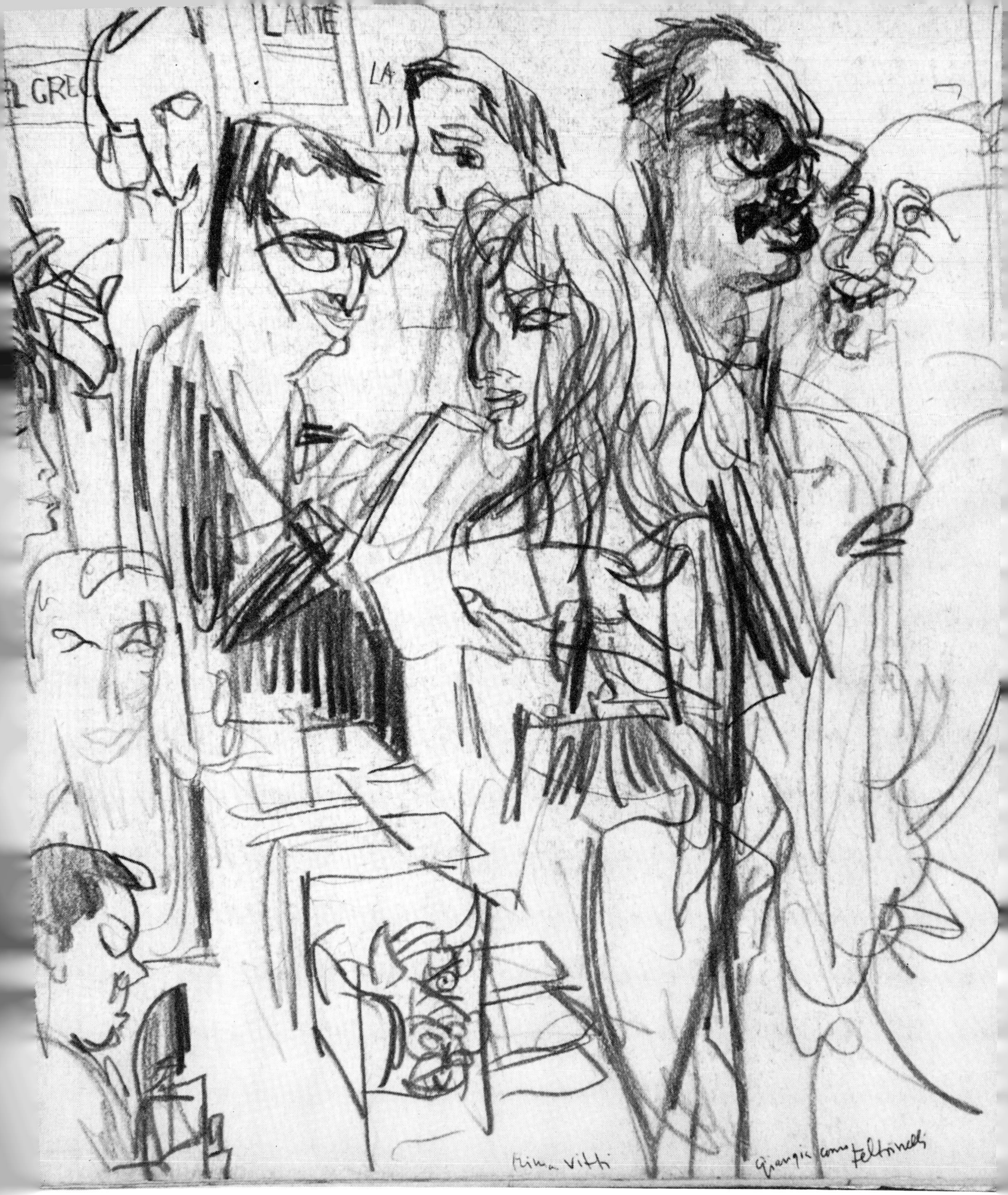

Giangiacomo Feltrinelli, Rome

– or, as believed by my Italian friends, his intellect and connections placing him at the head of his movement, the not unusual urge in such people rose to prove his worth in a minor 'direct action'.

Above **Nassau**'s brightness, the whitest high-stepped imperial-colonial **Government House** – beflagged mast, striped box and white-topee-ed red-accented black sentry – aloof. But inside – **Sir Francis and Lady Cumming-Bruce**, and their bush-blouse/foulard/white upturned moustache guest, groomed to perfection – cosy.

The Union Jack pennant over the Rolls's bonnet, Sir Francis's panama hat and her *battistes* – on the way to **the Lyford Cay snorkelling party**; yet only we three float unadventurously face down for a while – the rest sit poised, glasses in hand, on the waterside pavilion terrace under a yellow canopy, a jot superior. Their indubitable decorativeness and exclusivity is not of *Vogue*'s idealization – they are of a much earlier vintage, impressively 'mature'; impressively not only because most studiously costumed, but also because their features, modelled into repose-masks denoting the infinitely *riches* – assuredly not *nouveaux* – are beyond desires, except for vanity-feeding – somehow high clerical. Appearance must be their main preoccupation – although the host, a Scandinavian/American billionaire, is supposed to fly to his New York headquarters every other day for his empire-tending.

A predominant massive back-view – roll-brimmed, many-colour-banded panama, striped vented jacket, fingers/wrists smattered with shiny accents, black socks/shoes – reveals for greetings a Roosveltian facial enormity largely dark-glassed; next, identically monster-shade- and floppy-hat-masked (only a sharp/long nose visible) but a many-stringed attention-demanding necklace, large-patterned loose Hawaiian blouse over narrow-trousered crossed legs: straining emphasis on her preserved feature – a 'distinguished' ankle; and a few more imperishables under panamas. But, demonstratively apart, a young person, bare-footed and in disarray.

Back in Government House's coolness, the Bahamian *ambiance* left behind, I am steered to books by J. G. Bennett, *Energies Material-Vital-Cosmic* and *The Dramatic Universe*, and to Gurdjieff's maxim, 'Man, a cosmic apparatus for the transformation of energy.'

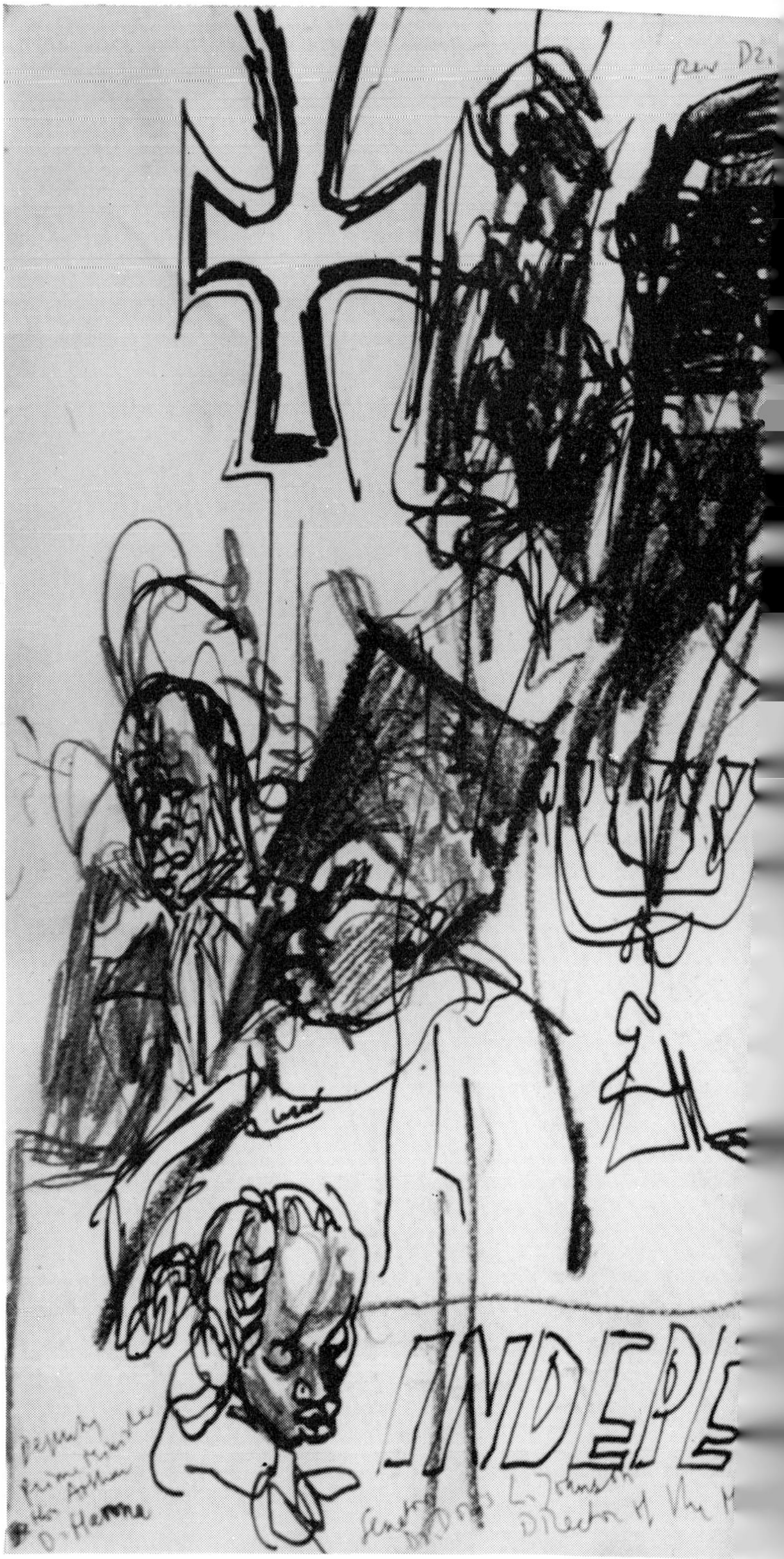

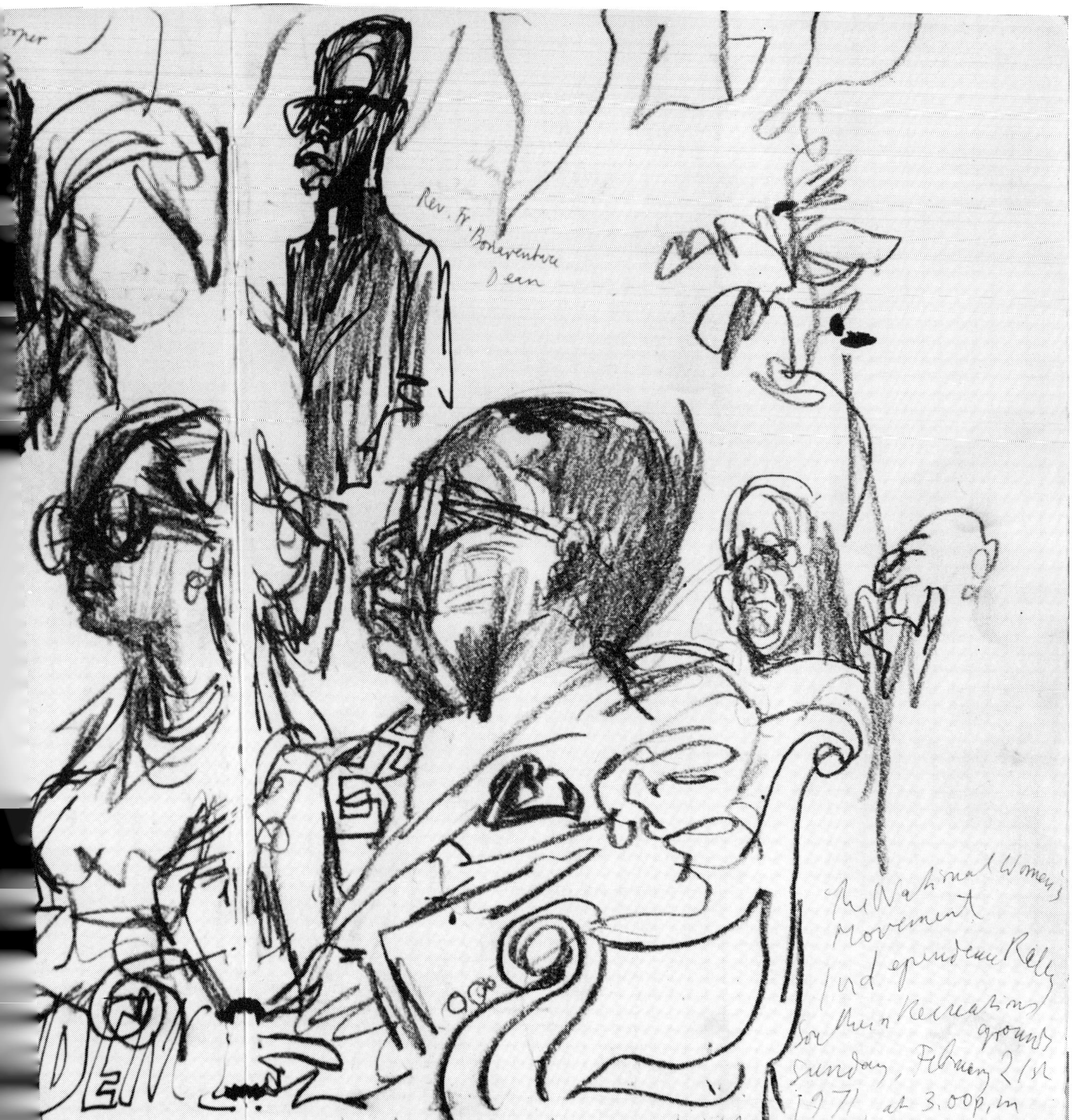

Bahamas Independence Rally, 1971

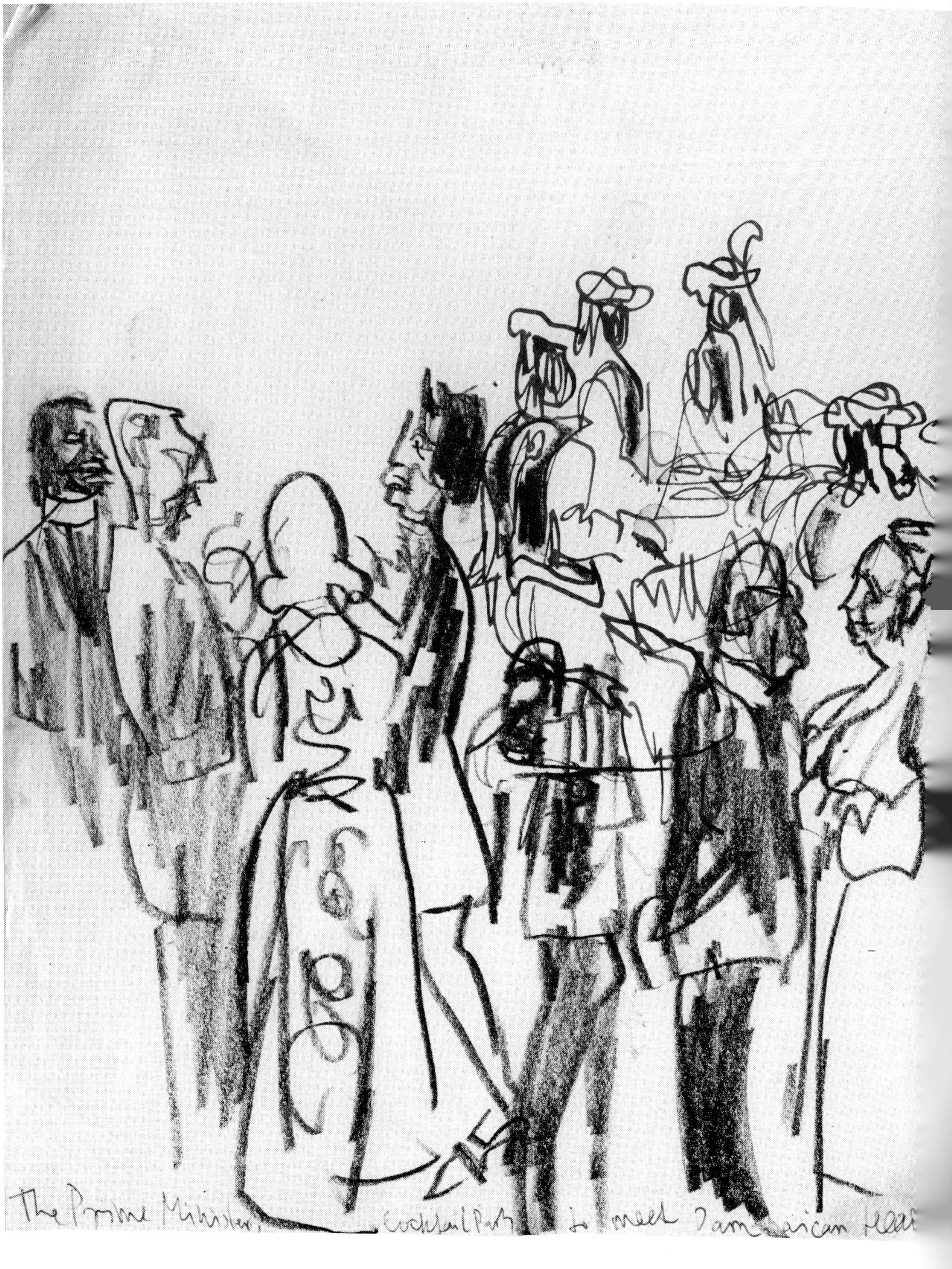

The Prime Minister's Cocktail Party to meet Jamaican

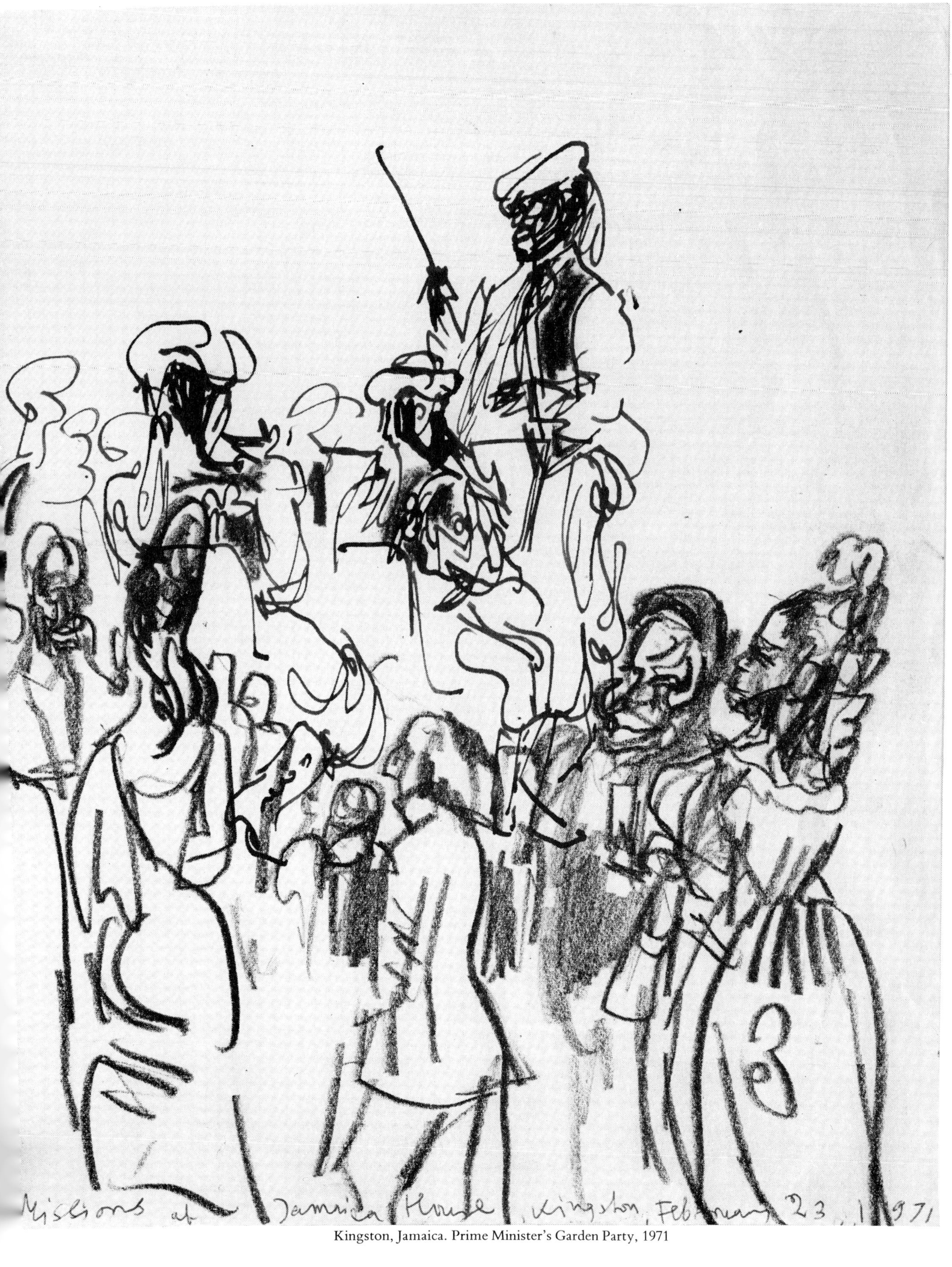

Kingston, Jamaica. Prime Minister's Garden Party, 1971

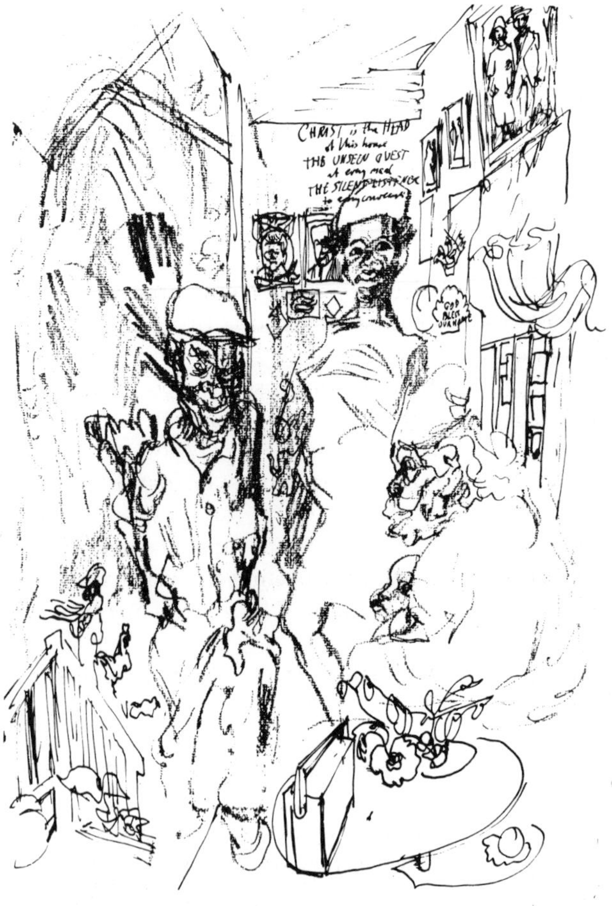

Barrie's parents' home, Jamaica

A Great Dane, a leash, a straw-thatched giantess strides/weaves through the black studs' Hyde Park paddock. One evening she enters the studio, the Dane in front and **black Barrie** behind – the selected begetter. Tempestuously they cohabit; I may take her to a show – Barrie replacing her at their son's cradle; tempestuousness swells her into a matron; Barrie, a dancer/choreographer/actor, now my friend – and *partouseur*. London (theatre and family) repels him – Barrie joins Jamaican Television.

In the greenest palmy/balmy **rurality of Jamaica** Barrie approaches a foliage-embedded homestead's weathered fence – a lyrical black she-sylph at the gate. She towers above him, but arches down to him, loves the rogue – they whisper endlessly: he, a London-trained womanizer-chameleon, for her purity a romance-shy wooer (or a convert?).

We – the threesome – stroll, steel-band-beckoned, into the Jamaica-embellished country fair: she, between us (shorter), **a Caribbean fairy-belle**, holding our hands.

No sharp-descent curtains. Rather the quagmire left after the hippy exodus exudes new 'models' for me: was **Heathcote Williams** their continuation, or a novel phenomenon?

Teresa's period of expansion: she would bring along, or take me to, the new heroes – she a muse – the most sublime among them, Heathcote; and others: **Snoo Wilson**, tailing her into the studio (I taken aback) as if an outsized pick-up punk-bruiser, on that occasion pink/purple-thatched; another time followed by three lovely/varied girl comics to rehearse in my studio his *Everest Hotel*; or **Simon Callow**, at that time bulldozing the fringe at the murky old Half Moon as Brecht's Hitler, to re-enact the grotesque's ascent in imitation of that production, climbing to the top of my studio's scaffolds, clown's black patch under false nose, for my painting of all his Hitlers on one unrolling 12 foot stretch of paper.

Or **The People Show '79**, an imposingly inconsequent performance – the theatre the nearest to my heart: a chain of enchanting astonishments without predictability-tedium – transferred at Teresa's bidding bodily to my studio to paint an almost equally disjointed 'portrait' of the show: its opening – the bare anorexic acrobat-dancer suspended by her feet (this torture reconstructed at the studio for a few minutes) under the sinister surveillance of a huge-hairy-headed Mexican actor; above, the comic/possession-burdened Christ figure – an American genius-performer; to the left a black Aphrodite/priestess; also a newspaper-reading emeritus thrillingly bursting into arias; a mindless, jiggling pair; an indispensable prophet character; a pianist-conductor, **Mike Figgis.** Or **the Ardens** and a Trotskyist **'Tito' Gerassi** – dissidents within the West – Teresa's New York University harvest, led in by **Conor Cruise O'Brien**'s wisdom and our joint book, *The United Nations: Sacred Drama*; or **John McGrath** extricated by her from the next seat at the New York showing of *Hair*.

Her conquests, and my profits, stretched from **Calvin Lockhart** of the Bahamas, a black cinema star, **Perry Henzell** of Jamaica, the maker of *The Harder They Come*, **Frankie Dyman**, a lovable Caribbean rogue, to **John Dunbar**, **Ed Victor**, **Richard Neville*** of *IT*, *Friendz* and *Oz*, to the experimental film-maker **John Du Cane**, now in Thai prison, to **Jim Haynes** of the Traverse Theatre in Edinburgh and the Arts Laboratory in London, *Suck* of Amsterdam and '*Hello I love you*' in Paris.

But **Heathcote uppermost** (well before knowing him his *AC/DC* twice watched/acclaimed by Caryl) dominating my ambience and painting – some half-a-dozen large pictures evolved round his able-bodied slimness shrewd/innocent-featured under bushiness – all *malgrè-lui* grace, unhampered by his third-hand droopy-dusty garments, many drawings and an eight-fold issue of the *Chronicle* carrying larger-than-life full-length Heathcote with little China, his daughter, perched on his shoulders – continuity attained.†

Heathcote uppermost – dominating the 'alternative' anarchy which emanated from the Notting Hill free state of Albion: ruled by him; graffitoed by him (POWER IS LOVE GONE BAD over blind walls and fences); entertained by him, a stripped-to-the-waist fire-eater; pamphleteered by him – mostly in fervour and bile against the neighbouring Queen, but also in adulation of elephants. His sallies: to disrupt/drum into his own play at the Royal Court Theatre Upstairs, thus enforcing improvised endings; to lead with this very Berber-

*His *Oz* dramatically underlined by the Old Bailey obscenity trial, in which I, a defence witness/expert on art, when cornered by the prosecutor's 'So, as you define Art, it can comprehend everything from Mickey Mouse to Rembrandt?', declared (widely reported): 'Indeed, yes.'

†And pursued: the latest 'Memoir' inclusion has China, now 16, evolving from Heathcote and her baby-self.

drum an invasion of my studio by an Algerian music-and-dance troupe: their carpets/cushions laid, their mother cum baby, instruments, turbaned selves, domesticated in an instant, the session to last many hours – and a painting 10 by 9 feet to emerge; to become a monkey over the feeble aforestation of the South Bank, leaping/swinging from branch to branch seeming not to touch the ground.

Or this 'scene': Teresa and he (a bit tipsy) go for a bite to the National Film Theatre, leaving me at work; return soon in disarray: he, a principled equalizer, had gone into the 'ladies' – a commotion ensued, in which he knocked down a commissionaire and was consequently thrown out. Teresa, undecided between dis- and pleasure at Heathcote's abominations compromised by tenderly calming him, while I, rather lost, fussed over my papers at the other end of the studio, but overhearing from Heathcote: 'Does he want to join in?' His angelic amorality blends unforced with sophistication; even his Eton and classy upbringing does not embarrass him in face of his chosen way of life: he once brought to my studio his sweetly conventional mother and sister – without excuses.

Or: to begin with, an enforced inmate, Heathcote's domestication in a mental home, to which he would repeatedly return to stay at will. He took us there once: his progress throughout the building was that of a redeeming Messiah. He shone with bliss-dispensing goodness: they were all past receivers of his meticulously diversified gratifications. A cluster of the oldest, and isolated, women were made happy/delivered by their love for him, by his embraces.

June 1973: a Leicester Square teeth/mouth hospital, a walk in-out little painless roof-of-the-mouth speck scraped out. But next day a panic call: the analysis has found the growth **malignant** – instant appointment made with **Dr Coffin**(!). He sits me in his surgery chair and, without touching me, pronounces operation-readiness of bed and action for tomorrow – no time to be lost. Please, enlarge – what will be done? And he, rings run round my face (not touching), defines the cutting out of most of my left upper jaw and cheekbone, with the healing of what would be left of my face and the return to some sort of ordinary functioning in a year or so.

Walking along the Harley Street railings after this was mostly given to self-observation. My phlegmatically short-range optimistic side, true to itself, kept me watchful and sorting out possible escapes. I went into a telephone box and

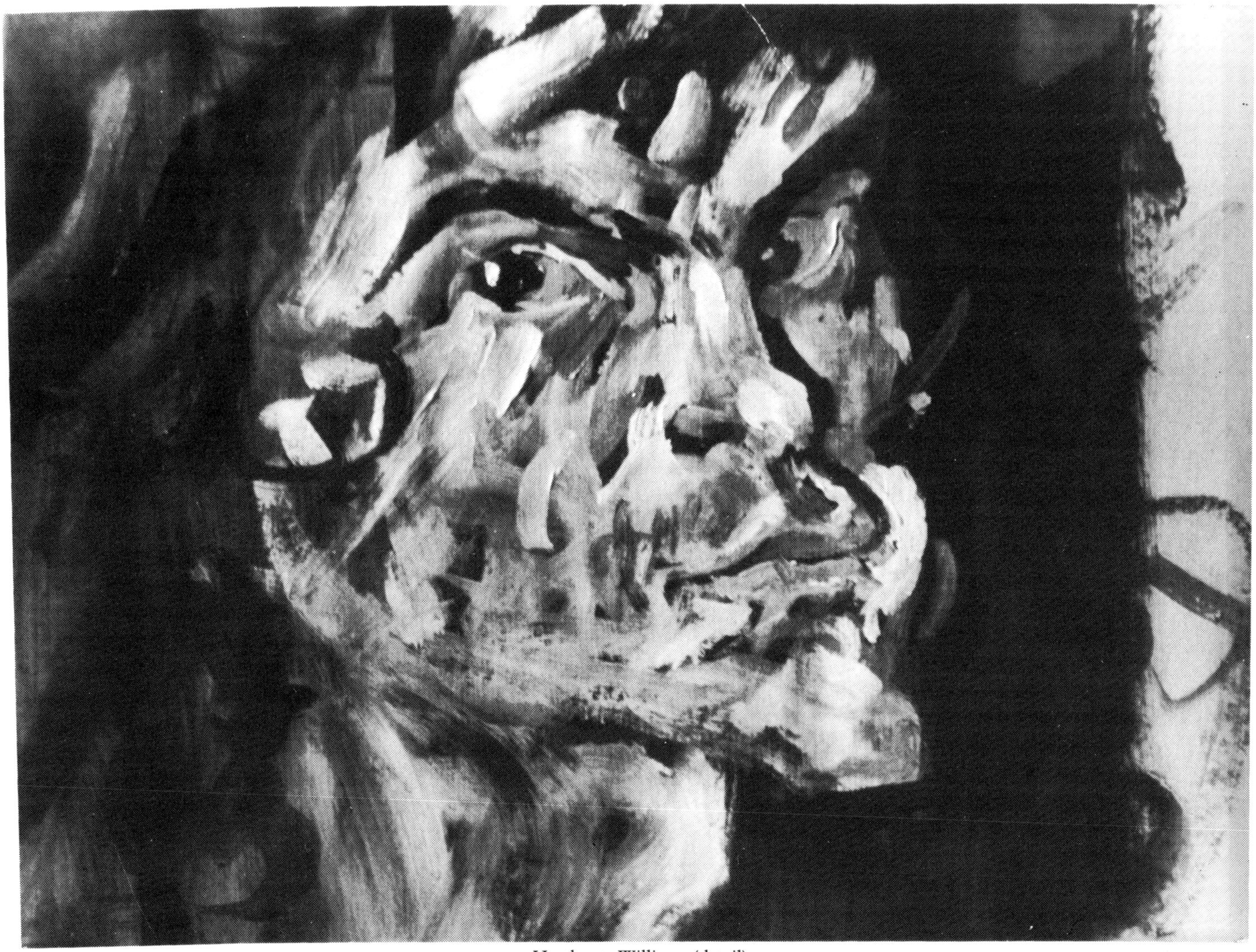

Heathcote Williams (detail)

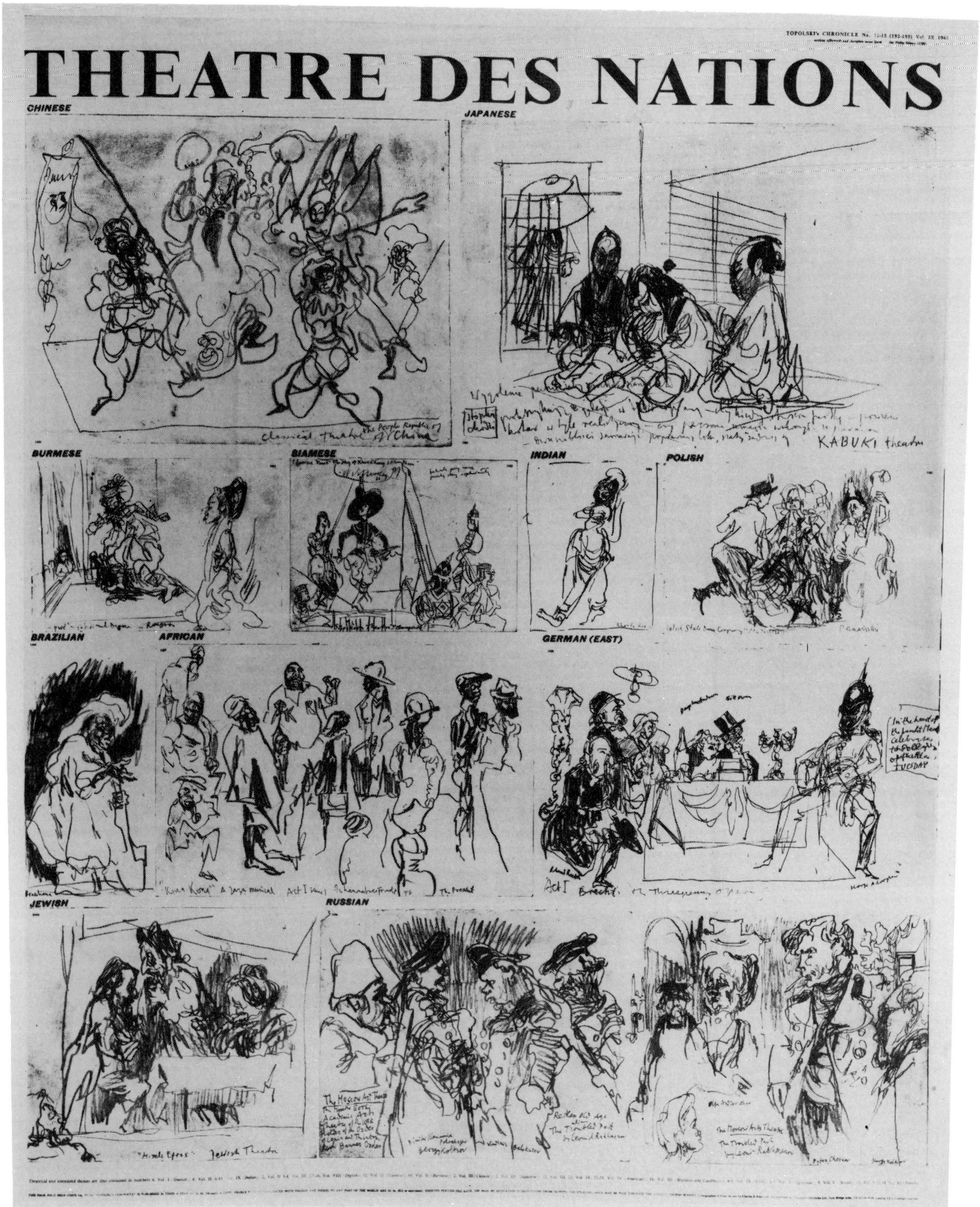

Théâtre des Nations (from *Topolski's Chronicle*)

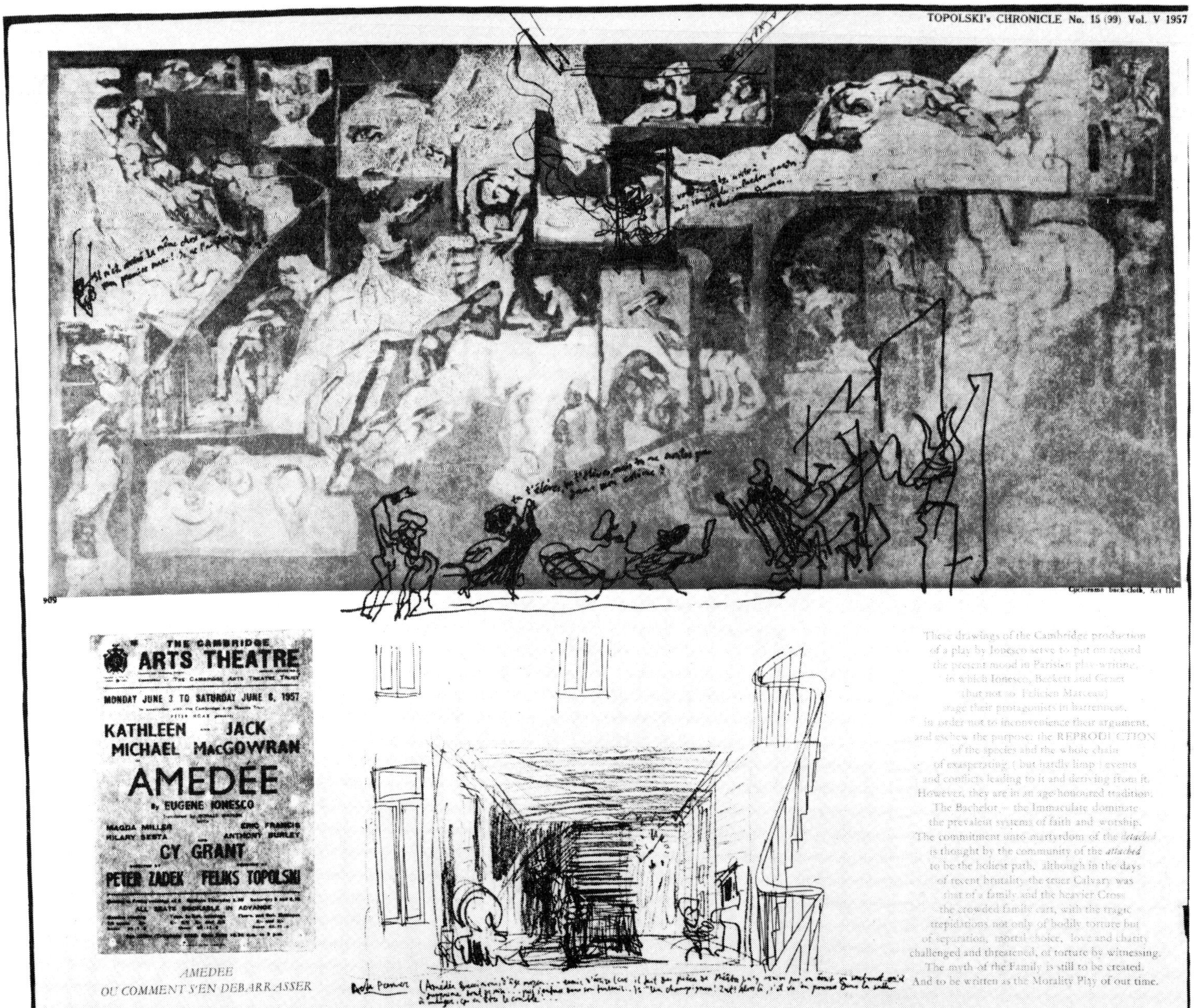

Ionesco's *Amedée* designed by Topolski, sketched in performance, 1957 (from *Topolski's Chronicle*)

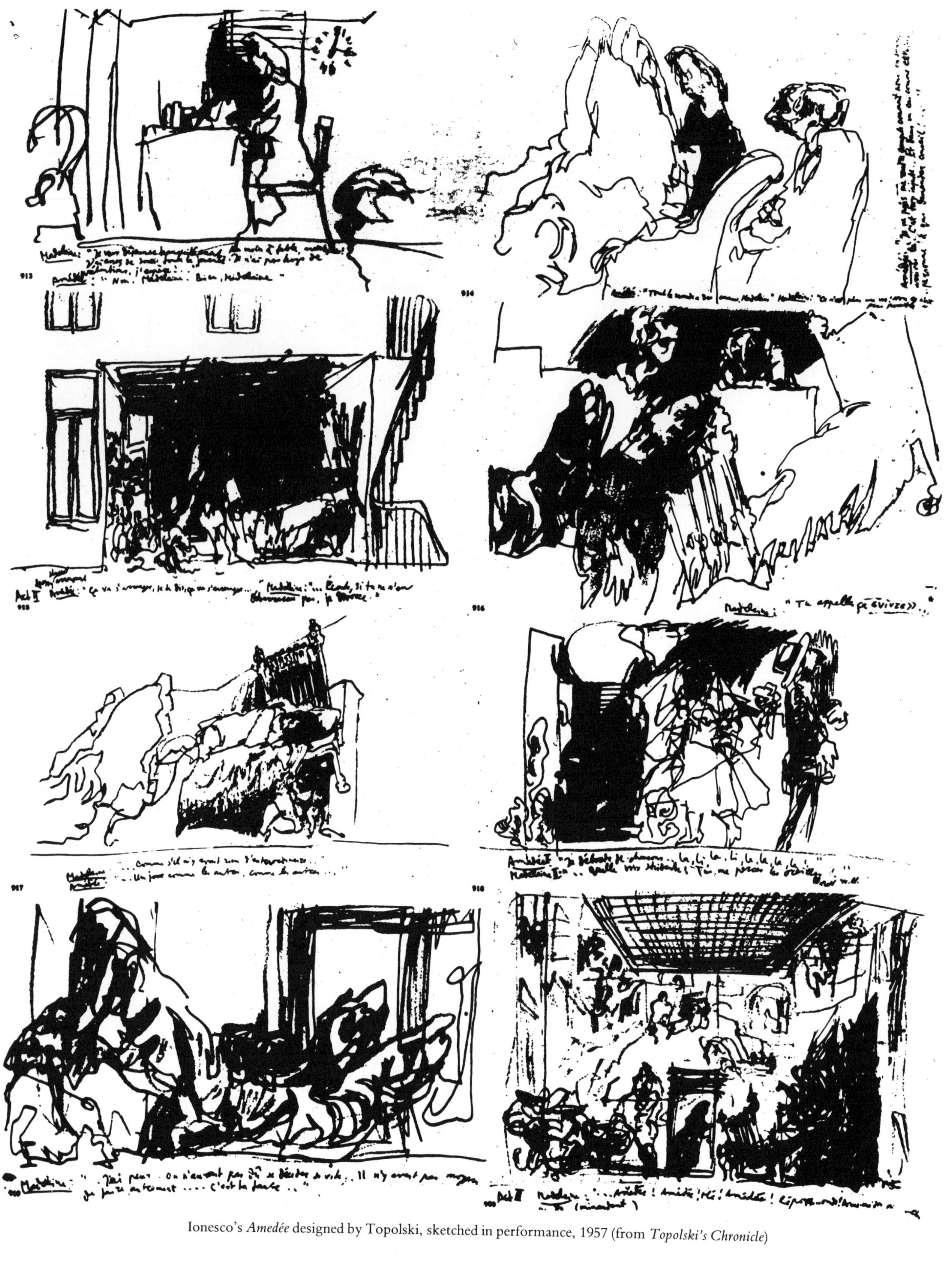

Ionesco's *Amedée* designed by Topolski, sketched in performance, 1957 (from *Topolski's Chronicle*)

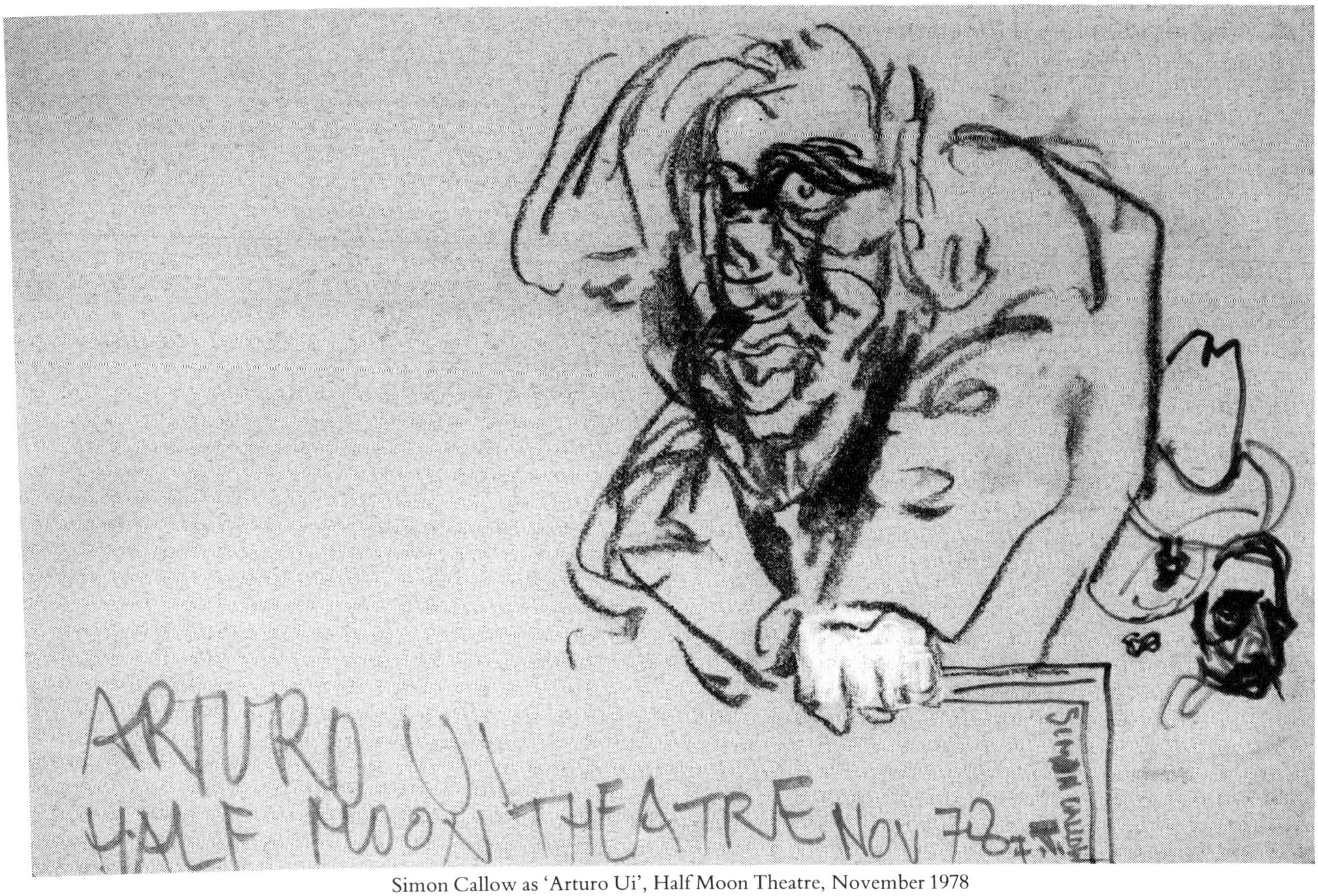

Simon Callow as 'Arturo Ui', Half Moon Theatre, November 1978

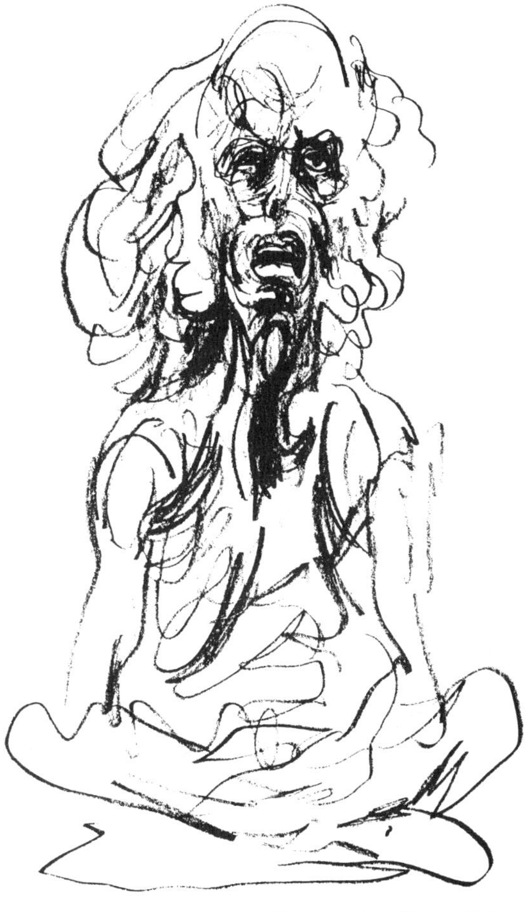

Julian Beck of the Living Theatre, New York, 1968

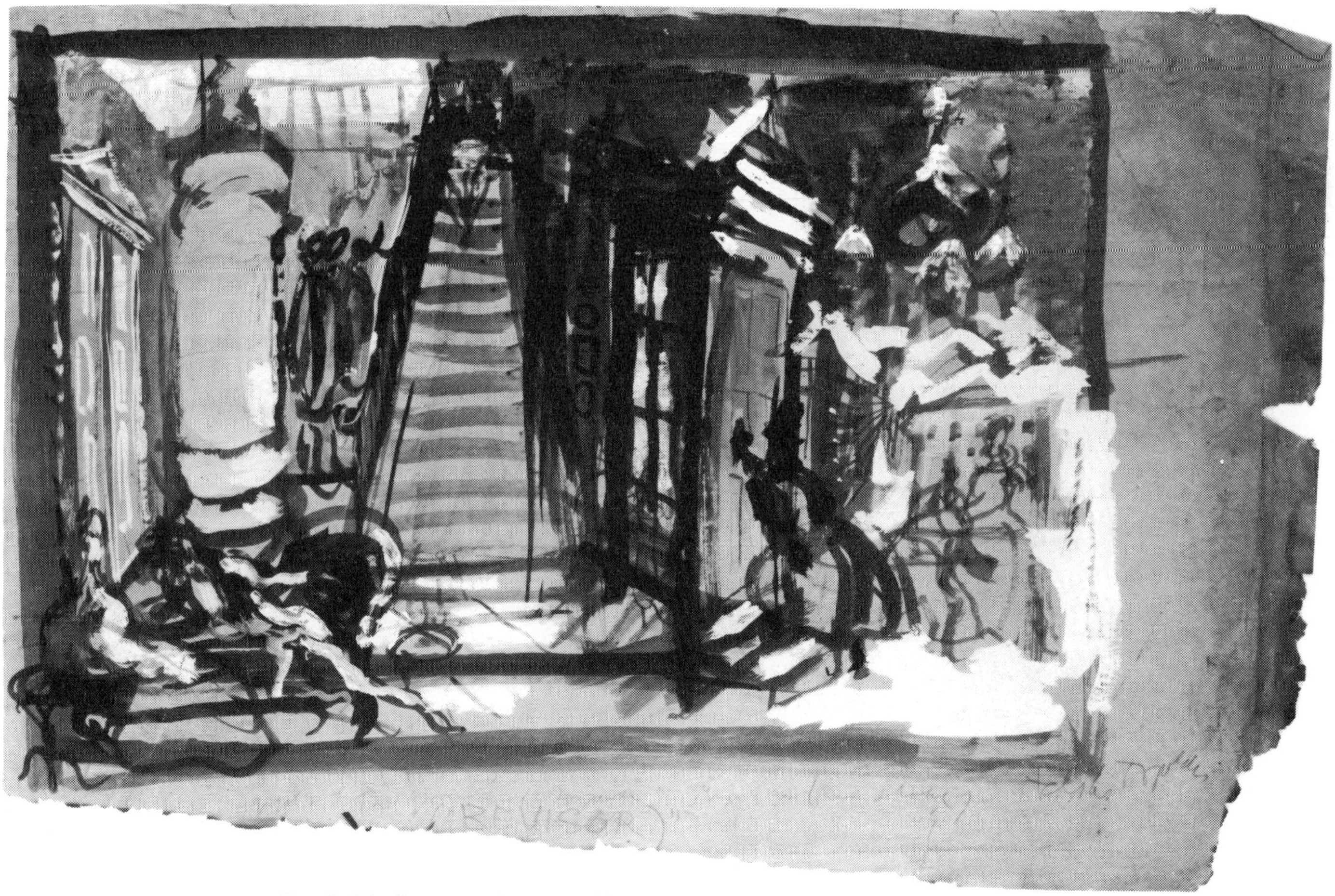

Gogol's *The Government Inspector*, Old Vic Production, designed by Topolski, 1945–6

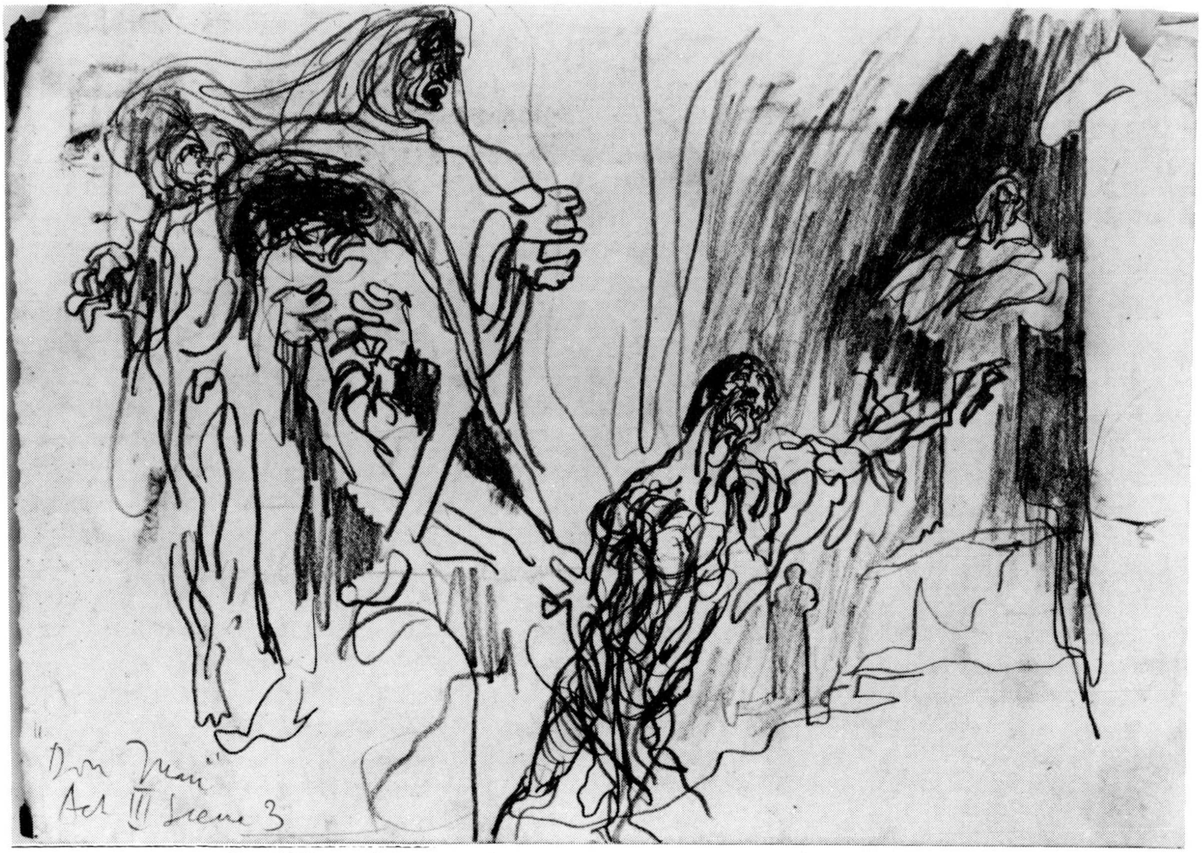

Ronald Duncan's *Don Juan*, designed by Topolski, 1952 (sketch in performance)

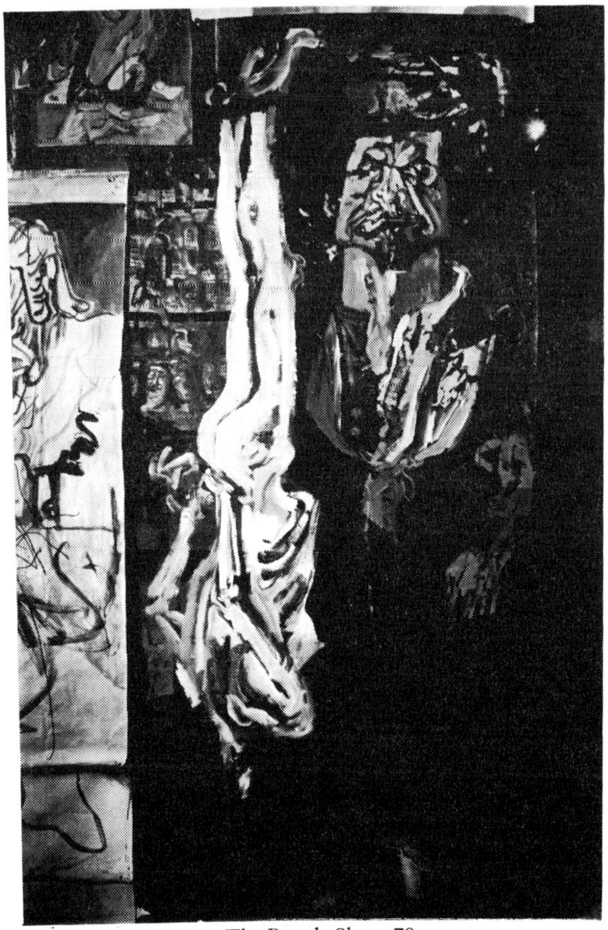

The People Show 79

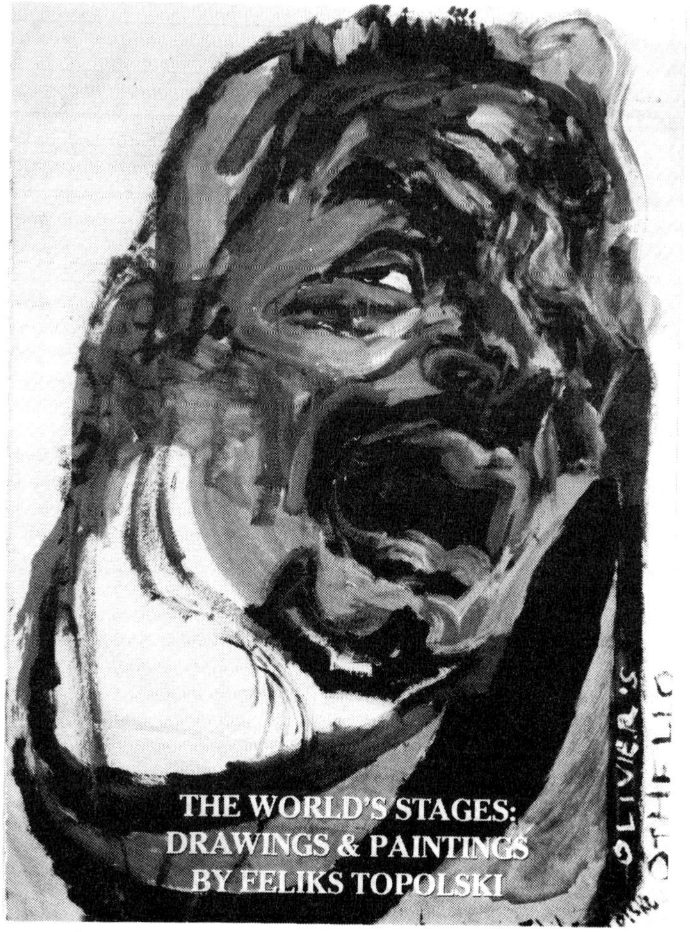

Olivier as 'Othello' (catalogue of exhibition at National Theatre)

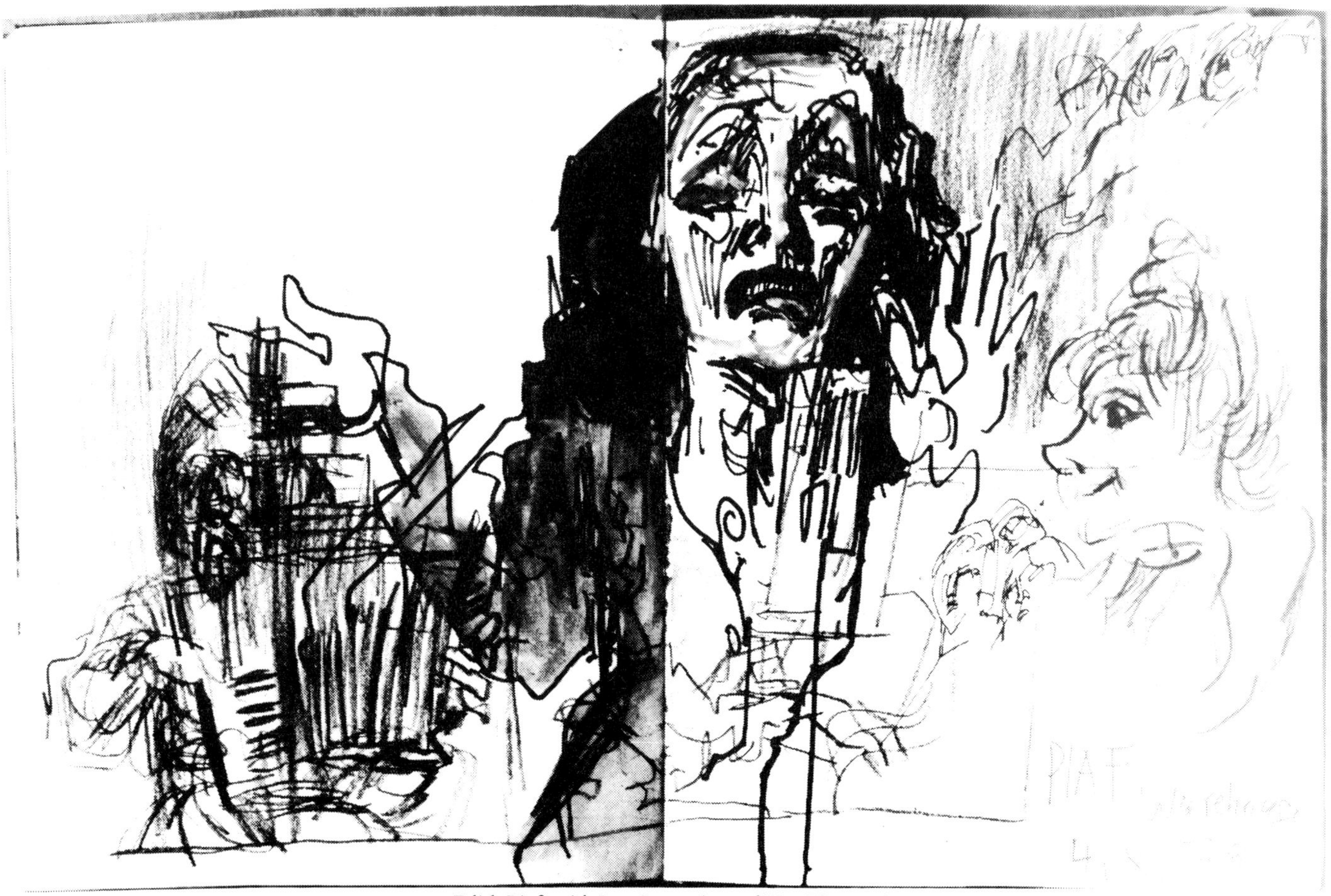

Edith Piaf, with Jane Lapotaire and Zoë Wanamaker

TOPOLSKI'S CHRONICLE No. 11 (23) Vol. II 1954

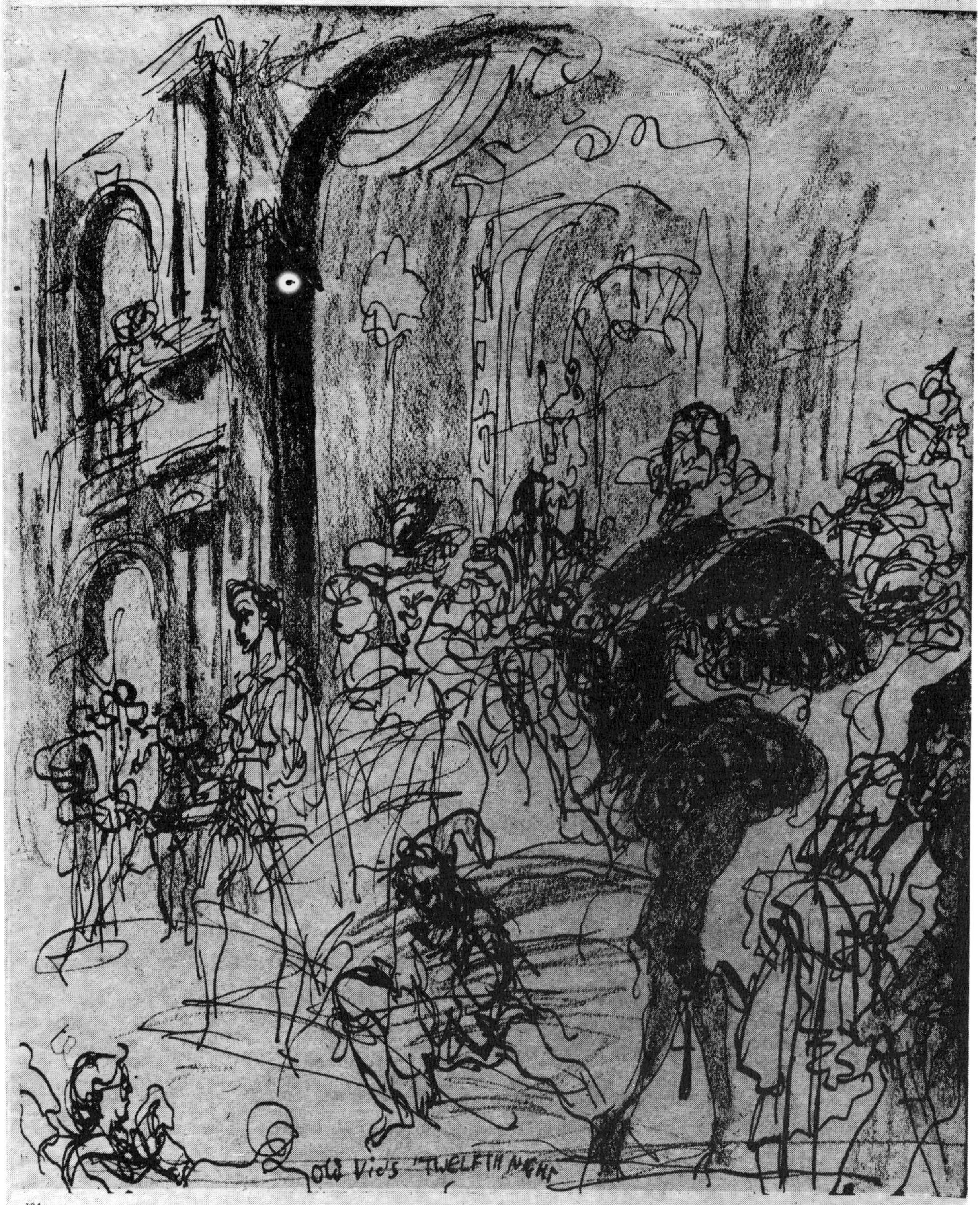

194

ENGLISH THEATRE

English Theatre (from *Topolski's Chronicle*)

talked to my Egyptian osteopath; I talked to my son. He, **Daniel**, produced a chain of medical consultations, while I refused Dr Coffin's eager helpfulness.

The worth of telling all this is in the complete absence of fear or defeat, probably ricocheted off such minutiae as the comicality of the name Coffin and his untesting over-readiness to chop and saw. We learned within a few hours about the practice of counter-measures and in no time Daniel set up a respectable '**concilium**' at the Marsden Cancer Hospital composed of a leading surgeon known for not rushing things gladly and the hospital's great radiotherapist. Mr Coffin was there too.

I was given a series of treatments, no more mention of an operation. And, secretly (a layman-patient must be excused his illegitimate musings), assumed that there had been, at the initial lab-test, a mistake, and that my therapy – and later checks – had to be performed for the profession's 'face'.

So for a lazy breast-stroke **Serpentine** swim into the lowering sun: grey sky/dark greenness/silvery water in front; eyes closed, thus a negative: sky dark, freckled light greenness; eyes closed under water – realities return as a 'photo'.

Blue-hot summer afternoon over Hyde Park's green pastures, that is to me a Promised Land patch (not to everyone's taste, but to mine), tree- water- cafeteria- bound, the stage for the black-and-white harmony's summer-long *fête-champêtre*. **The Rastafarians** play ball – a wild manhood's costume ballet – and a multitude of groups picnic/play/pose thickly flung over the undulating grass – all and each animated by amity.

The dominant mood is, rightly, of mating: activators – the English pale-skinned girls; black boys seen receiving coolly their just deserts; but the pasture, set here for some years, shows delightfully the aftermaths: the crop of naked coffee babes ring round young families – there take place happy multi-hued encounters/embraces of mothers/friends/cousins/sisters; a joyful father (black, almost naked but eye-catching in his adventurous selection of shorts/socks/sandals) prances with a many-coloured mini-parasol aloft. And the vivacity and variety of pulchritude on offer spills on to the terraces of the cafeteria – a pair of fine pink legs protrudes from under the balustrade of the highest level, the face almost hidden – she markets the best of her.

They are very truly **black**, when nude (in the Lido corral) against the pink/brown/grey others; the in-curve of the spine, the high head, the largest mightily flopping feet. '**Pashas**' draped up to and around their dark glasses, set in a tight group (one guide/adviser always in suit and tie) on wiry seats, ponder from above (and close to) pink female topless bodies laid out on their backs or bellies on the asphalt. Teenage **girls** on the

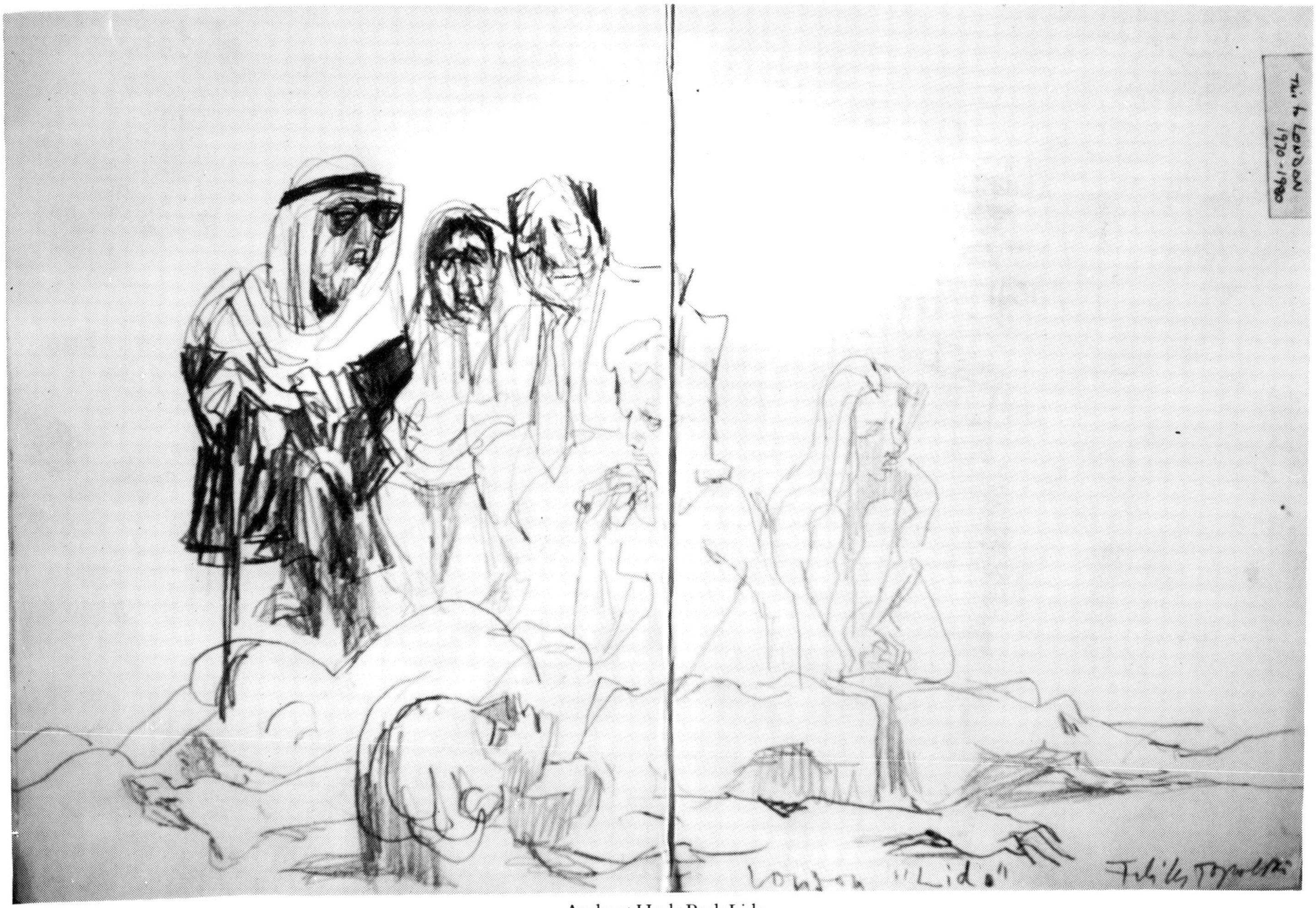

Arabs at Hyde Park Lido

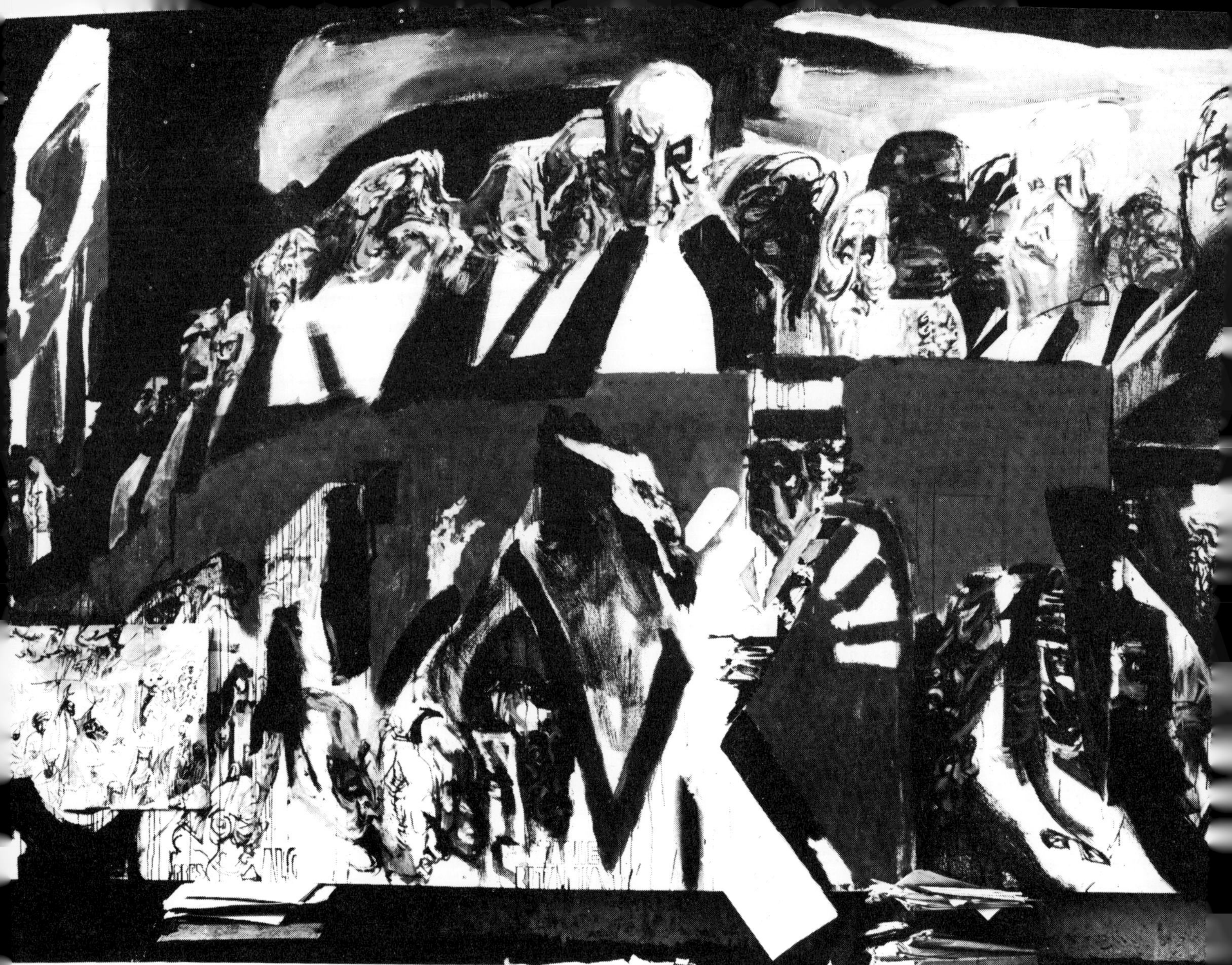

The International Court of Justice at The Hague (Polish National Museum in Warsaw)

move, breast-baring, from year to year increasingly decorative though remaining uncouth; **boys** ever aggressively calamitous.

In opposition, **the aged**: restlessly constant to-and-fro shaky prance on the diminished legs of the old male body – for no distinguishable purpose unless, oddly, to be seen.

The *passé* beauties: Marguerita (Lady) Strickland, Cliff Darnley's daughter, who modelled shatteringly – was it just before or at the beginning of the war? – for a large cigarette advert: 'This Exquisite Moment', now parades along the length of the shore, a one-person cortège trailing bags, floating rugs shawls umbrella, wide-winged-hatted coal-black-locked, make-up-masked – a bizarre but endearing apparition. Halima, a Polish painter, glimpsed once (unacquainted then) from a slowed-down open car high at a window – a *négligé* temptress, arms lifted at her morning toilette – now to me, wide-berthing her, a 'Hello, Feliks': a large cadmium-orange-haired Rabelaisian grossly patterned mound among flat-down bodies; and perhaps myself, who entered the Lido in May 1935, paying my tribute at least once a summer ever since, then in my twenties – now a cranium-exposed flabbily fleshed monstrosity with an ever-darting eye.

The Hague, 1975; at the invitation of **the International Court of Justice** I am staying a week with its President – pampered, accommodated with desired changes of seats/angles, my large sheets of paper/pencils/paints shifted/safeguarded throughout long days' sessions, the judges also sitting singly for me.

All this in anticipation of a major – in size and conception – painting – a group portrait to dare to revive the great Dutch tradition. Fifteen judges displaying faces/manners of fifteen nations brought to emphatic old age's judicial dignities.

Somewhat inaptly they are faced/opposed by a discordant motley of North African states, each served by French and Belgian lawyers in full regalia, and countered by elegant Spaniards about to lose their last colonial foothold. The theme is **L'Affaire du Sahara Occidental** – its carving, its hidden mineral riches sharpening the issue.

But the judges' and the pleaders' daily dallyings recorded in massive reports, and crowned by the sensible verdict underlining the glory of international legal *concorde* – are instantly annulled by an explosion of the native force turning the territory into a battlefield.

On my return to London, I paint at speed, over the largest

canvas in hand, a mock – but monumental – tale of it all, to the inclusion of the dominating the Court peace-dame emblem painted by Besnard and dated *26 juillet 1914* – that is weeks before the outbreak of World War I.

The officially proposed painting has been forgotten – my private one found its way to the National Museum in Warsaw.

More than 20 feet long: the sketched-out tale of the three of us (my children Daniel and Teresa – and myself) lined up in a Land-rover, **voyaging from London to Poland's Jagiellonian University in Kraków;** it is now, perhaps undeservedly, in their Museum. In one way such a story picture, stripped of its aesthetic pretences, foreshortens lengthy literary narratives – perhaps then to describe the picture, turning its simplifications to advantage, will tame the epic dimensions of the experience.

The painting begins with a monster-hovercraft Channel crossing and our threesome-in-profile guided by 'THE BEST SALAMI IMPERIAL' and 'GUTE FAHRT', arrowed to Hanover and onward along the straight-lined/sign-posted **Autobahn**, which cosmetically **tops/erases** – the **Belsen** mass-graves and the dying, the boiling-over **escapees-slaves** of all Europe revengefully treading across smashed Naziland, **the last hurried battles** yielding the green army's defeat – all rising from under the asphalt in my memory; and in reality in the unchanging sinister high-hatted green shapes of the border guards of both Germanies.

Then West Berlin's confusion: **the Nazi faces** (brutalized by ageing into horror masks) in civilian (still leathery) clothes, General Senger modifying from a military commander to a benevolent pedagogue; but also **old Dr Hans Cürlis** materializing for belated fraternization and a comic double interview (German television with an interpreter, filmed by a Polish television crew).

Cürlis, pink aged cherub, blissfully tipsy, charms, upsets Germany's image of overall abomination. We two sit, almost holding hands.

The East German border cuts us down to measure. The guard, boxed high and monstrously Prussian-costumed with Russian trimmings, stops us and mimes for a 'souvenir' – puzzlement. But he sign-explains unmistakably: a **bribe-tip** for the passage is demanded – a bottle of whisky from the kiosk conveniently placed at the back to be put into that dustbin underneath his watchbox.

'TRANSIT WARSZAWA'. In Polish: 'PEACE! WORK! SOCIALISM!', 'PROGRAMME OF THE PARTY – PROGRAMME OF THE NATION!', red-lettered, hugely stretched above the flat ex-German land; the country folk awkward, stuck fast into this flatness – the by now aged winners of the pitiless race to take over. 'HEARTS THOUGHTS DEEDS FOR PEOPLE'S POLAND!' and red/white bunting fail to animate the square-coated citizentry of wintery Głodno. The sheepskin-coated/hatted (a strange medieval shape) people of Koło uncommunicative in lone pursuits – unaffected by the market square-binding 'XXX YEARS OF PEOPLE'S POLAND', by the more modest 'YOUTH TACKLE DIFFICULT TASKS', by the crysome full moon.

But Poland's level-spread misty rurality awoke tenderness – the film of this journey faithfully records the mood, with the battered Land-rover rolling tiny in long shot under the highest sky (although, when the director sweated over this, we thought it cliché-phoney). The triumphal chariot – the Land-rover – rode (in a parable of Returns – to beckoning prospects – to the staged apotheosis), accompanied by today's equivalent/parody of the historiographers and savants attached to mighty voyagers/conquerors – the film crew.

A poorly modernized heraldic mermaid (sword raised and shield) over the Warsaw approach road.

The first film-shot in **Warsaw**: the Land-rover disgorges the three of us at the foot of the Zachęta, the palatial 1900 *salon d'art*, and I, my index finger obeying the director's orders, point clumsily (out of character), retrace for their inattentiveness the tight circumambulations of my pre-war past: the rotund church in front of us backed by my Mikołaj Rey school and, not far beyond, my home; twisting round, but visible, Mazowiecka Street – high *bohème* café society's *paseo* from Garliński's gallery, past Mortkowicz's publishing and bookshop to the Ziemiańska café – the noon-to-three essentiality. In later years the parade (bowing, hat-waving,

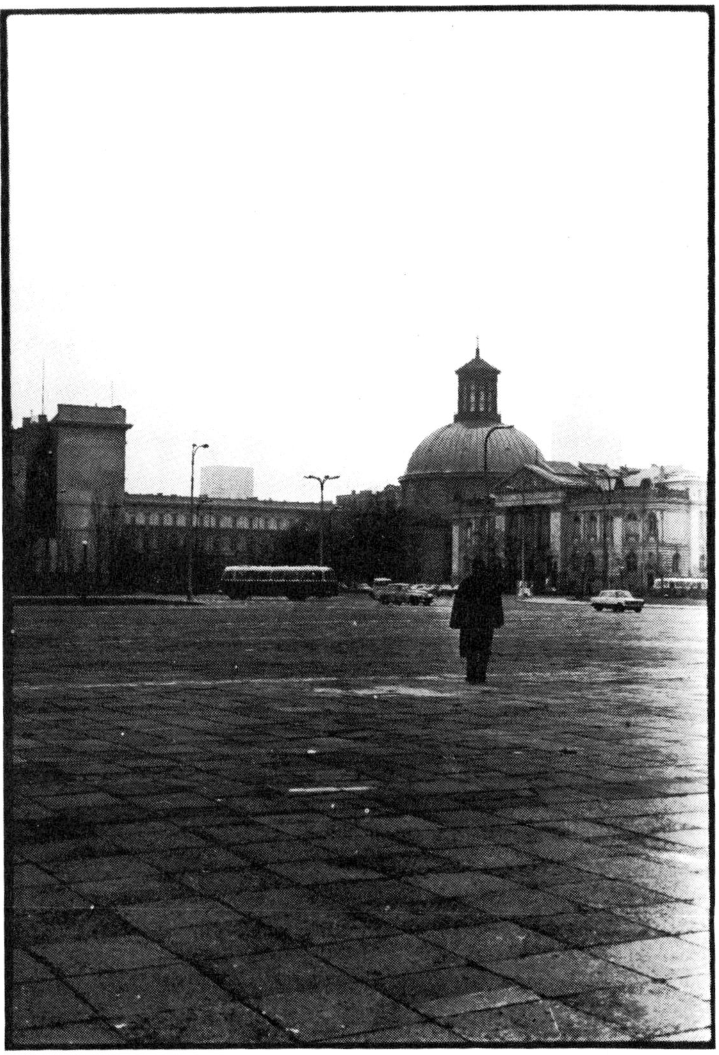

In Warsaw, 1974

agitated encounters, street photographers recording) extended to Marshal Piłsudski Square with the *Literary News* vitrine, a weekly-changing sensation, and the IPS, the modern art pavilion, exhibiting and, as a gathering-centre (with my two-walls, 14 metres mural as décor), competing (and winning) with the Ziemiańska. To complete the round, the exuberants would cross the square's emptiness for the Europejski Bar and rumbustious hours over vodkas and spicy snacks.

Now, unearthily there looms the Stalinesque immensity of the Palace of Culture, given to Poland by the incorrigible Russians as a gesture of friendship, with the minutest attention to ornamental details based on researches into Polish folklore motifs. It is much in use, and, above all, fulfils architecture's duty to mark history. Warsaw, smashed to the ground, lost its bricks-and-mortar continuity, but by the coincidence of its fate and fervour it re-invented/-accented and, above all, re-created, within a few years, its massif of half a millennium.

The earliest bastions and crumpled walls were remade, even re-invented; but the seventeenth and eighteenth centuries' Royal Castle, the churches, the palaces, and burghers' 'Old Town', whole streets of the nineteenth century, returned, brick by brick, soon gaining patina to make it all look older than sadly washed London and Paris.

And the Palace of Culture led in new areas of kowtowing to the pseudo-classical mode of Moscow, yet often echoing also the Warsaw of the turn of the century. Then – with a modicum of political, thus aesthetic liberation – the surviving architects of the 'modern' school began to erect their 'complexes', followed by the penetration of Western commercialism with a Swedish-built high-rise hotel. Even the war destruction has its commemoration: a broken rough-edged fragment of an arch embracing the unknown soldier's tomb is all that remains of a colonnade which linked two wings of the Saxon Palace, also gone. Thus is raised from the dead (topped by congested post-war layers) the life of the city, of Poland.

In the meantime Warsaw works; the statues – pre-war (Kiłinski, the shoemaker hero of the 1793 Uprising) and new (Dzierżyński, a Pole and Lenin's first ruthless adjutant-suppressor of counter-revolutionaries; the Ghetto Defenders' monument on the acreage of mouldy rubble) – the fake palaces behind intricate railings and stamping sentries, are prosaically circled by citizenry – fur-hatted/chested ladies, men carrying attaché cases pronounced to my eye; all backed by high restless cranes.

King Sigismundus the Third's column, crushed to the ground by the Germans, has been lifted to stand as before, in the Castle Square. The Royal Castle, rebuilt from scratch into the approximation of its shape-before-last, already roofed and clock-towered, but still its redbricked body unclothed with plaster into a mere replica – now a vast originality.

There is a queue. We move in with it (and out of it Daniel picks up a girlfriend for life) into the immense staircased openness, astounding in its harsh redness and shadowiness. It will be 'finished', as the art-historian-and-decorator demand of a 'period' museum, but now soaring raw-brick walls embrace/enhance the fierce outsized creations (objects, mechanized conglomerations, banners) by war-seared artist Hasior. Soon after, the same collection, 'displayed' neatly to an exhibition designer's formula in the bright foyer space of London's Festival Hall, left its passion behind.

Preserved by the Germans for their high-ranking officers, the old hotels, Brystol and Europejski, parade in their lobbies Warsaw's winter fashions: the ladies' costly accessories come deviously from the West – the bracelets and ear-rings, watches, extravagantly framed and coloured spectacles, bootees; but the lavish fur coats thrown open in the swing of their *entrée* and the stunning fox tail fur hats are made by the old craftsmen of Chmielna Street.

The yet more striking élite gathers at SPATIF, nominally the theatrical profession's club: 'everybody' comes here, preferably after theatre hours.

The theatre. Poland's forte. Szajna's *Dante* – the relentless spectacle which – already at the door – begins to pound sensitivities with tortured suspended figures. Sadly their subsequent fearsome animation in the initial mute advance down from the balconies and along the bridge over the audience is instantly made lame when spoken – thus actorish – conventions take over. And, as with Hasior, when transplanted to London *Dante*'s great impact (in its best elements) was no more.

The Iron Curtain, a trifle; culture jet-travels and I cannot be sure whether the Polish Romantic Słowacki's *Balladyna* in Warsaw's National Theatre production – whirling motorbikes and high-boot nudity round the rustic tragic sisters – followed affectations of the West or was their parallel.

But the way in which the national stereotypes in the plays by the Romantics and by Wyspiański of the turn of the century are now staged is breathtaking; the enchained and Hamletish leaders of revolts, the poet-intellectual parading in peasant-feathered square hat, the moustachious magnate in purple and furs, the bare-footed village girl at a fence – scanning distances for hope (stage-glimpse, touching to me), the good Russian, the patriot priest, the patriotic Jew in black silks, the array of archangels, seers, apparitions of kings and the ancients of Poland's prehistory. . .

Poland's receptions rosier and rosier. The weaving of friends' warmth and of the culture officials' enticements grew to a peak in this year.

The tides. The years leading to 1974 generated plenty in me and brought a multitude of responses and promises. Some books (*Shem Ham and Japheth Inc.* got itself on the 'best books of the year list' in one of the Sunday papers); rather extravagant, thus unrealized, projects, as for instance the concept of a fleet of tented travelling art-circuses, each carrying an identical packaged multi-media spectacle engendered by a filmed circular painting – this pressing into realization what was to become my *Memoir of the Century*; multiplying travels; the new marriage and a dream tower-home.

But the 1974 journey to Poland swelled this tide extravagantly – old friends and new explosive people were there in plenty; and I shared out my Polishness, unshackled, between these and those around me in the West.

Culture's manipulations in the West tend to be dominated

by the power of money markets; in parallel Poland's art is more or less controlled by fluctuations of political stakes. These reach down to the fates of single artists, pampered to the extreme while they fit into the frame of 'high-level' motivations/humours, to be, more or less, ejected when they cease to be needed. More or less, because the networks of dependencies are not too efficient, individual whims slackly controlled.

And this was the time when I myself became (inexplicably to me) an object of *favours*, to the point of discomfort when offered a choice of country mansion/castle from a thick register of minutely recorded post-aristocratic estates (photographs attached).

And so: on this visit, with a number of my works already in the collections of the National Museum in Warsaw, a retrospective exhibition was plotted to take the main areas there or the whole of the *Zachęta,* with the directors and myself, plans in hand, trotting round.

Then the art-book publishing bosses made a contract with me for a tri-lingual 'Monograph' to be designed by me along perhaps extravagant lines: a great number of pages, colour plates, fold-ins, pockets for accumulating later supplements. Simultaneously: conferences with Andrzej Wajda as the possible director of a feature film on a peripatetic artist's view of the century – and sessions with Irena Harasimowicz précising the script. And, at the National Theatre, advancing projects with director Dejmek to stage the most unruly and inspired play by Stanisław Witkiewicz (Witkacy), *The Cobblers.*

All this unceasingly recorded by Tomasz Pobóg-Malinowski's film crew, to the devoted inclusion of a party *monstre* given in my honour by my old Artillery Officers' School colleague, Jerzy Blikle – the only tolerated (three-generations-old *pâtisserie* favoured by De Gaulle when in Poland) hero of private enterprise, thus almost the only private host – at which 'everybody' was present; of our attendances at theatre rehearsals; of our visit to Antoni Słonimski, the veteran poet and nonconformist chairman of the Polish PEN club.

Crows flap without haste over horizontality. 'FOR PEOPLE'S POLAND THE HEARTS THE THOUGHTS THE DEEDS' but: my childhood's two- or one-horse peasant carts still keep going on remote roads. Same shape, but the war corrupted the wholeness of their modesty: used lorry tyres bulge over old squeaky wheels; and the little country horses have disappeared, replaced by the tall, perhaps post-army breed. But they still roll to and from the markets and, when our car is about to overtake each of them, there takes place invariably a hieratically unified inward turn of the two heads and shoulders of the tightly seated man and woman, to look behind, almost cheek to cheek – perhaps a baby laid in the straw at the back – a true Family.

'OUR WORK FOR YOU THE FATHERLAND' – we enter – the expectancy mounting almost as in my young days – the last stretch of the road, narrowed and shadowed by tall poplars, the Vistula keeping us company on the right.

The new Kazimierz is on the official tourist lists, thus tidied up, prompted by 'what foreigners might think'. The

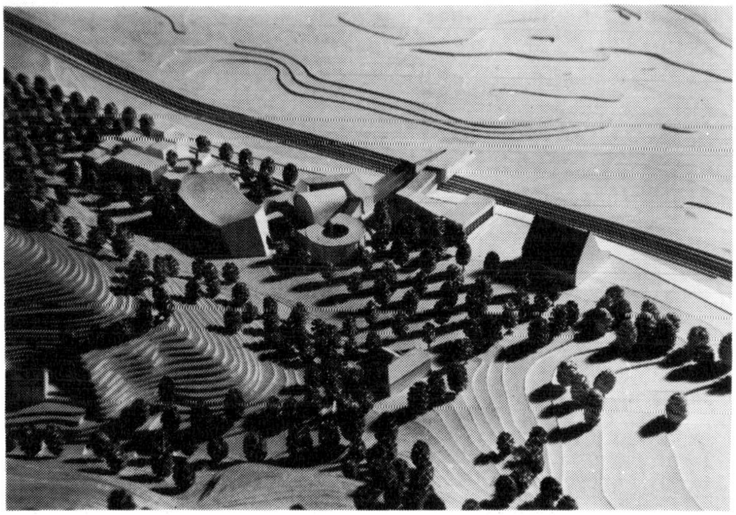

Model of proposed *Memoir* project in Kazimierz

market square, neat under the besoms' constant application, does not fill up any more with the weekly country market, relegated, and with it the peasant carts, to muddy spaces out of sight. The village people hug the walls, watchful. We are received, in the hush of respectful etiquette, at the Architect's House built since the war and fitted in among the façades of the square in 'modern' accord.

And here comes the documentary film's insertion of **Madame Maria Kuncewiczowa**, a marvellous writer (and mother of Witold), who spoke prettily about me in my youth to the camera from her Kazimierz home. She and her husband, as the revered patrician-citizens of the village, pressed on the local authorities and on me as well that the search for my *Memoir*'s location should end there. This was supremely attractive to me: my formative art student's years were tied to Kazimierz – and to close the circle by setting my ultimate pictorial synthesis there was made even more irresistible by the enthusiastic collaboration of the architect-in-residence **Jerzy Kowarski**. During my previous visit the two of us evolved a project, outrageously ambitious in scope, scale and engrossment into the landscape. We had the complete support of the authorities – the *Wojewoda* (Governor) of Lublin province travelled to Kazimierz to dine with us in celebration of the completion of a 3 metre square maquette.

And this time, the film camera ever at our side, we stopped in Kazimierz on our journey from Warsaw finally to survey the site.

The village's pre-war beauty has almost recovered. River-bound, with its churches and its cushioning against Three Crosses Hill, it folds into tender wholeness when looked at from the ruin of a sixteenth-century granary, which was to be meticulously revived as my roughing-out and reference-gathering quarters; and the village's reality was to intertwine/blend with the sequence of my Kazimierz in the twenties painted on a crenellated wall bridging the road leading to Kazimierz. Otherwise, **panoramic imagery** was to wind **almost free-standing** – no 'architecture', only mini-supports – through the landscape of orchards (incorporating them) backed by green hills; but, in accord with the moods of memory, ranging from lyrical and leisurely to most brutally apocalyptic, it would rise/fall/narrow/enlarge/turn into loops, circularity, while meandering along the river shore for about 200 metres to a growing series of 'addenda' shapes intended to multiply with the demands of the growing 'diary' of the present – thus open-ended towards the harsh finale of chalkpits.

And I was to divide the coming years between this and London's smaller version.

Rurality breeds different slogans: 'LET US MAXIMIZE CULTIVATION OF FODDER PLANTS', and preserves its essentials: the straw-clad roofs amongst trees; the whitewashed churches; the roadside crosses; the kerchiefed old women – ears and eyes on misdeeds; young men – a swift comb out of the pocket to be repetitiously run through their (nowadays) long hair; the fighting geese; the stream-edging willows – and the squeaking carts.

Sandomierz of gentle Renaissance domestic shapes. And – in front of them and of our parked car – three classically riff-raff drunkards sway/wrestle/swear, to be speedily collected by the motorized *Milicja*.

But 'PEACE TO THE NATIONS OF THE WORLD' and instant change to darkening rusty skies, smoke- and fire-fed, of the colossal '**HUTA LENINA**' industry.

And promptly another change: the old streets of Kraków opening on to the high long walls of Wawel Castle, tightening again to reveal the model square of staid and unmolested European tradition, well filled (unlike self-consciously provincial Kazimierz) with market stalls under umbrellas, vigorous crowds, a generous provision of pigeons. And the memento-filled music-and-cabaret cellars.

Now **the Jagiellonian University** (one of the oldest in Europe) and **the Doctorate Honoris Causa** ceremonially crowning this abundance of favours.

Dark tints of the interiors and the double lines of old portraits offsetting violet-pink or black robes, some crossed with expressive chains, one ermine-caped. Respectful aura of the guests in the rising pews (amongst them Norman Reddaway, the British Ambassador, and his wife, having sweetly flown from Warsaw for the occasion). Even the fussing of the film crew, working out the finale of their picture, adds to the gravity. It may seem arrogant that – seated between two beadles holding tall maces, in front of the Rectorial podium, robed and bereted and highly exposed, awaiting my turn in the sequence of speeches – I try surreptitiously to note down the scene.

The *ex cathedra* speech bestowing the title on me was delivered in Latin. My speech was in Polish:

'Facing this intimidating body of high priests of one of the most respected temples of learning, I, the so-called professional artist, am inclined to feel like an exposed swindler, for in our time the terms 'profession' and 'craft' do not easily encompass pretenders groping over the wildernesses of their fancies, comically heroic in their vulnerable arrogance.

'I must therefore look for the grounds to justify my presence among you, because, although you have attired me in your stately vestments, I am, at the best, a person *hors concours* of the Academy.

'Thus:

'A highly ambitious Anglo-American television series has recently been made (and subsequently a large volume published) which embraces the totality, let's say, of Promethean humanity's progress. I may add that it was created by the remarkable popularizer of learning, also the author of a book on the poet and painter William Blake – Professor Bronowski, a Pole by origin.

'One of the hour-long programmes was built round a collection of portraits which I painted and drew for this purpose. Wandering within their improvised exhibition, Bronowski evolved his theme: I quote, "Topolski's portraits do not so much fit the face as explore it; the artist is tracing the details, almost as if by touch; and each line that is added strengthens the picture but never makes it final. We accept that as the method of the artist. But what physics has now done is to show that that is the only method to knowledge. There is no absolute knowledge . . . All information is imperfect. We have to treat it with humility. That is the human condition; and that is what quantum physics says."

'Assuming that this certification text persuades you to treat me as *de facto* your equal, I move on: in consequence of that quote, I fancy that (in common with learned investigators in any field) the artist-explorer, guided by his creative instinct, is indispensable. Fixity is death and humanity, deprived of rebirth by the cyclic rhythm of seasons of the year, must wade onward through the unknown. The awkward, cautiously advancing colossus sends forward the scouting antennae of sensibilities: inventors, discoverers, artists, philosophers, prophets. A lonely, risky and most often ungrateful role, because it is those who come later, the cultivators/consolidators, who will reap the harvest.

'So many apologies!

'But do I have an original theme up my sleeve, worthy of the occasion?

'For the advanced in years there remain, as solely his own, fewer and fewer thoughts which, perhaps by the law of statistics, have not also occurred quite independently to someone else. A few examples:

'In my early days in England I would surprise and shock the English by saying that their country was exotic to me – for them the exotics began across the Channel. This dictum was contained in my reportage printed in the Warsaw *Wiadomości Literackie* (*Literary News*), in 1935 I believe. Thus the proof exists that the thought occurred to me before Federico Fellini stated the same in an interview a few months ago.

'In an address which I gave in the forties (this too was fortunately registered in print) I said, while reflecting on governmental patronage, "Without the Sistine Chapel, Michelangelo would not have fulfilled himself." Many years later, Malraux wrote in *The Voices of Silence*: "Were it not for the Sistine Chapel, the myth of the Renaissance would be less effective."

'But perhaps still untouched themes beg for attention; for example: a wise patronage of art that is not dominated by

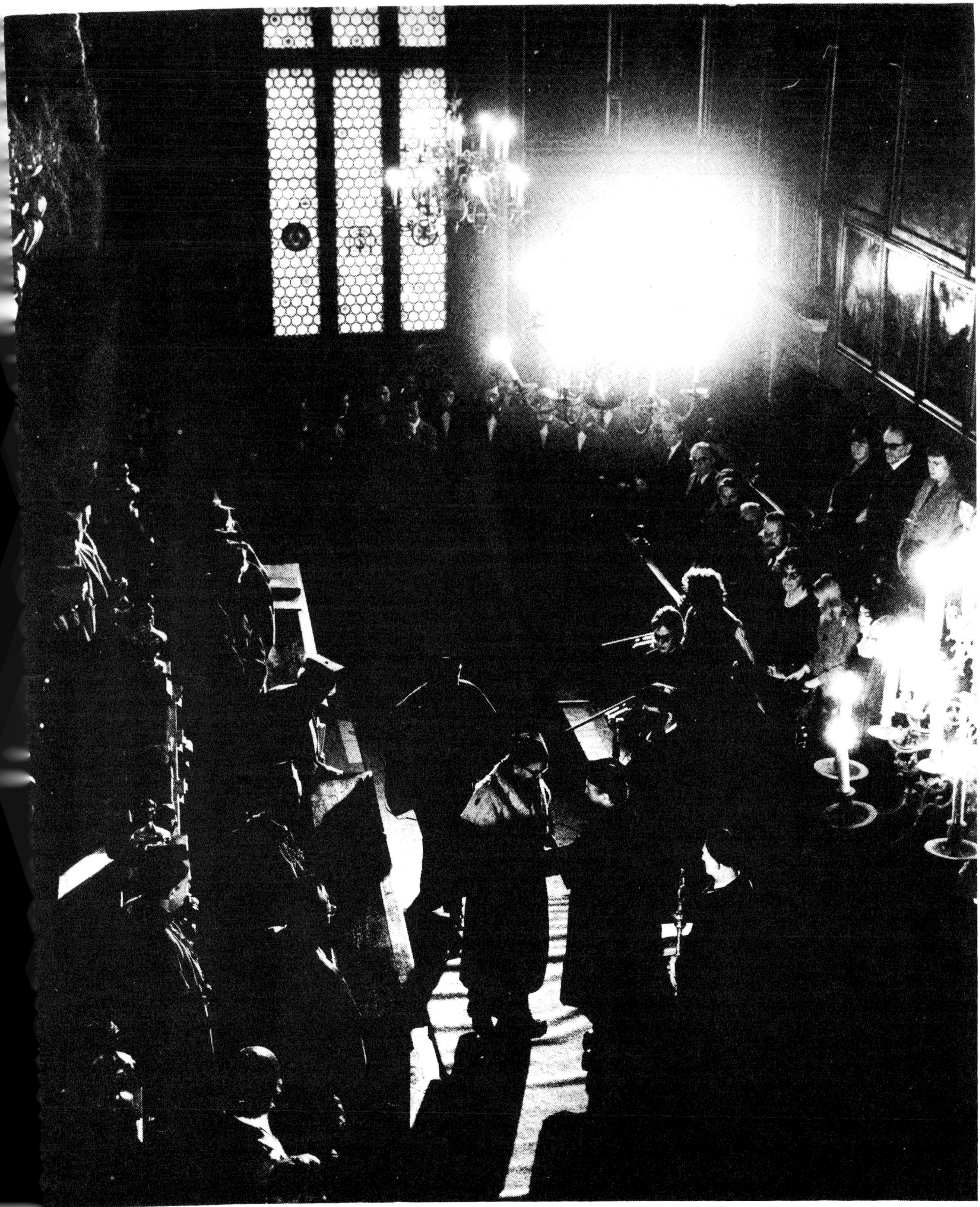

Granting Doctorate Honoris Causa of Jagiellomian University of Kraków, 1974

itinerant *objets d'art* and museums of expensiveness hung up in rows; a risk-taking, hence a fruitful patronage, providing artists with the equivalents of Sistine Chapels so that they may rise above themselves. Or: the alleged freedom of the artist shackled by the commercialism of the Western world and by his self-created bonds of ephemeral dogmas; also abstractionism as the religious art of capitalism. And most gladly: my rare position – a fully formed Pole, who ventured into the world, not driven out by history, and fell in with another country without the bitterness of an *émigré*. Hence one who looks not wholly from the inside nor wholly as an outsider. The centuries-old theme of foreign-mania and novelty-mongering – seen from both sides – deserves to be dusted off.

'But the academic robe and biretta are beginning to weigh heavily . . . And I notice restlessness in the glints of eye-glasses and in the mounting fatigue in the eyes of my English children; also the nervousness of the film-makers at the ending of their stock. Therefore, bravely and prudently, I reject rhetorical temptations, solemnly thank you for the conferment of this distinction, and revert to my point of departure, ending with a citation from José Ortega y Gasset: "Science and Culture are in concert the tools of life." '

This distinction by the University, therefore, one presumes, outside fluctuations of political tides, rests undisturbed. But all, I repeat ALL other prospects, victims of dependence on the inconstancy of official promises, evaporated.

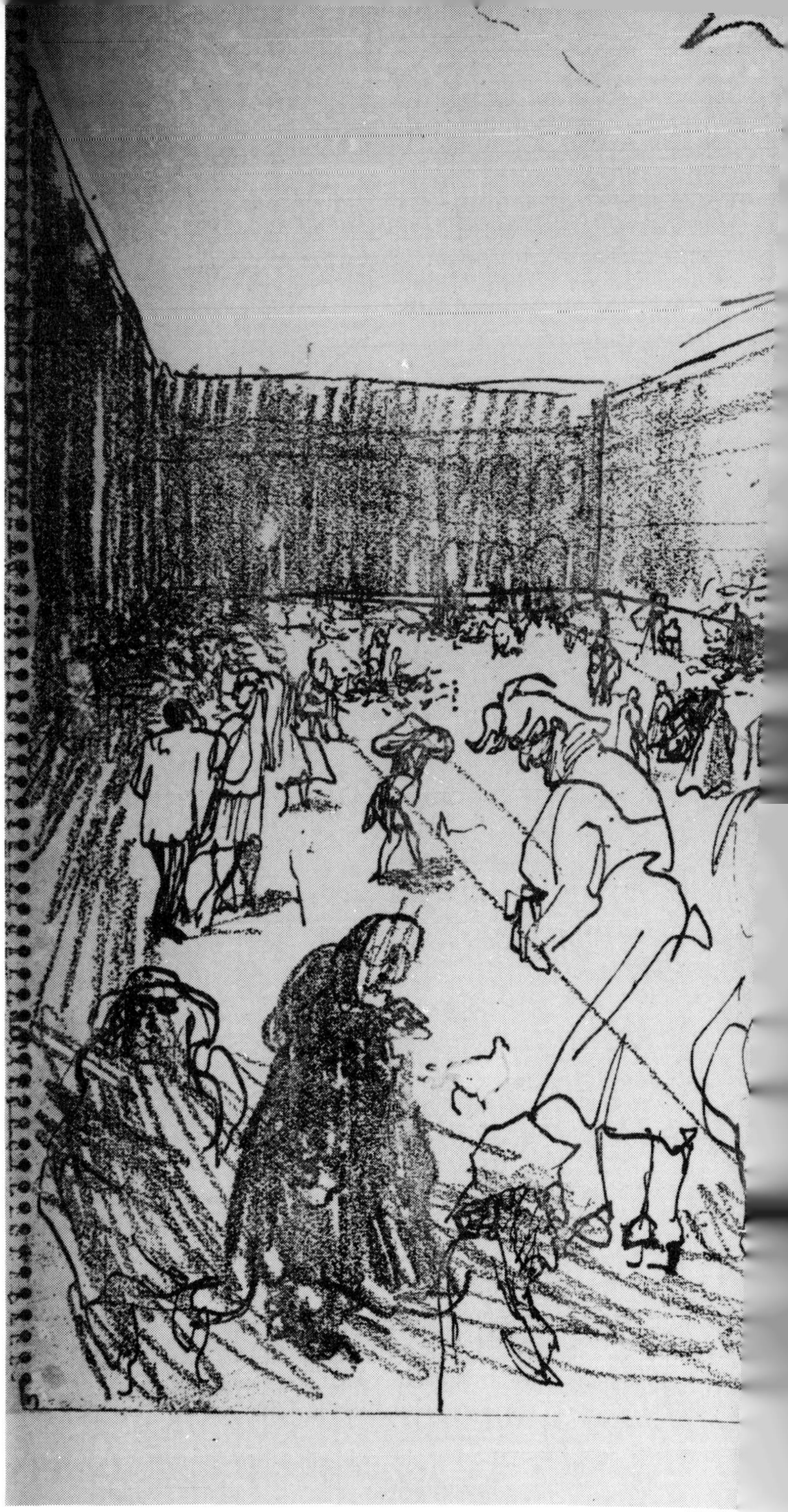

Oświęcim (Auschwitz) had to fall in at the outset of the return journey – memento which renders empty any daily pursuits. It can't be omitted – the children have to see it.

The perennial memory of the realness of Belsen in 1945, of the dead, of the dying – differentiated in victimization/torture/murder, of the murderers; and of the other *Lager*, bomb-smashed (and charred-body-filled) the night before our entry-'liberation', made this exhibit-cum-souvenir stall (yes, yes, necessary) for me an unbearable tag.

But: we went in under '**ARBEIT MACHT FREI**'; we moved through some blocks, through the tidied-up museum of slaughter. Under the slushy snow the adjoining Brzezinka (Birkenau *Lager*), less of a curator's favourite, was, in its shabby broken state, nearer the bone.

Remote Tatra-exit from Poland (an earlier journey) toughly blocked by the frontier guards, prying for irregularities, proposing to confiscate our funds – and piling up threats. But miraculously there appears a traveller of consequence aware of my *bona fides*. . .

Crossing Czechoslovakia's Eastern protrusion – **Prague** left for another time* – rushing against dusk in search of short cuts to the Hungarian border we lose ourselves in vacant back roads. Our monstrously outlandish pale open Bentley (though perhaps echoing pre-war Czech swelt Tatras) crushes through scrubs to a standstill. Locals emerge out of already dark (by then) wilderness. Helpful. They, meticulously but it seems clandestinely, prescribe our route. But, deeper in the now thickening forest, now pathless, we rouse up ourselves: they are helping us at risk to smuggle us – the supposed fugitives – across the frontier! The tussle to extricate from this laid-out secretive escape and to manoeuvre on to legality of the sleepy and distrustful outpost. . .

*Prague: that bridge-balustrade punctured by saintly clusters congealed in supreme rapture gesticulating heavenward – or about to fly. And then, in accord, the sudden rush of blackened sky, the launching in rapid succession of the lightnings of amassed thunderbolts of downpour – the grand sculptured perspectives storm-tossed into life.

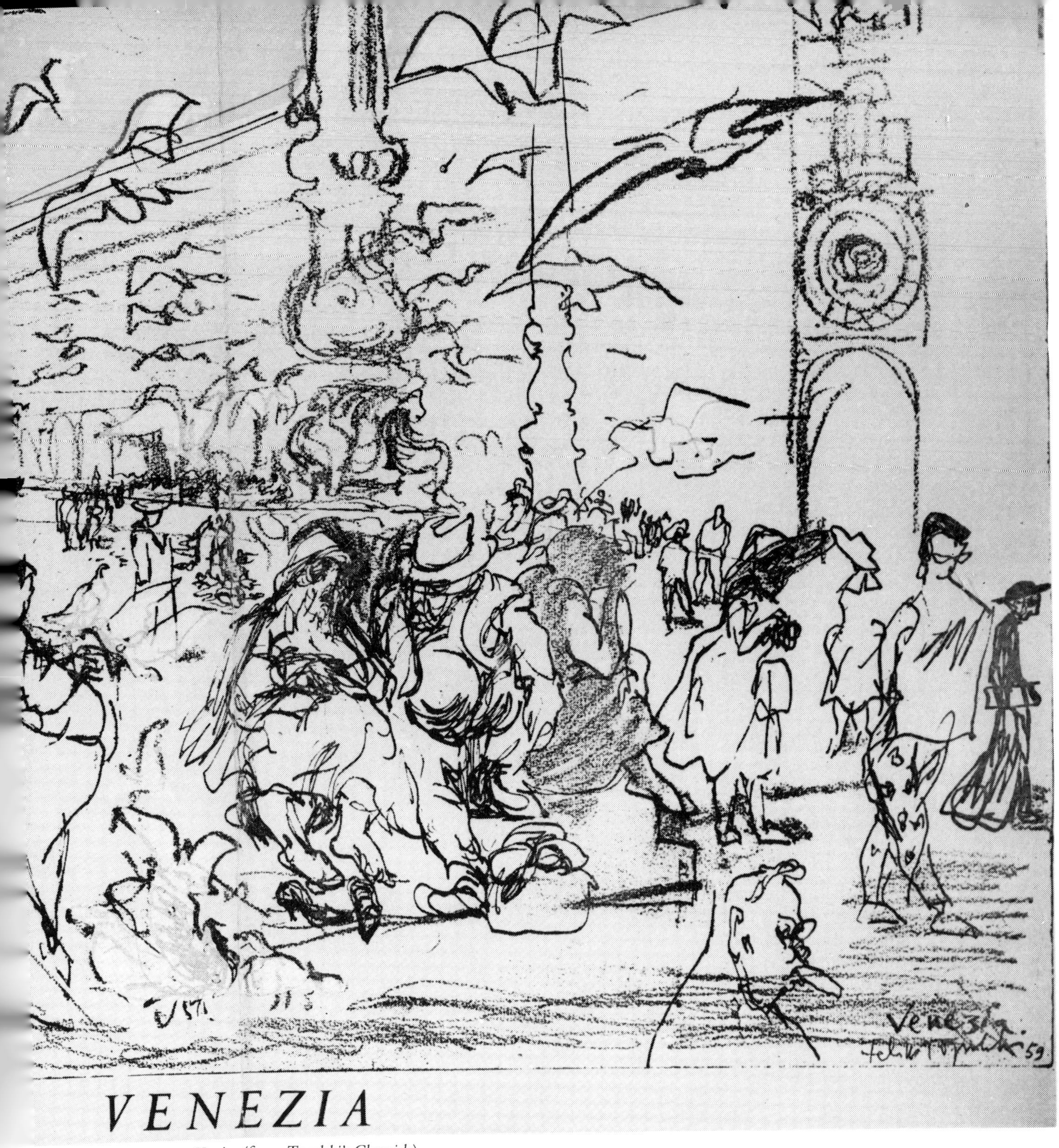

Venice (from *Topolski's Chronicle*)

Budapest, then: distressed dusty people, still posturing over mouldy not ruins, but expired flamboyance-vistas of the Habsburgian past. The mirrored, chandeliered, gilded but soiled interiors of dead Grand Hotel epoque still muster old frail dummy-waiters patch-betailed, who in pretence of uninterrupted gentility refuse a table to a black visitor.

The Balkan Cauldron. The Balkans at the time of my childhood – a cauldron of boiling discords rushings into tribal combats – the origin, apparently, of World War I. And these competitive riches of enchanting postage stamps: Bosna and Hercegovina, Makedonija, Croatja, Srbija, Dalmacija. . .

Amazing to find now one single richly landscaped country, populated by a handsome breed . . . No room to take more in this accelerated dash, after the amassment of the Slavonic joys and ordeals, to the so close and utmost untrammelled bliss of **Venezia**.

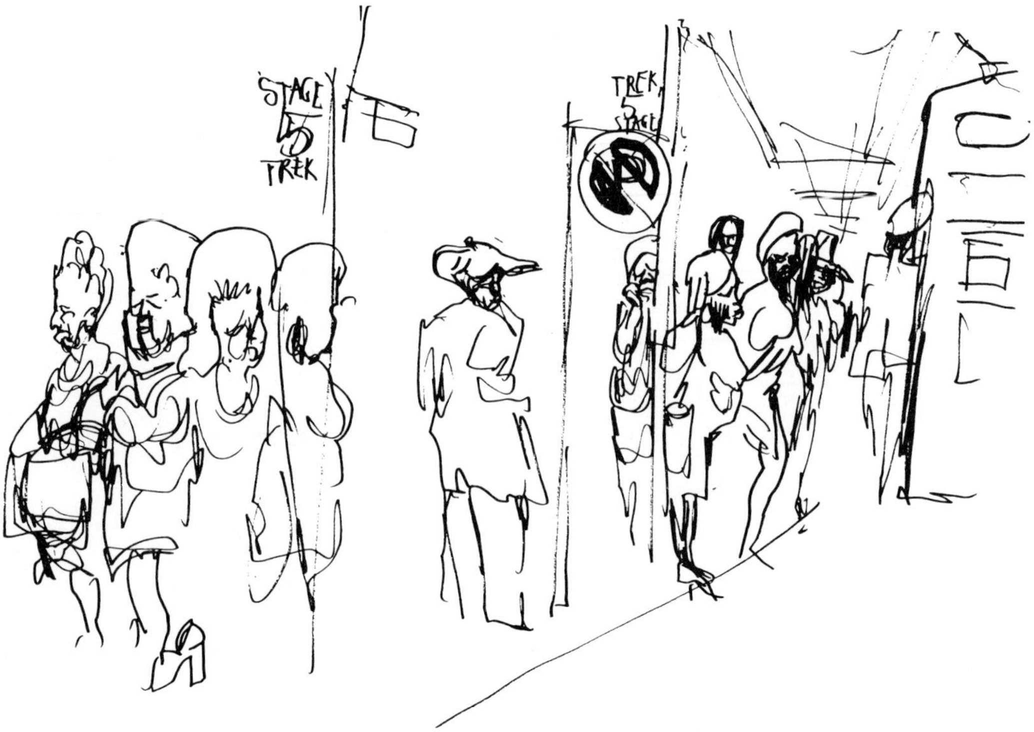

South Africa, Johannesburg apartheid bus stops

In London, pre-departure, two black actors from **South Africa** play at black humour under monstrous menace. After the show, in the adjoining pub, although I am reliably introduced, they artfully dodge my asking for contacts. And so does Fugard.

Enmity and delay at **Johannesburg** airport; a drive through apartheidal streets (the divided bus stops give the flash of heavy white housewives' prosperity and, better to look at, blacks); my white liberal hosts' foreboding intonation when listing accessible but meaningful themes for my drawing – in prominence, Soweto, the new and notorious shanty township, forbidden to the whites, yet to be stealthily penetrated. We talk, after a formal gourmet meal served by well-groomed black servants, moving to the open-plan sumptuously modern drawing room – the vegetation merging with *objets d'art*, paintings and books of highest (but *comme-il-faut*) selectivity.

The morning paper runs front-page headlines on the top event, already in progress, coming this day to its climax: 'HERE COMES THE BRIDE! The wedding of this or any other year: **Princess Dlalisile, daughter of King Sobhuza of Swaziland, marries Mr Vusi Tshabalala, son of the Soweto tycoon**.' The planning of my stay last night had not included this. And I see why. With their best anti-apartheid intentions this bestrode and confused the clean black–white good–bad cause, it blurred all sorts of edges. But my predilection for blurred borderlines was awakened – I pressed and they, good people, obliged and moved fast. A black journalist drove me (some sort of credentials manufactured instantly) into Soweto and the wedding's fantasia.

Once through the expected shanty outskirts, tidal multitudes storm massive perspectives of yellow–blue–white tenting. '**Soweto Tabernacle – All Welcome**!' and 'Princess Arrives!' Closer into the higher strata: through the jostle of uniformal yet individualized white and red togaed women, by top-hatted or war-painted magnificences, by roped off monumental groupings of even higher eminences – into the inner immensity, filled up with the highest dignities – and choraling. The many-tiered wedding cake rises whitely behind the seated Swazi Princess Dlalisile (eyes flashing) high coiffured and jewelled and tented by a white veil; cream tailored to elongated perfection, somewhat *blasé*, the Soweto tycoon's heir; the bridesmaids black and two white (blonde Paula Vilarres, brunette Jennifer Katzenellenbogen); the ladies (dashingly hatted and courtly) and gentlemen (morning coats) of the families – behind them the Swazi ministers, wild beasts' skins over bare painted torsos, heads feathered, shield- and spear-armed (costliest wrist watches visible) – all attentive to the speakers: the black Mayor of Soweto Peter Lengene, the White Mayor of Johannesburg Dr A. D. Bensusan (both in lounge suits and chains of office) and supremely elegant (button-holed morning coat and stylish whiskers) King Sobhuza of Swaziland. The privileged black and white public; the reporters and flashing cameramen; the interminability – as proper.

In the evening, properly, the ultra exclusive reception at the top hotel of Johannesburg. Shimmer of ostentation and food-champagne amassment on a scale nowadays achieved only in such places, serving an incongruously motley crush – the white upper strata, attempting style and superiority, and their younger and modern-liberal bearded and dowdy counterparts losing to flamboyant eccentricities (both female and male) of black bareness serving as the dashing base to tribal conceits of

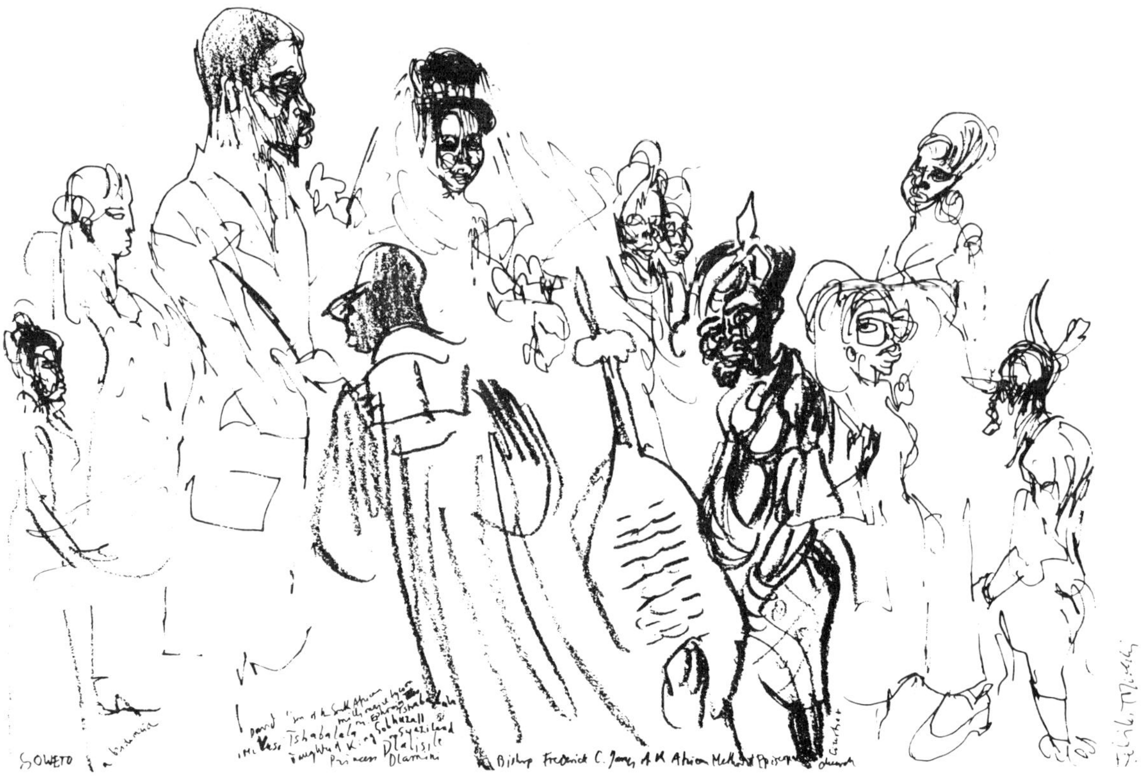

Soweto, wedding of Mr Virsi Tshabalala and Princess Dlalisile

drapes, jewels, feathers. **Apartheid's suspension** has its price – affordable by the rich and the ruling.

The lobby below: the regular apartheidal guests sunken into armchairs – only their disapproving grimaces raised while diagonally from above descend, static on escalators, postured and silhouetted, the frieze of *Incroyables* of the Third World.

The apartheid got blurred when, emboldened after a few authorized visits to the township, we chanced being driven by a white painter friend to **Sydney Kumalo, an acclaimed black sculptor,** who, though respected widely and made rich (because there contemporary art is in generous demand), has to obey the law and live in Soweto. Stretches of oppressed shanty shacks lead to a high white-walled compound. Kumalo opens the door, friendly although we are not preannounced – and although yesterday hoodlums broke in and beat him up; there are stitches across his face.

Bulky, shaven-headed, youngish, he stands calm within his – truly – palace. The white architect acclaimed as best (and they are here daringly advanced and unhampered by the saving syndrome)* designed this uncompromising blend of modernity and Kumalo's sculptural soft-weaving sandstone that spreads in mounting and *en suite* variations – a whimsy of opulence, filled nonchalantly with treasurable objects and his impressive works.

The hoodlums would naturally be local; 'clone' manufactured, Soweto grows/rots into as organic a city as any other.

Some venturings into Soweto are formalized: 'Wes-Randse Bantoesake Administrasieraad/West Rand Bantu Affairs Administration Board Permit. F. Tepolski [*sic*] representing African Self Help visiting Day Nurseries.' Flat Soweto steams – **a mad coquette** blocks the road (hair plaited in with coloured threads, wrists and ankles adorned likewise) barefoot, bare-breasted – her rags elegantly tatty.

In the slummiest depth an up-to-date and thus sad **Roman Catholic chapel:** neat Sunday school boys round a fastidious vicar (very dark glasses) who says, 'The Pope, when Archbishop of Milan, inaugurated and blessed it all.' Not far, hoardings: 'Born to Wonder'; and another, 'Jesus Saves'; and 'Oh Man life is great'; and 'Pushkin Vodka'.

The old retireds, Mr and Mrs Kgerochdira, at 1722 Dube, Soweto. As anywhere else from Newcastle-on-Tyne to Turin to Salzburg to Seattle to Chile, the worldwide standard interior of proletarian well-off culture. Television and radio central to souvenir bric-à-brac: plastic, crochet, lace, decorated vases filled with feathers/leaves; life-well-spent expressions on their faces (he was a chauffeur), reclining in hospitable serenity towards a calling neighbour, younger and rather forward in her worldly manner, smart-trouser-suited in 'electric' blue, a pink beret stylishly cascading.

Close by, a school filled with uniformed girls; and an open-air bar (but fenced for security) with rumbustious insubordinate drinkers. Well, a city.

An old scribble of mine emerges quoting from *Realism* by Guicciardini (the name, the title don't give me any clue as to what this was) in Latin, '*Foris ut moris, intus ut Libet*'; below,

*Yet an old Polish architect friend who emigrated to South Africa cannot go on – the everyday falsity of living on the backs of the enslaved, however liberally, defeated him. Soon he left for the West, as did many others I met there.

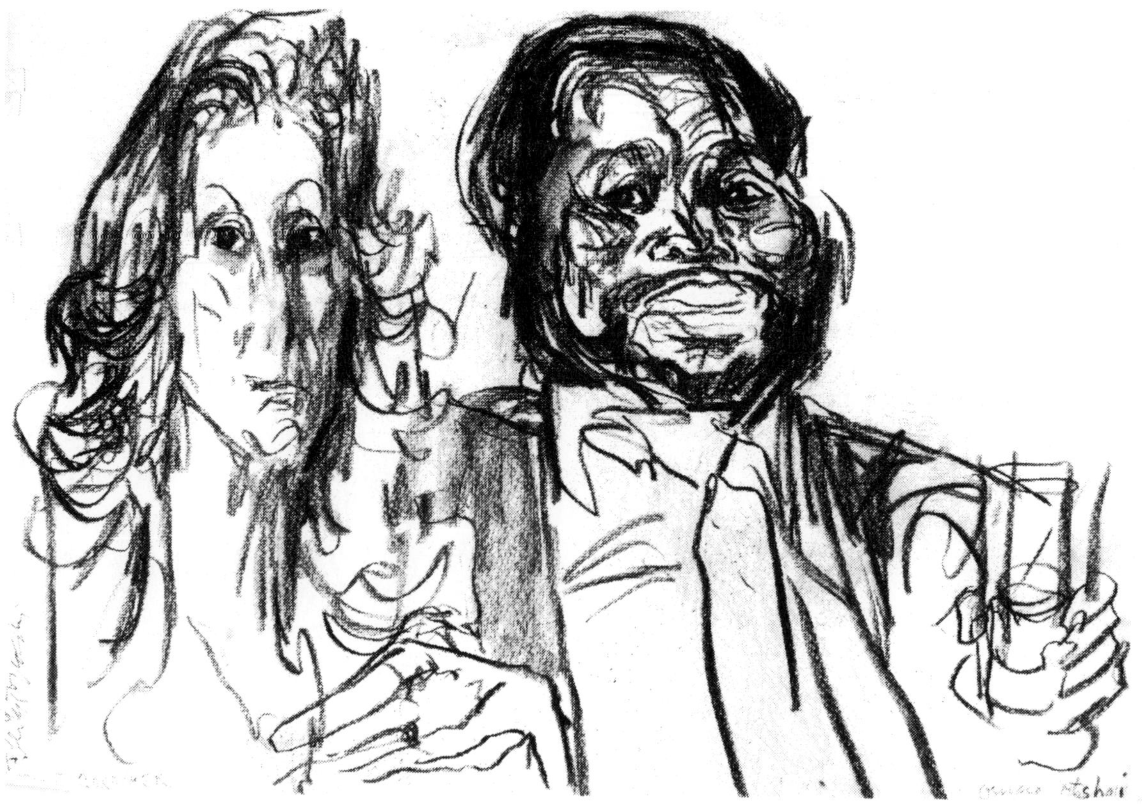

Nadine Gordimer and Oswald Mtashai

an interpretation: 'Speak with the many, think with the few.' Thus this is a perfect recipe for survival under oppression (I touched before on this theme with the Persian word *Ketman*, written about by Miłosz), but equally serviceable in the complex/stressful existences of border-worlds, such as the whites' South Africa, which divide, strip, reveal, bare – but not to full disclosures. Tensing for danger, for decision in speech or action to be brave, false or non-committed; apparent, or not. The daily intercourse strains, challenges, may be deadly – yet within the convention of 'normality'. But all this against the background of the rulers' constant façade of superior assurance . . . Already on the plane to South Africa I had seen the accumulation of those emphatic faces of power-arrogance.

Dutch Reformed Church, Sunday, 3 February 1974, service for the opening of Parliament – here they all are: thin-lipped men, white-hatted women, condemned, in their supremacy, to await the worm's turn. They disgorge from their 1982 *Kerk* framed by the black-hatted-coated white pastor to the right, a nonchalantly watchful black in light working clothes to the left.

A few corners away, paradoxically, **the Congregational Mission Church (1902);** iron-barriered outside steps carry dressed-to-the-nines black women and their daughters, also in white hats – but larger.

Johannesburg Cathedral: organ music and the processionals, with a black boy cross-carrying, loosen tear glands: human unity, in spite of the lurkings of antinomy present there, under the Church Establishment's protection. Outside, up the Cathedral's stairs steps Pride: corset-straight middle age hidden by sunglasses, false yellow curls, propped breasts – short dress awind over her valuables – the unblemished legs that gave her status. Down below a black legless beggar.

Playing to the full this divisive world: **the Jewish golf club** – slavish copy in manners and clothing of British-American styles; **the Britons** – their Club conducted matchlessly along the line stretching from London's Pall Mall and St James's to Tierra del Fuego (now dying), Bombay (now dead), Australia, Canada – and American imitations. Here the 'coloured' wine waiter, or is he the *maître d'hôtel*?, handsomely done up in white, with blue collar and cuffs and a dark sash, conducts black 'boys' in white pants down to half-calves round the tables; the unedifying ritual mused over from the walls by handsome representatives of the animal world.

I have little to say about Mrs Suzmann, a leading and brave Liberal MP – who refused on the phone to remember that she had once sat with me on a plane in friendly animation, and refused, on the phone, to see me or to help to get an entry to the Parliament – and, sadly, not much about my visting gentle, friendly, impressive **Nadine Gordimer**.

I let myself, as ever, be dominated by my duty to draw – yet Nadine's face's fleeting moods, contained in narrowness of beauty, kept escaping me: I fidgeted over some four drawings, one of two heads, another including a black poet, Oswald Mtashai, also present (were they challenging the law of the country?), missing – with my drawings failing – a good conversation round me. Pressure of her impressiveness making me tumble into self-consciousness? Or perhaps, her own evasive self-consciousness? Or (a fancy perhaps in justification of my bad drawing) South African pressures provoke subconscious attempts at the dismantling of passport features/definitions? My imaginings apart, she is the finest person of no apparent fear. . .

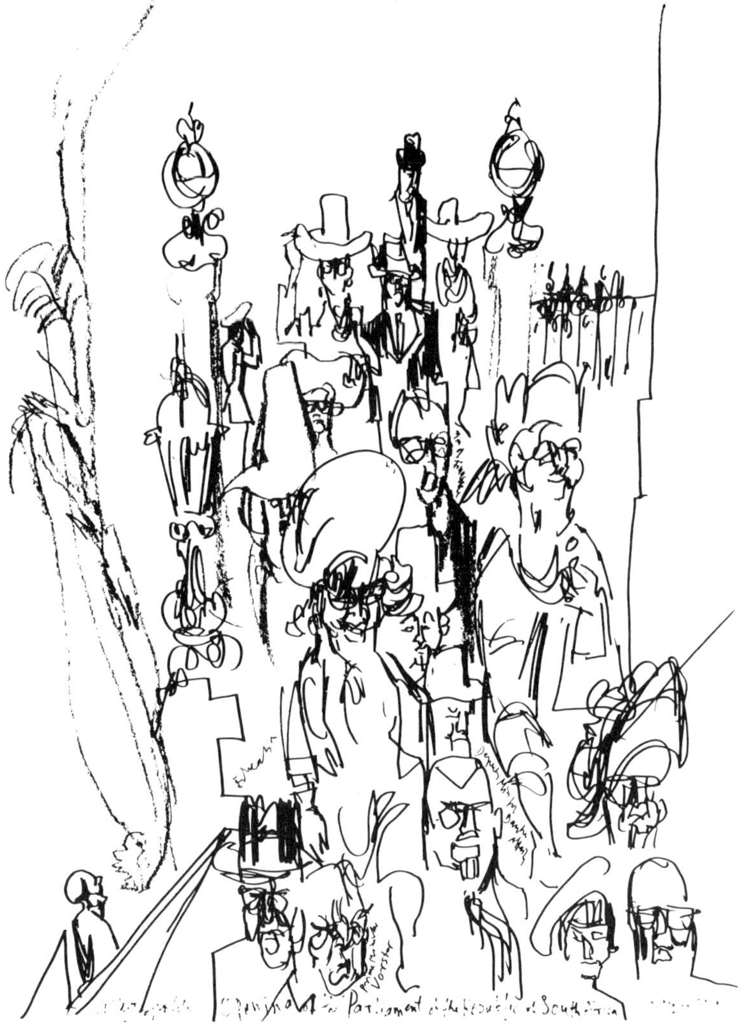

Cape Town. Opening of Parliament

Cape Town was different. The masters, liveried-chauffeur-driven, edged each evening in patriotic formality round the stunning views of the Bay topped by Table Mountain and Devil's Peak to their mini-lives, leaving the town centre to anarchy and fear.

Racially entangled **District 6**, while being condemned and eliminated, exuded the most inflammable tension over crashing bricks and plaster, telephone wires collapsed – the ruins, thus its inhabitants, in transit: not subdued but, brought to backs-to-the-wall vexation, flashing-eyed, beggarly swagger-fantasy dressed, unpredictable – these fully battling (though in retreat) but stumbling over life's finity (hunger, age) – the dying and the dead; all against the background glare of vast waters filled with hope-selling (not for them) shipping.

The opening of the Parliament of the Republic of South Africa: below the sweep of the ceremonial staircase a few black labourers' heads just protrude, a token presence of the originators of human habitation on this spot. Up the stairs will climb the top-hatted ribbon-crossed figurehead and his *équipe*. Before then, the ruling élite descends side stairs in tight formation to fill up the House – and I, placed below at the entrance, receive/absorb the stream of faces, a telling symposium. The Afrikaner features grow massive with age in both women and men, and this travesty is garnished into ostentation by spectacles, ambitious hats, *frisé* locks and whiskers, *maquillage*, jewellery. They vary, of course, but being the most powerful selection with their spouses and invitees, uniformity dominates.

I am helpfully informed: the Deputy Minister for Bantu Affairs grins toothlessly; Education – black-hatted blankness; Finance – the smoothest baldy; Mrs de Toit – senator – the more-than-standard diamond-strewn protrusion. I am led forward to intercept and draw **Mr John Vorster, the Prime Minister** – black hat white-silk-lined in hand (a little feather peeps from above the ribbon), a sort of jewelled miniature coat-of-arms pinned on his tie, heavy Dutch face (palest irises, thin mouth screwed to the left, white side whiskers); to draw J. H. Abraham, Commissioner-General of the Transkei – not fitting into the prototype – huge glasses camouflage shrewdness, nose bulges over fixed, open-mouthed joyfulness, the stiff collar runs amok, bound by hugely zigzagged tie over unruly chest; they close on me, and there is one more to scribble, Dr Hilgard Muller, Minister of Foreign Affairs, who springs away completely from the serial bulkiness into the internationally neat, pipe-grinding diplomat-module for political export.*

Not far, a main square and, seated, J. C. Smuts, 1870–1950; another face, another time.

Cape Town's Maynardville Theatre shows Welcome Msomi's *Umabatha* by **the Zulu Theatre Company**. There is a plot, standard international costumes – bogus Westernizations – but it all thuds to life's fury with the Zulu's war dances. The friendly wing of the master race, the audience, responds from below with relaxed confident calm to this rush at them of threatening clamour, of brandishing spears, of fearsome paint: the elderly couples, the school-blazered neat girls – perfectly safe behind the convention-boundary of the stage. During the interval I witness, in the dressing rooms, an advanced stage of **confrontation**: the towering black hero-performer stands erect, his grand tribal regalia merely in the service of his blindingly glistening nakedness, his feathered head touching the ceiling; and, seated demurely, facing him, the 'civilized' and of best intentions, white, rather old-spinsterly patroness of the theatre. Her mien can't help but contain a *soupçon* of condescension, disarmingly excusable – because (one cannot hold back the thought, of pressing obviousness, of the defensive device necessitated by her inner disquiet) of the essential incompatability-clash confusion between unresolved/suppressed superiorities within this non-apartheid interlude.

Rise-flight askew over lofty nature to **East London.** Onwards by car: **King William's Township** and the landscape laid out for peasantry – their women in tall turbaned ease, babes peeping from the drapes, extravagant facial make-ups of unrestrained joy, long pipes, necklaces,

*But on the cricket terraces, when turning round and looking up from my lower seat, the range of the developing stages of the Afrikaner face, before 'dignity' struck it, was completed. Boys of ten are large and fat, their elder brothers and fathers – fat and large; but beside them their cousin-neighbours grow into giant brutality, side-whiskered, beringed, sun-glassed – power is there.

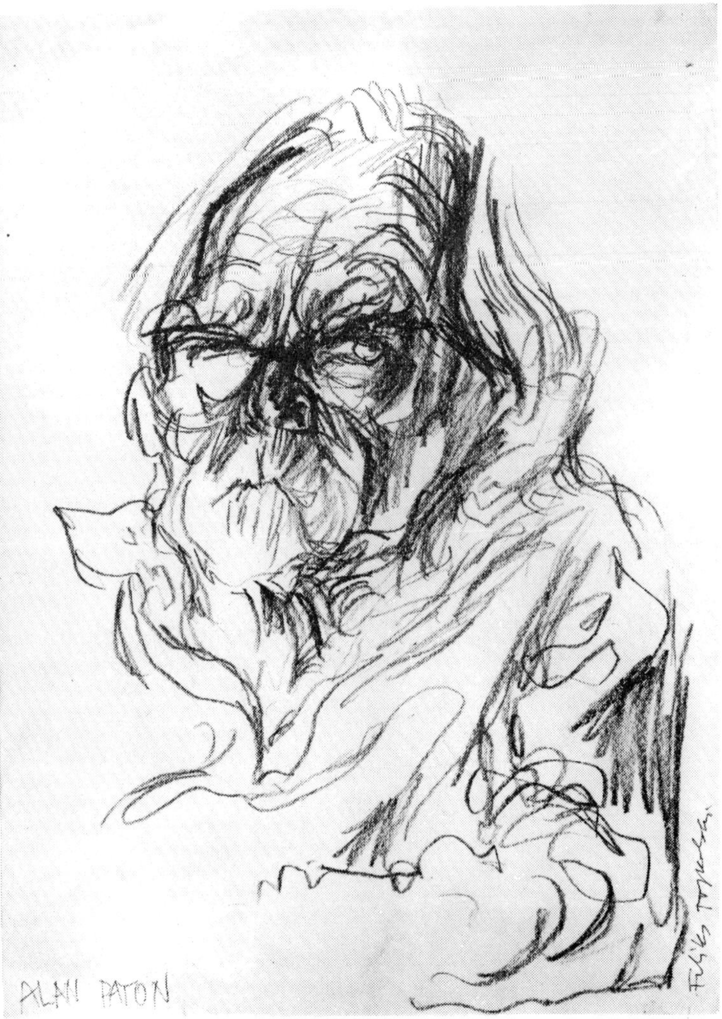

Alan Paton

ear-rings, bangles, teeth.

A web of secrecy – by the way of the Priory of Our Lady mission, an intense girl in sari and a black Reverend – gets us into **Welcomewood**, a notoriously despicable enforced **Resettlement Camp** near Dimbaza. Our guides are brave, and so are we, since there is no admission of whites – punishments severe. The grimness of tiny family-shacks crowded in a barbed-wired terrain of a hopelessness reduced by now for media-blunted Western sensitivities into melodrama-stereotypes, but REAL here, of defeat, want, trap. Drawing one must try, though, for once – to be convincing – this should really be a photographer's documentation job. But, in a flash, police in a jeep, **the crime of drawing** into a haversack – and our priest-guide in a haggle with the two, luckily black and rather rustic, policemen. Either he creates a satisfactory version (missionaries?), or, simply, they prefer to shirk the entanglement of the arrest. The drawing, although not advanced enough, will be reproduced in the States and England.

Nature widens, deepens – descending clouds shed distant showers, chase shadows; indeed, immeasurable landscapes with figures. It is **Transkei** now. Stilled vultures float over craggy bridge-clasped valleys, minuscule swarms of circular kraals pass by – and this everlasting rusticity emanates, of a sudden, five dreary townees (ties, hats) lined up at a STOP sign, surely for transport – to 'jobs'. The highway thus claims attention – and gains it to the full further, with a policeman gesturing over a freshly wrecked machine. And further bus-stops, and Bata, heading for Umtata, beggars claiming to be clowns on all fours at the feet of a black-shawled trek of women, moving into the distance in harmony with the kraals shed by a bounteous hand (same sizes as the resettlement huts – better, or dignified by their time-honoured rusticity?); and again the land recedes-speeds into hilly shoals shadows-stained, rises into the highest extra-azures. An abrupt closeness: a blanketed shape skids down a steepness at us, throws off the drapes, and *voilà*, the lean dust-powdered erect nudity stamping/swaying in his version of rock'n' roll. We had entered the tourist-land. And so Umtata gives municipal 'architecture' as background to a leaning-on-a-stick dandy of inimitable style: multi-layered hat on one ear, a long flaring-out tailored flamboyance over the pantaloons wide rainbow-striped, spreading bare toes protruding.

Tsolo-Maclear. The backcloth turns grey, skies descending, vultures amassing; from flat-topped mountain's misty steamy spaces emerge horsemen under umbrellas. Then, in the deserted stretch, there materializes a she-marvel, the wandering pilgrim or apostle or prophetess – a **holy beggar.** She may be all this – her timeless presence, manner and dress has the assured authority of enduring illumination. First, we see on the horizon her (and her acolyte boy's) backs; we overtake them, stop, reverse to drive at them full face – and turn again to follow and overtake (while they stroll in constancy of direction): their monumental progress, and our pathetic enslavement to our metal-capsule's unfeeling speed-supremacy and sealed-off non-communication.

She progresses carried by dust-sweeping blue-white robes; her supports – a large two-branched cross and the boy; layers of accessories, badges, offerings – the testimony and the tale of years on the road; her head-dress – white, stiffened high, floating/blowing down her back, topped by a half bird half crescent, marked in front heavily with red criss-crossed symbol. All of it draped iconlike, around her blackest old physiognomy of rapture and spellbound surrender. Hers the truest rite of passage.

Now, not long to wait for the elemental emphasis: the verticals (Mount Freie?) take over, rains storm downwards in swathes on Basutoland's (or is it Griekwalandoos's?) Keneja River which responds in ominous brown turmoil lifted-crawling at speed – a giant endless caterpillar – up and high over our cracked-open road. We have to turn back, short of petrol and daylight for this unplanned detour.

But, after the dramatic night-blunderings and a short sleep on a samaritan pub's table, sea-shore Bizana (blue mountains afar. Nearer, round kraals and frivolous trees, nearest, 'MOTOR REPAIRS') and change of country attire and mood into marketplace jollities: a female, round, round-hatted, colour-dripping, offerer of fruit – the opposite of the abstemious saintliness on the mountain road. Jollity prances through Natal – a boy: bright turban, enormous ear-rings, orange garment horizontally striped across chest and sleeves, long staff, accumulation of belts, puffed up blue pants tied with ribbons under the knees; a girl: hair in many-coloured plait-

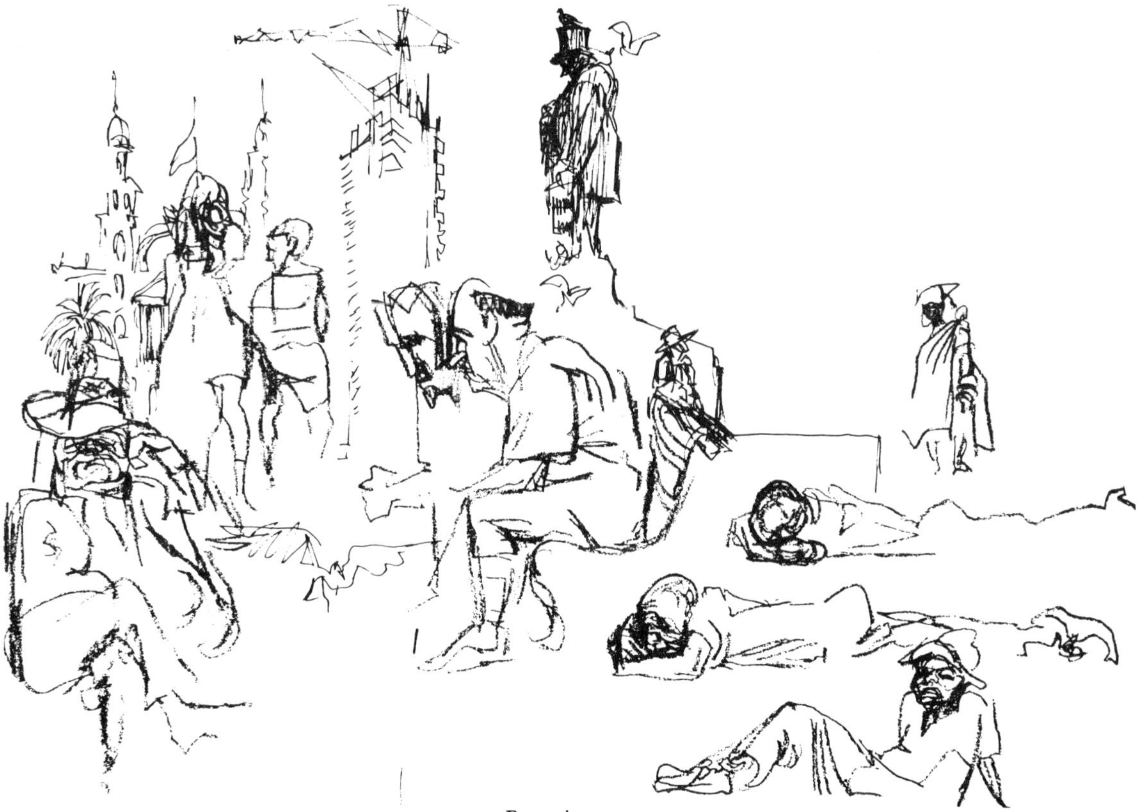

Pretoria

strips, surmounted by a pancake forehead-overhanging piece, wrappings round calves and forearms, indecipherable folds and sashes clasping a suspended baby, and an umbrella in hand. It reaches tourist-brochure antics of 'rickshaw' men on **Durban's Marine Parade.**

Alan Paton, fiery, alert, my contemporary (he had looked me up in *Who's Who* to be ready for my visit) – emanating inquisitive and volatile energy, undiminished, I suppose as with me, because forgetful of his surface deterioration. Lucky, though, in his ancient face having taken on the life-lasting features of an eagle ever after the same prey.

A key **Progressive Party** meeting: Alan Magid for the Provincial Durban Council; Ray Swart for Parliament; Lawrence Gander – the supremo; and many other dedicated stern faces, wide-eyed girls interpolated. Even this 'whites only', while outside the blacks, plentiful and pressing. They are not a uniformly down-trodden mass; the abundant diversities loaded with vigour, resilience, set off by the Afrikaner solemnity (even by Britons, even by Jews), are not only **indestructible** but **advancing**: their suppression is an act of retreat.

Stadsraed van Pretoria prohibits 'shortcuts across lawn' in the main square and the blacks are not allowed to sit on the benches. But they spread (richly miscellaneous) over the grass, lazily watch the formal British-costumed (ribboned straw-hats) schoolgirls and elder bare-legged blondes rounding the nicely put-together centre-point: bearded armed frontiersmen crouching below a rock upon which stands, much larger in scale, a homely benevolently peaceful whiskered fatty, extra-tall top hat, frock-coat, wide high-office sash, stick in one hand, roll of papers in the other, wide crinkly trousers – a play-focus for pigeons, one always posted on his hat's top.

Pretoria is the capital city, so I enter a poshness of bannered, colonnaded, old-gun-sprinkled, garden-befurred, demi-nude-statued, governmental architecture maziness and finally the Palace of Justice – to meet a legal celebrity, Graham Greene-recommended, a noble-faced man of reasonableness and optimism. How can it be? How does he fit in?

On the way out, I slide into the lavatory and tiptoe round the tall back – black suit, black hat, black umbrella stuck under an arm – of an old peeing judge (echo of Nuremberg lawyers).

Both men seem incongruous in present-day South Africa – rooted perpetuators of old ways?

Yet the bizarreness of South Africa continues for the time being. The airport fences the heavy-calved-bellied-chinned spectacled bush-bloused from the equally comfortable coloured: saris accompanied by small bulgy men, their self-importance accented by an array of formal black: whiskers, city hats, overcoats and umbrellas.

Stop in **Nairobi**. Uhuru Highway, Kenyatta Avenue, Kenya Export Promotion Council, Standard Bank, Motor Racing – the reverse (the rule of the black) also functions.

Addis Ababa, an earlier mixture of exotic monarchy (at that time): villaginess and encroaching hotel-civilization. Along the latter's strained communication lines my bag (all drawings of South Africa in it) disappeared.

The hotel has absorbed cosy-palatial pavilions, until quite recently within the Emperor's compound – so, under my window, amongst **trim Imperial gardens,** the stylishly helmeted military on guard (green trimmings, black trousers, white gaiters) do their in-step duty blown over by green–yellow–red flags – the vultures stationed above seem a décor-feature, not a premonition of things to come very soon. Because the wide straight avenue, named for some of its length 'Winston Churchill', parades – to a tourist's eye – benevolence. The black-tinted beauty of the Ethiopian features and bodily poise carries the white homespun drapes with endless inventiveness, clearly not affected, but of individualized harmony within parochialism. The pedestrian flow includes cows, goats, turbaned Arabs, white double nuns, chic policemen, bicycle racers. The bazaar-web transacts vociferously.

No overall tensions, but, moving deeper, natural diversities; sequences of unconnected tonalities. I must not stray from my abhorrence of academic-critical smugness in chopping living evidence into classified systems, affording prominence not to the remarkable but to the phenomena which slot into continuity patterns. With the knowledge now of the soon-to-come upheaval, I must not fall for stalking out early 'trends'. I can, at the best, list the encountered, not sought-out, contradictions.

So, for instance, a visit to Haile Selassie Hospital, Room 110: **Prince Merit Byena** – an astonishing sight. A noble commanding coal-black head encrusted with a white plaster cage, raised on the cushions, sharply alert and discursive. Around, courtly ladies and hand-kissing 'clients' – the constant procession of obeisances, uninterrupted for us. We occupy in this small space/ward a different dimension, his voice and language (and tremendous eyes – the head rigidly boxed in) passing smoothly in and out from one to another. The miserably trivial caption for this scene is: he slipped on his residence's marble staircase and damaged the top of his spine. Not much later, I will visit him at an English nursing home – a horizontal escapee from his country in revolt.

Another fossilized era: a gentle English colonial house (a chimney-shelf of honoured photographs), autochthonous confidantes and domestics of enchanting, white-draped picturesqueness encircling a majestic **Mrs Stamford**, the respected widow-relic of British Imperial generosity.

A rural monastery. A timeless group under the trees: in their white drapes, they lean forward on long staffs, attentive to seated older-and-priestly readers of scripts (larger volumes on

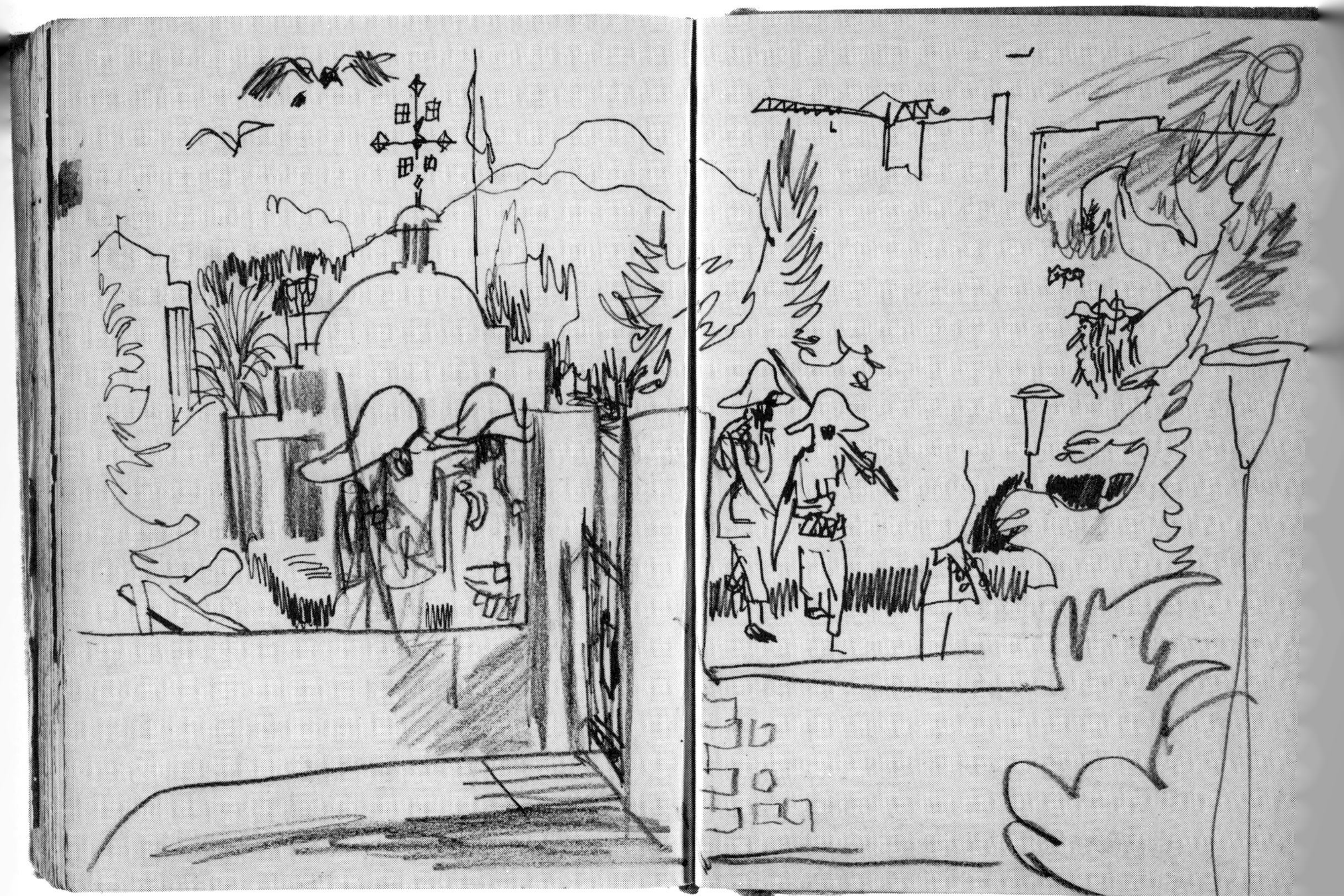

Ethiopia. Addis Ababa, Imperial gardens

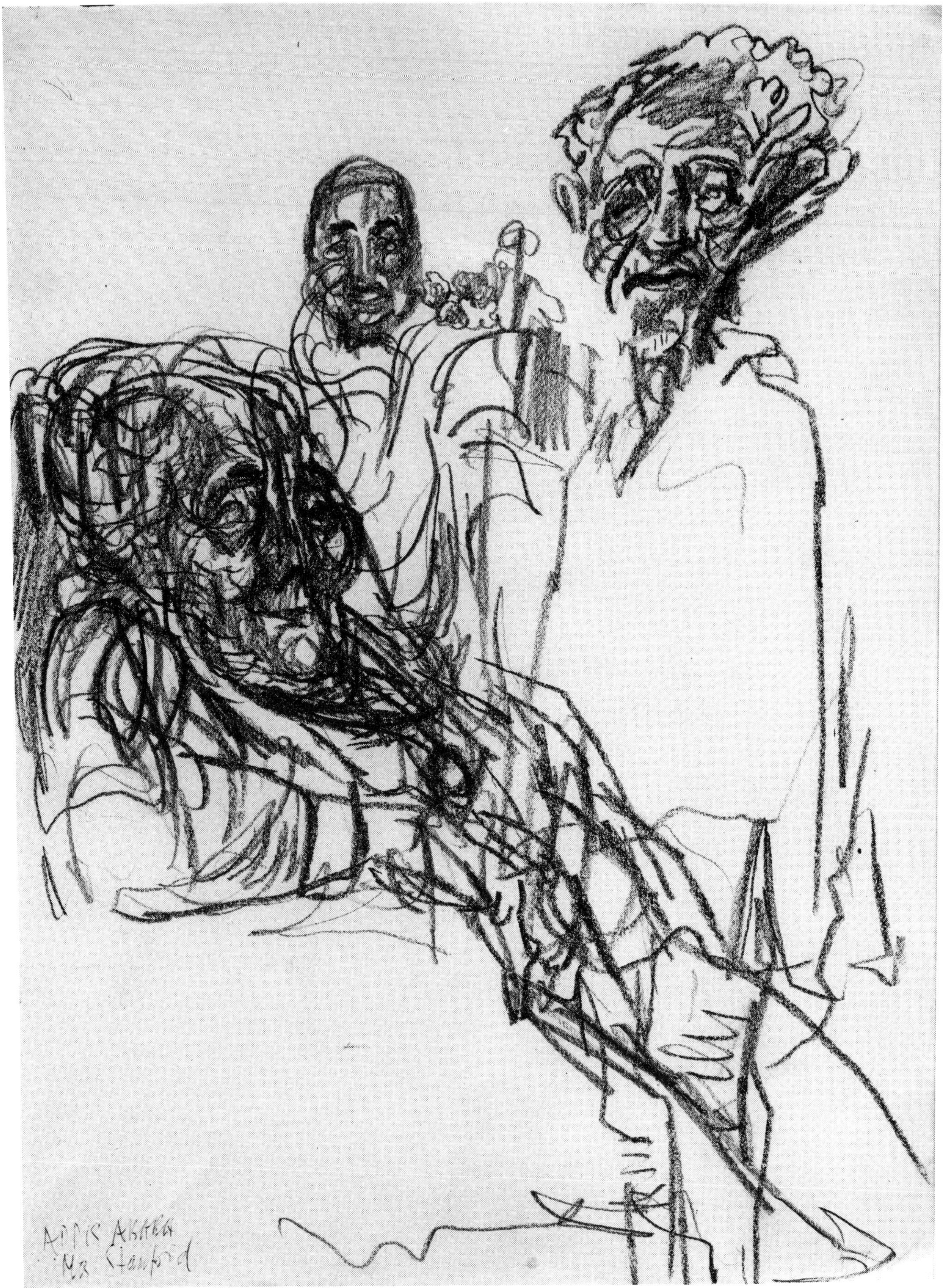

Mrs Stamford

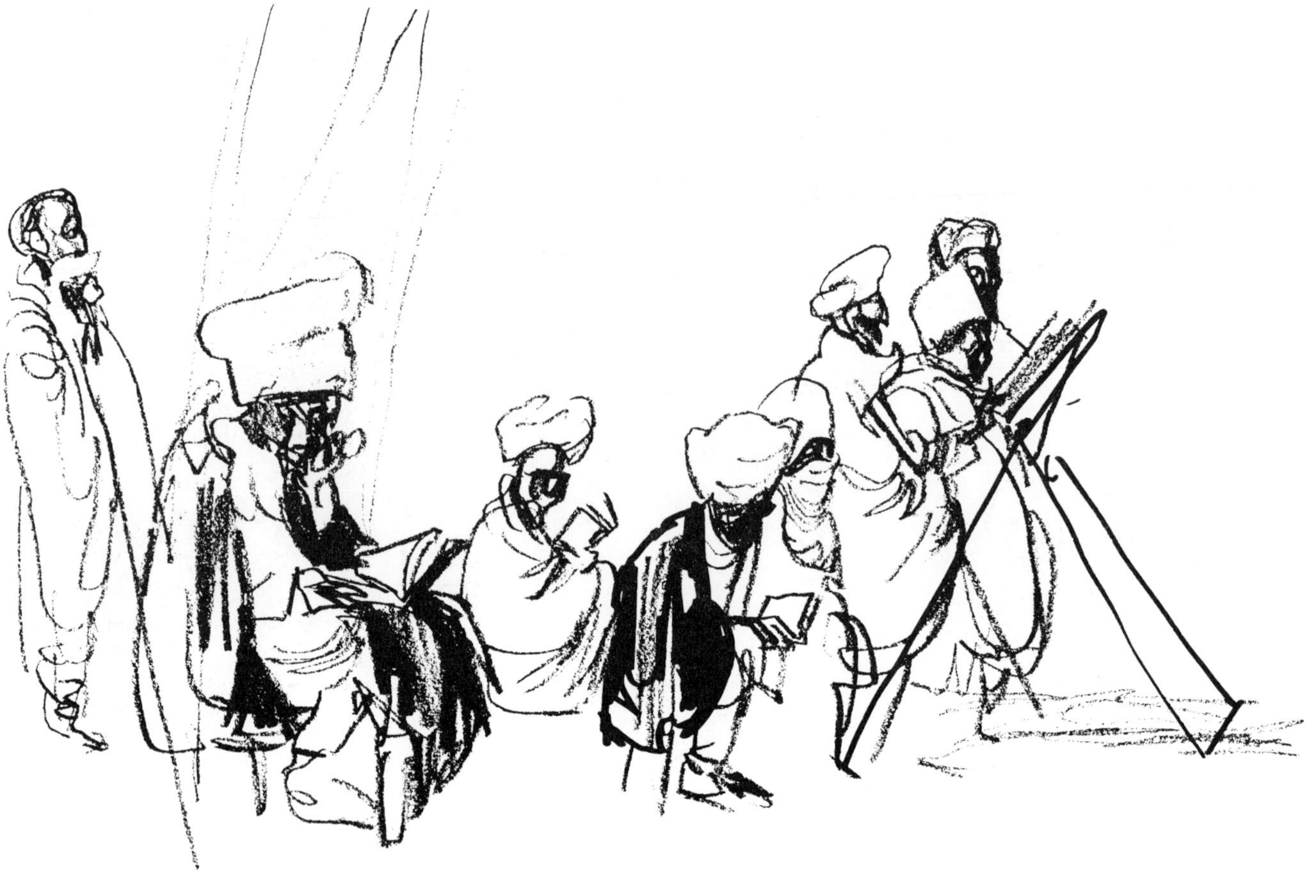

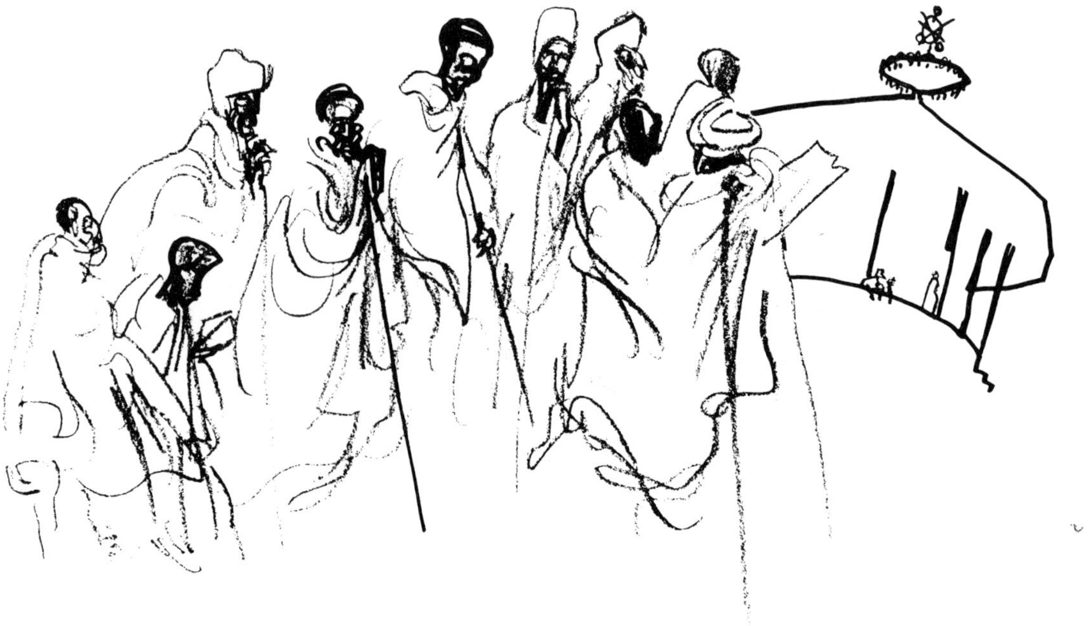

A rural monastery

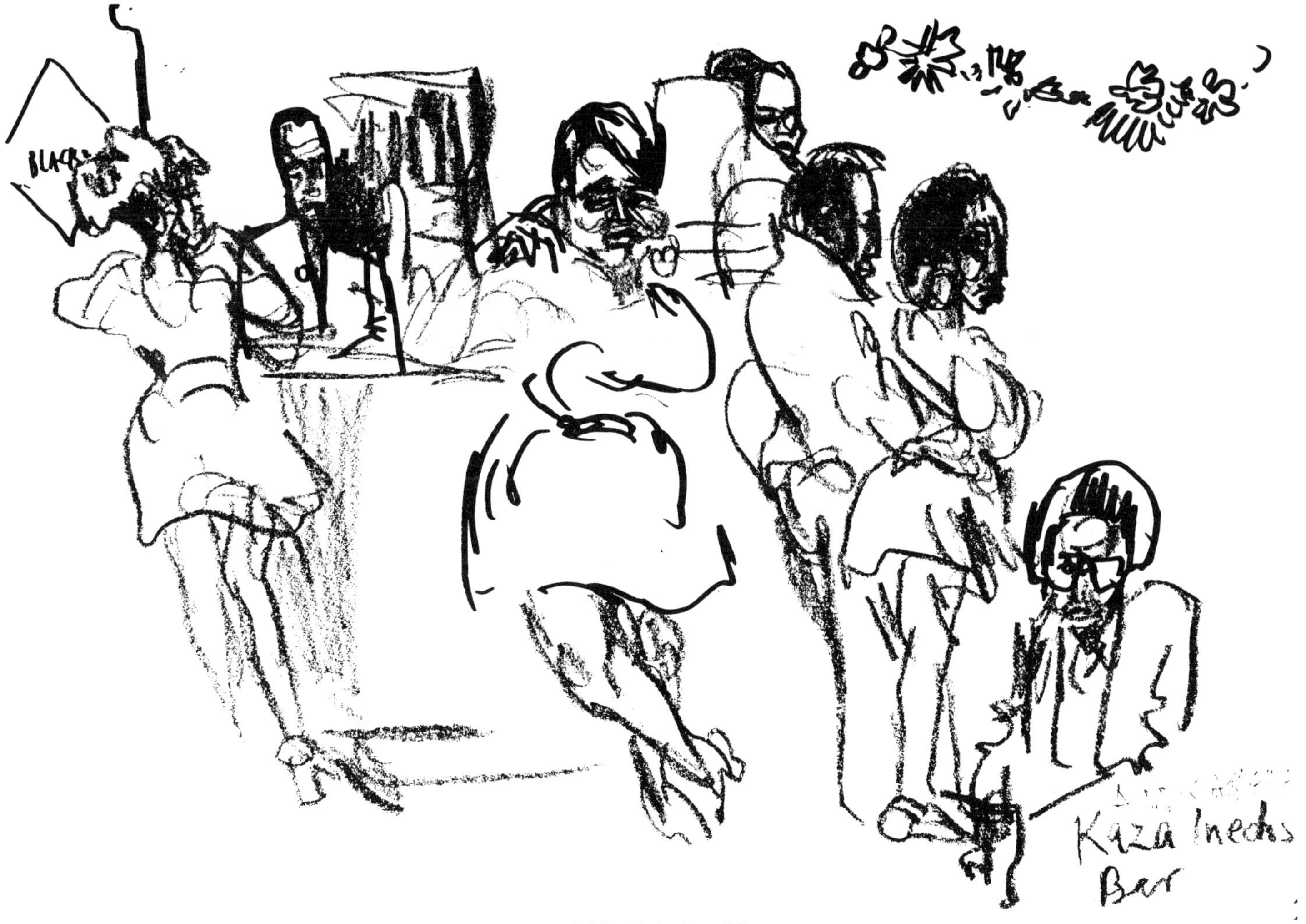

Addis Ababa Low life

easels) – these in black and white; there are lambs close by, a round rustic temple, a timber bell tower. Then a modest Service: a personage, embroidered cape over his shoulders, performs with a chubby cross in the left hand, an incense censer in the right; two small boys facing him: one squatted with a monster drum, the other caped too, with an intricate sculpture-crucifix; enclosing them, turbaned figures with ritualistic rattles. The overall calm of it all must have been passed on from the beginning of their cult.

The deepest roots: in the capital itself, a huge sonorous interior: their liturgy in which ancient crowns, robes, colours, faces, sounds emerge from the murky temple's labyrinthine interiors, the hither-and-thither **hieratic procedures**, undrilled and chaotic, yet converging – the histrionic beggars completing the cautionary imagery of earliest legendary Christianity: the elevated and the outcast. But young tramps on the outskirts of holiness detach themselves and threaten me. The scene has seeds of violence.

What's left out? The bourgeoisie and their decorous outings. The restaurants gave pleasure in contrast with the hotel's misery and costly standard: the carpeted low sitting, those stylish people, the enormous brass trays of foods.

And what else? A Polish girl pours out obviousnesses: a Warsaw university student fell for a fellow student, an Abyssinian; but, married to her, and having returned to Addis Ababa, he also returned to his tradition of manly dominance (a routine which runs through this tale); besides that, the fate of uprootedness, and her having matured in a 'people's democracy', make the Imperial poverty hateful. Yet he comes to meet me – a charming, lively, clear-headed (not indoctrinated but enlightened) young man denouncing in fluent idiomatic Polish the Ethiopean rulers' criminality. So, a sample of **young thinking**, of young Africans back from their studies in Eastern Europe.

They fill me in on **the low life:** Victory Bar, Kaza Inechs bar – fine to draw. Straight prostitution set in lined-up misery-huts, profits curtailed by the midnight limit.

And next morning (my case appears, surely by miracle) in the Ethiopian Airways plane the stewardesses loll in the laps of the passengers, like those barmaids last night.

From Tarkovsky backwards into Russia. Tarkovsky's theme: the ruthless dogmatism of modern science-modelled men set on exterminating 'irregularities'. But from under the surface of rot, bursts of survival, forceful or tender, fed on infirmity – these are his poetic verities.

His *Stalker* is lifted beyond film-making in two sequences of purest creativity: the long 'pan' over jetsam and flotsam of decomposing stricken life – organic and artifacts – in deadly unity, shallowly laid evidence under the sheet of palpitating waters – a slowest melancholy survey (half buried there amongst undulating weeds are an icon, a revolver, syringes, banknotes) ended with a living human hand – not fisted but loose-poised over the liquid surface, in vague readiness.

The other, tragically optimistic: a wrapped-up victim child-mutant, speechless and limbless, leans in bleakness over a table – sets a casual-melancholy gaze at a glass on it – her eyes, having gained energy from deprived regions, put the glass in motion – and over the edge to tumble down ever so slowly. It is all calm, or resigned, or rather of humble promise. Then her cheek rests on the table – all atremble with the passage of a train. It is the slowest 'shot'.

Andrei Tarkovsky, a cinematic poet, moulds his films unbound unpredictable, never less than epic; how does he get his funding and his crews and casts in supposedly dogma-enslaved Russia? Seen at a public London confrontation, a surprisingly restless, almost fidgety but demonstrably able-bodied and able-brained little slim person, adorned with fripperies (rings, chain at his belt), bedecked in brown-to-beige-to-yellow colour scheme and the lock of very black hair askew, demanding mannered attention; surprising not only visually (why should one expect a pensive White Russian rather than a rumbustious Cossack-type of the Ukrainian steppes?) but also in his somewhat lightweight talk, somewhat self-contradictory – changing tune without any attempt at explanatory footnotes, but wheeling along – in fact in accord with the shape/progress of his creations which puzzle, loose themselves in changed rhythms, filibuster through illogicalities to reach poetic truths. In his introduction, he flounders into freedom and Hamlet clichés, challenges opera as nonsense and plays on this, that he was trapped into directing *Boris Godunov* for Covent Garden – to me an inexplicable and pathetic commitment for this declared and proven freest artist.

Tarkovsky at my studio. How come? No high-flung connections. Admiring his films above anyone else's, I attended his subjugation to rather futile questions/answers, watched his and his wife's aloof departure, bodyguarded by Lindsay Anderson and his London distributor, without daring to accost him. Deliberations followed at the Zanzibar over tactics of approach: Ernie Eban, a vocational researcher, offered to trace his address (but announced failure after some days). Maurice Hatton weaved out an argument about plotted secrecy and the security belt being extra-tight after the Taganka director's most recent predicament, blown up by the media: thus no hope. I wrote a plain letter – and there they were.

Such a much-desired head-on meeting entangles insolubly. Our 'globality' sets obstacles of its own making: the worst – the **middle-persons** planted in-between, reductive in their interpreting (indeed, they don't translate), in their flaccid air-media questioning style which puts in our mouths flaccid themes/answers. We settle in this privacy but under the omnipresent pressure of interviewing routines, so that our (Teresa's and my) authentic appreciation reaches him, translation-flattened (my Russian unserviceable when I wish to dwell on subtleties), as trot-out compliments; and the conversation thus tramelled, though preceded by great hopes, proceeds unworthily.

Caryl does better. She enters later (only to glimpse the MAN and collect the car outside) while we are settled mercifully at posing/painting, conversation secondary – radiantly anticipatory; says at him, 'You're a genius' and departs not expecting any translation or answer.

What scraps remain?

Besides the obvious, yet not expected to come out (again and again) with such throwaway unconcern, dismissiveness of obtrusive/oppressive rulers, the confirmed substance of Russianness – love of his land; there is no such devotion anywhere else (the Poles use theirs as a weapon, yet don't mind staying away; the Chinese?) – perhaps the pull of Russia's immensity, its gravitational force.

His wife's blossoming from my distant caricature view of her at the public meeting into an indispensable-for-a-Russian-abroad sample of his Motherland.

But best contact in conversation was made probably in minute asides and feelers, gratified by all-round laughter. Amongst other laughs (my turning attention to his wife's grand calves and high-laced fancy two-leather boots; my detecting in *Nostalgia* – apparently wrongly – two instances of in-bed shoe-wearing), to justify my NO to any, even his, *Boris Godunov*, I narrated my Brook's *Boris* nightmare escape (over another dead body): a great laughing success.

The ever-swelling growth of this monstrosity – the opera – suited indeed to the nineteenth-century's royalty-infested aesthetic pretensions paired with the need for pompous display of 'circumstance'; and the staying power of its multiplying snob public. It swells onward, consuming vast resources, on the widening ripples of 'popular appreciation' and the continuing requirement of background for official ostentation.

My weariness with the medium had its negative climax precisely with *Boris Godunov* directed many years ago at the same Covent Garden by the gaining-prestigious-ground Peter Brook.

The Opera interior has an odd low-barriered double row embracing the stalls with a narrow *promenoir* behind. We sat in the front one, but why some girl and I got ourselves lured into that trap I cannot recollect. Brook had been praised for this production of unbelievable heaviness (he was already stepping on the praise-ladder) – somehow the Russian operaticism combined with Brook's ambition to prove himself within these *passé* challenges combined into an unbearable slow-motion ponderousness. The only appropriate word is 'Teutonic' – – the Teutonic boyars in *basso molto profundo*. The torture of having to endure this procedure hemmed on the rack of the front seats! The noisy intrigues mount to conclusive clashes (oh how terribly slow in coming) and murderings; the dead multiply, strewn all over the stage – and we, beyond forbearance, thrash, stepping on people's feet, out of the row – still another dead body on the floor of the dark passage blocks our way – we step over it and totter to the exit. A pause, still dazed: what was it? This last body was surely a reality, not on the stage? But we plunge

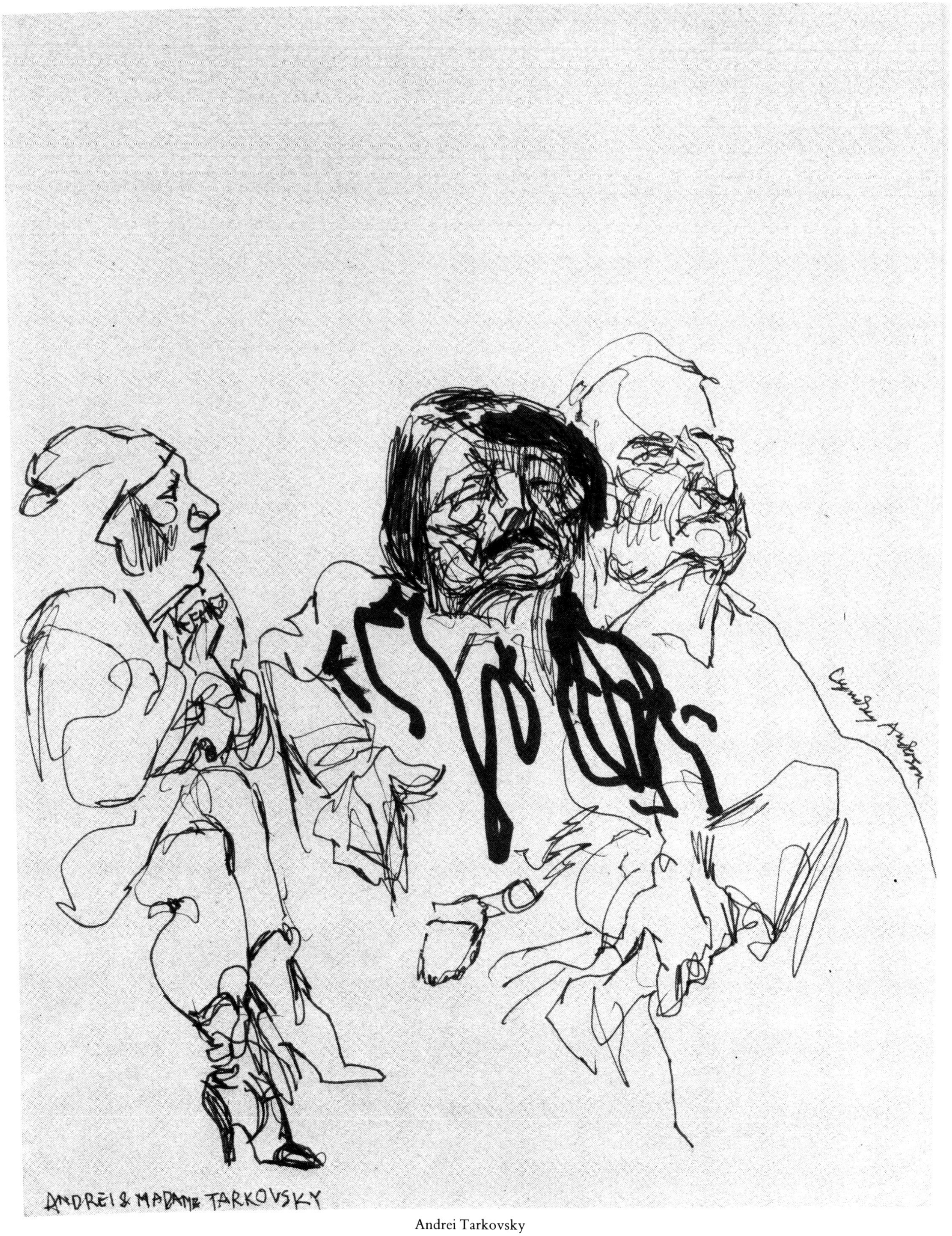

Andrei Tarkovsky

into the open air, mean but safely out of *Godunov*'s reach, certain that the last body must have been of one of us who had tried to escape but had failed to make it . . . fainted? died? We were beyond charitableness.

And so, Tarkovsky's counter-tale about George Steiner's high-powered lecturing/preaching, bringing on an instant epidemic of faints in his audience.

And the truly best came, Russian/Polish/Western matters put aside, and also our probings into his completed and projected films, when, properly, his interest arose confronted with my *Memoir*: the actual thing barred from viewing by builders, he went one by one over sixty photographs recording it fully for my gift contract with the Greater London Council; here he was reaching towards me through my work and finding it worthy of attention. And the truest closeness emerged when I put before him sketches for a sculptural feature within my labyrinth: here were two artists/craftsmen deliberating, no more politeness-driven, a tangible problem in hand – his advice, technical and imaginative, was keen and useful. At last we met. The idea for this sculpture – a monkish self-immolatory figure – came to me two days before seeing his *Nostalgia* and its burning finale.

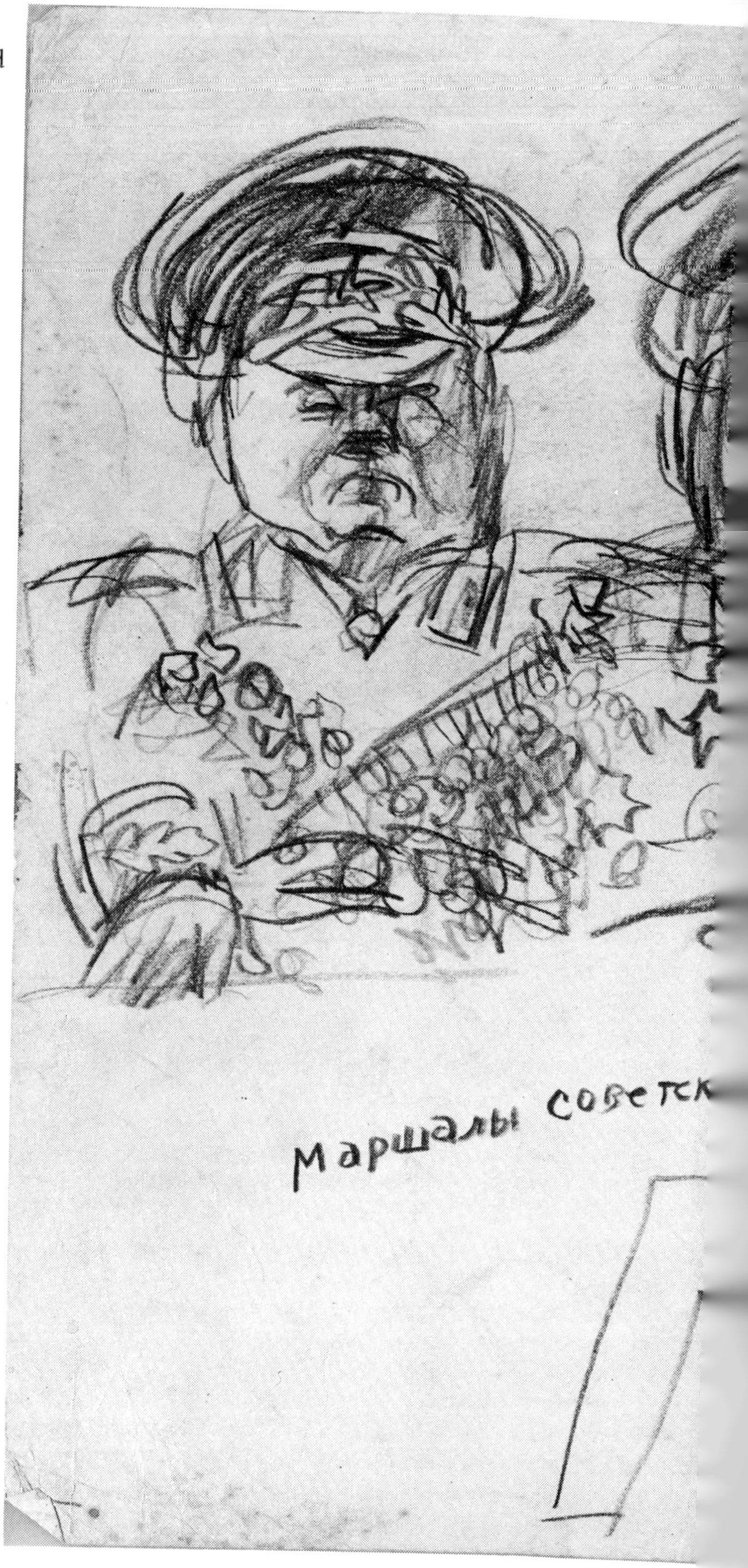

Brook's *Boris Godunov* was my last opera.

No, wrong! There was still to come ***Figaro* at the Bolshoi.** But that was in the way of duty. **CBS Television** proposed to make a film-reportage entirely out of my drawings of some event/place – in other words a translation of my ***Chronicle* into film** – this to be a 'pilot'.

The idea materialized between Frank Stanton, their head, and myself. We combed West and East for revolutions, disasters, ceremonials, international gatherings – sensational or momentous, but a rare historical lull persisted worldwide and we settled to the seasonal, in which category the most exotic seemed Moscow's 1 May. High-up sky-is-the-limit decisions within mammoth organizations invariably slide down the realization-line passed from hand to hand of ever-assertive lesser '**executives**' and '**experts**'. The pure and faultless concept began, when delegated to local sub-bosses, to get entangled in the imponderabilia of co-opted professionals eager to trap me on the unfailing issue of cost-saving.

In consequence, endless curtailments followed.

The concept of the script was mine; the text was written by me in a sort of rhythmical prose to be read by me. But even that final stage was muckraked: 'professionalism', as the cover for sins of second-ratedness, reduced to routine conventionalism my more ambitious formulations; but the vital damages to the text were two-fold: crude censoring-pressures from London sub-bosses/underlings, impossible to bypass, to twist the impartiality of my wording towards shabby journalistc Cold War innuendos; and then, when I managed to persist (my drawings, the comment; the text, a mere accompaniment), they (the professional authority) decided that my try-out reading was far too spluttered with foreign accent and engaged for it a Polish actor-in-exile who hammed it with falsely emphatic intonations and pauses at odds with my wording, cunningly achieving anti-Soviet

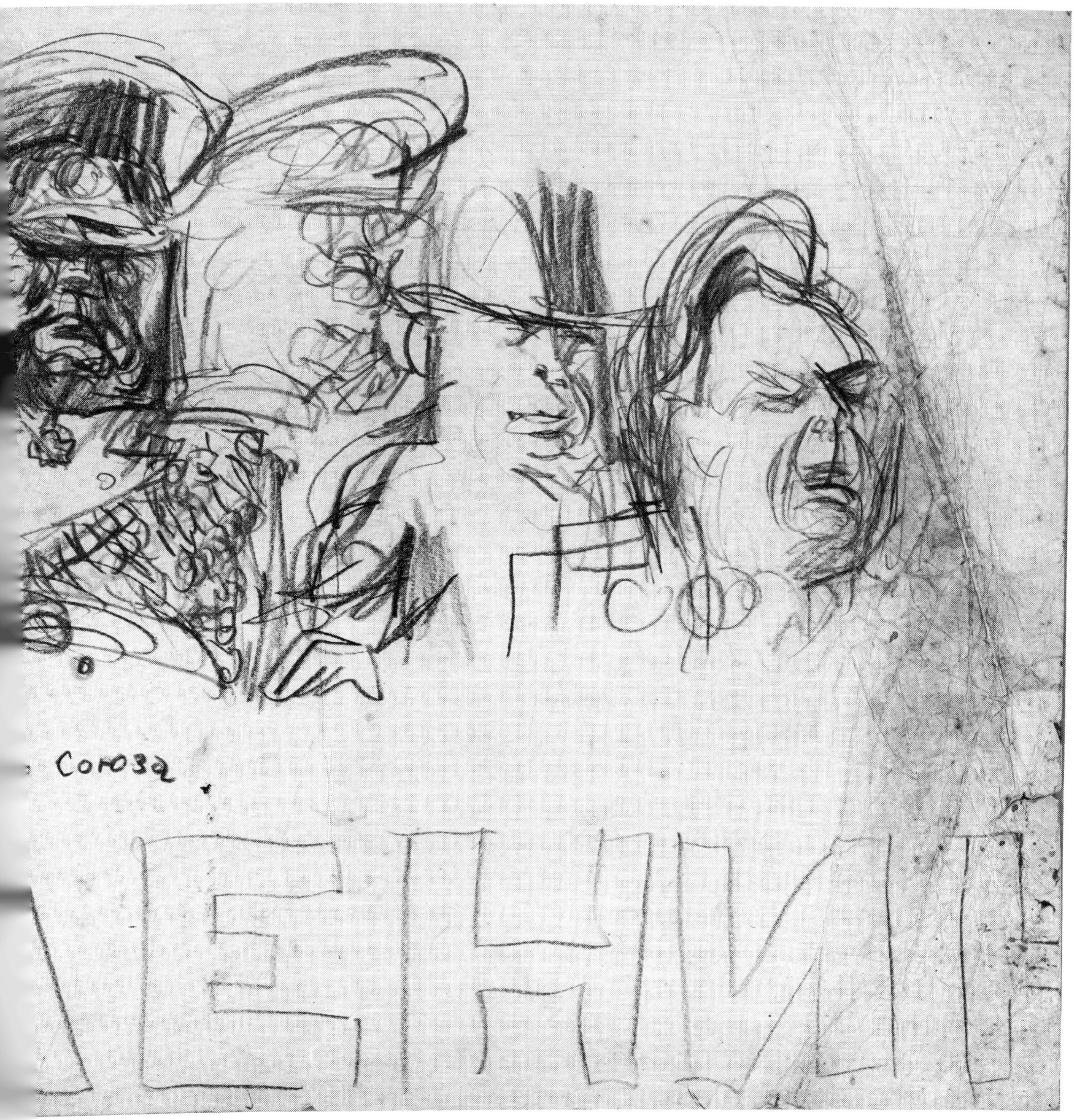

Moscow. The first of May, 1969. Lined-up leaders (from CBS TV film on Moscow)

tone. The film, in its crippled state (even attempts at animation added behind my back), was shown in the States at Christmas 1969.

As a drawing film-maker I hoped to reflect, however fleetingly, the immense fanning out of Russian variations: in land, sky and people. (A thought: perhaps this unruly kaleidoscopic richness has to be governed by a *nahajka* (knout) but which may also, by rebound, breed resilience. *Ruskaya Sherokaya natura* – 'the impetuous Russian nature' – is there, in every nook of living, battling, creating, alongside the atrophy between the rulers and the people.)

It began grandly with **the First of May** Red Square celebrations: the intricate bureaucracy of gaining passes and exact, graded and security-bound, seats in the terraces, fiercely checked, were soon overcome by my dare-stepping out to the fore (my pass now dominated by my sketchbook, my meagre justification/shield) into the path of the arriving Soviet dignitaries, and along and along (astonished at myself and indeed at the slacker control at this elevated stage, yet acting as if by right) to assert my drawing presence just below Lenin's Mausoleum lined on top by the rulers of the land.

Elated, I drew continuously: the medal- and gold-weighted uniformed Marshalls-of-all-the-forces/colours, Goering-modelled, the farthest possible from Revolution tradition, climbing up and settling on various levels of this marble base – forming a *tableau vivant* of power structure crowned by mostly black-hatted and black-coated supremos: Brezhnev, Kosygin *et al.* These drawings, given this unparalleled demonstration of ostentatious might, amongst the best I have done in spite of plastic sketchbook pages and sliding greasy crayons enforced by CBS experts, were later – most of them – heavily retouched without my knowledge, thus obliterated, by my CBS Television 'bench experts'.

And the parading Volga-flow of many hours, precision-drilled and millions-strong (it must have been), could not be dismissed as a march of enslavement: these young people (mingled with, also, before and after) are in continuity with their predecessors, victorious over the German military invincibility as Russians; they are genuinely in patriotic step.

But outside mass celebrations and formal guidances: in the shallows of officialdom, my driver, a true **Russian *zhulik*** (a ruffian-dodger), led me fearlessly astray. He took me (his host after some function) to the posh restaurant of the Nacionalny Hotel. We ate and drank choicily and I drew the scene intermittently. Our youngish waitress, of true White Russian generosity in shape and bearing, grew interested, commented – and then demanded to be included. A guffawing/teasing bargain was struck: for her approximate likeness in the drawing, she pulled me by my hand off my chair (in a room crowded with people of obvious 'consequence') to a fulsome and long-lasting kiss/embrace behind an all-exposing column.

Next evening, now off-duty but still in charge of an official car, he took me well outside the town's touristy area to a Moskva-river boathouse-nightclub. An abundance this of vodka-floated uncontrolled fun.

Ever-suspicious 'Russia-observers' might propose that this driver knew about and catered for visitors' appetites for unguided irregularities. But I prefer to think that, having sensed in me a spirit of camaradely insouciance, he loosened up to team with me in his naturally Muscovite risk-taking fulfilments.

And it ended badly for him. He did not conform to the rules at the smooth store exclusive to foreigners, but, his endearing flamboyance encouraged by our previous feats, swaggered into this holiness and over-acted in our *duetto* (there was intermingled a matter of his desire for an exclusive pair of shoes), so that a frontal clash with the management forced his identification. Next morning another driver was waiting for me and knew nothing about my friend. However, the morning after, he was there at the hotel's entrance: spies or no spies, he was not lurking but posted openly to catch me, a dismissed but undaunted 'brave', to assure me about his *sans-souci* future – and still plotting my role in securing for him those only-for-foreigners shoes.

I must not slide facilely into exaggerated assumptions about the Russian people's unruly boisterousness resulting in/fostered by Ivan-the-Terribles. The measure of boisterousness in societies cannot be weighed solely against the varying governmental systems, and, quite possibly, having been persuaded to expect conformity, the visitor is given to underlining trivial acts of nonconformism. Be that as it may, in the comparatively unrestricted West, boredom is the norm, even in protest, while nonconformism too often verges on hooliganism. But in Soviet Russia the dissident or a mere ruffian strike a note of romantic style.

A group of gracefully vigorous and challengeful-in-their-work literary and painterly young men and women, met by me several times at their homes then, emanated a presentable journalist (he abandoned architecture as too inflexible in his country) fluent in English (English wife) and fluent-worldly altogether: a few months later he visited my London studio. Our brimful conversations held no hesitations dictated by concerns over discordant cultures' touchy touchlines; his detached cynical ease (none of the anticipated Russian earnestness of firm convictions one way or another) best instanced by this: 'Oh, there is now in Soviet Russia **a fashionable rush to dissidentism** – it is not done NOT to have been in prison', said in Western high-brow intonation/mode of chicanery – but strained to the darkest limit.

He came two or three times to London at shortish intervals and once I took him to Moura Budberg, at that time travelling a lot to Moscow to see theatrical productions for Peter Daubeny's World Theatre.

She liked the smooth Russian, but wondered later at the frequency of his London trips; this ease, she thought, in view of travel restrictions, raised questions.* And I told him jokily just this to provoke some convoluted evasion – and jokily he reparteed with no pause: '**Yes, I am a spy**'.

These becoming overall Russian pages – a detour: **Andrei Voznesensky**, 'number two' poet of Russia, sat motionless in the ring set at the centre of the **Albert Hall** in London on a

*There were around London then lurking gossipings about Moura-spy.

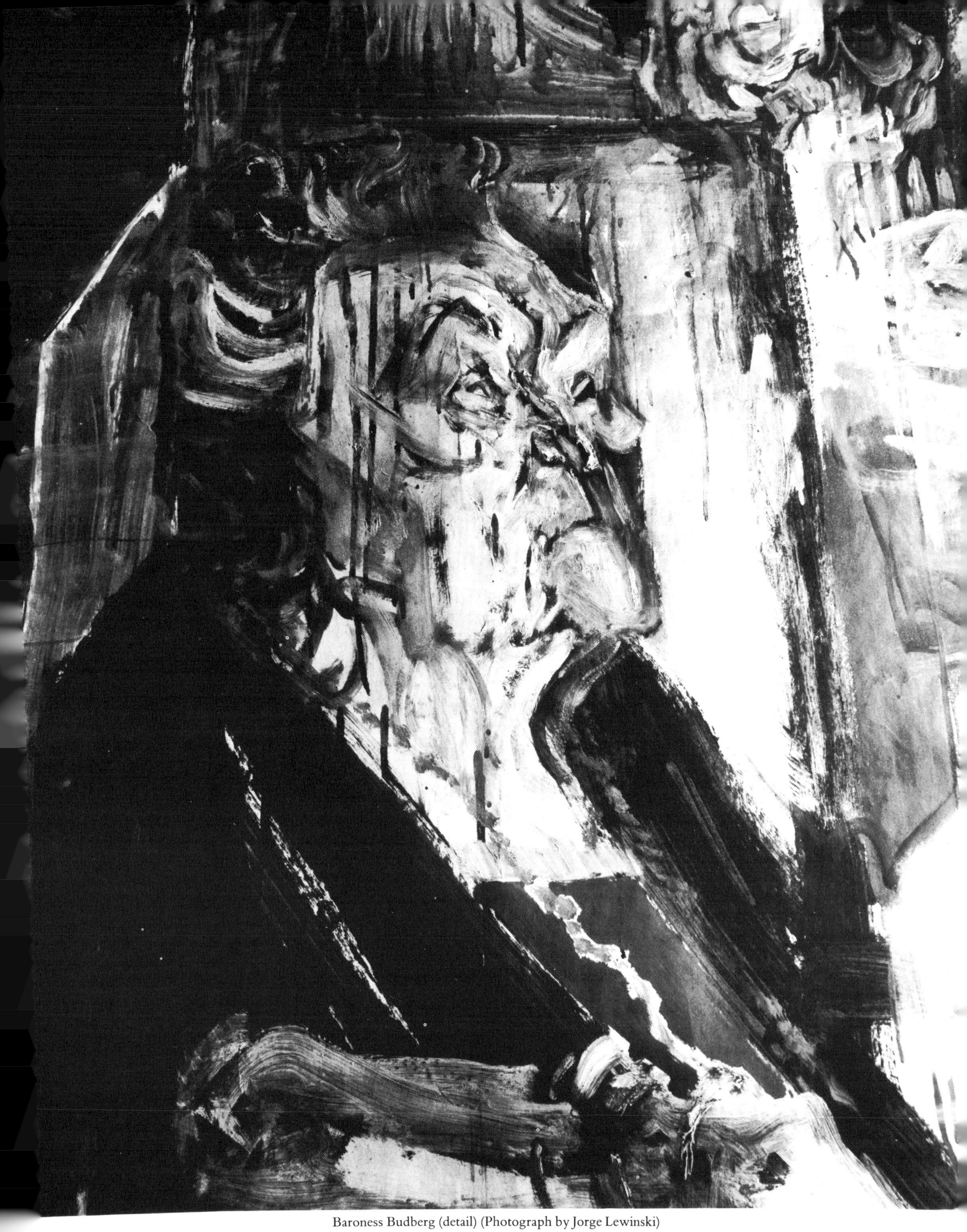

Baroness Budberg (detail) (Photograph by Jorge Lewinski)

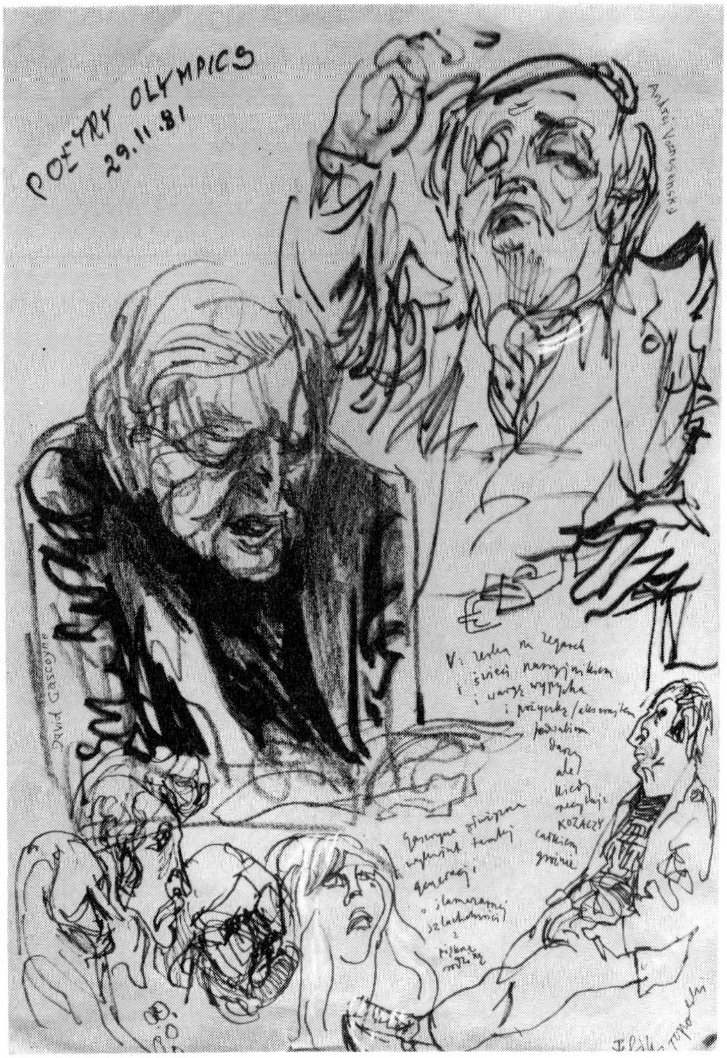

London Poetry Olympics, 1981. Andrei Voznesensky reciting

memorable night on 11 June in 1965 when 3000 hippies (with thousands more clamouring outside), stoned and chorally festive, celebrated, as never before or since (but possibly like the impromptu audiences in Pushkin Square in Moscow) International Poetry. Dozens of poets delivered themselves of their poems, but Voznesensky did not open his mouth; a young plain and bony-faced Slav, plainly suited, he had been forbidden, it was whispered,* to participate in this orgy of uncontrolled verbal decadence, and so his sheer presence stood for an act of bravery.

Allen Ginsberg, swayingly 'high', spluttered close-bending over/on to the Russian's face his translation of a Voznesensky poem; who sat stiffened.

A double-leap ahead: last year, or was it two years ago, Michael Horowitz began his poetry Olympics, worthy but far from matching those right-time/right-place Rites at the Albert Hall.

But Voznesensky was there, nearly twenty years older, wiser – and corrupted; corrupted by time? By too many stays in the West? By and with Russia herself in her embourgeoisifying progression? Or decked into a dummy Westerner by his Soviet sponsors – a showpiece? His being aged balding and massive could have been acceptable, but hardly his manipulating what there was: the tuft of yellowed hair (surely dyed) 'borrowed' across the skull, the flashing necklace/medallion, the pouting lip, mannerisms sneaked from many sources (why business executives' fitful flips of the cuff for time-checking?), the whole wrapped in velours and foulards. But this mummery did fade out when the original fiery poet stood up to boom/declaim; or was it a rusty duplicator's duplicating job? self-copy-cat's job?

This ageing poet and Tarkovsky – my (appearing mean) listing their vanities needs a differentiating comment: Andrei the film-maker carries a manhood's natural dose of flamboyance; Andrei the poet blots his truth with Western marketplace titbits, exemplifies Soviet Russia's relinquishing of world leadership as an experimenter in revolution (manners included) to reduce itself lamely to consumerism.

These trends of personal greed and vanity – sardonically named in present Poland '**little stabilization**' – more significant than the leaders' pronouncements, re-establish the force of the 'human nature' dictum – and the triumph of the West's non-ideology. The latest news: China's People's Army, that perfect body within Mao's purist faith, now rids itself of plain, symbolically unadorned tunics (both officers and lower ranks), for tailored and epauletted outfits (as the Russians did before them) – and, simultaneously and unavoidably, of the Chairman's 'thoughts'. The final nail. . .

Turn back, turn back to Moscow. The film year was 1969.

Before that, there was a few days' stop in Moscow – short but crowded – on the way to Mongolia's Ulan Bator and Mao's China – that was in 1966.

London–Moscow in Aeroflot. The Soviets are no longer clumsy baggily squared stubborn boors. Now, average tourists returning to Sverdlovsk, they exhibit bourgeois appetites.

Further back. A major motoring **trip en famille** to Eastern Europe, but from Warsaw to Moscow by air. It is **1962** and this is our round of Moscow and Leningrad settled in peace: from the Airport – an open lorry in front of us carrying a hatted plump gent sunk in a branching-out armful of flowers – 'return from holiday', we are told; military lorries in plenty, women roadworkers and СЛАВА – glory – TO this or that along the road; old Moscow townscape signposted by Stalinist spires (the University, the Metro entrance), masked with hoardings – strip-cartooning and dating their cosmic conquests, giant-captioned: 'WE FIRST IN THE WORLD'; beyond, slogans/adverts of Communism's joyousness above preoccupied pedestrians; the military: back-to-Tsarist stiff epaulettes, the naval ratings: stylishly never changed; cranes everywhere, housing conceived in immense uniformal perspectives (unrestricted by private parcelling; Hausman did the same in Paris), fronted by its nicely decrepit mid-nineteenth-century counterparts and bulbous onions of

***Pablo Neruda** chickened out, having promised to come, presumably not so much under orders, but under the good Communist's inner command. I tracked him down reading his poems grotesquely in a *comme-il-faut* Belgrave Square *salon*, his huge bulk overhanging a tiny phony-Rococo table (little politely diplomatic flags flanking his thick volume: Union Jack and the Chilean), his tightly/shinily shoed feet concluding immensely swelling-out ankles.

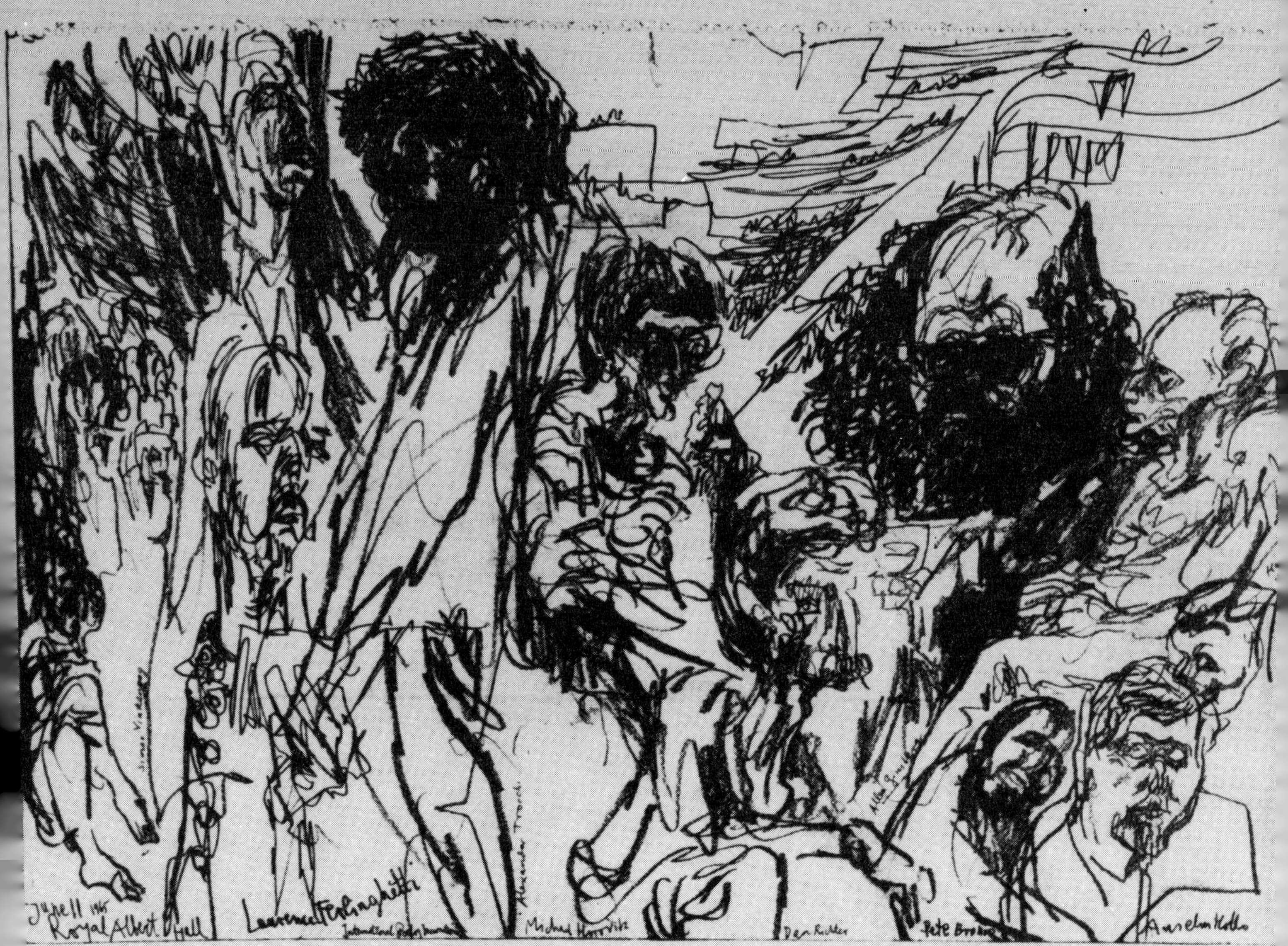

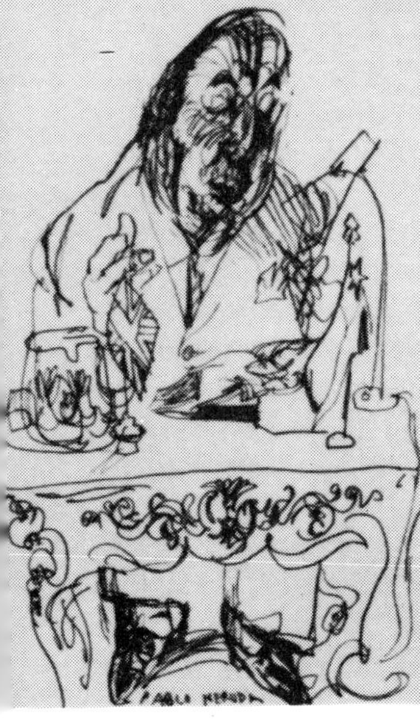

INTERNATIONAL POETRY AT THE ROYAL ALBERT HAL LONDON

Pablo Neruda promised but failed to come. He was trac down at a more formal reading in Belgrave Square. No the poems reproduced here were recited at the Albert

WHAT HAPPENED AT THE ROYAL ALBERT HALL?

Though it came about spontaneously in the best tradition of "happenings", the international poetry presentation at the Royal Albert on the evening of June 11 crystallized out of a very contemporary ferment: that's to say, it was no fluke. It was sudden and perhaps . . . if we are to judge from the level of the production . . . over-hasty; that it took place when it did and not perhaps a few months later and more expertly as part of a wider and more coherent strategy—this is to be explained by a few chance coincidences: the presence of so many foreign poets in London, the happy impulse of two young poets, the availability of the hall, etc. But, just as we have to look farther than the Sarajevo murder for the cause of the First World War, so do we have to look beyond these coincidences for the reason behind what happened at the Royal Albert Hall.

One might say it was in the air, has been since after 1945, this felt need on the part of poets, artists, thinking individuals in general for a coming together internationally of individuals in an immediate way, transcending politics. In another place, I called this growing protest and the various calls for some kind of direct action the "invisible insurrection", and I argued that at its most articulate, this (r)evolt is against the whole gamut of traditional responses which is unconscious for the most part, hallowed by convention, and quite inadequate for the complex world which has been thrust upon us by the relentless evolution of our own technology. During the last two decades there have been many international cultural festivals, but the manifestation at the Royal Albert is remarkable in that, conceived, plotted, and undertaken in ten short days, the thousands came and many were turned away at the door.

The impulse to bring all these people together to participate in an "evening of poetry was regarded by some of us as a kind of experiment in human festival, a practical demonstration of the immediate availability of creative people of very different backgrounds to the idea of cultural experiment. And the toleration they showed of some very indifferent poetry during more than four hours was surely evidence of the audience's general appreciation that something was being achieved, something significant and to do with human solidarity, just by our all being there at all in such a place, poets so very different, all together, participating. This concordium was above all a happening, conceived joyfully and seriously in the spirit of play. The idea caught on, the various poets boarded the "shameless bandwaggon" (cf.—programme notes), and set about demonstrating that the greatest concert-hall in all England was hardly big enough to contai who, at the shortest notice, w from all over in answer to th eous gesture of international For myself, I think it is not question of choosing to co-op discovering oneself in and of ible insurrection" by virtue practical posture. The (r)evol place at the level of symbols question of our ever meeting of reaction head on in a wa terms. But it is happening aware of it, you are (pro fact To quote again from the p notes: "Self-evident for real the words . . .

ALEXANDER TRO

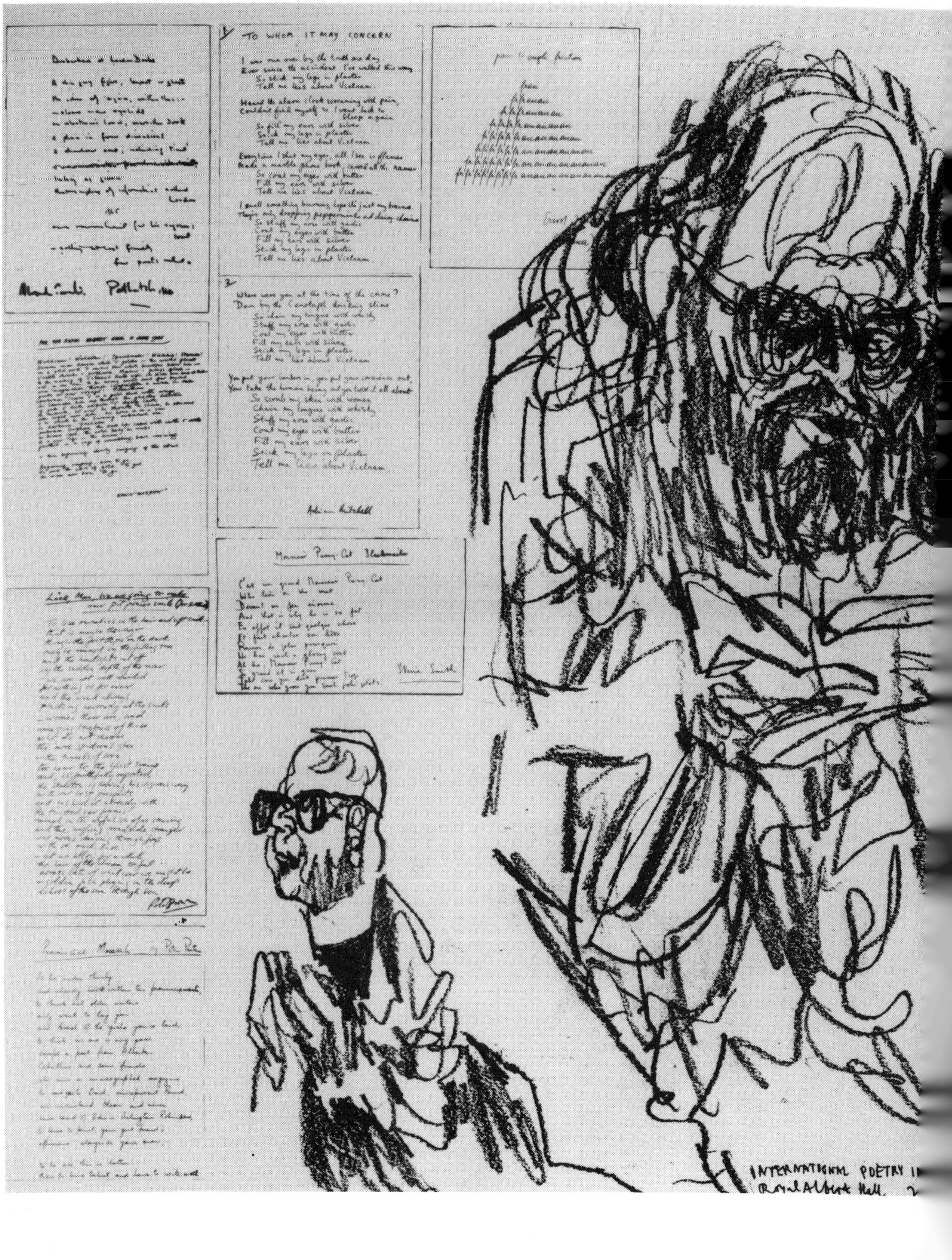

TO WHOM IT MAY CONCERN
I was run over by the truth one day
Ever since the accident I've walked this way
So stick my legs in plaster
Tell me lies about Vietnam.
Heard the alarm clock screaming with pain,
Couldn't find myself so I went back to sleep again
So fill my ears with silver
Stick my legs in plaster
Tell me lies about Vietnam
Every time I shut my eyes, all I see is flames
Made a marble phone book, carved all the names
So coat my eyes with butter
Fill my ears with silver
Tell me lies about Vietnam.
I smell something burning, hope it's just my brains
They're only dropping peppermints and daisy chains
So stuff my nose with garlic
Coat my eyes with butter
Fill my ears with silver
Stick my legs in plaster
Tell me lies about Vietnam.
2
Where were you at the time of the crime?
Down by the Cenotaph drinking slime
So chain my tongue with whisky
Stuff my nose with garlic
Coat my eyes with butter
Fill my ears with silver
Stick my legs in plaster
Tell me lies about Vietnam
You put your bombers in, you put your conscience out,
You take the human being and you twist it all about
So scrub my skin with women
Chain my tongue with whisky
Stuff my nose with garlic
Coat my eyes with butter
Fill my ears with silver
Stick my legs in plaster
Tell me lies about Vietnam.
Adrian Mitchell
Monsieur Pussy-Cat Blackmailer
Stevie Smith
INTERNATIONAL POETRY I
Royal Albert Hall.

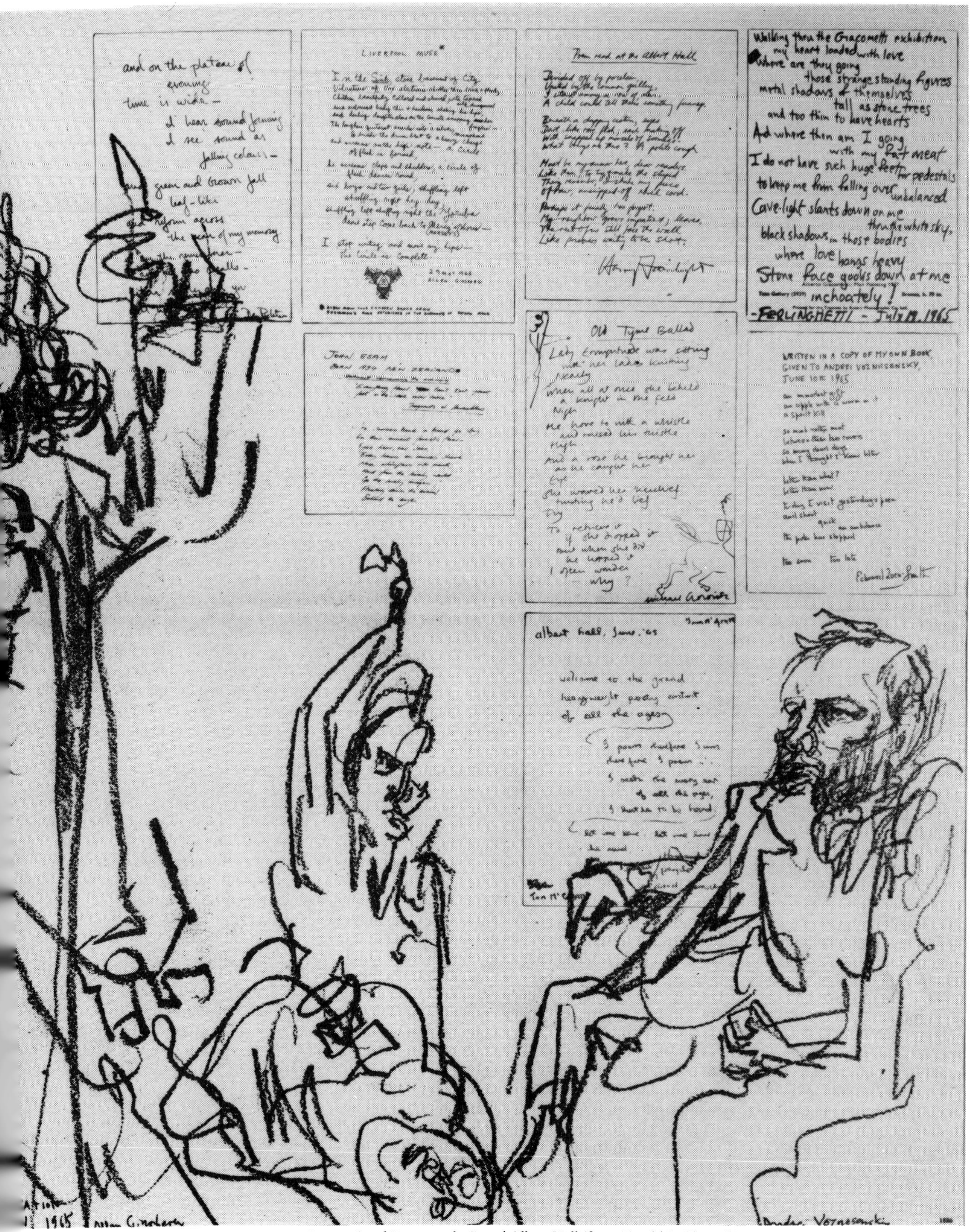

International Poetry at the Royal Albert Hall (from *Topolski's Chronicle*)

in décor and in manners – though the latter pauperized; the giant newest ones are shaped for now. The close-up faces at a stand-up bar: weary or pausing peak-capped men, as anywhere else; a heavy kerchiefed woman, as only in Russia; a lone soldier, simply still, or melancholy? But his blouse trim and well pasted with red-starred insignias of some valour and epaulettes marked with one bar, his faultlessly looked-after cap pulled in the unchanging traditon of Russian-Ukrainian panache deep over the right ear, a cultivated lock of hair on the left compensating. No, no sadness, but just a pause within his role. The packed-with-Seriousness exhibitions. The packed theatres: a first night at the Mayakovsky with the stage-box displaying a group of weighty personages: formal younger men as courtiers – a majestic woman (an 'honoured' actress? a critic?) dominates, while below in the stalls rows of modest up-turned-nosed profiles of the 'ordinary'.

At a friendly artist's МАСТЕРСКАЯ – studio. **Shmarinov** is an 'academic' illustrator of assured status – the occasion, as always in Russia, has this ceremonial hospitality and grouping, which falls into the 'conversation piece' category of an earlier, but not provincial, precisely Russian mood. There is present, amongst the elder friends and family, a young son – proudly showing (to his father's approval) his, a jot unconventional, but always 'responsible' work. They are all warmly **KULTURNYJ** people – the word embraces much more than 'cultured'; it encompasses education and cultural awareness, but also behaviour, quality of living. It may be simply a useful replacement, in the egalitarian society, of 'gentlemanly'.

And so, at dinnertime in the Leningrad Hotel in Moscow, a very young, very sprightly officer (in a field-belted tunic and tall boots) who comes to our table and with formal phrasing and bow asks for permission to invite our daughter Teresa to dance, is KULTURNYJ. But possibly a high-coiffured peroxided ear-ringed girl, accompanied by a high-ranking be-medalled officer, is not.

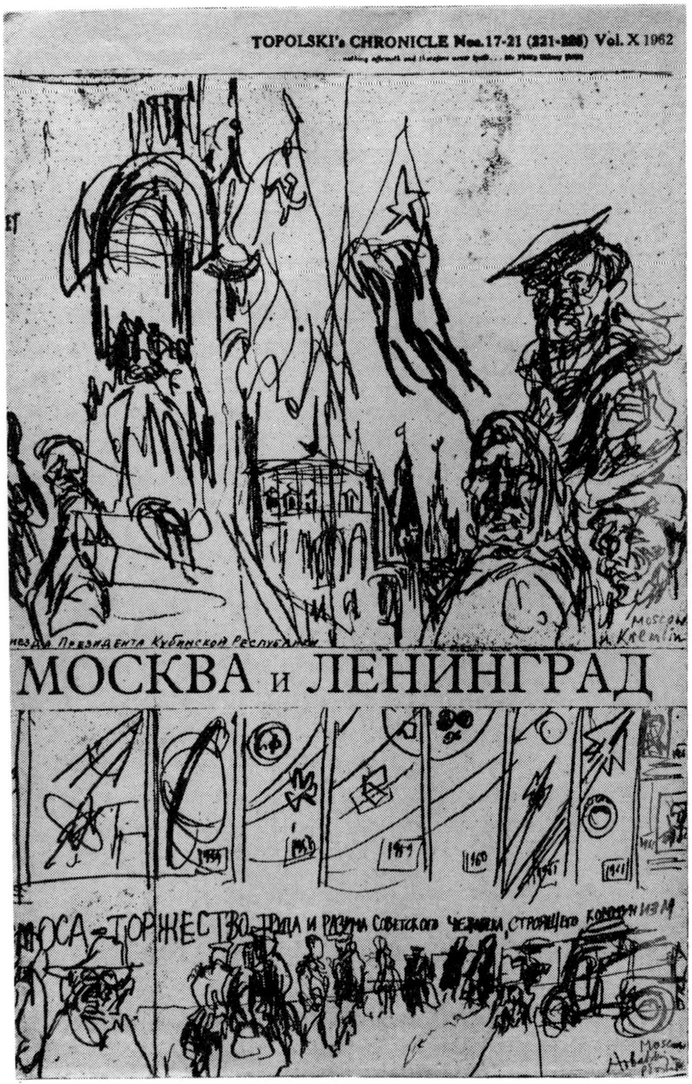

Moscow and Leningrad (from *Topolski's Chronicle*)

religion, and still to the fore, also nicely shoddy, kiosks (АРБУЗЫ – water melons); all backed (this is Tercena Street) by another giant sky-piercing edifice, explained by fiercely red 'UNDER THE LEADERSHIP OF LENIN'S SOMETHING . . .' and 'THE WORLD IN FRIENDSHIP'. The strangest blending of sentiments, yet it holds for Moscow now.

The Kremlin accessible for the business of enthusiasm: gatherings over anniversaries; international (friendly) meetings of the Energy Institute and such (prolonged speeches under Lenin's giant icon); arrivals of Presidents of, say, the friendly Cuban Republic (appropriate banners); the Kremlin theatre – Uzbek or other folklore groups from distant Soviet Republics peforming mainly for their flat-faced sons/brothers soldiering in the Moscow garrison. Outside, under Red-Star-topped Spasskaya tower, stand, hands in pockets, three tattered boys unyielding in their 'up to no good' posture – not far from a militiaman on duty and Lenin's black tomb. And the boys' 'alternative' posture is emphasized topographically by the multitude shuffling, from the opposite end of Red Square, in an orderly queue on to the Mausoleum; the queue snakes round the Kremlin's walls endlessly – its faces/shapes are (even obvious tourists') those of pilgrims. Hotels: still (or more so) museums to the turn of the century –

Leningrad's Hermitage and the Winter Palace are *nouveau-riche* fantasies of the newly Westernized Tsardom, therefore beating in scale anything of the time. For kerchiefed worker-women, students, children, this is their church-going: 'Culture' seems to be their faith. And, as such, it has to be intolerant of irreverence: an elderly, genteel-in-bearing, I-should-say lady, attacks me, having spotted in my drawing-in-progress the scribbly suggestion of herself, with loudest accusations of being 'nie KULTURNYJ'.

There is a *vernissage* at the Russian Museum. Cameras, blinding lamps amongst enormous gesturing statues dominated by the compulsory Lenin. Further, the invitees thicken round the pictures – a 'cultured' crowd, as at any private view anywhere else, perhaps more earnest, though, and better defined. I am put in the hands of a particular artist because, I imagine, he specializes in reportage painting – he shows here a series of large able line-cum-colour compositions on the theme of some (I forget) distant tundra-reclamation scheme – his recent commission.

He invites us to his studio. And a three-tiered theatre unfolds: Teresa, struck suddenly by fever, is laid down and anxiously tended; our plane back to Moscow has to be caught by a taxi-start from the hotel, quite a distance away – so we watch the clock; the host, immersed in his '**social realism**'; an

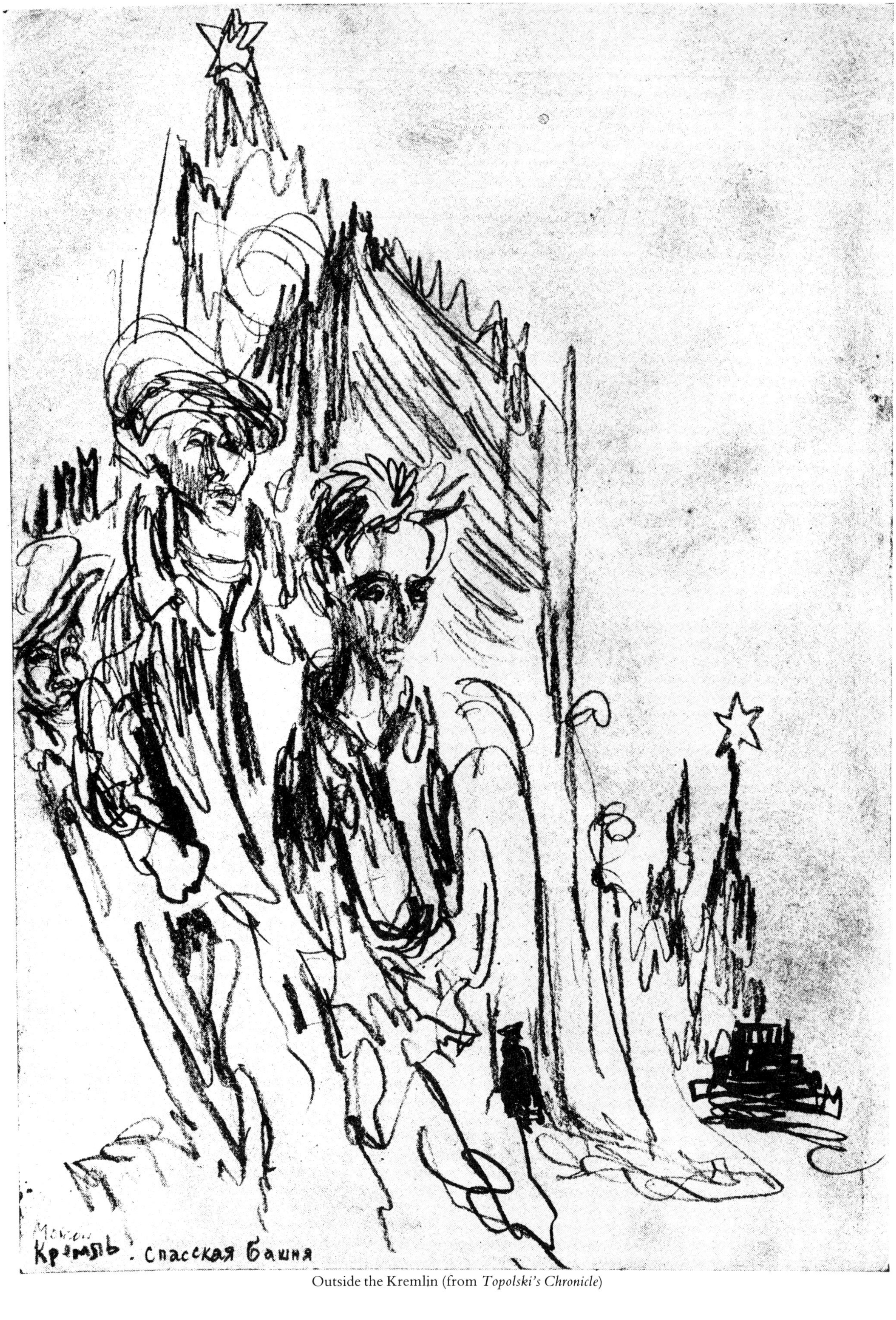

Outside the Kremlin (from *Topolski's Chronicle*)

untroubled maker of approved art – but my eye reaches, in this very lofty interior, a high-up ledge propping a surround of paintings: **abstractions** strong in colour and compositional definition. Knowing that Soviet artists paint now in private their aspirational West-echoings, I ask, rather thrilled at his assumed-by-me duality: 'Are they recent?' 'Oh, no, I painted these thirty years ago – and abandoned all that.' So much for confrontation with an, undoubtedly leading, surviving FORMALIST.

And all this delays us dangerously. Collecting our luggage at the hotel delays us further. And when the minutes count, an old wrapped-up-in-shawls **babushka** at the wheel of our taxi will surely not be fast enough. But here comes to the fore (my refrain, as before and since) the stubborn indomitability and bountiful goodness of Russian Womanhood: she grasps our predicament (to the inclusion of Teresa's state), drives like a fury, leaps out of her taxi and leads us at a gallop ruthlessly through all the barriers and officialdom's obstructions. Without her. . .

I end this Russia-in-reverse on **the war's aftermath**. The location: the large staircase mounting to the Nuremberg Trial's courtroom; the scene: a modest dialogue between a small neat girl in Russian soldier's uniform and myself in British khaki, both perched on a half-landing window-ledge. We talk for a long time, my hesitant/halting Russian somehow almost keeping pace with her unhurried fluency. And almost from the outset she sets the tone, the rhythm, the intimacy, non-existent in our ever-tentative confrontations, emotions- and words-skimpy, hence hasty in mockery-chopped abbreviations: non-existent yet not unfamiliar, because, yes, she immerses the two of us in Chekhov's unhurried melody. She is gravely serious. Her words are her responsibilities, so that everything she says advances her life, and so mine. There is no trace of flirtatious banality, of small talk – our dialogue is earnest; and we reach out, but gently, towards the essence. There is no plot, no contest, but a tending of this honesty between us; for me echoing a theatre-dialogue past – for her, her present; an authentic 'meeting of souls' (however much mine is inadequately trying to rise to her excellence). I assume, moved and swept along, that the gravity of this girl soldier, generously donated in unhurried detailed comprehending of values, is the substance of *Matushka Rossiya* – '**Mother Russia**'.

London at present. My panic and escape into stand-offish evasion at an interviewing girl student's common-run question on **my beliefs**: 'A private matter, not unlike the voter's right to secrecy, or the no-entry nature reserve.' But I truly meant that, hemmed in by *idées-reçues* – implanted demands to fill in categorizing questionnaires, each of us strains to retain an unpestered backyard, the truest to oneself, for unformed unthought-out hesitations.

My tendency is to dodge questions on faith in Jesus's or in Marx's gospels, since they provoke defined answers, and to riposte with undefined reversal-thesis: humanity's history is

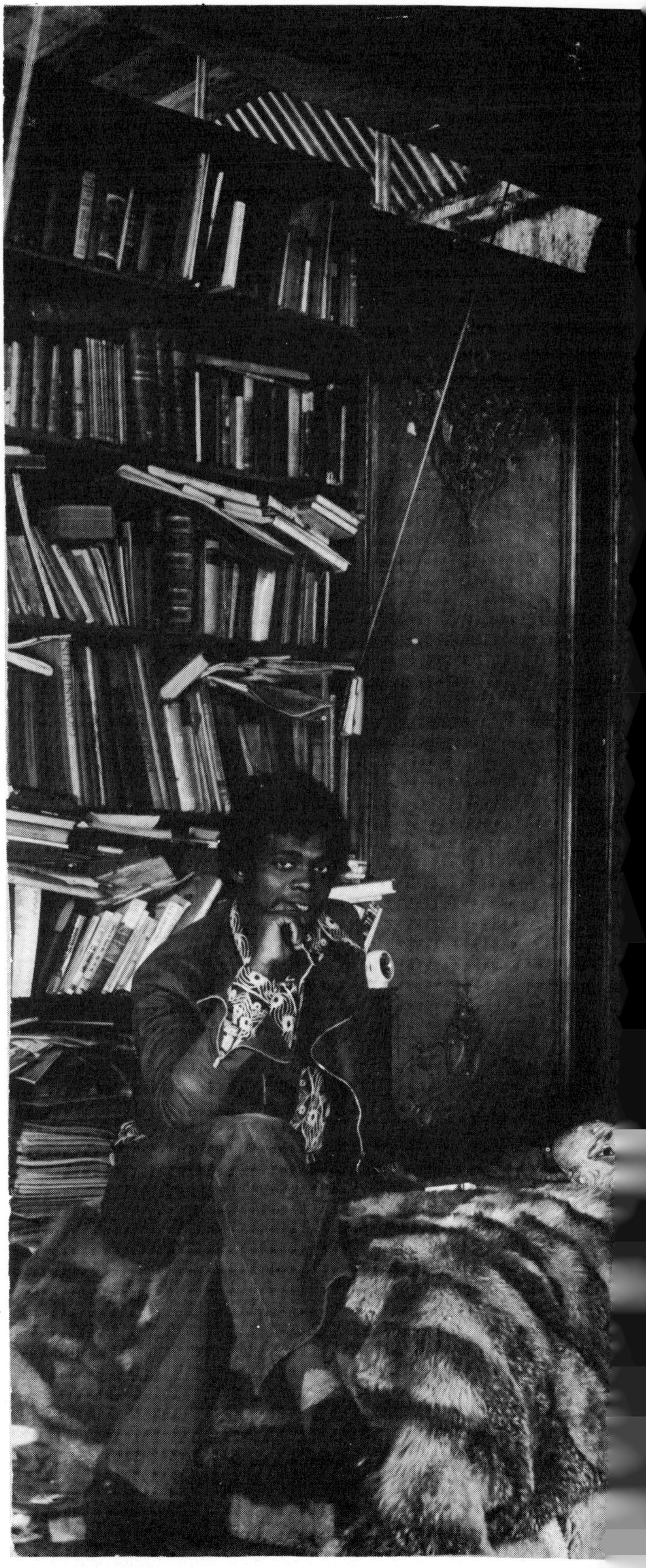

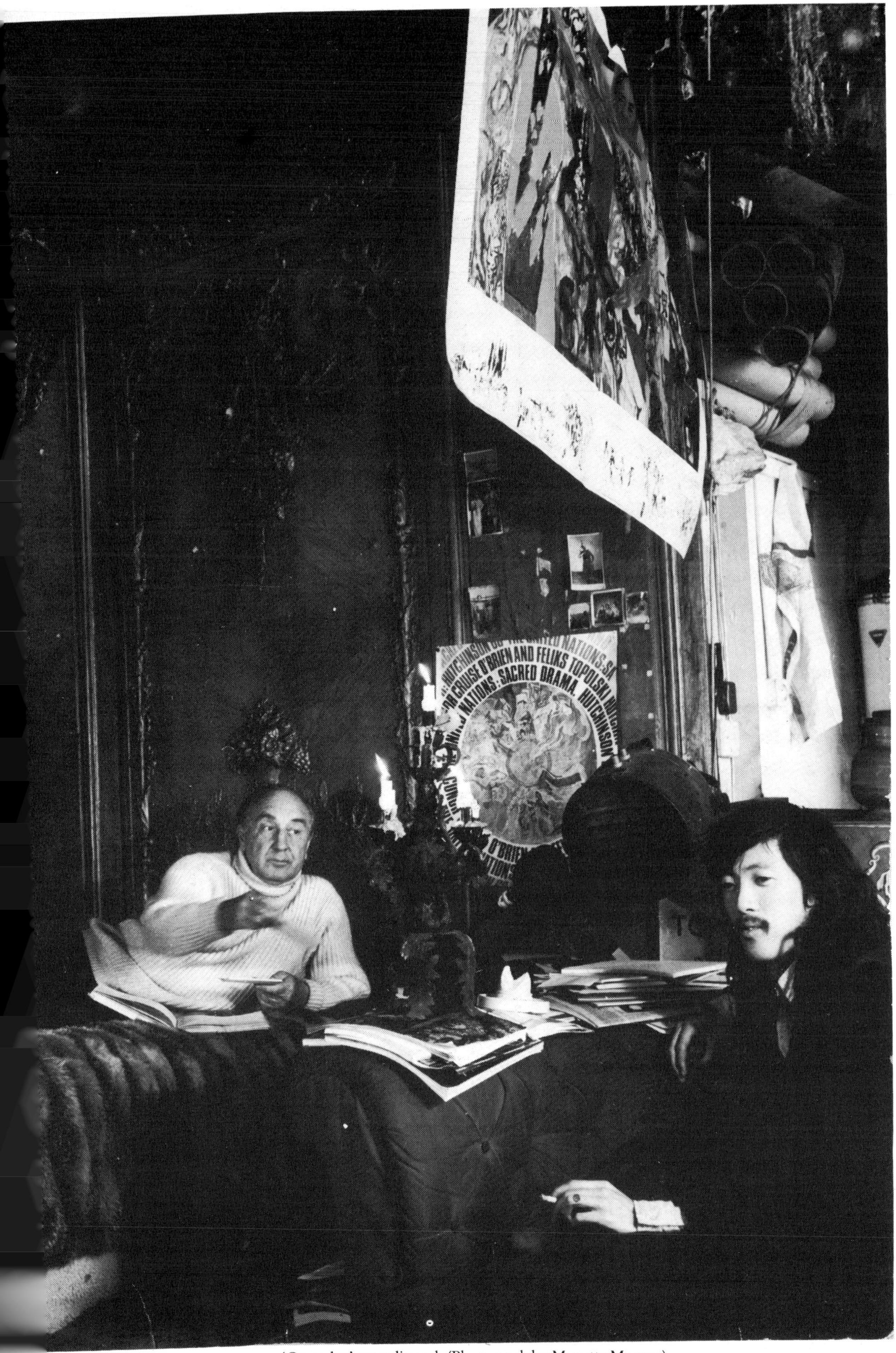

'Open day' at studio arch (Photograph by Mayotte Magnus)

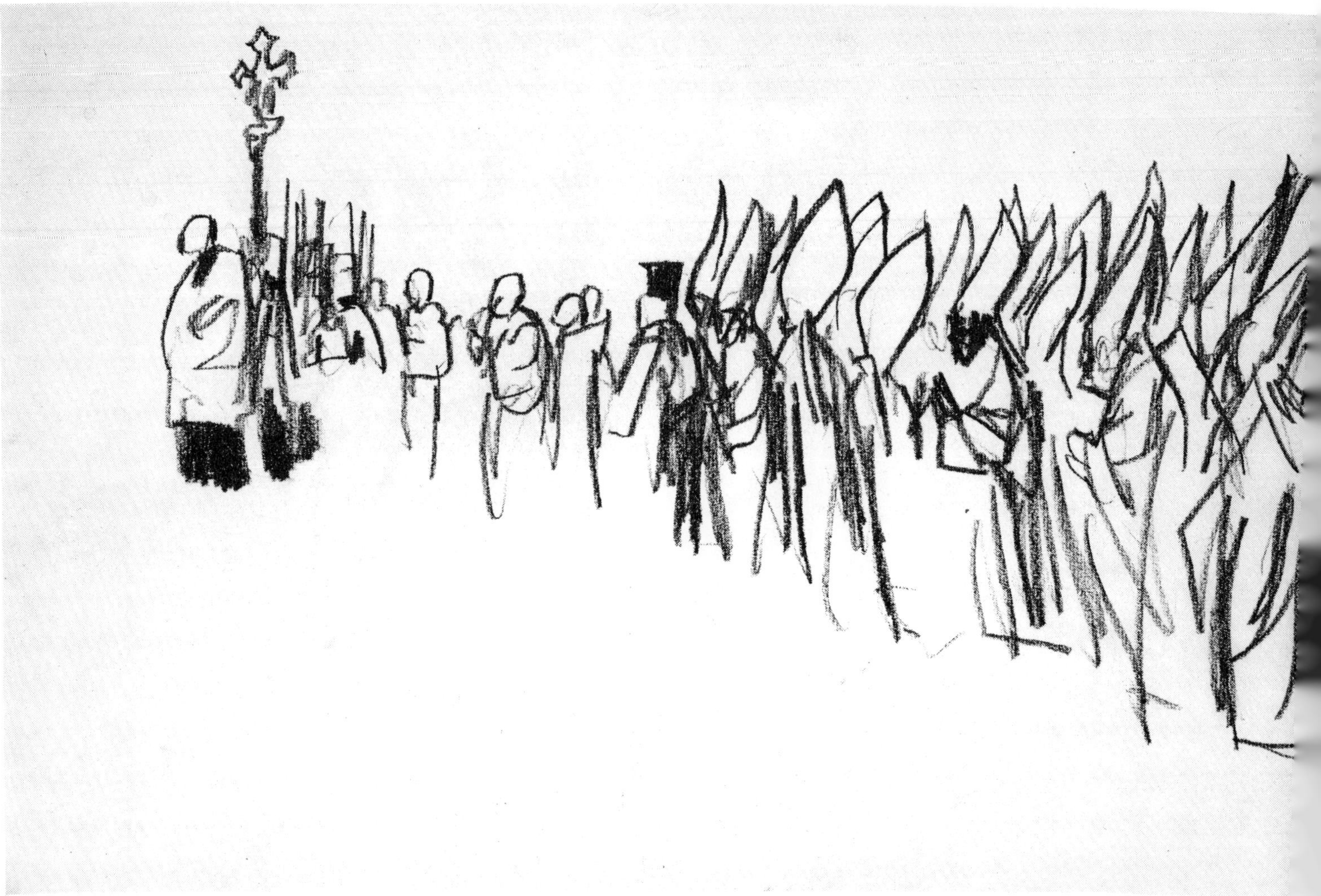

Pope John Paul II's inauguration in Rome. Cardinals' procession (from *Johannes Paulus Papa II* portfolio)

shaped by clashing faiths, not by the reasonableness of ploughmen: the reality of murderous mass movements confirms/shapes the gods, makes the gods real. And so we live under insecure skies thunderous with ideas/gods, thus have no need to declare beliefs: the gods come at us – even if innocent bystanders – our rulers, propellers of our fates.

This new Poland. In my sceptical between-the-wars the young of all strata and all register-denominations were steadily turning away from religion; but under the Nazi oppression only the churches illuminated Polishness – and so under 'Stalinism' and for years after; yet the 'intelligentsia', settling in 'small stabilization', did not go along with obscurantist Catholicism – and in later years I did not in my encounters come across any *réligiantes*: these were by then mostly the moribund 'uneducated'. Then recently political restlessness has grown with the new generation leaning once more on the Church's uncensurable network – **Catholicism as patriotism** revived. And, with the Polish Pope, this *soi-disant* 'counter-reformation' sweeps the country: former steeled atheists roll their eyes, as if spellbound, sanctimoniously droning the articles of their cult: the Motherland-cum-Mother-of-God, the Pope's Polishness, Poland's crusading role. They (those of them who did not travel West) prop their stand with fantasies of the-West-as-Utopia and with the hate of Russia the powerful, but also the 'inferior'.

There are signs that **the Solidarność** revolution – which it was, although differently staged from its nineteenth-century models – is being defeated (by novel means) – and may be similarly followed by the drying out of its intoxications.

When, at the height of its thrust, my friends from Poland clashed in my studio – the reasonable moderates against the inflamed romantics – I found myself first siding with those (mostly older) who referred to the geography of enclosed Poland and to its unquestionable destiny within the power/economics game. Their younger opponents tended to posture, to cash in, as it were, on the West's sympathy (and political machinations) – in short, to stay here lip-serving revolution while the elders were packing up to go back next day.* But eventually, again true to myself, my indecision left me in the crossfire: my revolutionary parentage spotlighted my present non-commitments – their revolution was unreasonable too – and failed, a descendant of a long line of failed nineteenth-century revolts (all over Europe), each of them stepping on to barricades or into battles against the odds and in spite of the advocates of reason; even in spite of those revolutions which were corrupted in their own victory.

*Poland, my people, keep me at bay: the hate/fierceness of yes-or-no demands exclude the no-man's-land-dweller; unavoidably both sides confuse by an admixture of nit-picking latent envies within their mutual condemnations. For non-committed me it is daunting enough to confront here in London's neutrality the explosive visitors from over there.

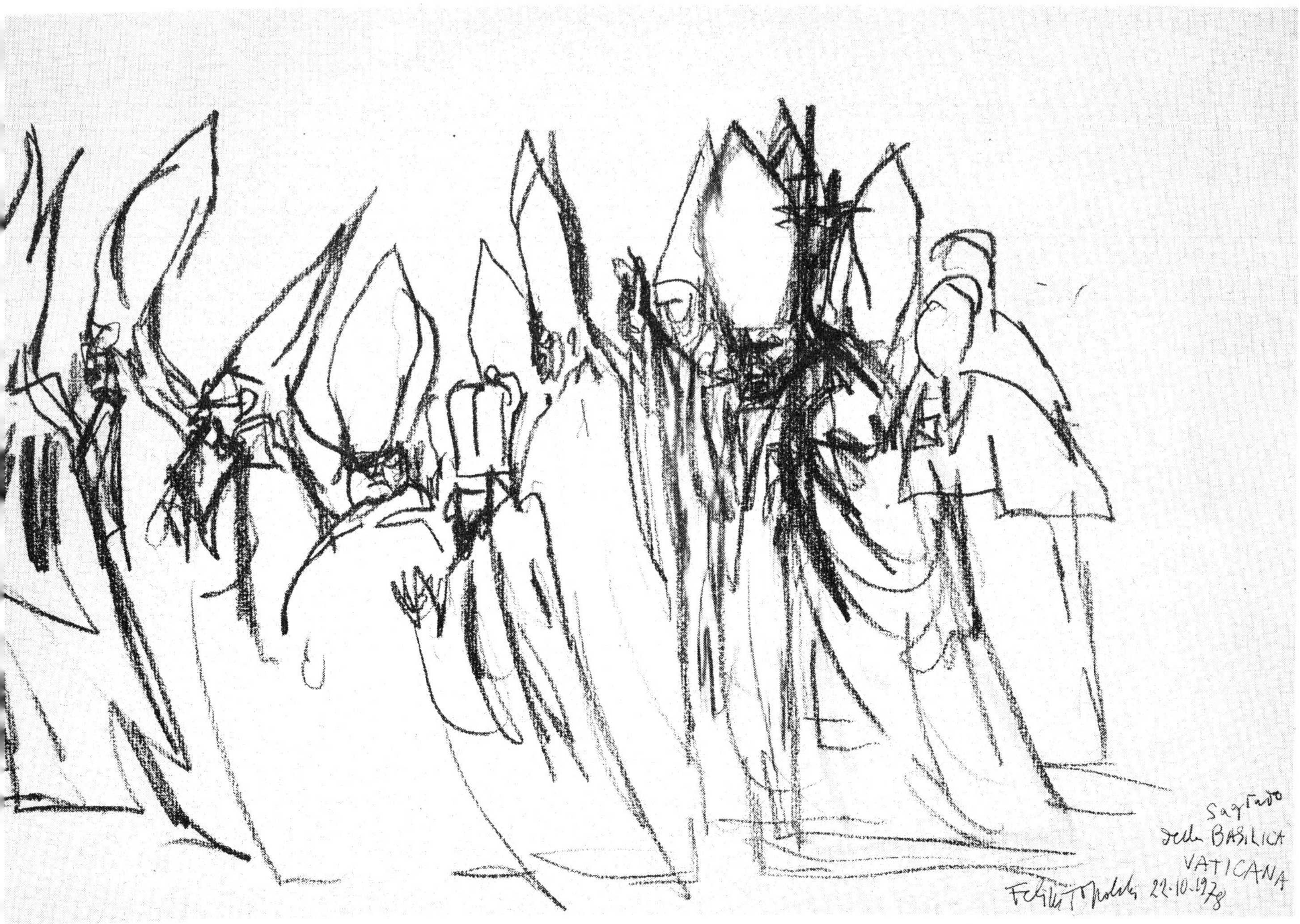

Hence there asserts itself once again the truth of beliefs/ gods directing humanity's story – and actions thus prompted have to fulfil themselves, caution out of the way.

Back to the palpable – my proper field: witnessing the **Pope's inauguration in Rome.** Will this 'faithful' report help take stock of the facts of history or drift into prejudicial assertions?

So: *Suo Sanctitas, Johannes Paulus Papa II, Die* XXII *Octobris* a. 1978.

The immediate imponderables on arrival in Rome: in distant streets, outside the **Città del Vaticano,** the **Brigati Rossi** skirmishing with the **Guardia Civile**; the ring round the new Pope of **Polish clergy,** instantly formed and hermetically closed, suspicious, unyielding negative or misleading.

The paraphernalia of glory and worship, as set – and unchanging – in Renaissance Italy at its peak: Jesus and his Father subservient to the earthly powers of the church.

This curving soaring ostentation, this triumphal power of the Vatican Baroque walls in the faith-bowed-down tens (or hundreds?) of thousands. The masses – the extras (amongst them Polish pilgrims stretch their neatly controversial banners: WSPÓLNOŚĆ, WYZWOLENIE, 'unity, liberation') – fill up the intimidating space of **Piazza San Pietro** ringed by far-sweeping colonnades; closer, the curving wings of St Peter's (the flamboyant saintly statues interpolated by armed soldiery silhouetted on top against obligingly celestial blue, safeguarding the eternal and the temporal destinies of the Holy Father); and, in this embrace the steps up to the Basilica grade not the more righteous and saintly, but **the parade of vanities;** the 'Black' nobility of Papal Rome, uniformally cloaked, gold-chained, white tie/collar-supported heads, pride-marked whether thin or heavy, distributes the invitees in gradation of their earthly splendour: Juan Carlos of Spain and his Queen, the whole earth's other Kings/the shawled Grand Duchesses/Princes/rulers democratic or dictatorial, be-ribboned and be-medalled, and their be-feathered, tarbooshed, turbaned attendants, their ambassadors of all colours and their inflated ladies; also the Italian princesses Orsini, the grand Bali of the Order of Malta, the highest clergy of all denominations and colours, Middle East military high-peaked hats, axelbands, white-wrapped stiff tubulerations – gold–black floatings, rainbow-streaked robes/ fezes on very black skin. The grandiose fuss of Vatican protocolarized priorities and the full palette of chest-crossing ribbons or orders chained at the neck; feathered tricorn and exotic headgear; robes/flesh-tones subdued, there follow the

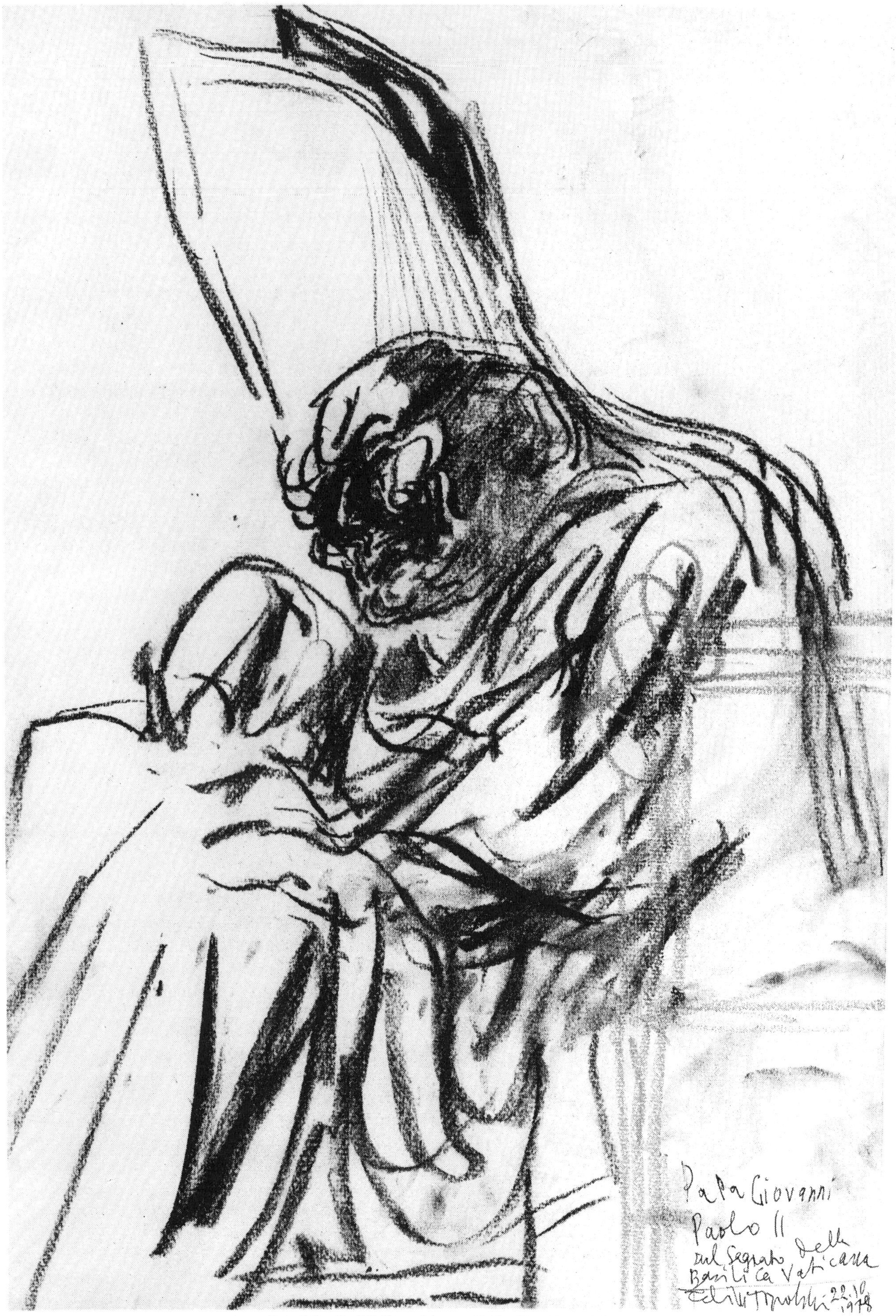

Pope John Paul II (from *Johannes Paulus Papa II* portfolio)

sser ranks, but still within the selective hierarchies: the mbassies (amongst these by fluke and without glitter I and ıgfrido Maovaz holding my coloured pencils), the ring of ıighty Swiss Guards (feathered helmets, halbards, orange-lue-red striped) confirming the sphere of prestige; beyond, :ill given some distinction, the amassed nuns; the select riors and Prelates – and a small clutch of young Cracovian easants from Wojtyła's rurality (boys – red-blue and peacock :athers, girls sequinned corsets, gaudy necklaces).

The Pope varies his head-wear; enthroned, and crowned vith the highest red-lined mitre, his innovation, having lismissed the many-crowned tradition, he embraces one after .nother his lined-up cardinals, who store somewhere out of ight their somewhat smaller mitres, in which they ›rocessioned initially; and prostrate themselves in turn in ;carlet skull-caps; he pays singular attention to his senior ?olish Cardinal, Wyszyński, his 'kingmaker'. And there kneels to him also the conspicuous figure of an Eastern patriarch. The chorus of nuns punctuates this prolonged ritual with a refrain of a few monotonous notes, not to be forgotten. The Pope, now in white skull-cap and, it seems, a different cape, descends a few steps to a makeshift altar bearing a tall grandly carved crucifix (still high above the multitude, ever surrounded) to swing the smoky censer and to conduct *La Santa Messa*, putting to the test the might of the Roman Catholic Church by holding subdued the variegated unique assembly of the lay rulers at the protracted function, alien to most of them.

Most of the many drawings I did then (my preoccupation engrossing, I wondered, as often, at the staying power of the 'privileged' round me – there, but also at conferences, at the opera – undiverted but duty-glued) had him in profile; the distance was considerable and now and again I had to apply my Japanese-made mini-telescope while pencilling with the other hand.

And so I welcomed the next day's **special audience for Poles** – given an assurance by a Polish clergyman in the Pope's entourage of a front seat. Sadly, for no reason (I only talked to him on the phone, but passed on my 'credentials'), he failed me – I had to wrestle unaided with the devilry of the faithful mob, but here, unlike some years earlier at the Holy Sepulchre where I won the sympathy and physical support of an Arab Legionnaire, I was alone amongst – to all intents – enemies. This horribly engineered vast new Nervi-designed hall, divided by ropes into sections for more and less important pilgrims, was brutally controlled by Italian bullies obviously trained for the job of giving no quarter to any one of His Holiness's flock. Indeed, having battled for a reasonable seat, I was dislodged (my purpose disregarded) and, from my now-distant place, I envied those personae, irrelevant in my view, roped in closeness to the Pontiff; and again my 'monocular' had to serve. The white Pope, edged by Polish prelates in black and purple, spoke in sermonizing parables and at great length, then offered his compatriots a walkabout, followed by his patron-cardinal, a postively haughty figure in red-edged black, red skull-cap and red sash. We, the roped-off devouts, squabbled/crashed over the chairs and one another.

I was determined to have another try. The Polish courtier-prelates or whatever their rank slighted me again: ('Ha, an artist? – never heard the name; special assignment from London? – try to phone later.')

And so this time a general public audience on the 25th, the day after this when, in the centre of Rome, leaning for no particular reason against the wall of a public building (the State Bank?) sketchbook in hand, I watched, staged for me, a squealy rush/stop; a demi-ring of army-carriers dropping down, all tense speed, all crouching, tuft-bereted/webbed/automatics-dangling panicky curly-haired **youngsters-in-uniform** – in a few moments turned sloppy – a false tip-off. But the traffic, the pedestrians, unconcerned.

Even the British Embassy did not help. Placed well, I started a promising drawing before *Il Santo Padre* Giovanni Paolo II entered, edging/framing the empty space on the page reserved for him with garlands of multi-denominational robes/hats, telling old faces, but, at the instant of his arrival, pitilessly chased down the length of the soulless Nervi un-nervation, I filled in a lapidary Pope – with what, again, I could see of him through my glass.

In the mood of immediacy of the experience and preoccupation with the drawings, I painted at speed a 9 by 6 foot painting – the Wojtyła-Wyszyński embrace within accumulated props/perspectives/clergy/rulers/military-terrorist diversions; the work (nothing sycophantic about it) is now at the Museum of the Jagiellonian University (the Pope's) in Kraków, the Vatican Museum having been unkind to it. A Polish priest stationed in Germany, who came to London prospecting for a 'sacred art' exhibition, was impressed by my Papal painting and proposed it (a colour transparency assisting) for the Vatican. A long apologetic anc embarrassed letter from him arrived after a while: the curator of the Vatican collection 'appreciated my art' but would like me to paint for them something smaller and – here my priest hesitantly gave a longish list of **censoring/aesthetic restrictions**.

And still more to tell. My *Memoir* having reached the present, it turned on the following 12-foot-high canvas scroll into a *Diary*, with the current dated sequences beginning, as it happened, with the Enthronement of the new Pope.

But into the early hours before my morning flight to Rom‹ I had front-rowed at Andrew Logan's Clapham Common tentified '**Alternative Miss World**' – unholy function: transvestites, fading aggressive ladies, scatological and stimulatory *braggadocio*. An irresistible theme in the medieval picture convention of duality: Heaven/Hell images to inaugurate my *Diary*. The Pope seated high in profile, towering above a soaring triangle of the great function's saintly vanities, Vatican yellows dominant, counterpoints th‹ red pyramid of vices.

The painting will evolve onward – other dates, other images; but back to His Holiness: I was quite discomfited, while painting, at the emerging mood of his features – **irascible, fervent**. As it is in the nature of my act of painting to let go, to accept what shapes itself, that is, up to the point when there is nothing more I can add; correcting, touching up, would, with me, be reductive/destructive. Thus this image of an irate Pope had to stay, however contrary to the benign Pastor he appeared to be – then. But very soon after, his first upsettingly harsh admonishments were dealt to the Central American priesthood; then his unbending commands. I don't claim pictorial prediction of his later revealed characteristics – it would be utterly against my mind's habits and it was, to me, a chance slip of my brush; but the coincidence I think worth telling.

The pressures of Now. **Vanessa**'s motor-cycling foray on my studio, helmeted, battle-wrapped – a swift yet majestic she-warrior out of futuristic legend – but to shower me for hours with Workers' Revolutionary Party phraseology and leaflets ('Sex I left behind'). Have all passions passed over to women (The Furies)? Because it was not John Arden, but his wife Margaretta d'Arcy, who came to beflame me over uniting Ireland, the sufferings of the IRA in Ulster's prisons.

ULSTER. Jimmy (trim-bearded/squat/bourgeois-vain suit) will be devoted – of course irritating, suspected of funk and risk-dodging; and it may be so but, in sum, he leads me deeper, and more persistently and hazardously than expected.

I brief him with my idiosyncrasies and targets but to start with have to yield to his patriotism: to **Belfast** along a roundabout hilly way for its admirable general view; and the road helpfully serves up my first **Army control-point** – lacking precision routine. The emptyish roads curve over the noon sun-sleepy landscape and Jimmy points out in passing, indifferently, a broken-up building turned a pleasing **grass-overgrown ruin** by a mere ten years: an innocent roadside pub, The Black Mountain, one of the first to be smitten; new standard housing already nestling to it closely, Catholic, because those early battles dislodged the Protestants from here. The victors we pass: flower-patterned Grandma, teenage girls in pairs (pants up-to-date-shaped and hair/cosmetics as directed by London women's mags). Another bend and the promised 'general view'. The urban sprawl blast-flattened and creater-sprinkled, industrially hugging its river – the anomalous unimpeded sun out of blueness falsifying the Belfastian ambience.

As asked, scrupulous Jimmy drives me into the front lines – through a shoppy back street filled with the morning bustle (also round the corner the renewed home-craft of two-wheeled bright yellow folksy carts – in preparation, against the odds, for tourists); and already, at this hour, the oldsters (to maintain the legend of Irish supremacy in liquor and talk) wave bottles, giggle toothlessly – do their duty as local colour. But younger men, expressionless under 'IRA are Anarchists' 'Digby Fishy' 'Tommy Seamy', after sleeping off their night-skulks and -sports. The legendary **Falls Road**, pauper of a street of Catholic denomination. **Mighty boulders** jut up along the gutters defending houses from explosive-loaded cars;* behind, virulent-profiled lads, leaning against the walls, propped against ugly entrances and corners, loosely but fiercely, punctuate Republican, Sinn Fein clubs – the Legal Arm of the IRA bordering on illegality – a Provisionals' shopfront, slovenly barricaded 'Art Shop – Sinn Fein' an 'IRA area' between the orange ball of a beacon and the round-triangle 'School'. But also there ambles/shambles everydayness, sweating out an unavoidable but rare clergyman.

And at the end of the long flatness an authoritarian immensity, but makeshift, but heavy with meaning: a high-stretched (very high – some 30 feet up on iron girders) **wire fortress** – the police station, almost abutting (the steady traffic, road-sign-drilled, looks after itself in between) on **the Mill Town Catholic Cemetery** that displays a patch for fallen IRA fighters. On the corner a menacing thickening of springily squatted youths (as if ever awaiting a sign) – though perhaps just labourers taking their midday break? Jimmy parks among all this for my drawing – I shall learn tomorrow that this was an almost-heroic act.

Again along the Falls Road. In a tight side street, within appropriate concrete obstacles, a **road-check patrol** settled to search cars and humans – for a short while, a co-ordinated and tensed routine: soldiers down on their haunches, lurking 'to cover', and those who act. A massive armoured vehicle ('Pig') soon collects them – and again a calm industrial lining to the commercial front.

Now for balance we U-turn through/under corrugated iron blockages on to the neighbouring **Protestant Shankill Road**,

(slogans, slogans:

TO REPRESSION!

BERNADETTE IN – PRISONERS OUT

FUCK THE POPE

FUCK SLOPPY

but the Falls Road answers:

VOTE POLITICAL

PROVOS IRA

NO REBELS HERE → VICTORS

on sheetings tracing deadened streets, on rods propping rotted fences, and protruding above black rags, torn and theatrical, flutter in the wind); hacked-up rubble accented by lone column chimneys of burnt-out factories: the same grey bustling about people extirpated (like their opposites) throughout the last eleven years' baseness of dark insidious murders and wrongs.

The Belfast religiosity-map leaps/thrusts/presses back-forth from year to year – corrugated sheetings march along streets' centres, demarcate/shut out more menacing closenesses, cut athwart, fall over and rise in another configuration because stabilizations do not keep pace with events – a war not only of humans but of housing.

Occupations, oppressions, blacks/whites, anarchy of the young/oldsters' law-and-order governments, and bombs and hostages, but here:

First time I see, and disbelieve my eyes, **a neighbourhood**

*Those rocks decoratively, bizarrely and gravely lounging along the wretchedness of the Falls Road are heedlessly sculptured for matters of life and death: almost shameful to use them as an argument over the infamy and futility of 'art' mounting ranks of pebbles in museums – playful 'nature-aping' is left behind by this vehement concreteness. Art is Artifax, that is the gift for creating imagery given to humanity, and let us be grateful.

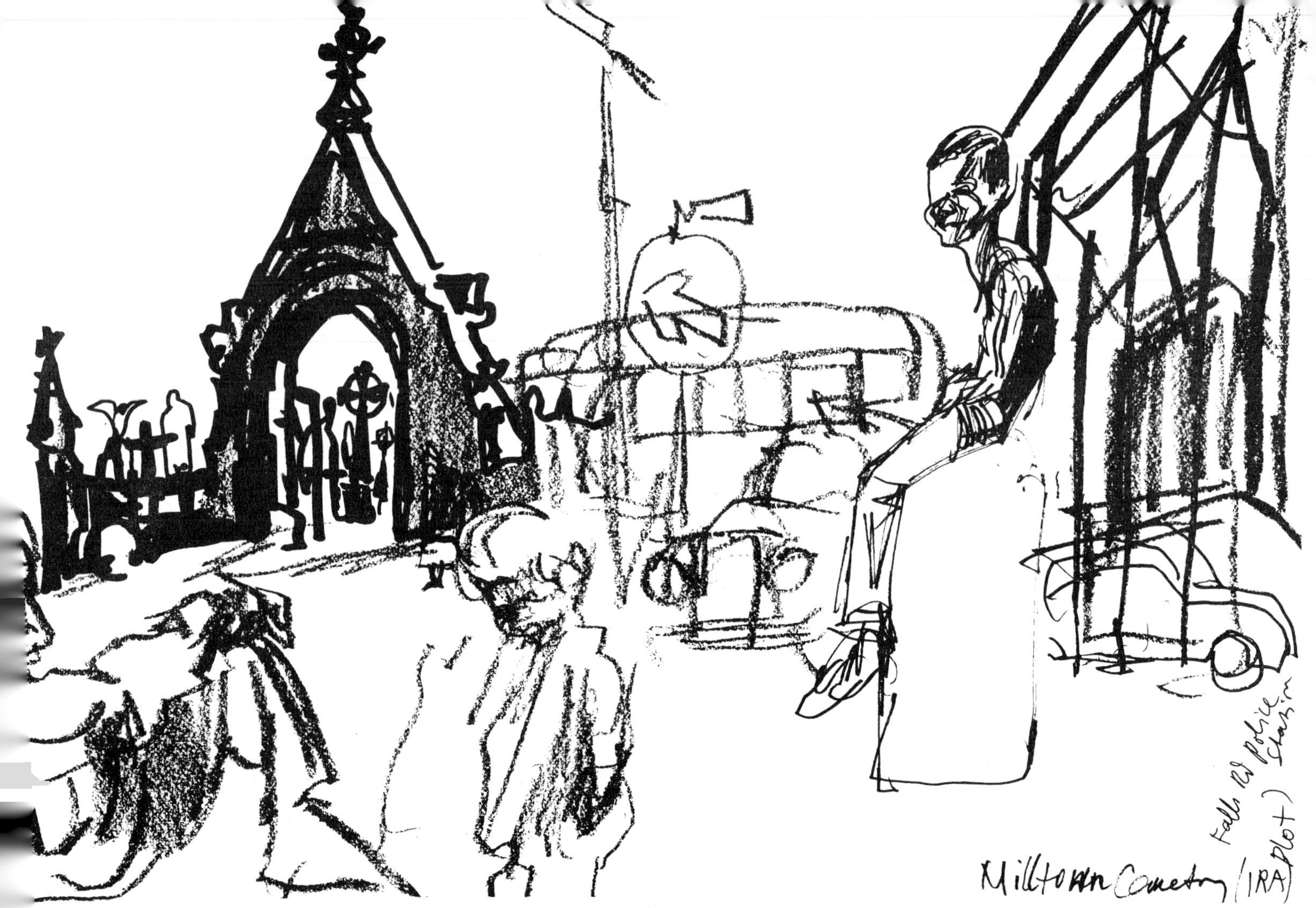

Northern Ireland: Belfast. Police station and Milltown Catholic Cemetery

at civil war. Not even over a balk, but from parlour to cellar, from house to house, from left-side to right-side pavement, from one street to the next. People, tribally entangled, supposedly circle one another in hate, calling upon **two Jesuses**; or is this only a verbal cover for the history of oppression and privileges? Several random conversants assure of their lack of interest in the struggle and in Republicanism. And the IRA Provisionals, armed for ceaseless fighting, seem pressed lately (a new revelation for them, or the necessity to reload stale batteries with present-day-ness?) towards **social revolt**.

But another death-dealing pointer: the imitation US Mafia(?) – these acquired skills/facilities bring out the cancer of **protection rackets**.

The bathetic truth may be that the working class on both sides of the shaky sheeting are not fired by calls for holy war or social justice, but, immersed in their miasmic sub-existence, fall on life-death tensions however provoked. But Britannia rules, with the middle classes' approval, over all this on the principle of the democratic '**business as usual**' ideal (in commerce, administration and the arts), patrolled by the military.

The range and grand gestures of a civil war do not exist here – the murderers steal in without the accessories of picturesqueness. They will, if caught, act their heroic parts – only then.

. . . also the supporting systems of permanent barriers, closed at 6 pm, and of concrete blocks, and gratings/grills shutting off inroads of heretics/dissenters, or 'shopping precincts' in mid-town with uniformed 'searchers' fingering the housewives. Above all, the burnt-out bombed-out stretches of the once-inhabitation – but, invariably, not in the centre, not in the well-to-do suburbia.

We circle this once-modest town – now a battlefield – enter the perplexed normality of universal-municipal everydayness: the dejection and distress of the Belfast-scape moves along its likeness to provincial/suburban England routinely engaged in shopping, children's play, church- and pub-going; it all becomes deliberate in this civil war's border/no-man's-land burnt out and sheathed in corrugated iron walls; and to get into **the wire-barricaded Hotel Europa,** the car the documents and ourselves are subjected to search/control. Inside the ceremonious listlessness/sluggishness of standard British provincialism, the dining room filled with rattling-away old crones on some conference, served – by Asians – Northern Irish food.

I put to Jimmy the list of my **potential contacts** with the extreme left/right of both denominations. It makes him uneasy. And me clear that my *cicerone* was well chosen: non-engaged, a majority representative, conditioned to keep within the routine paths of his business and complacency over the volcanic terrain. And in consequence, he has to know precisely (but always acting normality, because of 'jobs'; because of the watching world; because of investing foreigners; because of 'business as usual' – the call of the Britain that held out under the German bombardment) the schedule/disposition (and frequent changes) of explosive, sensitive spots: those presently threatening, those historically prominent, marked by exploded mines, or, otherwise, those necessary to the dominant workadayness. All these his survival stakes.

We set out. He points, seemingly with some pride, to non-monuments in their bedraggled littleness, bare of patina, picketed by traffic and anti-traffic signs, scrawled over by insipidly spiritless graffiti. And because he knows but is an outsider (thus unnoticeable – he and his car), with a sense of duty too towards my stint, he plunges into the neighbourhood of the notorious **Interrogation** (torture) **Centre** at Castlereagh Headquarters in Latis Drive (keeping a prudent distance): suburbia of exemplary detached housing cum gardens; and within it, neatly, a calm steel-netted green enclosure with casual gatekeepers – the tidy pleasurable perspective of greenery outside carries **green-blazered schoolgirls** leaping homeward.

Next stop outside **the Unionist Party Headquarters** in the shabby Newtownards High Street (East Belfast – the other side of the river): a man knocks at the locked door lengthily, but unpressing. This time **skipping schoolboys in green,** green kerchiefs round their necks (like *Konsomols*' red, *Hitler Jugend*'s brown); and sad-rumbustious drunkards overflowing out of the Ulster Arms perform, filed through by armed (but no confidence) **RU Constabulary**: the man along the right pavement, the woman along the left. The street fades into slums, abandoned shops and railings locked against the narrow Catholic depth; and a hefty two-towered church – from which, they say, the first shots were fired in 1969.

And again through **IRA Provisionals'** and **Sinn Fein** domesticated positions. Again the Falls Road: another section – roofs crashed open from the inside by the fists of bombs. The small St Paul's church divulges the faithful – up to babes-in-arms and an unremarkable man propelled on wheels – all almost static, passive and brooding; an ambulance arrives, and motions of loading.

Tomorrow Jimmy will say, 'You were **lucky** – there was a shot the moment before we arrived and a man was mortally wounded.'

I ask for a range of newspapers – but see that, though Jimmy acts readiness to oblige, to ask for a Protestant paper in a Catholic area would be either hopeless or dangerous; that, at the hotel, I'll be given London papers only, because this eliminates problems. In a leading bookshop (close to the University) guidebooks on Belfast do not exist – only on Ireland overall. Thus the trifles of compromise co-exist with no compromises – **a thin wedge to killings** behind the counter, on doorsteps and in parlours.

– **Woodstode Road,** Catholic because cleared of Protestants together with their burnt-out houses – yet at the edge of the fallow rubbishy emptiness ('NO REBELS HERE') a mean bricky prayer-house has survived ('Healer Saviour Baptizer' in Victorian calligraphy) amongst a few cut-open bared interiors of poverty.

– One side of **Mountpottenger Road** – the Catholic underdogs' one-storey terrace, redbrick, white window-

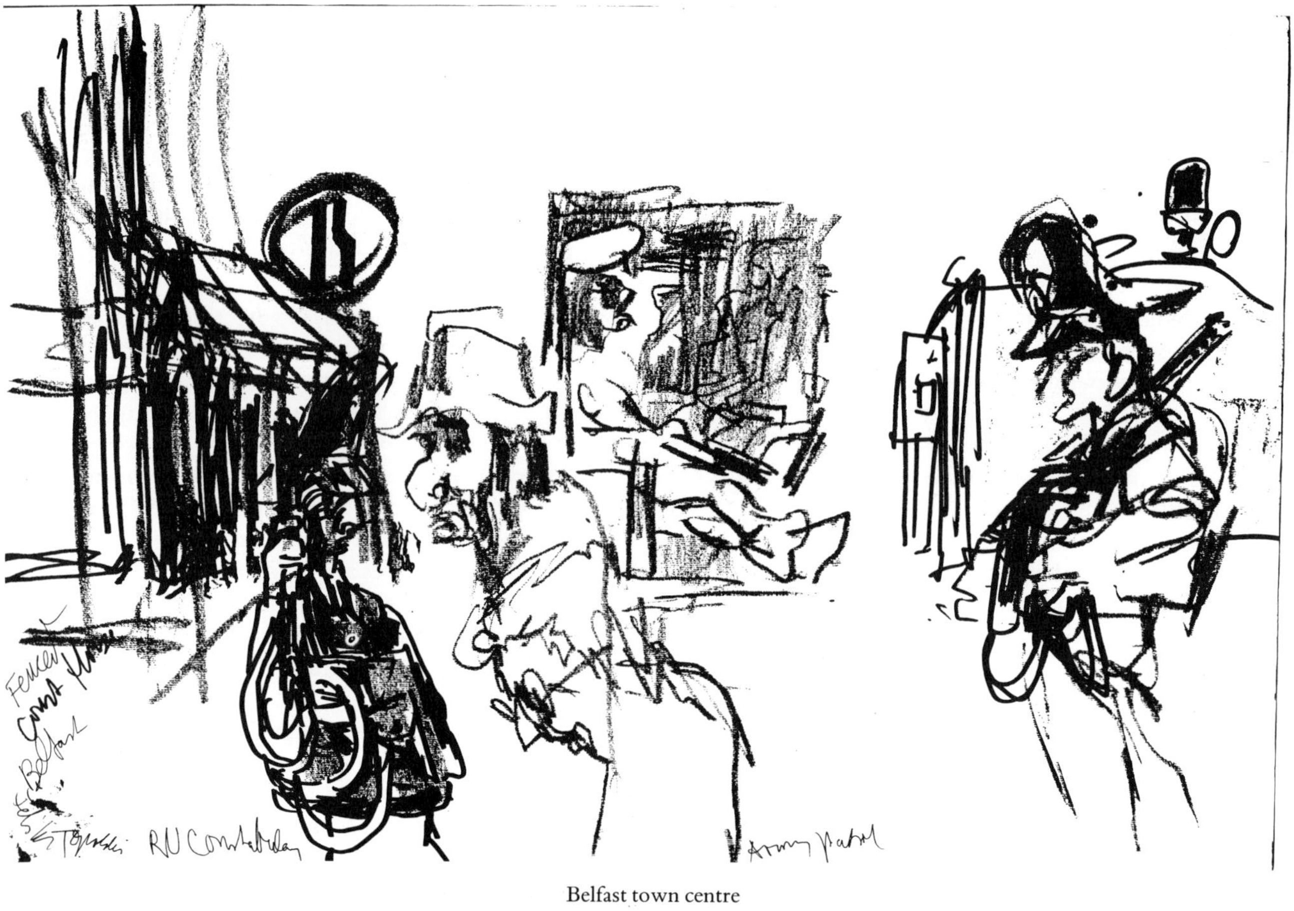

Belfast town centre

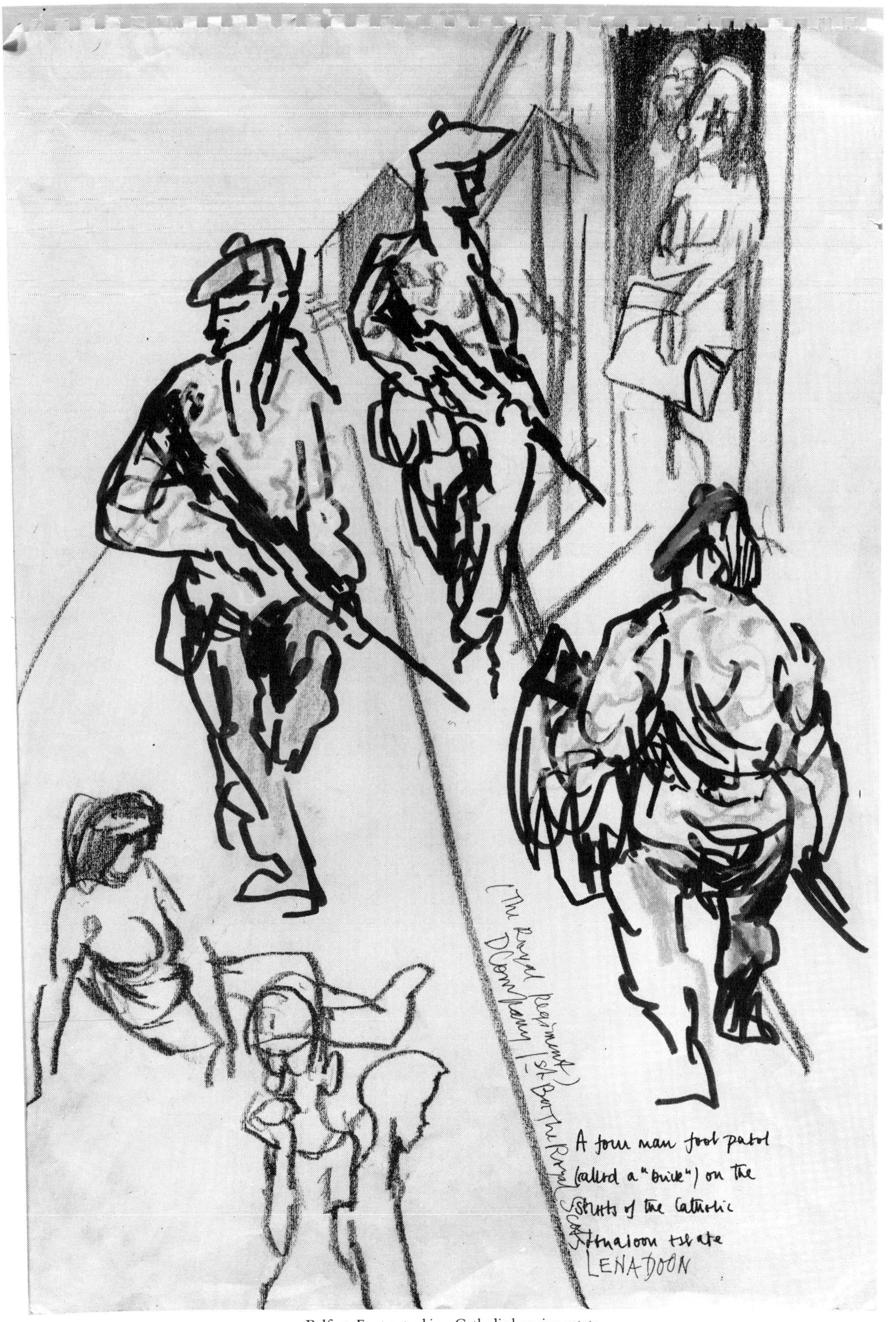

Belfast. Foot patrol in a Catholic housing estate

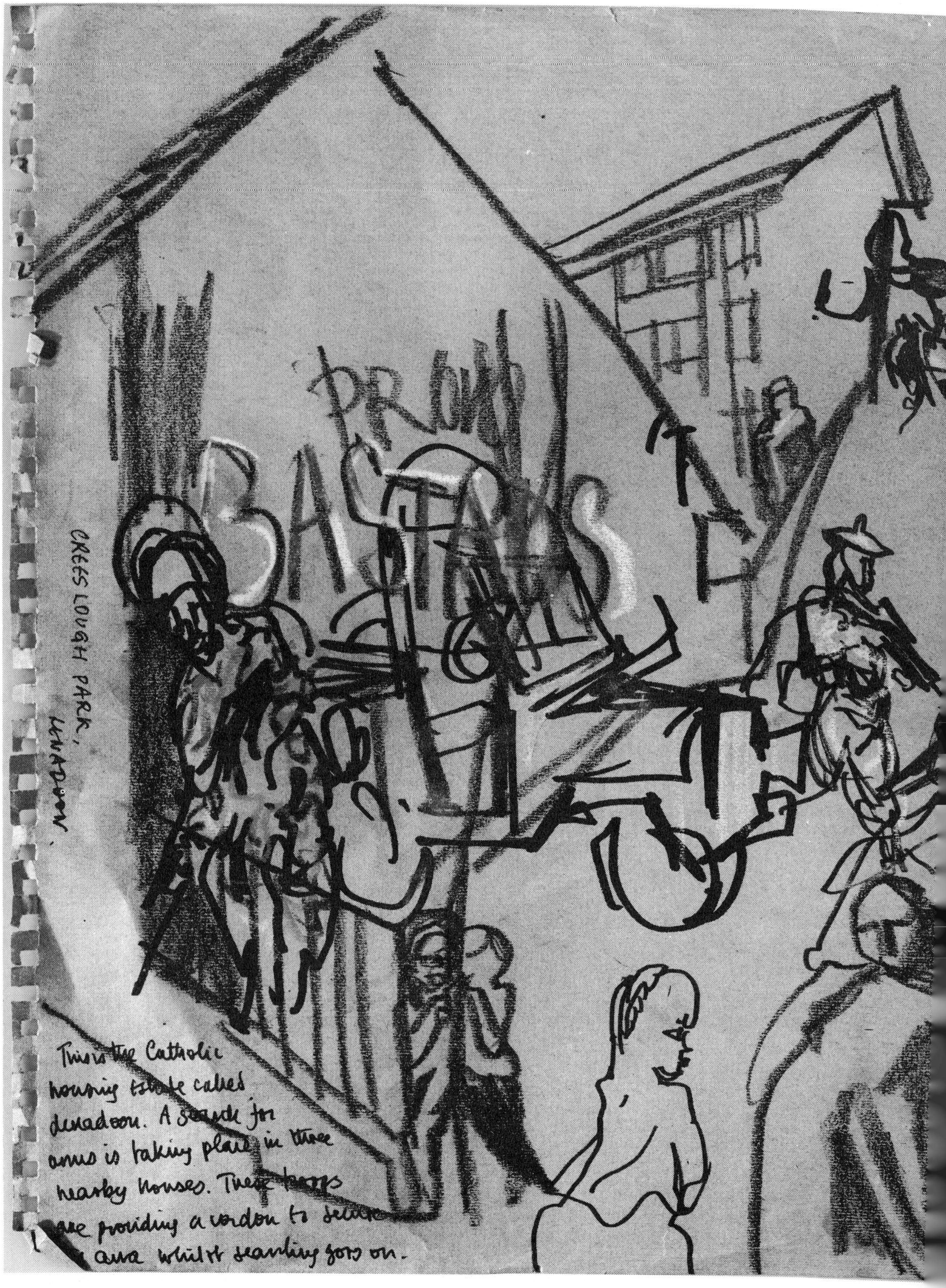
CREES LOUGH PARK, LENADOON.
This is the Catholic housing estate called Lenadoon. A search for arms is taking place in three nearby houses. These troops are providing a cordon to secure the area whilst searching goes on.

Arms search operation at a Catholic housing estate

edges, ins-and-outs of the timorous aged, and volatile girls (swift hair) after a purchase; but, narrowly, on the opposite side, the harsh-walled 'Siccoro Engineering Works' lets out, the shift ended, a phalanx of **workers – Protestant all,** according to the owner's order.
– St George's Market normal (except for **frisking**); a funeral limousine outside transports perhaps a normally deceased.
– **Donegal Square,** the City Hall and the 'Black Man' statue (no one knows who he was). A generous sprinkling of young stationary girls: no prostitues here, Jimmy says, only massage parlours; oddly these girls are waiting for their lovers. An old man seated on the steps of an insurance building looks after an infant on a pram (as in China – babysitting ancients) – old women swagger in the uniforms of traffic wardens or '**searchers**'. The circling Land-rovers crested with warriors uselessly camouflaged.

I have been warned that drawings should on execution instantly be posted to London: do not carry them about, do not leave them in your hotel room; warned of many 'possibles' – rightly, because '*la mort court*'. **The pubs**, for instance, **traps for strangers:** divided by denomination, a stranger is suspect, therefore cornered, questioned, pushed out, beaten; but Jimmy leads me into an exception, **'The Crown Bar'** in Great Victoria Street, the preserved sample of Victorianism with an eye on tourists. Beyond the counter, partitioned intimacies; overstated old Celtic mugs floating in the drunken racket, and Jimmy's accelerating prattle.

Through it all there trundle along, pretending 'normality', the official-cultural fancy-tasks, just now the Belfast Civic Festival, subsidized and 'promoted' by a leaflet titled 'Belfast Alive'; the Miss Britain and sports contests; the Arts Council dripping calculated grants; the local BBC pseudo-patronizes; and the local poets rage/thunder (in Xeroxed brochures), perhaps trend-conscious, but their ardour battle-fired.

The intellectual republican socialisms forge ruthless revolutions, but protest – in accord with the principles of democracies' humanitarian laws – over interrogation tortures, political prisoners not separated from criminal, courts without juries . . .

One more survey: **after six** the barriers lock, the people dig in (excepting the drunkards laid here-and-there in the roads), and the smothered city asserts itself, abandoning its mirage of daily ordinariness.

I possess, anyway, routes-contacts in **all directions,** able to lead me – by way of Sinn Fein towards the Provos – into the conspiratorial territory of Falls Road (the surface of which I had traversed the day before in a 'civilian' car driven by an average everyman, stopping at my request, but at a nervous distance from my targets).

Seamus Lynch would have led me along the edges of the legal IRA. Enoch Powell had sent out letters, and so there await me the Unionists, the Grand Master of the Orangemen's Order, and predominantly farming and fishing charms. Gerry Fitt (SDLP) would have guided me amongst the mellower Catholics. And John Cushnaham within the Alliance Party.

I bypass these beckonings, which would haul me in by pressures aiming at conversations/engagements and divert m from being a watcher and a drawer. And so I rode with everyman, and yield now (because pre-cornered by London arrangements and because it is a mechanical, non-pressuring set-up) to **the Military 'facility'**.

A Major picks me up (in mufti and in a civilian car: 'They are all known to *them* anyway, and in any case when Command ordered a hundred replacement Fords, they arrived in an identical brown. Delivered us on a plate, straight into their hands!), drives to the outskirts, past barriers, barricaded gates, controls, to **Headquarters, Northern Ireland,** becaus today a monthly reception for 'celebrities' is taking place – this time for Mr Dennis Faulkner, brother of the late Prime Minister killed a short time before (but in a hunting accident); and me, a supplementary 'personage'. The military bureaucracy deployed over corridors, behind bevies of doors labelled by rank, name and administrative-informative function, disgorged prominent figures (the tallest a Colonel-Lieutenant, the shorter ones less star-studded, and the smooth Mr Faulkner) and propels us all in urbane contortions through those functional entrails into the grand hall-stairway, freshly knocked together, without marks of history, to ascend past the dullest paintings and to deposit us in faceless Rooms. **The Rooms,** comforting themselves with military prints, are packed with uniforms, bowings and scrapings, the basic exchanges cut short by reshuffling. The staff officers: one suggests, as a marvellous subject for me, the shadowy **'Pig'** interiors crowded with armed soldiers at the slit-openings; another prepares me for the **armoured** dashes through the Catholic Falls Road: 'The only way . . .' (not knowing that I had been reconnoitering it already in an unarmed civilian 'guise'); still another, a chief of propaganda, tells how he dared, ringed by soldiers, to jump out briefly and got a 'Fuck Off' from a fierce 'not really old' woman.

These are their only approaches to the terrain. But my social feeler-exchanges with **Faulkner** (who are our common acquaintances . . . with whom/where throughout the world . . . how in Brazil's yachting clubs community . . .?) – also touch on local anecdotes/friends in avoidance of the overhanging theme of helplessness (this goes too for others at the gathering) in the face of the here and now. But some voices break through – **helplessness**, because they already had a parliament, which failed, to be replaced by a simplified rule. Try again? Surrender? Comparisons with the British exits from Palestine or India – 'Those were Colonials, here we have our own people'. 'The Republic doesn't want Ulster – endless shindies and Paisley's jingoism – no!'

Now I am led to a roomful of pinned-up maps and statistics: the briefing. I am to be turned over to **D Company, First Battalion, The Royal Scots,** for their regular patrolling in Catholic areas. Difficult work – the military being the main target of attacks.

Driving to my assignment, through today's universal bustling ugliness of pseudo-well-being, I voice my pre-arrival theory. Youngsters, always and everywhere, played at gang wars, while now here (I have seen photographs and films of Irish riots, with twelve- to fifteen-year-olds to the fore)

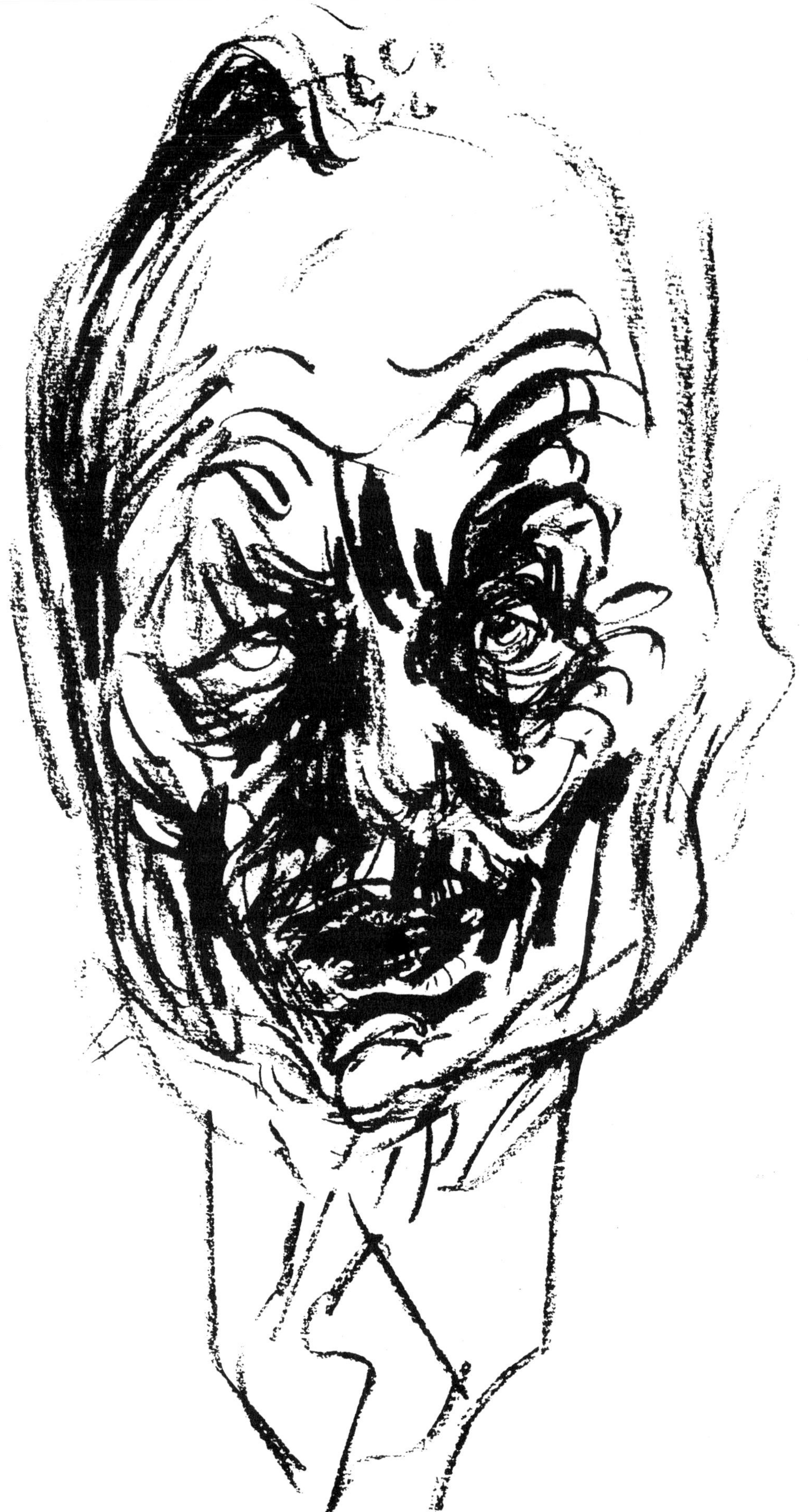

Enoch Powell

suddenly the make-believe takes 'flesh': happiness itself – their hands which fought with sticks are filled with real well-oiled rifles, glory is offered to their games by the 'media'; ringed by television and press reporters, they make history, fuelling vanity in the service of a CAUSE reduced to the juvenile level, one side of the street against the other. The religious war? Fanned by the ambitious-cum-parochial leaders and fitted to the wits of a child-boy with a stick? The major says it was so, but that street battles belong to the past – the toll-of-life was too high – coming into the open harmful for them; also, the weapons and the methods have improved (probably co-ordinated with those elsewhere) – are **more 'sophisticated'**. Now **a single 'pro'** with a bomb, or one sharpshooter at a window of a terrorized household, ambushes a calculated and timed victim. Invisible and unpredictable. Or a driverless bomb-carrying car is set off at a building – hence these protective rows of giant rocks along the gutters.

'Very few army and police about,' I say. His predictable response: 'Low-profile policy . . . less intensification . . .' But later it seemed conceivable to me that, in fact, 'the Armed Forces' are tactically under siege.

We drive through a range of checks into a sprawling military complex: an expectantly large hospital, custody sheds, NAAFI hut – and ranks of barracks. **Captain Thompson,** Company D, First Battalion, the Royal Scots, takes me over; I am wearing my blue-denim bush-blouse bought for China – as khaki is taboo, I was warned, for Ireland too – to appear an unblemished civilian, but here is the reverse: my blue denim off and **a military camouflage-khaki jacket** on, precisely, for me not to differ and tempt . . .

Now, for the latrine, where I fitfully disentangle out of memory an abridged list of associations with the past: all those humbling inveiglements of an 'an eye-witness' on to the side of the current overlords – in French Indo-China and 'American' Vietnam, in Malaya, in Israel, in Japan. Also a pause for a touch of stupefaction – or for tightening up in readiness (professional) for what will take place?

Two open Land-Rovers **in convoy;** in the leading one, the driver, and I next to him, the Captain and a private perched, weapons alert, in the back; in the second one, four more men.

The procedure demands, first, calling for orders at the regimental headquarters at **Woodbourne Camp in West Belfast.** The patrol wheels into the town centre – does not merely progress but demonstrates and provokes: streets drift by their normalities, but for that instant of our passage, as if in ostentatious defiance, their ordinariness takes on an extra edge.

Woodbourne Camp, a transient makeshift citadel, corrugated-iron-sheeted, barbed-wire-wrapped, studded round with concrete blocks and watchtowers – we approach it quite fast. A few yards from the entrance the brakes screech and, simultaneously: my captain, bawling at me 'Don't get out', jumps to the ground together with both crews; they all, each for himself, bend double in evasive zigzags and, **in a furious run,** throw themselves behind the entrance blocks, weapons aimed back at the street-vistas and the nearest blank-looking houses; and only then the two Land-Rovers (and I) fling into safety. Seconds. Unprepared for this manoeuvre, I ask my driver (helmeted and visored) for its meaning. Simple: vehicles entering these fortresses offer **the most vulnerable targets** for potential sharp-shooters at windows and on roofs close by. A leap and scattered run reduces the risk for all but the driver who at the wheel of an open, totally exposed, car is handicapped for a few seconds, and me a veritable 'sitting duck' rooted (by command) at his side, displaying my old mug over the military blouse – **a possible high-ranking rarity** for a gunman. I chose not to talk about this to the captain, who, I imagine, thought it better to have the 'old boy' driven in, rather than to risk his falling about and tripping the others.

Hideous tightly packed barracks, men listless (between duties); Scottish city-boys, produced and subdued by urban penury, even when fully rigged out, do not exude power. Significant that, with their shortcomings, they do not plunge into compensatory bullying extremes. The officers, within this wired stockade, being of a 'higher' order, underplay it: eat from the same pot – carrying filled-up plates from the cook-house across the muddy passageways to **the officers' mess-hut** 'personalize' their contacts with the men, are eager to show their dormitories. They send me up a ladder to one of the feebly knocked-together **towerlets** above rising parapets, containing a soldier on the lookout in three directions for possible attacks from amongst the prosaic crumbling terraces of Belfast.

Now the day's **routine**. We load in and whirl out at speed. First: a **corrugated wall**, which separates Protestant from Catholic areas, a wall over 20 feet high smudged with acclamatory slogans crossed by intimate hate-love bulletins, widely towering over a sordidly bedraggled no-man's-land. The soldiering opens here with **a foray** on to this silent wasteland in dust clouds of whirling turns and halts, men leaping out, galloping to covers of crumbled corners, flat-downing/crouching – trigger finger at the ready. And into this nth rehearsal-display filter, hushed and impasssive, yet leisurely, **the littlest boys** propelled by the military allure – the military, on this stage-like patch, seem to perform, so that with the entry of those kids, with their quotidian familiarity, **the counter-action** of two groups differing in size and rhythm creates a dramatic truth: ARTificial-symbolic, as though the action were not real.

Next the patrol rides on to a new Catholic housing estate, this time with urgency on an **'arms search'** operation – an informer the sole activator. Two more patrols (also two open Land-Rovers each, their men's dark berets with white and red feathers differing from our khaki ones) wind in unison with us to surround and cordon off the area – some troopers going down steepness into the complex of tidy semi-detacheds, standard garden-plots attached. Fences, blots of greenery, a rich variety of road signs multiplied by the effusion of inner-estate ones – courteous well-being of the lower middle class with no trace of destruction or of ominous barriers, crammed with pram-mums, young girls cycling, shopping movements hither and thither, women in pregnancy, or those in make-up and tightly bottomed frocks/trousers – their body-mime signalling – but emphatically not to the soldiery. The uninterrupted flow of **an ordinary afternoon,** although the tumult of the armed invasion cuts in and rounds off a slice of the estate with its ready-for-anything **fury of runs and 'taking-cover';** the uniforms, camouflage-patterned for muddy fields, not for neat street combats, increase the bizarreness. Time passes, the 'strategically held' estate (machines and pointed guns) functions. Small boys begin to climb over our vehicles. The 'search' takes place in the cluster of houses behind me. I draw. It is clear that success – that is, cornering **hidden IRA men** or finding **a cache of arms** – could result either in an explosion of gunfire, panic and victims – or in smuggling out the seized without upsetting the routine of pseudo-indifference.

Because the acting of pseudo-indifference is a safety device for those masking their passions – republican, unionist, religious, revolutionary – but a safety-valve, which serves the majority, Catholic and Protestant, masking their **genuine indifference**.

Captain Thompson proposes: it is early afternoon, the pubs should be quite empty, therefore a **surprise check in search of arms and suspects** if carried out now – 'may make it easier to draw'. 'Suffolk (Catholic) Bar' is a newish low-spread building, not in the tradition of corner-hugging but, in the manner of a roadhouse set in open (bombed-out?) terrain. As always (regulations?) clamourous ride-in, leaps, guns stuck out threateningly and all, but for one driver, seven (I with my sketchbook) march across and in and, **spread in a half-circle,** assess the situation: unexpectedly, the large low single interior is densely filled up by men only – possibly more than a casual afternoon (a meeting?). The throng tightens away from us unbudging, all the faces turned at us, long long silence. Inertly and mindlessly it goes uppermost through my head that drawing here/now – the object of such concentrated attention – would be ridiculous, **the nearness of bloodshed** unfocused. Even when Thompson (not relaxing his combat-posture) whispers to me that perhaps not, we should back out, that 'THEY may get irritated', I agree, taking it that the nonsense of drawing was the central issue. Another instant of strained taut immobility, and (**guns ever-pointed**) we **retreat** – backward. Outside, Thompson tells me that recently, in a similar numerically unequal confrontation, the locals disarmed and massacred a patrol; and that here the disparity was even more **desperate**.

It is all repetitious – routines form repetitious contrasts; the refrains prolonged and dull – the verses, bursting one-liners.

We are still amongst **the Catholics** on the Lenadoon Estate, but in the old terraces of cosy folk-housing. Men absent – probably in that pub – women and children in gestures and groupings of normality; our soldiers, stroll in file, as though carelessly, as though reconnoitring, as though (because I do not believe in the reality of this particular operation) at the ready. Once again the kids press forward and impose a mock-fraternization; **mothers** with elder daughters shadowed in doorways, **passive,** evoke the image of the Italian village encompassed by battle with its cowering women in dark openings.

This time the patrol climbs above the city to set **a surprise Road Block,** such as the one which stopped me before, as a civilian. Askew across the road our two Land-Rovers leave a narrow passage – searches of people and vehicles, whispered reports into microphones (to the patrol's leader? or further?). People in cars and lorries, passive, stiffened. The routine for survival – or not.

A short stop at a Library, where **a policeman** was **murdered** – foolhardily parked on that spot, with me perched in the front seat, and drawing. A caption written by Captain Thompson under my drawing of the location showing one of our soldiers standing duty on its porch:

> The patrol is checking that there are no problems in the Library. This was the scene where Constable MAGILL of the RUC was murdered and three other police, one an unarmed policewoman, were seriously wounded on 9 April 1980. The police had been called out to the Library after some vandalism had taken place. About 60 shots were fired from the other side of the road, fourth upstairs window along from the left – a range of 80 metres from three weapons.

The most recent **murderous narration** – as always, punctuated by prosaic circumstances, concluded by a bullet or a bomb: the dead body of an old man, shot in his street because he blurted something out, had been lying for nearly a week on a yellow line, because the dead are made into **booby-traps**.

Again **the officers' mess,** gin-and-tonic and well-brought-up exchanges, but with the running emphasis on lying-in-wait and unpredictable terror. Do I sense in their hospitality a veiled discomfort (perverse/tragicomical) at not dishing up an ugly incident for me.

They have been here since February, will leave in two weeks, will pack up their household goods, the souvenir-objects which flimsily warmed up their home-aura – the most treasured a carefully detailed picture belonging to their Colonel, which I deciphered as Calcutta – the leave-town of my days round '44, and apparently his. Their replacements will hardly differ, will step into the same timetable within the same time-honoured structure of patronizing caring gentlemen and gratified privates-commoners.*

*Why don't the trade unions consider breaking into this. Why does a voting democracy stand on feet of clay: institutionalized hierarchies.

I rush to catch **the departing 'pig'**; if missed, my whole patrol (and the dangers) would have to be revived to take me back to the centre.

The armoured charabanc with **shuttable slits** (shut at every entry/exit/stop) filled up: soldiers of various formations – timid cockiness in spotty faces, a plump female soldier (green forage cap and skirt, shirt-and-tie), her rolling eye a stalking/ questing hook; then, when in contact, she acts 'fed up', will flee the service (her contract ends in the summer) – to what? typing. Her future life to be sustained on memories of those 'pig' transports amongst the uniformed 'boys'. Two men at the back slit aim their guns at everydayness; two helmeted in front operate an additional net-obstacle over the front slit. This defensive ponderousness is wheeling along streets which I traversed before, stopped in and drew in comparative ease – this incommunicado norm is telling.

The 'personnel' passengers are dropped off, one by one, each with full display of **caution**.

The ignominy of the day: the driver, though I beg to be comfortably dropped across from my hotel, combatively U-turns and confuses the rush-hour traffic (because dramatize they must, the wretches, in the sweat of their privileged equipment) to reach the Europa's barbed-wire fence and barriers and control-hut, and spits me out with my haversack on to the hands of **dazzled 'friskers'**.

At some later hour, below my window, huge roars and tramping and slogan yelling: an immense processional surge goes by, swinging flags of many colours – from **Union Jacks to green-white.** I am confused: a reconciliation? or an impending clash for surely these are the youngest playing at war, now done up with the glory of tribal-tinted rags wrapped round their bodies? Until a correct guess, confirmed later: this ecstatic unity in **Ulster patriotism** is caused by this afternoon's victory, in International Football, of Northern Ireland over Scotland, one to zero.

Evenings at the Europa Hotel – an oasis of safety – agitate with varied pursuits; for all its closely guarded security, the late hours seem to swell with a great many more clients than this establishment could house – its barbed-wire fences assuring **Belfast's upper strata** jollifications.

Sometime around eight in the morning a knock catches me under the shower. Breakfast? I open the door – and there stands (a spill-over from night passions?) a seemly, buxom, shoeless (stockinged rustic feet), black-eyed-haired, small-breasted, true '**Miss Northern Ireland**'. And blushing/giggling that she got the room number wrong and, immovable in the doorway, good-naturedly and graced by her peasanty speech, she asks for my name. 'Lovely name', and, so (because still towel-wrapped), I offer her breakfast if she returns in a while. And she does come back. A Catholic, had a job but, restless, left it; she has a five-year-old child by an imprisoned terrorist, but also a Hindu boyfriend, who hopes to open a restaurant in Derry. One of the sphere of girls who dance themselves into this sealed hotel's discothèque.

Jimmie, stylishly pink-shirted, arrives to drive me into the depths of the country to catch **Paisley**.

Folk-speech at my side, gratingly toneless, drones bullet-shooting, wheel-crushing, bomb-exploding anecdotes – outside our car runs the shoppy-homely '**cultural desert**' circulated by housewives self-rendered graceless by spectacles-frizziness-frocks, short of solemnity – updating those proud black-shawled women of Ireland; and old boys heavily spectacled; with the young up against corners/fences or squatting on doorsteps in lackadaisical preparedness; the small kids inattentive, unpredictable. And the rare Police-Ulsterman in distended **bullet-proof black waistcoat** and armatured peak cap seems hucksterly and trivial. But the growing **flatness of reality fuels the need for drama** (traceable all over the globe): in consequence *Ulster Bank* and *Allied Irish Bank* and the *Newsagent* (it is dangerous to ask for the wrong paper) and *Royal Ulster Society* and *Boot's* must bear passionate graffiti; and armoured/armed slit-eyed rolling fortresses. Now the car plunges into inconsequential greeneries interpolated with torpid cottages – every township repeats the chainstore-stamp, combatively barrier-bound for battles, circulates 'pigs' – grey and khaki. But strawberry girls stand alongside the open road.

Dungannon just gutted, a barred CONTROL ZONE (two soldiers, male and female, backed by a bronze Private of World War I diverts the traffic to Armagh: puffed up Cathedral, '**PROVOLAND**' on fences, Military Police to-and-fro in front of the palatial **Women's Prison** (**Margaretta d'Arcy** is there, having rushed from London to surrender herself in lieu of a fine). We circle smoking debris, one remaining wall announcing 'NO SURRENDER', and emerge at last into lush greenness towards Six Mile Cross – an expanding of **Paisleyite territory**.

A pre-Paisley church sits beautifully amongst gravestones, backclothed by green-grey distances, and garnished 'artfully' yet with a modicum of dignity by black-green shrubberies trimmed into bulgy geometrics. Across the road a steep plot, its weary grass bearing a white contour of the projected chapel, behind it a freshly concreted Community Centre; the dissonance of **sectarianism on the move.** An open-air semi-circular row of empty chairs and benches; and at the road's turn a modest police assistance of two drives into view. They and Jimmie fall into camaraderie and he photographs me flanked by the two to parallel (my thought) that distant snap with a Malayan patrol. Charabancs and cars agglomerate the faithful – I walk with them into the circle and face a young good-looker, his ambitious three-piece suit edged by a dog collar. I announce my drawing purpose. 'For whom?' 'For myself (true), but also maybe for the *Telegraph*.' 'No, not for that paper.' He demands a promise 'no *Telegraph*', otherwise I shall be forbidden to stay. I promise (and later learn that the local *Telegraph* is his taboo, not the London one). At the centre of the semi-circle: **a pulpit** hung with crocheted velvet. At its side, falling about in the wind, a microphone and easel holding plans and costings (both, throughout the occasion, repeatedly retrieved by helpful hands). The chairs are reserved for the worthies who will make their late arrivals, but, behind me (I sit on a single bench alongside the chairs), the plot fills up, already thickly, with **goody agelings** in their Sunday best: flowers (artificial) sprouting on veiled hats and over their dresses;

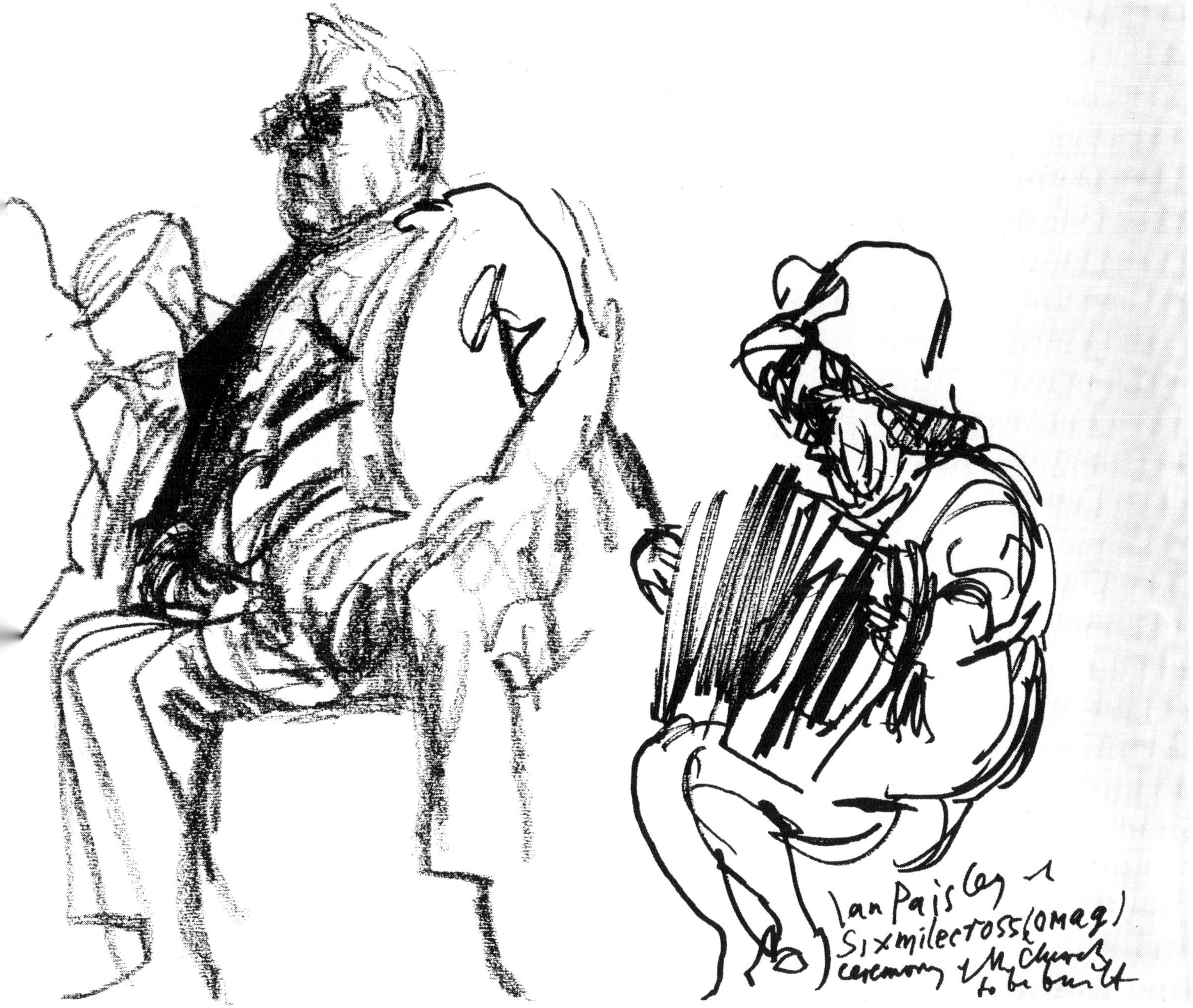

Ian Paisley

gloves, parasols. The bare hillock turns into a bed of choice flowers grown locally on Presbyterian fertilizers. The solitary younger female next to me came challenging her background ('If they knew. . .'), is a Catholic, but curious about Paisley and in accord with many of his ideas. 'Which ideas?' 'His devotion to his country.'

The little gathering buzzes in the sun, waiting. The board and the easel fall over again and again. The microphone stand keeps overturning. The young Pastor fusses, drills the photographer and greets the now-arriving **high-ups**, climbing out of their cars: bowings, groupings, exchanges, still more flowery attire of the ladies. The aura is celebratory-pleasurable, playful-peaceful, county – well-being not peasanty, just a provincial garden-party: revering their **household prophet,** carefreely. The two policemen are out of sight, unnecessary. . .

There he is: **a giant**; heavy, strength-filled – even his belly pronounces not neglect, but thrust. His vast physiognomy – monumental and of the seventeenth century, belonging to the gallery of Wesleys and Cromwells – downs over the gathering.

A lot of time passes in the boredom of ritual addresses by a string of pastors, biblical quotes, choral prayers (Paisley yawns wide-openly and often) and chants (with one of the hatted rounded dames accompanying on an accordion); then the lengthy arranging of Paisley handling a spade for a photograph, so that the later inauguration ceremony can proceed undisturbed. And finally, warmed up by pressing speakers, a collection.

At last Paisley steps forward – it is a pity that, almost continuously from now on, he dims his impact by dark glasses (obstructing my drawing as well) because, when removed, the mighty flesh-folds over his eyes, aiding the grabbing aggressive snout, make the mountainous facial geography of this thundering preacher, supposedly self-made pretender, unsupported by holy anointments.

Two white vapours appear on the sky, unblemished for some days, as he begins by apologizing for reminiscing about his earliest performances, carries on from there with perhaps an hour-long ramble, ending 'This much for private matters', passing suddenly on (adroitly lifting his voice to a limitless **roar**) to sectarian and political hopes-prognostics. From this, still only the groundwork, the *Leitmotif* of the oration emerges, propelled manfully and mightily '**Don't hem me in!**', swelling in strength, modulating, yet ever more assailing, threatening – 'DON'T HEM ME IN!!' 'DON'T HEM ME IN!!!'

Having ended and sat down, he is easily able to return to the microphone and add an 'afterthought' – again, but softly, concluding – '**Don't hem me in.**' Now the ceremonials. Paisley, spade-holding, summons the congregation in big voice big gestures – they spring up to converge on him.

I think I could retrace the map of every city I have walked, except for my own Warsaw which was turned into dust and raised from it, confusingly reshaped; and for London, which is a memory-atlas of impenetrable density.

I get a patient listener-driver for an erratic trip, pin-flagging the living map of London with my memorizing.

14 Hanover Terrace, our 'stately' home within Regent's Park, facing the lake: the best of London, one thought (a formal Regency town house in countrified landscape), disregarding the safeguards of a freehold to satisfy one's appetites within a treacherous 'Crown lease'. It symbolized a **dominant split**: family and artist's workshop; to have had it all under one roof would have impinged on, stifled habits embodied in the fortified solitariness of a studio. The Little Venice studio percolates throughout this story, less so the house. But it reflected thoroughly Marion's and my shared life-drift and perhaps also my opportune readiness to adjust to what befell me: the interior-planning and collecting-games, the Regency-fitting decorative black serving pair, but, at the same time, doing the house agin convention to deserve a *House and Garden* feature entitled 'Topolski versus the Prince Regent'; playing with the paraphernalia of a sort of way of life, not entirely committed (the uncommitted painter at his studio on a parallel course) yet fulfilled between the two of us, pressed by the queuing-up demands. Between the two of us? Surely it was Marion, maturing into a wise matron, who structured and promoted that life; surely I was not much more than its coy decorator, trimmer of outward frills – with the added supply of funds, which were easily flowing – corrupting commissions plentiful. Marion the enthusiastic, thus spoiling, mother, and the children growing in falsely 'aristocratic' ease into amateurish dilettantism; and myself – ever immature, though Marion, now a *savante*, in her new strength supported and conducted my moves as an artist – my *Chronicle* uppermost.

The car rolls south. Regent's Park, though for ourselves a great slice of life – and gratifying – was in essence for me an *hors concours* extravagance, even geographically, with the strip of London separating it from the south side of Oxford Street always disregarded – a nuisance-distance to traverse.

Who were those lovely precious **pansy-dandies**, faultlessly diversified in minutest play on changes within the strict conventions of gentlemanly clothes; and so in manners; and so their Mayfair rooms round Berkeley Square and 1935–6? **Tony** would take me on those rounds, my early preciosity satisfying/matching, memorably, the leather or chintzy chairs, the ambitiously draped windows, the *objets d'art* and awe-inspiring photographs in tasty frames on consoles and chimney-pieces, the drink-postures, the tweeds/house velvet jackets/the waistcoats and woollen socks, extra extravagancies (never washed but hung in rows to air), handkerchiefs in cuffs and those (matching? not matching?) in top pockets and so on . . . but I don't remember the names. Except (perhaps because this was elsewhere – in Kensington, a bit out of the way, and art-diverted) the Yeoman's Row(?) studio of **Oliver Messel**; he, a chic smoothy non-bohemian, grouped round with only an iota less graceful liegemen and patrons, within a sumptuously unworkable fantasy on the theme of *fin-de-siècle* atelier-décor – and gracious towards me.

What Duchess received me in **Grosvenor Square**? At what address did **Lady Colefax** hold her salon? What happened to the paintings by Freud and Lowry and Macbride bought at the Lefèvre Gallery, still in New Bond Street; to a sumptuous **Burra**, brought to my old studio, rolled up, by – an itinerant dealer then – Mr Corcorane, which I loved to distraction and bought from him for peanuts because it was only two-thirds of the picture documented in colour in a Penguin booklet? I saw it not long ago, still with one third missing, in a Cork Street gallery, priced monstrously. I challenged the gallant salesman on the painting's incompleteness – who, a quick professional scoundrel, took my 'no danger' measure at a glance and bullied me out.

The times of collecting: I will always regret not buying from the **Leicester Galleries**, which held two of my shows when in Leicester Square, a very tall narrow and juicy-brown Doré, which bothered old Brown and Philips, filling up their staircase's steep ceiling. They hated it even more than my ahead-of-its-time/pre-pop 12 foot by 9 foot *The East*, though Nehru came in person with Lady Mountbatten to buy it 'for India'; and, though press and sales were good and GBS came to look at my portrait of him, they ended our association.* Another clash (these tales of mishaps move well outside the West End) took place at my exhibition in **Dublin's Waddington Gallery.** Its owner, who begot the present dealing-genius and resettled for him in London, saw my enthusiasm for Jack Yeats's paintings (old Yeats gave me the run of them) and, as his dealer, worked on me to buy one. Successful in some measure, my exhibition did not enable me to go ahead with this deal. Waddington's selling-arguments

*It begs to be added that, before this, my first showing of oils in London (there had been one at **Knoedler's** in New York) was held at **Wildenstein's** with critics' aplomb and sell-out proposing a straight path upward – but the New York Wildenstein himself soon commanded a 'new policy' excluding one-man shows by living artists; but the firm in final gesture recommended me to the Leicester . . .

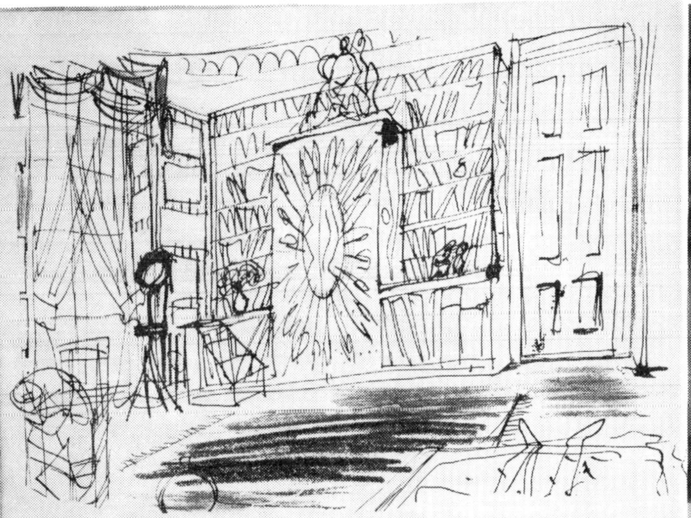

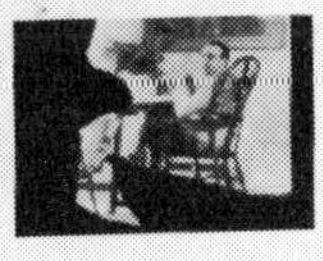

FELIKS TOPOLSKI

VERSUS

THE

PRINCE REGENT

When Feliks Topolski recently moved into one of the graceful houses that form the pristine colonnaded terraces round Regent's Park, he faced a challenge and at once accepted it. Although Feliks Topolski likes Regency houses, he is opposed, and very strongly, to the idea that the interior decoration—his own background—should automatically become Regency too. Often we are tempted to have correct rather than personal decoration: we feel safer that way—safer from the criticism of our friends. Feliks Topolski is not tempted by safety. As an artist, he is used to criticism, and to not being swayed by it; he never lies awake at night wondering whether or not his guests approved his drawing-room colour scheme, or found his dining-room murals too daring. For him, his rooms are the backdrops to the stage whereon his life is set—a life with many scenes and acts and intervals. To gather round him a host of objects reflecting facets of his past, present and, in sketch form, his future, is more important to him than to uphold the canons of West End decoration. These four pages show how he has arranged and decorated his new home—painting much of it himself—to suit his own and his family's needs and feelings, ministered to, but not enslaved by, a gracious Regency building.

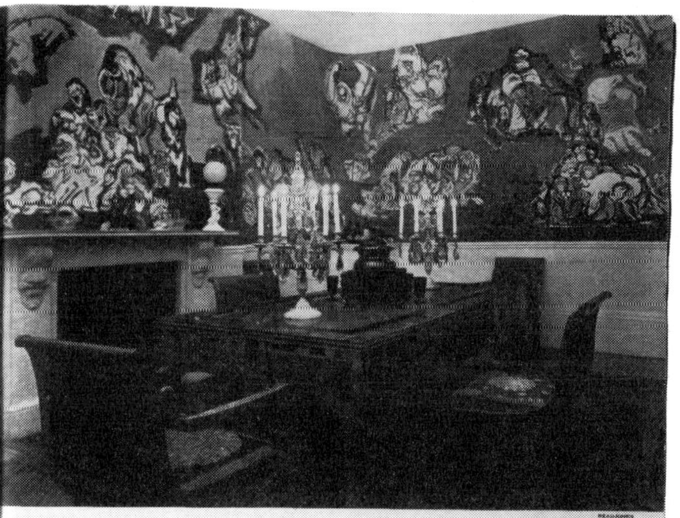

The dining-room, as an unexpected background for the formal French furniture, has a mural of monkeys, by Topolski. The marquetry table is centred by a rare ruby Bristol punch set

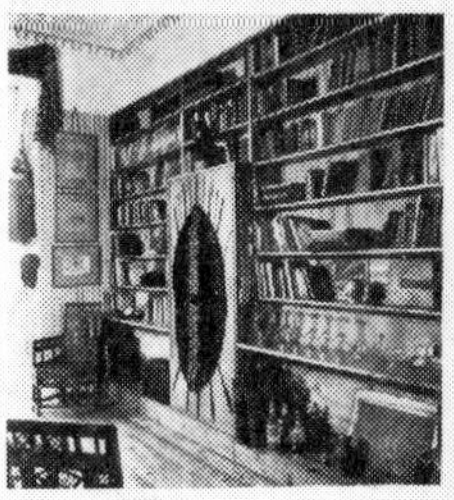

Above The "Travellers' Room" (sketched by Topolski opposite), has simple shelves, a striped wallpaper, Regency bamboo chairs, and a pelmet made from an Indian sari. Ronuk resurfaced the honey-coloured floor

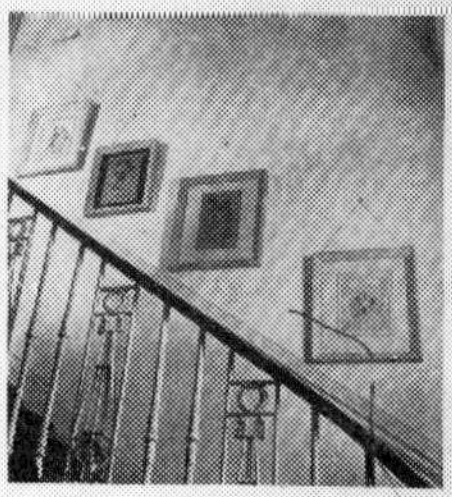

On the walls, above the delicate Regency bannisters, the progression of drawings of famous people is by Topolski. Above are to be seen Winston Churchill, H. G. Wells, George Bernard Shaw, and Pablo Picasso

Continued overleaf

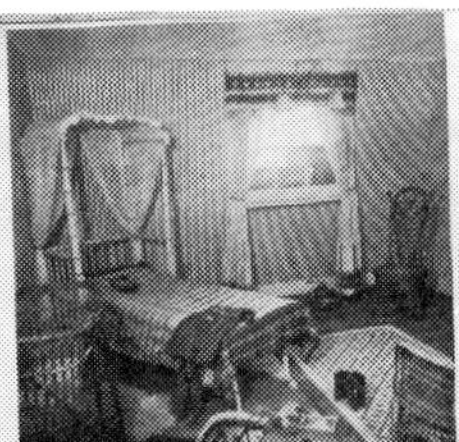

Cane, bamboo, and a carved, wooden bed painted by Topolski to resemble bamboo, are used in the candy-striped nursery. White bedside rug is of sheepskin

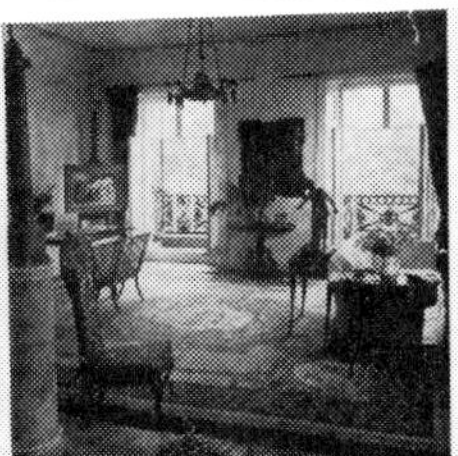

With its balcony overlooking the prettiest part of Regent's Park, is the study end of the big room shown opposite. Native spears are used to make curtain rails

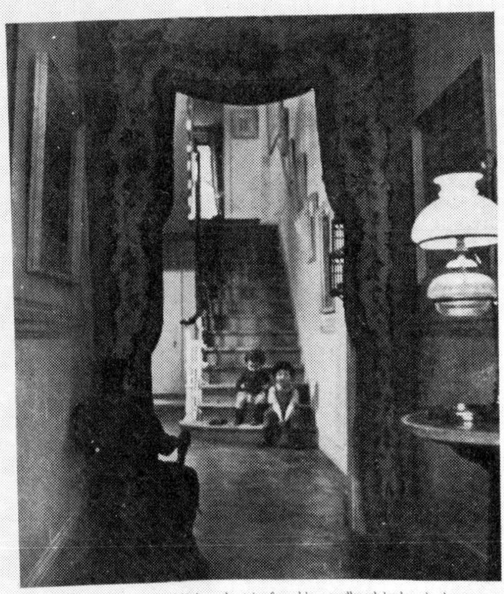

Teresa and Daniel Topolski sit on the stairs, framed by a needlework lambrequin. An early Portuguese chair, made of pressed leather, resembles a monumental old man

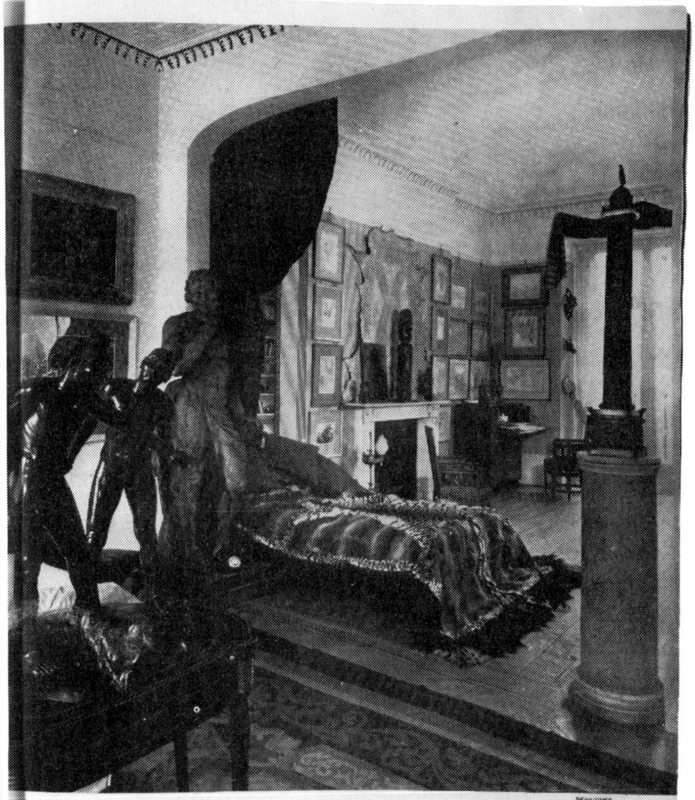

A turbulent harmony of skins, bronze, marble, bark and Indian saris, gives the L-shaped room a unique Topolski flavour. This is the other end of the "Travellers' Room": the bed cover is animal skins; the bark curtains were a present from the King of Buganda. The Regency cornice, originally white, is now thrown brilliantly into relief by Topolski's painted background of super-glossy carmine, all the way round the room

Pages from *House and Garden* April-May 1950

were preposterous – but, in view of his rapid rise, worth relating as a dealer's recipe. Jack Yeats's pictures he made into a perfect investment – he held forth – by raising their price automatically by £100 yearly. He (and his son) must soon have accelerated the tempo, since Yeatses are now selling at many thousands apiece. If I remember, that was 1947 or –8; the price given me was £200 or £250, which I sadly did not meet, and earned the fierce hatred of the dealer.

Back in Mayfair and to happier deals. In a Bond Street arcade there was a tight staircase leading up to a crowded junky room – my future treasure trove. I found my way there because it had downstairs a tiny appetizer-window filled up by an astonishingly seductive painting; I went out of my way several times to look at it (it seemed grand and costly with its beautifully carved wide black frame of seventeenth-century Dutch provenance) to be drawn, unable to resist any more, up those stairs to face **little Wengraf**. And the painting became mine to dip into the arcane mysteries of writhing Flemish nudes in astonishing foreshortenings – until the theme of it dawned on me as Diana and Actaeon, reducing its fascination.

With our parting, the painting remained with all of the Hanover Terrace goodies in Marion's hands and soon moved into the back rooms of Messrs Leggatts, Old Master dealers; Leggatt himself, met by chance (as it happened, at a reception for Mrs Thatcher, then in Opposition), reacted to my disinterested curiosity with diplomatically offensive reserve – they, superdealers, must undergo secret instruction in commercial Masonry. Similarly lesser Wengraf provisions – Tiepolo and Rowlandson drawings, a mighty table – I think from the Duke of Devonshire's Library – are being dispersed; and, equally, old patriarch Affia's junk-diggings (in still-junky then South Moulton Street), from Eastern dresses to unplaceable sculptures to a miniature of the Place Vendôme column with Napoleon in his field greatcoat – a rarity, as this realistic non-imperatorial statue stood up there for only a few years.

A great deal of meticulous planning: either to turn the jigsaw of unpremeditated accumulations into my own visual philosophy – or, the opposite, scouting for right-for-the-slot objects. Rather humdrum house-setting dilemmas, except that my painting proper was abandoned while brushing in between the leafery of the drawing room ceiling-mouldings trad red background – hours/days of neck/arm/back-straining – or, more rewarding, covering the walls and ceilings of the dining room with a brown-blue oligarchy of ape-rulers and monkey-subjects – to match the Bessarabian carpet, uncomfortably stood upon by Empire-provincial chairs round the eighteenth-century table, Marion's ambitious dishes mounting by lift from the sombre 'country' kitchen below. Next to it, the stuffy and musical West Indian social life, almost continuous, slackened Olive's and Roy's services – still greatly rewarding, with me attending their basement parties, being taken out by them to **West Indian joints,** Roy's inspired kites being flown by him and my children in the Park, **their wedding party** (well into their life with us) – a striking event in my studio's garden; and the inauguration-act of ultra-flamboyance: their friend Cesar, a black bearded giant, fierce in his army-surplus outfit, riding on his motor-bike **up to the door of 10 Downing Street** (no barriers there yet) to deliver Number Two Volume One of my *Chronicle* – Churchill its subject.

The first-floor room crossing the whole house played at reflecting still another **divisiveness:** the two french windows and balconied front brought in the park; planted on an Aubusson and papered with my Coronation *Chronicle*, it proposed to evoke a **mock-European aura,** with an unruly ensemble of furniture, objects, pictures (old – and mine), statues – up to a 9 foot wood-carving of a faunish pseudo-classical nudist, who stood guard smirkily by the arched division of the interior (which still managed to include my working table). The rest, with a single window facing the backs, had **attributes of a traveller.** And the emphatic mark, backing to the faun and framing the arch, for exiting out of the home ground, was in a loosely draped, generous length of **bark cloth**, Ugandan earth-dyed. I told elsewhere the tale of the Kabaka of Buganda's bark cloth as prerogative 'entitlement', and its periodical replacements.

The front-to-back overall room was duty-bound – I hate the purpose-bedroom concept – to embracing and surveying as much as possible of the home-terrain from the vantage of the bed, which jutted out here along the divide borderline. But, already in the traveller's quarter, it was covered by a patchwork of exotic skins made for us to my design – its back against a mirror (Fowler's) framed in bamboo. The carpet was Chinese, the bookshelves' centrepiece door was decorated with a threatening rosette of African assegais and arrows backed by a shield, and the rest (and the chimney-piece and the window's edge) crowded with **round-the-world trophies.**

The prolonged haggle, the great price and transport problems over a Sarawak headhunter's sword, and a collection of marvellous folk figurines left with money for postage in the care of an ADC to the Governor of Madras, which never arrived – taught me that the widest and cheapest source of exotic trophies (at that time – probably no more) is London: generations of Imperial servants, soldiers and explorers (reduced or dead) sweating out their spoliations on to England's junk heaps.

On the walls (blue- and white-striped – a vague bow to Regency) tightly hung my world- and history-wide drawings; but, propped on the bookshelf, my favourite: **a Japanese drawing** of, the precise costumes tell, an eighteenth-century Western gentleman (trader?) and his servant pouring him a drink; Dutch or English – there is, beautifully drawn and observed, the racial duality of the West: the tall, vague-faced Master, and the other tiny, Cockney-hooked (nose meets chin), shrewd faced.

Upper storeys carried a majestic Burra, a Lowry, a Freud's still-life and, recommended by him, Desiderio Monzù. But, with me out, and in anticipation of the end of the house's tenancy, Marion began to disperse its contents.

This throwing to the winds of half of my life's accumulation by other hands does me well: I could not have brought myself to do it – and the present, no more acquisitive, fares better unburdened – my architect wife's preference for uncluttered and shiftable spaces in concord; except that the paper avalanches irrepressibly descend and tend to fill those spaces.

The earliest of Mayfair: next door to little Wertheim gallery showing my drawings, a quaint entrance to John Lane The Bodley Head, publishers of my *London Spectacle 1935*, opened straight from Vigo Street *en face* of Savile Row, into a little dark hall, in which, perched provisionally as it were by the edge of a small table, young and smooth Allen Lane was working out his first Penguins.

My first publishers, my first gallery, parading through exhibition rounds, strolling to made-to-measure and hairdressers' right addresses – hair cuts 'in the know' upstairs through the corner hat shop in Jermyn Street – Olivier a client; Savile Row's Anderson and Sheppard – all by recommendations, pre-war Mayfair to be crossed from to the Café Royal and its plentifulness.

Early war and the Blitz, enrichment alongside thrills and risks; Tony's shaky *pied-à-terre* in Albemarle Street ceded to me by him, and its predatory radius – the Players' Theatre underneath, a supplier of fun and friendships; the night-clubs, cabarets and theatres with Theodora, Betty and Baron (Marion occasionally), the shelter-crawling – grand and plebeian, the radius reaching out to the limits of the Blitz – until stricken in Soho.

After the war, the West End's concentrated 'by appointment' demeanour of dealers, thus their clients, began to diffuse – to pour outward; even theatre-land ceased to hold together – the walks turned into underground/bus-rides, eventually car-rides – to, ageing contributing, eliminations, more static observations – and work-posts clasping the river's opposite shores at London's pivot.

Since the war, the stumbling, unconvincing return to past gestures.* The time of retreats/clashes, reflected in costume. Post-war attempts at recapturing the past (I thought then that the bush-blouse, the best solution if one doesn't look back, should dominate – yet rediscovered only now; the time lag of thirty years): the *élégantes*' Edwardian styles were given the first knock by the upsurge of proletarian assertions – 'Teddy Boys', the mock-Edwardians, confused, the self-assurance of exclusivity gone. Later came the hippy mock-uniforms: war surplus, but also second-hand red-coats; trailing ball-dresses and dusty feathery hats for girls. Coincidences these were not. The Imperial aura gone, the wars disgraced, truer equality by denim elegancies proclaimed – the young propelled the changes by costume-mockery.

This is prompted by a **1983 May-stroll** over London's **sacred top art-market's quarter-mile.** In Old Bond Street there is a showing of my drawings/paintings and my son Daniel's photographs to match the publishing of our common book given to our South American journey; ignored by 'serious' critics – they did not come. The gallery has no standing, but this could not be reason enough for the virtual boycott. The exhibition itself? Art-work's quality is easily dismissable, but not when unseen.

But a tentative counterpoint emerged in the Jermyn Street – Christie's area of smartly unostentatious Old Master dealers' shops: an acclaimed exhibition of **Gustave Doré**, turned by selection and precious framing into a high-price commodity. Never mind; Doré percolates through with his vulgar-brutal-naive-prodigious-popular nonconformism. And a few quotes from the catalogue introduction by a Samuel F. Clapp:

> First, he was an Alsatian. Edmond de Goncourt writes: 'He is an Alsatian, and an Alsatian, even with talent, is an inferior Frenchman or German.' Secondly, he annoyed the Establishment by successfully avoiding any academic training or apprenticeship at the drawing academies or at private ateliers which young artists were expected to attend. This was unthinkable and not to be condoned. Moreover, the awards at the Salon were largely dictated by academicians who disliked painters who strayed from the Academies or neglected their apprenticeship. Thirdly, and most importantly, he committed the cardinal sin of being popular. In an age in which popular taste was considered vulgar, this was truly unforgivable. The English critic P. G. Hamerton (1866) provides a good example: 'The very popularity of Doré is in itself a circumstance to be noted against his chances of recognition by the highest class. True critics have such a well-grounded distrust of the popular judgement in art, that if the people applaud heartily they at once conclude that the work must have some glaring abomination in it that has fascinated the vulgar world.' With the exception of the very first two works which Doré, at the age of sixteen, exhibited at the Salon, and with the exception of three drawings for Dante's *Inferno* which were shown at the Salon in 1981, Doré did not contribute any drawings to the Salon until 1866. Nor is there any drawing in this Exhibition known to be datable before 1861. Doré's illustrations in the 1850s were drawn on wood-blocks. He began etching only around 1870, doing pure watercolours in 1873, and showing his sculpture in 1877; consequently, before 1860 he could be known only as an illustrator and caricaturist. Another criticism of Doré was that he was arrogant. According to de Goncourt, 'He has a terribly disparaging character, he recognizes no talent in any contemporaries, however gifted they may be, except in himself.'
>
> However, his difficulties in his country were not all of his own making. The problem was not so much that officialdom discriminated against him during the Second Empire, but that his work did not suit the taste of the bourgeoisie. The official organizations did not in fact have real artistic direction . . . Doré was on excellent terms both with the Court, he was one of a very few painters invited to the Sézries at Compiègne . . . and with the Emperor's cousin Princess Mathilde, who frequently invited him to her artistic salon.
>
> The problem was that the new patrons, the bourgeoisie, set the prevailing taste. Having established themselves materially under the Second Empire, they did not want anything that deviated from the image of an ideal, moderate and settled society . . . Conversely, following the surrender at Sedan and the fall of the Second Empire, Doré's popularity at Court and prosperity under the old régime

*Harold Acton entered, without prerogatives for me of his legend, gracefully boldened into premature middle-old age, formalized by conventional black-hatted elegance – somewhat overtaken by the whimsies of manners, but proper for the Florentine squire in the seclusion of his haughty time capsule, a visiting absentee from the Metropolis; this and his past of roaming Peking with my Jaś Tarnowski and with (or against) Sir Francis Rose, hardly in step with his writing – an appreciative introductory essay to a book of my work.

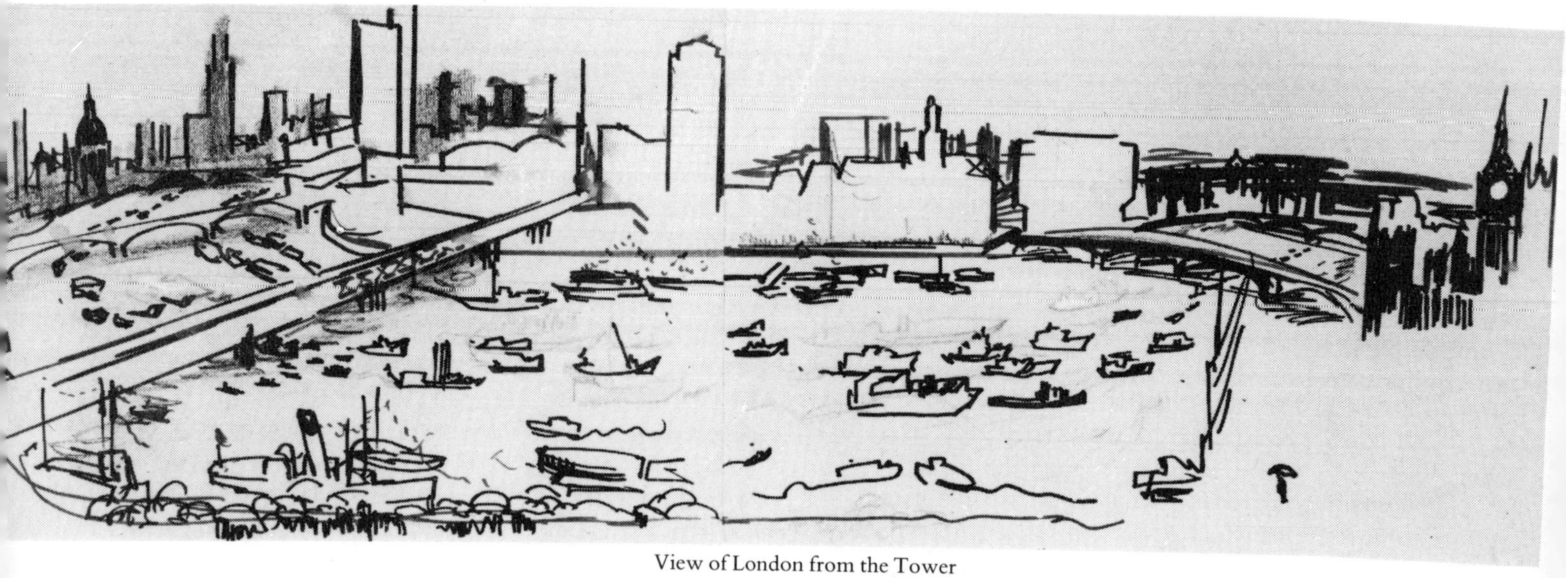

View of London from the Tower

worked against him . . . As M. Jean-Marie Moulin observes, 'Those who have had the experience of working on the Second Empire in the area of the arts have felt the scorn (sometimes tinged with indulgence) that has surrounded the period . . . the causes of this ostracism, sometimes even fury . . . are deeper than one would think.' Despite all this, Doré received increasing acclaim in the 1870s, which was publicly recognized when he was made an Officer of the Légion d'Honneur in 1879.

Blake is not threatening because he is safely 'mystical' and because his drawings are not detailed . . . Doré has been criticized for not interesting himself in daily events or politics, like Daumier and others. However, he regarded journalism and caricature as superficial and emphemeral and as for politics he believed 'An artist should keep to his art and have no political opinions.'

It has been fashionable to emphasize Doré's lively social life . . . Millicent Rose even refers to him as a playboy . . . He had an enormous impact on his time . . . by making use of new technologies, he socialized art . . . Influenced by technological progress during the last hundred years, art criticism, it has been said, has placed undue emphasis upon the avant-garde. Now the time has come to reconsider this artist who was more concerned with what was enduring than with what was new.

I do not childishly attempt to identify myself with this nineteenth-century self-monumentalizing outsider. I propose only to point out the repetitiousness of institutional power/pressure; the monstrous, though ephemeral, influence of word-spinning **authorities**; the aftermath when some later generation's priests of current establishment take as subjects for their and their trends' *engrandissement* the 'neglected' or 'misjudged'.

My impregnable territory has been defined: the accessible workshop and showroom in the manner of old masters (before art middle-men arrived); the *Chronicle* adding another public dimension bypassing the art scene, and my panoramic labyrinthine endeavour formed to fit my need for open-ended painting, not pictures. I have held to these with no concern for academies – right, left and centre, 'modern' and political – and the Royal Academy.

M**y South Bank studio-arch** drew in its own circle. And so I studded my **Chronicle's hundredth issue in 1957** with the collage: the sheet's outer side is bordered by large figures of my contrasting visitors – London's ever-present brackets: an Under-the-Arches dosser (and so was intermittently I) and Colonel Pomeroy of the Welsh Guards (who descended first time on my Little Venice studio during its farewell exhibition and whom I drew and painted repeatedly – now Viscount Harberton), spanning the anguished view of St Paul's and the Thames, harassed by giant activities of the building trade; and the Lambeth cockney and young Teddy styles linking the two. The other side of the broadsheet: unhampered yet by later (enforced by architectural fashion, which also smashed the lovable shot-tower) pedestrian bridges (about to be eliminated in turn by the new Trustees): the view from Waterloo Bridge of my studio surmounted by the distant Big Ben, helicopters coursing between their landing stage outside my back window and the Heathrow Airport (sadly too rubbed out now); the Royal Festival Hall with its domestic fossilized ballet and equally trad concerts; but also its surprises when borrowed for a ceremonial occasion: robed Queen Mother heading procession of the Academics along red strip laid between JAZZ TODAY announcements; but then mixed patterns of different visitors to Book Exhibition, to Lycée Français prize-giving, to the National Film Theatre, and the then rising 'Flower Children' drifting to the 'open day' at my studio.

In the past few years, with **my second marriage**, the survey point was lifted to the other side of the river and up to **a tower-pyramid** with its two folly-watch-turrets guarding the endless balcony – the daily news parade given wider action-horizon.

This elevation above stately (as seen from here) London and its river, nailed down on the left by St Paul's Cathedral and Big Ben on the right; and, behind, Whitehall and

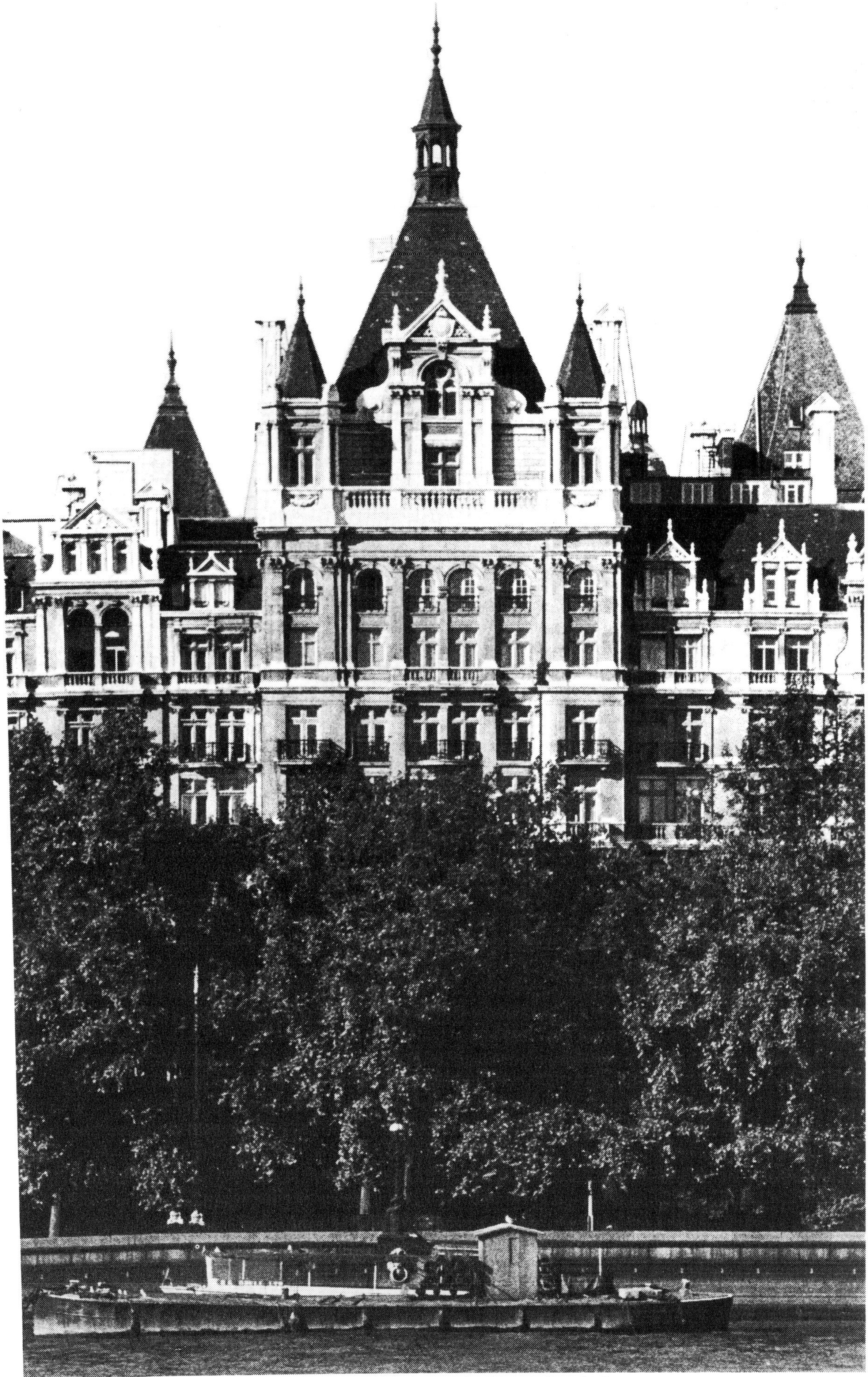
The Tower (Photograph by Amanda Saunders)

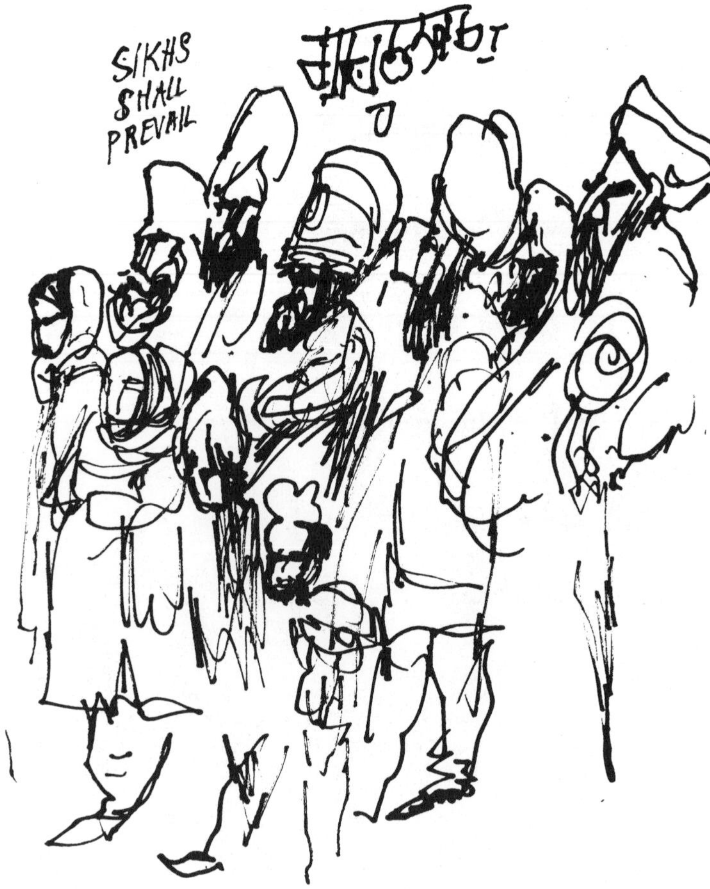

Sikh demonstration

Buckingham Palace, tempts to survey only from this height, perched on my grandly balustraded balcony, no more to particularize and record face-to-face, the events which thus blur into seasonal repetitiousness, whether calendar or protest-dictated.

The river brings processionally the Queen of the Netherlands in a flotilla of mean motorboats, hers edged with watermen in red; or bursts up with routine fireworks; or boat-races of one kind or another, while across on a dully garden-furnished patch bands play, and further to the left, in front of the concreteries of the National Theatre, buskers and street shows fill in the 'enlivening' programme. There would be regular features: Changing of the Guard or Trooping the Colour, but also the trot of the Marathon, and clap for women runners; the National Front's shaven heads outnumbered by police helmets; the Sikh's turbans; the antis . . . But also, vertically down: on the grass, the pairs, the Indian families, the gardeners; on the benches, the down and outs; speeding: civil servants and typists; daily rush-traffic: all new cars tail-to-tail. This detached viewing, the almighty's out-of-focus mistiness – the habitual mixer, the counter of buttons ascends to abstraction, hence the higher sloth.

Whitehall Court – the grandstand to review London's day-to-day embroiled history. Craftily the Police channel/split/misdirect the marchers, who aim at the rewarding route of Whitehall, into streams weaving by the Embankment, and round my stand: many hours, many miles lasting Peace demo criss-crossed and U-turned on itself over Westminster Bridge, and '**Whores for Peace**' banner paraded-wasted before nobody-me on my doorstep.

Tense wavelets of police from shadowy Whitehall toward Trafalgar's crowds – and a choral scream and a great tumult (barks, fists in unison) of hurried, almost at a run, stampede of shaven skulls/scratched-scarred brute young mugs grimaced for a brawl; no political urge here – solely the hate-mob hotted up by the rhythmic micro-roars of a heavy gent in their midst: '**Sieg Heil**!'*

Then: the swell for the miners; the town paralysed by the teachers, anti-apartheiders, anti-nuclears – all ignored by the current rulers, thus losers.

The trade unions' Victorian embroidered-patchwork standards, beflagged slogans voice their vote-agreed message along the Embankment low down below my balcony.

Across the river, in the out-of-the-way domestication of miserable Jubilee Gardens, mill in turn the unemployed marchers, the homosexuals, the funfairs, the fireworks at the day's end (with the dutifully Shell-windowed Queen), the grant-thirst students, the schoolchildren protesting against their milk-cuts (this years ago, when Mrs Thatcher, as the Education Minister, presented for the first time her stern self), the racial minorities with their extra white-skinned girlfriends, the strikers of various denominations; all these if denied my Whitehall view, filter or assemble by **my South Bank studio** with or without bands, exclamatory vocally and accented by banners.

Whitehall Court: voracious of townscape, 1884 elephantine prima-donna-fabrication holds the centre of the London stage (the Thames – the footlights), overdressed, necklaced with balconies, tiara-ed with a fouling-the-skyline row of pyramids.

Inevitably my now (haste haste) last stand takes place within the largest of these roof-pyramids – the whole of London in solemn rotation purring beneath and up to all four horizons manufacturing clouds-smokes-rains-rainbows; sun-moon-stars; jets-gulls-pigeons-helicopters-tugs-pleasure and rowing boats-plunge suiciders-*son et lumière* effects – almost (but updated) as in the *Illustrated London News* fold-in print of 1880 on my kitchen wall – 'Bird's Eye View of London as Seen from a Balloon'.

The South Bank having been put aside, I pick my visible nostalgia spots East–West–North.

Down the River, the Temple – vital duality (surely not hypocrisy) well embossed; a Royal occasion at the Inner Temple makes the outsiders to the daily privilege of gowns/wigs, reduced by the rooted uniformity of their three-piece suits, blossom here into personages, robed, ruffed, ribboned, bechained, bemedalled, led – this restitution of the old, the fat, the faded gagas into the dignity status of Age, Portliness, Profundity. Formalized to the minutest details, the occasion fulfils its predictable ritual.

So, for instance: **the Honourable Society of the Inner Temple Grand Day** in the Inner Temple Hall – white ties, decorations/ribbons.

*The National Front, one hears, dismissed of late its bully-cohorts and along with other parties crowds the not very roomy forecourt of mid-ideologies designed to seduce the largest slice – the mid-slice of the voting nation.

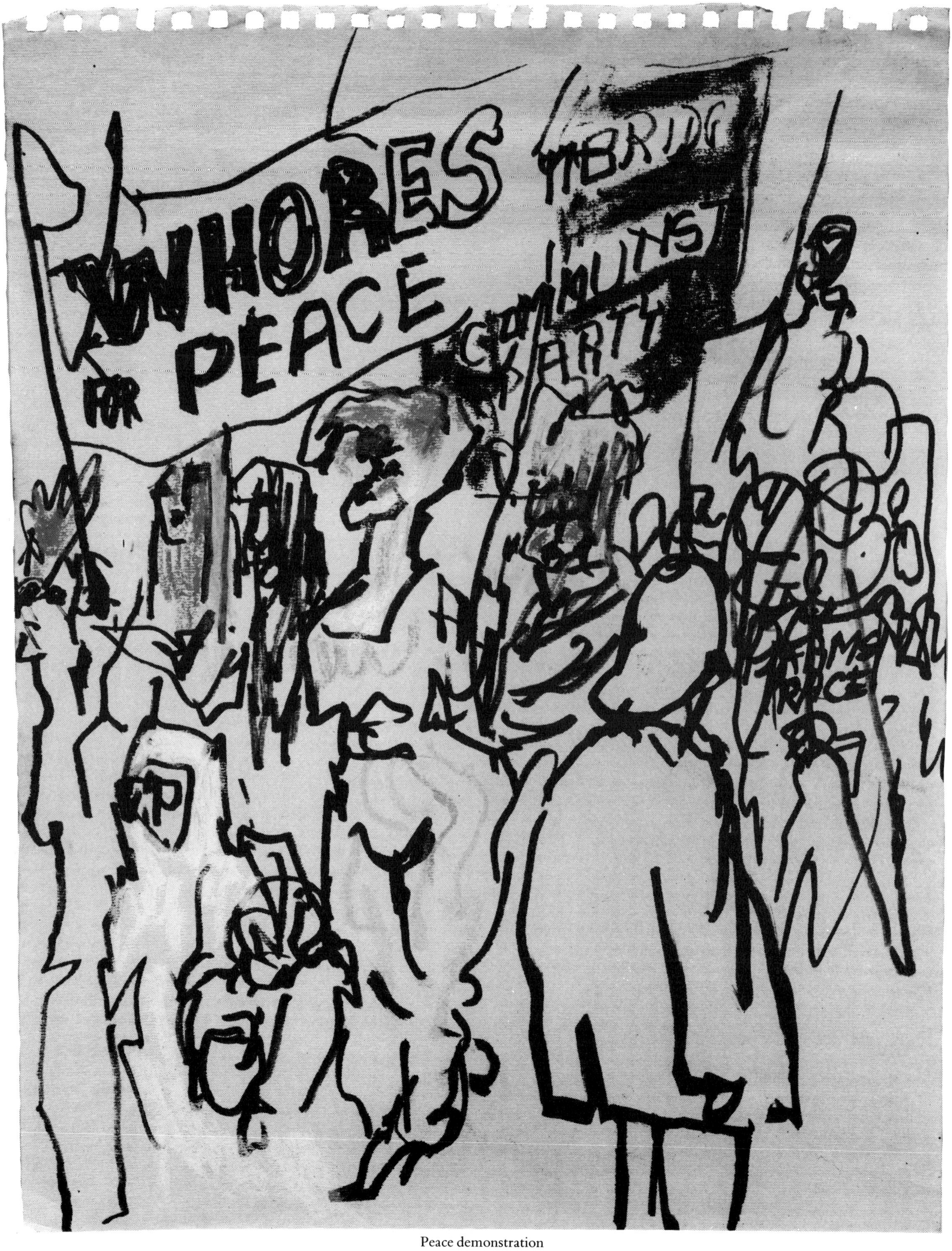

Peace demonstration

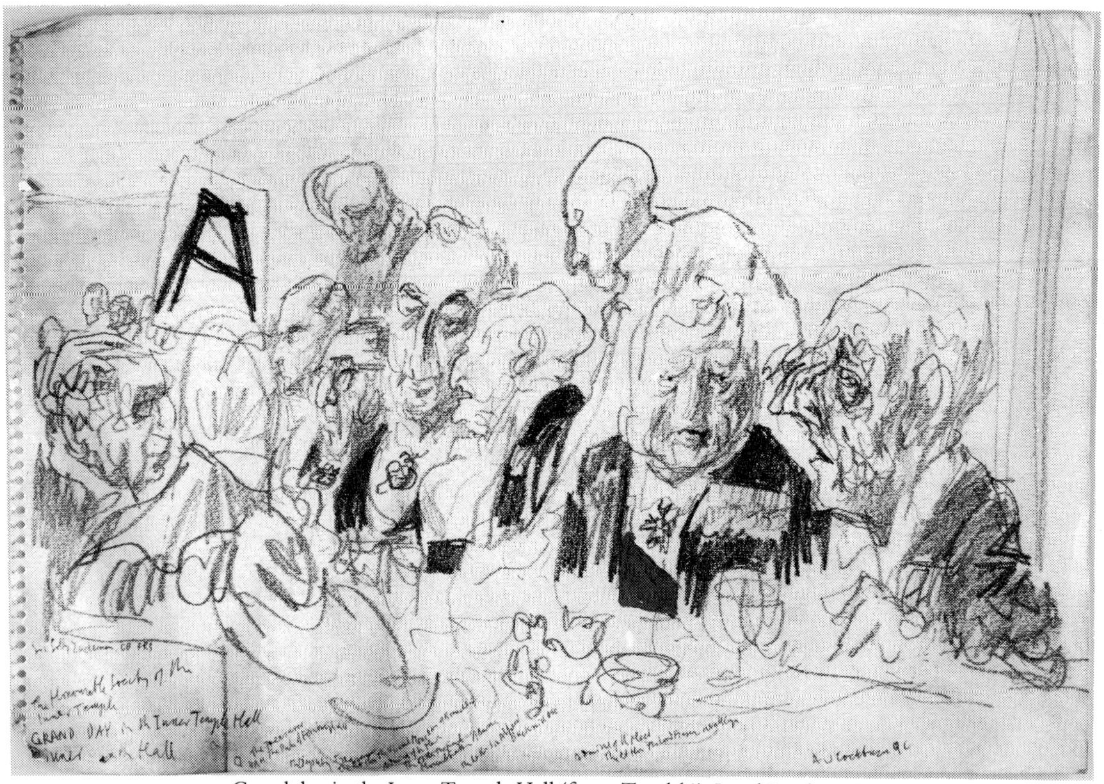

Grand day in the Inner Temple Hall (from *Topolski's Legal London*, 1961)

The top table: The Rt Hon the Lord Chancellor The Viscount Kilmuir – lucky distinction of the jabot under a bold black-accented Roman head; the Treasurer, HRH The Duke of Edinburgh, young and slim; but next a low-bulging heavy-spectacled Deputy Treasurer The Rt Hon The Viscount Monckton of Brenchley; Admiral of the Fleet The Rt Hon The Earl Mountbatten of Burma – I stop at him: his extra-huge head designed in extra-aristo convention, set on immensities of something surely top-unique at the neck and extra-decorative diagonal ribbon, dwarfs into shrunken vulgarity almost the rest of the table, however adorned; they may be beefy or hook-nosed/chinned-cum-bushiest eyebrows, or posh Jewish like Sir Solly Zuckerman CB FRS; though, without Mountbatten, their head-wagging top-drawerism could make them stand in for tribal elders.

But a few steps away, in privacy, but still within the noble precincts, an unceremonious **libertine** unpredictability is attained. The gathering, unselective, even extravagantly mixed in ages and spheres, has however a 'civilized' framework – at least to begin with: glasses in hand, noncommittal tediums, a wining-dining drill. But then sudden nudity and its anti-convention of no bars: long-lasting, ebbing and flowing, tolerant of any anarchy or inadequacy, bizarre of incidents and coincidences, nebulous pile-ups – inconsequential.

Yet these free-wheeling hosts must have selected their 'mixture' with some sophistication.*

I climb up the beamed steep-walled tower-top to survey inland London. **Horse Guards Parade** across Whitehall (an early march: River Plate Victors, 23 February 1940 – the latest, 10 October 1982, 'Sikhs shall Prevail'), prancing, drumming, trumpeting, once to rivet me, then justified by victory, now the paper tiger monarchy's parade ground is upset by the imposition of the ICA, to which the noncomformists make pilgrimages, hoping to receive **an alternative enlightenment** to conform with. In 1980 I submitted, foolishly, to the test of its pretence at ultimate assessment with my *Chronicle*'s retrospective.

Thus one of my principal routes, as seen from my Tower, embraces Trooping the Colour, the Mall (with an intruder/heresy: the Institute of Contemporary Arts) and, out of greeneries and from behind the gilts of Victorian statuary, **Buckingham Palace**. *The pomp* of the ICA – a Modernity establishment, and *the circumstance* of the paper-tiger Monarchy complement each other as contemporary Western cardboard imitation-Janus of faith and power – camouflaging

*An orgy *monstre* in a distant suburb of plutocratic opulence conformed to stricter conventions: a large 'family' household, teenage children present (not visible later); all this a sectarian logical conclusion of the fanaticism of the Ile de Levant nudist colony. At first a principally dull conversation piece within *nouveau-riche* tastelessness, buffet provisions and drinks abounding. Then (there are rows of wall-hooks provided) nudity and fancy peep-at-cunt-and-tit demi-nudity (defused though by plain nakedness), began to sprinkle the gathering, but the reserved decorum of glass-in-hand small talk continuing. A suburban routine party (those fully dressed now in minority), except that '**invitations**' are not to dance, but for '**upstairs**'. A nicely mature and polite lady, wife of a multinational boss, and I, obstinately dressed, climbed upstairs to find rooms with floors entirely fitted with mattresses overflowing with ebbing buttocks, obliging legs, unoccupied erections in search of availables. The two of us upright (Virgil and Dante among the damned) inquisitively yet calmly commenting, surveying – observing for a moment a smaller room, as if exclusively given to elder male shapes, heads busy at their female partners' crotches.

I push through spare naked ladies crowding the landing into the lavatory, unzip and pee. All round me an instant outburst of outraged shocked voices: I was committing a supreme *faux pas* – this was meant to be 'ladies only' in their strict *savoir faire*.

Back in the shadowy palpitating rooms to continue 'escorting' my elegant lady in our superior outsiderism, but can't find her – until: there she is, throwing off the last bits of clothing and falling on her back (narrowly accommodated) with an erect stranger above her.

A nice touch: on a sofa placed in the salon's centre there sat grandly – respect surrounding them – **the veteran 'swingers'** – by age or invalided out; an *hors concours* pair, once legendary party givers, ceremonially present, she terminally wasted, awaiting the end with dignity. Mere young '**performers**' lowering their voices, lining up to pay homage.

I spy out sidling up the stairs an outsider (though a legend in his own right), a master at sniffing out a party going, even (he lives in Paris) across the Channel; Jim – an outsider because his late-hippy bearded style, his loaded haversack, mark a wanderer among these obvious householders.

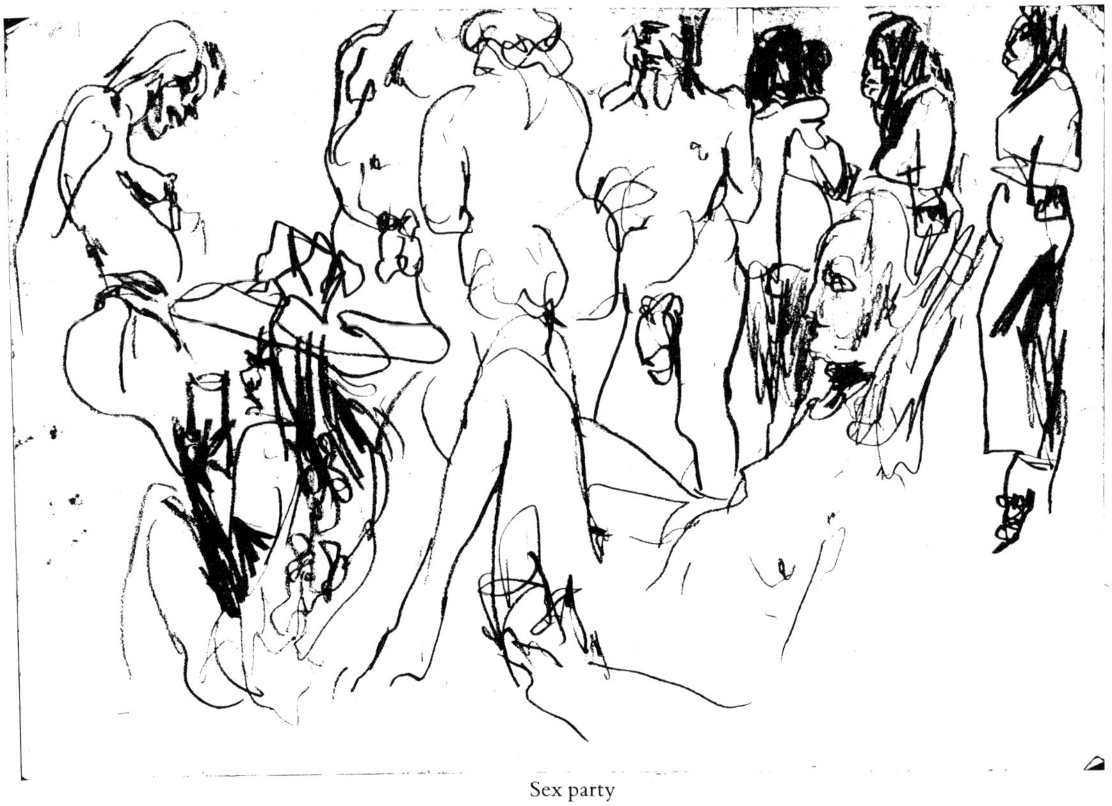

Sex party

multinational commerce and multi-armed democracies. (Their adversary: imperialism idealism-draped.)

EIIR

To Mark the Silver Jubilee of the Queen the Master of the Household has received her Majesty's Command to invite .... to an Evening Reception to be given at Buckingham Palace by the Queen and the Duke of Edinburgh on Wednesday, 20th July, 1977

Tight parking in the precincts to step out clashing with the boxing champion Henry Cooper (Caryl tells me) out of the next car – and (my 'Coronation Gallery' dormant to the left) the red-carpeted climb between the handsome lines of liveried flunkeys – to emerge into the black and white mass of lesser physicality (than that of the lackeys) with their deteriorating women, floating drably, yet consequentially, along vast distances of gilt-framed oily imagery – mostly dullened by familiarity of recognition. The glass-topped containers of memorabilia, drawings, etc., placed at intervals, reduce the private party effect to that of a museum private view.

Now somewhat commotious divide: enter, each on his/her own, in the walkabout routine, **the Royals**. The divide wavers on three counts: those manoeuvring forward for the honour/reward of a word or a handshake (Lord and Lady Grade noticeable), the others holding on to their front-line luck, and those who back out as a mark of old acquaintanceship or detachment.

The rooms are open *en suite* and in continuous circle – thus the above Royal Family function will go on endlessly. But with conventionalized diversions: the rather depopulated Music Room presents the red-coated brass at its mellowest. State Dining Room – 'buffet and small tables' – contains most of **the recognizables**: to the fore Tony Armstrong Jones, no more the Princess's husband but a favoured guest Viscount Snowdon; and all 'personalities' anxiously selective in casual encounters. Ball Room played to by platform-raised Joe Loss Band with the ball-usual tunes; **the Queen Mother** rotating devotedly in the arms of a ballet-dancer in fashion.

City-state 'democracies', surveyed by gods-myths furnishing solutions, satisfied the Greeks but could not conceive **the almighty vote-democracy**. How was it that Poland's gentry, from smallholders to magnates, gained the right to elect kings out of the whole of Europe's lists of candidates, thus vote-selling corruption leading to selling out the country to surrounding oligarchies? A morose guidance for the eventual triumph of the one vote one man principle, nay, dogma of faith lip-served even by those who flaunt it.

The gods of Olympus now materialized into flesh: royals, stars of many denominations orbit the firmament of the Palace rooms. The ordinaries will deepen their worship by means of the media, be assured of their participation by a four-yearly vote, and held orderly by permanent institutions. But even these select hold one vote each on par with some 50 million of the excluded – the mighty vote idealizes each citizen, whatever their background prejudices, education-conditioning, status, beliefs – inherited, born out of contrariness, revolt.

But these **flesh-gods** are not, as those of the myths, issued from human quirks, but by the materialist accountancies secreted in their *comme-il-faut* made-to-measure pockets. The summit held by this meek little woman made-up into averageness, but the property-richest, or almost, in the world. And in this superior stance she manages, unconsciously, to disrupt her own domain by accelerating the current tide of worldwide divisions into the newest haves and have-nots.

The graces (and pretences) are marred by a mundane discord in which I am enmeshed: this modest hostess was also my landlady: the Crown Commissioners (now I believe serving another cause as well), the delegated managers of her immense wealth, aim recently it seems at an imitation of amoral, amok-driven, gold calf-worshipping multinationals – naturally without her descending to be aware of the social disruption caused in her name.

My case may be proving little but it is spread over thirty-five years as her tenant, thus its hesitant relating should carry some sense. Britain's comforts of the thirties and post-war up to the seventies were accessible. A fluid mid-sphere of earners (myself) could, along with the country's opulent, lease a house in the Royal Crown Regent's Park, feast in best eateries, clothe in Savile Row – yes, property was the hidden divider, but the Crown-leased terraces housed the nobility alongside barristers, writers (H. G. Wells, Connolly, Pinter) and painters like myself.

But now, in the multinational oily days we are all swept away with impunity. The Crown leads the ruthless elimination drive in establishing the fantasy top sphere by charges unrelated to the country's life. Our stay in Hanover Terrace, the last twenty years' lease having seemed somewhat high but bearable at £1,200 yearly, the privilege of continuing would cost now £1,500, but after £400,000 obligatorily spent on repairs and a premium of £175,000. Thus at the Royal command those lovely domestic terraces will, if at all, be filled up solely by the new international rich – with the wide abyss yawning between them and the rest of Britain; thus under the royal lead the monstrous step is made towards **the unbridgeable.**

Although I am aware that I have no right and no competence to allude to India's internal politics, it is impossible to contain my attitude to **Indira Gandhi** within a purely private sphere.*

To digress for the sake of spot-lighting the 'conditioning' of my attitude: I was brought up in post-First World War Poland, re-created after 150 years of division and enslavement. The republican democratic constitution of the country released pent-up self-rule objectives which reached, after half-a-dozen years, a disorganized stalemate brought about by a surfeit of political parties. The man who, almost single-handed, created free Poland, and who then stood back from the voted-in system, a former Socialist and a selfless patriot: Piłsudski – eventually took power (not unlike de Gaulle later), was greeted enthusiastically, and his benevolent dictatorship functioned well – before it deteriorated under the pressure of his lieutenants – and successors.

I met Indira in 1949 when invited by Panditji to India. I stayed with them for almost two months. Later, whenever she came to London, we met. And, when returning from China in 1966, I stopped in New Delhi and worked for long hours at drawing her while she carried on her daily business or in long uninterrupted dialogues.

I am enumerating all this in support of my constant respect for her and for the gravity and humility with which she was facing her duties. Even as a young woman at the side of her father she impressed with her seriousness, yet unmarring her naturalness and humour.

Our London meetings, mostly at my studio, were always enchanting. On one occasion I arranged a visit to the home of a leading black writer, Jan Carew, who gathered young Caribbean intellectuals for Indira so that she could get acquainted at first hand with the problems and aspirations of their world. Her dignity, charm, ease and alertness captivated; her grasp of Third World perspectives impressed.

And an incident:

A pair of English playwrights, John Arden and Margaretta D'Arcy, and their children involuntarily crossed some isolated 'out-of-bounds' border while travelling in North India. They were arrested and imprisoned without much chance of gaining legal procedure – or freedom. I learned about this and instantly cabled Indira. They were released within days.

But my most implanted memory is of our long conversation in 1966. Indira was discouraged by her opponents' manoeuvres, by gain-chasers. There was no trace, as ever, of self-seeking – she seemed seriously keen on resigning, perhaps the only paradoxical trace of selfishness: to find peace.

It would be presumptuous to suppose that my isolated voice influenced her, when arguing that at that juncture she was irreplaceable, and that my humble view was that it was her duty to carry on. I am recording this only to establish my conviction that, if ever there was a ruler devoid of self-interest, but anointed, as it were, with a sense of mission (an inherited mission since she, retiring and shy, had initially to force herself into the great role), it was she.

I wrote to her a few weeks ago and the reply confirmed for me, as I trusted, her unchangingly pure stand. Her 'strong' government (excesses at the peripheries of power regrettably taking place) seemed to me what India needed.

Party games, which under cover of democratic ideals bring forth power-seekers and threaten anarchy, have been positively curbed before, if there was a truly noble personage on call.

South America at Daniel's bidding promises to be hard. It had to come, but it materializes as *his* fulfilment with me harnessed to its commitments: six relentless months of stupendous geography, the book contract, the television film-making network of fixed dates.

This last begins already with a commandeered farewell-party-performance at my studio, stolen by Tambimuttu spectacularly vomiting over the fur-covered sofa.

Then, my inner 'system' perhaps vetoing the looming

*Written on request for contribution to an issue of the *Illustrated Weekly of India*, 20–26 November 1977. Now, in 1987, I exchange Christmas cards with Rajiv Gandhi.

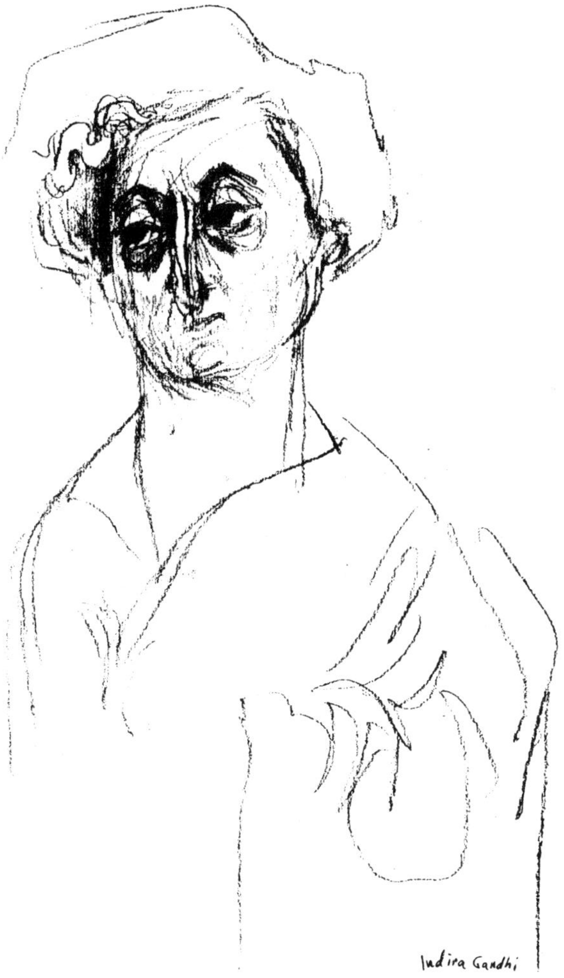

Indira Gandhi (from *Topolski's Chronicle*)

departure date, the doctors whisk me to a hospital in panic over blood appearing in my urine – and propose cancelling my journey, or at best delaying it. Daniel goes ahead, lands in Paraguay and, with the Somoza assassination, is picked up in the streets of Asunción, gaoled, given three days' fullness of Latin-dictatorial inhumanity, and freed thanks to a note smuggled out to the British Ambassador. Propelled by schoolboy-cum-Oxford magic of nomenclature (unlike me: I go for living entanglements), he chooses as his target the bleak southernmost tip of the continent at Tierra del Fuego and wills out of it his best photographs and writing.

I, still in London, hold prolonged consultations with Professor Macdonald, who reluctantly recognizes my travel obligations but warns me about rough roads in the Cordillera which may shake my innards into a crisis, and insists that, if that comes, I shall make my instant way down the mountain slopes and get on a plane to England. I leave nearly six weeks after Daniel for Santiago, to meet him at the Hotel Foresta, which he will reach travelling north the length of Chile.

Before our departure for South America we naturally wondered how to confront it. The most tempting – yet obvious – idea was to embody the mood of discovery, to assume entering unknown lands, facing their peoples, habits, structures as bizarre and astonishing (in differences and similarities for the European explorer), fraught with inexplicable threats from nature and gods; thus hopeful of sharpening our reactions to exotic elements of otherness, perhaps blurred under the layers of contemporary universality.

Of course, we were swamped instantly by the give/take of everydayness, the multitudes of encounters, offerings, trivialities; but – given thought – at least the 'received ideas' may be stealthily but honourably evaded, for the best, through PEOPLE – *they* are not in the guidebooks, not herded/chopped into intricate categories/systems/statistical entities.

The difficulties of the voyage: habitually we both prefer to journey alone, for the same simple reason: two people tend to turn inwards (in conflict or accord), with their backs to what they came to see; singly, one is admitted and merges into the foreignness.

The father–son watershed. This voyage, extra-difficult, framed-in by prescribed footsteps of 'received ideas'; yes, Daniel finds his 'explorations' through hardships and human encounters which instantly grow as events into his life; I always pursued/participated in history-in-the-making. My early travels were quests for conflicts – changes – restlessnesses of the global map: wars/liberations/ destructions/revolts/congresses, not for static or archaeological geography. And happened mostly before the tourism-onrush – and so were explorations, adventures; the rare fellow 'passengers' military/diplomatic/a few 'delegates'. Later, 'businessmen'. Then, soon, tourists, led in by rather brave loads of blue-rinse-groomed American moms. There was a division: those keen on absorbing, and those (ordinary conscript soldiers and refugees) catapulted out, hating 'overseas' and longing for their backyards. Now ALL package-travel, and blot and 'invade'/bend the globe; and you fall into a propelled crowd, barred from contact/merging with other worlds. The sing-song of the guides everywhere, the mass production of souvenirs, the scavenging-robbing. Hence this time I battled ceaselessly against being subjected to the predictable.

And then, there comes to the fore the element of Father-versus-Son.

A traveller, well-provided with introductions, descending on the fabric of a city/nation, is a pest, tearing out/chewing over snatches of 'insight', senseless bundles of threads. The pestering pest demands and gets attention but does not give it; yet then, instantly, he opinionates and misquotes, with literary garnishings. On his flight back he lists his scraps: the *Junta* General and his entourage, some Foreign Ministry dignitaries, the voice from a slum-window, the bird's-eye-view of volcanoes, earnest gatherings of academics, artists, schoolchildren's ceremonies, a market for mystery cures, hotel-reception squabble, the curfew hour, thefts, ruins of Incas and of *campesinos*' huts, *hacienda* glimpses, a military and folklore parade, taxi-drivers' conversation . . . a lot and nothing.

London–Santiago. Sorrowfully, more, funereally, I am without curiosity whipped along, because already off the Gatwick train some tendon (in my good leg) cracks and, in pain, I follow routines.

The fearsome flight (chopped into hate close-ups: Germanic blond giant hems me in with his soft-porn reading matter, bare belly emerges, an unbuttoned robustness) of more hours than bearable to think; but the grand sunrise, countered though by the straining at the port-hole on Rio touchdown for the multi-advertised, unparalleled beauties of the bay – of which no trace; only cloudy drizzle.

I move seats, for the last lap, next to a girl – truly a Miss Latin America lovely – wishing for the elating aura of my descent on Chile to have this demi-goddess as a motto; but she (eighteen-year-old classical singer, half orphan, five languages, Austro-Belgian – South America only adopted to start new life with torn bag and plaster on her bare feet) departs, also into rain, at São Paulo.

I remain almost alone, eye-to-eye with darkly animalistic, tight-knitted (as I imagined those pitiless machos) youngster, who has earlier been trying to pick her up (without any smile) with a Coca-cola temptation, and who now saw, from a further seat, her and my farewell embrace. I seek comfort therefore within my three-seat lair and, furtively drawing him, ponder the possibilities of vengeance by my first Latin enemy – I presume, the appropriate mood for entering South America.

At the port-hole: we are surely closing on Chile, yet all still flatly polite, agriculture patched and, equal politeness, sown with cotton-wool cumulus bundles; but on comes the captain's voice about the Andes. I roll over to the other side and – bizarre magnitudes, convulsing alienness: tightly, defensively, in endlessly gnarled ramparts, stands the jagged army – multi-ranked in black depths, unbroken and invincible, topped by white helmeted horizontals under azureness of indifference. Slowly, meaningfully this invincible barrier presses at us (our wide-winged machine static) and mounts upward, the threat, ever closer; then, hard to bear, the massive attack opens its chasms, lifts its cragginess above us – engorges us. But we, the plane as if waking up, leap forth and down and miraculously enter and then slowly, over improbable calm flatness, circle Santiago airport (the Andes retreat and hide in greyness): peopled balconies and randomly spread carpet, really meagre, rolled out and brush-dusted by busy dots – not for us, but for the President of Brazil. Just the same, some youth greets me, extricates me from commotion and causes, amazingly, my luggage to be passed from hand to hand without (but only just) searchings; I ride into the town through reasonable suburbs along a reasonable roadway, reasonably punctuated by universal hoardings (BIENVENIDO SANTIAGO DE CHILE) and telepoles – as anywhere else; but to fly to it over half the world . . .

Daniel-watching is high-tension theatre; his is a heroic mould and purpose – his able-bodied ever-preparedness and his Homeric head-neck fit his ever-search, ever-taking challenges, against his inattentive impatience, often surfacing – naturally, within the limiting world around him.

He is in permanent haste, seeking out and running with equal dedication several parallel races: athletic – social justice – appetites of all kinds – camaraderie – heights and distances – hardships . . .

He presses towards fullness of life, infuriated by red light for him – green light for other traffics, selecting at speed – if the alternatives are the mountain peak or tasting the subtleties of the passage – the former.

Of course, I have been, and still am, susceptible to diversional appetites, and may search for and find similarities between us. But in contrast, I recognize that I tend to be pedestrian. And so, when with him, I consciously stand back in recognition of his top-form manhood, hold back my speech and my actions, do not stir my latent aggressiveness (in the earlier days of the journey with some peevishness); and I appreciate the attention directed at him mainly.

But, in consequence, he most often does not comprehend my intention, and takes over my territory, assuming my stepping-down a weakness, mere sybaritism, signs of old age . . .

Then, unavoidably, now and again, when I think I see a mistake or omission on his part, I break through with advice, which he then takes (having framed me into limitations imagined by him) as impositions.

And tied to this the last consequence of his commendably aggressive spirit: he has to be without doubts – chinks in his fighter's armour – so he tends to put blame in difficulties on others (mostly me). Thus it may be said, that he lacks detachment, that is a sense of humour (though plentiful in high spirits). But let's be clear: I say amen to all this, since these are the prerogatives of men of action.

A continent of statues. Is it right for me not to know anything about this – possibly the grandest statuary-folly ever (Rome's Victor Emmanuel memorial? But does it not fall into the mausoleum category?): its viewing contains the harshness of the Andes as the background, the vast city-bred neon announcement 'SIEMENS', whatever it may mean, the diminishing perspectives of bronze horsemen interrupted by a shapeless modern 'form' and closed by some obelisk or other – fossils of past commemorations. And the immense IT: sprawling, in the manner of the untrammelled Santa Lucia hill, this, albeit many-symboled monument, washed all over by mini-waterfalls fought by the upward-reaching vegetational vigour. It has an onward intention, stated by a vessel's prow somewhat led by water-stamping super-beings (perhaps female) some winged yet part-submerged, and out of the mid-deck of this near-craft there rises a rock surmounted by the handsomest naked immense male (though unfairly G-string-equipped) shouldering a banner and Roman-saluting distances of planted greenery and blue-tinted mountains – accompanied by another, smaller (but well-muscled) one, rather outshone; and more, after the bare length of obedient waterfall activity (yet there are also at far edges the counter-demonstrations impossible to interpret – the dolphins rising from the floods and spouting BACK at the hero-in-the-centre strong protest streams of water), a surprise – a calm, seated male, nude again (but covered in places), not pensive, but rather a reserve player waiting his turn on the plinth. After this, rounding off the scene of extravagancies, an ornithoid ending: either a symbol of deserved glory or *memento mori*, or both, as they most often pair off: a perched eagle (or vulture?), wings spread, threatening (the reserve player?) or doing the job of an emblem rounding up this colossal, one guesses, allegory – of Chile? of South America? of the past, the future?

Would some meaning come out of obscurity, if I added that I shared the bench at the foot of this enstoned eloquence (and, no mistake, an impressive creation) with a young mother and child. They appeared to be taking all this (and presumably the political present) for granted; this was their daily walk and rest; the mother's face was finely boned in the mestizo handsomeness, neither melancholy nor resigned, its mood, the gravity of sheer living.

Valparaiso. The Chilean elderly seem to be emphatic Europeans, hence somewhat *passé*. The three-piece-suited old thing, topped with a mask frilled with spade-beard cum glued-upward rich moustache all in unblemished white, but updated with large darkest spectacles. The public benches in the tree-shadows would accommodate another species – possibly also *émigré* from Europe, but self-consciously draped in a local poncho, although capped by a Breton beret (his 'stand'), posing yet unresolved, as if waiting for the final transportation. The old women bent double as if overacting; the poor marked by set-on-chairs public-view decomposition. All amid exorbitant fountains and stone (starch-collared, yet in Roman folds) finger-raising dignitaries – public benefactors.

But wagonetting steep up, or serpenting by road, give the grand ocean-horizon which must propel those urchins' living-impetus, the drunken joy-dance of this bulky, bottle-holding-to-us, proletarian, the three workers, macho-featured against ocean-shipping and the ultimate edge of land, and the cracking beauty of those old streets – the points of tenderness and pride.

Down again to the edge of the waters: the rocky bay billows huge winds, storming waves and gulls' shrieks at the bulky-boat-filled fishermen's anchorage of San Pedro. Some boats cut outward into the high foam, some return, some men lounge and gossip over the grounded ones under the flutter of multi-coloured flaglets; whiskered San Pedro himself (painted bright) lines up with old discardeds along the ocean wall. This 'tableau', a candidate for the list of the world's unperishable (I hope) wonders. But further, the shore of rich vacationers begins with the Hotel O'Higgins – pride-inflated flags and soldiers jogging by command.

Ages-sanctified hence unerring-in-style, the demi-world – rubbed out or corrupted into unbalance in the 'West' – is alive here in Latin America. My early Europe still cherished it – the Toulouse-Lautrecian shady-*louche*-lovely confidence in being a part of the indivisible whole, not puritanically threatened and thus turned unsavoury.

Take the shabby turns behind Valparaiso's main square – all fits into city patterns of yesterday – the sailor's traditional pleasures; girls (many yellow-haired to satisfy nostalgias) take position in the doorways and lean on elbows out of the windows (as of old) of Hotel Glory and Hotel Mocamba; or begin to file into Bar El Mar (it is still early) to be treated to bottles of beer by the giant black merchant sailor from Virginia, an early customer. Daytime tradings draw to an end: donkeys are loaded and led away, old men and old dogs get out of the way in the shadows of the stilled cranes, a sole lay preacher delivers his last street-corner plea and marches off with his bandsmen and hymns, replaced by men with hunter's stealthy eyes.

Brazilian President's visit to Chile punctuated by an exhibition of Brazilian art: Museo Nacional de Bellas Artes de Santiago, as turn-of-the-century culture-palaces go, fine: statues/lamp-pedestals line staircases up to the extra-flamboyant stucco-glass-iron largesse, perfectly framing upper-cum-diplomatic *vernissage*-conceits, with, on the balcony above, heavies in mufti, massive hands on the banisters in the stance of readiness.

The *vernissage* – a stage; sculptures – the props: grand nudes and sprawling apotheoses to be circled in pursuits of politesse; abstractions applying their holes to framing maquillaged faces. The two Presidents too busy for this ceremony, their wifely stand-ins densely bedecked with bric-à-brac of opulent status (the husband-rulers prone to be abruptly ousted), have the look of potential rich refugees, weary under the load of their possessions; even their make-up seems to be adding to the burden, weighing on their features. No one looks at the pictures . . . The *contredanse* of influential connectings sustains itself on masterly *canapés* and *Pisco-Sours* – art (selected, travelled, catalogued and platitudinized) stays portentously spaced on the walls in its degraded blankness, as indispensable pretext for contemporary 'functions'. The tragi-pessimistic protest paintings of most recent years hang muted, turned merely fashionable.

Down below in the *Museo* two leading artists, Rodolpho Opazo and Ricardo Yrarrazaval, show work – which grows out of the ripples of the Mexican revolutionary *Angst* theme – ignored by the ceremonial élite upstairs. But an attentive look at their exhibition and dinners in their well-feathered studios confirm their 'alibi'-status as part of a 'Western'-oriented culture-class upheld by the double vow of negating the Allende Left and the *Junta* Right.

The same is true of GRUPO CIEN: their aims – *Busca Rescatar Nuestros Valores Culturales* – tell all. Prosperous but also cultivated suburbia; gardens and drive-shaded grand-and-modest house of Hernán and Carmen Goñi Edwards: pictures, books, worthy CIEN people. Selectively gathered, having declared their individual 'antis' they are (ecologists, sociologists, architects, musicians, historians, etc.) oddly demonstrative of their noble ancestry, supported by portraits and photographs – nailed within the confines of Chilean archaeology/history as if raised above and superior to their neighbour, but sprinkled with tolerance-factor. José Piñera, plump, previously an ambassador, is now anti-government, but also the father of the present Minister of Work; the young man, Belisario Velasco, who was head of the Radio, has just been freed from political exile in the north; these two don't seem to be members, but are present and proudly pointed out. Indeed, political tolerance/variability merely ornaments, for us the visitors, this patriotic masonic 'lodge' – the key is professionalism in the service of *los valores tradicionales de la cultura chilena*.

And when, the next day within the citadel of Edificio Diego Portales, **General Fernando Matthei** (*Junta de Gobierno, Gabinete Fuerza Aerea*), as Teresa warned, a charmer, treats us to tea and to an invitation to film as and what we choose without any restrictions and, on the way out, we drive past the toothy whitewashed walls of the prison with shut, black gates queued up to by the dark crowd of callers, the Orwellian world-schema proves a poor, sickly joke.* Here, the Latino-Indian hotch-potch of unruly, out-of-hand, over-breeding, multi-divided multitudes, both greedy and resigned, only bewilder; and ourselves: held in nooses of puzzlement and confusion.

*BACK IN LONDON
Coca Rudolphy comes to my studio.
Coca, 5 foot svelte
Santiago actress, daughter of
retired Admiral who
wouldn't believe IT
until
SHE was tortured.
Coca tells (the drawing-room tone, even
titters of politesse, but a lot of
illustrative body-twists):
she was never afraid
She watched her step/her answers for consquences
She heard her own screams – detached

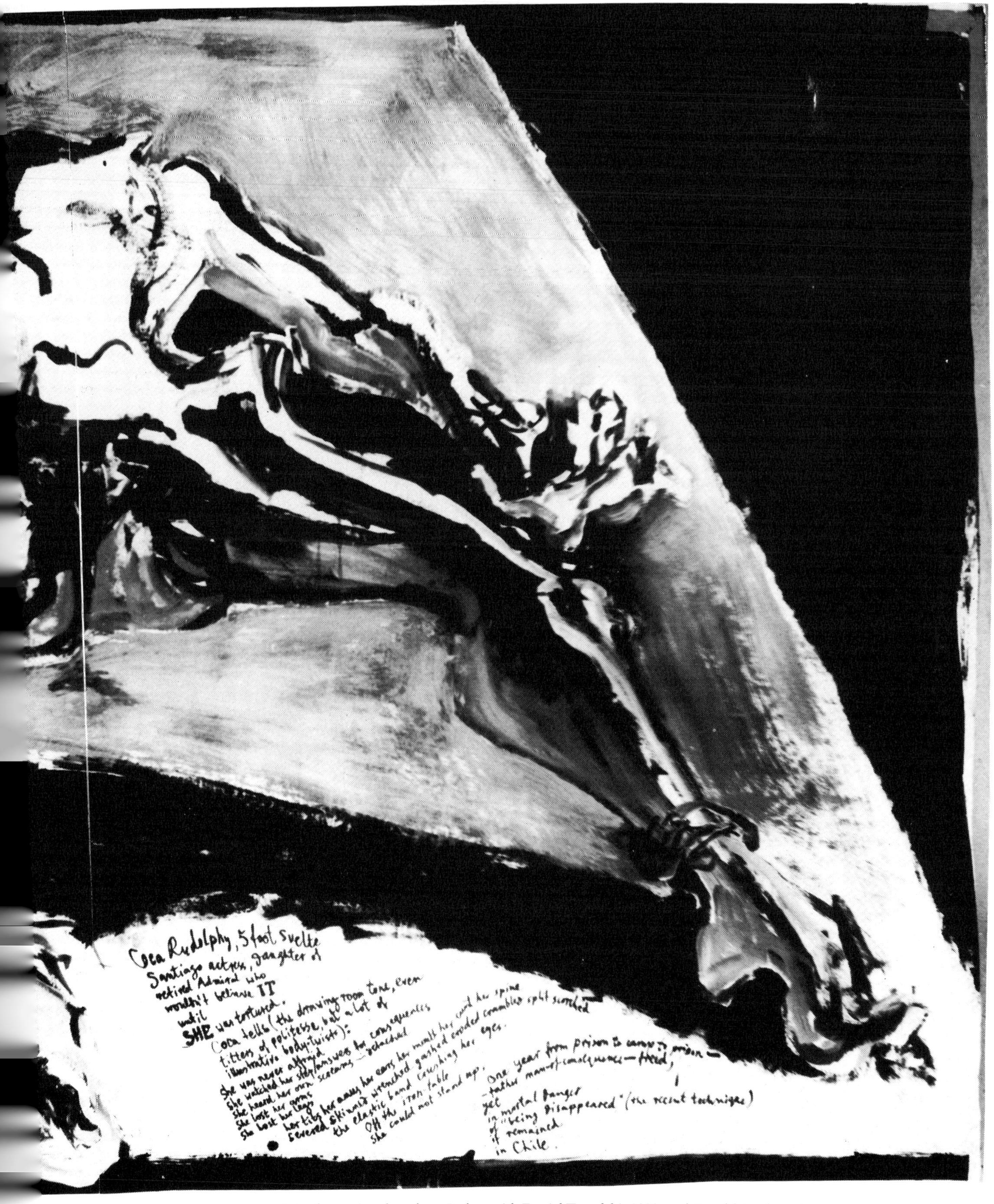

Chile (from *Travels with my Father*, with Daniel Topolski, 1983, and *Topolski's Chronicle*)

She lost her arms
She lost her legs
Her tits her anus her ears her mouth her cunt her spine
severed skinned wrenched gashed eroded crumbled split scorched
the elastic band crushing her eyes.
Off the iron-table
she could not stand up.

One year from prison to camp to prison –
father man-of-consequence – freed,
yet
in mortal danger
of 'being disappeared' (the recent technique)
if still
in Chile

We fly by small airforce planes and helicopters – volcanoes smoke amiably – and drive over the length of Chile, filming with Eduardo Vega Bezanilla of the Chilean Foreign Office assisting, and **Teniente** (Lieutenant) **Christian Pabst García**, whose great-uncle was the great film-maker Pabst – perfectly modelled, in his British-cut airforce uniform, on an ideal English flying officer – in charge of organization.

A Homeric glimmer: four of us in the early hours, in the resthouse of *Producción de Cobre Comerciable* in Calama. The troubled hero and three councillors. The hero – an airforce *Teniente* – is concerned, as the ancients, with honour. He is not politically restless, but he is an aspirant to loyalty and purity of serving. He serves his orders from the top devotedly (in this instance, to guide/liaise our expedition to success), but the Commander of this distant garrison blocks them by refusing a necessary helicopter and, at the *Teniente*'s protests, abuses him; this happens behind a closed door, but the hero emerges paled and shattered.

A trivial matter, probably fuelled only by the local Commander's steaming ambition, but in our night-converse, it opens up vistas of fundamentals.

The *Teniente* takes up an uncompromising knightly stance: he felt doubly offended – as an officer performing his duty, and by the dishonour creeping into the upper ranks of his Service; and he sees as the only way out – to resign from the Service.

The youngest among us, a product of untroubled English public school and Oxbridge, with the inevitable admixture of humanist-socialist ideals never tested by oppressive realities, agrees – perhaps on wrong premisses; and applauds the *Teniente*'s proposal to report the case in person to his uppermost *Junta*-superior, which he thinks his duty, however destructive to him.

Now the turn of the opposite and the practised view: a youngish career diplomat, with several worldwide postings behind him, masterly in promotional up-stepping, in private a connoisseur both of the arts and of living. Again the politics, that is, generalized grievances over social injustice, are of no concern – his assessments and advice concentrate on personal interplay within seemingly monolithic systems.

No, no, he says, this is a very minor incident – a subordinate must suffer, now and again, a dressing-down by a superior officer, and cannot win by referring to a higher, far-away authority – rank *oblige*, and, if he reports the matter, the local Commander has many answers/arguments at hand, the most useful being 'security reasons'.

My untoward role – because of the unexpectedly forceful but, in my view, blinkered boosting of the drama by the English voice – tends to be that of an arbiter. The *Teniente*, handsome, very much of one piece in his uniform and manner, a professional soldier, cannot be imagined as a freelance drifter/manipulator within his country. I state the need for calm assessment of the measure of his grievance as against his 'professional career'; I proffer doubts about his reaching his *Junta* General at all. And my final plea is for sleeping on it.

Next day he is less keen on discussing the matter; the next and the next, it is not mentioned any more, but the martinet in him is visibly on the increase.

That night of agitated clashing exchanges – their histrionic heights, the overdrawn characters growing into conflicting protagonists – verged on the epic, perhaps more Racine than Homer, with pedestrian duty standing in for honour. It was all touchingly, pathetically there – even in, or perhaps because of, its minimal singularity. Well above this dry telling.

Thirty-six hours by train – **Antofagasta, Chile to La Paz, Bolivia.** On what rests this tableland? – with appeals (no adverts) hugely scribbled over crumbling wall-bracket misery-shacks, thrown about the widest aridity (AYOAYO Station, *Elevación 3868.3 m*); the infrequent churches do not amend it and the tourists sour it.

Over flat dryness reaching humped horizons there feed/starve slaty donkeys and handfuls of llamas. How did the Third World get lifted and suspended at such heights?

At the station-stops, Indian women, baby-loads on their backs, squat among their tenting skirts to shit under low clouds. Burdened, they sway-trot along over the sooty grey cracked earth that at random sprouts mud-hovels and then levels them, when the animals and people move on.

On the train a bowler-hatted woman sets her belongings on the seats and herself on the floor in between; beautifully composed, she needleworks. But the train attendants chase her out.

La Paz. Morning: oppressiveness and pain and bad drawing heightened by police registration – shabby crowded procedure, but no monolithic drama: a girl official, handling hollow formalities, assisted by grim-grimacing gun-clenching girl soldiers, bursts into joy at my pince-nez suspended on a string.

Posters – toothy dictatorial face – lure citizens YO DEFIENDO TU SECURIDAD TU FAMILIA Y TU PROPRIEDAD. San-Francisco-churchy Indian murmurs pleading to blood-shedding white-skinned saints in 3-D tableaux, within garish, golden-lacquer-garnished *nouveaux-riches* conquistadors' show-off, yet honestly tragic since made by their 'naive' Indian pupils: local ardent new believers, whose martyrs, truly suffering and richly bleeding, are the link with their fierce, distant tradition.

The whole wall-space – untrammelled by taste – crowded with baroque opulence, in which vulgar/touching paintings are only subservient accents. The Museum (a handsome old palace) feeds today's glorification of pictures alone – lines of 'colonial' holy images, torn away from the churches where the décor of worship matters, falsify the truth. But good to see this determined-to-kill angel-bowman – I return to him – the Indo-Spanish painter's gifts lifted on **the fierceness**. Same fierceness in a half-café exhibition next door: anger-protest, favoured in Latin American art now, animates these ugly, ardent pictures – but the little painter, his work soaked in brave challenge, stands there, humble-shaped and black-suited (a poor man's attempt at respectability) – perhaps already defeated by age, and parochialism – and repression or perhaps his last stand if, forced to take it, would be more like his pictures. And, as an artist, he offers humanity against the Museum's modern visiting-show of miserable modern French prints – the disease of chic idiom wandered here too.

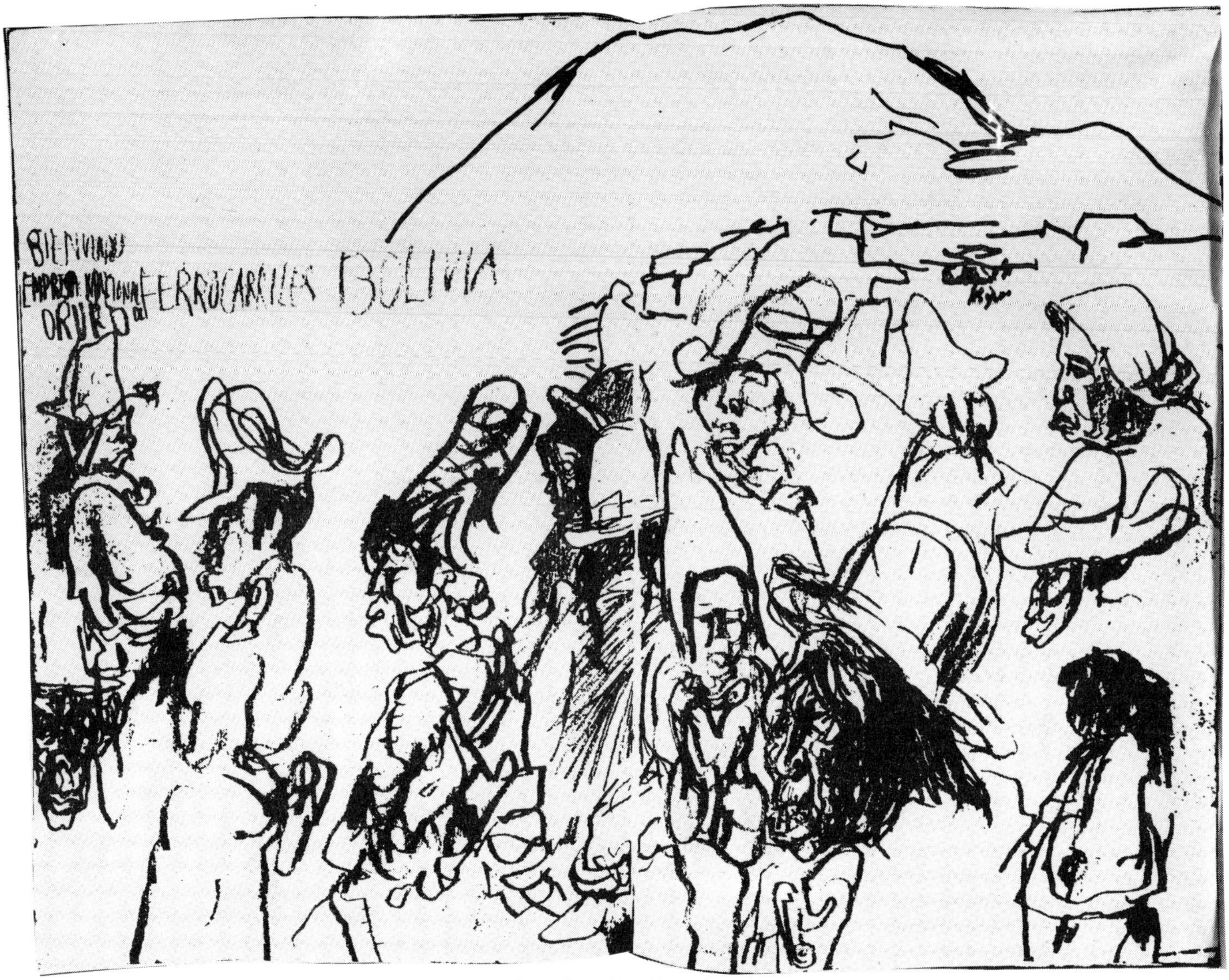

Bolivia (from *Topolski's Chronicle*)

And then Gonzalo Montes, an average La Pazian, and his lament over Bolivia's fate under terror (and his children's – barred from the shut-down university), and the promise of the coming revolt by the 'good military'.*

After the showpiece of La Paz – the steep **upper Indian town** – the Ambassador produces his surprise: we pick up his wife (drop Daniel, seduced by the Sunday *paseo* cum military band), change to a Land-rover and soon get on rough roads, skirting speedy-steep rivulets with the bustle of washerwomen of style and a wide-spread display of drying weavery. The highest bend and all this vigour abruptly ceases – the frontier crossed into inanimate deathly otherness.

Bolivia's **Valley of the Moon** is as the pre-exploration of the moon imagined it to be: shatteringly unearthly. The enormous (height and expanse) bunching up of precipitous stalagmites, sharply straining upward, as if to meet ghostly stalactites above, no longer there – the earthly fossilized leftovers of gigantic inter-planetary interplay. We sweep and turn and roll up and down over rocky dry beds, are caught/fringed by those monstrous jagged obelisks/needles until even the Land-rover cannot battle further.

We back out, turn round within a trickle of a rivulet, reach in a roundabout struggle a minimal road – and then, soon, the next unpredictable, yet metaphorically correct, change: out of the wilderness there shapes itself, to sit confidently on top of it, the golf-club of **the exclusives**: the mighty, the upper strata and the diplomats.

The usual chic appendages – pavilions/umbrellas/banners/caddy boys/bright-checked clothing and bright voices/clatter of balls; a Japanese group (distant 5 feet-high bright dots) at their aloof and segregated game. But of course we entered this smoothness from the back; now we exit along a narrowly – but neatly – provided network of 'facilities' and find, among another spell of tender villages, a country inn with the right balance of exoticism and familiarity.

Bolivia–Peru. The full coach from La Paz leaves us (no one raises the alarm) on the far shore at the lake-ferry; the two of us, facing an empty sheet of **Titicaca**, and with the ferry not returning for us, miraculously activate a huge boat – and find the bus waiting. Then a late entry into **Copacabana**:

*A routine publisher's party in London: and a routine introduction to the jacket designer for a book of poems, who declared himself the brother of my La Paz friend, Gonzalo: 'Yes, his children are back at the university, open now; everything is much better.'

Fleetingly, the choking spasm of – hurt? collision? let-down? That brother in La Paz had been reached through hard journeying – the Bolivian predicament in distant isolation settled in memory, and this London encounter quenched that feeble mirage, a reminder of the trivial accessibility of any nowhere; pulled down the whole voyage to the level of **a trip**.

charming; candles and carbide-lamps light up the market; the changeless courtyardy inn – and harmony.

Passport-stamping offices are closed, hence out of Bolivia illegally on a wobbly bus. Daniel at once knits a friendship-for-ever with a Peruvian youth, still breathless having run out of Copacabana hopefully for a mile to catch us in case we halted (the two of them will circle Lima after *chicas*, evening and night).

The frontier attempts to eliminate solely the two of us (the stamp-absence) from the packed bus, but Daniel, true to himself, battles us through into Peru and, later, again bravely, in the midst of a Peruvian village (our bus will not go further) squashes me into a *collectivo*, and himself stays behind in uncertainty.

The *collectivo* contains a bourgeois-Brazilian pair with a kid (each of these journeys has a maniacal minor – this one flamboyant: shouts and blows on a whistle), Daniel's Marco of Lima and a peasant couple – she, the bowler, he, a cap refined in the US manner, and (it takes me aback) there appears in his callused hands an immense smooth and shining SEIKO radio or recorder or all-in-one. As programmed by the nature of this highland, a fierce storm (lightnings and deluge) comes and goes – but the road turns river; tin replaces thatch; slogans garland the roadscape as in Bolivia, but aggressively 'democratic'; here and there, within minimal municipal greens, busts of determined Peruvian heroes pop up.

Puno. The darkening, the murky traffic led by amassing telegraph poles, the drab slogan-walled station approaches; the *collectivo* dispatches me with my bags under the rain in the mud, young Marco, Daniel's new friend, at my weary side – we cross to the dismal Ferrovia Hotel, its un-'reception', stair-and-room décor: the almost life-length flashback (but sluggishly realized, and in spite of travellers' monotonous 'This is *exactly* like . . .' being my taboo) to the depth of parochially autumnal Ruthenia, then eastern Poland – only cadet officer's uniform, the sword and the tart at my side, missing . . .

Much later Daniel arrives, having altruistically stayed behind to be rescued by a coachful of Australians; and we dine in this almost (but less and less so) pre-war provincial Polish hotel's salon-dining room – stretches of murky-white tablecloths, unpopulated except for our two-tabled little cluster of Daniel's road-acquisitions: two English boys (diplomacy and oil) from Santiago, the Peruvian Marco, shy and acclaimed – and, after a while, Daniel's friend of the last ten minutes: a giant American girl.

Now, with the accompaniment of fluting/drumming/whistle-blowing by four nylon-folk-costumed musicians, all analogies disappear: this is Puno, Peru, harmlessly harmonizing its band's barbarous artlessness with our inescapably jaunty touristiness gelling (a sudden realization) into the modern peripatetic folksiness.

Puno town. . . . ACCION POPULAR VIVA EL INICIO DE LA LUCHA ARMADA 'VIVA PCP' . . . 'A BAJO . . . VIVO GOBIERNO'; and the loudspeakers; and Plazas de Armas; and the gesturing statues – *Cornel don* Francisco Bolognesi, *heroico Defensor de Arica*; and in Parque Pino (the 1881 statue of *soldado* Manuel Pino, fringed with torsos of moustachioed *cornels*) wide-spread stalls laid with 'Literatura Soviética' alongside 'Mao-Tse-Tung' (his star already fallen in China) and posters *Revistas* **China**; with a bus named 'Jesus Nazareno' receiving Indians and soiled high-loaded **gringos**. All under the inconsiderate skies.

Young *gringos* at dawn in haste – giggling groups – apparently cultivating superiority over the humble *Indios*, deservedly get outwitted – robbed at the station by the dozen – and now mockery turns to indignation.

'The most spectacular train journey', **Puno–Cuzco**, is to begin: *Jefe de Estación*; *Damas 1ra*; *Damas 2da*; the bell – one, two, three – inevitability stills all momentarily – and the train begins to roll, as if over, as if into (so close it is) the frieze of miasmatic misery – yet with the touch of picturesqueness – and musicians, crowded in gluey dampness, busy with the mucked-up basics of selling, buying, devouring under the slogans of socialism – until the rails divide, the scene thins out, the finale – a rot-edged, mummy-like, man spread-eagled in the mud. Mud persists, raised/shaped into pitiful hutments, though some feeble treelets try to align the misery – perhaps to provide some frontier-front in the warfare between tourists and the poverty-inflicted local robbers. The flatness stays with the train (though climbing mountains are sketched at far edges), only at intervals punctuated by crucified mounds.

A hamlet and its stop-hut – and the train settles to nap in midday's empty stupor. Those beauties sung by the guidebooks have not materialized as yet, as I vaguely expected: the thinness of the undertaking, fuelled by the exclamatory archaeologizing of the PR travel agencies, mobbed by the soiled youngsters of the world; and mounting animosity of autochthones, humbled and revengeful; and of nature on its own angry trail.

A weary look round over the long first-class coach: a plump egocentric, carefully made-up (perhaps even powdered into whiteness) for his role of, one assumes, a 'safe-conduct' man of affairs (elaborate sports cap always on, not angled but responsibly straightforward, huge darkest glasses, thin black line over meaty lips, above a self-indulged chin and respectable newspaper); but the even plumper commercial gent opposite open and cheery and full of advice on Bionorm (glucose) tablets and Cuzco hotels.

At La Raya (alt. 4319 m) *PLA Proletarios Unios*. On the flats the still bowler-hatted and crinolined women circle, chickens at their heels, their placid herds of cows, sheep, donkeys and llamas; why all over the land do they leave their horses to pasture fully saddled? At Tejidos, or is it Checacupe, a patchwork clown-beggar mixes millennium-style medievalisms; he and a pale-maned and bearded high-loaded wandering *longus* inscribed with '. . . *something* DEL PERU MAO LENIN' left behind, while the train floats downwards with a foaming river. The hot springs bring the greener lands (so what?) and, under the rain, with village kids at a gallop, the mood clears, although the tourists (a furious Frenchwoman, comic Germans, the Swiss and Americans indistinguishable) frame the passage in bathos. Perhaps THEY are the central theme for us.

All this is not bad at all – knocking about against folk-youth gambits/deeds/pleas/haggles surely gives more than the fly-over routines of queuing – customs-barriers – eye-on-the-luggage – taxi-chase. But **the Cuzco–Lima flight** will go better: Daniel's pick-up girl (while, indeed, queuing to send me off) tends me throughout; her sister and brother-in-law, Police-Major in Lima, muster my luggage on arrival and drive me in their broken-down Volkswagen to my hotel room-plus-bath.

Cuzco. Scholars and their thick prestigious books, mindlessly bound by the academic dogmas of the day. Their subsidized travels fructify with rigorous 'studies' of
dating
singling out names
stringing up influences and derivations
throwing in handfuls of 'formal' clichés.
Having worked for ten years on their book, Professor George Kubler – on the architecture, and Professor Martin Soria – on the sculpture and painting – of South America, don't give any notion (and they are not supposed to) of the **undivided wholeness** of these three arts here and of their worship-full blood-soaked **purgatorial Indo-Spanish blend.**

Cuzco cathedral. The marketplace carries on inside the entrance – barriers sorting out, at varying prices and with some argument, touristy desires; fine – no need for putting on airs, there will soon be dignity abounding. The awesome scale opens into twin cavern-immensities: ambushing *vacua*, and plenty more diverting openings – to accost and compel the errant *campesinos* at every turn with holies of holies, and their demands. There are also steps down into the *memento mori* desserts.

The black shadows dissolve the heights, and there is no colour – gold (caked over plentifully) is no painter's colour, but the declaration of euphoria, both of pride and of worship; pictures and polychromed statues, however exorbitantly gesturing and bloody, are only signposts to lined-up adoration-points; the lighting lifts out accents, mercifully not neonized to ban murky mysteries.

Mercifully the tourists, humbled and in tight groups, cannot submerge this giant piece of man-made ecology, though the faithful, presumably only the Indians, are absent at this hour.

Thus the Indian was won over by Christ's irresistible might; but how and when did the transition begin from the cathedral to the marketplace and its rewards? and what code now holds Cuzco and its tourists in accord? – many if only sporadic brutalities? only the fear of the police?

The questions more pressing on this continent than elsewhere, with the answers suggesting themselves thickly.

Pablo Neruda:

Entonces en la escala de la tierra he subido
entre la atroz marana de las selvas perdidas
hasta ti, Macchu Picchu

Then on the ladder of the earth I climbed
through the lost jungle's tortured thicket
up to you, Macchu Picchu

Translation by John Felstiner

My curse or blessing is the urge to battle against emotional glueyness, defending my supposed watchful validity. I just managed to beat it down the few times it began to flood over me: mostly in the face of nature's magnitude.

Thus I may be prejudicially armed against **Neruda's sonorities**. And he must have seen his Macchu Picchu when still unpolluted by the tourists' invasion. Polluted, or, to me, (watchful, not kneeling to), revived into this century in its grotesque *contredanse* of not-quite confrontations. The myth city gripped in the Cordillera's fierceness, raised from the dead, becomes a stage for the futile antics of **non-pilgrimages**. And, properly, these circumambulating cortèges – not imagining any need for a ritual and the climax of an altar – are redeemed (but not aware of) with the only available/left-to-us act of worship (sacrifice?): the copulating young pair (meaningfully German/Polish) on the highest pinnacle above Macchu Picchu.

Lima. The overblown prestige of archaeology worldwide ('antiquarianism' is my term) perhaps points to a fear of facing the present, and here is pathetically obvious: the officially cared-for pile of old stones – and, across the road, poverty.

Quito. Plaza Independencia – Palacio de Gobierno – standard capital city accents, their repetitiousness, country after country, diminishing the impact; the two dressy guards (mestizo and black, bayoneted rifles and, oddly, spurs) coo with groupie girls, and let me casually into the *palacio*'s courtyard to look at Oswaldo Guayasamin's mural in Latin America's academic manner. Outside, the banners, the military band; and, in the square, the world-over embenched, time-killing retireds.

The pedestrian progress, cobble-impeded, files narrowly, unstriking; but a few rare men suddenly blossom with *hidalgo*-haughty handsomeness – though these lean towards thickly feathered dark lip-nostril emphasis. Quito women (unlike those of Lima) uniformally ill-formed even in their brief youth – yet those male beauties seem to delight in them.

Differently: **the campesinos** even though subdued by the city; their Indian faces as I always imagined; minutely solid, yet elegant in their most-apt attire – unvaried, but for colour, from childhood to old age; men coquettishly pigtailed, women burdened, but in a stylish trot – let them stay such forever. And also the blacks: high-raised outside/above the rest – **separate**. And that separatedness shows in the reciprocal disdain of the divided – the dividing-line not to be crossed over.

Also in the Plaza (a day of anniversary ceremonies) the *Sesión Solemne de Concejo Municipal de Quito* with the emphatic/bloated Spanish power-faces lined up (the world's ambassadors present, in turgidity) for **Jaime Roldos Aguibra, Presidente Constitucional de la República de Ecuador**, to step up to a pulpit (an Airforce ADC in attendance) and, his worry-eyebrows working up and down, deliver a longish address on the achievements and happy prospects of his government. A few months later he and his masterful wife will be **killed** in a mysterious aircrash.

Out in the square again, now in full celebration, the cathedral steps mounted tightly with a girls' and boys' choir cum mime, well attended by the placid onlookers below – interspersed with **restless young men** shiftily assessing the tourists' shoulder bags and cameras.

Alan White, **the British chargé d'affaires**, and the hospitable Spanish wife of the head of the British Council take me to **Señor Galo Plaza Lasso**, the former (before intermediary upheavals) president of Ecuador, internationally respected figure of South America. Cannot wish for more: cloud-capped mountain chains accompany or cross us, eucalyptuses give way to high cacti; *campesinos* in their market finery frieze the roads; and the warning-reminder – a crossroads holy statue hedgehogged with improvised nailed-on plastic symbols of revolutionary labour – pink arms holding hammers.

But beyond, the grace of the remoteness of rurality (costumes and gestures in accord with the land), till one reaches almost by chance the walls of the *estancia* and enters another era – the unhasty vague Indian domestics within a cobble-stoned quadrangle held by the silence of three-winged old-print sedateness. The anticipated/imagined colonial Spain opens up. There is, in the coolness of the lobby and the antechamber, the assurance of style: the past accumulated in harmonious layers exists by its seigneurial right. Yet then the huge galleried interior, rebuilt by the host, serves for his entry: and there (I am the last to hold to the uniformity of a standstill-past) this majestic relic presents his contemporariness by his faultless correct (a shade *comme-il-faut* eccentric) anglicized country casuals of wools/cashmeres/silks; but also his has-been presence in political vulgarities: behind him high on the wall a pair of immense full-length portraits – identical in size, identical in details: black tails, white ties, red–blue–yellow ribbons across the chests – his father an earlier (beard and curved moustache), and he the later (young and smooth) president; logically and properly bad paintings, in accord with the surrounding array of dedicated photographs of the world's mighty. These speak of his commitment to the international UN *contredanse*. But now he is back: 'I've always been a farmer.' Though not quite. His role as an incorruptible elder statesman, with a variety of top international engagements behind him, makes him needed still. And he tells us, with some satisfaction, that he acts constantly as an intermediary at the highest level and that, recently, during a gathering of several South American leaders, he was selected to give a key speech.

We move to a pretty lean-to greenhouse (plants and birds), his wife properly secondary; and, after leisurely drinks, we eat deliciously, with an Indian girl, starchly folklorish, serving, and hear of his endless squirish activities. Indeed, he is convincing, his grace and handsomeness and worldliness contributing when he holds forth on salvation through **paternalism** (though the term is avoided). He is even more convincing on our long drive over his 2,600 hectares of mountainous estate. The grand vistas, horizons lost in clouds, tender with the decorative peasantry hieratic at cultivation and crafts, securely bowing to the father figure. There are many questions though, and the answers don't carry beyond his presence.

An over-smoothly suited person, overstated in facial hair-décor and self-assurance – an old town **café macho** type – proposes to show his family's collection as the first step on the way to his millions: he had heard the National Gallery of London is paying out for religious art.

The boorishness of his 'contemporary' manner ceases at the steep steps to the old door in a shabby lovely street-frontage behind Plaza San Francisco. The shady narrowness opens on to a courtyard's unerring gentility and the family group at the top of the galleried stairs: he now unrecognizable – a respectful young offshoot.

Whether they had dressed up for the occasion, or it was their habitual formality, they and the gravity of their greetings blend with the salon to which we are solemnly led. It is gladdening – greatly – being my kind of archaeology: putting my finger on the still-warm pillow of alien living.

None of the traveller's usual *entrées* into interiors – international modern – sumptuous and/or kitschy, palatial, academic, artistic, collector's – or plebeian-rustic. The authenticity of this continuity, unblemished, unselected by taught sophistications, layer upon layer, of **the Spanish-colonial** citizen's family home; generational overlapping, naturally temporarily stilled and living in the paternal-grandpaternal period: the soft-centred chairs circling the walls and the tiny plinth-table – the carpet underneath and the flower vase on top, his/her youth portraits. He, the grandfather, tiny relic, is the master, and ceremonially conducts our reception; his wife is elegantly shrivelled – but speechless with panic in her eyes throughout; the others of all ages (all minute) assist in respectful silence.

We sit out the prologue of dignified exchanges; nothing is served as, I imagine, we are not proper visitors, and after a quarter of an hour the inspection/enchantment moves on.

Most of the rooms are entered from the continuous roofed balcony, to the accompaniment of a multitude of courtesy gestures, but some interconnect. Thus the family cortège which follows us, by winding in and out through their familiarity, enacts in revealing performance, each dramatis persona stunningly dependent on/activating the others; their class-world, their interwoven existences, the tragicomedy of Quito, are platitudes as anywhere else, fossilized, yet living and in the making.

This is not fancy. The art objects ARE, and they belong to all the rooms, closely filling up the walls, the tops of sideboards, cupboards, side tables. The rooms are tight, some windowless and filled by a bed (I guess at the occupier of each), some strangely of no practical use, as if forming the pauses/chapels for the contemplation of a bric-à-brac – dominating saintly image boxed in gaudy domesticity, while the main dining room has hardly space to squeeze between the wall and banks of chairs. The pieces of furniture, accumulated around the turn of the century, seem, by trial and error of years of utility, to have found themselves the habit and cosiness of placing: the lesson of amassment of artefacts and humans in harmony.

The procession is permeated, of course, with anxiety over the impression the collection will make. Most of the paintings and statues are just run-of-the-mill colonial-Indian religious images, but I am always attracted to their innocent bloody passions.

The patriarch has been guiding us through all this liturgically, yet with a good dose of sales-patter dramatization. Now we return to the salon to sit round again, but this time for the moment of truth: a dialogue between me and the initial young man; the old recede, as they should, when the contemporary news-media 'vibes' bring out the greed for quick gain. He retells his pathetic misconception and my little speech closes the matter; I have to make it clear that the National Gallery in London and the museums in general are not after religious paintings as such but after single works by particular artists, mostly independent of their subject matter. Only then are they prepared to pay vast sums. I also give some shaky advice, raise the matter of regulations about exporting antique art-works and assure them that we have no adverse opinion of their collection.

There is a show of good manners while we leave . . .

A telephone call: Carmen something (an Ecuadorean name) **in Polish**. Soon this timid young girl comes to my hotel rooms – her mother Polish, her father an Ecuadorean, who came to Poland on some educational exchange scheme, and stayed on. She, Carmen, brought up in Poland to reach a diploma in painting at the Warsaw Academy of Art, urged by her father to visit his country and his family, came to Quito. And the painful clash between her Bohemian-European ways and her conservative grandparents, who, disappointed in not confronting an imagined blonde of traditional manners, wanted her to wear (*passé* for her) longish dresses and stay under their guard while they searched for an appropriate husband. And so she sidestepped them, fell in love with, and married hastily, a young Ecuadorian architect cum musician, who played the night-clubs and soon surfaced his macho instincts; they were parted now.

There arose an instant compatibility between us, both of idiomatic Polishness and our common profession. We took a bus: swaying in its congestion, paying those tiny sums of sucres, being part of the ordinariness of Quito – a feeble but still real pleasure for me, contrasting with those detached car/taxi rides. Then some walking after centre-of-town businesses, bypassing my routine stops (the British Embassy and the sumptuous Quito Hotel) and, at her command (since she wanted to show me her precious sites), emerging low down, below the scarp of smartness, at the homely old church in the village square. The church contained her favourite naive paintings, but it was puzzlingly closed and I wanted to see her work before dark.

But, before this, I was to see her special offering. We took a precipitous path behind the church, edging among the pine trees, the immense gorge and the colossal mountainscape crowning great distances below and afar. The path wound round stony edges, until unexpectedly, we stepped into the ruins of a grandiose *hacienda*. She was preparing me for it: it was haunted; a friend she brought there after dark backed away in haste, intimidated; her patron and master(?) had lived there until some twenty years earlier, but now abandoned, open to the elements and vandals, crumbling yet persisting, it became sublime, with odd inner half-open darkened twists, life-invoking graffiti. Its solitariness on that bulwark in face of the aloof prospect of huge distances – their centre advancing at us in the shape of densely wooded, threatening prominence. And the vultures.

Then we zigzagged upwards on foot (beyond my invalidated prowess and training, but done) to her house on top of the village, and her room, suspended, still higher, over the same stupendous depth, the window taking it all in.

All this, from the outset, and culminating in her room (her drawings, spreading to meticulously obsessively patterned immensities bigger than her floor space, outstripped the modesty of the term, being complete works impossible to be achieved differently, or stretched out into further media); all this carried the accompaniment – a flow of her confessional talk; she was there, in Quito, on her own. And the tale was of doubts, regrets, unfulfilment; of longing for Poland and her milieu there – the strongest regret and, somewhat hopeless, emotion; of 'jobs' only, and wrong steps and reaching the edge of 'composure'; conscious of losing grip on herself, apprehensive.

She took me (it was dark already) on short walks, to me immense, to La Galería, an art gallery of fashion where we found a Peruvian sculptor, preparing his *vernissage* for the following day – with sumptuous women probing ahead for choice purchases (such is art patronage intensity there), to another (miles away) closed already, to a vegetarian eatery run by a stylish Polish-Jewish woman, mostly for selectively jeansy young North Americans, with concerts thrown in.

Next day Daniel arrived and, at a meeting arranged at the Quito Hotel lobby, he unhesitatingly pointed to the shape among others at the entrance: 'Here is your Polish girl.' Such was the Polish physical prevalence in her mixed origin.

My departure nearing, I tried clumsily to leave her with more support. I took her for supper to a charming old Polish diplomat-collector; to another with the German dandy-bookseller-publisher and his worldly German businesswoman friend. I sent her some literature and wrote to her, and several months later sent a telegram, but never had any reply. And my Polish diplomat told me on a visit to London that also, after one meeting, he lost sight of her. She did not reappear.

Sequel:

Two days later, officially invited as guests of the British *chargé d'affaires*, in the be-pennanted limousine within a formal cavalcade we arrive in front of Carmen's village church, which was closed to her modest call, now open, but

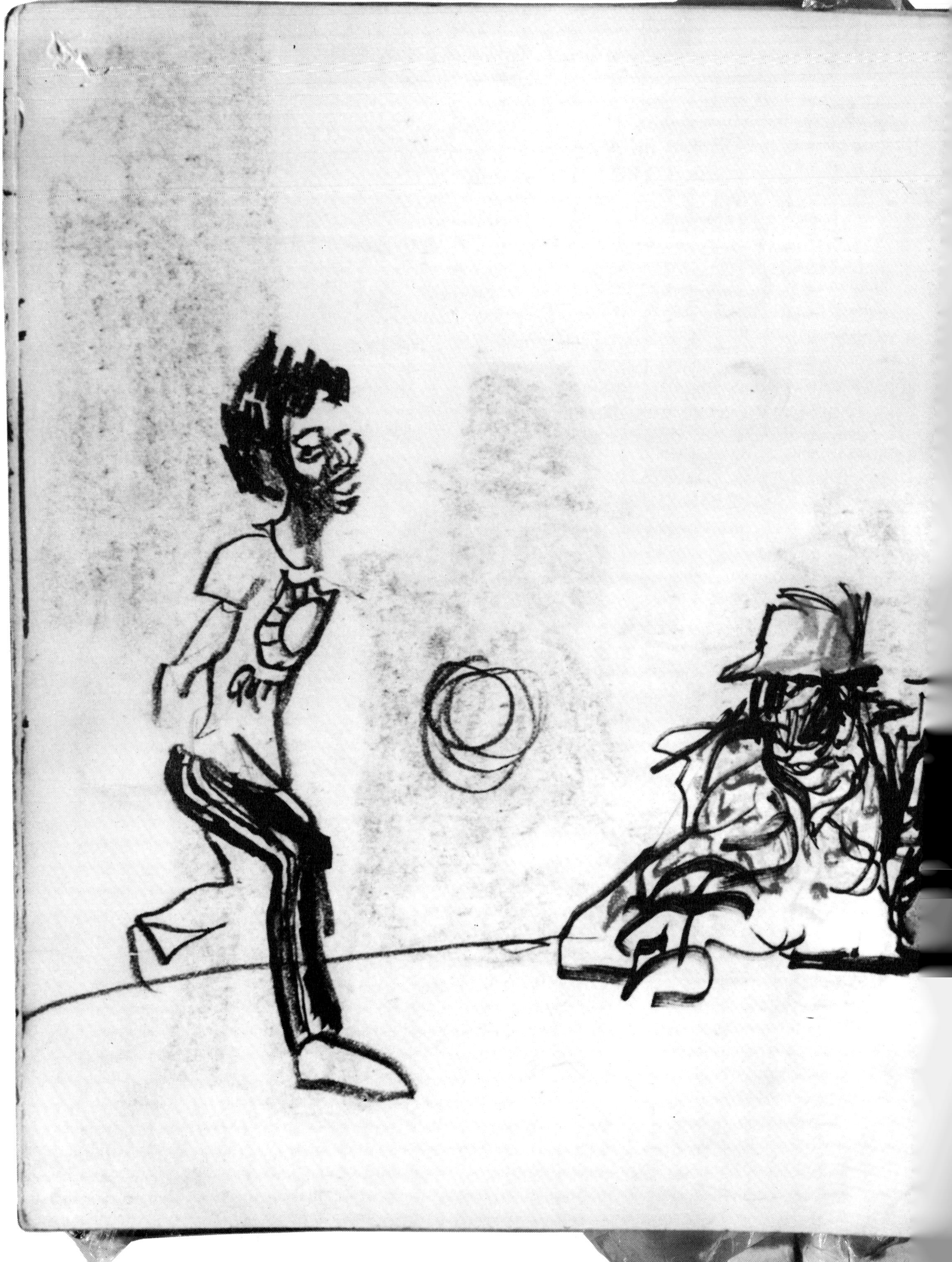

Ecuador (from *Travels with my Father*, with Daniel Topolski, 1983)

ceremonially, and **for pride**. We enter it between the two lines of presidential guards, soon after comes the Vice-president (now President), and finally, trumpeted in and escorted by adjutants, the President. As San Francisco monastery was the other day the mere backcloth of the past to the orchestration of revolutionary banners, slogans, songs and speeches, so the gold-glittering altar has a serving role in the spectacle of earthly power: the long table in front of it, garnished with the top men of the country (behind them stand erect their adjutants and attendants), faces the congregation of courtly worshippers – *Cardenal Arzobispo de Quito*, a minute figure, being late, hurries and trips upon the steps to the altar, habitual for him in hieratic ascensions, but now blocked by the live demigods, amongst whom there is a chair for him. Consequently, this ritual of longsome speeches of self-congratulation and practical promises superimposes hollowly over the claims of eternity exuding all round it.

Bogotá (before Daniel's arrival). Again and again, this vigil-wait for Daniel. Santiago was easy, though he, after his imprisonment in Paraguay, had to cover immense distances with only the approximate date of meeting as a point of contact. Santiago was easy because I was already involved in engagements, and, returning to the hotel on my second afternoon, I found him in my room, more or less on the date we had proposed a month earlier. The joy at uniting in victory over stretches of time and swelling bulging oceans and continents milling with unpredictable humans: the emphatically supremely convincing confirmation of kinship. These treasured moments, these endorsing encounters we repeated, thanks to the fragmentation of our South American expedition, several times. The holy moment passes, becomes confrontation, in all its nuances: discords, alliances, manoeuvres, tripping on trivialities.

Again, another compressed, therefore more anxious wait, in La Paz, close to our departure, in the hotel room. Daniel, having heard of the great impact on me of the Moon Valley, arranged to be taken there in the morning in a car by some young Bolivians he had come across the night before. He should have returned hours ago. Bags were packed and we were due at the bus-stop. And, unavoidably, my imagination raced with visions of tragedy, of the boys (nothing easier), for the sake of his camera, throwing him into the sharp-edged ravines of that deserted world; I imagined his impaled death, the search of his body – the full-scale paternal tragedy woven out.

And then he strolled in – not only debonair, but also having had a haircut, and offering an amazingly *sang-froid* tale: the boys had failed to come, yet, shortness of time and distances brushed aside, he made it on the back of a lorry and a bus. This was, after the torture of my imaginings, a veritable breathtaking resurrection.

The Peruvian wait was hard indeed. These Andean Cordillera passes held terrors, such as the most recent cutting off of the heads of two camping young Germans – by wandering bandits? by *campesinos*? But Lima's reuniting was defused by a television director's fussing presence, and true tenderness reappeared only in Ecuador. I lived in old Quito long enough – that is some ten days – to feel domesticated, yet anxious. Daniel being late and not in touch; his over-Andes trek treacherous and unpredictable – Lima to Quito. Days went by, my messages at the hotel mini-reception trying to direct him to me from hour to hour; and when, unusually for me, I sat one evening, flattened somewhat, in a dreary café attached to the hotel, suddenly he stood on top of the back-door steps, sprightly and not damaged.

Then, finally, Bogotá, as from then on we did not part until it was I who left – Rio for London.

Again the vigil-wait, this time differently tense, his lone passage taking him through most violent, knifing-to-death country. Again the great joy, underlined by the tale of Colombian imprisonment and clashes with the military.

And then his nightly walks in Bogotá within **the killer quarters** – days were enough for me – held me in tension. But it had to be: this was the errantry for one of the heroic breed, however drug-and-gutter-bound Bogotá's life-death arena was. Also, it may be so, those hours were his own, free from all obstructions.

The repellent sordidity, grazed against, mostly heard of, read about, of murder and torture, is not ennobled as by 'the grandiose roles played by the people of Greek tragedies', but now here is 'committed' prosaically on these stages ill-shaped for violence: the low muddy *barrios*, the barbed wired or mining-torn slices of abysses, all under climatic onslaughts, all passed by/through on our South American way. All vultures' pastures. No scope for gestures of glory.

The Caribbean coast's Baranquilla, its reputation as drug-trade junction, its outskirts shabbily, damply dozing at noon, even as we skirt its edges on the road to Santa Marta, has its allure: those gap-roofed and Coca-Cola-marked mini-shadows packed tightly with hammocked people-in-waiting for the sun's decline to mercy; their stillness, imposed, seemingly under the surface plotting ambushes bottled up for later kills. But now, sun at its highest, the man-beasts languid (even those, helmeted and armed, crouching within their posts), the stilled palm trees fringing the low boggy horizon, only an occasional S-shaped umbrellaed black girl-stroller passes in slow motion turn-of-duty. The allure resides in this dusty-damp-decomposing calm underlined by the girl's slow progress – the promise of (now dormant) brutality; the circling condors, butterfly-interpolated, add a metaphor.

This route of smugglers and ruthlessness, along which we are rolling in a rusty vehicle they use (within the cocoon of artificial breeze), now traverses the vastness of swamp-land invaded by industry-polluted ocean lagoons, blanketed by crippled broken timbers and cacti, brooded over by white ibises – the only creatures left in what used to be one of nature's major reserves.

Santa Marta – *Perla de América bienvenida* – approaches: roads, hills outlined by battle-ready chains of camouflage-

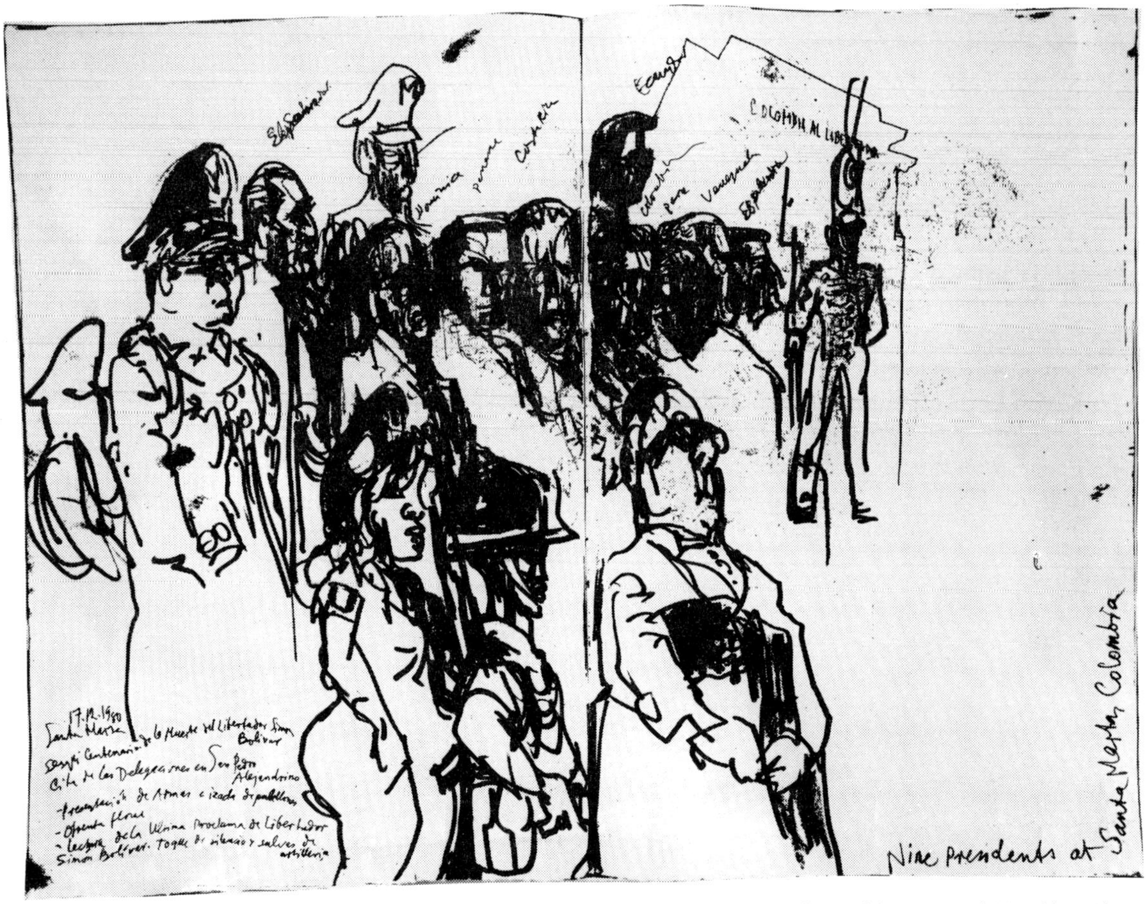

Nine Presidents at Santa Marta, Colombia (from *Travels with my Father*, with Daniel Topolski, 1983 and *Topolski's Chronicle*)

fatigued and sub-machine-gunned soldiery – on foot, in vehicles – tin or wide-brim or forage-capped. And, through Santa Marta, more uniformed varieties: girl-traffic-policing; girls, appliquéed with orange, on parade duties. All accumulating in crescendo to giant-cacti-bound hotels-*de-luxe* turned into billets for nine of South America's Presidents (gathered for the 150th anniversary of Bolivar's death) among banners and fences – all over a holiday-postcard *bienvenida* bay.

The credentials-campaign tosses us into the night – the huge press tent has ceased to issue them at this hour and we are driven into the darkened woods, along roads still lined by armed shadows at the ready, up to a random point among the thickness of the forest where a little table lit by a carbide lamp is perched close to the road with a *sans-souci* girl in mufti behind it; she IS the bureau for those security-bound admissions. Yes, we are on the list; badges/passes are distributed by her, but I am refused, because I have not brought the essential: a passport photograph of myself to be filed. But Daniel steps forward, pencils a beard on to a spare photograph of himself (cleanshaven as well as I) and offers it to the girl: '*Mi padre.*'

South American military fashions. The military versus the civilian government – a shaky axiom: Napoleon and, till the First World War, most European crowns were, so to speak, military; and since then, Corporal Hitler, Marshals Piłsudski and Pétain, Generals Franco, de Gaulle, Eisenhower, Amin and Jaruzelski. And are Vietnam, Belfast and Afghanistan militaristic or not? Soldiers in the north-west quarter of this globe are less seen because the ultimate weapons are concocted in secrecy.

Militarism, to simplify: the South American states are run by the ruling class with the military as their tool, excluding the *campesino* and the city proletariat who are the revolutionary material and the excuse. The European nationalisms are millennia old. Tribe language/territory divisions justify Europe's national passions, sustained against internationalisms of Christianity – a thousand years' assault – and today's Marxism. But Spanish-speaking (Portuguese Brazil is a separate matter), Spanish-mestizo-ruled Latin America eulogizes Bolivar, their unifying hero, yet splits into numerous discordant and warring countries – artificial creations based on former colonial provinces. The original tribal inhabitants are not included in this game; the ruling class belongs to the Spanish tradition, with the countries often complementary in their resources; yet our oft-repeated question, 'What about the United States of South America?' is always shrugged off, even at Santa Marta during the rally of nine Presidents of the continent.

All this, without Europe's or Asia's justification, is in need of exaggerations and verges on the grotesque: mental and physical. And so the academics and cultivated aristos within each country tend to overvalue the characteristics of each as unique and superior to those of their neighbours, to isolate the archeological pre-conquest past presented as a border-to-border independent case. But the visual demonstrations of national identities (here this awful word is apt) had, for a century and a half, to be modelled on a fragmented Europe, as indeed their whole way of life tends to be: sporting and naval outfits, male manners and tweeds from Britain; Paris for women; army drill – Prussian.

But I am too rash. These are of our time; in the second half of the last century – witness the old prints, and, above all, the statues – the clashing armies and their commanders wore those touching French-inspired kepis and frilly Napoleonic epaulettes (I say touching, because this shape was for me always connected with Latin American heroics); these and the top-hats plus whiskers and the banners; and to find all this there – also in some ceremonial guards' uniforms – helped to link 'my' legend with reality, often terribly bleak.

And so each city in each of these high Andean countries is heavily populated by monuments, most of them probably erected at the beginning of this century, since, somehow, the architectural styles of the past seem to have arrived greatly delayed. Their themes are heroic deeds and victorious leaders, while across the borders similar heroes raise their swords and win – possibly in the same encounters. Multitudes of them, since obviously aggressive and plentiful arguments for so many patriotisms are sorely needed. In La Paz there crouches/attacks, bayoneted gun in hand, an ordinary infantryman or partisan in bronze; all true to my history pre-vision: he wears the Frenchified kepi, but also sandals over the huge bare feet of a universal *campesino*.

The banners: Ecuador's and Colombia's oddly are identical, both the colours and their distribution, the yellow stripe being wider than the blue and the red; only the heraldic emblems differ. But no one seemed to know why the stripes vary . . .

Uniforms but primarily the hats: in Chile, ultra-modern and West-orientated, the airforce (and its uniforms to the last stripe) is modelled on the British. But across the frontier into dictatorial Bolivia and amazingly the military headgear matches their oppressive role: stiffened wired-upward structures with peaks flat over the eyes, they are exact replicas of Germanic shapes. And then one learns that in the early Nazi days, impressed Bolivians invited Roehm, still Hitler's favourite then to come and redesign the drill and outfits of their forces!

The sheer contrariness – the need to differ (even the trends in political systems may respond to this?) – strikes the eye on entering Peru: the police-cum-military cap is a negative to the Bolivian verticals – here the horizontals tend to be enforced: the peak stands far forward and so to the top – wires are out, democratic softness prevails!

Ecuador, enriched lately and patronized by the States, goes for the toy policeman *à la* USA, and plays at toy guardsmen at the presidential palace. Colombia, though, accepts Europe's traditions and has the palace guards in their 1900 German-copied *Pickelhauben*. Colombia staged the meeting of nine Presidents of Latin America which was dominated naturally by the military parade of their representative units. Brass helmets, hussar-shakos, endless varieties of colour-schemes, of stepping drills, here on display was the pathos-ridden pomp of Latin America's competitive insistence on enforcing differences – the designers' field-day.

However, all this faded out. Wherever one went, in whichever country, when there were conditions of emergency, battledress and matter-of-fact equipment were worn, and the soldiers took on a uniformal US-model look.

December 24: **flight** (over flat Cali) down **to the Tropics** thickening around and through the flood network (the accompaniment – drunken buoyancy and radio-continuum knobbed to the loudest ever-present song/guitar monotony – by young machos, mini-bottles of whisky opening to the dull rhythms; the same crowd, swollen by local 'connections', will go on on the Amazon-facing terrace until well into Christmas night; will, in falling-about embraces, roll out on to the road under the traffic or on to zigzagging motor-bikes. Are they drug-smuggling Mafia underlings, or, as Daniel prefers, any Christmassy 'citizens' – students?) to **Leticia**.

Picturesque customs' searches, although still in Colombia (Bogota–Leticia–Brazil is the route of sin); messy-charming-dusty village – '*Residencia Alemanas*': under the propped-up roof the languorous patio with Germanic females, and the roomlets – windows on to the corridor, on each the golden FELIZ NAVIDAD; and that café terrace, viewing the double *paseo* of demi-clothed demi-blood beauties on high heels and motor-cycles, and the goings-on of tourist-seduction for Amazon tours – all this and the drunkards and the shy Indians, with the grand colour-changing river cyclorama; also at night the Christmas show on a garlanded platform by the shore (same 'famous' songsters – but now in person), while the tourists in the hotels settle over their miserably European holy dinner.

The Amazon in the straw-roofed boat ersatz exploration – but fine, though bothered with Anglo-holidayish pranks.

My resistance and protestations at phoney 'experiences', dictated imitations (*ergo* 'tourism') moving into the lead; but these are each tourist's own unique happenings – and so, having in my remote past 'truly' gone through much of those trials, I tend to misbehave when roped in now, but have to recognize some value emerging in such testimonies.

Over Callaru's dark tributary, butterflies painted in wettest watercolours, rather gigantic and challenged by equally gigantic bumblebees to jousts over the shore-scum; the bizarre-shaped blood-sucking (from legs only) flying bugs; in full moon, mosquitoes few and less bellicose, but making their entry under the nets. And the band of village children, in the morning, tracking me at shitting posture. As everywhere, there stands out among them a child-coquette, playing knowingly the game of hide-and-seek to the camera and the sketching-pad.

I fall on my face a lot, but form attachment with Camille, **the mulatto boy** in our crew, with whom I exchange drawings each of the other and swim and taste the calm of the days' village doings. Of course he is beautiful, at first reservedly proud – then unreservedly companionable, tolerant of my (for him) oddities – a perfect friend, brusquely lost for ever at the landing back in Leticia. The network of

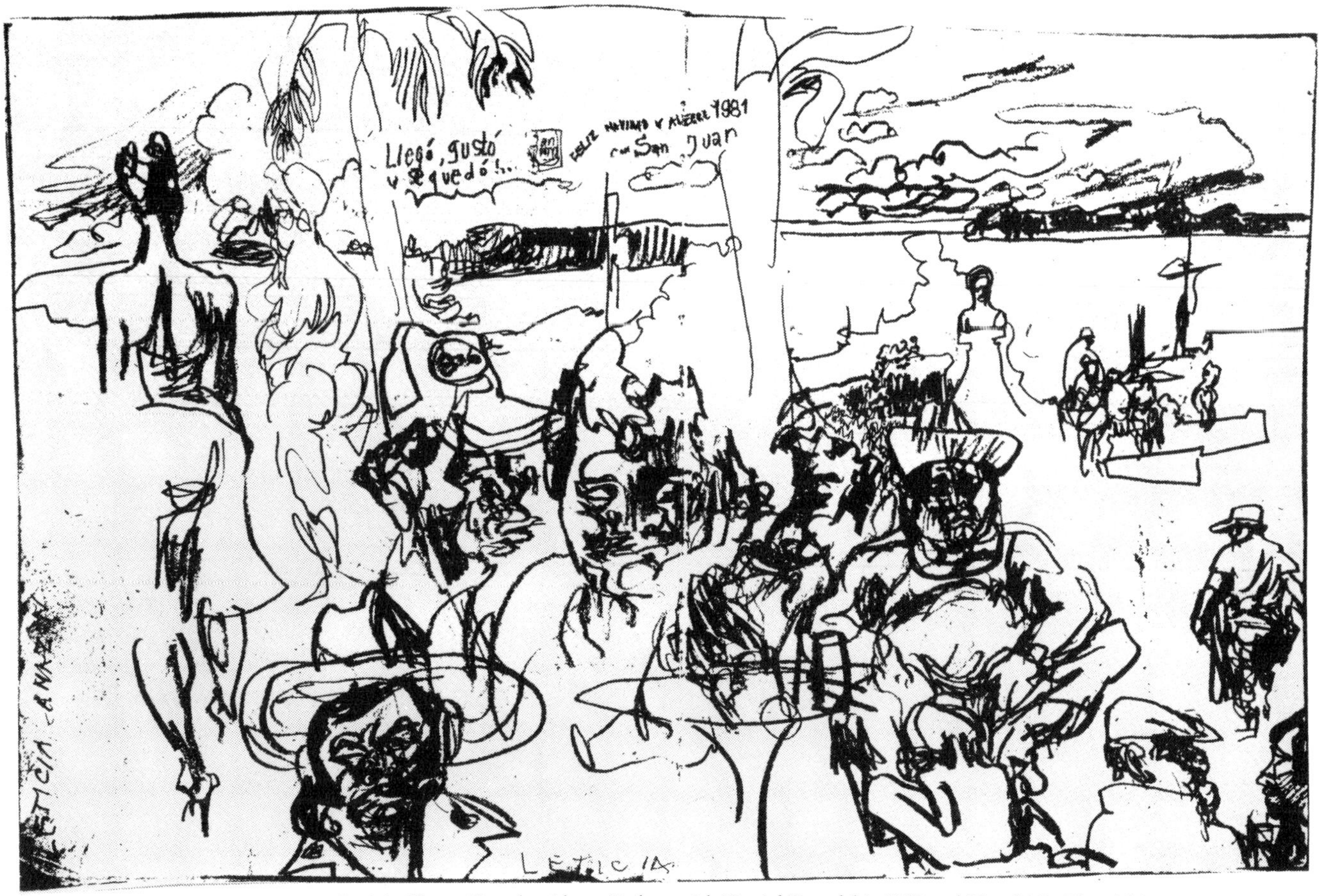

The Amazon at Leticia (from *Travels with my Father*, with Daniel Topolski, 1983 and *Topolski's Chronicle*)

relationships in this world: he is a schoolboy from Cali, holidaying with his uncle, the white owner of the boat.

Over the village creek a dugout carries a fishing man: a few paddles, then the same hand shoots the spear steeply through the surface. But we, the swimmers, do not encounter predatory creatures, and, back in the boat, in progress over the black, narrow, almost static waters, all is lyrical and, oddly, without expansive ostentation in this, most tropical, passage: water – black-brown, between and under high thicknesses of vegetation – green, and within it a rarely glimpsed flower – always purple, no other. The silence of the still depths, yet composed of the past giant struggles: the overturned bulky white-grey trunks – some blocking our way. And in this closeness the sky's moods are of no importance.

The fitful vegetal, carpeting/invading from bank to bank the tributary's width, ensnares the boat; cutting, crashing, being caught (the damaged motor anxieties) by this virginal-seeming membrane offers the reverie of primary exploration – until: IMMENSITY, of sky-meeting, speeding – bright vast waters – disdainful of the idea of being discovered; of bad-tempered, purpose-changing clouds, cascading, rainbowing, sun-dressing.

Surprisingly, having been prepared for a world of zoological abundance, there are no wild creatures except for mosquitoes, a few parrots and **semi-domesticated monkeys**. I had to find them, shamefully, in the zoos (no ant-eater even there) – one of them, outside Manaus, set up by the army with a proud legend stating that the animals were all collected during military exercises in the jungle . . . what sort of exercises?

Manaus. After dark on the Amazon's banks under the Panorama's balcony (*'Peixadas e Comidas tipicas – Linda vista a Rio Negro – Educandos'*) a group of machos pressurize heavy ladies for a night's erotics.

Manaus-Santarém flight broodings inhabited by my aggros – an undefined malaise, wrestled against so as not to fail in carrying out this harsh deed to its completion; fencing off the overwhelming camaraderie of the television crew and its director's and Daniel's prattling up of the shapeless air-hostesses, while we rush down on to the deeper virginal Amazonia . . . and it pizzles – I check upon myself: pseudo-self-assured – built on cracking foundations of laziness – undeservedly amassing attention and prestige – pseudo-intellegentsia member – PSEUDO. And the essence: bursting abcesses of ageing ignominy. And so, imponderabilia, they propel the unwilling, contrary me over the burning continent of beastlinesses which underline my insufficiency.

The guilt is Sudamérica's. Sudamerica is an expanding **chronic disease** – its assaults hit soften subdue the brain, the

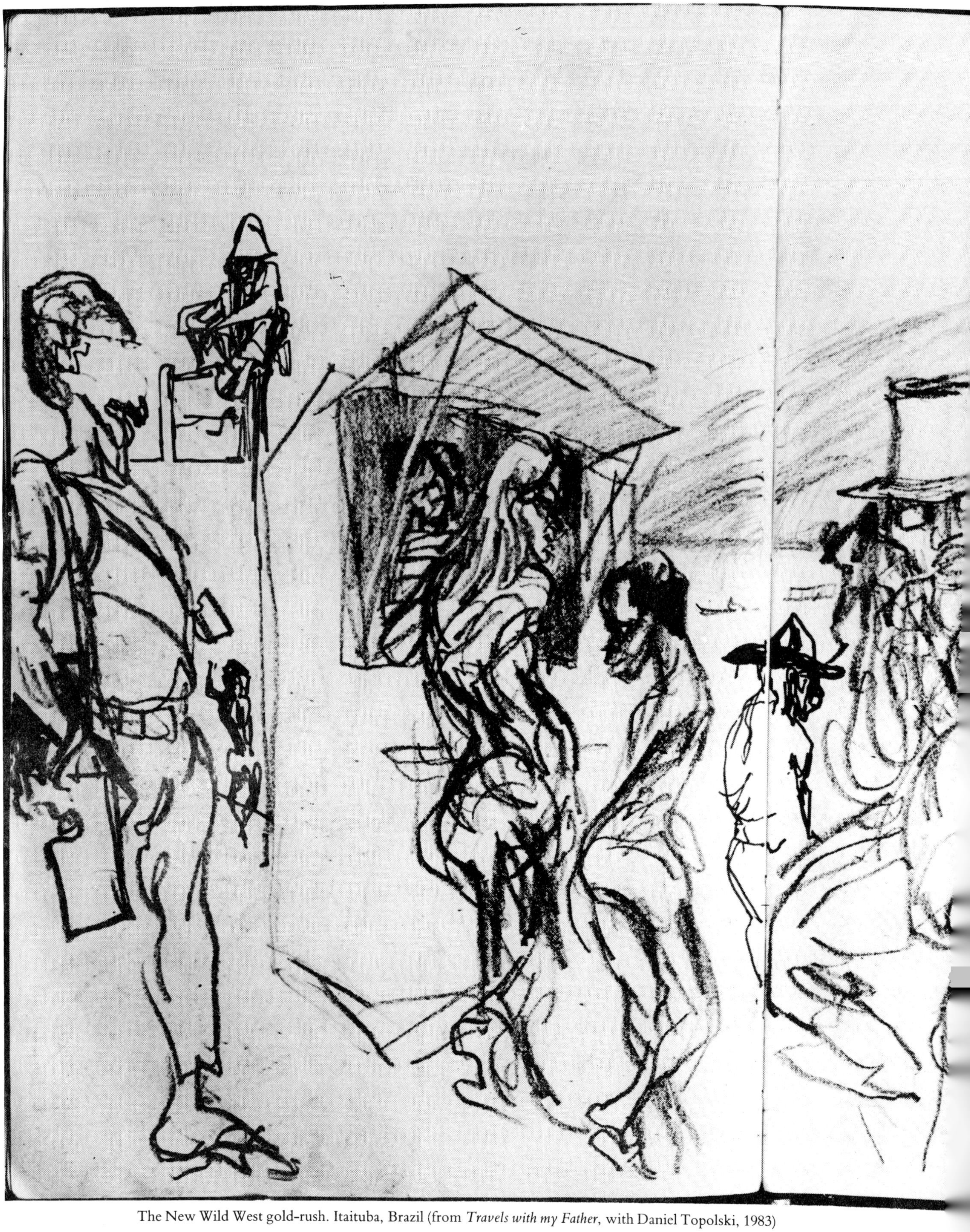

The New Wild West gold-rush. Itaituba, Brazil (from *Travels with my Father*, with Daniel Topolski, 1983)

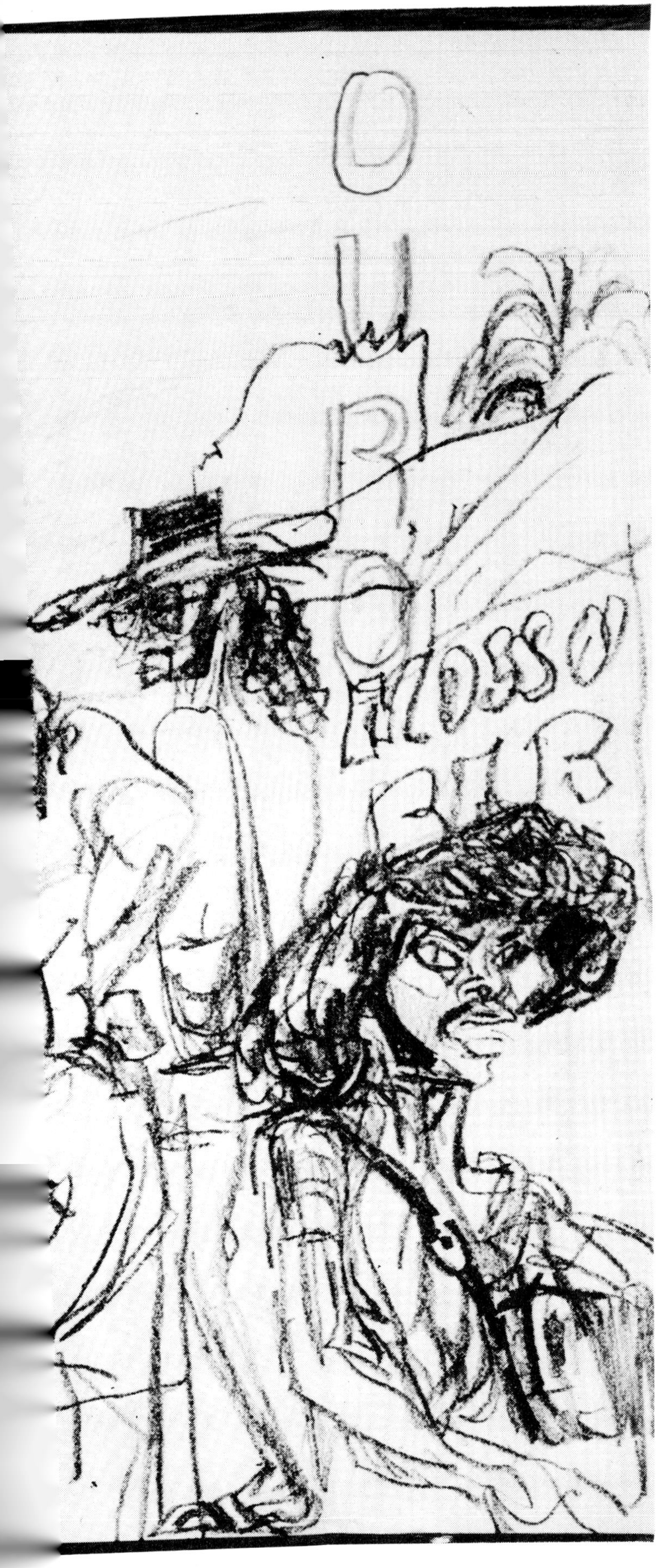

limbs: in progress, contradictions swell/petrify, refuse to identify/circumscribe problems, pursue solutions – confuse . . . The infected recoils into hate/haughtiness towards what he encounters, but then, defeated by the multitudes and immensity, begins to show symptoms of his inadequacy: ambulances/hospitalizes in the tourist-buses-hotels of 'received ideas', to come out shamed and weary and giving ear to laments, grievances, accusations (silence of the Indians); falls into the violence/knifery statistics; falls falls on to his face (a side-effect) on the steps of Bolivar's house, off the Amazon stilt-house ladders; in the Andes lets his weight fall and his arse-hole cry. He will take the air-way over the ocean to escape, but the disease stays with him and grows.

Out of the clouds: the villagey **Santarém** stop, and a homely-foresty track up to the horizon; the tinted Jesus-pendulum at the driving-wheel; a Coca-Cola 'Brahma Shop' with a waiting Mercedes-Benz. And now, barbed-wired claims followed by tele-wired poles; some industry in the bush, thatched roofs, an umbrella over a bicycle and, below, in a stream, an old car settled for cattle-like washing. Into any village – kids, huts, palms, a dog; but the road forks, so ALTA, and a long-nosed soldier gets out and an average man in a black sombrero gets in – and we drive up a ramp of the chic-modern tropical fortress, the Equatorial Palace Hotel, Santarém. Among peasanty shacks, not even hill-raised, sits this dramatically fortified castle of today – approachable and tempting, yet repelling (because conflicting two contemporary aims: one – to incite/entangle for the stripping of money, hence to bow in the opulent jeansy semi-bareness; and two – to defend against the ever-present danger of the barging in of (equally jeansified) savagery and revolution).

The sudden low leap (by means of a tiny hired avionette) among the drama of clouds and under, over rivers and jungle, with unmeasurable distances around – into **the New Wild West gold-rush**. And in this stormy closeness – everything: the aura of nowwhere, milling with bizarre heroes-*aventureiros* who read comics, interwoven, until the afternoon of the day of our arrival, with OURO-buying makeshift money-changers. One senses a law-of-the-jungle fierceness crouching-in-wait, pushing up, under the thin layer of villagey thriftiness liable to be washed away at any moment, as if by those frequent swelling deluges from above. On the edge, the *TransAmazonica*, humbly rosy and muddy, lined with **bordello hutments**, drunkenly and desperately attended. But in the town of **Itaituba** itself they queue, also desperate (identical bags over the shoulder) at the sole, governmental, low-rate OURO exchange (others suddenly forbidden trading), new government obstructions destroying their expectations of riches. And that even more **heroic Indian girl**, who hoovers for gold 21 m under the surface of the river among piranhas and crocodiles. Rough world of rough-ians lined up against the air-strip barrier (as we, charlatans of privilege, embark on our further flights) longing, earth-bound, watching. Our game duller than their daydreams – in pseudo-luxury we fly to our next senseless stop: Belém.

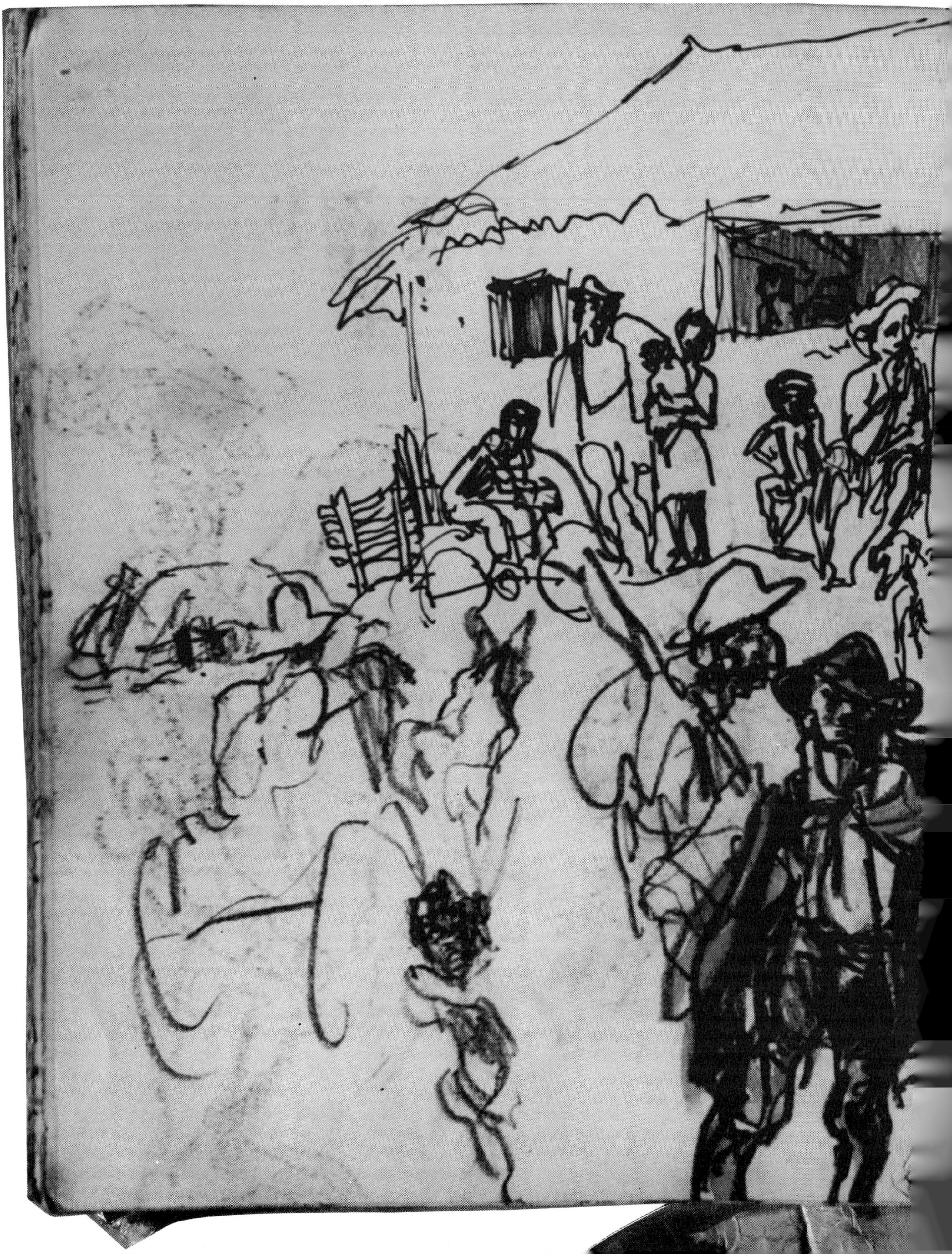

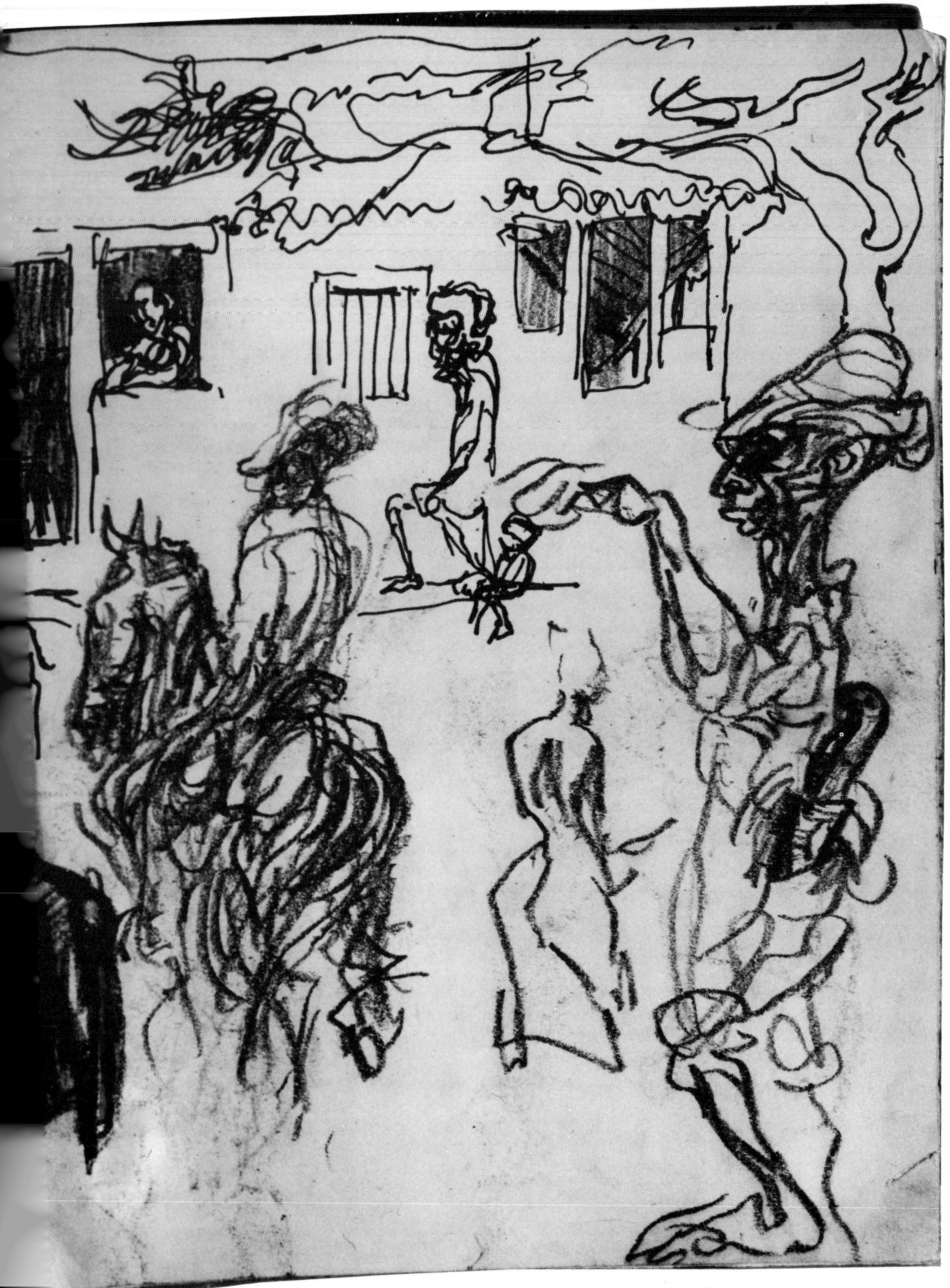

Brazilian Vaqueiros (from *Travels with my Father*, with Daniel Topolski, 1983)

Daniel is right to have brought us to **the vaqueiro country**. The faces, for a change, true rurality with fine family steadfastness, set in a gentle landscape, and manhood flourishing with harsh horsemanship.

But to me, topping all this, is the *vaqueiros*' marvellous rusty-coloured leathery outline – their capes floating at speed, hats, bony small horses – all this touches my old devotion to the seventeenth-century Thirty Years War shapes in Callot's drawings and Rembrandt's *Polish Rider*.

Nostalgically tender, we speed away (a fearsome pig-boar trots-wobbles across our road, eagles overhead, those tall palmy far-spread forests) into thunder-lightnings of proper magnitude; but the finality-like deluge passes – we pass through it – and that's all of Teresina.

Quote from the transcript of the BBC **Television film**: *World About Us*:

FELIKS: In this relationship between son and father – which we were conscious of from the beginning, since it is how we chose to go, the two of us, rubbing against each other, finding a way to harmony through disharmony – I felt at first a lot of disharmony in the the sense that I had been still in my old shape of competitiveness with what Daniel is obviously better at: getting to grips with life and being springy on his feet, as it were. So possibly, because of that, in some way I had a sense of playing second fiddle and feeling that this was not as good a journey as my former journeys were. But then came my collapse. I got this awful accident, this failing of my right foot, which made me fall about. It started in Bogota. The foot wouldn't hold me so I was falling on my face a great many times. During one single walk around Bolivar's house, I fell three times, and I had to lean on Daniel, and he held my hand, and it became part of the whole game that really I was a cripple more or less. It has gone now, luckily, but I was a cripple and the potential of a cripple father being led and taken care of, and with great tenderness, by the son, produced a new situation, a sort of crossroads in my life, and in our attitudes to one another. In other words, I accepted the situation of an older man with his limitations, his muscles not being on top form and relying on the younger man, and I think this created **a harmony** which I never experienced before; and I hope now, when I am better, this close harmony will go on, because I feel happy in it. I feel that I am settling to the beginning of harmonious old age, close to my son.

A counter-current wells up in me irrepressibly and more often with the spreading effusiveness of multi-media-disseminated, multi-parroted laudations of everything consumable – from chewing-gum to conveyanced-round 'sights'. Brazil – the heading for the chorals of unbroken superlatives – forces into my focus its defects rather than its indubitable assets.

Rio's self-image: a permanent holiday – its citizens religiously chant the litany of their beaches' names – their articles of faith.

The travel brochures' assurances about the best-in-the-world beaches crowded with unsurpassed beauties – I see more beauty at the homely Serpentine Lido in London.

The Sambão dance school's carnival-rehearsal: push-button prancing/clamouring and push-button (drums stop) end of gaiety; these are, it seems, routine traditions only. The São Paulo theatre's *Macunaima*, satirizing modern Brazil's falsities, does a carnival spot: the tight group of gaudily costumed actors mechanically floats across the stage with mechanical/fixed grins and flat record-like miaowing of those eversame tunes.

The Rio beaches are packed, but this one is empty. Why? Because the other day a Naval Captain was knifed to death here. Police still linger around. The realization of how the *favelas* (the deprived, mostly black, slums) are strategically hovering above rich Rio; how the robberies and murders descend on the beaches of the ever-holidaying privileged breed: in my experience, with torrential rain falling as well, it all had the symbolic mark of a terrible prophetic judgement – not only for Rio.

My last of South America. Daniel's gesture, after our Rio airport parting, when he went off with the Brazilian brothers Carlos and Georgio, abandoning me in the queue at the passport barrier, a gesture of returning alone solely to give **an intimacy wave** and then run off.

Eton–Harrow at Lord's, for me not many years ago (1967?–8?), was top-hatted and picnicked off the carriages at noon – an *insouciant blasé* party displaying their repast's extra exclusivity as if on stage encircled by the grandstands: Alec Douglas Home, Harold Macmillan, their ladies, their daughters, sons, granddaughters and Eton grandsons.

This year (1983) demonstrates the disintegration of style, yet also appears to begin the reversion. With the Tories rampant the return to decorum, no longer timid, can be observed at 'optional functions' such as Trooping the Colour which provoke dressing up to decorum's fullness. Abnegation seems to dominate here though: announced vocally, the boys dishevelled to make some case or other (shirts hanging out, shaggy hair bound with a string), but wait, most of these seem to be somewhat exotic in features and their girls ditto – is their case that of a refusal, unlike their erstwhile-foreign fathers, to be imitation Englishmen? In comparison, a group of leather-dressy punk boys and girls (in the members' friends' enclosure too!) seem elegant, thus correct.

There is only a single carriage on display where fifteen years ago our rulers were perched, but populated at lunchtime by unpublicized faces and unambitious clothes, though, indeed, there stand out amongst this 'cream' public a few school blazers, morning coats, some, with the air of defiance, top-hatted.

Behind the grandstand and blocked by a carpark a *maidan* serves for amassed but separate 'inner' groups picnicking. In contrast with the dark-haired outer elements, the upper and

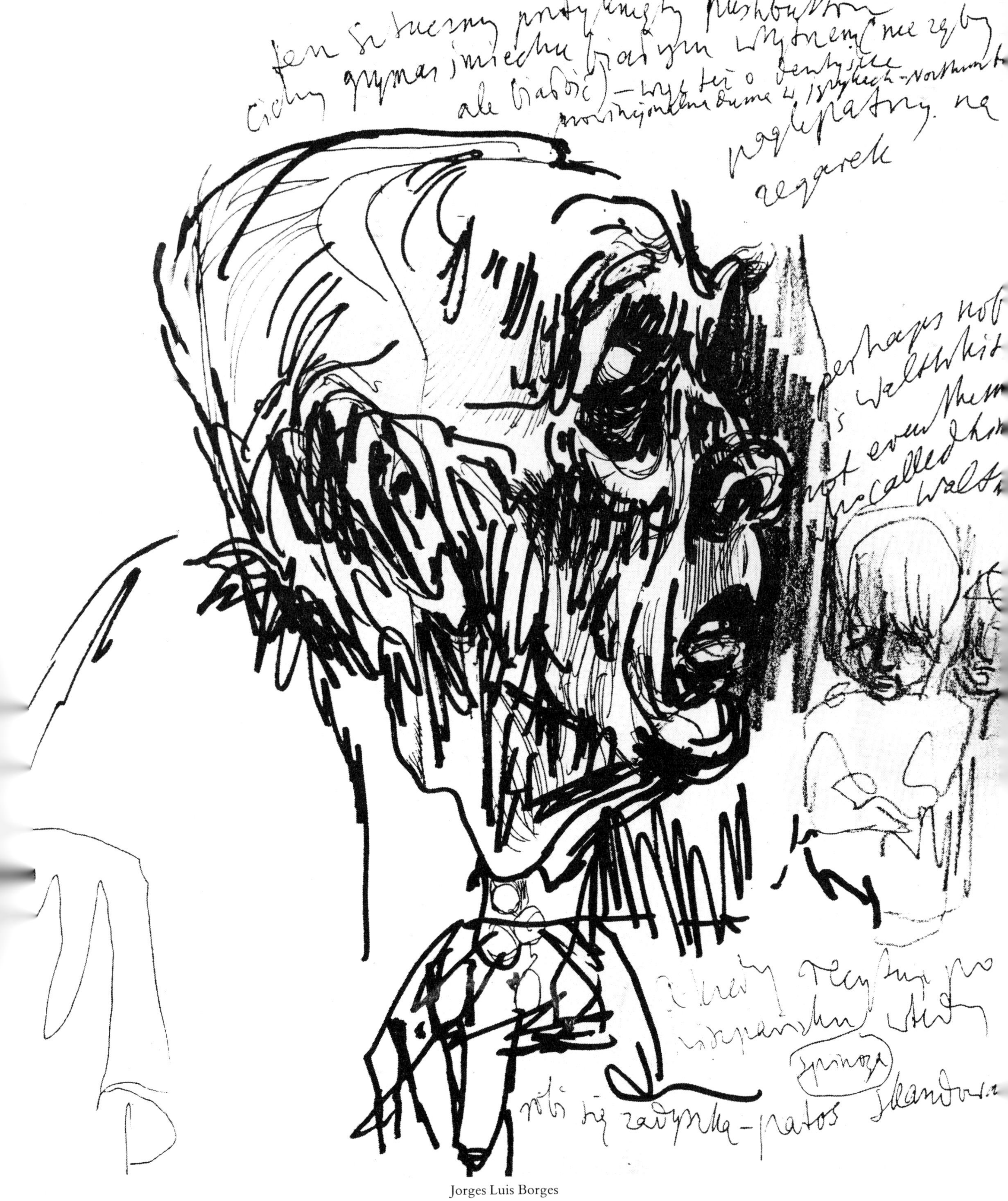

Jorges Luis Borges

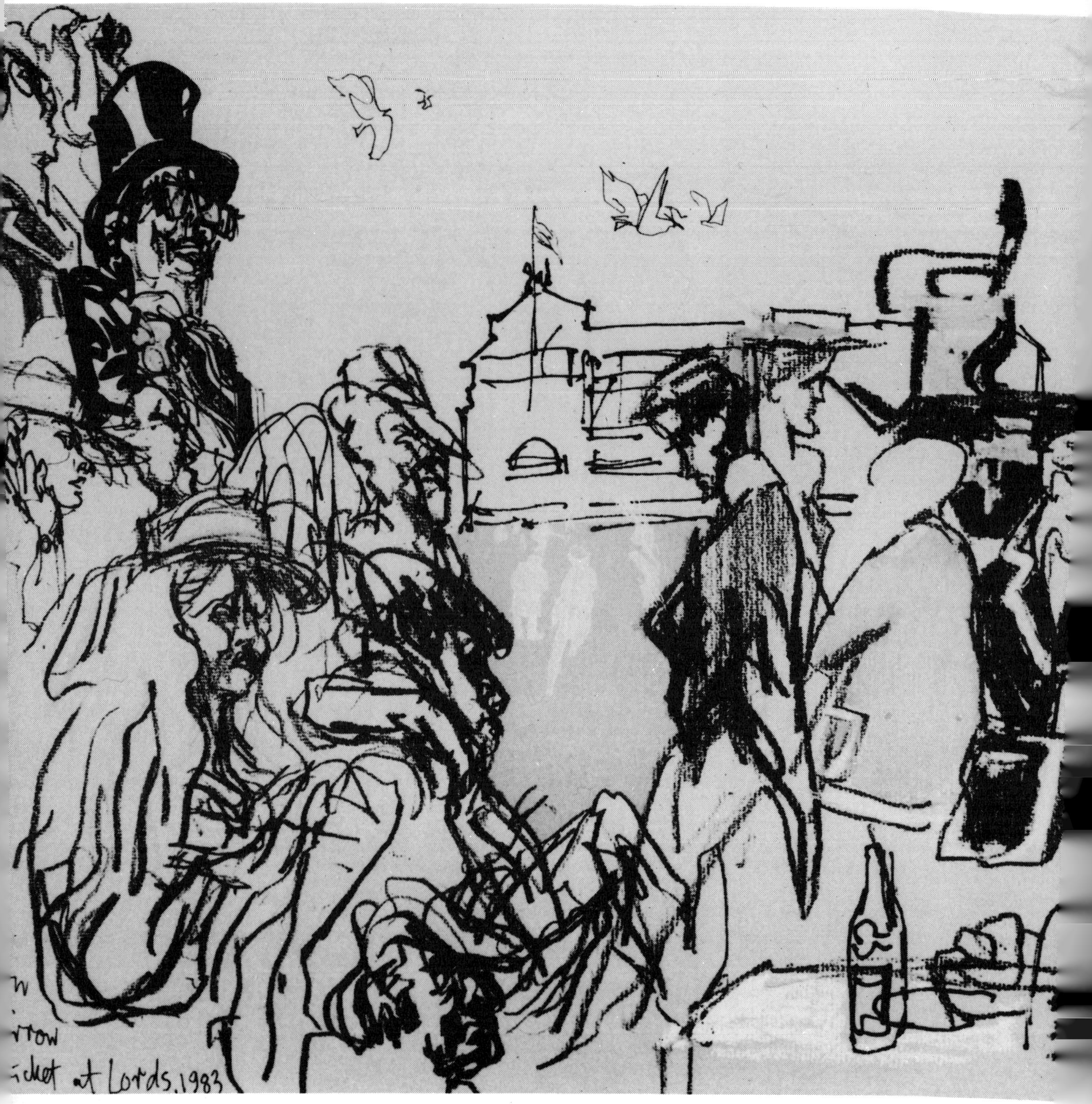
at Lords. 1983

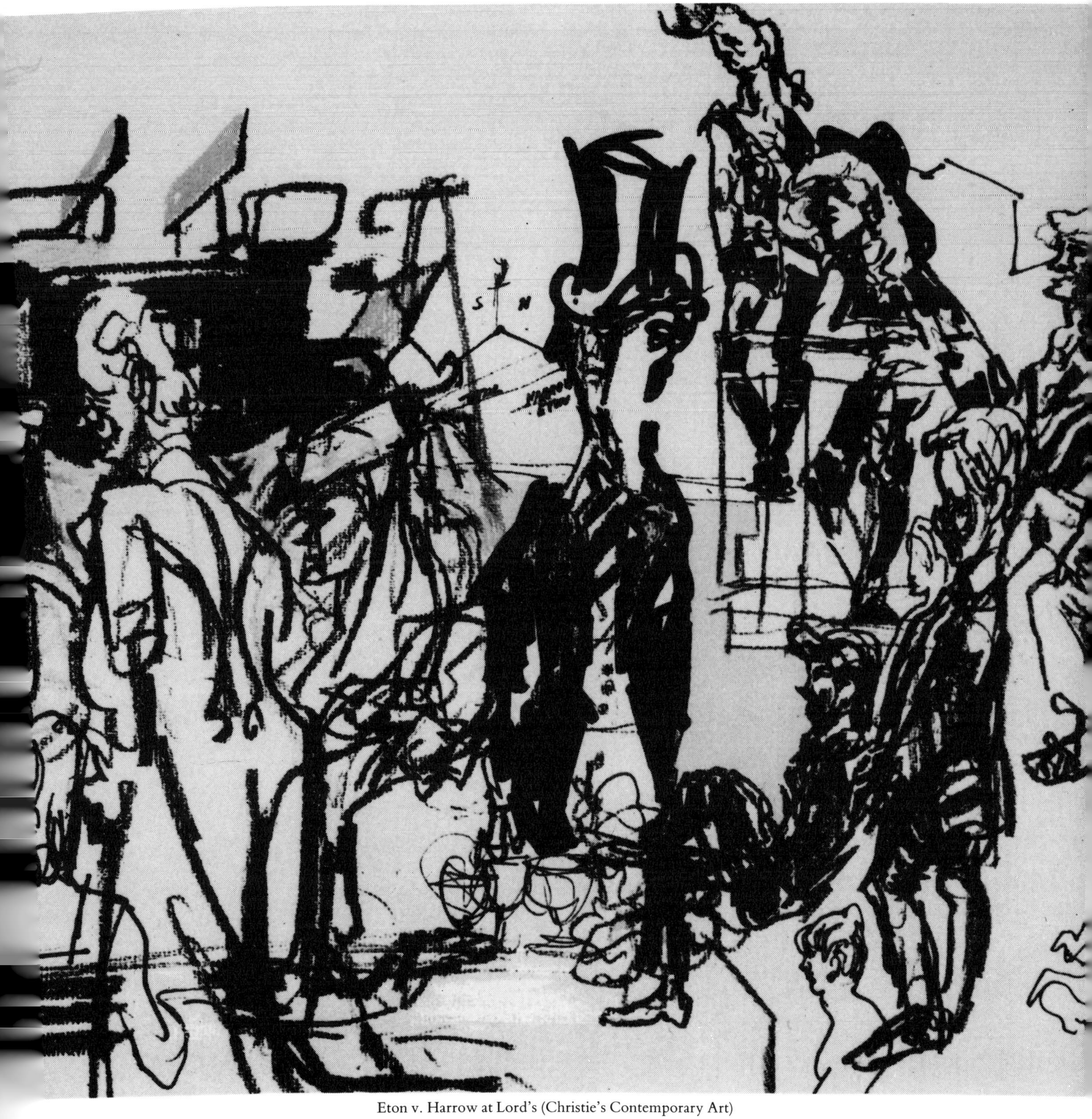

Eton v. Harrow at Lord's (Christie's Contemporary Art)

upper-middle young seem to have closed their ethnic ranks: their girls, keenly followed by the boys, tend to be smaller now, pink and blonde and chubby and the shortest of noses; it is a cosy breed, but not of the elegance in demand now – for this, with its anorectic extreme, watch the parade of unclassy teenagers at **the Serpentine Lido**. Those girls are remarkably and attractively standardized: their heights vary but, under pale straight hair their faces are Twiggy's, their bodies narrow, arms/legs slim and nicely coltishly graceless in movement, feet long narrow flattish – the left one developing a bunion at an early age, the skin, until polluted by the sun, of the Nordic whiteness considered supreme since antiquity.

The confidence of the Upper Strata returning, but their inbreeding reducing their young to dumpiness, it is predictable that Johnny-aristocrat will be back at the stage door to invigorate his breed.

Circularity – or, closer, girdling the new with the remotest past by the means of longevity, welcoming newcomers – ever-increases in orbit, evermore propelled by the rush of time, as if hurriedly strapping life's bundle for departure.

A small, tender, distant link alongside a sample of my everyday London: **Andrzej** steps up to Caryl and me while we park in The Cut for Michael Horowitz's **Third International Poetry Olympics** at the Young Vic. Andrzej, a very young Pole, brought up in Poland, and a close friend for the past four years since he emerged in London as the creator of the theatrical Cherub Company, by now blooded as a director of productions at four Edinburgh Festivals and in London, unaided yet stubborn. To give him more shape: his itinerant diplomatic parents supplied him with a world grasp – and grace of bearing – but he worked out his own transit from Poland to London's Central School of Drama, which made him bilingual and got him on to the Young Vic's stage – whence he moved to form his company. But, in the meantime his father was pushed out from the Service and out of Poland by the shameful 1968 anti-Semitic official ruse, to settle in Denmark, which offered shelter to such victims. His Gentile mother visits her son regularly in London and cooks exquisite Polish suppers for, among others, ourselves and my daughter.

And so, on the way to rehearse his company in his next production, of all things *Cyrano de Bergerac*, at the Upstream Theatre round the corner, he came up to us and said: 'Feliks, I just dropped in your letter box a cassette I made for you from a record I brought from Poland – I collect ancient Polish theatricals – with Leszczyński playing Cyrano before the war – which gave me the idea of doing the play – and, on the other side, Ordonka's songs. You told me once that she was something or other to you in your youth, so I thought . . .'.

Young Andrzej, in his twenties, in 1983, as the intermediary to recollections of **adolescence around 1923–4**. Hanka Ordonówna – **Ordonka**, THE star of the QUI-PRO-QUO cabaret of that time, sings in her pretty-pearly way in my tower-rooms over the Thames and evokes . . .

Schoolboys not admitted, I would pocket my school-cap and, on my father's ticket, take the seat in an open side-box, which in that long narrow interior gave the closest view of the stage. QUI-PRO-QUO changed its exquisite programme every month and brilliantly assisted my formative years – a supreme academy of the highest standards in ungovernable wit and wide-open view of humanity, winged by women of beauty and of richest gifts, and by inspired comics. It had to be all this also because the best serious writing men – poets mostly – of Poland teamed for this manifestation; and because, to underline its attraction, the chic and unerring charmer-compère and director of a visiting Hungarian company, Fryderyk Jarosy, defected, and stayed with QUI-PRO-QUO (having learned the language and paired with one of its girls) as its funny-accented augmentation.

But Ordonka: the ideal – in structure and in inner force: the palest of skin (and hair) over the slimly spun-out, wisely active shins, arms, toes, fingers; the extended shoulders; the tiniest head, face; all of this blended to communicate the A to Z of female moods. Naturally, the first impact of this allure on a schoolboy remains the strongest in my memory (though afterwards a long chain of her varied and subtler acts – all converging in her endowments – advanced my maturing sex-enlightenment) – flimsy and even unworthy of the general timbre of that theatre as it was: a solitary monologue, but as if in the presence of a lover, round a large bed with its headboard facing the audience; and she, acting masterfully the gamut of teases, rejections, acceptance (this being really an early striptease, but performed by a true artiste – with a *soupçon* of mockery), and shedding her *négligé* garments – until agonizingly dropping in unison the slip-straps and herself on to the bed, out of sight.

QUI-PRO-QUO's drolls: Dymsza – a Warsaw cockney, compact, combative of fist and tongue and tilted cap; and bony Krukowski, the bowler hat seated on prolonged nose and ears – the master of Jewish *shmontzes*; both faded away, though seen again in post-war Poland. But Mira Ziminska – clowness on lovely legs – now travels the world as head of Mazowsze, the vast folklore troupe (engaging me when in London in *duettos* of remembrances, her costumed dancers in respectful circle around us): in the early thirties she and all of them became friends with me, using my gifts. All except for Ordonka – whom I never met. Ordonka married Miś, the best looking of the handsome countly Tyszkiewicz family, but was separated from him in the years of the brutally enforced Polish diaspora over the face of Russia.

He and I fell into brief companionship in Moscow, besieged by the Germans, days before the evacuation east of the government and the Diplomatic Corps. This would have swept me along as well (and entirely reshaped my future), if I had not, on the orders/intervention of the then British Ambassador, Sir Stafford Cripps, been flown to Archangel to embark on a crossing to Britain which I expected to be speedy, since I had been entrusted with urgent messages and was carrying drawings of 'stop press' value for *Picture Post*.

And so I let Miś Tyszkiewicz wangle my 'British Warm' off my back, thus exposing me to two months of wintry Arctic seas: **the cruiser SS *Suffolk***, accompanied by two destroyers, was not embarking on the return trek home but on a duty tour patrolling the peripheries of the North Pole and engaging the enemy: an armed landing on the Isle of

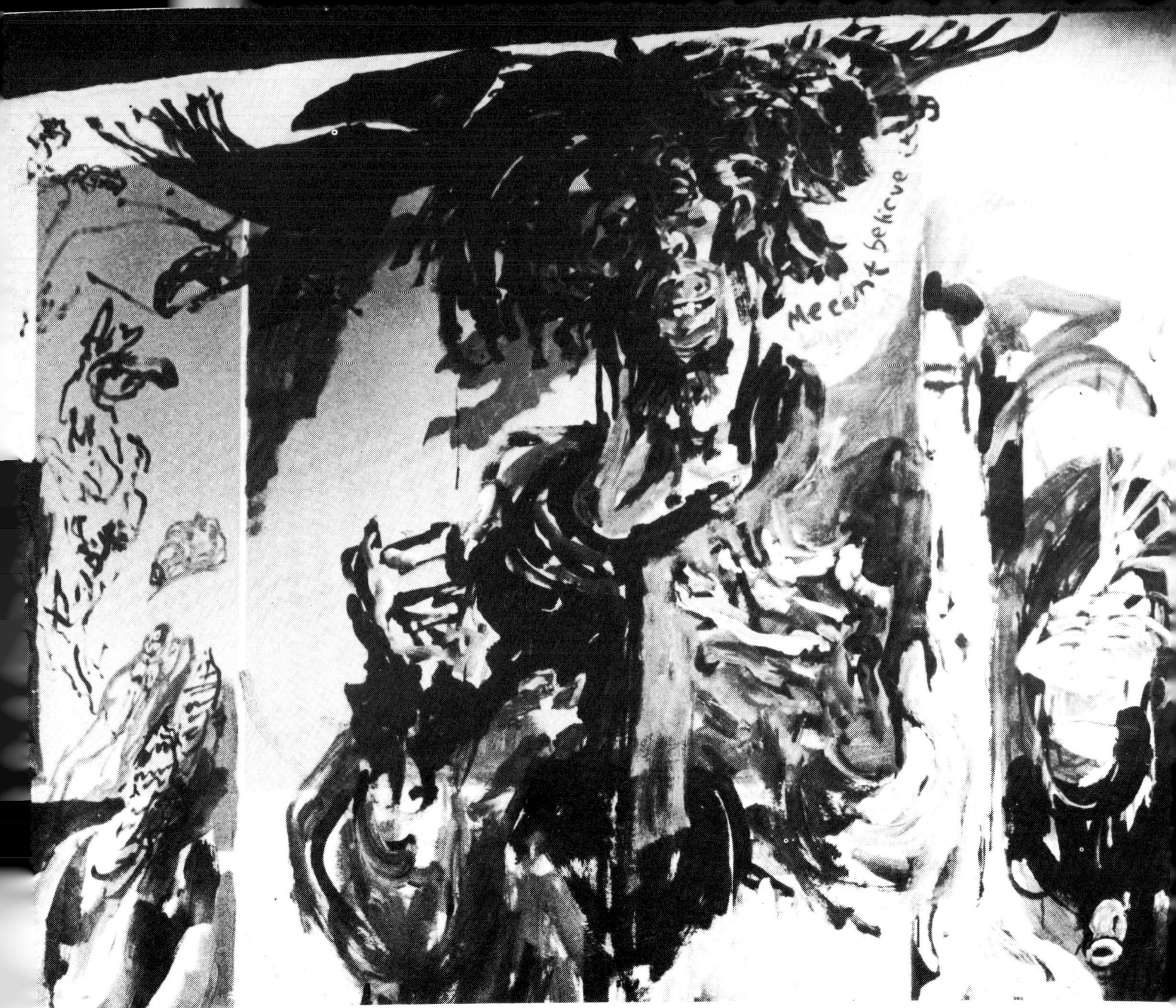

Michael Smith, detail (Photograph by Caryl Topolska)

Bear, suspected of nesting a German meteorological station, and a night attack on a German convoy deep within the North Cape of Norway, with a race against dawn dodging the revengeful planes, were to be the elements of our routine. For me, out on the decks or on the bridge, an issue duffel-coat had to suffice against the cold.

Tyszkiewicz and Ordonka became reunited in Palestine.

The Young Vic then: the limply begun Poetry Olympics – the handsomely drab interior filled with the tolerant young – shot up into thrills when conventional flat readings were brushed aside by Kevin Coyne (singer-poet) and Mountbatten's Plimsoll Group, but volcanically and triumphantly by the Rastafarians: Zephania's all-movement rapping musical verses; and, more 'mind-blowing', the grunt-and-fury, high-then-buckling, static-but-in-attack **Michael Smith**. OK, they have all on their side: the militant cause set to unique rhythms, and to their unique physique. For today they are unmatchable.

Whenever lifted by my enthusiasms, no more a slug, I charge headlessly at my target – this time, the show concluded, I rush the Rastafarian brave to net him for painting at the studio. Only later I may wonder what impact this thrusting oldie (hairless, featureless, styleless, statureless and slovenly) may have made on the accosted.

I got him to my studio, painted him – some 8 feet high and still his longer leg not fully in the picture: the fiercest in Rastafarian protest 'me say me caann't believe it' rhythms – my most explosive image. His assessment: 'Not vital enough, man . . .'

His aggression into this chapter's thicket of gentle memorabilia – a spiky branch sprouting forth, but to be snapped by its own gales.

A few weeks later the news came, 'Michael Smith **stoned to death** in Kingston.'

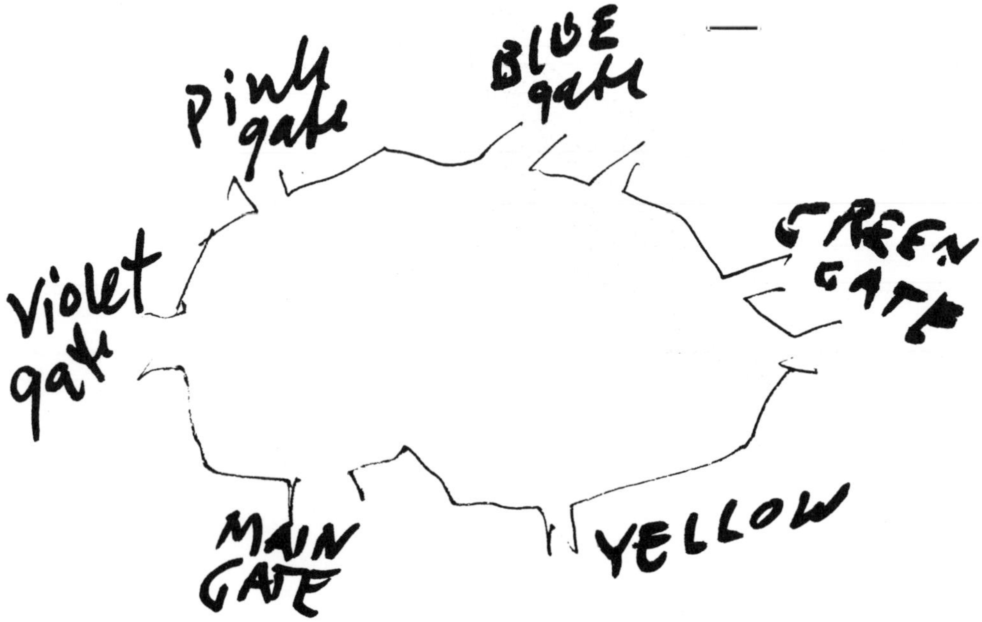

Greenham Common. Gates

January 1984. These may be times not of the novelty of feminism but of a rapid return to antiquity's majesty (minus gestures and draperies) and to the mastery of **goddesses**.

Greenham Common: smothered in tales of bellicose feminism excluding, often by acts of hostility or humiliation, male fellow-travellers; of skirmishes at the fences with the Police and the Army; of expulsions and arrests. I had been given the key-name at the Main Gate, and warned that I must guard myself from exuding my 'customary charm' as any trace of it might raise anger/unpleasantness.

Teresa drives and, stripped for action, we carry only essentials, prepared for harsh encounters/dangers. Equatorially unblemished skies undermine my excursions into grey-grim confrontations (Ulster, and now Greenham) with false vacationality. The winter sun imposes a mood of 'ceasefire' – only a few (the 'skeleton' crew?) women campers fuss over cookers, bend 'benders': their plastic patchwork hillocks of tents must be hiding their main force, napping; soldiers, cordoned behind double coils of barbed-wire fencing – the stilled zoo-beasts. A feeble forest by the Green Gate blinks with colours of hanging blankets, humpy teepees, layers of flimsy drying garments. A scribbled 'Women only' ominously warns – but ponchoed, many-sweatered emerging girls wave to me.

At the Violet Gate, though, a nice, solitary girl, unaffected in her firmness, corrects me – 'women': and two 'women' teenagers going the rounds, cropped and stripe-tinted hair, ignore my existence.

My lifelong mountebank postures – having arrived at old age and old shape without my altering my ways, and thus perhaps appearing monstrously ridiculous – now coincide with the entry of hard-eyed young women; in consequence I am undermined in my entirety, have been conditioned/attuned to receptivity in women; my reflexes and advances wholly repelled, I am paralysed.

In different terms, my ingrained and perpetual rejection of groupings of any kind may have found strength and justification in relying on so-called personal intercourse, thus with me mainly in communion with women rather than with men friends. This ceases to be – women become another 'fascist' group, depriving me of my allies.

My daughter drove me back and, on the way, gunned down every remark of mine, on the grounds of my facetiousness, irresponsibility, male angles – forcing me, I am sure, into untrue-of-me exaggerations by her committed interrogatory tone.

Two days after Greenham Common, my studio was visited by Jane Hickman and Eileen Meredith, solicitor partners, of whom the former is the Greenham Common Women's lawyer currently conducting their case in New York. Attractive women-people, but keyed up for catching men (me) at sinful displays of habits of advances and such, thus reducing me to watching my spoken/mental steps, to a ridiculously defensive and apologetic stance, to the neglect of authentic dialogue. So much for confronting this congregation of belief.

At the other end of my studio, simultaneously, there gathered (a chance of my 'open studio' policy) a cluster of young men, more still arriving, telling me that they had come to meet Christof, and flopping down on the sofa, on the floor, in a tight impenetrable ring – backs to me and to my pictures all around them. **Squatters** (under my arcade) of **ideology**. They improvised, in disregard of the aims of my 'openness', a conspiratorial session; they shuffled/distributed 'literature'

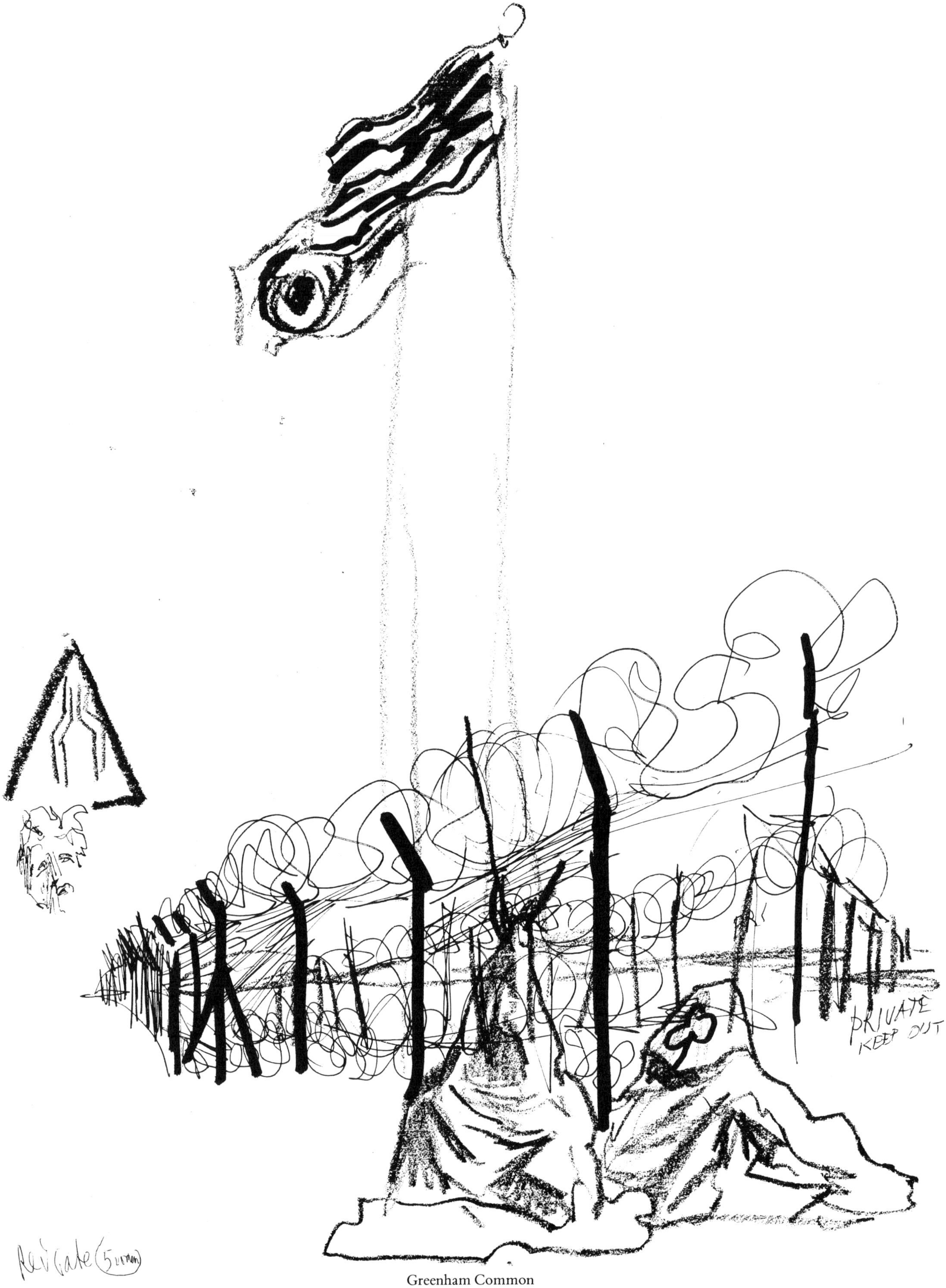

Greenham Common

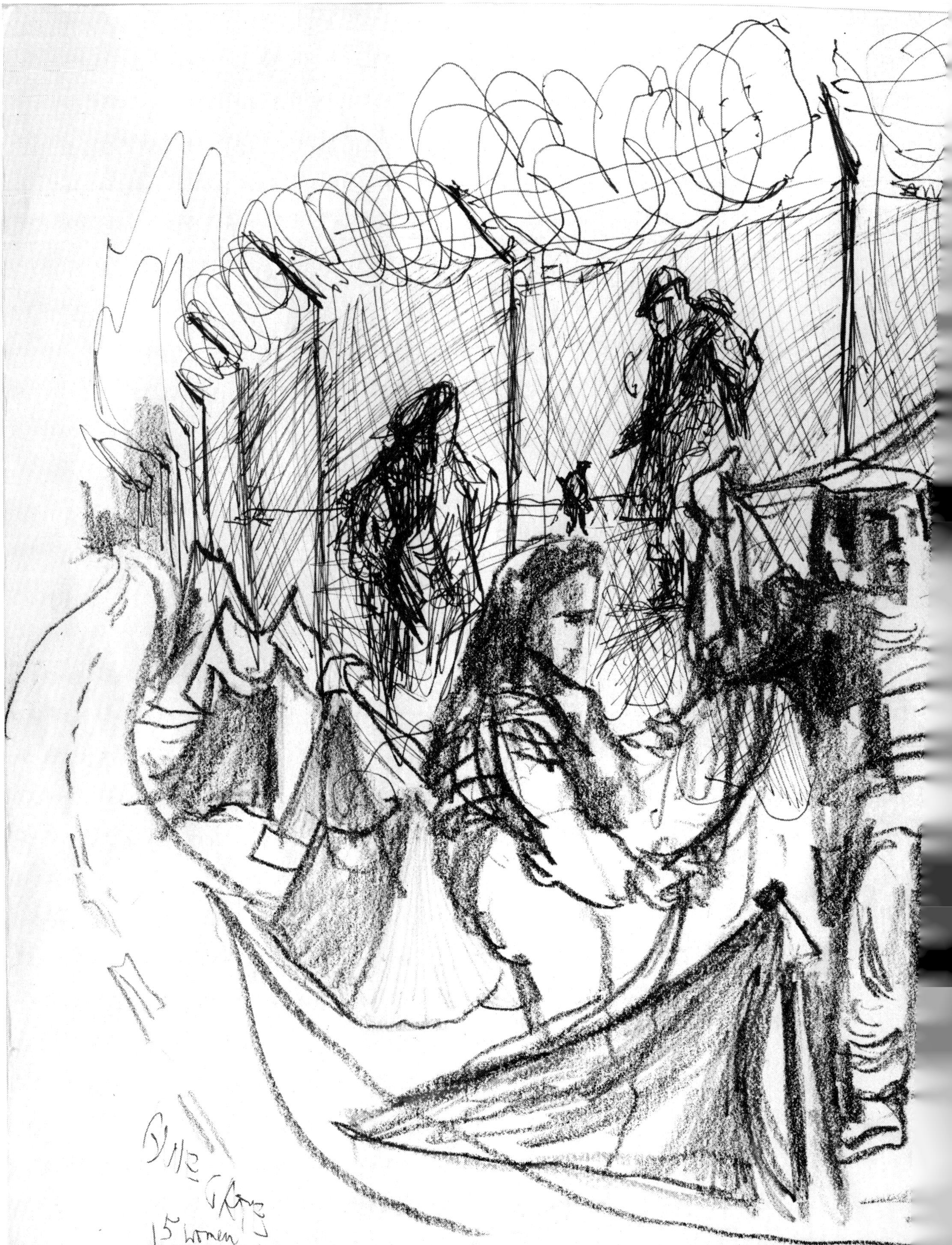
15 Women

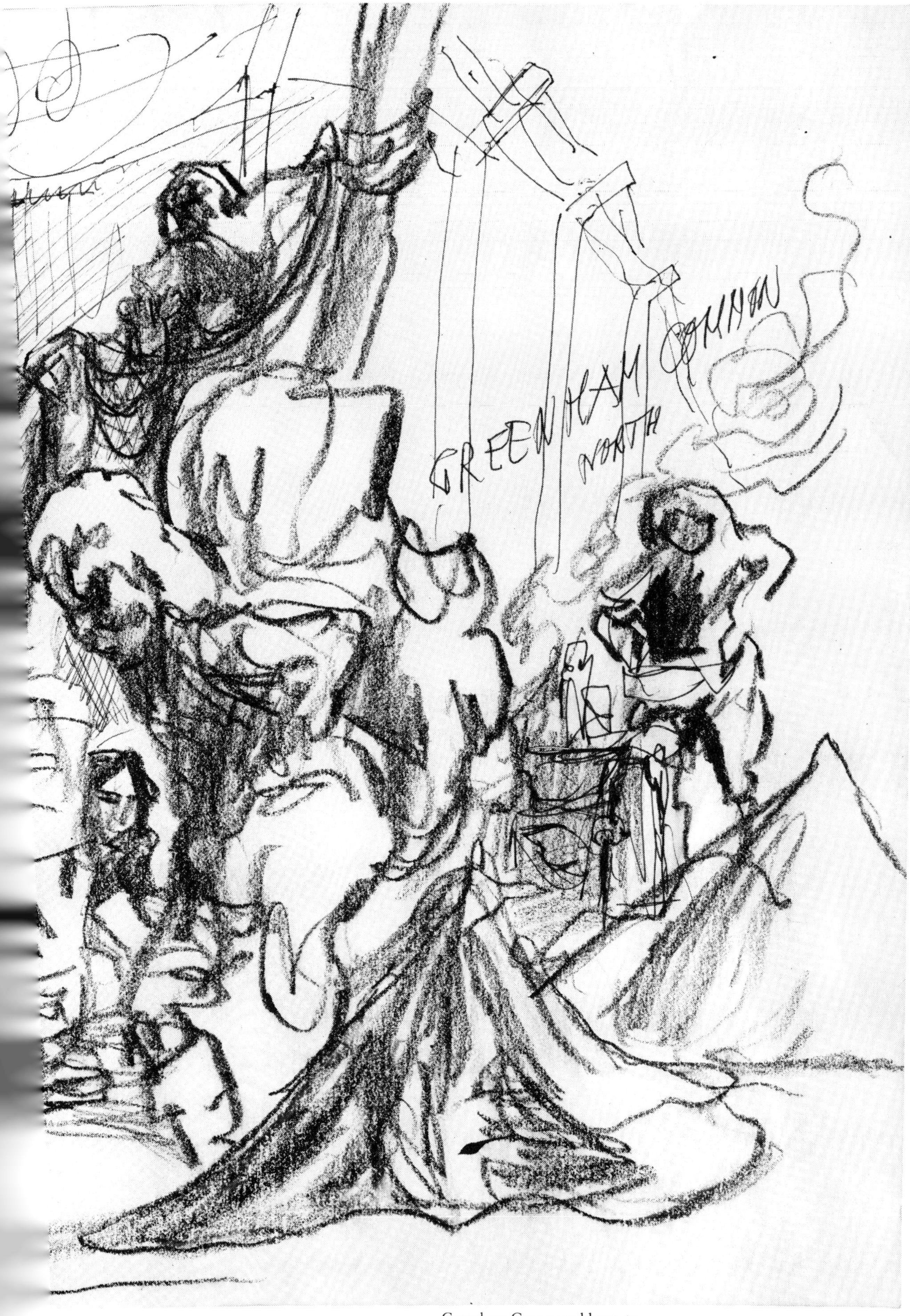

Greenham Common: blue gate

(hand-outs, posters, stickers), plotting the next 'Stop the City' demonstration. I hated the scruffy dullards, their ignoring my art, their (in good cause) regimentation.

But (being a lifelong mountebank) I resent most of all 'sophisticated' facetiousnesses: two days later, an assembly at the **Institut Français** to celebrate the forty-fifth birthday of the literary bilingual magazine *Adam* filled up with the cultured, as if the last stand of creative individualism. It should be my world, demonstrating a medley of variegated values – it is, emphatically, not. Or do I fail to be receptive? Or is this 'occasion' a mere broken plank tossed sickeningly on a sluggishly receding tide? This blinkered and gutless 'élite' gathers only coynesses. One after another, they doubtfully entertain with 'poetic' word-acrobatics; a faded star (the highest heels, dangling ear-rings, hand senselessly wandering along the hairline, face battling against unflattering light) recited in up/down modulations an endless snobbish dated piece by Rosamond Lehmann on meeting the blessed Cocteau. And, inserted in between, French clichés and intonations. And musicalities: four singing comics, as well as three morning-coated blowers on curved horns, reducing Mozart to umpha-umpha. And the obedient (oh how weary) herd.

Thus yet another, this one a funereal, breed.

Half-century of London is an A to Z topography stuck thickly with rusty memory pins rather than a selective line up of chronology. Today into the old Land-rover (its roof sawn cut to make it openable): into the past cars, all second-hand, almost all drop-heads or open – the American Auburn, Armstrong Siddeley, handmade Bentley, miserable saloons, chain of Austin Champs – for a modest Saturday ride westward: Caryl's shopping, my drawing the King's Road *paseo*.

But this would, at the outset, overlap with the range observed from the South Bank and the Whitehall Tower: so the inward direction, driven by Teresa in the Moke, after a Richmond Park Sunday walk. The Putney shore of the river: many long hours, weathers and time-of-the-year disregarded, of duty-bound parental watch over Daniel's oarsmanship from his Westminster School sculling (it was I who set him rowing, with the Regent's Park lake at our windows, and then a Weybridge Junior race, in which he beat the record by one full minute, decided his sporting future) to his double Oxford blue, and, now, year after year of coaching Oxford to victories. Daniel's first Oxford–Cambridge coach, when challenged on the unusually light weight of this candidate, stood by his choice: 'The boat goes faster with Topolski in it.' Indeed, Daniel's will-power cemented in rowing. But the superhuman effort which goes into such a race can be observed only from a close-following motor-boat – a sympathetic punter on the shore has a dull time of it.

The World's End housed me, Park Road sheltered me studio-less, Cheyne Walk's house boats hosted erratic explorations. Further down along the Embankment Gerald Scarfe combines showpiece residential opulence with protest-cartooning.

And the foremost: George Weidenfeld, aided by literary experts, politicians and their confidante ladies, academics/decorators/publicists/lawyers, sprawls his lordship-bulk, achieved beyond measure, yet ever carrying a forehead-fold of insecurity – what else am I forgetting?

Probably my last with him: he excuses himself – yet a sort of typical of him demonstration-disclosure in front of me – phones Lady Falkender and embarks on a prolonged dialogue by a 'different George', this time in elegant phraseology, classics-quoting, to no obvious business afoot, caressing/impressing with high culture/civilized (we need such!) reliability. Soon to be listed for the Labour peerage.

The luckiest of men: the holy Buddhists erected straight across the river, to comfort his contemplatory metaphysical needs somewhat laid fallow, a convenient pagoda.

Further, grim Dolphin Square and forgettable encounters: one, a very tall Serbian, has been a guerrilla fighter, tells me (why do I remember this?) about a forward, yet lacking in inches, art-dealer of Brompton Road, who, having lured her into his gallery's basement, gained his access to her by tripping her expertly into horizontality.

Back into Chelsea: a latter (Falklands) day's Sunday service with the Chelsea Pensioners from which I emerge into the Kings Road – and to the studio to start an apotheosis-painting of today's Anglo-Anglican bellicosity in battle- and mohican-attires.

But attempting to try to disentangle summarily the lifetime of entanglements within the web of side streets up to Sloane Square and beyond, there was to be listed a Sloane Avenue Polish countess, and an unblemished Chinese 'hostess'.

In between, forgotten connections with a studio off Fulham Road, opposite Sydney Street, and another by the Stamford Bridge football grounds. In between, dotted with villagey shoppings, friendly Polish ex-dancers and retired Generals, the early home in Collingham Road SW7 (opposite the church), tea with Ivy Compton-Burnett, vodka with Baroness Budberg, drinkless talk with C. P. Snow, with declining Maurice Collis, with James Laver and Veronica Turleigh, for *bigos* and Jewish carp in the Polish Hearth Club.

Now across the Park . . .

But for the wood – no trees: this procedure reducing a long life into a directory must be arrested.

An *enfant terrible* of English letters declared the other day: '**Motivation is out**.' It was for me always out, but my blessed temporary editress, who principles/shapes her own writing on it, showers me relentlessly with 'Why? Why? **Why?**' This one yesterday: 'Why all these pieces were not included in Daniel's and your book on South America?' drew out of wearied me the fobbing off: 'The publishers tricked us into shrinking the book', and gave me a guiltily sleepless night, because, of course, I cheated; there would be a dozen answers why – the most potent, yet the least measurable, the gut-reason. 'Why,' she would insist, do I go on, not about South America, but about the private view at the Hayward (just because it happened next?), with

Matisse's inventions in new taste blotted out by the amassed invitees, thousands of non-formulated non-declared whys.

Close by, beckoning with its neon-vulgarized huge 'Topolski', offers itself, free of charge, my *Memoir*. But none of the Hayward stooges/crowd/extras percolated in there, and I had no urge for a 'Why?' Back to the pretences-propelled opening (don't don't ask 'Why'): there cuts through the private viewers, to me singularly visible singularly aloof, Caryl. Tall and straight ('Centurion's back'), battledressed for her routine architect's day of climbing scaffolded domes of the V. & A., she cuts through the opening crowd because almost alone in attending to the pictures on the walls; because complete in this that no 'Why?' can be directed at her; that no 'Why?' can arise between her and me.

Any sense ('why?') in going on after this declaration of, after all, faith? Except for relating the facts of daily engagements. Caryl, in her calm wisdom, bails out from the Cherub's *As You Like It* first night and is replaced by Teresa – of ultimate otherness. She wears her mother's jacket (part of a jupes-culottes ensemble which I designed before Teresa was born); auburn-dishevelled over restless-featured intelligence and small-aggressive, she challenges all round her to be on the *qui vive*; she knows and gathers everybody and appropriates every moment. I am always some steps behind her, breathless; but also tempted to cheat on demanded attention with side glances.

We sit through Shakespeare on young Andrzej's inspired shoestrings and, for the love of him, net in **Adam (Count) Zamoyski**, and the four of us set off for **the Zanzibar** under Teresa's membership wing. Adam is important. The Zamoyski saga could have been told earlier, but since he, a very young scion, is of today, 'Why not' now.

The Zamoyskis tower amongst the grandest families of the past Poland: the largest estates before Communism, blood connections with the Spanish Royalty; and Adam's mother, being the Princess Czartoryska, adds to his, surprisingly not at all obsolete, stature.

A small stature: I once painted a series of sort of family-tree portraits – I promise, without any snob-promptings – as the large pictures varied greatly in the choice of models, the concept relying on bizarre conglomerations of compositional twists. It resulted in several pictures and was started by an impromptu idea (telling this will help perhaps) when an art student wandered into my studio, named Victoria von Preussen; a straight descendant of the Ottos, Frederick the Great and the more recent Emperors Wilhelm I and II (marked as the last in the family-genealogy diagram contained in a German Encyclopedia, copied and pasted in the painting); she was be-jeaned and torn-plimsolled. Irresistible material: even old jeans were pinned by me on to her painted legs while she led Frederick's white horse, followed by the Wilhelms and Crown Prince of 1900.

Zamoyski's painting has at the centre his father **Stefan**, Ordynat (that is the head of the family), an elegant, small, yet monumentally featured man devoted with dignity to his country's, thus his family's, past glories; Adam at his side, then a somewhat hippyish, long-haired, unruly contemporary offshoot; behind, the much more flamboyant and disruptive younger brother of Stefan, **Andrzej** – in the painting given to heroic gestures of earlier centuries, yet leaping up to emphasize his mock-leadership – in underpants, trouserless (as he tended to appear in the streets), he merely imitates (in conscious irony-in-defeat) the top-figure of the sixteenth-century Hetman Zamoyski, red robes flowing, horse-riding to real deeds.

Andrzej was a very close friend-nuisance. Indeed, his background, his features and his height, his flamboyance and his *esprit*, would have destined him, in centuries more propitious for such values, to be a history-shaping leader. Now, a younger son, engulfed, through his marriage, within English countrified aristocracy, he escaped into outward eccentricity, embracing over-ambitious (in their brilliant range) projects in which he tried to net the high academy (he encamped for this purpose in a farm at Kidlington just outside Oxford), the arts and politics. An enchanting man, but unpredictable, and an embarrassment to the guardians of the aristocratic façade – his brother and his wife.

He stayed with me in Little Venice often upsetting entirely but disarmingly my work and habits. But also, pestered by his relations, sharpening the edges of his behaviour – until, not going here into details, they united (the usual excuse being the well-being of his children) in certifying him out of the way. With his brilliant readiness to accept a challenge, he fought cunningly within this impossible situation; he, if I remember, was more than twice in and out of mental homes, trying all the time to engage public figures and opinion on the scandalous system of certification – and the resulting maltreatment of the 'insane'; but principally carrying an attaché case fatly filled with documents, to get his being certified annulled. There was no more of fantasy Andrzej – this ever-extending preoccupation encompassed him, until, still ostracized by his people, barred from his children, not making any headway – and whatever else there was (why? why?) he killed himself.

In the following years my dinners with Stefan were entirely given to his confessional deliberations over his guilt. Until Adam grew on to the scene and, after Stefan's death, became The Zamoyski of a modern mould: clear-headed, enterprising, both serious and playful. And, though brought up in England, greatly attached to his Polishness, but devoid of *émigré* stuffiness.

So this was the crowning of that evening: Teresa, a friend of both handsome young Poles, at ease with them, presiding as it were; Andrzej (Wiśniewski) gathering our reactions to his first night; Adam and he greatly contrasting, yet in accord over Poland. And all attended/attuned (not patronized) on equal terms by me – the conversation keen and flowing. Kisses on both cheeks all round.

Thunder? End of a haughty July day darkens into **pandemonium**, close and brutal – surely man-made. Ungladly we step out on our ten-storeys up balcony to endure the predictable officialdom's rejoicing. But the pathetic slips into enchantment this time. Perhaps because these fireworks explode for us: our yearly celebrations coagulate – the eighth wedding and this tower's anniversary, my seventy something year, her thirty something, in all some

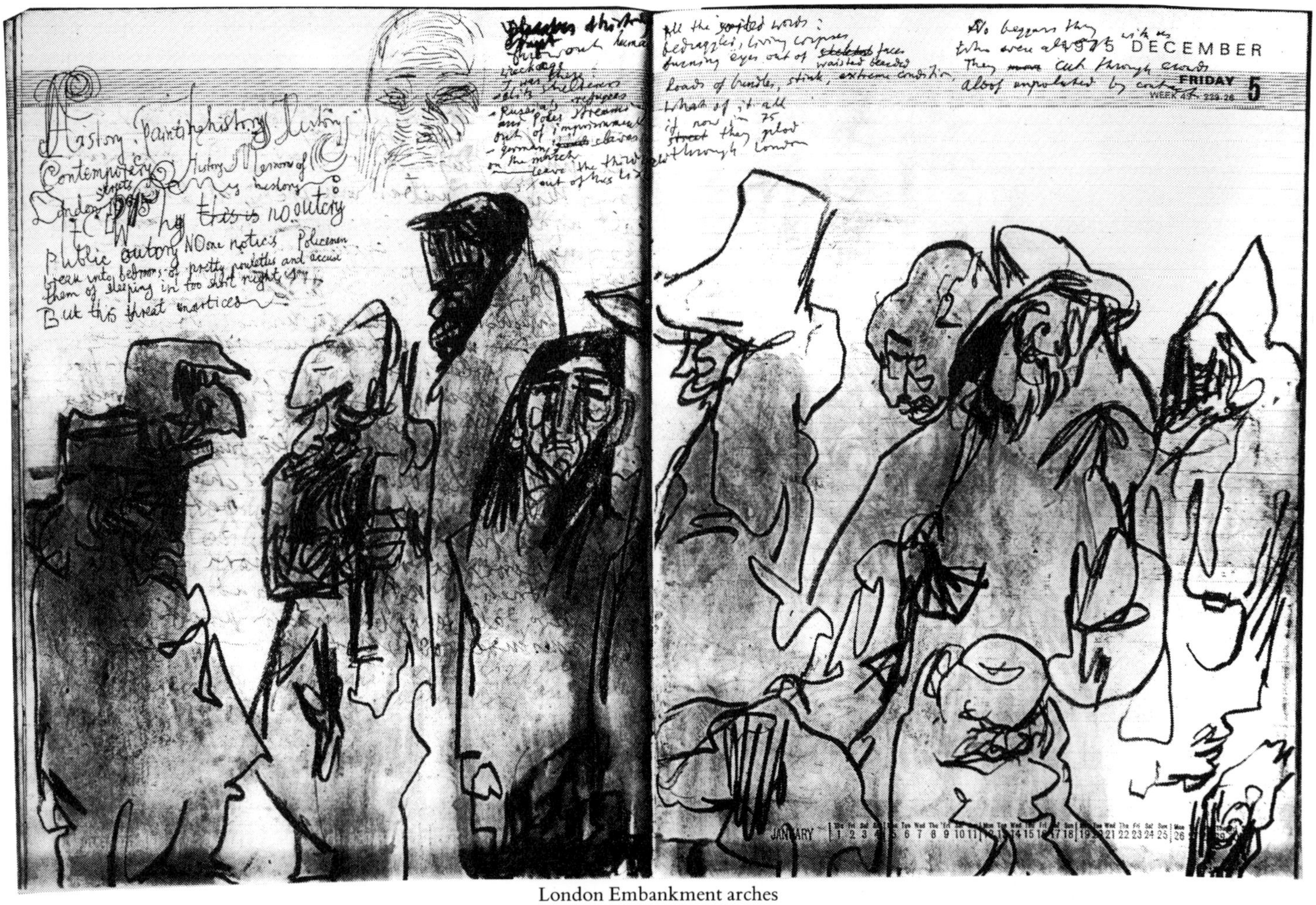

London Embankment arches

hundred and twenty worth of starry bursts; they fire up to visionary clarity London's horizon of darkness, superimpose on and turn into marvel of variations the web of lights – criss-cross mapping, spotting, reflecting, three elements conflicting.

Today's view from St Thomas's window – a grey bad April down-turn of the River, crossed askew by the business of Westminster Bridge, boxy-boats scattered, banked on the right by now-dead monster GLC and, at the centre, my comic-proud tower-pyramid above (to me) a forest of them, growing upward out of the bush of Victorian restlessness. My stare, tenderness-smudged, pleases in this treasured finality-viewing. It doesn't wish any further ones beyond it.

Back to my July South Bank led to by reverberating, **sordid Hungerford Bridge**, its girders-crossed and trains-commuters-punctured progressive revealings of our mighty mysterious-seeming tower behind, but the stage of attacks and murders – also the sinister, so shamelessly exposed as to be unnoticeable, shady mass of dossers' lairs under its arches.

Indexitis/indexication is nothing else but the ageing (thus accumulating) mind's tendency to ramble, jet-propelled by associations of memory. This may string/mould the past into a meaning, but may also be a futile inconsequential listing.

For instance: **the fires** in my studio.

Because I am writing this there, buried under the cacophony of labourers' choppy voices, banging tools, crashing glass – several front-window panes having been cracked/blown out when a few nights ago (in August 1983) a mystery man – burned to death without disclosing his motives – set on explosive fire a vast 'sculpture' of piled-up car tyres in the shape of a full-size submarine, planted by the combined subsidies of the Arts Council and the GLC on a footbridge close by; the fierceness of petrol- and rubber-fed flames pushed through my 60-foot long studio to smash some panes of the back window as well – glass-splinter witnesses present in the oddest nooks and crannies of the interior. In the past I spent the nights here, and wonder how my flesh would have received such an attack.

This hauls from memory a night's sleep in the mid-1960s shattered by roaring flames licking my back window. It is not just a window; it (like the front one) fills up the arch-curve with a 20-foot height in the centre and a 30-foot width; and it was my Austin-Champ jeep, parked tightly alongside, which was on fire.

And the ultimate, still in the period of my studio nights, but when absent in New York: that morning, about to depart for a London flight, my son tells me on the phone about the burning of the studio. This is 1968, my trunk is full of drawings gathered in the States (the Chicago Convention and riots their dominant subjects) – materials for a book and promises of paintings – and the urge to get on with it makes me refuse to be dominated by the disaster.

It is the night after when, driven to the studio from the airport, my abhorrence demands not getting there, not becoming immersed. From a distance I watch for a long while the broken furtively lit arch-interior busily populated by the rescue team – recognizable shadows on the ceiling of Marion, Daniel and Teresa – and turn back to the house, where they would arrive, sooty and exhausted, several hours later. I never told them about this cowardice, and my evasive behaviour and the repeatedly claimed lack of distress (on the contrary, a sort of relief at the decks having been cleared for the 'next') amazed, but mostly annoyed them, since their stupendous and meticulous efforts at saving, sorting out, more scraps than reasonable from the tragic piles of the burnt, singed, dissolved-in-mucky-water life's accumulation, seemed almost ignored by me. But my pressing for the matters in hand and ahead demanded almost ruthless dismissal of the fire's aftermath, which muscled in for priority attention with, beyond my family's anxieties and devotion to my almost-demolished past, the 'media' and the flood of condolential letters and calls unwittingly pushing me under. Complete strangers still engage me in routine ever-identical exchanges on that fire.*

Does this enumeration carry any message? One supposes that each of the fires mirrored the mood of its date: that the early sixties carried the wave of dissolution of fossilized and over-confident social structures; that the hippy 'loving' challenge was edged with an emerging brutalism (not unlike Victorianism's Seven Dials lining), sweeping over the approaches to the South Bank art-fortresses, with attacks and murders on my very own Hungerford Bridge and under its Charing Cross arches. The 1968 fires, probably a deliberation, rode still on that crest.

And the last of 1983? The further stage, now worldwide and sky high, in liberation, through mightier weaponry, for a single person's assertions.

The world-spread tide of nomadic hippydom receded. Astonishingly their younger brothers and sisters have no clue of this yesterday, **haltered** within the prescribed Western staleness.

My young visitors (art students mostly), from Germany-Poland-Holland-Italy-the States, fire at me questions, conditioned by career-money preoccupations – and old unbridgeable divisions.

Invariably they ask: how have I been paying for my global travels? how to acquire the trick (as it must be) of self-advancement? how did I meet my young wife? – their curiosity-range marking the revived constraints of generational, class fences. Yes, they travel, but having bought regular return two-weeks holiday-passages with judiciously earned money – and they are amazed when told about their free-wheeling predecessors' lawless casualness.

They show me their drawings and colour transparencies. Of course their work reflects the current mode of furious 'new realism', remarkably forceful for mild-mannered beginners in tackling size/texture/strength/movement and in the aura of PROTEST. Indeed, the anger of the acclaimed 'school' is their advantage. But, on reflection, this anger linked with between-the-wars German art lacks its *raison d'être*. Those earlier images sprang from *unsponsored* outrage; the present pleiades are powered by offshoots of the official 'Cultural Blitz' operation, co-ordinated with the allied tactics of the rest of the Atlantic (multi-national) deals, the immense propaganda/sales/prestige machinery engaged. But the results are still a formal abstraction, however brilliant the brushwork over lapidary shapes – the inner core missing.

At the height of American abstraction-expressionism I proposed it to be the ideal capitalist faith-iconography in its not-upsetting blankness of content; but the art establishment rushed ahead to harness in time the potential challenges. The young coming to my studio, most able performers in this harsh enlarged idiom, also **pretend protest**; or perhaps NO: their life-style settling-bottling within the sybaritic doctrines is in itself a self-inflicted oppression. Theirs and their masters' art protests not against some or other injustice but against themselves. An echo of the young Dubliners' cries nearly forty years ago. And do I myself dare even now, on the surface so close to them (**an ignored progenitor**?), to stay a sideliner? Yes, I do, because of my – not forty, not fifty, but nearly sixty years' – content-consistency (often lonely, therefore erratic) in the watch of human comedies amassing into the epic.

Malraux claimed that: '. . . the fact that the word "painting" is linked with "picture" has paralysed us.' This labyrinth, uncurbed, unframed, non-picture painting is my answer to this. (Given earlier in this book but never mind.)

A bizarre idea: painting throughout my life the same 'panorama' – varying/enlarging/broadening in themes/ experience – from the Warsaw 14 metres-long parade of personages to the present attempt at an overall summation zig-zagging 600–700 feet . . .

The *Memoir* evolves naturally out of accumulated and overflowing testimony. Its raw material: experiences understood or enigmatic/on-the-spot drawings/to-and-fro associations/dreams – never documentation of events unwitnessed. It is a painting, not a potted history – thus its chronology is skeletal, as it oscillates between images and abstractions of memories. The work is open-ended, in constant progress . . .†

The facts of my life, spread over the globe and woven into the history of this century, were pinned down by me in

*Hugh Casson told me that he circled my burnt-out studio, finding in the piles of detritus outside and carrying away some half-surviving scribbles.
†*Memoir of the Century*. Extracts from introductory piece for chance visitors.

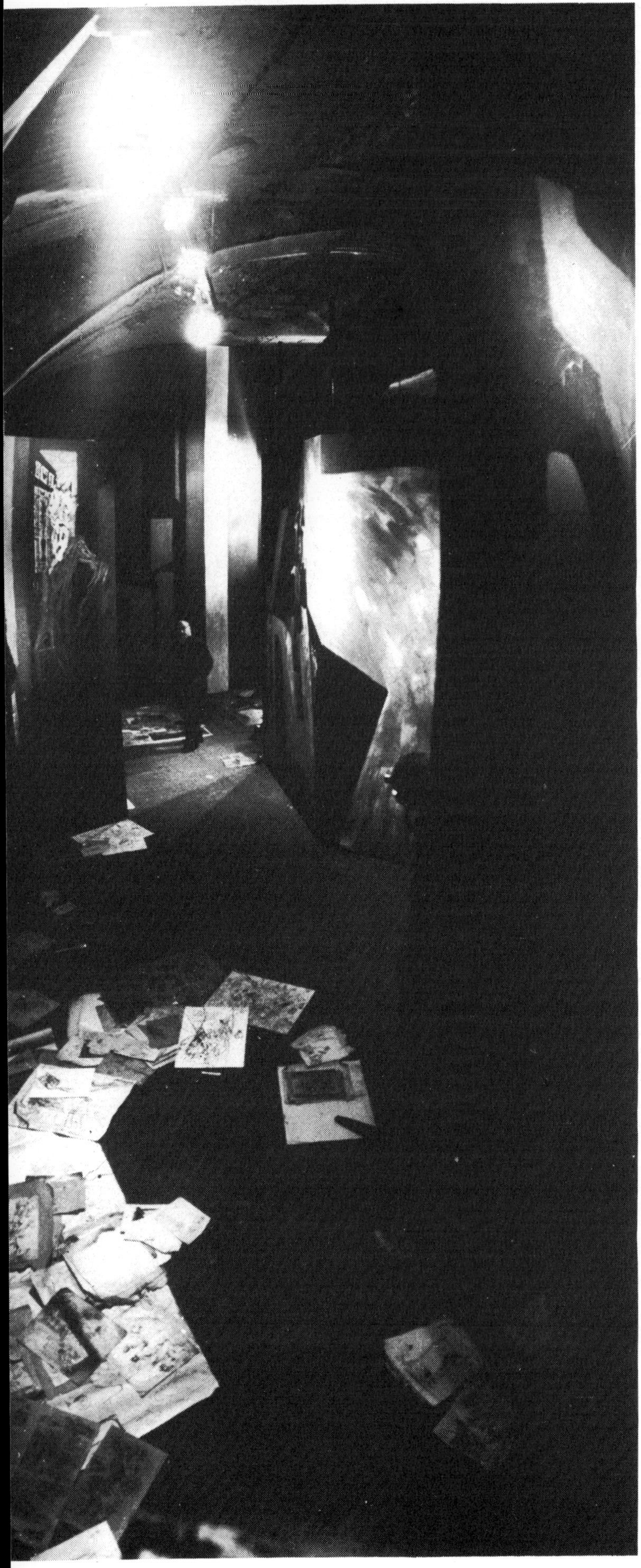

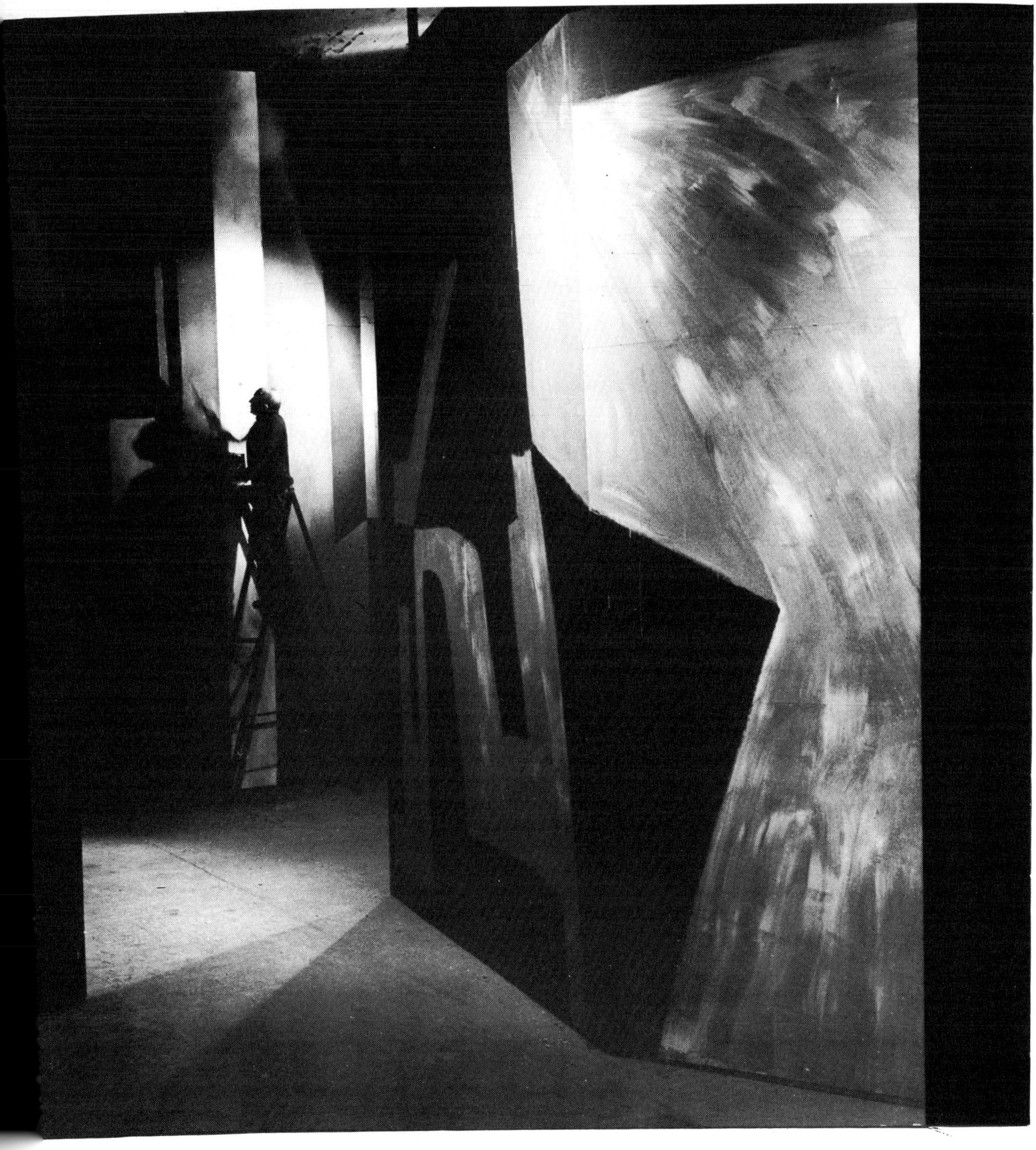

Memoir of the Century in progress (Photographs by Daniel Topolski and Amanda Saunders)

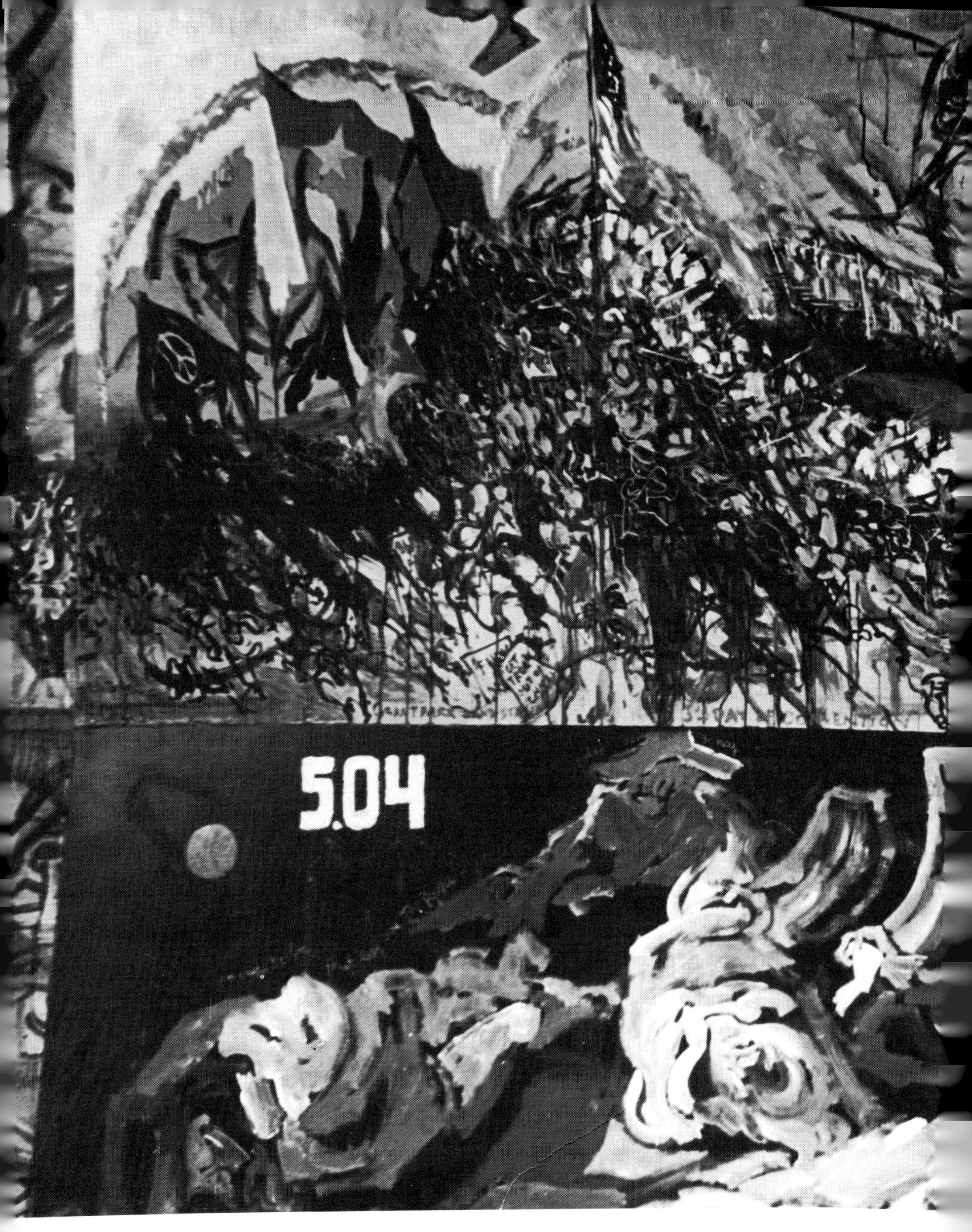
5.04

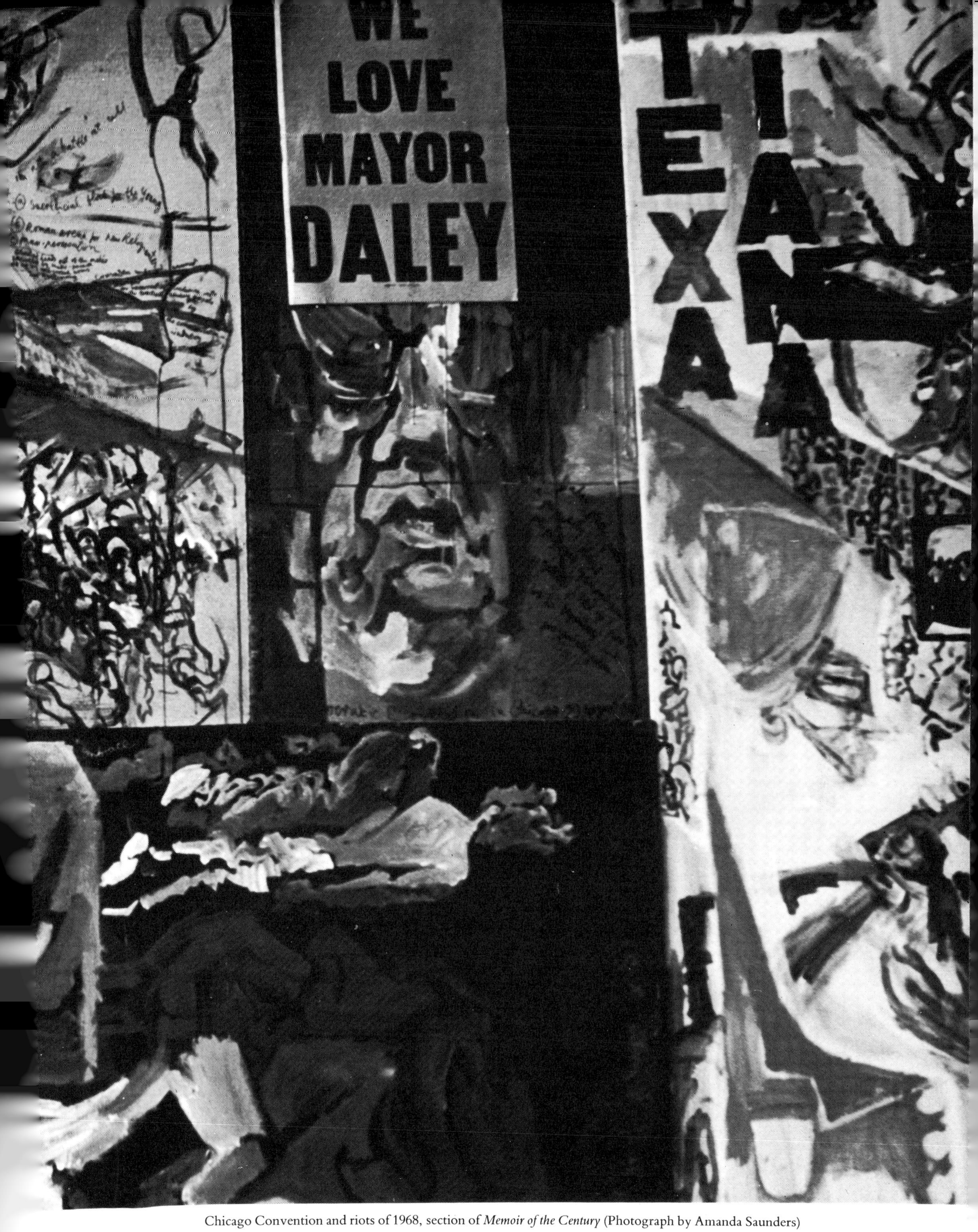

Chicago Convention and riots of 1968, section of *Memoir of the Century* (Photograph by Amanda Saunders)

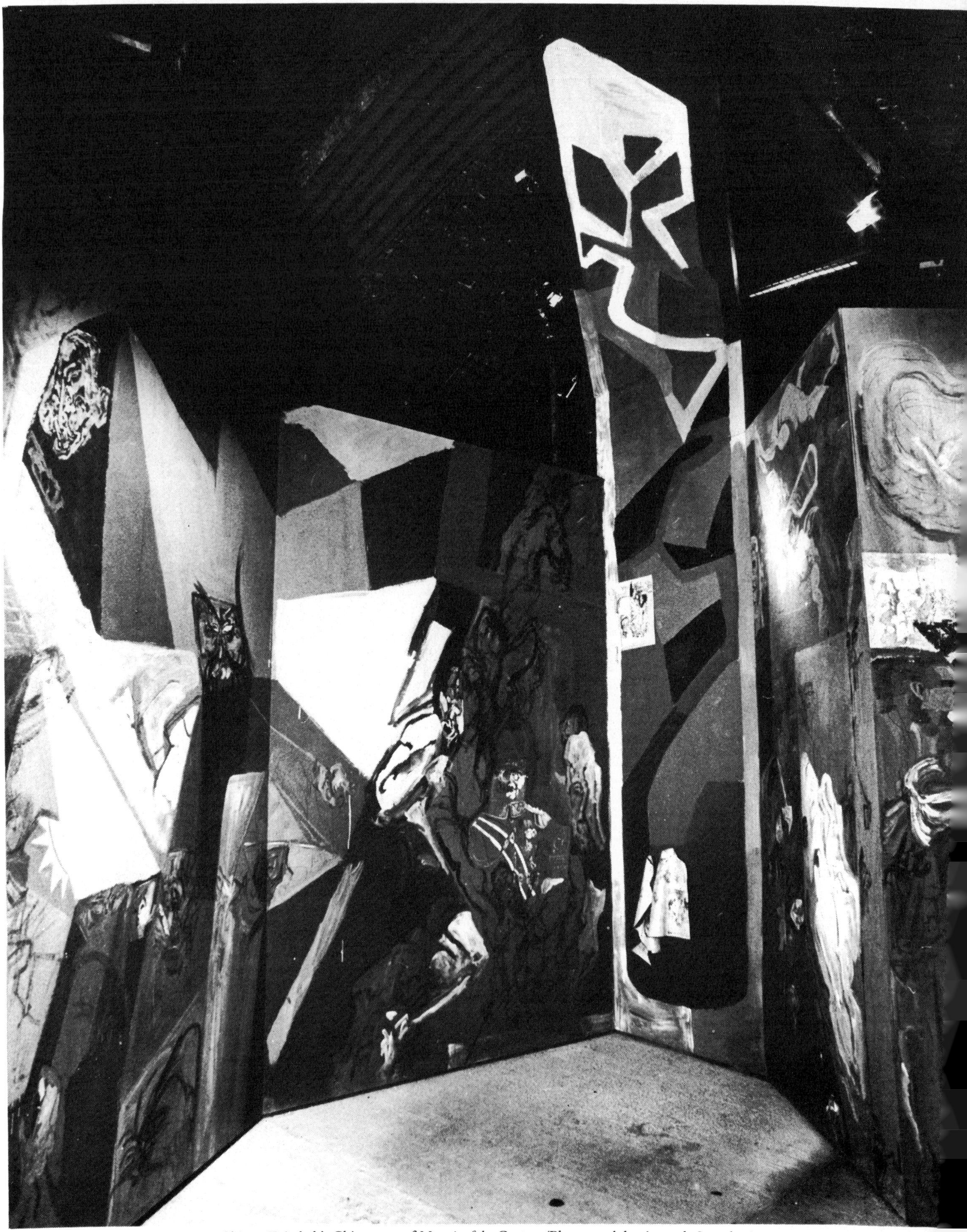

Chiang Kai-shek's China, area of *Memoir of the Century* (Photograph by Amanda Saunders)

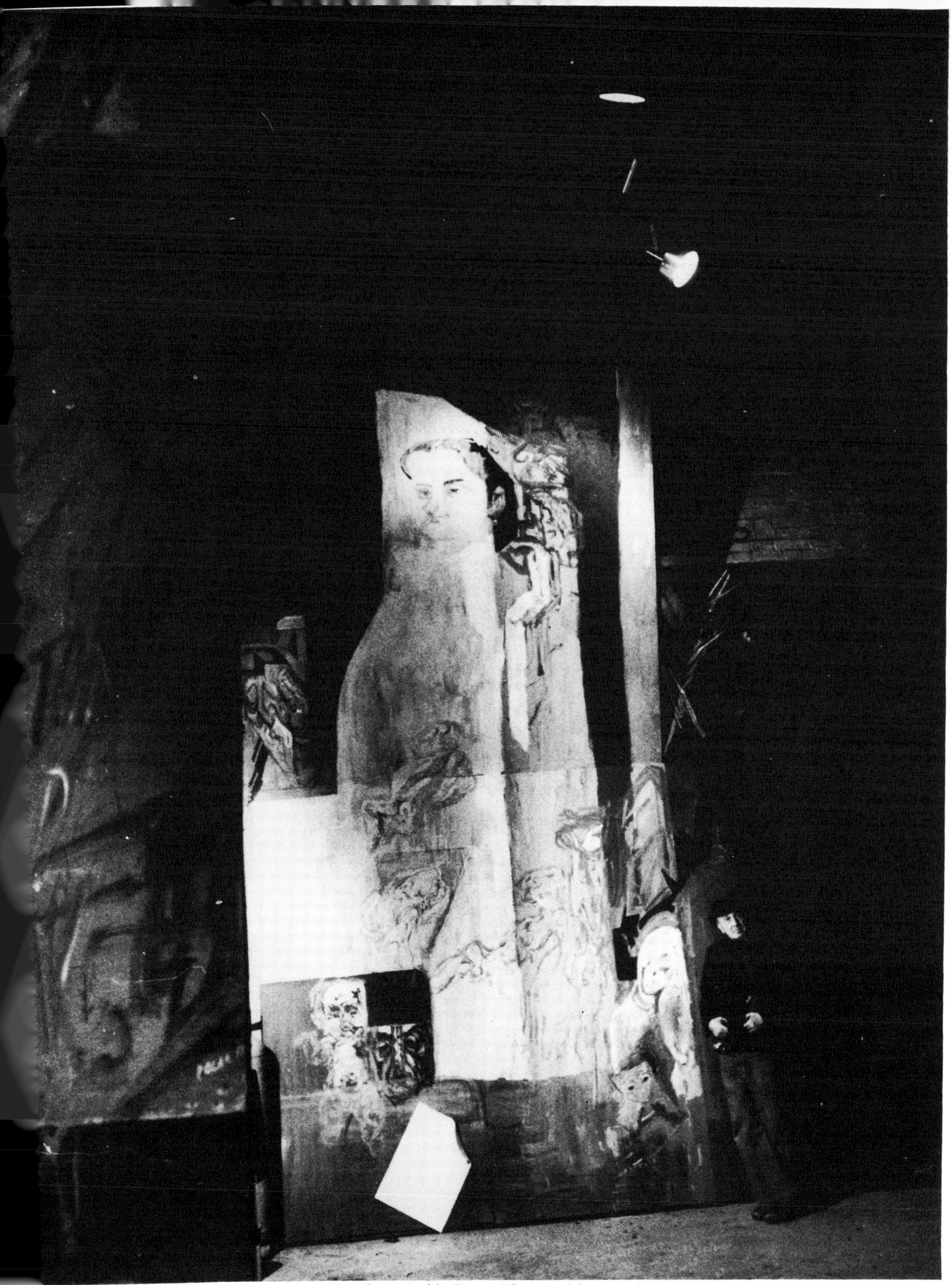

Earliest section of *Memoir of the Century* (Photograph by Amanda Saunders)

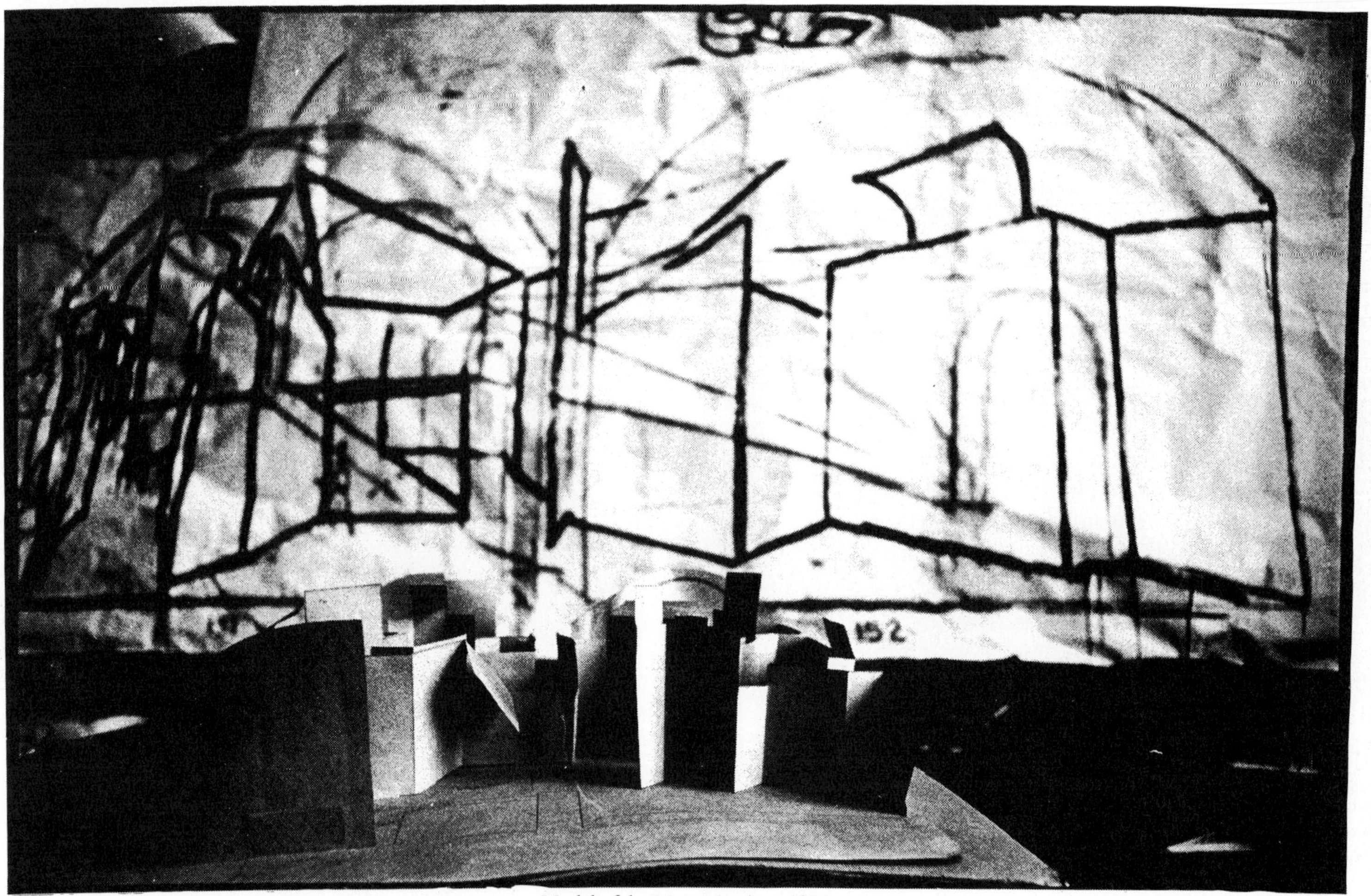
Model of the *Memoir* project, 1974

drawing on the spot from very early days. These drawings, masses of them, are the main fodder of this *Memoir*. But the *Memoir*, being a painting, develops its own form, the images and story-telling merging with the unifying movement of colour.

So two levels emerge: first, being a panoramic progression, it aims at reaching you as a sort of elemental, abstracted-from-reality, epic-scape; next, closer scrutiny may give hints of the human-scale tragicomedies.

And further: the sketchbooks serve me in shaping the painting, but the onlooker faces only the painting and, ideally, I would wish to provoke in him freewheeling imaginings, detached from an explanatory habit of mind.

Yet having declared this ideal, I recognize the need for a modicum of guidance over what is, after all, a pictorial tale. The happenings, the faces, emerge and demand to be identified. But my descriptions and naming must be reticent, for fear of deteriorating into trivializing gossip.

And one more point: I don't work consecutively, but move about, returning to add passages and balance abstract against figurative elements. So now, starting at the left, I hasten to say that the first sequence is possibly the least progressed of all . . .

. . . There is no ending. The *Memoir* reaches the present, becomes the Diary and continues from day to day to be cut short only by nature's will.

My speech (or parts of it) on 15 May 1984 in reply to the Duke of Edinburgh's formal opening of the *Memoir*, to which he gave, more or less, such finale: 'If, at the end of this century, you will wish to go on into the twenty-first but your aged legs refuse to work, I shall carry you across . . .'

It dawned on me only last night that, this being on many counts a personal culmination, I should respond with more than conventional phrases. The obvious theme is GRATITUDE. The growing monolithic state patronage of the Arts falls into the hands of entrenched coteries or tends to favour large groups, more easily digestible in democracies than single makers of art; but single artists shape the art of the day.

My predilections make me a loner, aware of but unswayed by changing trends, thus not favoured by committees – Left or Right.

But, *but* the spirit of a varied patronage by Popes and Princes, not playing power-games but reaching out for 'what they liked', happily still lingers. And in this free area rest my gratitudes:

A brief chronology:

Hardly out of my Warsaw Academy of Art, I was asked by Professor Karol Stryjeński, the Head of the then Polish equivalent of the Arts Council, to paint some 40 feet of the walls of their headquarters meeting hall – his personal decision.

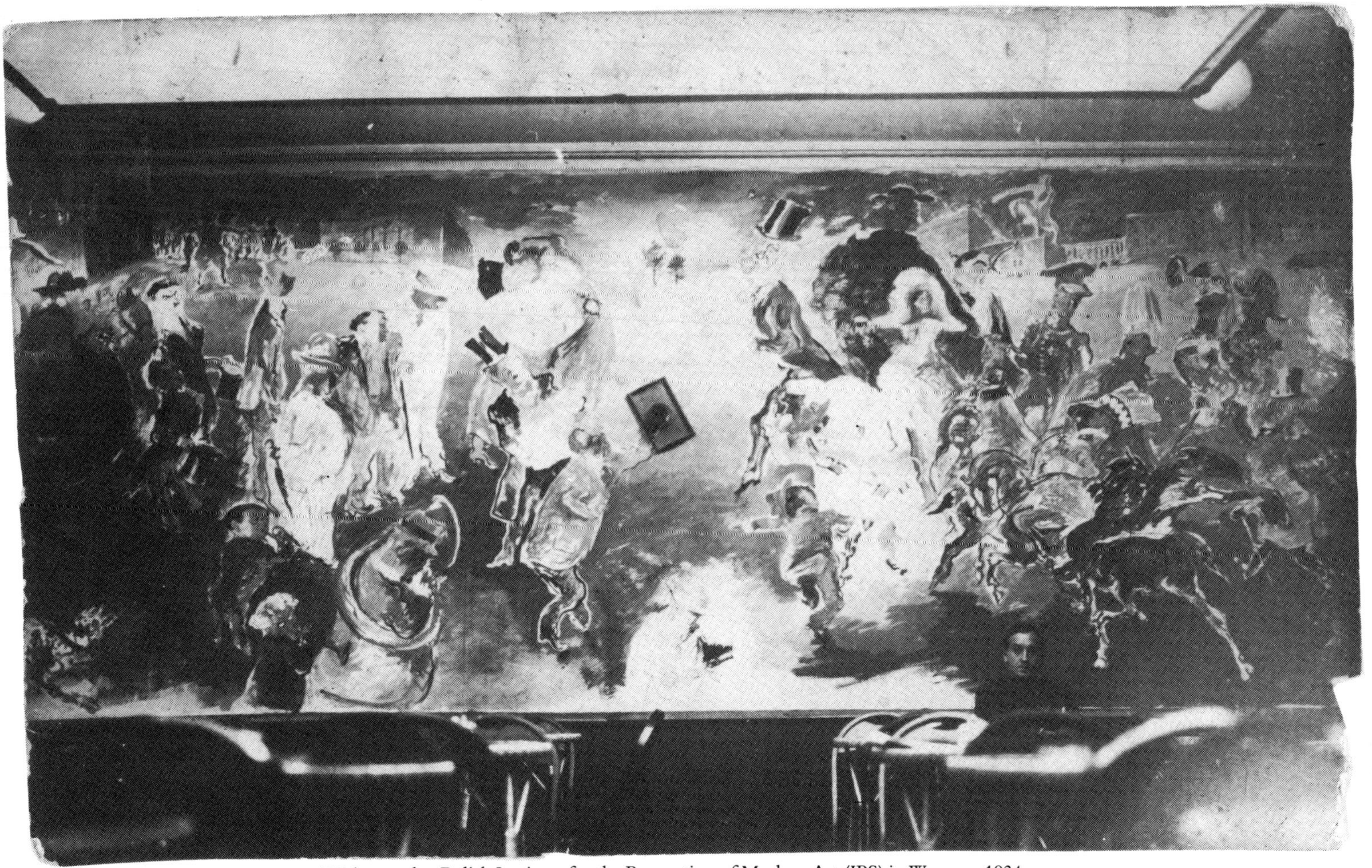

With mural at Polish Institute for the Promotion of Modern Art (IPS) in Warsaw, 1934

Soon after the war, I painted in London – thwarted by lack of space – the largest canvas I could squeeze into my studio, called *The East*. It was acquired by Pandit Nehru, to be followed by angry questions in the Indian Parliament.

Then came the uniquely enlightened and unprejudiced committee of 'The Festival of Britain 1951', under Gerald Barry's leadership. My gratitude is due to their assigning the largest space on the South Bank for my – at last – full-spread (60 feet by 20 feet) summary of recent round-the-world travels.

A few years later the Royal, thus untrammelled-by-committee-cautions, command gave me a gallery in Buckingham Palace to cover with a Coronation fantasia – a true Palace revolution, since, within this corseted-in-tradition edifice, I was free to paint what and as I saw right – rather a loosely flowing irreverent contemporary work. And it is still there.

And, finally, my life-long draughtsman's travels, over the globe and its drama, needing an extra-large area for its painterly summing up, my chance settling in the South Bank arches (two arches from my Festival mural) brought the GLC's generosity . . . and the ultimate solution: I gave my *Memoir* to London . . .*

*Now patronized by the South Bank Board and the Minister for the Arts.

Film-making on 'nostalgic' Paris, setting pre-war drawings against the present.

– The main thing: Paris is as it was – undamaged – lovely peeling streets behind St Germain, Place de Furstenbourg . . . and, when mad/tremendous modernity of Pompidou implants itself, it sits among old façades countering them – without boring planners' insistence on curtailing the new to match the old, yet constantly bulldozing it round the corner.

Paris was Europe and still is, unlike London, carrying on its École de Paris tradition of internationalism without priorities for the French: le Pompidou created by an Italian and an Englishman, directed by a Swede, and presenting a collection with Picasso, a Spaniard in the forefront. Theatre and film makers carry Russian, Polish, German, English names; in literature the celebrated prizes are given to Russians, Irishmen, Polish Jews writing in French.

– Caryl: 'Roller-skate disco to dance, what art-market currently to art.'

– Colonialism *à rebours*: as in England: a peaceful conquest/penetration by those formerly colonized. The square in front of Pompidou, less the obvious fun fair, more an Eros fair – the biology of attractions: young men of Africa and Asia enact the Sabines' story with young women of Europe and North America.

– The envy and the wish – the desire of Mediterranean plump brunettes to become Nordic – achieved: after the period of peroxide, *voilà*, now the young *Françaises* are truly natural blonde – tall – slim (perhaps the warriors, German and American, helped?).

– The Art-market: end-of-period production in quality, even quantity, lags behind the selling organization. Endless lines of little art-boutiques are parallel in misery with the lines of instant sketchers of portraits and Sacré Coeur views in the Place du Tertre. Also, le Pomidou, both an unfair competitor and diminisher of impact/values through over-exposition in its amassment and bureaucratization – but in itself a supreme folly. As everywhere: ritual without content; each period demands symbolic edifices/temples, and the Pomidou does this – to be occupied by high priests ahead of justification by current art.*

– Paris was a discovery – we, the foreigners, would sink into its unique harmonizing of disharmonies (organic-human-unhypocritical) – the whole range of sensuosity (gluttony, brothels on all levels from open confident pub-like to *'fiv'-o-clock maisons de rendezvous'*) – to gentle first communion girls† trotting to St-Germain-des-Prés tripping over Café Flore homosexuals. NOW the hordes of tourists tramp Paris underfoot. They may offer a new theme for a draughtsman of manners, but the life of Paris/France seems throttled – or, worse, bending to tourists' trade.

Various views:

– An American bohemian domesticated in Paris: enthusiasm for Paris/France, but not for the French; change: generational, the French soften their xenophobia – the English language penetrated and reduced their sense of superiority, the world's young mixing, no more defeat-complex.

– An American black girl student and her two black US friends: they hate Paris, maltreated everywhere including their hotel – she raped twice. Brutality.

– Young aristocratic Frenchwoman: distressed at the social standstill: no more salons, cocktails, visiting. Culturally stays in the *cul-de-sac* of opera and ballet, detesting/mocking Pompidou and all that; her *savoir-faire* retarded: mentioning toilet-paper makes her speechless with embarrassment. But she can't resist the disco . . .

– The bohemian-chic of the Left, returning from the funeral of Pierre Goldman, miserable – because of the shrinking of their numbers in their cultural milieu – 10,000; they compare this with parallel funerals of the past and claim that, besides reduction of the Left, the crowd was almost entirely and significantly made of the May '68 generation now in their thirties. The young are not interested in politics – they concentrate on their egos.

A telephone call. *Pani* – Mrs – Wanda Piotrowska with her precise gentlewoman's vocal neatness strings a tale of horrors. She is grateful because I am the only person, *'mój Felku'*, left; she is apologetic, because lost. And she weaves into her polite lament praises of God's Will in cornering her into the ultimate defeat – because she has suffered defeats throughout these forty-some years, groomed to perfection to meet them, always calling on God, with just a timbre (not a word) of excuse for Him.

I thought she was about two years older than me, but today she said with a little laugh that there were only a few months between us when she, **Wanda** in Lewszowo, an eleven- or twelve-year-old **tomboy girl**, gambolled barefooted, scratch-kneed into my spotty boy's heart.

Lewszowo was a modest manor lording it on a slice of Ruthenian land, then parcelled out among veteran Piłsudski Legionaries – General Berbecki set in it, with his old adjutant, my stepfather, given the adjoining plot – the two run as one by the General's family.‡

And so the General's household and our summerly contributions were most harmonious; my horse-riding with the boys (possible only in the rain, since our retired-military horses worked the fields) memorable; and our moonlit (surely) August evenings *en famille* on the veranda perfect for my mooning after Wanda's vitality, her elder sister Alicja romantically poised in beauty – intimidating.

There were later, over the years, rare meetings with Wanda in Warsaw, which she remembers better. Then my departure from Poland. And after a long lifetime of war and of London, a voice on the phone – and the shock confrontation, through this graceful quite ancient stranger, with my own old age. The life I led sought, to begin with, the company of my elders, but then imperceptibly shifted from them, but never to settle among my contemporaries; now among the younger, thus identifying with them, I tend to a false security of agelessness. Wanda – a *memento mori*.

I knew most of her tale of past woes, yet I listened once again – aware of her need to outpour it, always gentle-voiced – to her compression of it into an awesome list which my memory could replenish. But, this being the tale of Poland's martyrdom encapsulated within one family, it should be written over a thousand pages by a master – and a Polish patriot. I am not the first, nor enough the second, but must not slight Wanda – and so in inadequate unconstrued phrases:

The apocalyptic Huns and their aftermath stamped upon this single batch of people thus (and I only go by chaotic words from Wanda): Bronek: in the army, in prisoners' camp, insanity; Wiktor: underground-cum-parashooting East-West, caught, tortured, hanged; Sławenty: guerrilla battles, paralysed; sister and a cousin, insane. The General and

*The West is shaped now by middlemen, not by makers/explorers/cultivators and benevolent patronage. The Pompidou folly is not the Eiffel industrial fanfare, but a temple/altar for ritualizing society manipulations – by administering predigested/categorized canned and enshrined have been revolts, as private and museum sales . . .

In fact, the act of propel-elating humans up diagonal walks is this ritual, the elevation above popoular-trad vulgarities on the piazza below. The supposed purpose – showing works of art – is significantly of little impact: they do not belong (dull *passé* screens reintroduced), diminished into insignificance by not measuring up to giant girders; in fact their presence (plus publications, videos) seems to be a sly argument for the might of PR-ism (star-selectivity essential here), without which they would not reach their present myth and market heights.

I will not enter the capitalist plot argument as the whole middleman system may have blossomed organically – its manipulations (practised by selective displays and the avalanche of books/periodicals/projections/postcards-prints, aimed at conditioned pre-orientated *idées*-to-be-*reçues*), the natural flowering out of 'sincere' convictions/ideals of 'dogma' conditioned delusions. And the speed at which the 'protests' are engulfed into mercantile seduction – engulfed and soon brusquely brushed out of the way for the next 'movement'. But directed it must be.

†But also: Eugenio d'Ors searched (in our book) in vain for young girls: they did not exist because hiding in *Les Salons Cosmétiques* being made-up into women; today *la jeune fille* dominates.

‡To put the reader into the picture of Polishness: far from a military caste (except for a number of high-ranking professionals, schooled in Tsarist Russia and Austria), the nucleus of its army's 'top brass' emerged from the Legions – sanctioned under the Austro-Hungarian Empire, in need, on the brink of the First World War, of fighting men – a patriotic-cum-socialist sub-military organization (anticipating upheavals which would almost certainly bring unification/independence), composed pre-eminently of the strata of 'intelligentsia' idealists, from students to professionals to landed gentry. Their officer-corps, grown out of their civilian maturity, carried into the regularized army – and, later, into the Government – *sui generis* flexibilities and liberalities. No match for the Junkers.

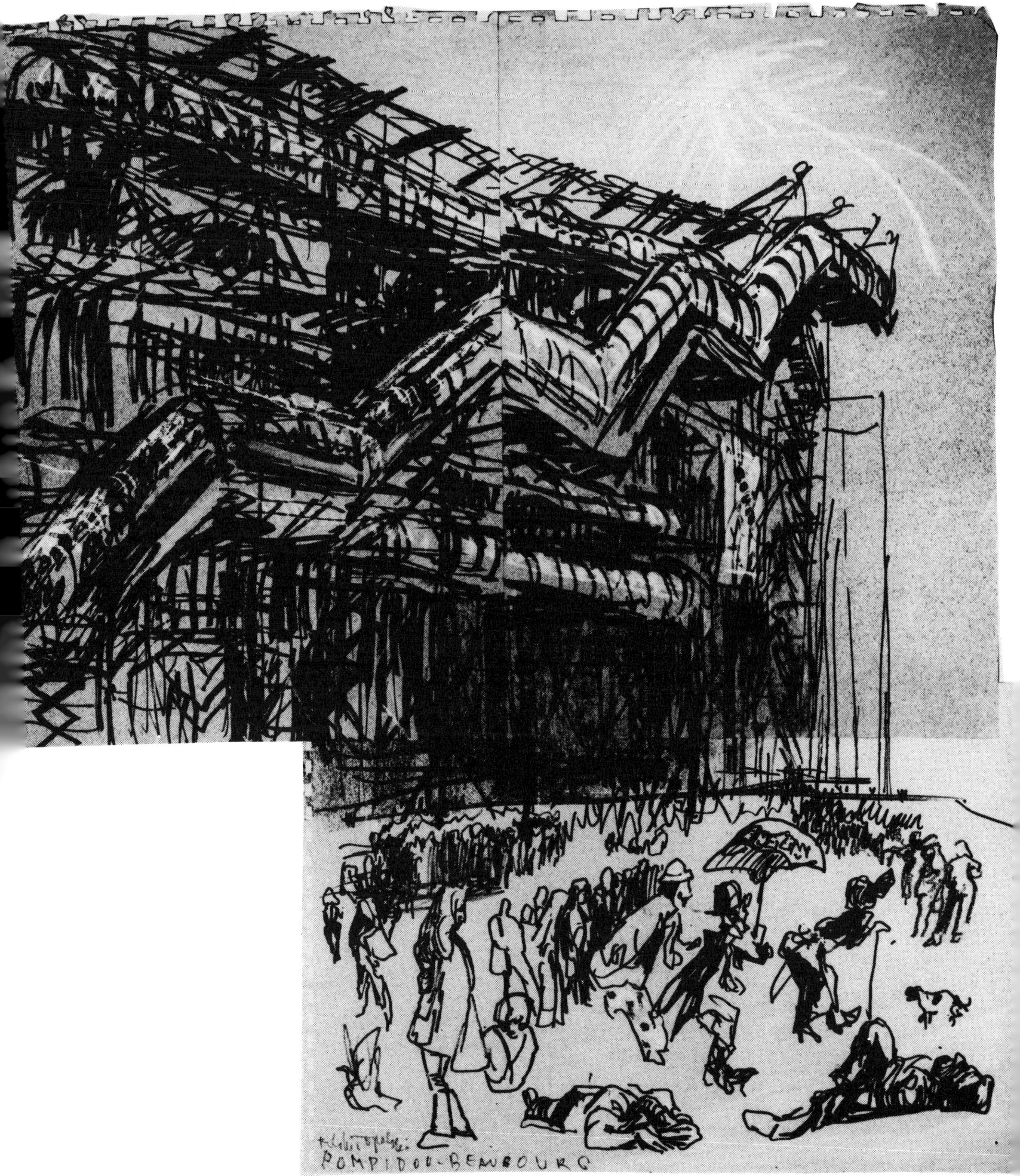

The Pompidou Centre (from *Topolski's Chronicle* in Quarto)

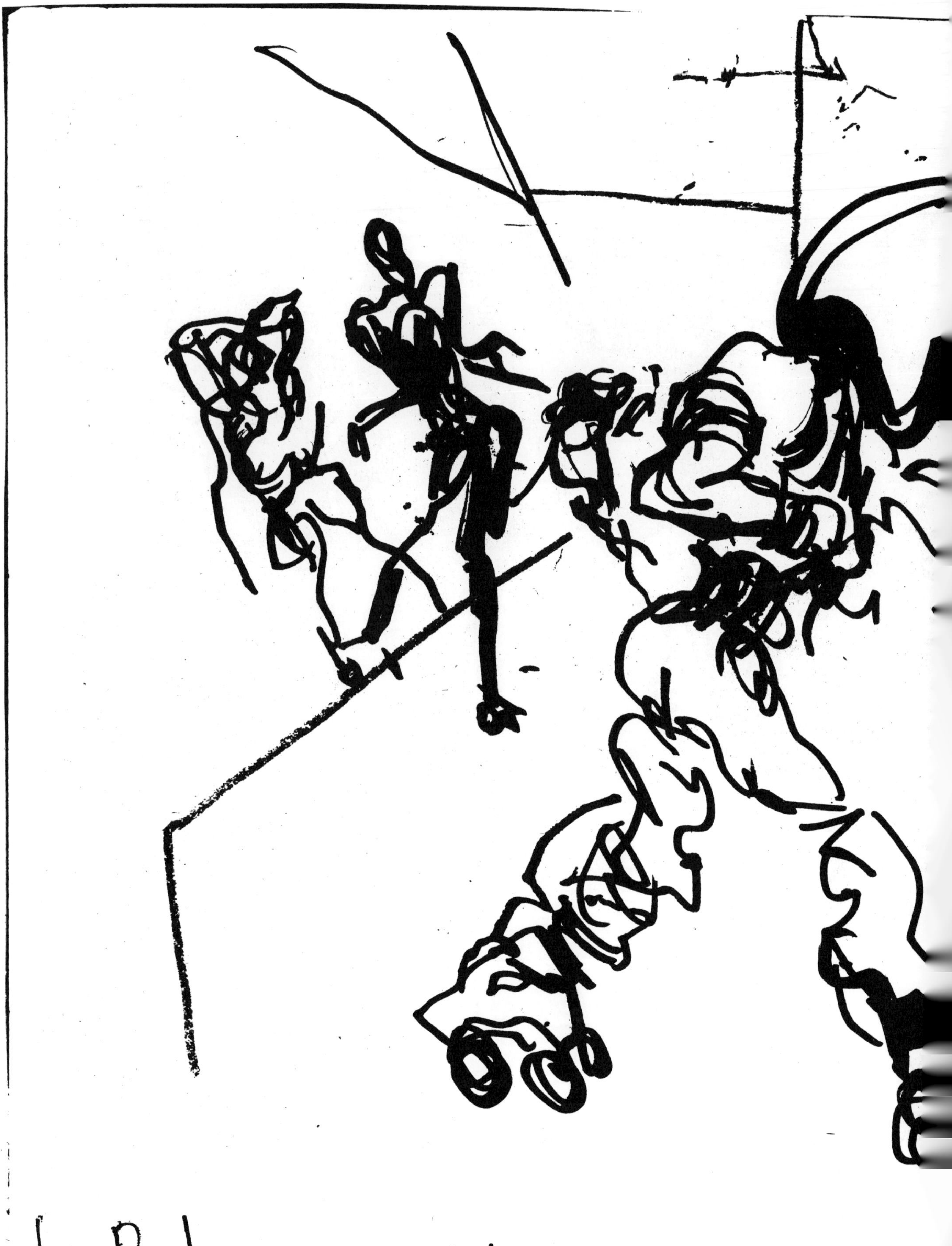

Le Palace-Roller-Disco

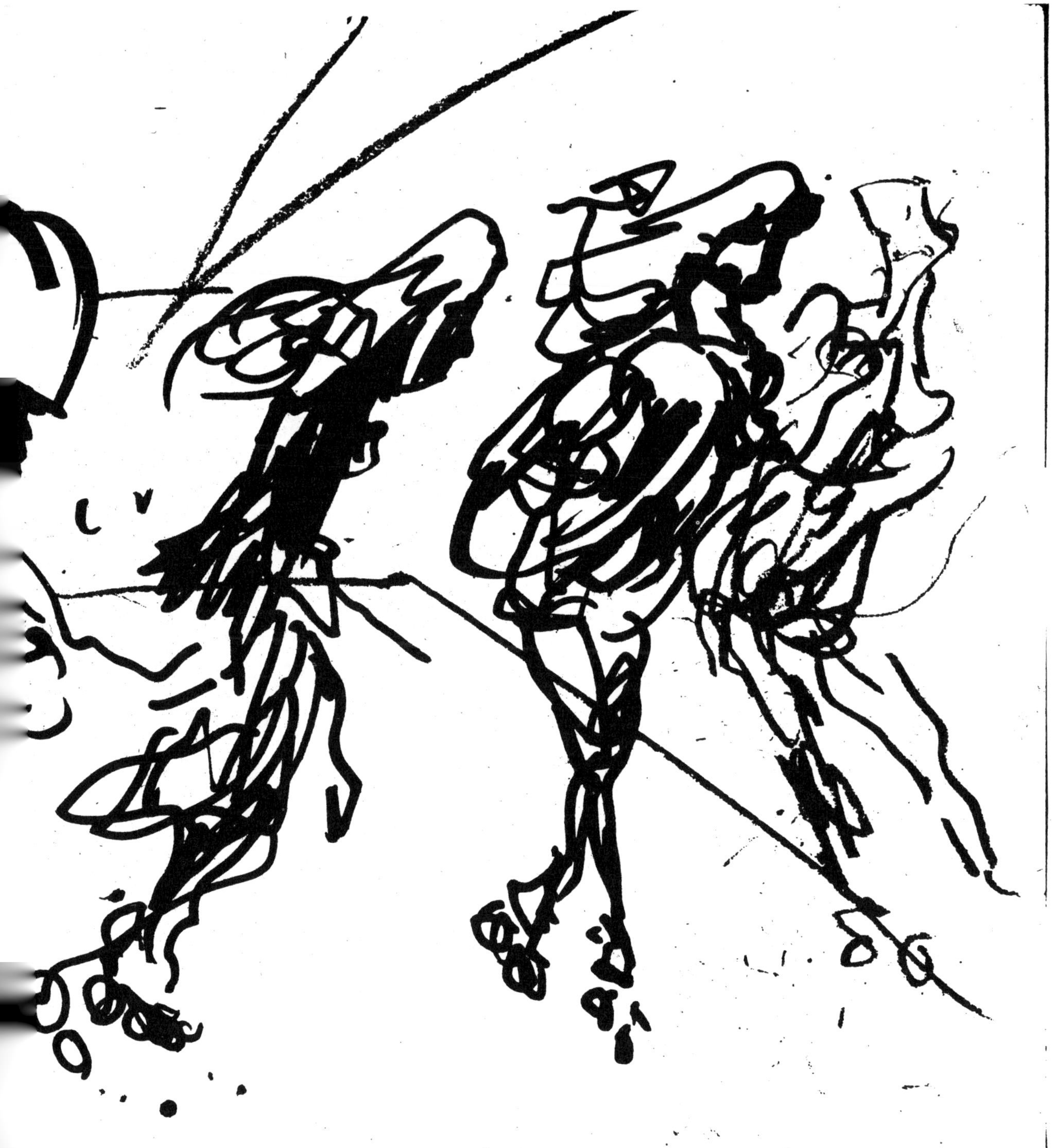

Paris: Le Palace-Roller-Disco (from *Topolski's Chronicle* in *Quarto*)

his wife, separated and deported, having found each other back in Communist Poland, and been given a small house in the formerly German township of Gliwice, poverty enforced took sub-tenants in those years of the panicky but also greedy onrush of expatriates from the Russia-appropriated Eastern territories – soon the General found on his doorstep with crashed skull, and not much afterwards gentle Zofia murdered in their rooms – one can only guess at the released savagery conjuring up this short-cut to property.

But Wanda, widowed by her also-military husband, was saved/stranded in London.

Now, even in final degradation/defeat, she keeps appearances – General Zamorski, with whom she has shared for many aged years those two rooms in Wimbledon, is only an acquaintance; they are always addressing each other as 'Pan', 'Pani'.

It was troubling, but also touching, to see these two old people, at one time of the privileged, washed by the worst of fates into Wimbledon suburbia (when first visited in London), accommodated to their minimalities, wrapped in *savoir-faire* biscuits cum tea: she made up into old-age primness (the tomboy rubbed out utterly), two little Pekinese in the crook of her arm, a little finger drawn away from the cigarette-holder; he, from an unbending Minister of the Interior in the Poland of the Colonels to a restorer of modest paintings, a devourer of books, a lone walker. Yet this meekness cannot have been easy to settle for.

That call of my old country, of my aged generation apt to pull me back down where I should belong, if not for the quirky stepping-onward of my present.

At my first encounter with this lost pair, I drew them, documentarily as it were, with their dogs, their plants, their hospitable biscuits, photographs of their pinnacle and of the formalized entombments; and a very large painting emerged (surprisingly chosen for the collection of the National Museum in Warsaw): black upon black cut by a white divide, scattered with indefinite shapes of the Berbecki clan – he in full square-hatted zigzag-braided uniform, Zofja borne in a funeral, a hanged form: all somehow bracketed in the obviousness of Wanda a child-promise, and Wanda declined. As shamelessly described, kitsch of an unacceptable story-telling kind, but, as often with me, these elements were my private/secret scaffoldings for, I intended, a picture of indecipherable (by the onlooker) but absorbing mood; the disclosures here serve this tale, not the picture-gazers.

But this is not all; by chance, by instinct, with the painting moving as it were to the right, there erupted at the final edge a clashing vertical band of colour-gaudiness – soon, in the process of painting, to be justified almost only as an emblem – thus to remain unreadable, since further definition would have leapt shamefully away from tragic dignities. Old Wanda does not gladly acknowledge the young presence in England of this great-niece of hers, who, like many of the youngest adventurers from today's Poland, came to my studio. This new breed of a few years ago (the latest style of romanticism is a different matter), coached to dodge the German terror and then the restrictive régime, reached its pinnacle in her: she was furnished to the fullest with all the attributes of body and soul to be a World's Miss Make-it. Her deeds brave and cynical astonished; her juggling with men/husbands (I was best man at one of her weddings), her undercover excursions to Poland, her new-model gold-digging. So, absurdly, entered the blood-continuity the stride of the present, sweeping me away from contemplatory dangers.

Then, with elemental suddenness, the vegetational wretchedness of a helpless old exile, burdened/choked by funereal memories of his kin, thrust General Zamorski into an ignominious crowding-at-the-exit by the way of geriatric deprivation of self-control, with his mind working, fiendishly humiliating to a man of action, a politician and an artist.

She tells it all (and about having to move out of their lodgings; 'God' knows where to) neatly: her gentlelady's upbringing did not include breaking down into tears or rising to shouts of despair – the opposite is proper: calm and calmer-still registering of terminal indignities, punctuated by the subservient refrain about God being a merciful witness.

The blows dealt by history pathetically merged now with nature's order of decline; pointedly this latter brutality, reserved for survivors, proves the least bearable.

Long corridors, a long ward to the furthest bed against the wall; the bed's flatness ahead makes me whisper confusedly to old Wanda who guides me, 'he must have got up' – but no, he's there on his back, an inch or two of him under a blanket – a cadaver's measure. Even, when her fussing lifts his eyelids over unfocusing greyness, the skin hangs rigid over nose/cheek bones, over twisted gaping hollow-red orifice. If not dead yet, he's ready and it is death's fault at being late.

But. The right arm supports or shields the head – indicates the desire for hiddenness: anger? thus still living? At ancient Wanda's prattling (coy, rejuvenated by his contrasting plight)? Or, drawing me out to speak? He breathes/stutters, 'I hear a strange voice!', not in curiosity, but as if 'strange' signified unwanted.

I dial their Wimbledon number – the buzz of termination.

The Faithful

A letter awkward in syntax and hand:

Dear colleague Feliks! 53 years have gone past (over half a century) since our ways parted after finishing the School of Officers of the Artillery Reserve at Włodzimierz Wołyński . . . On the 1.IX.1939, 4.00 a.m., the Germans' VIIIth Army struck at us. Fierce fighting took place over the River Warta where our artillery regiment operated. On the 2.IX.39 in the afternoon on the observation post I was wounded in the face and left hand. They covered us with hellish fire – *bursting grenades*, then the 2nd battery was almost completely destroyed. On the night of the 3rd/4th.IX.39 took place the retreat to the main line of resistance in the region of Szczercowo, where the fighting lasted till the night of 6.IX.39 – our infantry charged with bayonets a few times – the Germans were fleeing like mad, they were frightened of hand-to-hand fighting. Unfortunately the immense superiority of German tanks and aircraft forced us to retreat towards Warszawa. And there on 13.IX.39 at night, in the region of Ożarów-Strzykuły, German tanks gave us hell, my mare killed under me crushed me, broke my left leg and the warring ended for me . . .*

Or in a third letter:

> Our regiment was posted to protect the frontier in the region of Wicluń on the Warta and here the combat with the Germans began at 4.00 a.m., 1.IX.1939 – and on 2.IX.39 at noon near Działoszyn on the Warta I was, already, wounded on the observation post; and on the night of 14.IX.39 near Ożarów close to Warszawa in an encounter with German tanks the horse under me was killed and crashing on top of me broke my leg – and the war was finished for me . . .

I read Czerniak's first letter cursorily with the impatience dealt out to the plentitude of such coming from Poland, like this one mostly concluding with some time-consuming request. But the second and the third (and then a Christmas card, compressed – also further periodical letters all worked out in clumsily naive phrases) repeated mulishly and flatly his whole two-weeks war chronology, which gradually grew on reading and rereading into a meek everyman's capsule of unchallenging duty/devotion. His minute battle-tests, his anonymity (blotted out from my memory, even) given a lift by the eminence of his comrades in prison camps and paradoxically by the 'error' bombing by the Allies – perhaps a stronger trial than his former battles; then, back in Poland, his falling into the routine of acceptance. And so, those few September days stay in sharpest detail above the rest of his life – the climax.

But this is not my theme. On reaching the lines '. . . dear colleague Feluś you must be proud that the Regimental Standard of our 30 PAL (30th Light Artillery Regiment) was decorated with the *Virtuti Militari* cross . . .' there came the jolt demanding a reshuffle of some ingrained truisms.

No need to restate my consistent 'out-of-step'-ism, most emphatically surfacing when pressed into conformity – military conscription service responded to as make-believe – an opportunity for a display of disrespect and skill at truancy. But there is a need to restate the division amongst believers: – the faithful and humble servers of ruling dogmas/systems; – the Promethean challengers against odds, who hold my surface sympathies.

And I recognize, but at a distance, the needs and the strengths of group-ties – although becoming uncomfortably conscious of a mass of alikes gathering round me into a growing grouping of lackadaisical stoics.

And here calls this conformist voice of pride in loyalties; of unquestioning belonging: 'Proud of my 30th Light Artillery Regiment . . .'.

Memories begin to swell up. That knightly bony stern Major who lodged me in his quarters, a mere cadet officer on short regimental 'practice'; the row of faces above the high silver-zigzagged collars of the officer corps, whom I drew one after another (wounded, killed, captives in 1939?); my riding in manoeuvres at the head of the reconnoitre patrol (Czerniak's second injury) – ever self-consciously dodging the prescribed barks of command with feeble gestures to my men to indicate 'halt', 'dismount'; but elated when at a trot emerging from some woods to descend on a village below with the clatter of hoofs/sabres/rifles, imagining myself to be riding into trouble against Cossacks, Tartars, or Swedes of 300 years before; or dug into the slope of a sandy hillock, field-glasses at my eyes (Czerniak's first wound – his field-glasses saved his sight).

Would it help to throw in quite another, yet also 'service', letter? – **A letter from a Major** late the Royal Sussex Regiment – a calm record of a family's decimation in the service of their country. When in the Middlesex Hospital, having been wounded in the London Blitz, I befriended the Staff Nurse Catherine Macpherson. Soon after, she joined the Colonial Nursing Service, sailed for Singapore and disappeared. Her brother's letter tells how 'She sailed the day her elder brother was killed in the Indian Army on the Abadan landings to squash the Iraqi rising. Catherine . . . was lost at sea in the Banku Straits on the S.S. *Tanjong Penang* in mid-February 1942, sailing from Singapore . . . I believe into captivity.'

My drawing of her is in the Major's hands together with 'an etching by the Scottish painter James Patterson of my uncle, 2nd Lieutenant John Cooke Macpherson, who was killed at the battle of Loos . . . Like my sister who was lost presumed killed, John Macpherson was never seen after leaving the trenches when the Gordons went into the attack on the day so many of Scotland's young men were killed . . .' '. . . I count myself fortunate in having this one drawing as a reminder of an elder sister who was full of fun in the days before the last war, and who I saw for the last time late in November 1940, just before I sailed for overseas service . . .'

Indeed, they all served. And truly she was full of fun – a dark strapping girl, marvellous in her dark-belted uniform, starch-collared and -head-crowned.

All these half-thoughts at night, kicked off by this simple man's 'pride in the 30th Regiment'. And that pride is apt to penetrate/tear apart the cynic's jesting garment impregnated against vulnerability, to render me open to such yieldings/affections. (Even though knowing these affections generate/pair almost invariably with generalized counter-hates, -disdains.) But what an immense estate of feelings, hence of harvesting full living, full dying.

If yielding, it ought to be assumed that devotion, loyalty, harmony, hierarchy, unity (mystical–physical) – in faith and practice, in conversions – that all these, even the communion of two, are participatory, tribal in essence, in other words spring from belonging – in short are variations of love.

But this argument counters my 'ways'. From what urges springs my stubborn contradiction? To what does it lead except solitude? Is it simply enslavement to the *Zeitgeist*'s

*Czerniak's second letter contained this aside: '. . . in October 1941 we were taken to a **penal camp in Lubeck**, where, besides us, there were French officers, amongst them Captain Blum, son of the French Premier, also Yugoslav and Belgian officers, amongst them twelve generals, a few Czech officers, also – Captain of Artillery, the son of Stalin, Jacob Dżngaszwili, by profession an engineer-architect . . . On Palm Sunday Lubeck was bombed and by the same token our camp also suffered.'

elevation of singleness unaided? The doubting Thomas's ultimate fate.

In all: am I on the point of *volte-face*? Will I flop into one of many crowded pools, love all the old soldiers, march in protest, become a Buddhist?

No. The obvious: in my late seventies aggressive muscularity retreats: legs give up running, arms' tendons snap, above all thinned juices betray an overall cooling off. But, appetites diminished, the needs for aids grow: sentimental indoctrinatory proneness emerges – a beckoning slope. And, as in the High Street I pass untempted by any supermarket trove of popular promises/goodies, I skip off-the-peg loves/hates.

Weltstädte, die an einem Flusse liegen, haben oft an ihrer linken Seite etwas Besonderes, Unerwartetes. Es ist nicht immer vordergründig, wie das Jugendstil-Hotel Gellert in Budapest. Manchmal muß man es suchen, wie die Studentenlokale und Boutiquen an der Rive Gauche in Paris oder die urigen Gaststätten des Trastevere in Rom. Die Londoner South Bank scheint sehr auf Fassade angelegt. Da ist das imposante Gebäude des Greater London Council, also des Groß-Londoner Stadtrates, und seit dem „Festival of Britain", das im Jahre 1953 dieses etwas verkommene Viertel sanierte, der neue Komplex mit der imposanten Royal Concert Hall im Mittelpunkt. Steigt man im betriebsamen U-Bahnhof Waterloo aus, gewissermaßen von rückwärts kommend, erlebt man eine breite, verkehrsreiche Straße und riesige moderne Bürohäuser. Geht man dann unter den Backsteinbögen der Hungerford Railway Bridge flußwärts, gelangt man über Treppen in die großzügig angelegten Bauwerke der Konzerthalle, die auch tagsuber in ihren Erd- und Tiefgeschossen mit wechselnden Präsentationen und Cafeteria-Betrieb Gäste anlockt und betreut. Weiter liegt da die Hayward Gallery, zu deren Ausstellungen sich die Besucher kilometerlang ge-

FELIKS TOPOLSKI

Von L. Fritz Gruber
Fotos Calle Hesslefors

This enforced scanning the past. **Autobiographical wooings** began much too early in my life, easily each time brushed out of the way – for pressing forward. Then George Weidenfeld angled me twice: the first time I simply didn't deliver and the contract was dissolved; the second time his cleverly schemed bait-advance came in small doses following completed chapters, with Antonia, then Pakenham, just out of Oxford, star of his firm, coming to my studio once a week to sit side by side over my current scribbles, phrase by phrase argued out and put by her on to the typewriter – the manoeuvre ensuring that the quaintness of my English, agreed to be preserved, did not get wildly incomprehensible. This worked beautifully until, the advance having been paid out, my urge towards current (far-flung and full-time) pursuits won again.

Obviously this time the autobiographical age and engagement descended upon me harmoniously because it works in concert with my painted *Memoir*. Unless, unless the act of painting this labyrinthine vastness demanding my extreme 'forward' determination, the writing (not my natural medium, thus literally legerdemainist by comparison) may have come still too soon; it may be reducing my painting drive by diverting attention/energy to the allurements of the past, before merely a useful archive. In fact, sadly, it happens, unavoidably wrapped in other imponderabilia/excuses: the *Memoir* has slowed down. The torn shoulder-tendon, the cut knees, the ever-limping maintenance services contribute; but this among recent enticements: why just yesterday? nostalgia hardly ever in my range?

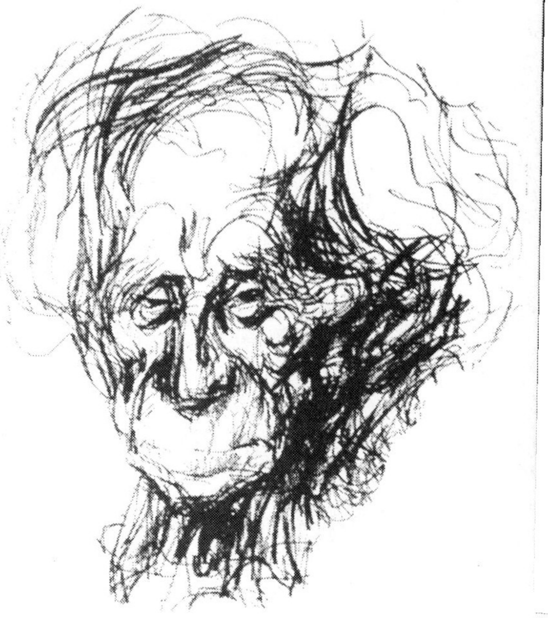

A sudden small plain aged woman stands shy in mid-studio (the door is open). In hardly audible Polish, visibly emotion-bound, she declares that she looked after my children – Teresa just a few months old – in Wales and in the transitional Harley Place.

But within this insignificant presence were carried tensions above those of a mere caller. This was clearly of the greatest import to her – perhaps a pilgrimage to regain herself as the very young thin girl, shyly daring, clearly linking her stay with us to her lone but in hope (our hope) best days. This became instantly apparent.

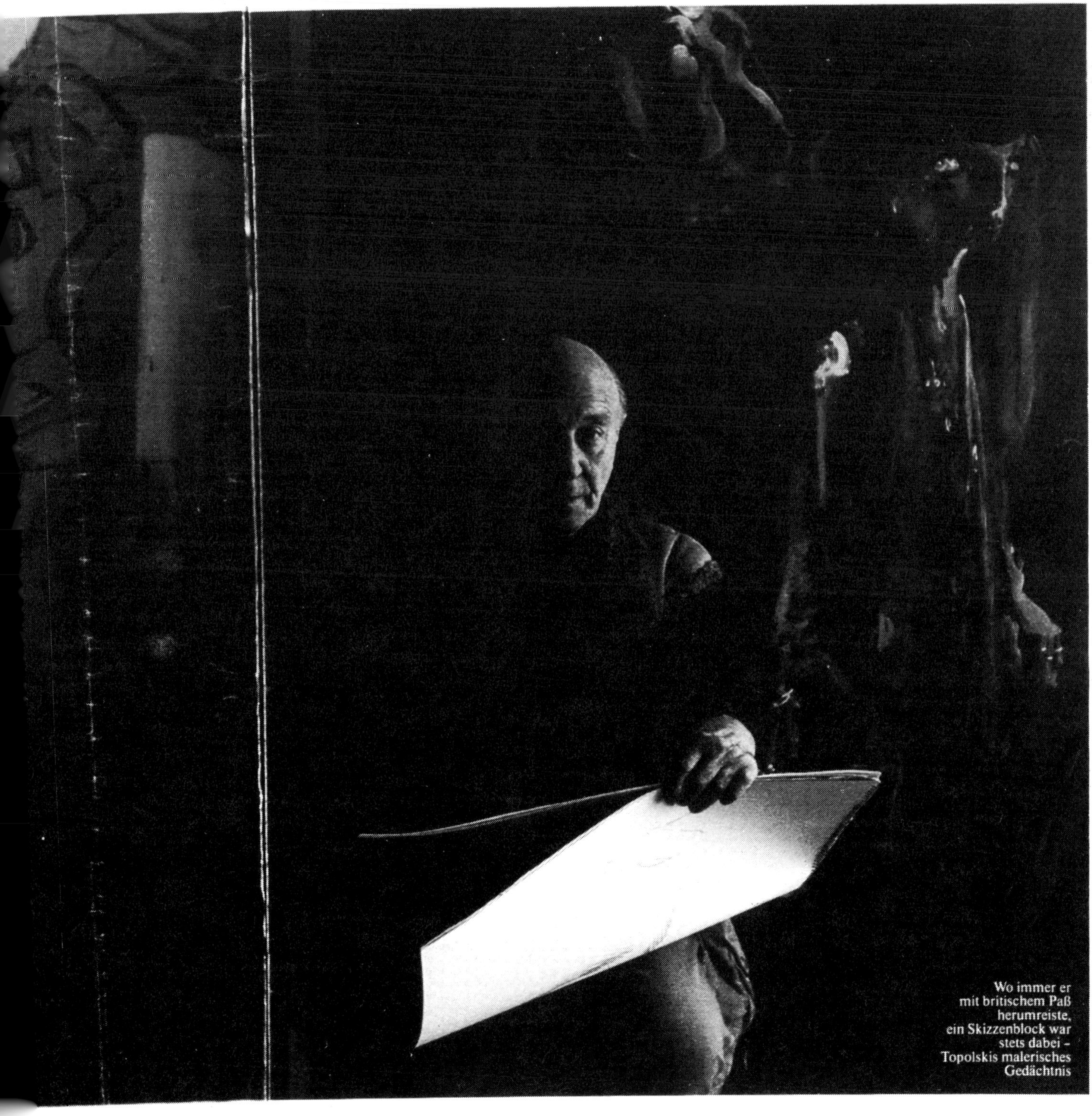

Pages from *Frankfurter Allgemeine Magazin*, 6 September 1985

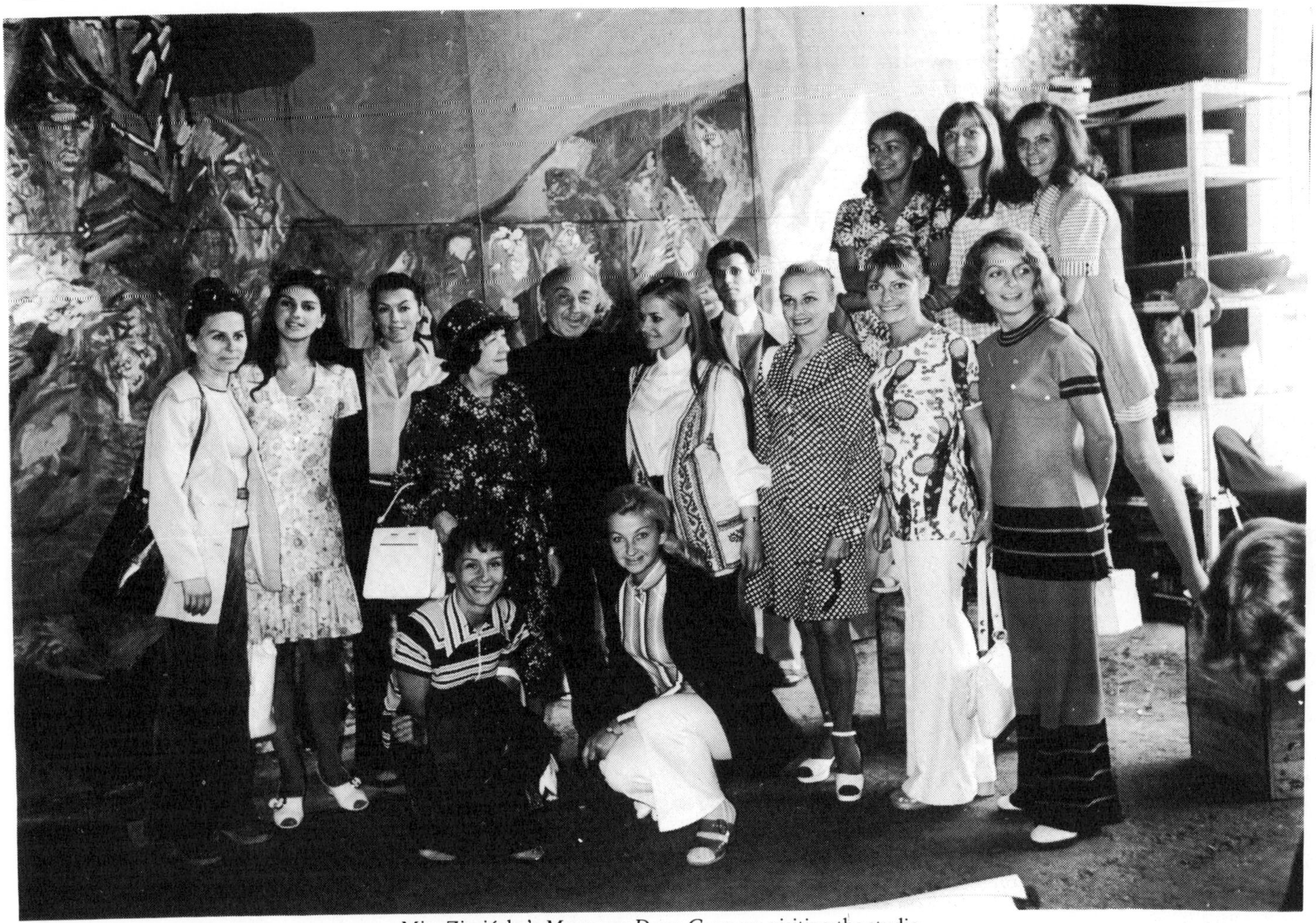

Mira Zimińska's *Mazowsze Dance Company* visiting the studio

Her first was asking for Marion – and, on being told that Marion died only a month or so ago, she, although held by visible timidity, took it as a blow, tightened in pain.

Yes, as it came out later and only in meek hesitant wording, this was a pilgrimage back to the glorified-by-memory year – Marion, the young and noble personification of it all.

This woman bracketed thirty-some years – the bulk of given-to-us time, started about then, having rolled by, with its promises, non-fulfilment, disintegrated – almost.

The rush of most distant beginnings, to clash incongruously against vaporous conclusions – because the whole cause and effect ballast rubbed out.

She must see the children, particularly Teresa. And her bottled-in vintage tenderness gushes out: she is precise about their ages, looks, baby-characters – she always trembled for Teresa's defencelessness. I tell her that the child's disadvantges in the face of the then bully-brother steeled her to fearlessness.

Within moments **Maria becomes important.** She goes to see Teresa, though her English non-existent: Teresa accepts the visit reluctantly – yet a miraculous joy rises between the two: she loves Teresa, Teresa gains a friend in Marion's memory; then they come to me and, without a trace of affectation, affection mounts – Teresa next morning takes her to Marion's grave.

All this contains at some point Daniel as well. Maria's emotional trust repays her richly.

But those thirty-some years were also hers.

This tale is filled up between her and me. She, a soldier, came to England and us, after the tragic dispersal of the Polish army in Italy and enforced interruption of her just-begun Economics studies. There was this young Italian artist and astronomer(!) in reserve, as it were; and, since her bad English would not support well her further studies in England, she escaped to Rome and marriage.

On the surface a happy ending, but, with three untender children and a lifetime with a man who ignored the family for his own concerns, she was defeated. And her memories of us: she meticulously watched, assessed our squabbles, suffered for Marion and the children; when, with us for a time separated (I remembered none of this), she would bring the children for every full Sunday to my studio, assured by Marion that the children need me and that I am really a good man.

And this up-down, restless, year-long, messily housed/divided married slice of life – parallel to her own, later – grew into her privately tended possession – thanks to Marion, apparently (to her) already a shining matriarch, and Teresa, the unblemished-yet innocence.

The average Poles, aged with me, come of late to claim closeness; even if adequate in mind and body, merely fit, in the years of German oppression, for being marshalled into passivity, victimization – perhaps surviving.

Yet there were some who stood up to death for shielding their Semitic and half-cast countrymen. Then the guerrillas . . .

And this summer, 1986, brings Jan Karski to my door.

I met him first and last in 1942–3?: he was then a modern warrior – pentathlon-modelled, not a hefty legendary knight, but ever on the leap – if necessary into self-immolation (once when caught he cut his wrists to escape self-betrayal under torture). There were such couriers, emissaries, crossing enemy lines by land and by air between London's Polish Government and their Underground Command.

But he was unique: he, a gentile, smuggled himself into the Warsaw ghetto; and, much more of a trap, the Bełżec extermination camp – to add eye-witnessing to the evidence of the documents which he was to carry across: his mission of proving to politically entangled, thus disbelieving leaders of the West that the systematic preplanned mass-murder of the Jewish race had begun, thus to set off world-wide defensive crusade.

In England he confronted Eden (Churchill would not see him), several Ministers, and Jewish influentials; in the States, Roosevelt *et al.* – to no avail.

Bathetically only in recent years he, now a professor at Georgetown University, is given the widest hearing in the States – and Israel.

Although compressed into modesty of professorial two-piece-and-tie, he, now even more unique, a hero-veteran thinned to the shape and features of holiness, speaks wisely and widely – the anticipated traumas-complexes of Polishness withered.

In my present world of, at the best, stoicism, his appearing even if also in the guise of a stoic, upsets my ill-balanced composure.

It was no surprise, when first adrift in Washington's indifference, at his finding in good Pola Nireńska, an itinerant dancer, a wife of comforting reassurance in her Polono-Jewishness.

I just read what a survivor of Oświęcim, Elie Wiesel, wrote of Karski: 'A brave man? Better: a just man.'

What follows happened and does happen repeatedly in **'influential circles'**. The titles/initials are true of that occasion; but the unpremeditated omission of full names, instinct-dictated, is right, as it lifts the record of a particular luncheon into a telling parable:

Flatly related Lord Forte's 'informal cellar luncheon', Caryl's illumination: **an anti-nuclear shelter!**

There – I had not realized it – the supposed 'cellar' coquetry, wine-racked sumptuousness, is the preview of tomorrow's everydayness of the mighty: this descent in a steel-upholstered lift – the only and prolonged insinuation into the depths – into this moles' fortress, fitted for feasting; and these bottle-bristling enclosing walls; and these glass-in-hand 'choice' men, elect for (ghastly) survival.

In retrospect (I owe it to Caryl) the function was an exercise in the sinister: the herding in between drink and food for the eight-minute film on the 800-million-pound (and ever-multiplying) Forte empire underlined the platitudinous stolidity of procedure. The Forte food was justly unemphatic, so that the effect of long-lasting underground existence was perfectly simulated within these two hours, with the langour of the infinite resulting in patience and amiable uniformity – the conditions essential for underground Ark-dwellers. The long table held the ring of passive busts, circled by the lackeys in slow motion. Then, with the coffee, the ritual articles of faith – the *Credo*.

15th June 1982
Cafe Royal, Cellars

MR ROCCO FORTE	MR WILLIAM ARMSTRONG
MR ALAN WHEATLEY	~~MR L. ROSSO~~
SIR JAMES CARRERAS	MR CLIVE CLARK
FELIX TOPOLSKI	The Rt. Hon. ALAN HARE
MR. ANDREW FAULDS, MP	LORD DENHAM
GENERAL SIR JOHN HACKETT	H.E. The Portuguese Ambassador, Sn. J. DE FREITAS-CRUZ
LORD FORTE	The Rt. Hon LORD THORNEYCROFT
The Rt. Hon. LORD CARRINGTON	His Grace, THE DUKE OF WELLINGTON
LORD GARMOYLE	LORD GEORGE BROWN
MR KENNETH FLEET	~~SIR DENIS MOUNTAIN~~
MR E. HARTWELL	LORD DELFONT of STEPNEY
MR ANTHONY STAFFORD	MR ROBIN COMPTON
MR CHIANDETTI	DoTT. V. SCHIAZZANO

MR J. PETERSEN

Lord Forte's cellar luncheon guest list

One after another the speakers murmured (audibility not needed as their *status quo* texts were choral and known): The Rt Hon. Lord T. of the Right, as demi-host, also praising/blessing the deserving amongst us; the Hon. Lord George B. of the Left muttering his consent; General Sir John H. in accord, with witty adornments; the Hon. Alan H. offering his City confirmation; and the Rt Hon. Lord C. mumbling the expected.

His Grace the Duke of W. pink-facedly and gracefully kept silent; and so did Andrew F. MP because his views might not have been compatible (he had recently been sent out of the House by the Speaker); and Lord F. and Lord G. and the two Lords D. and Sir James C. and HE the Portuguese Ambassador Sn J. de F. and Dott. V. S. of the Italian Chamber of Commerce and Mr Robin C., Chairman of Time-Life International, and Mr F. T., Artist – because the *word* was in no need of further confirmation.

These, presumably, are on the list to be saved at Armageddon – men only.

The ruling classes' invigoration, before our time, by genetic cross-hatching with American heiresses and chorus girls, is now effected by **flamboyant Manchester** (via Oxbridge) **boys**; not through bedroom progeniture but through pace-acceleration.

The unruly yet phlegmatic tendencies of the aristo-dandies got a boost from this admixture. From my observing standpoint this – both gutsy and shrewd – penetration originated with **Baron** (his Christian name turned *nom-de-guerre*) Nahum. He chose to be a dashing 'social' photographer, thus blockbustering high-and-wide: his real charm and enthusiasm given to connecting – seductive. This enthusiasm gave a certain fillip to a lot of my English/London life. War service cost him his arm but did not diminish his living-fervour – perhaps overtaxed, he died suddenly; unless the death of his well-loved twin-brother brought this about. His stoic joy-message, carried unfalteringly through the war, may then have lost its *raison-d'être*.

Then came on the scene his Manchester nephew, **Anthony Blond** – his replacement, even better equipped for the same energizing mission with his manner-schooling of 'classiness' – and more. His medium, well trodden, 'gentlemanly' publishing, but evolved, as his life, extravagantly. He can, without causing any ripples on the dignified surface of the profession, leap from one self-created 'house' to another (partnerships/logos changed), from one way of life to another. He would one day inveigle from my studio, with a wink, a young black painter – and at another time hold a faultlessly elegant dinner party at his conventionally pretty **Belgravia house** (but overflooded with Indian village-paintings, trophies of a recent trip – for sale) – his hostess a lovely little Lady something, his wife to be. Unconventional within conventions, they would wed in Ceylon, the guests flown in from the West.

Last night (14 October 1984), he held a party on publication of a book on the Beatles under a new imprint and at his newest surprise home.

My love of the dockland, sparked on my first, up-river, arrival in London, made me roam the river-overhanging warehouses north-and-south in search of an ideal architectural frame (as I always saw it) for settling in. I was, as uncomfortably often, too far ahead: it was impossible then to trace the suspicious and unwilling landlords of abandoned beauties or to bypass the blankness of 'condemned' decisions and official indecisions; one, eventually cornered, was fenced with crippling restrictions at £17,000 – at that time greatly above my means. It was a soaring crane-jutting sooty beauty thick of blackened brick and hefty beams, open on every one of some five/six levels to majesties of the river, Tower Bridge and floating craft.

Now **dockland conversions** lead the home-fashion and Anthony is there at the acceptable moment, though in an immense storage block, not quite on the Thames.

Five storeys' breath-choking climb up narrow-industrial-metal-steep stairs (the new lift out of order) and there: low-deep-bricky-gutted-ungainly spaces thickly stacked with shadowy humans – Anthony's vast accumulation, as far as perceivable, of: the low – the high, the brainy – the shapely, the oldest – the youngest, the leisurely – the professional, the freelance – the salaried, the on-the-make – the powerful, the present – the have-beens. . .

The murky crowd, undaunted by (or broken in to) this future-spelling austerity vacillates out-of/into shadows, out-of/into brutal streaks of the few bare bulbs' glare; for me it is dipping and surfacing, it is blundering from one pool of light to another, from one inconsequentially revealed-as-known, or puzzlingly not-quite-familiar face to another emerging suspended momentarily, dateless (age forcing some still further into a bad-dream domain) to fall into the mire of the forgotten.

Am I tired beyond alertness? Am I, within this old-bricked blankness, mesmerized by this out-of-place out-of-logic simultaneous **congesting** of many of my (parallel to Anthony's) long life's encounters?

All right when I come upon Jerome Burne of *Time Out* with Polly Toynbee – my bubbling about her father, Philip, and her response not hooking on to one another (the echoing din), facial beamings notwithstanding; all right when I move to a ginger-pigtailed little Irish-Guinness squire, Gareth Browne, with, from both of us: 'We meet in incongruous circumstances.' Even when Kingsley Amis's outline traces a tentative bee-line at me. But then the mix-up at one go of fifty years of 'social betters': the gums-teeth large woman bends over me, horsing about my non-ageing; and three more elongated faces form a choral to intone on this theme – all apparently well set in my past, but closed to me. Then, the sadness of it, a Mayfairite caryatid, who once set me atremble with desire; a brave but failed restoration job; the ancient and sole refrain of ours revived unavoidably: 'I'm lunching tomorrow with Annabelle'; 'Give her my love' etc. . . . There is Charlie, disrupting the uniformity, bulging, Henry-the-VIII-bearded and proud of the likeness, a recent acquisition of mine; but back to the enfeebled past: another well-ankled *passé* person insists on intimacy and on leading me to a long parasoled she-grandee with a man matching her height and costume-distinction: 'We've just been talking about France

. . .' to which I: 'What made you come to this warehouse to talk about France?'; 'Curiosity.' Then the everywhere-present Guardee Michael Alexander of the sixties Chelsea set, leading a blondie facelessly silhouetted against the blinding spot of light – she insists that long ago I asked to paint her; would I now? She wants to reinstate our unconsummated connection of the past, of which I have no recollections and no present stirrings. Then a bearded everyman of the Albert Hall poetry days – not remembered. Then Ed Victor, now an imposingly whiskered grand agent, late of shoestring *INK*. And in the midroom, kisses from another couture-chic unremembered 'close' friend; and still another. They multiply; they culminate into a mixed pantomiming-metaphor – (I much in on the act) on the themes of generation/class-passing, their stubborn futility embattled to-the-end; and above all of the expectation of **the universal threat**.

A link/precedence: not long before, Lord Forte's lunch-gathering for the country's supremos (why me there?) – the luxury at ease in the long-lift-descent depths (underground nuclear shelter?) under the Café Royal. Blond's forward instinct paces the same way: designers' frilly interiors expected to become shambles, the gracious life must move, undiminished, into unadorned shelters. So this is a successful dress rehearsal (how pitiful) for carrying on beneath the surface-disaster: glass-in-hand, small-talk, 'How-well-you-look', transferred into grimness without a hair turned. And the theme of the occasion is comfortably just-*passé*: the Beatles – and the guests (significantly the upper strata prevailing) are also faded, though packed into the future, though a rock band in the corner tries to boost up the morale . . .

Teresa, my Beatrice – the superior outsider to this purgatorial hollowness – leads me out. Yet accosted once more – properly, to ease re-entering the present – by a youthful-pretty serving wine around the place, a schoolgirl in fact: 'I came to your studio the other day with Abigail – she's working on her 'A' levels now – chars for a pop group . . .'.

Marriages are conquests. This hinged differently. This found its strength elsewhere. The year is easy to spot – the all-vital studio wrenched from me and smashed, leaving the Regent's Park Nash edifice, a mad choice, a Taj Mahal, a monument to Marion the mother, nonsensically useless for a painter. **A mucky sculptor's shed** borrowed for a roof over doubtful-to-come inspirations – the concrete floor's centre given a camping mattress cum blanket: the true necessity.

Caribbean dancers arrived in London: a colossal folk-troupe evolved by foreigners, as often the case, an older-than-me Warsaw acquaintance, and an American girl. But all this only sets the stage for my entering their London lodgings, the Pole fussing in narrow untidiness of unpacking round the bed, on which squatted **a fantasy-come-to-life girl**, bare legs held by the arms, back cushioned against the wall – the whole folded up with the ease of a flamingo, the body-and-face detailing – the subtlest.

That evening, the company held a loud-and-fast-rhythms party, and, throughout, the oblong girl towering, with me in lower being's adoration, stamped/swayed at each other in courting premonition. In silence they left, in silence they reached his hired lair, in silence they bared themselves to deep murkiness and, no self-consciousness in this primeval encounter, but in the nature of things, he went worshipfully down at the feet of this erect masterpiece. The act of possession/submission does not stay in memory, perhaps because of my compulsive, levelling-out, non-stop promiscuity.

That short-lived lair held an uninterrupted chain of encounters – a black dancer, only days later (remembered blackness round the flaring pink of her cavity – and my failure); an English white (skin) red (hair) equivalent to Greek Hera models, this remembered as one of my – and her – greatest nights, never equalled, though perpetuated with variations of numbers and set-ups for years; and, in contrast, a dark Welsh speedy-limbed Artemis; and Indian – spared; a Polish countess (her mother though a theatrical bombshell).

The American had left, but at one time she stayed in London for a while with another American girl: a punting expedition on the Thames crowned by her flights/dives from the high barges – and loving. Yet, when she went away, I bedded her friend.

As with my life's other solemn segment, all this did not encroach on my special devotion – given to long pauses, but rooted well. There was a harmonious stretch in New York; and, later, she and her husband living in Dublin, but her marriage cracking, we would meet in London. Until our tightening closeness demanded a step forward: she came to London to stay with me as a marriage try-out. On the first evening we sat on my studio doorstep, in bliss; then a blissful night. Next day, a modicum of anxiety entered – exclusions, replacements, were not for me, and, when she went out for a few hours, a note of **relief** replaced intensity.

We understood each other to a fault – we settled to lasting attachment without, not within, bounds. She moved to the States and tested 'glamour', but, a car (or was it an air?) accident (the battlefields of the rich) prompting, she made her ultimate move. With her in London, we continued to be unbinding lovers, yet much more: she emerged as a fully inspired playwright, a profound being, and in continuity a loyal friend. My earlier adoration of her form became all-embracing **admiration**. Our intimacy settled into mutual respect in friendship. And there was for her also a settled home.

It has become a ritual (of how many? thirty years?) of bodies and minds in embrace, at intervals but never ceased, confirmatory and in accumulation progress. Her plays, ever-astonishing, born in a high pitch of inventiveness, one after another, jetted into the cold space of indifference – I merging my meticulous reading of them, scene after scene, brought by her as they emerged, and vocalizing, as was her need, my minutest, however tentative/slight receptivities; and I could trust, equally, her responses to my work and problems. But the outrage of the impassable barrier laid against her creations being realized in the theatre!

She would enter, precede me, but turning her face to me in greeting grace, simultaneously her height achieving in those few steps the ease of longsome advance, the shoulders rounded for intimacy, the narrowest legs, rising up from unparalleled ankles, for directness. All this unchanged by a lifetime of years, except for her toes grown clawy to sustain this elevation, and the skin slackened over the durable slimness, which in a few weeks, when stricken by the brain tumour, trephined and tortured by treatments, became fleshless thinness. Her last at my studio: she uncovered her tormented body, took off a headscarf, revealing the shaven – a red scar to the side – skull, and there stood before me this ultimate medieval *memento mori* finality – and culmination, when, prone now, I laid on top of her, thus our failed bodies becoming merged in a reverential offertorium.

After that, only a telephone call bringing her gratitude, the voice fading away.

I don't think what follows is treachery/bad faith, but the innate contrariety steeled in my youth by the code of the anarchic faith: the principle of a-sentimentality. Detection of encroachment of it instantly/instinctively countered. Thus non-commitment, guarded/defended, became a self-denying virtue. And, conversely, I am weakened, irresolute, defeated, when cornered by convention's **guilt-pressures**.

I was compelled to put all this down, and so, my contrariety alerted, proceeded to soil its threatening clean nobility. A recent bigger than life and unfinished nude of a girl (unfinished because of the cold which sent her under blankets) was marked by an uncanny likeness to my American lover when young. I could not resist this spoliation: the girl's hair was dark so I lightened it, and, not only painted into the composition the other tormented nude as seen by me at her end, but also told the girl – pressing for my completing the picture of her – all.

The influx of faces/names/events cannot stop – this book's **finity is an imposition.** But the eye witness's urge may be naturally drying out, thus marking **this life's limitations.** Myself of the near past would fidget/press (this is the beginning of 1985) to be at the Sudan/Ethiopia border; perhaps in Cambodia or Afghanistan or Nicaragua; at Indira's post-mortem . . . though less, or not at all, at the Falklands skirmish; in cross-road China; in the Reagan-adulatory US and at New York art-marketing; or even in Solidarność-split Poland.

No good to embark on trying to establish whether the 'themes' of today, or my slowing down, account for this demise. Whichever, this closes the book more firmly than the publisher's date-line.

But now, April's weeding-time. The senility and deaths of the older than I were expected; those of the younger (Clement's, Michael's) are malevolent or sacrificial calamities.

And, generationally confused, I did not link my encroaching encripplement with my contemporaries' deaths, such as of the nearest to me, Marek, absorbed till the last in headstands and ever-rampant eroticism.

But Marion's terrible deterioration, a shock after years of not seeing her: first at her new home (where she read attentively and approved my chapter on her), then my dutiful stays at her hospital bedside, lulled defeated by those alien immobile bone-stretched features, shut-eyed open-mouthed – absented; and then each time, when startlingly alerted by my stirring to leave, this deadness cracks open to take me in – an astonishing eye-and-smile noose/bondage – to no-escape togetherness?

The consecutive funerals of these two – incorrigibly/foolishly I stand my ground – came the closest to my open-ended *Memoir* concept of being 'cut short only by nature's will', thus also to a pretext for ending this written version . . .

Teresa takes me to Marion's grave. The muddy shivering forest of rockery rises/lowers in united discords: marble vanities provoke more attention than Portland stones.

But Marion's, still a clumpy and thus tender outline (a small pot of greenery just now being set in by Teresa and two-sticks' cross – Daniel's doing) most strangely landscaped round by, black-marble-regimented in faithful-unbending formations, the Poles, almost solely the old-age defeated officers of the Polish exiled forces, carried in deep ranks into the eternity of patriotic readiness.

And all this past agitation, now arrested into silence, with, oddly, an Anglo-Irish and declared leftist Marion, as if in the lead, confronts (only one step across a path) large and high-lifted full-square Karl Marx. Only he matters for the stream of gapers and faithfuls pilgrimaging to him, their backs to his disciple Marion and the defenders of old Poland.

My instant action-draughtsmanship (a roving eye to selectivity to seismographic line on paper) – supposedly, when pure (that is unhampered by aesthetic trimmings), a rarity; supposedly firmly 'creative' as against photography-enslavement – began to lose ground. Also the nourishing remoteness is gulped out.

The avalanche of apparatuses, high-paid widest-distributed, ever ready to click the fleeting, less-and-less predictable-visible incidents, valid (no more need for confrontation) by unpredictability. Armies, mass-conflicts replaced by push-button explosions, kamikaze hits, assassinations, hostage-snatches . . . A sudden inflammation, a pile of crashed metal, a blurred bleeding back of a head stand by their location-date captions – the fastest draughtsman will never attend this factuality.

Even so, if by a miracle witnessing/involved, the facts of 'action' register by their triviality within the matter-of-fact indifference.

Perhaps my receding gifts interlock with the world of unostentatious modernized anarchist.

Post scriptum

Slowing down days – thus attention-brewing. Slower stepping, hesitant at puddles, stopping at pavements' unevennesses – pretexts to catch breath but more a vista of dossers, of chugging tugboats, or a girl's full measure – in the past neglectfully hurried by. Minutiae revealed and relished at the welcome neglect of wider sweeps.

Yesterday: my studio: I wade on to the nature-like (thirty-three years' layered) paper-hillscape paper-cascading, its vulnerability in repose under the morning light. Krystyna, poetess-printer, comes with some proofs and pours out the rapid salt-and-pepper dose, in our native tongue-idiom, of the

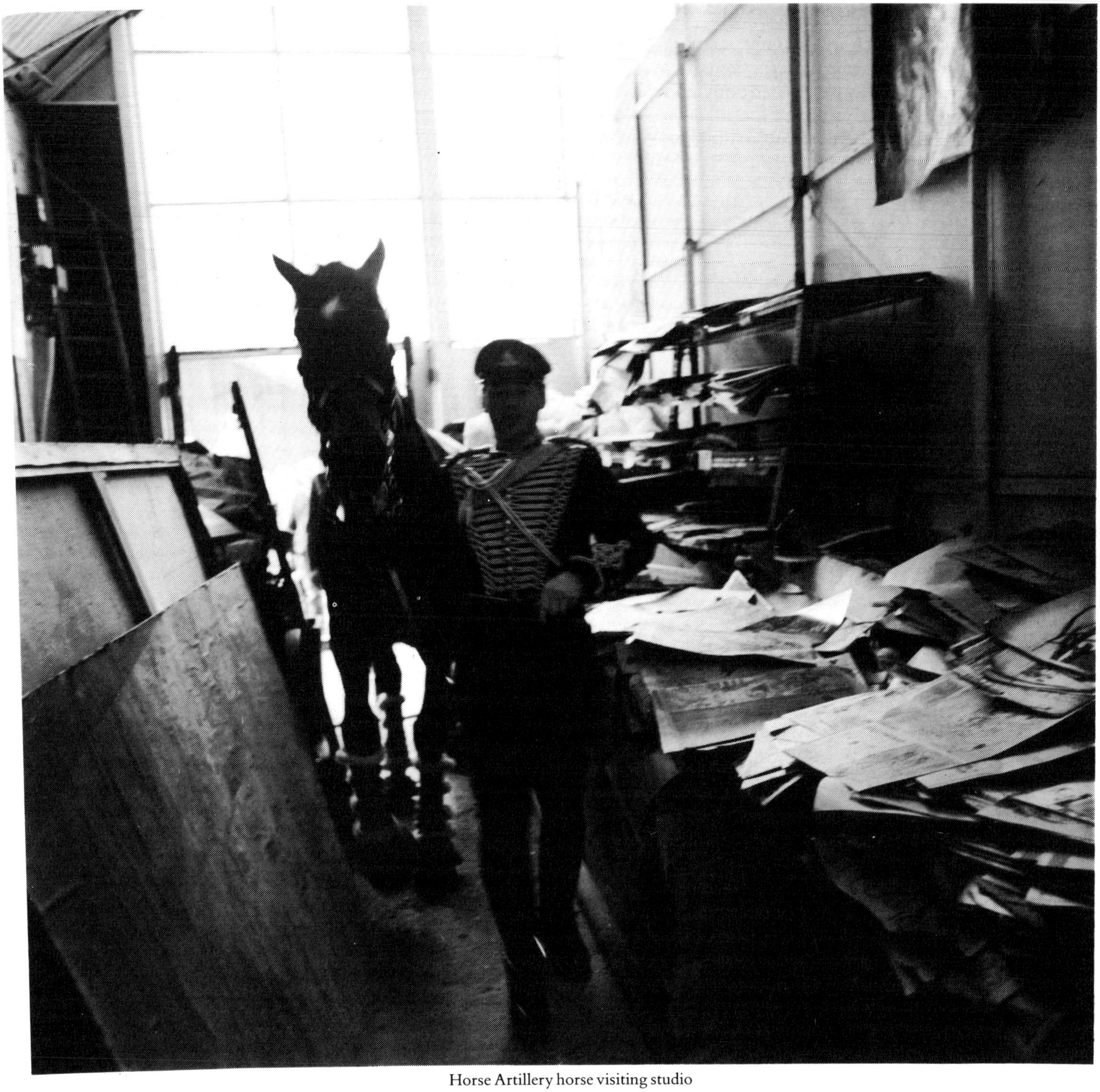

Horse Artillery horse visiting studio

latest worldwide Polishness. Afterwards, calm – effortless slight pleasures at touching up a rot-damaged *Arturo Ui* painting.

The end-of-the-day strong arm of my wife; the back-number comfort amongst gallery girls plotting her exhibition (her modesty), watchful of their diversities, of the changes imposed by years on their familiar looks (and costuming); but also of the background pretty busyness of a Nigerian kinetic artist activating, hammer-and-wires, her gesturing winged figures.

Our drive-search for the polluted Diorama; my richly adorned pee over the rubble (eyes awander): the blissful little drizzle, an imposing Industrial Revolution façade, now blinded but erect; an inconclusive fence being painted by a graceful-dancing young man – an umbrella in his left hand; the extinguished basement behind me – but in one of its windows there group and labour under out-dated light a cluster of arts-crafts youngsters.

The Diorama, an old glory disfigured by early developers, just about blotted out by the bitty smartness (of false Regency and Lasdun's sleekness) and speed (of the arterial inconsequences), gives us glimpses of a touching squat sub-culture. Lovely keen dust-paint camouflaged boys toss about old Diorama plans, wish to bring it back to life. I, ever a panorama addict and doer, and having read this morning about the Polish 1890s 'Racławice Panorama' having been rescued and reinstated in a new rotund edifice, love them. . .

The midnight slice of an erratic Godard on television

moves me with the glimpses, masterly explorations of his *tableaux vivants* staged out of Old Masters' great paintings; the arrested turns of heads, the tacit profiles; the ancient colours/crushed folds/lengths of brocades as pedestals to the Olympian torsos. Great creations, an impact of rarity, this gift at the end of an almost retired's day.

MEMOIR OF THE CENTURY

Sections and details

Photographs by Amanda Saunders and Marcus Harrison

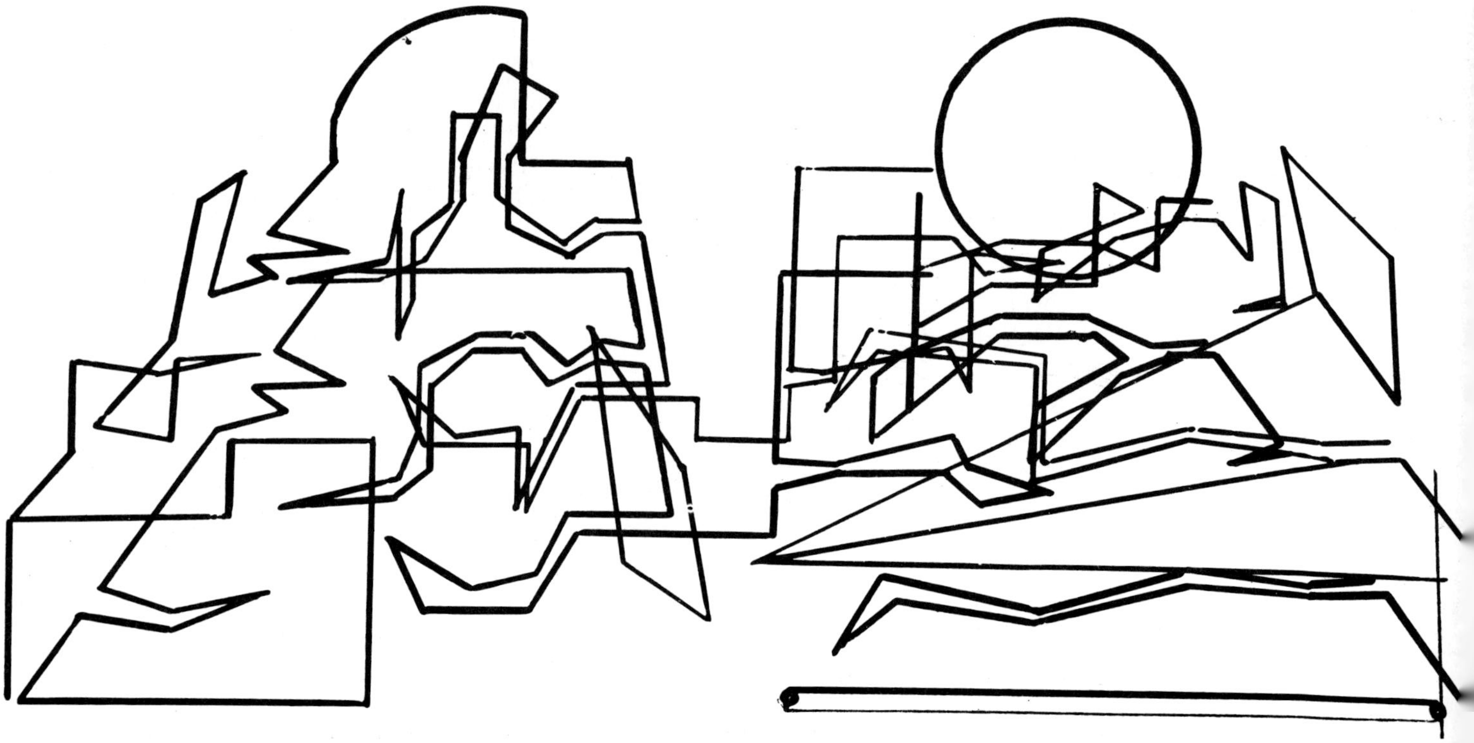

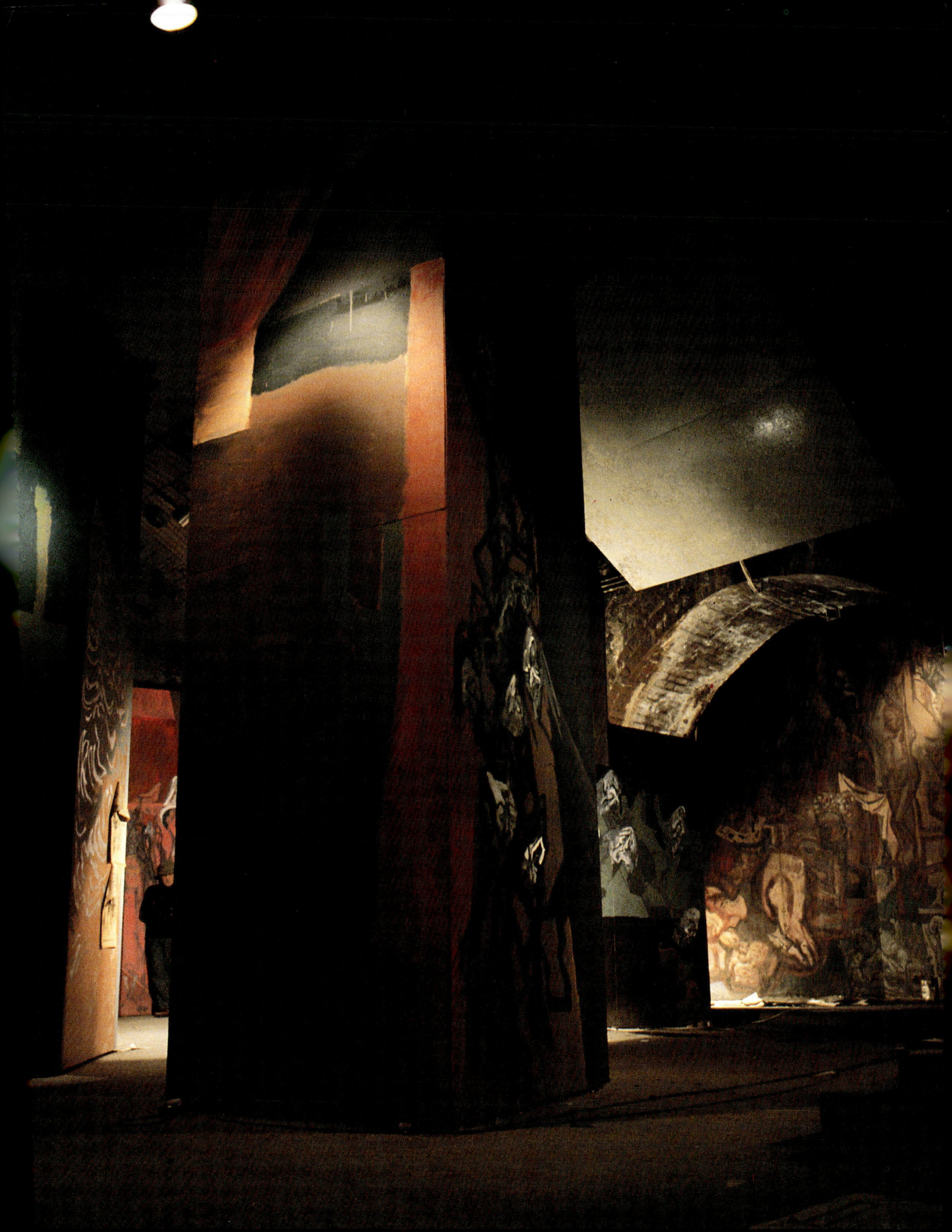

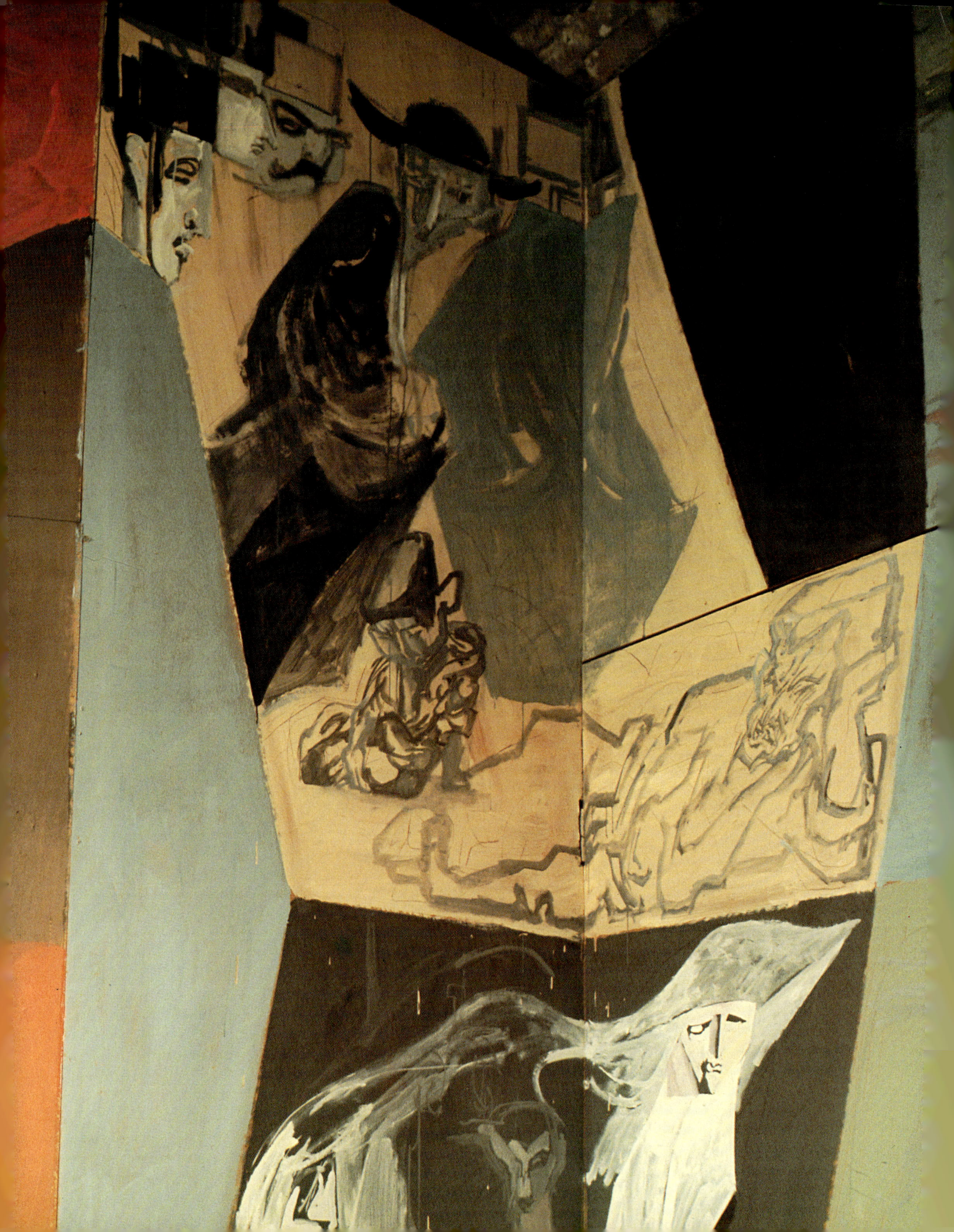

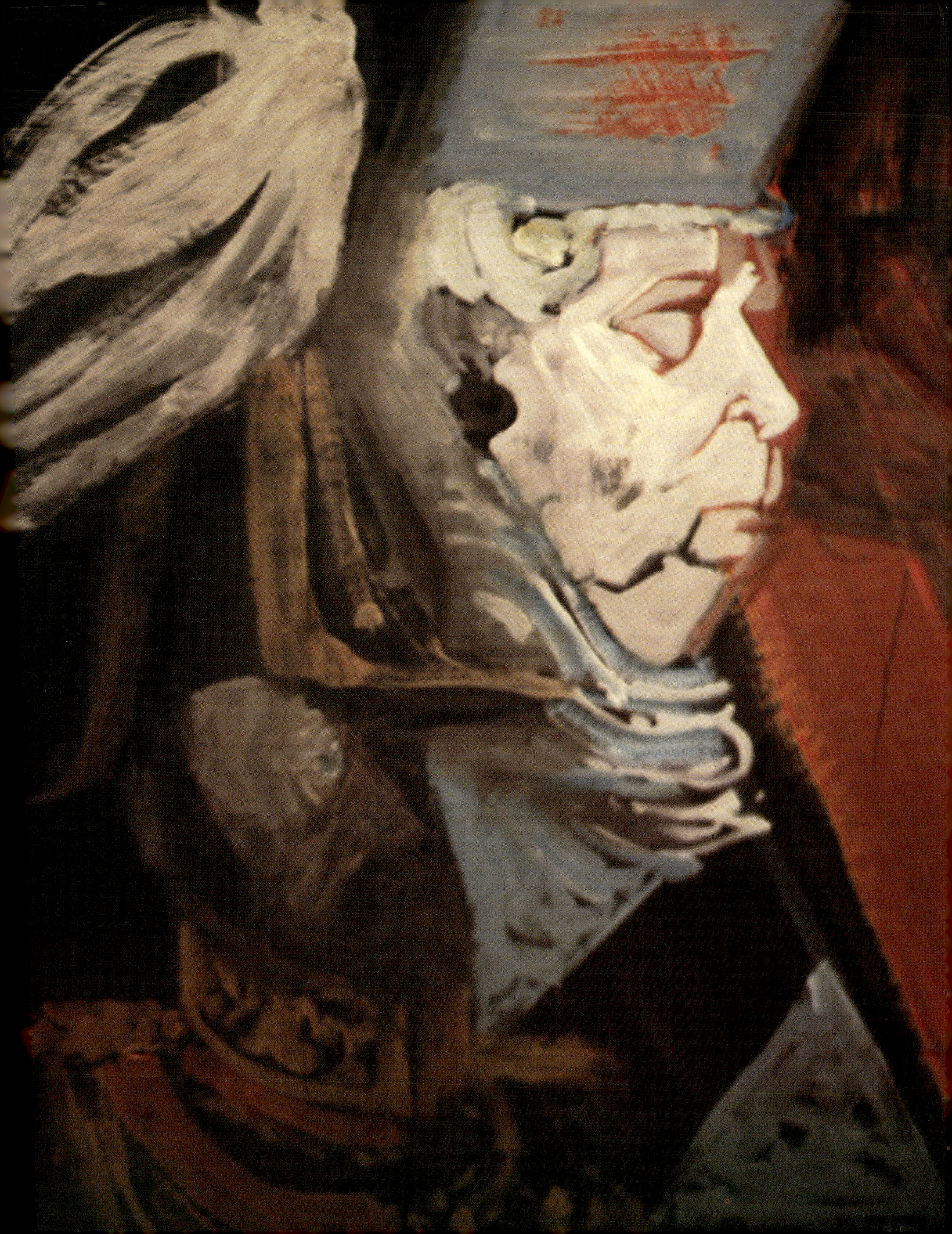

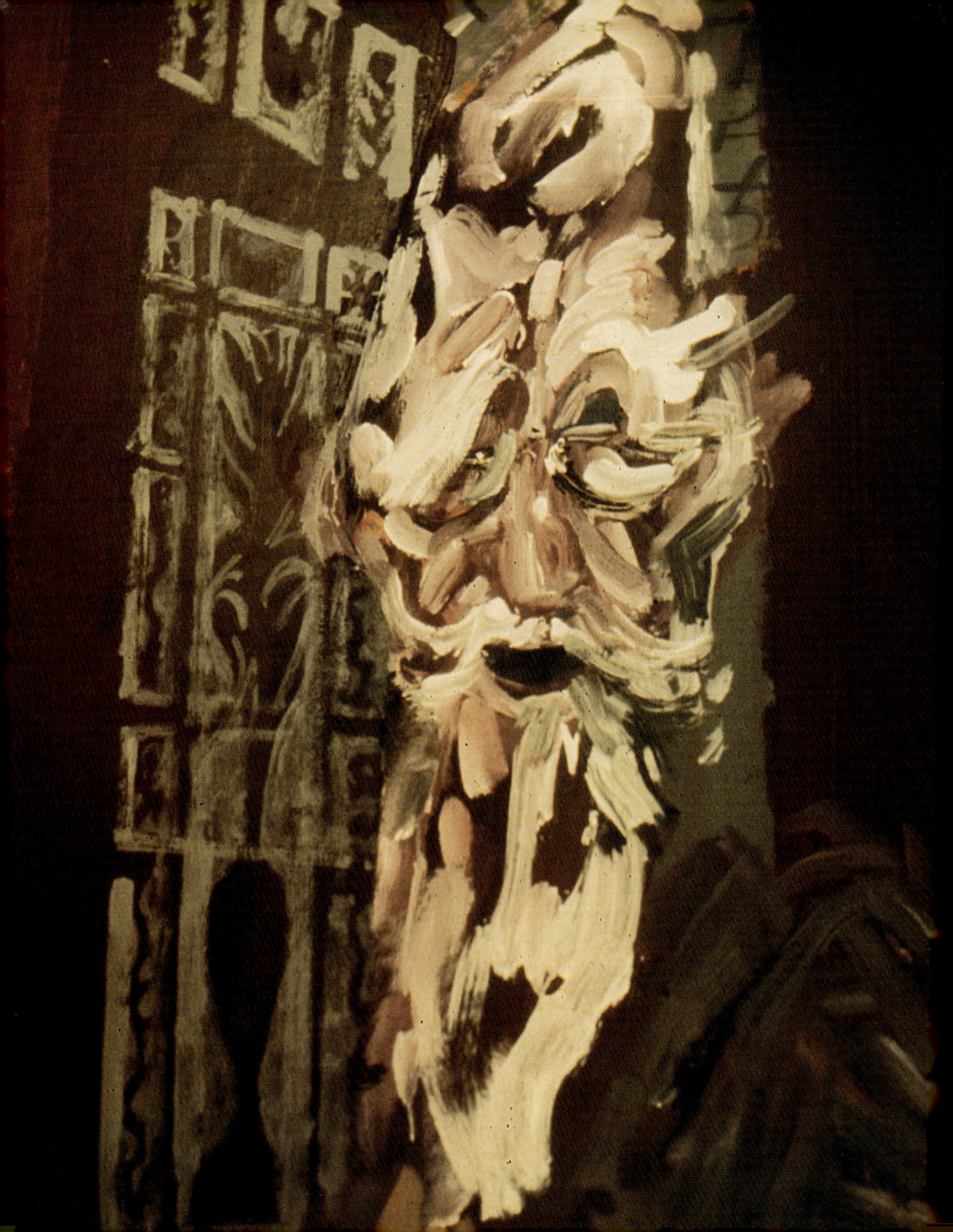

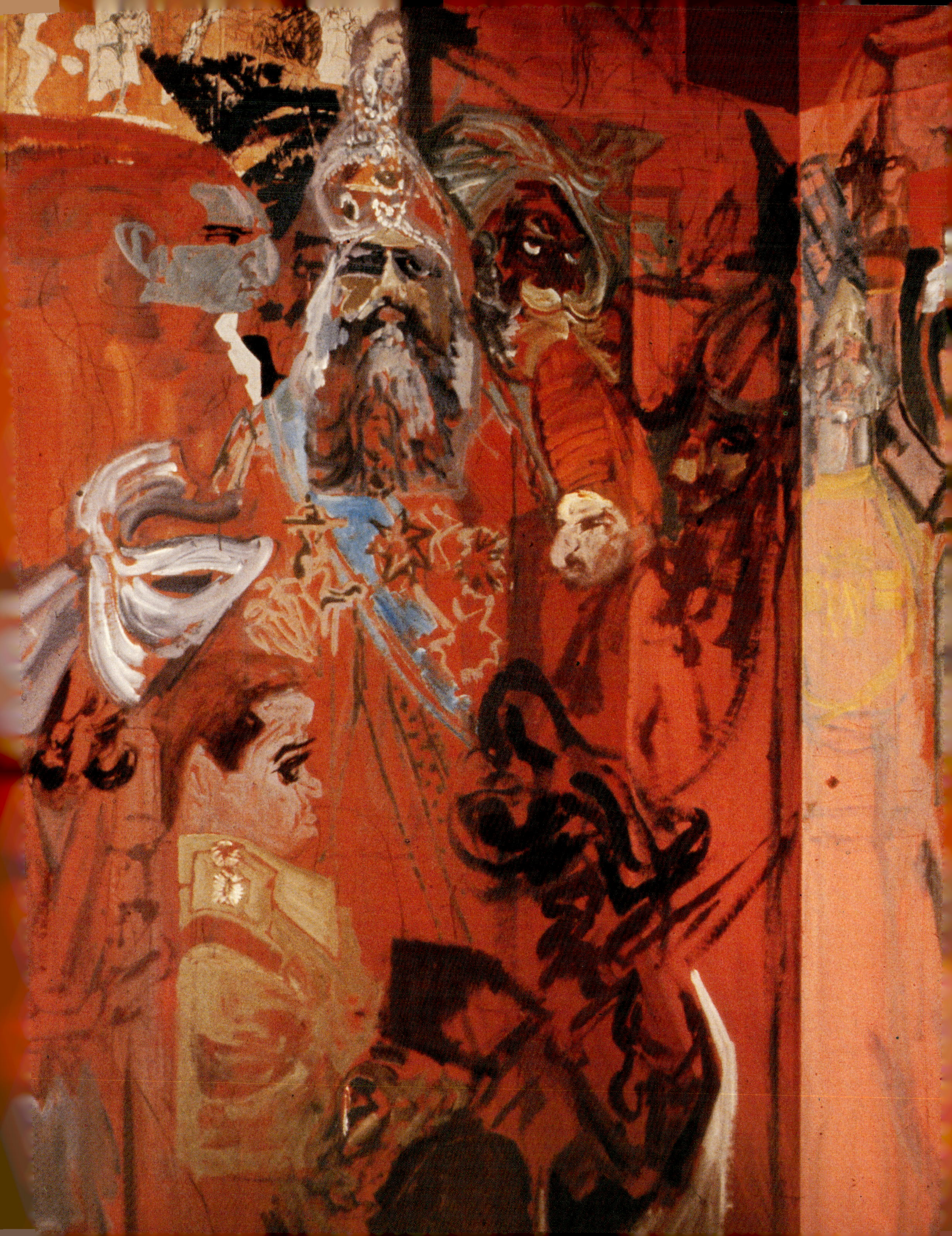

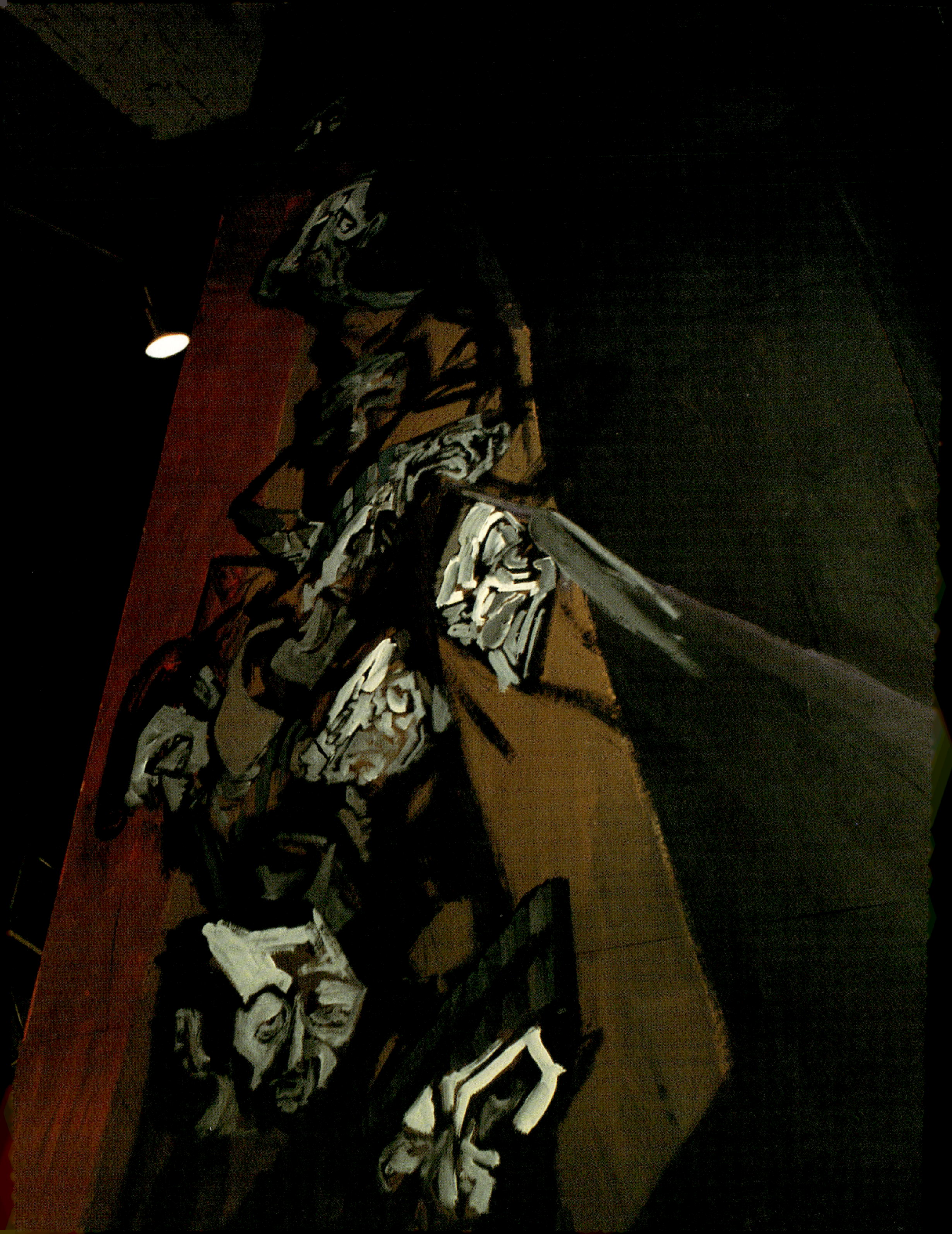

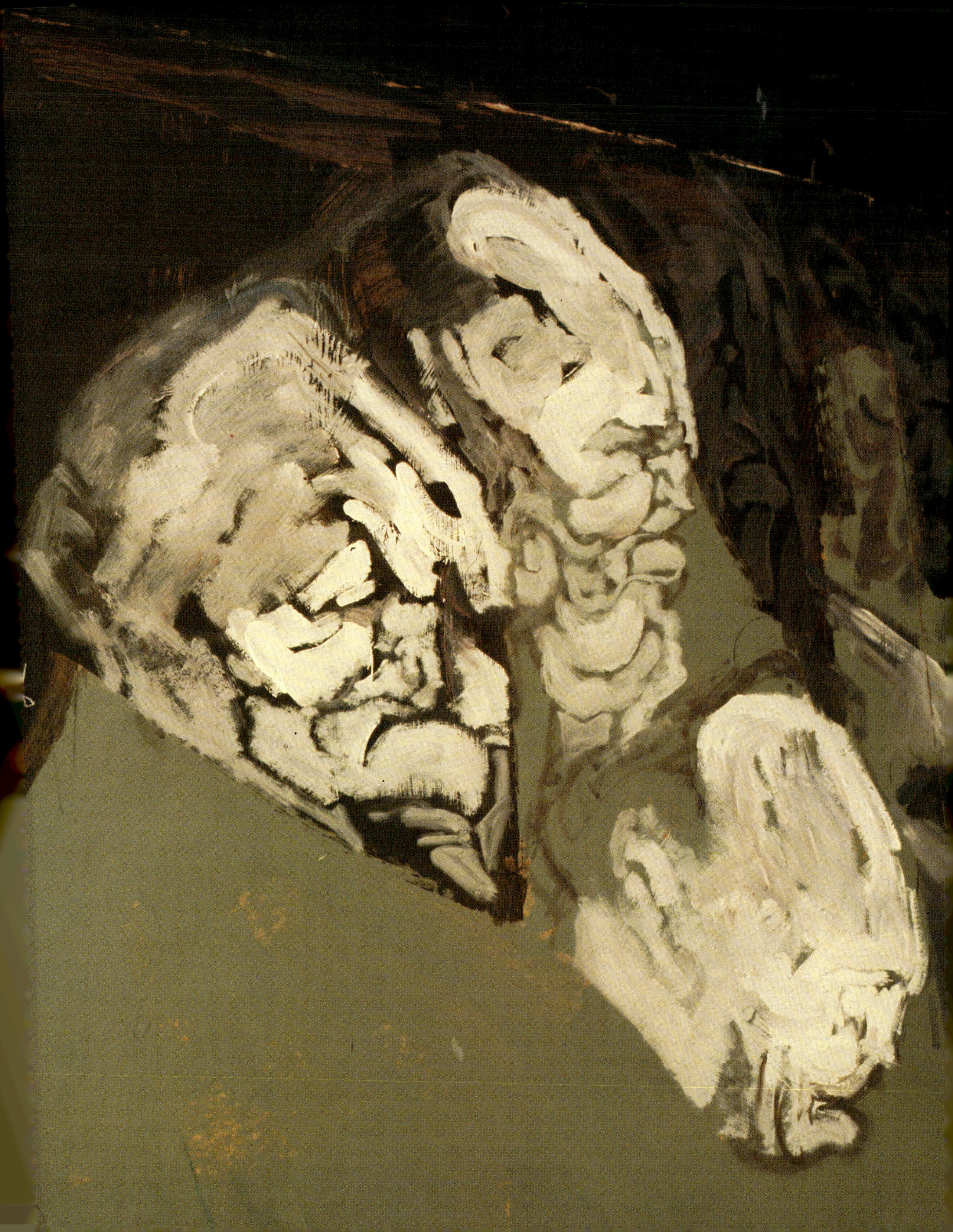

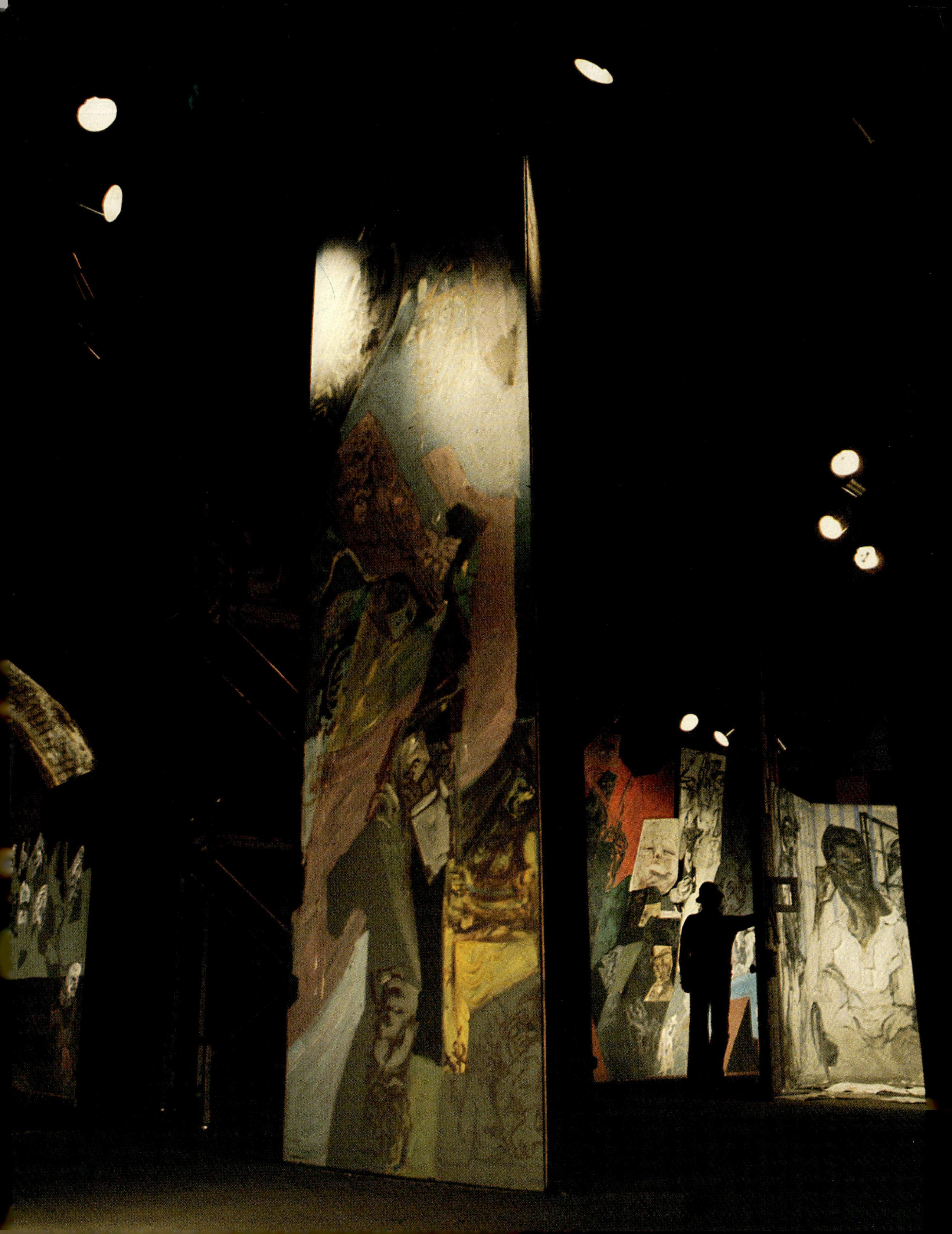

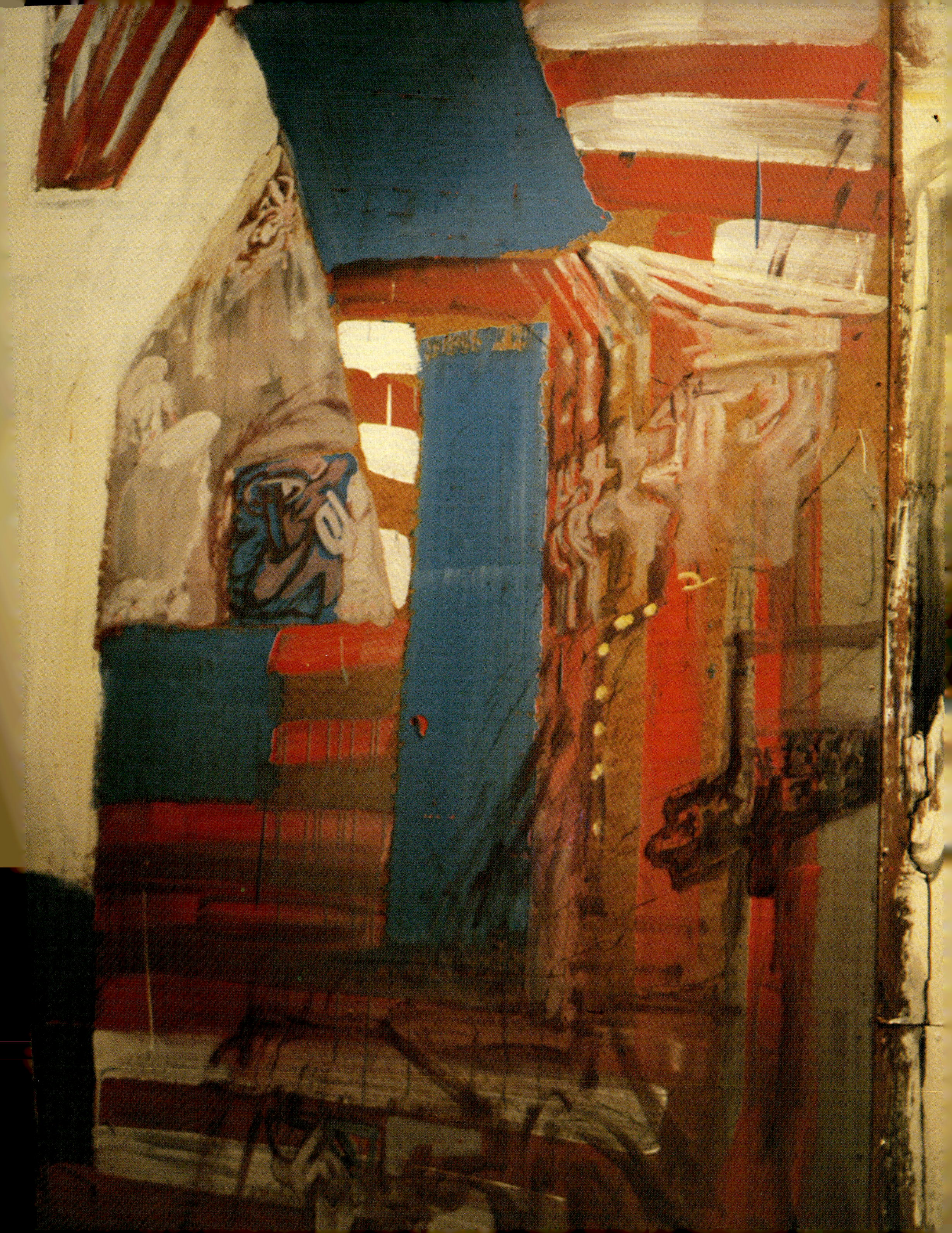

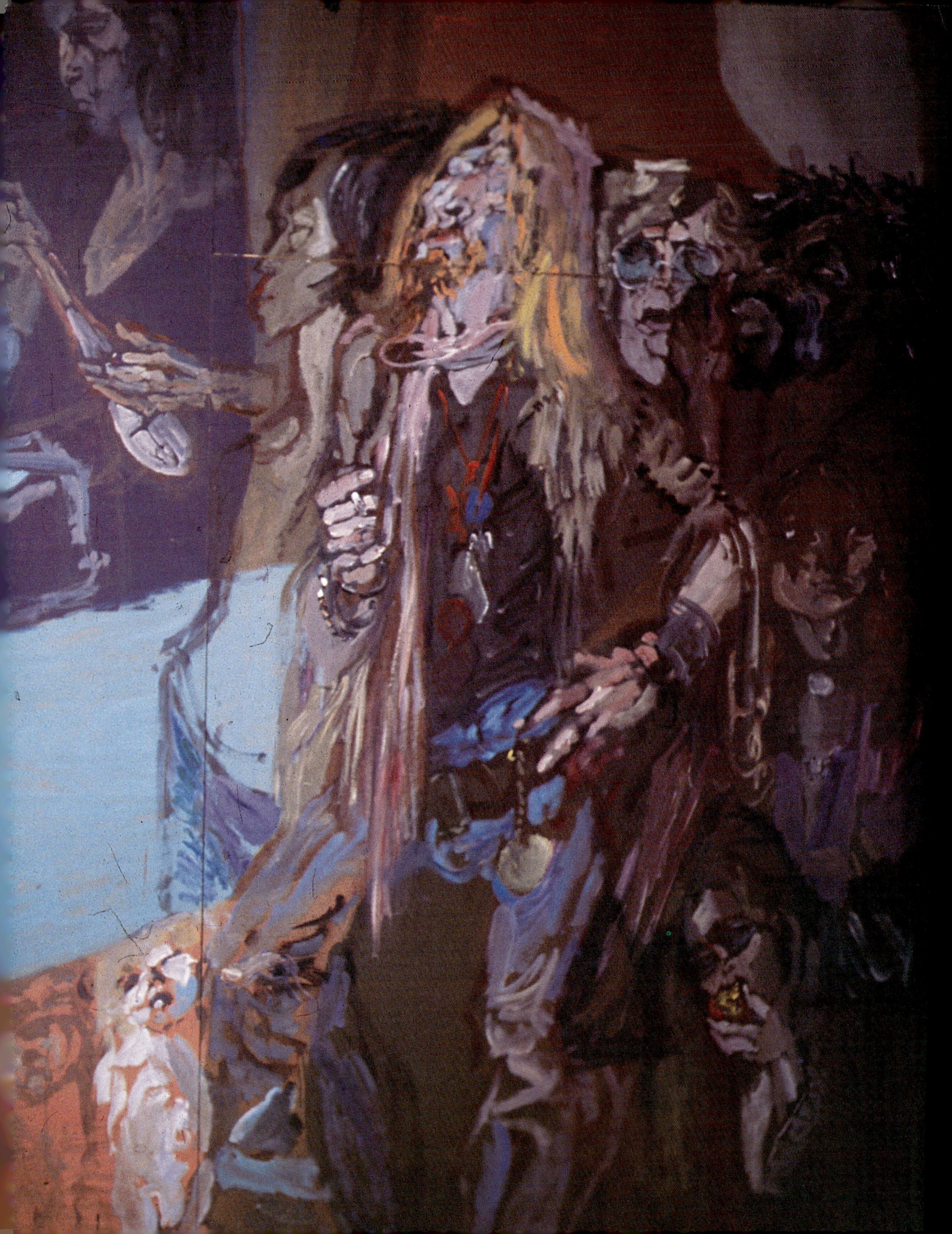

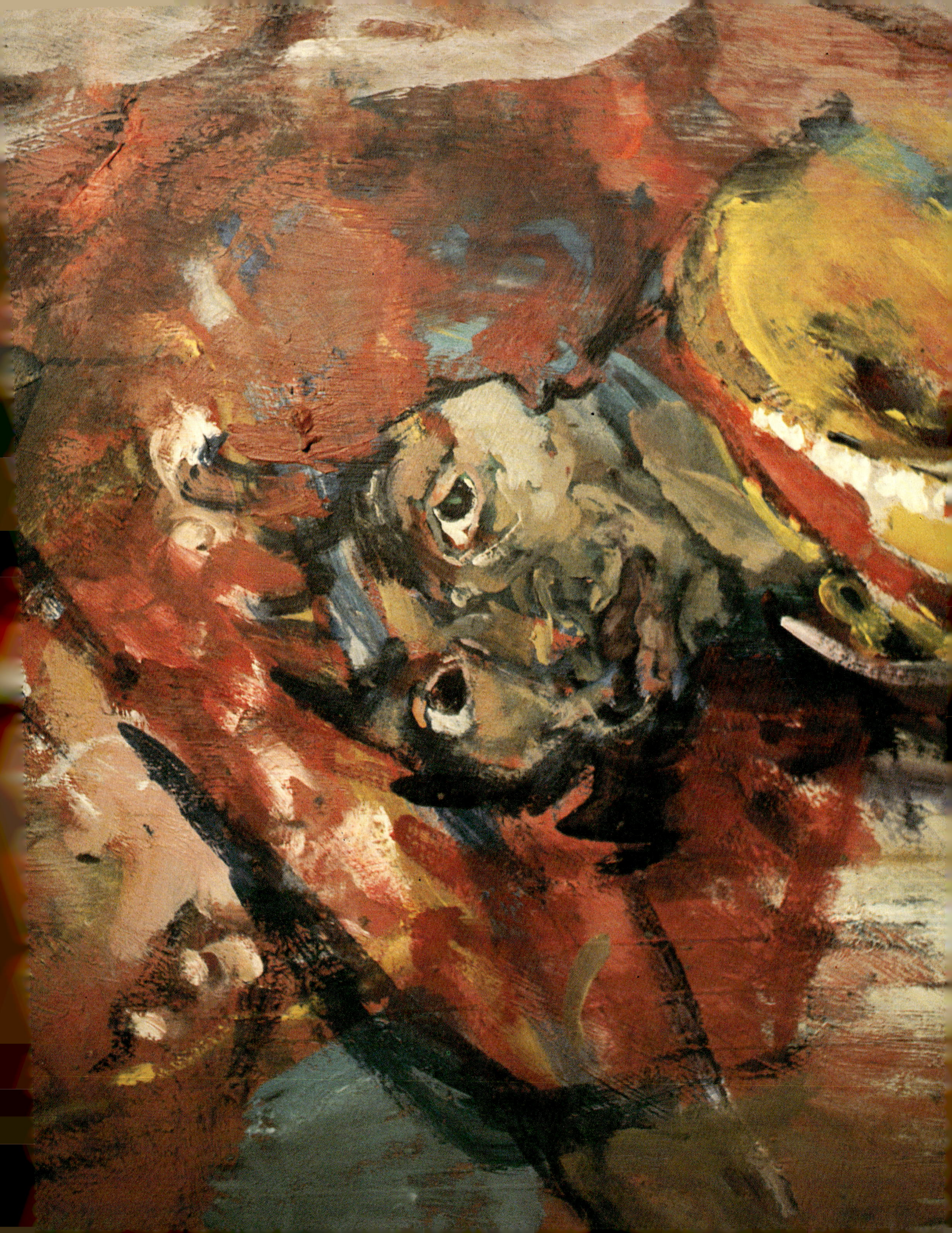

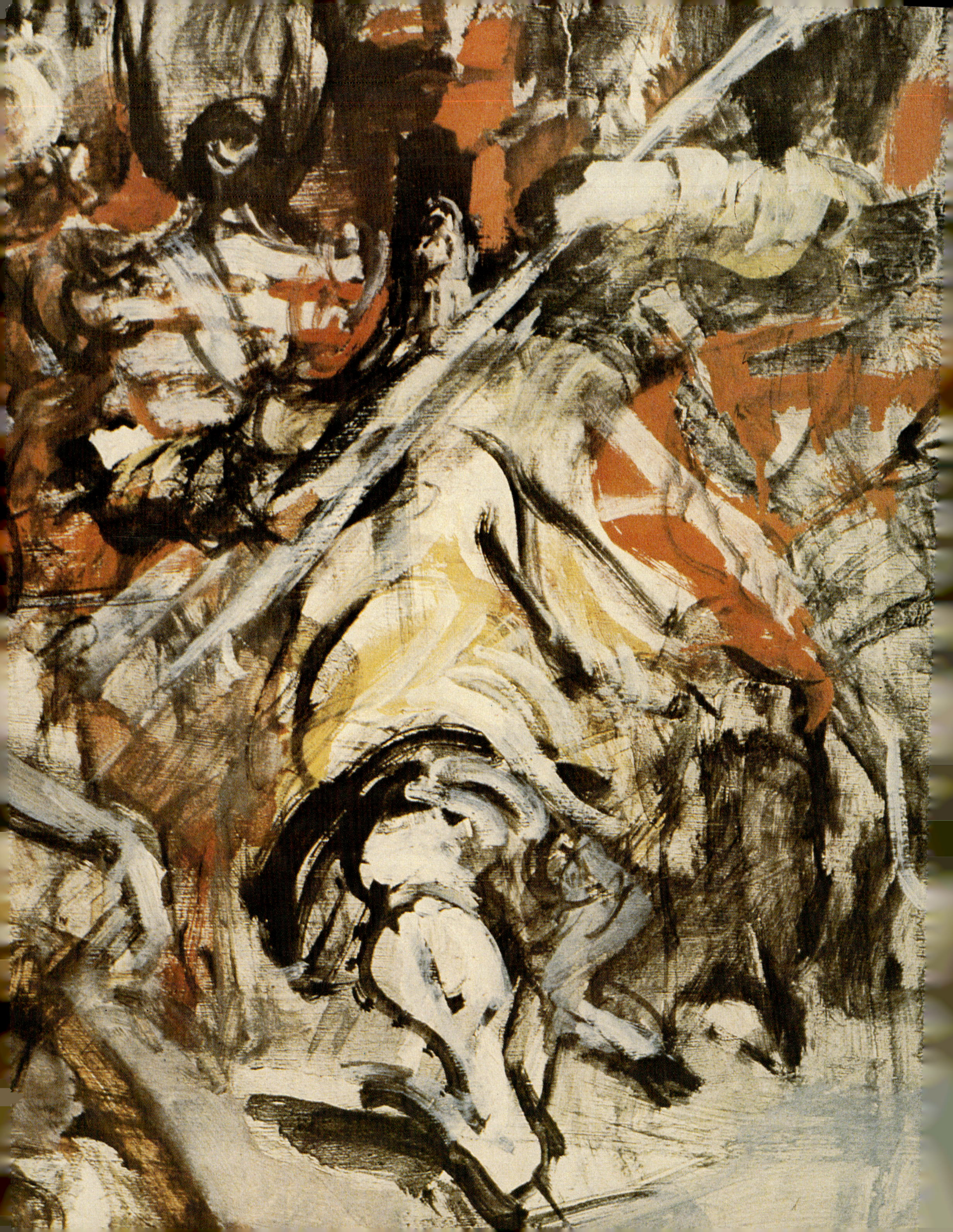

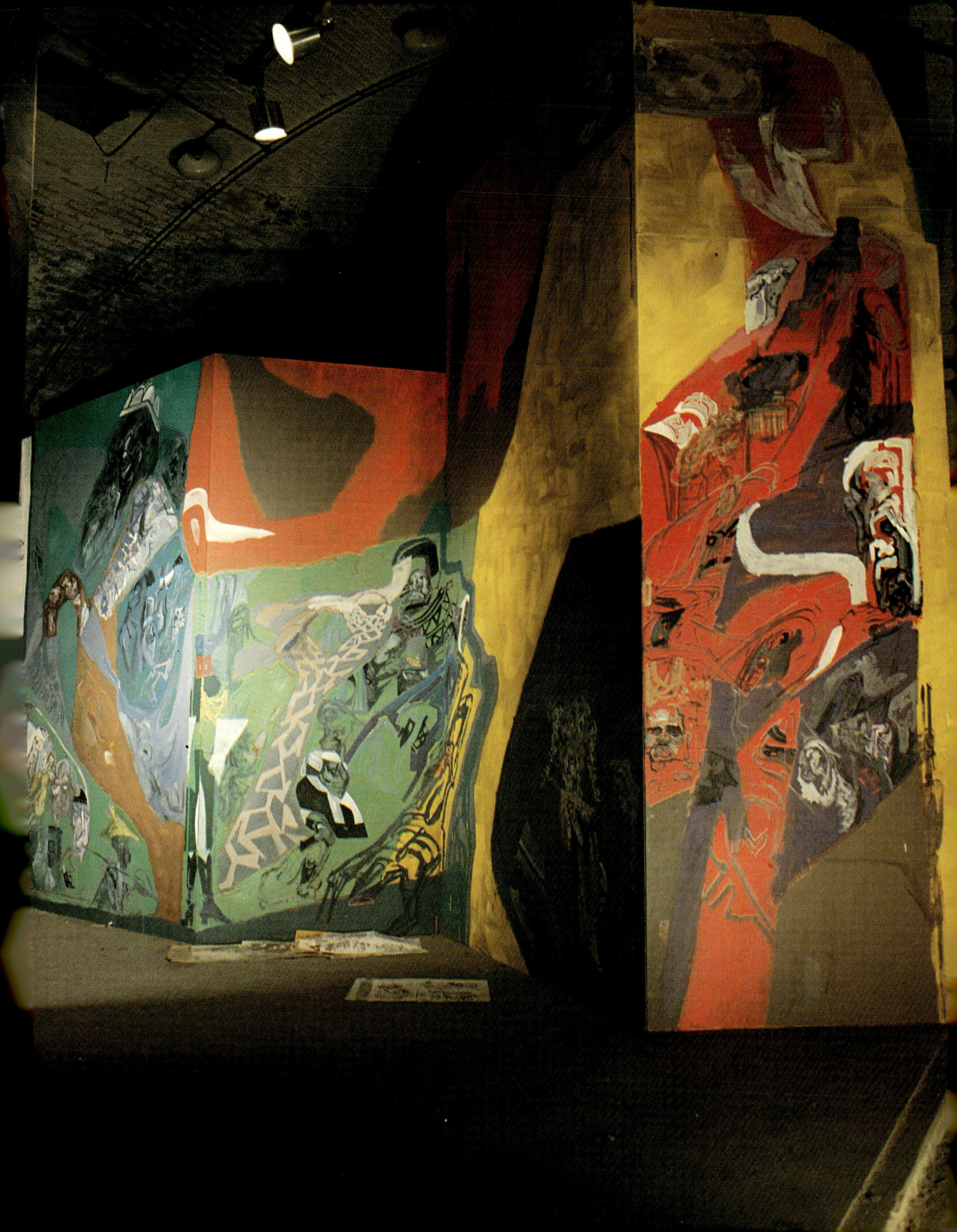

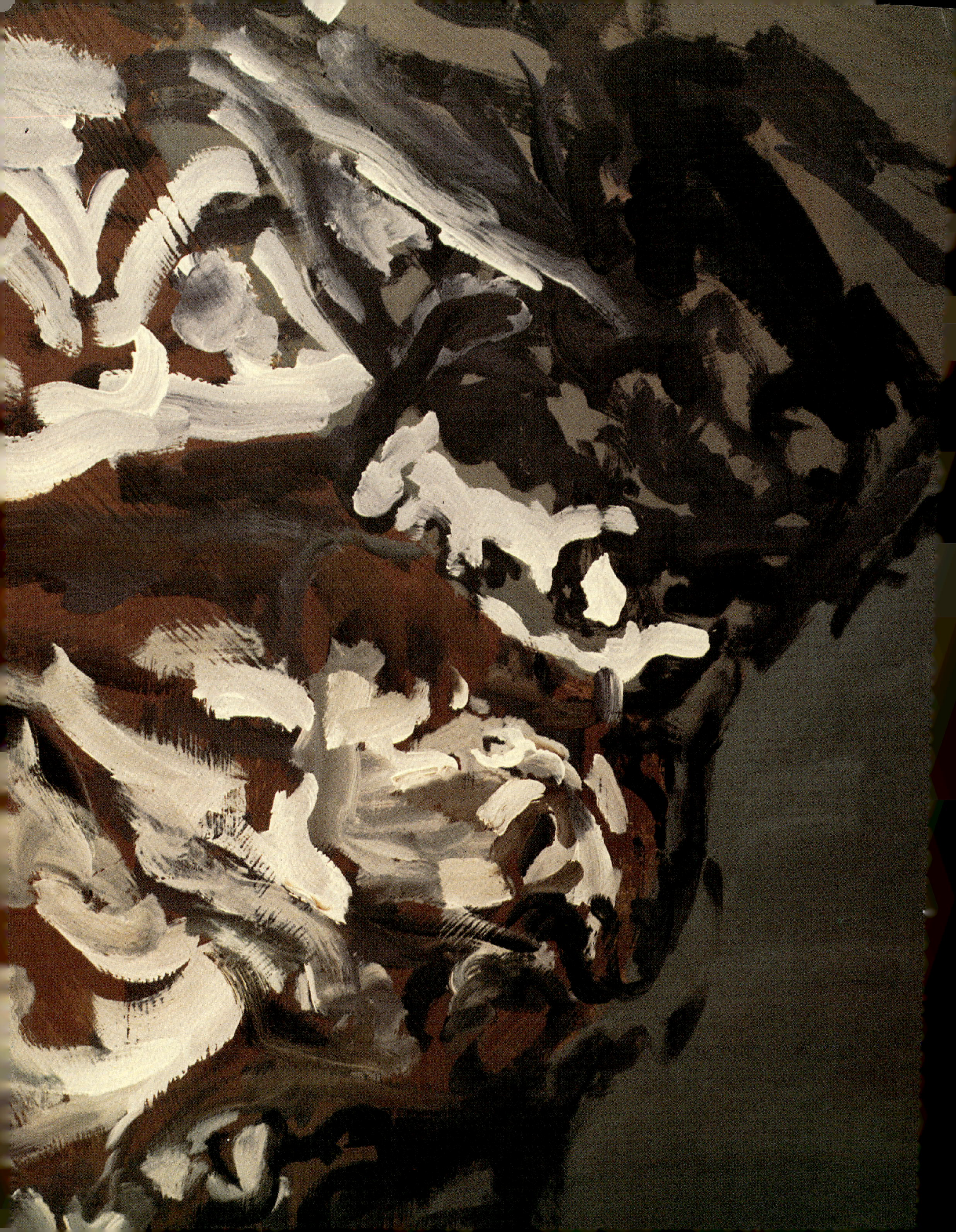

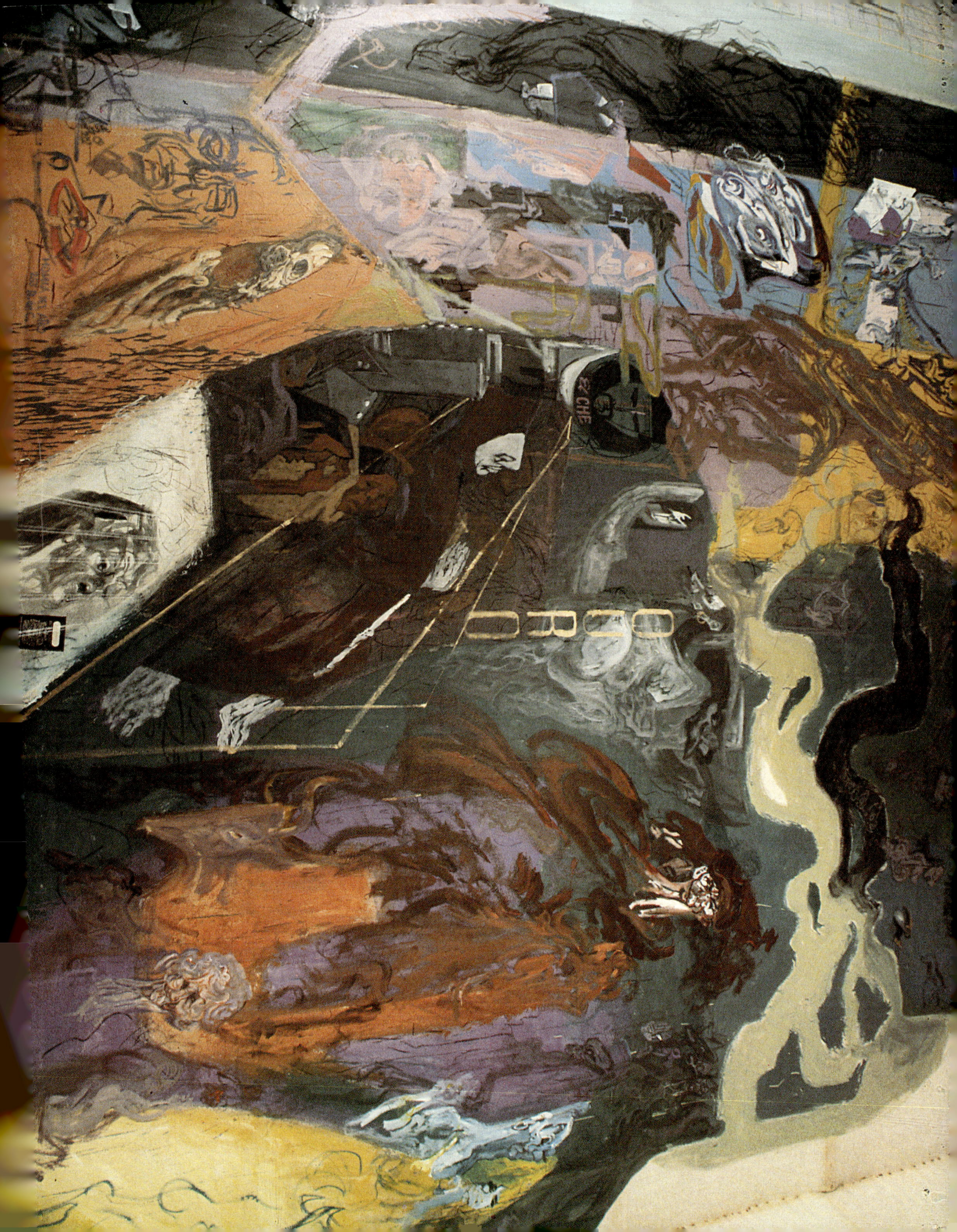
ORCO

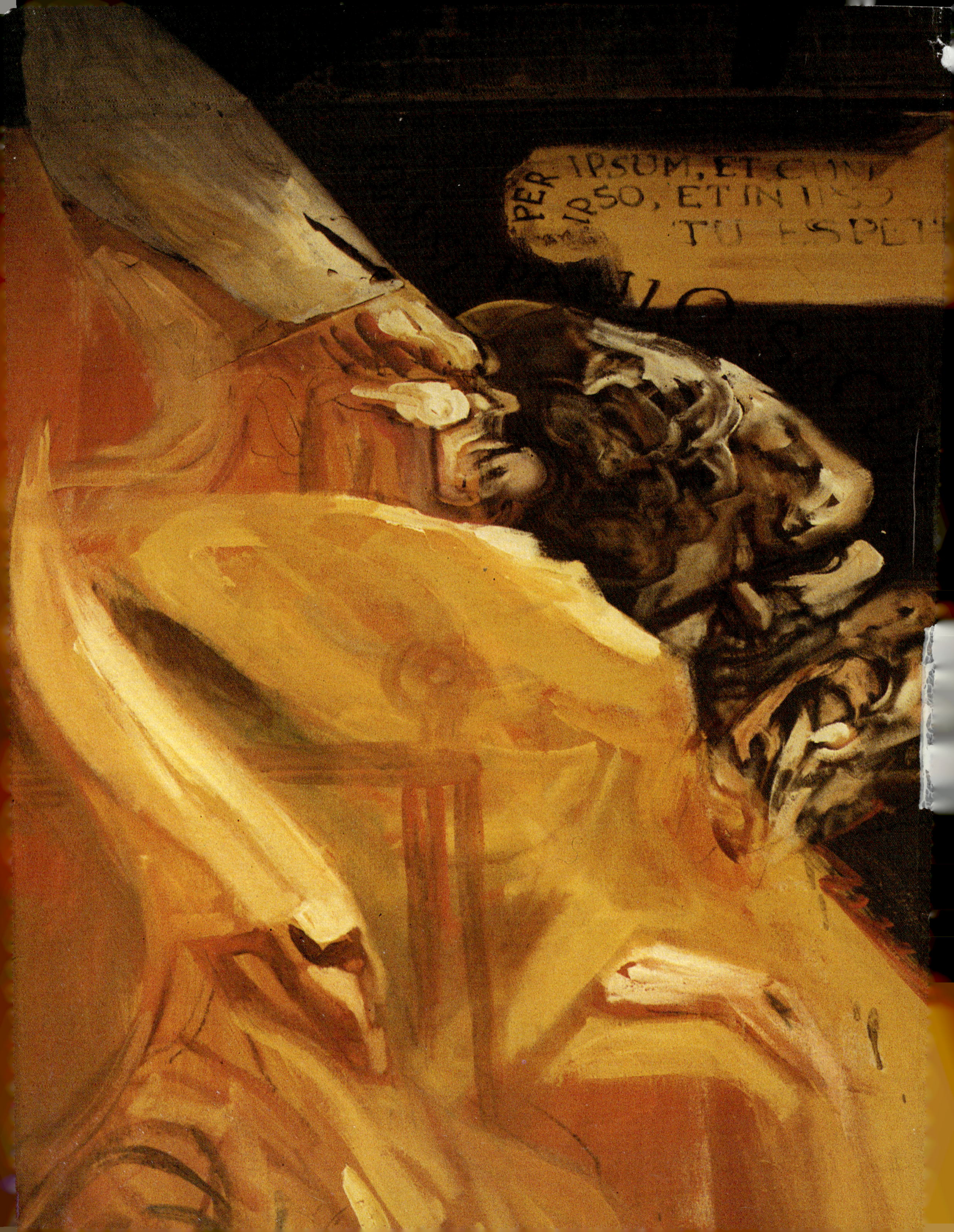
PER IPSUM, ET
IPSO, ET IN